World Music

THE ROUGH GUIDE

Also available in Rough Guides music reference series:

The Rough Guide to Classical Music on CD

Forthcoming:

The Rough Guide to Jazz
The Rough Guide to Opera
and more!

Published October 1994 by Rough Guides Ltd, 1 Mercer St, London WC2H 9QJ.
Distributed by the Penguin Group:

Penguin Books Ltd, 27 Wrights Lane, London W8 5TZ
Penguin Books USA Inc., 375 Hudson Street, New York 10014, USA
Penguin Books Australia Ltd, 487 Maroondah Highway, PO Box 257, Ringwood,
    Victoria 3134, Australia
Penguin Books Canada Ltd, 10 Alcorn Avenue, Toronto, Ontario, Canada M4V 1E4
Penguin Books (NZ) Ltd, 182–190 Wairau Road, Auckland 10, New Zealand

Typeset in Bodoni and Gill Sans to an original design by Henry Iles.
Printed in the UK by The Bath Press, Avon.

720pp, includes index

A catalogue record for this book is available from the British Library.
ISBN 1-85828-017-6

World Music

THE ROUGH GUIDE

Editors

Simon Broughton, Mark Ellingham,
David Muddyman and Richard Trillo

Contributing editor

Kim Burton

MO12182713

THE ROUGH GUIDES

ACKNOWLEDGMENTS

After four years in the making, this book owes a big debt to a great many people – above all our many contributors (see p.671 for the role call), who took on the endless rewrites and updates with good humour and even enthusiasm! We are also very grateful for support on the project to Jak Kilby, Graeme Ewens, Dave Peabody, John Clewley, and all the other photographers who scoured their files on our behalf; to the infinitely wise and helpful Ian Anderson and Ben Mandelson; to Phil Stanton of World Music Network for coming in at just the right minute with a CD; to Gaylene Martin of Partridge & Storey for masses of help, especially in the early days; to Charlie Gillett for the much-missed *Foreign Affair* and *World of Difference*; to WOMAD for inspiration over the past decade and arranging many an interview; to Apple maestro Henry Iles for confidence, design and scanning; to proofreaders Kate Berens and Margaret Doyle; to Susanne Hillen and Viv Antwi for pulling off the production (and a relaxed attitude to the final, final, final revises); to Tania Hummel for checking and chasing; to Melissa Flack for the instant map; and to Jerry Williams and Judy Pang for inspired and lightning layout.

The book couldn't have happened, either, without the enthusiastic support of promoters and record labels, big and small. Many thanks on this front to: Roger Armstrong and John Crosby at GlobeStyle/Ace, Paul Fisher at JVC, Danielle at Virgin, Iain Scott at Triple Earth, Nick Gold and Jenny Adlington at World Circuit, all at Piranha, Ned Sublette at Qbadisc, Adrian Faiers at Tumi, Alf Goodman and Robin Broadbank at Nimbus, Bernard Kleikamp at Pan, Susan Taylor at Canyon, Jody Yebga and Pat Naylor at Ryko, Miles at Topic, Sally Reeves and Jodie Boulting at Hannibal, Ian Green at Greentrax, Andy Morgan and Janet Craig at WOMAD, Tatiana Spencer and Amanda Jones at Real World, David Flower of Sasa Music, all at Silex, Brenda Dunlap, Anthony Seeger and Michael Maloney at Smithsonian/Folkways, Bing Broderick at Rounder, Judith at Green Linnet, Máirie Harris at Gael-Linn, Fiona MacAlister at Heart Beat, Virgil at Adastra, Carina Grace at Solid, Gail Marriner at Cooking Vinyl, Emyr Glyn Williams at Ankst, Rhys Mwyn at Crai, and Elin Owen at Sain, Mike Harding at Touch, Claire Stanhope at CSA, Klaus Schruff and Ulrich at CMP, all at Trikont, Dominic at All Saints Records, Stefan and Michel at Mukalo, Yorick Benoit at Run Productions, Martin Jenkins at Black Crown, Kate Bartlett at Greensleeves, Holly at Ariwa, Morag White at Larrikin, Laurie Staff at Harmnia Mundi, Gerald Seligmann at HEMIsphere, Yorick Nenoist at Run Productions, Tam at BMG Ariola, and all at Saydisc.

SIMON would also like to thank Kate for living with the non-stop music and the late nights and acting as carrier pigeon.

KIM would also like to thank, in the Balkans, Spaso Berak, Professor Nikolai and Dr Dimitrina Kaufman, Himzo Tulić, Kiril and Vasil Natev, Agim Vellaj, Roberto Pla, Drago Vovk, Spiro Konduri, the Hajrić and Polić families, Krasimira Peneva and family, Svanibor Pettan, Spartak Kondi and family; and for editorial help, Martin Jenkins, Peter Barbaric, Clive Bell, David Toop, Alf Goodrich and Phil Wilson.

DAVID would also like to thank Katherine Pierpoint, Sam Dodson, Iain Scott, Salih of Melodi Music, Aki Pattalisof Trehantiri, Jameela Siddiqi, Aki Nawaz, Ravi, and Marc Dubin.

RICHARD would also like to thank Jean Trouillet of World Network for disarming enthusiasm and advice; John Collins for Ghanaian information; Ian Thomas and Lois Darlington of Stern's for queries answered and CDs borrowed; Lou Edmonds; Jenny Cathcart for helping on French interviews; João Mendes; Caroline Shaw for kind lusophone support; Phil Bunce for Songa humour and Malawi help; John Storm Roberts of Original Music; Nick Dean of Natari; and Peter Moszynski. Lastly, and crucially, all my thanks and love to Teresa, David and Alex, who endured the editing and enjoyed the music. Who wants a dance?!

MARK would also like to thank: Natania Jansz, for reading and living with the book – and suggesting it might all work out; Henry, for laughing at the problems; Kim, for saying yes and doing such a great job; Simon for endurance rarely seen off mountain ascents, for keeping me at the task, and introducing me to the Wagi Brothers; and Manuel Dominguez for the original idea.

"FOUR FIFTHS OF THE WORLD
CANNOT BE WRONG."

Hijaz Mustapha

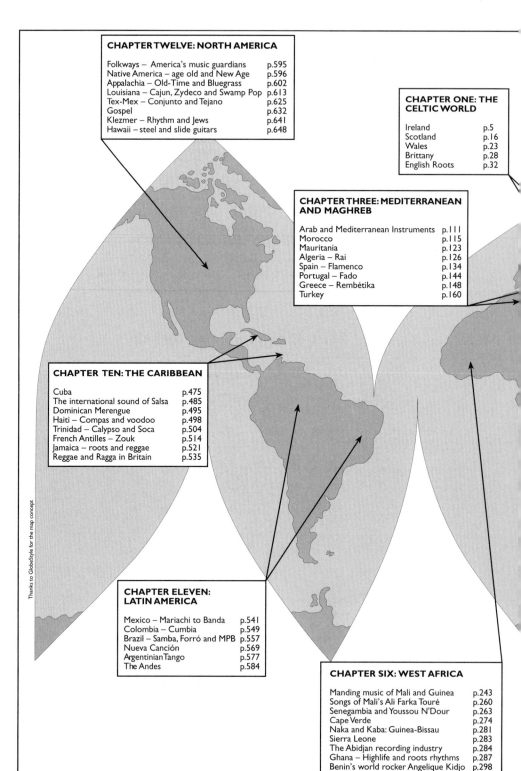

Thanks to GlobeStyle for the map concept

CONTENTS

INTRODUCTION

T he idea of this book is to provide a way into sounds that, in large part, are unfamiliar. If you just heard Youssou N'Dour on the radio, Ladysmith Black Mambazo on a Paul Simon record, or Margareth Menezes supporting David Byrne, and you liked the sound of it, read on. This is the guide that tells you where to go from there – and more.

Although many of the music styles that we have featured are long established in their home territories, WORLD MUSIC as a concept is less than a decade old. The name was dreamed up in 1987 by the heads of a number of small London-based record labels who found their releases from African, Latin American and other international artists were not finding rack space because records stores had no obvious place to put them. And so the world music tag was hit upon, initially as a month-long marketing campaign to impress on the music shops, the critics, and buyers that here were sounds worth listening to. The name stuck, however, and was swiftly adopted at records stores and festivals, in magazines and books, on both sides of the Atlantic. The Germans caught on, too, coining the more lively weltbeat.

There's a purist argument that world music is a "ghetto" term, and another that the term is next to meaningless, so broad is its interpretation. Alternatives abound: roots, international, ethnic. But the music industry feels at home with the world music tag, and whatever we think about it, at least we all know what the term means, don't we?

Or do we? When we started work on this book, some four years back, the task seemed relatively simple. We would compile a guide to twenty or thirty of the most interesting musics in the market. We'd ignore western Classical music and Anglo-American rock and soul and rap and jazz and country – all of which are covered in depth elsewhere – and we'd delve into the rest. We would write about those diverse and wonderful musics emerging on the new crop of labels: zouk, soukous, cajun and zydeco, rai, qawwali, rembétika, taarab, gypsy bands from Transylvania: that kind of thing. We would deal, too, with artists little known in the West but megastars in their own orbit – people like Juan Luís Guerra (whose recent album sold five million worldwide), or the Indian movie singer Asha Bhosle (the world's most recorded artist). We would call in the experts – record producers, music commentators, the more accessible musicologists – and put together a 300 page book.

It wasn't long, however, before we realized such modest aims were unrealistic. If we were going to feature salsa and merengue, then we'd have to include samba, forró, tango, cumbia and vallenato; if we had Bulgarian singers and Hungarian dancehall bands then why not flamenco or fado? Cajun and zydeco led to old-time and bluegrass and klezmer; the African section turned into virtually a book on its own. We started venturing into the Arab world, India, Central Asia, the Far East, the Pacific, Celtic music . . . the parameters constantly shifted.

Part of the reason for this – and for the end result, a 700-page book on just about every strand of global popular music – was the huge and unprecedented surge of interest on the part of record labels and record buyers. Although much of the mainstream music press, with its hankering for the next big thing, lost interest in the world music tag almost as soon as it had pronounced its appearance, music listeners certainly did not. World music has been the single biggest growth area in record stores in the 1990s and, coinciding as it has with the move from vinyl to CD, there has been a glorious roll of releases.

Where once it was very hard to find recordings of bands from Zaire or Mali, Cuban son or Mexican conjuntos, Finnish fiddlers or Indonesian pop, there are now fantastic recordings readily available. And it's not just the best contemporary groups from around the world that have appeared on disc in the west – a plethora of CD releases of classic and archive material has made accessible the whole history and development of regional styles as well as their legendary musicians. Important collections of Indian, Turkish, Greek, Tex-Mex and calypso music – to name just a few examples – have made it onto the shelves.

The 1990s have also seen an explosion of world music clubs, concerts and festivals throughout Europe and North America, bringing all this music to a live audience. Much of the credit for this is due to the WOMAD organization, who produced their first, pioneering festival – bringing together groups from Burundi, China, Egypt and Ireland – in Somerset, England, in 1982. Today they organize a whole roster of festivals in locations as far flung as England, the US, Spain and Japan, and their influence has permeated into "world stages" at dozens of rock, folk and jazz festivals around the world.

How the guide works

The guide consists of thirteen chapters, arranged according to regions that make broad musical sense. Each chapter then breaks down into a series of features on specific countries or genres of music. At the end of each of these sections, you'll find a selective discography: not an exhaustive listing, by any means, but one that covers most of the top recordings and the writer's personal choices. In each discography, we've highlighted a star disc (see DISCOGRAPHY HIEROGLYPHICS, opposite) as a way into the music.

There are some quirks, inevitably, but each has a reason. We decided for example, to bundle the Mediterranean with North Africa to emphasize the links between flamenco and Moroccan music, and between Greek and Turkish styles. In addition, we feature musical satellites alongside their sources, so you'll find British ska and reggae in the Jamaica section, bhangra in with India, and the like. All artists and music styles are detailed in the index, if you'd rather dip and browse.

Throughout the book, we have tried to highlight influences and sources but of course the musical map can be as arbitrary as any national border. Salsa originated in Cuba, took off in New York, and was re-exported to the Caribbean and Latin America. Much Caribbean music developed from the imported African slave populations, while Zaire's dominant soukous music emerged out of the Latin rumba that was so popular on colonial radio in the 1940s and 50s.

This cross-fertilization is, of course, one of the reasons why the music covered in these pages is so damn good. We have put together THE ROUGH GUIDE TO WORLD MUSIC to spread the word and to fill in some of the often hard-to-find background. If we do nothing else, we hope that the features in this book will open your ears to music you hadn't previously considered, and expand your listening in areas you always knew you liked, if you could only remember that name . . .

DISCOGRAPHY

Each section in the guide is followed by a discography, with reviews of the best and most accessible recorded music – mainly on CD but also on vinyl and (in some cases) on local cassettes. The cassette industry is a thriving part of the music scene in much of Asia and the Middle East, where our recommendations are slanted towards famous works – which are often bootlegged repeatedly – rather than titles on a particular label.

The bulk of the recommendations, however, are on CD, the format of just about every new release available in your local record store – and for hundreds of re-releases, too, often combining a pair of original vinyl albums.

We have used two hieroglyphics:

⟨D⟩ All releases on CD are preceded by this symbol. All other recommendations are at time of writing on vinyl or cassette only.

⟨D⟩ Each discography has one "star" CD, signified by this larger CD symbol. This is not neccessarily the greatest disc ever (if such a beast was possible to define!) but, if you're approaching a particular music for the first time, we reckon it is the best initial purchase, either because it's wonderful or representative or both. In general, we have opted for a contemporary disc by a group or musician playing today.

HIEROGLYPHICS

THE CELTIC WORLD

The Celtic World. It's a dubious concept in terms of politics and populations. But in music and culture and language, at least, it's alive and it's real. Ireland, Wales, patches of Scotland and England, Brittany, Galicia and Asturias in Spain: all share a Celtic bond, which manifests itself most extravagantly and enjoyably at a series of music festivals held across Europe in the summer months. Show up at any one of these and you're likely to be entranced by the traditional music on show and the diversity of its incarnations: as "roots"-style folk, as folk-influenced rock, as any number of Celtic world fusions. At the British festivals, at least, you're likely to see a fair number of English roots bands, too; although not strictly (and often not at all) Celtic, they get an honorary place on stage and – by extension – in this chapter.

The interest in Celtic culture, and music in particular, owes a large debt to the folk music revival of the 1960s, spearheaded by singer-songwriters and kick-started internationally by Bob Dylan. The new folk fraternities – singers, players and bands – in Britain, Ireland and France, especially, began to investigate their own roots more thoroughly, and to unearth a rich and exciting Celtic tradition.

The impetus came most forcefully from Ireland, where the Celtic traditions had been camouflaged for a while in the towns, with showbands playing pop hits and Irish country and western, but had been kept very much alive in the rural areas and village bars. In the early 1960s Seán Ó Riada, a visionary composer and harpsichord player from Cork, lit the bonfire by investing his predominantly classical orchestra, Ceoltoiri Chualann, with a distinctly Irish roots feel. He died in 1971 but from the ashes of his band master piper Paddy Moloney emerged to form The Chieftains, who were to put a significantly greater degree of emphasis on the Irish tradition. The freshness of their sound, the rarely heard virtuosity of the instrumentalists and the canny marketing prowess of Moloney and Claddagh Records conspired to sell this trailblazing phenomenon across Britain and points beyond, where it had an astonishing knock-on effect inspiring other musicians to seek out their own roots.

Scots, particularly, found their own Celtishness nestling restlessly beneath the surface and quickly fired it back into action via a barrage of flying fiddles, blazing bagpipes and Scots *wha hae*. Many of the groups who gained some notoriety as a result threw passion and Celtic fervour recklessly before any acknowledgment of technique, but the best of them – like Silly Wizard, The Tannahill Weavers, and Runrig – performed valuable work in shedding Scottish music of a suffocating preoccupation with kilts, parlour music and Moira Anderson. The Battlefield Band gave the bagpipes a new life beyond Burns Night and Hogmanay, while the Boys Of The Lough have given the Scots Celts an influential voice in the folk music world right into the 1990s.

Through the 1970s and '80s, though, the baton remained very firmly with the ebullient youth of Ireland. Crucial to developments were Planxty, initially envisaged as a foil for the charismatic singing of Christy Moore, but soon much wider in scope, as the purity of Liam O'Flynn's *uilleann* piping and the vision of Donal Lunny's arrangements showed the way to a new music rooted in history. Other bands of breathtaking ability flooded out of Ireland in Planxty's wake – the Bothy Band, De Dannan, Moving Hearts and Clannad among them – and the Celtic legacy has been appropriately rampant ever since, finding new voice in the

1990s with the like of Altan, Four Men And A Dog, and Déanta.

It is a passionate giant of a tradition that has reawakened in varying degrees seemingly wherever the Celts set foot all those centuries ago. It even reaches into England, where the brilliant young Northumbrian piper Kathryn Tickell is never slow to point out the Celtic roots of her music. Cornwall, too, has its Celtic roots and is the most vocal English county in distancing its own cultural history from the rest of the country. You have to dig, but records of Cornish music in the native tongue are still to be found, just as they are in the Isle of Man, a couple of hours on the boat out of Liverpool.

There are some good things happening in British roots music, too, that have nothing at all to do with the Celtic past. All sorts of wonderful mixes – of English country music with reggae and bhangra, for example – and an honorable folk-rock tradition, built on the work of people like Ashley Hutchings, who set sail with bands like Fairport Convention and Steeleye Span.

For a long time Wales was the country the Celtic revival forgot – a nation steeped in music which apparently had no music to call its own beyond the predominantly classical tradition of the Eisteddfod choirs. The sternly puritanical Methodist revival of the eighteenth century all but wiped out the ancient Celtic traditions and took a sledgehammer to the Welsh language, too. However, the language has survived and Welsh culture has been invigorated over the last decade or two, with bands like Ar Log investigating their own Celtic tradition and others ploughing an individual furrow with Welsh language rock.

A more fervent outpost of Celtic music exists in Brittany, in northwest France, where the Celts fled in the fifth and sixth centuries following the Anglo-Saxon invasion of Britain. The Breton language survives in many areas

CELTIC ✈ GLOSSARY

Biniou Breton oboe.

Bombard Breton bagpipes.

Bodhrán Large Irish frame drum played with a small stick or the hand.

Bouzouki Plucked string instrument of Greek origin adopted and adapted by Irish musicians.

Box Slang term for accordion.

Ceilidh (Ceili) Communal dances, invariably including a ceilidh band.

Ceol Celtic word for music.

Clarsach Celtic harp.

Crwth Old-style Welsh harp.

Eisteddfod Welsh music and cultural festival.

Fest-Noz Breton dance or ceilidh.

Fleadh Literally an "orgy" but used now for music festival events – orgies of music.

Fonn mall "Slow air" in Gaelic; used of an instrumental performance of a song melody or lament.

Gaeltacht Area where the Gaelic (Irish) language is spoken.

Gwerin "Folk" in Welsh; a **gwyl werin** is a folk festival.

Hurdy-gurdy Drone instrument with melody strings bowed by a wheel. Known as a Vielle à Rone in France.

Jig Irish folk dance in 6/8 time; a slip-jig is in 9/8.

Kan ha diskan Unaccompanied Breton dance singing.

Mouth music Unaccompanied Scottish dance singing.

Northumbrian pipes Small bagpipes from the English county of Northumbria.

Pibroch (Piobaireachd in Gaelic) The original form of Scottish bagpipe playing; pilbroch songs emulate the form of piping.

Reel Irish folk dance in 4/4 time.

Sean nós This means "old style" in Gaelic and is used of the vocal tradition from the west of Ireland.

Session Informal music performance, often taking place in a pub.

Set Traditional group dance.

Setting Arrangement or ornamentation of a traditional melody by an individual musician.

Strain Section of a tune, usually eight bars long. A tune may have two or more strains.

Strathspey Scottish dance style noted for its peculiar rhythms.

Telenn Breton harp.

Triple harp Traditional Welsh harp.

Tin whistle Small metal six-holed fipple flute.

Twmpath Welsh dance or ceilidh.

Uilleann pipes Irish bellows-blown bagpipes.

For more on the Celtic instruments, see the "Instruments and Players" box on pp.12–13.

here, and the Bretons have retained colourful traditions of song and dance quite distinct from the rest of France. In recent years, their sense of identity has received a major boost through the efforts of charismatic harpist Alan Stivell, whose folk-rock band achieved international success. More recently, the Breton guitarists Gabriel Yacoub and Dan Ar Bras have won much acclaim.

Pockets of Celtic tradition also survive in parts of Italy and Turkey, but the greatest Celtic bastions in southern Europe are on the Atlantic coast of Spain, in Asturias and Galicia. Bagpipes of many different shapes, styles and sizes are still played and maintain a particular stronghold in these areas, and the all but extinct hurdy gurdy has also enjoyed a renaissance there in recent years. Spanish bagpipe schools have come into existence at a rate to make a Scotsplayer deeply jealous.

Throughout these territories, the Celtic links may appear historically remote and obscure, but their spirit remains instantly identifiable in the music. Characteristic of all the strands are the vibrant weaving of tunes, whether led by pipes, fiddle, or squeeze box, and the often complex arrangements, backed by a lively rhythm section of drums, guitar or bombard. There are no hard-and-fast rules to determine the origins of this Celtic tradition, but its purity, feel and explosive vitality are pretty much unmistakable.

CELTIC AND BRITISH FESTIVALS

· ·

The Celtic bonds have been emphasized in recent years by the emergence of numerous international festivals, most notably at Lorient, in Brittany, which has been a real focus through the past decade. A rather wonderful feature of many of the larger events is that you can wander into a bar and hear snatches of Erse (Irish), Welsh, Gaelic, Manx, Breton and Gallego – often in the same conversation.

The best source for festival information is the London-based magazine *Folk Roots*, which published in its April issue a vast festival supplement with details of a couple of hundred-odd roots events.

FRANCE

Lorient Festival Interceltique
First two weeks of August.
This Breton festival alerted Europe to the Celtic upsurge. Over the last decade, it has hosted consistently memorable events, featuring musicians from Galicia to Galway, Cornwall to the Côte du Nord. Further information: Festival Interceltique, 2 rue Paul Bert, 56100 Lorient. ☎01033-97212429.

St-Chartier
Nearest weekend to July 14 (Bastille Day).
The "Rencontres internationales de luthiers et maitres sonneurs" (international meeting of instrument makers and master pipers) is held in and around the château of St-Chartier, close to the town of La Chatre, in the Indre *département*, 175 miles southwest of Paris. Although St-Chartier is ostensibly a festival of pipe and hurdy-gurdy music, in reality the net gets cast somewhat wider. There are daytime and evening concerts and informal sessions in the village cafés and around the campground. If you want to buy pipes or other Celtic instruments, this is the best place to meet makers, virtually all of whom seem to have stalls here.
Further information: Michèle Fromenteau, 141 rue National, 36400 La Chatre. ☎01033-54060996.

IRELAND

Fleadh Cheoil
August bank holiday weekend.
This "orgy of music" (as the title translates) is Ireland's premier gathering of traditional musicians, from all around the country and from America, too. They arrive, ostensibly, for a series of competitions involving different instruments, but it all soon turns into a street party, which goes through the night every night for a week every summer. The fleadh is held in a different town every year – follow the bodhrans and you won't believe your eyes or ears.
Further information: Comhaltas Ceoltoiri Eireann, 32 Belgrave Square, Monkstown, Co. Dublin. ☎01 2800295.

Galway Arts Festival
Second and third weeks of July (usually!).
Galway is a hive of music throughout the summer and provides a useful base to explore the hot spots of Irish music in Clare and Connemara.

THE CELTIC WORLD

Things reach a climax with the Galway Arts Festival, where a small army of traditional musicians congregate, quiet times are unknown, and concerts of traditional music take place in every other pub till the small hours (and they don't get much smaller than in Galway).
Further information: Galway Arts Festival, 6 Upper Dominick St, Galway. ☎010353-9163800.

SCOTLAND

Ceolmhor Lochabair
First weekend of May.
A significant recent addition to the Celtic festival calendar, this is held in the picturesque surroundings of Fort William, close to Ben Nevis in the Scottish highlands. Scots, Irish and Breton musicians all turn up in force.
Further information: Ceolmhor Lochabair, Marcos An-Aird, Fort William, PH33 6AN. ☎0397-700708.

Shetland Folk Festival
End of April/early May.
Seasickness on the notorious boat trip to Shetland is justified by the music and partying that attract the hordes to this Lerwick-based festival. It is not exclusively Celtic but the crack is always mighty.
Further information: Kevin Jones, 5 Burns Lane, Lerwick, Shetland, ZE1 0EJ. ☎0595-4757.

ENGLAND

Cambridge Folk Festival
Last weekend in July.
This is Europe's premier folk festival and it's always a treat: broad and contemporary in outlook, including a lot of young new Celtic and British bands, trad folkies, bluegrass and world roots groups.
Further information: Festival Office, 6 East St, Sidmouth, Devon, EX10 8BL. ☎0296-393293.

London Fleadh
June.
A major showcase for Irish bands from all points of the compass, with lots of traditional stuff amid the heavyweight rock-led headliners. A day event, it is held at a perennially packed out Finsbury Park.
Further information: Mean Fiddler Productions, 28a Harlesden High St, London NW10 4LX (☎071/284 4111) .

Sidmouth Folk Festival
First week of August.
Now a staggering forty years old, Sidmouth is the grandaddy of all folk festivals, pioneering world music of all shapes and sizes, with a particular

favouritism towards Celtic folk. Recent guests have included Le Gop and Vermenton Plage from France, Liam O'Flynn and Dervish from Ireland, Catriona MacDonald and Ian Lowthian from Scotland, and England's Big Jig. A superb event that occupies the whole of this seaside town in Devon throughout the week.
Further information: Festival Office, 6 East St, Sidmouth, Devon, EX10 8BL. ☎0296-393293.

WOMAD at Rivermead
Mid/late July.
WOMAD have done more than anyone to promote world/roots music and they always fly the flag at Reading with an adventurous line-up, including the best of Celtic/British acts, alongside everyone else from Haiti to Mongolia. WOMAD also hold a festival most years at Morecambe Bay, Lancashire (August bank holiday), as well as at various global locations – in Spain, Japan and elsewhere.
Further information: WOMAD, Mill Lane, Box, Wilts SN14 9PN. ☎0225-744044.

WALES

Pontardawe
Third weekend of August.
The leading Welsh festival near Swansea has a long and proud history of adventurous booking, doing much to encourage the latent Celtic traditions and going out of its way to attract the best of folk music from further afield. It always features a strong Irish and Scottish representation as well as upcoming bands from France, Italy, Spain and elsewhere.
Further information: Festival Office, Cross Resource Centre, High St, Pontardawe, Swansea, West Glamorgan SA8 4GU. ☎0792-830 200.

Gwyl Werin y Cnapan
Second weekend in July.
This is the biggest folk event in Wales, though hardly known outside, and it always features a powerful line-up of bands from Wales and the rest of the Celtic world. Takes place at Ffostrasol, Dyfed.

PORTUGAL

Oporto Interceltic Festival
Last week in March.
Promising Portuguese festival featuring leading acts from Scotland, Galicia, Ireland and Brittany as well as artists more local to Portugal's second city.
Further information: Mundo da Canção, Rua Formosa 49-3° (sala 7), 4000 Porto, Portugal. ☎010351-2-319596.

IRISH SOUL

IRISH TRADITIONAL MUSIC HAS FED INTO THE MAINSTREAM FOR DECADES – AND IT'S NOT LYING DOWN YET AWHILE

Alan Parker's engaging film "The Commitments" centred on the activities of a young Dublin soul band. Soul bands in the James Brown mode are thin on the ground in Ireland, much less Dublin city, but soul musicians . . . that's another story, as Nuala O'Connor explains.

Nothing, it would seem, connects the young urbanites of The Commitments to native Irish traditional music culture, but Irish soul singer Van Morrison thinks otherwise. He identifies, rather loosely, "soul" as the essence of Irish and Scottish traditional music.

Native-grown Irish "soul" thrives in the cities, towns and rural fastnesses of the country. Kept alive by a combination of historical, political, and cultural forces, Irish traditional music remains today one of the richest music cultures in the western world. From an exclusively rural pre-industrial base traditional music culture set down roots not only in the cities and towns of Ireland but also among the large immigrant Irish communities in Britain, North America, and Australia. Mass communications media and international travel have ensured that these dispersed musical communities are linked by an extensive network of festivals, competitions, concerts and informal comings and goings. Long after much traditional music in the industrialized west has ceased to exist in any meaningful way, Irish music continues to re-present itself, not as a museum piece but as a living and breathing bridge between the past and the future.

Which is not to say that there it's all plain sailing. Argument rages as to the authenticity of the current manifestations of traditional music. Some see innovation as the death knell of the tradition; others see renewal and reinterpretation as the only way forward. Time will tell.

COME DANCE WITH ME IN IRELAND

Most of the instrumental music the visitor will hear in Ireland is **dance music**. Originally played in kitchens, barns and at crossroads, for weddings, wakes and seasonal celebrations, it was for centuries the recreational and social expression of Irish people and nowadays it evokes the same response as it did then – get up on your feet! A vital feature of the music is the demands it makes on the listener to get actively involved. Nothing cripples traditional music faster than polite applause from a seated audience, and in some ways the division between performer and audience is an artificial one that works against the fullest expression of the music. In the loose and convivial setting of the pub session, where a more satisfying range of responses may be employed, enjoyment can get more physical with toe tapping, finger drumming and shoulder shrugging, and of course dancing.

The melody of any dance tune is but bare bones to a traditional musician; it's dependent on performance for flesh, blood and soul. Ornamentation, decoration and embellishments are the way in which the performer breathes life into the music. It's a kind of controlled extemporization in which the player re-creates the tune with every performance. Technical mastery is only half the story, for the skill with which musicians decorate a tune is the measure of their creative powers and often even accomplished players will play the *settings* of established master players.

Nearly all Irish tunes conform to the same basic structure: two eight-bar sections or *strains*, each of which is played twice to make a 32-bar whole, which is then repeated from the top. In a session one tune is followed without any appreciable break by another couple, and after a brief pause for refreshment the musicians break into another selection of two or three tunes.

The majority of dance tunes are **reels and jigs**, but every musician must be able to play hornpipes, polkas, slides, mazurkas, *scottiches*, and highlands. At the last survey in 1985 the number of jigs, reels and hornpipes in the national repertoire stood at over 6,000. Although formal classes exist, the tradition is an oral one, with tunes being handed on from player to player in performance, and the repertoire is constantly changing as new tunes are added and others shed. And the arena in which this takes place is the session.

DANCE TUNES

•••••••••••••••••••••••••

U ntil well on into this century the house dance or crossroads dance was the most popular form of entertainment in rural Irish communities. The dances were either group dances now known as "sets", based on quadrilles where two sets of two couples danced facing each other, or solo dances performed by the best dancers in the locality. Rural depopulation, church interference, the commercial dance halls, the radio and the record-player nearly killed the custom off, but over the last ten years the country has witnessed a quite phenomenal revival in "set dancing". The crossroads dances have not reappeared but increasingly pub venues are making space available for dancers.

The dance tunes are the jigs, reels and hornpipes known to every traditional player. Not every player can play for dancers though, or wants to. In dancing, the dancer and not the piper calls the tune, and playing for dancers requires special skills. The beat must be rock steady, the tunes are played at a slower tempo than is usual in a session, and the player is restrained from excessive improvisation and personal expression. Nonetheless, the recent set-dancing craze has involved more people than

Crossroads dance in Co. Wicklow

ever in an active relationship with traditional music. Sets can be got up with as few as four people (the "half set"), and it's now possible to find set-dancing sessions in pubs all around the country. Anyone who knows the steps is welcome to join in, and if you don't it's always possible to turn up at a local set-dancing class and learn from scratch.

THE SESSION: MUSIC AND CRACK

The **session** is the life-blood of traditional music, and with the session goes the associated notion of *crack*. Crack is hard to define and impossible to plan for, and when it happens is obscurely described as being "ninety" or "mighty", as in "there was a mighty session last night in X's and the crack was only ninety". Music, conversation, drink and people combine in mysterious fashion to produce good, or even great, crack.

As a rule sessions take place in **pubs**, the temples of Irish traditional music culture. Many pubs and bars hold pay-on-entrance sessions or gigs (after which a "real" session might happen) but they also cater for musicians who need a place to meet and play informally. In this case the pub owner is usually into the music and not just out to make a fast punt. Under this

arrangement the musicians are not paid, but neither are they under any obligation to play, or even to turn up. It's possible to arrive at a pub known for its sessions only to find that on this particular night no one is in playing mood. The venues of sessions are as changeable as their personnel, and situations can change overnight. A change of ownership, a row, or too many crowds can force the musicians out to other meeting places. Nevertheless, summertime is a good time for sessions, particularly in the west of Ireland, and a few inquiries locally will usually yield the necessary intelligence.

At first sight sessions may seem to be rambling, disorganized affairs, but they have an underlying order and etiquette. Musicians generally commandeer a corner of the pub which is then sacred to them. They also reserve the right to invite selected nonplaying friends to join them there. The session is not open to all comers, although it might look that way, and it's not done simply to join in with no form of introduction. More than one session has been abruptly terminated in full flight by the insensitive or inebriated ignoramus insisting on singing "Danny Boy" or banging away inexpertly on the *bodhrán* (Irish frame drum) in the mistaken belief that his or her attentions are welcome. The newcomer will wait to be asked to play, and may well refuse if they consider the other musicians to be of a lower standard than themselves.

Good traditional sessions can feature group playing, solo playing, singing in Irish and English or any combination of these: it all depends on who's in the company and where their musical bias lies. Singers may gang up and keep the musicians from playing or vice versa. The **all-inclusive session** often occurs at festivals during the summer when large numbers of musicians congregate in one place. These can be unforgettable occasions when it seems the music just couldn't get any better and all its treasures are on display.

Originally all this music was unaccompanied and a single fiddler, piper, flute-, whistle- or

---

JOHNNY DORAN: LAST OF THE TRAVELLING PIPERS

· ·

One of the greatest *uilleann* pipers of all time was **Johnny Doran**, who worked as a travelling piper throughout Ireland during the 1930s and '40s, until his untimely death, aged 42. He has had a huge influence over almost every subsequent Irish piper, including all the great modern players such as Davy Spillane, Finbar Furey, and ex-Bothey Band piper Paddy Keenan.

Doran (right in the photo below, with Pat Cash and his son) was born into a piping family and grew up in the village of Rathnew, Co. Wicklow. He moved with his family to Dublin and in his early twenties embarked on the life of a travelling piper, setting out each spring in a horse-drawn caravan to play at crossroad dances, fairs, races and football matches. It was that caravan that caused his death, crushing him after a wall collapsed on its roof; Johnny was left crippled and died two years later, in 1950.

Doran was recognized as one of the greats in his lifetime, and his arrival in a village was treated as a considerable honour. As one writer of the time put it, he was "a man of tremendous personal charisma and capable of sending out a musical pulse which utterly captivated the listener". Although Doran never made a commercial recording, he played on a handful of 78s made by the Comhairle Bhéaloideas Éireann (Irish Folklore Commission) and reissued by them on a cassette, "The Bunch of Keys".

What's special about Doran's playing is the rhythmic backing that supports the melody. His rhythms are continually varied and masterfully accentuated and the two recorded versions he left of "Rakish Paddy" reveal the truth that traditional musicians never play the same thing twice. "The Bunch of Keys" also includes recordings of reels, jigs, hornpipes and airs, all played with astonishing virtuosity. As an outdoor player, he played in a legato or open-pipe style, although as the music historian Brendan Breathnach observed, his style was essentially personal: "It always strikes me he was playing for himself, in response to some innner urge or feeling, and he went over and over the tune until he got the whole thing out of his system."

accordion-player played for the dancers. The single decorated melody line was the norm in playing as in singing, and the music had no rhythmic or harmonic accompaniment. Nowadays there are few traditional musicians who play exclusively solo and unaccompanied, but all good players can and will play solo on occasion. However, western ears are now attuned to playing and singing with a chordal backing, and over the past fifty years this has inevitably found its way into traditional playing and singing.

AIRS AND GROUPS

The instrumental repertoire is, as already described, mainly made up of dance tunes. But there is also a group of instrumental pieces known as *Fonn Mall* – "slow airs" – played without accompaniment and usually to hushed

Sharon Shannon

Seán Ó Riada: the genius of Irish traditional music

attention. Most of them are laments or the melodies of songs, some of which are of such great age that the words have been lost. The **uilleann pipes** (see instruments box on pp.12–13) are particularly well suited to the performance of airs, as their plaintive tone and ability to perform complex ornaments cleanly allows them to approach the style of *sean nós* singers (see p.10).

Playing airs offers the musician challenging expressive possibilities. Just listen to the great "box" (accordion) player **Tony MacMahon** play "Port na bPucai" (The Ghosts' Tune), a haunting and exquisite air supposedly taught to fishermen in the Blasket Sound by fairy musicians at the dead of night. Or listen to **Davy Spillane**, one of the country's younger pipers, reworking the conventions of the slow air in his own composition "Equinox", which incorporates electric guitar and low whistle. To listen to a solo player, whatever their instrument, is to get close to something old and fundamental in the tradition.

Playing in **groups** or with accompaniment is a prominent feature of traditional music performance today. Most concerts that charge for entry feature at least two musicians playing together, and frequently more plus a singer or two. One of the most exciting exponents of this style is the band **De Dannan**, which in its heyday featured three women singers who have now all gone on to solo careers in commercial rock: Mary Black, Dolores Keane, and Maura O'Connell. When they were in full song, driven by the band's virtuoso instrumentalists, it was physically impossible for the audience to stay seated as the crack topped the ninety mark. De Dannan carries on the tradition today with two remaining original members, Alec Finn and Frankie Gavin.

Ireland's best-known traditional band, **The Chieftains**, carry on the virtuoso tradition, too. This group was the spearhead of the 1960s revival of Irish traditional music – indeed, the revival is largely down to the efforts of the group's founder, composer and arranger, **Seán Ó Riada**. Living in the *Gaeltacht* (Irish-speaking area) of Cuil Aodha, renowned for its singers and passionate devotion to music, Ó Riada hit on the idea of ensemble music-making using traditional instruments like the pipes, fiddle and whistle. It was a brilliantly obvious innovation and, over the past three decades, The Chieftains have developed the concept of ensemble playing to the point where it has become universally accepted and adopted. In addition Ó Riada brought his genius for interpretation to bear on choral, liturgical and orchestral music. The choir he founded in the 1960ss is still going strong and can be heard every Sunday in the church in Cuil Aodha as well as at sessions and concerts.

A recent newcomer to the ensemble scene is **Sharon Shannon**. Playing furiously energetic dance music, Shannon is a mesmerizing accordion player who can also turn her hand to the fiddle. Having spent a few years playing with **Mike Scott and the Waterboys**, she recently went on the road with her own band. Her first solo album mixed well-known and much-played tunes like "The Silver Spire" and "O'Keefes" with Cajun, Swedish, North American, and new material in traditional style. In contrast **Altan**, another bright young band, led by fiddler Mairéad Ní Mhaonaigh and flautist Frankie Kennedy, concentrate on bringing to light little-known traditional material.

These and a handful of other bands are full-time professionals, but much group playing is organized on an ad hoc basis. Many traditional musicians have day jobs and use music to supplement their income. Others seldom if ever get paid for playing. From time to time small

CLANCYS AND DUBLINERS

· ·

Singing folk songs to instrumental accompaniment became universally popular in Ireland in the 1960s with the triumphal return from America of **The Clancy Brothers**. The Clancys had taken New York's Carnegie Hall and the networked Ed Sullivan Show by storm and they were welcomed home to Ireland as conquering heroes. Their heady blend of rousing ballads accompanied by guitar, harmonica, and five-string banjo revitalized a genre of folk song that had been all but scrapped. Hundreds of sound-alike ballad groups decked out in a motley selection of ganseys – The Clancys' hallmark was the Aran sweater – sprang up.

The ballad group fashion eventually petered out, but it had laid the foundations for a revival of interest in popular folk singing that has remained strong. Another great group of this era, one still going strong, was **The Dubliners** (pictured below in the '60s). As well as fielding two unique singers, Luke Kelly (who died in 1984) and Ronnie Drew, they boasted two fine instrumentalists: banjoist Barney McKenna and fiddler John Sheehan. Moreover the Dubliners were resolutely urban and their repertoire and approach to performance was gritty, energetic and bawdy. Songwriter Elvis Costello once remarked of North London Irish folk-punk band The Pogues that their music was "the promise of a good time", and this was ever so of the Dubliners.

No surprise then to see the two bands coming together to record one of the best-known and most raucous of folk songs, "The Irish Rover". This deadly combination produced an explosive single which is crack on vinyl.

tours which cover the traditional music circuit around the country are organized. The line-up depends on who's available and willing to travel at the time.

SEAN NÓS AND
THE VOCAL TRADITION

It's the **songs in the Irish language** that are at the heart of the music of Ireland, and of these the most important belong to a tradition known as **sean nós**, literally "in the old style". An unaccompanied singing form of great beauty and complexity, it is thought to derive in part from the bardic tradition which died out in the seventeenth century with the demise of the old Gaelic order. It makes great demands on both singer and listener. The former requires the skill to vary the interpretation of each verse by means of subtle changes in tempo, ornamentation, timbre and stress, while the latter needs to possess the knowledge and discrimination to fully appreciate the singer's efforts. To the untutored ear it can easily "sound all the same", with its slightly nasal tone and unemotional manner of performance, but perseverance will lead to great rewards.

Different areas have slightly differing sean nós styles: the songs of Connemara, for example, have elaborate melodies that lie within a small vocal range, whereas those from Munster are simpler but have a wider range. The sean nós repertoire is made up of long songs which have an allusive and delicate poetic style. Connemara's **Joe Heaney** and **Maighréad Ní Dhomnhaill** are two of the greatest of all singers in this style.

There is a more recent tradition of Irish-language singing which resembles the English-language style. These songs include lullabies, ballads, drinking songs, love songs and nonsense songs.

The majority of Irish people today are English speakers and much unaccompanied song is in that language. The repertoire, constantly being revised and renewed, contains imported Scottish and English ballads like "Barbara Allen" or "Mattie Groves", as well as native **compositions in English**: love songs, carols, emigration songs, and rebel songs. There are plenty of singers around to sustain this tradition, and they can frequently be heard at concerts or in the singers' clubs which are a feature of big cities like Dublin and Cork.

Dolores Keane and Mary Black

In addition the tradition of **informal singing**, especially in pubs, is still widely found in Ireland, despite the gutting of lovely old bars and the abominable karaoke. This kind of music-making blurs the distinction between performer and listener in a most satisfying way. It isn't so much that everybody sings, although there can be group singing; it's more that the absence of artificiality and the spontaneity of the event involves everybody present.

Even younger singers like **Mary Black** or **Liam Ó Maonlai** are accomplished unaccompanied singers. Ó Maonlai in particular is a proficient sean nós singer and is as much at home at a traditional session in the west Kerry Gaeltacht as at a stadium gig with his pop band, The Hot House Flowers.

SHAMROCK AND ROLL

Since the 1960s Ireland has had an indigenous rock scene which owes little or nothing to traditional music. Indeed it can be difficult to identify anything recognizably Irish – either musical or lyrical – in much Irish rock. Ballad singing, the Irish language, and traditional music in general were associated with values considered narrowly nationalistic and repressive by young people who looked to America and Britain as exemplars of cultural freedom. Both Bono of U2 and Philip Chevron of the Pogues speak of having Irish culture forced down their throats when young and rejecting it, although both have revised their opinions in the meantime and drawn on the ballad tradition in their own work.

ALTAN

. . . .

In the 1990s, Altan, more than any other band, have come to be seen as the flagbearers of Irish traditional music, taking the place of the old guard of the Chieftains, Clannad, and the like. Which is fair enough, for they have recorded what is perhaps the decade's best album to date, "Island Angel", a gloriously fresh reworking of old songs and airs.

At the heart of the group are fiddler and singer Mairéad Ni Mhaonaigh from Donegal and flautist and whistle player Frankie Kennedy from Belfast. Mairéad learnt to play through her father, Proinsias, a traditional fiddler in an area rich with them, but, unlike earlier generations, had an early enthusiasm for rock artists like David Bowie. Planxty, however, inspired her to look again at Irish traditions, as did British folk-rock bands like Fairport Convention and Steeleye Span.

These were all sensibilities brought to bear when she and Kennedy went into the studio to record a first set of jigs and reels. However, the sound of Altan was and is resolutely traditional. Mhaonaigh and Kennedy both feel Irish musicians play best when they stay within the Celtic traditions, and although they play Scottish tunes (notably from Cape Breton Island), they don't try and incorporate blues or Cajun (of which they are fans). They don't plan their albums a lot, either, taking songs and airs from the oral tradition, in time-honoured fashion. And their roots are reinforced by the fact that Mairéad sings mainly in Gaelic – naturally enough, as it's her first language.

Mairéad reckons Irish traditional music is in a healthier state in the 1990s than it has been for years. "More people are playing than ever – learning instruments, seeing they can have a good time. It's not everywhere, of course, you still have to search it out, but it's there alright. And if we've proved anything, it's that you can stay in the tradition and appeal to a modern audience without using an exotic style for effect." And the reason for that appeal? Mairéad suggests the synthesizer has a big hand in it, with its too-perfect sound, and that Irish music represents a return to real and raw sound. "Musicians playing honestly, without any compromise at all. That's what we strive to do. Listening to a lot of the old musicians in Ireland gives me a real buzz – the same buzz I get from hearing John Lee Hooker or Mick Jagger. It's the heart talking."

While the rock'n'roll revolution was taking place in the 1960s and '70s, however, a revival of interest in traditional music and singing was also happening. Ireland is a small country so it was inevitable that a certain amount of **crossover** took place, although the traffic was mostly in one direction, as rock musicians raided the storehouse of Irishry to lend a Celtic air to their songs.

The most influential figures in blending rock with traditional music, from the 1970s on, have been *bouzouki* and keyboard player **Donal Lunny** and singer **Christy Moore**, the founders of **Planxty**, a band which really changed the way young Irish people looked on the old folk repertoire. Their arrangements of old airs and tunes, and Liam O'Flynn's wonderful uilleann piping, opened a lot of ears and inspired a lot of the new Celtic groups of the last two decades.

In 1981 Lunny and Moore made a more radical attempt to fuse traditional and rock music with the launching of **Moving Hearts**. Their objective was to bring traditional music up-to-date by drawing on all the apparatus of rock, yet without compromising the folk element. It was a tall order, but they came as close as any Irish band has ever done. The line-up included two pipers, saxophone, bass and lead guitars, electric

INSTRUMENTS AND PLAYERS

· ·

We've included mention of the best instrumentalists on the Irish music scene in this round-up of traditional instruments. If you get the chance to see any of them at the festivals, don't miss it.

THE HARP

There are mentions of harp playing in Ireland from as early as the eighth century. Indeed, in Irish legend the harp is credited with magical powers and it has become symbolic of the island (as well as of Guinness). The old Irish harpers were a musical elite, as court musicians to the Gaelic aristocracy, and had a close acquaintance with the court music of Baroque Europe; the hundred or so surviving tunes by the greatest of eighteenth-century harpers, **O'Carolan**, clearly reflect his regard for the Italian composer Corelli.

The harp these players used was metal-stringed and played with the fingernails. Today's harpers play (with their fingertips) a chromatic, gut-string version, which one of its best exponents, **Maire Ni Chathaisaigh**, describes as "neo-Irish". Maire has been notably successful in adapting dance music for the harp, drawing on her knowledge of and love for the piping tradition to breathe life and passion into her music.

Be warned that there is also a bland, anodyne type of twee Irish music played on a gut-strung instrument, often as accompaniment to ersatz medieval banquets held at tourist locations around the country. About as traditional as green beer, it should be given a wide berth.

UILLEANN PIPES

"Seven years learning, seven years practising, and seven years playing" is reputedly what it takes to master the *uilleann* (pronounced "illun") pipes. Perhaps the world's most technically sophisticated bagpipe, it is highly temperamental and difficult to master. The melody is played on a nine-holed chanter with a two-octave range blown by the air from a bag squeezed under the left arm, itself fed by a bellows squeezed under the right elbow. As well as the usual set of drones, the uilleann pipes are marked by their possession of a set of regulators, which can be switched on and off to provide chords. In the hands of a master they can provide a sensitive backing for slow airs and an excitingly rhythmic springboard for dance music.

The pipes arrived in Ireland in the early eighteenth century and reached their present form in the 1890s. Taken up by members of the gentry, who became known as "gentlemen pipers", they were also beloved of the Irish tinkers or travellers, and two different styles evolved, the restrained and delicate **parlour style** exemplified by the late **Seamus Ennis**, and the **traveller style** which, designed as it was to coax money from the pockets of visitors to country fairs, is highly ornamented and even showy.

Some of the most acclaimed musicians of recent years have been pipers: Seamus Ennis, **Willie Clancy**, and travellers **Johnny** and **Felix Doran**, all alas now dead. Today **Liam O'Flynn** is regarded as one of the country's foremost practitioners and has pushed forward the possibilities for piping through his association with classical composer Shaun Davey and with the band Planxty. Other contemporary pipers include **Finbar Furey** and **Davy Spillane**, who learned much of his technique from travelling pipers.

THE BODHRÁN

The *bodhrán* is an instrument much in evidence at traditional sessions, and a recent addition to the dance music line-up. It is not universally welcome, partly because it looks like an easy way into playing – and it isn't. The great piper Seamus

The bodhrán (left) as played by De Dannan

Ennis, when asked how a bodhrán should be played, replied "with a penknife". The bodhrán is a frame drum usually made of goatskin and originally associated with "wren boys" or mummers who went out revelling and playing music on Wrens Day (Dec 26). It looks like a large tambourine without jingles and can be played with a small wooden stick or with the back of the hand.

When played well by the likes of famed Galway musician **Johnny 'Ringo' MacDonagh, Donal Lunny, Mel Mercier**, or **Tommy Hayes**, the bodhrán sounds wonderful, a sympathetic support to the running rhythms of traditional music. Since it was introduced into mainstream traditional music in the 1960s by the great innovator **Sean Ó Riada**, it has developed by leaps and bounds, and new techniques are constantly being invented. Many traditional ensembles now regard it as de rigueur.

FLUTES AND WHISTLES

It's the **wooden flute** of a simple type that is used in Irish music, played mostly in a fairly low register with a quiet and confidential tone which means that it's not heard at its best in pub sessions. Played solo by such musicians as **Matt Malloy** or **Desi Wilson**, its clear flow of notes displays a gentler side to the rushing melodies of jigs and reels.

While anyone can get a note, though not necessarily the right one, out of its little cousin the **tin whistle**, it can take a long time to develop an embouchure capable of producing a beautiful flute tone, and so piper Finbar Furey has introduced the **low whistle**, which takes the place of the flute when there is no proper flute player around.

In the right hands, those of **Packie Byrne** or **Mary Bergin**, for example, the whistle itself is no mean instrument, but it's also suitable for the beginner. If you're interested, make sure you get a D-whistle, as most Irish music is in this key.

FIDDLES

The fiddle is popular all over Ireland, and each area has its own particular characteristics: Donegal breeds fiddlers with a smooth melodic approach but lively bowing techniques, whereas the Sligo style, exemplified in the playing of the great **Michael Coleman**, is more elaborate and flamboyant.

THE BOUZOUKI

At first sight it might seem odd to include the bouzouki on a list of traditional Irish instruments. Nevertheless, its light but piercing tone makes it eminently suitable both for melodies and providing a restrained chordal backing within an ensemble, and since its introduction to the island by **Johnny Moynihan**, in the late 1960s, and subsequent popularization by **Donal Lunny**, it has taken firm root. In the process it has lost much of its original Greek form, and with its flat back the Irish bouzouki is really closer to a member of the mandolin family. Along with other string instruments like the guitar and banjo, which provide supporting harmonies in a "folky" idiom, bouzoukis crop up at sessions all over the country, and some of the best accompanists are bouzouki players.

---

bouzouki, drums and percussion. Their gigs were memorable events, feasts of exciting music that seemed both familiar and new at the same time. Unfortunately the band was too large to survive financially and folded in 1984. Since then there have been a few reunions which have played to crowds of fans old and new. Their 1985 album, "The Storm", released after their break-up, is a landmark in its pioneering use of rock and jazz idioms to rethink the harmonic and rhythmic foundations of Irish music.

Davy Spillane, one of the pipers with Moving Hearts, continues the exploration. He tours and records with a rock line-up and worked with Van Morrison on his album "A Sense of Wonder" while still with the Hearts. More recently, he collaborated with Elvis Costello on "Spike The Beloved Entertainer" and with the Senegalese singer Baaba Maal.

Other groups working in the borderlands of rock include the aforementioned **Altan, Four**

Men and a Dog, Alias Ron Kavana and **Déanta**, each of whom maintains a traditional core repertoire, using rock mainly for its image and sound. "Traditional music with balls" is how the Four Men classify their likeably unclassifiable mix, which is one of the most danceable sounds on the circuit today. They have some great players, too, including Conor Keane on accordion and veteran guitarist Artie McGlynn, whose career takes in the Clancys, Planxty and a spell with top '80s band Patrick Street. Ron Kavana, who is responsible for the recent series of trad reissues on the GlobeStyle Irish label, has a somewhat different approach, combining Irish material and instruments (including pipes) with African and Latin rhythms, and an energetic delivery hailing back to his R&B days.

Clannad are another band who have moved with grace between the trad and pop worlds, and have had a fair amount of success in film

THE CELTIC WORLD

music, fusing Irish tradition into an atmospheric sound. Their former singer, **Enya**, has moved further into the rock sphere, with a kind of Gaelic new wave sound.

Most recently – and with huge success, both in Ireland and Britain – **The Saw Doctors** have broken into the pop mainstream with a string of hit songs about Irish village life. The band, a mix of young and old musicians, using fiddles and accordions and other trad instruments, are from the west of Ireland, and their music owes much to their roots there. It also owes a good deal to the showband tradition of Irish pub bands from the 1960s on. Showbands have a pretty dreadful history but the good Doctors could just be the one great exception. Time will tell.

Less obvious, perhaps, is the influence of sean nós on Irish rock singers. That voice, primitive and complex at the same time, is as much a part of the Irish tradition as any array of instruments, and it can be heard in the best of the music by **Sinead O'Connor, Van Morrison, Dolores Ó Riordan** of The Cranberries, and, not least, in the The Pogues' singer, **Shane McGowan**.

The Pogues, a band of London Irish who emerged in the early 1980s playing a chaotic set of "Oirish" standards and rebel songs, deserve special mention in any feature on Irish music. Originally known as Pogue Mahone ("kiss my arse" in Gaelic), they were inconoclasts to the core, bringing a punk energy to the Irish ballad. They were also blessed with one of the finest Irish songwriters of recent years, Shane McGowan, who captured the casualties and condition of Irish exile in London in a series of superb new ballads.

The Pogues, said fan and producer Elvis Costello, "saved folk from the folkies". Perhaps. Certainly they helped bring a new audience, and a new generation of musicians, back to look at its roots. However, my guess is that the "rock meets traditional" path is a bit of a cul-de-sac, and that what's to be gained and explored, by and large, has been. In its place is something a lot more exciting and broad – the World Music scene. This global ocean is the perfect place for traditional music to flow, picking up and shedding influences along the way, in sessions and at festivals. And the Irish are in poll position to inhabit the world stage in traditional music.

◤ DISCOGRAPHY ◢

COMPILATIONS

Various *Treasures of My Heart* (GlobeStyle, UK). This is a fabulous sampler of GlobeStyle's Irish Series – a projected ten or so compilations of material rescued from the great Topic record label by the musician Ron Kavana. Each of the main series CDs has a thematic angle and there's not a duff track to be heard throughout. Initial titles are:
Leaving Tipperary: Irish Music in America.
Kerry Fiddles.
The Gentleman Pipers: Classic Irish Piping.
In the Smoke: Irish Music in '60s London.
The Rushy Mountain: Music from Sliabh Luachrar.
The Wandering Minstrels: Irish Dance Music.
Hurry the Jug: Songs, Lilting and Storytelling.
A Living Thing: Contemporary Classics.
The Coolin: Irish Laments and Airs.
Sleeve notes are admirably copious, too, providing an excellent overview of the various strands of Irish music.
Various *Bringing It All Back Home* (BBC, UK). Music from a TV series which documented the journey, development and influence of traditional music. Songs in Irish and English, dance tunes, airs, laments, piping, fiddling, whistling, group and solo, country music, and trad-meets-classical. The pick of the crop.
Various *Our Musical Heritage* (Funduireacht an Riadaigh, Ireland). With its accompanying book this three-cassette anthology of singers and instrumentalists, compiled by Seán Ó Riada from 1960s radio programmes, is an indispensable guide to all aspects of Irish traditional music.
Various *Fiddlesticks* (Nimbus, UK). Convincing proof, if it were needed, of the quality of Irish fiddling. Recorded at a festival of Donegal fiddlers in 1991, this disc features great ensemble playing plus solos from Tommy Peoples, Seamus and Kevin Glackin.

Various *Dear Old Erin's Isle* (Nimbus, UK). Superb recording of a 1992 Cork festival which brought together some of America's best Irish musicians, including old-timers like piper Joe Shannon and melodeon player Tom Doherty, and young fiddlers like Eileen Ives and Liz Carroll.

SINGERS

Beauty an Oileain *Music and Song of the Blasket Islands* (Claddagh, Ireland). The Blasket Islands – off the southwest coast of Ireland – are renowned for their music and singing and this album testifies to a passionate involvement. Taken from a variety of sources, from the 1950s to the '90s, these remarkable songs, tunes and airs evoke the soundscape of a life and lives long vanished.
Maighread Ni Dhomhnaill *No Dowry* (Gael Linn, Ireland). Singing in Irish and English by one of the great traditional singers. Here she is in wonderful voice, unaccompanied, and accompanied with understated skill and sympathy by Donal Lunny.
Joe Heaney *Irish Traditional Songs In Gaelic and English* (Ossian, Ireland; cassette only). Heaney is one of the greatest sean nós singers, from Carna in the Connemara Gaeltacht. This selection includes classics of the sean nós repertoire as well as Irish traditional material in English. Someone once said of Heaney, "he opened his mouth and the voice came out like an iron bar".

INSTRUMENTAL

Mary Bergin *Feadoga Stain: Traditional Music on the Tin Whistle* (Gael Linn, Ireland). A landmark recording by a master musician. On two slow airs and a "rake" of dance tunes, Bergin is accompanied variously by Johnny "Ringo" MacDonagh on bodhrán and bones, and by Alec Finn on bouzouki and mandocello. Yet to be surpassed.

Ⓒ **Maire Ni Chathasaigh and Chris Newman** *The Carolan Albums* (Old Bridge Music, Ireland). Guitar and Irish harp join together on arrangements of harp music by the great Turlough Ó Carolan, the so-called "last of the old Irish harpers". Ó Carolan's music interfaces the old Irish harp repertoire with the Baroque music popular in Ireland in the seventeenth and eighteenth centuries. These tracks crack with life in superb and precise arrangements.

Ⓒ **Michael Coleman** *Michael Coleman, 1891–1945* (Gael Linn, Ireland). The great Sligo fiddler at his best, digitally remastered, on a superb double CD.

Johnny Doran *The Bunch of Keys* (CBE-Gael Linn, Ireland). The classic 1940s recordings of Doran on uilleann pipes. Available on cassette only.

Ⓒ **Seamus Ennis** *The Wandering Minstrel* (Green Linnet, US). Like Doran, the late great master-piper, Seamus Ennis still influences traditional players of all instruments today. This recording of a major figure in performing, collecting and pre-serving traditional music offers piping at its best.

Ⓒ **Paddy Glackin** *Rabharta Ceoil In Full Spate* (Gael Linn, Ireland). Glackin is a superb fiddle player, with a strong Donegal influence in his style and selection of tunes. Here he is accompanied by arranging-wizard Donal Lunny, and joined by brothers Kevin and Seamus on fiddle and Robbie Hannon on uilleann pipes.

Ⓒ **Martin Hayes** *Martin Hayes* (Green Linnet, US). Rooted in the Clare style of fiddle playing learnt from his father and uncle, both famous musicians, Martin Hayes also draws on blues and jazz influences. Superbly expressive playing, at its best on the unaccompanied tracks.

Ⓒ **Noel Hill and Tony MacMahon** *IgGnoc na Graí* (Gael Linn, Ireland). Recorded one memorable night at a session in Dan Connell's pub in Knocknagree, County Kerry. Hill and MacMahon, on concertina and accordion or "box" respective-ly, play for a group of set-dancers. Wonderful music and atmosphere. Almost as good as being there.

Ⓒ **Eileen Ivers** *Eileen Ivers* (Green Linnet, US). Eileen Ivers is a young Irish-American fiddler – and already among the best in the business, with a well-judged balance between tradition and innovation. Her slow air playing and electrifying tune play-ing mix superbly with African percussion, making for an album of wonderful tonal moods.

Ⓒ **Seán Ó Riada** *Ó Riada* (Gael Linn, Ireland). A live recording by this seminal arranger and player who set traditional Irish music on its current revival.

Ⓒ **Brendan Power** *New Irish Harmonica* (Punchmusic, Ireland). New Zealand-born harmonica player, Brendan Power adds his name to a small but illustrious list of harmoni-ca master players. In his case virtuoso technique combines with a sympathetic approach to traditional music informed by jazz and blues. All the "bent" or "blued" notes are effortlessly expressed, while the ornamentation intrinsic to traditional music is perfectly executed.

Ⓒ **Sharon Shannon** *Sharon Shannon* (Solid, Ireland/Philo, US). One of the brightest stars on the traditional music horizon, this young woman is a virtuoso player of both box and fiddle. She plays both on this exciting album featuring a range of music from old traditional to Cajun, French Canadian, and contemporary trad. Some fine trad and not-so-trad musicians (including Adam Clayton of U2) accompany.

GROUPS

Ⓒ **Altan** *Island Angel* (Green Linnet, US). The deep root of the Ulster tradition, particularly that of Donegal, makes for an album both coherent and fresh. Regional style restated in con-temporary idiom comes through on great tunes and five beautiful songs from Mairead Ni Mhaonaigh, who also plays masterfully on fiddle.

Ⓒ **The Bothy Band** *The Best of the Bothy Band* (Green Linnet, US). One of the great bands of the 1970s, featuring fiddler Kevin Burke, flute virtuoso Matt Molloy, and Donal Lunny.

Ⓒ **The Chieftains** *Chieftains Four* (Shanachie, US). An all-time favourite slice of Chieftains, from 1973.

Ⓒ **Clannad** *Dúlamán* (Gael Lynn, Ireland). A 1976 album of fresh, syncopated, jazz-influenced arrangements from this high-ly influential band.

Ⓒ **Déanta** *Déanta* (Green Linnet, US). Stunning debut from this Country Antrim band of young virtuosos.

Ⓒ **De Dannan** *De Dannan* (Polydor, Ireland). The mighty Galway band at their awe-inspiring best. Flying dance music and great singing from Mary Black, Dolores Keane and Maura O'Connell.

Ⓒ **Four Men & A Dog** *Shifting Gravel* (Topic, UK). One of the best new bands on the circuit, the six Four Men stay close to traditions in their material, but play it with a voice and energy of their own, led by bodhrán player extraordi-naire, Gino Lupari.

Ⓒ **Moving Hearts** *The Storm* (Son, Ireland). This instrumental compilation released after the demise of the ground-breaking contemporary traditional band has a heady mixture of tradi-tional and contemporary tunes on a grand collection of instruments: saxophone, pipes, percussion, electric guitar, bouzouki and bodhrán. One of the bravest attempts to marry rock and trad idioms.

Ⓒ **Planxty** *Planxty* (Shanachie, US). The 1973 debut that inspired a new generation of players.

Ⓒ **The Pogues** *Rum, Sodomy and the Lash* (Stiff, UK) and *If I Should Fall From Grace With God* (Pogue/Island, UK) . The two most irresistible stashes of Poguery. *Rum* features their original London Oirish punk-roots sound; *If I Should Fall* is a more mixed bag with a touch of Latin and Balkans in the rhythm, and the beautiful "Fairytale Of New York" duet between Shane MacGowan and Kirsty MacColl.

Ⓒ **Van Morrison and The Chieftains** *Irish Heartbeat* (Phonogram, UK). Van employs that legendary Irish soul to wonderful effect on traditional material.

THE CURSE OF THE WHITE HEATHER CLUB

SCOTTISH MUSIC HAS SURVIVED ANDY STEWART

Scottish music has entered the 1990s in remarkably fine health, with a bedrock of Celtic groups – led by the Boys of the Lough, Silly Wizard, The Tannahill Weavers and Runrig – storming through traditional material in a blaze of bagpipes and flying fiddles. Colin Irwin wonders how we could ever have imagined there was no more north of the border than Andy Stewart and the Bay City Rollers.

Legendary fiddler Scott Skinner

There used to be a British television show – still fondly remembered by people who buy Max Bygraves and Val Doonican records – called "The White Heather Show". This, the British public were gleefully informed each week, was the sound of Scotland, all men in kilts, led by the likes of Andy Stewart and Jimmy Shand, with their accordions and sentimental songs of the highlands. The show ran for many years, and – let's not be mean – probably gave an awful lot of people an awful lot of pleasure. It also damned Scottish music with an image of banal glibness from which it looked like never recovering.

While Jimmy Shand's gung-ho accordion playing became an institution and the nation hooted along with Andy Stewart's "Scottish Soldier" and "Donald Where's Your Troosers" (a British number one in the 1960s and the '90s), Scots musicians were donated a legacy that was to dog them for the next two decades. To make any credible headway beyond the shackles of an image decimated by kilts and highland flings, they were forced to deny the very thing that provided their one claim to be unique in the first place – their Scottishness.

For two decades even the best exponents of a purely Scots music had teetered on the edge of ridicule. The excellent **Ian Campbell Folk Group** (who included future Fairport Daves, Swarbrick and Pegg, while Ian's sons, Aly and Robin, went on to form UB40) had flirted with commercialism and pop sensibilities – as virtually every folk group of the era was compelled to do – and was too often unfairly bracketed with England's derided Spinners

as a result. It was a similar cross borne by others of the period, particularly **Robin Hall and Jimmie MacGregor** (remembered in Britain for the awful "Football Crazy" novelty hit) and **The Corries**, both of whom were too closely associated with the curse of the White Heather Club. Yet The Corries, especially, laced their blandness with bold enterprise, inventing their own instrumentation and writing the new unofficial national anthem, "Flower of Scotland".

Pop and rock, of course, always had a thriving tradition of Scots bands but mostly their origins were incidental, or laid on as thick as the tartan on the Bay City Rollers' trousers. It was to be the late 1970s before Scots musicians investigated their own musical history with any real sense of purpose. **The Boys of the Lough** led the way, initially driven on by the instinctive brilliance of their Shetland fiddler Aly Bain, and they were followed by **The Battlefield Band**, who consciously attempted to hack away the old Scots cliches.

Then **Alba** did the unthinkable and introduced bagpipes to a contemporary rock line-up, paving the way for a rush of groups like **Silly Wizard** and **The Tannahill Weavers** to sweep Scots music into the Eighties with pride. Scots bands could at last draw on their evocative national fund of music, free of self-consciousness, and the results were encouraging. In the 1990s, the Scots variant of Celtic music has found contemporary-sounding champions in bands like **Runrig** and **Capercaillie**, who have blended mass rock appeal and techniques with ancient inspirations, while even out-and-out rock bands like **Deacon Blue** and **Simple Minds** have drawn liberally on traditional Scottish modes of melody and instrumentation.

THE SCOTTISH TRADITION SERIES

. . . .

Scottish traditional music — in its deepest, darkest manifestations — has been superbly documented in a series of archive recordings produced by Hamish Henderson and others at Edinburgh University's School of Scottish Studies. The highlights of this collection have recently found their way onto a series of (to date) sixteen CDs, which, if you're seriously interested in the roots of many of the musicians covered in this article, are nothing less than a treasure trove.

The first volume in the series, **Bothy Ballads**, is one of the most important and fascinating. These narrative songs were composed, sung and passed around the unmarried farmworkers accommodated in bothies or outhouses in late-Victorian and Edwardian days. The songs were often comic or satirical, such as warnings about skinflint farmers to be avoided at the hiring markets. Under the bothy system, workers would move on from farm to farm after six-month "fees", so the songs were in constant circulation and re-invention. They include some gorgeous ballads and instrumentals.

Music from the Western Isles (volume 2) is another intriguing disc: Gaelic songs recorded in the Hebrides, including some great examples of **"mouth music"**, the vocal dance music where sung rhythms are employed to take the place of instruments. There are pibroch songs on this disc, too — the vocal equivalent of the pipers' airs and laments. On volume 3, **Waulking Songs from Barra**, you enter another extraordinary domain, that of Gaelic washing songs, thumped out by women to the rhythms of their cloth pounding. Played this blind, you could imagine yourself to be thousands of miles from Scotland. More amazing vocal traditions are unleashed on volume 6, **Gaelic Psalms from Barra**, with their slow, fractured unison singing.

An equally compelling vocal tradition is that of the Scottish **Travelling Singers**, showcased on volume 5, **The Muckle Sangs**. This is a delight, including virtually all the greats, Jeannie Robertson, Lizzie Higgins and the Stewarts of Blairgowrie among them.

Fiddle music is also outstandingly represented in the series, with several volumes devoted to the art. Volume 4, **Shetland Fiddle Music**, features classic players such as Tom Anderson and George Sutherland, who were to exert such influence on the likes of Aly Bain and Catriona MacDonald (see box on Aly Bain). Volume 9, **The Fiddler and His Art**, is a fine overall compilation, showing the different styles prevalent around the country.

Finally, as you'd expect, the Scottish Tradition has recordings of some of the finest **pibroch pipers**, among them George Moss (volume 15), and pipe majors William MacLean, Robert Brown and R.B. Nicol (volumes 10, 11 and 12). *The Scottish Tradition Series discs are available on CD and cassette from the Scottish label Greentrax (Cockenzie Business Centre, Edinburgh Rd, Cockenzie, East Lothian EH32 0HL; ☎ 0875-814155).*

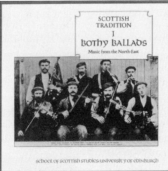

SCOTTISH TRADITION
1
BOTHY BALLADS
Music from the North-East

school of scottish studies university of edinburgh

"The White Heather Club" is now well and truly buried, and at last some of the traditions are being aired, too, in their older forms. The dance music of **Bob Smith's Ideal Band** has had a couple of albums devoted to it, and the extraordinary *strathspey* rhythms of legendary fiddle player **Scott Skinner** have had belated exposure, too. Also getting a fresh listening – especially with the releases of the Scottish Tradition Series (see box) – are the repertoires of **traditional Gaelic songs**, like the wonderful **Cathie-Ann McPhee**, still current in the Scottish rural outposts, and those of the old **travelling singers** – people like the **Stewarts** of Blairgowrie, **Isla Cameron**, **Lizzie Higgins** and, the greatest of them all, Lizzie's mother, **Jeannie Robertson**.

THE PIPES OF WRATH

Bagpipes are synonymous with Scotland yet they are not, oddly enough, a specifically Scottish instrument. The pipes were once to be found right across Europe, and pockets remain, across the English border in Northumbria, all over Ireland, in Spain and Italy, and notably in eastern European countries like Romania and The Czech and Slovak republics, where bagpipe festivals are still held in rural areas. In Scotland, bagpipes seem to have made their appearance around the fifteenth century, and over the next hundred years or so they took on several forms, including quieter varieties, both bellows and mouth blown, which allowed a diversity of playing styles.

The highland bagpipe form known as **pibroch** (*piobaireachd* in Gaelic) evolved around this time, created by clan pipers for military, gathering, lamenting and marching purposes. Legend among the clan pipers of this era were the MacCrimmons (they of the famous "MacCrimmon's Lament", composed during the Jacobite rebellion), although they were but one of several important piping clans, among which were the MacArthurs, MacKays and MacDonalds, and others. In the seventeenth and eighteenth centuries, through the influence of the British army, reels and *strathspeys* joined the repertoire, and in the early nineteenth century a tradition of military pipe bands had emerged, and with it a network of piping competitions.

The bagpipe tradition has continued uninterrupted to the present, although for much of this century under the domination of the military and the folklorists Piobaireachd Society. Recently, however, a number of Scottish musicians have revived the pipes in new and innovative forms. **Alan McLeod** succeeded in knitting the pipes into a framework of instruments, playing as a teenager with the band **Alba**, and his lead has been consolidated by the **Battlefield Band**, whose arrangements involve the beautifully measured piping of **Duncan McGillivray**, and **Iain MacDonald**, who had previously piped along with rock instruments in the band **Ossian**.

Alongside all this came a revived interest in traditional piping, and in particular the strathspeys, slow airs and reels, which had tended to get submerged beneath the familiar military territory of marches and laments. The century's great modern-day bagpipe players, notably **John Burgess**, received a belated wider exposure. His legacy includes a masterful album and a renowned teaching career to ensure that the old piping tradition marches proudly into the next century.

FOLK AND CELTIC REVIVALS

The Scots' first forays into a new "traditional music" grew out of the folk and acoustic scene in mid-1960s Glasgow and Edinburgh. It was at Clive's Incredible Folk Club, in Glasgow, that **The Incredible String Band** made their debut, led by Mike Heron and Robin Williamson. The Incredibles took an unfashionable glance back into their own past on the one hand, while plunging headlong into psychedelia and other uncharted areas on the other. Their success broke down significant barriers for them and others, both in and out of Scotland, and a quarter of a century on Robin Williamson is still tinkering

DICK GAUGHAN Handful of Earth

around with his Celtic roots, with perhaps less gusto but just as much guile.

In their wake came a succession of Scottish folk-rock crossover musicians. Glasgow-born **Bert Jansch** launched "folk super-group" **Pentangle** with Jacqui McShee, John Renbourn and Danny Thompson, and the flute-playing Ian Anderson found rock success with **Jethro Tull**. Meanwhile, the folk clubs in Glasgow and Edinburgh gave rise to an interesting mix of traditional and pop artists. Among the latter, Barbara Dickson, Gallagher & Lyle, Rab Noakes and Gerry Rafferty went on to mainstream success, while a more traditional Scottish sound was promoted by the likes of **Archie, Ray and Cilla Fisher**, who sang new and traditional ballads, individually and together, the **McCalmans**, who employed bodhráns, mandolins and traditional material, and, perhaps most crucially, **Dick Gaughan**.

SHETLAND MAGIC: ALY BAIN

· ·

Aly Bain has been a minor deity among Scottish musicians for three decades. A fiddle player of exquisite technique and individuality, he has been the driving force of one of Scotland's all-time great bands, **Boys Of The Lough**, throughout that time, while latterly diversifying roles as a TV presenter and author. In these guises, he has been instrumental in spreading the wings of Scottish music to an even greater extent. First and foremost, though, Bain is a Shetlander and his greatest legacy is the inspiration he has provided for a thriving revival of fortunes for Shetland's own characteristic tradition.

Aly was brought up in the capital of Shetland, Lerwick, and was enthused to play the fiddle by Bob Duncan – who endlessly played him records by the strathspey king **Scott Skinner** – and later the old maestro **Tom Anderson**. Duncan and Anderson were the last of an apparently dying breed, and the youthful Aly was an odd sight dragging his fiddle along to join in with the old guys at the Shetland Fiddlers Society. Players like Willie Hunter Jnr and Snr, Willie Pottinger and Alex Hughson were legends locally, but they belonged to another age and the magic of Shetland fiddle playing – one inflected with the eccentricity of the isolated environment and the influence of nearby Scandinavia.

By the time the teenage Aly was persuaded to leave for the mainland, Shetland was changing by the minute, and the discovery of North Sea oil altered it beyond redemption, as the new indus-

trial riches trampled its unique community spirit and sense of tradition. The old fiddlers gradually faded and died, and Shetland music seemed destined to disappear too.

That it didn't was largely down to Aly. After a spell with Billy Connolly (then a folk artist, before finding comedy success as a professional Glaswegian) on the Scottish folk circuit, Aly found himself working with blues iconoclast Mike Whellans, and then the two of them tumbled into a link-up with two Irishmen, Robin Morton and Cathal McConnell, in a group they called Boys Of The Lough. The last thing Aly Bain imagined was that he'd spend the next quarter of a century answering to this name. But he did, and his joyful artistry, unwavering integrity and unquenchable appetite and commitment to the music of his upbringing kept Shetland music alive in a manner he could never have imagined. Even more importantly, it stung the imagination of the generation that followed.

These days, Shetland music is buzzing again, with its own annual festival a treat of music-making and drinking that belies the impersonal industrialization of Shetland. There are young musicians pouring out of the place, among whom **Catriona MacDonald** – who was also taught by Tom Anderson, in his last days – is the current cream of the crop. She is adept at classical music, and is fast becoming an accomplished mistress of Norwegian music, and her mum went to school with Aly Bain – which in Shetland these days counts for an awful lot.

Gaughan's passionate artistry towers like a colossus above three decades. He started out in the Edinburgh folk club scene with an impenetrable accent, a deep belief in the socialist commitment of traditional song, and a guitar technique that had old masters of the art hanging on to the edge of their seats. For a couple of years in the early 1970s, he played along with Aly Bain (see box feature) in **The Boys of the Lough**, an Irish-Scottish band that was knocking out fiery versions of trad Celtic material. Gaughan became frustrated, however, by the limitations of a primarily instrumental (and fiddle-dominated) group and subsequently formed **Five Hand Reel**. Again playing Scots-Irish traditional material, they might have been the greatest folk-rock band of them all if they hadn't marginally missed the Fairport/Steeleye Span boat.

Leaving to pursue an independent career, Gaughan became a fixture on the folk circuit and made a series of albums exploring Scots and Irish traditional music and re-interpreting the material for guitar. His "Handful of Earth" (1981) was perhaps the single best solo folk album of the decade, a record of stunning intensity with enough contemporary relevance and historical belief to grip all generations of music fans. And though sparing in his output, and modest about his value in the genre, he's also become one of the best songwriters of his generation too. An amazing man.

EWAN MACCOLL: THE MAN FROM AUCHTERARDER

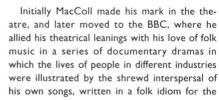

T he single most gifted, influential and inspirational figure in modern British folk song was a man from Auchterarder, Perthshire, called Ewan MacColl. He was enthused with the unique spirit and dignity of Scottish music by his parents, both lowlanders, and became a superb ballad singer, devoting himself to the music with such zeal and political sense of purpose that it still colours people's thinking years later.

He is perhaps best remembered now as a gloriously evocative songwriter – with the ability to switch from tender love songs to crushing political venom without apparent change in demeanour. But it was his revolutionary championing of indigenous folk song that caused such a furore, and played such a fierce role in the preservation of folk song wherever it came from. Singers and musicians, decreed MacColl, should only play music of their own country: a rule he gained much notoriety for imposing at his own folk clubs. It seems a ludicrous notion in hindsight but with American music sweeping the world in the late 1950s/early '60s it may well have saved large swathes of traditional British folk music.

Initially MacColl made his mark in the theatre, and later moved to the BBC, where he allied his theatrical leanings with his love of folk music in a series of documentary dramas in which the lives of people in different industries were illustrated by the shrewd interspersal of his own songs, written in a folk idiom for the series. These eight "radio ballads" were major breakthroughs for folk music, and from that point on MacColl was a central figure in the evolution of British roots music. He continued to perform with his American wife Peggy Seeger almost to his death in 1989, his hatred of the Thatcher government inspiring him to ever greater heights of savagery in his songwriting.

Elvis Costello made his public debut down the bill at a Ewan MacColl gig. Shane MacGowan of The Pogues says the only time he ever set foot in a folk club was when MacColl was appearing. And Elvis Presley recorded one of his songs – the Grammy Award winning "First Time Ever I Saw Your Face". They should be thinking about building some kind of statue up there in Auchterarder.

GAELIC ROCKING

Scottish music took an unexpected twist in 1978 with the low-key release of an album called "Play Gaelic". It was made by a little-known group called **Runrig**, who took their name from the old Scottish oil field system of agriculture, and worked primarily in the backwaters of the highlands and islands. The thing, though, that stopped people in their tracks was the fact that they were writing original material in Gaelic. This was the first time any serious Scottish working band had achieved any sort of attention with Gaelic material, although Ossian were touching on it around a similar time, as were Nah-Oganaich.

Runrig have since marched on to unprecedented heights. They slowly chipped away at prejudices, conducting their own musical experiments adopting accordions and bagpipes, sharper arrangements, electric instruments, full-blown rock styles, surviving the inevitable personnel changes and the continuous carping of critics accusing them of

One-time Mouth Musician Talitha MacKenzie

Gaelic rockers Capercaillie

selling out with every new market conquered. They even made one epic concept album, "Recovery", which effectively related the history of the Gael in one collection, provoking unprecedented interest in the Gaelic language after years of it being regarded in Scotland as moribund and defunct.

Runrig are now a long way from the gentle little ceilidh group that started out playing to tiny audiences in the highlands, appearing in front of rock audiences at concert halls around the world where only a partial proportion of the audience are jocks in exile. Their own Gaelic input is marginal these days, but they started a whole new ball rolling.

Although few made the connection, because of their geographical remoteness and isolation from the rest of the scene, Runrig were basically making a logical step on from the work of those classic Edinburgh/Glasgow bands whose names roll off with such ease you imagine there's an umbilical link binding them together: **The Corries** and the **McCalmans**; the **Whistlebinkies** and the **J.S.D Band**; **Silly Wizard** and **The Tannahill Weavers**; **Alba** and the **Battlefield Band**; **Ossian** and **The Boys Of The Lough**; **Mouth Music** and **Capercaillie**. Not all of these, by any means, sung in Gaelic, but in each the Gaelic element was strong within the music, in the use either of traditional material or instruments.

Among the ranks of these bands, each with their own agendas and styles, are some of Scotland's most important and influential contemporary musicians. **Silly Wizard**, especially, featured a singer of cutting quality in **Andy M. Stewart** (and did he need that M.), while **Phil and Johnny Cunningham** have subsequently gone on to display a pioneering zeal in their efforts to use their skills on accordion and fiddle to knit Scottish traditional music with other cultures. **Mouth Music**, too, were innovative: a Scots-origin duo of Martin Swan and Talitha MacKenzie, who mixed Gaelic vocals (including the traditional "mouth music"

THE CELTIC WORLD

techniques of sung rhythms) with African percussion and dance sounds. The band have recently crossed further over into the dance world, with a new vocalist, while **Talitha MacKenzie** has gone solo, radically transforming traditional Scottish songs, which she clears from the dust of folklore with wonderful multitracked vocals and the characteristic Mouth Music African rhythms. On a more roots front, **The Whistlebinkies** were notable for employing only traditional instruments, including fine *clarsach* (Celtic harp) from Judith Peacock.

These bands' collective success has paved the way for more tolerance and encouragement for the "purer" Scots musicians and singers: clarsach player **Alison Kinnaird**; singers **Savourna Stevenson, Christine Primrose,** **Arthur Cormack**, and **Heather Heywood**; and the amazing **Wrigley sisters** from Orkney – teenage girls playing Scottish traditional music in the 1990s with unlimited technical accomplishment and attitude with a capital A.

Above all, though, the Runrig baton has been grabbed by the excellent **Capercaillie**, who themselves have risen from Argyll pub sessions to flirt with mass commercial appeal, reworking Gaelic and traditional songs from the West Highlands. As yet, they don't appear to have compromised their ideals one iota on the way, and don't look as if they intend to, either. Not while the fulcrum of the band revolves around the arrangements of Manus Lunny and the gorgeous singing of Karen Mattheson. It'll be a long time before Scots Gaels are forgotten again with people like them around.

◢ DISCOGRAPHY ◣

In addition to the discs below, note the Scottish Tradition Series (Greentrax, UK), detailed in the box on p.17. This series, now up to sixteen titles, is by far the most important source of traditional Scottish music – and many of the discs are a treat.

TRADITIONAL

Ⓓ **Aly Bain** *Aly Bain and Friends* (Greentrax, UK). One of the bestselling Scottish albums of modern times, compiled from a TV series Bain produced on traditional Scottish music.
Ⓓ **John Burgess** *King of the Highland Pipers* (Topic, UK). The greatest modern exponent of bagpipes demonstrates his art to devastating effect through *piobaireachd*, strathspeys, hornpipes, reels and marches. Not for the faint-hearted!
Ⓓ **Cathie-Ann McPhee** *The Language of the Gael* (Greentrax, UK). This superb 1980s recording, re-released on CD, is some of the best Gaelic singing you're ever likely to hear.
Scott Skinner and Bill Hardie *The Music Of Scott Skinner* (Topic, UK). An essential Scottish roots album, featuring rare and authentic recordings by the elusive genius of the fiddle — and the weird strathspey style in particular – dating from 1908. Some of the quality is understandably distorted, though the collection is well supported by modern interpretations of Skinner's style by Bill Hardie.
Bob Smith's Ideal Band *Better Than An Orchestra* (Topic, UK). Neatly described on the sleeve as "a fantasia of music and fun from the Glasgow of the Thirties" – and that's about the size of it. There's some wondrous playing among the showbiz.
Belle Stewart *Queen Among The Heather* (Topic, UK). One of the legendary Stewarts of Blairgowrie, Belle is a gloriously colourful singer with an evocative array of travelling songs. Another excellent album on Topic, **The Travelling Stewarts**, features other members of her family, including the great Jeannie Robertson and her daughter Lizzie Higgins. June Tabor is among the younger singers who regard this as a crucial collection – and who's to disagree?
Ⓓ **Various** *Cape Breton Island* (Nimbus, UK). Vibrant, live recordings of Scottish fiddling as preserved amongst the many Scots of Cape Breton Island, Nova Scotia, including the revered Buddy McMaster. A rich collection of strathspreys, reels, jigs and marches for pipes and fiddles, with piano accompaniment (a characteristically Scottish combination) and lots of stamping feet.

Ⓓ **Various** *The Silver Bow* (Topic, UK). This collection of Shetland fiddle tunes was notable for bringing together the old maestro Tom Anderson and his star pupil Aly Bain. They played both individually and together on the album and the effect is never less than enthralling.

SINGERS AND FOLKIES

Ⓓ **Eric Bogle** *Something Of Value* (Sonet, UK/Philo, US). Bogle emigrated from Scotland to work in Australia as an accountant, but when he reappeared he was hailed for writing one of the great modern folk songs, the anti war epic "The Band Played Waltzing Matilda". His writing isn't matched by his singing but that's well cloaked here by all-star support.
Ian Campbell Group *The Singing Campbells* (Topic, UK). Ian and family sing old and new ballads. Unaccompanied and great.
Ⓓ **Archie Fisher** *Will Ye Gang, Love* (Green Linnet, US). Mid-1970s album of old and new ballads by the scion of the Fisher family.
Cilla Fisher and Artie Trezise *Cilla and Artie* (Topic, UK). Almost worth including just for Cilla's imperious vocal performance of the late Stan Rogers' "The Jeannie C", this album, released in 1979, has a freshness and friendliness that holds good today.
Ⓓ **Ray Fisher** *Traditional Songs of Scotland* (Saydisc, UK). A third exquisite album of Fisher ballad singing.
Ⓓ **Dick Gaughan** *Handful Of Earth* (Green Linnet, US). A majestic album that could make you laugh, cry and explode with anger with every twist and nuance of Gaughan's delivery. When *Folk Roots* magazine asked people to vote for their favourite album of the 1980s, this won by a street – and deservedly so. A mix of traditional and modern songs, its dynamism and relevance is no less formidable over a decade on.
Bert Jansch *Early Bert* (Xtra, UK). Jansch never bettered this album, originally released as "Nicola".
Ⓓ **Ewan MacColl** *Black And White* (Cooking Vinyl, UK/Green Linnet, US). This posthumous compilation, lovingly compiled by his family, showcases MacColl's superb technique as a singer, his gift for choruses ("Dirty Old Town"), his colourful observation as a lyricist ("The Driver's Song"), and his raging sense of injustice {"Black And White", written after the Sharpeville Massacre of 1963). A fitting epitaph to one of the all-time greats of British folk song.

Andy M. Stewart, Phil Cunningham and Manus Lunny
Fire In The Glen (Shanachie, US). Two former members of Silly Wizard combine with an Irishman in a formidable celebration of Scottish traditional music. Phil Cunningham's brilliance as an accordion player is demonstrated on any number of albums, but it's especially impressive placed against the wonderful, wonderful singing of Andy M. Stewart.

CONTEMPORARY GROUPS

Battlefield Band *Anthem For The Common Man* (Temple, UK). The best release from the most consistently innovative Scottish group. Highlights are the explosive piping of the outstanding Duncan McGillivray and the blossoming of Brian McNeil and Alan Reid as songwriters (just listen to "I Am The Common Man" and "The Yew Tree").

Boys of the Lough *Good Friends – Good Music* (Transatlantic, UK). The album which saw the Boys decide to step beyond the confines of British and Irish tunes – already soundly mastered on a series of fine albums – to share their style with guest musicians from other cultures. It worked brilliantly.

Capercaillie *Delirium* (BMG, UK). A group who tend to get very upset when they're written off as Scotland's answer to Clannad, and quite right too. They have in Karen Mattheson one of the supreme singers around today, and their delicacy of touch is also matched by a thriving fire in their bellies that has brought them to the attention of rock audiences. *Delirium* includes "Coisich a Ruin" (Walk My Beloved), a Gaelic work song that achieved UK chart success.

The Easy Club *Skirie Beat* (Rel Records, UK). An admirably ambitious and sadly underrated group, the Easy Club took the baton from the more thoughtful Scots bands of the '70s and ran with it at a pace, injecting traditional rhythms with a jazz sense. MacColl's "First Time Ever I Saw Your Face" never sounded like this before.

Five Hand Reel *Five Hand Reel* (RCA, UK). Three Scotsmen (Dick Gaughan, Bobby Eaglesham and Dave Tulloch), an Irishman (Tom Hickland), and an Englishman (Barry Lyons), in full-blooded stride early in their career. They could be dauntingly erratic on stage and record, but when they got it right, as here, they were stupendous.

Mactalla *Mairdih Gaol is Ceol* (Topic, UK). Impressive collection of songs and tunes by a group comprising many of the best Gaelic musicians around – Blair Douglas, Arthur Cormack, Christine Primrose, Alison Kinnaird and Eilidh Mackenzie.

Mouth Music *Mouth Music* and *Mo-Di* (Triple Earth, UK). Gaelic songs meet ambient dance and African sampling. One of the best Celtic fusions around and arguably surpassed by Talitha MacKenzie's recent solo album *Sòlas* (Riverboat Records, UK).

Ossian *Borders* (Iona, UK). The band's finest hour: singing, harps, bagpipes, accordion, fiddles, all gel perfectly.

Runrig *Alba* (Pinnacle, UK). An excellent "best of" compilation of this most dynamic Gaelic band, who have now made it well beyond Scots or folk frontiers.

Silly Wizard *Live Wizardry* (Green Linnet, US). A great double CD live set from 1988. Also available on video.

The Tannahill Weavers *The Best of The Tannahill Weavers 1979–89* (Green Linnet, US). The band's own selection from their first decade.

Various *The Sampler* (Topic, UK). Mid-price sampler of Topic's Scottish artists, including Alison Kinnaird and Battlefield Band.

HARPS, BARDS AND PUNKS

THE FORGOTTEN CELTS OF WALES

Welsh music tends to conjure up images of miners raising the roof of their local chapel – and, indeed, despite the near obliteration of the mining industry, male voice choirs remain a dominant feature of Welsh rural life. But Welsh music extends out into village halls, clubs, festivals and pubs, where Saturday nights often resound with impromptu harmonies. In quieter venues, harp players repay their musical debt to ancestors who accompanied the ancient bards, while modern folk draws directly from the broader Celtic musical tradition. There are exponents of Welsh-language rock, too, who have traded in their dreams of commercial success for unabashed nationalism. William Price and Chris Sharratt report from the valleys.

The Welsh word "gwerin", the closest approximation of "folk", has a much wider meaning than its English counterpart, taking in popular culture as well as folklore. In a Welsh *gwyl werin* (folk festival), you're as likely to encounter the local rock band as the local dance team, and the whole community will be there – not just committed specialists. If you're roaming around Wales, look out, too, for the word *twmpath* on posters – it's the equivalent of a barn dance or ceilidh and is used when Welsh dances are the theme of the night.

It's often said that the Welsh love singing but ignore their native instrumental music. Certainly, Welsh folk song has always been close to the heart of popular culture, acting as a carrier of political messages and social protest, while traditional Welsh music and dance have had the difficult task of fighting back to life from near-extinction following centuries of political and

WELSH HARPS

·······················

Historically the most important instrument in the folk repertoire, the **harp** has been played in Wales since at least the eleventh century. In recent years craftsmen have recreated the ancient *crwth* (a stringed instrument which may have been either plucked or bowed), the *pibgorn* (a reed instrument with a cow's horn for a bell) and the *pibacwd* (the primitive Welsh bagpipe). Some groups have adopted these instruments, but their primitive design and performance means they rarely blend happily with modern instruments.

The simple early harps were ousted in the seventeenth century by the arrival of the **triple harp**, with its complicated string arrangement (two parallel rows sounding the same note, with a row of accidentals between them), giving it a unique, rich sound. The nineteenth-century swing towards classical concert music saw the invasion of the large chromatic pedal harps that still dominate today, but the triple, always regarded as the traditional Welsh harp, was kept alive, as a portable instrument, by gypsy musicians. It has been making something of a comeback in gwerin circles over the past decade.

religious suppression. Unlike their Celtic cousins in Ireland, Scotland and Brittany, folk musicians in Wales have learned their tunes from books and manuscripts rather than from older generations of players, and even amid the Celtic music boom of the 1970s, bands concentrating on Welsh tunes remained virtually unknown.

Language has also been more of a divider in Wales than in other Celtic countries. Rock and folk are both great pillars of the Welsh language but English speakers have not received the same encouragement to explore their own folk culture within the Welsh framework. The preservation and nurturing of Welsh-language songs, customs and traditions is vitally important, but the folklore of English-speaking Gower and South Pembrokeshire and the rich vein of industrial material from the valleys is actually in much greater danger of disappearing.

BARDS AND EISTEDDFODS

The **bardic** and **eisteddfod** traditions have long played a key role in Welsh culture. Medieval bards held an elevated position in Welsh society and were often pure composers, employing a harpist and a *datgeiniad*, whose role was to declaim the bard's words. The first eisteddfod appears to have been held in Cardigan in 1176, with contests between bards and poets and between harpists, players and pipers.

It was a glorious but precarious tradition. Henry VIII's Act Of Union in 1536, designed to anglicize the country by stamping out Welsh culture and language, saw the eisteddfodau degenerate, and the rise of Nonconformist religion in the eighteenth and nineteenth centuries, with its abhorrence of music and merry-making, almost sounded the death knell for Welsh traditions. Edward Jones, Bardd y Brenin (Bard to the King), observed sorrowfully in the 1780s that Wales, which used to be one of the happiest of countries, "has become one of the dullest".

Folk music, however, gained some sort of respectability when London-based Welsh societies, swept along in a romantic enthusiasm for all things Celtic, revived it at the end of the eighteenth century. Back in Wales, in the 1860s, the National Eisteddfod Society was formed, the pre-runner of today's eisteddfod societies. These days three major week-long events dominate the calendar: the **International Eisteddfod** at Llangollen in July, the **Royal National Eisteddfod** in the first week of August and the **Urdd Eisteddfod**, Europe's largest youth festival, in May. The National and the Urdd alternate between north and south Wales.

Eisteddfodau have always tended to formalize Welsh culture because competitions need rules, and such parameter-defining is naturally alien to the free evolution of traditional song and music. When Nicholas Bennett was compiling his 1896 book *Alawon Fy Nghwlad*, still an important source of Welsh tunes, he rejected a great deal of good Welsh dance music because it did not conform to the contemporary high art notion of what Welsh music ought to sound like. Despite this frequently heard criticism, eisteddfodau have played a major role in keeping traditional music, song and dance at the heart of national culture.

GWERIN SOUNDS

The most influential traditional Welsh musician of recent years is the triple harpist **Robin Huw Bowen**, who has revived interest in the instrument with appearances throughout Europe and North America, and has done tremendous work making unpublished manuscripts of Welsh dance music available.

Bowen started out in the late '70s with a pioneering roots band called **Mabsant**, who introduced a jazz sensibility to the Welsh folk tunes Bowen unearthed. In a somewhat similar vein, the current pacemakers are **Bob Delyn a'r Ebillion**, whose blend of contemporary Welsh and Breton (they have a Breton player in the band) influences veer more towards the rock field. Formed around the nucleus of Tym Morys and Gorwell Roberts, one-time buskers of old Welsh songs, they are probably the best known

SIÂN JAMES

cysgodion karma

SCD 4037
ADD

The bizarrely named Bob Delyn

band on the circuit and certainly one of the most accessible, full of melodious intent and dance riffs. Another new band, making a strong showing with young audiences in the north, is **Moniars**; they have a raucous electric bass-and-drums approach to Welsh language song.

On the more traditional gwerin scene, the acknowledged father of Welsh folk is politician, songwriter and Sain Records founder **Dafydd Iwan**. He began as a singer-songwriter in the Dylan/Pete Seeger mould in the mid-1960s and has been popular and prolific ever since, providing a musical voice for the nationalist movement. Another singer-songwriter, **Meic Stevens**, is also producing good work on the borderlines of folk and acoustic rock.

Tudur Morgan, from the excellent (and sadly defunct) group **4 Yn Y Bar**, has also been involved in some notable collaborations, including working with Irish musician/producer Donal Lunny on "Branwen", a song and music cycle based on the Welsh Mabinogi legend.

Singer/harpist **Siân James**, from Llanerfyl in mid-Wales, has produced two albums so far which have won the acclaim of Welsh and English speakers alike. She has a strong clear voice which her record company has been promoting as a "Welsh Enya" – a claim that's not far off the mark. Her influences are certainly eclectic. She makes sporadic appearances with the rock-oriented **Bwchadanas**, and has even cropped up playing harp with the London roots-reggae band, One Style. A name to look out for.

Another folk-based pacesetter among the women is **Julie Murphy**, born in Essex but now a fluent Welsh speaker, whose Welsh-language work alongside Breton singer **Brigitte Kloareg** in the band **Saith Rhyfeddod** has led to a promising bilingual collaboration with young English hurdy-gurdy expert Nigel Eaton. Another quality Welsh-language singer is Cardiff-based **Heather Jones**, who works solo and with fiddlers Mike Lease and Jane Ridout in the trio **Hin Deg**, who blend Welsh song with Welsh/Irish fiddle music.

Close harmony songs in three or four parts were a traditional feature in mid-Wales, where the *plygain* carol-singing tradition still survives at Christmas. Small parties of carol singers, each with their own repertoire, would sing in church from midnight to dawn on Christmas morning. The group **Plethyn**, formed in the 1970s to adapt this style to traditional and modern Welsh songs, still perform occasionally, and member Linda Healey was also involved in the Branwen project.

Wales' busiest band is probably **Calennig**, from Llantrisant in Glamorgan, who blend fiery Welsh dance sets with English-language songs from the Valleys and Gower. They tour regularly in Europe, America and New Zealand and have helped to popularize Welsh dance with a punchy collection of twmpath tunes and up-front calling from Patricia Carron-Smith. From the same town come Welsh-language band **Mabsant**, again regulars on the international festival circuits, whose strength lies in the powerful voice of Siwsann George, also a fine solo singer, and soulful sax work from Steve Whitehead.

On the straight folk circuit, **The Hennessys**, led by broadcaster, TV personality and songwriter Frank Hennessy, have a huge and well-deserved middle-of-the-road following in the Cardiff area twenty years after joining the procession of Irish-influenced trios in the folk clubs. **Huw and Tony Williams**, from Brynmawr in the Gwent Valleys, are popular names, too, though their following, like other English-language performers, is greater away from home than it is inside Wales. Huw's songwriting – notably songs like "Rosemary's Sister" – has been embraced by Fairport Convention and a string of other big-name performers. In Wales, he's best known for his Eisteddfod-winning clog dancing.

Traditional dance in Wales has been revived over the past fifty years after a long period of religious suppression. It plays a big part in the folk culture of Wales, and the top teams are exciting and professional in their approach. Dances written in recent years, often for eisteddfod competitions, have been quickly absorbed into the repertoire. **Cwmni Dawns Werin Canolfan Caerdydd**, Cardiff's official dance team, are the leading group, and their musicians are recommended for a hearing as well. **Dawnswyr Nantgarw**, from the Taff Vale village that was the source of the country's romantic and raunchy fair dances, have turned Welsh dance into a theatrical art form: concise, perfectly drilled and very showy.

Dawnswyr Gwerin Pen-y-Fai, from Bridgend, have an adventurous band full of good session players, while Anglesey-based **Ffidl Ffadl** also boast an excellent musician in fiddler Huw Roberts, formerly with the early 1980s bands Cilmeri and Pedwar yn y Bar. **Dawnswyr Brynmawr** also have a capable band who play for twmpath dances as Taro Tant.

IT'S NOT UNUSUAL – WELSH-LANGUAGE ROCK

Wales has thrown up a few big name pop and rock artists over the past thirty years. **Tom Jones** and **Shirley Bassey** are the stuff of legend, while rock names have included Velvet Underground composer **John Cale**; producer and guitarist **Dave Edmunds**; hard rockers **Man**; the whimsical **Green Garside** of Scritti Politti; balladeer **Bonnie Tyler**; the awful **Shakin' Stevens**; folk-punk band **The Alarm**; and, most recently, dance remixers **K Klass**.

It's a strong but short list, by British standards, and Welsh groups are often left debating why they don't get more of a look in. Their response has been twofold; either bands have knocked hard on the door of the British music establishment, singing in English and playing on the London gig circuit (as all of the above have done at some stage of their career), or they have turned their backs on commercial success, singing in their native tongue, launching Welsh record labels, and in the process cultivating what is now a thriving Welsh-language music scene.

Whilst English-language Welsh bands have usually enjoyed success by making their nationality an irrelevance, Welsh-language bands have purposely expounded their strong national identity. Commercial, they aren't, but nonetheless a Welsh-language rock scene has been a definite fixture, ever since the early days of that most pernicious London export, punk. The **punk** explosion of 1976 carried with it a DIY ethic that was ideal for the growth of a Welsh scene, and bands like **Trwynau Coch** set up their own labels to cater for their own markets.

In the '80s, the home-grown Welsh language scene began to consolidate. Caernarfon punk band **Anhrefn** (Disorder) set up **Recordiau Anhrefn**, a label devoted to "dodgy compilations of up and coming left-field weirdo Welsh bands", as one of them put it. It was a case of enthusiasm for the burgeoning Welsh-language scene, rather

The rather wonderful Gorky's Zygotic Mynci

bands and it introduced their music to a Europe-wide audience.

Midway through the '90s, Welsh-language rock music has a solid infrastructure of bands, labels and venues. Styles, as in English rock, cover pretty much the range, from the techno-rap of **Llwyrbr Llaethog** to the Fall-style avant-garde rock of **Datblygu** and the eccentric, psychedelic guitar melodies of **Gorky's Zygotic Mynci**, who can claim the Velvet Underground's John Cale as one of their biggest fans. The latter, with vocals and sound that at times recall the great Young Marble Giants, are perhaps set for mainstream success, and if they make it, it'll be interesting to see how much they can retain Welsh-language songs. The same applies to **Catatonia**, whose haunting female vocals and jingly guitar sound have already given them a couple of indie hits.

The process of success and singing in English isn't perhaps as inflexible as it has been in the past, and the market is at last established enough for bands to record alternative versions, with Welsh and English vocals. Recently, **Mike Peters** from The Alarm made a Welsh-language version of his "Back into the System" album, along with all-Welsh band The Poets.

And for all that the Welsh-language rock scene is a local one, it is not parochial. Bands have been forging links in Europe and getting established on the festival circuit with the help of CRAG, a European Community initiative designed to help music from minority languages. Welsh language bands are on the march!

than hit-making. The scene was developing nicely and before long Radio One DJ John Peel – to many, the standard bearer for underground rock in the UK – started playing Welsh-language bands on air and having them in for sessions. This was an important catalyst to new Welsh

---

DISCOGRAPHY

For Welsh music by mail order, try Cob Records in Porthmadog (☎ 0766/512170).

FOLK/ROOTS

Ⓒ **Aberjaber** *Aberjaber* and *Aberdaujaber* (Sain, Wales). Two albums by a defunct but fine band formed by Cardiff jazz/roots/world musician Peter Stacey, Swansea harpist Delyth Evans and Oxford music graduate Stevie Wishart (viol and hurdy-gurdy), who experimented with Welsh and original instrumental music.

Ⓒ **Ar Log** *OIVIV* (Sain, Wales). A compilation of their last two studio albums.

Ⓒ **Robin Huw Bowen** *Telyn Berseiniol fy Nghwlad* and *Helar's Draenog* (Teires, Wales). Two self-produced albums of dance music and airs for the triple harp.

Ⓒ **Calennig** *Dwr Glan* (Sain, Wales). Rocky Welsh dance sets and songs tinged with Breton and Galician influences.

Ⓒ **Cilmeri** *Cilmeri* (Sain, Wales). Long-defunct but well-respected north Wales six-piece, the first band to put a harder Irish-style edge on the music of Wales.

Ⓒ **Bob Delyn** *Sgwarnogod Bach Bob* (Crai, Wales). The new sound of Welsh folk: Celtic harp meets the bardic beatbox.

Ⓒ **Delyth Evans** *Delta* (Sain, Wales). Solo album of Celtic harp music by Aberjaber's harpist.

Ⓒ **Dafydd Iwan ac Ar Log** *Yma O Hyd* (Sain, Wales). Compilation of two great mid-Eighties albums which celebrated legendary joint tours around Wales by these performers.

Ⓒ **Siân James** *Distaw* (Sain, Wales). Original, modern and traditional songs from the harp and keyboard player with a wonderful and at times spine-tingling voice.

Ⓒ **Tudur Morgan** *Branwen* (Sain, Wales). An album of songs and music based on the Mabinogi legend.

Ⓒ **Pedwar Yn Y Bar** *Byth Adra* (Sain, Wales). Four piece, also now defunct, which arose from the ashes of Cilmeri and added American and other international influences to Welsh music.

Ⓒ **Saith Rhyfeddod** *Cico Nyth Cacwn* (Fflach, Wales). 1994 album by bagpipers Jonathan Shorland and Ceri Matthews.

Ⓒ **Various** *Carolau Plygain* (Sain, Wales). Few albums are available of Welsh "source" performances, the older generation who handed down their songs, but this album of Christmas carols from mid-Wales is a gem.

WELSH-LANGUAGE ROCK

ⓒ **Various** *O'R Gad* (Ankst, Wales). A great introduction to modern Welsh-language rock, featuring Catatonia, Gorky's Zygotic Mynci, and other bands on the Ankst roster.
ⓒ **Anhrefn** *Rhedeg I Paris* (Crai, Wales). The godfathers of Welsh-language rock. Raw and noisy.
ⓒ **Catatonia** *For Tinkerbell and Hooked* (Crai, Wales). Two highly promising EPs by this quirkily hard-edged pop band.

ⒸⒹ **Gorky's Zygotic Mynci** *Tatay* (Ankst, Wales). Debut LP from this young Carmarthen band. A strange and adventurous brew which spins off into touches of psychedelia before coming down to earth with a Robert Wyatt cover (in Welsh, of course). Altogether rather wonderful.
ⓒ **One Style** *Right to Say* (Crai, Wales). A real oddball, this: a Welsh and Jamaican roots reggae band, including Sian James on harp!
ⓒ **Mike Peters** *Noli Mewn i'r System* (Crai, Wales). Welsh-language version of "Back into the System" from the Alarm's former frontman, now looking to more acoustic roots.

THE BRETON ACCENT

SPURRED ON BY LORIENT AND THE PIONEERING ALAN STIVELL, BRETON MUSIC IS IN BON SANTÉ

Brittany, France's northwest province, is host to the largest annual inter-Celtic gathering of them all, the August Lorient festival. This, however, is just the most public face of a music that plays an integral role in local festivals and stands as a symbol of the French Celts' independent-minded traditions. Raymond Travers forages through the Breton hinterland in search of festou-noz and the like.

reton music, which draws richly in its themes, style and instrumentation on the common Celtic heritage of the Atlantic seaboard, has been for centuries a unifying and inspiring part of the culture of the province. Despite the intermittent efforts of a reactionary clergy to stifle its popularity, it survived the union with France and the general suppression of indigenous art and language.

However, attempting to pin even an approximate date on the origins of traditional Breton music is a haphazard business. No literature survives in the native tongue from any period prior to the fifteenth century, although we do know that wandering Breton minstrels, known as *conteurs*, had enjoyed great popularity abroad long before this. Many of the songs which they wrote were translated into French, being otherwise unintelligible to audiences outside Brittany, but unfortunately both versions have vanished with time. Only a number of Norse and English translations, probably dating from the twelfth century, escaped destruction. These works tell of romances won and lost, acrimonious

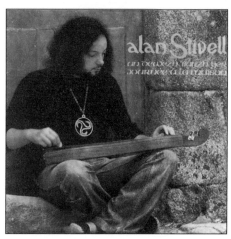

Alan Stivell: the man with the Breton harp

relationships between fathers and their sons, and the testing of potential lovers.

The historical record of Breton music really begins with the publication of **Barzaz-Breizh**, a major collection of traditional songs and poems, in 1839. It was compiled by a nobleman, Hersart de la Villemarqué, from his discussions with fishermen, farmers and oyster-and-pancake women, and in view of the scarcity of other literature in the native language has come to be acknowledged as a treasure of Breton folk culture. Though serious doubts have frequently been raised as to its authenticity – many sceptics believe Villemarqué doctored those parts of the material he found distasteful, and even composed portions of it himself – it is unquestionably a work of linguistic brilliance and great beauty, and its appearance triggered the serious study of popular Breton culture.

As for the traditional instruments on which the music is played, perhaps the most important is the **bombard** – an extremely old and shortened version of the oboe which, depending on the condition of your brain on any given day, sounds either like a hypnotic trance-inducing paean to the gods, or a sackful of weasels being yanked through a mincer. The **biniou**, the Breton bagpipe, dates in its current form from the nineteenth century, although several types are still in use, distinguished by the length of the chanter.

The **telenn** or Breton harp was also a native instrument long ago. Its influence had declined to a barely peripheral level until **Alan Stivell**'s appearance on the scene in the 1960s inspired a resurgence. His international hit, "Renaissance of the Celtic Harp", heped introduce Breton – as well as Irish, Welsh and Scottish – traditional music to a worldwide audience, and subsequently stimulated interest in less accessible material.

FEST-NOZ ACTION

The most rewarding setting in which to witness traditional Breton music is undoubtedly a **Fest-Noz** ("Night Feast") – a night of serious eating, drinking and dancing, similar to a ceilidh. During the summer months, such events are very common, attracting hordes of revellers from miles around. Though they are often held in barns and halls in the more isolated parts of the region, discovering their whereabouts shouldn't present any problems, as an avalanche of posters advertising them appears absolutely everywhere. Once the evening gets underway, the dancers, often in their hundreds, whirl around in vast dizzying circles, hour after hour, sometimes frenzied and leaping, sometimes slow and graceful with their little fingers intertwined. It can be a bizarre and exhilarating spectacle – and a very affordable one too, with very modest admission fees.

Traditionally, the most common form of festou-noz music is that of a **couple de sonneurs**, a pair of musicians playing bombard and biniou. They play the same melody line, with a drone from the biniou, and keep up a fast tempo – one player covering for the other when he or she pauses for breath. This is defiantly dance music, with no vocals and no titles for the tunes, although there are countless varieties of rhythms, often highly localized and generally known by the name of the dance.

There is a purely vocal counterpart to this, known as **kan ha diskan**. This is again dance music but is performed by a pair of unaccompanied "call and response" singers. In its basic form the two singers – the *kader* and *diskader* – alternate verses, joining each other at the end of each phrase. As dances were in the past unamplified, the parts were (and are) often doubled up (or more), creating a startling rhythmic sound. The best singers might also give the dancers the odd break with a *gwerz*, or ballad, again sung unaccompanied.

Over the past couple of decades, these traditional accompaniments have been supplanted more and more by four- or five-piece **bands**, who add fiddle and accordion, and sometimes electric bass and drums, to the bombard, and less often the biniou. The tunes have been updated and given a more rock sound, while the ballads have given way to more folk-style singer-songwriters, with guitar backing. Purists might regret the changes but they have probably ensured the survival of festou-noz, with participation by pretty much all ages. They have also nurtured successive generations of Breton musicians who move on to the festival and concert circuit.

BARDS AND BANDS

The godfather of the modern Breton music scene, **Alan Stivell** started the ball rolling in the mid-1960s with one of the first folk-rock bands in Europe. He played harp, bagpipes and Irish flute, alongside **Dan Ar Bras** on electric and acoustic guitar, on a repertoire that drew on wider Celtic traditions. Both artists are still performing and recording, individually. Stivell's efforts are increasingly esoteric, while Ar Bras, who played with Fairport Convention in 1976, is a fixture at that band's Cropredy reunions, and produces mellow acoustic solo albums.

The other key figure from Stivell's band was **Gabriel Yacoub**, who led **Malicorne**, the best-known Breton band of the 1970s and '80s, through a series of experiments with folk-rock and electronic music, often using archaic instruments. Latterly, he has played as an acoustic duo, with his wife Marie Matheson.

Folk rock, however, has been just one direction for Breton music in the 1980s and '90s. On the concert circuit, the biggest Breton names tend to be the singers, among whom the most famous is **Andrea Ar Gouilh**. Her recent output includes

THE CELTIC WORLD

BRETON MUSIC FESTIVALS

I n addition to the pan-Celtic extravaganza of Lorient (see p.3), Brittany has a network of local festivals, where you'll always find some kind of band, most commonly one of the many local *Bagadou* – bombard and biniou marching bands – whose rat-a-tat-tat military drumming can be heard for miles around. There are also a few smaller, specifically music festivals. The best of these are:

Le Printemps de Chateauneuf-du-Faou (Easter Sunday). An intimate festival in this small town near Carhaix. Breton singers and musicians only – and usually the very best.

Festival de Cornouaille, Quimper (mid/late-July). A colourful festival of music and dance, mainly traditional Breton, but with the odd foreign guest.

Tombées de la Nuit, Rennes (early July). This is the best opportunity to hear modern, electric Breton sounds. Performers are encouraged to retain a Breton identity but they plough just about every musical field going. Most years, there are also a few fellow-Celtic acts.

a return to Breton roots with a recording of old songs taken from the Barzaz-Breizh, though her concert repertoire is as likely to include a rendition of Bob Dylan's "Blowin' in the Wind", which sounds rather marvellous sung in Breton. **Youenn Gwernig**, a druid and singer, is another name to look out for at festivals. He lived for many years in New York and delivers his own ballads in a deep booming voice, sometimes accompanied by his two daughters who sing Brooklyn English translations. Equally weird is **Kristen Nikolas**, a wandering poet who makes his own idiosyncratic records, in Breton, in foreign studios, while the most compelling name has to be that of the duo **Bastard Hag e Vab** (Bastard and Son), who have been stalwarts of the live circuit for years.

Other notable Breton singers include **Bernez Tangi**, who for a while fronted a fine band called Storlok; **Yann Fanch Kemener**, well known among Bretons but is somewhat inaccessible to others with his unbelievably long traditional *gwerziou*; the singer-songwriter **Gilles Servat**, who sings in both Breton and French, mixing his own protest songs with renderings of Breton poems; and a trio of younger fest-noz performers, **Jean Do Robin**, **Claude An Intanv** and **Anni Ebrel**, who are slowly gaining recognition and who write some of their own material.

Fest-noz singers are sometimes accompanied by harpists, among whom the best contemporary players are **Ar Breudeur Keffelean**, virtuoso twin brothers who also have a group, **Triskell**. The more mystic '60s side of the tradition is encapsulated by the suitably bearded and misty-Merlin-type, **Myrzhin**, harper of the mysterious.

If you have a more casual interest in Breton sounds, though, you're likely to find some of the bands rather more rewarding. A fine fest-noz act to look out for is **Strobinell**, who have a line-up of bombard, biniou, violin, flute and guitar, and make occasional forays into a looser, jazzier groove. Another, always visually entertaining group is the mega-ensemble **Klik Ha Farz**, whose members wander around the hall as they play. They use a bass drum in conjunction with traditional instruments, rather in the manner of Gallego and Portuguese groups.

For the electric fest-noz sound, complete with full rock drum kit, the best exponents are **Bleizi Ruz** (Red Wolves) and **Sonerien Du** (Black Musicians). Bleizi Ruz, who started out some twenty years ago playing traditional songs, play less at fest-noz these days and more on concert stages. They are probably the most successful folk-rock fusion group still on the circuit and have recently added synths and drum machines.

Musically, the most adventurous band of the last decade has been **Gwerz**, who made several records of traditional songs and ethereal instrumentals, using bombard, biniou, uilleann pipes, and guitars. Their singer, **Eric Marchand**, has recently been collaborating with Indian musicians to interesting effect. Also making crossovers from a Breton base are **Les Pires**, a zany instrumental quintet comprising violin, accordion, clarinet, double-bass and piano, who play essentially middle-European dance music.

Strangely enough, while these musicians are looking out, some of the most interesting new "Breton" sounds have been emerging from

Kornog stalwarts Soïg Siberil, Jean-Michel Veillon, Christian Lemaitre and Scots interloper Jamie McMenemy

bands of mixed nationality. **Etre-Vroadel** (EV), Brittany's most popular rock band, are a mix of Finnish and Breton musicians who use the bombard and cover traditional material.

More folk-oriented, and purely acoustic, are **Kornog**, who feature Scots singer, mandolin and bouzouki player Jamie McMenemy, alongside three Breton instrumentalists, among them Soïg Siberil, who played guitar in Gwerz. They have rearranged Breton material quite radically for guitar, fiddle and bouzouki, slowing down the tempo to highlight solo playing and adding the occasional Scots ballad. At time of writing, they're the Breton band to watch.

DISCOGRAPHY

A few Breton discs – mainly of the more rock-crossover variety – find their way into international sections of record stores abroad. For the real roots stuff, however, you'll need to go to Brittany and in particular to Ar Bed Keltiek, a record store with branches in Rennes, Quimper and Brest, or, best of all, to Le Chant de l'Alouette (4 rue des Etats, 35600 Redon, Brittany; ☎99 72 44 94), run by musician Jakez Le Soueff – a living Breton encyclopedia on all matters musical, who will track down any recording that exists. These shops are also good for information about forthcoming gigs and events.

COMPILATIONS

ⓒ **Various** *Celtic La Compile* (Le Cire Jaune, France). An eclectic 18-track compilation of Breton music of just about every style: sentimental balladeers, marching bands, loud rockers, quirky accordions and bagpipes – it's all here.
ⓒ **Various** *Dans* (Iguane, France). Traditional dance tunes given new life with superb new arrangements and restrained electrification.
ⓒ **Various** *Gwerziou et Chants de Haute-Voix* (Keltia Musique, France). Unaccompanied Breton songs by the region's top artists. The best example of the genre available.

ARTISTS/BANDS

ⓒ **Dan Ar Bras** *Acoustic* (Green Linnet, US). A recent release from the ex-Stivell, Malicorne and Fairport guitarist.

ⓒ **Barzaz** *An den Kozh dall* (Keltia Musique, France). A classic 1992 release of mellow, intense acoustic music, with some lovely flute playing.
ⓒ **The Chieftains** *Celtic Wedding* (RCA, UK). The Irish band turn their hand to traditional Breton dance tunes. A fresh perspective and highly accessible.
ⓒ **Gwerz** *Live* (Gwerz, France). Electric and acoustic material from perhaps the best Breton musicians of the last decade, now pursuing individual projects.
ⓒ **Kornog** *Première: Music from Brittany* (Green Linnet, US). An excellent live album from this adventurous Breton (and Scots) band, formed by ex-Gwerz guitarist Soïg Siberil.
ⓒ **Patrick Molard, Jack Molard et Jacques Pellen** *Triptyque* (Gwerz, France). An innovative release of jazzy interpretations of Breton traditions.
Pennou Skoulm *Pennou Skoulm* (Slog, France). Traditional dance music from a group who regularly appear on the fest-noz circuit. Cassette only.
ⓒ **Les Soeurs Goadeg** *Moueziou Brudez à Vreiz* (Keltia Musique, France). Alan Stivell produced this disc of old-time Breton singing in 1975. Goadeg, a trio of sisters, were into their 70s at the time, and the album showcases their highly traditional gwerziou (ballads) and kan ha diskan singing.
ⓒ **Alan Stivell** *Journée à la Maison* (Rounder, US). A good compilation of Stivell's Breton Celtic harp folk-rockery – more accessible than the recent esoteric output.

THE NEW ENGLISH ROOTS

A LONG WAY FROM MORRIS DANCING AND INCEST BALLADS

Not so long ago, confessing even a passing affection for English folk music was about as un-hip as being a trainspotter. Folk's image of incest ballads sung with fingers planted firmly in the ear, singer-songwriters parading their hopeless love affairs and, of course, the dreaded morris dancers didn't exactly denote credibility and relevance. Over the past decade, though, there has been a sea change, as a new generation of musicians delved into English (and Celtic) traditions, knocked them around with a wonderful disregard for notions of purity, and came out with what the labels and press started calling "roots". Colin Irwin owns up to being a fan.

T he beginnings of folk's re-creation as roots began towards the end of the 1980s when a bunch of young musicians, too unselfconscious to be tarnished by the dictates of cultural fashion, adopted the pattern of English folk song as a basis for their own attacking styles. As ever, it was the Irish who showed the way, with the London-based Pogues knocking pub and club audiences with their punkish balladry, but it wasn't long before bands like **The Men They Couldn't Hang** tossed their caps firmly into the English end. And before long there were many others, notably the irrepressible **Billy Bragg**.

The evolving relevance of folk song in England hit Bragg the moment he set foot inside the Trowbridge Festival. Bragg, all Doc Martens and political cred, had been coaxed into this cosy corner of Wiltshire as much out of curiosity as pioneering spirit. The archetypal articulate boot boy let loose in a tradition he and most others of his generation believed long moribund . . . the incongruousness of the meeting was lost on no-one.

The first thing Bragg heard at Trowbridge was the extraordinary sound of **Blowzabella** – pipes, hurdy-gurdies and all – belting out his own meisterwork of socialist ideology, "Between The Wars". The song was nestling at the time in the Top 10, sharing airtime on Radio 1 with the likes of A-Ha and Duran Duran, and here, down in Wiltshire, right before his own eyes, it had become – a folk song. Billy Bragg was, as he put

it, totally gobsmacked, and a few pints to the wind later, his preconceptions had gone out of the window, as, like others of his ilk, he discovered a fire and a passion to which more mainstream areas of music merely paid lip service.

Since then "Between The Wars" has become something of a standard, covered by the Oyster Band and every other roots outfit,

Blowzabella kicking out the jams

and Billy Bragg a connoisseur in the field. He has shared a compilation album with the great Norfolk traditional singer **Walter Pardon**; he's sung on stage with the legendary **Watersons family** from Yorkshire; he's toured and recorded with such giants of the genre as **Dick Gaughan**, **Roy Bailey** and **Leon Rosselson**.

Just one musician's CV, sure, but Bragg's activities are symptomatic of what has been happening across the country through the 1980s and '90s, with a steady harvest of English roots music in a variety of unlikely areas. **Kathryn Tickell**'s splendid Northumbrian piping has been used to good effect, for example, on two Sting albums. And **The Levellers**, who a few years ago might have been considered conventional, if rowdy, folk-rockers, have acquired a formidable reputation as roguish champions of the rock alternative. And all this while the old standard bearer of the English folk-rock genre,

Richard Thompson, continues to measure out the benchmark of the style with incomparable distinction.

But more than this, the reassessment of all things folk/roots has focused attention on the **real traditional music** of England – traditions that have managed to survive forty years of pop and rock, ten of Thatcher and karaoke boxes, and now look set up for many years to come. The sound of Billy Pigg playing "The Lark In The Clear Air" on Northumbrian pipes may not be everyone's idea of ecstacy, but, to these ears at least, it beats the socks off Madonna.

NORTHUMBRIAN ROOTS

Nowhere is this living tradition more in evidence than in the border lands of **Northumbria**, the one part of England to rival the counties of the west of Ireland for a rich unbroken tradition. No thundering Billy Bragg or Levellers here – just the rich splendour of a countryside that has constantly been interwoven with its indigenous music. The changing times may have dissipated that music's importance to the local communities, but it has never come close to eradicating it. Whether it be sheep-farming in the moorlands

or raucous nights in the pubs in the mining communities, the old music has survived as a backdrop.

Sometimes bleak, sometimes tragic, often wildly happy, Northumbrian music has remained an integral root of the local character, and names like **Jack Armstrong**, **Joe Hutton**, **Billy Atkinson**, **Jimmy Pallister**, **Tommy Edmondson**, **Willy Taylor**, **Tom Clough**, **Billy Conroy**, **George Hepple** and **Billy Pigg** are revered locally for their role in perpetuating that tradition.

Much of this proud tradition is due to the proximity of Scotland and its history of country dance bands, and to the influence of Irish migrants. As a result, outstanding accordion players, fiddlers and even mouth organists have consistently abounded, though the instrument that really gives the area its unique role in English music is the **Northumbrian pipes**. One of the smallest and least intimidating members of the bagpipe family, these pipes are also more versatile than most of their Celtic relatives and as a result blend in more easily with other instruments. **Billy Pigg**, who died in 1968, is still regarded as the king of the Northumbrian pipes for the vibrant orginality of his playing, his prolific writing of tunes and the

Pub session at Sidmouth – England's most enjoyable gathering of folkies

high profile he gave the instrument in particular and Northumbrian music in general.

His influence remains strong and there's a clear line between him and **Kathryn Tickell**, the lady who – still in her 20s – has astounded pundits with the skill of her playing and the success she has achieved with it. Tickell's current influence in the perpetuation of the legend of Northumbrian music is incalculable and her importance is likely to be felt for generations to come, but it would be wrong to ignore the role of many others, both musicians and enthusiasts, who have promoted the music of the area with fanatical zeal.

The **High Level Ranters** from Newcastle for years kept the flag flying with their local songs. "The Lambton Worm", "Blaydon Races", "Keep Your Feet Still Geordie Hinnie", "Dance To Yer Daddie": this was the staple diet of the Ranters, who also did much nationally to focus attention on the area's mining songs. The Ranters' **Colin Ross** acted as an ambassador for the Northumbrian pipes at a time when most people looked at the instrument and fled, and over the last few years his work in the band has been admirably continued by **Alistair Anderson**, originally noted as a vigorous concertina player, but now recognized as a piper and, especially, as a composer. He is best known for his "Steel Skies" suite, a tour de force directly inspired by Northumbria and rooted in music centuries old. "It was written to be played by musicians steeped in traditional music and its development from the tradition was evolutionary rather than revolutionary," Anderson said of the work. "I hope it retained the spirit of the music it has grown from, while opening up some new musical ideas on the way."

The **Northumbrian Pipers Society** have also worked wonders to keep interest in the

THE K FACTOR

·······················

I f there's one musician who has personified the upward trend of English roots music in recent years, it has to be Kathryn Tickell (and a sharp blow to the ear to anyone who pronounces it "tickle"). More than anyone else, she has reformed the stuffy old image of folk music, inspiring a legion of others in her wake.

Young, mini-skirted, funny, and entirely well-adjusted in mind and deed, Kathryn has successfully blended technical expertise with progressive ideas and youthful vitality. After all, she spent some vital formative years playing with Asian and reggae musicians and feels no incongruity about applying some of their ideas and values to her own heritage of Northumbrian music. She's also a fan of classical, bluegrass and jazz music which suggests that future influences in her work will stretch wide indeed. On her 1993 album, "Signs", she dipped into Greek, Cajun and Irish music, as well as continuing the reworking of Northumbrian material.

The one thing she hasn't compromised on is the temptation to include a singer in her band, arguing that instrumental music for its own sake should be sufficient to overcome the prejudices of concert audiences. And why not? With her own piping (and sometime fiddle playing), and accomplished backing from Ian Carr on guitar,

Geoff Lincoln on bass and the superb young squeeze-box player Karen Tweed, the Kathryn Tickell Band is as hot as they come.

instrument alive, to the extent of helping to open a pipe museum in Newcastle. A number of border festivals have doggedly and successfully concentrated on local music, to the extent of including (somewhat controversially) competitions for various instruments in the manner of the Irish fleadhs. They've provided a healthy incentive to young musicians in the area, and a new breed has indeed emerged, numbering among its ranks outstanding musicians such as the pipers **Becky Taylor** and **Pauline Cato**, the piano-accordion player **Lynn Tocker**, and the superb teenage fiddler **Nancy Kerr** (daughter of celebrated singer-songwriter Sandra Kerr). It's nice to be able to talk already of a post-Tickell generation.

You'll catch some of this music at the main English folk festivals, though to hear it at its best there's no beating the local events, above all the Rothbury Traditional Music Festival. Alternatively, take a trip around the pubs and clubs of Hawick and Jedburgh, Alnwick and Morpeth, and check things out.

THE RURAL TRADITION

Not that Northumbria is the only area where the tradition has survived unbroken. Not by a long chalk. Indigenous music flourishes in East Anglia, Sussex, Cornwall and Humberside – although, admittedly, not always amid great public awareness of its existence.

East Anglia might seem an unlikely setting for a roots scene but scratch around and you find surprising riches. In Suffolk, things revolve around a wonderful banjo player, **John Howson**, who organises great pub sessions – and has made some fine recordings. Over in **Norfolk**, there's more diversity and regular pub sessions for local musicians. Two of the greatest traditional singers in the entire folk tradition were from this area: farm labourer **Harry Cox** from Yarmouth and **Sam Larner**, a fisherman, from Winterton. Larner was 79 when he made his first record but his subsequent output, and that of Cox, gave the 1960s folk revival a huge source of material and inspiration. It's a legacy that survives today at clubs and pubs in the more rural areas and particularly through the singer **Walter Pardon**, who has lived all his life in the same cottage at Knapton, Norfolk. He was discovered in the 1970s by the late Peter Bellamy, along with a fund of long-neglected songs handed down to him through generations.

It's much the same story in Sussex, home of the late great **Scan Tester**, who played dance music in local pubs with his Imperial Band from before the World War I right up until his death in 1972. Much of the traditional repertoire has come through his hands, and his own renderings are still a delight to be heard on the compilation album "I Never Played Too Many Posh Dances". Sussex is also the base of the **Copper Family** of Rottingdean, the finest example of the living folk tradition in England. Their patriarch Bob Copper has written two books about rural life, and the family's 1971 quadruple album, "A Song For Every Season", remains one of the milestones of the folk tradition. That the Coppers still sing regularly at Peacehaven and that the group is now built around Bob's children John and Jill and *their* families is evidence enough of the durability of the music.

Another celebrated family, the **Watersons** from Yorkshire, are also still going strong with recent reinforcements from teenage daughters. Joining ranks with one of folk music's most revered sons, **Martin Carthy**, by virtue of his marriage to Norma Waterson, gave them a new lease of life and with a fresh influx from a new generation there is no greater example of the link between old and new. Their daughter Eliza Carthy is already involved in a promising career, singing and playing with the Northumbrian fiddler Nancy Kerr.

And up in **Shropshire**, another area where you'll find the music intact if you look hard enough, you'll come across **Fred Jordan**, a rugged farmworker who sings like an angel and has become a fixture at festivals up and down the land. He has been responsible for a fund of material, but has always been willing to learn new material to augment the stuff handed down in his family and is now just as likely to perform songs of a music hall flavour like "Grandfather Clock" as he would "The Seeds Of Love".

The one record that is still cited as the biggest influence in traditional music circles is "English Country Music". This was put together in 1965 by **Reg Hall** and **Bob Davenport**, issued in a limited edition of 99 copies and sold out within a fortnight. Among the primarily Norfolk musicians featured were the fiddler **Walter Bulwer**, **Billy Cooper** on dulcimer, **Reg Hall** on melodeon and fiddle, **Daisy Bulwer** on piano, **Mervyn Plunkett** on drums, and **Russell Wortley** on pipe and tabor. It was, astonishingly, the first ever recording of English traditional instrumental music and it fired in a variety of young musicians a feel for their own tradition that has led them into all manner of development and experimentation.

LORDS OF THE DANCE

orris dancing is at the very heart of clichéd English imagery. It hasn't yet been rescued from ridicule by roots music, and, who knows, perhaps it never will be. However, for all its apparent absurdity, it's quite amazingly popular, and there is, after all, something spectacular and heart-warming about the sight of the men in their whites waving bells and hankies, re-enacting some obscure fertility ritual.

The history of morris is ancient and cloudy. Nobody's quite sure how it evolved, or indeed if it's a specifically English tradition. Nonetheless, with its related offshoots, it has evolved as an eccentric culture entirely its own. Long-held customs that women are not allowed to dance the morris have been the subject of fierce debate, with female dance teams emerging at a frantic pace with variations of morris, rapper and clog.

The "serious" teams, meanwhile, preserve their own territorial traditions with a protective discipline that seems positively archaic, but are rigorously encouraged by the Morris Ring, the movement's unofficial governing body.

Although these days morris dancing is widespread throughout the country, its spiritual home is in the Oxfordshire area where local dancers still gather in the village of Bampton every Whitsun to welcome the summer. May Day is the traditional start of the morris season and even if you can't stomach the dancing, it has always provided excellent music. Rod Stradling and Reg Hall have played with Bampton Morris, the Albion Band used to have their own morris side, and the outstanding singer and melodeon player John Kirkpatrick is also an ace dancer. You may laugh, but it's serious stuff.

ELECTRIC AVENUE

It all sounds unbelievably mundane now, but back in 1971 folkies thought the world had stopped when **Martin Carthy** plugged in his electric guitar on stage. Dylan thought he'd been given a hard time with all that "Judas" baiting when he went electric at Newport Folk Festival a few years earlier, but at least he was raping his own songs. Martin Carthy, the doyen of English folk musicians, was doing it with a national treasure.

The idea of a band playing traditional English music with all the trappings of a rock band had initially been discussed by **Ashley Hutchings** and **Bob Pegg** at Keele Folk Festival at the end of the '60s. Having coaxed the folk singer Sandy Denny into their ranks, Hutchings propelled **Fairport Convention**, then perceived as a Muswell Hill interpretation of Californian soft-rock, full-tilt into an English folk direction. The move was to invest their guitarist **Richard Thompson** with a unique songwriting style of his own that has served him brilliantly for over two decades, and it turned their "Liege And Lief" album into a momentous bit of musical history.

But Fairport were seen mainly as a rock band playing with folk music, and Hutchings wanted to pursue the idea of an electric folk band to the limits. He quit Fairport Convention specifically to form that beast, engaging the most respected musicians on the folk club circuit to see it through. The result was **Steeleye Span**, initially involving Maddy Prior and Tim Hart and the Irish duo Gay and Terry Woods, whose presence instantly scuppered any purist notions of Englishness. They made one album, "Hark The Village Wait", before the Irish contingent quit to form their own band (Terry later re-emerging with The Pogues) and Steeleye really got underway with the induction of Martin Carthy and fiddler Peter Knight on the seminal "Please To See The King" album.

Steeleye went on to a glorious career, exerting a positive influence on the whole genre which had spawned them, even if some of their ideals became blurred in the process. Carthy was a relatively early casualty (though he did return briefly for what was conceived as their last throw of the dice) and Hutchings himself abandoned ship to launch another new vehicle for his vision, the Albion Country Band, when he saw the pressures of success diluting intent. None of the Steeleyes had ever envisaged that worldwide tours and hit singles would ever become part of the equation for traditional music.

The **Albion Country Band** were something of a folk supergroup, featuring various ex-Fairports, Richard Thompson and Martin Carthy amid its ever-evolving incarnations. In the early '80s, Hutchings changed the group's name to the **Albion Dance Band**, and shifted the music accordingly, deciding that the future lay with "English Country Dance", a music rooted in history yet which didn't have to be rigidly structured – and indeed provided admirable scope for development.

Many other folk-rock bands emerged in the wake of the Steeleyes' success. Most of them were awful, though the other half of that original Keele thought-tank, **Bob Pegg**, achieved great critical acclaim if little commercial success alongside his fiddle-touting, singing wife, **Carole Pegg**, with the volatile **Mr Fox**. One of their offshoots, **Five Hand Reel**, later took the notion of electric folk to new areas of authenticity with the Scottish traditional singer Dick Gaughan; and there was a brief flurry of folk-rock excitement during the Eighties when two respected folk figures, **Bill Caddick** and **John Tams**, combined to create the **Home Service** from the remains of one of Hutchings' Albion enterprises, merging Steeleyesque ideas with a full-blooded brass section.

The ubiquitous Ashley Hutchings tries out one band too many

But bands like the Home Service were impossibly expensive to maintain and with the record industry moving on to new toys, the folk-rock movement collapsed amid grumbling about insensitive drummers and going up one-way streets backwards. The one really enduring group were the **Oyster Band** (see box), a wonderful outfit who dipped liberally into folk and pop traditions, and hit on a more rock sound in collaboration with **June Tabor**.

Tabor herself deserves much more than an Oyster footnote. Since her 1976 debut, she has played with most names in the folk-rock world, including the Albion Band, the Fairports, Martin Carthy, and with Maddy Prior and the guitarist and songwriter **Nic Jones**. She has perhaps the finest voice around on the folk circuit and is as much at ease with trad or rock arrangements and songs – truly a national treasure.

WILD IN THE COUNTRY

If the 1960s were dominated by protest music and the singer-songwriters, and the '70s by Steeleye/Fairport folk-rock, then the '80s were the domain of **roots dance music**. Working from a new and wonderful fusion of influences, these new roots bands might, a few years ago, have been labelled folk-rockers, but most of them wouldn't understand the significance of the term were it to bite them in the upper groin region.

The moving spirit behind this new roots scene was one **Rod Stradling**, a long-time iconoclast on the folk scene who had been involved since the early 1970s in a series of hugely influential bands. The first of these, **Oak**, concentrated on English country music, inspired by that seminal 1965 album, and were followed by the **Old Swan Band**, who affected defiant attitudes as an antidote to the Celtic music that obsessed the English folk scene of the time. Then came the **English Country Blues Band**, with bottleneck and slide-guitarist Ian A. Anderson, who laced their dance music with blues and slowly transmuted into **Tiger Moth** – a raucous electric band who still appear from time to time as **Orchestre Super Moth**, mixing it with all manner of World Music influences.

Stradling, however, in the late 1980s concentrated his considerable energies on yet another new band, **Edward II & The Red Hot Polkas**. This was his most ambitious and

THE OYSTER BANDITS

. . . .

Over the last decade, the **Oyster Band** have dominated the English roots music scene.

The group started out purely as an informal dance band of flexible personnel and erratic style after meeting at Canterbury University in the 1970s. The full incarnation often had as many as thirteen musicians on stage, though a more manageable acoustic group, Fiddlers Dram, splintered from it to play club gigs and in 1979 unexpectedly hit the jackpot with a #3 novelty single, the best-forgotten "Day Trip To Bangor". Fame and fortune notwithstanding, the group's three mainstays – Ian Telfer, Alan Prosser and John Jones – were more interested in exploring the relatively uncharted territory of roots dance music, and Fiddlers Dram were cast to the wind.

As the Oyster Band, their first big achievement was the neatly titled album "English Rock'n'Roll: The Early Years 1800–1850", an exciting, improvised statement of intent and a clear milestone for English dance music. The band's line-up settled with Telfer (actually a Scotsman!), Prosser and Jones joined by Ian Kearey and Chris Taylor. A tight multi-instrumental unit, they were keen to take risks, fusing folk with all sorts, and gained a following among rock as well as folk audiences, especially from the mid-1980s, when they added a drummer, Russell Lax, and turned more electric and guitar-orientated.

"Being English can be the kiss of death," commented John Jones. "You've got to overcome so many things to actually make it feel radical and different and genuinely alternative." Whatever, they have managed it. Jones still pumps away on his trusty melodeon and sings in a Yorkshire accent, Telfer leaps around dementedly as he plays fiddle, and Prosser waggles his head like a nodding dog in the back of a Ford Capri while he weaves intricate guitar patterns. Yet the Oysters have crossed over to an astonishing degree, sounding as vital as any thrusting young rock band yet maintaining the respect of their original folk audience.

They've made some cracking albums along the way, too, and have been instrumental in breaking down many of the remaining vestiges of prejudices against any folk-based music in their eternal quest for the ultimate English roots album. All this and they still fill a dance floor in seconds.

defiant idea to date, mixing English country dance music, sublimely, with reggae. You can't take such liberties without getting up somebody's nose and Edward II certainly did that, but their work with reggae dubmaster the **Mad Professor** at the mixing desk is possibly the single most significant leap for English country music. You have to like reggae music in the first place, of course, but the idea of merging the music of last century rural England with the sound of the modern cities was a

masterstroke, and for all its audacity a logical one. The band's first album, "Let's Polkasteady" in 1987, was a veritable earthquake in roots circles, and over the next few years, latterly sans Stradling, they have moved on to develop an arresting Caribbean-English fusion.

Stradling saw the Polkas as essentially a dance band, albeit somewhat more modern in vision than the Ashley Hutchings' Albion incarnations. Subsequently people with ever

A Leveller in ascending mode

a radical left/green band as any the rock world has thrown forth, playing benefits for free and living on the road.

Up north there has been a lot of good action, too. The **Tansads** from Wigan, based around John Kettle and his brothers, produced a committed and tasteful funk roots, with tongue-in-cheek lyrics, guitar, accordion and brass. The **Whiskey Priests** from Newcastle are another great creation: all flat caps and mining songs, but more Pogues than Lindisfarne in delivery. Equally wonderful was the brief appearance of the Deighton Family, Yorskhire and South Moluccan by origin, who were equally at home playing "All Shook Up" as "Handsome Molly".

Other stars in the new dance roots firmament include **The Barely Works**, who took on the gauntlet of musical anarchy and invested it with a colourful conglomerate of melodies and styles. Put together around Chris Thompson, who had already made a small mark on the folk revolution with the splendidly ramshackle **Boothill Foot-Tappers**, the Barelys offered a richly joyous resume of everything from bluegrass to eastern European gypsy music. Barriers and prejudices were decimated in the

wilder hair and stranger instruments took on the baton. **Blowzabella**, erratic but never dull, carved out a starring role, introducing English country dance to rhythms from the Balkans and beyond, with Nigel Eaton cranking things out on hurdy gurdy. They have split, alas, but continue to perform in various combos.

Other notables included **Flowers & Frolics**, who played more traditional dance material – jigs, polkas, hornpipes, and the like – in a somewhat Oyster Band mode, and the **Cock & Bull Band**, from the unlikely roots home of Milton Keynes. They continue to produce thoughtful dance music with a wide and exotic range of instruments, including mandocello and appalachian dulcimer, and an excellent French pipe player, Jean-Pierre Rasle.

And then from Brighton there are the anarchic, aforementioned **Levellers**, who play a defiant roots music to predominantly

Drummer Tim Walmsley hogging the Barely Works limelight

rock audiences and assert that "being called a folk group makes us very angry". They mix in all manner of Celtic and English influences with often bizarrely recycled instruments, including of late a kind of didgeridoo, to produce a powerful, moody sound, highlighted by astute, political lyrics. As part of the New Age traveller world of alternative 1990s England, they are as committed

full-blooded wake of a trio of fascinatingly oddball albums. They split in 1993 after a long trawl of gigs and festivals, though have reappeared sporadically of late, and in violinist Alison Jones, accordionist Sarah Allen and tuba player Alice Kinloch, boast musicians likely to stay on the cutting edge of roots (and haircuts) for a while to come.

This revival of roots music has had a bonus in the rebirth of **traditional music** among young musicians at the all-important ground level. In addition to the previously noted duo of **Eliza Carthy** and **Nancy Kerr**, with their duelling fiddles and vibrant voices, **Chris Wood** and **Andy Cutting** have been leading the charge for a couple of years. Cutting first made his name as a precocious teenage melodeon player with Blowzabella, and his partnership with the exquisite Kent fiddle player Chris Wood has been likened to that of Martin Carthy and Dave Swarbrick, such is their natural fluency and innovation. This has lately taken the form of embracing French-Canadian music.

The **Lakeman Brothers** from Devon, all teenagers, have been stunning festival audiences with their virtuosity on a variety of instruments and a style that openly embraces jazz and rock, as well as the English tradition, with an encouraging debut album, "Three Piece Suite" (including a Billy Joel song!), emerging from their own beautifully named Crapstone label, which isn't a comment on the music but the Devonian town from which they hail.

The **Young Tradition Award** has actively encouraged this trend, with outstanding musicians like **Simon Thoumire**, **Catriona MacDonald** and the brilliant young piano-accordion player **Luke Daniels** emerging as genuine forces in its wake. And, of course, talent is self-perpetuating. For each glamorous young star who comes on the scene to pick up a bit of publicity and sell a few records, another few hundred may be tempted to pick up a fiddle or an accordion or an acoustic guitar or whatever to see if they can give it a go.

English roots music's increasingly cosmopolitan nature also bodes well for the future. Edward II's experiments with reggae were but a drop in the ocean of musical cultures now second nature to most urban areas of the country. It is surely only a matter of time before the Asian bhangra and ghazal traditions (see Chapter Five) get a wider grip on English music. It has already been happening to a limited degree since the late '80s when the English Punjabi band **Alaap** – the first major bhangra band – started mixing cultures and traditions, and took a further leap when the much-vaunted ghazal singer **Najma Akhtar** released an acclaimed fusion album, "Qareeb", and

New generation fiddlers Eliza Carthy and Nancy Kerr

followed it with one or two folk festival appearances.

The best shots in this direction, to date, however, have come from the mesmerizing **Sheila Chandra**. She may have initially come to attention in the early Eighties with a gimmicky exoticism surrounding her Asian-rock band **Monsoon**, but her solo work in recent years has been as challenging and innovative as any. Her albums "Weaving My Ancestors' Voices" and "The Zen Kiss" are visionary melting pots of culture and tradition. "I became aware that the ornaments that British folk singers used were the same as those in the North Indian vocal tradition," she says. "Then I realized I'd also heard this in Islamic vocals, Andalusian vocals and the music of Bulgaria. Suddenly it became crystal clear."

With such clarity around, the future for English roots music looks rich indeed. And as for the present, well, with the range being presented at festivals, and the maverick diversity of the current crop of roots bands, I'd say English folk music is in safe hands. Most pleasing of all, perhaps, is that you can wander into a pub in any English city and hear a band mixing styles, cultures, traditions and instruments, and (probably unknowingly) utilizing the enduring values of that splendid "English Country Music" LP from the dark and distant past of 1965.

COMPILATIONS

Ⓒ **Various** *The Folk Collection* (Topic, UK). This budget-priced compilation is a healthy introduction for the uninitiated. It goes beyond English music, including Patrick Street and Four Men And A Dog from Ireland, and Dick Gaughan and Ewan MacColl from Scotland, but the tracks by Richard Thompson, Martin Carthy & Dave Swarbrick, Maddy Prior, June Tabor and Nic Jones give it a formidable English bias.

Ⓒ **Various** *Folk Heritage I* and *II* (Music Club, UK). A compilation that admirably reflects the history of the British folk scene, while providing enough modern evidence of a continuing tradition to give it contemporary relevance. Among the more intriguing inclusions are the Silly Sisters (the brief alliance between Maddy Prior and June Tabor), the visionary multicultural band Blowzabella, and the brilliant London-based Irishman Ron Kavana.

Ⓒ **Various** *The Cutting Edge* (Cooking Vinyl, UK). Subtitled "A Selection Of Contemporary British Roots Music", this was Cooking Vinyl's trailblazing flagship for the new dawn of roots music in the '80s. Many influential young guns of the movement are here, including the Oyster Band, Rory McLeod, Edward II & the Red Hot Polkas and the amazing Deighton Family from Yorkshire.

TRADITIONAL AND REVIVAL

Alistair Anderson *Steel Skies* (Topic, UK/Flying Fish, US). A great album from this concertina player and piper, inspired by his native Northumbria and rooted in music centuries old.

Ⓒ **Eliza Carthy and Nancy Kerr** *Eliza Carthy & Nancy Kerr* (Mrs Casey, UK). Astonishing 1994 debut by two teenagers of immaculate roots pedigree. They play duelling fiddles with rare verve and the defiant simplicity of their arrangements is fresh enough to recall an earlier golden age. There's also one song, "The Wrong Favour", which indicates the arrival of Carthy as a major songwriter.

Ⓒ **Martin Carthy and Dave Swarbrick** *Life And Limb* (Special Delivery, UK). One of the seminal duos of English acoustic music, who were huge in the folk clubs in the '60s before going on to higher-profile glories playing guitar and fiddle respectively with Steeleye Span and Fairport Convention. They re-formed as an occasional touring outfit at the start of the '90s and this little gem emerged to show their rapport undiminished by the passing years.

The Copper Family *A Song For Every Season* (Leader, UK). This was originally a four-album boxed set, released in 1971 in sync with Bob Copper's book detailing the life and times of Britain's premier singing family in rural Sussex. It was later re-released as a single album under the same title. Both stand as glorious monuments to the family who have provided much of the country's fund of traditional folk song.

Ⓒ **Old Hat Dance Band** *Old Hat Dance Band* (Mellophone, UK). A wonderful country roots outing from a band of former Old Swans, Oysters and the like that revolves around the Suffolk trad scene stalwart John Howson. The music is good-time, foot-cranking stuff, played by an array of instrumentalists – virtuosos all – including trad dulcimer player Reg Reader, fiddler Chris Wood and concertina man Mel Dean.

Ⓒ **June Tabor** *Aqaba* (Topic, UK). The finest female singer in the land at her stark best, full of suppressed passion and vocal subtleties. Her sullen mood music won't get you dancing round the living room – but few performers come more powerful than this.

Scan Tester *I Never Played to Many Posh Dances* (Topic, UK). Wondrous double album of 52 tunes from the legendary concertina and fiddle player who inspired many of the young breed of English country musicians. There's an excellent companion book of the same title by Reg Hall.

Ⓒ **Kathryn Tickell Band** *Sign* (Black Crow, UK). Released in 1993, this album marked a quantum leap in the career of the golden girl of Northumbrian piping. She tackles a variety of styles – including Cajun and Greek – and her band is thrillingly ambitious.

Ⓒ **The Watersons** *For Pence And Spicey Ale* (Topic, UK). A vintage collection from the Yorkshire singing family, with Mike, Norma and Lal Waterson reinforced by Norma's husband Martin Carthy. Unaccompanied harmony singing is what they are most widely recognized for, and they rarely sound better than here.

Various *English Country Music* (Topic, UK). The famous collection put together by Reg Hall and Bob Davenport in a limited edition of 99 copies, which subsequently fired up a whole generation of young players and would-be folk-rockers. It features, among many other delights, the hammer dulcimer playing of Billy Cooper.

ELECTRIC AND CONTEMPORARY

Ⓒ **The Albion Country Band** *Rise Up Like the Sun* (EMI, UK). Ashley Hutchings' exploding vision of an "English rock music" in its all-time-greatest line-up, featuring Martin Carthy and John Kirkpatrick.

Ⓒ **The Barely Works** *Glow* (Cooking Vinyl, UK). Dazzling musical anarchy swirls around the Barelys' instinctive lust for bizarre tangents and the paradoxically well-ordered songwriting of Chris Thompson. Too many different styles to meet any particular criteria of sound with its mish-mash of banjos, fiddles and accordions, but this is the most immediate of their three albums.

Ⓒ **Blowzabella** *Pingha Frenzy* (Some Bizarre Product, UK). A wonderful testament to the band recorded live in Brazil (where else?) in 1988.

Ⓒ **Billy Bragg** *Talking With The Taxman About Poetry* (Go! Discs, UK). The man who arrived barking during the mid-80s to take up the cudgels of folkarama and restore some much-needed pride. All bristling working-class dignity and matey cockney pride, Bragg almost singlehandedly rehabilitated English singer-songwriters, and this album, originally issued in 1986, was an important step for him, bridging his move from world to personal politics.

Ⓒ **Sheila Chandra** *The Zen Kiss* (Real World, UK). Traditional English melodies crossed with Indian, blues and gospel delivery and techno sampling. Gorgeous and fascinating.

Ⓒ **Sandy Denny** *Who Knows Where The Time Goes?* (Hannibal, UK). A magnificent four-album anthology issued as a memorial to the greatest English singer produced by the folk movement. Denny had two influential spells with Fairport Convention, leaving to form her own band Fotheringay, though she was pursuing a solo career when a fall down some stairs tragically ended her life in 1978.

Ⓒ **Edward II and the Red Hot Polkas** *Let's Polkasteady* (Cooking Vinyl, UK) **and** *Wicked Man* (Pure Bliss, UK). *Polkasteady* launched Stradling's vision of reggae and English roots; *Wicked*, recorded sans Stradling, moved to an arresting Caribbean-English fusion which those hysterical souls at Folk Roots greeted as "the first sighting of 21st Century music".

Ⓒ **Fairport Convention** *Liege and Lief* (Hannibal, UK). By popular consent, this was the greatest ever Fairport album, and the veritable progenitor of folk-rock. The line-up included Ashley Hutchings and Sandy Denny, both of whom quit the band (though Denny was to return) after the recording.

Ⓒ **Home Service** *Alright Jack* (Fledg'ling/Hokey Pokey, UK). The last of the major folk-rock bands and one of the most progressive, combining an excellent brass section with a strong John Tams/Bill Caddick front line and some fiery material. Economic restraints blunted their edge and they missed the golden era, but this was an exceptional album.

Ⓓ **Nic Jones** *Penguin Eggs* (Topic, UK). One of the golden boys from the '70s English folk revival, captured here at the point of his graduation from straight interpreter of traditional songs to innovative performer, arranger and outrageously fine guitarist. Sadly he hasn't performed in public since a horrendous car crash in 1982, but this is a glorious reminder.

Ⓓ **The Lakeman Brothers** *Three Piece Suite* (Crapstone, UK). Debut album by a young Devon-based band of virtuosos, who bring jazz and rock influences to bear on the English tradition.

Ⓓ **The Levellers** *See Nothing, Hear Nothing, Do Something* (China, UK). Isolated from the rock tradition by their maverick independence and socially aware material, The Levellers have created their own niche with their dedication to an alternative lifestyle and folk leanings. This is a wonderfully rag-taggle collection of obscure B-sides, live cuts and alternative versions.

Ⓓ **Oyster Band** *From Little Rock to Leipzig* (Hannibal, UK/Ryko, US). An exemplary compilation documenting the band's rise from their ceilidh roots to their more rock-oriented 1990s sound.

Ⓓ **Steeleye Span** *Please To See The King* (Mooncrest, UK). The crucial 1971 album which effectively launched folk-rock: Martin Carthy strapping on an electric guitar for the first time, Maddy Prior's voice soaring gloriously, Peter Knight full of guile and daring on the fiddle. It has aged well.

Ⓓ **The Tansads** *Up The Shirkers* (Musidisc, UK). Seven-piece band from Wigan sporting a colourful collection of ages, cultures and hairstyles, built around the fierce songwriting of John Kettle, the passionate vocals of his teenage brother Andrew, and the cooing counterpoints of Janet Anderton. A peculiar bunch, but a great live act and a formidable representation of English roots music, 1990s style.

Ⓓ **Richard Thompson** *Watching The Dark* (Hannibal, UK/Ryko, US). Triple CD compilation charting the great English guitarist-songwriter's career, from Fairport to life with Linda to solo albums, and with a few oddities thrown in along the way. Thompson's influence on the whole English roots thang has been massive across three generations, and he's touched crucial elements of rock as well.

FROM THE BALTIC TO THE BALKANS

This chapter doesn't cover a geographically or ethnically unified area: far from it. The pieces that follow relate, very broadly, to "Eastern European" territories – stretching the term a bit beyond to west and east – and these regions are as ethnically diverse and geographically varied as they come. So, too, of course, is the music, which is amongst the world's most sophisticated and beautiful, quite at odds with the current state of turmoil in much of the region.

A lot of the music discussed here is real folk music which still exists in an original form. Traditional music survives on the fringes of twentieth-century civilization in remote parts of the Baltic and eastern Europe which became fringes as a result of political circumstance. The regimes of communist eastern Europe had varying attitudes to their traditional cultures but they all preserved in one form or another rich musical traditions that have been lost in the west.

In Transylvania, for example, the isolationist policies of Romania's Nicolae Ceausescu, combined with the unique ethnic mix of the region, have left the richest folk culture in Europe. The distinctive singing of Bulgaria has been the most spectacular international success, but there are plenty more unfamiliar sounds, ready to emerge.

As the countries of eastern Europe are painfully breaking up into their constituent ethnic groups, national music has also become a powerful force as a statement of identity. This is true of most of the region – and most obviously and tragically so in the former Yugoslavia.

But this chapter goes beyond the Balkans to include the former Soviet Union, thus ranging in effect from the Baltic to Baikal. The diverse nationalities that made up the Russian and then the Soviet empire have ethnic links which take them way beyond the realms of this "European" chapter, and into Asia. But their common history

means that like the Baltic and Balkan countries Georgia, Armenia and all the former Soviet Republics are using their distinctive national voices to break out of Russian domination.

In another of Europe's fringe areas, the mountain fastness of the Alps, this chapter covers the collision between a conservative traditional culture and the radical trends of punk and contemporary jazz to reveal some of Europe's most surprising sounds. Brazilian-Bavarian music and Alpunk: its all here!

The range of music throughout the territories of this chapter is really astonishing: the haunting sounds of Ashkabad from Turkmenistan or the "throat singers" of Tuva, the radical vocals of Värttinä from Finland, the dissonant majesty of Georgian choirs, the wild and melancholy sounds of Transylvania, the rhythmic jazz virtuosity of Bulgaria's Ivo Papasov and the punkish drive of Attwenger from Austria. There are some extraordinary vocalists, too, like Mari Boine, Márta Sebestyén, Nadka Karadzhova and the Bulgarian choirs, and politically charged singer-songwriters, like the late-lamented Vladimir Vysotsky, who was the conscience of Russia through the Brezhnev period.

All these artists and traditions show that the extreme diversity of central and eastern Europe should be a source of richness and strength for a very long while.

Outside their strictly geographical settings the musical styles of eastern Europe are also proving a potent force. The powerful singing of Bulgaria has been used in commercials and feature films, while British-based groups like Orbestra, The Ukrainians and 3 Mustaphas 3 demonstrate that these traditional east European forms can be used to create wonderful music far beyond its original context. And in many cases this new international attention means that local music gains strength at home.

Ashik (Ashug) Turkish or Azeri (Ashik) or Armenian (Ashug) wandering minstrels.

Balalaika Three-stringed Russian folk instrument with triangular body. Popular since the eighteenth century.

Cimbalom Hungarian hammer dulcimer found in village bands and Budapest restaurant orchestras.

Contra (kontra) Three-stringed viola playing the chords in a Transylvanian band.

Csárdás Hungarian couple dance.

Doina Romanian song with rhapsodic form and melancholy character.

Domra Russian three-stringed mandolin. Forerunner of the balalaika.

Duduk Armenian oboe with a plaintive sound.

Dudy Czech bagpipes.

Gajda Balkan bagpipes.

Gadulka Bulgarian fiddle with three or four strings, played vertically in front of the chest.

Gusle Serbian and Montonegrin one-stringed fiddle, played - by a **guslar** - to accompany epic songs.

Hammer dulcimer Instrument with a trapezoid sounding box and strings struck with two hammers, common in Hungary (cimbalom) and Romania (tsambal).

Hardingfele (Hardanger fiddle) Norwegian folk fiddle with four "sympathetic" or drone strings.

Hora (horo, kolo, oro) Ring-dances, ubiquitous in Romania, Bulgaria, and ex-Yugoslavia, all of which have different forms.

Hurdy-gurdy Drone instrument with melody strings bowed by a wheel.

Jodl Yodel – a song without words for calling across Alpine valleys.

Joik Song of the Sami people, often improvised and epigrammatic.

Kantele Finnish zither and national instrument with over forty strings in its most developed form.

Kaval Long wooden Bulgarian and Macedonian rim-blown flute.

Ländler Central European dance with moderate 3/4 beat.

Maqam (mugam) Arabic scale in which a whole piece or suite of pieces may be played.

Nai Romanian panpipes.

Nyckelharpa Swedish keyed fiddle.

Polka Dance from Bohemia in 2/4 time.

Polska Swedish dance in triple time.

Rebec The first known European string instrument, rather like a lute, played on the knee and depicted in angel hands in numerous medieval frescoes. It has many modern offspring in eastern Europe.

Saz Long-necked lute of Turkish origin.

Schrammelmusik Viennese music originating in the wine taverns in the nineteenth century.

Spelmanslag Swedish folk ensemble.

Stubenmusik Alpine string ensemble music.

Tambura Long-necked, round-backed Bulgarian or Macedonian lute with three or four double courses of strings.

Táncház Contemporary Hungarian folk dancing movement.

Taraf Romanian village ensemble.

Tsambal Romanian hammer dulcimer.

Tapan, (tupan) Barrel drum played in Bulgaria and Macedonia.

Zither Plucked or strummed instrument with strings strung along a wooden sounding board. Various forms across Europe.

Zurna (surna, zurla, curla, pizgë) Loud, simple oboe found in Turkey and throughout the Balkans.

THE MIDNIGHT SOUND

SCANDINAVIA'S FINN-LED FOLK REVIVAL

The music of the countries on the northern rim of Europe, long overlooked, is beginning to make its mark on the World Music community as young musicians explore their roots and reinvent their traditions. Magnus Bäckström and Phillip Page unveil the northern folk scene, one of the freshest and most exciting in Europe.

T he Scandinavian countries, with their high living standards and well-developed social security, are very much part of the industrialized western world. Yet, like other countries on the geographical fringes of Europe, they have preserved a distinctive folk music in the long northern shadows as part of their twentieth-century culture.

Much of this music goes back a long way, but in the last few years there has been an explosion of creativity, with young musicians rescuing music that had been in danger of dying out. They have given it a fresh new sound, promiscuously mixing in all manner of influences from all manner of places to produce one of present-day Europe's liveliest folk music scenes.

The most ancient music is associated with animal herding, the age-old way of life in the region. Animal horns, from cows or goats, were used to signal across the mountains and valleys in all the northern countries and this music, and the vocal herding music closely related to it, are the ancestors of "modern" Scandinavian folk music. Right across the region, however, it is the violin that is the most important instrument, along with its regional varieties like the Norwegian Hardanger fiddle. And it's often not so much the melodies themselves as the particular ornaments and accents that are added to them by individual musicians that gives the music its special identity.

There is an identifiable Scandinavian sound behind much of the music, though it displays a great variety of forms, styles and attitudes. On the one hand many folk musicians exhibit nostalgia for the turn-of-the-century National Romantic era; on the other there's a more radical feeling among the post-war generation who came to it via the Vietnam protest movement of the 1960s and the struggle to find their own identity against Anglo-American cultural domination. And more recently there's been a revival of interest in local roots traditions and experiments with World Music fusions. Finland is where the most dynamic musical culture is developing now.

FINLAND

Culturally, Finland is the odd one out of the Scandinavian countries – sandwiched between Sweden and Russia with the Baltic Sea to the south. The language is unrelated to the neighbouring Germanic languages of Scandinavia, but with its close cousin Estonian, belongs to the Finno-Ugric group, which has its roots amongst various non-Slavic tribes on Russian territory.

A country of 188,000 lakes, endless forests and vast open spaces, Finland has developed quickly since World War II, catching up with the other Scandinavian countries in the standard of living and surpassing them in economic growth. Considering the small population of Finland – a mere five million – the number and quality of its musicians and groups is staggering, as is their energetic approach to their traditions. On the current World Music scene it is the Finnish groups like Värttinä and JPP who are making the biggest waves with their iconoclastic reinterpretations of traditional culture.

The musical character of Scandinavia is often on the dour side, and Finnish music has perhaps the most melancholy sound of all. You can hear it even in some of the more modern tunes as played by the late master fiddler Konsta Jylhä. But then again a lot of Finnish music is

Old-time Finnish kantele group

as fast and joyful as any. It has an interesting mix of influences from Russia and Sweden (there is a strong Swedish cultural influence in Finland) and ranges from the dance melodies of slow fiddle-waltzes and wild polkas, both often accompanied by a pumping harmonium – one of the characteristic sounds of Finnish folk music – to the ethereal sound of the kantele.

The zither-like **kantele** is the national Finnish instrument and dates from ancient times. In the Kalevala saga, Väinämöinen, the mythical hero, subdues his foes by playing on his kantele, made from the jawbone of a giant fish strung with a maiden's hair. The instrument was originally five-stringed – you still find these today – but it has developed variants over the years that range up to giant chromatic kanteles that can be used to play western classical music; the melodies and accompanying chords are plucked on the rows of strings. The kantele appears in various forms all along the Baltic coast. In Estonia it is the **kannel,** in Latvia the **kokle** and in Lithuania the **kankles.** It has a magical, silvery tone that seems to carry both the listener and the players away into the vast forests of Karelia or the depths of the Baltic sea.

The usual north European waltzes, mazurkas and marches all have their Finnish forms, as does the Swedish polska (see p.49), although with a much more even beat than in Sweden. But nowhere in the Nordic countries does the polka (without the s) have such importance as in Finland, and Finnish polkas are often "exported"

into Swedish or Norwegian folk music. The vocal repertoire and the songs of the national epic, the Kalevala, are also central to the tradition.

Kaustinen, a small village in the middle of Finland, east of Vaasa, is well known for its traditional culture and high percentage of folk musicians. Since 1968 it has hosted the largest folk music festival in the country. Kaustinen is also the home of the **KMI**, the Kansanmusiikki-instituutti (Folk Music Institute), an important archival and research centre, established in 1974, which has produced some fine recordings of Finnish musical traditions. The Jeppo district in the Finnish–Swedish area in the west is famous for its minuets, still played and danced in a living tradition.

The maestro of Finnish folk music, the Kaustinen fiddler **Konsta Jylhä**, is almost a national hero. He died a few years ago, but his many compositions, of which "Konstan parempi valsi" waltz is one of the most loved, are still often played and belong in the standard repertoire of Finnish folk musicians. Another character of a different kind was **Teppo Repo**, who carried on the ancient tradition of herding music playing various flutes and horns as well as the kantele.

Today the Kaustinen scene is literally swarming with exciting and talented young players and bands. Top of the list is fiddle group **JPP** (Järvellan Pikkupelimannit). With a line-up of anything from four to nine fiddlers (sometimes as many as thirty), backed by acoustic bass and harmonium, this band has gone way beyond the traditional *pelimanni* (folk musician) style to

JPP hit the road with their customized tour bus

VÄRTTINÄ

Värttinä evolved out of a youth group that started performing north Karelian folk music in the 1980s. Now in a slimmed-down form, with four female vocalists and an instrumental group, they are one of Finland's most dynamic ensembles, winning their audience in rock clubs as well as folk festivals.

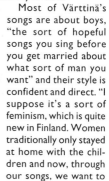

"We don't wear national costume," explains their leader, Sari Kaarinen, "because it's old fashioned and people will think that we are singing and playing that boring old folk music."

Exuberant and aggressive, they sing the music of the Finno-Ugric people of Karelia and Ingria. These districts (most of which are now in Russia) have a distinctive vocal tradition with strong irregular rhythms very different from the rest of Finland. Värttinä learn their repertoire from old collections and recordings of music made early this century and from the groups of elderly women singers that still perform this music in Russia. Some of the most beautiful are old Ingrian dance songs that have their own particular harmonies. They've also travelled farther afield to learn tunes from Finno-Ugric people like the Mari and Setu much deeper inside Russia.

"We are singing these songs in our own style for today. Although our lives have changed, they haven't changed that much and these songs are still suitable. We have the same joy and sorrows as a hundred years ago. You can hear from these songs that people wanted to celebrate and escape their poor hard life. Where we are different is performing with instrumentalists. The tradition in Finland is that women sing and men play – but not together! I think there's a national feeling too. Now that Finland is going to join up with the rest of Europe, perhaps people are keen to have something that is specifically Finnish and they can say is ours."

Most of Värttinä's songs are about boys, "the sort of hopeful songs you sing before you get married about what sort of man you want" and their style is confident and direct. "I suppose it's a sort of feminism, which is quite new in Finland. Women traditionally only stayed at home with the children and now, through our songs, we want to say you must be strong, and show that women always have been very strong in our culture."

Miinan Laulu (Miina's Song)

Red and blue roses growing on a rock
That is what a young girl's suitor should be like
If only I could stamp that rose into the ground
If only I could attract that handsome boy

My sweetheart was playing the accordion
And I went to hear it
The accordion was put away
And we started kissing

You fool, you paid a mark
I only paid a kopeck
You lay in bed under a blanket
I lay on the floor

I am a small girl
Like the string of a fiddle
When I walk down the road
Boys fancy me

Old woman, give me that handsome boy
And give him without a quarrel
As I will take him anyway
And will not let him stay a boy.

create an adventurous and highly distinctive music. They have become one of the most important groups in the country. Central to their success are fiddlers Mauno and Arto Järvelä (uncle and nephew) and harmonium player Timo Alakotila. Their newly composed pieces, mostly written by Arto or Timo, are notable for their melodic elegance and cheeky harmonic sideslips that pull the rug from underneath their listeners before returning them to the home key at the last possible second. Combined with Mauno's genius for precision they have taken JPP into a league of their own.

Another fine group, closely associated with KMI, is **Tallari**. Popular and widely respected, their aim is to research, present and preserve the multitude of Finnish musical traditions, mixing fiddle, kantele, harmonium, clarinet and mandolin with rare and ancient instruments such as birch-bark and jouhikko (three-stringed lyre).

New on the scene, and making quite a splash with a punchy repertoire that includes Balkan and bluegrass flavours, is the wild and fiery quintet **Troka**, featuring JPP's Timo Alakotila on harmonium and Matti Mäkelä on fiddle, plus second fiddle, bass and accordion.

Other Kaustinen bands include **Salamkann** (Lightning Kantele), featuring KMI director Hannu Saha on kantele; thrash folk group **Folkkarit**; and **Spontaani Vire**, a quartet of accordion, clarinet, fiddle and the harmonium of young virtuoso Eero Grandström.

Further south in Helsinki the Folk Music Department of the **Sibelius Academy** has been in operation since 1983. The spirit here, as established by founding director **Heikki Laitinen**, is also one of adventurous innovation, with roots firmly planted in tradition and an openness to all manner of influences. Several outstanding groups have emerged from the department, one of the earliest (in 1983) being **Niekku**, a six-musician band (five of them women), who used a wide array of folk instruments in a sparse, almost ambient setting; they were pioneers in the "New Finnish Folk" movement.

Rising from the ashes of Niekku is accordionist **Maria Kalaniemi** and her band, which includes some of Finland's best young folk musicians. A virtuoso of the free-bass accordion, Kalaniemi's playing is fluid and sensitive, her repertoire vast, and her compositions and arrangements a sheer delight. She has quickly become one of Finland's most prized young musicians.

Two other forward-looking bands with their origins in the department are **Pirnales** and **Ottopasuuna**, the former taking the kantele to new levels of sophistication in their collaborations with kantele master **Martti Pokela**, a true revolutionary, and the latter specializing in digging up obscure tunes from the Finno-Ugric tradition and giving them unorthodox arrangements. Their unusual instrumentation of saxophone, clarinet, fiddles, mandolin, and percussion allows a unique framework for experimentation.

The most astonishing group, and the most internationally successful to have emerged from the Academy, is **Värttinä** (see box), four female vocalists and an instrumental backing group who have revitalized Finno-Ugric tradition with a distinctively modern style and an exuberant and aggressive approach. A household word in Finland, they have developed the distinctive polyphonic singing tradition of Karelia, the region of eastern Finland that extends into Russia.

Karelia, the "land of destiny", holds a great place in Finnish culture as the area where the Kalevala, the evocative national myth which deals with the forging of the mysterious Sampo and the struggle for its control between the imaginary lands of Pohjola and Kalevala, was preserved in the oral tradition.

Among the more experimental groups is **Piirpauke**, who have been creating their particular brand of global fusion since the mid-1970s. They combine Finnish folk with African, Asian, Arabic, European, Latin and Caribbean sounds, and their most recent CD includes Andalucian singing and Senegalese percussion.

A cultural fusion that has really taken root in Finland is **tango**. As the Finns would have it, the twin capitals of tango are Buenos Aires and Helsinki. The melancholy side of the Argentinian dance really seems to have taken hold of the Finns' northern spirit, and tango clubs are regular fixtures all over the country. JPP can play a mean tango, and listen out especially for accordionist **Pedro Hietanen and his Heavy Gentlemen**!

SWEDEN

Fiddling is at the heart of Swedish folk music. The instrument was introduced in the middle of the seventeenth century by six French violinists employed at the court, and within fifty years it had spread all over the country replacing the bagpipes as the leading folk instrument. A large majority of Swedish folk musicians play the fiddle, which means some six or seven thousand round the country.

The district of Dalarna, northwest of Stockholm, is the liveliest centre of Swedish folk culture. Here you find strong regional dialects, costumes worn on special occasions, local traditions and a real sense of cultural identity. Every village has its own ensemble (*spelmanslag*) and music is played for all sorts of occasions. The valley around Lake Siljan is the musical heart of Dalarna and it's said that if you meet two people from Rättvik, one of the local villages, three of them will play the fiddle. This is the district where most of the major folk events take place and where you'll find the leading musicians.

The living legend of Swedish fiddle music is **Päkkos Gustaf**, but the most dynamic fiddler was the great **Hjort Anders** (1865–1952), who was wont to step into a small country church and play a wild "Devil's Polska" just for the hell of it.

Veteran Swedish fiddler
Hjort Anders

Younger fiddlers include Björn Ståbi, Pers Hans, Kalle Almlöf, Jonny Soling and Per Gudmundson. None of them play the tunes straight. Indeed, it's the ornamentation and accents brought to the basic material that reveal the character of the individual musician. As this facility for improvisation is so important it's no coincidence that the relationship between Swedish jazz musicians and folk music is close. Just listen to a recording of the jazz pianist **Jan Johansson**. With his soulful and sensitive improvisations on Swedish folk tunes, he sounds like a real fiddler on the keyboard.

Sweden's other great area of musical interest is Uppland, just north of Stockholm. This is the home of the **nyckelharpa**, a relative of the hurdy-gurdy that is unique to Sweden. Like the hurdy-gurdy, it uses keys to stop the strings, but rather than "bowing" the strings with a revolving wheel, it is bowed by hand. It has a characteristic bumble-bee sound, from drone strings that vibrate behind the melody, and has been dubbed the "sitar of the north". It has become the most popular instrument after the fiddle, especially the chromatic instrument developed by the late Eric Sahlström, Mr Nyckelharpa, in the 1950s. Leading modern players include Åsa Jinder, Väsen's Olov Johansson, and Peter Hedlund. You're likely to see at least one of this trio if you hit on one of Uppland's popular summer nyckelharpa festivals.

As everywhere, the accordion has found its way into the traditional music scene, too, despite the objections of the purists who point out that it cannot reproduce the typical Swedish microtones and ornaments of the violin. More recently the folk revival has seen the rebirth of the Swedish bagpipes, old herding instruments like the cow and goat horns and the spelpipa, the herding flute. These are now a regular part of the musical scene, alongside saxophones, synthesizers and many African and South American instruments.

In traditional Swedish music individual musicians come first, although they all perform in various ensembles which vary from occasion to occasion. Since 1980 more and more fixed ensembles have become established. The leading contemporary folk groups are **Groupa**, **Norrlåter**, **Väsen** and **Den Ful**. In many contemporary groups you find combinations of Swedish traditional elements with African or Caribbean ingredients, plus influences from rock and jazz.

One of the more eclectic contemporary bands is **Hedningarna** (the Heathens), a quintet with two Finnish female singers and three male instrumentalists. Their electro/acoustic mix with synthesizers, samplers, electric bagpipes, hurdy-gurdy, Arabic oud (lute) and percussion and an elaborate stage show has made them a hot property in Swedish music circles and abroad. **Väsen**, a trio of guitar, viola and nyckelharpa, featuring Olov Johansson, is another exciting band; they perform powerful versions of traditional material, along with their own songs.

There are in fact two distinct ages of Swedish folk music. The older tunes tend to be in minor-keys and are often described as "blue" or melancholy. But that's not the whole story. Although to modern ears tunes in the minor generally sound sad and those in the major happy, the old Swedish tunes use particular scales which predate the tempered system used by western classical music. The unwary ear may simply hear them as out of tune, but one of the striking features of the Swedish folk revival is the care taken by young musicians to play these ancient scales correctly. And as far as the emotions go, an old Swedish fiddler interviewed by a folklorist around the turn of the century told him, "You see, in this part of the country we can be merry in the minor too!"

The newer folk music of Sweden (perhaps 150 years old) is shared with all north Europeans in the form of the waltzes, polkas and mazurkas that form the backbone of the European folk tradition – although the Swedes add their own style of ornamentation brought in from the older layers of traditional music.

The most common dance in this repertoire is the **polska** – not to be confused with the European polka. Whereas the polka has a two-beat rhythm, the polska has an intricate and fluid triple beat with complexities similar to those found in Balkan rhythms. Compared with the um-pa-pa rhythm of a waltz, the three beats of the polska have an emphasis on the first and

THE NÄCKEN AND THE DEVIL'S POLSKA

· ·

The fiddle plays a major role in Swedish folklore through the Näcken, a troll and master-fiddler that lives in streams, waterfalls or lakes. There are special Näck-tunes, which require a special tuning of the fiddle-strings, though the folklore stipulates that to learn the magic touch of the Näcken you must hang your fiddle under a bridge across a stream three Thursday nights in succession. The Näcken will then play on your fiddle and put his magic into your instrument. The last Thursday night, though, he will put his own instrument next to your's and you have to pick the right one. If you pick the Näcken's fiddle you are his forever – but pick your own, and with the new Näcken touch you'll become rich and famous.

Another Swedish musical legend is that of the Devil's Polska, from Horga, a small village and great folk music centre in the district of Hälsingland. At a barn dance, so the story goes, all the village youth gather to dance to the local fiddler. Suddenly the door swings open and a dark-dressed stranger appears. He asks to borrow the fiddle and starts to play a special polska. The tune and the playing are so wonderful that no one can keep from dancing and no one can stop – not even when they see the stranger's goat hooves and they realize the devil himself is leading the music. He keeps playing until all the dancers drop down dead – or according to some versions the dead bodies themselves keep on dancing until the skulls roll down the hill. The Horgalåten (Horga tune) is still one of the best-known and most-played tunes in Sweden, though the dramatic effects seem to have been lost!

---

third pulse: pa-um-pa. Swedish musicians tap their feet on the first and third beat of the bar (a habit which they've also brought to the waltz). The sound of the Swedish polska as played by two violins can be very strange and other-worldly. The rhythmic patterns are particularly distinctive.

About eighty percent of the repertoire of Swedish folk musicians is made up of polskas or their more modern variant, the hambo. Other tunes are Swedish versions of the waltz, polka, schottisch and march. The Swedish march, though, has more the feel of a rolling wheel than of a proud and angry army marching to war. Their purpose was often to accompany people walking long distances, not to fight but to find work. Nowadays they are played as concert pieces, but are still used for ceremonial occasions and weddings.

NORWAY

If Norway's indented coastline were straightened out, it would stretch halfway round the world. It's not surprising that amongst the far-flung pockets of settlement, with their 272 dialects of the Norwegian language, a distinctive musical culture exists. It survives at its best in the isolated villages of the Telemark district, west of Oslo, and the mountainous, fjord-riven districts of Hardanger and Voss on the west coast.

In the east, too, close to the Swedish border, the town of Röros is the centre of another area with rich folk music traditions. Norway is unsurpassed in the Nordic countries for its tradition of vocal music, with many prominent singers. Compared to Sweden, where the music exists in a more modernized form, contemporary Norwegian folk music is based far more on traditional forms and instruments.

In addition to the usual waltzes, polkas and mazurkas there is a distinctive Norwegian dance called the **halling**. This immensely energetic male solo dance has the acrobatic ingredients associated with cossack dancing and lots of opportunity for improvisation in the steps and the music. The high spot of the dance comes when the dancer attempts to leap and kick a hat from a stick held by a girl who is herself perched on a chair. A halling has an even two-beat rhythm with a sort of floating feeling to the music.

Other common dances are the somewhat calmer walking dance called the *gangar*, and the *rull*, *springar* and *pols*, all of which are couple dances. The gangar and springar are connected with the Hardanger fiddle repertoire and the pols with flatfele music. The springar, the most widespread of all the Norwegian dances, is nominally in 3/4 time, but the rhythm is so flexible that the three beats rarely have the same length.

The most typical Norwegian sound comes from the **Hardanger fiddle (Harding fele)**, with its very bright tone and set of buzzing drone

THE SAMI AND MARI BOINE

• •

The Sami, or Lapps, live in northern Norway, Sweden and Finland, preserving their own language and a culture related to other arctic peoples. As the indigenous people of arctic Scandinavia, their relations with the colonizers have often been problematic, although, following a political struggle in the early 1980s, originally focussed on plans to combat a planned dam, their rights and way of life are now enshrined in the Norwegian constitution.

Central to Sami music is the joik, an improvised and highly personal style of singing in a sort of epigrammatic form. Often describing nature or animals, joiks illustrate the close relationship that the Sami people have with the world around them. When Sami people sing joiks for each other they don't applaud but simply sing a joik in return.

Contemporary Sami music has seen some dramatic developments over the past few years, with several artists forging an international reputation. Nils-Aslak Valkiapää from Finland performed the opening song at the 1994 Winter Olympic Games in Lillehammer, Norway. His recordings break new ground in Sami music-making, incorporating diverse elements such as symphony orchestra, synthesizer and jazz/folk fusion with the help of the Finnish group Karelia. Angelin Tytöt from the village of Angeli in Finland are a trio (sometimes a duo) of young girls, joiking and singing with guitar and percussion.

It is Norway's Mari Boine (aka Marie Boine Persen), however, who has made the biggest impact outside Sami land with her modern electric band. This singer has been an articulate spokesperson for

Mari Boine lays down some Sami rhythms

Sami culture, both in her music and in interviews. As she explained: "I used to think men oppressing women or governments oppressing people realized what they were doing and were just cynical. But then I realized that often they are unaware and are filled with fear. I feel I have to find my way

to their hearts to let them know what they are doing. It's the only way to change things. That's why I feel my music is important.

"Our first relationship is to nature. You are part of nature, not the master of nature. This also gives us a strong sense of solidarity – you are about other people. Money is not important and power is not important. It's more your personality, the human being that is important."

Mari Boine's music is dominated by her strong and urgent voice, plus a few carefully selected instruments from peoples all over the world, notably the native South Americans, chosen in part due to their history of even harsher colonization. Most distinctive is her drum. She uses an African drum, but the combination of drum and voice goes back to ancient Sami culture and pre-Christian shamanism.

"The colonizers brought Christianity and told the Sami they had to forget their primitive religion – and music was part of that religion. A lot of people of my parent's generation don't accept the music, they say it's devil's music and what you sing when you're drunk – the colonizers also brought alcohol. When I started to use a drum some people got worried and said, 'Is she a Shaman?' So I decided I couldn't use a Sami drum.

"I think your voice is a mirror of your soul and how you feel inside. When I began I was singing pop songs and ballads and didn't sing from the heart. Over the last ten years I've been fighting this feeling of being inferior to Norwegian or western people and my voice got stronger as I decided I wouldn't let anyone oppress me and that I have a value as a Sami. Western culture makes a distance between you and your body or heart. In Sami culture you think of everything as a whole."

Gula Gula (Hear the Voices of the Foremothers)

Hear the voices of the foremothers
Hear
They ask you why you let the earth become polluted
Poisoned
Exhausted
They remind you where you come from
Do you hear?
Again they want to remind you
That the earth is our mother
If we take her life
We die with her.

strings. This developed out of the standard violin and is more or less the national instrument of Norway. It is usually highly decorated with inlay on the fingerboard and around the instrument itself. (Some Swedish fiddlers call it, perhaps enviously, the "tatooed fiddle.") The bright tone comes from tuning it higher than the normal violin, and the four sympathetic strings that vibrate beneath the bowed strings give it a fuller tone suitable for unaccompanied dance music. In the hands of a good player a single instrument can sound like a pair, and a pair sounds practically orchestral. Hardanger fiddles are found in the southwest and up the west coast of Norway. The ordinary fiddle, or **flatfele** (flat fiddle) as Norwegians call it, is found in the northern and eastern parts of the country.

The most famous performer on the Hardanger was Torgeir Augundson, universally known as **Myllarguten** (Miller's Boy). He died over 100 years ago but his legend lives on. Today the Björgum and Buen families dominate the scene: **Hallvard T. Björgum**, son of the late **Thorleif H. Björgum**, and the brothers **Knut** and **Hauk Buen**, are all leading fiddlers, while **Annbjørg Lien** a disciple of Hauk Buen, is a dynamic young player on the scene. **Sven Nyhus** and **Hans W. Brimi** are the leading representatives of the flatfele tradition.

Of the contemporary folk groups, **Slinkombas** have done the most interesting work, but unfortunately they now only exist on record. The singer **Tone Hulbaekmo** is another major figure, having reached a wide audience with his imaginative arrangements of Norwegian traditional songs and his reintroduction of the Norwegian harp.

FESTIVALS AND PARTICIPATION

FINLAND

Kaustinen Folk Festival, held each year in mid-July, is the oldest and largest folk music festival in all the Nordic countries. The week-long event showcases lots of Finnish musicians alongside players and dancers from all over the world.

Other festivals include **Joensuu Song Festival** in Karelia, the **Ikaalinen Accordion Festival** and the **Finnish WOMAD** (both in June), and the **Etnosoi!** world music event in Helsinki (Nov).

In the Swedish-influenced regions of Finland you also get *spelmansstämma* (see below).

SWEDEN

The most typical Swedish folk music event is the **spelmansstämma**, which might be translated as "folk festival" but is really more of a jam session than a concert programme. There is usually a concert ingredient but it's in the informal sessions or buskspel (playing in the bushes!) that the most exciting music takes place. Since the 1970s spelmansstämma have mushroomed, with many of them becoming tourist events, but three remain outstanding occasions: **Bingsjö** (early July), a small village in Dalarna, where some 10,000 people gather for the 24-hour festival; **Delsbo** (early July) in Hälsingland district; and **Ransäter** (early June) in Värmland district.

There are two big international festivals in Sweden: the **Rättviksdansen Folk dance Festival** held in Rättvik, Dalarna (late July); and the **Falun Folk Festival** (FFF; mid-July) held in Falun, the capital of Dalarna. FFF presents a hundred-plus concerts of music from around the world, with Swedish and Dalarna music a major ingredient.

For those who want to learn to play or sing Swedish folk music there are many week-long **summer courses**, and foreign participants are common. Most Swedes speak good English. There are also a few longer winter courses. Further Information from **SSR.** (the Swedish fiddlers' Association) Box 387, 791 28 Falun, or Folklore Centrum, Wollmar Yxkullsgatan 2, 118 50 Stockholm (010 468 643 4627).

NORWAY

The main organized folk events are **kappleik**. These are local, regional and national competitive festivals – rather like sports events – where musicians, singers and dancers enter different classes. The biggest kappleik is the national **Landskappleiken**, held in a different location each year at midsummer.

Förde Folk Music Festival is a new international festival, held at Förde, near Bergen, showcasing Norwegian folk music (early July). There are also jam sessions and dances outside the official programmes.

DENMARK

Denmark has a lot of music festivals, but hardly any highlight Danish folk music. The best bets are the **Tønder Folk Festival** (August) and the **Skagen Festival** (June), although both have an Anglo-American slant.

Most of the discs below are marketed by Digelius Music (Lalvurinrinne 2, 00210 Helsinki; ☎358/0 – 666-375) and are available by mail order from them (along with around 10,000 other World Music titles). Selected titles are distributed in Britain through Topic, Direct and Sterns, and in the US through Green Linnet and Distribution North America.

FINLAND

ⓒ **Various** *Entiset Etniset* (KMI, Finland). The real stuff: archive recordings of Finnish folk music from the 1930s to '50s.

ⓒ **Various** *Kuulas Hetki* (Olarin Musiikki, Finland). The subtitle, "Ensembles and Soloits of the Sibelius Academy Folk Department", may not sound compelling but this is a superb and adventurous compilation, featuring tracks from JPP, Ottopasuuna, Maria Kalaniemi and the bizarre Turkilla Prostitutus.

ⓒ **Various** *Tulikulkku* (KMI, Finland). The cutting edge of contemporary Finnish music – a recent release put together as a fiftieth birthday tribute to Heikki Laitinen, founder of KMI.

ⓒ **Arto Järvelä** *Polska Differente* (O Art, Finland). A fine solo outing from the JPP fiddler, with all star guests.

ⓒ **JPP** *Pirunpolska* (Olarin Musiikki, Finland). A collection of favourites from Finland's number-one folk group. "Pirun polska" means the Devil's polska, so beware!

ⓒ **Konsta Jylhä and Kaustisen** *Purpuripelimannit Finnish Folk Music Vol I* (Finlandia, Finland). Recordings from the early 1970s by the legendary fiddler and his band.

ⓒ **Maria Kalaniemi** *Maria Kalaniemi* (Olarin Musiikki, Finland). Finland's dynamic young accordionist plus combo in an imaginative mix of Finnish and Swedish tunes and tango.

ⓒ **Karelia** *Best of Karelia* (Bluebird Music, Finland). An intriguing blend of folk, jazz, and electronics. Like a trip through the Karelian countryside.

ⓒ **Pedro's Heavy Gentlemen** *Tango* (Fazer, Finland). Pedro Hietanen's a big lad, he's got a great moustache, and he plays exquisite tango.

ⓒ **Troka** *Troka* (Olarin Musiikki, Finland). Fiddles, accordion, harmonium, bass, addictive rhythms and melodies plus a great sense of fun add up to one of the hottest albums in Finnish folk history. A band to watch.

ⓒ **Värttinä** *Oi Dai* (Spirit, Finland). Finland's leading contemporary band features all-female vocalists and some wild instrumental playing. Oi Dai is rhythmic, fast and powerful with some tricky Karelian beats; ⓒ *Seleniko*, the band's fourth album, is less frantic, more varied and again altogether delightful.

SWEDEN

ⓒ **Various** *Årsringar, Svensk folkmusik 1970–1990* (MNW, Sweden). A double CD spanning twenty years of Swedish folk music – traditional, contemporary, young, old, instrumental and vocal – including Lena Willemark, Ale Möller, Filarfolket, Norrlᵃter and more. The best introduction to Swedish folk music today.

ⓒ **Various** *Suède–Norvège: Musiques des vallées scandinaves* (Ocora, France). A traditional collection of songs and dances, featuring some of Scandinavia's finest fiddling from the Frifot trio and others.

ⓒ **Forsmark Tre** *Västgötalåtar* (FMP, Sweden). Beautiful and catchy melodies on fiddles, accordion, nyckelharpa and synths. This trio, although relatively unknown, has had a great influence on Finnish musicians.

ⓒ **Frifot** *Frifot* (Caprice Records, Sweden). Traditional and contemporary Swedish folk music performed by three top musicians: Ale Möller, Lena Willemark and Per Gudmundson.

ⓒ **Hedningarna** *Kaksi!* (Xsource, Sweden/China Records, UK). Already recognized as a milestone in Swedish progressive folk with its unique combination of electric bagpipes, oud and acoustic instruments, this is an exhilarating record.

Hjort Anders Olsson *Hjort Anders* (Sonet, Sweden). A double album of pieces from a major figure in Swedish folk music. Legendary folk fiddling at its best. Now deleted but worth finding if you can.

ⓒ **Väsen** *Vilda Väsen* (Drone, Sweden). An acoustic trio with a huge, wild and powerful sound who are clearly having a lot of fun. Their follow-up, ⓒ *Essence* (Auvidis Ethnic, France), is more relaxed, but the tunes are just as catchy.

NORWAY

ⓒ **Various** *Norwegian Songs and Dances* (Playasound, France). Much better than you'd imagine from the title: traditional and contemporary material recorded by many of the country's top groups and musicians.

ⓒ **Thorleif H. Björgum and Hallvard T. Björgum** *Skjöldmöjslaget* (Sylvartun, Norway). Two of the Hardanger fiddle giants on their best album. Wonderful rhythms and intricate playing.

ⓒ **Bukkene Bruse** *Bukkene Bruse* (Grappa, Norway). Impressive young trio featuring Annbjørg Lien on Hardanger fiddle and modern arrangements of trad tunes.

ⓒ **Hans W. Brimi** *Bal gamle dörrer* (Heilo, Norway). Pols-tunes and more on flatfele by one of the living legends of Norwegian music.

ⓒ **Mari Eggen and Helen Høye** *Sprell Levande* (Grappa, Norway). A brilliant album of fiddle duos played with real spirit and depth.

ⓒ **Annbjørg Lien** *Annbjørg* (Kirkelig Kulturverksted, Norway). Strong set from an up-and-coming Hardanger fiddler.

Slinkombas *Slinkombas* (Heilo, Norway). Norway's top folk musicians on a legendary recording, with singing accompanied by flute (sjöflöjt) and Hardanger fiddle.

SAMI MUSIC

ⓒ **Mari Boine (Persen)** *Gula Gula* (Real World, UK) and *Goaskinviellja/Eagle Brother* (Verve, UK). *Gula Gula*, with its distinctive sound and powerful message, introduced Mari Boine to the world. *Goaskinviellja/Eagle Brother*, carries on in similar, if anything still more highly charged, vein.

ⓒ **Angelin Tytöt** *Giitu* (Mipu Music, Finland/Topic, UK/Green Linnet, US). Three girls from a Sami village in the north of Finland perform traditional joiks with percussion and folky guitar, produced by Värttinä's Sari Kaasinen.

ⓒ **Nils-Aslak Valkeapää/Seppo Paakunainen/Esa Kotilainen** *Winter Games* (DAT, Norway). Features the joik performed at the 1994 Olympic Games. Ailu (Nils-Aslak) is accompanied by two of Norway's top players on sax, keyboards and flutes, giving a rich impression of Samiland.

DENMARK

Karlekammeret Polcalypso (Olga Musik, Denmark). One of the more spectacular contemporary folk fusions to come out of Port-of-Copenhagen.

Svenska Nils (released on a private label by H.J. Christensen, Kalundborg, Denmark). Traditional music in a recording held in high esteem by the younger Danish folk musicians.

NOWT SO QUEER AS VOLK!

ALPINE FOLK AND THE PHENOMENON THAT IS ALPUNK

Behind the stereotypical image of Alpine music – lederhosen, cowbells and red-faced farmers puffing away on tubas – lurk more subversive talents. Christoph Wagner makes for the mountains and reveals unexpected developments from Germany, Austria and Switzerland.

Punk yodelling, hardcore thigh slapping and jazz fusions? There are some mighty strange goings-on in the mountain fastness and bastion of bourgeois values at the heart of Europe: the Alpine regions of Germany, Austria and Switzerland. And all the more strange, for this is a legendarily conservative society, where the dangers of the mountain environment have long made a virtue of experience and tradition.

Tradition, of course, remains. There are authentic old-style Alpine musics, sometimes very different from one valley to the next – and a variety packaged into a predictable thump by commercial bands, who play in the hotels and restaurants. But of late, beneath the snowline, things are beginning to move as young musicians have started to reshape the traditional folk music.

BAVARIAN FUSIONS

Munich in Bavaria is the home of **BavaRio**. As the name suggests, this group presents a combination of Bavarian melodies with samba rhythms from Brazil – and this isn't the latest World Music fusion dreamed up by the marketing boys. The sound was born from a real historical migration. On an extended visit to Brazil, Wolfgang Netzer, the leader of the band, came across a sound that sounded strangely familiar to him and touched childhood memories of when he used to be a member of a schuhplattler dance group slapping thighs and lederhosen. The music had been taken to Brazil at the turn of the century by a wave of Bavarian immigrants: ländlers, polkas and waltzes mingled with the sound of the Brazilian south, where there is a Bavarian community to this day.

Back in Munich, Netzer developed the music by adding South American instruments to the traditional Bavarian *stubenmusik* instrumentation of hammer dulcimer, harp,

zither, guitar and bass. With Brazilian *cavaquinho*, *viola caipira* and Latin American drums on the one hand, and a button accordion, dulcimer, tuba and zither on the other, BavaRio make a real link between the two cultures. Their eponymous album ranges from tracks that sound like "The Third Man" gone mildly tropical to some crazy Bavarian dance music in Brazilian rhythms.

BavaRio hanging out in their Alpine hothouse

Another Munich group, **Die Interpreten**, is doing a similar tightrope act with variations on Bavarian folk music. They bring their jazz background plus a range of saxophones to traditional melodies. Once they've got hold of the mainly sedate dance tunes and subjected them to lively intonation and overblowing techniques it sounds as though jazz saxophonist Albert Ayler were lost in a Bavarian beer tent. This is eccentric music that is surprising and refreshing, although it sometimes borders on parody.

The best-known alternative Bavarian group is **Biermosl Blosn**, three brothers from the Well family who play trumpet, horn and accordion and irritate local right-wing politicians by writing satirical lyrics to traditional tunes and producing records with titles like "The Yodelling Horror Monster Show". Their most notorious performance was on local TV in 1980, just before Bavarian president Franz Josef Strauss made his New Year speech, when they played the Bavarian anthem with new words directly attacking his politics. Since then their music has not been played on Bavarian radio or TV. They've now founded another band called **Well Buam** (Well Boys) which leaves politics alone and concentrates on blowing hot dance music.

In a gentler mood is the music of **Fraunhofer Saitenmusi**, who play in an Alpine New Age style with harps and zithers, and **Rudi Zapf** (a former member of BavaRio) and **Georg Glasl**, the best-known solo stars of the new Bavarian scene. Zapf plays the **hammer dulcimer** and includes virtuoso arrangements of classical music and jazz as well as music from the Alpine folk tradition. On the album "Musikalische Weltreise" (A Musical World Trip) he joins up with **Evelyn Huber** and **Ingrid Huber-Zapf** (family and friends!) to perform arrangements of pieces from all over the globe, from China and Ireland to Greece and Venezuela, alongside local tunes.

A simple version of the hammer dulcimer was already in use in the Alps in the Middle Ages, but the zither is much younger and was introduced by vagrant musicians in the eighteenth century. On his concert zither Georg Glasl makes renaissance music sound as if it were composed for this instrument, and classical compositions take on a real folk quality.

These attempts to develop Alpine folk music by opening it up to other styles should be seen against the background of a growing interest in the music from amateur players. In Munich alone there are hundreds of traditional *stubenmusik* ensembles playing just for the fun of it. Many of these are disciples of **Sepp Eibl**, one of the

Dance fiddler Hans Kegel from Appenzell

most influential figures of the authentic Bavarian folk revival. His group favours tunes from the richest period of Bavarian folk music, the mid-nineteenth century, reconstructed from archives and musicians' notebooks. The music of this authentic movement is a far cry from the commercial dilutions of Alpine music.

Many of the young musicians hold traditionalists like Eibl in high esteem, but the majority seem sceptical as to whether purity of tradition alone is enough to ensure the survival of Bavarian music. Wolfgang Netzer speaks for most of the young generation when he says the search for authenticity can only be a temporary measure. "Genuine folk music means vitality.

A traditional Bavarian Beer garden band

Life goes on and one cannot keep re-hashing what was made a hundred years ago. It won't make it better. When it was made a century ago it was very powerful stuff, but when you re-do it today it loses that intensity."

SWISS IN SPACE

The desire for a new impetus is shared by the musicians of **Appenzeller Space Schöttl**, one of the most prolific bands of the Alpine music movement in Switzerland. The name is a joke about the idea of something as technologically advanced as a space shuttle coming from Appenzell – an area known only for its cheese. Töbi Tobler plays the local hammer dulcimer of the Appenzell region and Ficht Tanner plucks bass. Their music is rooted in the Appenzeller world: they learned the local tunes from the old dance fiddler, **Hans Kegel**, now in his eighties, and they play with him at the "Rössli" Inn in Appenzell on the major festivals of Landsgmänd (a political gathering), Vechschau (a cow market) and Chilbi (a religious feast). But in twenty years of playing, Tobler and Tanner have also had brushes with jazz, blues and rock music and now mix it all up in their *schöttl* (the name puns

Bavarian Dancefloor
Boarischer Tanzbodn
Live mit den Well-Buam

on its German meaning, "shake"). No recordings of the band exist: "There's enough plastic in the world!", they say.

The Tessin region of Switzerland on the southern slopes of the Alps belongs to the Italian language area and is the home of **L'Orchestrina**. They come from Lugano and their leader, Pietro Bianchi, is a versatile instrumentalist who has studied meticulouslythe music of the Tessin Alps. Playing a wide range of instruments, the quintet combine strands of Tessin folk music developed over the course of five centuries: the songs of the wandering bards of the Middle Ages, the music of the village fiddlers, and the brass band tunes that became popular in the nineteenth century. With energetic fiddle playing, mandolin, accordion and hurdy-gurdy, L'Orchestrina shake the dust from weary old melodies.

BAT OUT OF HEURIGER

In Austria there are two centres of the Alpine roots music revival: the highly conservative cities of Vienna and Linz. In Vienna the old tradition of Schrammelmusik now belongs to the tourist heuriger and wine taverns on the fringes of the city and in the Vienna Woods. But Roland Neuwirth's

Extremschrammeln tries to bring the form up to date, often using a classic schrammelmusik line-up of two violins, guitar and accordion with musical additions from blues and jazz. His lyrics satirize the way of life in Vienna but retain the fatalistic melancholy typical of the city.

In Linz, in the cider-growing region further up the Danube River, two groups, **Urfahrer Durchbruch** and **Die Goaß**, have been bringing traditional music back to the inns and pubs in a wild and direct form. They form the nucleus of **Attwenger**, a hardcore Alpine music ensemble who are a sort of Austrian version of The Pogues. With the weird sound of a button accordion from the Steiermark mountain region played through a wah-wah pedal, gunshot drum tracks and electronic hiphop rhythms, they try "to find the meeting point between folk music and punk". Markus Binder, the drummer, explains: "We take typical elements of the old tradition and try to amplify these. Old and new styles are contrasted, fresh and hard, by using reduced instrumentation arranged in an expressionistic and dense manner."

Unlike other bands such as **Brodlahn** and **Die Verkochten Tirolerknödel**, who combine traditional tunes with sophisticated jazz-rock production and neoclassical arrangements, Attwenger look at both punk and traditional music as expressions of rebellion in everyday life. They sound as though they sport safety pins through the bellows of their accordions, and their songs have deliberately mystifying titles.

Despite their punk gloss, Attwenger take their influences from the music of their home region where a number of unique dances have survived: the Schleiniger, Innviertler Ländler and Aberseer Ländler. They turn these local specialities into hot dance-floor numbers with rap rhythms and an aggressive beat. Their success shows they must be getting something right. Attwenger have made a despised regional folk music popular again on Alpine dance-floors, and who knows, perhaps New York will soon be dancing schuhplattlers to the Attwenger beat. The New Alpine World Music is ready to take off.

■ **DISCOGRAPHY** ■

TRADITIONAL MUSIC

Sepp Eibl und Freunde Musizieren (Trikont, Germany). Traditional music from Bavaria, ländlers polkas and more played in authentic style on double-neck guitar, harp, zither, violin, clarinet and accordion.

ⓒ **Thalia–Schrammeln** *Music from Old Vienna* (Naxos, Germany). A good introduction to the bitter-sweet world of Vienna's typical schrammelmusik.

Various *Austrian Folk Music Vols 1 and 2* (Arhoolie, US). A good overview of the different regional styles of Austrian music played by different ensembles.

ⓒ **Various** *Jüüzli: Muotatal Yodel* (Chant du Monde, France). Not the trained sounds of enthusiasts but real field recordings of yodelling to call the cows back home.

Various *Originale Volkmusik aus der ganzen Schweiz* (Mono Editions, Switzerland). An album covering all the regional styles, accompanied by an interesting illustrated booklet (in German).

NEW TRADITIONAL MUSIC

◫ Attwenger *Most* (Trikont, Germany). The first and best album by these Alpunks, featuring traditional dance tunes played with hip-hop drum rhythms. Head-banging ländler-beat from the wildest of the Alpine groups.

BavaRio *BavaRio* (Trikont, Germany). A mixture of Bavarian dance music and samba from Rio de Janeiro blending traditional instruments of Bavaria and Brazil.

Biermosl Blosn *Jodel horrormonstershow* (Mood, Germany). Authentic Bavarian Tanzl music with new lyrics – often very funny, apparently, for those who can decipher the dialect.

◫ Fraunhofer Saitenmusik *Zwischenklänge* (Trikont, Germany). Bavarian "chamber music" style folk with a New Age touch. Pleasant sounds.

◫ Die Interpreten *Nicht ganz sauber!* (Trikont, Germany). Bavarian dance tunes meet jazz. Good, rough-edged playing on saxophones and drums.

◫ Well-Buam *Boarischer Tanzboden* and *Santanz* (Trikont, Germany). Hot versions of traditional Bavarian dance classics as the Well family get on down. A lot of fun and highly recommended, whether you have your own lederhosen or not.

◫ Rudi Zapf *Hammer Dolce* (Trikont, Germany). The champion of the hammer dulcimer plays everything from Baroque classics to jazz.

IN SEARCH OF GÓRALE

POLISH HIGHLAND MUSIC AND ITS NEIGHBOURS

Music played by hoary old mountain fiddlers is part of the popular image of the Polish highlands. Dressed in tight embroidered trousers and round hats with wide brims, these fiddlers pop up on tourist postcards and murals decorating the mountain resort of Zakopane in the Podhale region. Simon Broughton set out to find them.

The Podhale region lies in the foothills of the Tatra Mountains where the *górale*, fiercely independent mountain farmers, live in lush meadows and winding valleys. Their music is rather different from that heard elsewhere in Poland and with its sawing string sound is part of a culture that stretches along the Tatras and Carpathians to Transylvania. Podhale musicians, however, are always Poles, not gypsies. The distinctive górale style with men singing in forced high voices and a string band with lots of open fifths is found on both sides of the Tatras in the Polish Podhale and northern Slovakia.

The composer **Szymanowski** and his artistic circle, who frequented Zakopane from the 1920s, popularized the *górale* (highland) culture and drew inspiration from it. He described the work they were doing as "an emergency ambulance service for Tatra culture", and their mouth-to-mouth resuscitation seems to have been remarkably successful for musical life around Zakopane seems to be flourishing today.

Going in search of **Podhale music** one Saturday, I came upon two weddings and a funeral

within a few kilometres of Zakopane, each with a band of five or six musicians. This is a fairly typical-sized ensemble, all of which feature a lead fiddle, two violins playing chords to fill out the middle, and a cello sawing out the bass. Having been to several outstanding wedding parties in Transylvania, I imagined Podhale might be a bit of an anticlimax. Not a bit of it. The musicians

Podhale wedding band outside the church

FESTIVALS IN POLAND, THE CZECH REPUBLIC AND SLOVAKIA

POLAND

Particularly in southern Poland and the highland region it is still possible to hear village bands at weddings and other celebrations. But there are a number of festivals which are a focus for this sort of music. These include:

Kazimierz Dolny This beautiful town west of Lublin has an annual week-long festival of folk bands and singers (late June or early July).

Zdynja Annual festival of Łemk music and culture held in the Beskid Niski south of Gorlice (July). The Łemks are an ethnic minority related to the Ukrainians, and this is probably the best opportunity to hear their authentic music.

Zywiec This noted beer town hosts an annual festival of local Silesian Beskid folklore (August).

Zakopane Annual festival of highland music which in recent years has taken in groups from all over the world (late August or early September).

CZECH REPUBLIC

Straznice The biggest folk festival in the Czech lands is held in this village in south Moravia (last weekend of June). There are three purpose-built stadiums in the castle grounds. There's also a chance of hearing music during the wine harvest at the local wine caves.

Domazlice Festival of Chod folk music – the Bohemians on the western borders who have preserved the strongest regional identity and music, including *dudy* bagpipes (August).

Strakonice An international festival of bagpipes is held biennially here in southern Bohemia, with players from all over Europe (end of August).

SLOVAKIA

Vychodna The annual festival of Slovak folk music in this northern Slovakian village rivals the gathering at Straznice (see above) but is more national in character (end of July).

Svidnik This town, an ugly modern sprawl in the beautiful region of Carpatho-Ruthenia, hosts a summer "Ukrainian" folk festival (end of June). Like the Łemks just over the border in Poland, the local Rusyns are an ethnic group related to the Ukranians. Łemk groups come over to perform.

---

were first class, many were young and there isn't the tendency to modernize the bands and use PA systems that so often spoils the music in Transylvania.

Village weddings in Poland are often held in the local fire station. These are usually imposing buildings with tall towers and a large room suitable for a wedding feast. The górale people are notoriously closed to outsiders and I was warned that strangers might be positively unwelcome at a wedding. But at the one I ran into, in the village of Kosielisko, the hosts couldn't have been more hospitable or welcoming. Tread carefully and the rewards will probably be rich – people here are proud of their traditions and are flattered that outsiders find them, and especially the music, interesting.

At the Kosielisko wedding, the party went in a series of horse-drawn carts to the church. At the front, two outriders on horseback (pytace) declaimed verses in typical górale style. Next came the musicians, crammed into a cart and playing all the while, followed by the bride and the rest of the company. The musicians played the couple into the church and then climbed up into the gallery to play music for the communion and a wedding march at the end of the ceremony. Back at the fire station the band had a bite to eat before playing for most of the night. During the course of the evening one musician would take a break and another take his place so the music continued almost without interruption.

The most typical **górale songs** begin with a couple of lines declaimed by a man towards the band, who then take up the song into a dance. Another man then takes the chosen woman onto the floor and dances with her before handing her over to the man who started the song. The most common highland dances are the **ozwodna,** with an unusual five-bar structure, and the faster and more regular **krzesany.** Both feature the angular melodies typical of Podhale music. As well as the typical Podhale songs and dances the music also includes Slovak and Hungarian tunes and Polish waltzes, but always with a distinctive Podhale accent.

Robin Broadbank of Nimbus Records will shortly be producing a CD of authentic Podhale music. It is one of the few areas of eastern Europe that recording companies haven't yet discovered, so this will be doubly welcome.

CZECH REPUBLIC AND SLOVAKIA

Most of the folk music records in the Czech and Slovak Republics are of "folklorique" ensembles. The records from the Vychodna festival, which are easy to find in Slovakia, tend to be rather self-conscious but give a good cross-section of Slovak regional styles. There are also a few records of real village performers which are amongst the best recordings of traditional eastern European folk music.

Various *Anthologie Chodske Lidove Hudby* (Supraphon, Czech Republic). A two-record set of songs and bagpipe music from the Chod region in western Bohemia.

Various *Anthology of South Bohemian Music* (Supraphon, Czech Republic). Field recordings of old songs, instrumental music and customs made in the 1950s. A bit specialist for most tastes.

Various *Ej, hrajte, hudci, hrajte* (Opus, Slovakia). A fantastic disc of village performers from all over Slovakia beginning with some highland music identical in style to that of the Polish Podhale region.

Various *Uz Terchovci Idu* (Opus, Slovakia). Similar idea to the record above, but with more organized ensembles. Not as good.

Samko Dudik *Samko Dudik* (Opus, Slovakia). A rare reissue of recordings made in Brno in the late 1950s of the legendary Dudik-family band. Samko Dudik (1880–1967), greatly admired by the composer Janaček, led an eight-piece orchestra of strings and cimbalom that was one of the best examples of Moraviann music.

Karmína *Old Czech Folksongs and Ballaids* (Bouton, Czech Republic). A lively contemporary group, often to be found performing on Prague's King Charles Bridge, who use medieval and folk instruments.

POLAND

Good recordings of traditional music have been very hard to find, but recently the Polish record company Polskie Nagrania have started releasing some outstanding collections on CD.

⊙ **Various** *Songs and Music from Various Regions* (Polskie Nagrania, Poland). With musical selections from bands all over Poland, this is the best overall introduction to Polish folk music. Includes some great music from Podhale and the Nowy Sacz regions.

Various *From the Tatra Mountains* (Morning Star Records, US). In the absence of good modern recordings of Podhale music, this collection of music played by groups who emigrated to the US in the 1920s is very useful. Strangely enough, a lot of the tracks sound more modern than the music you hear in the Tatra region today!

⊙ **Various** *Polish-American Dance Music* (Arhoolie, US). A similar collection of old American 78 recordings from 1927-33, including a couple of Podhale tracks.

⊙ **The Sowa Family** *Band Music from Rzeszów Region* (Polskie Nagrania, Poland). The Sowa family from the village of Piatkowa are obviously quite a remarkable family band with a tradition going back 150 years. This is a great album of polkas, waltzes, sztajereks and wedding tunes.

A MUSICAL MOTHER TONGUE

HUNGARY'S MAGYAR AND GYPSY TRADITIONS

"It's very important for us Hungarians to play our music, dance our dances and to know our musical mother tongue. Without these things we lose our identity." So Simon Broughton was told – and it's true. In eastern Europe, where everybody's music stands as a national label, it has an especially potent force for Hungarians.

The Magyars – like the Romanians to their east – are a cultural island with a distinctive language unrelated to the sea of Slavs around them. Like the people, the music is now thoroughly "Europeanized" but it remains highly distinctive. In very large part, this is down to the Hungarian language, which is invariably stressed on the first syllable, lending a strongly accented dactylic rhythm to the music. Its infectious sound has been surprisingly influential on neighbouring countries and it's not uncommon

to hear Hungarian-sounding tunes in Romania, Slovakia and southern Poland.

BARTÓK, KODÁLY AND ROOTS EAST

The composers **Béla Bartók** and **Zoltán Kodály** were not the first to investigate systematically the peasant music of Hungary, but they were the most famous and influential. On their collecting trips with an Edison phonograph at the turn of the century, they revealed the "real" Hungarian folk music as opposed to the popular salon tunes played by gypsy orchestras that were taken to be folk music until then. Both men were fine ethnographers as well as composers and by using folk material in their own work they not only found their individual voices but brought the folk music to the attention of an international audience.

Bartók with his cylinder recorder in 1908

Kodály's interest was in Hungarian music and the creation of a truly national style. Bartók's concerns were more international, rooted in the peasant music of all the nationalities of eastern Europe and beyond. By 1918, when the war brought his expeditions in eastern Europe to an end, he had collected over 3,500 Romanian tunes, 3,000 Slovak, 2,721 Hungarian, plus Ruthenian, Serbian and Bulgarian pieces. In 1981 Hungaroton released an LP of Hungarian songs he had recorded on cylinders between 1906 and 1917. The recording quality is, of course, very poor but there is an incredible sensation of hearing something quite remarkable from another world.

What Bartók and Kodály discovered on their expeditions to remote Hungarian villages was a music that was earthy, fresh and hitherto unknown. More than that, it was distinctly Hungarian and in its oldest layers stretched back to the Magyars' roots on the fringes of Europe between the Volga and the Urals. The Hungarians are not of Indo-European stock like most Europeans but belong to the Finno-Ugrian linguistic group, who lived over 4,000 years ago in the Volga-Kama region. In a long and complex series of migrations the Finns and Magyars moved west, with the Finns turning right up to the Baltic and the Magyars left towards the Carpathian basin.

Much research has been done to see if there are musical connections between the Hungarians and Finns but virtually none have been found; not surprising, perhaps, as the tribes are thought to have split around 4,000 years ago. Kodály, however, found a link between the oldest Hungarian songs, with their pentatonic (five-note) tunes and descending pattern, and songs of the Mari (or Cheremis) people, a Finno-Ugrian group who still live close to the ancestral home around the Volga and Kama rivers in the Russian Republic. Kodály came up with a substantial

number of Hungarian tunes that had direct equivalents in these eastern territories: musical fossils apparently dating back to a shared past 2,500 years old.

The link was not as straightforward as it seemed, though, as similar tunes have been found amongst several other Turkic tribes. It seems more likely that this music rubbed off while the Magyars were on their migrations, which brought them into close contact with Turkic peoples. All the same, Kodály's conclusion about the importance of this musical link in defining the national heritage is still valid: "Time may have wiped away the eastern features from the face of the Magyar community, but in the depths of its soul, where the springs of music lie, there still lives an element of the original east, which links it with peoples whose language it has long ceased to understand, and who are today so different in mind and spirit." For those seriously interested in the music of this little-known area of Russia and the links with Hungarian music, Hungaroton have released a box set called "Folk Music of Finno-Ugrian and Turkic Peoples", collected on field trips by László Vikár.

THE "NEW STYLE" AND GYPSY BANDS

The Hungarians' musical history evolved as they settled in the Carpathian basin (around 896), adopted Christianity about a century later and began to come under the influence of European culture. In 1526 Suleyman the Magnificent put a stop to that and Hungary endured 150 years of Turkish rule. Most of the Hungarian music familiar today has its roots in the eighteenth century when the country rebuilt itself as part of the Hapsburg Empire. The close contact with central European culture brought music with a regular metric structure for dancing and marching instead

Magyars getting on down in the countryside

of the free speech rhythms of the archaic style. Solo bagpipers used to play these new tunes for village dances but were gradually replaced by the new **gypsy orchestras.** The medieval-style drone accompaniment gave way to the central European harmony of the string bands.

Just as bagpipes mean Scotland, so gypsy bands mean Hungary in the popular imagination. When nationalist composers like Liszt composed their Hungarian Dances and Rhapsodies in the latter part of the nineteenth century they took as their models the music of the urban gypsy orchestras much as you can hear it in Budapest restaurants today. The majority of this repertoire, often showy and sickly sweet, was formally composed in the nineteenth century.

Following Bartók's lead, folklorists tend to dismiss this urban gypsy style in favour of authentic "peasant music". Yet the music the gypsies play is no less Hungarian, and it has more in common with peasant music than the folklorists like to admit. Hungarian folk song was often an influence on popular songs, and even in the remotest parts of the country urban songs have become part of the oral tradition and serve the function of folk songs. In the Transylvanian village of Szék you can still hear a *csárdás*, which pops up in Brahms' Hungarian Dances, often cited as prime examples of gypsy-style fakery.

Gypsy bands started to appear in Hungary from the middle of the eighteenth century and their fame spread. "The Hungarian has a musical score which can compete with that of any nation with regard of perfection. . . . This score lives and travels in the form of the Hungarian gypsy," wrote one observer in 1858. Most of the early gypsy bands seem to have been located in western Hungary and were often invited to perform at aristocratic celebrations.

In addition to society gigs, the gypsies also performed at recruiting ceremonies where young lads were enticed into the army with **verbunkos** music (from *werbung* – the German word meaning "recruit"). The Hapsburgs only introduced universal conscription in 1868, so before that the men were lured with dancing, music and the promise of a carefree life. This music is strongly rhythmic, consisting of a slow dance followed by a fast one. The steps were developed from the showy men's dances of the village.

The Hungarians, always searching for a musical identity, found it in the verbunkos music. It formed the inspiration for Liszt's "Hungarian Rhapsodies" and typified the Hungarians abroad. A German officer saw the dance in 1792: "It expresses the character of the nation in an extraordinary way. The true Hungarian dances have to begin really slowly and then continue faster. They are much more becoming to a serious moustached face than to a young lad no matter what forced capers they do. The whole art of the dancer is to be seen in the artistic movement of his legs and the rhythmic clicking of his spurs."

The most famous gypsy band leader was **János Bihari**, born in 1769, the same year as Napoleon, and known as the Napoleon of the fiddle! "Like drops of some fiery spirit essence, the notes of this magic violin came to our ears", wrote Liszt. Bihari's band usually consisted of four strings plus a cimbalom, the hammer dulcimer so common in gypsy bands. According to the stories he lived in a princely style playing at banquets and celebrations across the land, but died neglected in 1827 having squandered his wealth. Several of his compositions, however, can be heard in the repertoire of gypsy bands in Hungary today.

Sadly, these days, in Hungary itself, it is very hard to find real village music in the way Bartók and Kodály did. The music was disappearing in the early years of the century and they knew it. Perhaps the best areas to try – at traditional weddings and so on – are Szabolcs-Szatmár county, rather out on a limb in the northeast and in the south of the country bordering the former Yugoslavia. The band in Bogyiszló (near Szekszárd) is worth hearing, and there is an excuse for music as strange masked figures take to the streets at the Busójárás Carnival in Mohács at the beginning of March. The music in Mohács is basically Serbian and Croatian, while the Bogyiszló orchestra has the plucked tamburas typical of the Slavonian region over the border and plays Serbian kolos alongside the purely Hungarian stuff.

GYPSY FOLK

The music played by Hungary's ubiquitous **gypsy bands** is Hungarian rather than "gypsy". The millions of gypsies scattered throughout the world are often musicians but there is no music common to them all. In Hungary, oddly enough considering the number of musicians, the gypsy communities' own folk music hardly uses instruments at all. Most of the gypsy musicians who play in the urban bands don't actually live amongst the (generally poorer) gypsy communities, as they play exclusively for a non-gypsy audience, and often they don't know the traditional gypsy folk music.

The gypsy folk music repertoire includes slow songs about the hardships of life and faster dance songs. Although there are no instruments, the songs are accompanied by rhythmic grunts, the tapping of sticks and cans and imitations of instruments in a "doobie-doobie-doobie" sort of way called "oral-bassing". It's a wild, improvised sound peculiar to gypsy music, heard to good effect on an album from Hungaroton called "Gypsy Folk Songs from Hungary".

Recently a gypsy group called **Kalyi Jag** (meaning Black Fire in Romany) from Szatmár county in northeast Hungary have started performing traditional gypsy music on a professional basis. Most of the songs are traditional and the group plays spoons and watering can as well as the guitar – which has found its way into most gypsy communities in recent years. Kalyi Jag have made two records and proved quite successful on the tánchaz scene playing modern music with a distinctive gypsy character.

THE TÁNCHÁZ

Budapest is one of the best places in Europe to hear really good folk music, and the place to go is a **tánchaz** – literally a "dance house", named after traditional village dancing places. The atmosphere at a tánchaz is a cross between a barn dance and a folk club but without the self-conscious folksiness of its western counterparts. The dress may be blue-jeans and trainers with the odd Transylvanian jacket or skirt, but for the most part the clientele – teachers, doctors, lawyers –

know the music and can dance it well. Once again this is a statement of identity. In a world where everybody wears the same blue-jeans or Benetton clothes, this music and dance comes with a Hungarian designer label.

The tánchaz movement started in the 1970s as a reaction to the regimented folklore of the state ensembles. Following in the footsteps of Bartók and Kodály, musicians like Ferenc Sebő and Béla Halmos collected music from the villages, learnt it and brought it back to Budapest. But whereas Bartók and Kodály had been interested mainly in songs, this new generation was interested in the traditional dances. The idea was to bring the music back to the grassroots rather than present it on stage and, despite the urban setting, keep it closer to its original form.

Despite having virtually no official support, the movement grew from strength to strength and for many years had a political force. The wellspring of Hungarian tánchaz music was in neighbouring Romania where the Hungarian minority of Transylvania has kept a living folk tradition to this day. Tánchaz musicians often travelled there in very difficult circumstances to collect music and dances. In Transylvania the two-million-strong Hungarian community was under threat from the Ceausescu regime, yet at home the subject was taboo as the government refused to condemn a "fraternal socialist" country. The tánchaz musicians were a sort of

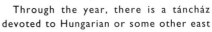

TÁNCHÁZ IN BUDAPEST

E very year around the end of March there is a huge festival of tánchaz groups in the sports stadium in Budapest. It's an all-day marathon and after the scheduled events the real fiends usually decamp to the tánchaz in Almássy tér for an all-night session. If you have the stamina, this is the best part, especially as groups from Transylvania and elsewhere are now a regular feature of the festival. The tánchaz at Almássy tér is like a scrappy student union building but the music is of the highest quality. Close your eyes and it will take you to another world.

Through the year, there is a tánchaz devoted to Hungarian or some other east European music virtually every night in Budapest. They usually begin around 5 or 6pm with dance classes, often for kids, and the real thing gets going from around 8pm. There's usually a bar and light snacks available.

For details, check in *Pesti Műsor*, the Budapest what's-on magazine, under the "A művelődési házak programja" (Houses of Culture) listings. The word együttes, which crops up frequently, means "ensemble".

MÁRTA SEBESTYÉN

· ·

"When I was seven or eight years old I was already singing folk songs, but not the ones I'm singing now. I didn't know the style. But I won a folk-singing competition in school and the first prize was this disc of original folk-song recordings just released from the archive of the Academy of Sciences. I put it on and I was shocked at the sound of an old woman's voice from Moldavia or Transdanubia. It was a completely new sound and I simply copied it note for note so suddenly here was this child singing with the voice of an old woman!"

Since that first contact with authentic folk music, Márta Sebestyén has found her own style and gone on to be the leading singer on the Hungarian folk scene. In 1991 she was awarded the prestigious Liszt prize for her work,

which has also included roles in Hungarian rock musicals. She has a strong stage presence – I once saw her silence a restive rock crowd with a simple unaccompanied folk song – and her repertoire includes Romanian, Slovak, Serbian and Bulgarian songs. Central to her art, however, is the music of Transylvania, which she has been visiting for the past decade or so to collect material first hand.

"More and more, I have learnt from personal contacts. Of course, at the beginning I had to study the recordings and then go and see these

people, because it's silly to go somewhere before you know what to expect. And even when I knew many of the songs from field recordings it was amazing to go there personally and hear the songs in different forms, with different ornaments. It's like a living river, you never put your legs in the same water.

"On that first visit, I learnt some beautiful songs from an old lady in Gyimes. I didn't have a tape recorder but luckily I have quite a good memory and I can recall exactly the melodies, the tone of voice, what we ate – everything. I visited her again recently but now her man has died, her health is bad and she doesn't feel like singing those songs. Now she sings very sad laments which are very personal to her. That's why it's important to try and catch these things, because they die with the performer. Maybe her laments will become mine one day."

And, as to why it's important to sing these folk songs now: "It's a question I'd never ask myself. It's silly to lose something that has survived for so long. It's important to take care of nature and the environment and also to look after music. It's not simply nostalgic, but also contemporary. Now we have TV and video but the human soul still needs to sing and to play and not just put on a record and listen to it. We still have emotions, Thank God."

conscience of the nation, reminding Hungarians of the rich culture and plight of their brethren over the border.

By the late 1980s the reformist Hungarian government had given up the "fraternal" stance and joined in condemnation of Ceaus,escu's policies, and the tánchaz movement lost its potency a little.

But since the Romanian revolution of December 1989 there has been a regular flow of Transylvanian groups playing in Budapest and bringing a welcome rough-edged note of authenticity.

Tánchaz music falls into two types. One is music from Hungary proper which, with less of a living tradition, has usually been learnt from archive recordings or written collections and arranged by the groups in the manner of folk bands all over Europe. But the most popular music comes directly from the village tradition and that means Transylvania (or occasionally the Hungarian communities in Slovakia). If at first the tunes all sound similar, keep listening. The better you know this music the more rich and varied it becomes. In the right hands it has a beauty unrivalled in Europe.

Táncház dances are played in sets, generally moving from slower tempos to fast – beginning perhaps with a verbunkos or Lad's Dance, giving the chance for the men to show off, and ending with a fast and furious csárdás. It's the *primás*, the first violinist of the band, who keeps an eye on the dancers and judges when to make the move and tempo change into the next dance. When it's done well it's a thrilling sensation.

The csárdás is the most famous Hungarian dance tune and you won't spend five minutes at a Budapest táncház (or a Transylvanian wedding) without hearing one. They can be fast or slow, "whirling", "quivering" or "leaping" – and there are all sorts of regional variations. All of them are couple dances which can reach great virtuosity, but at their most basic it's two steps left, two steps right followed by a turn. The music has a regular four-square rhythm with a distinctive spring.

The best-known names on the current táncház scene are **Márta Sebestyén** (see box), a truly remarkable singer (and not just of Hungarian music) and **Muzsikás**, the group she has often performed with. They have released four excellent records and tour regularly. Also recommended are the **Kalamajka**, **Téka** and **Jánosi** ensembles who specialize in the Hungarian and Transylvanian repertoire, and **Vujicsics**, who play fantastic music from southern Hungary and the former Yugoslavia. Other singers to watch out for are **Éva Fábián** and **András Berecz**.

DISCOGRAPHY

FIELD RECORDINGS/ ANTHOLOGIES

Béla Vikár made the first cylinder recording of Hungarian music as early as 1895 and, with the work of Bartók and Kodály and their successors, the Hungarians have led the field in ethnomusicological research. Field recordings (including those of Bartók, complete with his transcriptions) have been issued on the old state record label, Hungaroton, but few as yet have been re-released on CD.

Various *Anthology of Hungarian Folk Music Vol 1* (Hungaroton, Hungary). A superb, five-album collection of original Hungarian dance music, ranging from Transdanubia in the west all the way to the distant world of Gyimes and Bukovina in the east. The other volumes in this comprehensive series are a bit specialist for most tastes.

Various *Hungarian Folk Music 3* (Hungaroton, Hungary). Four-album boxed set devoted to the ancient layers, the new European style, instrumental music, and folk customs. The best overall introduction to the music, well presented with translations and transcriptions of the material plus some good photos.

Ⓒ **Various** *Hungarian Folk Music from Szatmár Region* (Hungaroton, Hungary). A new release of four great gypsy bands from the northeast of the country including some Jewish repertoire. Terrific stuff.

Ⓒ **Various** *Traditional Music from the Carpathians* (Quintana/Harmonia Mundi, France). A variable selection of music from over the border in Ukraine from Hungary's new independent record company. Just a shame they couldn't have taken a leaf out of Hungaroton's book and provided decent sleeve notes.

Ⓒ **Various** *Croatian Folksongs and Dances* (Quintana/Harmonia Mundi, France). Recordings of Croatian village bands in Hungary made between 1953 and 1985. One of the very few releases of this sort of music.

Ⓒ **Various** *Gypsy Folk Songs from Hungary* (Hungaroton, Hungary). A comprehensive collection of real gypsy folk music, recorded from performers around the country.

ENSEMBLES

Bogiszló Folk Orchestra *Bogiszló* (Hungaroton, Hungary). A lively record of one of the best village bands with a strong Serbian influence.

Kalamajka Ensemble *Bonchidától-Bonchidáig* (Hungaroton, Hungary). Good perfor.iances from one of Hungary's best táncház groups.

Ⓒ **Jánosi Ensemble** *Original Folk Tunes in Bartók's Music* (Hungaroton, Hungary). A nice idea: examples of tunes Bartók used in his compositions in the form he might originally have heard them in Transylvania.

ⒸⒹ **Muzsikás** *Márta Sebestyén* (Hannibal, UK). The best ever Muzsikás album, giving the Hungarian and Transylvanian repertoire the full táncház treatment. All the band's other albums come highly recommended, too; they include Ⓒ *The Prisoner's Song*, Ⓒ *Blues for Transylvania*, and Ⓒ *Máramaros*.

Sebo Ensemble *Music in Folk Dancing Rooms* (Hungaroton, Hungary). Here you have all the táncház greatest hits. A spirited double album of staple repertoire from all over the country.

Ⓒ **Vujicsics** *Serbian Music from Southern Hungary* (Hannibal, UK). A very skilled group who play fast, furious and virtuosic Serbian material. Márta Sebestyén sings.

Táncház compilations. Every year Hungaroton release a record (and latterly CD) of selected groups from the Budapest Táncház Festival. These give a good overview of what's happening on the dance-house scene. The *13th Dance-House Festival* CD was released in 1994.

Note: Some of the best recordings of Hungarian music are listed in the Transylvania discography on p.73.

A CULTURAL FAULT LINE

THE WILD SOUNDS OF ROMANIA AND TRANSYLVANIA

Romania lies right across a cultural fault line that separates central Europe from the Balkans. In the dramatic form of the Carpathian Mountains it sweeps across the country in a swathe that sharply divides the musical styles on either side. Of course such borders are rarely impermeable; the same Romanian language is spoken on either side and there are plenty of musical cross-fertilizations. Reflecting the divide, however, two articles follow, dealing first of all with Transylvania, the western province within the Carpathian Mountains and a treasure house of folk music, then with the legacy of Ceausescu and the music of the provinces of Wallachia, Moldavia and the Banat.

All these strands of Romanian music are extraordinarily varied and archaic, preserving almost archeological layers of musical development, from the "medieval" music at the extremities in Gyimes and Maramures, to the "Renaissance" sounds of Mezoség and the more sophisticated music of Kalotaszeg: a range from the atavistic and primeval to the delicate and beautiful. Simon Broughton, Transylvanophile to the core, is hooked.

THAT OLD TRANSYLVANIAN SWING

If you want to experience a real living European folk tradition, there is no beating Transylvania, Romania's westernmost province. Home to an age-old ethnic mix of Romanians, Hungarians and gypsies, the region's music is extraordinary: wild melodies and dances that are played all night – and then some – at weddings and other parties.

THE TRANSYLVANIAN MIX

Transylvanian villages, although often collectivized in the Ceausescu years, remained relatively resilient to the changes and ravages of those years. The dictator had demolition plans – but the revolution came just about in time. The region's music, certainly, survived intact and it is still a part of everyday life the way it must have been hundreds of years ago all over Europe. The older men and women know the old songs and still use them to express their own personal feelings.

The composers found Bartók and Kodály found Transylvania the most fertile area for their folk-song collecting trips in the first decades of the century, and they recognized that the rich mix of nationalities here had a lot to do with it. Transylvania has been home to Romanians, Hungarians, Saxons, gypsies and other nationalities for hundreds of years. For these communities music is part of their national identity, yet it is also part of a distinct and unified Transylvanian instrumental musical culture. The Romanian music of Transylvania is closer to the Hungarian than it is to the Romanian music outside Transylvania. And the Hungarian music of Transylvania sounds much more Romanian than the music of Hungary proper.

In fact within Transylvania the Romanians and Hungarians share many melodies and dances. It takes a very experienced ear to tell the difference and even then a particular melody may be described as Hungarian in one village and Romanian in another village over the hill. The Romanian dances often have a slightly more irregular rhythm than the Hungarian, but often the only difference between one tune and another is the language in which it is sung. There's a recording of an old man from the village of Dimbău (Küküllődombó) singing perhaps a unique example of a song with the first half of each line in Hungarian and the second half in Romanian!

The character of Transylvania is much more central European than the other parts of Romania. The Transylvanian Romanians tend to consider themselves more "civilized" than their compatriots in Moldavia and Wallachia. The architectural styles belong to the Austro-Hungarian Empire (of which the region formed a part) and the medieval Gothic buildings look straight out of the world of Grimm's fairy tales.

The music of Transylvania sounds much less Balkan than that from over the Carpathians. It might seem wild and exotic, but it is recognizably part of a central European tradition with added spice from its geographical location.

The traditional ensemble is a string trio – a violin, viola (called a *contra* in Romanian, *kontra* in Hungarian) and a double bass, plus a cimbalom in certain parts of Transylvania. The *primás*, the first violinist, plays the melody and leads the musicians from one dance into another while the contra and the bass are the accompaniment and rhythm section of the band. The contra has only three strings and a flat bridge so it only plays chords, and it's the deep sawing of the bass and the rhythmic spring of the contra that gives Transylvanian music its particular sound. Often the bands are expanded with a second violin or an extra contra to give more volume at a noisy wedding with hundreds of guests.

WEDDING PARTIES

Music in Transylvania serves a social function – nobody would dream of sitting down and listening to it at a concert. In some areas there are still regular weekly dances, but everywhere the music is played at weddings, sometimes at funerals and at other occasions, including when soldiers go off to the army, around Christmas.

Wedding parties last a couple of days and if you're lucky you'll find yourself in a specially constructed wedding "tent" built from wooden beams and tree fronds. The place is strung with ribbons and fir branches, tables are piled high with garish cakes and bottles of plum brandy and various courses are brought round at regular intervals. There's a space cleared for dancing and on a platform is the band of musicians sawing and scraping away at battered old fiddles and a bass making the most mesmerizing sound. The bride

and groom, stuck up on their high table, look a little fed up while everybody else has the time of their lives.

The wedding customs vary slightly from region to region but generally the band has to start things off at the bride's or groom's house, accompany the processions to the church and possibly play for one of the real emotional high spots, the bride's farewell song (*cîntecul miresei*) to her family and friends. Whilst the marriage takes place inside the church, the band plays for the young people, or those not invited to the feast, to dance in the street outside. Once the couple come out of the church there's another procession to wherever the wedding feast is being held – either in the village hall or the "tent" erected at the house of the bride or groom. There the musicians will have a short break to get something to eat and then play music all Saturday night, alternating songs to accompany the feast and dances to work off the effects of the food and large quantities of plum brandy. There are even particular pieces for certain courses of the banquet when the soup, stuffed cabbage or roast meat are served!

Late in the evening comes the bride's dance (*jocul miresei*) when the guests dance with the bride in turn and offer money. Things usually wind down by dawn on Sunday; people wander off home or collapse in a field somewhere and then around lunchtim the music starts up again for another session until late in the evening.

With the trend toward larger and larger weddings all sorts of instruments have started to find their way into the bands. Most common is the piano accordion, which, like the contra, plays chords, though it lacks its rhythmic spring. Very often you hear a clarinet or the slightly deeper and more reedy **taragot** which sounds wonderful in the open air. Sadly, however, because young people have moved away to work in towns, they often demand the guitars, drums and electric keyboards of the urban groups at the banquets – along with appalling amplification, which is increasingly brought in, too, by traditional acoustic bands.

Some band leaders might regret the trend but they are obliged to provide what the people demand. They may play traditional melodies but with the newer instruments the quality of the music is often lost. Paradoxically, the combination of guitar and drum kit is far less rhythmic than the contra and bass in the hands of good musicians. Other groups like the marvellous **Palatca** band stick unswervingly to

---

Wedding song
Yesterday you were among the girls
Today you are among the wives
Tomorrow among the old women

Funeral song
From one world to another
From one country to another
From the land of longing
To the land without longing
From the land of pity
To the pitiless land!

Village dance in Maramures

the traditional line-up and are recognized as
one of the great bands of Transylvania.

GYPSY BANDS

The Pălatca band, like most of the village
musicians in Romania, are gypsies. In the
villages, gypsy communities all tend to live
along one particular street on the outskirts, and
it's amazing how often you find these streets
are called Strada Muzicantsilor or Strada Lăutari
– both of which translate as "Musicians' Street".
The gypsy musicians will play for Romanian,
Hungarian and gypsy weddings alike and they
know almost instinctively the repertoire
required. Children often play alongside their
parents from an early age and grow up with the
music in their blood.

There's no doubt the gypsies have some special
aptitude for music, and perhaps the job suits
their social position rather on the edge of village
life. Playing music, too, can be an easy way to
earn good money. The best bands command
handsome fees, plus the odd chicken and bottles
of plum brandy "for the road", but they certainly
have their work cut out over the weekend. It's also
an indication of the value of music in this society
that the musicians are not only well rewarded but
also well respected. When the old primás of the
Pălatca band died all the people he had played
for in the village came to pay their respects.

It's difficult to highlight the best bands – there
are dozens of them – but in addition to the Pălatca
band I have heard great music from bands in the
following villages of central Transylvania (the

names are given in their Romanian form with the
Hungarian, where appropriate, in brackets):
Vaida-Cămăras (Vajdakamarás), Suatu
(Magyarszovát), Soporu de Cîmpie (Mezőszopor),
Sîngeorz-Băi and Sic (Szék), a virtually one-
hundred percent Hungarian village and one of the
great treasure houses of Hungarian music.

A glance at the engagement book of one of
these bands will show them booked for months
ahead. Yet most of them confine their playing to
quite a small area as travel is relatively difficult.
Some tunes are widely known right across
Transylvania but many are distinctly local and
a band playing too far from its home village
will simply not know the repertoire. It will be
interesting to see what happens now that local
bands are travelling to Hungary and beyond
on tour. Foreign audiences demand a variety of
styles which the táncház groups from Budapest
can readily supply. But if the village bands
from Transylvania start doing the same thing
then the music's strong local identity can only
break down.

THE HUNGARIANS

There are about two million Hungarians in
Transylvania and seven million Romanians, but
it is the music of the Hungarian minority that has
made most impact outside the region. The
Hungarians consciously promoted the culture
of their brethren in Transylvania to highlight
their suffering under Nicolae Ceausescu.
Hungaroton, the state label, produced a large
number of excellent recordings while Budapest-

based groups like **Muzsikás** have toured extensively and acted as cultural ambassadors for the music.

Kalotaszegi fiddler Sándor Fodor

Transylvania has always held a very special place in Hungarian culture as it preserves archaic traditions that have disappeared in Hungary itself. While Hungary was occupied by the Turks for 150 years and its villages destroyed, Transylvania remained an independent principality with its own cultural identity. The old medieval settlement patterns changed very little under Ceausescu's isolationist policies. It really does feel like Tintin territory at times.

Although the effects of the Ceausescu regime on traditional culture are generally acknowledged to have been disastrous, the paradox is that a traditional culture has survived here unparalleled anywhere else in central or eastern Europe. As a minority, the Hungarians felt particularly threatened, and there was a deliberate move to wear their traditional costumes, sing their songs and play their music as a statement of identity, even protest. These days, national costume and dances are much more visible amongst the Hungarian minority than the majority Romanians. But amongst all the peasants there was a feeling that their own culture was something they knew and could trust, unlike the slogans and lies of the regime.

The regular visits of folklorists and táncház musicians, have also helped reinforce the musical culture. Transylvanian music is the staple diet of the Budapest táncház clubs, and once the peasants saw these educated city folk taking an interest they took more of an interest themselves. Now there are two opposing trends at work in Transylvania: the continuing interest in this unique tradition and the inevitable effect as the country catches up with the century.

REGIONAL STYLES

Within the overall Transylvanian musical language there are hundreds of local dialects: the style of playing a particular dance can literally vary from village to village. But there are some broad musical regions where the styles are distinct and recognizable.

Bartók gathered most of his Romanian material in the area around **Hunedoara**. The area is still musically very rich though, strangely enough, a recent musical survey found that virtually the entire repertoire had changed.

Further north is the area the Hungarians call **Kalotaszeg**, and which is home to some of the most beautiful music in the region. This area lies along the main route to Hungary and central Europe, and the influence of western-style harmony shows itself in the sophisticated minor-key accompaniment – a development of the last twenty years. Kalotaszeg is famous for its men's dance, the *legényes* and the slow *hajnali* songs performed in the early morning as a wedding feast dies down. These have a sad and melancholy character all their own. One of the best of all recordings of Transylvanian music includes both these forms, featuring the gypsy primás **Sándor Fodor** from the village of Baciu (Bács). There is also some fine Romanian music in this area around the Sălaj district, which can be heard in the villages or on a very fine Romanian recording of *jocuri Sălăjene* (dances from Sălaj) by a small ensemble from Zalău.

Probably the richest area for music is known to the Romanians as **Cîmpia Transilvaniei** and to the Hungarians as **Mezoség**. This is the Transylvanian "heath", north and east of Cluj – a poor, isolated region whose music preserves a much more primitive feel with strong major chords moving in idiosyncratic harmony.

Further east is the most densely populated Hungarian region, Székelyföld (Székely land). The Székelys, who speak a distinctive Hungarian dialect, were the defenders of the eastern flanks of the Hungarian kingdom in the Middle Ages, when the Romanians, as landless peasants, counted for little. Rising up towards the Carpathians, their land becomes increasingly

PRISLOP FESTIVAL

· ·

There's a good opportunity to hear the contrasting musical styles of Maramures, Suceava (in Moldavia) and *Bistritsa-Năsaud* (in central Transylvania) at an annual festival held at the end of August on the Prislop pass, where these three counties meet. The official part is a little self-consciously folkloric, as organized groups run through their stuff on stage. But informal music gets going a bit further down the hillside and in the last few years there's also been the rare chance to catch ensembles from across the border in Ukraine.

wild and mountainous, and the dance music is different once again with eccentric ornamentation and very often a cimbalom in the band.

For Hungarian speakers the songs are fascinating as they preserve old-style elements that survive nowhere else. In one village I heard a ballad about a terrible massacre of the Székelys by the Hapsburgs in 1764, sung as if it had happened yesterday. Fleeing this massacre, many Székelys fled over the Carpathians into Moldavia, where they preserved music and customs that are no longer found in Székelyföld itself. During the Second World War 14,000 Székelys were resettled in the south of Hungary. In those outer reaches the string bands of Transylvania have given way to a solo violin or flute accompanying the dances.

MOLDAVIA AND MARAMURES

The Hungarian inhabitants of neighbouring Moldavia are called the **Csángós** and they occupy the remote pastoral regions east of the Carpathians. Strictly speaking this isn't Transylvania at all and the music – with its archaic "pipe and drum" style – sounds wild and other-worldly, ruptured across the divide between Transylvania and the Balkans.

Hungarian records of the Csángós often feature music from the Gyimes valley, where you find peculiar duos of violin and *gardon* – an instrument shaped like a cello but played by hitting its strings with a stick. The fiddle playing is highly ornamented and the rhythms complex and irregular, showing the influence of Romanian music. Csángó songs are also of interest to Hungarians for their archaic qualities. The extraordinary Csángó singer **Ilona Nistor** from Onesti (formerly Gheorghe Gheorghiu-Dej) in Bacău county has a growing reputation.

On the other side of Transylvania, sandwiched between Hungary, the Carpathians and the Ukrainian border, are the regions of Maramures and Oas, both areas of distinct regional character. Village costumes are not just worn for best but for everyday life and the music includes magic songs and spells of incantation against sickness and the evil eye. You can still find traditional Sunday afternoon village dances, either on the streets or on wooden dance platforms. From birth, through courtship and marriage to death, life has a musical accompaniment.

The music of **Maramures**, while recognizably Transylvanian, sounds closer to that of Romanians outside the Carpathians. As often happens in the highland regions of Romania, here the music is played predominantly by Romanians, not gypsies. With an instrumental group of violin, guitar (called a *zongoră*) and drum, it has a fairly primitive sound, lacking the beguiling harmonies, and with a repeated chord on the zongoră played as a drone. Hundreds of years ago all the music of Europe probably sounded something like this.

THE CEAUSESCU LEGACY

At a reception for foreign dignitaries, so the story goes, former president Ceausescu summoned a string trio to play after dinner. The banquet was lavish but the music was lousy, as the cellist was not allowed to sit down in the dictator's presence and had to scratch around standing up. If Ceausescu had known anything about music he might have hired a *taraf* or village ensemble. Those guys can play even a double bass ploughing a furrow down a muddy street in a wedding procession and do so most weekends!

Nicolae Ceausescu's 25 years of dictatorship are still present like a dark shadow over Romania, and as the country painfully tries to catch up with the rest of Europe the effects of an inefficient centralized economy and a feared secret police are hard to shake off. The legacy extends, too, to some of the country's folk music, which was manipulated into a sort of "fakelore" to glorify the dictator and present the rich and picturesque past of the Romanian peasantry on which Ceausescu's future was to be built. Official policy sought to create the "New Man" – an agricultural and industrial proletariat – and this was behind the much-publicized "systematization" policy which involved razing villages and resettling the inhabitants in shoddy "agro-industrial complexes".

The musical equivalents of these monstrosities were the huge sanitized displays called *Cîntarea Romaniei* (Singing Romania), which were held in regional centres round the country. Thousands of peasants were dressed up in their garb and bussed out to picturesque hillsides to perform songs and dances. These were filmed, appallingly edited, and shown on television every Sunday. The words of songs were often changed – removing anything deemed to be religious or that questioned the peasants' love of their labours. These were replaced with bland patriotic sentiments or hymns to peace.

This gave folklore a pretty bad name amongst the educated classes, though the peasants were hardly bothered by it at all. They just did what they were told for Cîntarea Romaniei and got on with their real music in the villages. The fact is that traditional music still flourishes throughout Romania – probably more than anywhere else in Europe – not thanks to Ceausescu but despite him. The isolation of the country and its almost medieval lifestyle have preserved traditions that have been modernized out of existence elsewhere. Luckily village systematization didn't progress very far. Only a dozen villages were destroyed (in the Bucharest area), although the impact of collectivization and forced resettlement of peasants badly affected traditional culture in some of the central provinces. Since the revolution some musicologists have even hazarded a beneficial effect of Cîntarea Romaniei in reviving ballads, *doinas* and other forms which were dying out. They are now concerned to get back to the original style beneath the "fakelore" and, as one put it, "to rediscover the Christian dimensions of Romanian folk music".

As Romania catches up with the west, some kind of preservation will doubtless become necessary if the music is to survive. However, it isn't ready to wither away just yet – and its great joy is its total spontaneity and authenticity. It has a life, function and identity all its own, and it can absorb outside influences with some ease. I've heard the Lambada played by village bands in Moldavia and it had already taken on the local character of the region.

LEFTOVER RITES

Many of the ritual customs that survive in Romania, particularly around Christmas and New Year, have their origins in pre-Christian rites. **Carol-singing** takes place just before Christmas as bands of singers go from house to house with good-luck songs (*colinde*). The custom is something like wassailing in Britain but the songs are nothing like the religious carols of the west. These are pagan songs for the celebration of the midwinter solstice: Christ does not feature, and the tales instead are of such things as legendary battles between folk heros and lions or stags. What is remarkable is so many of the pagan texts have survived undisturbed. In performance they have a fiery or war-like character rather than a pious or religious one and are sung with a strong, irregular rhythm. The tradition predominates in the western half of the country.

The coming of **New Year** is traditionally celebrated with masked dances and the **capra** or goat ritual. The goat is both a costume with hair and horns and a musical instrument as the animal's wooden muzzle is articulated so its jaws can clack together in time with the music. The ritual goes back, like similar customs all over Europe, to ancient fertility rites as the old year suffers its death agony. The noise of bells and clappers was supposed to frighten evil spirits and drive them away. The goat is also mirrored in the devil figures painted in local churches.

The **goat dances** are most thriving in Moldavia where the custom has expanded into full-scale carnivals with music, costumes and political satires bringing its message very much up to date. In the towns, groups of costumed youths have taken to leaping on board trains and intimidating passengers with performances.

During Whitsun week, the **Calusari**, another ritual dance, was performed as an invocation of fertility. It was danced by an odd number of men with a wooden sword and sticks and was famous for the complexity of its steps. Rival groups would often dance in competition. Now the Călușari has been taken up by regional ensembles and forms a staple part of choreographic displays. There's an annual Călusari festival in the town of Slatina, near Craiova in the south of the country.

THE TARAFURI OF WALLACHIA

As in Transylvania most village bands in Wallachia are comprised of **gypsies**: the groups are generally named **Taraf** and then their village name. These *lăutari* (musicians) are professionals who play a vital function in village life at weddings and other celebrations. Yet their music sounds altogether different from that of their Transylvanian counterparts over the Carpathians. The word *taraf* comes from the Arabic and suggests the more oriental flavour of this music. Songs are often preceded by an instrumental improvisation called *taksim*, the name again borrowed from the Middle East.

The lead instrument is, as ever, the fiddle, which is played in a richly ornamented style. The middle parts are taken by the *tsambal* (cimbalom), which fills out the harmony and adds a plangent rippling to the texture. At the bottom is the double bass, ferociously plucked rather than bowed Transylvanian style. In the old days you'd always find a *cobza* (lute) in such bands but their place has given way to the tsambal, guitar and accordion. The gypsies are never slaves to tradition; the young ones particularly are always keen to try new instruments and adopt modish styles. The staple dances are the *hora*, *sîrba* and *brîu* – all of which are danced in a circle.

In Romanian the verb *cînta* means both "to sing" and "to play an instrument", and the lăutari of Wallachia usually do both. Whereas in Transylvania the bands play exclusively dance music, the musicians in the south of the country have an impressive repertoire of **epic songs and ballads** which they are called on to perform. These might be specific marriage songs or legendary tales like "Sarpele" (The Snake) or exploits of the Haidouks, the Robin Hood brigands of Romanian history. One of the tunes you hear played by lăutari all over Romania is "Ciocirlia" (The Lark), which has also become a concert piece for the stage ensembles. Reputedly based on a folk dance, it's an opportunity for virtuoso display and culminates in high squeaks and harmonics on the solo violin to imitate birdsong, followed by the whole band swirling away in abandon on the opening theme.

Considering the wealth of village musicians in Romania it's remarkable that two of the very few recordings available feature the same taraf from the village of **Clejani**, southwest of Bucharest. Mind you, it's a village with fifty professional musicians whose reputation has spread throughout the area. The appearance of the so-called **Taraf of Haidouks** from Clejani at the 1991 WOMAD festival caused a sensation as they played their wild and unmistakable music into the night and when finally forced off stage split into smaller groups to engage in persistent busking for the rest of the festival. Their disc, "Taraf de

Taraf of Haidouks

I don't sing to boast of it
But my heart is bitter
I don't sing because I know how to sing
I'm singing to soothe my heart
Mine and that of the one who is listening to me!

LOST SHEEP

The pastoral way of life is fast disappearing and with it the traditional instrumental repertoire of the *fluier* (shepherd's flute). But there is one form – a sort of folk tone poem – that is still regularly played all over the country: the shepherd who lost his sheep. This song was referred to as early as the sixteenth century by the Hungarian poet Bálint Balassi. I've heard it on the flute in Moldavia, the violin in Transylvania and on the violin and gardon in Gyimes. It begins with a sad, doina-like tune as the shepherd laments his lost

Haidouks", is extraordinary, packed full of truly virtuoso playing with incredible performances on violin, tsambal and accordion. It includes the "Ballad of the Dictator", composed to a traditional melody by the 70-year-old fiddle player Nicolae Neascu, which tells of the dramatic fall of Nicolae Ceausescu. A new addition to the age-old ballad tradition.

Other Wallachian villages famous for their gypsy bands include Mirsa, Dobrotesti, Sutesti and Brăila. In Moldavia and Bucovina, the village bands have survived less well, as the musicians tended to be Romanians rather than gypsies. Given the pastoral traditions of these regions it is quite common to hear a shepherd's flute in place of a violin in an ensemble. There's also a tradition of brass and wind bands.

Taragot player from Taraf de Carancebes in the Banat

THE DOINA

The **doina** is a free-form, semi-improvised and much older song tradition. With poetic texts of grief, bitterness, separation and longing, it might be called the Romanian blues. Very often different texts are sung to the same melody, which may then take on a contrasting character. It is essentially private music, sung to oneself at moments of grief or reflection, although nowadays the songs are often performed by professional singers or in instrumental versions by gypsy bands. Old doinas of the traditional kind can still be found in Oltenia, between the Olt and Danube rivers in the south of the country. This one is typical:

I don't sing because I know how to sing
But because a certain thought is haunting me

flock. Then he sees his sheep in the distance and a merry dance tune takes over, only to return to the sad lament when he realizes it's just a clump of stones. Finally the sheep are found and the whole thing ends with a lively dance in celebration.

Some of the professional bands have adopted the lost sheep story and embroidered it so that during his search the shepherd meets a Turk, a Jew, a Bulgarian, and so on. He asks each of them to sing him a song to alleviate his suffering and promises to pay them if they succeed. No one succeeds until he meets another shepherd who plays a *ciobaneasca* (shepherd's dance) and cheers him up. In the end he finds his sheep devoured by wolves.

THE PIPES OF PAN

Romania's best-known musician on the international stage is **Gheorghe Zamfir**, composer of the ethereal soundtrack of the film "Picnic at Hanging Rock". He plays *nai*, or panpipes, which are thought to have existed in

Romania since ancient times – there's a famous Roman bas-relief in Oltenia. The word *nai*, however, comes from Turkish or Arabic, so perhaps an indigenous instrument existed as well as a similar one brought by professional musicians through Constantinople.

In the eighteenth century "Wallachian" musicians were renowned abroad and the typical ensemble consisted of violin, nai and cobza. But by the end of the following century the nai began to disappear and after the World War I only a handful of players were left. One of these was **Fanica Luca** (1894–1968), a legendary nai player who taught Zamfir his traditional repertoire. Nowadays, Zamfir plays material from all over the place, often accompanied by the organ of Frenchman Marcel Cellier.

In other hands, the nai has become largely associated with tatty urban orchestras.

THE BANAT BEAT

The Banat, Romania's western corner, is ethnically very mixed, with communities of Hungarians, Serbs, Germans and gypsies living alongside the Romanians. The province's largest town, Timisoara, is famous as the birthplace of the revolution that brought down Ceausescu, and the protests there were due largely to the presence of these ethnic minorities.

The music of the Banat is fast, furious and a relatively new phenomenon, having absorbed a lot from the *novokomponovana* music of neighbouring Serbia. It is extremely popular played all the time on the national radio stations and by gypsy bands everywhere. I suspect it's simply the attraction of this fast, modern-sounding urban music with saxophones and frequently erotic lyrics. The Silex recording of the **Taraf de Carancebes** is a great introduction to this virtuoso style.

As Romania slowly catches up with the rest of Europe, its rich musical traditions are bound to disappear. Doubtless the music will be maintained in an organized form, but the great joy of Romanian music now is its total sponteneity and authenticity. Let's hope that in the next few years, more of these amazing bands are recorded and able to tour before one of Europe's great musical traditions is lost.

◼ DISCOGRAPHY ◼

TRANSYLVANIA COLLECTIONS

ⓒ **Various** *Musiques de Transylvanie* (Fonti Musicali, Belgium). This is the best overall introduction to Transylvanian music, with a very good selection of pieces and performances.
Various *Hungarian Music from Northern Mezőség* (Hungaroton, Hungary). Four discs featuring music from the villages of Bont,ida (Bontsida), Răscruci (Válaszút), Buza (Búza), Fizesul Gherlii (Ördöngösfüzes) and Suartu (Magyarszovát). Collected by Zoltán Kallós and György Martin, these are earthy performances of music that has become all the rage on the Budapest tánchaz scene.
ⓒ **Various** *La Vraie Tradition de Transylvanie* (Ocora, France). A selection of peasant music from Maramures and Transylvania.
ⓒ **Various** *Musiques de Mariage de Maramures* (Ocora, France). One of the few recordings of Maramures music, captured at three village weddings.
ⓒ **Various** *Romania – Music for Strings from Transylvania* (Chant du Monde, France). A fine collection of dance music played by village bands. Good to see Romanian music in a first-class release like this. Highly recommended.

TRANSYLVANIAN GROUPS

ⓒ **Szászcsávás Band** *Folk Music from Transylvania* (Quintana/Harmonia Mundi, France). This is the real thing – a gypsy band from the predominantly Hungarian village of Ceuas (Szászcsávás). Great recording, wild playing plus some interesting Saxon and gypsy tunes.
ⓒ **Sándor Fodor** *Hungarian Music from Transylvania* (Hungaroton, Hungary). Music from Kalotaszeg including some Romanian dances. One of the essential Transylvanian records.

ⓒ **Béla Halmos** *Az a szép piros hajnal* (Hungaroton, Hungary). One of the leading musicians of the Budapest tánchaz scene with a collection of music from various regions of Transylvania.
Mihály Halmágyi *Hungarian Music from Gyimes* (Hungaroton, Hungary). Dance, wedding and funeral tunes played on fiddle and gardon. Strange and wild music. A great performance of the shepherd and his lost sheep with a running commentary.
ⓒ **Muzsikás** *Máramaros* (Hannibal, UK). A fascinating CD from the top Hungarian group exploring the lost Jewish repertoire of Transylvania. They are joined by two wonderful old gypsy musicians on fiddle and cimbalom.
ⓒ **Ökrös Ensemble** *Transylvanian Portraits* (Koch, US). Another comprehensive guide to the various styles of Transylvania. The fiddle-playing of Csaba Ökrös on the last track is stunning.
Ferenc Sebo *Folk Music from Lőrincréve* (Hungaroton, Hungary). Extraordinarily rich and beautiful music from the Maros-Küküllő region south of Cluj performed by modern players re-creating the music as collected before World War II.
ⓒ **Taraful Soporu de Cîmpie** (Buda, France). From the village of Soporu, one of the fine gypsy bands from the Cîmpia Transilvaniei.

ROMANIAN GYPSY GROUPS

ⓒ **Taraf de Carancebes,** *Musicians of Banat* (Silex, France). A five-piece gipsy band including saxophone, trumpet, clarinet, accordion and bass. Some stunning virtuoso playing which is enough to explain the popularity of the Banat style.
ⓒ **Taraf de Haidouks** *Taraf de Haidouks* (Crammed Discs, Belgium). This is brilliant – an essential recording of

virtuoso playing by Romanian musicians from Clejani in an ensemble of fiddle, accordion, tsambal and bass. Their earlier recording, as ⓒ **Les Lautari de Clejani** *Music of the Wallachian Gypsies* (Ocora, France), is another fine, if slightly less colourful, collection of songs and dances.

ⓒ **Trio Pandelescu** *Trio Pandelescu* (Silex, France). This highly recommended trio features hot accordion playing from Vasile Pandelescu plus tsambal and bass. Brilliant music-making with delicate moments of real poetry and all the requisite fire.

ROMANIAN VILLAGE RECORDINGS

Various *Ballads and Festivals in Romania* (Chant du Monde, France). A scholarly collection of long ballads and a few dances from Wallachian villages. Good recordings and full texts in French.

ⓒ **Various** *Village Music from Romania* (VDE-Gallo, Switzerland). A three-CD box produced by the Geneva Ethnographic Museum. Archival recordings of specialized interest made by the musicologist Constantin Brailoiu in 1933–43 on his travels around Moldavia, Oltenia and Transylvania.

THE VOICE MYSTERY

BULGARIA'S STRANGE POLYPHONY

After wine, footballers and attar of roses, music has become Bulgaria's best known export, with the distinctive singing style to the west of its women singers popular in the west on disc, in concert, and popping up in commercials, film soundtracks and even a Kate Bush album. At home, the music traditions are very much alive, whether at social occasions or at the great quintennial festival at Koprivshtitsa. Kim Burton checks in.

Bulgarian music is instantly recognizable. Both its matter and manner are powerfully individual. To foreign ears one of its most immediate characteristics is the vocal timbre of such singers as **Nadka Karadzhova, Yanka Rupkina** and **Konya Stojanova** – the soloists on the popular **"Mystère des voix Bulgares"** album recorded by Bulgarian Radio's women's choir. Their rich, direct and stirring sound has rather oddly become referred to in the west as "open-throated". In fact the throat in this style of singing is extremely constricted and the sound is forced out, which accounts for its focus and its strength and which allows the complex yet clean

Mystery voice Nadka Karadzhova

ornaments that are such a striking feature of these singers' performances.

Another western misconception about the "*Mystère des voix Bulgares*" album was to categorize it as "folk music", when the compositions, for the most part, were highly sophisticated modern choral compositions. The only "village" songs on the record are those slow, heavily ornamented solo numbers with titles about lambkins and the like. These are traditional women's songs and used to be sung at the social events called *sedyanki*, evenings when the unmarried girls would gather together to sew and embroider, gossip and compare fiancés, or sung to guests on the occasion of various festivities. Their ornamentations, although subtly varied with each performance, are always thought of as a vital part of the tune, and the only time you will ever hear a song without them is when the singer is too old to manage them.

Much Bulgarian music, both sung and played, was traditionally performed without harmony, or with at most a simple drone like that of bagpipes. Nonetheless, in some districts a most extraordinary system of polyphonic performance grew up. In the Shop district near Sofia, women in the villages sing in two- and three-part harmony – though not a harmony that western ears readily recognize, as it is full of dissonance and tone clusters and decorated with whoops, vibrati and slides. The singers themselves say that they try to sing "as bells sound". In the Pirin district, in the southwest, the villagers sometimes sing two different two-voiced songs with two different texts simultaneously, resulting in a four-part texture. This polyphonic style of performance is normally the domain of women, although in Pirin men also sing in harmony, albeit with a different repertoire and in a rather simpler and more robust style.

The rhythmic complexity and speed of Bulgarian music is also striking – for the Hungarian composer Béla Bartók the discovery of these irregular rhythms was a revelation. The most widespread is probably the *ruchenitsa* dance, three beats arranged as 2–2–3, closely followed by the *kopanitsa* (2–2–3–2–2). More complex patterns are by no means uncommon. These rhythms, so foreign to western ears, are ingrained in Bulgarians, who snap their fingers in such patterns while queueing for a bus or hanging around on the corner of the street.

RITUAL MUSIC

Even though Bulgaria is a small country – the population is just nine million – there are several clearly defined regional styles. The earthy, almost plodding dances from Dobrudzha, in the northeast, are quite different in character from the lightning-fast dances of the Shop people, and the long heart-rending songs from Thracian plain contrast with the sweet and pure melodies from the northwest. In the remote mountains of the Rodopi, in the south, you can still hear the distant sound of a shepherd playing the bagpipes to his flock of a summer evening, and in the villages or small towns of the valleys groups of people sing slow, broad songs to the accompaniment of the deep *kaba gaida*.

The yearly round of peasant life was defined by the rhythm of the seasons, sowing and harvest, and many of the ancient rituals, intended to ensure fertility and luck, survive, though more in a "Well, we always do it this time of the year" way than in the belief that they will produce any kind of magical effect. These customs include Koleduva, when groups of young men process around the village asking for gifts from the householders; Laduvane at the New Year; and the

springtime Lazaruvane (St Lazarus Day), the most important holiday for young women, who take their turn to sing and dance through the streets. All have particular songs and dances connected with them – usually simple and repetitive and almost certainly very old.

The most startling of these rites, **Nestinarstvo**, from the villages of Bulgari, Kondolovo and Rezovo in Strandzha, has died out in its original form, in which its exponents would fall into a trance and dance on hot coals to the sound of bagpipes and drum to mark the climax of the feast of saints Konstantin and Elena, but is sometimes presented at festivals and folklore shows. The wild and stirring music remains the same.

These days the two most important rites of passage in Bulgarian life, whether in the country or in the town, are getting married and leaving home to do military service. Both these occasions are marked by music. Every moment of a **wedding** – the arrival of the groom's wedding party, the leading out of the bride to meet it, the procession to the church and so on – has a particular melody or song. The songs sung at the bride's house the night before the wedding are the saddest in the whole body of Bulgarian music, because the bride is leaving home, never to live again in her parents' house.

Parties to see the young men **off to the army** are more cheerful. In towns, the family of the recruit hires a restaurant and a band – normally some combination of accordion, violin, electric guitar, clarinet/saxophone and drum kit which plays a promiscuous mix of folk, pop and other melodies – and the guests eat, drink and dance. In the country the feast is often held in the evening, and out of doors.

On one such occasion I witnessed in the village of Mirkovo, the main street was jammed with trestle tables and the guests were entertained by a little band of two clarinets, trumpet and accordion, who played the slow melodies called *na trapeza* (at the table) while the guests ate. Later the young soon-to-be soldier, glazed of eye and rather unsteady on his feet, was led round and presented with gifts of money, flowers or shirts. (Shirts in fact play a great role in Bulgarian folk life. At weddings each member of the party wears a handkerchief pinned to their breast, but the more important relatives sport an entire shirt, sometimes still in its cellophane wrapping.)

After all the food had gone, the band struck up a set of local dance tunes, and everyone rushed to join in a *horo* – a ring dance – whose leader capered and leapt, all the while flourishing an enormous flag on a long pole. Bulgarians, especially villagers, love dancing, and at the end of a festival or similar event, if the band starts to play for pleasure, you can see people – from grannies to young children – literally racing across the grass to join the circle.

BANDS AND INSTRUMENTS

Most Bulgarian bands that play at weddings and so on use modern, factory-made instruments, often amplified with more enthusiasm than subtlety. Around the town of Yambol in the Strandzha area, in the east, however, people prefer the old folk instruments, and if they can afford it will even hire a professional band from Sofia to come and play them.

Such a band will almost invariably consist of *gaida* (bagpipes), *kaval* (end-blown flute), *gadulka* (a bowed stringed instrument) and *tambura* (a strummed stringed instrument), sometimes with the addition of the large drum, the *tapan*. These instruments were always common throughout the country and after the war, when the state founded its ensembles for folk songs and dances, they were the ones chosen to front the new "orchestras". As a result they have undergone certain developments and refinements to aid reliability of tuning and tone, while some players have brought their skill to a quite unbelievable peak of virtuosity.

The gaida is the best known of all these instruments. Although of simple construction – a chanter for the melody, a drone, mouth-tube, and a small goatskin for air

– it's capable of a partly chromatic scale of just over an octave and in the hands of a master such as **Kostadin Varimezov** or **Nikola Atanasov** its wild sound has an astonishing turn of speed and rhythmic force. These players also have the ability to use the potential the gaida has for rich ornamentation to perform beautiful versions of slow songs and other na trapeza melodies. In the Rodopi mountains they have a huge bagpipes, the deep-voiced *kaba gaida*, which accompanies singing or dancing, sometimes alone and sometimes in groups of two, three, four or even more. There is one group called literally **Sto kaba gaidi** (One hundred bagpipes) and although this could be thought excessive the sound is undeniably impressive.

Like the gaida, the **kaval** was originally a shepherds' instrument, and some of its melodies, or rather freely extemporized meditations on certain specific motifs, go by such names as "Taking the herd to water", "At noon", "The lost lamb". The modern kaval is made of three wooden tubes fitted together, the topmost of which has a bevelled edge that the player blows against on the slant to produce a note. The middle tube has eight finger holes and the last has four more holes which affect the tone and the tuning. They are sometimes called *Djavolski dupki* (the Devil's holes), and there is a tale that they they were made by the Devil, who was so jealous of the playing of a young shepherd that he stole his kaval while he was sleeping and bored the extra holes to ruin it. Of course they only made the instrument sound sweeter and the Devil was, as is usual in folktales, thoroughly discomfited.

The great Hundred Bagpipes Ensemble

The school of kaval playing that has grown up since the war, led by **Nikola Ganchev** and

Stoyan Velichkov, is extremely refined and capable of all manner of nuances of sound. The sound is sweet and clear (the folk say "honeyed"), the low (*kaba*) register is rich and buzzing, and in the last ten or so years a new technique called *kato klarinet* (clarinet style) has appeared – the instrument is played as though it were a trumpet producing a sound indeed very like the low register of the clarinet.

The **gadulka** is a relative of the medieval rebec, with a pear-shaped body held upright on the knee, tucked into the belt or cradled in a strap hung round the player's neck. It has three, sometimes four bowed strings and as many as nine sympathetic strings which resonate when the instrument is played producing an unearthly shimmering resonance behind the melody.

The gadulka is exceptionally tricky to play – there are no frets, not even a fingerboard, the top string is stopped with the fingernails, and the whole thing is liable to wriggle out of the learner's grasp like a live fish. This makes the gadulka players' habit of showing off by playing virtuoso selections from the popular classics all the more startling. **Mihail Marinov** and **Atanas Vulchev** are notable among older players, and **Nikolai Petrov** is an important member of the younger generation.

The **tambura** is a member of the lute family, with a flat-backed pear-shaped body and a long fretted neck. Its original form, found in Pirin and in the central Rodopi, had two courses of strings, one of which usually just provided a drone while the melody was played on the other. These days the common form of the instrument has four courses tuned like the top four strings of a guitar, and in groups it both strums chords and runs counter melodies. It has thus changed its form and its role in Bulgarian music more than any other instrument, as chordal harmony is not typical of village music and was only introduced by academically trained composers in the course of this century.

Around the end of the nineteenth century factory-made instruments like the accordion, clarinet and violin arrived in the country and were soon used to play dance music and to accompany songs. Modern accordion style was pretty much defined by **Boris Karloff** who played very elegantly and wrote a number of tunes – notably "Krivo Horo" – which have become standards. More modern accordionists worthy of note include the gypsy **Ibro Lolov**, **Traicho Sinapov** and **Kosta Kolev**; the latter, also well known as a composer, arranger and conductor, plays in a

unique style which contrasts in its restraint and care with the high-speed acrobatics of some of the younger players. By far the most brilliant of these is the young **Petar Ralchev**, a Thracian who, unlike some of the speed-merchants, combines new ideas with a lot of taste and, more importantly, a lot of soul.

STATE CONTROL

Nowhere in Europe has politics had so much influence over music. In the 1950s, after the communists had established themselves in power,

Trio Bulgarka with singing pal Kate Bush

they set up the State Ensemble for Folk Songs and Dances under the leadership of **Philip Kutev**, an extraordinarily talented composer and arranger whose style of writing and arranging became the model for a whole network of professional and amateur groups across the country. His great gift was the ability to take the sounds of village singers, drone-based and full of close dissonances but essentially harmonically static, and from this forge a musical language which answered the aesthetic demands of western European concepts of form and harmony without losing touch with the atmosphere of the original tunes. If you compare his work with the attempts of earlier arrangers to force the tunes into a harmonic system which they really didn't fit, his success is as obvious as their failure. It's his heritage that is heard on the "Mystère des voix Bulgares" recordings, and those of the **Trio Bulgarka** and the instrumental group **Balkana**.

It is impossible to overestimate the tight grip that the Communist state had on every aspect of Bulgarian life, and this is as true of music as of anything else. What began as a praiseworthy attempt to preserve and enrich folklore became a straitjacket to which all musicians had to conform or else stop working as musicians. It reached such ridiculous extremes as prescribing a certain percentage of Russian songs to be played in the course of an evening's entertainment in a restaurant to demonstrate the eternal friendship of the Bulgarian and Soviet peoples. And the musicians couldn't ignore this insanity because there were people around whose job it was to make sure that they were doing it. One musician told me how he had had to audition all his new songs and dances to "The Committee of Pensioners" before he was permitted to perform them on the radio. If they were "not Bulgarian enough" then permission was refused. Even if it was granted, the style of performance had to be acceptable. "Once they told me that I was playing too fast, and that Bulgarian music is not played so fast. This was a tune that I myself had written, it was I that was playing it, and I am a Bulgarian musician. How could they tell me the way to play my own song? But they could. I tell you, Bulgarian music used to be behind closed shutters – but now the shutters have been opened."

That, certainly, is the intention. Shortly after his election as leader in 1991, Filip Dimitrov observed that "Bulgaria is practically the only country in the Balkans in which there is no connection between today's popular music and folk music. You find it in Serbia or Greece, but not Bulgaria since the war. That's the effect of the Communist Party trying to impose its rigid patterns so the music has nothing to do with everyday life." The new government policy, in as much one exists, is to let folk music find its own role and place again with state support where necessary.

This doesn't mean that the people working in the field of folklore during the communist years were all apparatchiks – nor that they failed to produce immensely beautiful music. The network of regional professional ensembles, fed by a stream of talent trained in schools set up to teach folk music, meant that there was time, money and opportunity available for people to develop the approved language in their own way, and many composers created their own individual style. Amongst arrangers and composers, Kosta Kolev is one unmistakable voice, and the work of **Stefan Mutafchiev** and **Nikolai Stoikov** with the Trakiya Ensemble in Plovdiv was very inventive.

The series of regional competition-festivals held around the country and culminating once every five years at the vast gathering of amateur music groups at Koprivshtitsa (see box), the mass-production of folk instruments, and the encouragement shown to amateurs, has managed to keep music alive in the villages. Unfortunately this has been at the cost of alienating a lot of people, particularly the young city-dwellers, by means of insisting on propagandist songs with titles like "Mladata Traktoristka" (The young girl tractor-driver) and referring to them as "contemporary developments in folk creativity". Recent years have seen a move away from state control and also funding, but fledgling private companies are beginning to play a part in developing a new folk-based popular music. All the same, most of the bands involved hail from smaller towns like Yambol or Plovdiv rather than the capital Sofia.

The festival at **Koprivshtitsa** is particularly important, not merely because of its size (there are literally thousands of performers bused in from all over the country) but because it is the only one devoted to amateur performers. Practically the only recordings of genuine village music that the state record company Balkanton has ever released are from this festival, and they are among the most beautiful and valuable commercial recordings of Bulgarian songs and dances ever made.

WEDDING BANDS

The wedding bands are a fascinating example of the formerly "underground" folk music that is currently an extremely important part of

Bulgarian village dancers strut their stuff at Koprivishtitsa

KOPRIVSHTITSA FESTIVAL

. . . .

Imagine a cross between a pop festival and a medieval fair: 18,000 people singing and playing music in the mountains of central Bulgaria surrounded by traders exploiting the new free-market potential, the smell of grilling kebabs, beer tents, plastic-trinket sellers, stalls with the latest in Bulgarian CDs, and gypsies weaving through the crowds with performing monkeys and dancing bears. This is the festival that takes place every five years on the hillside above the picturesque village of Koprivshtitsa.

It began in 1965 as a showcase for Bulgarian folklore financed by the Ministry of Culture. The Bulgarian communists were generous in supporting their own idea of folk music: state song and dance troupes presenting a "rich national heritage" abroad and professional dance ensembles going into villages to show the locals how Bulgarian dances should be performed. But Koprivshtitsa was one of the better ideas. Here the music was performed in something like its raw style by ordinary villagers.

The 1991 festival was a microcosm of Bulgaria itself: a confused halfway house between a centrally controlled state and a market economy where private cafés have sprung up to serve the petrol queues. The competitive element in which performers were awarded insulting pseudo-gold medals had gone but the former jurors were still there at their tables observing and taking notes for research purposes. The Ministry of Culture, strapped by the severe economic crisis, only came up with half the money needed, and the festival was saved by other government departments providing transport, tents and medication free of charge.

Bulgaria is host to a large Turkish minority population who were persecuted by the former regime. Officially there were no Turkish groups participating in the festival although the organizers intend to invite Turkish, gypsy, Jewish and Armenian performers next time round – if they get the funding – in 1996. Going off in search of a kebab, though, I stumbled across a clutch of Turkish musicians at the centre of a ring of dancers playing zurna and tupan drum. For a few leva, you could have the dubious thrill of the zurna blown directly into your ear – "ear fucking" as they put it. With the rhythms insistently pumping out, the dancers were in fact in a sort of sexual frenzy. Some of the men had beer bottles tucked into their wide waistbands and, thrusting their groins, they carefully controlled their movements until the climax of the dance, when the beer frothed over and sprayed the crowd.

Its supporters say the Koprivshtitsa Festival shows Bulgarian music at its most authentic. I don't see that performing a mid-winter dance on a concrete platform in August, with men dressed in woolly bear-suits in a temperature of 30°C, is remotely authentic, but the music, if not the event, is genuine. The performers may have been assisted by "consultants" but this is village music as performed by the villagers, not arranged and cleaned up by professional ensembles. Still, I suspect that nowadays most mid-winter rituals in Bulgaria are performed at Koprivshtitsa in August rather than at their proper time. Beware too the endless "folk plays" full of butter churns and spinning wheels that pop up between the musical numbers. It's clear that the social changes since the war have changed the nature of village life for ever.

Unlike Romania, where folk music has kept its original function in spite of the regime, in Bulgaria it has rather lost its true meaning, thanks to sponsorship by the state. Now it needs to find a natural life again, but I wonder if it can do so when the link between the music and everyday life is broken. It may have become permanently festivalised!

The best music at Koprivshtitsa happens off-stage away from the dreaded PA systems. You can find little groups just singing to themselves, or solitary bagpipe and fiddle players on the hillside. This is where the music belongs and where it sounds at its best. There's no doubt, either, after a visit to Koprivshtitsa, that there is incredible musicality amongst ordinary people. Would you find 18,000 people who can perform like that in any other country? And Bulgaria has a population of only nine million.

For the moment the Koprivshtitsa tradition endures and many of Bulgaria's professional musicians go to the festival to keep in touch with music at the roots. As Elena Stoyin, an eminent musicologist and one of the now redundant judges told me, "We are a small and poor country, but we are rich in these traditions and happy that people are preserving these things themselves."

Simon Broughton

Bulgarian musical life. Unlike the musicians mentioned above, who were approved by the state (though none the worse for that), they existed outside the framework of official music making, hired to play at weddings, the seeing-off of recruits and various village festivities. Because they did not have to pay much attention to the communist ideal of workers and peasants marching into a glorious dawn in order to record or get on the radio (as semiprofessionals the airwaves were not open to them in any case) they were free to experiment with instrumentation, mixtures of folk instruments like gaida and kaval with electric guitar, synthesizer and kit drums, rock and jazz rhythms, and foreign tunes.

As the state monopolist recording industry in Bulgaria didn't allow the formation of a commercial style, some of these musicians simply learned songs from Serbian and other radio broadcasts and pirate cassette tapes and performed them to a public that responded to their directness and energy. Others, particularly in Thrace, went further and began a far-reaching reinvention of their local music. It was only in the mid-Eighties that officialdom picked up on the existence of this music, and through the efforts of some far-seeing musicologists was persuaded to recognize them as worthy of public support. A triennial festival was set up in the town of **Stambolovo** (hence the wedding bands' alternative name of *Stambolovski orkestri*) and the results issued on the Balkanton record label. The festival presented the new music in maybe a slightly bowdlerized form – bands were subjected to the "assistance" of approved musical directors – but the recordings were a revelation nonetheless.

Clarinettist **Ivo Papasov** (see box) is the best known of these musicians abroad, thanks to the work of Hannibal Records who managed to record him and his electric band after a long struggle with the bureaucracy. He started out with the Plovdiv jazz-folk ensemble, and in his own later work has flirted with jazz and produced some startling transformations of traditional Thracian and Turkish music. His family is of Turkish origin, and even in the period just prior to the fall of the Zhivkov regime, when the very existence of a Turkish minority in Bulgaria was denied (the Balkans suffered greatly under the Turkish Empire for over five hundred years and the

Jazz-folk virtuoso Ivo Papasov

attempt to whip up anti-Turkish feelings was part of an ultimately unsuccessful attempt by the communists to retain power by playing the nationalist card), you could get homemade recordings of Papasov playing Turkish melodies with a small band of the type common today in Istanbul. Now that under the new government Balkanton has released tapes and records of "Turkish music from Bulgaria", we can look forward to hearing something very interesting from him. His second Hannibal release, "Balkanology", begins with a Turkish dance and also includes Macedonian and Greek material.

There are many other bands of this type, often composed of gypsies, using the new freedom in all kinds of ways. The orchestras **Sever**, **Juzhni Vetar**, **Shoumen** and **Trakiiski Solisti** all have fresh and intriguing ways of interpreting their traditional music. Some have now made commercial recordings; others are still only to be heard live or on homemade tapes sold in the markets of the small towns where they live.

NEW SOUNDS

It is not only the wedding bands that have lately been pushing back the boundaries. Some

IVO PAPASOV

· ·

With a huge gut and unwieldy frame, Ivo Papasov seems an unlikely source for some of the most nimble and virtuosic music you'll encounter anywhere in the world. After seeing him in concert, though, you'll be left in little doubt that he's one of most interesting clarinettists around. He and his band race through numbers based on the complex rhythms of Bulgarian folk dances, grafting on jazzy improvisations for clarinet, saxophone, accordion and keyboard. He is also one of the few jazz musicians to have been in prison for propaganda.

"It was in 1982 when there was a campaign to make Bulgarian Turks change their names. I was often playing at Turkish weddings and the police came, arrested us, beat us and took us to prison. I was in prison 20 days and then was to be sent to a labour camp. They wanted to make an example of me, but a friend of mine, a prosecutor, managed to get the judgement changed and I was released."

Ivo Papasov is a Bulgarian Turk from Kardzali close to the Greek and Turkish borders. "I am from Thrace where Orpheus was born. It is an area very rich in music." He has an immense following in Bulgaria, not just among Turks and Gypsies but amongst young people as well. It's now easier than it was for him to give concerts, but he's most famous for playing weddings for those who can afford it.

"They are big weddings – maybe 1,000 or 1,500 people with lots of eating, drinking and dancing. They last more than 24 hours, starting in the morning at the bride's house. There's eating and drinking and money is bestowed or maybe a car or a house. In the late afternoon when it's cooler there's a dance outside and then more eating and drinking till morning."

Ivo cites some of the greatest jazz clarinettists and saxophonists as influences – Benny Goodman, Charlie Parker, David Sandborn – but alongside them is Petko Radev, the Bulgarian clarinettist, also from Thrace, who plays traditional music as well as first clarinet at La Scala, Milan. Always keeping his background in mind, Ivo Papasov is one of the many musicians in Bulgaria who is brilliantly forging contemporary music out of traditional forms.

Simon Broughton

---

of the bands that play purely traditional instruments have been making experiments. The UK label Black Crown has released a record of the band **Loznitsa** called "Moods", featuring both the old master of the gaida **Nikola Atanasov** and the incredible young kaval player **Georgi Zhelyaskov,** which is a good representation of the new trend. Particularly worth investigating is the work of the kaval player **Teodosi Spasov**, who has not only recorded a very beautiful and practically avant-garde folk album, "Dulug Put" in collaboration with composer Mutafchiev, but also played to great acclaim with the well-known Bulgarian jazz pianist **Milcho Leviev** on his first concert in Sofia after twenty years of exile. Spasov's album, "The Sand Girl", is a very successful folk-jazz fusion from one of Bulgaria's most exciting young players.

The future of Bulgarian music is highly unpredictable. At the time of writing the country seems to have survived a painful transition to democracy, but its economic problems are exacerbated by the UN sanctions imposed on its neighbour and natural trading partner Serbia. It will probably be impossible to sustain the network of festivals of music, dance and folk art as there simply isn't the money to support them. Koprivshtitsa will almost certainly survive, given its importance, but even the wedding bands are likely to find hard times ahead as people have less money to spend on their marriage festivities. On the other hand, increased opportunities for travel, and exposure to influences and techniques from the rest of the world, are having their effect.

The last couple of years have seen the appearance of several small private labels which are playing a part in the development of a new folk-pop – or rather, several types of folk-pop in which gypsy musicians and singers are often prominent. Some of it is heavily influenced by Serb *novokomponovana narodna muzika* (see p.87) – orchestras **Kristal** and **Eros** are good examples – other bands like **Palantiri** and **Rodopi** show a clear debt to Papasov, though usually without his hair-raising virtuosity and with, some might say, better taste.

From the Black Sea coast **Orkestar Slunchev Bryag** delivers a sort of gypsy-influenced Bulgarian pop-soul with gaida, kaval and gadulka instead of a horn section. Yet other musicians, almost too many to mention although singer **Daniel Spasov** stands out, are gently updating the Kutev sound; the Subdibula label specializes in this area. In con-trast, the Bulgarian ROD label has gone into the villages to record their "Magic Water" series, which presents traditional and often intensely local music, beautifully performed by amateurs, although their enthusiasm for presenting everything they tape sets a challenge to the non-musicologists among us.

All in all, it seems that Bulgarian music will continue to be as thrilling and inventive in years to come as it ever has been.

DISCOGRAPHY

GROUPS

ⓒ **Bisserov Sisters** *Music from the Pirin Mountains* (Pan Records, Holland). One of the best vocal trios from Bulgaria backed by the Trio Karadzhovska on kaval, gadulka and tambura. A good introduction to the Pirin sound.

Boris Hristev and Orkestar Rodopi *Orkestra Rodopi* (Bofirov Music, Bulgaria). A grand spicy mixture of modern Thracian song and dance led by accordionist Hristev. Guest kaval master Teodosi Spasov makes his presence felt on a couple of tracks.

ⓒ **Loznitsa** *Moods* (Black Crown, UK). A tight band of excellent musicians playing material from all over the country with vocals by Kalinka Vulcheva. Well produced.

Orkestar Sever *Albaniya '93* (Payner, Bulgaria). A cassette-only recording of one of Bulgaria's hottest gypsy-led bands. Miladin Asenov's synthesizer playing has to be heard to be believed.

ⓒ **Ivo Papasov** *Orpheus Ascending* and *Balkanology* (Hannibal, UK). Both albums are splendid examples of Ivo's irrepressible style. The virtuoso clarinettist and his band play all sorts of goodies from their wedding bag. Fast and furious: gypsies love it, musicologists despair. The *Balkanology* album includes more ethnically diverse material and, with the allusion to Charlie Parker, perhaps a touch more jazz.

Daniel Spasov *Byala Mariya* (Subdibula, Bulgaria). A capella ballads, electric-Africa grooves and sizzling folk instrument arrangements jostle one another on an astonishingly powerful release of northern Bulgarian songs from a young singer to look out for.

ⓒ **Trio Bulgarka** *Balkana* and *The Forest is Crying.* (Hannibal, UK). The three singers – Yanka Rupkina, Stoyanka Boneva and Eva Georgieva – perform a capella and accompanied by one of Bulgaria's best instrumental groups, the Trakiiskata Troika (Thracian Trio). The two albums include some Bulgarian favourites re-recorded for a western audience.

COMPILATIONS

ⓒ **Various** *Le Mystère des voix Bulgares Vol I* (4AD, UK). Classic melodies and arrangements given a hauntingly beautiful performance by the Women's Choir of the Radio. Indispensable. There are three further volumes, but this is the best.

Various *Koprivshtitsa '76* and *Koprivshtitsa '86* (Balkanton, Bulgaria). Recordings of some of the best amateur musicians and groups in the great quinquennial festivals at Koprivshtitsa. They are hard to find but are among the most beautiful and valuable commercial recordings of Bulgarian songs and dances ever made.

Various *Popular Clarinettists from Thrace* (Balkanton, Bulgaria). A cracking collection of superb playing from six of Bulgaria's best clarinettists, including Petko Radev and Ivo Papasov. If you can find it, get it!

ⓒ **Various** *Stambolovo '88* (Balkanton, Bulgaria). A selection of wild and wonderful experiments by some of the wedding bands who took part in the 1988 Stambolovo festival. They came from all across the country and give some idea of the diversity of Bulgarian styles and their modern development.

ⓒ **Various** *Two Girls Started to Sing . . .* (Rounder, US). Real field recordings made in 1978–88 in village locations round Bulgaria. This is music as it is really lived and performed. Good notes, too.

ⓒ **Various** *Village Music of Bulgaria* (Elektra-Nonesuch, US). Excellent selection of material including a stunning performance of the Rodopi song "Izlel e Delyo Haidutin" by Valya Balkanska, which was the first Bulgarian song in space when it travelled on the spacecraft *Voyager* as one of its examples of Earth culture.

BALKAN BEATS

MUSIC AND NATIONALISM IN THE FORMER YUGOSLAVIA

It's hardly necessary to say that the former Yugoslavia has a complex ethnic and cultural mix – three years of civil war have underscored that. The extraordinary mosaic of nationalities, languages, customs and beliefs involved in the conflict gave the region great musical riches, and when the fighting at last dies down many of them will remain, even if only in exile. Inevitably, too, distinctive national styles are now being pressed into service by the nationalist politicians and hence promoted more than ever. Kim Burton tracks the new republics.

Almost overnight, it seems, Yugoslavia changed from being a cheap holiday destination for those with a mild taste for exotica to being associated with brutality and internecine slaughter of a degree not seen in Europe since the days of World War II. The Balkan countries as a whole owe their reputation as a flashpoint for conflict to their complex and interwoven mixture of races and religions, and what was Yugoslavia had probably the most diverse ethnic and cultural mix of them all.

Before Yugoslavia became a single country in 1918 it had a complex and often bloody history of invasion and foreign control, resulting in what is now the major cultural divide within the country and one of the primary causes of the current conflicts. From the fourteenth century onwards the east and south were part of the Ottoman Empire, while Croatia and Slovenia in the west were part of the Holy Roman Empire and later Austro-Hungary.

As a result, what was Yugoslavia and is now a collection of internationally recognized and unrecognized independent states consists of not only Catholic Slovenes and Croats, Orthodox Serbs and Macedonians, Muslim Albanians and Bosnians, but also Turks, Hungarians, gypsies, Vlachs and many other small communities. Each of these groups has its own music – distinctive and yet a part of the ethnic mix. And while the pure traditional music is dying out it's being brought up to date in the form of *novokomponovana narodna muzika* (newly composed folk music), heard everywhere in cafés, bars and taxis.

Between the traditional and contemporary styles are various professional and semi-professional groups working outside the recording industry who play for money at social occasions like weddings, Saturday-night dances and village feasts. The rather different task of deliberately preserving old songs, dances and crafts is undertaken by the amateur ensembles known as *Kulturno-Umetnička Društva* (Cultural-Artistic Societies) or KUDs, which receive state support in the form of finance or artistic direction from well-known performers or academics, and these days they hope for business sponsorship as well.

Some KUDs concentrate on their own local music while others attempt to present styles from all over the country. In the past there were attempts to inculcate a pan-Yugoslav ethic, but in the years immediately preceding the outbreak of the fighting, like practically everything else in Yugoslav society, KUDs had been used as a means of asserting ethnic and local identities. Most villages and factories still boast a KUD, and larger towns may have several. They perform at folklore festivals, sometimes record for the radio and occasionally make tapes or records for small local labels. These are often well worth hearing as they give an idea of the contemporary village or small-town sound. Professional folklore groups like the Belgrade-based **Kolo** are impressively drilled but rarely as soulful.

SLOVENIA

Slovenia, which was the most westerly and developed member of the Yugoslav federation, is now a fully recognized independent state. It achieved independence from Yugoslavia in 1991 after a ten-day war with the Federal Army leaving sixty dead. This relatively benign secession, by Balkan standards, was largely thanks to the (again relative) cultural homogeneity of Slovenia compared to the other republics.

Commercial forms of Slovene popular music reflect the country's historical links with the Alpine region and the Austro-Hungarian Empire. In other words: cheerful waltzes and polkas played by accordionists, trumpeters and clarinettists in knee-breeches, and romances sung by women in dirndls. Most of these songs are newly composed and all tend to sound much the same. Indeed, the official festival competitions such as that in Ptuj are likely to disqualify entries that stray too far from the accepted formulae or show dangerous signs of originality.

It's this sort of music you are most likely to hear on the radio or performed live. Its beginnings lie in the history of Slovenia as a province of the Austro-Hungarian Empire from the fourteenth century until 1918. Slovenian conscripts posted far from home learnt the tunes from their fellow soldiers from Vienna, Prague, or Budapest – the popular music of central Europe. Young musicians even now can play melodies learned by their grandfathers or great-grandfathers far from home on the marches of the empire.

The current style was more or less invented about forty years ago by the **Avsenik brothers**, Slavko and Vilko, who are also immensely

The Pale Moon: old-time Slovene instrumentalists

popular over the border in Austria and southern Germany and have gained any amount of gold discs. Practically every other band has copied their style and line-up of accordion, trumpet, clarinet, guitar and brass bass with a vocal trio. Such bands perform at weddings and other celebrations and, during the summer, at the so-called *gasilske veselice* (firemen's merrymaking), held at weekends and holidays at the local fire station, where there is some space to set up stalls selling food and drink and enough open ground for dancing.

Other, older styles of music such as the so-called **velike goslarije** (big bands) of cimbalom, stringed instruments and woodwind exist only in much reduced form. The northeast's **Beltinska Banda** is the best of the surviving groups.

Traditional, unaccompanied singing in harmony – once very widespread – is now rarely to be found in the villages and there are very few players of older traditional instruments such as the bowed zither and panpipes.

Slovenia is the only republic where there is a deliberate movement independent of the state to revive or preserve old music – perhaps because it's the only one in which the music is not still living and growing. The work of the wife-and-husband team of **Mira Omerzel-Terlep and Matija Terlep**, who collect and reconstruct old instruments, research old songs and perform them, is the best example of this kind of initiative. As well as making a series of field-recordings, some of which have been released by the German company Trikont under the title *Das Bleiche Mond – Bledi Mesec*, they have recorded a series of four discs which give an excellent idea of the way things used to sound. Another well-established revival group with a stronger instrumental bias is **Trinajsto Prase**, a trio of conservatory-trained musicians whose outlook has something in common with the Hungarian tánchaz movement (see p.62).

Accordionist **Tine Lesjak** has recorded some of the dance, song and military repertoire from the days of Austro-Hungary in a tribute to the older style of playing, and in the last few years many young people, inspired by the new national movement, have started to learn the *citra* (folk zither).

CROATIA

Croatia, like Slovenia, has been formally recognized as an independent country but due to the large numbers of Serbs living on Croatian soil has been unable to make a clean break. At the time of writing the Serb-inhabited areas which declared themselves autonomous in 1991 are still policed by UN forces and show no signs of ceasing their defiance of either Zagreb or their one-time sponsors in Belgrade.

Culturally, Croatia looks to the west, although its music is far less western than that of Slovenia. Musical styles in Croatia are generally attractive and cheery, with none of the complications found further east, but ultimately with less depth as well. There are plenty of KUDs, which often play in their local village bars, and some high-quality professional groups that perform arrangements of folk material somewhat after the Bulgarian model.

The group **Lado** is probably the best and most versatile of these.

The peasant musicians themselves, particularly the women, tend to hide themselves away, as if their singing was faintly shameful and certainly old fashioned. Some even go so far as to hide their abilities from their husbands. One such group of singers was studied by a musicologist (female herself) who was forced to sneak in the back door to record them while someone kept watch for returning menfolk. It is hard to hear anything spontaneous. However there is a wealth of festivals featuring amateur groups that are worth hearing. A couple of rock bands from the capital, Zagreb, have used folk tunes – notably **Haustor** and the eccentric **Vjestice** (Witches), who brew up a striking mixture of punk, South African jive and Croatian folk. With the rise of the new nationalism some of the old songs have come back into fashion, but on the whole the new government seems to see the fostering of national identity based on folklore as a strategy of the disgraced communist regime and prefers to present Croatia as a modern and thoroughly western-oriented society.

The most typical ensemble is the **tamburica orchestra**. The *tamburica* is a plucked and strummed string instrument that comes in various shapes and sizes, from the tiny mandolin-like *prim* to the large *berde*, the size of a double-bass. Dances are accompanied and encouraged by the whistling of the men and a high-pitched squealing from the women. Slower songs are sentimental and betray the sticky-sweet influence of Vienna, while the fast ones are extremely lively with scurrying inner parts and counterpoints. The best-known singer is Krunoslav Slabinac, known as **Kico**. The real stronghold of the tamburica is Slavonia, the region to the north and east of Zagreb, though it extends into central Croatia and the Vojvodina in northern Serbia, where the elder statesman is **Zvonko Bogdan**. Close by, in the area known as Medjimurje, the lyrical songs have some qualities in common with those of neighbouring Hungary, and recently have become very popular in Croatia as a whole.

Around Zagreb, in the hills of the Zagorje, the music is almost indistinguishable from that of Austria, and most of the newly composed songs are in this vein, while along the Dalmatian coast small male voice choirs called **klape** perform smooth harmonies in an Italian style.

Utterly different and quite startling is the music from the coastal area of **Istria**, where they not only sing and play using a very unusual local scale, but also harmonize it in parallel seconds. They even have instruments dedicated to reproducing such harmonies. The *rozenica* or *sopile* is a type of large oboe and is always played in a pair, one large and one small. The much smaller *šurla*, two pipes played with a single mouthpiece, allows one player to play two parts at once. After a period of acclimatization it can be quite attractive. The Istrian bagpipe, the *diple*, works on the same principle and is still to be found along the Dalmatian coast and inland into Herzegovina. For hardened discord lovers there's a Folkways album of songs and religious music made on the Istrian island of Krk in the early Sixties.

BOSNIA-HERZEGOVINA

Bosnia-Herzegovina, in the centre of former Yugoslavia, is the area where Turkish influence has lingered longest and where the ethnic diversity has led to the most bitter fighting. It has a population of about five million, three million of whom are Muslims, most of the remainder being either Catholic Croats or Orthodox Serbs. The capital Sarajevo was an extraordinary melting pot of Catholics, Orthodox, Muslims and Jews until it was pounded by Serbian shelling in the spring of 1992. At present it is impossible to guess what the future

GlobeStyle's great but tragically titled album

of Bosnia-Herzegovina and its rich and varied cultures will be, although some sort of division into ethnic zones seems unavoidable.

The most typical form of urban music in Bosnia is the **sevdalinka** or love-song. (The name is derived from Turkish "sevda" – love – but in the Bosnian dialect it has come to mean a love that is yearning, hopeless, and painful.) The broad, ornamented melodies often use oriental scales and chromatic inflections.

The lyrics speak of star-crossed lovers, faith or faithlessness and breathe an atmosphere of regret and resignation. I have heard tales of listeners who were so moved by a particularly impassioned performance that they left the room and shot themselves out of grief.

The roots of sevdalinke came with the Turkish invaders. The Bosnians accepted Islam much more readily than did the other inhabitants of the Balkans, possibly because they had been Bogomils, a Christian sect proclaimed as heretical and attacked by both eastern and western churches. As a result the towns of Bosnia became centres of Islamic culture, and it is believed that some oriental religious melodies known as *ilahije* were adopted by the townspeople and fitted with new lyrics to become sevdalinke. This does not mean that all sevdalinke were introduced from the east. Many Slav songs have entered the repertoire as well, and the melody of the celebrated "Kad ja podjoh za Bembašu", the unofficial anthem of Sarajevo, may be of Jewish origin.

Each of the towns of Bosnia or Herzegovina has its own sevdalinka tradition, and their subjects relate to their home-town's particular quirks of history or geography. Zvornik, for example, on the River Drina between Bosnia and Serbia, was known as the Gate of Bosnia and was, in the time of Turkish rule, the point from which armies were despatched to put down revolts and uprisings in Serbia. As a result many of the sevdalinke from Zvornik deal with loss and with lovers who are never to meet again. One famous song says: "The Drina flows from hill to hill, not with rain or white snow, but with the tears of the maidens from Zvornik."

In contrast, Sarajevo, the capital of the province, was the home of rich land owners and merchants who carefully guarded the honour and marriage prospects of their daughters by keeping them hidden away from undesirable suitors. So many Sarajevske sevdalinke speak of thwarted love. The story goes that young women, forbidden to meet or even see their lovers, would sing of their love through the barred windows of their walled gardens to the young men strolling in the dusk through the narrow lanes of Sarajevo.

The following is a typical lyric:
A red rose has blossomed
In the lane, there is but one left.

Through that lane my sweetheart passes
And with his horse he tramples the flowers.
Let him, O let him trample them
If he but pass this way more often.

Traditionally the singers would perform to the accompaniment of the *saz*, a stringed instrument of Turkish origin with a pear-shaped body and long neck. The sound is quiet and contemplative and fits the mood of sevdalinka perfectly, but it is a dying art and in Bosnia before the war there were perhaps only thirty *sazlije*, mostly of the older generation. Among the most notable of the older singers are **Hasim Muhamerović**, **Emina Ahmedhodzić** and **Muhamed Mesanović-Hamić**, some of whom accompany themselves on the saz.

Far more common these days is the performance of the same songs to the backing of a typical folk orchestra of accordion, violin, clarinet and guitar with a different sort of harmony and less rhythmic subtlety, but retaining the supple and mournful beauty typical of these songs. The old sazlije look down on this style, but there is no doubt that performers such as **Safet Isović**, **Hanka Paldum**, **Zaim Imamović**, the late **Himzo Polovina** and others are part of the long and sophisticated tradition.

Although there are many other types of music in Bosnia apart from sevdalinke, the one you're most likely to hear is a style known to the locals as **Izvorna Bosanska muzika**, which means roughly "roots music". This is a fairly recent development of the village music from the area around the small market town of Kalesija in the eastern part of the republic. At one time performed at village celebrations known as *sijela* (sittings), marking the end of harvest time, ploughing, sowing or on feast days, and now more often at the Saturday night dance in the local house of culture, it is usually performed by a small group of a couple of singers, two violinists and a player of a *šargija* – the village equivalent of a saz.

The sound of the music is quite startling to western ears as the idea of harmony and consonance is totally different to that of western Europe. Essentially it involves two voices singing together in very close harmony – so close, indeed, that the western ear perceives a grinding dissonance where the Bosnian hears a charming consonance. It's an extremely old way of singing and widespread in the Balkans, stretching from Istria to eastern Bulgaria, but the Bosnian bands have developed it in a very interesting way, being remote enough to preserve it but close enough to trade routes and small towns to acquire modern instruments and adapt them to the old music.

It was around the time of the First World War that such string bands of this type made their first appearance, and the taste for the music has more recently been taken to parts of western Europe by *gastarbeiters* (those working abroad – mainly in Germany). This has provided the impetus for many local record companies to record the music, giving it an unusually wide distribution for what is a rather obscure form of village music. It means you can find practically pure folkloric performers like the **Jelić sisters**, the very lyrical group of **Mohamed Beganović** and the almost punkish energy of **Zvuci Zavicaja** (Sounds of Tradition) next to **Kalesijski Zvuci** (Sounds of Kalesija). The latter's "Bosnian Breakdown" album on Globestyle is an astonishing mixture of local singing and fiddling styles with a hot village-dance rhythm section.

Village band from western Serbia

SERBIA

What is a folk song – the traditional tune sung only by enthusiastic revivalists or a more modern tune sung by ordinary people as part of their lives? The state of "folk music" in Serbia illustrates the dilemma more than any other area of ex-Yugoslavia. It's still possible to find, in more remote areas, survivals of ancient songs and dances as part of some half-understood ritual, yet when most Yugoslavs talk about "folk music" they are generally referring to songs written this year or last and performed in nightclubs and on television by singers wearing glittering and often skimpy costumes. This *novokomponovana narodna muzika*, with its high media profile, its stars and scandals, hit-parades and its own magazine, *Sabor*, is an extremely important strand in Serbia's (and southern ex-Yugoslavia's) musical life.

Novokomponovana is a transformation of traditional village and small-town music into a musical form simultaneously answering the needs of modern urban working-class life and the requirements of the commercial music industry. Referring back to older styles, it roots itself strongly in the culture of villagers or immigrants to the towns and in its mass-production it underwrites a huge recording industry. It is often compared to country and western music in the US, and the two do have a lot in common. Both use a band of traditionally sanctioned instruments, accordion and clarinet in the case of one, fiddle

and steel guitar in the other; both use a formalized performance practice derived from true folk roots; the lyrics of both deal with similar subjects, mainly love and its betrayal; and finally, the vast majority of both is deeply trashy.

Still, there are little gems nestling in the rubbish and, ephemeral as they are, some are masterpieces in miniature. **Miroslav Ilić**, **Saban Saulić**, **Saban Bajramović**, **Semsa Suljaković**, **Vesna Zmijanac** and **Hanka Paldum** are not only great stars but also fine singers, and some are distinguished interpreters of sevdalinke. At the pop end of the spectrum is **Lepa Brena**, whose posters stare down from bedroom walls all over the Balkans. She presents herself as a girl of the people made good, and like the majority of her colleagues comes from Bosnia.

It's from urban Bosnian music, with its Turkish influences, that modern novokomponovana draws its style, and the guardians of national and artistic purity call it kitschy, unoriginal and, most bizarrely, sadomasochistic – this last in reference to the Turkish-derived elements.

Serbian music is generally cheerful rather than stately, joyful rather than lamenting and is well represented by the fast two-beat dance called the kolo, meaning a wheel or circle. As its name suggests, it's danced by a group holding hands in a ring. The upper body hardly moves at all; all the hard work is done below the knee and the feet weave the most intricate patterns. A kolo is liable to break out on most social occasions and is inescapable at a wedding, whether the music is being supplied by a live band, a single musician or just recordings. At one time the village bagpiper was essential, but

FROM THE BALITIC TO THE BALKANS

THE VLACHS

·······················

The northeastern corner of Serbia, an area known as the Vlaška Krajina (the Vlach Marches), is home to a little-known people, the Vlachs. Formerly nomadic shepherds, they speak a language closely related to Romanian but their origin remains obscure. They retain a unique mixture of customs, some of which are clearly pre-Christian and connected with ancient cults of the forest and the sun and moon, and most of these rituals involve music. In one area, at the Whitsun Rusalija festival, women used to fall into trances to the sound of music and prophesy, and perhaps still do.

The funeral rites known as *pomana* designed to comfort and provide for the departed on their long journey to the other world are most interesting. At set times following the death, funeral feasts are given and the dead relative is invited to attend.

> *Grandfather, come to supper*
> *For we have readied all*
> *That all may eat.*
> *We pray to God, grandfather*
> *That He may let you come.*
> *The sheep are bleating*

> *Come and release them, grandfather*
> *For there is no one to look after them.*
> *Do not forget, grandfather, your courtyard*
> *Where you grew old*
> *And whence you have departed.*
> *May God forgive you*
> *May God give you our words.*

There is an enormous body of music to accompany the rituals: at the vigil, the funeral procession, the burial and the wake, and the French record company, Ocora, has released an excellent recording of village music from the Krajina which includes wedding and dance music as well as funeral music from ensembles that range from bagpipe and fiddle duets to large brass bands.

Modern Vlach music bears a strong resemblance to that of Wallachia in southern Romania in its rhythm, harmony and modality. Music for dancing is speedy and energetic, often in 6/8 time, but with a certain melancholy aspect that is more evident in the songs. Vlach music is very popular, not only among the Vlachs themselves, and most Serbian accordionists will have several tunes in their repertoire.

---

nowadays there are few, if any, to be found, and his place is usually taken by an accordionist.

The most typical peasant instrument today is the *frula*, a small recorder-like flute. It was originally a shepherds' instrument with a pure and piercing tone used for pastoral improvisations and to accompany dancing. The accordion was introduced before the First World War, so the old people say, and has now become the foremost instrument. Most families will have one tucked away somewhere, often a child's size. The most usual type has five or more rows of buttons, allowing extremely rapid trills, slurs and repeated notes reminiscent of the articulation of the frula. Modern virtuosi play with breathtaking speed and precision.

One of the most extraordinary is **Mirko Kodić**, who plays with astonishing skill and passion, and is not afraid to mix the frula with the synthesizer and *sa-sa* (a more syncopated rhythm than kolo, of southern origin) with rock and roll. A less iconoclastic but equally fine player is **Ljubo Pavković** who leads the *narodni orkestar* of Radio-Television Belgrade,

while an older generation is represented by **Tine and Radojka Zivković**.

The southern areas of Serbia were freed from Turkish control considerably later than Belgrade, and the music and dance of towns like **Leskovac and Vranje** have a much stronger oriental flavour than the purely Slav music of nothern and central Serbia. Vranje is also the centre for one of the main schools of brass band music inside Serbia, the other two being in the Vlach country (see above) and around Čačak. These bands are now the most popular village ensembles and have replaced the traditional instrumental groups. They normally play local music, the straightforward kolo or the more complex and syncopated *čoček* dance. They also normally play the latest Eurovision Song Contest entry and, these days, the Lambada. The most famous bandleader, **Bakija Bakić**, died a few years ago but his son carries on the family tradition and has recently regained the status of number-one band from **Fejat Sejdić**, voted top orchestra six times

Jova Stojiljkovic and his Brass Orkestar

since 1979 in the annual brass band festival held in late August/early September in the village of Guča, near Čačak. On a wild and crazy Globestyle disc there's a recording of **Jova Stojiljković and his Brass Orkestar** from Golemo Selo village in the Vranje area.

MONTENEGRO AND
EPIC POETRY

The romantic figure of the blind travelling minstrel accompanying his tales of past heroes on the **gusle**, a type of one-stringed fiddle, features prominently in Serb art and literature as a symbol of national identity and culture unbroken by five centuries "under the Turkish yoke". Like all nationalist myths there's a fair amount of truth in it and, although even this particular epic tradition, the most developed in Europe, may only stem from the sixteenth century in its present form, it deals with legends from the remote past as well as historical events dating as far back as the fourteenth century.

Although the tradition of the **sung epic** flourished throughout Croatia and Bosnia as well as Serbia, it was particularly identified with the tiny mountain kingdom of Montenegro, which in its remote independence and old-fashioned patriarchal society retained the conditions in which it could flourish. It is in Montenegro that most present-day (rarely blind) *guslari* are still found.

The poems, which may be thousands of lines long, are intoned in a strained and pinched voice rather than sung. The melody is more a set of patterns to carry the words and aid the performer's memory than it is a tune, and a listener who doesn't understand the words will come away with the impression of unvaried and wearisome monotony. But it is in the words that the interest lies. They speak of entirely legendary subjects; or historical figures become legendary, like the prince Kraljević Marko whom they transform from a minor nobleman of doubtful loyalties into a mighty warrior against the Turks, aided by his horse Šarac, who could speak and drink wine like a man; or the *hajduks*, eighteenth- and nineteenth-century social bandits who took to the hills and swept down to rob and murder rich travellers, at the same time providing an unofficial resistance to Ottoman rule. The most important of them is a loose cycle of poems that cluster around the battle of Kosovo Polje when the Serbians were conquered catastrophically by the Turks in 1389. These tales of fate, heroism and treachery set the agenda for much of Yugoslav literature.

Even now epic poems are still composed about contemporary subjects. They are normally about trivial subjects, such as the untimely death of a promising young footballer, but in 1991 a tape by **Djordjije Koprivica** appeared on sale with a new epic called "Devil's Kolo on Goli Otok" (words by Zarko Sobić) which deals with the infamous prison camp of that name (Bare Island) used to hold people suspected of Stalinist loyalties in the period after Tito's

MUSIC AND THE WAR

• •

The importance of music and song for the Balkan peoples has been illustrated in bitter fashion by the break-up of Yugoslavia. Music has become a sort of shorthand for political attitudes and a sense of nationhood. In some cases prisoners-of-war and civilian internees have been beaten and forced to sing their captors' nationalist songs. The fact that prisoner and guard sometimes share the same songs, the same tunes, with words that differ only in the substitution of "Serbian" for "Croatian" or vice versa, only underlines the misery and horror of civil war.

The rise of national feeling in all parts of former Yugoslavia was mirrored in the field of music. As it became more acceptable (or at least politically valuable to nationalist and factional leaders) to express "patriotic", separatist aspirations, old songs were revived and new ones written.

In Serbia old melodies from the period of the Balkan wars, such as "The March to the Drina", became brass band favourites, and the singer Predrag Gojkovic released a widely successful album of old and new patriotic songs called "Ko ti kaze, ko ti laze", Srbija je mala (roughly "Whoever says Serbia is small is a liar"). A little later tapes of famous četnik (the World War II Serbian royalist resistance movement led by Draza Mihajlovic) songs appeared for sale on the streets of Belgrade. In Croatia songs that had been banned under Tito because they were identified with the Croat fascists, the Ustaše, began to reappear, sung in bars or used as instrumental interludes in pop tunes; while Slovenian DJs had been leavening their western-leaning diet of rock and house music with local recordings of polkas for several years. The Bosnian SDA (Party of Democratic Action, with a largely Muslim membership) released a cassette of "SDA Songs", and was promptly sued for plagiarism by the Serbian star Miroslav Ilic and his co-writer in a move which had obvious and unpleasant political undertones. The limits of style in new-composed folk mean that nearly every song bears a close resemblance to a hundred others.

As normal life collapsed with the outbreak of fighting in Croatia and later Bosnia-Herzegovina, musical life and the music industry collapsed along with it. Each Bosnian Serb gun battery shelling Sarajevo had its resident guslar who regaled them with epics as they watched the city burn. In 1992 the brass band festival at Guča in Serbia and the Folklore Review in Zagreb were both given a heavy nationalist spin by the respective governments.

In Montenegro the choice of a new national (or republican) anthem caused a fierce political argument — should it be the war-like café song "Onward, onward, let me see Prizren" from the court of Nikola I, the last king of an independent Montenegro, or the folksong "From Lovcen Mountain the Vila Called", or should one be newly composed? This could seem like a farcical "Operetta War" (the court of Montenegro inspired Lehár's "The Merry Widow", but unfortunately the passions inspired are all too real. The words of "Onward, onward" not only carry a lot of emotional baggage, but also imply specific political and territorial claims. The arguments expressed centred on musical style rather than lyrical content, but the political subtext was quite clear.

As the war became more intense, ghosts from the past began to move in. At first the songs had approached patriotism via sentimentality ("The dawns are more beautiful in Serbia", "The stars in Herzegovina shine more beautifully"); now they spoke of war, duty and sacrifice. In Serbia the title četnik was hijacked by the leader of the ultra right-wing Radicals, Vojislav Šešelj, whose paramilitary forces have been responsible for some terrible atrocities. So too were their songs, which had been kept alive in exile. The melody of "Ko ti kaze" turned out to be closely related to that of a četnik song, "From Topola to Ravna Gora General Draza's men are on Guard" which was among "The 12 Most Beautiful Cetnik Songs" on a cassette of that name, along with "Draza is alive, he will not die (while there are Serbs and a Serbia)". Such songs would have earned a jail sentence ten years before, but now they helped feed the growing current of Serb nationalism.

Although many Serbs looked upon these developments with distress, others perceived them as proof that what they saw as the long suffering of the Serbs, first under the Turks and then under the communists, was coming to an end. In Croatia the same thing was happening but as though reflected in a mirror. "I sit on the threshold, in my own street, I'll not let anyone take my Croatian home. Vukovar is the pride of all Croats, Osijek and Vinkovci stand like brothers. The whole of Slavonija has said No! Croatia takes pride in that." The words come from an anonymous cassette which also includes titles such as "Bombs will fall on Belgrade" and "No Belgrade ever again". The openly fascist HOS, in an uneasy relationship with the government of Franjo Tudjman, took up the Ustaše revival with a vengeance, wartime flag, Hitler salutes and songs like "The Ustaša March (The brave Croat Ustaša Army carries out its duty)" included.

As the war in Croatia subsided into an uneasy armed truce, fighting broke out in Bosnia-Herzegovina. The Serb population in the countryside, subject to a barrage of propaganda from Belgrade and persuaded to fear the imposition of an Islamic state and what they called the return of the Ottoman Empire, took up arms, besieged Sarajevo with heavy artillery and began to drive non-Serbs out of their homes. Their fears and ambitions were ancient ones, illustrated in the cycle of epic poems that cluster around the battle of Kosovo in 1389, conventionally thought of as marking the point of no return in the Turkish conquest of the Balkans. Briefly, the day before the battle the Serbian Tsar Lazar is visited by St Elijah in the form of a bird, who offers him a choice between victory and an earthly kingdom, or defeat and a heavenly one. Lazar chooses the heavenly kingdom, and is killed along with his knights, but the reason for defeat is laid at the door of the treacherous Vuk Brankovic who led his forces over to the Turks at the critical moment. The poet surveys the carnage on the battlefield and comments "All was honourable and holy, and according to God's will."

Here we can see the root of the whole complex of myths that drive the Serb insurgents in this war. Serbia is a holy country, favoured by God. Its whole history is one of suffering and defeat, yet defeat can never be final, and the struggle for freedom must be continually renewed. Treachery is only to be expected, so they look for it everywhere. Next to traitors (usually the opposition within Serbia, the west, and off-and-on, depending on his political manoeuvring, their patron President Miloševic of Serbia itself) the greatest enemy of the Serbs is the Turk (that is to say, Muslims: even now the Bosnian Serbs may refer to Bosnian Muslims as Turks) who plan to destroy Orthodox Christianity. And the guslars telling and retelling these tales on the front line strengthened these beliefs day by day.

While the Serbian nationalist cliché runs "Wherever Serbs live, there is Serbia", Zagreb's Drazen Zanko claims that "Everyone must know that this is our country, wherever Croats live." Some lyrics finally degenerate into a gazetteer. "Drina, Timok, Danube and Morava, that's your Serbian state" suggests Zeljko Grgujevic in his song claiming legitimacy for the Croat-run territory of Herceg-Bosna, opposed by Gordan Krajišnik who lists Serbian-held areas in Bosnia and Croatia: "Knin, Grahovo, Petrovac, Drvar, Kljuc, Celinac, Banja Luka and Prijedor, we have freed our corridor." There has been no let-up in the perversion of folk music and folklore for political reasons. Šešelj has acquired a tame shaven-headed folk singer called Dzej who appears at his rallies.

Meanwhile in Bosnia, whose territory has suffered most in the fighting, in the cellars of RTV Sarajevo where a tiny recording studio has been set up, between the outbreaks of shelling and mortar fire, both rock and folk musicians produce songs with titles such as "Where are you now, my friends, when Bosnia is dying?" and "I Sew a Green Beret" [symbol of the Muslim forces]. Some, for example "Help Bosnia now" and "Sarajevo, heart of the world" are sung in English with the intent of drawing the attention of the world to the suffering of Bosnia, but unfortunately when they enter the western marketplace their unfashionable Eurorock style and often inexpert technique has meant that they've sunk without trace.

break with the Soviet Union. It was only with the rise of political nationalism that it was possible to discuss it in public without the risk of arrest, and this recording shows the epic form is still fulfilling its old function of providing a public place for national discourse.

MACEDONIA

The cultural territory of Macedonia extends well outside the borders of the ex-Yugoslav republic into northern Greece and southwest Bulgaria, areas known respectively as Aegean and Pirin Macedonia. Although the three Macedonias make up one single folklore area, the political situation is immensely complex. The Macedonian people did not officially exist until after World War II, when the communist government formed the republic of Macedonia and recognized a Macedonian nationality as a separate people of Slav stock. The Bulgarians used to claim that there was no such thing, that the Macedonians were actually Bulgarians, and that Vardar Macedonia (the Yugoslav republic) should really be part of Bulgaria. But the post-communist government has set aside any claims to the territory and recognized Macedonia as an independent state. The Greeks, who refuse to recognize the existence of any Slav minority in Greece, have only recently abandoned attempts to veto EC recognition of the Macedonian republic, and continue to put obstacles in the way of the young state, imposing an economic blockade.

The Macedonians themselves are quite confident of their separate identity although in the usual tangled Balkan fashion the republic also contains a very large Albanian minority as well as Turks, Cincars (Vlachs), Albanians, gypsies, Serbs and other nationalities. (The French for a fruit salad is a *Macedoine des fruits*.) The musical make-up of the area, of course, reflects its ethnic mixture, and the tormented history of the region has had its influence as well. The Macedonians refer to their country as *Jadna Makedonija*, (Sorrowful Macedonia), and many songs and dance tunes have an undercurrent of grief or defiance.

As usual the music of the towns differs considerably from that of the villages, but there is one thing they have in common: the extraordinary complexity of rhythm. Most music in the world can be understood as combinations of beats of equal length or of long and short beats in the ratio of two to one. But in Macedonia it's much more complicated. In western music, a bar of triple time – such as a waltz – has three equal beats; but in Macedonia it may be a bar of 7/8 divided up as 3–2–2 (eg. the dance tune "Potrčano oro") or 2–2–3 ("Staro Komitsko Oro") or 2–3–2 ("Baba Djurdja") and so on. The dance song "Pominišli libe Todoro" is in 22/16 played as 2–2–3–2–2–3–2–2–2–2! At one village session a clarinettist reduced me and some local musicians to jelly with a really complex tune, adding "These mixed rhythms are real buggers aren't they?" and laughing proudly. It's good to know that even Macedonians can get confused. Yet these tunes really swing. It's better to feel them than count them, and they make perfect sense when you know the dances they accompany. In the villages dancing is still an important social activity and everybody from toddlers to grannies ends up in a big circle jigging happily to rhythms that would make many western musicians break out in a cold sweat.

The most typical village instrument is the **bagpipe**, known as the *gajda*, although despite sayings such as "Without a gajda it's no wedding" it's now less common than it used to be. The finest contemporary gajda player is **Pece Atanasovski**, the leader (until his recent retirement) of the folk orchestra of Radio Skopje, with which he has made many recordings. The class that he runs each summer (write to P. Atanasovski, Vostanička 92, 91000 Skopje, Macedonia) is a fine place to learn about the music and dance of the Macedonians. Other traditional instruments are the double-course *tambura*, yet another Balkan variation on the strummed string instrument, and the kaval, slenderer and longer than the Bulgarian model, made of a single piece of wood and often played in pairs.

Festivals and weddings are often marked by the appearance of the wild-sounding ensembles of **zurli** and **tapan.** The zurla is a primitive oboe with a piercing nasal sound only bearable out of doors. They are always played in pairs with the second zurla holding a drone. The tapan, a large cylindrical drum, is the only instrument with sufficient volume to compete and it drives the dance along with a flurry of explosive syncopations. Towards the end of the party, young men carried away by drink and emotion approach the musicians to press banknotes to their foreheads and get the zurla played directly into their ears.

After the Second World War the state sponsored the creation of professional ensembles such as the folk orchestra of Radio Skopje – invariably excellent – and the ensemble **Tanec** – of sporadic quality – which performed arranged versions of folk melodies. In contrast to similar ventures elsewhere in eastern Europe, the music remained close to its roots and lost none of its native beauty and emotional content. Many village KUDs are keeping this tradition alive and well.

Traditional urban music was performed by groups known as **calgii**, of oriental origin. The classic line-up is violin, clarinet, *kanun* (Turkish plucked zither), *ud* (lute) and a percussion section of *def* (enormous tambourine) and *tarabuka* (small hourglass drum). They played for dancing and *na trapeza* ("at the table") during and after a feast. The sound of a čalgia is romantic and passionate, sometimes tinged with typical Macedonian melancholy, sometimes fiery and mysterious. The only two čalgii of traditional type remaining belong to the official groups of Radio Skopje and Tanec. One clarinettist who has worked with both is **Tale Ognenovski**, now approaching 70 but one of the most influential musicians of the post-war era. He is also a master of the style that has succeeded čalgia.

The new groups have a line-up of clarinet (more recently saxophone), accordion, guitar, bass and drum kit, replacing the oriental instruments. It is more direct and less dark-hued than most čalgia, but still attractive. You hear it everywhere – on the radio, in buses and taxis, providing dance music and backing up singers. **Miroslav Businovski** is one of the more talented clarinetists and the Skopje group, **Uzun**, have attempted to fuse folk and pop idioms. Even more interesting than their experiments is the music of the Macedonian and Albanian-speaking gypsies.

ELECTRIC GYPSIES

Gypsies arrived in the Balkans about 600 years ago from their original homeland in Rajasthan and rapidly became known as fine musicians. Since then they have supplied musical talent out of all proportion to their size (there are up to one million in a population of some twenty million in ex-Yugoslavia). In some places they are practically the only musicians left who can be engaged for weddings and feasts, and so hold a virtual monopoly over local musical life. They are particularly concentrated in Macedonia.

The gypsies owe their position to their undoubted skill as performers and their low social

Gypsy musicians at a festival

status. As foreigners of suspect origin they were forced into jobs that were thought to be dirty or dangerous, either physically or for magical reasons or both: for example executioner or metal-worker. Music is a job in the second category, the magical.

In the Balkans, an instrumentalist, gypsy or not, is considered to be in contact with the unseen and risky world of spirit forces. A travelling musician is still more of an outsider. Even now there is much racism directed against gypsies although they probably had more guaranteed legal rights in Yugoslavia than any other country in the world, with a Romany-language newspaper and radio station: the settlement of **Suto Orizari** outside Skopje (the setting for Emil Kusturica's film "Time of the Gypsies") is the largest gypsy town in the world. The gypsies are adaptable and were the first to adopt the clarinet and violin, instruments that require more time and skill to master than was available to the peasants, and now they have laid claim to the synthesizer.

In the bars of Šuto Orizari you can hear the modern music of the gypsies, which provides an interesting contrast to the rather tired cabaret style of **Stevo and Esma Teodosievski**, previously Macedonia's best-known and most influential performers. It's the rare phenomenon of a gypsy music intended for a Romany audience, though many non-Romanies come to listen. The typical orchestra these days contains electric guitar, synth or electric organ, drum kit, maybe a saxophone and a singer. The one indispensable piece of equipment is the echo unit, which is invariably turned up full and often the cause of a quarrel between singer, keyboard-player and saxophonist as to who needs it the most and who has the right to adjust it. The music is highly coloured, passionate, even erotic, and may sound very Indian, particularly in vocal quality. The gypsy language is related to Hindi: Indian film musicals are popular with the gypsy population and their songs have rapidly spread throughout Macedonia.

The clarinettist, saxophonist and composer, **Ferus Mustafov** from Strumica is the greatest virtuoso in this field, although some prefer the more oriental style of the older **Medo Cun**. He was allegedly discovered playing in a restaurant when a group of pop artists on tour dropped in for an after-show supper. They were so impressed they arranged a recording session for him, and the rest is history. His music is a fascinating fusion of Macedonian, Turkish and Romany and many of his tunes have become standards. He frequently plays, accompanied, it must be said, by a band of dubious quality, at the Skopje restaurant Velčevo Meanče.

A younger clarinettist is **Tunan Kurtisev** whose party trick is playing in the styles of every Yugoslav clarinetist of note and then launching into his own mocking improvisations. One of his tunes pays explicit tribute to the origin of his people. Quite clearly inspired by Indian music, he calls it "Majka Indija" (Mother India).

Gypsies are also prominent in the field of new-composed folk in Macedonia and Serbia, where **Saban Bajramović** is the outstanding example, as well as in the brass bands and sometimes in the folklore ensembles, where they are often drummers: these days most players of zurla and tapan are gypsies – though some older musicians say that they have simplified and coarsened the subtleties of rhythm that are at their greatest in this very exacting style of playing. Nevertheless, the music recorded by today's greatest zurla player, **Mahmut Muzafer**, on a cassette called simply "Ora", is as subtle and complex as anyone could wish.

◢ DISCOGRAPHY ◣

Even when Yugoslavia was still a single country the production and distribution of records and tapes was a fairly erratic business, and recordings would appear, vanish and resurface in unpredictable fashion. The war has naturally worsened matters, so with the exception of Slovenia all the local recordings below should carry the rider "If you can find it". Some recordings of the music of Serb and Croat minorities in Hungary are listed in the discography for that section (see p.64).

Unfortunately none of the new-composed folk music is available on a western label. Any amount of cassettes, however, can be found in shops catering for the Yugoslav immigrant workers and refugees, particularly in Germany, Switzerland or Belgium. The area around main railway stations is often a good place to look.

Kalesijski Zvuci *Bosnian Breakdown* (GlobeStyle, UK). Recorded shortly before the outbreak of the war, the title has gained a terrible irony, but this music from eastern Bosnia is as powerful as ever. Two tunes in traditional style and the rest with electric guitar and drums.

Ensemble Pece Atanasovski *Danses de Macedoine* (Auviclis, France). A selection from over twenty years' worth of recordings by the master bagpiper and his colleagues. Includes fine examples of village dance music, čalgia, and zurla and tapan duets.

Ferus Mustafov i orkestar Mustafe Ismailovica (RTB, Yugoslavia). Oldish (mid-1980s) but hot dance music. A head-down gallop through Serb, Macedonian, gypsy and Vlach style tunes with inimitable energy. One side features clarinet, and the other saxophone, with an excursion on the trumpet as well. As good as any of Ferus's recordings and better than some.

Jova Stojiljkovic "Besir" and his Brass Orkestar *Blow 'Besir' Blow* (GlobeStyle, UK). Dance music from southern Serbia performed by a village brass band. Lots of čoček and plenty of kolo give a pretty good idea of what you might hear at a wedding or all-night party.

Various *Bez Sevdaha Nema Milovanja* (Diskoton, Bosnia). Outstanding two-cassette collection of sevdalinke by various well-known singers, accompanied by a small band from Radio Sarajevo. If you can find it, this is the best possible introduction to a wonderful style.

Various *Bosnia: Echoes From An Endangered World* (Smithsonian Folkways, US). Covering more or less the whole spectrum, with a focus on Muslim performers, from sevdalinke accompanied by the radio orchestra to a muezzin's call to prayer, it includes an outstanding performance by Himzo Polovina accompanied by saz.

Various *Da si od srebra, da si od zlata* (Croatia Records [formerly Jugoton], Croatia). Probably the best and widest selection of traditional Croatian music generally available.

Various *Der Bleiche Mond – Bledi Mesec* (Trikont, Germany). Recent field recordings of Slovenian instrumental music in the old style. Features unusual instruments like bowed zither,and ivy-leaf . . .

Various *Folk Music of Yugoslavia* (Topic, UK). A splendid choice of village music from all over the country by Wolf Dietrich. It includes some startling cuts – check out the Macedonian Robanovski brothers on clarinet and violin – and some nice Bosnian singing.

Various *Super Veselica* (Sraka, Slovenia). Polkas and waltzes, trumpets, clarinets, the odd ivy leaf and all the accordions you could ask for. An evocative disc, just like a slice of Sunday afternoon Slovene radio.

Various *Yougoslavie 1 (Les Bougies du Paradis), 2 (Sous les Peupliers de Bilisht)*, and *3 (Bessa ou la Parole Donnee)* (Ocora, France). Three invaluable records of the music of some of the Yugoslav minorities; Vlachs, Tosk Albanians, and Gheg Albanians, very rarely heard outside its native surroundings. Highly recommended.

ALBANIAN EPICS

SONGS FROM THE LAND OF CLEAR SPEECH

Albania, isolated from the outside world for many years by geography, history and politics, has some of the richest and most startling music in the Balkan area, claims Kim Burton.

Albania is a small country with a tiny population: around two and a half million Albanians live inside the borders, with another million or so across the border in Kosovo and in western Macedonia. Since the final break-up of the Ottoman Empire at the time of World War I, the circumstances of the two groups have been very different, and only since the fall of Enver Hoxha's hardline Stalinist regime have they been able to meet one another at all freely. However, on the whole what is true of music within Albania remains true for that outside.

Called by its inhabitants *Shqipëri* (which, alas, doesn't mean "the eagles' country" as romantic travellers believed but "the land of clear speech"), Albania still retains certain elements from its past as a tribal society and Albanian concepts of honour, hospitality and family duty are immensely powerful. Its music falls into two major and very different stylistic groups which reflect the division of the population into northern Ghegs and southern Tosks and Labs, separated by the River Shkumbin. Gheg music is rugged, heroic and single voiced while Tosk and Lab music is softer, more lyrical and polyphonic. In addition, the usual Balkan distinction between the music of the village and the music of the town holds good.

What unites all these styles is the weight that both performers and listeners give to their music as a means of patriotic expression and as a scaffolding for their oral historical tradition. Many composer-performers quite openly say that this is their main purpose, and that although under Hoxha they were forced to sing songs in praise of the Party "these days no-one wants to hear them". At concerts the audience breaks into applause and furious whistles of approval at a line in a song that reflects their feelings, and if their approval is strong enough will rush the stage to hand small gifts to the singer.

Even out-and-out pop music, usually on an Italian Europop model, and a relatively new development in a country where in the 1970s singer Sherif Merdani was given a twenty-year jail sentence for performing The Beatles song "Let it Be", fulfils this role. The hit of 1993, a rather sentimental song called "Jon" (Ionian), was about the attempts that many made to cross that sea to Italy, and the family break-ups it caused. My landlady in Tirana wept silently as she listened to it on the radio.

ON THE ROCK OF THE NORTH A BOY IS CALLING

The most serious musical form of north Albania is the epic poem. The oldest type, known as Rapsodi Kreshnikë (Poems of Heroes) and accompanied by the singer on the one-stringed fiddle, the *lahuta*, sounds very similar to the music of the Montenegrin and Serbian *guslars*, and is the province of old men. Indeed, Albanians describing this sort of music will sweep their fingers across their upper lip with a flourish to express the luxuriant growth of moustache thought necessary for the singer.

This tradition is particularly identified with the inhabitants of the northern highlands, but another ballad tradition is found throughout the Gheg area, with particularly important schools in Dibër

Sharki player Altush Bytyci from northern Albania

O, OUR KOSOVË

•••••••••••••••••••••••

There is a very large Albanian (Gheg) population in the formerly autonomous Yugoslav province of Kosovo (Albanian Kosovë), which was brought under direct Serbian control in 1989 following claims made by the Serbian minority (or rather, made for them by the nationalist factions in Belgrade) of violent intimidation by Albanian terrorists. Currently the province is run by the Serbian government as a police state in which ill-treatment of Albanians is commonplace. In Macedonia, where there is a sizeable Gheg population and a smaller one of Tosks, the situation is currently far calmer.

The music of the Kosovars is much the same as that over the border in Albania itself, although as it was given a good deal less government support it has perhaps remained closer to its roots. Before it was closed down by the Serbian authorities, Radio Television Prishtina used to churn out immense amounts of cassettes featuring popular singers like duos Resmije and Rifat Kida or Mahmut Ferati and Milaim Mezini plus many recordings of the elder statesman of Albanian song, Qamil e Vogël (Little Qamil) and his collaborators. Recently there have been attempts to develop a more "poppy" approach, notably by Besnikët and the Albanian-speaking gypsy Mazllum Shaqiri ("Lumi"), who has spearheaded the search for a contemporary way of singing old songs.

The recent crackdown by the Serbian authorities has led to the jailing of some singers accused of performing politically motivated heroic songs and of course a rise in the number of clandestine performances of such songs. By the late 1980s many professional musicians were refusing to risk performing them in public for fear of arrest, and café bands whose custom it was to perform songs in both languages by employing singers in shifts found themselves playing to an audience that listened in shifts as well according to its ethnic allegiances. Since then, matters have become even worse. A recording industry of sorts – quite a prolific one, in fact – is based around the *gastarbeiter* communities in Germany, and plenty of cassettes of local singers in exile find their way back to Kosovo. However, following the break-up of Yugoslavia and the severe economic problems of Albania itself, the future of Albanian music in Kosovo, indeed the future of Kosovo itself, is anyone's guess.

(Debar) and Kerçovë (Kičevo) in Macedonia. Here the singer is accompanied by the *çifteli*, a two-stringed instrument related to the *saz*. One string carries the melody while the other is used mainly as a drone. The tales tell of heroes such as the fifteenth-century warrior Skanderbeg, leader of the struggle against the Turks, and their semihistorical, semimythical events are bound up with the constant Albanian themes of honour, hospitality, treachery and revenge (on a Topic recording there's an excerpt from one about the ill-fated American-backed uprising in the 1940s). The performances can be highly emotional with compelling shifts of rhythm and tempo quite unlike the epics of their Slav neighbours.

Both traditions serve as a medium for oral history in what was until quite recently a preliterate society (there was not even a generally agreed alphabet until the early 1900s) and also preserve and inculcate moral codes and social values. In a culture that retained the blood-feud as its primary means of law enforcement until well into this century such codes were literally matters of life and death. Song was one of the most efficient ways of making sure that each member of the tribe was aware of what obligations he or she was bound to.

The çifteli is also used, together with its big brother the *sharki* and the tambourine-like *def*, to accompany dances and lyric songs, whose imagery is drawn from country life. ("You are the flower of the mountain . . . the morning dew. . . .") Since the Second World War bands of massed çiftelie and sharkie have become popular with Albanians both inside and outside Albania and the same repertoire of songs old and new is also performed by small bands based round clarinet and accordion at weddings and feasts.

In the countryside it's still possible to meet with shepherds who play for their own amusement using various homemade wind instruments of the type common to shepherds and cowherds throughout the Balkan area. More unusual is the *zumarë*, a double "clarinet" made from two tubes of cane or the hollow bones of a bird tied side-by-side and provided with a simple reed at one end, and with a flaring bell of cow or goat horn at the other. The tone is piercing and rousing, yet most of the tunes are melancholy and contemplative. The player uses circular breathing, taking air in through the nose while blowing out through the mouth using the cheeks as a kind of reservoir without needing to stop for breath. Children learn the technique by blowing through a straw into a glass of water, keeping a continuous stream of bubbles.

The songs of the northern city of Shkodër, always the most cosmopolitan of Albanian towns and the centre of intellectual life, are very different to the music of the peasantry. Lyrical, romantic and sophisticated, with oriental-sounding scales and a constant interplay of major and minor, they bear an affinity with the *sevdalinke* of Bosnia and the neighbouring Sandzak, but differ from them in their extreme and typically Albanian restraint and the exceptional fluidity of rhythm and tempo. The earliest descriptions of such groups, which date from the end of the nineteenth century, suggest a remarkable sound: violin, clarinet, saz, def, sometimes an Indian-style harmonium and percussion provided by rattling a stick between two bottles; these days the accordion and guitar have replaced the more exotic instruments, but the intimate approach of the singers remains the same. Among the most important are **Bik Ndoja**, **Luçija Miloti**, **Xherdet Hafizi** and the handsome **Bujar Qamili**.

In the capital, Tirana, and central Albania in general, much of the popular music has a noticeable gypsy flavour, exemplified in the hot clarinet-led band of the gravel-voiced **Myslym Leli**, whose tapes are sold semiofficially in the street kiosks, and unofficially on every street corner. Mixed with influences from the eastern Mediterranean pop, this forms the basis for the nearest approach to an indigenous pop music that Albania has so far developed, to be heard in the work of **Merita Halili** and glamour queen **Parashqvili Simaku**, both of whom are presently living outside Albania and performing for the large emigrant audience in the United States and western Europe.

THE MANY-PETALLED ROSE

The music of the Tosks and Labs of southern Albania is very different – so different that it has led to claims by some Greek musicologists that it is not of Albanian origin at all but Greek. Certainly the territory in which it is found extends into Greek Epirus, and there is a sizeable Greek-speaking minority in southern Albania, but as it is quite unlike musical styles from the rest of Greece such claims seem intended to bolster political and territorial arguments of the type endemic in southeast Europe.

Lacking the determined heroic ethos of the north, this music, both vocal and instrumental, is relaxed, gentle, and exceptionally beautiful. It has a highly developed polyphonic structure of up to four independent parts, depending on the area from which it comes. The Labs have a saying that "One traveller is alone, two will quarrel, but three will sing." The most complex and strangest of the vocal styles, some fine examples of which are to be heard on the Chant du Monde recording "Albanie: Polyphonies Vocales et Instrumentales", stems from around the port of Vlorë in the southwest. Each singer has his or her own title – taker, thrower, turner or drone – and a separate part to play in the web of independent lines and sustained notes which create a rich and moving sonic world decorated with falsetto and vibrato, sometimes interrupted by wild and mournful cries. Much of the power of this music stems from the tension between the immense emotional weight it carries, rooted in centuries of pride, poverty and oppression, and the strictly formal, almost ritualistic nature of its structure. The force of these songs is extraordinary and unparalleled in any other Balkan music.

famille
Lela de Permet

Polyphonies vocales et instrumentales d'Albanie

In some areas, mixed groups of instruments (violin, clarinet, *llautë*, def, and often these days accordion and guitar) and singers are found. The most important centres are the city of Korçë, home of the great **Eli Fara**, now yet another emigrant but still one of southern Albania's most loved female singers, and the remote mountain town of Përmet, one of the great musical centres of Albania and birthplace of two of the country's most important musicians, clarinettists **Laver Bariu**, who still lives there, and **Remzi Lela**, now living in Tirana and leader of one of the few groups to have recorded and toured abroad, La Famille Lela de Përmet. Albanians say that the most beautiful of Përmet's songs are those sung for the bride at weddings. "The bride stands in the middle of the room, arrayed like the Morning

Star", they sing. "The many-petalled rose passes down the lane, the boys and girls follow after her."

Instrumental music in the south obeys more or less the same rules as the vocal music. Southern Albanians use many string instruments of the lute family related to the Turkish saz and Greek *bouzouki* to perform dance melodies and rhapsodic meditations on slow airs, but the glory of their instrumental music is the *kaba*. A kaba (the word is Turkish meaning "low" or "deep") is a half-improvised melancholy form led by a clarinet or violin supported by a drone from accordion or llautê and usually followed by a dance tune to release the tension. The melodies, ornamented with swoops, glides and growls of an almost vocal quality, sound both fresh and ancient at the same time, and exemplify the combination of passion with restraint that is the hallmark of Albanian culture.

DO YOU REMEMBER, COMRADES, WHEN THE INSTRUCTIONS ON FOLK MUSIC WERE ISSUED?

Enver Hoxha, 1974

The communist government took control of musical life just as it did of every other aspect of life in Albania. As well as organizing large orchestras of traditional instruments "in the spirit of collective labour" they used to support local amateur groups in a network of festivals which culminated in the huge quinquennial festival at Gjirokastër, on the understanding that every group included a song in praise of Enver Hoxha and the Party.

Now there is no money for such activities the only organization actively involved in the promotion of music is Albanian Radio-Television (RTSh), which is hoping to reorganize the festival network in collaboration with private sponsors. The Artistic Director of RTSh, Zhani Ciko, has hopes for a rather more natural set-up in the future, and says that it would be better to have no festivals at all than to have them organized along the old lines. Mind you, he also says that they "try to favour the popular spirit and select and protect the national culture". Old habits, it seems, die hard.

Apart from the occasional concert at the Palace of Culture it can be difficult to find live music at the present time. The country is so poor that those usual Balkan venues for bands – cafés and restaurants – can't afford to employ musicians, and in addition many of the best-known singers are now living abroad, performing for the exile community. The best chance is to keep your eyes and ears open at the weekend in the hope of happening on a wedding celebration, which normally begins late on a Saturday evening and continues until the middle of Sunday afternoon with the arrival of the bride at her new home. If you have no head for hospitality then make sure you're not spotted hanging around outside, as you will invariably be invited in to help with the celebrations; as a guest you will be expected to eat, drink and dance in the newly-weds' honour.

DISCOGRAPHY

Famille Lela de Përmet *Polyphonies vocales et instrumentales d'Albanie* (Indigo/Harmonia Mundi, France). Beautiful and approachable songs and instrumental music from the Përmet and Korçë regions of southern Albania. Wailing and sliding clarinets give this music an enchanting mournful sound.

Various *Albania 1: Canti i Danze Tradizionale* (I Suoni Cetra, Italy). If you think you might like polyphonic singing, this is the disc to track down. One whole side is devoted to recordings from the archives of the Academy of Sciences in Tirana, and the instrumentals from all round the country on the other side are pretty hot too.

Various *Albania – Vocal and Instrumental Polyphony* (Le Chant du Monde, France). More music from the southern half of Albania, starting with an astonishing song from Vlorë and ending with a very lovely one from Përmet. A beautiful introspective sound.

Various *Folk Music of Albania* (Topic, UK). The first commercial western recording of music from Albania, this dates from 1966 but is still probably the best introduction to the musics of Albania with a lot of splendid performances by all manner of groups.

Various *There Where the Avalanche Stops* (Touch, UK). Recordings made at the 1988 Gjirokastër festival. Volume 1 includes some beautiful ensemble singing from the Lab tradition, music of the Greek minority, a remarkable evocation of natural sounds with flute, bells and voice and a great performance of one of the north's most popular songs, "Këndon bylbyli". The sleeve notes don't mention it, but it features some of the best-known singers and musicians including Korçë's Eli Fara. A second volume is promised.

BALTIC TO BAIKAL...

THE MUSICS OF RUSSIA AND THE NEW REPUBLICS SPAN CONTINENTS

From the Baltic to Baikal? The old Soviet Empire was immense – and its music encompassed all influences from central Europe to the Mongolian steppes. Simon Broughton blithely extends the geographical range of this chapter by just a few thousand miles to tour the ethnic music of Russia and the new republics.

It may seem outdated to lump the countries of the former Soviet Union together, particularly when the people and cultures are so widely different – and often ethnically closer to countries outside the old Union. But their shared experience of communist ideology dictated from Moscow, and the sudden rise in national consciousness with the break-up of the empire, mean that these countries have a lot in common. In particular, at present, each has an exaggerated awareness of its indigenous culture and national traditions – and of course these are not neatly contained within the borders of the fifteen former republics of the USSR but dispersed in an impossible jigsaw of around 130 nationalities. Never have music and culture counted for so much, though sadly the motivation is often simply to demonstrate the differences with their neighbours. But better with a balalaika than the barrel of a gun.

"National" music and culture was nominally encouraged by communist policy, but within tightly controlled limits. The idea was to demonstrate the fraternal ties of multicultural nations in the achievements of socialism. Each of the republics had its sanitized state ensembles strutting their stuff in vastly overblown folklore shows. Many, like the various Red Army Choirs and Georgian and Armenian Dance Ensembles, have toured widely and gained enthusiastic fans in the west. Their performances are spectacular and fine for what they are, but they have very little to do with the real local music and dancing.

The former Soviet Empire, however, was so large – covering over thirteen million square miles and stretching halfway round the world – that local traditions often survived in the isolated areas. Over the past few years, members of the Dmitri Pokrovsky Singers have collected and recorded wonderful traditional songs from old performers. Soviet musicologists have always studied these things, but with Boris Yeltsin's proclivity for ancient Russian traditions it seems they will be increasingly heard – and the new independent states are likely to be equally keen to promote their own cultures.

Nowadays, in addition to the numerous ethnic conflicts, the big problem is money. The newly independent republics have huge economic problems and naturally enough music and culture come behind basic essentials. The same is true in Russia and at the moment the rich archives of

The Dmitri Pokrovsky Singers

the former state recording company, Melodiya, are in peril due to lack of investment. But in the enterprise culture new bands will appear with a wider range of music than ever before.

The possibilities are certainly exciting, as the countries of the former Soviet Empire are still musically unexplored. Witness, for example, the recent arrival of Tuvan throat music (of which more later) on the world scene, which WOMAD unleashed to capture the imagination of thousands of festival-goers. As well as a rediscovery of the traditional music, there's a strong interest from contemporary groups in regional musical styles and, out of the ferment, we are likely to hear some remarkable sounds in the next few years.

THE BALTIC FRINGE

The countries of Lithuania, Latvia and Estonia enjoyed a brief period of independence between the wars until they were annexed to the USSR in 1940. Independent again, since 1991, their orientation is firmly west rather than east, particularly as the Balts hold Moscow responsible for holding up their economic development and prosperity. Musically, too, their traditions – each of which are quite distinct – belong to the culture of northern Europe rather than Russia.

The music played a fair part in the independence process, which was popularly labelled the "Singing Revolution". In 1988 half a million people gathered in and around Tallinn's Lauluväljak, or "Song Square", to express their support for the Estonian Popular Front. For years, say the Balts, singing is all that the authorities allowed them, and on this occasion singing and dancing went on throughout the night. In August 1989 a human chain was formed across the entire length of the three countries in a peaceful protest. They sang a melancholy song, "Rise Up Baltic States", written specially for the occasion in all three Baltic languages. They sang again in 1991 in the streets of Vilnius and Riga as Russian troops moved in and shed blood. Ancient folk songs about tilling one's own land or not suffering under cruel masters served as protest songs.

The most popular manifestations of Baltic music are the huge song festivals, held in all three countries, which date back to the growth of the national movement in the nineteenth century. Estonia held the first song festival in Tartu in 1869 to celebrate the abolition of serfdom, and association with political protest and the demand for freedom was always present if muted. Latvia followed suit in 1873, while the Lithuanians came on the scene late, in 1924, during the short period of independence for all the Baltic states between the wars.

These festivals are huge displays of national consciousness, garlanded with flags and folk costumes. At the twenty-first Estonian national song festival in 1990 one third of the population gathered together to sing. For the first time since the war there were no communist slogans and there was fervent singing of previously banned religious and patriotic songs like "Eesti Vabaks" (Estonia be Free): a year later, it was.

Germany and Poland have been the strong cultural influences on the region, but the three countries preserve their own distinctive musical forms. Estonia and Finland are related linguistically and musically and all three republics share a *baltic zither* – known variously as the *kankles* (Lithuania), *kokle* (Latvia) or *kannel* (Estonia), and as the *kantele* in Finland – which is important in the accompaniment to traditional song.

In Latvia, in particular, there has been a conscious revival of kokle playing. A Latvian legend maintains that the strings of the kokle represent the rays of the sun and the instrument itself is the incarnation of the human soul, so expressive is its tone.

Lithuania also boasts one of the world's extraordinary polyphonic singing traditions called *sutartine* – dissonant and punchy snatches of folk poetry sung by women or played on wooden trumpets. The practice is now rare, but many examples were recorded before the war.

The best occasion to hear a wide variety of Baltic music is at the annual "Baltica" folk festival, held in rotation, each July, in each of the Baltic capitals – Tallinn, Vilnius and Riga. On disc, traditional Baltic music is hard to come by at present, though it probably won't be long before the new countries fill the gap, so integral is it to national pride.

On the spot, you may have more luck – and you should look out for albums by some of the new bands, too, who are experimenting with fusions in the manner of Värttinä in Finland. The Latvian band, **New Moon**, for example, use the kokle and other ethnic instruments to create a U2-like sound. Crossing over further into rock, there is even a ska-punk band in Lithuania, called **BIX**. The Baltic states had always been at the forefront of "Soviet Rock" and in the 1970s had spawned a couple of folk-influenced bands, the Estonian **Vantorel** and Latvian **2XBBM**.

BELARUS

The Belorussians are Slavs living in the vast flat lands between Poland and Russia. They maintain a traditional repertoire of agricultural songs, dances and laments, for which choral singing is central – as indeed it is right across the Slavonic territories to eastern Siberia.

The Belarus choral singing style, as practised by groups of old grannies, is a bit of an acquired taste but it is available on disc for the curious in a UNESCO ethnographic recording of villagers

FROM THE BALTIC TO THE BALKANS

singing and playing traditional music and Partisan songs from World War II.

If you delve around, you might also unearth some of the pop versions of Belarus folk songs, which were big hits in the 1970s from a group called **Pesniary** – one of the snappily termed VIAs (vocal-instrumental ensembles) with which the Soviet authorities hoped to stave off "subversive" western rock. One of the Pesniary combo was married to the famous Soviet gymnast Olga Korbut and the couple – a kind of musical-athletic ensemble – were promoted as Soviet life at its cleanest. They later emigrated to the US.

These days, Belarus has a couple of rather more decent rock bands, **Bazylki** and **Ulis**, who incorporate folk elements into their material.

British band The Ukrainians get back to their roots

MOLDOVA

The territory of the Moldavian Republic (formerly Bessarabia) was annexed to the Soviet Union in 1940 with the historical justification that it had been part of the Russian Empire from 1812 to 1918, when it was joined to Romania. For the moment Moldova is a member of the CIS, and the nationalist movement for reunification with their Romanian brothers across the River Prut suffered a heavy defeat in a recent referendum.

The region's traditional music is directly related to Romanian music with a strong tradition of gypsy *lăutari* in village bands. It is yet to surface on western recordings.

UKRAINE

Ukraine has a rich repertoire of traditional music: carols, agricultural songs, and – a uniquely Ukrainian form – the *duma* or Cossack Song. Dumas are historical epics that are thought to derive from ancient laments, although the texts are usually about the struggles against the Turks and Tartars or the seventeenth-century war of liberation against the Poles. Their melodies often have an oriental flavour in keeping with the subject matter of Cossack slavery under the Turks. The traditional performers of these songs were blind itinerant musicians accompanying themselves on the *bandura*, the Ukranian lute-zither.

Traditional weddings in Ukraine were – and, in some country areas, still are – elaborate affairs lasting a couple of days. They are complex musico-dramatic events with monologues, dialogues, songs, dances and instrumental pieces. The most distinctive musical ingredients are the sad ritual songs sung by the women commenting on all aspects of the nuptial process.

The Ukraine's traditional music is quite well represented on disc, with recent Silex recordings of local choirs and village bands, and a window on past glories in Arhoolie's releases of Ukranian musicians from the 1920s. The latter's disc featuring **Pawlo Humeniuk** ("King of the Ukrainian Fiddlers"), is glorious, even for those normally shy of old "archive" recordings, and the music is a reminder of the close connection between traditional Ukrainian and Jewish *klezmer* music.

An unlikely but inspired example of how contemporary Ukrainian folk might develop comes from a British group, **The Ukrainians**. This trio – two of whom are of Ukrainian descent – evolved from a rock band, The Wedding Present, but now play traditional instruments like accordion, mandolin, fiddle and balalaika, along with a rock drum kit. They went back to old recordings of Ukrainian country dances to use the rhythms of the dancers' feet in their rhythmic backing, and they sing in Ukrainian, sometimes using old melodies, sometimes their own authentic-sounding compositions.

Ukraine's own leading rock bands, **Collegium Accessor** and **VV**, actually have some traditional elements. The former are a magnificent psychedelic-folk outfit; the latter might be called a local version of The Pogues.

RUSSIA

The Russian Republic, the largest in the old Soviet Union, has always been politically and culturally dominant in the region. Its population numbers around 130 million, of which over 80 percent are ethnic Russians.

Russian folk music was long considered serene and melodious but recent research suggests this is not the whole truth. In fact most of what were considered to be authentic Russian folk songs – and dutifully performed by state folklore ensembles and Red Army choirs – turn out to be nineteenth-century fakes composed by urban songwriters of the day. So classic Russian songs like "Kalinka", "Dark Eyes" and the "Volga Boat Song" have more to do with gypsy romance than authentic folk tradition.

The "real" Russian folk tradition only began to be discovered in the 1970s when musicologists and students went out into the villages to explore the unpolished and often pre-Christian culture of rural Russia. The music was much more original and varied than people had supposed. The songs range from the terrifying howling of the *plachi* laments to the *chastushki*, satirical songs often with accordion or balalaika accompaniment, and the *khorovodi*, funky foot-stomping round-dances.

The best-known performers of ethnic Russian songs are the **Dmitry Pokrovsky Ensemble** who have recorded for Peter Gabriel's Real World label and the German label, Trikont. Their Trikont recording, "The Wild Field", features a very wide repertoire, including Cossack songs, harvest and wedding songs, religious music and a bizarre instrumental track of jew's harp, whistle and clanging rhythms hammered out on a sickle. (There's probably not much else to do in Russia with a hammer and sickle these days.)

A group from a different end of the spectrum are St Petersburg's **Terem Quartet**. Their music doesn't try to be authentic or traditional. It is just wild, eclectic and great fun. The members of the band all trained at the (then) Leningrad Conservatory and play their instruments – accordion, two *domras* (Russian three-stringed mandolins) and a huge bass balalaika – with astonishing virtuosity. Their repertoire includes Russian popular songs, pastiches, and their own compositions. They have recorded for Real World and are regulars on the WOMAD festival circuit. They are brilliant on record and even better live.

The Terem Quartet are in many ways typical of St Petersburg, which has a radical and

The Terem Quartet work out

satirical tradition. These qualities also distinguished much of the city's pop and rock scene, which falls largely outside the scope of this book, but is worth mentioning in a traditional context as its roots were at least partly grounded in traditional music – European (mainly German), gypsy and Jewish. The scene also had roots in a kind of western folk music – the so-called Bards' Movement of the 1950s and '60s: poets who played the guitar and sang their often highly satirical verses for small student and intellectual audiences. Key figures among the Bards included **Alexander Galich**, a professional playwright, eventually forced into exile in France; **Bulat Okudjava**, philosophical and lovesick and one of the few with real melodic invention (his albums have been released on the French Chant du Monde label); and, most importantly, **Vladimir Vysotsky**.

Vysotsky, from Moscow, was a truely titanic figure, whose work was ardently followed by all elements of the Russian population from young punks to war veterans, and was a major influence on the development of Russian-language rock. He started writing songs in the '60s and, purely through privately circulated and copied cassettes, was known right across the country. His main inspiration was *blatnye pesny* ("delinquent songs"), a street-level song culture dealing with women, drinking, fighting and jail. Musically his songs were very simple but Vysotsky brought his own intelligence and philosophical imagery to the form and his legacy of almost a thousand songs is an encyclopedia of post-war Soviet life. He died in 1980, still without an official album release in Russia, although he was subsequently given official approval by Gorbachev, and Melodiya issued a series of twenty or more of his albums.

In the late 1970s and the pre-glasnost '80s, rock music was a genuine focus of dissident

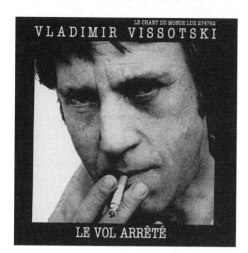

LE CHANT DU MONDE LDX 274762
VLADIMIR VISSOTSKI

LE VOL ARRÊTÉ

opposition to the Soviet regime – so much so that the state set up its own pop groups, or VIAs (vocal-instrumental ensembles – see Belarus). On the "real" subversive scene, meanwhile, cult underground bands like **Time Machine**, **Aquarium**, **Zoopark**, and **Kino** became household names despite having no records, no press, and no radio or TV appearances. Musically these bands weren't particularly original – a mix of Bob Dylan and the Sex Pistols, by way of progressive rock – but the lyrics were something else: songs about apathy, conformism, hypocrisy, disillusionment and alcohol abuse all reflected one basic human condition – alienation.

This lyric, "The Calm" by Time Machine, was a typical – and by western rock standards, highly poetic – contribution:

My ship is a creation of able hands,
My course is a total disaster.
But just let the wind pick up
And everything around will change,
Including the idiot who thinks otherwise.
An answer ready for every question,
Night has always made right,
But no one believes that
There's no wind on earth,
Even if they've banned the wind.

Since the demise of Soviet power, the Russian rock scene has largely moved away from politics and towards the western styles of the moment – yes, there is Russian house, along with Russian reggae, new wave, industrial, rap, and the rest. More recently, there's also been a growing interest in ethnic-pop crossover, probably stimulated by the current trend in World Music. Bands in this field include **Yat-ha**, a duo of sampling keyboard player and throat singer from Tuva, and **Cholbon**,

who play progressive rock in Yakutian shamanistic style!

For those seriously interested in the authentic ethnic musics of the Russian fringes, there are an exemplary series of CDs on the French Inédit label and several interesting discs from the Dutch label, Pan. One of the best Inédit albums is called "Songs of Women of Old Russia" and contains an incredible collection of pieces from European Russia and from a community in deepest Siberia. These latter women, from a village near Lake Baikal, are descendants of prisoners sent to exile in tsarist days and, living in isolation amongst their predominantly Mongol neighbours, have kept the old Russian music intact. Another Inédit disc, "Music of the Tundra and the Taiga", is devoted exclusively to the ethnic groups of Siberia and includes the astonishing sounds of a quintet of jew's harps played by Yakuts and a group of the shamanistic Tungus people from the very far east, imitating the sounds of the forest!

Among the Pan material is a selection entitled "Mother Volga" which presents music of the Mari and Chuvash people, who are Finno-Ugric and Turkic in origin, rather than Slav. Hungarian musicologists have traced distant musical links to the Mari which must date from before the migration of Hungarians from the Volga region in the seventh century.

Tuvan singer Kaigal-ool Khovalyg of Huun-Huur-Tu

The ethnic music that has had most (and most improbable) attention on the world scene, however, is from Tuva, a small autonomous Russian republic on the Mongolian border, with a concrete marker declaring it the "Centre of Asia". The Tuvan's music is an other-worldly "throat singing", known as *khoomei*, and also heard in Mongolia itself. By virtuoso movements of the larynx, tongue and jaw, a singer can create melodies from the harmonics or overtones of the fundamental note that he is singing. In this way one singer can sing both melody and accompaniment.

A pioneering recording was made in 1987 by Ted Levin for Smithsonian Folkways, and things have mushroomed since then with many more, including a wonderful Real World recording and a sort of Tuvan crossover album from Sainkho Namchylak on Cramworld. Each of them offers a window on a strange world of intimate songs to sheep and goats, quite unlike anything else you'll ever hear.

TRANSCAUCASIA

The Transcaucasian region of Georgia, Armenia and Azerbaijan is the former-Soviet Union's richest musical area. The Georgians and the Armenians are amongst the oldest Christian nations in the world, having converted early in the fourth century, and they both have rich and different traditions of church music. Their folk and urban music is fascinating and colourful, too, for western ears, and a lot of recordings are now available.

Georgia has a great and highly distinct tradition of polyphonic choral singing. You can still hear these songs performed impromptu and with the help of large quantities of wine at al fresco parties and weddings across the country. The choirs may vary in size from a trio to large ensembles and the singers are usually men. The style of the songs varies, to the trained ear, across the country with the most complex polyphonic songs to be found in the western regions of Guria and Mengrelia. The Svanetian region, remote and isolated in the foothills of the Caucasus Mountains has kept some of the oldest traditions

in its distinctive three-part songs. These are often accompanied by the *changi*, the Svanetian harp, which looks like it's come straight off a Greek vase. In the eastern region of Kakhetia are some of the richest, most sonorous songs, while further south you find long, lyrical *orovels*, originally sung while ploughing. These are closely related in name and sound to the *horhovel* songs of Armenia, suggesting a close link in agricultural life.

There are half a dozen fine collections of Georgian choral music on western labels, including excellent performances by the best-known of Georgia's professional ensembles, the **Rustavi Choir**.

Another music to be heard on every car radio-cassette player in Georgia, or in the bars of downtown Tbilisi, is prosaically called "urban music". But to anyone with a slightly sentimental streak it is marvellously intoxicating. The melodies are hummable and catchy and sung in simple harmony with accompanying guitars. The most famous song of this type is "Suliko", a sad ballad of lost love made immortal by being Stalin's favourite song. There are several groups playing this type of music – and it appears on a couple of western records – but, if you're in town, search for a record of the **Tsisperi Trio** in Tbilisi's record stores and you're away.

Old-time Armenian ensemble

Armenia is known for its wild and passionate virtuoso instrumental music with drums and clarinets – a style that has spread throughout the Transcaucasian region. Also typically Armenian is the soft and soulful sound of the *duduk*, a reedy woodwind instrument usually played in

DIAL-A-TUNE GEORGIA

· ·

In the road that winds uphill from the Metekhi church in old Tbilisi there's a place on the right, next to a wine shop, that looks like a cross between a tea house and a taxi firm. You can't miss it because above the entrance are vivid paintings in the naive style of Georgia's most famous painter, Pirosmani. The pictures show musicians with pink and bulging cheeks blowing into oboes and striking drums. A notice in Georgian and Russian declares it to be the "Centre for Players of Oriental Instruments'.

Going in it's much quieter than you expect. No puffing cheeks or wild drumming. Not an oriental instrument to be seen. Just a few guys sitting around reading the paper or playing dominoes. A man at a desk by the door is on the phone and jotting down notes in a ledger.

However, should a call come in to say, "We're just having a little get together to celebrate my son's engagement. Could you send some of your lads round to get things going?" they'll be round, faster than a kiss-o-gram. For Georgians, music is an essential ingredient of any celebration. You can see them at the weekend dining al fresco in local beauty spots, often with instrumental trios wandering from group to group in turn. This office in Tbilisi is here to provide the music for weddings, birthdays – any sort of celebration.

The "oriental" instruments are *duduks* (a soft reedy wind instrument), clarinets and drums that the Georgians have picked up from their Transcaucasian neighbours to the east, the Armenians and Azeris. The tunes can be wild dances on the clarinet and accordion with the insistent rhythm beaten out on the drum. Or it can be a soft and reflective song accompanied by a couple of duduks. The instruments themselves, by the way, are kept in the lockers which line the walls – so they can be grabbed quickly if the musicians are needed in a hurry.

---

pairs, with the second instrument providing a steady drone. This is a plaintive, reflective sound, which can be extraordinarily beautiful. Both are reasonably well represented on western discs.

Another important tradition is that of the *Ashugs* – troubadours who appear also in Turkish and Azerbaijani music (where they're called *ashiks*). The word comes from Arabic (meaning "lover") and describes someone who is a musician, poet and storyteller. The most famous of these troubadours was **Sayat Nova** (1712–1795) who lived in the cosmopolitan world of Tiflis (Tbilisi), the Georgian capital, and became court musician to King Heracles II. Some of the repertoire of Sayat Nova and more recent Ashugs has been recorded by Ocora with traditional ensembles of *kamancha* (3-stringed fiddle), *kanun* (zither), *tar* (lute) and *duduk*. All these instruments belong to the world of Turkish and Persian music and Armenia, as a Christian country right on the fringe, is unique in absorbing them so intrinsically into its culture.

The predominantly Muslim Republic of Azerbaijan, currently in the throes of a fierce sporadic war with neighbouring Armenia over Nagorni Karabakh, has its closest linguistic and cultural links with Turkey, although the influence of Persia has again been important. The music shares the forms and styles of the Middle East with long inflected vocal melodies and heavily improvised instrumental styles. The pieces are often long and complex.

The most developed musical form is the *mugam*, which refers to the musical mode as in Turkish *makam* or Arabic *maqam*, but has also come to mean the formal cycle of vocal and instrumental pieces as well. The instrumental ensemble is typically tar, kamancha and daf (frame drum). The mugam begins with an instrumental prelude on the tar and continues with a sequence of vocal pieces interrupted by instrumental improvisations. Ocora, Pan, Chant du Monde, King and Inédit (featuring the singer *Alem Kassimov*) have all released recordings of classical Azerbaijani music.

CENTRAL ASIA

The music of the five central Asian states – Kazakhstan, Uzbekistan, Turkmenistan, Kyrghyzstan and Tadjikistan – falls into two broad types. Linguistically the Uzbeks, Kazakhs, Kyrghiz and Turkmen are central Asian Turkic groups, while the Tadjiks speak a language related to Persian. Musically, though, the picture is more complex as influences have been picked up from neighbouring cultures.

In the south and east of the region, the Uzbeks and Tadjiks share a closely related musical

THE VOICE OF ASIA FESTIVAL

. . . .

For most westerners the huge expanse between the Black Sea and the Bering Straits evokes only half-formed images of the Gulag Archipelago, the Trans-Siberian railway and endless steppe. I was aware there was a lot more to it than that when I landed in Alma-Ata, capital of Kazahkstan, to join a jury for the first *Azia Dauysy* ("Voice of Asia") festival. But the vastness of the land and the incredible wealth of nations, languages, cultures and musics only began to dawn on me as I took off from the same airport a week later.

The brief for the festival was "popular music within the context of Asian culture", which I and the more aggressive members of the jury took to mean that all the music should incorporate Asian rhythms and melodies in a "rock" or "pop" context. Many of the 45 contestants seemed to feel the brief would be satisfied by singing a disco number while wearing traditional Uzbek or Kyrghiz costumes. They were promptly eliminated in the first round. When the semifinalists were announced, we were told that those eliminated included the most popular singers in Kazakhstan and had to undergo a press conference explaining our criteria.

For me, the highlight of the festival was the Friday-night semifinal under a full moon. The twelve groups and solo artists included Yakuts, Kyrghiz, Mongols, Kazakhs, Uzbeks, Turkmens, Tuvans, Dagestanis, and Russians. The musical mix was fascinating. Tuvans and Mongols utilized the traditional "throat singing", voicing a low drone and an overtone at the same time, accompanied by a feedback guitar. The Yakuts' chanting was like North American and Eskimo music but led into dense heavy metal. Traditional songs were adapted very effectively to rock instrumentation by the Kazakhs and Uzbeks. They would mike up traditional hand drums to augment the drum kit and play the indigenous single-string fiddle and dombra with a contact pick-up through an amp. The singers from the southerly Islamic republics like Turkmenistan and Tadjikistan sang local versions of Turkish pop music and were less influenced by western "rock" formats, although one brought on a harem of dancing girls between verses of his derivative disco number.

I asked repeatedly, for the local equivalent of a wedding band. I wanted to see the tradition brought up to date rather than the rock groups converted (sometimes clearly reluctantly) to tradition. I was told there was nothing interesting in this area, but I found un-named tapes for sale in the market which featured amazing traditional music. We had seen the local ensembles attached to the museum and they were impressive and interesting, but the anonymous performers on the cassettes were even better.

The basic instrument is the dombra – a two-stringed lute – a cousin to many other similar instruments found from the Adriatic to the Gobi Desert. The thrilling vocals on these tapes are a cross between an Asiatic cowboy lament and a Eurasian bardic wail. Long-held notes of immense power are interspersed with rapid-fire verses. A glimpse of showmanship from the dombra player at the Conservatory, where he suddenly whipped the instrument towards the audience like a baton, spun it in the air and brought it back for the next stroke à la Hendrix gave us a flavour of a live performance by one of these Robert Johnsons of the steppes.

A group called Kars from Tashkent, the capital of Uzbekistan, won the Grand Prize. They had great confidence and abandon playing traditional music on modern instruments. This was Uzbek music with a future. One Russian jury member felt the prize shouldn't be awarded. He had earlier regaled me with stories of the time he had interviewed Tina Turner for Russian TV, so I could see where his prejudices lay. There was a certain unease among the radicals on the jury watching the crowd boogey frantically to the most superficial pop-disco imaginable. Were we shoving some rigorous foreign criteria down their throats to serve some abstract ideas of our own?

Hearing the crowd cheering and singing along with the best numbers of the six finalists on the last night removed any such doubts. Uzbek and Kazakh flags waved in the night air while fireworks exploded over the stadium and the winners wept with joy. It is hard to see such groups every day. They often play in restaurants or, more rarely, at concerts, and recordings may never come out except on private bootlegs. The music industry is primitive, but the musical vitality of every part of it is moving and impressive. I can't wait to go back.

Joe Boyd

cultural traditions of this crossroads city in Uzbekistan, and includes songs from *sozanda* (female entertainers) and the music of Islamic and oriental Jewish communities. **Ashkabad**, a group from Turkmenistan, have recorded for Real World and show just how much wonderful music there must be waiting to be discovered in central Asia. These musicians are heavily in demand at local weddings and their sound is languorous and melodic with some beautiful violin playing and a distinctly Middle-Eastern beat.

The Ashkabad disc is a clear sign that western producers are now exploring what is going on in the former Soviet Union (see also the Voice of Asia Festival box), while the musicians are beginning to tour abroad. There are exciting

Ashkabad – from the centre of Asia

culture linked with Afghanistan to the south and with the Uighurs in Chinese Turkistan to the east. The Turkmen have connections with Iran over their border to the south. In the traditional cultures of all these peoples music plays a major role, particularly in pastoral and nomadic life.

The music is as yet hardly known in the west, although there are a few inroads. Smithsonian Folkways have issued a fascinating recording from Bukhara, which gives an amazing picture of the

prospects of new fusions being thrown up as contemporary bands explore and re-work the traditional sounds.

Thanks to Art Troitsky for his contribution on Soviet rock and the Bard Movement. If you're seriously interested in Russian rock, check out Art Troitsky's books Back in the USSR: The True Story of Rock in Russia *and* Tusovka *(Omnibus Press, UK).*

■ DISCOGRAPHY ■

Among the most interesting discs available is an ongoing series from a Dutch label, Pan Records. These focus on various regional traditions and are organized by Vyacheslav Shchurov, a folklorist from the Moscow Conservatory. They are well recorded and give a fascinating insight into a wide range of musical styles. Several of them appear in the discography below.

GENERAL ANTHOLOGIES

ⓒⅮ **Various** *Musics of the Soviet Union* (Smithsonian Folkways, US). This is a basic introduction, featuring quality recordings from several different republics.

ⓒⅮ **Various** *Voyage en URSS* (Chant du Monde, France). This six-CD set, licensed from Melodiya, includes ethnographic recordings from right across the former Soviet Union. However, it is eccentrically arranged, very patchy, and suffers from a lack of basic information about the music.

BALTIC REPUBLICS

ⓒⅮ **Dzintars** *Songs of Amber* (Rykodisc, US). The only internationally available disc. Although a lot of the music

comes from folk sources, it is not traditional music, but classical singing.

BELARUS

ⓒⅮ **Various** *Byelorussia* (Auvidis/Unesco, France). Includes recordings of villagers singing and playing traditional music as well as a couple of Partisan songs from World War II.

UKRAINE

ⓒⅮ **Ensemble Berehinya** *Vorotarchik (The Gate-Keeper)* (Pan, Netherlands). These performances of traditional Ukrainian vocal and instrumental music are from a professional folk troupe but they provide a good idea of the music, including a spirited Cossack song as a finale.

ⓒⅮ **Pawlo Humeniuk** *King of the Ukrainian Fiddlers* (Arhoolie, US). Glorious 1920s recordings of a master fiddler with various ensembles.

ⓒⅮ **The Ukranians** *The Ukrainians* (Cooking Vinyl, UK). A wonderful album by a British band, part-Ukrainian in origin, featuring songs inspired by old-style dances. The group use a mix of traditional and rock instruments.

Various *Musiques Traditionelles d'Ukraine Vol 1* and *Vol 2* (Silex, France). These two albums feature local choirs and village bands, with some wonderful instrumental tracks.

RUSSIA

Dmitry Pokrovsky Ensemble *The Wild Field* (Real World, UK) and *Faces of Russia* (Trikont, Germany). *Wild Field* presents music from the area of southern Russia bearing that name; *Faces of Russia* is a better disc, featuring a much wider repertoire, including Cossack songs, harvest and wedding songs, and religious music.

Terem Quartet *Terem* (Real World, UK). Virtuoso renditions and pastiches of Russian popular songs from this sophisticated and highly entertaining St Petersburg quartet.

Huun-Huur-Tu *60 Horses in my Herd* (Shanachie, US), **Shu-De** *Voices from the Distant Steppe* (Real World, UK) and **Sainkho Namchylak** *Out of Tuva* (Crammed discs, Belgium). These are all fascinating discs of Tuvan "throat singing". For a first listen try Huun-Huur-Tu, who are refugees from a state ensemble, spectacular players, and the deepest singers you're likely to encounter.

Various *Chants des Femmes de la Vieille Russie* (Inédit, France). An incredible collection of women's pieces from European Russia and deepest Siberia.

Various *Document: New Music from Russia* (Leo Records, UK; 8 CDs). Leo is basically an avant garde jazz label (and a wonderful one, at that) but this challenging set earns a place in a guide to World Music because a lot of its music stems from folk and traditional sources. "Dearly Departed", sung and played by a St Petersburg quintet, is a patchwork of choral songs performed with great intensity over an ensemble of accordion and jazz instruments creating a sound world that is distinctly Russian and simultaneously ancient and avant garde. Another piece, "Thracian Duos", features Anatoly Vapirov on saxophone and Sergei Kuryokhin on piano with a series of duets and improvisations on Bulgarian folk music with a shade of John Coltrane.

Various *Musiques de la Toundra et de la Taïga* (Inédit, France). Music from the ethnic groups of Siberia, including a quintet of jew's harps played by Yakuts, and Shamanistic Tungus people from the very far east, imitating the sounds of the forest!

Various *Mother Volga* (Pan, Netherlands). Sounds from the Mari and Chuvash people – distant relations of the Hungarians.

Various *A Peacock Once Went Flying* and *Play, Vanya* (Pan, Netherlands). Two high-quality ethnographic collections from the south of Russia. The "Peacock" is purely vocal music featuring various village ensembles. *Play, Vanya* is predominantly instrumental. Amazing that all this could still be recorded in the 1970s and '80s.

GEORGIA

Rustavi Choir *Georgian Voices* (Elektra Nonesuch, US) and *Georgia* (World Network, Germany). "Georgian Voices" is the best introduction to Georgian singing, with songs from all regions of the country performed by one of the best known of Georgia's professional ensembles. "Georgia", on the excellent World Network label, includes the added bonus of an instrumental duduk trio.

Shavtvala Gogona and the Kolkheti Ensemble *Oh, Black-eyed girl* (Pan, Netherlands). A sweet-voiced ensemble and a fine collection of music that includes some more urban songs and instrumental tracks.

Tsinandali Choir *Table Songs of Georgia* (Real World, UK). A powerful collection of songs from the wine-producing region of Kakhetia. The sort of rich harmonic experience that traditionally accompanies the glories of Georgian food and wine.

Various *Georgie: Chants de travail – Chants religieux* (Ocora, France). Less polished but perhaps more authentic performances, recorded on location.

Various *Georgia: Polyphony of Svaneti* (Chant du Monde, France). Vivid recordings of music you can still experience at svaneti celebrations.

Various *Soinari, Folk Music from Georgia Today* (Welt Musik, Germany). A fine introduction to urban songs, including the famous "Suliko", plus some traditional polyphonic songs as well.

ARMENIA

Djivan Gasparian *I Will Never be Sad in this World* (Land Records, UK/Opal, US). This is unremittingly slow and melancholy – but mesmerizingly if the mood takes you.

Richard Hagopian *Armenian Music through the Ages* (Smithsonian Folkways, US). Virtuoso ud playing from an American-born Armenian, performing songs and instrumental pieces that reflect more of the classical tradition.

The Muradian Ensemble *Hayastan* (Van Geel, Netherlands). The playing is glorious and the selection of pieces quite beautiful. Quite frankly, this is a great disc – period. There's another volume, equally good, entitled *Muradian Ensemble*.

Various *Armenie: Chants Liturgiques du Moyen Age et Musique Instrumentale* (Ocora, France). A varied selection of Armenian instrumental music, including duduks and religious chants.

Various *Armenie: Musique de tradition populaire et des Achough* (Ocora, France). Traditional chants and Ashug troubadour songs.

AZERBAIJAN

Ensemble Dede Gorgud *Heyva Gülü* (Pan, Netherlands). Rural bagpipe music and Ashug melodies.

Alem Kassimov *Mugam d'Azerbaïdjan* (Inédit, France). A fine recording of classical Azerbaijani music.

Various *Azerbaïdjan* (Chant du Monde, France). A cross-section of Azerbaijani folk music.

CENTRAL ASIAN REPUBLICS

Ashkabad *City of Love* (Real World, UK). Lyrical and accessible music from Turkmenistan. Hear how central Asian music can swing.

Various *Asie Centrale* (Ocora, France). Two-CD set featuring the classical music of all five central Asian states.

Various *Badakhshan* (Pan, Netherlands). Songs and mystical poetry from the Pamir Mountains.

Various *Bukhara: Musical Crossroads of Asia* (Smithsonian Folkways, US). This 1990 recording gives an amazing picture of the cultural traditions of this city in Uzbekistan. It includes *sozanda* (female entertainers) and the music of Islamic and oriental Jewish communities.

Various *Voix de l'Orient Sovietique* (Inédit, France). A disc which brings together music from central Asia, plus Azerbaijan, Armenia and Georgia.

MEDITERRANEAN AND MAGHREB

The Mediterranean basin is a region of hot climates and strong emotions. Passionate expression comes across in the music, with love the foremost topic for song lyrics and drinking and religion equal second. Although this chapter includes disparate types of music, ranging from Mauritania to Turkey and from flamenco to Algerian *rai*, a common thread of long historical roots and Arab influence runs through many of them. Gypsy traditions also run through several of these musics, most notably flamenco, Greek and Turkish.

Not all the pieces sit comfortably together: Turkish music, for example, is a distinctive bundle of styles, many of which owe little to Arabia. And the urban blues of Portugal, the *fado*, has a deep folk history still waiting to be properly uncovered: not much Arabic here, perhaps, but its parallels with the lowlife of Greek *rembétika*, 2000 km to the east, are clear enough; and, in turn, the Greek musical heritage owes much to influences from the Levant and Egypt. The common instruments of the Mediterranean basin are described in some detail in the first feature.

The chapter then begins in Morocco, the heart of the Maghreb – the western Arab world. As well as old indigenous styles, the classical *andalous* music, developed in Moorish Spain, remains a popular, highly stylized form with great influence throughout the Arab-speaking world. Inspirational music of the *Gnaoua* brotherhood, using a lute and castanets, is unique to Morocco.

From across the straits of Gibraltar we feature the flamenco of Andalucía, with its panoply of brilliant artists and audible and obvious associations with the *andalous* and Berber music of Morocco. Rhythmic strings, percussive dancing and inflamed, mesmerizing vocals is an apt description of flamenco, but it could apply to many of the musical forms in this chapter, including Mauritanian. Both Moroccan music and flamenco have strong links with Mauritanian music and the three together emphasize a Moorish, as distinct from Arab, cultural sphere all too often forgotten. The Mauritanian musician caste, the *iggawin*, were not only accomplished performers but also the griots of their community – this chapter's link with West Africa.

The Algerian *rai* phenomenon, with its worldwide stars Cheb Mami, Chaba Fadela and above all Khaled, originated in the folk music of the hinterland of Oran, the main port city of western Algeria. With Khaled performing worldwide to packed houses, and still massively popular at home (on cassette), he is one of this chapter's true stars of World Music.

In contrast, Portuguese *fado* is a style with a limited international following, which deserves more. Traceable back to the country's multiple identity as the poor cousin of western Europe, and an old imperial power, it branded the lyrics of the ballad onto African folk roots and served it up as a song of lament and fatalism. The *fado* is still performed and a number of archive recordings are now available on CD.

Turkey has arguably the most variety in its music of any country in this chapter. It has many links with music of the Balkans and also with Iranian and Middle Eastern music, but many of its traditions originate in the grasslands of central Asia, its itinerant poet-musicians, the *ashiks*, having long been famous for singing in the tea houses along the silk road. The Ottoman and Byzantine eras were times of great musical exploration and this, combined with numerous folk styles – from Macedonian in the west to Kurdish in the east – have all been strongly imprinted on the music of modern Turkey.

The music of Greeks living in Turkey had a great influence on the music of urban Greece in the 1920s and 1930s – most especially on *rembétika*, music of the underworld cafés of Athens and Pireás. The singers would write songs in their own slang about their loves, their struggles and their hashish. A blend of this rebellious tradition, together with inspiration from the country's regional folk musics, has found reformulated expression in the "new wave" movement of *néo kíma*. Our interview with multi-instrumentalist Ross Daly touches on many of the themes in the Greece and Turkey features.

MEDITERRANEAN AND MAGHREB ✈ GLOSSARY

Most of the specific instruments mentioned in this chapter – and Chapter Four – are described in the article following.

Amanédhes Proletarian café music of early twentieth-century Greek-occupied Turkey.

Andalous Moroccan, classical music derived from the traditions established during the Moorish occupation of Andalucía.

Arabesk Popular Turkish music with predominantly Arabic, rather than Turkish, melodies and style.

Ashik Literally "one in love", an Anatolian troubador (Turkey).

Cante Jondo Literally "deep song", the profoundly emotional style of flamenco singing.

Chaabi Arabic popular music covering a wide mix of styles.

Chir al-milhûn See *milhûn*.

Dhimotiká General term for Greek folk music.

Fado Portuguese urban "blues", summed up by its literal meaning, "fate".

Fasil Semiclassical, light Turkish vocal music.

Flamenco Vocal and guitar-based music of partly gypsy origin: its heartland is the southern Spanish province of Andalucía.

Gnaoua Moroccan religious brotherhood, whose members are descendants of African slaves.

Halk "People" in Turkish-and thus Turkish folk music in general.

Iggawin Mauritanian musicians.

Maghreb Literally "the West", in Arabic, meaning the western shores of the Arab-speaking world, in practice from Tunisia to Mauritania, as opposed to the Middle East.

Mevlevi Classical Turkish style associated with the Sufi Mevlevi sect (of whirling dervish fame), using the same modes and instrumentation as Ottoman classical music.

Milhûn A semiclassical form of sung poetry related to *andalous*.

Moussem Moroccan popular religious festival.

Neo Kima Greek, "new wave" music of the 1960s–80s, whose exponents opposed the junta and took inspiration from the Latin *nueva canción*.

Nuba Classical Moroccan musical suite.

Ozan Music of the Turkish *ashiks*.

Ozgun Literally "genuine music" – the more progressive wing of Turkish pop.

Rai Algerian "rebel" music. Originally an acoustic folk style from around Oran, it is now a very hi-tech sound, with electric guitars and synthesizers, and is characterized by lyrics of dissent from conservative Islamic values.

Rembétika Urban "blues" style of early twentieth-century Greece, based partly on a drugs subculture, partly on Turkish influences.

Sevillana Flamenco song and dance style, popular throughout Spain, but originating in the city of Sevilla.

Smyrneïka Style from Smyrna, now Izmir.

Türkü Folk-infused Turkish urban pop music.

Wahrani Algerian music – a more socially acceptable blend of Egyptian sounds, classical *andalous* and *rai* (Algerian).

WIND, STRINGS AND THUNDER

INSTRUMENTS OF THE MAGHREB AND MIDDLE EAST

The instruments of the Mediterranean basin and the Middle East are part of a common, musical family that gives the region its sound. David Muddyman, David Lodge and Marc Dubin sort out the definitions. Beware: certain names crop up regularly in Islamic lands but might refer to different instruments – in much the same way as "guitar" can refer to an electric bass or a Spanish classical instrument. To add to the confusion the same instrument may go by different names.

LUTES

The word lute comes from the Arabic *al 'ud*, which simply means "the wood", which the instrument is made from. The **oud** has been part of Arabic music since its early use as an accompaniment to poetry of the wandering Arab minstrels. After the arrival of Islam it played a central role in the formulation of Arab music, used by mathematicians and philosophers during the golden age as the instrument to define the scales, and in effect Arab music itself, much as the piano came to be used in Europe. From it was derived the guitar.

Sudanese star: Abdel Aziz el-Mubarak on the oud

It is said the oud owes its special tone to the birdsong absorbed by the tree from which its wood is derived – mahogany, coconut, lemon and olive among many. It was introduced to Europe via Moorish Spain in the eleventh century, retaining its five or six pairs of strings, but acquiring a longer neck and becoming the lute. In **Turkey** it's known as the *ud*, a fretless lute with eleven strings (five pairs and one single).

In **Morocco**, apart from the Arab-style oud – used in the classical Arab orchestras, and for accompanying chaabi-singers – the commonest lute is the **gimbri**, an instrument of sub-Saharan origin, very similar to instruments like the Mandinka kontingo, the Wolof khalam of Senegal, and the tidinit from Mauritania. It has a sound box covered in front with a piece of hide and a rounded, fretless neck with two or three strings. The body of the smaller treble gimbri is pear-shaped; that of the bass gimbri (also known as *sentir* or *hadjouj*) is rectangular. The Gnaouas often place a metal strip covered with rings on the end of the neck to produce a characteristic buzzing sound that resonates with bass strings. Chleuh Berbers also use a lute they call *lotar* which has a circular body, and three or four strings plucked with a plectrum.

The **Greek laoúto** is a long-necked lute found thoughout the country. While very similar to the fretless Western lute and the oud (called *oúti* in Greek, and found only in Anatolian refugee communities and in Thrace) the laoúto adds a long fretted neck and four double courses of metal strings tuned to perfect fifths.

There are several lute-like instruments in **Turkey**, the commonest of which is the **saz,** a long-necked lute, usually with seven strings (two pairs, and one set of three) played with a very thin plectrum. Several variations include the *divan saz*, with eight strings; the *cura saz*, with six strings; and the *baglama*, with seven strings on a shorter neck and a large bulbous body. The tambur lute, noted for its deep tone, has a very long neck with three strings and a large, almost rectangular body. The *cümbüs* is a twelve-stringed, fretless, banjo-type lute

Bouzóuki

with a large resonating metal bowl covered with skin or plastic, which substitutes for the Turkish ud when louder instruments are being played. Its smaller, fretted version is called the *saz tambur*.

A lute-like instrument familiar in Greece, through the watered-down music played in tavernas, is the **bouzoúki**, a long-necked lute with four pairs of strings. In its early form, which had three pairs of strings, it was similar to the Turkish saz, but the Greek virtuoso Manolis Hiotis added the fourth pair in the early 1950s to help him play even faster, an innovation which was soon adopted as standard in Greece. At the same time, the older fretboard, which could play Arab-related modes, was replaced by a guitar-style fretboard, suitable for the western scale. The instrument became famous as the principal sound of rembétika, along with the baglamás, a small, usually homemade version of the bouzoúki, favoured by jailed rembétes.

The **Moroccan buzuk**, although closely related to the Greek instrument, is nowadays usually electric, with anywhere from four to ten strings and, unlike the eastern Mediterranean version, is tuned in the western manner.

BOWED INSTRUMENTS

Across the Maghreb and Middle East, the most popular bowed instrument is the **rabab** (or rababa), a spike fiddle, rather like a viol, with the bottom half of its long, curved body covered in hide and the top in wood with a rosette sound-hole. It has two strings and in Moroccan andalous music it tends to lead the other musicians. Moroccan Chleuh musicians also use an archaic single-stringed rabab with a square neck and a sound box covered entirely in skin. In Arab classical music, the rabab is often replaced

nowadays with a violin, though the older instrument is still made and used. In Egypt there are many types of rabab, the most common having two strings and a sounding body made of an unlikely combination of coconut wood and fish skin. In Turkey, it finds a role in classical and Mevlevi dervish music.

Also often heard is the three-stringed **kamenjah**, originally a Persian fiddle adopted by the Arabs and, again, held vertically on

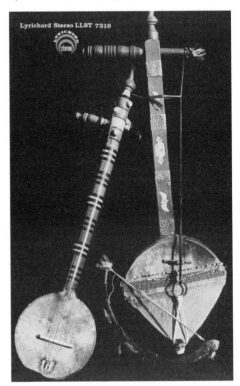

Moroccan rabab and lotar

the knee. It has an oblong wooden body and a short neck. In Turkey, it's called *kemançe* and originated with the shepherds of the Black Sea coast. The related *keman*, formerly a round-bodied version of the kemençe, is now the Turkish name by which the European violin is known.

In **Greece**, the closely related *líra* (plural *líres*) is found in two forms: an island version called *kemanés*, which is pear-shaped, fretless and normally played with a small bow; and a flat-backed, bottle-shaped type from the Pontus called *kementzé*. The líra has three metal strings tuned in fifths (G,D and A) and since the centre string is just a drone the player improvises only on the outer two. The hand playing the fretboard stops the strings with the fingernail pressing against the side of the strings rather than with the fingertips as with a violin. Tiny bells are often attached to the bow which the musician jingles for rhythmical accent. These Greek fiddles are commonly traced back to the island of Crete but they are also found on several islands in the southern Aegean, and occasionally in Macedonia.

Finally, the **yayli tambur** is a bowed version of the Turkish tambur lute, its tone somewhere between a cello and double bass.

ZITHERS AND DULCIMERS

The **kanun** (or *qanun*) is a flat trapezoid box played over the knees, with anything from seventy to a hundred strings (although as few as 42 in Turkey) arranged in courses of three and plucked with plectra attached to the fingernails. It is said it takes half a lifetime to learn to play, and another half to tune the thing, which is done with a system of levers, introduced in the eighteenth century. It is believed to have been invented by the great Arab philosopher Al Farabi, although a similar form of zither is known to have been used by the Phoenicians.

In **Egypt** the kanun commonly has 24 treble gut-string chords (72 strings) played with two plectra. Tuning it to quarter-tones produces a soft yet brilliant tone. The kanun-player enjoys a high status within the musical community and is generally the leader of the classical orchestra or *takht*. It's known in Greece as the *kanonáki*, but it is uncommon there.

The **Greek sandoúri**, a hammer dulcimer with up to 100 strings or more in courses of two or three, played with a pair of small beaters, was also hardly known until they were imported in

some numbers by Anatolian refugees after 1923. Nowadays, the sandoúri has enlarged the traditional guitar/violin duo to a threesome in the Dodecanese islands.

OBOES

Among wind instruments, the oboe-type **shawms** are the commonest kind in the region. Among them is the **ghaita**, sometimes spelled *rhaita*, a very loud instrument popular throughout the Muslim world, especially at weddings. It usually has a conical pipe made of hardwood, ending in a bell often made of metal. Its double-reeded mouthpiece is encircled by a broad ring on which the player rests his lips in order to help the circular breathing needed to obtain a continuous note. It has six to eight finger holes at the front and one at the back.

The Turkish *zurna* (*zirne* in Kurdish) is a virtually the same instrument. Also Turkish is the small, oboe-like instrument with a very large reed, called *mey* in western Turkey and *düdük* in the east and the Caucasian republics. It has a much sweeter, more melancholy tone than the zurna. NB: The düdük is also the name given to a simple duct flute which you see on sale at markets throughout Turkey.

FLUTES

Flutes are known by various names but there are two main varieties – the classical *ney* which is very hard to play and the more folk-oriented recorder-type *kaval*. **Moroccan** flutes (*nai, talawat, nira, gasba*) use a straight piece of cane, open at both ends, with between five and seven finger holes, and a thumb hole at the back.

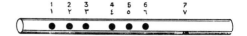

Oriental flute

The **Turkish** ney is made from calamus reed or hardwood, with six holes in front and one at the back. The **Egyptian** *nay* is found in many different sizes with two to seven finger holes. It's played obliquely, with great difficulty: continuous breathing produces the breathy tones which, according to Hollywood anyway, produce the archetypal "sound of the desert". The nay is an essential member of the takht ensemble, often also played as a solo instrument and is extremely popular in Sufi trance music.

In **Greece**, the Thracian variant is called the *kaváli* and in Epirus it's known as the *tzamáras*. The *sourávli* is a similar-sounding duct flute recorder, formerly found on Crete and one or two other islands. The Greek shepherds' *floyéra* is an obliquely held end-blown flute that provides dance music in more isolated villages.

Lastly, the **Kurdish** shepherd's flute known as the *blur* is made from a branch of mulberry or walnut, with seven or nine finger holes.

CLARINETS

Various kinds of **clarinet** are found across the region. The **Greek** *klaríno* and the **Turkish** *klarinet* are the keyed type, virtually identical to the European instrument. The klaríno was introduced to Greece in the early 1800s and is now one of the most popular melodic instruments.

The single-pipe **Egyptian** *mizmar* is a type of clarinet, played with nonstop breathing to give a continuous sound. It comes in many shapes and sizes, but they all derive from the ancient form still used by the Bedouin today. The *saiyidi mizmar* from Upper Egypt has been slighly elaborated into an outward-tapering wooden trumpet with six finger holes, and blown with full cheeks to the front.

The **Arab** *arghul* is a double-pipe clarinet, sounding almost like a bagpipe at times, and consisting of two parallel wood or cane pipes, each with a single-reed mouthpiece, five finger holes, and a horn at the end for amplification. The long simple pipe gives a constant bass drone; the other, shorter pipe has finger holes for the melody line, tuned to give an exciting off-beat "harmony". In Morocco the *arghul* is known as the *aghanin*. The slightly different instrument played in Turkey in the environs of Ererli on the western Black Sea is the *çifte* (the Turkish arghul proper being found only in a small area near the Syrian border).

BAGPIPES

The **bagpipe** arrived in some form in **Greece** from Asia in late Roman times. Today the instrument is found in two forms – the usually solo *gaída*, found throughout the Balkans, and the *tsamboúna* (or *askómandhra*). The gaída sound is produced by a single reed, called a *bibíki*, similar to that used in the clarinet

attached to the two pipes, the shorter of which has six or seven finger holes in front and one behind, and the longer of which is used purely as a drone. The chanter and drone pipes are separate, at opposite ends of a goatskin bag, as with the Scottish bagpipe. The tsamboúna is a simple bagpipe with a fuller, deeper sound than the gaída, found on Crete and a number of other islands. Its the drone pipe and melody pipe, with five finger holes, are joined and set in wax in a half-opened, larger section of reed or wood.

The very similar *tulum* is a **Turkish** bagpipe found in Rize and Artvin provinces, near the Georgian border. It generally has two pipes, each with five finger holes, inserted into a goatskin bag which the player inflates before beginning.

PERCUSSION

Rapid hand-clapping and the clashes of bells and cymbals are only part of the vast repertoire of Arab and Turkish percussion (Greek music makes much less use of percussion).

The **darabouka** is the commonest Arab and Maghreb drum, made of pottery, shaped into a cylinder, swelling out slightly at the top. The single skin, beaten with both hands, often needs to be heated before a performance to give the right tone. In **Turkey**, a similar drum goes by the names of *deblek*, *dümbelek* or *darbuka* (*demblik* in Kurdish) and can be made of wood or metal as well as pottery.

The **Egyptian tabla** is the same, goblet-shaped drum played across the knee. It has two main sounds, commonly recognized in Egypt as the dark *dum* and the light *tak*, between which there are several secondary sonorities. In Egypt it traditionally has a body of clay, and a skin made from Nile perch, although it is generally replaced today by a more robust aluminium and plastic version which sacrifices the deep, mellow sound for sheer volume, making it ideal for working in Cairo clubs. In **Morocco**, a round wooden drum with skins at both ends (beaten with a stick on one side and by hand on the other) is called the tabl but is quite different from the *tabla*. It is used only in rural, Berber music.

Other Moroccan drums include the **taarija** (a smaller version of the darabouka, held in one hand and beaten with the other like a tambourine); the treble and bass **tam-tam bongos**, played with either hands or sticks; and the **guedra**, a large drum which rests on the ground.

In **Egypt**, the **riq** is the leading percussion instrument, and puts the player firmly in charge of the rhythm, though the riq-player is traditionally held in low social esteem because of the instrument's associations with belly-dancing. The precursor of the tambourine, the riq is smaller, made of wood with an animal skin, with five to eight cymbals. The *duff*, basically a riq with no cymbals, is a double-sided tambourine, often square in shape, which has to be supported so that it can be beaten with both hands. The slightly larger *bendir* found across the region is round and wooden, 40 or 50 cm across, with two strings stretched under its skin.

Turkish drums include the large, double-sided drum called **ramzalla** or *davul* (*daoúli* in Greek) beaten each side with different-sized sticks to create a bass-and-snare-drum-like effect; the small **küdüm**, which are kettledrums played in pairs, with sticks (known as *nakkara* in Egypt); the Kurdish **def bass drum** and the **tef frame drum** which has added snares or metal rings inside the frame; and the **erbane**, a Kurdish tambourine.

Cymbals include the small Turkish cymbals called **zil** and the brass finger cymbals called **sagat**, which are widely used in Egypt; and a small Moroccan cymbal played with rods called the **nakous**.

Other percussion instruments include the pretty little **kabik** – wooden or metal spoons of Turkey – and the Moroccan double castanets used by the Gnaouas, made of metal and called **garagab**, or *karkabat*.

MARKETS, MOUSSEMS, MOSQUES

MUSIC OF THE KINGDOM OF MOROCCO

From the formal repertoire of classical andalous to the innovations of electric chaabi, David Muddyman reviews the breadth and depth of Moroccan music.

From the towering minarets that dominate the skyline of every Moroccan town – and control the ritualized lifestyles of devout Muslims – the **muezzins** call the faithful to prayer at sunrise and four more times every day. It's an unforgettable sound weaved into the aural scenery wherever you go. For visitors who've come the short distance from Europe to Morocco, the cultural change is dramatic and the music has a mesmerizing effect. Go to the centre of any town and you're likely to hear a mélange of half a dozen styles as the sound-systems of a dozen or more market stalls vye for your ear-space.

Public festivals or **moussems**, both religious and cultural, take place all over the country, while in summer, the marriage season, you'll frequently come across weddings. None would be complete without a procession around town led by musicians. The wedding band, which normally consists of oboe-style instruments, called ghaita, and drums, ends up outside the groom's house where the party breaks into dancing.

Late afternoon is the time to sit outside a café, sip hot, sweet mint tea and let the sounds permeate through you. Occasionally, cafés have live music, especially during Ramadan, when they open at dusk and stay busy all night.

THE BERBERS

The **Master Musicians of Jajouka** are Berbers, the ancient inhabitants of much of the Maghreb before the Arabs came and the first tillers of Moroccan soil. In the eighth century they retreated to the mountains in the wake of the Islamic invaders and although the countries of the Maghreb tend to be thought of as Arab, Berber influence is everywhere and most Moroccan music outside the big cities is Berber in origin.

Berber music is quite distinct from Arab-influenced forms in its rhythms, tunings, instruments and sounds. It is an ancient tradition that has been passed on orally from generation to generation. There are three main categories of Berber music: village music, ritual music and music of the professional musicians.

Village music is essentially a collective performance. Men and women of the entire village will assemble on festive occasions to

BOWLES, STONES, AND THE PIPES OF JAJOUKA

• •

One of the first westerners to record and document the music of Morocco was the writer and composer **Paul Bowles**. In the 1950s he secured funding from the American Rockefeller Foundation and the Library of Congress to spend a year recording as many examples of the different styles of Moroccan music as possible. An account of part of his travels in the Rif Mountains, entitled "The Rif, to Music", is included in his book *Their Heads are Green, Their Hands are Blue* (Peter Owen/Ecco Press). A funny and often frightening tale, it recounts some of the difficulties he had with the bureaucracy of a divided country, administered at the time by the French and Spanish authorities. The authorities feared that his recordings would show the primitive, primeval face of Moroccan society while they were trying to modernize it. Many of the recordings made by Bowles and his assistant, Christopher Wanklyn, have been made available through the Folkways label and the Library of Congress. The best, the double album "Music of Morocco" (Library of Congress, US), is hard to find nowadays, but some libraries still have copies.

During the late 1950s and early '60s Tangiers was a city where just about anything was possible, procurable and permissible. It attracted many artists, musicians and writers, including Joe Orton, William Burroughs, Brion Gysin, and the

The original Brian Jones Jajouka album

Rolling Stones. In 1968 the Stones' Brian Jones was introduced to the **Master Musicians of Jajouka** in the foothills of the Rif Mountains. For centuries the Master Musicians have enjoyed royal patronage and protection. Their awesome sound is produced by a multitude of double-headed drums and by the dark drones and melodies of the ghaita, or rhaita, a double-reed pipe or shawm similar in sound to the oboe. The leadership of the group is passed down from father to son. The present chief, Bachir Attar, inherited the post when his father died in the late 1980s.

Jones recorded the Master Musicians with the aid of psychedelic sound trickery and produced his strange "Pipes of Jajouka" album. The heady concoction of hypnotic rhythms, wailing pipes and Jones' heavy sound treatments gave what for many was close to a mystical experience – especially when stoned immobile on kif. For many years this was the only record available of Moroccan music and many people went looking for lengendary Jajouka on the Marrakesh-express trail. Although the Rolling Stones returned there in the mid-1980s to use Jajouka on their "Steel Wheel" album, the Master Musicians' next "solo" recording didn't emerge until 1990 when American bassist and composer **Bill Laswell**, travelled to Morocco. Using the latest digital technology, he produced an album of purity and power.

dance and sing together. The best-known dances are the *ahouach*, in the western High Atlas, and the *ahidus*, performed by the Chleuh Berbers in the eastern High Atlas. In each, hand drums (*bendirs*) and flutes are the only instruments used. The dance begins with a chanted prayer, to which the dancers respond in chorus, the men and women gathered in a large ring in the open air, around the musicians. The ahouach is normally performed at night in an open square of the kasbah; the dance is so complicated that the musicians meet to prepare for it in a group called *laamt* set up specially for the purpose. In the *bumzdi*, a variation of the ahouach, one or more soloists perform a series of poetic improvisations.

Ritual music is rarely absent from any rites connected with the agricultural calendar – such as moussems – or major events in the lives of individuals, such as marriage. It may also be called upon to help deal with *djinn* (evil spirits) or to encourage rainfall. Flutes and drums are usually the sole instruments, along with much syncopated hand-clapping, although communities engage professional musicians for certain events.

Village ahouach in the High Atlas

The **professional musicians**, or *imdyazn*, of the Atlas Mountains are itinerant, travelling during the summer, usually in groups of four. The leader of the group is called the *amydaz* or poet. He presents his poems, which are often improvised and give news of national or world affairs, in the village square. The poet may be accompanied by one or two members of the group on drums and *rabab*, a single-string fiddle, and by a fourth player, known as the *bououghanim*. This latter is the reed player, throwing out melodies on a ghaita, and also acts as the group's clown. Imdyazn are found in many weekly souks in the Atlas.

RWAIS

Groups of Chleuh professional musicians, from the Souss Valley, are known as **rwais**. A rwai worthy of the name will not only know all the music for any particular celebration, but also have its own repertoire of songs – again commenting on current events – and be able to improvise. A rwai ensemble can be made up of a single-string rabab, one or two *lotars* (lutes) and sometimes *nakous* (cymbals), together with a number of singers. The leader of the group, the *rayes*, is in charge of the poetry, music and choreography of the performance.

A performance will start with the *astara*, an instrumental prelude, played on rabab, giving the basic notes of the melodies that follow (this also makes it possible for the other instruments to tune to the rabab). The astara is not in any particular rhythm. Then comes the *amarg*, the sung poetry which forms the heart of the piece. This is followed by the *ammussu*, which is a sort of choreographed overture; the *tamssust*, a lively song; the aberdag, or dance; and finally the *tabbayt*, a finale characterized by an acceleration in rhythm and an abrupt end. Apart from the astara and tabbayt, the elements of a performance may appear in a different order. The arrangement and duration of the various parts are decided upon freely by the rwais.

One of the most impressive collections of rwai music is the four-CD set produced by the Maison des Cultures du Monde, in Paris, in conjunction with the Moroccan Ministry of Culture. The collection includes performances by many of Morocco's finest rwais.

THE ARABIC INFLUENCE

Morocco's classical music comes from the **Arab-Andalucían tradition**, and is to be found, with variations, throughout the Maghreb. It is thought to have first evolved, around a thousand years ago, in Córdoba, Spain (then ruled by the Moors), and its invention is usually credited to an outstanding musician from Baghdad called **Zyriab** (see Chapter Four). One of his greatest innovations was the founding of the classical suite called *nuba*, which forms what is now known as andalous music, or *al-âla*. There are, however, two other classical traditions, *milhûn* and *gharnati*, each with a distinctive style and form. Andalous, far from being the scholastic relic you might expect, is very much alive, popular and greatly loved. Television, which plays an important part in the Moroccan music scene, broadcasts nightly programmes of andalous classics during Ramadan, and people who don't have their own TVs congregate at a local café that does.

Originally there were 24 nuba directly linked with the hours in the day. Only four full and seven fragmentary nuba have been preserved in the Moroccan tradition. Complete nuba would last between six and seven hours, are rarely performed in one sitting and are usually chosen to fit the time of day or occasion. Each nuba is divided into five main parts, or *mizan*, of differing durations. These five parts correspond to the five different rhythms used within a suite. If a whole nuba were being performed then these five rhythms would be used in order: the *basît* rhythm

(6/4); *qaum wa nusf* rhythm (8/4); *darj* rhythm (4/4); *btâyhi* rhythm (8/4); and quddâm rhythm (3/4 or 6/8).

Traditionally each mizan begins with instrumental preludes – *bughya*, *m'shaliya* and *tuashia* – followed by a number of songs, the *sana'a*. There can be as many as twenty sana'a within a given mizan although for shorter performances an orchestra may only play three or four before going on to the next rhythm.

The words to many sana'a deal, though often obliquely, with subjects generally considered taboo in Islamic society like alcohol and sex – perhaps signifying archaic, pre-Islamic and nomadic roots – although others are religious, glorifying the Prophet and divine laws. The fourteenth sana'a of the basît mizan in **Al-'Ushshâq** tells of the desire for clarity following an active night entirely given over to the pleasures of sex and wine:

> *Obscure night steals away*
> *Chased by the light*
> *that sweeps up shadows*
> *The candle wax runs*
> *as if weeping tears of farewell*
> *And then, suddenly and behold,*
> *the birds are singing*
> *and the flowers smile at us.*

When the Arabs were driven out of Spain, which they had known as Al-Andalus, the different musical schools were dispersed across Morocco. The school of Valencia was re-established in Fez, that of Granada in Tetuán and Chaouen. The most famous orchestras are Fez's, led by **Abdelkrim Rais**; Tetuán's led by **Abdesadak Chekara**; and Rabat's, which was led by the great **Moulay Ahmed Loukili** until his death in 1988 and is now under **Haj Mohamed Toud**.

Other cities, however, such as Tangier and Meknes, have their own andalous orchestras and are just as fanatical about the music as the major cities. The **Orchestra of Tangier** have their own clubhouse, in the old city kasbah, where musicians sit with enthusiasts and play most evenings, in between sucking on their mint tea. Many of them seem to live only for their music. "Les fils de detroit" as they call themselves ("Sons of the Strait" – of Gibraltar), organize their own informal concerts in the kasbah museum and often play free for the local people.

A typical andalous orchestra uses the following **instruments**: rabab (fiddle), oud (lute), kamenjah (violin-style instrument played vertically on the knee), kanun (zither), darabouka (metal or pottery goblet drums), and taarija (tambourine). Each orchestra has featured unusual instruments from time to time. Clarinets, flutes, banjos and pianos have all been used with varying degrees of success.

MILHÛN AND GHARNATI

Milhûn is a semiclassical form of sung poetry - a definition which sounds a lot drier than it really is. Musically it has many links with andalous music, having adopted the same modes as al-âla orchestras and, like them, uses string instruments and percussion but the result can be quite wild and danceable.

The milhûn suite comprises two parts: the *taqsim* (overture) and the *qassida* (sung poems). The taqsim is played on the oud or violin in free rhythm, and introduces the mode in which the piece is set. The qassida is divided into three parts: the *al-aqsâm*, being verses sung solo; the *al-harba*, the refrains sung by the chorus; and the *al-drîdka*, a chorus where the rhythm gathers speed and eventually announces the end of the piece. The words of the qassida can be taken from anywhere – folk poetry, mystical poems or nonsense lines used for their rhythmic quality.

Al-Thami Lamdaghri, who died in 1856, was one of the greatest milhûn composers. He is credited with many well-known songs including "Al-Gnawi" (The Black Slave), "Aliq Al-Masrûh" (The Radiant Beauty) and "Al-'Arsa" (The Garden of Delight):

> *Open your eyes*
> *Taste the delights and the generous nature*
> *Of this heavenly garden*
> *The branches of the wonderful trees intertwine*
> *Like two lovers meeting again*
> *And totter about, heady with happiness*
> *The smile of flowers,*
> *Mingled with the tears of the dew*
> *Recall the melancholic exchange*
> *Of a sad lover and his joyous beloved*
> *Birds sing in the branches*
> *Like as many lutes and rababs.*

The milhûn orchestra generally consists of oud, kamenjah, swisen (a small, high-pitched folk lute related to the gimbri), the hadjouj (a bass version of the swisen), taarija, darabouka and handqa (small brass cymbals). As well as musicians, an orchestra will normally feature a number of singers. Some of the best known are Abdelkrim and Saïd Guennoun of Fez, Haj Husseïn and Abdallah

The Gharnati Ensemble of Rabat

Ramdani of Meknes, and Muhammad Berrahal and Muhammad Bensaïd of Saleh.

Gharnati, the third music of Arab-Andalucían tradition, is mainly played in Algeria but there are two important centres in Morocco – the capital, Rabat, and Oujda, near the Algerian border. As with al-âla, gharnati music is arranged in suites or nuba, of which there are twelve complete and four unfinished suites. Again pieces are divided into five mizan, each with its own rhythm, and each having its own set of songs or sana'a, many of which sing of love. The order of rhythms is *msadder* (4/4); *btâyhi* (4/8); *darj* (6/8); *insirâf* (5/8); and *makhlas* (6/8).

The gharnati orchestra consists of plucked and bowed instruments together with percussion: the usual ouds and kamenjahs supplemented by the addition of banjo, mandolin and Algerian lute, the kwîtra.

Music in orthodox Islam is frowned upon unless it is singing God's praises. As well as the chants of the Koran, which are improvised on a uniform beat, the **adhan**, or call to prayer, and the songs about the life of the prophet Muhammad, there is another entire range of prayers and ceremonies belonging to the Sufi brotherhoods, or *tarikas*, in which music is seen as a means of getting closer to Allah. These include the music used in processions to the tombs of saints during moussems.

The aim is for those present to reach a state of mystical ecstasy, often through trance. In a private nocturnal ceremony called the *hadra*, the Sufi brothers attain a trance by chanting the name of Allah (*zikr*) or dancing in a ring holding hands. The songs and music are irregular in rhythm, and quicken to an abrupt end. Some brotherhoods play for alms in households that want to gain the favour of their patron saint.

BROTHERHOODS

The **Gnaoua brotherhood** is a religious confraternity whose members are descendants of slaves brought from across the Sahara by the Arabs. They have devotees all over Morocco, though the strongest concentrations are in the south, particularly in Marrakesh.

The brotherhood claim spiritual descent from Sidi Bilal, an Ethiopian who was the Prophet's first muezzin. Most Gnaoua ceremonies, or *deiceba*, are held to placate spirits, good and evil, who are inhabiting a person or place. They are often called in cases of mental disturbance or to help treat someone stung by a scorpion. These rites have their origins in sub-Saharan Africa, and an African influence is evident in the music itself. The principal instrument, the *gimbri* or *sentir*, is a long-necked lute almost identical to instruments found in West Africa. The other characteristic sound of Gnaoua music is the *garagab*, a pair of metal castanets, which beat out a trance-like rhythm.

Gnaoua trance musicians

Jilala are another brotherhood who are devotees of Moulay Abdelkader Jilal. Their music is even more hypnotic and mysterious than that of the Gnaoua and seems to come from a different plane of existence. The plaintive cycling flute (the *qsbah*) and the mesmeric beats of the bendir (frame drums) carry you forward unconsciously. It is said that while in a trance many people, including the celebrated Moroccan writer Mohammed Mrabet, have withstood the touch of burning coals and the deep slashes of a Moroccan dagger, afterwards showing no injury or pain.

Nowadays, Gnaoua music can be heard at festivals and in the entertainment squares of Marrakesh and elsewhere. Gnaoua music, featuring the wonderful **Mustapha Baqbou**, has been superbly recorded by Bill Laswell and issued on Axiom.

CHAABI

All of the foregoing musical forms have had their impact on the most popular music of Morocco – **chaabi**, which means simply "popular" and today covers a bewildering mixture of styles. The music that takes this name started out as street music performed in the squares and souks, but it can now be heard in cafés, at festivals and at weddings. Many towns have café-meeting places where the locals sing songs in the evenings (some cafés keep their own instruments for musicians who can't afford their own) and, at its more basic level, chaabi is played by itinerant musicians, who turn up at a café and bang out a few songs. These might include a milhûn song, followed by a Hamid

Zahir, maybe an Egyptian song of Uum Kalthoum, followed by one from the latest cassette by leading bands Nass El-Ghiwane or Jil Jilala (see below). Café songs usual finish with a *leseb*, which is often twice the speed of the first part of the song and forms a background for syncopated clapping, shouting and dancing.

During the 1970s a more sophisticated version of chaabi began to emerge, with groups setting themselves up in competition with the commercial Egyptian and Lebanese music which dominated the market (and the radio) at the time. These groups were usually made up of two stringed instruments – a *hadjouj* (bass gimbri) and a lute – and a bendir and darabouka or tam-tam as percussion. As soon as they could afford it, they updated their sound and image with the addition of congas, buzuks, banjos and even electric guitars. The hadjuj and bendir, however, remain indispensable.

Their music is a fusion of Arab, African and modern western influences, combining Berber music with elements taken from the Arab milhûn and Sufi rituals, Gnaoua rhythms and the image of European groups. Voices play an important part, with the whole group singing, either in chorus or backing a lead soloist. Lyrics deal with love as well as social issues, and occasionally carry messages which have got

Gimbri player Mustapaha Baqbou

their authors into trouble with the authorities – even jailed. The three most popular groups of this kind are from Casablanca – Jil Jilala, Lem Chaheb and Nass El-Ghiwane.

Jil Jilala, which means "Generation of Jilali", was formed in 1972 as a Sufi theatre group devoted to their leader, Jilali. Their music is based on the milhûn style, using poetry as a reference (and starting) point. More recently they have worked with Gnaoua rhythms and they occasionally use a *ghaita* in their line-up. The group's central figures are the conga-player and lyricist Mohammed Darhem, and Hassan Mista, who plays an amplified, fretless *buzuk*. They are rhythmically accompanied by two bendir players – Moulai Tahar and Abdel Krim Al-Kasbaji – and have recorded with a variety of hadjuj players, including Mustapha Baqbou.

Nass El-Ghiwane, the most politicized of the three chaabi-fusion groups, lays great emphasis on the words of its recitatives and verses and chorus. The band's music, again, combines Sufi and Gnaoua influences while the words may lambast a lazy government official or talk of social injustices. Originally a five-piece band of banjo, hadjouj, bendir, tam-tam and darabouka, the band was fronted by lead singer **Boujmia**, a man with a soaring, powerfully melodic voice. He was killed in a car crash in the early 1980s and the rest of the group have continued as a four-piece ever since. There has been a retrospective cassette from Boujmia's time released in Morocco on the Hassania label, which includes "The Table", the song that made them famous:

Where are they now?
The friends who sat at my table
Where are they now?
All the friends that I loved
Where are the glasses?
Where are the glasses we drank from?
Friendship can be bitter
But it was also sweet to sit at my table

Lem Chaheb is probably the Moroccan group best known abroad, through its work with the German band Dissidenten (two of whose members play and record with them). Featuring the virtuoso figure of guitarist and buzuk player Lamrani Moulay Cherif, they are also the most westernized of the three big names in electric chaabi.

In the 1980s another generation of groups emerged which combines traditional and modern influences, this time based in Marrakesh but concentrating on Gnaoua rhythms. The most successful of these is **Muluk el Hwa** (The Demon of Love), a group of Berbers who used to play in the Djemaa el Fna in Marrakesh. Their line-up is totally acoustic: bendir, tam-tam, sentir, buzuk, garagab and hand claps. The only album available in Europe is "Xara Al-Andalus" (Erde Records, Germany),

One of Lem Chaheb's numerous cassettes

LOOK FOR ANOTHER LOVER

．．．．．．．．．．．．．．．．．．．．．．

Some chaabi artists have remained firmly traditional in their use of instruments, but forward-looking in their musical approach. One such example is the sensational singer **Najat Aatabou**. She is proud of her Berber heritage and uses traditional Berber rhythms (even though she now sings in Arabic or French), but is very outspoken about certain traditional values and often expresses her criticism in her lyrics. The inequality between men and women and the injustice of traditional family rules are two of her recurrent themes, but she is still more than capable of writing beautiful love songs. When her ensemble use electric instruments they blend beautifully with more traditional oud and bendir.

Aatabou's first release, the eye-opening "J'en ai marre" (I am sick of it), sold 450,000 copies. Her second release, "Shouffi Rhirou" (Look for Another Lover), and every subsequent release have sold more than half a million copies, and she is now a huge star throughout the Maghreb and can fill large venues in Europe. A wonderful compilation CD, "The Voice of the Atlas" (which includes "Shouffi Rhirou"), is available on GlobeStyle records.

a collaboration with the Spanish group Al Tall. The album features medieval Valencian music and Arabic poetry from Andalucía, which deals with subjects still relevant today – the whims of rulers, exile, love and wine.

Nass El Hal, formed in 1986, offer two shows – one using a traditional acoustic line-up with buzuk and violin, the other with drum kit and electric guitar. Their repertoire included peasant harvest and hunting songs, and religious dances.

Other groups of note include **Izanzaren**, from Casablanca, and **Shuka**, who play everything from al-âla to Gnaoua music.

OTHER FUSIONS – AND RAI

Moroccan music is an ideal starting point for all kinds of fusion experiments, and in the 80s and 90s they have come thick and fast.

The most successful, perhaps, has been that of the Berlin-based **Dissidenten**. Before their collaboration with Lem Chaheb, they had worked with Mohammed Zain, a star player of the nai (flute) from Tangier who belongs to a Sufi sect, and Gnaoua gimbri players Abdellah el Gourd, Abderkader Zefzaf and Abdalla Haroch. Their albums with Lem Chaheb have placed a genuine Moroccan element into a rock context.

A number of Moroccan singers and musicians have also crossed over into 1990s dance music. **Yosefa Dahari** is a name to look out for in this respect, with her work (sung in Maghrebi and English) on the Worldly Dance Music label with David Rosenthal and Gil Freeman. **Hassan Hakmoun** is another – a New York-based gnaoua musician who mixes it in the city with all manner of ideas and musicians. Also resident in

New York these days is Bachir Attar, a young scion of the Jajouka troupe, who has recorded with jazz saxophonist Maceo Parker under the productive genius of Bill Laswell.

Over in Britain, **Sidi Seddiki**, Rabat-born but a Londoner since childhod, has produced perhaps the finest blend of Moroccan music and western pop to date: strong, catchy songs, drawing on chaabi, and using a superb classical flautist. Belgium, meanwhile, is the base of blind multi-instrumentalist **Hassan Erraji**, who has released a trio of jazz-flavoured discs with his multicultural groups Belcikal (now disbanded) and Arabesque. he is well worth seeing live, too, with his startling juggling with the bendir.

The **Spaniards** have concentrated mainly on Arab-Andalucían music. There have been several notable collaborations between flamenco musicians and Andalucían orchestras, such as that of **José Heredia Maya** and **Enrique Morente** with the Tetuán Orchestra (Ariola, Spain), and **Juan Peña Lebrijano** with the Tangier Orchestra (GlobeStyle, UK).

Rai has always been a music that Moroccan kids could identify with, and there are now many good Moroccan rai singers including **Cheb Kader**, **Cheb Mimoun,** and the mysterious **Chaba Zahouania**. The latter is said to be forbidden by her family from being photographed – a fact that record companies have capitalized on by using alluring models for the cassette sleeves. The influence of rai is also heard in the music that originates in the Oujda area, the closest Moroccan town to the Algerian border. Listen out for **Rachid Briha** and **Hamid M'Rabati**.

DISCOGRAPHY

CLASSICAL MOROCCAN MUSIC

⊙ **Juan Peña Lebrijano and the Orquesta Andalusi de Tanger** *Encuentros* (GlobeStyle, UK). A stunning cross-cultural blend that combines the passion of flamenco with the beauty and grace of andalous music.

⊙ **Orchestre Moulay Ahmed** *Loukili de Rabat Nuba Al-'Ushshâq* (Maison des Cultures du Monde, France). Six-CD set. The only problem with this is the price (£75/$120). It's quite an experience, finely presented and with informative notes.

⊙ **Ustad Massano Tazi** *Musique Classique Andalouse de Fès* (Ocora, France). Again, beautifully recorded and presented. Includes "Nuba Hijaz Al-Kabir" and "Nuba Istihilal".

⊙ **Various** *Maroc: Anthologie d'Al-Melhûn* (Maison des Cultures du Monde, France). A three-CD set containing performances from many of Morocco's finest milhûn singers. A good introduction.

CHAABI AND CONTEMPORARY

⊙ **Najat Aatabou** *The Voice of the Atlas* (GlobeStyle, UK). A superb collection of some of Najat's best-loved songs, including "Shouffi Rhirou" which has been covered brilliantly by the 3 Mustaphas 3.

⊙ **Hassan Erraji** *Nikriz, la Dounia* and *Marhaba* (Riverboat, UK). Erraji is an oud-player, who fuses his classical training with accessible jazz. "Nikriz" is a real showcase for his talents; "la Dounia" has a starker, and more Arabic content; "Marhaba", the latest, is more song-based, upbeat and very listenable.

⊙ **Lem Chaheb** *Lem Chaheb* (Club du Disques Arabe, France). A compilation from the late 1980s. The band's usual line-up of guitar, buzuk, percussion is augmented by trumpets and synthesizers provided by two members of Dissidenten.

⊙ **Sidi Seddiki** *Shouf!* (GlobeStyle, UK). A fine debut album of chaabi meets pop from a London-based musician.

ⓒ **Yosefa Dahari** *Yosefa* (Worldly Dance, UK). Just what the label says: dance music with English and Maghrebi songs. A bit of an exotica product but one with promise.

GNAOUA AND JILALA

ⓒ **Various** *Gnawa Night – Music of the Marrakesh Spirit Masters* (Axiom, UK). Gnaoua music at its evocative best, recorded by Bill Laswell.

ⓒ **Various** *Moroccan Trance Music* (Sub Rosa, Belgium). Not for the faint hearted, this is intense gnaoua and jilala music, combined with some of Paul Bowles' personal recordings.

INSTRUMENTALISTS

ⓒ **The Master Musicians of Jajouka** *Apocalypse Across the Sky* (Axiom, UK). Without the electronic trickery of Brian Jones' seminal album, the power and clarity of these remarkable performers stands out all the more on Bill Laswell's outing.

Hmaoui Abd El-Hamid *La Flûte de l'Atlas* (Arion, France). Hypnotic and haunting.

TOP TEN MOROCCAN CASSETTES

In Morocco, cassettes of all kinds are readily available in any market – and you can buy videos of many artists, too. The following are a personal top ten to ask for (in order of priority).

Nass El-Ghiwane *Nass El-Ghiwane* (Hassania, Morocco). The only remaining recordings with singer Boujmia. Powerful and hypnotic.

Najat Aatabou *Najat Aatabou* (Hassania, Morocco). A traditional line-up of oud, violin and drums accompany Najat's magnificent voice.

Jil Jilala *The Candle* (Disques Gam, Morocco). Poetic introductions to a set of atmospheric songs.

Abdelkrim Rais and the Orchestra of Fez *Vol 5* (Fassi Disques, Morocco). "Nuba Maya", which is featured on this cassette, has some of the most beautiful melodies in the andalous tradition.

Hamid Zahir *Hamid Zahir* (Tichkaphone, Morocco). From the old school of chaabi singers. A rich textural orchestra of traditional instruments and vibrant drumming carry Hamid through an uplifting selection of songs and fiery lesebs.

Lem Chaheb *Lem Chaheb* (Nissim, Morocco). This early tape includes the wonderfully infectious "Nari Nari" which was later covered by Dissidenten as "Radio Arab" – the Moroccan equivalent of the Byrds' jangling guitar sound.

L'Haj L'Houcine Toulali *L'Haj L'Houcine Toulali* (Tichkaphone, Morocco). Popular milhûn at its best. His orchestration is some of the best and the melodies stay with you for a long time.

Orchestra Faysel *Orchestra Faysel* (Forkafane, Morocco). A very odd mixture. Synthesizer, drum machine, buzuk and bendir lead the trance dance Berber beats. If the Velvet Underground had been Moroccan, they might have sounded like this.

Mohamed Bajaddoub *L'Age d'Or de la Musique Andalouse Vol 2* (Disques Gam, Morocco). Beautiful arrangement of andalous suites. Very inspiring stuff.

Nass El Ghiwane *Chants d'espoir* (Hassania, Morocco). From the late 1980s, a haunting collection of long narratives that draws you in even though you may not understand the lyrics.

BLACK AND WHITE WAYS

MUSIC OF THE MOORS

David Muddyman listens to the music of a country on the far western shores of the Arab-speaking world.

Mauritania is a huge territory on the west coast of North Africa, between Morocco and Senegal, the meeting place of West Africa and the Maghreb. Most of it is desert, traditionally barren camel and goat-herding country. In recent years droughts have caused a steady flow of nomads towards the cities. Now over ninety percent of the population lives in or around the cities and the population of Nouakchott, the capital, has increased from around 20,000 in the 1960s to nearly half a million today.

The country's name comes from its dominant ethnic group, the Moors (Maures in French), broadly divided into "white" Bidan (who claim ancestry from north of the Sahara) and "black" Haratin whose physical ancestry lies in Saharan and sub-Saharan Africa and who were traditionally vassals of the Bidan noble class. But social status in Mauritania is considerably more than a question of skin colour. Until recently Moorish society has had a strict hierarchical class system with musicians – *iggawin* – occupying the lowest rung beneath the warriors (hassans), merchants and others. Being a hereditary caste, their skills are handed down from father to son, or mother to daughter. Marriages almost always take place between people of the same class. The men always have the word *ould* between their names, meaning "son of", and likewise women are *mint* – "daughter of". Compared with most Arabic-speaking countries, the women of Mauritania have more freedom, reflecting their Berber (indigenous, pre-Arab, North Africans) and African heritage.

One traditional task of the iggawin was to follow the warriors into battle singing of their bravery and encouraging them into battle. At other times they would entertain their patrons with praise songs about the great deeds of their ancestors or act as social historians, poets and jokers. This is much like the role of the *griots* and *jali* in West Africa (see p.245). Before the days of radio it was also their job to act as newscasters, touring the villages reciting news from the outside world to musical accompaniment. They also sang epic songs which were used as teaching stories for the entertainment of children and adults alike. Today, however, professional musicians can be employed by anyone in return for money or other gifts. Since the advent of the tape recorder it has been traditional for patrons to allow the recording of the entertainment for their own use, the recordings passing into the ownership not of the musicians but of the patrons. Many songs of the iggawin repertoire are Middle Eastern in character and others are simple enough for the audience to take up the chorus.

There are different sets of instruments for men and women. The traditional male instrument is the *tidinit*, a small hourglass shaped lute with four strings, two long strings on which the melody is played and two short ones which provide a drone-like accompaniment. This is very similar to the other lutes found in West Africa, such as the *Wolof khalem* and the *Mandinka ngoni*. In recent years it has increasingly been replaced by the electric guitar. The main instrument used by the women is the *ardin*, which looks like a back-to-front kora. It has a body made from half a large gourd covered with skin. A curved wooden pole is inserted through the body and between 10 and 14 strings are attached to the pole by means of leather thongs. Other instruments used by the iggawin are the *t'bol*, a large kettledrum, and, occasionally, the *daghumma*, a long hollowed-out gourd covered by a net of beads which acts as a rattle.

BLACK, WHITE OR SPOTTED

Moorish music is based on a sophisticated system of modal music which derives from Arabic music traditions. Male musicians will tend to play in one of three "ways" (the "black way", "white way" and the "spotted way"). Within each way there are strict rules that must be observed, such as the succession of modes that a musician must play in a strict order. Each way consists of five modes, the first four corresponding to either the life cycle or to a mood or emotion. It is believed that the fifth mode refers to a higher state of consciousness and, according to life cycle, the time after death. The modes are called *karr*, *fagu*, *lakhal*, *labyad* and *lebtayt*. Female musicians are not bound by the same rules and use all the different ways at once.

One of the most successful musicians to have emerged from the Moorish tradition is the female singer **Dimi Mint Abba**. Since winning first prize in Tunis at the **International Umm Kalthum Song Contest** in 1977 she has won international acclaim as well as remaining a favourite at home. Dimi was born in 1958 to distinguished musical parents. He father was asked to compose the national anthem when Mauritania gained independence from France in 1960. During her childhood Dimi would sing and accompany her father and mother on the t'bol, and from the age of ten she was taught to play the ardin by her mother. In 1976 she was invited to sing on Mauritanian radio, and people first discovered what a stunning voice she had. In 1976 she won a song contest held by Mauritanian radio and this led to her being entered for the Oum Kalthoum Contest in Tunis. Since then she has toured Africa and Europe and has gained a reputation as one of the Muslim world's greatest singers.

While in Europe in 1990 she recorded an evocative album for World Circuit. At the time she was touring with her husband **Khalifa Ould Eide**, who played guitar and tidinit, and two daughters from a previous marriage, **Zeyrouz Mint Seylami** and **Garmi Mint Abba**, who dance, sometimes with remarkable eroticism, and play drums. The song that won the Oum Kalthoum Contest, "Sawt Elfan" ("Art's Plume"), is included on the album. Written by Ahmedou Ould Abdel Qadir, it tells how the artist's work, in many ways, is more important than the work of the warriors:

Art's Plume is a balsam, a weapon and a guide enlightening the spirit of men.
Indeed, it is the world of truth living between the flickerings of visions
and the folds of the imagination.
Indeed, between the flickerings of visions, the fold of the imagination,

and the eyes of the impossible,
Winged songs in rapture float aboard a vessel
of hopes!

Other recordings of Mauritanian music are available. There are three albums of traditional music available on Ocora records and another four on Safari Ambiance. The Ocora selections feature a double album, "Hodh Oriental", of music played in "the black and white ways"; the other, "Musique Maure", features a wider variety of sounds. The Safari Ambiance albums are much harder to find. Three feature **Saidou Ba**, a musician who plays the hadou (or hoddu, the African guitar) in a style reminiscent of the blues; the other features **Bacar Cheike Drame**.

Of the modern singers making records, the most interesting is **Tahra**, who made the curious album, "Yamen Yamen" in 1989. With songs sung in a mixture of Arabic, French and English and a hi-tech Moorish-tinged backing, on first hearing anyone would be forgiven for having no idea where this comes from.

Dimi Mint Abba and Khalifa Ould Eide with Dimi's daughters, Zeyrouz and Garmi

DISCOGRAPHY

Khalifa Ould Eide and Dimi Mint Abba *Moorish Music from Mauritania* (World Circuit, UK). Beautiful and evocative. If you haven't seen them on tour then this goes some of the way to giving an insight to their special sound. Notice the flamenco-style hand-clapping here (though the direction of influence is likely to have been from Moorish to flamenco).

Tahra *Yamen Yamen* (EMI, France). An intriguing album of Mooro-tech with Jean-Philippe Rykiel on synth.
Various *Musique Maure* (Ocora, France). A pleasant and diverse, if not exactly earth-shattering introduction.
Various *Mauritanie Vols 1 and 2 – Anthologie de la Musique Maure / Hodh Oriental* (Ocora, France). Concentrate on the black and white ways for solo instruments and voice.

THURSDAY NIGHT FEVER

ALGERIA'S HAPPIEST HOUR

Andy Morgan, with help from Mark Kidel, uncovers the roots of rai, Algeria's young music of dissent, and looks at its future prospects in the light of the country's shifting fortunes.

It all started with a blackbird and a jealous musician. Back in the ninth century AD, in the city of Baghdad, a distant predecessor of Saddam Hussein by the name of Khalif Haroun el-Rashid fell in love with the singing of a freed slave called Zyriab, known as "the Blackbird". The chief musician of el-Rashid's court, Ishaq el-Mosili, was bitterly envious and the Blackbird had to fly for his life. He travelled the length of the Arabic world and fetched up in Córdoba in southern Spain, where he dreamt up and composed the *nuba*, the 24 long suites governed by different modes and rhythms which form the basis of classical andalous music.

After the expulsion of the Arabs from Andalucía in 1492, Arab musicians found jobs in the various courts of North Africa, where they continued to play in the strictly regulated and measured Andalucían style. By the early years of this century, after four centuries of evolution, the classical andalous style had acquired local colourings and variations. In eastern Algeria, around the town of Constantine, it had become **maluf**, in the western part of the country around Tlemcen and Oran it had become **hawsi** and **andalous**. This "classical" music was played for the elite of muftis, pashas and other dignitaries.

Andalous orchestras would tinkle away on their ouds, rababas and daraboukas in the palaces and homes of the gentry, singing of days long gone and pausing for a little mint tea and sherbert. It was a refined style which used the symbolic language of classical Arabic religious and secular poetry as well as the more populist form of poetry called *chir al-milhûn*.

One of the first Khaled cassettes

TELL IT LIKE IT IS

Meanwhile out in the streets of the coastal regions of western Algeria, local **country musicians** were doing their thing for the masses. Dressed in long white jellabas and turbans, these cheikhs (the same word as "sheikh", meaning "honorable sir") used classical and chir al-milhûn poetry set to a very basic two- or three-chord rural music with strong pounding beats. They were accompanied by players of a hard rosewood desert flute, the *gasba*, and a small metallic drum called the *guellal*. Their stage was any busy marketplace such as the *tahtaha* of Medina Jdida, Oran's Arab quarter, where they performed among magicians, story-tellers, political agitators, beggars, teeth-pullers, snake-charmers and the rest of the motley crew that frequented such places. Their audience, mostly illiterate farmers and shepherds in from the sticks, would shout out "Ya rai" when they got excited, akin to someone at an R&B gig hollering "Oh, yeah" or "Tell it like it is". The word *rai* means "opinion", "advice" or just plain "discourse".

The cheikhs, however – men such as Cheikh Hamada or Cheikh el-Khaldi – were somewhat stuffy and retro. They were from society's "guardian" class, men with strong standards of morality and decency. Their repertoire consisted largely of innocuous love ballads or tales of old heroes and Muslim saints. They were looked on benignly by the colonial French authorities, who sought to discourage any kind of subversion or lewd talk in the local arts. Many cheikhs led a comfortable coexistence with their French overlords and were even collaborators, generally loath to step out of line. Hamada, to be fair, was an exception, and became a stern critic of the colonial administration. One of his sons was executed by the French.

The early decades of the century were a time of great change and social upheaval in Algeria. A new urban underclass of poor factory and brewery workers, illiterate and rootless for the most part, was gradually coming into being. No-one seemed prepared to sing about the stresses of poverty, rural immigration, colonial misrule, unemployment, overcrowding, crime, prostitution and the other daily concerns of this new group of people. No-one that is until the cheikhas, the women singers, hit town.

The town in question was **Oran**, capital of the colonial province of Oranie in western Algeria. A modern seaport, known as the "little Paris" of North Africa, it had had a reputation for being one big fun-house ever since the Spanish invaded it centuries ago and kept women there to entertain the troops. The city was divided into separate quarters – French, Jewish, Spanish and Arab – each with its own atmosphere and music. The Jewish preference was for the classical hawsi music of Tlemcen. Their stars were Saoud L'Oranais, Larbi Bensari and Reinnette L'Oranaise, who performed every night in the cafés and "cabarets" of the quarter. Muslims were forbidden by the French administration to sell alcohol in their own cafés so they crossed to the Jewish and Spanish quarters to get it. French officials went to the Jewish cafés to get their shot of oriental dancing and maybe a little something else. The various communities, between whom music was often the best point of contact, coexisted peacefully enough, hustling for their daily bread. It was in this steamy seafront world of hash dens, cantinas, Moorish cafés, bars and bordellos that the cheikhas established their dominion.

In the topsy-turvy society of 1920s Oran, Muslim women were the exploited of the exploited. If you had the misfortune to be born poor and female you had to learn survival in hostile surroundings. The constant struggle to preserve female honour was lost by many unsuspecting young women and social ostracism was the usual result. And if they had in mind a singing or dancing career then polite society would turn its back on them.

The cheikhas who adopted the rural rai style of the cheikhs were generally the daughters and wives of peasants or manual labourers. Known as the "women of the cold shoulder" – because they had a Madonna-esque approach to clothing and were beyond the pale of "decent" society – they had a lot to say and very little to lose. Quickly ditching the classical and poetic language of the cheikhs, which was purely men's talk anyway, the cheikhas adopted a patchwork of Oranian street slang, interwoven with bits of French and clichés of the chir al-milhûn canon. The cheikhas gave up their surnames when they went public and were known instead by nicknames or birth place names.

THE PIAF OF RAI

One particularly outré young woman called Saadia, from the country town of Relizane in Oranie, was gathering notoriety and pre-eminence among the new breed of female singers. An orphan, she had survived an uncomfortable youth and ended up dancing with a troupe of cheikhs. From dancing she graduated to singing. Having taken refuge from a rain storm in a café during a local function one day, she was recognized by a group of French "fans" and with her limited French she started ordering rounds, crying "Remitti pan ache, madame, remitti!" ("Another shandy, barman, another"). She became known as **Cheikha Remitti**, the Piaf of rai.

Cheikha Remitti was truly fearless. With her gruff, booming voice, nurtured by cigarettes and booze, she poured out her heart to her mostly male audiences without any frills or fancy wordplay. She went from venue to venue surrounded by a male retinue of *gasba* (flute)-players, *guellal* drummers and a *berrah*, a kind of master of ceremonies who took donations from the audience in return for dedications and requests. In common with other cheikhas Remitti deliberately cultivated a mystique of sulphurous, exotic living, tempting other women to throw caution to the winds and follow her ways. The directness of her songs hit the average Muslim listener like a bolt between the eyes. Instead of singing "My beautifully coloured bird is nestling in your fig tree" she would sing "It was a single bed and my lover and I slept in it/He scratched my back and I gave him my all" (from "A Habib el-Chatar").

Not surprisingly much scorn was heaped on her head. Only at the all-women wedding "parties" could women let themselves go in such a way. The *meddahates* – groups of women musicians – were (and still are) an essential part of the three-day wedding feast. Outcasts, unmarried and therefore able to sing of carnal love, they share some elements of the modern rai repertoire. But to behave that way has always been unacceptable in any other context.

The cheikhs considered Remitti immoral, even criminal, for her inappropriate behaviour. And the French authorities dismissed her and her like as an all-round, unsettling bad influence. The underground agitators and mujaheddin of the emerging independence movement considered her brand of rai anti-revolutionary and apolitical, drugging the people with retrograde thoughts of debauchery and alcoholic oblivion. Remitti could not have cared less and continued defiantly to celebrate the everyday woes and occasional pleasures of the workers and peasants who flocked to the cafés where she performed. In

N'sel Fik (You belong to me)

Sahraoui: Oh lord, I was speechless, your look stunned me, my love.
Refrain: I love you, apple of my eye, I adore you my love.

Fadela: Oh lord, I was taken aback by his beauty and my heart fell for him.
Refrain: I love you...

Sahraoui: Oh lord, without the suffering caused by your love, none of this would have happened to me, my beauty.
Refrain: I love you...

Fadela: Only God can appease my pain, humane only to silence my suffering.
Refrain: I love you...

Sahraoui/Fadela: Part of you belongs to me, no... All of you belongs to me.
Refrain: I love you...

Fadela and Sahraoui (Translated by Nourredine Gafaiti and Andy Morgan).

Chaba Fadela and Cheb Sahraoui

1936 she made her first recordings for Pathé and her fame gradually spread.

By this time, 78rpm records by the great Egyptian artists Umm Kalthoum and Mohammed Abd el-Wahab were beginning to find huge popularity all across the Maghreb and new styles of city music were evolving. In Oran the Egyptian sounds were blended with a little classical andalous and a pinch of rai and the result was *wahrani*, a new urban hybrid whose greatest exponent was Belaoui al-Houari. His new Oranian folklore quickly became the rage and was an important forebear of modern pop rai.

Ever since the early 1930s, the battle for an independent and free Algeria had been gathering pace. In the mid-1950s the volcano of revolutionary fervour erupted and insurrection gripped the country. The cheikhas were quick to add their voice to the protesting chorus. In the words of Remitti: "The FLN (Front de Libération National) didn't have to contact me. Straight after the uprising of November 1st 1954 I began to sing about the armed struggle. For we, the generation of Cheikhs Hamada and Madani, were prepared for the armed struggle. We had been following the revolutionary speeches of Messali el-Hadj. Cheikha Kheira Guendil was the first, I believe, to brave the colonial police and sing about a free Algeria in public."

HICK MUSIC GOES POP

With the eventual capitulation of De Gaulle and Algerian independence in 1962 there was a brief period of nationwide jubilation, street-partying and riotous merrymaking. Very soon, however, a cloud descended on the young nation. The Marxist theoreticians of the new Boumedienne regime were not partial to outspoken libertine musicians championing sexual freedom and the good life. Their cultural policy was to promote a respectable "national" musical genre and not surprisingly they opted to place the classical andalous style mixed with a little of the local chaabi music of Algiers on this vaulted pedestal. Rai was, after all, hick music, sung by a bunch of hooligan yokels with stiff Oranian accents who were unworthy of any role in the sacred Algerian patrimony.

In **Oran**, things were seen a bit differently. One artist in particular, Ahmed Saber, continued to parody the shortcomings of the new government in songs which mixed rai, wahrani and a little rumba. He dared to criticize Ben Bella, the hero of the revolution, and spent several periods in jail for his recklessness, eventually dying in poverty in 1967. Boumedienne shut the regional TV station of Oran, prohibited alcohol and put a ban on large concerts or gatherings of rai musicians. Rai was locked behind closed doors.

This was not an unfamiliar place for rai to find itself. Rai was always most comfortable in small gatherings such as marriages, circumcision feasts or simple family get-togethers in which the singer would improvise stories about the lives of the people present, all of whom she or he knew personally, and the berrah would go around cajoling "tips" out of the audience. In these surroundings rai could be poured out uninhibited without fear or recrimination. Apart from anything else, the gasba flutes and guellal drums of the traditional rai orchestra were totally unsuited to large concert halls.

This last fact hadn't escaped the attention of the younger generation and especially of two young musicians from Oran, multi-instrumentalist (but mainly trumpeter) **Bellemou Messaoud** and singer **Belkacem Bouteldja**. Independently, both dreamed of updating the rai sound to make it more suitable for the swinging youth of the mid-1960s who were getting hooked on the latest sounds from Europe and America. The French *beau mec* Johnny Halliday played the Regent Cinema on Oran's seafront strip and dozens of hopeful "rocker" combos with names like The Students or The Vultures (the latter fronted by the Ahmed brothers, later key rai producers) began boogieing to the beat of The Beatles, James Brown and Otis Redding.

Rai had to be made danceable to retain its appeal. Bellemou and other musicians started experimenting by substituting the gasba with sax or trumpet and the small guellal with the much larger, booming tabla drum. Around the same time, Bouteldja was customizing an accordion so that it could play the quarter-tones so characteristic of Arabic music in general. They recorded some 45rpm singles together.

Led by Bellemou, the post-revolutionary generation of young musicians started to formulate a modern "pop- rai". Their influences ranged from rock to flamenco. Spanish artists had been visiting Algeria for decades to play for the large Spanish community of Oran, which included many refugees from Franco's dictatorship. Their music was very popular, especially with the young Bellemou who had studied at the Spanish music school in his hometown of Ain Temouchent.

After a few years with their new sounds on the Oran wedding and café circuit, Bellemou and Bouteldja had achieved local fame, not to say notoriety. Trumpets, saxophones and accordions in rai music? They left audiences speechless. Cheikha Remitti, jealous and proud by nature, was furious at her baby being stolen from her. "I built the house and they stole the keys and moved right in", she declared angrily. In the slip-stream of Bellemou's and Bouteldja's success a new generation began turning to the rai hybrid to provide a soundtrack to their lives. Among these "midnight" children were two child singers from Oran who were becoming a popular attraction at wedding and circumcision feasts. Fadela's family house in the seedy former Jewish quarter was a stone's throw from the municipal theatre and she had always had her heart set on a stage career. Khaled Brahim's father was a policeman and he came from the Eckmuhl district in Oran's new town. They were to become known as **Chaba Fadela** and **Cheb Khaled**.

The 1970s were a bad time for the youth in Algeria. The previous decade had exacerbated the problems of poverty, homelessness and unemployment which had plagued the country since independence. When President Chadli took over from the long-standing leader Boumedienne in 1977, corruption became almost endemic. The young people of cities like Algiers and Oran, too old for school and too young for military service, existed in an aimless limbo, denied sexual freedom or the chance to travel abroad and continually preached to about religion and morality by the authoritarian central government. Frustrated though they were, they were not oblivious to the general radicalization of third world culture which was implicit in the music of Bob Marley and the plight of the Palestinians. Most importantly the groups of the Moroccan new wave such as Nass el-Ghiwane and Jil Jilala, who were busy moulding a hard, modern style of Arabic music with lyrics that confronted the worst injustices of modern living, were becoming popular all over the Maghreb.

The mid-1970s also witnessed another development that was to be crucial to the pop rai boom of the '80s. For decades, record producers in Algeria had released their material on 45rpm vinyl singles which were relatively expensive to produce. After 1974 cheap cassette recorders became readily available and the vinyl era rapidly ended. Producers sprang up like flowers after a freak flood, ranging from two-bit sharks with a microphone and a beat-up cassette player, to the likes of brothers **Rachid and Fethi Baba Ahmed** and the talented arranger Mohammed Maghni, who were often survivors of 1960s rock groups and strove to develop new sounds and styles.

CASSETTE CHEBS

The contradictions of Algerian society are typical of any post-colonial society. Algerian teenagers are tuned into global culture, and satellite dishes

RAI SOUNDS, WRY METHODS

Musically, rai is a melting-pot, an evolving mix of sounds from local traditions, along with the influences of rock, soul, funk and reggae. With the arrival of the cassette era, in the effort to cut costs – mixed perhaps with the genuine desire to be utterly modern – human percussion sections were dispensed with and the drum machine took their place. Saxes, trumpets and accordions were also dumped in favour of the all-powerful Roland DX7 or some other synth. But traditional elements, such as the rythmically free introduction (*istiqbar*) with its meandering line, and a number of complex traditional rhythms for the main body of the song, have mostly been kept.

World Music buyers are most familiar with the elaborate, creative productions of **Rachid Baba Ahmed**. Based in Tlemcen, a traditionally oriented town near the Moroccan border, Rachid has one of the few 24-track studios in Algeria, and the sound he produces is exceptional, uncharacteristic of rai in general. His most famous hit was "N'sel Fik" by Chaba Fadela. His current stars are Chab Anouar and a singer disingenuously called Khalid...

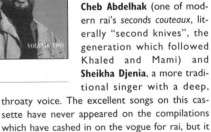
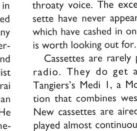

Rachid Baba Ahmed

Most of the cassettes sold in Algeria and in the French cassette shops are made with limited technical means and low production values. Many of them sound quite rough. Oran studios generally function with no more than four tracks, and there is rarely space for more than one vocalist and a couple of musicians. The classic Oran rai sound was developed by the trained musician and self-taught engineer Mohamed Maghni. He combined a lead vocal, bass guitar and sometimes lead guitar, synth, drum machine and darabouka (clay drum).

Six-song cassettes have mostly been produced by an *éditeur*, a man who will in most cases also own one or more cassette shops: some éditeurs own studios as well. Singers are used to getting one-off payments for recording a cassette and, while no singer is tied to a single éditeur, certain artists like Cheb Mami and Chaba Zahouania have worked fairly regularly with Boualem of Disco-Maghreb, one of the most successful men in the business.

The rai produced in France is tamer, even if it is better produced: the sounds may be sweeter, but something of the music's soul has been lost. **Cheb Kader**, the first "cheb" to be groomed for success in Paris, was born in Morocco and spent most of his youth in Paris. He has a ʳood voice, but this over-produced rai has lost its sting, merely providing exotic stuff for the disco floor. One of the best releases of the 1980s was a collaboration between **Cheb Abdelhak** (one of modern rai's *seconds couteaux*, literally "second knives", the generation which followed Khaled and Mami) and **Sheikha Djenia**, a more traditional singer with a deep, throaty voice. The excellent songs on this cassette have never appeared on the compilations which have cashed in on the vogue for rai, but it is worth looking out for.

Cassettes are rarely played on Algerian state radio. They do get air play, however, on Tangiers's Medi I, a Moroccan commercial station that combines western with Arab sounds. New cassettes are aired in Oran through being played almost continuously and very loudly from the open cassette shops.

Mark Kidel

feature as prominently on the skyline as minarets. TV's lure of sexual liberation has had an unsettling effect on a society held together by a mix of unquestioning faith and widespread acceptance of double standards. While young men and women may flirt in public, women are controlled by men, marriages are still arranged and virginity is a prerequisite.

The shock value of modern rai is not so much its content, but a refusal to "contain" potentially explosive material. By bringing the unspeakable out into the street, rai threatens the social order. The younger generation finally abandoned the double standards, and the rai phenomenon reflects a complete breakdown of the old order.

For the emerging new generation of chebs, royalties were unheard of. Candyfloss contracts were confected and then ignored. When Cheb Khaled eventually hit the big time, a number of producers claimed to have an exclusive deal with him. His reply was "My only contract is with God". At least the total lack of interest on the part of state radio and TV towards rai no longer hindered its development. A million-and-one cheap cassettes carried the sound instead.

Conscious of the fact that any singer with the prefix "Cheb" or "Chaba" to his or her name would provoke fantasies of rebellion and saucy

Khaled

living in the minds of prospective customers, producers insisted that their artists adopt the title. "Cheb", which means "young", "charming" and "attractive", served to differentiate the young turks of pop-rai from the older generation of cheikhs and cheikhas. Some singers, however, like the silver-tongued casanova Houari Benchenet, stuck with the politer wahrani style and flatly refused to comply.

The modern rai era was born when Chaba Fadela recorded "Ana Mahlali Noum" ("Sleep doesn't matter to me any more") in 1979. All the elements that had made the rai of the cheikhas so controversial – the plain speaking, the realism,

KHALED

. . . .

Khaled's crowning as **"King of Rai"** isn't just a tape and tinsel marketing gimmick, but an honour bestowed upon him in 1985 at the first ever rai festival in Oran. With his immediate likeable personality and deep, baleful voice, he evokes the spirit of profound North African blues in a way no-one else seems able to.

His early influences were mostly oriental – Umm Kalthum, Farid el-Atrache, as well as such European luminaries as Piaf, Aznavour and even Jacques Brel, "one of my idols". Rock'n'roll was less of an influence – though he admits to having worn bell-bottom trousers in the late '60s. His own career and songs are at least partly the result of family circumstances:

"I have never smoked in front of my father. I can't drink in front of him. It's the truth! You have to have respect, okay, but I also have my own life... . I'm living in France with a woman who is not my wife. If someone does that in

Algeria, it's a catastrophe before the parents' eyes. Rai speaks about that mentality – can't do this, can't do that, this sin, that sin. I'm sick of sin, sin, sin. I'm a real believer, even too much of a believer, but one mustn't condemn someone to death for having fun. I've studied the Koran and as far as I'm concerned he who wants to pray has his mosque in front of him, and he who wants to have fun goes his own way and that's all there is to it.

People say I've been assimilated into European society, " he shrugs. "But music is a journey – you can't stay in one place." He hasn't been home for three years, partly, to be fair, because he is a highly provocative figure for fundamentalists who have demonized him for his red-wine-and-women lifestyle. "I'm not frightened for myself, because I have people to protect me, but if a bomb should go off or something, others might get hurt."

the love of life, the lack of concern for accepted mores – were also at the heart of modern rai. Plus ça change, plus c'est la même chose.

PRESENT AND FUTURE SHOCKS

Khaled (then still Cheb Khaled) was signed in 1991 to a worldwide recording deal by the legendary French label and Polygram subsidiary,

---

Hada Raykoum (So That is Your Desire)

So that is your desire,
So that is your law,
So that is your opinion,
So that is your choice.

A delectable girl wants to marry
But she also thirsts for freedom.
She loves the wild life,
And in vain she waits
For her husband to show some passion,
Or a mite of foolhardiness.

She married only to divorce,
So that she could eventually enjoy her body.
Sacrilege! Her husband has dozed off
And suspects absolutely nothing.

Lyrics by Khaled, translated by Andy Morgan.

Barclay. Even when Barclay finally took on the challenge of spreading the rai-gospel throughout the world, the idea of investing large amounts of cash in the career of an Algerian singer was viewed as a huge risk by many. In the event, the pay-off was handsome. The first Barclay album, "Khaled" (1992), featuring the smash hit "Didi", went gold in France (over 100,000 sales) and sold respectably in many other countries. The follow-up, "N'ssi N'ssi" (1993), featuring songs from the soundtrack of Bertrand Blier's film "1-2-3 Soleil" sold less well but compensated by earning Khaled a Cesar (the French equivalent of the Oscar) for best soundtrack album. Although his international advance has been patchy – astounding success in India on the one hand and slow, arduous development in the US on the other – in France he's a one hundred percent crossover success, a "name" who gets invited onto chat shows and sells out the massive Zenith venue in Paris for two nights in a row.

While Khaled and a few others have taken steps to control their music, many saw no reason to deviate from the time-honoured ways of rai

production and marketing. Back in Algeria two names have risen nearly to the point of challenging Khaled's supremacy – **Cheb Hasni** and **Cheb Nasro**. Even in 1991 these two crooners dominated the market and sales of 400,000 per cassette were not unheard of. If their lyrics were very much in the same vein as those of Khaled and the first-wave singers, their taste in sound leaned towards the smooth, the seductive and the unashamedly tacky. Hasni and Nasro are inheritors of the record-'em-cheap-and-sell-a-load school of production. Their international ambitions are evidently non-existent and outside the North African diaspora they are virtually unknown. Among the younger generation of Algerians, however, both at home and in France, they are the tops.

FISHING THE RIVER

"Rai stands at a historical crossroads": it would be convenient if it were that simple. But it does appear at first glance that the style's very existence in Algeria is threatened. The journalist Bouziane Khodla, writing in Révolution Africaine, had this to say: "Rai really is only expressing genuine and deeply held frustrations. It stems apathy and says yes to life. We condemn the fact that such a part of our national heritage is censored by those who only want to dampen the ultimate Thursday night fever."

But given the fact that Hasni, Nasro, Sahraoui, Fadela and others like the young Cheb Anouar, protege of producer Rachid Baba Ahmed, still live and work in Algeria, how can rai possibly exist, and even occasionally flourish, in a country where only the army stands between the outlawed Islamic fundamentalists (the Front Islamique du Salud – **FIS**) and total power; where an 8pm curfew is in force in many cities; where the murder of foreigners (those few who remain) is on the increase; and where gangs of "fundamentalists" roam about abusing and even physically attacking women who don't observe sharia law.

The answer is simple: rai and the fundamentalists fish in the same river. Their shared anti-establishment constituency is the young, the working class, the unemployed, the illiterate, the dispossessed, the fed-up. The FIS is a heterogeneous movement whose strength comes from the fact that it is the only credible alternative to the detested Front de Libération National (FLN) who have ruled the country since independence. The young generation who voted for FIS in the annulled elections of December 1991 are not automatically to be labelled "barbes", prepared to grow beards, or exchange their jeans for jellabas. They just wanted to tell the FLN how badly President Chadli and his cronies had forsaken the trust and confidence of the people. In his song "Le Consulat" ("The Consulate"), Cheb Hasni sings "My country is a flower which they have devoured". There's no doubt who he means by the devourers.

Although serious-minded grass-roots fundamentalists may deplore and physically threaten people in the rai scene, the FIS leadership is a group of very astute political movers and the last thing they want to do is alienate the youth vote by openly denouncing rai. Even when the then-legal FIS ran the local council of Oran in the early 1990s, they allowed a rai festival to take place. While the ruling FLN made sure that the music never got near national TV or radio until the mid-1980s, the influence of the FIS on rai has, so far, not been half as damaging.

So what does the future hold? If the FIS eventually take over in Algeria, becoming the establishment, then their current passive acceptance of rai music may be swiftly denounced by hardline clerics. Latent racism impedes the French major labels from developing the careers of rai artists on French soil, so that avenue doesn't appear to be broadening. Meanwhile, the cassette producers, who to their credit were partly responsible for the tremendous success of pop-rai, now pine for the glory days of the 1980s when the top-ranking artists could sell over 100,000 copies of each cassette. Even with minimal or nonexistent investment in production facilities and marketing, real fortunes were made.

Today in Algeria, rather than investing in new talent – which, despite all barriers, still abounds at weddings and other functions in the west of the country – the jaded éditeurs prefer to churn out yet more cheaply produced cassettes by Hasni, Nasro or Tahar – too many titles by too few names. Moreover, just when Khaled is pushing the frontiers of the rai sound by using top overseas producers and session-players, the Arab producers for the most part still hold doggedly to the cheap, well-tested synth and drum-machine fomula. It is already starting to fail. In France, the lure of cheaply produced, badly packaged cassettes is not as strong for the new generation of *beurs* (descendants of North African immigrants) as it was for their older brothers and sisters. The beurs know only a European lifestyle of high-rise living, unemployment, hyper-markets – and CDs.

The producers face a change-or-die ultimatum which few show signs of heeding. Ask any of the Arab cassette-shop owners in Paris how business is going, and you get sighs, bowed heads and tales of woe. Nevertheless, it is with the few younger, beur producers who are aware of the need for change – who can adapt rai's sound to the tastes of the new generation, and take on board the notions of marketing and publicity – that hope must lie. As one prominent rai producer said recently: "The beurs are rai's best hope."

Many thanks to Nourredine Gaffaiti, Rabah Mezzouane and Mohammed Maghni for information.

DISCOGRAPHY

There's a fair amount of rai available on CD these days, though for the latest releases appear first (and in some cases only) on cassettes issued in France or Algeria. If you want to track these down, get yourself to in Paris and scour the cassette shops near the Barbes Rochechouart metro station, or the shops, Bouarfa (32 rue de la Charboniere) or Laser Video (1 rue Caplat).

ⓒ **Chaba Fadela and Cheb Sahraoui** *You Are Mine* (Mango, UK). The ubiquitous husband and wife team perform one of their many versions of "N'Sel Fik" on this solid collection, one of two albums by the duo released on Mango in the UK, the other being Fadela's "Hana Hana".

ⓒ **Cheb Khaled** *Hada Raykoum* (Triple Earth, UK). This is pop-rai in its raw mid-1980s state with Khaled singing like the rebel he was reputed to be. For a more sophisticated Khaled style, try also his most recent albums, ⓒ *Khaled* (Barclay, France), rai's biggest international hit, produced by Don Was and featuring the bombastic bass-driven "Didi", which has swept across borders to reach new audiences, and ⓒ *N'ssi N'ssi* (Mango, UK), another Don Was production which brings rai into a World Music fusion with New York recorded jazz and funk-inflected sessions.

ⓒ **Cheb Khaled and Safy Boutella** *Kutche* (Stern's, UK). This collaboration between the King of rai and the roving Algerian jazz musician and film-score composer Boutella was a revelation at the time of its release (1987) for the quality and subtlety of its sound. Features sharp and shimmering versions of Khaled standards such as "Shab El Baroud" and "Chebba".

ⓒ **Cheb Mami** *Let Me Rai* (Totem/EMI, France). The superb voice of Mami is at times shanghaied by bland production: at other times it's done full justice to by subtle use of violins and accordion. A mixed bag, but significant for the fact that it reveals the musical ambitions of the most realistic pretender to Khaled's throne.

① Bellemou Messaoud *Le Pere du Rai* (World Circuit, UK).This album should be included in any self-respecting rai collection simply because it features the music of one of pop-rai's pioneers, though its fine moments are sadly accompanied by a rather flat production.

① Cheikha Remitti *Rai Roots* (CMM/Buda Musique, France). Really interchangeable with the Michel Levy-produced CD, "Ghir El Baroud", this compilation features the diva of folk-rai in all her lustful, rasping, pounding glory. A nut with an acquired taste but hypnotic once cracked.

① Cheb Tati *El Hammam* (Blue Moon, France). Remarkable for the fact that many of these tracks were produced by UK dub master Dennis Bovell, managing to clearly demonstrate what even the casual rai listeners soon learn for them-selves…the curious fact that rai and reggae have a fundamen-tal rhythmic affinity.

① Various *Rai Rebels and Pop-rai Rachid Style* (Earthworks, UK). These compilations feature the work of Tlemcen-based producer Rachid Baba Ahmed, in whom many hoped they had at last found the Lee Perry of rai. Although Rachid hasn't fulfilled his early promise there are some seminal tracks here including Fadela and Sahraoui's rai standard "N'sel Fik" and excellent contributions by Cheb Khaled and Cheb Anouar.

CASSETTE ONLY RELEASES

Cheb Anouar *Laaroussa* (Étoile d'Évasion, Algeria). The young Anouar – whose contribution to the Earthworks compilation "Pop-rai and Rachid Style" stood out a mile – has always been among the most promising artists in Rachid's stable. Here his husky singing style is aptly accompanied by a simple violin driv-en backing-track, with very pleasing results.

Cheb Djellal *Le Prince de la Chanson Maghrebien* (Boualem, Algeria). A much underrated singer from Oujda on the Morocco-Algeria border. This set demonstrates to full effect Djellal's pared-down menacing Moroccan-rai style with its hypnotic call and response vocal arrangements, without a tacky synth sound in earshot. Absolutely captivating.

Cheb Khaled and Chaba Zahouania (MCPE, Algeria). The king of rai has often teamed up with the genre's most durable and impressive female star for a quick cassette release or two. Zahouania is one of the rare singers who has successfully mas-tered both the folk-rai style of the cheikhas and the pop-rai of the chebs and chebas. This recording features a great tribute to one of Algeria's all-time heroes "Sidi Boumedienne".

Cheb Zahouani *Moul El Bar* (Bouarfa, Algeria). Grim-faced Zahouani, with his "local hard man" looks, sings in a rasping no-nonsense style to hard bass heavy rhythm tracks. Wicked.

A WILD, SAVAGE FEELING

THE ROOTS AND REVIVAL OF FLAMENCO

Flamenco is one of the great musical forms of Europe, with a feeling few "folk" cultures can match. A decade or so ago, however, it looked like a music on the decline, preserved only in the clubs or peñas of its aficionados, or in travestied castanet-clicking form for tourists. But in the 1980s and 90s, flamenco has returned to the Spanish mainstream, with styles infused by jazz, salsa, blues and rock making their way in the charts and clubs, and a new respect for the old "pure flamenco" artists. Jan Fairley investigates the state of play.

Scratch a hot night in Andalucía, even on the much-maligned Costa del Sol, and you'll find flamenco. "You carry it inside you", said a man in his sixties sitting next to me at a concert in the local municipal stadium in downtown Marbella. There was not a tourist in sight, it was 2am, the sky was deep blue-black, patterned with stars, the stadium cluttered with families enjoying the most pleasant hours of the Andaluz summer, flapping their fans until dawn, children asleep on laps.

Flamenco is undoubtedly the most important musical-cultural phenomenon in Spain, and its huge resurgence in popularity has seen its profile reaching out far beyond its Andalucían homeland. It owes this new-found influence in part, perhaps, to the southern-dominated socialist governments – Prime Minister Felipe Gonzalez is from Sevilla, as are many of his associates. Perhaps, too, it is down to Spain's unconscious desire, now it is part of the EC, to establish a national identity that challenges European stereotypes. The sanitized kitsch flamenco, all frills and castanets, exploited as an image of tourist Spain during the Franco period, has been left far behind by a new age expressing the vitality and attitudes of a younger generation of traditional flamenco clans.

In the 1980s, the Spanish press hailed **Ketama** (named for a Moroccan village famed for its hashish) as creators of the music of the "New Spain", after their first album which fused flamenco with rock and Latin salsa. Since then they have pushed the frontiers of flamenco still further by recording the two "Songhai" albums in collaboration with Malian kora-player Toumani Diabate and British bassist Danny

Canarón, Paco de Lucía and Juan Peña El Lebrijano

Thompson. **Pata Negra** ("black leg" – the tasty bit of an Andalucían leg of smoked ham – and an everyday term used for anything good), caused an equal sensation with their "Blues de la Frontera" album.

This revival is no longer confined to the purists who kept old-time flamenco alive in their peñas or clubs. On radio and on cassettes blaring from market stalls right across the country you hear the typical high-pitched treble tones of commercial flamenco singers like **Tijeritas**. The European success of the flamenco-rumba of the **Gipsy Kings**, a high-profile gypsy group from southern France, has further opened and prepared the ear of European popular audiences for something more powerful. Rumba, which has come back to Spain from Latin America (and so is known as a music of *ida y vuelta* – "go and return"), is one of the many fusions of the Spanish music taken to the new world with the conquistadors and their descendants, where it has mixed with African and other elements.

The impetus began at the end of the 1960s, with the innovations of guitarist **Paco de Lucia** and, especially, the late, great singer **El Camarón de la Isla**, (see feature box on p.138). These were musicians who had grown up learning from their flamenco families but whose own musical tastes embraced international rock, jazz and blues. Paco de Lucia blended jazz and salsa onto the flamenco sound. Camarón, simply, was an inspiration – and one whose own idols (and fans) included Chick Corea and Miles Davis, as well as flamenco artists.

ORIGINS

The **roots of flamenco** have evolved in southern Spain from many sources: Morocco, Egypt, India, Pakistan, Greece, and other parts of the Near and Far East. How exactly they came together as flamenco is a subject of great debate and obscurity, though most authorities believe the roots of the music were brought to Spain by gypsies arriving in the fifteenth century. In the following century, it was fused with elements of Arab and Jewish music in the Andalucían mountains, where Jews, Muslims and "pagan" gypsies had taken refuge from the forced conversions and clearances effected by the Catholic kings and Church. The main flamenco centres and families are still to be found today in quarters and towns of gypsy and refugee origin, such as Alcalá, Utrera, Jerez, and Cádiz, and the Triana barrio of Sevilla.

There are two theories about the origins of the name flamenco. One contends that Spanish Jews migrated through trade to Flanders, where they were allowed to sing their religious chants unmolested, and that these chants became referred to as "flamenco" by the Jews who stayed in Spain. The other is that the word is a mispronunciation of the Arabic words *felag* (fugitive) and *mengu* (peasant), a plausible idea, as Arabic was a common language in Spain at the time.

Legendary gypsy singer Manolo Caracol

Flamenco aficionados enjoy heated debate about the purity of their art and whether it is more validly performed by a *gitano* (gypsy) or a *payo* (non-gypsy). Certainly, flamenco seems to have thrived, while preserved and protected by the oral tradition of the closed gypsy clans. Its power, and the despair which its creation overcomes, seems to have emerged from a precarious and vulnerable life, from a people surviving for centuries at the margins of society from which they have to earn a living but which in return offers them no social status. Flamenco reflects their need to preserve, and aggressively, their self-esteem.

These days, there are as many acclaimed payo as gitano flamenco artists. However, the concept

MEDITERRANEAN AND MAGHREB

of an active inheritance is crucial. The veteran singer **Fernanda de Utrera**, one of the great voices of "pure flamenco", was born in 1923 into a gypsy family in Utrera, one of the *cantaora* (flamenco singer) centres. She was the grand-daughter of the legendary singer "Pinini", who had created her own individual flamenco forms, and with her younger sister Bernarda, also a notable singer, inherited their flamenco with their genes. This concept of an active inheritance is crucial. Even the members of Ketama, the Madrid-based flamenco-rock group, come from two gypsy clans – the Sotos and Carmonas.

If flamenco's exact origins are obscure, it is generally agreed that its "laws" were established in the nineteenth century. Indeed, from the mid-nineteenth into the early twentieth centuries flamenco enjoyed a **"Golden Age"**, the tail-end of which is preserved on some of the earliest 1930s recordings. The original musicians found a home in the café *cantantes*, traditional taverns which had their own groups of performers (*cuadros*). One of the most famous was the Café de Chinitas in Málaga, immortalized by the Granada-born poet Garcia Lorca. In his poem "A

las cinco de la tarde" (At five in the afternoon), Lorca claimed that flamenco is deeply related to bullfighting, not only in sharing root emotions and flashes of erratic genius, but because both are possible ways to break out of social and economic marginality.

Just such a transformation happened in 1922 when the composer Manuel de Falla, the guitarist Andrés Segovia and the poet Garcia Lorca were present for a legendary *Concurso de Cante Jondo* (Deep Song Gathering). A gypsy boy singer, **Manolo Caracol**, reportedly walked all the way from Jerez and won the competition with the voice and the flamboyant personality that was to make his name throughout Spain and South America. The other key figure of this period, who can be heard on a few recently remastered recordings, was **Pastora Pavon**, known as La Niña de Los Peines, and popularly acclaimed as the greatest woman flamenco voice of the twentieth century.

In the 1950s several crucial events in flamenco history took place, establishing for the music a culture beyond its aficionados in the café cantantes. In 1954, the Spanish label

DUENDE

·······················

Duende is one of those mystical, indefinable words that goes deep to the heart of Spanish culture. Garcia Lorca wrote that duende could only be found in the depths of abandonment – " in the final blood-filled room of the soul". Its power is likened to the moment which transcends time – a moment of immortality.

Mario Pacheco, founder of the best contemporary flamenco label, Nuevos Medios, says "Some artists have it, others don't. It's a quality that has nothing to do with training or technique. It's dragged crying and spitting from the bottom of the soul – a very brief moment of pure communication that takes you out of time. That moment is part of Spanish culture: the audience waits for it in flamenco as they do in the bullfight. The artist becomes what they are singing, they are there, but at one moment they disappear, they are not there – it's beyond words, impossible to describe. You are totally taken up by it then. It's that powerful."

Carmen Linares

Hispavox recorded all the flamenco greats on the "Antología del Cante Flamenco"; two years later the first national contest of Cante Jondo was launched in Cordoba; then in 1958 a Chair of Flamencology was established at Jerez. Each of these events brought media attention (and respectability) and they were accompanied by the appearance of numerous *tablaos* ("clubs" – heirs of café cantantes), which became the training ground for a new and more public generation of singers and musicians.

THE ART OF FLAMENCO

In addition to tablaos, flamenco is played at fiestas, in bars, and at *juergas*, informal, more or less private parties. The fact that the Andalucían public are so knowledgeable and demanding about flamenco means that musicians, singers and dancers found even at the most humble local club or festival are usually very good indeed.

At that local fiesta in Marbella, **Tina Pavon** from Cádiz sang *fandangos* and *alegrias* (literally happinesses) and *malagueñas* from Málaga: part of the light *cante chico* and intermedio repertoire which pave the way for *cante jondo* (deep song). This is the profound flamenco of the great artists, whose *siguiriyas* and *soleareas* are outpourings of the soul, delivered with an intense passion, expressed through elaborate vocal ornamentation. Tina Pavon's improvised sculpting of phrases, which draws attention to certain words and the emotions they evoke, had people on their feet shouting encouragement.

To invoke such a response is essential for an artist, as this "talking it up" lets them know they are reaching deep into the emotional psyche of their audience. They may achieve the rare quality of *duende* – total communication with their audience, and the mark of great flamenco of any style or generation. Duende is an ethereal quality: moving, profound even when expressing happiness, mysterious but nevertheless felt, a quality that stops listeners in their tracks. And many of those listeners are intensely involved, for flamenco is not just a music; for many it is a way of life, a philosophy that influences daily activities. A flamenco is not only a performer but anyone who is actively and emotionally involved in the unique philosophy.

For the musicians, this fullness of expression is integral to their art, which is why for as many famous names as one can list, there are many other lesser known musicians whose work is startlingly good. Not every superb flamenco musician gets to be famous, or to record, for flamenco thrives most in live performance. Exhilarating, challenging and physically stimulating, it is an art form which allows its exponents huge scope to improvise while obeying certain rules. Flamenco guitarist Juan Martin has remarked that "in microcosm it imitates Spanish society – traditional on the outside but within, incredible anarchy".

There is a classical **repertoire** of more than sixty flamenco songs (*cantes*) and dances (*danzas*) – some solos, some group numbers, some with instrumental accompaniment, others a cappella. These different styles or *palos* of flamenco singing are grouped in "families" according to more or less common melodic themes. The basic palos are soleares, siguiriyas, tangos and fandangos, but the variations are endless and often referred to by their place of origin: *malagueñas* (from Málaga), for example, *granaínos* (from Granada), or fandangos de Huelva. The Andaluz provinces of Cádiz, Sevilla, Málaga and Granada are responsible for most of the palos, although contributions came from other parts of Andalucía and from the bordering regions of Extremadura and Murcia.

In all of these palos, the most common **beat cycle** is twelve – like the blues. Each piece is executed by juxtaposing a number of complete musical units called coplas. Their number varies depending on the atmosphere the *cantaor* (creative singer) wishes to establish and the emotional tone they wish to convey. A song such as a *cante por solea* may take a familiar 3/4 rhythm, divide phrases into 4/8 measures, and then fragmentally subdivide again with voice ornamentation on top of that. The resulting complexity and the variations between similar phrases constantly undermines repetition, contributing greatly to the climactic and cathartic structure of each song.

SONGS AND SINGERS

Flamenco **songs** often express pain, and with a fierceness that turns that emotion inside out and beats it up against violent frontiers. Generally, the voice closely interacts with improvising guitar, the two inspiring each other, aided by the *jaleo* – the hand-clapping *palmas*, finger-snapping *palillos* and shouts from participants at certain points in the song. This jaleo sets the tone by creating the right atmosphere for the singer or dancer to begin, and

CAMARÓN DE LA ISLA

José Monge Cruz – known throughout his career as **El Camarón de la Isla** ("The Shrimp of the Island") – died on July 2nd 1992. Flags were immediately dropped to half mast in his home city of San Fernando, near Cádiz, and that morning every single Spanish newspaper, even the Basque journal Egin, which holds little love for the socialist stronghold of Andalucía, carried Camarón's photo and obituary on their front pages. The leading Madrid daily, *El País,* devoted no less than four pages of homage to his memory. "Camarón revolutionized flamenco from the point of absolute purity", it concluded.

Only 41 years old when he died, El Camarón (the name referred to his bony frame and the delicious shrimps of Cádiz – the "island") was acknowledged as a genius from the moment he first sang publicly at the end of the 1960s. His high-toned voice had a corrosive, rough-timbred edge, cracking at certain points to release an almost ravaged core sound. This vocal opaqueness and incisive sense of rhythm, coupled with near-violent emotional intensity, made him the quintessential singer of the times, with a voice that seemed to defy destiny.

Even at his gentlest, Camarón's voice would summon attention – "a fracture of the soul", critics called it – and he would phrase and match cadences in astonishing ways, yet always making the song appear as if it was composed for exactly that manner. To his guitarist-collaborator, Paco de Lucía, the voice "evoked on its own the desolation of the people. My soul left me each time I heard him – he gave to flamenco a wild, savage feeling." It was a verdict which was echoed elsewhere in almost Christ-like terms. As one of the obituaries put it: "Camarón's despair was our consolation. His desperation soothed us. The infinite sadness of his voice gave us tranquility. He suffered for us. His generosity liberated us from misfortune."

Of mythical standing in his lifetime, Camarón will no doubt become a flamenco saint, for he seemed to live out the very myths of the music that sprung from him. The anguish of his singing dogged his life and he supported it through enormous numbers of cigarettes, hashish, then cocaine, and then heroin. His death leaves an unfillable void in the flamenco world.

---

bolsters and appreciates the talent of the artist as they develop the piece.

Aficionados will shout encouragement, most commonly "¡olé!" – when an artist is getting deep into a song – but also a variety of stranger-sounding phrases. A stunning piece of dancing may, for example, be greeted with "¡Viva la maquina escribir!" (long live the typewriter), as the heels of the dancer move so fast they sound like a machine; or the cry may be "¡agua!" (water), for the scarcity of water in Andalucía has given the word a kind of glory.

It is an essential characteristic of flamenco that a singer or dancer takes certain risks, by putting into their performance feelings and emotions which arise direct from their own life experience, exposing their own vulnerabilities. Aficionados tend to acclaim a voice that gains effect from surprise and startling moves more than one governed by recognized musical logic.

Vocal prowess or virtuosity can be deepened by sobs, gesticulation and an intensity of expression that can have a shattering effect on an audience. Thus pauses, breaths, body and facial gestures of anger and pain transform performances into cathartic events. Siguiriyas which date from the Golden Age, and whose theme is usually death, have been described as cries of despair in the form of a funeral psalm. In contrast there are many songs and dances such as tangos, sevillanas and fandangos which capture great joy for fiestas.

The *sevillana* originated in medieval Sevilla as a spring country dance, with verses improvised and sung to the accompaniment of guitar and castanets (which are rarely used in other forms of flamenco). **El Pali** (Francisco Palacios), who died in 1988, was the most well-known and prolific sevillana musician. He combined an unusually gentle voice and accompanying strummed guitar style with an enviable musical pace and ease for composing the popular poetry of the genre. In the last few years dancing sevillanas has become popular in bars and clubs throughout Spain, but their great natural habitats are **Sevilla's April Fería** and the annual romería or pilgrimage to **El Rocio**. It is during the Sevilla fería that most new recordings of sevillanas emerge.

Another important and much more seasonal form are the *saetas*. These are songs in honour of the Virgins carried on great floats in the processions of Semana Santa (Easter Week), and they are, traditionally, quite spontaneous. As the float or *paso* is passing, a singer will launch into a saeta, and the procession will stop for the duration, perhaps offering accompaniment with drums or hand-clapping or shouts of encouragement.

Camarón – or more fully **El Camaron de la Isla** – was by far the most popular and commercially successful singer of modern flamenco. Collaborating with the guitarists Paco and Pepe de Lucia, and latterly, Tomatito, Camarón raised cante jondo, the virtuoso "deep song", to a new art. He died in 1992, having almost singlehandedly revitalized flamenco, inspiring and opening the way for the current generation of flamenco artists.

Among the best **contemporary singers** are Enrique Morente, the aforementioned Fernanda and Bernarda de Utrera, El Cabrero, Juan Peña El Lebrijano, the Sorderas, Fosforito, José Menese, Carmen Linares and El Potito. **Enrique Morente** is considered one of the great artists of his generation through his renovation and adaptations of modern and classic poets. **Carmen Linares** is one of the really major figures of the 1990s. She commands all the cantes and her deep, rich voice expresses melodies with complex attack and searingly intense emotion. Rigorous and uncompromising, she works by innovating from within the tradition. **El Potito**, just twenty years old, is one of the voices to watch – and already being compared with the late, great Camarón.

FLAMENCO GUITAR

The flamenco performance is filled with pauses. The singer is free to insert phrases seemingly on the spur of the moment. The **guitar accompaniment**, while spontaneous, is precise and serves one single purpose – to mark the *compas* (measures) of a song and organize

rhythmical lines. Instrumental interludes which are arranged to meet the needs of the cantaor (as the creative singer is called) not only catch the mood and intention of the song and mirror it, but allow the guitarist to extemporize what are called *falsetas* (short variations) at will. When singer and guitarist are in true rapport the intensity of a song develops rapidly, the one charging the other, until the effect can be overwhelming.

The flamenco **guitar** is of lighter weight than most acoustic guitars and often has a pine table and pegs made of wood rather than machine heads. This is to produce the preferred bright responsive sound which does not sustain too long (as opposed to the mellow and longer sustaining sound of classical guitar). If the sound did sustain, particularly in fast pieces, chords would carry over into each other. The other important feature of the flamenco guitar is a diapason placed across the strings to enable retuning. This was an important development for the relationship between guitarist and singer, for before its introduction a singer had to strain to adapt to the guitarist's tone.

Paco de Lucía

The guitar used to be simply an accompanying instrument – originally the singers themselves played – but in the early decades of this century it began developing as a solo form, absorbing influences from classical and Latin American traditions. The greatest of these early guitarists was **Ramón Montoya**, who revolutionized flamenco guitar with his harmonizations and introduced a whole variety of arpeggios – techniques of right-hand playing adapted from classical guitar playing. Along with **Niño Ricardo** and **Sabicas**, he established flamenco guitar as a solo medium, an art extended from the 1960s on by **Manolo Sanlucar**, whom most aficionados reckon the most technically accomplished player of his generation. Sanlucar has kept within a "pure flamenco" orbit, with no straying into jazz or rock, experimenting instead with orchestral backing and composing for ballet.

The best known of all contemporary flamenco guitarists, however, is undoubtedly **Paco de Lucía**, who made the first moves towards "new" or "fusion" flamenco. A payo, or non-gypsy, he won his first flamenco prize at the age of 14, and went on to accompany many of the great traditional singers, including a long partnership with Camarón de la Isla. He started forging new timbres and rhythms for flamenco following a trip to Brazil, where he fell in love with bossa nova, and in the 1970s established a sextet with electric bass, Latin percussion, flute and saxophone. Over the past twenty years he has worked with jazz-rock guitarists like John McLauglin and Chick Corea, while his own regular band, featuring singer Ramón de Algeciras, remains one of the most original and distinctive sounds on the flamenco scene. Of his fusion, he says: "You grab tradition with one hand, and with the other you scratch, you search. You can go anywhere and run away but must never lose the root, for it's there that you find flamenco's identity, fragrance and flavour."

Other modern-day guitarists have equally identifiable sounds and rhythms, and fall broadly into two camps, being known either as accompanists or soloists. The former include **Tomatito** (Camarón's last accompanist), **Manolo Franco** and **Paco Cortés**. Among the leading soloists are the **Habichuela brothers**, Pepe and Juan, from Granada; **Rafael Riqueni**, an astonishing player who is breaking new ground with classical influences; **Enrique de Melchor**; Gerardo Nuñez; Vicente Amigo; and **Ramón El Portugues** from Extremadura. The latest prodigy is **Jerónimo Maya**, acclaimed by the Spanish press as the Mozart of Flamenco when he gave his first solo performance, aged seven, in 1984.

NUEVO FLAMENCO

One of flamenco's great achievements has been to sustain itself while providing much of the foundation and inspiration for new music emerging in Spain today. In the 1950s and '60s, rock'n'roll displaced traditional Spanish music, as it did indigenous musics in many parts of the

world. The work of Camarón de la Isla (see box), however, began a revival of interest, and in the 1980s flamenco almost reinvented itself, gaining new meaning and a new public through its fusion with jazz, bossa nova and salsa, blues and rock.

Purists, of course, hated these innovations but, as José "El Sordo" (deaf one) Soto, Ketama's main singer, explained, they are based on "the classic flamenco that we'd been singing and listening to since birth. We just found new forms in jazz and salsa: there are basic similarities in the rhythms, the constantly changing harmonies and improvisations. Blacks and gypsies have suffered similar segregation so our music has a lot in common."

Paco de Lucía set the new parameters of innovation and commercial success, and was followed by **Lolé y Manuel**, who updated the flamenco sound with original songs and huge success; **Jorge Pardo**, Paco de Lucía's sax and flute player, who was in fact originally a jazz musician; **Salvador Tavora** and **Mario Maya**, known for their flamenco-based spectacles. Meanwhile, **Enrique Morente** and **Juan Peña El Lebrijano** both worked with **Andalucían orchestras** from Morocco, and **Amalgama** recorded with southern Indian percussionists, revealing perhaps unsurprising stylistic unities. Another interesting crossover came with **Paco Peña's** 1991 "Misa Flamenca" recording, a setting of the Catholic Mass to flamenco forms with the participation of established singers like Rafael Montilla "El Chaparro" from Pena's native Cordoba, and a classical academy chorus.

The encounter with **rock and blues** was pioneered at the end of the 1980s by Ketama and Pata Negra. **Ketama**, as noted before, used

Pata Negra brothers Raimundo and Rafael Amador

RECORDING A JUERGA

·······················

The word *juerga* has no exact equivalent in English but implies a get-together of flamenco singers, guitarists and aficionados: an informal occasion, with an atmosphere of spontaneity, exuberance and gaiety, in which some of the most inspired and cathartic flamenco can happen. It is quite the opposite of a performance or "act"; indeed, the distinction between performers and listeners blurs as all involved contribute, if only by shouts of encouragement.

When an opportunity came to record a juerga in Andalucía for the Nimbus label, I jumped at the chance. I'd been hooked on flamenco for several years and had amassed a large collection of records and cassettes. And with few exceptions the recordings that seemed to give the best impression of flamenco's richness and intensity were not studio recordings but those rare and much-copied tapes generated by some unknown soul who had set up a cheap cassette recorder in a bar or backroom where a juerga was happening.

My Nimbus collaborator, Phil Slight, had been intimately involved with the flamenco scene in the town of Morón de la Frontera. He contacted **Paco del Gastor**, one of the most sought-after accompanists, and found him immediately enthusiastic about the idea of a juerga recording in Morón, his home town. Paco arranged for the use of one of the flamenco peñas (clubs) and started recruiting gypsy flamenco singers from across Andalucía to take part in our two planned juergas. They included José de la Tomasa from

Sevilla; María la Burra and María Solea from Jerez; Manuel de Paula and Miguel Funi from Lebrija; Gasper de Utrera from Utrera; and Chano Lobato from Cadiz. After some warming up, both sessions went with a typical juerga swing. Like good jazz musicians, flamencos of this calibre are so immersed in their art that there is no need for rehearsal or trying out arrangements, even though they might not have worked together before.

The juerga recording in progress

The **recording equipment** used was an unobtrusive portable DAT recorder using a single point soundfield microphone for Cante Flamenco and spaced omni-directional mics for Cante Gitano; there was to be no mixing, no re-takes, no editing, nothing to freeze out the essential elements of spontaneity and surprise. Apart from some re-ordering of songs the CD that emerged ("Cante Gitano") is just as it happened, captured on the wing in the Andalucían night.

Robin Broadbank

rock and Latin sounds, and added a kind of rock-jazz sensibility, a "flamenco cool" as they put it. **Pata Negra**, a band led by two brothers, Raimundo and Rafael Amador, introduced a more direct rock sound with a bluesy electric guitar lead, giving a radical edge to traditional styles like bulerías.

Collectively, these young and iconoclastic musicians have become known, in the 1990s, as *nuevo flamenco*: a "movement" associated in particular with the Madrid label Nuevos Medios. They form a challenging, versatile and musically

incestuous scene, in Madrid and Andalucía, with musicians guesting at each others' gigs and on each others' records. Part of Ketama crop up, for instance, along with the astonishing guitarist Tomatito on the new album by **Duquende**, who is perhaps the most powerful singer of flamenco's "new wave".

The music is now a regular sound of nightclubs, too, through the appeal of young singers like **Aurora**, whose salsa-rumba song "Besos de Caramelo", written by Antonio Carmona of Ketama, was the first 1980s number

FLAMENCO DANCE

Most popular images of flamenco dance – twirling bodies in frilled dresses, rounded arms complete with castanets – are *sevillanas*, the folk dances performed at fiestas and, in recent years, on the disco and nightclub floor. "Real" flamenco dance is something rather different and, like the music, can reduce the onlooker to tears in an unexpected flash, a cathartic point after which the dance dissolves. What is so visually devastating about flamenco dance is the physical and emotional control the dancer has over the body: the way the head is held, the tension of the torso and the way it allows the shoulders to move, the shapes and angles of seemingly elongated arms, and the feet, which move from toe to heel, heel to toe, creating rhythms. These rhythms have a basic set of moves and timings but they are improvised as the piece develops and through interaction with the guitarist.

Flamenco dance dates back to about 1750 and, along with the music, moved from the streets and private parties into the café cantantes at the end of the nineteenth century. This was a great boost for the dancers' art, providing a home for professional performers, where they could inspire each other. It was here that legendary dancers like **El Raspao** and **El Estampio** began to develop the

Dance engraving by Gustav Doré

spellbinding footwork and extraordinary moves that characterize modern flamenco dance, while women adopted for the first time the flamboyant *hata de cola* – the glorious long-trained dresses, cut high at the front to expose their fast moving ankles and feet.

Around 1910, flamenco dance had moved into Spanish theatres, and dancers like **La Niña de los Peines** and **La Argentina** were major stars. They mixed flamenco into programmes with other dances and also made dramatic appearances at the end of comic plays and silent movie programmes. **Flamenco opera** was soon established, interlinking singing, dancing and guitar solos in comedies with a local flamenco flavour.

In 1915 the composer Manuel de Falla composed the first **flamenco ballet, "El Amor Brujo"** ("Love Bewitched"), for the dancer Pastora Imperio. **La Argentina**, who had established the first Spanish dance company, took her version of the ballet abroad in the 1920s, and with her choreographic innovations flamenco dance came of age, working as a narrative in its own right. Another key figure in flamenco history was **Carmen Amaya**, who from the 1930s to the '60s took flamenco dance on tour around the world, and into the movies.

In the 1950s, dance found a new home in the tablaos, the aficionado's bars, which became enormously important as places to serve out a public apprenticeship. More recently the demanding audiences at local and national fiestas have played a part. Artistic developments were forged in the 1960s by **Matilde Coral**, who updated the classic dance style, and in the 1970s by **Manuela Carrasco**, who had such impact with her fiery feet movement, continuing a rhythm for an intense and seemingly impossible duration, that this new style was named after her (*manuelas*).

Manuela Carrasco set the tone for the highly individual dancers of the 1980s and '90s, such as **Mario Maya** and **Antonio Gades**. These two dancer-choreographers have provided a theatrically inspired staging for the dance, most signifcantly by extending the role of a dance dialogue and story – often reflecting on the potency of love and passion, their dangers and destructiveness.

Gades has led his own company on world tours but it is his influence on film which has been most important. He appeared with Carmen Amaya in "Los Aranos" in 1963, but in the 1980s began his own trilogy with film-maker Carlos Saura: "Boda de Sangre" (Lorca's play, "Blood Wedding"), "Carmen" (a reinterpretation of the opera), and "El Amor Brujo". The films featured Paco de Lucía and his band, and the dancers **Laura del Sol** and **Christina Hoyos** – one of the great contemporary dancers, who has herself created a superb ballet, "Sueños Flamencos" (Flamenco Dreams).

to crack the pop charts, and **Martirio** (Isabel Quinones Gutierrez), one of the most flamboyant personalities on the scene, who appears dressed in lace mantilla and shades, like a cameo from a Pedro Almodovar film. Martirio's songs are Almodovar-like, too, with ironical, contemporary lyrics, full of local slang, about life in the cities. They are basically sevillanas, with a splash of music hall, but the voice is as flamenco as they come.

Martirio's producer, **Kiko Veneno**, who wrote Camarón's most popular song, "Volando voy", is another key artist on the scene. His own material

is basically rock music but it has a strongly defined sense of flamenco, as does that of **Rosario**, Spain's top woman singer of the moment, who has brought a flamenco sensibility to Spanish rock music.

Other more identifiably nuevo flamenco bands and singers to look out for on the scene include **La Barbería del Sur** (who add a dash of salsa); **Wili Gimenez** and **Raimundo Amador**; **Radio Tarifa**, who mix Arabic and pop sounds onto a flamenco base; and, a new arrival, **José El Frances**, from Montpelier in France.

DISCOGRAPHY

ANTHOLOGIES

ⓒ **Various** *Magna Antología del Cante Flamenco* (Hispavox, Spain). A superb ten-CD anthology, with a volume from each major centre of flamenco.

Various *Gran Antología Flamenca* (RCA, Spain; 10 LPs). A who's who of singers and guitarists, recorded at the end of the 1970s, and including pieces from every flamenco centre plus flamencoized folk tunes and songs from the Americas which have travelled home. Still available on vinyl!

ⓒ **Various** *Antologia de Cantaores* (EMI, Spain). A near-definitive 25-CD anthology of singers. Volume 3 features La Niña de los Peines.

ⓒ **Various** *Grands Cantaores du flamenco* (Chantdu Monde, France). Another bumper series of singers, with over a dozen discs, to date, including Carmen Amaya (Volume 6) and Manolo Caracol (Volume 7).

Various *Early Cante Flamenco – Classic Recordings from the 1930s* (Arhoolie, US). Some of the earliest recordings by figures who dominated the first half of the twentieth century: Pastora Pavon "La Nina de Los Peines"; her younger brother Tomas Pavon; Manuel Vallejo, one of the first non-gypsy singers hailed as a king; and the great voice of the flamboyant Manolo Caracol.

ARTISTS

ⓒ **Camarón de la Isla** *Autorretrato* (Philips, Spain). A compilation showing Camarón's genius at both ends of the flamenco scale, the deeply traditional and infectiously commercial. Includes the fabulous tango, "Soy Gitano", sung with the Royal Philharmonic Orchestra, as well as some heart-stopping unaccompanied solos like "Las doce acaban de dar".

ⓒ **Agustín Carbonell El Bola** *Carmen* (Messidor, Spain). One of the best young guitarists.

ⓒ **Carmen Linares** *Cantaora* (Riverboat, UK) and *La luna en el río* (Auvidis, Spain). Flamenco singing rarely comes richer or more emotional than this. Linares, a contemporary of Camarón, is the woman of her generation with a fierce edge. See her live if you ever get the chance.

Garcia Lorca y La Argentina *Canciones Populares Españolas* (Sonifolk, Spain). The great Spanish poet played piano and La Argentina sang on these ten songs, recorded in 1931. A true classic.

ⓒ **Paco de Lucía** *Almoraima* and *Sirocco* (Philips, Spain). Two landmark albums that set new standards for solo flamenco guitar.

ⓒ **Enrique Morente** *Negra, si tú supieras* (Nuevos Medios, Spain). Innovative arrangements of lyrics by modern and classic poets.

ⓒ **Enrique Morente with Sabicas** *New York and Granada* (BMG, Spain). One of the last Sabicas recordings – recent but classic.

ⓒ **El Pelé** *Poeta de esquinas blandas* (Pasión, Spain). Terrific singing from Pelé and superb accompaniment from the young Vicente Amigo.

ⓒ **Manuel Soto El Sordera** *Grands Cantaores du Flamenco* (Chant du Monde, France). Music to bring tears to your eyes from one of the great singers. Includes a breathtaking live recording of a Holy Week saeta.

ⓒ **Tomatito** *Barrio Negro* (Nuevos Medios, Spain). A superb solo album from Camarón's collaborator.

ⓒ **Fernanda et Bernarda de Utrera** *Cante Flamenco* (OCORA, France). Brilliant recording made for French Radio from the granddaughters of the legendary "Pinini". The recordings include the Cantinas de Pinini, siguiriyas, bulerias por solea and fandangos. Paco del Gastor accompanies on guitar.

ⓒ **Various** *Cante Flamenco* (Nimbus, UK). The best of both worlds: live recordings of an intimate, emotionally intense juerga, plus the climax of a large-scale public recital.

ⓒ **Various** *Cante Gitano* (Nimbus, UK). José de la Tomasa, María la Burra, María Solea and Paco and Juan del Gastor recorded live at a juerga (see box on "Recording Flamenco"). Exemplary stuff.

ⓒ **Various** *Noches Gitanas* (EPM, Spain). A fine four-CD set of live of traditional flamenco.

NUEVO FLAMENCO AND CROSSOVERS

ⓒ **Various** *Los Jóvenes Flamencos Vol I* and *II* (Nuevos Medios, Spain/Hannibal, UK). Essential and definitive compilation albums of the young flamenco singers and groups of the '80s and '90s, including Ketama, Pata Negra, the late Ray Heredia, Aurora and the jazz edge of Amargos and Benavent: a roll call of top musicians and producers. Nueuos Medios have recently released a third volume.

ⓒ **Amalgama y Karnataka College of Percussion** (Nuba, Spain). A fascinating collaboration between a young flamenco group and percussionists from southern India.

ⓒ **Vicente Amigo** *De mi corazón al aire* (Sony, Spain). A fine solo outing from this virtuoso guitarist.

ⓒ **La Barbería del Sur** *La Barbería del Sur* (Nuevos Medios, Spain). Infectious, salsa-tinged sounds.

ⓒ **Duquende** *Duquende y la Guitarra de Tomatito* (Nuevos Medios, Spain). A wonderful combo with this great singer sharing lead with Tomatito's guitar, backed by Juan and Antonio Carmona of Ketama.

ⓒ **Pepe Habichuela** *A Mandeli* (Hannibal, UK). A mix of tradition and innovation from this highly reputed guitarist, with electric bass and jazz on some tracks, while others are as pure as they come.

ⓒ **El Indio Gitano** *Naci gitano por la gracia de dios* (Nuevos Medios, Spain). El Indio has a voice like bitter chocolate which can deal with everything from tangos to granaínas. Backed by the jazz-swing guitar of Gerardo Nunez.

⊙ **Ketama** *Ketama* (Hannibal, UK). Groundbreaking album that introduced rock and blues to the flamenco sound.

⊙ **Lolé... y Manuel** (Gong Fonomusic, Spain). The finest album from this highly imaginative '80s duo: musicians from flamenco families who challenged the traditional scene before the current generation.

⊙ **Paco de Lucía** *Solo quiero caminar* (Philips, Spain) and *Live ... One Summer Night* (Phonogram, UK). Two glorious albums from Paco and his sextet, with the jazz and Latin influences given full rein.

⊙ **Juan Peña Lebrijano y Orquestra Andalusi de Tanger** *Encuentros* (GlobeStyle, UK). Juan Peña, a gypsy from Lebrija, encounters Paco Cepero's guitar and the stately and haunting music and Arabic chorus of the Orchestra of Tangier in a re-fusion of the music of Andalucía with that of the Maghreb.

⊙ **Martirio** *Estoy Mala* and *Sevillanas de los bloques* (Nuevos Medios, Spain). The radical fringe of flamenco rock, with lyrics exposing the hypocrisy society and Catholicism lay on women, and life at the margins of modern Spanish society. Uses local untranslatable slang with verve and humour.

⊙ **Gerardo Nuñez** *Flamencos en Nueva York* (Accidentales Flamencos, Spain). Simply one of the best guitarists around.

⊙ **Paco Peña** *Misa Flamenca* (Nimbus, UK). A "flamenco mass" created by this Cordoban guitarist, with the classical Academy of St Martin in the Fields chorus.

⊙ **Pata Negra** *Blues de la Frontera* (Hannibal, UK). Flamenco meets rock and blues – an intoxicating mix. The band details read like a checklist of musicians who were to emerge in the nuevo flamenco movement.

⊙ **El Potito** *Andandao por los caminos* (Sony, Spain). First album from the latest voice tipped as a "new Camarón".

⊙ **Rafael Riqueni** *Flamenco* (Accidentales Flamencos, Spain) and *Mi tiempo* (Nuevos Medios, Spain). The first is just guitar; the second with a string quartet.

⊙ **Radio Tarifa** *Rumba Argelina* (Música Sin Fin, Spain). Rumba and flamenco injected with Arab rhythms from an adventurous new band from Andalucía.

⊙ **Songhai** *Songhai* and *Songhai 2* (Hannibal, UK). These two CDs are among the most satisfying encounters of World Music crossovers. On the first, Ketama meet Malian kora-play-er Toumani Diabaté and, with the help of British bassist Danny Thompson, interchange leads and interweave rhythms to devastating effect. *Songhai 2* features Ketama and Toumani Diabaté along with fellow Malian, singer Kassemady Diabaté, jazz bassist Javier Colina (in place of Thompson), and flamen-co's first violinist – Bernardo Parrilla!

CHASING THE FADO

PORTUGUESE BLUES

Paul Vernon was living in San Francisco where he frequently dropped into the Purple Heart Thrift Store, a barn of a place run by Vietnam veterans. Among the usual gritty pile of old records was an English HMV with an unfamiliar name: the legend below read "acc. Viola e Guitarra". Realizing he'd found some kind of ethnic folk recording, he dug deeper and assembled twenty-seven 78s. Now a lot closer acquainted, he tells the story of fado.

Back home, after that first foray into the pile of 78s, I cranked up the gramophone and let the needle drop. The sound knocked me sideways. I felt like I'd discovered the lost chord. To explain the elusive and haunting beauty of the fado is no easy task. It's deceptively simple, like quicksand. The listener is enmeshed in a fado song before quite knowing how or why. It sounds like a bowlful of echoes from everywhere – though the most resonant are, not surprisingly, Brazilian and Cape Verdean.

The literal dictionary definition of the word *fado* is "fate". The meaning invested in this small word by the Portuguese, however, is rich, deep and complex. The music, at least in Lisbon, could be defined as an urban café style and parallels can be drawn with rembétika, blues and original tango. Like rembétika, its subject matter is life's harsh reality. Like rembétika again, its instrumental accompaniment is largely stringed – in this case the Portuguese *guitarra* (12- or 10-string guitar) and *viola* (Spanish guitar) – but unlike rembétika its approach is more about the graceful acceptance of destiny than a garrulous resistance to it. The fado speaks with a quiet dignity born of the realization that any mortal desire or plan is at risk of destruction by powers beyond individual control.

A song listing from one of those old 78s

When I arrived in Lisbon, following the path that led from my stack of unsleeved fado 78s, I hardly dared hope I'd find what I was looking for. But I did, and moreover I found it in cafés and on the street. Not just as music but also as poetry, as speech, as an attitude and ultimately a whole way of life – a coping mechanism that the Portuguese have employed, for over a century and a half, as a means of making sense of life's quirks. "The fado is life", one man told me in a Bairro Alto café – and it's true.

DESIRE AND INSULT

So how and where did fado start? There are many theories and almost all of them contain some essential truths, for the fado is an old tree of music, with deep and tangled roots formed over a longer time frame than many folk art forms. It is half as old again as the blues, but with an international exposure less than one tenth of that form. What you find, therefore, is a very long tradition which, culturally isolated, has remained almost completely unchanged at the core. Portugal's early imperial expansion ensured that the home country was exposed to a broad wedge of other cultures, principally African.

The Portuguese style of imperialism was a disturbing mixture of arrogance and humility – arrogance in assuming that parts of the world were just waiting to become Portuguese, humility in Portuguese readiness to settle, to mix and to leave the home country for good. Intermarriage was common and the goal of Portuguese citizenship through achievement – becoming *assimilado* – was a permanent fixture in the culture of Portuguese-colonized peoples. By the beginning of the nineteenth century a substantial African and mixed-race population, often from Brazil (which became independent in 1822 and was soon substantially richer and more important than Portugal), was firmly ensconced in the Alfama district of Lisbon.

The dances most commonly associated with this cultural group were the *fofa* and the *lundum*, a song and dance exchange for a couple in which lewd comments, expressions of desire and outrageous insults were traded. It was described with contemporary horror as "the most lascivious thing I ever saw". Later, elements of lundum and fofa came to be known as "the fado". With a fundamental ingredient of the fado identifiably African in origin, it seems certain that the term was first applied to a guitar-accompanied African dance form with a rich emotional appeal.

The next factor to consider is the long Portuguese tradition of poetry and literature, both academic and folk. In folk terms both the quatrain (rhyming couplet) and *modhina*, or ballad tradition, were part of Portuguese culture long before the early nineteenth century. The popular folk quatrain was used in many forms by a largely rural community to celebrate specific calendar events, preserve folklore, tell childen's stories and declare undying love – all the usual concerns of a pure folk form and arguably the lyrical genesis of the fado, which seems to have all but dropped the strong lyrical meat of its old African precursors like lundum in exchange for something more soulful.

These three basic ingredients – dance, modhina and quatrain – supplied rhythm, form and content. At some point lost in the fog of history the parts gelled together and matured to form the fado. This is not to ignore the evidence of latter-day pop-fado or tourist-fado – these more glamorous styles have evolved and remain intact – but the central structure of the original form is still living and breathing.

Maria Severa is where the enigmas really begin. According to most dependable contemporary accounts, she was the first great exponent of the fado and the originator of the female *fadista* tradition of wearing a dramatically draped black shawl while performing. Born and raised in the Alfama district of Lisbon (the wrong side of the tracks) she and her mother ran a small tavern in which the embryonic music was performed. In 1836, Maria Severa's fado was heard by the Comte de Vimioso and they entered into what observers of the time referred to as a "tempestuous love affair".

The impact on Lisbon society of this scandalous, high-profile "mismatch" was considerable, with the result that the fado received widespread public attention for the first time. Sheet music was published, newspaper articles were written and the whole matter was hotly debated by the Portuguese at every level. As with any new music that appears to threaten the status quo, people quickly took sides and dug their heels in. The controversy was not dissimilar in essence to the emergence of the tango in Buenos Aires.

For how long before these events the fado had been an identifiable song is uncertain. There is some evidence to suggest it was known in Brazil a few years earlier, in 1829, but it is clear that the fado we hear on record from at least as far back as 1910 – the fado that is still nightly practised in Lisbon – is the same fado that emerged from this nineteenth-century scandal.

But the fado lives not *just* in Lisbon. There is another side to the story, the fado of Coimbra, which shares the origins and keeps the basic form, but is recognized by both devotees and critics alike as essentially divorced from the barrel-house style of Lisbon.

CHERISHED ILLUSIONS

Coimbra, the old university town of Portugal, is a place of deep and unbroken tradition. Here among the narrow streets and university buildings, Portugal's heritage of literature, song and poetry has been quietly and lovingly nurtured for more than five centuries. Those who practise the fado de Coimbra are a very different breed from the bus drivers, barbers, labourers and shoeshiners who use it in Lisbon for cathartic purposes.

The 1920s and '30s saw a remarkable flowering of the Coimbra style, fortunately pre-served on record. A group based around Dr Antonio Menano, including singing doctors **Edmundo de Bettancourt** and **Lucos Junot**, *guitarristas* of astonishing virtuosity such as **Artur Paredes** and **José Joãoquim Cavalheiro**, produced a body of music that documented the Coimbra fado in its true glory. They also interpreted other Portuguese song forms from rural regions such as the Beirra Baixa and Alentejo. Their efforts spawned vigorous debate in music journals of the time and their recorded legacy affords a glimpse of a culture that would otherwise have been irretrievably lost.

While Coimbra fado retains the same form and instrumental accompaniment, its attitude is markedly different. It has been called a more refined strain of fado, but this empty phrase does not accurately reflect the majesty and emotional summits – like a fusion of blues and opera – that a good singer can reach. Certainly a Coimbra fado would be deemed unseemly if it were not highly rehearsed and stylized. Rodney Gallop, writing in 1936, succinctly defined the difference: "It is the song of those who retain and cherish their illusions, not of those who have irretrievably lost them".

Coimbra fado is nevertheless full of longing, and it is that spirit which lies at the very heart of the fado, be it from Lisbon or Coimbra. There is a Portuguese word, *saudade*, that has no direct equivalent translation in English. The closest definition is "yearning". Its emotional parallel is the Spanish *duende*, but the direction it takes is different. It's perhaps the Portuguese equivalent of whatever it is that fuels deep Mississippi or Texas blues – a measure of the understanding that passes between performer and audience. (*Saudade*, or *sodade*, is also discussed in the piece about Cape Verdean music on p.275)

Both the Lisbon and Coimbra strains of fado must possess saudade if they are to be considered genuine: a singer will not last long before a Portuguese audience without it. Audience behaviour is actually crucial to a live performance and the rules for the audience are at least as strict as for the singer. In the typical Lisbon situation, no audience will suffer a poor performance to the end, nor tolerate interruption during a good one. Noisy patrons are physically jostled from the room, and poor singers rudely halted in mid-song.

It's a serious business for all concerned and anyone experiencing the genuine fado for the first time will need to bear these simple rules in mind, especially when fiery debate breaks out. At the end of a song it is perfectly acceptable to indulge in applause, whistling, stamping, shouting, table-banging and beer-spilling. Indeed they're all expected. For especially fine renditions the phrase *fadista!* (pronounced "faaadeeshta") is especially appropriate.

The term *fadista*, like most things Portuguese, has deeper layers of meaning than just "singer of fados". From the mid-nineteenth century until at least the early 1900s it was a term applied to a picaresque section of Lisbon society. Fadistas were the Portuguese counterparts of Athenian *mánges* – people whose dress, attitude and pocket knives spoke eloquently of their disdain for ordinary society. A contemporary description is worth noting for its refined sense of outrage: "*Fadistas* wear a peculiar kind of black cap, wide black trousers with close-fitting jacket, and their hair flowing low on the shoulders – they are held in very bad repute, being mostly vauriens of dissolute habits". (Catherine Charlotte, Lady Jackson in *Fair Lusitania*, 1874). Whether Lady Jackson ever heard the music of these dissolute good-for-nothings she does not say, but her attitude persists to this day. The Lisbon Tourist Office still issues grim warnings

A Bairro Alto fado club

about the footpads and muggers lying in wait in the Bairro Alto for your watch, wallet, spectacles.... It seems churlish to shatter their delusions with the tales of honesty, friendship and humanity that underlie most visitors' experiences. If you don't have the chance to visit, do your ears a favour by turning to the discography, where you will find a music of unsurpassed beauty.

AMÁLIA RODRIGUES

U nlike Maria Severa, who never had a chance to leave any recorded examples of her art, Amália Rodrigues had – and continues to have – an immeasurable impact upon the direction of the fado through her recordings. Like Severa, Amália Rodrigues was born into the poverty of the Alfama district. Her mother was an orange-seller and an early photo shows mother and child at the dock-side peddling fruit. A strikingly beautiful woman with a powerful personality, Amália's greatest talent lies in her voice. Astonishing range and control allow her to produce music of great beauty and emotional depth. She needs only to be heard at her best to be appreciated.

In a long career that started in 1939, Amália's style has defined and crystalized the fado. If you've had only a passing acquaintance with the music, it's likely that it is hers you have heard. You may have listened to some of the later, more popular pieces with orchestral accompaniment. There are, however, early recordings that not only illuminate the roots but also reflect the heights to which a real fadista can rise.

Amália Rodrigues' early records are intense, heartfelt, deeply traditional and strikingly innovative. They represent a pinnacle of development in fado's history. If the legendary blues man Robert Johnson had been a Portuguese woman, he would have been Amália Rodrigues.

Tudo isto é Fado (All this is Fado)
You asked me the other day
If I knew what fado was.
I said I didn't know,
You said you were surprised.
Without knowing what I said,
I lied then,
And said I didn't know.

Vanquished souls,
Lost nights,
Strange shadows
In the Moorish quarter.
A whore sings,
Guitars weep,
Ashes and fire,
Pain and sin.
All of this exists,
All of this is sad,
All of this is fado.

If you want to be my man
And always have me by your side,
Don't speak to me of love
But tell me about fado.
Fado is my sentence,
I was born to be lost.
Fado is everything I say,
And everything I cannot say.

Amália Rodrigues, composed by Aníbal Nazaré F. Carvalho, translated by Caroline Shaw.

Amália Rodrigues

It's still not easy to find examples of the fado in your average record store, but large stores should have some of the following.

VINTAGE RECORDINGS

Ⓒ Armandhino *Armandinho 1928–30* (Heritage, UK). Twenty virtuoso *guitarra* solos from a master musician.

Ⓒ Various *Portuguese String Music 1908–31* (Heritage, UK). A mixture of Portuguese and Portuguese-American instrumentals.

Ⓒ Various *Fado de Coimbra 1926–30* (Heritage, UK). Instrumental and vocal music from this exclusively male (and surprisingly academic – notice all the doctors) tradition.

Ⓒ Various *Fado de Lisboa 1928–36* (Heritage, UK). Superb and emotive vocal and instrumental café music.

Ⓒ Various *Fado de Lisboa Vol 2 1928–30* (Heritage, UK). Twenty recordings by female artists from the café and theatrical traditions.

CONTEMPORARY ARTISTS

Ⓒ Fernando Machado Soares *Fernando Machado Soares* (Ocora, France). Modern recordings of the Coimbra style.

Ⓒ Carlos Paredes *Carlos Paredes* (Nonesuch, UK). Solo *guitarra* virtuoso.

Ⓒ Amália Rodrigues *Monitor presents Amália Rodrigues* (Monitor, US). This is Amália at her very best, recorded live at Paris-Olympia in 1960.

Ⓒ Various *Un Parfum de Fado* (Playasound, France). At least ten volumes of contemporary fado have been issued in this excellent series features the top current singers.

SONGS OF HASH AND HEARTACHE

REMBÉTIKA AND THE FOLK MUSIC OF GREECE

Greek music has had a bad press for years. Zorba the Greek, Nana Mouskouri and interminable "Souvenir from Greece" cassettes are partly to blame. But, as David Muddyman and Marc Dubin discover, if you scratch under the surface the music of Greece is as rich and varied as anywhere in the world. Song translations are by D. Papatzaneteas.

Within the folk music, or *dhimotiká*, of Greece there is a wonderful mix of east and west. Many of the older songs were invariably in eastern-flavoured keys or, more properly, modes *(dhrómi* or *makámia)*, which often have links with the music of Turkey and Iran. Much of the dance music of the *koumpanía* groups in mainland Greece and the folk music in Macedonia or Thrace is still played in a modal way, but the music of the west, especially the Neopolitan-Italian-tango forms popular between the world wars, has infiltrated many styles of Greek music. This oriental flavour is most evident in **rembétika** and **amanédhes,** two styles that were popular in the first half of this century, and revived in the 1970s.

MAINLAND FOLK MUSIC

The music of **Epirus** has many links with lands across its borders, especially Albania and Macedonia. Although it is becoming much harder to find traditional players in the region, there are many fine records available, particularly "Chants Polyphoniques et Musique d'Epiré" (Ocora, France) and "Songs of Epirus", part of the series released by the Society for the Dissemination of National Music.

There are three main types of music still to be found in Epirus – dance tunes, drinking songs and *mirolóyia* or laments. Drinking songs are normally sung either with no instrumental accompaniment, or possibly just a drum or tambourine, whereas dance tunes are normally played by a group of four or five players. These ensembles would often consist of *klaríno, laoúto* or guitar, violin and the *défi* (a form of tambourine).

In the **Peloponnese** and the central mainland there are groups – koumpaníes – similar to those of Epirus. The main folk music of the region is *paleá dhimotiká*, traditional folk ballads sung to dance rhythms such as *kalamatianó, tsámiko, hasaposérviko* and *syrtó*. The klaríno has largely replaced the traditional instruments of the region like the *gaïda* (bagpipe) and the *karamoúza* or *pípiza* (forms of rustic oboes) and the clarinets used are of the simple type which aids rapid fingering and allows graces notes, the little trills and flourishes that do nothing to the main melody but give it a characteristically Balkan sound. One of the best modern exponents of this style is **Yiorgos Mangas**, a clarinettist in his thirties.

A professional itinerant musician, he spends the summers on the church and open-air village festival circuit, and plays the Athens clubs in the winter. Like many of the musicians in this area, he improvises in a modal way and is a master of the *taxími*, the free-rhythm introduction which sets the mood for the dance piece to follow.

Yiorgos Mangas on clarinet

The music of **Macedonia and Thrace** still reflects a long association with the Ottoman Empire. Both were still in Turkish hands until as recently as 1912, and the music here is louder and less lyrical than in the south and has an oriental feel. The Thracian *kavál* is identical to its Turkish counterpart; so too is the northern gaïda. In Macedonia you also find the *zournás*, a very loud, screechy double-reed oboe similar to the Indian *shan'nai* and the *zurnas* of the Islamic world. Zournás are found at local festivals, as is the *daoúli* a deep-toned drum similar to the Turkish *ramzalla* and Albanian *tupan*. The klaríno and *toumbeléki* (lap drum) are not unknown, but even in their relatively gentle presence the dances are fast and hard-stamping. Occasionally the Turkish *kemençe*, very similar to the *líra*, can be found playing the *barfalidigo*, a chain-dance popular at Macedonian weddings. The kemençe also accompany songs by guests gathered at the courtyard of the bride's house after the church service. They are performed with a series of round dances which can last hours.

FOLK OF THE ISLANDS

The largest of the Dodecanese are Rhodes and Kos, both of which are close to the Turkish coast. Despite this proximity, Turkish influence on the music of the islands is minimal. Today the standard form of instrumental music is a duet between vióli and laoúto.

Other instruments found on the islands include *pinávli* or *floyéra* (flutes) and tsamboúna (bagpipe). Most of the island musicians are semiprofessionals, music supplementing their income as craftsmen or farmers. They are often called upon to play at weddings, or at local *panyiri* – village feasts in honour of the patron-saint of the local church.

Crete is the most promising area in Greece for hearing live music outside of festival time. Although primarily agricultural, there are several large towns on the north coast, making it rich in both urban and rural music traditions. The traditional Cretan ensemble has one líra player and one or two laoúto players. The líra player is usually the leader of the ensemble and the source of new compositions and improvisations. The rhythmic accompaniment of the ensemble comes from the laoúto, which are rarely used to their full potential; but a good player will coax a pleasing chime-like tone from his instrument. These ensembles play highly syncopated music which accompanies lively dances, providing most of the music heard around the island.

The **Ionian islands** were never occupied by the Turks, unlike the rest of Greece, and they have a predominantly western musical tradition. The indigenous song-form is Italian both in name (*kantádhes*) and instrumentation (guitar and mandolin). It is most often heard these days on the islands of Lefkádha and Zákinthos.

AMANÉDHES

Early this century, across the Aegean Sea in Smyrna (now Izmir) and Constantinople (now Istanbul), music cafés were a popular diversion. Groups played a style known as *cafe amanes* or amanédhes, after the interjecting refrain "Aman, Aman", "Alas, Alas" or "Mercy, Mercy", which was used not only as a chorus, but also as a means of giving the singer time to think of new lyrics or exotic embellishments. The music was graceful and engaging and the singing required considerable skill, and echoed the vocal styles of Persia and central Asia. The instruments most commonly used in amanédhes included violin, *kanonáki* (zither), *sandoúri* (hammer dulcimer), *oúti* (lute) and *saz* (a long-necked lute from which the Greek *bouzouki* was derived). The female singer often played castanets and danced on stage. Some of the great singers of this era were Rosa Eskenazi, Rita Abatsi and, in America, Marika Papagika.

Rosa Eskenazi

Rosa Eskenazi, a Greek Jew, was perhaps the most famous of all Greek singers. Born in Istanbul around the turn of the century, she moved with her family to Thrace and then, in 1922, to Athens. In Athens she started singing in cafés for tips, until she was discovered by the influential composer and recording executive **Panayotis Tundas**. He encouraged her to expand her *smyrneïka* repertoire with popular songs from the Greek mainland. She later found

> **Among the Beauties of Athens**
> Among Athenian beauties,
> One stands apart
> In flaming hearts.
> Black hair she has,
> Black eyes she's got,
> Upon her cheek a beauty spot.
>
> Aman, Aman, crazy I shall be.
> From the first time I saw her
> She's done bad to me.
> And I'm wasting away
> from the love in my heart,
> And without her I'll never be cured.
> **Skarvelis (1933).**

fame with rembétika songs like "Young Butcher", "Little Mary" and "Among the Beauties of Athens", recording many discs in the US during the 1940s. She died in 1981.

Rita Abatsi was Rosa Eskenazi's chief rival among female singers. She too was born in Smyrna, in 1913, and started singing at an early age. In the 1930s she was part of a famous trio with fiddle-player **Dhimitrios Semsis** and guitarist and tanbur-player **Aghapios Toumboulis**. Abatsi's style and arrangements incorporated rhythmic syncopations and *glissandi* (vocal slides) which became her trademark. She was one of the most prolific of all the singers of the 1930s and 1940s, and many of her 78 recordings have survived on a reissued album by EMI and Adherfi Falirea (the label formerly managed by the Athens shop, Pop Eleven) including "The Turkish Slipper", "Gazeli Neva Sabah" and "Kalogria", written by the great composer Papazoglu. Rita Abatsi died in 1969 at the age of 56.

Marika Papagika was born around the turn of the century on the island of Kos. Her recording career really started when she emigrated to America in 1918. Most of her best recordings were made with the violinist **Athanasios Makedonas** and with her husband, Kostas, playing sandoúri. Her first recordings were mainly old rural folksongs and sentimental west European-style songs, but she soon moved on to sing in the Smyrna-style, with songs like"Katinaki Moy", "Idhes Dhio Kyparissia" and "O Lagos", for which she became famous. Her success highlighted the demand for Greek music within the Greek-American community and she paved the way for many other artists to record in America.

It is interesting to note that, at the time, the popular records played at 78rpm were normally 10-inch discs, but the average Greek record was 12 inches, which made it possible to extend performances from three minutes to four.

REMBÉTIKA

Modern Greek music emerged at the end of Ottoman rule – which effectively gave birth to the Greek state – and with the rise of a new urban culture. In musical choices, the upper and middle classes leaned towards the light Viennese and Italian styles of classical music, while at the other end of the social spectrum Greek and Byzantine traditions prevailed, mixed with central Balkan and Eastern influences. These trends were intensified by the influx of refugees from Asia Minor as the result of the disastrous events of the early 1920s.

In 1919 the Greeks, in the grip of the *megáli idhéa*, a nationalist ideology calling for the reconstruction of the Byzantine Empire, landed in Asia Minor as a prelude to annexation of large parts of the defeated Ottoman Empire. By 1922 they had been repelled by troops led by Mustapha Kemal (later known as Atatürk) and fled back to Smyrna. This humiliation resulted in the exchange of religious minorities, ratified by the peace treaty of 1923. Turkey was to accept 390,000 Muslims resident on Greek soil. Greece, however, was faced with the resettlement of over 1,300,000 Christian refugees. As a result of this, huge shanty towns grew up around Athens, Pireás and other cities. These new refugees brought their music with them, and this had the most pronounced effect on the urban music of Greece, for it was often only the poorest class of workers who had constant contact with the refugees and their culture. The musicians of these two cultures were constantly "borrowing" musical ideas from one another.

Rembetíka had been around in some form since the turn of the century. It had always been the music of the poor and the dispossessed, and combined musical styles of the eastern Mediterranean with lyrics telling of the plight and joys of their lot – often partly in Turkish. Perhaps the best definition of rembetíka is given by Gail Holst in her excellent book, *The Road to Rembetíka*: "What was special about the rembetíka song was the combination between traditional musical forms of the eastern Mediterranean and the words of the songs, which dealt with the life of the urban underworld and the less reputable elements of society." The word itself has no certain derivation, though the old Turkish word *rembet*, meaning "from the gutter", is the most likely.

Rembetíka has its origins in an oral tradition where improvisation played a part in both the music and the lyrics. Songs always started with an instrumental prelude, the *taxími*, where a good musician showed his ability. These taxími would let people know which mode the song was in, setting the mood of the song to come, and they could last from one to twenty minutes depending on how the musician was feeling. After this the song would start, often with the singer improvising lyrics, sometimes to a familiar tune, maybe mentioning people in the audience and possibly touching on recent events of local interest. Some songs are attributed to a particular composer or musician but, in many cases, musicians improvised both the music and the lyrics as they sat together.

Rembetes at Piraeus, 1937

TAKE ME TO THE TEKÉDHES

In the 1920s and 1930s rembétika could be heard in the many *tekédhes* of Athens, Pireás and Thessaloníki. These were hash dens where the workers, the out-of-work and the *mánges* – the Athenian "spiv" or "wide boy" subcultures – would meet to drink sweet coffee and enjoy small *narghilés* (water pipes) of the best hashish from Bursa or Syros. Sometimes a lone man would get up and do the slow *zembékiko* dance.

Three great figures – Batis, Artemis and Stratos – were associated with this early rembétika and they are commemorated in a wonderful old song of the time:

Secretly in a boat I went
And at Thrakou's cave I came out,
I saw three stoned men
Stretched out on the sand.

It was Batis and Artemis,
And Stratos the Lazy One:
Hey, you Stratos! Oi, you Stratos,
Fix us a good narghilé.

So old Batis can smoke,
Who for many years has been a dervish,
So Artemis can smoke too,

Who brings us stuff wherever he goes.
He sends us hashish from Constantinople
And all of us get high.
And Persian tobacco
The manges smokes quietly.

The trio all frequented the same tekédhes and, along with Markos Vamvakaris, they formed arguably the greatest of all rembétika groups. By the mid-1930s they were playing every night in the tekédhes around Pireás and Athens.

Batis was the clown of the group – not a particularly good singer or musician, but very popular with the mánges for his quick wit and generosity. He was a used-car salesman and always had a few drachmas to spare when the others were broke. **Stratos**, the group's singer, later went on to perform with mainstream stars like Tsitsanis and Papaioanou. **Artemis** (Anestos Delias) was the only member of the group who had any musical training. His father had been a well-known sandoúri player in Smyrna until 1922. Artemis was adept on guitar and bouzoúki by the time he was sixteen, when he started to write songs. In his short career his few compositions – like "In the Baths of Costantinople" and "The Show-Off" – all became classics. Sadly, by the time he had teamed up with the other members of the groups he was taking hard drugs and on the way down. In 1934 he wrote the song that could have been his epitaph, "The Junkie's Lament":

From the time I started to smoke the dose,
The world rejected me.
I don't know what to do.
Wherever I stand, wherever I'll be,
People bother me.
My soul can't stand it,
"Junkie", they are calling me.
Sniffing certainly led me to the needle
Until my body slowly melted and became weak.
Nothing was left in this world for me to do,
Because the drugs have led me
to die in the streets.

In 1943, at the age of 29, he was found dead in the street outside a tekédhes with his bouzoúki in his hand.

MARKOS VAMVAKARIS

Markos Vamvakaris, the "grandfather of rembétika", was born on the island of Syros in 1905. His father played the gaïda (bagpipe) in cafés to supplement the family's income, and Markos often accompanied him on a dog-skin drum. When he was eight, the family were so desperate for money that Markos had to leave school and work in a cotton factory. He hated this and soon left to sell newpapers on the street and run errands for local shopkeepers. At the age of fifteen he stowed away on a boat bound for Pireás. Pireás was a rough port full of criminals, tramps, prostitutes and hash. When he arrived he got a job as a dock labourer and then in a slaughterhouse. It was whilst working in the slaughterhouse that he first heard the bouzoúki and vowed to get a bouzoúki himself and learn to play. Within six months he was writing songs and playing in the tekédhes where he met other musicians like Stratos, Batis and Artemis.

The **Pireás Quartet**, as the four of them became known, atracted huge crowds at the tekédhes they played, many of whom tended to get overexcited by the music. Fights often started and, many nights, the police were called in to break up the crowd. Markos opened his own café where they could play, but the police wanted information about drugs from him before granting him a licence. Having failed with the café, Markos, Batis and a pianist, Rovertakis, went on a tour of Markos' island, Syros. Following that tour he wrote probably his most famous song, "Frankosyriani", about a Catholic girl from the island of Syros:

Markos never considered himself a singer – he usually left that to Stratos, who had a much

I have a flame ablaze in my heart.
It's as if you've bewitched me,
Sweet Frankosyriani
I'll come to meet you again on the shore,
I'd like to satiate myself on caresses and kisses.
I'll take you to Pateli, to Neohori.
We'll be fine at Alithini,
And romancing at Biskopo,
My sweet Frankosyriani

Markos Vamvakaris (right)

sweeter voice – but when Columbia wanted to release a record by him they persuaded him to have a go, and were pleased with his gruff, metallic style. Subsequently, he sang on nearly all his records and the gravelly style became an archetype that many other singers copied.

The late 1930s were a difficult period: the German army had started its rampage over Europe and Greece was being run by the dictator Metaxas. Metaxas clamped down on hash-smoking and many musicians sought refuge in Thessaloníki. Here they had a certain amount of freedom because the police chief, Vassilis Mouskoudhis, was a rembétika fan and allowed the musicians to smoke in peace. Mouskoudhis became so popular on the music scene that he was even best man at Vassilis Tsitsanis' wedding.

Metaxas ordered the record companies to stop recording hashish songs and make rembétika respectable entertainment. This, coupled with the new Greek passion for Italian kantádhes, resulted in enomous changes to the rembetic tradition. And with kantádhes came the major and minor scales of accordion, piano and guitar, none of which could play the quarter-tones required for the old "roads".

So the oriental flavour of rembétika started to disappear. The old style of prewar music that Markos had popularized in rembetic circles was going out of fashion. He and his brother

Vassilis Tsitsanis

had a brief flurry in the late1940s with the now famous **Kalamata** group, which also included famous musicians such as Papaianou, Hadzichristou, Mitsakis and Manisalis. But really their time had passed. Postwar Greece was looking for new heroes and new ideas. Some of these came in an unusual guise.

CLOUDY SUNDAY

One of the new heroes was **Vassilis Tsitsanis**. He did not have the usual background of a rembétis: his father was a leather and silver craftsman who sometimes played the bouzoúki but forbade his son to touch it. Vassilis inherited the instrument on his father's death, however, and quickly became adept. He originally came to Athens to enrol as a law student at the university, but it was soon apparent that his future lay with music. A shy man, always smartly attired in English sports jackets, his sad eyes feature in all the photographs of the time. He is said to have looked sad even when smiling, yet he was adored by millions and when he died in 1984 the streets of Athens filled with a crowd of 200,000 people and innumerable bouzoúkis.

Tsitsanis substituted love themes for drug lyrics, and made the rembétika sound softer and the words more pleading. With this mellowing he reached a far wider audience than the prewar singers ever had. He made his first recording – "This is Why I Wander the Streets of Athens" – in 1937, and he continued to record during his military service in Thessaloníki between 1938 and 1940. By the time of his release from the army in 1940, he was a prolific composer and a master of improvisation. He remained in Thessaloníki and – as all the recording studios were closed – opened a small ouzo bar where he sang nightly. By this time he had started to integrate the rembétika form with Italian kantádhes, which was increasingly popular. During Greece's occupation he wrote some of his most beautiful songs, including "Cloudy Sunday", a thinly veiled lament for his desecrated homeland and demoralized countrypeople. Although it wasn't recorded until 1948, the song quickly spread by word of mouth, becoming an anthem of the dispossessed:

Cloudy Sunday, you look like my heart
Which is always overcast, Christ and Virgin,
You are a day like the one when I lost my joy.
Cloudy Sunday, you make my heart bleed,
When I see you rainy, I can't have a moment peacefully,
You make my life black and I sigh heavily

Concert poster for Marika Ninou

REVIVALS

Through the efforts of groups of real enthusiasts rembétika has had several revivals, first during the time of the military junta in the late-1960s when students identified with its rebellious nature and the hashish themes of the prewar style. There was a second burst of enthusiasm in the first few years after the fall of the junta in 1974, when small, illegal clubs spouted and tried to emulate the smoky, prewar days. Several groups sprang up, most notable of which were **Ta Pedhia apo Patra** ("the Boys from Patras"), but they had all disbanded by the end of the 1980s. Even the music written by Stratos Xarhakos and Nikos Gatsos – which is probably the best original rembétika written in the last 30 years – sounds too clean. Rembétika is essentially a music of nostalgia and regret: it loses its immediacy in a world in which individuals have relatively more freedom of choice.

Once in a while, though, an old star gets out his bouzoúki and plays in some of the less over-amplified clubs in Athens: a few have made quite successful comebacks, like **Mihalis Yennitsaris**. And occasionally an old man will get up to dance a slow, passionate *zembékiko* while the younger generation, who have less passion but a more sexual and gangling style, laugh because they don't understand. As remétika historian Gail Holst expresses it "The young men were talking to the birds; the old man to the stars."

NÉO KÍMA

The first **néo kíma** (new wave) music emerged in small Athenian clubs during the early 1960s. Most of these clubs, which initially concentrated in the Pláka district, were closed down during the 1967–74 military junta, and most of those that survived degenerated into expensive, glitzy, plate-smashing nightclubs. But their legacy remains an important source of inspiration.

In part a reprise of the forms of rembétika, as well as a politicized folk movement with connections to trends such as *nueva canción* in Latin America, néo kíma's young, improvisatory composers identified strongly with the Greek Left, whose revolutionary songs they revived and adapted.

Though not directly associated with the néo kíma movement, **Mikis Theodharakis** and **Manos Hadzidhakis** – the two best-known modern Greek composers – had much in common

In the mid-1940s Tsitsanis started working with **Sotiria Bellou**, the beginning of a partnership that led them both to stardom. She was a formidable-looking women with cropped hair and a voice to match. Her greatest skill was in rendering tragic songs which less powerful singers would have sentimentalized.

The other great female singer associated with Tsitsanis was Marika Nikolaidou, better known as **Ninou**. Her voice was softer and more sensuous than Sotiria's. She worked with Tsitsanis until her emigration to America in 1953. He, meanwhile, contin-ued to work until the end of the 1970s, and always with star billing.

The mid-1950s saw the emer-gence of the *arhondorembétes* – the rembetic-style musicians who got really rich. These were mostly bouzoúki players with impressive techniques like **Hiotis**, who was responsible for adding the fourth pair of strings and changing the tuning, thus enabling him to play faster. By this time "rembétika" bore little resemblance to the bluesy, gasping sound of the 1930s and 1940s. Middle-class trend-setters would go to bouzoúki joints – a highly expensive night out – and people would throw thousands of drachmas at the musicians, paying to dance badly and smash plates.

REMBÉTIKA IN ATHENS

. . . .

Over the past few years rembétika has become popular in Athens again, although it is no longer the music of the poor and dispossessed. Today's audience is the middle-class intelligentsia and the music is played by groups of talented, predominantly young, musicians. There are two principal clubs in Athens with the music starting around midnight. There is no entrance fee, but food and drinks tend to be pricey and there may be a minimum charge. Both clubs are small so reservation is advised.

Reportaz (☎923 2114), on the corner of Diakou and Tzireon near the Temple of Zeus. Don't be put off by the kitsch decor featuring *karaghiozis* puppets; the music is good. There's a dining area downstairs and a tiny bar above.

Stoa Athanaton (☎321 4362), in a great location in an alleyway off Athens' fish and meat market halfway between Monastiraki and Omonia. It's just behind the intersection of Athinas and Sofokleous. All-night sessions in a rather exclusive upstairs taverna.

with its spirit. Theodharakis' international reputation owes as much to his political turnabouts as to his compositions. It's perhaps fairer to judge him by his astonishing settings of poetry by Odysseas Elytis and his 1960s work with the **Horódhia Trikálon** (the Trikala Choir) and vocalist **Maria Farandouri**, which are certainly more representative than his overplayed soundtrack for Zorba the Greek. Farandouri, like Theodhorakis a member of the Greek-Turkish Friendship Society, also appeared on a few albums during the 1980s with Turkish protest musician **Zülfü Livaneli**. Hadzidhakis, who died in June 1994, mostly steered clear of political statements; instead he launched his own record label during the 1980s, Sirios, to provide a forum for various non-mainstream musicians, including his own "disciples".

To outside ears, the contemporary Greek music scene tends to begin and end with these highly arranged, quasi-symphonic instrumental works. Only the Cretan composer, **Ioannis Markopoulos**, relies on recognizably Greek vernacular forms; his material is described as *éntehno*, which translates approximately as "art composition". He employed authentic folk material and instruments but in juxtapositions that you would never have heard in their natural environment.

Perhaps the first musician to break out of the bouzoúki mould was Thessaloníki-born **Dhionisios Savvopoulos**, who appeared in

1966 with his first album, "To Fortigo", quickly carving a niche for himself with his maniacal, rasping voice and elliptical, angst-ridden lyrics, his persona embellished by shoulder-length hair and outsized glasses. Solo-guitar accompaniment soon gave way to twisted orchestration on his subsequent records. Because his material was not overtly political, Savvopoulos was one of the few "protest" artists able to perform under the junta, and he became something of a password among the generation coming of age under its doleful sway. Savvopoulos gave due acknowledgment to the gypsy influence on Greek popular music, and served briefly as head of Lyra records in the late 1980s. Yet some critics found his music pretentious and unlistenable; and many others ceased to give him serious consideration after his much-publicized return to the Orthodox Church.

Other guitarist/composers, in a country not usually known for them, include **Notis Mavroudhis** and **Kostas Hadzis**, a gypsy guitarist whose recent collaboration with mainstream vocalist **Haris Alexiou** featured wonderful duets in Romany.

An earlier, explicit tip of the hat to the gypsies was made by **Nikos Ksidhakis and Nikos Papazoglou** in their landmark 1978 release, "Ih Ekdhikisi tis Yiftias" ("The Revenge of Gypsydom"), a classic, now available on CD. The opening track, featuring a deceptively serene Savvopoulos, gives way to spirited, defiant lyrics and rhythmic melodies, both a homage to and a send-up of the sort of music beloved of the itinerant truck-drivers who peddle cheap bedding and plastic buckets around the countryside. The two Nikos, joined by **Manolis Rasoulis, Dhimitris Kondoyannis** and **Sofia Dhiamandi**, followed this up a year later with "Ta Dithen", another successful effort edging more explicitly into the territory of urban folk and even rembétika without completely forsaking gypsy culture.

Ksidhakis' genius is more as an arranger, and a magnet for other talent, than a composer. After a relatively long silence broken only by "Proti Vranhia sti Athina" with **Glykeria** – a singer much maligned for her glass-breaking voice, but credited with reviving many old folk and rembetic standards – Ksidhakis came back with a vengeance in 1987 on "Konda sti Dhoxa mia Stigmi", accompanied by **Ross Daly** and top vocalist **Eleftheria Arvanitaki**. There's not a wasted note on what's simply one of the best Greek discs ever, one of the first Lyra releases popular enough to get issued as a CD. Most of the tunes are firmly based on mainland and urban traditions, and have a strong gypsy flavour, but the lyrics – by turns mythically symbolic and

suggestively ambiguous – have distanced themselves from the straightforward appeal of Ksidhakis' first two collections.

Also from northern Greece came **Himerini Kolimvites**, a group of architects from Thessaloniki and Kavala led by Aryiris Bakirtzis, whose eponymous first album has acquired enduring cult status in the decade since its 1981 release. Rembetic, mainland pop and even island models are set on their ear with rich, drunken harmonies drawn out on both bowed and plucked strings, and utterly surreal lyrics. Disappointingly, their later releases haven't live up to that debut.

Less easily categorized is the work of **Stamatis Kraounakis and Lina Nikolakopoulou**, whose 1985 "Kykloforo keh Oploforo" was a thoughtful, if somewhat slick, exploration of the boundary between rock, jazz-cabaret and Greek styles. More pop-oriented, but similar in approach, **Thanos Mikroutsikos** and Nikolakopoulou featured Haris Alexiou on their 1991 record "Krataei Hronia Avti ih Kolonia".

The road to folk and Byzantine revival and/or adaptations seemed in some cases to lead from the realm of film soundtracks and "art" extravaganza so much in vogue during the 1960s

YIORGOS DALARAS-THE GREEK BRUCE SPRINGSTEEN

•••••••••••••••••••••••••

Any look at contemporary Greek music would be incomplete without mention of **Yiorgos (George) Dalaras**, a musical phenomenon of the last twenty years, who has been dubbed the Greek Bruce Springsteen. Born in 1950, the son of a Piraeus rembétika-player, Dalaras is the king of *laiki* – pop – but also spans the whole range of Greek music. He has released over 40 LPs, ranging through the dhimotiká folk repertoire to the works of Theodorakis, Hadjidakis and Markopoulo; he even taught himself enough Spanish to do passable covers of Latin American and flamenco standards, with the American blues guitarist Al Di Meola. He's versatile enough, too, to have performed solo on four tracks of Hronis Aïdhonidhis' highly recommended "Songs of Thrace and Asia Minor" album. In Greece, his concerts pack 80,000 at a time into football stadia.

Yiorgos Dalaras's Latin album with Al Di Meola

and 70s. Instrument-maker and arranger **Hristodhoulos Halaris** did a version of the Cretan epic "Erotokritos" back in 1976, with Nikos Ksilouris and Tania Tsanaklidhou as vocalists. His 1980 soundtrack for "O Megalexandhros" was disappointing, but introduced **Hrisanthos**, a male singer with a distinctive high-register voice.

Halaris has gone on to concentrate exclusively on Byzantine chants, beginning with the controversial "Ih Melodhi tou Pathous", hymns of Constantinopolitan composer Petros Peloponnisios, whose instrumentation caused outrage in some circles.

Medieval – rather than Byzantine – Constantinopolitan was the emphasis of **Vosforos** (**Bogaziçi**), a group coordinated in Istanbul from 1988 to 1992 by **Nikiforos Mataxas** to preserve and play Ottoman classical, devotional and popular music. The specific appeal and pertinence to Grecophiles was demonstrated by the contents and packaging of their first album, "Vosforos", subtitled "Greek Composers of the City" (ie Constantinople), and concentrating on the contribution of Greek and other non-Turkish musicians to the Ottoman courtly tradition. The formality of their second, double album "Bogaziçi in Concert at the Palas Theatre, 15 March 1988", was broken only by a few light zeybek dances.

More modest in scale and aims is **Dhinameis tou Egeou**, which started out as three musicians – Hristos Tsiamoulis, Ioannis Zevgolis, and Mihalis Klapakis – in their namesake first album, and acquired two more on later discs. Despite some ill-advised noodling with bells, sitar and Egyptian ney (flute), they are one of the more accessible folk/island/*smyrneïka* revival groups, and their original compositions – especially on "Ihos Veeta" – are often as interesting as the older material, a good omen for the future.

DISCOGRAPHY

Most of the Greek releases below are available in Britain (or worldwide by mail order) from *Trehantiri* (367 Green Lanes, London N4; ☎0181/802 6530). In Greece, an excellent shop is *Tzina*, at Panepistimíou 57, near Omónia Square, Athens.

EARLY REMBÉTIKA

CD **Various** *Greek Oriental Rembetika 1911–37* (Arhoolie, US). An essential rembétika compilation, with great names like Rosa Eskenazi, Andónis Dalgás, and many more. Includes Rosa's "Why I Smoke Cocaine". A must.

CD **Various** *The Greek Archives* (FM Records, Greece). This looks set to become the classic collection of rembétika: a series of (so far) twelve CDs covering every aspect of the music – and other Greek styles and traditions, too. Particular rembétika gems, so far, include the first three volumes, covering the music in America, from 1920–45 and 1945–60 (vols 2 & 3) and volume 12 of "unknown recordings".

CD **Various** *Greek Orientale* (Polylyric, Greece). A superb collection of smyrneïka-style songs from the 1920s and 1930s, including songs by Rosa Eskenazi, Rita Abatsi, Marika Papagika and Semsis. Good sleeve notes in English and translations of many lyrics.

CD **Various** *Historic urban folk songs from Greece* (Rounder, US). A collection of archive recordings of top rembétes. Really terrific stuff, mostly from the 1930s.

Andónis Dálgas *Periorismena Atitypa yai Syllektes* (Lyra, Greece). A varied, well-edited collection of the gifted Constantinopolitan singer.

Anestos Delias *1912–1944* (Adherfi Falirea, Greece). Collection by one of the best songwriters of the 1930s, better known as Artemis. Performed by the famous quartet of Stratos, Markos Vamvakaris, Batis and Artemis.

Vangelis Papazoglou *1897–1943* (Adherfi Falirea, Greece). A double album of classic songs from the 1920s and 1930s written by Papazoglou and sung by most of the top stars of the era, including Stellakis, Rosa Eskenazi, Kostas Roukounas and Rita Abatsi.

LATER AND CONTEMPORARY REMBÉTIKA

Sotiriou Bellou *1946–1956* (Margo, Greece). Early work by the "Greek Billie Holliday", the first somewhat better: both without the electric backing of later years.

Marika Ninou … *at Jimmy the Fat's* (Venus/Tzina, Greece). Poor sound quality since it was a clandestine live recording, but still a classic. Ninou sings live with Tsitsanis in the early 1950s, including two cuts in Turkish.

CD **Vasilis Tsitsanis** *Yia Panta 1937–1940 Vols 1* and 2 (EMI, Greece). A CD-release of two early Tsitsanis albums, mostly with Stratos on vocals. CD *Vasilis Tsitsanis 1938–1955* (EMI, Greece) is a good Tsitsanis collection with Sotiria Bellou, Marika Ninou and Stratos singing.

CD **Stratos Xarhakos and Nikos Gatsos** *Rembétiko* (CBS, US). Soundtrack to the namesake film, available as a double LP or, in slightly edited form, on one CD. Virtually the only "original" rembétika to be composed in the last 30 years.

CD **Mihalis Yennitsaris** *Saltadoros* (Trikont, Germany). One of the last surviving composer/performers from the early days appears live on this German collection with singer Maria Nalbandi and the group Prosekhos.

FOLK MUSIC

CD **Yiorgos Mangas** *Yiorgos Mangas* (GlobeStyle, UK). Studio- recorded gypsy-derived klaríno music from one of the less well-known clarinettists. A fairly good introduction and widely available.

CD **Hronis Aidhonidhis** *Songs of Thrace and Asia Minor* (Minos Matsas, Greece). The best and most accessible collection available, featuring Thrace's top folk singer, plus accompaniment by Ross Daly and solos by pop stalwart George Dalaras.

CD **Ross Daly** *Selected Works* (RCA, Greece), The best place to start for budding Daly fans, with good notes. His latest album, CD *Anki* (RCA, Greece), was released in late 1994. Daly's local cassettes, *Anadhysi* (Sirios, Greece), *Okto tragoudhia keh ena Semai*, *O Kyklos sto Stavrodhromi* and *Hori* (all three on BMG Ariola, Greece) are all worthy of investigation.

ⓒ **Yannis Parios** *Ta Nisiotika Vols 1* and *2* (Minos Matsas, Greece). Parios sparked a renewal of interest in *nisiotikó* (traditional, island) music – maybe not the most authentic renditions but easy on the ear.

ⓒ **Various** *Grèce – Chants polyphoniques et musique d'Epiré* (Ocora, France). One of the best recordings from Epirus. Klárino, frame drums and bells for the dances, polyphonic vocals on the ballads and laments.

Various *Greek Music from the Island of Crete* (Lyrichord, Greece). A good mixture of ballads and dance tunes, played on líra, laoúto and bagpipes.

Various *Songs of...* (Society for the Dissemination of National Music, Greece). A 30-strong series of LPs, each covering the traditional music of one region or type. All contain lyrics in English and are easily available in Athens at the Musicological Museum.

ⓒ **Various** *Takoutsia, Musiciens de Zagori: Inédit – Grèce - Epiré* (Inédit/Auvidis, France). Drinking songs, dance tunes and dirges, performed by one of the last working clans of Epirot gypsy musicians. Wonderful.

ⓒ **Various** *Armenians, Jews, Turks and Gipsies in Old Recordinhgs* (FM Records, Greece). This imaginative release is volume 8 of the new "Greek Archives" series (see above).

NÉO KÍMA

ⓒ **Kostas Hadzis and Haris Alexiou** *Alexiou Tragoudhaei Hadzis* (Minos Matsas, Greece). Hadzis by himself is disappointing: but with Alexiou, singing in Greek or Romany, it's Greek flamenco.

Notis Mavroudhis and Nikos Houliaras *Ekdhromi* (Zodiac, Greece). Rare guitar-voice duo: one side contains haunting versions of Epirot folk songs, the other original pieces.

ⓒ **Dhinameis tou Egeou** *Anatoliko Parathiro* (Sirios, Greece). The latest from five folk revivalists.

ⓒ **Himerini Kolimvites** (self-produced, 1981). First, cult-status recording by a group of architects from Thessaloníki and Kavála, milking rembétika, pop and island traditions for surreal lyrics and rich melodies.

ⓒ **Stamatis Kraounakis and Lina Nikolakopoulou** *Kykoforo keh Oploforo* (Polydor, Greece). Perhaps most representative of the "pop" wing of New Music trends.

ⓒ **Nikos Ksidhakis and Nikos Papazoglou** *Ih Ekdhikisi tis Yiftias* (Lyra, Greece). Groundbreaking recording of the late 1970s, still much loved in Greece.

ⓒ **Nikos Ksidhakis and Eleftheria Arvanitaki** *Konda sti Dhoxa mia Stigmi* (Lyra, Greece). One of the best Greek discs of the last twenty years, featuring superb Ksidhakis arrangements and compositions.

ⓒ **Nikos Papazoglou** *Synerga* (Lyra, Greece). Recent offering from the composer-performer, returning to his introspective earlier style .

ⓒ **Domna Samiou** *Seryiani* (Sirios, Greece). "New" traditional music by a folk music collector, interpreter and revivalist.

ⓒ **Dhionisios Savvopoulos** *Dheka Hronia Kommatia* (Lyra, Greece). Retrospective anthology of the composer's best decade.

ⓒ **Mikis Theodharakis and Maria Farandouri** (Minos Matsas, Greece). A good album, representative of their long collaboration.

ⓒ **Vosforos** *Greek Composers of Constantinople* (EMI, Greece). First and best exploration of the Anatolian dimension of Greek music.

No Purist
An Interview with Ross Daly

Ross Daly is an Irishman, born in England, who trained in classical music, studied sitar and rabab in Asia, and then, pausing in Crete, became entranced by the sound of the líra or three-string Cretan spike fiddle. He mastered the instrument while living on the island in the 1970s and '80s, and also spent time in Turkey learning the kemençe, a Turkish equivalent. More recently, Daly coordinated "Lavirinthos", a workshop dedicated to the interpretation of music from past and present Greece and Turkey – and occasionally beyond. A long-time Grecophile, he is currently based in Athens, where he spoke to Marc Dubin.

Your interest seems to have begun with Cretan music and expanded ever outwards.

That's true. But when I began studying all these instruments, I didn't intend to become a specifically Cretan líra-player. I never felt the desire to confine myself to a given tradition – and not being Cretan, I couldn't be a Cretan líra player anyway. What I can offer involves following a course related to my own life and travels. So I'm interested in music ranging from Cretan folk to Turkish classical, plus certain kinds of Persian and Indian music. I've always made it clear that I'm not trying to do anything "authentic". I'm not a purist. But neither did I set out with the intent of popularizing things. The fact that my approach to traditional music became popular surprised me.

So how did you start out in Crete?

I started out with a number of people in Iraklion, the first nucleus of Lavirinthos, by playing Cretan folk standards in the way that we felt best. We also played my own compositions and those of other members of our group. These were based on Cretan forms, since we – mostly Cretan musicians – were performing exclusively in Crete then. We expected to have somebody throw a tomato at us, but that never happened, and audiences liked it very much, much to our surprise.

The Cretans are very conservative musically, but what I've always tried to do is play a piece, especially an old one, as I understand it. I study its history and origins, so I know what the traditional sound is today, and what it would have been thirty, forty, or seventy years ago. Once I have as clear an image as I can, I start doing personal experiments. I've noticed that in most musical traditions, the whole approach to the music changes every forty to fifty years. For example, people involved with Turkish classical music are extremely conservative, not tolerating any change whatsoever. They treat the recordings of Nezat Atlig's orchestra or any of the well-known contemporary Turkish classical orchestras as an absolute standard. However, if you listen to recordings from the 1930s of the same pieces, the sound is quite different, and if you go back further to the recordings of Tamburi Cemil Bey – who died in 1916 – you hear again an entirely different style.

Many Greek and Turkish melodies travel well, with verses in Greek, Turkish or even Slavic languages.
In my opinion there are no ethnic boundaries, only regional ones, and even outside of these music travels. For instance, around Izmir there are Greek and Turkish versions of "Tsakitsis/Çakiçi", about a famous turn-of-the-century bandit, and any Greek or Turk who was raised there can hum the respective lyrics for you. There was also an old oud player here in Athens called Ioannis Souris, born in Anatolia. He remembered a lot of old songs, so they used to get him on the radio to be recorded. Halfway through a song, which he'd started in Greek, he'd switch to Turkish, go back to Greek, then back to Turkish, and the station staff used to get annoyed with him because they wanted only the Greek lyrics! And he'd say, "Okay, I'll skip the Turkish ones", but he'd get carried away and keep changing back and forth.

Formerly, when these people lived together, it was common to sing in two languages at once. Another example of how music belongs to regions and not to ethnic groups is the Black Sea. The Pontic Greeks, who now mainly live near Thessaloniki, play a music which originated along the Black Sea and which they consider to be theirs. But if you listen to the music of the Laz, coastal Muslims speaking a language like Georgian, or that of the Hemsin, Armenian-speaking pagans converted to Islam who live just inland along the Black Sea, it's difficult to tell the difference. So music tends to be regional: whoever lives, or was living, somewhere, has a tradition which doesn't respect linguistic or ethnic or religious boundaries. It's true of the entire Caucasus. The songs of Bulgarian, Greek and Turkish Thrace are also very similar.

How do the gypsies fit in?
If you consider the Greek folk music of the central mainland, the Peloponnese, Epirus and Thrace, its instrumental music – especially clarinet – is almost entirely derived from gypsy culture. The exception is Epirot polyphonic song which the gypsies don't participate in, but all Epirot instrumentalists have historically been of gypsy origin.

Just as some people say flamenco isn't Spanish folk, but Andalucian gypsy music, most mainland Greek music can be described as Greek gypsy music. So it's sad that their huge contribution is ignored and even denigrated. Many Greeks, if they want to disparage a particular music, call it tourkoyfftika, "Turkish gypsy," two of the worst pejoratives combined. But Turkish gypsy clarinet is extremely beautiful, not at all what's played in Athens nightclubs.

With your extensive travels in Greece and Turkey, you're well placed to evaluate the health of traditional music in each country.
The majority of folk music played in Greece or Turkey is extremely low-quality in all respects. Despite this, you find amongst all this atrociousness some good musicians playing dreadful stuff, who in different circumstances would be playing more interesting material. There are many reasons for this, but mainly overdependence on western European and American cultural prototypes. A Greek child showing musical talent may start off with a traditional instrument, but as soon as possible he'll be channelled into classical piano or strings, and be sent to an odhío, those terrible music schools which have sprouted up all over Greece.

You're describing part of the general ksenomanía (craze for foreign things) in Greece, but that doesn't really explain rock drums and bass guitars at "traditional" village festivals, or clarinettists at Turkish weddings.
Formerly in Greek or Turkish culture, the whole spectrum of society – from the least to the most educated – drew on the same, implicitly understood tradition. There was an interchange of ideas and activities between members of every class.

Now, only those deprived of the opportunity to study classical music end up playing traditional instruments. The highly educated no longer concern themselves with this music. So the folk idiom has become the preserve of "deprived" people and audiences demand heavily electrified, bad-taste material.

Not enough people from all levels of society take an informed interest in Greek music. I doubt if there is one Greek in ten today who can tell you what Greek music actually is. They've become alienated from their own heritage, existing in a cultural limbo while trying to become "Europeans" under duress. And it's not only true of Greek folk. The many Greek rock groups of recent years haven't the slightest idea of what rock is!

So the outlook for any musical tradition in Greece is poor. What about Turkey?

The Turks have certain advantages. They've collected huge amounts of material and there are also very good schools in Turkey for the study of Turkish classical or folk music, and you can find extraordinary recordings in radio station archives. At least in Turkey, people who concern themselves with Turkish music know very well what it is. I've met, for example, a solicitor in Istanbul who played oud extremely well and expressed disenchantment

with his profession. So I said, "Why don't you work as an oud player?", and he said, "The standards are pretty high; if I worked professionally, I wouldn't be up to them." As an oud player, he could run rings around anybody in Greece! Turkish standards are high, the criteria exist and are common knowledge, so you can't fool anyone.

In both countries, hasn't quality music become a specialist taste, with performers playing to an elite and urban-based audience?

That's unfortunately true. But because the Turks have done very thorough collecting of material, if there is mass interest later, it's all there, ready and waiting. In Greece, something is irretrievably lost every day – archival recording just isn't being done.

The Turks at least admit that a certain body of work is their music, while the Greeks are so confused about what is "theirs" that people now equate Greek music completely with Hadzidhakis and Theodorakis. They're good, I like them – up to a point. But they're just the tip of the iceberg, a very recent phenomenon with roots in European or even Latin American music. Bouzouki is only a small part of Greek music, the more recent years of an urban tradition.

RONDO À LA ATATÜRK

MUSIC OF TURKEY

Millions of tourists visit Turkey on holiday but the music remains very little known in the west. Ferhat Boratav and David Muddyman go on a musical tour from ashiks to arabesk.

A visit to Turkey can be a noisy experience. The distinction between private and public space is very different from that in the west and people simply assume that their own musical tastes enjoy universal acceptance. Probably the first sort of music you'll hear will be either *arabesk* or *taverna* – in the market, in taxis or on inter-city bus journeys, where the passengers are hostage to the driver's musical tastes.

People in Turkey certainly listen to music – hit songs from singers on opposite sides of the

musical spectrum like Ibrahim Tatlises and Sezen Aksu can sell in the millions – yet it is extremely difficult to witness music-making. The *dogunsalonu* is where marriages take place, and still provides the bread and butter for many a musician. But increasingly, in many events that in other countries would have obligatory live music – festivals and religious or public holidays – Turks are content with a rudimentary sound system and a couple of cassettes.

The gap between a music industry that sells millions of cassettes and the dearth of live music is not due to a lack of musical talent, but rather to a long process where what is considered civilized and modern has been forced upon authentic traditions and tastes. This process has created its own style and aesthetics, but leaves Turks alienated from their musical roots.

RONDO À LA TURK

According to historical accounts, Turkish ears first heard western music in 1543 when the French king, Francois I, sent a group of musicians, among other gifts, to the Ottoman court. The sultan, Suleyman the Magnificent, decided that this music would corrupt the virile spirit of the Turks and ordered them back. The Ottoman's answer was to send their janissary (mehter) bands with their troops to the gates of Vienna. Their musical impact was more lasting than their military might, with *alla Turca* music featuring trumpets, drums and cymbals appearing in compositions by Haydn, Mozart and Beethoven.

All this is now history. The janissary bands have beaten a retreat and now just play regularly in the courtyard of the military museum in Istanbul. Elsewhere western music has made a successful comeback, although there is a sort of musical schizophrenia in Turkey right now.

Turkey, and before it the Ottoman Empire in its final decades, underwent a profound process of modernization which left no tradition untouched. The certainty with which the director of national radio and TV and the humble cassette vendor alike divide their music into "classical Turkish", "popular western music", "popular music with Turkish lyrics" and "folk music" has no relevance to what your ears will hear.

The problem lies with the cultural policies of the Turkish republic founded in 1922 and their aspirations to western models. In the 1930s, the founder of modern Turkey, Mustafa Kemal Atatürk, was proudly exclaiming that Ottoman court music was "just Byzantine" and the real music of the Turks could be found among the common people of Anatolia. Unfortunately the state was under a misapprehension about the nature of that music.

Under the leader's guidance, the republic's musicologists began to comb the villages in pursuit of real Turkish music. They found it, and corrupted it: melodies were standardized, lyrics purged of "vulgarities", instrumentation regimented and spontaneity ruled out in exchange for the precision of group performance. The rebellious songs that heartened the Turkoman nomads against the pacifying efforts of the centralized state, and likewise the religious dissidence shimmering in the hymns of the Shiite Alevis, were too strong and suspect. For a short period, real folk music suffered a strict ban on the radio, while the content of the popular tradition was reshaped and eventually lost altogether.

Religious music met an even worse fate. The institutions that housed the mystical Sufi orders like the Mevlevi (whirling dervishes) and served as informal conservatoires for both secular and religious musical training were closed down and their members persecuted with secular zeal.

Ironically, Kemal and his close circle of friends were very fond of traditional music, in both its popular and courtly varieties. Some of the best singers and players were invited to perform during long evenings around the table at the presidential palace. Mustafa Kemal had a penchant for the tunes of his native Thessaloniki and the measured rhythms and dignified steps of the men's zeybek folk dance, and sometimes he led the songs.

But all that was in private. In public the reformers had their aims clear: to reach the "level" of contemporary western civilization. Margot Fonteyn came to Ankara to teach modern ballet, Paul Hindemith established the conservatoire, Béla Bartók and Zoltán Kodály were invited on folk music collecting trips.

LET THERE BE HALK

Fortunately the *halk müzigi* – Turkey's folk music – was more durable than Kemal. It remains a living tradition, although there are signs of decline caused partly by the broadcasting and recording industries. Folklore groups have recently been founded in many areas, sometimes with state assistance, to preserve a dying art. Halk müzigi can be divided into four very rough categories: rural music, Kurdish music, *ozan* and *türkü*.

In general, the folk styles of all the Turkish provinces are very similar: the most striking differences are found only around the Black

MEDITERRANEAN AND MAGHREB

Sea, close to the Syrian border and in the predominantly Kurdish east.

Village music is made primarily at celebrations such as weddings and annual festivals. Weddings often last for three days, and from mid-morning to midnight the whole district reverberates with loud dance music from *davul drum*, *zurna* (an oboe) or *klarnet* (clarinet). Dances are performed by segregated groups of men and women, hands and arms linked to form a long line. Wedding music, together with dance tunes and children's songs, are all forms of *kirik hava* or "broken melody", characterized by incessant but very danceable rhythms.

In the area around Trabzon and Rize on the Black Sea, *kemançe* (fiddle) music is very popular. The kemançe is not only used at weddings and other festivities, but also for personal enjoyment, and shopkeepers and barbers can sometimes be heard playing to themselves when there are no customers about. Kemançe music has an exceptionally fast tempo, marked out by drums or foot stamping. Two good kemançe cassettes are "Kayana/Laziko" by Yusuf Cemal Keskin and "Muhabbet Alami/1" by Hüseyin Köse. At celebrations on the coast between Rize and the Georgian border it is also possible to hear a bagpipe called the *tulum*. A good example of this music can be heard on "Pestamalli Kiz" by Rizeli Mustafa Sirtli.

THE LOVERS OF LOVE

A very old folk tradition that thrives to this day is *ozan*, the music of the folk-poets of Anatolia, who are usually referred to as *ashiks*, meaning "the ones in love". The ashiks have wandered the plains of Anatolia since around the tenth century, putting music to the words of legendary poets like Yunus Emre, Pir Sultan Abdal and Sefil Ali, as well as writing their own songs. Ashiks belong to the Bektasi/Alevi faith, which combines wisdom with warmth, and stresses unity, understanding and equality between men and women. Despite this – or perhaps not surprisingly – many ashiks have been the subject of mistrust and contempt from orthodox Sunni Muslims and secular authority. The most recent serious outburst was the burning in 1993 of a hotel in Sivas where an Alevi conference was taking place: at least

twelve people died, but no arrests have been made.

Ashiks accompany themselves on the *saz*, a long-necked lute, with three sets of strings, said to represent the fundamental trinity of the Muslim faith: Allah, Mohammed and Ali. There are flourishing Ashik cafes in Erzurum and Kars, in eastern Turkey where the spontaneity and wit are nourished by appreciative audiences. The ultimate experience (provided your Turkish is up to it) is a contest between two good ashiks where they both play a song and compete with alternating lines, improvising witty jibes and mixing them with sayings from ancient poetry. The audience judges the players on humour, the beauty and aptness of the poetry, and instrumental improvisation. But the judgement is never conclusive.

Today a large number of ashiks make cassettes, and even more play the villages and towns of central Anatolia. One of the greatest of this century was **Ashik Veysel**, a blind singer who died in 1974. There are still several tapes of his available locally, and many of his compositions are sung by other ashiks and the more commercial singers of türkü (see below). His best recordings are available on the French Ocora label, and are the only ones made in a village setting – those recorded in the sterile environment of the Radio Ankara studios are like hearing a caged bird sing. Veysel allowed these recordings to be made on condition they should not be released before he died, because he feared for his safety due to the way some of the lyrics could be interpreted.

Ashiks are normally soloists but there is one ozan supergroup, **Muhabbet**, which combines the talents of some of the best ashiks in Turkey today. Arif Sag, Musa Eroglu, Muhis Akarsu and Yavuz Top alternate between releasing solo cassettes and playing with the group. As a group they have released eight cassettes and dozens more as solo artists. Of the many other ashiks available, Ali Ekber Çiçek, Murat Çobanglu, Feyzullah Çinar and Mazlumi ve Asim Mirik are all worth hearing.

Türkü takes elements from all of Turkey's music traditions to form a folk-infused urban popular music. It takes melodies from the folk tradition, and plays them on a mixture of folk, western and Arabic instruments. The weekly halk müzigi chart features predominantly türkü music, and stars like **Belkis Akkale**, Burhan

Çaçan, Besir Kaya, and Nuray Hafiftas are constantly battling for top positions.

POPULAR MUSIC AND ROCK

Traditional music was first broken down by the classical repertoire, but by the late 1940s and early 1950s western-style popular music was firmly established in Turkey. In the late 1950s the first rock bands appeared and some of the leading names – **Erkut Tackin, Cem Karaca, Erkin Koray** and **Baris Manço** – are still around. One of the most popular figures was a young star of Turkish classical music, **Zeki Müren**, who appeared in glitzy costumes on stage, exploited his feminine physique and started a parallel career in film musicals.

The rockers, on the other hand, faced two options. The majority softened their style to create a popular light music. The so-called "superstar" **Ajda Pekkan** was, and still is, the heroine of this genre. A smaller group in the rock scene searched for a way of combining the protest element with a sound that would appeal to the masses. Surprisingly enough, that sound was folk music. In the late 1960s rock bands like **Apaslar** (the Apaches), **Kurtalan Express**

and **Mogollar** (the Mongols) borrowed rhythms and melodies from folk songs and dances and successfully reproduced them on electric guitars and drums. The protest against worldly values and the espousal of a mystical love for nature in the lyrics were typical of their lead singers – Cem Karaca, Fikret Kizilok and Baris Manço. Bootlegged cassettes of their albums are still widely available in the flea markets today, especially on Taksim Square, Istanbul.

Since the 1980s this tradition has been labelled *özgün muzik* (genuine music). This might seem a complete misnomer – although in contrast to their predecessors they usually include folk instruments in the bands – but their supposed authenticity is to be found in their militant political attitudes rather than their musical style. **Selda**, **Ahmet Kaya** or the groups **Kizilirmak** and **Ezginin Gunlugu** are the leading names on the left of this tradition, and although there is a common belief that the protest tradition is a monopoly of the left and the Kurds, there are also equivalent voices among the Islamists and Turkish nationalists.

A trio of singer/composers, Mazhar, Fuat and Ozkan, better known by their acronym **MFO**, have been around since the 1960s, but reached

KURDISH MUSIC

· · · · · · · · · · · · · · · · · · · ·

O f Turkey's population of some 55 million, around ten million are **Kurds**. Their folklore and national identity are preserved with the help of the *dengbej* (bards), *stranbej* (popular singers) and *cirokbej* (story-tellers). A dengbej is a singer with an exceptional memory, effectively the guardian of the Kurdish national heritage, since he must know hundreds of songs for which there is no written notation. Dengbejs sing the Kurdish myths and legends, sing about the struggle for freedom, and also have in their repertoire love and entertainment songs. Sadly some of the best Kurdish dengbej, like Sivan Perwar and Temo, now live in exile abroad.

The main instruments used in Kurdish music are wind instruments, such as the *blur* and the *düdük*, found in the mountainous regions where they take advantage of the echo from the hills, and string instruments such as the *tembur* and the *saz*, used in the towns.

A big contribution to the *özgün muzik* genre is now coming from Kurdish sources (the ban on Kurdish has recently been lifted). Sivan Perwer, a Kurd living in exile in Europe, is one of the leading exponents of this mixture between universal form and national content. Because musical folk traditions have been and still are important to Kurdish ethnic identity and national claims, Kurdish musicians have been closer to their traditional sources and found it easier to adapt it to their purposes.

By far the most famous Kurdish musician is the leading arabesk performer Ibrahim Tatlises, who releases regular cassettes in Turkish. When the ban on Kurdish music was lifted, people had high hopes for his role as a mouthpiece for the Kurds. This hasn't happened, indicative of a wider failure of Kurdish music to achieve any popular impact. Tatlisis has performed in Kurdish on stage but made no recordings and openly declares he is reluctant to sing for a limited audience, preferring the mass appeal of the Turkish market.

a peak in the 1980s breaking sales records with songs about all aspects of modern life: summer loves in the resort of Bodrum; the mismatch between a rich intelligent girl and the bullying macho of the neighbourhood; and corrupt officers and officials. Another group, **Bulutsuzluk Özlemi**, is an interesting band with a political orientation, whose songs dwell on urban alienation, prison and the struggle of youth against tradition.

All these musicians consider their music pure rock; but they are the people of a country where, in every town, daily prayer calls from the mosque are heard in the five different modes of classical court music. The groups' modern output carries traces of this background. Another group, **Mozaik**, discovered this "infiltration" when they played one of their compositions to a Turkish classical musician. He listened and announced to the rockers that they had unwittingly composed a piece in nikriz mode, one of the few exclusively Turkish modes of the Ottoman musical tradition.

There are deliberate attempts as well. MFO is reworking some of the old Sufi hymns for a new album, and they have recruited a singer from the most venerable amateur classical music association of Istanbul. Another rock musician, Serder Ataser, is doing the same thing to mystical Alevi songs and türkü. In both cases the intention is to leave the traditional voice and instruments as untouched as possible. Their predecessors had less faith in their musical sources and tried to disguise them with a symphony orchestra or rock band. Now the new generation is rediscovering and exploring its roots.

The new Turkish pop movement has, in the last few years, been led by Sezen Aksu, one of the two Turkish artists (the younger Deniz being the other) to be played on MTV. Aksu's music is essentially western in sound, but with distinct arabesk echoes and Turkish folk drums and pipes included in her videos. The hot property at the moment is Tarkan, in his twenties, whose new release "A.Acaibsin" ("You are Strange") has sold over a million copies.

ARABESK AND TAVERNA

Until 1990 the "supervisory commission" of state-run radio and TV had a total control of what was played on the media. Anything they considered impure, amoral, subversive or alien was banned and this affected music right across the spectrum. This meant that arabesk, Turkey's most popular music during the 1980s, was not heard on the media because of its foreign, Arabic elements and was virtually an "underground" force.

Arabesk appeared in the late 1960s and gets its name from its predominantly Arabic, rather than Turkish, melodies and style. With real Turkish music absent from the airwaves for so many years, audiences tuned in foreign stations and developed a taste for popular Arabic styles. The growth of the music mirrored the rapid urbanization of the 1970s, as people from the provinces flocked to the cities, bringing their musical tastes. The biggest stars are **Orhan Gencebay**, **Coskun Sabah** and **Ibrahim Tatlises** and, at the height of the arabesk boom in the late 1980s, their racy, tuneful releases and fatalistic lyrics accounted for around three-quarters of all cassette sales. The more youthful **Küçük Emrah** is also massively popular.

Arabesk was heard everywhere – spilling out from shops, in taxis and buses, but not on radio or TV – and in the late 1980s there was a deliberate government campaign against the music, because the lyrics were seen as too downbeat and the overall sound simply un-Turkish. There was even an attempt to win over the audience to officially approved arabesk songs, which of course bombed.

The situation changed dramatically with the arrival of independent radio and TV in the 1990s. Arabesk is now a mainstay of commercial stations as well as state TV who are belatedly trying to compete. Although the style is now on the wane, perhaps having lost the appeal of official disapproval, it still holds its own, and recently some of the older names, like Adnan Senses and Kibariye, have resurfaced. Kibariye is a gypsy performer reflecting a general return to a more rootsy sound.

Taverna is a fairly recent innovation, the offspring of Greek taverna music and Turkish cabaret, drawing to some extent on folk music and arabesk but even more disposably a "Muzak". In recent years, taverna sales have been catching up with arabesk, and stars like **Cengiz Kurtoglu**, Metin Kaya and Karisik are constantly topping the chart. Not long ago, Karisik managed eight cassettes in the top 25 at one time.

WHIRLING CLASSICAL

Turkish **classical music** is a product of the Ottoman civilization. Based on modal systems or *maqam*, analogous to the western scale system, and formulated over five centuries ago, the traditional classical repertoire in Turkey today is selected almost entirely from notated sources preserving the works of such notables as the fifteenth-century composer Abdüladir Meragi (died 1435), the eighteenth-century Prince Cantemir and Sultan Selim III. The instruments normally used by classical ensembles includes tambur lute, ney flute, rebab or kemançe fiddles, keman or violin, kanun zither, oud and küdüm kettledrums.

One of Turkish classical music's principle components is the music of the Sufi **Mevlevi** sect (also known as the whirling dervishes). Jalal al-Din Rumi, the founder of the Mevlevi movement in the thirteenth century, believed in music as a spiritual and meditative aid to contact with God. The ritual involves a **spinning dance** (from which the whirling dervishes got their name) with the left hand turned down towards the earth and the right hand towards heaven, symbolizing the dancer as a medium between the two. The music is dominated by the ney, the wooden flute which has a mystical role in Turkish music, with tambur lute, rebab, fiddle and percussion. The sound is delicate and inspirational. The best-loved Mevlevi composers are Köçek Dervis, Mustafa Dede (seventeenth century), Dede Efendi (eighteenth and nineteenth centuries), and Rauf Yekta (nineteenth and twentieth centuries).

After the founding of the republic, classical music in its religious form was banned from public performances until 1946, when a secularized festival was established in Konya to mark the anniversary of Rumi's death. Now public concerts, incorporating pieces with a clear "Mevlevi" style, are given in theatres, concert halls and in radio broadcasts, often with large ensembles of over thirty instrumentalists and singers. One of the most famous ensembles is the Istanbul Municipal Conservatory's Klâsik Icra Heyeti, which often gives concerts around Istanbul, and on Sunday mornings these and other such performances may be broadcast live on Radio Istanbul. The single most important Mevlevi musical event is the annual **Mevlana festival** in Konya (December 3–17) although occasional performances in the Galata Mevlevi Hanesi in Istanbul are more intimate and more atmospheric.

Despite the gradual relaxation of government restrictions, there's little positive encouragement for the best classical musicians to stay in Turkey. **Kudsi Erguner** and his ensemble choose to work in Paris; Ihasan Ozgen and group **Bogaziçi** (Bosphorous) spend much time in Athens; and **Necdet Yasar** and ensemble are installed at the Turkish Music Research Centre of Maryland University in the US.

FASIL

The *fasil* or semiclassical style is a night-club version of classical Turkish music, essentially a vocal suite of light orchestral pieces. The music has a distinctly gypsy flavour, and every short rest is filled with flourishes and improvisations from the stars of the orchestra – the sort of expression that's frowned upon in strict classical circles.

The main instruments used in fasil are *klarnet*, *keman*, *oud*, *kanun*, *darabuka* and *yayli tambur*. You can hear informal gypsy groups playing this kind of music in restaurants around Istanbul. One of the best ensembles is the superb **Erkose Ensemble**, whose music is some of the only *tzigane* (gypsy) music from Turkey widely available on record. Other, well-known artists of the *fasil* genre are *klarnet*-player **Mustafa Kandirali** kanun-player Ahmet Yatman, oud-player Kardi Sençalar, and vocalists Suzan Bizimer and Kemal Gürses.

In Britain, there is an excellent Turkish record/cassette shop with a good stock, ten-day special-order service and reasonable prices: Melodi Müzik, 121 Green Lanes, London N16 (☎ 0171/359 0038). Similar stores exist in many big cities in Europe, the US and Australia. Most recordings are still available only on cassette or vinyl.

FOLK

Belkis Akkale *Türkü Türkü Türkiyem* (Sembol plak, Turkey). Possibly the greatest türkü singer at her best. Almost all of the traditional instruments of Turkey are in here somewhere. Cassette only.

Diyarbakirli Besir Kaya *Derman Kalmadi* (Özdemir, Turkey). Türkü music of düdük, saz and ney blend beautifully with bass guitar, kit drums and Besir's soaring voice. The sound of modern Turkey and very danceable. Cassette only.

Ⓒ Erkose Ensemble *Tzigane* (CMP, Germany). An instantly appealing introduction to the fiery world of Turkish gypsy music. With swirling clarinet, violin, lute, zither and percussion, this is a tight, virtuoso sound.

Ⓒ Mustafa Kandirali *Turkey* (World Network, Germany). Dubbed the "Benny Goodman of Turkey", Kandirali is the top "belly dance" clarinettist and gives a wild performance with a small ensemble.

Muhabbet 5 (Zirve, Turkey) and *88* (Pinar, Turkey). Two albums that show the combined talent of four of the greatest saz-players. All have deep resonating voices, which add soulful respite to the wash of fine saz interludes. Cassette only.

Ⓒ Talip Özkan *L'art vivant de...* (Ocora, France). The leading saz-player, with a fine selection of his "living art" from various parts of Turkey, on saz and tambura. Intimate and reflective.

Arif Sag *Halay* (Nora, Turkey). Arif Sag has for many years been one of Turkey's favourite singers, releasing dozens of records and tapes, both solo and as a member of Muhabbet. This tape features complex rhythms, superb saz-playing and solos from many Turkish folk instruments. Cassette only.

Yayuz Top *Deyisler-1* (Sembol plak, Turkey). A fast and vibrant tape from another member of Muhabbet. The flutes and saz play melodic interchanges over pulsating rhythms. Cassette only.

Ashik Veysel on *Voyages d'Alain Gheerbrant en Anatolie* (Ocora, France). The only recording of Veysel in a village, and much more expressive then studio releases. Superbly supported by his constant companion Küçük Veysel, who sings in unison with the master. A CD re-release is on the way.

Ⓒ Various *Turkish Folk Songs and Instrumental Music* (King, Japan). Accessible türkü introduction, with some good instrumental tracks too.

Ⓒ Various *Song Creators of Eastern Turkey* (Smithsonian/Folkways, US). A sample of contemporary ashiks, complete with good notes and translations – an excellent way into a fascinating but difficult troubadour music.

Ⓒ Various *Folk Music in Turkey* (Topic, UK). An excellent selection of many styles of Turkish folk music. Produced in Britain as part of a series covering Balkan music.

Various *Türküler Gecidi* (Türküola, Turkey). Another wonderful hit-parade from the world of türkü, featuring Belkis Akkale, Burhan Çaçan, Mahmut Tunçer and others. Cassette only.

KURDISH

Sivan Perwar *Vol 9* and *Vol 11* (Kurdistan Yekitiya Humermenden, Germany). Arguably the finest Kurdish singer. Both collections contain Sivan's powerful voice and saz accompaniment, backed by düdük and blur, together with western keyboard and classical Arab oud and kanun. Cassette only.

CONTEMPORARY

Sümeyra *Kalinlarimizin Yüzleri* (Yeni Dünya, Turkey). Female özgün singer with one of the most soulful voices in Turkey, accompanying herself on the saz. Cassette only.

Ruhi Su *Zeybekler* (IMECE, Turkey). One of the greatest özgün singers with a selection of old west Anatolian ballads sung in Ruhi's forceful style. Cassette only.

Selda *Selda* (Uzelli, Turkey). Selda is equally at home singing özgün and türkü. This collection features both and includes the wonderful "Dost Merhaba". Cassette only.

Ⓒ Various *The Best of Turkey* (Atoll, France). A cross-section of the big names of Turkish pop including Baris Mançe, Cem Karaca, Zeki Müren and Ibrahim Tatlises.

Ⓒ Various *The Other Side of Turkey* (Feuer and Eis, Germany). An excellent introduction to the leading figures on the more progressive, politicized wing of Turkish rock, including Mozaik and Bulutsuzluk Özlemi.

Ⓒ Ibrahim Tatlises *Fosforlu Cevriyem* (Bayas, Germany). It's perhaps hard to recommend one arabesk release over another. This is a live recording with all the essential attributes: intense, pained vocals, wild instrumental flourishes and lots of reverb. One of the few recordings on CD in a very disposable market.

TURKISH CLASSICAL MUSIC

Bogaziçi *Türke Müziginde Rum Bestekâlar* (Columbia, Turkey). A mixture of Greek and Turkish musicians playing music of the Byzantine, Ottoman and Mevlevi traditions. Beautiful recording of courtly classical, "art" and sacred music.

Ⓒ Kecskés Ensemble *Ancient Turkish Music in Europe* (Hungaroton, Hungary). Ottoman music from the sixteenth to eighteenth centuries, recorded by fine Hungarian musicians, including military pieces, vibrant dances and sedate court music.

Ⓒ Kudsi Erguner Ensemble *Whirling Dervishes from Turkey* (Arion, France). A master ney-player and one of the most prominent Turkish classical musicians, here performing Mevlevi ritual music with singers and instrumentalists.

Kudsi Erguner and Süleyman Erguner *Sufi Music of Turkey* (CMP, Germany). A meditative rather than ecstatic set from the ubiquitous Erguner family, here represented by two brothers on simple ney and frame-drum. Whale music for Sufis.

Mevlana *Mistik Türk Müzigi Saheserleri serisi vols 1–6* (Kent, Turkey). One of the best sets of Mevlevi music. Any of them will provide a good introduction to the beautiful celestial music of the Mevlevi, though early volumes may prove difficult to find. Cassette only.

Ⓒ Nesrin Sipahi *Love Songs of Istanbul* (CMP, Germany). Sharki is a dark and emotional type of song, with many compositions dating back to the eighteenth century. Backed by the Kudsi Erguner ensemble, this is the only recording available.

Ⓒ Turquie *Musique Soufi* (Ocora, France). Two LPs (or one CD) of quiet, evocative Sufi invocations that haunt and hypnotise. The instrumentation is simple – ney, frame drum and voice – which gives the space required for each voice to penetrate the soul a little.

THE NILE AND
THE GULF

I t is difficult to approach the Arab musical world without misconceptions. The western media tend to caricature Arab musical culture as a series of wailing voices and belly-dance rhythms. Yet delve into Arab music and you'll find a wide range of styles. To compare the brassy haze of Nubia with the avant-garde jazz of Lebanon, Bedouin rhythms with religious incantations, or city pop with working-class blues is to get a feel for the weft and warp of the Arab musical canvas.

Because of the elevated place given to the word in Arab culture – and poetry being considered the highest art form – the role of the singer has been to take the word to the people. Arab song, nearly lost after 500 years of Turkish influence, was reborn this century into a tumultuous modern age of radio, video and cheap cassettes. Its singers and writers, through the language and emotional power of popular song, have been influential in determining the identity of nations, expressing the hopes of their people and on occasions threatening the states themselves. Music has thus retained its unique power in the Arab world, and it offers listeners a window onto its personality.

This chapter kicks off with a survey of Arab music, covering its classical roots and early themes and the diversity of artists from the modern cities, ranging from Beirut on the Mediterranean to Kuwait in the Persian Gulf. One of these modern traditions is covered in the feature on Palestinian music, deeply stained by the stresses of Israeli occupation. The feature that follows homes in on four of the great singers in the classical tradition, whose voices and personalities have left an imprint on Arab culture with which there are few parallels anywhere in the world. The most remarkable of these artists

was Umm Kalthum. As the author writes: "This was a woman who truly had the Arab world in the palm of her hand… who, apart from Allah, is the only subject about which all Arabs agree."

The Arab music industry works hardest and fastest in Egypt. There's a major feature on the popular sounds of the Cairo streets – gritty *shaabi* and pop-style *al-jil* with its Nubian variants.

From Nubia we travel south up the Nile to Sudan and a wilder zone of unpredictable musical twists and nuances. Sudan encompasses everything from polite *oud*-playing to abandoned dervish sessions, salacious songstresses and camped-up swing bands. Musically, the second biggest country in Africa is an extraordinary feast, wrecked by the ruthless tyranny of the Khartoum government – a large space to watch.

The final feature is on Ethiopia, source of the Blue Nile, which, although having little in common with the other countries mentioned, has no more in common with any others in this part of the world. Indeed it's a great pleasure to listen to sounds so dissimilar from anything else, and so completely engaging. Ethiopian music is hard to compare: there's a good simile in the notion of walking down an unfamiliar staircase in complete darkness, a lopsidedness that leaves you clutching for a solid wall. Fortunately, a stack of highly enjoyable CDs is now available to test out the route, and the country is wide open to visitors for the first time in twenty years.

When this book was first planned, a piece on Somalian music was part of the picture. For lack of a clear picture of what is happening in the country this has had to be shelved in this edition. For a taste of the music, meanwhile, check out the fine CD release from Original Music (US), "Jamila: Songs from a Somali City", a collection of love songs from Brava, on the Kenyan border.

4

For full details about instruments, turn to the first feature in Chapter Three, "Mediterranean & Maghreb".

Al-jil Egyptian electric dance music developed in response to foreign pop imports.

Azmari Traditional Amharic musician (Ethiopia).

Dalauna Common Palestinian song-form.

Daloka Sudanese urban women's tom-tom drums.

Dervish Sufi ecstatic, who can achieve trance through dance. The word has a Turkish/Persian origin and literally means a religious mendicant or *fakir*.

Eshista Sexy Ethiopian wedding dance – a common pop rhythm.

Felahin The farming and peasant class of Egypt and Palestine.

Kashif Erotic Sudanese wedding dance.

Kebero Ethiopian drums.

Krar Ethiopian harp, sometimes known as the Harp of Apollo because of its resemblance to the classical instrument.

Maqam Complex scales on which classical Arab music is based.

Masenqo Ethiopian one-string fiddle.

Masmoudi Slower Egyptian pop rhythm in 8/4.

Matsoum Egyptian pop rhythm in 4/4 time.

Mawal Improvised *shaabi* vocals.

Merdoum Sudanese vocal and drum style from Kordofan, popularized by Abdel Gadir Salim.

Meyjana Common Palestinian song-form.

Mijwiz Palestinian shawm, a kind of oboe.

Mulid Festival to celebrate the saint of a mosque, in Egypt often a massive affair.

Nubia Region spreading from southern Egypt to northern Sudan, flooded by the dam-Lake Nasser.

Qawaali Palestinian praise-and-debate-singers, famed for their skill in improvising lyrics and retorts (the same root as Indian qawwali).

Rajaz Poetic metre, likened to the rhythm of a camel's hooves.

Raks sharki Egyptian dance and music traditionally performed at weddings, known in the west as belly dance.

Saiyidi Folk music of the upper Nile valley (the name applies to the musicians) famous for clever wordplay. The rhythm is used a lot in *al-jil* pop.

Samaai 10/8 rhythm, much used in classical song.

Sam-ennawarq Ethiopian tradition of double entendre (literally "wax and gold", after the casting process).

Sawahili Egyptian folk music (literally "coast") from the Mediterranean coast.

Shaabi Broad Egyptian song-style (literally "popular" or "vulgar"), ranging from light song to street-wise, class-conscious comment.

Shababi Short Palestinian flute.

Simsimaya Egyptian guitar-like instrument used in *sawahili* music.

Sufi Member of an Islamic brotherhood with a saintly leader.

Sut el-Khalije Gulf Arab music of fishermen.

Takht Traditional Arab ensemble of four or five main instruments, including *oud, rabab, riq* and *kanum*.

Tchik-tchik-ka Ethiopian dance style, very mobile in the chest and shoulders.

Washint Ethiopian flute.

Zar Sudanese women's drumming cult.

Zikr Egyptian Sufi street festival.

PARTNER OF POETRY

MUSIC OF THE ARAB WORLD

The Arab world is perhaps the largest culturally homogenous region on earth. Its 200 million people are bound by devotion to a common language, the most popular voice of which has long been poetry and song. As well as a tradition of classical song found throughout the Arab world, there are also the regional forms of the indigenous peoples, and of the nomads and invaders who have swept across the region. David Lodge tours the Arab musical world through time and space.

Musical expression reached a peak of importance between the eighth and twelfth centuries. But this period was followed by a long era of stagnation under Ottoman rule. Arab society subsequently emerged in the twentieth century in nationalistic fervour, against a background of political instability and war, demanding the return of territory and identity from the colonial powers. During this struggle, Arab culture has also had to confront a new ideological challenge with the west – the technology and permissive values that seem to go hand in hand. It is in such a climate that Arabs this century have undergone a musical renaissance.

Classical Arab music, like a giant canvas stretched across the Arab world, is enjoyed throughout society and transcends all age and social barriers. The musical arena is today dominated by a small number of great classical singers who are adored by the masses. Their popularity has given these giants of the stage enormous cultural significance. They are arguably more influential than presidents, swaying the moods of society at large by touching the lives of almost every individual with their poignant lyrics and sultry melodies. From humiliation in military defeat to the personal wounds of love, their music has provided sustenance during long periods of pain and introspection. Typically, for over an hour at a time and in highly charged melancholy tones, singers dwell on the themes of tragic fate, or love – forbidden or unrequited – beckoning the listener to wallow in metaphor and listen as the lyrics unfold to the story of his or her own life. As Umm Kalthum sang in "Enta Umri" (You Are My

Life, lyrics by Ahmed Shafik, composition by Mohamed Abd el-Wahaab, 1965):

> *Your eyes brought me back to my lost days.*
> *They have taught me how to regret the past and its wounds.*
> *What I experienced before my eyes saw you is wasted time.*
> *How could they count it as my age?*
> *You are my life, whose morning started with your light.*
> *You are, you are, you are my life.*

MUSIC AND THE HUMAN SOUL

Love, wine, gambling, hunting, the pleasures of song and romance, the brief pointed elegant expression of wit and wisdom. These things he knew to be good. Beyond them he saw only the grave.

Arabic original, anonymous

From a thousand years or more before Islam, the nomadic Arab tribes had firmly established the hedonistic character of their music. In nomadic days, music was primarily a job for **women**. Female singing slaves were brought to the cities to entertain the noble houses and caravanserais, both as prostitutes and artists. And they would accompany warriors onto the battlefield, banging *duff* and *tabla* and singing war songs of *rajaz* poetry while the combat ensued. En route they would be always at the ready to stir the spirits of the soldiers wherever they stopped. At tribal nuptials the women singers and musicians led the celebrations. And they were there too on the *haj* to Mecca – which was in those pre-Islamic days a pagan pilgrimage – where they would sing and dance around the *kabba*. The principle **male performers** were *mukhanathin* – transvestite slaves – from whose ranks came the majority of male musicians well into the early days of Islam. They suffered the wrath of the more orthodox Muslims, and ridicule from society at large, but their skills were nurtured in the protective courts of certain less pious caliphs who appreciated their outrageous antics at feasts and banquets.

With such decadent roots, it is hardly surprising that when Islam arrived in the seventh century, the singing and the playing of musical instruments were considered sins, and swiftly banned. Yazid III, a noted Umayyad caliph, warned in 740 AD, "Beware of singing for it will steal your modesty, fill you with lust and ruin your virtue." Unlawful instruments were destroyed, singers were considered unworthy witnesses in court, and female slaves who turned out to have a vocal inclination could be taken back to market and exchanged. Still today in Islam there is no music. The call to prayer by the *muezzin*, while being a supreme example of the complex *maqamat*, the Arabic scales on which Arab music is based, is not considered music. This is because the emotional input of a sheikh in the recitation is guarded by strict rules about pitch and tempo, which determine mandatory rhythmic and phonetic styles. A celebrated Cairo court case in 1977 ruled, "The holy Koran contains the words of God, who recited it in a manner we do not comprehend. Koran recitation is an act of compliance and does not involve any innovation." To enduce *tarab*, enchantment, through delivery of the Koran is a sin, indicative of the fear in Islam of the influence of music on

ambassadors, the Arab poets wrested the limelight from the brilliant cultural centres of Baghdad and Damascus. With the arrival of Islam, the Koran's rich language, rhythm and rhyme struck a chord with the Arabs, and it soon became the textbook of all artistic creation. Today the special place of poetry in Arab music is proudly guarded. Songs are judged primarily on their words, and music without them is considered a "religion without a scripture". Tragic in love, devotional in worship and abusive in the back streets, by bringing these words down to the masses, the modern-day lyricist remains a poet of the people.

Soon after the birth of Islam in the seventh century, Arab music gained a suitor from an unexpected quarter. The Arab musical world was under the protection of the caliphs' court in Baghdad, where away from the jurisdiction of the Islamic purists, enjoyment and creativity reigned. This was the hedonistic world of Harun el-Rashid (786–809) and the Thousand and One Nights. This environment proved to be a highly productive one, nurturing such visionaries as the musician and theorist Ishaq al-Mawsili (767–850), famed for knowing every line of poetry ever written in Arabic, and whose antics are celebrated in fable. It is said he once found himself in the charge of a previously deaf and dumb consul, whom he succeeded in inciting to tears at the beauty of his voice. In the same era, Al-Farabi wrote his "Great Book of Music", a major treatise on rhythms, scales and modes – musical theory by far the most advanced

Camel hoof rhythms from a tribe on the move

human nature. Music in the Islamic Arab world is a singularly secular pursuit. (see the article on *qawwali* on p.222 for a different view.)

Denied figurative expression in Islamic art, the Arabs reserve special importance for their **language**, which has been the control point of their culture throughout history. In pre-Islamic nomadic times, the poet was magnificent; a spokesman on policy, judge in dispute, a voice to praise heroes and scorn enemies. As cultural

of its day. This was an age of great advances for the Arabs, an era of intellectual order and discovery that abounds with tales of superhuman feats, and which pushed Arab culture to the forefront of medieval art and science. At a time when Europeans were clubbing each other on the dark plains of Christendom, the Arabs were living in their "golden age", worrying about the power of imagination and the effects of music on the human soul.

SCALES AND RHYTHM

•••••••••••••••••••••••

The modes or Arabic scales were produced during the golden age of the
Arabs and largely remain to this day.
Melody is organized on a series of *maqamat*
(melodic modes), any given one of which
(*maqam*) has a distinctive scale, a certain register and compass, one or more principal notes
and typical melodic phrases. Each mode then
has its own ethos and is often associated with a
particular mood, season or body humour. Safi
el-Din, in the ninth century, devised one for
every hour of the day. Today there are estimated to be about forty in use in Egypt, and about
twenty others elsewhere. All are divided not
into twelve semitones, as in western musical
theory, but 24 quarters. The large number of
modes, all of which are relative to one another,
means an Arab singer has a highly complex job
in moving from maqam to maqam. Yet in performance the maqam are rarely adhered to: in
practice musicians each find their own way of
scaling the range, an ability that has been called
the "maqam phenomenon".

Rhythm theory is complex but easier to get a fix
on. Perhaps the most basic rhythm is *rajaz* – the
metre of a camel's hooves on sand. With this
beat nomadic Bedouins developed "al-Huda", the
caravan song, capable of distracting their beasts
from the burden of heavy loads so effectively
that, so the story goes, the animals would arrive
frisky after a long journey to the rhythm of the
drum, and then drop dead of fatigue.

The subsequent flowering of music has produced a sophisticated range of rhythms, and the
old camel song is no longer very high up the list.
Today, rhythm patterns vary greatly in length,
from the shortest of two beats to the longest of
88 beats. Of the 111 rhythms, or *iqa*, recorded
in the Middle East and Egypt alone, only about
ten are commonly used. Among these are the
matsoum in 4/4 time, the most broadly used
rhythm in pop music, where it's frequently
slowed down, mid-song, to make the *masmoudi*
rhythm, which is 8/4. You'll hear both of these in
Egyptian al-jil. Classical song tends to use the
samaai, a 10/8 rhythm.

EMERGING TRADITIONS IN THE TWENTIETH CENTURY

The trumpeting bands marching at the head of
colonial advances into Egypt in the 1850s,
and the tantalizing operas of Verdi and Mozart
playing in the new Cairo Opera House, were a
rude awakening for an Arab world that had, for
500 years, been shrouded under the Ottoman
mantel. Intellectual and artistic life ignited as
this sudden clash with modernity shook the
Arabs out of a deep-rooted complacency.
Egypt, fired by a nationalistic drive for
independence from 2000 years of foreign rule,
emerged to lead the quest for an Arab
renaissance, and soon was recognized as Arab
cultural heartland and the focus of musical
innovation. The Turkish flavour was soon out
of favour and the sound of Arab music was
heard again in the streets and theatres. In
attending this rebirth of music and song, and
attempting to bring Arab music into the modern
age, the Cairo music scene struck a dynamic
balance between tradition and the seductive
promise of western advances.

Arab culture was vulnerable to the
sophistication and technical know-how of
Europe. Despite having invented a musical
notation as early as the middle of the ninth
century (in "The Philosophy of the Arabs" by Al
Kindi), the Arabs abandoned the idea and their
music was never commonly written down. By the
late 1800s, musicians had moved a long way
from established theory. In 1932 at an
extraordinary pan-Arab conference in Cairo
(supported by Bartók who was by this time
taking a great interest in Arab music), Arab
musicians gathered to take stock of their musical
output. They found a wide diversity from one end
of the Arab world to the other. Thus began a
campaign to rekindle an interest in tradition,
and to search its roots for guidance.

The west, far from being viewed as a potential
menace, was seen as a source of inspiration. Arab
music has shown itself far more open to outside
influence than the music of neighbouring Persia
and India. Composers were keen to make the most
of western advances, many of whose root ideas had
passed from Arab hands a thousand years earlier
– like the *rabab* fiddle which had evolved into the
violin, and the concept of harmony which gradually

crept back into Arab composition. Entirely new instruments were greeted with unguarded enthusiasm. For example, the introduction of the cello – which one western musician at the conference thought would "overwhelm the Arab ensemble and bring on tears" – was welcomed by Egyptian musicians who thought *that* was the very reason to have it. Electric guitars, oboes and the double bass were added to the traditional five-piece Arab *takht*, which soon became a full-blown orchestra. Studios were re-equipped with the latest technology, and composers plagiarized melodies from Beethoven to Bartók, giving them form with a jazz back-beat or Hollywood rumba. In many songs of the 1960s there's a strong hint of western classical melodies, most notably in the works of **Mohamed Abd el-Wahaab** and his poet-mentor **Ahmed Shawki**, who were largely responsible for pioneering this innovation in Arab music (in "Nahr Khaled", listen out for Verdi's "Rigoletto", Beethoven's "Fifth" and Tchaikovsky's "Marche Slave"). Yet this was no imitation. Foreign themes were woven into the dense layers of drones, unisons and parallel octaves of the lush Arab orchestra, and the "eastern feel" was maintained.

Mohamed Abd el-Wahaab

Despite this modernizing trend over the last hundred years, many traditional themes hang over in Arab music from its distant heritage. Arabic music still centres on the singer, whose vocal ornamentation and improvisation skills enrich the song from "merely a chicken, without the nice fat which gives it taste", as one local saying puts it. The live *hafla* (party) atmosphere, with repeated shouts of praise and demands for encore from the audience, is still vital to the performance. Music continues to be the partner of poetry, while vibrant rhythm, fine melody and ancient instruments remain pivotal to the Egyptian sound. Ironically, in the computer world of today's generation of "classical" composers, sampled sound and Arabic programmes are maintaining the traditional character in their contemporary music, and manage to fool even the critical Arab listener.

Along with technical advances came the media, which has played a dominant role in the music of the Arab world. The big western music companies were in Cairo early in the century, and before long rogue entrepreneurs were touting village café-goers with the new phonograph, which they would operate for a fee. The piercing voices that emerged from the whirling

NON-MUSIC OF ISLAM

• •

A Koran reciter who wants to broadcast on the radio will first have to be judged worthy by a committee of religious scholars. He is tested on the complexity and subtlety of the *maqamat*, and in his agility in dispensing, through it, the words of God. By protecting the Arabic "scales" throughout the ages in this way, a religion which shuns music has in effect kept the music alive. Today "non-music" still plays this role by continuing to demand only the most perfect rendition of ancient Arabic modes from the most able voices – a sure defence against encroaching western influence. The full resonance of the call to prayer from some of the finest and most accomplished singers in the world is sheer delight.

There are two types of **Koran recitation:** *tartil*, a musically simple rendition of Koranic

text adhering strictly to the rules of reading, and *tajwid*, which is musically elaborate and involves intricate melodic and cadential formulae and ornaments. Here there is room enough for individual styles, and many popular reciters have crossed over to pursue very profitable careers in the secular field (most notably Sheikh Sayed Darweesh).

Religious, but non-Koranic, **devotional chanting** lies between the secular song and Koranic recitation. A musical ensemble will be led by a western-style conductor, and the solo singer of the secular field is replaced by a chorus of twelve men. Religious chanting is performed during Ramadan, at local weddings and at Sufi celebrations around mosques on the birthday of the saint.

COPTIC MUSIC

T he Coptic Christian faith in Egypt is the most true to the ancient traditions. The Coptic language is closest to that of the pharaohs, and the Copts declare themselves to be the true Egyptians.

Certainly the melodies and rhythm of Coptic liturgical music supports this, being most closely linked to that of the *felahin*, the farmers of the Nile delta who have been toiling the soil for millennia. Some go so far as to say the extrapolated syllables of Coptic song recall the hymns of the ancient Egyptian priests. If this is so, then the melodies passed on by oral tradition, and the use by the Coptic Church of triangles and small cymbals, are the closest thing to the music of the pharaohs.

contraptions at their feet seemed to pronounce that life was never going to be the same again. Yet the three-minute phonograph was hardly suited to the tradition of the long Arab song, and music had to wait for radio in the late 1920s before it discovered the new opportunities offered by technology. Film, and later television, provided a stage for popular song, which found an expanding record-buying public.

By the 1920s the whole Arab world was listening to the same Arab music for the first time. With its mass appeal, a superstar industry developed fast. Through these publicly adored giants of song arose the cult-hero poet-lyricists

Cairo cassette stall

like Ahmed Ramy and the "prince of poets" Ahmed Shawki, spreading revolutionary new messages that implied the right to personal fulfilment and expectations alongside the duties of family and Islam.

But what proved the most revolutionary of media innovations was the least spectacular. The humble cassette appeared in the early 1970s and put the music industry into the hands of the public, turning its control over from the businessmen to the streets. Suddenly everyone could make music, and it sometimes seemed nearly everyone did. Coinciding with a period of dramatic social change, the cassette offered a format for a new wave of popular aspirations and opened the floodgates to songs moving away from acceptable musical standards. It allowed the working class for the first time to voice their discontent, and with a contemporary breed of urban folk music they have successfully embarrassed traditional Egyptian good taste. Similarly, the arrival of youth culture in the 1980s, with pure pop music, opened a Pandora's box of western gadgetry. In providing a vehicle for these musical movements over the last twenty years the cassette has broken the long conservative domination of the music business.

With the sudden demise of the old stars in the early 1970s, the old guard, failing to pass on the tradition, stood by helplessly as the new street music filled the void. Abd el-Wahaab, who carried the torch for classical song until his death in 1991, insisted:

"There should be a definite distinction between the great singers, like Abd el-Halim Hafez and Umm Kalthum. In Europe, they are not attempting to replace the "old" with the "new" or classical with modern, as is happening now in Egypt. The new-wave singers have damaged the music scene with their songs."

When traditionalists and Muslim fundamentalists alike accuse the new music-makers of embracing the "disease of Americanization", even pop music defends itself against criticism. They insist that this synthesis of Egyptian themes with modern needs shows a way forward for Arab culture. This, they say, is music as it has always been, a mirror of the popular disposition.

THE ARAB CITIES – A CULTURAL MAP

Culturally, the Arab world can be imagined as two giant wings of the Middle East and North Africa, separated by the body of Egypt. The two major schools of Arab music in Baghdad and Andalucía were separated at birth, when the brilliant pupil Zirab was evicted from the cultural centre of ninth-century Iraq by other musicians jealous of his skills. At Cordoba, in Moorish Spain, he established schools of *haute couture* and beautification, and developed a "Hispano-Arab" music, unaffected by Greek theory, that remains the purest Arab form to this day. The mood of Baghdad with its Persian-Greco-Turkish heritage meant that these two regions have always followed very different paths, and have continued to do so into the modern age. Egypt as cultural buffer zone between the two has its own cosmopolitan society, and tells its own story.

Within these broad areas of cultural style, each region, approximately corresponding to national boundaries, flies its own distinct musical colours. And, of course, within each country there are multiple genres, each with its own sounds, rhythms and voices. What follows here is a brief country-by-country sketch. As the commercial industry of Cairo becomes artistically discredited, the music from other parts of the Arab world may point a way forward for an Arab musical renaissance.

In Beirut's heyday after World War II, **Lebanon** was known as the "Paris of the Middle East", home to artists and intellectuals escaping despotism elsewhere. In this cosmopolitan centre they produced a brief flowering of Lebanese

Two of the many faces of Fairuz

music and arts. Since 1975 Lebanon's cultural prestige has faded as the 17-year civil war drove many Lebanese into exile, and the music industry was re-established in Paris. Lebanese music represents the most western of Arab musical moods. One singer in particular, who has held the Lebanese identity together through decades of instability and division, is the revered star **Fairuz**. With her brilliant family of musicians, the **Rahbanis**, she has nurtured Lebanese culture and kept alive the hope of exiles for a return to their homeland. They have consistently shunned purism and take on influences as diverse as Mozart, Latin American rumbas, flamenco and Balkan folklore to colour themes drawn from Arabic legends and heroes. Today, Fairuz's son Ziad continues the tradition with experimental Arab jazz. With the end of the war and the return to some kind of battered normality in Lebanon, his work, at the forefront of the Arab search for musical direction, is inspiring fresh talk of a modern Lebanese renaissance. **Syrian** music is closely linked to Lebanese – and also Cypriot; regions which share the hard *dabka* rhythm, similar dances and a similar lyrical romanticism.

War and exile has been a stimulus to musicians in **Palestine** which, since 1948, has been devoted almost exclusively to the theme of the return of their homeland. Refugee camp singers adapt traditional ballads with words crying for Palestinian statehood; the youth of the intifada defied the occupation with resistance songs. Recently, avant-garde groups, the most famous of which is **Sabreen**, have been influenced both by their immediate neighbours, and from the west, developing a more eclectic style that contains messages of hope and forgiveness. In an area of the Middle East so politically charged, it's not unusual for music to be treated by adversaries as threatening propaganda. Because Palestinian artists often worked in the studios of Tel Aviv, songwriters have had to develop a symbolism of language which deceives the Israeli censors. Much Palestinian music was formerly banned in Syria and Jordan, which have had their own delicate diplomacy to think about. Palestinians resorted to airplay on their own radio network, broadcasting into the occupied territories from secret locations in the refugee camps of Lebanon. Now the Palestinians can look forward to a recognized homeland they will be more able to define their own media and produce music which embraces revived aspirations.

Nowhere else in the Arab world do the arts get more state support than in **Iraq**, a country which links cultural heritage closely with the leader and his political prestige. The region's status as the cradle of Arab culture and home to its "golden age" in the eighth and ninth century is sufficient to give the art of Iraq unparalleled credibility. Great theatre, music and poetry festivals in **Baghdad** and Babylon draw artists each year from across the Arab world, and in this way Iraq's role as cultural guardian is re-affirmed. Iraq has produced some great artists this century, most notably the world's finest oud player, **Munir Bachir**. Iraqi music shares some characteristics with that of Iran and eastern Turkey: a strong voice is greatly valued and it is typically masculine and pushy, unlike the softer tones of Iraq's Arab neighbour-states. But while music has often been used cynically to excite public opinion (witness the Kuwaiti singers during the Gulf War forced to sing pro-Iraqi songs on Baghdad TV), the folklore of the outlying regions continues to document its own version of events. In Iraq folk music remains a vibrant and living medium of communication, often the only uncontrollable avenue for the expression of discontent.

Conversely the folk music and traditions of **Kuwait** have given way to the modern state and a hi-tech recording industry. Massive investment in state-of-the-art studios and a modern media infrastructure has allowed Kuwaiti musicians and composers to develop a distinct musical identity with a rich, sweet "Gulf sound", a classical Bedouin music

Kuwaiti cassette from Abdullah Roueshid

increasingly popular throughout the Middle East. The Iraqi occupation of Kuwait led to a flourish of patriotic songs, most memorable of which was "Allah Homma el-Terag" (I pray that God resolves our pain), sung by Abdullah Roueshid before a group of tearful, tiara-clad Kuwaiti girls – a bizarre spectacle repeated nightly on the TV networks of Kuwait's Arab allies for the duration of the conflict.

The **Saudi** singer **Mohamed Abdu** has probably done more for Gulf music than any other, and the Saudis are justifiably proud of their music heritage. On the opening notes of the famous "Ga'ni el-Asmar" (The dark one has come) by female Saudi singer Etab, in Egyptian discos, Saudis are given full range of the dance floor. Holding hands, they sweep across the floor, turning in unison at each end with bended knees and gracefully choreographed swishes.

Oman is home to the *sut el-Khalije* – a kind of Arabian blues majoring on oud, drums, hand-clapping and, sometimes, Arab bagpipes. It's the music of the fishermen who used to ply the Arabian coast for a living before the oil era.

Note that Morocco, Mauritania and Algeria are covered in Chapter Three: "The Mediterranean and Maghreb".

THE ARAB WORLD

Most of these artists live and record in Cairo. Some of their recordings may be on CD but cassettes, available at Arab-owned stores in big cities, are much more widely available. Sut el-Beirut (Egypt/Lebanon) is the most important label, but most of the cassettes in the local stalls are actually bootlgs.

MAGHREBIA

Samira Said *Al Gani Al Samrr* (A night of fun). Accomplished modem classical singer from Morocco, one of Cairo's popular stars of the moment, and getting poppier by the release. *Khaifa* (1992) and *Ashaa* (her latest) indicate an artist who deserves to be picked up by a record company in Europe.
Warda *B'twanas Beek* (I feel comfortable with you), *Tabaan Ahbab* (Of course we're in love) and *Harramt Ahebak* (I'm Through With Love), which sets some songs to a modern, oriental dance beat, are typical of the output of Warda, originally from Algeria. She used to copy Umm Kalthum, but she's changing style, often performing concerts without an orchestra. She remains one of the Arab world's great musical hacks.

LEBANESE

Fairuz *Al-Gomma al-Hazeenah.* Fairuz is a Christian, and as well as secular material, has recorded much, beautiful church music, as on this album. She has numerous releases: ask for her by name.
ⓒ **Various** *14 The Very Best of Dabkeh* (Voice of Stars, France/Lebanon). A compilation of rhythmic *dabka* tracks, quite widely available.

SYRIAN

ⓒ **Farid el-Atrache** *Best of Farid el-Atrache Live* (Voice of Lebanon, France/Lebanon). Check out this CD collection. His most famous work is "El Rabai" (The spring), a live recording featuring an astounding oud instrumental at the start.

Meada el-Hanawi *Various releases.* The output of El-Hanawi's slightly inane, modern/classical housewifely style is huge. Which is unfortunate as it always falls some way short of the Algerian singer Warda, whom she emulates.
George Wasoof *Yalli taibna s'neen fi hawak.* In this release (You are troubling us with your love), the Syrian megastar was well into his stride as a popular artist.

IRAQI

Try anything by **Sabah Fahkri, Kathem el-Sahar** (a rising star in the Middle East) or **Sadoun Gaber** or virtuoso oud-player **Munir Bachir**. And listen out, especially, for **Mosem el-Ghazali**, who created a stir by refusing to sing in public but who entertains princes in his palace with his stunning voice, considered by many to be the finest in the world.

KUWAITI

Abdullah Roueshid *Leila Omr.* Often plays minimal sets of just oud and voice, sometimes with flamenco overtones. Haunting.
Nabil Shu'eil *Ya Shams.* High, rather effeminate vocals and elaborate melody slide rapidly with the swinging strings from the orchestra.

SAUDI ARABIAN

Etab *Kef Ansa* (How can I forget?). A style strongly influenced by the Cairo industry where she records. This includes the eponymous dance track that made her famous around the Arab world in the mid-1980s.
Mohammed Abdu *Ba'ad* (Distant). The most influential of Saudi artists. "Ba'ad" is his most famous recording, produced in the early 1980s before Saudi music had reached a wider Arab public. This song did much to open up the market of Egypt to Saudi singers.

STRUGGLE FOR A MUSIC

PALESTINIAN SOUNDS OF THE INTIFADA AND AFTER

To a people struggling for statehood, cultural identity becomes as indispensable as bread on the table or a roof over the head. It is as hard to find a modern Palestinian song which doesn't touch upon the themes of loss of homeland, the struggle for self-determination, life under occupation or heroism and martyrdom as it is to find a country and western song that gives the thumbs up to Marxism. Andy Morgan listens to the music of a stateless people.

Before the great disaster of partition in 1948, Palestinian society comprised a multifaceted collection of creeds, religions and races, all of whom had coexisted in relative peace for hundreds of years – at least until the turn of this century. Christians from Nazareth and Galilee, Druze people from the Lebanon and the Golan Heights, small pockets of indigenous Jews, nomadic tribes who roamed the great deserts between the Mediterranean and the Gulf, Arab farmers and townspeople, Egyptians, Turks, Cypriots and Greeks – all were part of the cultural crossroads of the Holy Land.

Although the great city ports of Jaffa and Haifa were already sizeable commercial centres, most Palestinians were rural people who had either settled to become farmers (*felahin*) or who still pursued a nomadic, Bedouin lifestyle. The music of the felahin was mainly functional – songs for harvesting, tending the flocks, fishing, grinding coffee or making olive oil. There were also epic songs about old heroes and legends sung by itinerant storytellers (*zajaleen*), who travelled from village to village with their box of tricks and retinue of players. And finally, there were the Koranic incantations of the Mawaali.

The most important occasions for music and merrymaking were weddings and their associated feasts. After the immense platters of meat and rice had been cleared away the party-goers would sing and dance. The dances were collectively known as *dabka*, which literally means "foot-tapping". They consisted of precise steps and jumps performed by linked chains of dancers. The music was provided by village musicians who sang traditional airs, accompanied by traditional instruments such as the *shabab1* and *ney* (short flute and long flute), the *mijwiz* shawm, the *tabla* and *duff* drums, *rabab* (fiddle) and *oud*.

Certain songs became so ingrained and widespread that they mutated into distinct song-forms with fixed melodies and verse structures over which new lyrics could be improvised. In terms of their rooted structure and versatility, these song-forms are comparable to the twelve-bar blues or even, lyrically speaking, to the limerick. The most common types of song-form, then as now, were the *dalauna* and the *meyjana*. Singers were judged as much by their word-play skills as by their vocal prowess. The ability to juggle words and phrases to fit the form also brought local fame. Nowhere were these skills more pronounced than in the art of the *qawaali*. The qawaali were singers who engaged in a kind of musical debate, each participant often representing one of the families at a wedding where they would discourse on the virtues and qualities of their patron families, or argue over the relative merits of dark- or light-skinned women. These punning, rapping, word-tussling sessions were always sung rather than merely recited. In recent times certain qawaali, most notably Abu Leil and Haddaji Rajih el-Salfiti, have achieved fame across the whole of Palestine.

SONGS OF PARTITION

The tumultuous events of the late 1940s which led to the partition of Palestine and the creation of Israel in 1948 did not destroy the culture of the felahin. The many thousands of Palestinians who fled to the refugee camps of the West Bank and Gaza Strip took their musical traditions with them and kept them alive in their hostile new surroundings. The Arabs who stayed behind and continued to live in the new state of Israel, collectively known as "the Arabs of the 48", also clung tenaciously to their heritage.

Around the period of partition, the songs and dances of the felahin did not form part of the commercially exploited and recorded body of Arabic popular music. This area was dominated by the great Egyptian and Lebanese singers and songwriters of the day such as Umm Kalthum, Mohamed Abd el-Wahaab and Sayed Darweesh. The *felah* music was a "hidden" heritage, a common cultural bond among the Palestinian people but completely unknown outside their own sphere of existence.

Nevertheless Palestine did have a musical scene of sorts based in the northern Israeli towns of **Haifa and Nazareth**, the only active, cosmopolitan centres for Palestinian music-making until the early 1970s. In these towns, songs were composed, performed and recorded by talented musicians with their own highly individual style. This urban genre of music was performed by small groups consisting of a singer and a few instrumentalists and was far removed in its complexity and sophistication from the country "folk" style of the felahin. Instead, these city musicians were attuned to the sounds coming from **Damascus**, one of the great cultural centres of the Arab world where the intricate art of classical Arabic music was still revered and practised as it had been for centuries.

It was the versatility of the song-form that allowed the roots music of the felahin to survive the political upheavals of the late 1940s and develop a stage further. In the new climate of fear, anger and alienation, the gist of the improvised lyrics that accompanied the dalauna and the meyjana began to reveal a harder edge. Instead of songs about the slender stalk of wheat swaying in the wind like the lithe body of the dancing woman, the newly dispossessed sang about the power of the gun and the dream of nationhood. Heroes and martyrs of the struggle such as the great Arab leader Cheikh L'Hezedin el-Kassam, who vowed to be the first to shoot the God of the British colonialists, were lauded in popular song. Even non-Arab figures like Che Guevara became part of the new folklore. Every significant event in the life of post-partition Palestine – the Six Day War, the Yom Kippur offensive, Arafat's speech to the UN in 1974, the belligerence of Saddam Hussein and the intifada – has at one time or another been celebrated or mourned in song.

The first singer to score a hit with a collection of essentially Palestinian songs was **Mustapha Al Kurd**, whose cassette release "Kullee Amal" (Full of Hope) enjoyed fervent popularity all over Palestine in the early 1970s. He sung of the daily suffering of the Palestinians living under occupation, using a radical new concoction of local folk forms, Egyptian and Lebanese pop and western rock.

Mustapha Al Kurd, full of hope in the 1970s

The dearth of recording studios and commercial infrastructure accessible to Palestinians in Israel and the occupied territories meant that the growth of modern Palestinian pop was slow and arduous. At first, singers found their concerts and recordings subject to censorship but eventually the Israelis gave up trying to control the clandestine Arab cassette industry and recordings became readily available even if they had to be sold under the counter. In the late 1970s and early 1980s a new movement of political theatre began to make its mark. Playwrights were often forced to use highly symbolic language to convey their defiant message, and theatrical performances were subject to much closer scrutiny than the playing of music, which continued more or less unheeded in the privacy of Palestinian homes. The most internationally renowned of these theatre groups is undoubtedly **El Hakawatti**, based in Jerusalem.

LOVERS AND INNOVATORS

After Al Kurd's success in the early 1970s, Palestinians had to wait until the end of the decade before other groups made a similar impact at home and abroad. One of the most successful pop acts ever to emerge from Palestine are the prolific group **Al Ashiqeen** ("The Lovers"), who achieved fame, all too rare among Palestinian bands, all over the Arab world. The theme of their most famous cassette release, "Sirit Izz Deen El Kassam", is the colourful life of holy man and freedom fighter El Kassam.

The energy devoted to music-making intensified in the mid-1980s, especially among the youth of the occupied territories. The intifada uprising, a youth-led, stone-throwing revolt initiated in the Gaza strip in December 1987, fuelled the desire to express political woes in song, and bands sprouted up all over the West Bank. Singers, musicians and groups like Bassam Bashara, Walid abed Salim, Sabbar, Al Funoon Al Shaabiyeh and Riyad Awad have carried the hard-edged sentiments of revolt to a receptive audience. Bassam Bashara's hit cassette "Atfal Al Hijara" (Children of the Stones) is a typical example of the brooding, mournful and yet powerfully defiant style of singing and songwriting that epitomizes the best in modern Palestinian pop.

In recent times some groups have been experimenting by adding elements of jazz, western classical and Indian music to the traditional Arabic forms of Middle Eastern music. **Sabreen**, fronted by the charismatic Galillean female singer Kamilya Jubran, have pushed back the boundaries of innovation further than ever and enjoyed the kind of success that has almost turned them into a musical institution. In Beirut **Ziad Rahbani**, the talented son of Fairuz and the composer Rahbani, has earned himself the reputation as the most important figure in Middle Eastern music since the great Egyptian composer Sheikh Sayed Darweesh.

Lastly, two Lebanese singers have enjoyed continuous, deep-rooted popularity in Palestine over the last two decades, and any appreciation of Palestinian music would be incomplete without mentioning their names. The first is **Marcel Khalifa**, who has dominated Middle Eastern political songwriting since the mid-1970s with songs like "Alihdoud" (On the Border) and the beautiful elegy "Ahinu Ra Ckubs Oumi" (I Miss my Mother's Bread), which is based on a poem by the most famous of Palestinian poets, **Mahmoud Darwish**. The second is the great pan-Arabic diva **Fairuz**, certain of whose innumerable cassette releases – "Al Quds Al Filbal" (Jerusalem On My Mind) and "Raji'aoun" (I'm Going Back) have championed the Palestinian cause with great sympathy and eloquence.

Whether the newly autonomous districts of Gaza and Jericho will bring forth a renewal of defiant music or a mellowing of Palestinian music to include the blander, more commercial pop themes of love and self, remains to be heard.

Many thanks to Mohammed Hijazi and Rim Kalamé for information.

◣ DISCOGRAPHY ◢

Cassettes of Palestinian music are almost impossible to find outside the Middle East, and their availability is restricted to specialist Arab music and video stores in some major cities.

◉ **Various** *Palestine – Music of The Intifada* (Venture, UK). Features songs performed by a variety of West Bank musicians, who had to be smuggled out of Palestine to Berlin in order to record it. Even so far from the Middle East the release proved controversial and Venture received anony-mous angry complaints – even threats from Jewish groups in the UK.

Handala *Handala* and *Amani* (Sud-Nord, Italy). The only other recordings of Palestinian music readily available abroad. Although they don't give an especially accurate representation of Palestinian musical styles, they do provide a decent impression of the powerful emotions and political awareness that are at the core of modern Palestinian popular music. LP and cassette only.

FOUR SUPERSTARS OF CAIRO

KEY FIGURES OF TWENTIETH-CENTURY EGYPTIAN CLASSICAL SONG

The classical musical arena has always been dominated by a clutch of great classical singers enjoying huge popularity and influence. David Lodge profiles four of the finest.

At 25, **Sheikh Sayed Darweesh** (1891–1923) was a travelling actor fallen on hard times. At 30 he was hailed as the father of the new Egyptian Arab music, and hero of the renaissance. He rose to fame with his controversial "innovation" musical movement of the 1910s and '20s, in which he blended western instruments and harmony with forgotten Arab musical forms and Egyptian folklore. More importantly, he wrote words for the Egyptian people: dedications for the tradesmen, operettas for the hashish dealers, and daring anti-British nationalism for the masses, like "Bilaadi Bilaadi" (My Country, my Country), which became the national anthem.

My country my country,
my love and heart is for you.
Egypt, the mother of countries,
You are my wants and desire,

And your Nile has given so many gifts to your people.

After a composing career of just seven years, Darweesh died of a cocaine overdose, aged 32. He now lies in the Garden of the Immortals in Alexandria.

Abd el-Halim Hafez (1927–77) was known as the "Nightingale of the Nile". In a society that generally reserves true respect for the old, it surprised everyone when Halim Hafez took over the musical arena in his early twenties to became the golden boy of the nationalist revolution of 1952. He came at the right time with short patriotic songs that pleased President Nasser as well as the young generation of the day who embraced him as their spokesperson. By the 1960s his new, short, light songs, with their distinct melodic style, gave way to a partnership with Mohamed Abd el-Wahaab and a return to the long classical form. He was ill with bilharzia almost all his life, and involved the nation in his ongoing fight for good health with a vulnerability that charmed the nation. For men, he offered a rather camp alternative role in an oppressively macho society. And his little-boy-lost image had women crooning to mother him. He died in 1977, perhaps the last superstar of the great artists' era.

Mohamed Abd el-Wahaab (1910–91), "artist of generations", was the last remaining figure from the old guard and the most controversial and respected member of the musical fraternity. His achievements span a long career from the 1920s as a singer, to film star and eventually composer, a talent crowned when Umm Kalthum agreed to sing his "Enta Omri", a song which featured an electric guitar for the first time. As a composer, Abd el-Wahaab is remembered as the modernizer of Arabic music, liberating it, as his supporters see it, from the limitations of the *takht* ensemble and allowing it to embrace western-style tangos, waltzes and instrumentation. Others criticize his music for overt plagiarism. He stood by his vision for modernization of the music all his life, demanding that "the artist is the creator and has the full right to introduce new elements into his music as he sees fit. We must always be open to new ideas and not resist change. Change is inevitable in everything."

It is ironic that in his later years he became so contemptuous of other modernizers that he took his initiative a step further. In 1990 he released a classical song into a market awash with the bleeping synths of the new youth pop. This was the first occasion in 32 years that he sang his own composition. "Minrear Ley" (Without why) set out to test popular loyalty, but was viewed by many as the final gasp of a wounded musical genre. Its immediate success, however, goes some way to prove that, despite ending his life in the knowledge that he had failed to pass on the tradition to a new generation, his vision for Arab music lives on.

ALL ARABS AGREE

Umm Kalthum (1904–75) is indisputably the Arab world's greatest singer. Stern and tragic, rigidly in control, this was a woman who, in her heyday, truly had the Arab world in the palm of her hand. With melancholy operettas that seemed to drift on for hours, she encapsulated the love lives of a nation and mesmerized millions.

Rumour had it that Umm Kalthum inhaled gulps of hashish smoke before performing and that the scarf trailing from her right hand was steeped in opium. Her stage presence was

Give me my freedom, set my hands free,
I've given everything and kept nothing.
Your rope has made my hands bleed,
Why should I keep it when it didn't
keep me?
You, the one who is woken, falls asleep,
Remembers the promise, and wakes up.
And if a wound is cured, memory opens
another one.
So learn how to forget and learn how
to forgive
My darling; everything is fate

We haven't chosen to be born unhappy.
Our fate might put us together after meeting
became so difficult.
So if we denied each other and we met
like strangers,
Don't say that's what we wanted.
But that's what luck wanted.

From "Al-Atlaal" (The Ruins), written by Dr Ibrahim Nagy, composition by Riad Sunbati, 1966

charged by a theatrical rapport with the audience: a slight nod of the head or a shake of her shoulders and they were in uproar. She learned to sing by reciting verse at cafés in her village, and sometimes dressed as a boy to escape the religious authorities. It was to her training in religious chanting that she owed her stunning vocal agility and her masterful command of the complex *maqamat*. She was educated in the secular field by the poet Ahmed Ramy and of her total output of 286 songs, 132 were his poems. Her voice was the epitome of the Arab ideal – saturated with *shaggan*, or emotional yearning, and powerful enough on occasion to shatter a glass.

In her long career, she specialized in love songs that sometimes lasted an hour, improvising and ornamenting on a theme that would bring the audience to a frenzy. She was once asked to sing a line 52 times over, which she did while developing the melody each time. Of this ability she said: "I am greatly influenced by the music found in Arabic poetry. I improvise because my heart rejoices in the richness of this music. If someone went over a song which I sang five times, he would not find

The great, the legendary . . . Umm Kalthum

pride to them during their most difficult period in history. Nasser used her nationalist songs to keep the masses behind him, and timed his major political speeches carefully around her broadcasts. The less prescient Anwar Sadat once addressed the nation on the same day as her concert, and ended up without an audience, a mistake he only made once.

She remained a great campaigner for the traditional Arab song, leaving behind an orchestra, the Arab Music Ensemble, dedicated to maintaining the pure heritage (*al turath*, from the eight and ninth centuries). It's worth remembering that while Kalthum and her fellow classical musicians are today often considered "traditional Arab music", they were, in their day, part of a movement breaking away from tradition.

At Umm Kalthum's funeral in February 1975, attended by many Arab heads of state, over three million people followed her through the streets of Cairo. At 10pm on the first Thursday of every month, all radio stations still play Umm Kalthum in memory of her momentous live radio concerts of the 1950s and 60s. To this day, Israeli broadcasters seduce Palestinians to their stations with the music of Umm Kalthum, duly spliced with propaganda.

any one like the other. I am not a record that repeats itself, I am a human being who is deeply touched by what I sing." As a childless mother, her songs were her offspring given to the people. For these gifts they returned total adoration.

Apart from Allah, they say, Umm Kalthum is the only subject about which all Arabs agree, a fact that has always given her special political significance. She embraced Nasser's pan-Arab ideals and drew Arabs together by extending a

◗ DISCOGRAPHY ◖

Compact discs are wonderfully suited to the one-hour-plus of uninterrupted playtime required by classical Egyptian songs.

⊙ **Umm Kalthum** *Hajartek* (EMI, Egypt). This (Saudi-spelled) title is the passionately rendered song "Hagartak, yimkin ansa hawak" (I've left you and perhaps I will forget your love) – as essential as any. Another, equally melancholy song-album, also on CD, is ⊙ *Al-Atlaal* (The Ruins) (EMI, Egypt), her most acclaimed work, full of melo-drama and suspense. For "Enta Omri" (You are my life), she was greatly criticized on account of its electric instruments.

⊙ **Mohamed Abd el-Wahaab** *Vols I – X* (Club des Disques Arabes, France). A life's work is gradually appearing on CD, to the delight of suitably equipped fans (though with "Vol X" Club has only got as far as 1939). It may be some time before they get round to reissuing his final work, "Mingrear ley" (Without question), produced before his death in 1991.
⊙ **Abd el-Halim Hafez** You may get Halim on CD through spe-cialist importers, or from French or Arabic sources. "Safini Marra" (Be nice to me for once) was the song that launched his career. With "Ahhwak" (I love you) he modified Arab classical song to a simpler, lighter form. "Narr Habibi Narr" (Fire, my baby, fire) gave him superstar status on the film of the same title.

CAIRO HIT FACTORY

MODERN EGYPTIAN MUSIC: AL-JIL, SHAABI, NUBIAN

Since the 1920s, Egyptian culture has been broadcast to generations of Arabic-speaking people. Frequent visitor David Lodge takes the pulse of Cairo, the musical heartbeat of the Arab world.

E ven today, turn on the radio or television or go to the cinema in any Arabic-speaking country and it's almost certain to be an Egyptian show on offer. The star performers have invariably been drawn by the magnetism of this huge industry, and by no means all the great names are Egyptian. **Sabah**, whose singing career was eventually overshadowed by her licentious off-stage lifestyle, was Lebanese; **Warda**, once hailed as the new Umm Kalthum, is Algerian; **Farid el-Atrach**, the oud virtuoso, singer and composer, was a Druze Lebanese; **Faiza Ahmed**, the demure heavyweight of the 1960s, was Syrian; and **Samira Said**, the voice of modern classical song, is Moroccan (discography details on these artists can be found in the "Arab World" feature, p.176). And yet working with Egyptian composers and musicians, and singing in Egyptian Arabic, the lingua-franca of Arab culture, these singers are, to all intents and purposes, Egyptian. With unrestrained loyalty, they declare their hearts lie in *Misr* (Egypt), an emotional bond which also gives them access to the major Egyptian market and to an increasingly lucrative Arab-wide public of over 200 million.

The size and confidence of this ready market is partly responsible for the emphatic rejection by Egyptians of music from other countries – which means the streets of Cairo are blissfully unpolluted with western pop. The rejection of things foreign even extends to Arab neighbours; only in the last few years has it been possible to find cassettes from the Middle East in the kiosks of Cairo, while Algerian *rai* is a newcomer in 1994. Today, the city is a gathering point for music of diverse Egyptian roots, a musical playground of cross-cutting influences and inspiration. The brassy jazz of Nubia from the hot African south plays alongside the haunting clarinet of the desert Bedouin; the comical rap monologues of the

Nilotic Saiyidis mix with the heart-rending tones of classical song. In this unique auditory environment – at venues ranging from the giant Sufi *zikr* street festivals to football stadium extravaganzas, from the raw theatre of a working-class wedding to a belly-dance nightclub down Pyramids Road – Cairo offers Arab composers an extraordinary atmosphere for their inspiration.

MUSIC OF THE STREETS

When the heart throbs with exhilaration and rapture becomes intense and the agitation of ecstasy is manifested and conventional forms are gone, that agitation is neither dancing nor bodily indulgence, but a dissolution of the soul.
Ibn Taymiya, writer and theologian (1263–1328)

While the religiously orthodox have worked to keep music out of Islam, the Islamic mystics, the **Sufis**, have instead sought to harness its power and turn it to the service of God. According to the ninth-century Baghdad philosopher Abu Suliman al-Darani, Sufis believe that "music and singing do not produce in the heart that which is not in it" and that music "reminds the spirit of the realm for which it constantly longs". They taunt those who denounce music as a dangerous influence on human nature by declaring that if you have moral discipline, you need have no fear of it. The Sufis thus helped to nurture music through the ages when all around were doing their best to suppress it. This "heretical" alliance is most intensely displayed at the giant *mulids*, festivals to celebrate the saint of a mosque, when upwards of a million worshippers and hangers-on gather together in defiance of fundamentalists and authorities alike. The union of body and music is encapsulated in the *zikr*, a dramatic ritual which uses song and dance to open a path to divine ecstasy. Sufis explain the alarming spectacle of entrancement with a characteristic spiritual logic: "Music is the food of the spirit; when the spirit receives food, it turns aside from the government of the body."

Mulid folk band

nights, the city becomes a patchwork of pulsing coloured light and searing noise, as the elaborate ritual of the marriage party gets underway. First comes the "Hassabala" troupe, bugles and trumpets blaring (a style inspired by imperial British marching bands), who form a circle of up to 25 thundering wooden drums. Into this vortex of chanting and deafening rhythm go the whirling dancers and a stick-cracking folklore troupe from Upper Egypt. Unceremoniously, the music stops and the group dashes hurriedly into a waiting Toyota van which takes them hooting across town to their next appointment, possibly their fourth or fifth performance of the night. Once the bride and groom have been

To a binding hypnotic rhythm, heaving movements and respiratory groans, the leader conducts the congregation by reciting Sufi poetry, guiding them from one maqam mode to another. Bodies sway, heads roll upward on every stroke as they chant religious devotions with spiralling intensity. The *nay* (flute) played in a style depicted in the pharaonic tombs, alternates short, two-beat pulses on a simple melody line. Lifeless arms dangle, saliva slaps from open mouths, and eyes stare without seeing. Men collapse, convulsing, on the floor, while others run to lift them up, reciting to them verses from the Koran. The beat slows, and rows of sweating heads drop their gaze to the floor. Slowly, exhausted, the ecstatics return to the fray.

For the practising Sufi clans who have marched behind their flags and banners all the way from their village, the event is a display of clan loyalty, piety and pride. For the musicians who roam from one mulid to another throughout the year, turning popular village songs about secular love into an adoration of Mohammed the Prophet, it can also be a good living. In adaptation, these songs lose little of their earthly sexual passion: "It is he, it is only he who lives in my heart, only he to whom I give my love, our beautiful Prophet, Mohammed, whose eyes are made-up with kohl."

BRIDE AND HOME

A working class (*baladi*) wedding in a cramped alley in central Cairo is possibly the finest exhibition of spontaneous musical theatre you can witness anywhere. On Friday and Saturday

Cairo wedding

escorted away in a cacophony of noise, then out come the whiskey and hashish, and the real party begins.

A riotously made-up dancer laden with glittering sequins takes to the small stage,

Belly-dance music

cavorting with the master of ceremonies, lifting her dress a little, pushing out her leg, lying on the floor and gyrating, rubbing up against him, playfully controlling the arena. This is *raks sharki* – **belly dancing**. The dancer sings with flaying alto vocals – pop songs, classical songs, traditional songs all made raw and raunchy. The makeshift stage becomes a platform too for the guests who wave banknotes in their bids to stay in the limelight, to dance, sing or play the fool, with unselfconscious bravado and humour. More than just honouring the bride and her father, this stream of musical cameos is all part of the drama that provides an outlet for the tensions that build up in the tight-knit community.

It is on these occasions that men may choose to settle lingering disputes, dedicating their advice, threats and guarded insults via the stage to their rivals in a furiously fast interchange. Up leaps a boy with a fistful of banknotes held high: he makes his greeting, echoed by the MC in a rapid, musical rap. "Greetings to the police, especially the police of Saiyida Zeynab who are our friends, greetings to the youth of Alaa, greetings to the people of Hussein. We want this wedding to be nice with no trouble."

After a stream of passionate appeals to family and friends, and a short break of music from the five-piece band lining the back of the stage, another singer, dressed in evening suit and tie, takes over, slowly wailing "Ya leil ya ein" ("Oh! the night, Oh! my eyes!"), a wild improvisation that pierces the dark from a deafening, distorted PA.

MUSIC OF THE YOUTH

Until as recently as the late 1980s, from every taxi radio-cassette deck and every street corner kiosk, day and night, emerged the haunting voice of Umm Kalthum . While this music has far from disappeared, cassette shops and fast cars are today stocked up with other types of music and competition of a more commercial kind is rife among the hundreds of artists. The new sounds of Egyptian youth – *shaabi* and *al-jil* – are the music of two social revolutions shaping the nation's modern outlook.

Pressure for change in the musical world of Cairo had been building up for some time, and, over the past twenty years, the established order could do little more than look on as an entirely new Egypt unfurled before them. Since the mid-1970s Sadat's "open door policy" had welcomed western business, which gave birth to a new enterprise culture in the big cites. In addition, the Gulf states and Iraq provided new work for millions of Egyptian labourers, craftsmen and technicians who sent back their pay cheques to create, in effect, a new urban middle class.

With their new-found spending power, this rapidly expanding social group has reinvented Cairo in their own image, complete with take-out foodstalls, ear-splitting in-car hi-fi, "dunkin' donuts" and of course street-corner kiosks crammed with their music. Against these new social forces, the old guard was defenceless; by the time of Abd el-Halim Hafez's death in 1977 all the greats, bar Abd el-Wahaab, had already gone, and with the retirement of Shadia and Nagat soon after, there was no-one left to carry on the tradition.

It was time for folk music to reassert itself as Egypt's most vital form and, in a way, to reaffirm true Egyptian identity at a time of momentous and rapid change.

SHAABI – ART
FROM THE WORKERS

The humiliating defeat by Israel in 1967 shattered the pan-Arab dream of President Nasser, forcing Egyptians to face stark reality. From this abject poverty and humiliation they escaped into a new "light song", which drew on folkloric themes to reassert a proud Egyptian identity. It was a movement away from the serious classical hue of tradition and towards a more humorous, even salacious spirit. At first this was a middle-class initiative, with singers like Layla Nasmy and Aida al-Shah popularizing these forms for the respectable community. But soon, almost inevitably, it gave way to working-class singers with a more organic interpretation of the tradition, and with words from the present-day. This was the music of the shaabi (peoples') working-class areas of the cities – communities which rank with some of the most overcrowded in the world.

In 1971 the first singer to break into the mass market was the charismatic **Ahmed Adaweyah**. His lyrical irreverence, using the rough dialect of the streets, was the essence of his revolution. This kind of language had never been heard in song before. It is a weapon of the working class that affirms their own values while mocking respectable society, as in his song, "Setu" (composed by Farouk Salama with lyrics by Hassan abu-Atma), poking fun at a middle-class lifestyle:

Fast asleep he's fasting,
He doesn't want to bother.
And his granny and mummy are mothering him
With honey and butter.
Finally, but not that final,
He's a weapon without a bullet,
A failure at school and no good at work.

Full of metaphor and comical twists in conventional expressions, Adaweyah's lyrics stamped shaabi character into his songs and created that new expression for popular culture with the release of every cassette. His lifestyle and personality were steeped in the baseness of a poor and uneducated background – a working-class hero in direct conflict with middle-class aspirations.

His provocative social commentaries served to hang Egypt's dirty linen in public, which didn't go down well with the government and ruling class, fearful that it would reinforce the popular Gulf Arab image of Egypt as an uncultured society. In 1991 he received a surprise invitation to appear on TV for the first time to talk about censorship. His remarks were bleeped out. Songs with suggestive lyrics, or those that simply imply an immoral lifestyle, are banned. A contemporary of Adaweyah in 1992 sung "Her waist is like the neck of a violin, I used to enjoy apricots but now I would die for mangos!". This caused an outcry among the middle class, raised on the

sung poetry of Umm Kalthum. The cassette was nevertheless available everywhere, sold upwards of half a million, and, with its typically euphemistic fruitiness, became a favourite of the gay community.

Equally unpopular with the censors is the recurring lyrical theme of working-class pride. In a driving rap on his album "Akhar Sa'ar" (The Last Hour), **Shaaban Abd el-Rahim** affirmed the "Egyptian-ness" of shaabi music as real Egyptian music unadulterated by the outside world. Again, the cassette, and all others by him, were promptly banned. This is an example of the lyrics:

There is foreign music,
We sleep and dream, it's all foreign.
If we imitate, it will never help us,
Have nothing to do with foreign.
Thank God I can't find anyone to copy.
Listen to me, my country bumpkin,
All art comes from the workers,
And now all the people are saying,
Look, the ironing man is singing....

Similarly, in "Kadab ya Kheisha" (You're a liar Kheisha: *kheisha* is also the word for a floor mop), he reaffirms in a wailing *mawal* the values of loyalty in friendship, a quality he considers to be central to working-class culture.

I have a friend but it's a pity
As he turned out to be a liar.
I thought he was just as good as the other friends,
But he turned out to be very nasty,
He separates lovers.
When I found out about this I kicked him out
And closed the door on his face.
You're a liar Kheisha.
You got the best hairdresser* in town angry with you
You're a liar Kheisha.

[*Hairdressers are famous in Egypt for being unruffled and difficult to upset.]

As Japanese VCRs and American films became established in back-alley society, so the younger generation was seduced into a world of foreign, modernizing values – one where Shaaban's beliefs might seem no longer appropriate. Younger singers have a fascination with the musical gadgetry of the west, and synthetic sounds are challenging the claim that shaabi is the only authentic Egyptian music. Increasingly, on top of the traditional violins, *tabla* and squeeze-box, a western drum kit, organ, synthesizer,

SHAABI SUPERSTARS

haabi singers specialize in the *mawal*, a freely improvised vocal in which the singer impresses on the listener the depth of his or her sorrowful complaint. It's a form which is found widely in classical music, although in a more refined style, and bears comparison with other "folk-blues" like *fado* or *rembétika*. None of these artists has released any material on CD, nor is it very likely they will in the future. If you want to listen to them outside Egypt you'll need to check Egyptian and Arab-owned stores in big cities, or specialist importers. You may need to ask for a release by song, rather than album title, and it is common to find the same song on many different releases, or even the same release under different names.

Ahmed Adaweyah is undoubtedly the finest exponent of the thick, soulful tones of the shaabi voice suited to this singing, and he has many releases purely of mawal. But shaabi songs aren't all sorrow; the traditional progression has a fast rhythmic beat emerging from the improvisation, to take the song through chorus after chorus to climax

Ahmed Adaweyah - fruity irreverence

in a rousing dance tempo. As a shaabi singer becomes more famous, his jobs at weddings and festivals might be replaced by working the clubs and eventually private weddings in Egypt and the Gulf. With about a dozen releases, Adaweyah is still the most "Egyptian" sound on the market. "Zahma" (Crowded) was his first major hit, but "Al-Tarik" (The route) is one of his finest cassettes. There are also several tapes of his with the title "Mawal Adaweyah", each featuring a lengthy, heart-rending vocal improvisation.

Shaaban Abd el-Rahim is famous for his rapping wisdoms about his life, as he celebrates his rise from ironing man to superstar, and how,

despite selling upwards of 100,000 copies of each cassette, fame has yet to change him. He lives in his "village" on the outskirts of Cairo, where he maintains a traditional lifestyle and keeps chickens and goats on his roof. He may not be a millionaire but in his community he is idolized. A walk around the village or any of the shaabi areas of Cairo will see him constantly surrounded by a mafia-style group of devotees and extended family, for whom Shaaban is a working-class hero. Of his cassettes, "Akhar Saah" (The Final Hour) is highly recommended. But it is banned and almost impossible to get hold of; you'll have to search hard.

Kat Kut el-Amir is one of the originals. While his limelight was stolen by Adaweyah, he left a memorable song to posterity, one he composed and sang exclusively for el-Hag Ali, the biggest hashish dealer in Egypt in the 1970s, at his daughter's wedding – "Ya Gazelle el-Darb il-Ahmar" (You Gazelle of Darb il-Ahmar – an old quarter of Cairo).

Hassan el-Asmar is of the second generation of shaabi singers, jazzing up the music with a relentless bleeping synthesizer, and always identifiable by the sultry young female choruses that feature in his songs. "Mish Hasibak" (I'm not going to leave you) is the cassette to get.

Of the young *shaabi* stars, **Magdy Talaat** and **Magdy Shabini** are the most popular. Their releases, usually one each year, are advertised on TV, but otherwise they get no media exposure. Despite these limitations, their hugh success is an inspiration to hundreds of others competing in the market with dreams of fortune and fame. Try "Hobanha" (We love them) by Magdy Shabini and Elli Ayesni Negini (Whoever wants me come to me) by Magdy Talaat.

saxophone and sometimes an electric guitar are being added. As the shaabi stars attempt to reach a wider public with their increasingly slick product, production values are more and more critically assessed.

Many feel that even Adaweyah has let the shaabi movement down. It was strongly rumoured in 1991 that he was the victim in a drama involving a beautiful woman, a Saudi husband, a castration, and a few weeks in hospital; his recourse to drum machine and synthesizer on his latest release has caused it to be locally dubbed "Ahmed Adaweyah ba'ad il-amaleya" (Ahmed Adaweyah after the operation). Whether or not Adaweyah now walks with a different stride is neither here nor there; the story has established itself in popular folklore – a true rumour.

AL-JIL

Fed up with listening to the Beatles, Abba and Bony M in a language they couldn't understand, by the mid-1970s the youth of Egypt had decided they could do better. With the aid of samplers and quarter-tone programmes, Egyptian pop music, *al-jil* ("generation music"), was born. It wasn't quite this simple, but the sense of a revolutionary change was apparent. The dance music that they produced bears the clear hallmarks of the Arab sound: trained, controlled voices sliding through infectious happy melodies; distinctive, clear-as-a-bell backing chorus; and punchy techno-Arab beat.

Central to the movement was a young Libyan, **Hamid el-Shaeri**. Fleeing one of Gadaffi's anti-western purges, Hamid came to Egypt in 1974 and started working with Egyptians on a new sound. It wasn't until 1988 that one song stamped his seal on the market. This was the year of "Lolaiki", made in a back room and sold all over Cairo in millions. It was sung by a friend, Ali Hamaida, who to the great relief of many turned out to be a one-hit wonder (the song was okay once or twice, but all over town for a year...):
Without you I'd never sing,
Without you I'd never fall in love.
I have nobody without you.
You are my light and my sight,
My song is only for you,
Lolaiki [meaningless] lo lo lo lo lo lo lo lo lo
Lyrical themes of "boy flirts with girl, girl leaves boy, boy is miserable/finds new girl"

did little to win over the older generation, but the popularity of the new feel-good scene couldn't fail to impress upon the established cultural guardians the strength of this new youth movement. The rags-to-riches story of "Lolaiki" also impressed the back-street entrepreneurs, and the new industry exploded overnight. To the older generation, and music connoisseurs, the new music-makers were little more than businessmen selling cheap produce in the market. Gone were the intricate melodies, beautiful poetry, sympathetic use of maqamat and natural sounds, and in came the rasping synthesizer and the three-minute pop-song format. The official media turned against al-jil and, while western pop songs continue to feature on the radio and TV, the younger generation were for many years denied media access to their own music.

Al-jil singers are the first to admit they're in the business of entertainment, not art, but that is not to dismiss the genre's importance as a cultural force. In many Arab countries, people under 25 account for three-quarters of the population. More than merely giving people a tune to dance to, al-jil music has become a focus for young people breaking free from the constraints of traditional society. It finds ready markets everywhere from the Atlantic to the Euphrates, and by doing so it exports its visions of modernity to a wider Arab youth.

RURAL FOLK MUSIC

Egypt is a land of many environments. The archetypal image is that of the crowded towns, villages and farmland of the Nile valley, but mountain wilderness and arid desert cover 96 percent of the country. The diversity also ranges from the European colour of the northern, Mediterranean coast lands to the African resonances of the south. From each geographically distinct area comes a distinct music.

Folk music in Egypt still performs a vital role in recording a popular version of history. With their own characteristic rhythms, instruments and voices, there is music to accompany almost every event, from the harvest to circumcisions. There is social criticism in the monologues about village goings-on, worship in the festival songs for Ramadan, and mayhem in activities at weddings and mulids.

The Musicians of the Nile

Saiyidi is the folk music of the upper Nile valley. Saiyidis (the name applies to the musicians as well as their music) are famous for their clever use of words and for their playful monologues set to music. The music features two instruments in particular – the *nahrasan*, a two-sided drum hung across the chest and played with sticks, and the *mismar saiyidi* trumpet. The characteristic *rhythm saiyidi*, to which horses are traditionally trained to dance, is one of the most successful styles used in modern pop.

Among the best known of saiyidi stars are **Les Musiciens du Nil**. The "Musicians of the Nile", a name given to them for overseas promotional purposes, are known in Egypt for the lead singer **Met'al Gnawi**, the charismatic head of a gypsy family who were unexpectedly chosen by the Egyptian government to act as Egypt's official folk group abroad. His success astounds Egyptians who call him *rais* (president) in honour of his regular visits to western capitals. In Egypt he is well liked in his home town, Luxor, and otherwise is remembered for one song that tickled Egyptians' sense of humour, the saucy "Ya faraula" (My strawberry!: Egyptians are fond of using fruit in sexual allegory) which became a national hit.

Omar Gharzawi is famous for his monologues defending saiyidis and their culture – they are traditionally the butt of Egyptian humour. Other saiyidi names worth listening out for include **Sohar Magdy**, **Ahmed Mougahid**, **Shoukoukou** and **Ahmed Ismail**.

The folk music known as *sawahili* comes from the Mediterranean littoral, and is characterized by the use of a guitar-like stringed instrument, the *simsimaya*, though the style found in Alexandria features the accordion. Famous sawahili singers include **Aid el-Gannirni** from Suez and **Abd'l Iskandrani** from Alexandria.

As well as the various kinds of folk music, Egypt has two important ethnic musics – Bedouin and Nubian. **Bedouin** music comes from the desert, either from the western, Libyan desert, or the eastern arid zones of Sinai and the Eastern desert. The main instrument is the bedouin *mismar*, a twin-pipe clarinet which enables the player to produce a melody line and a drone simultaneously. Perhaps the best-known singer is **Awad e'Medic**.

NEW NUBIAN, OLD NUBIAN

Nubian music has its origins in the African south, among the now displaced Nubian people. The construction of the second Aswan dam in the early 1960s – which created Lake Nasser, the largest artificial lake in the world – effectively drowned their entire civilization. Over 100,000 people were forcibly removed. They put up a good deal of resistance at the time – and many poems and songs of the 1960s recount their anger and fear – but in the wake of the flooding of Lake Nasser, the communities moved south into Sudan and north into Egypt. Many Nubians travelled north to Cairo in

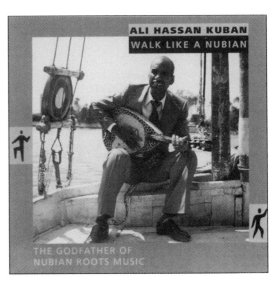

AL-JIL SINGERS

·······················

The singer is especially important to the success of the song, less these days for a good voice than for straightforward sex appeal. The singer and musicians typically have little say in the music-making process – there are very few singer-songwriters – and groups, although there were a few in the 1970s, have never caught on. Instead performers are supplied songs by a producer who has collected the melody, lyrics and rhythm from different sources and arranged them in a cynical formula dedicated to the mainstream conservative market. The financial rewards can be great; from a successful cassette, the singer gets fame and may earn spectacular money from headlining at live concerts in Egypt, the Arab capitals and private parties in New York, London and Paris, where tickets rarely cost less than £150 ($250).

The availability of al-jil music overseas is improving, but distribution is very patchy and, as with shaabi, you will most likely need to check Egyptian and Arab-owned stores in big cities, or specialist importers. Unlike shaabi, however, a number of CDs of al-jil have been released on the Blue Silver label (France). Order them through importers.

Hanan is the one female pop star in a musical environment dominated by men. She was classically trained, and began her career singing in the classical Arab Music Institute Ensemble, sponsored by the Ministry of Culture – which is something of an irony. Her highly controlled, squeaky voice sounds, at its best, stunningly wild. Try her "Besma" (I'm listening) cassette.

Ehab Tawfik is a protegé of Hamid el-Shaeri, whose treatment of the highly infectious melodies is the essence of Hamid's pop movement. "Ikmini" offers the most typical of al-jil sounds: this is his best cassette.

Amr Diab arrived in Cairo from Port Said by bus in 1984, and now turns up in a helicopter as the star billing at music festivals in front of 50,000 people. Today's sophisticated pop videos present him to his fans as a sensitive and serious pop star with an international lifestyle. He was the first singer to leap about on stage, where he makes the most of silk shirts, loose vests, and boyish good looks. "Habibi" (My darling) was his last big success.

---

search of work, but they never cease to dream of a return to their lost lands. Village music remains traditional, with ritual songs supported by a *duff* and hand-clapping.

In Cairo, **Nubian music** found two leaders, whose opposing voices exactly mirror the diverging paths of the city's Nubian migrants. **Ali Hassan Kuban** recalls overhearing a jazz band in a Cairo nightclub from the pavement outside and decided at once to add brass to his music. So came into being (at least apocryphally) the urban sound of Nubia. Although unknown in Cairo outside the Nubian community, Kuban's unique music has taken him on many European tours and put two CDs onto the World Music market. In Egypt, he campaigns tirelessly for the Nubian language, and insists that members of his musicians' cooperative sing in one of the two Nubian dialects. His brash, urgent musical style has inspired many others in Cairo, most notably Bahr Abu Greisha and Hussein Bashier. They specialize in wailing brass

which often gets totally out of control, but always lends a New Orleans feel to their unique sound.

Mohamed Mounir is a modern Nubian, the thinking person's pop star, having produced some of the most sophisticated modern pop music in Egypt. From the second generation of migrants in the 1970s, he came to study in Cairo already speaking Arabic as his first language. Mounir considers himself an Arab Egyptian and is highly critical of the popular Nubian movement for a return to the homeland. Concentrating less on Nubian nationalism than Kuban, Mounir sings of solutions to the problems of the wider Arab world – of which he feels Nubia is a part – such as the future of the Palestinians and the dilemma of Jerusalem. Mounir's home audience is dominated by students who appreciate his lyrics.

Thanks to Klaus Friederking for information in Tradewind.

ⓒ **Various** *"Yalla" Hitlist Egypt* (Mango, UK). An excellent introduction to shaabi, al-jil and Nubian styles, featuring songs by Mohamed Mounir, Ehab Tawfik, Shaaban Abd el-Rahim, Magdy Talaat, Hanan and others.

ⓒ **Soliman Gamil** *The Egyptian Music* and *Ankh* (Touch, UK). Instrumental works by a modern folk/classical composer. While the pieces on the earlier release have a "Sands of Arabia" veneer to them, "Ankh" eerily evokes – with the help of traditional instruments – a pharaonic world centuries before the arrival of Islam and the Arabs in Egypt.

ⓒⓓ **Ali Hassan Kuban** *From Nubia to Cairo* (Piranha, Germany). Tough, Cairo-Nubian music released to the world, and followed up on ⓒ *Walk Like an Egyptian* (Piranha, Germany). Both have excellent booklets.

ⓒ **Mohamed Mounir** *Mohamed Mounir* (Monsun-Line, Germany). A remixed compilation of 13 Arab-Nubian songs. The follow-up ⓒ *Wast el-Daira*, (Monsun-Line, Germany) presents him at his most intricate and sophisticated. Mounir's new cassette, *Iftah Albak* (Open Your Heart) promises to be another big seller, and earlier cassettes you might still pick up

include the beautiful, all-acoustic *El-Malek* (The King), *Kalemni* (Talk to me) and the early *Shababik* (Windows).

ⓒ **Les Musiciens du Nil** *Luxor to Isna* (Real World, UK). The rababa fiddle rasps and strange oboes and clarinets hoot and buzz through mostly instrumental tracks, interspersed with street-sound interludes. A document for posterity.

ⓒ **Mokhtar al-Said and El Ferka el-Masaya** *Amar 14: Jalilah's Raks Sharki 2* (Piranha, Germany). Confusing title for a CD of raks sharki, or belly-dance, compositions. Amar 14 – "the full moon", a euphemism for a beautiful woman – is the classic orchestral "oriental" sound, performed by al-Said and his Ferka el Masaya ("Orchestra of Diamonds"). By turns portentous and playful, this bubbles along with jangling riq tambourine.

ⓒ **Salamat** *Mambo El Soudani: Nubian Al Jeel Music from Cairo* (Piranha, Germany). Strong whiffs of Sudan drift through these thumping songs, dense with hysterical alto-sax, tenor sax and trumpet. With lyrics in Arabic, this is a less politicized, more good-time sound than Kuban's. Many of the musicians perform with both groups, though Salamat also have female vocalists.

YEARNING TO DANCE

SUDAN IS THE BRIDGE OF AFRICA AND ARABIA

Sudan, home of the "whirling" dervish and the pogo-ing Dinka, should be an exciting meeting ground for Arab and African musical culture. But religious dogma and civil war have combined to create a singularly inauspicious environment. Peter Verney, a long-time former resident of a country which leaves an indelible impression on all who touch it, surveys the scene and looks forward to a happier day when the country reclaims its position as one of Africa's great musical crossroads. Extra information is gratefully acknowledged from Helen Jerome and Moawia Yassin.

I t all came home to me when the mobile disco I was running in the shanty town around Omdurman was confiscated by the security police. Since 1989 a new military regime of "Islamic" absolutists – the **National Islamic Front** – has been clamping down on Sudanese musicians with a puritanical zeal that has forced many of the country's best-loved performers into exile or silence. Celebrated singers such as Mohamed Wardi and Mohamed al-Amin, branded as "communist" and under threat of death, have fled to Cairo, although the Sudanese

still play their politically tinged songs as a symbol of resistance. The massively popular lyricist and poet Mahjoub Sharif didn't escape detention, and became an Amnesty International prisoner of conscience. Even innocuous love songs are now banned from the radio, along with references to intoxication. Mixed dancing is out of the question. Only the uncontroversial "greats" such as oud-player Kabli have been left alone. The National Islamic Front also has its musical apologists, such as Hamad al-Rayah and the band Namariq, formed as the NIF's answer to the pro-democracy band Agd aj-Jelad, but the atmosphere is one of severe repression.

IT WAS NOT ALWAYS THUS

It was not always thus: **foreign artists** were once welcomed. Since the late 1960s, Ray Charles ("Hit the Road Jack"), Tina Charles (revered for "I love to love" and her approximation of Egyptian beauty), Bob Marley, Jimmy Cliff and Michael Jackson have all become Sudanese household names.

Their impact on Khartoum-based musicians is hard to overestimate. **Osman Alamu** pioneered Sudanese "jazz" when **Ibrahim**

Awad became the first singer to dance on stage, in the 1960s. The 1970s singer **Kamal Kayla** modelled his funk-shout style on the hugely popular James Brown, who, along with Hendrix and Santana, also influenced the eclectic **Zande Jazz** and home-grown heavy metallists **Eastern Breeze** from Gedaref – a town dubbed, with a slight excess of enthusiasm, "the Chicago of Sudan". There have been experiments with reggae and the occasional nod to country and western or blues – Kenny Rogers is popular with the people of neighbouring Ethiopia, with whom the Sudanese happily exchange musical enthusiasms.

Several army and police **"jazz-bands"** – often a young conscript's only access to instruments – continue to fuse African styles from Kenya and Uganda with spartan funk. This "jazz" is modelled on the Kenyan Shirati Jazz band and the Luo language bands around Lake Victoria: two or three intersecting electric guitars but no horns. What foreigners would recognize as jazz, in the horn-playing sense, is found in the seminal work of **Juma'a Jabir**, who once taught in the Army Music Section and later became a valued session player.

These days people keep their heads down. Silence shrouds artists like **Sherhabeel Ahmed**, an enlightened, charming singer and illustrator whose wife used to play bass guitar

Sherhabeel Ahmed with his bass-playing wife (left)

until it became impossible to continue in the political climate. When Sherhabeel sang Harry Belafonte's "Kingston Town" at Sudan Call, a 1985 famine concert echoing Live-Aid, it was a song he had covered for over a decade. Belafonte himself – representing the charity USA For Africa – was in the audience and was openly moved to tears.

DANCE AND TRANCE/ MALE AND FEMALE

• •

The **Sufi Muslim dervishes** brought the first wave of Islamic influence to Sudan several hundred years ago. Their appearance and behaviour made an abiding impression on British rulers of the "Anglo-Egyptian Sudan" in the nineteenth century. Within the religious tradition of *zikr*, the dervishes use music and dance to work themselves into a mystical trance. Undulating lines of male Sufi dancers seem to reach the heights of ecstasy with a physical grace that belies their age. Their tolerant spirit came to characterize the easy-going approach that prevailed in the country until quite recently, and laid the ground for a free-wheeling fusion of cultures.

The most spirited rhythms – in every sense – are mainly for women, in the psychotherapeutic *zar* **cult**. These sessions combine mesmeric drumming with incense, massage and a licence to release deep frustration. Under the guidance of the *sheikha az-zar*, gatherings last either four or seven days, drumming from dawn to dusk for different spirits that plague people and have to be brought out and pacified. These are occasions outside the bounds of life's ordinary rules, when women can smoke and drink and act out rebellious fantasies without having their religious piety called into question. The zar cult is older than Islam and works around and through it rather than competing against it. But like everything else that challenges the present government's fundamentalist social ideals, they are clamping down on zar, claiming it is anti-Islamic.

No matter how severe the social stresses, however, the songs themselves endure – the poetic ones and the vulgar ones – circulating in a culture where nearly any group of people can reproduce them by drumming or clapping or singing.

SONG AND DANCE

Lyrics come first in the Sudanese appreciation of music, whether they are made up on the spot, or relate an epic poem. The lyricists and poets are as celebrated as the singers themselves. Spontaneous songs of praise for the bride and groom are common at **weddings**. Along the Nile in the northern region, semi-settled nomads display their machismo by baring their backs for the groom to beat them with a camel-whip, working up a massive adrenalin buzz to the sound of massed women's drumming, then cooling off as the local bard strings together extended doggerel about the qualities of the newlyweds. Young unmarried women take turns to strut past the line of men, holding the worn-down whip handle aloft in a triumphant manner. Urban weddings are not as raw as this, but they remain probably the best place to hear musicians and witness the dove-like bridal dance or *kashif*, which can be powerfully erotic.

In the south, the **Dinka** – among other displaced victims of the civil war between the Khartoum government and the Sudanese People's Liberation Army – have an ever-growing list of new songs relating to war and liberation. They used to hymn their cattle, but, given the strong Christian influence, many songs are considered hymns to Jesus the Saviour, while others hail the SPLA guerrilla leader John Garang in equal measure.

The **Nuba** peoples of central Sudan also have modern songs of suffering and yearning for peace alongside their celebratory Kambala festivals.

In northern Sudan, poets like **Mahjoub Sharif** have long tackled political strife and been imprisoned for over-stepping the line. Sharif's lyrics have been used by leading singers Mohamed Wardi and Mohamed el-Amin. Metaphors from painful love are often reapplied to the state of the country; but sometimes only directness will do, as in Sharif's "Bullets are not the seeds of life":

Born are the beautiful children, hour by hour
With brightest eyes
And loving hearts you have bestowed upon
The fatherland, they will come
For bullets aren't the seeds of life.

In melodic terms, the attempts by former president Nimeiri (1969–85) to use singers to bind a huge unwieldy country into a nation were surprisingly successful. Tunes such as "Ana Sudani" (I am Sudanese) remained popular longer than the military dictator himself.

Words, in the strictest sense, are not always necessary. The Nubian *hm bee*, a regular wordless chant, is used to add weight to the stamping and clapping behind the singer. In western Sudan, too, animal and bird sounds are mimicked in the backing chants that flesh out complex, interweaving hand-clap rhythms. One bewitching example sounds at first like sampled sheep and goat noises with a belching chant of "rambo" pulsing though it. Meanwhile the singer is apparently urging his girlfriend to fetch him a packet of Gold Leaf cigarettes and asking when he can go to her house and refresh himself with cold water. (This is a man who knows what he wants, and doesn't bother with the usual simpering odes to a woman's eyes, forehead or other anatomy above the neck that characterize the less distinguished Arabic love songs.)

In terms of **instrumentation**, urban musicians introduced violins, accordions and horns after World War II, to go alongside the *daloka* tom-toms, stringed *rababas* (fiddles) and ouds of "classical" northern Sudan. Electric guitars and the occasional mandolin came to Sudan in the 190)s, and synthesizers in the 1980s, but the mode of playing of the old instruments is still detectable in the treatment of the new. A wealth of instrumentation is no guarantee of a good band, however, and while young impoverished bands like Eastern Breeze sounded good with homemade electric guitars, some of the rich kids with expensive imported equipment can be unbelievably dire and ponderous – or simply trite and derivative.

Sudan's traditional **dance styles** are varied: the slender Dinka cattle-herders in the south have perfected a vertical springing, tucking the legs up behind, similar to that of the Maasai and Samburu in Kenya, while northern Arab dromedary-herders leap and stomp to a loping, camel-like beat. In polite northern Sudanese society, dancing – other than religious or nuptial – is not really approved of, which can create an awkwardness unusual in Africa. Even in the discos – when there were discos to speak of – you'd find a group of men shuffling in a circle in their *jellabiyas*, swaying and snapping their fingers in the air, apparently the limits of choreographic versatility. But one can be surprised: in 1985 when the radio broadcast the news of the overthrow of Nimeiri, my neighbour Aziz, one of the Presidential Special Guard, now jobless but nevertheless elated, burst in and began breakdancing and moonwalking on my verandah with all the verve of a street kid.

MALE SINGERS

If the lyrical subtleties of Arabic are lost on you, then the best melodies or riffs for anyone's money come from the near-blind oud player **Mohamed al-Amin**, whose majestic bass voice rides a cascade of organ and violin, sometimes with a Cajun lilt or a hint of dub bass. He has a 1992 recording out in Cairo, but the one to track down is that of his 1982 concerts in London and Manchester. His revolutionary songs frequently got him in trouble, especially under Nimeiri's military regime. To avoid further spells in jail, he moved to Cairo after the 1989 coup, but returned in 1994. Never a prolific writer, his work is concentrated and even his rearrangements of old songs sound fresh.

Mohamed Wardi is a political veteran, a Nubian whose high, whiskey-smooth voice belies the content of his songs. His first hit was a song about the CIA's assassination of Patrice Lumumba in the Congo in 1960. His latest album, recorded in Egypt, unfortunately loses its Sudanese roots texture to Cairo studio gloss, but he has a massive back catalogue. He toured Britain in 1992.

Mohamed Wardi, Mustafa Sidahmed and Yusuf al-Mousli

Abu Araky al-Bakheit is the third great "nationalist" singer and musical innovator. Although he has stayed in Sudan rather than go into exile, he was silent during the early 1990s, refusing to comply with a government ban on certain songs – which applied to all artists – and saying he preferred to stop playing altogether. An indicator of his popularity is that, on his own terms, he is now performing again.

Agd aj-Jelad, a vocal group formed in the mid-1980s with politically conscious lyrics and roots rhythms, are now based in Egypt and back in the studio. Their most recent cassette appears

---

MOHAMED WARDI

· ·

The "golden throat" of **Mohamed Wardi** is appreciated right across the African Sahel region, as well as in the Arab world. Although this singer from Nubia in northern Sudan is now in exile, his music and its political message still manage to transcend the deep-seated hostility between northern and southern Sudanese, who have been engaged in civil war for three of the four decades since the country became independent in 1956.

Nowhere was this ability and commitment to humanity more clearly demonstrated than when he took his band to play at the Itang refugee camp in Ethiopia, where a quarter of a million southern Sudanese had fled to escape the war, in

1990. A video filmed by the SPLA guerrilla army captures the intensity of the delight that the refugees took in his concert, and the sense of solidarity that his music created.

From a makeshift wooden stage in the dusty wastes of the refugee camp, surrounded by people who had lost their homes, livelihoods and families, Wardi generated such an atmosphere that even the one-legged victims of land-mines were dancing on their crutches. And they knew the words to the songs of peace and liberation. The healing power of music was never more forcefully displayed, and for a while the prospect of reconciliation in this torn country seemed a little less forlorn.

Abdel Aziz el-Mubarak

Equally involved politically is **Mustafa Sidahmed**, a gifted, independent-minded singer whose songs in the 1980s broke new ground and avoided the clichés of his contemporaries. The recent collaboration of Mustafa Sidahmed, Mohamed Wardi and **Yusuf al-Mousli** in an album entitled "Tifil al-Alam ath-Thalith" (Third World Child) reflects on the worsening plight of Sudanese children. Regrettably the songs here are maudlin and reinforce the "victim" image of starving African babies, missing an opportunity to present a view with more insight.

Abdel Karim al-Kabli, now in his sixties, is one of those walking cultural memory banks, a folklorist who can talk in depth about the background of any number of Sudanese songs, and who plays oud in a variety of styles with deceptive ease. His avoidance of nationalist and political topics has allowed him to escape persecution by the regime.

to have avoided the fussy embellishments common in Egyptian productions, in favour of a forward drum sound.

Mockery of Sudan's new regime comes out of Canada, from **Hadi**, backed by the half of Wardi's band who asked for political asylum there. In one of Hadi's new songs, the chorus jokes about the beard of Hassan al-Turabi, the mentor of the Islamic hardliners now in power.

Two Sudanese artists who have no truck with political opinions have made considerable impact overseas in recent years – **Abdel Gadir Salim** and **Abdel Aziz el-Mubarak**. The rich, flowing texture of Abdel Gadir's All-Stars Band can be heard sumptuously recorded in a London studio on their World Circuit release. Listen out for the superb playing of saxophonist **Hamid**

ABDEL GADIR SALIM: HOT HORSE AND CATTLE MUSIC

· ·

Abdel Gadir Salim plays a blend of African sounds and Arabic lyrics, tinged with a unique kind of reggae, on instruments from all around the world. As Helen M Jerome found out in conversation with him and Sudanese journalist Moawia Yassin, he is creating a new kind of fusion.

Abdel Gadir Salim was born in Dilling, in the southern part of Kordofan province, in the west of the country. Tall, elegant and open, Abdel Gadir is not only a gifted oud player but a devoted student of Sudan's musical traditions. He is also the headmaster at a primary school in neighbouring Chad. He studied European and Arabic music at the Khartoum Institute of Music, learning different scales and the history of classical music.

He learned the basics of the oud from a friend who had been taught in the army. He didn't find it difficult, he says, "because when music enters the heart, everything is easy to learn". The violin he considers a far greater challenge – one of its greatest Sudanese exponents, Mohammed Abdalla Mohammadia, often plays in his All-Stars Band.

Before he went to the Institute, Abdel Gadir was composing city songs, what he calls "Khartoum songs". In 1971 a friend suggested he should consider his own area of Kordofan with its unique and beautiful songs and rhythms: there are over 100 types of song and dance in the western provinces of Kordofan and Darfur. He began playing folk songs, making a hit with the famous "Umri Ma Bansa" (I'll never forget you) from 1946, which is still in his set today.

Abdel Gadir mixes an urban sound with "Africanism". It is a new style, he explains, somewhere between pop and folk music, using an African sound, Arabic words, and international instruments. He composes the melody, but rarely the words. A friend often comes up with new lyrics, and if Abdel Gadir likes it he creates a melody. Old folk-expressions from Kordofan and Darfur are sometimes added, and Abdel Gadir will take out any poor lyrics and use his own.

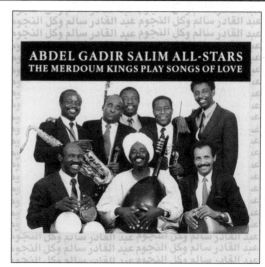

Talking about the country's regional styles, Abdel Gadir explains that the songs of southern Sudan are quite unlike those in the north, because they are not sung in Arabic and they use what he likes to call "hot drums and African rhythms" similar to those of Kenya and Uganda heard on the radio. In the west, in Kordofan and Darfur, the Arabic maqam scales are incorporated to some extent, but all the other music of Sudan is pentatonic, based on only five notes, like the black keys of the piano.

Abdel Gadir Salim's finest hour

The Nuba of southern Kordofan have their own language and use "hot, African drums". Among them live a populous, nomadic, cattle-herding Arab tribe from Yemen called the Bagarra (*bagarr*: cattle). Their songs are "hot" like those of the Nuba, yet they use the Arabic scales. The rhythms are supposed to reflect the faster movement of their horses and cattle. It is within this music that Abdel Gadir finds much of his inspiration.

Most of Abdel Gadir's songs have love themes, but they tend to be a good deal more to the point than, for example, Abdel Aziz's songs:

We'll meet at that place where the sand is smooth.
My soul is yearning to meet the one who departed.
That nice plant was planted in Al-Khiawy town,
But a love-broker prevented me ploughing it.
I wish he was dead...

From "Nitlaga, Nitlaga" (We'll meet) on "Nujum al-Lail"`

Abdel Gadir also keeps a few patriotic songs about and various folk numbers adapted to deal with problems like drought and famine. Moawia Yassin comments that these songs in praise of the homeland are institutionalized songs to address the shortcomings in society. But Abdel Gadir insists there is no problem with censorship from the government: "They like music. Everything is okay."

After the rain has come, the people of the village sing through the night for the success of the crops. Many local problems are dealt with in songs – some even tell parents to take their children for their tetanus injections – and other songs teach the children, or give praise and thanks, or instruct people to work hard. One song tells them "to go and fight and be strong... to go through the fire". These are true folk songs, without any accompaniment from the oud. Sudanese folk music is barely instrumental, says Yassin. "It uses throats, clapping hands, and rhythms with feet. It depends mainly on dance and instruments of percussion like the *tabla* and *nuggara*."

Singing alone, Abdel Gadir feels he can express his feelings most eloquently, but he needs his orchestra for a powerful dance sound. This sort of traditional music, with a band, has been in existence since the 1940s. "You need a big band for theatres, and for wedding parties," he says, and reckons that around eighty percent of their performances are in wedding houses. They also play at the theatre and on radio and television. But live performances maintain their reputation. It is difficult to make any recordings in Sudan as Radio Omdurman has the only studio in the whole country.

But he remains enthusiastic about the musical richness of the country. "Sudan is the middle of Africa, the bridge of Africa and Arabia. In Sudan we tend to hear just Arabic music and I think this is wrong. We must give African music a chance, it is so rich in rhythm, instruments and melody."

Osman Abdalla from the Nuba hills (not to be confused with Nubia), who was born in the same village as Abdel Gadir.

Hamid Osman also galvanizes the band behind Abdel Aziz el-Mubarak. Even those who think they don't like Sudanese music are taken with Hamid's *makossa*-flavoured sax solo on "Tarig ash-Shoag" (Way of Thorns). Abdel Aziz, who comes from the musical town of Wad Medani up-river from Khartoum (it has produced many famous singers), was the first Sudanese artist to play WOMAD at Glastonbury in 1988 – with a dozen musicians romantically resplendent in white *jellabiyas*. Next day they played London's Jubilee Gardens wearing tuxedos – as on the album cover.

Virtuoso oud player Hamza el-Din

The styles of Abdel Gadir Salim and Abdel Aziz el-Mubarak are very different. Abdel Gadir's rural style depends on folkloric tunes with an injection of the Arab maqam scale's half and quarter tones, and his lyrics are based on folktales sung in local accents. Abdel Aziz's music is purely pentatonic and his love songs are songs of the city; so while Abdel Gadir sings of a farm girl tired of waiting for her man to come and wipe the sweat off his face, Abdel Aziz is apt to proclaim his admiration for a woman's high heels:

Every pleasure in the absence of your eyes,
Is incomplete and does not touch me.
Every road that does not take me to you
Is a dark road that doesn't deserve a walk.

Darling all through my life
I have been longing for your smile.
From "Ya A'Asaal" on "Straight From the Heart", translated by Moawia Yassin.

Lastly, **Hamza el-Din** – a Nubian now living in Japan – is in a class of his own as an international experimenter. A virtuoso oud player, composer and ethnomusicologist, he trained in Cairo and Rome before moving to the US. He was heard at Newport in 1964 and Woodstock in 1969, later teaming up with Mickey Hart of the Grateful Dead and recording for Michael Nesmith's Pacific Arts label. In 1991 he re-scored his piece "Escalay" for the Kronos Quartet in San Francisco, and made a live album in Tokyo, "Nubiana Suite", with Japanese *wadaiko* and *shakuhachi* accompanists.

WOMEN SINGERS

For the sheer aching beauty of their voices, **Balabil**, a much-missed 1980s trio of women, were unmatched. Their recordings are almost untraceable, but one of the three, **Hadia Talsam**, has started recording again in Cairo with an all-star band, Kulu an-Nujum ("All the Stars").

The fortunes of women singers mirror the social trends of the last few years. Consider an extreme case, **Hanan Bulu-bulu**, the provocative Madonna of Sudanese pop. After the popular uprising that overthrew Nimeiri and his despised version of Islamic *sharia* law, Hanan Bulu-bulu reflected a new mood as she warbled and wiggled her way to fame at the 1986 Khartoum International Fair. Her notoriety derived from the video of her stage act, which borrowed the sensuous bridal "dove-dance" of Sudanese weddings and orchestrated the often saucy songs of the urban women's *daloka* or tom-tom tradition. But the backlash came soon after, as Islamic fundamentalists banned her concerts and beat her up for immoral behaviour, calling her "half-Ethiopian" – a euphemism for sexual licentiousness. She was by no means the best singer – her mewing little girl's voice and coarse repertoire never rivalled the poetic and emotional impact of other, more soulful, female artists – but she was a remarkable phenomenon nonetheless and she is apparently still performing.

Female artists like **Gisma** and the bluesy **Nasra** had earlier (in the 1970s and 1980s) pioneered a performance version of the erotic *kashif* wedding display, coupled with torrential drumming and facetious, worldly-wise lyrics. They were popular at private gatherings and were frequently arrested for the irreverent and revealing nature of their songs. For this they were either despised as prostitutes or regarded as realists. Home truths such as "Hey Commissioner, we know you keep the Toyota pick-up for the groceries and the Mercedes for picking up the girls" and "This *sharia* is driving us to drink" were never likely to endear them to the authorities. Most Sudanese women can drum and sing, and the less genteel urbanites delighted in reproducing Nasra and Gisma's coarse, salty treatment of the traditional *daloka* style.

Far more of a serious and respectable musician is the blind singer **Hanan an-Nil**, who in 1992 released "Al-Farah al-Muhajir" in Cairo. She accompanies her delicate, wistful songs on an electric keyboard – playing to far better effect than most other victims of the curse of the Casio.

Cheap, weedy electro-bleat and ping-pong percussion reached plague proportions in Sudan in the late 1980s, trampling on the subtleties of local rhythms. The same effect is likely from some of the recent Egyptian recordings, where a synthesized oriental-disco-orchestral backing frequently lets down the rest of the music.

DISCOGRAPHY

Few Sudanese musicians have had access to modern recording studios, and so far only a handful of CDs have been released. A good selection of cassettes is available from Natari in the UK and Africassette in the US. In addition to releases by the artists below, look out for the cassettes of Said Khalifa, Yusuf al-Mousli, Salah Ibn al-Badia and Kamal Terbas. For field recordings of zar and non-professional women's music, contact Sudan Update, BM "CPRS", London WC1N 3XX, UK (☎ and fax +44 422 845827).

ⓒ **Hamza el-Din** *Songs of the Nile* (JVC, Japan). Rhythmically interesting set of songs for voices, oud and percussion, but somewhat soulless in its sparse, studio bleakness. Recorded in Japan in 1982.

ⓒ⑥ **Abdel Aziz el-Mubarak** *Abdel Aziz el Mubarak* (GlobeStyle, UK) and *Straight from the Heart* (World Circuit, UK). The big sound of Khartoum – lush, ornamental and (perhaps surprisingly) really swinging.

ⓒ **Abdel Gadir Salim** *Nujum al-Lail/Stars of the Night* (GlobeStyle, UK). Recorded during a fleeting London show in 1989, this is much more faithful to the authentic live sound than the rather saccharine recordings that have been the Cairo industry's Sudanese cassette mainstays.

ⓒ **Abdel Gadir Salim All-Stars** *The Merdoum Kings Play Songs of Love* (World Circuit, UK). *Merdoum* is one of the vocal and drum styles of Kordofan, Abdel Gadir's homeland in western Sudan. Rougher-edged and raunchier than the more manicured tones of Abdel Aziz el-Mubarak – but no less apolitical.

ⓒ **Various** *Sounds of Sudan* (World Circuit, UK). Acoustic recordings of Abdel Gadir Salim, Abdel Aziz el-Mubarak and Mohamed Gubara, previously on three LPs. Acoustic el-Mubarak is certainly not what they're used to in Sudan. This is the only available recording of Gubara, an Arab *tambour*-player from the north with a high, searing voice. Good notes by Moawia Yassin.

ⓒ **Mohamed Wardi** *Live in Addis Ababa* (Rags Music, UK). First decent recording of Wardi's music, including Nubian songs.

ETHIOPIAN GROOVE

WELCOME TO THE LAND OF WAX AND GOLD

Ethiopia, one of Africa's most fascinating countries, musically and in every other respect, is once again open and welcoming to foreign visitors. An ancient mountain kingdom, it has considerably expanded in the last two hundred years but it remains Christian at its Amharic heart (the Amhara are the dominant language group, powerful in trade and government). Francis Falceto, long-time aficionado, tours the land of Ras Tafari and double entendre and offers suggestions on buying and listening in situ.

As you get off the plane at Addis Ababa you are greeted by a sign that is sublime in its optimism: "Welcome to Ethiopia, Centre of Active Recreation and Relaxation".

That sign, though, is no more or less the truth than all of the disaster-laden clichés that have been the common currency of Ethiopian reportage for the last ten years. A couple of decades ago, it was India that was viewed single-mindedly as the country where sacred cows wandered indifferently through cities crowded with people dying of starvation. Just as today, nobody is ignorant of the fact that India is a country of immense cultural achievements, so a similar evolution of thought needs to be made for Ethiopia. One of the keys to the rehabilitation of the country's reputation is the vitality of Amharic musical culture – the subject of this article.

The thirty years of civil war, followed by seventeen years of so-called "Marxist" dictatorship, which ended in 1991, have had a profound effect on musical life. Many popular artists quit the country for a precarious existence in exile. They include Aster Aweke, Ephrem Tamru, Kuku Sebsebe, Menelik Wossenatchew, Teshome Meteku, and more. Most went to the US, some to Sudan, others fled to Saudi Arabia or Europe. One of the country's pioneer record producers, Amha Eshete, shut up shop and left for America, after having cut some of the most beautiful Ethiopian songs ever heard.

During Mengistu's dictatorship, a continuous curfew deprived a whole generation of Ethiopians of any kind of nightlife. The streets of Addis were deserted after 10pm and only at a few of the luxury hotels were diplomats, western volunteer workers, Ethiopian apparatchiks and chic prostitutes allowed to carry on the standard nightlife pursuits of dancing and drinking until dawn and the end of the ceasefire. And even they were only allowed this at weekends.

To these restrictions was added a censorship as pedantic as it was bureaucratic, that picked through song lyrics before recording sessions could be licensed to go ahead, and put overseas visitors through painstaking inspections and the rubber-stamping of locally bought cassettes before allowing them to leave the country. All this has changed.

Despite the authoritarian interference, music was the only truly flourishing industry throughout this dark period in the country's history. With the advent of the cassette, music shops started to proliferate. They are concentrated almost exclusively in the old Mercato and Piazza quarters (named after the brief Italian occupation of 1936–41).

Music is omnipresent in Addis – honking out of battered tape decks in buses and taxis, drifting from stores and markets and especially audible when you visit the innumerable little restaurants (*tedjbets* or *bunnabets*), guesthouses and semi-private drinking parlours. These nerve centres of national vitality were always abuzz, throughout the years of dictatorship. And they too have multiplied since its demise.

TRAD/MOD

Traditional music always was and still is the basis of all Ethiopian styles. Even the most famous modern singing stars like **Tlahoun Gessesse**, **Mahmoud Ahmed** and **Neway Debebe** have two repertoires, one modern, the other rooted in tradition. And Ethiopians buy modern and traditional cassettes with equal enthusiasm.

Modern music descends directly from traditional. The modernity in question is essentially that of the "modern" western instruments which have been introduced. It was the more outward-looking elements of the military under Haile Selassie who were the first to introduce brass instruments in their **army bands** from the mid-1920s.

The Police Force Band

In a musical world of rasping brass sections, ripping blues, nasal-sounding waltzes, quirky funk or honking horns, the best recommendation one can make is to keep an eye open first of all for the **treasures of the 1970s**, either on cassette reissues or on copies made to order. It may be piracy, but it's also a norm that even the pirated seem to accept with equanimity.

Generally speaking, all the recordings of the **great pioneers** of this era are worth getting hold of: in the premier league Tlahoun Gessesse, Bezunesh Bekele, Hirut Bekele (no relation), Mahmoud Ahmed, Ali Birra, Alemayehu Eshete, Muluken Mellesse (who has, unfortunately, stopped singing since his exile to the US) and

Mahmoud Ahmed

Gradually, the performers tried out various traditional songs to create, by the late 1940s, real orchestras that could accompany fashionable singers. Thus the first "modern" orchestras were purely and simply the Imperial Bodyguard Band, the Army Band and the Police Band, trained initially by professionals brought in from Europe, among whom there was a significant Armenian contingent.

In Addis, you can occasionally come across the odd back-street shop full of old 45s from the 1970s in which these orchestras accompany stars like Tlahoun Gessesse and Mahmoud Ahmed. Progressively, private orchestras were developed, all of them evolving from an essentially military background.

These collectors' items represent a real golden age of Ethiopian music, even though by the 1980s they couldn't avoid a certain decline due to the constraints imposed by the dictatorship – including the indoctrination of musicians and difficulties of mere survival for the genuinely private independent orchestras, the only creative ones. It is still possible to find cassette copies of these old standards; indeed you can order them from any music shop.

The special characteristic of Amharic music is the use of a five-note, pentatonic scale with large intervals between some of the notes, giving an unresolved feeling to the music, like missing your foot on the stairs in the dark or waiting for a stone to hit the bottom of a well, and not hearing it.

These modes mean you can derive an intensity from performance that westerners would equate with soul music (compare, for example, the Washington-based exile Aster Aweke with Aretha Franklin). The limping asymmetrical rhythm of much of the music is also highly characteristic.

Ayalew Mesfin; and second-ranking and less prolific, Abebe Tessema, Frew Hailu, Menelik Wossenatchew and Getatchew Kassa.

Try to get your hands on the five **Ethiopian Hit Parade** LPs, extraordinary compilations which comprise, apart from certain stars already mentioned, forgotten meteors like Seifu Yohannes (who died young), Teshome Meteku (exiled in Sweden), collectors' items from the likes of Tebereh Tesfahunegn and Tewolde Redda and, in the strictly traditional department, musicians such as Kassa Tessema, Mary Armede, Asnaketch Worku, and Alemayehu Fanta.

Instrumental music also has its key figure in the shape of **Mulatu Astatke**, promoter and sole exponent of Ethio-jazz, otherwise known as the king of arrangers (alas, a somewhat dethroned king today) throughout this golden, pre-revolutionary age.

THE NILE AND THE GULF

Alemayehu Eshete in languid pose

You should also definitely try to get the recordings of **Getatchew Mekuria**, brilliant saxophone and clarinet player, as rippingly wonderful as he is unjustifiably forgotten (one LP and two 45s). A modernized cassette came out in 1993 through Mahlet Music Shop.

THE LAST RECORDS

The last records came out in 1978. Pressed first in India, then in Lebanon, Greece and finally Kenya, up to 3000 copies were produced in the case of big hits – serious numbers at the time. With the advent of the cassette industry and greater local technological capability, the Ethiopian market developed at a scarcely believable rate compared with what was happening in the western world. Manufacture of 20–30,000 became standard and certain cassettes sold more than 100,000.

During the dark years of the dictatorship in the 1980s, new singers emerged besides the veteran artists and most stayed in the country as it had become virtually impossible to emigrate. This was the finest hour for Ephrem Tamru, Aster Aweke, Kuku Sebsebe, Netsanet Mellesse, Amelmal Abate and some fifty other singers, male and female, who wore out the three or four genuinely professional orchestras who they shared in recording sessions at pains to create

new melodies and arrangements. Three historic groups are particularly important from this period – the **Wallias Band**, the **Roha Band** and the **Ethio Stars**.

But above all, after 1985, **Neway Debebe** became an idol, bringing a new freshness which reminded his public of the vocal prowess of the early Tlahoun Gessesse, a pioneer among pioneers of modern music. Neway, and a whole generation of young singers, renewed interest in the poetic style of *sam-ennawarq* (wax and gold), an old Abyssinian tradition of double entendre which has always fooled the censors, or at least allowed a safety valve whose presence they could sometimes ignore without incurring the wrath of the military chiefs. The meanings are made quite clear to the public through apparently innocuous love songs – though the following example, "Altchalkoum" (Can't take any more), written by Tlahoun Gessesse on the eve of an abortive coup against Haile Selassie (it was performed by him with the backing of the Imperial Body Guard Band, implicated in the coup attempt), fooled nobody and was quickly banned. It was banned again by Mengistu.

How long are you going to make me suffer?
I can't take any more, I've had enough.
I'm up to here with it, I'm more than up to here.
I can't take any more, how can I put up with it?
I can't put up with your torments
I don't know what more I can do.

With the arrival of a fragile democracy and the return of freedom of expression, it's not unreasonable to hope for a creative renewal for Ethiopian music: less of the one-two beat immediately danceable stuff, and a **renewal of inspiration** from the old style, rythmically formidable *tchik-tchik-ka*, with its unfettered lyrics, controlled synthesizers, and supreme horn sections. New talents are already jostling in an exciting field – Hebiste Tiruneh, Yihuneh Belaye and Chachi Taddesse to name but three. And the Abyssinia Band, the Medina Band and the Axumite Band are waiting in the wings.

Don't look for Ethiopian reggae. It really doesn't exist yet, unless you include a couple of experimental outfits with little following. It's true the word "rastafari" comes from Ras Tafari Makonnen, the title and surname of Haile Selassie, the last emperor of Ethiopia (who unwittingly started the cult on his visit to Jamaica), but rasta fetishism has no special meaning in Ethiopia, despite the admiration for Bob Marley common to the whole of Africa. There is a community of Jamaican rastas at Sheshemene, 200 kilometres from Addis Ababa. But they're viewed as an imported phenomenon. Nor is there any discernible relationship between Ethiopian music and reggae. At a pinch, the unusual local beat of Eritrea bears some comparison, but there's really no genuine historical or musical relationship there as this part of the world has never fuelled the African diaspora.

These comparative issues aside, **Tigrinya music** from Eritrea and Tigray, which is even less familiar in the west than Ethiopian Amharic music, is worth a detour for its repetitive, throbbing, camel-walk rhythms. There's a

ASTER AWEKE

By 1979, however, the revolutionary climate in Ethiopia had become intolerable for free spirits like Aweke's and she fled the country to the US. She eventually settled among the diplomatic and African exile community of Washington DC, where she set about re-establishing her musical career on the club and restaurant circuit. A formidable careerist ("I have never been in love"), she has cleaved a straight path to World Music stardom by never allowing her superbly vocalized and fiery lyrics to be swamped by arrangements.

Yaz-oh (Grab it, Get it on)
Ayee – get it on
Ayee – get it on
Ayee – like this, like that
Ayee – like that, like this
Ayee – get it on, grab it like this, grab it like that
Ayee – get it on, get it on, get it on
Ayee – come aboard and let's get it by dawn
Ayee – get it on here, get it on there
Ayee – get it on

Oh take me, my body is yours
But don't tell anybody, keep it to yourself
How can I keep it a secret?
I am in love with you

Alas, alas…
I go crazy when I can't have you
Alas, alas…
You say what?!
Take me, my body is yours
But don't tell anybody, keep it to yourself
'Cause love in the open never satisfied me

E thiopia's most successful World Music star, Aster Aweke was born in 1961 near Gondar, the ancient capital of the country. In the aftermath of the overthrow of Haile Selassie in 1974, she was already preparing herself for a life of music. Strongly influenced by an Addis musical idol of the time, Bezunesh Bekele, she more or less cut herself off over the next few years from her highly connected family (her father had been a senior civil servant in the Imperial government). She sang first in 1977 with various groups, then went solo and was "discovered" by Ali Tango for whom she released several cassettes and a couple of 45rpm singles. Her exceptional voice became well known, and she joined the famous Roha Band in 1978.

Aster Aweke, from "Kabu", translated from the Amharic by Danachew Abebe

stunning CD, "Kozli Gaba", by **Abraham Afewerki**, on Stile Libero/Virgin, Italy.

ALI TANGO

Every taxi driver in Addis knows the location of Tango Music and Video Shop, in the heart of the Piazza, on Adwa Avenue. The cramped surrounds are surprising in view of the importance and dynamism of this veritable laboratory of national swing. This is the home of **Ali "Ali Tango" Kaifa**, who has played an essential role in the Ethiopian music scene over the last two decades.

A smart talent scout and an inventive producer, he pioneered the cassette industry after having produced some fifty records, including cult classics like Mahmoud Ahmed's "Ere Mela Mela", Muluken Mellesse's "Jemeregne", Alemayehu Eshete's "Wededkuh Afkerkush" and Ayalew Mesfin's "Gunfan". He also "discovered" Aster Aweke, Amelmal Abate, Neway Debebe and now the teenage singer **Hebiste Tiruneh**, the first great success of the post-dictatorship era. An enthusiast for technology, Ali Tango was the first to use digital recording equipment and he has just opened a private studio – a high-performance set-up, even if it's not close to European standards.

Respected and envied godfather of a passionate industry, Ali Tango has always defended the freedom of expression of singers and independent orchestras – sometimes with great cunning during the dictatorship. And he enthuses over all the regional rhythms of Ethiopia – Gurague, Tigrinya, Gondar, Kotu, Oromo –and even takes an interest in Yemenite and Somali music – a rather unusual path in such a culturally self-sufficient country.

Lastly, but significantly, Ali Tango introduced the concept of affordable **video** rental before anyone else, with his western TV shows offering stiff competition to the indigestible diet of TV-Mengistu. Practically all the "Music Shops" have since become music and video shops.

THE LIVE ARTICLE

Although you can find musical entertainment at many of the international-class hotels, the best **live music venues** are the local *tedjbets* – where *tedj*, honey beer, is consumed – and the music bars or *azmaribets*. They're to be found absolutely everywhere and nothing is easier than having a look inside to see if you like the

Traditional musician playing the masenqo

atmosphere. Apart from a dozen or so main roads, the streets of Addis have neither names nor street numbers. To find their way about, people of Addis refer first to a district, then to a handy point of reference, like the post office or an embassy. It's difficult, therefore, to be precise about addresses: but the taxi drivers know nearly all the music places. As Ethiopians are absolute strangers even to the music of the rest of Africa, they're invariably amazed when foreigners show interest in their music. As long as your enthusiasm does not go unnoticed, which is unlikely, you can be sure you'll be adopted and guided, and introduced to all the best sounds and experiences.

You'll meet all sorts of musicians in tedjbets – *krar* players, players of the the *masenqo* one-string fiddle, *washint* players (flautists), *kebero* percussionists, even accordionists. These musicians are *azmari*, equivalent to the griots of West Africa or the wandering *taraf* musicians of Romania, privileged carriers of popular music, mediators of collective memory. They have an ambivalent reputation which is expressed by a mixture of suspicion towards bohemians and fearful respect for their freedom of speech and the power of the word. They are, in a way, professional amateurs, to whom one gives a tip to sing what one feels deep down, be it sadness, nostalgia, praises or veiled criticism.

Whether you find the atmosphere in your tedjbet bluesy or not, the alcohol flows freely and the atmosphere gets very hot, very quickly. Better put on your seat belt when the *eshista* or *tchik-tchik-ka* is unleashed: these are torrid dance styles in which the shaking of shoulders and chests would melt a statue.

Since the end of the curfew, the eating houses and *adarash* (café-club-hotels, brothels basically) along Debrezeit Road are slowly recommencing their former evening activities and have more memorable music on offer. You can always find traditional and modern musicians at La Villa Verde, especially at weekends. Don't neglect the Coffee House, one of the best clubs, near the Egyptian Embassy in Siddist Kilo district, and the Buffet de la Gare, which has been a sublime den of vice for many decades. The liveliest parts of town, however, are along Asmara Road and Bolle Road, in the Case Inces district and near Kirkos Church where you'll find the azmaribet belonging to Betsat and Abebe, an explosive duo, bursting with humour.

MUSIC SHOPS

If you're looking for recorded music in Addis Ababa, you'll find the city full of "Music Shops" – cassette-copying stores where you can get customized tapes for little money (the standard price for a cassette is about £2, or $3). At the entrance to the Mercato quarter, near the Great Mosque, the noteworthy Marathon Music Shop and Alem Music Shop stand out, as do Ambassel, Electra, Central Electronics, Ethio and Sheger, to cite only the most important stores from a list that could run to dozens. Not far from Mercato, the Piazza quarter is also the base for a number of bigger centres for music production, in particular Tango Music Shop on Adwa Avenue and Mahmoud Music Shop, belonging to Mahmoud Ahmed (but it's rare to find him there in person), on the corner of Cunningham Street and Adwa. Close by on the other side of the square is Ayalew, owned by Ayalew Mesfin, a singer who was a big star in the 1970s. He's always there, ready with anecdotes about the good old days and unofficial recordings of wild Ethiopian Radio sessions available for fans who call by. His group, the Black Lion Band, had one of the most rapid-fire horn sections on the pre-Mengistu nightlife scene.

To close this shopping trip, there are two stores situated outside the strategic centres of

Mercato and Piazza: the first, Ghion Video, by the entrance to the Ghion Hotel, belongs to the former lead sax-player from the Roha Band, Fekade Amde Meskel. The second, Selam Audio Video, not far from the station, is owned by the Roha's former guitarist, Selam Seyoum, a remarkable instrumentalist and also the living memory of modern Ethiopian music since he has written the first study of it for Addis Ababa University. He's a mine of information for anyone who wants to know more about the evolution of one of Africa's least-known and most engaging musical cultures.

FUTURE SHOCK

Ethiopian musicians are reeling from the effects of the changes since the flight of Mengistu and the onset of democracy in 1991. The end of the civil war resulted in a new country on their northern border – Eritrea – and the first taste of personal freedom for a whole generation. Travel is much easier than before, so musicians and bands are able

Krar, drums and washint from the Tukul Band

to play and record overseas – and return without a problem – and the opportunity to listen to other African and European music is beginning to have an effect on their own. Contemporary bands are also influenced in the same direction by the demands of Addis Ababa teenage culture, keen to make up for lost exposure to global youth fashions over the last two decades. Western music, reggae, and the sounds of Kenya and Zaire are all increasingly popular.

The **Abyssinia Band** was formed straight after the end of the war and is currently one of the hottest in Addis. As musician Abiy Solomon remarked, "We don't exactly want to be westernized – we're just trying to produce music of equal quality to the rest of the world. We're working hard to make the sound richer and change the traditional arrangements a bit to make them more modern." They are now experimenting with bubbling guitar tunes and writing songs in the seven-tone western scale rather than traditional pentatonic. Ironically, of course, it's pentatonic, polyphonic music that jumps, that the global audience is really attracted to, never mind what the young trendies in Addis yearn for. If Abyssinia Band and their like can bridge the two views, that would be some success to sing about.

Thanks to Caroline Swinburne for additional information.

◼ DISCOGRAPHY ◼

I f your local record store can't help, the best place to find recorded Ethiopian music, and have an unusual meal at the same time, is your local Ethiopian restaurant. If you don't have one yet, you may not have long to wait – they're opening all over the world.

CONTEMPORARY

Mahmoud Ahmed *Ere Mela Mela* (Crammed Discs, Belgium/Rykodisk, US). Reference point for one of modern Ethiopia's greatest voices. Recorded in Addis in 1975 with the Ibex Band – most of whose members went on to found the Roha Band – this was the first modern Ethiopian recording to be released in the west. A classic: one hit, you're hooked.

Aster Aweke *Aster* (Triple Earth, UK/Columbia, US). With *Kabu* from 1991 on the same label and the recent *Ebo* (Barkhanns/Stern's, UK/Abyssinian, US), Aweke is still one of the most popular voices in Ethiopia, although she emigrated to the US in the early 1980s. These CDs, recorded in the US and London, and notably westernized in the brass section arrangements, are still a formidable introduction to the Ethiopian feeling.

Alemayehu Eshete *Addis Ababa* (Dona Wana/Musidisc Stern's, UK/Shanachie, US). Alemayehu Eshete introduced the languid poses of rock into his country's music. But it's his profoundly Ethiopian, soul/blues style which knocks out his home audience. This CD, recorded in Paris, introduces some of the hits with which he's built his reputation. Listen to the pianist, whose keyboard style is unique in Africa. Guest clarinettist: big Ivo Papazov.

Netsanet Mellesse *Dodge* (Dona Wana/Musidisc/Stern's, UK/Shanachie, US). Netsanet is from the young generation of artists who have emerged over the past decade, despite the harassment of the dictatorship. His exceptional voice, served perfectly by the sophisticated arrangements of Yohannes Tekola – the trumpeter and leader of the Wallias Band – evokes Aretha Franklin in some minds, while others complain about sore eardrums.

Ethio Stars & Tukul Band *Amharic Hits* (Piranha, Germany). Two bands here: one a modern group based around the singer Getatchew Kassa, the other a traditional ensemble which has brought together some of the best instrumentalists in the business (particularly Kut Ojulu on bass *krar*). All produced by the dynamic Global Music Centre in Helsinki.

Various *Ethiopian Groove: The Golden 70s* (Dona Wana/Blue Silver/Stern's, UK/Abyssinian, US). 16-track compilation of golden oldies, bringing together artists not previously heard in the west (Bezunesh Bekele, Hirut Bekele, Ayalew Mesfin, Tamrat Ferendji) as well as the earliest recordings of Aster Aweke and two hits from Alemayehu Eshete. Finally available, an introduction to the golden age of Ethiopian music.

Roha Band *Roha Band Tour 1990* (Aman Int, US). Featuring the legendary Neway Debebe and two other singers, this is mainly an electric set, with several traditional pieces as bonus.

FOLK AND TRADITIONAL

Various *Music From Ethiopia* (Caprice Records, Sweden). Recordings made in Addis with Swedish assistance, bringing together traditional and modern songs. Includes some beautiful traditional examples (especially Lemma Gebre Hiwot, Alemayehu Fanta and Asnaketch Worku). The modern songs aren't representative of the best of Ethiopia but are still a reasonable showcase for what's around. Good accompanying booklet by Anu Laakkonen and Sten Sandahl.

Abraham Afewerki *Kozli Gaba* (Stile Libero/Virgin, Italy). Eritrean music (or to be more precise Tigrinya music) would merit a chapter of its own, so greatly does it differ from Ethiopian. It has a very specific rhythm, intoxicating and persistent. The first western outing for music from Africa's newest nation, this makes you want to get on the plane to Asmara tomorrow.

Various *Ethiopie: Polyphonies of the Dorze* (Chant du Monde, France,). This discography would be incomplete without paying homage to one of the most outstanding aspects of the numerous "tribal" musics found in Ethiopia. Part of the world musical heritage.

Various *Harp of Apollo* (JVC, Japan). Unpromisingly ethnomusicological packaging, but this repays a good listen: check out the wonderful voice of Tayech Berhanu on "Gurague Song" and the *kebero*-drumming of Getachew Abdi. Also features nice *tom* (thumb piano) playing and the young krar maestro Kut Ojulu.

Various *Music of Wax and Gold* (Topic, UK). Ethnic field recordings by the late, respected ethnomusicologist Jean Jenkins. Previously three LPs on the Tangent label, now available on one wonderful, bumper CD.

Various *Music of Northern Ethiopia* (cassette only, BCM Records, UK). Recorded by London University graduate Leslie Larkum on a recent research trip in Tigray.

THE INDIAN SUBCONTINENT

The Indian subcontinent is so vast and its cultures so varied that newcomers can be forgiven for feeling a little lost when first introduced to its musical wealth. Not only are the instruments, melodies and rhythms unfamiliar, but the ideas behind the music are often intimately connected with philosophical and religious concepts rooted in an intellectual soil having little to do with western approaches to time, matter and reality. Nor do the musics of India bear more than a distant family resemblance to one another. The range of folk music alone is enormous, and the music of Nepal is as different from that of Rajasthan as Scottish music is from Greek.

Indian music first became fashionably popular in the west in the late 1960s when, following the influential collaboration of the Beatles and Ravi Shankar, the sitar became a hip instrument. Where they led, the Stones, Traffic and a host of others soon followed in experimenting with Indian instruments. More of a hazy dabbling in guru-culture than a serious attempt to make sense of a centuries-old tradition, it was a fad which ended quickly, but it did introduce many people to the subtle intricacies of Indian classical music.

When venturing into the realms of classical and popular music it can be hard to see a link between the delicacy of the *alaap* of a North Indian *raag*, the awesome power of *qawwali*, the light, ephemeral, infectious sound of Bombay film music, and the soulful, evocative *ghazal*. The links are nonetheless real, and have as much to do with the phenomenal success of the Indian film industry and the reach of All India Radio as with the classic anthropological explanations of invasion and mass migration. In India only the privileged few own televisions, and so the principal form of entertainment for most people is the cinema. A film is judged by its music; indeed, it's usually the catchiness of the songs which draws financial support in the first place. For the majority of people the cinema supplies a musical escapism that allows them to forget their harsh lives. A side effect of the success of Indian movies is that the composers (or music directors as they are known) are put under enormous pressure by the industry's voracious appetite for songs. Some music directors have to work on as many as 30 films at once, each with six or more songs. As a result they're unable to rely on their own inspiration all the time, and they have to fall back on plagiarizing any and every style of music, from classical raag to western pop, tribal folklore and religious qawwali.

This chapter starts by looking at the *mahfil*, a modern version of a traditional performance practice which has gained new life through the efforts of aficionados anxious to preserve the richness of classical music and qawwali. Then follows a broad survey of the core tradition of Hindustani classical music and its instruments, with diversions to take in its cousin from South India, *karnatak* music, as well as the less demanding light classical styles of *thumri* and ghazal. The lucky-bag of Indian film music comes next, followed by a closer look at one of the styles it has plundered, qawwali, with a profile of one of its greatest exponents, Nusrat Fateh Ali Khan. Britain's *bhangra* boom gets an article next, followed by a short account of Indian folk music. Countries on the fringes of the subcontinent – Nepal and Afghanistan – boast equally rich folk traditions, and there's a short article on each.

Alaap Slow introduction, in free time and unaccompanied by drums, which introduces the notes of a raag one by one.

Alaappaana Karnatak equivalent of the alaap.

Bansuri Transverse bamboo flute.

Bhajan Hindu devotional song.

Caca Meditation songs from esoteric Buddhist tradition in Nepal.

Dhimay baja Giant drums used by the Newar people.

Dhol Large barrel-drum played together with the surnai in various folk traditions.

Dholak Double-headed drum played with the fingers used in qawwali and folk music.

Dhrupad The most austere form of classical singing.

Dutar Strummed two-stringed lute used in Uzbeki and Kazakh music.

Fakir Holy man who lives by begging.

Gaine Itinerant Nepalese professional musicians.

Gharana School of music (literally means "extended family").

Ghatam (ghardha) Large clay pot used as a percussion instrument.

Ghazal Light classical Indian song form introduced from Persia (Iran). The name is derived from an Arabic word meaning "to talk amorously to women).

Girah Additional verse inserted on the spur of the moment into the performance of a qawwali song.

Jugalbandi Instrumental duet.

Karnatak Classical music of southern India.

Kathak Elaborately refined Indian performance dance.

Khayal (khyal) A less austere form of classical singing than dhrupad (derived from a Persian word meaning "imagination").

Kriti Devotional song from south India – the most important form.

Madal Nepalese barrel-drum.

Mahfil Private instrumental and vocal performance (from the Persian word meaning "gathering" or "assembly").

Mohri Lead singer in qawwal.

Panchai baja Nepalese wedding band.

Pandit Teacher – an honorific title.

Party Group of qawwals.

Qawwali Sufi devotional music as performed by Nusrat Fateh Ali Khan and others (literally means "utterance" in Arabic).

Playback singer Singer on a film soundtrack to which the actor mimes.

Raag (Ragan) Scale pattern and melodic motif as well as certain philosophical and moral ideas used to generate a performance in that particular raag. Raga is the classical term; raag is colloquial.

Sarangi Bowed string instrument with sympathetic strings (in Nepal, a four-string bowed fiddle).

Sarinda Afghani bowed instrument.

Shehnai Type of large Indian oboe (the name comes from the Persian *shah* "king", and nai, meaning "flute").

Sarod Type of lute with metal fingerboard and sympathetic strings used in north Indian music.

Sitar Plucked string instrument used in Indian classical music with a metal fingerboard and a wealth of sympathetic strings (its name comes from the Farsi *seh-tar* – literally, "three-stringed").

Sufis The mystics of Islam.

Surbahar Bass sitar.

Surmandal Zither.

Surnai Loud folk oboe.

Taal Time measure – the equivalent of a raag in the sphere of rhythm (derived from *tali*, meaning "hand-clap").

Tabla Pair of drums played with the fingers and palms.

Tambura (also tanpura) Four-stringed instrument used to provide a drone.

Tambur Afghani lute.

Tarana Vocalization technique using syllables derived from esoteric Sufi tradition.

Teej Nepali women's festival.

Thumri Light classical song or instrumental piece.

Ustad Muslim equivalent of Pandit.

Veena Plucked string instrument. The most important of the instruments of karnatak music.

Zikr Sufi technique for achieving ecstacy by repeating holy names.

WHERE THE ELITE MEET

THE MAHFIL PERFORMANCE AND ITS MEANING

India has always shown respect to the initiate and the expert, and the demands made upon the listener are almost as exacting as those on the performer. The days when rich, powerful princes were knowledgeable patrons of the arts have passed, but their role is now being filled by rich, successful members of Asian communities at home and abroad, especially in London. Jameela Siddiqi grapples with the etiquette and rewards of hosting a mahfil.

I n the heyday of the Indian nobility, classical music was an art form reserved for the entertainment of the mighty. With the eclipse of the hereditary rulers and the loss of their patronage the musicians had to look for a new audience, which they found in the paying public. Purists and pandits argue that, with the passing of the golden age of classical music when a palace performance might have lasted all day and all night, music has been impoverished. As it must cater for a mass audience, not only in the subcontinent but also in the west, it has come to be performed in large concert halls instead of the intimate surroundings that its true identity as a chamber music demands. They claim the inevitable result has been coarser performances.

To some extent this charge is justified. Over the last fifty years or so the *alaaps* have got shorter, the same half dozen popular *raags* get played again and again in easily followed *taals*, and there is a widespread demand for *jugalbandi*, where two or more soloists come together for a duet or group performance. All these factors have compromised the quality and content of pure classical music, which although largely improvised, is supposed to function within very strictly defined boundaries.

LOVERS AND CLIMBERS

To combat this tendency the purists have tried to revive the old custom of arranging performances for an elite. This practice has come to be called **"hosting a mahfil"**, and an invitation to perform at one is an important milestone in the career of a promising young musician. But just as often, mahfil-holders invite well-known and already successful artists to play in private surroundings, although they are explicitly forbidden to perform anything that they may have previously performed in public, or anything that forms part of their public repertoire. It has to be different – it has to be the real thing. Time is of no consequence. If it takes 80 minutes to develop an alaap properly, then so be it.

There is a very active underground circuit of mahfil-holders, and it is virtually impossible to get onto it unless you know the right people. Critics of private mahfils charge that, in practice, genuine music-lovers are excluded, whereas social climbers with no real understanding of music con their way into the homes of the rich and turn up again and again simply to be seen.

However justified such criticisms may be, a mahfil is by and large a gathering of genuine devotees of music – they may be lovers of *khayal* or *thumri* or *qawwali*, but they have come because they are not satisfied with the atmosphere at large public concerts, and are more than happy to pay the price for a really memorable evening of music.

PREPARATION

The build-up to a mahfil is in itself a major performance. For the inner core of guest-listeners the evening has already begun as they rush back and forth with the final preparations – washing the hot-sweet betel leaves and wrapping them around sweet spices to make *paan* to be chewed, sucked and then spat out, improvising the necessary spittoons and preparing trays of fragrant nuts and spices for the musicians and guests.

The large drawing room still retains its grandeur – the furniture has either been moved back against the wall, or removed from the room altogether. The paintings remain on the wall. The fragrance of joss sticks fills the room – there is an air of excitement and anticipation. The "stage" is clearly marked with rich weavings and bolster cushions. Both musicians and audience sit on the floor, with no raised platform to separate performer from spectator.

Singer Shruti Sadolikar in the Nimbus front room studio

There is no amplification (it is considered vulgar). There are, however, a number of Walkmans and tape recorders of all shapes and sizes, strategically placed to record the evening's performance. The question of copyright is ignored, no matter how celebrated the performers are. The host assumes full rights over the evening's music, and the guests, with or without permission from the host, lay out their various recording machines.

The catering preparations have been under way all afternoon. A large number of helpers, usually female, crowds into the kitchen to prepare half-time snacks. These are in addition to dinner, to be served after the performance at around two in the morning. Most of the dishes for this meal have been prepared and brought in by the guests themselves, with the host providing certain staples.

Immense excitement surrounds this kind of event. It is a privilege to be asked to such evenings, either by the hosts themselves or by a third party who is prepared to introduce their guest as a good listener. Such an invitation marks one's coming of age as a serious music-lover.

GOOD AND BAD MAHFILS

The evening's costs are sometimes shared among the guests, who contribute to the collection which is taken up at the beginning of the evening; if the mahfil features qawwali then the listener gives the money directly to the singers. It is not unusual for qawwals to earn over £2000 (US3000) in a mahfil of about fifty listeners. Where qawwali is concerned the amount itself,

ideally, is insignificant – the gesture of getting up often and placing a small coin or note into the hands of the singer is a devotional act in itself. The right hand must be used and the money should never be given as though it represented the commercial value of a particular verse, but more as a humble gesture to emphasize the fact that the giver was sufficiently moved to rise up and present something to the musician.

All this is in sharp contrast to another kind of mahfil. There are a lot of mahfils where musical ability and knowledge of poetry are not the main objects of interest. These are known as **"nautch girl" mahfils**. At these the main attraction is a dancer, often classically trained but describing herself as an "actress" or "model". The all-male audience, who refer to the show as "classical" although they themselves have little acquaintance with true classical music or dance, shower the woman with money, and she in turn inclines to the biggest spender. This leads to an intense rivalry among those hopeful for her favours. Such mahfils are usually held in the basement rooms of seedy back-street hotels scattered about central London.

Far different from such gatherings are those where the audience don't merely recognize the forthcoming raag as the instrument is being tuned, but actually call out the name of the taal they would like the musician to use. And in the unlikely event that the tabla-player isn't too sure, there is any number of non-musicians in the audience (accountants, lawyers, typists, doctors, writers, housewives) to remind him of the taal and how to divide it.

The intensity of the music is sharpened by the interaction between audience and performer. Those listeners who are most apt to respond are soon noted by the musician, who is close enough to see the expressions on their faces and play to their emotions. There is no applause at any time, for clapping is considered undignified and only fit for large concert halls where there is no other practical way of showing appreciation.

Expensive and elitist it may be but the mahfil is probably the only way that a listener can recapture something of the spirit of the courtly "golden age" of Indian palace music.

RAAGS AND RICHES

CLASSICAL MUSIC OF INDIA AND PAKISTAN

The Hindustani classical music of northern India is one of the world's great art forms, astonishingly rich and intellectually complex but at the same time emotionally powerful and direct. Jameela Siddiqi, David Muddyman and Kim Burton explore its mysteries, and look at its less demanding cousins ghazal and thumri, and the southern karnatak tradition.

Alla Rakha with his son and pupil Zakir Hussain

The origin of north Indian classical music is shrouded in obscurity. There is a tendency in India to attribute the invention of any ancient art form to one of the many Hindu deities, and the resulting synthesis of myth and legend is often taken as literal truth. But in reality north Indian classical music as it exists today is the result of a long process of integrating the many and diverse cultural influences in India. Not only is there a rich and varied tradition of regional folk musics, but all through its history India has absorbed the culture and traditions of foreign invaders, the most influential being the Muslim Moghuls.

It is primarily the introduction of Turko-Persian musical elements that distinguishes north Indian classical music from its predecessor, *karnatak*, now restricted to southern India. The latter is a complex, rich and fascinating musical tradition in its own right, and even an untrained ear can usually distinguish between the two.

TEACHERS AND PUPILS

In the north, both Hindu and Muslim communities have provided outstanding artists. While it is true that music recognizes no religious differences – indeed it is something of a religion in its own right – it is customary for distinguished musicians of Hindu origin to take the title of *pandit* (and be known as a *guru*), while their Muslim counterparts add the prefix *ustad*, (meaning "master") to their names. An ustad may teach anything – not only his own particular art or instrument. It is not unusual for sitar maestros to teach *sarod* or vocal techniques to their pupils.

The teaching of north Indian classical music is a subject in itself. One thing that strikes a westerner is the spiritual link between teacher and pupil. Quite often the two may be blood relations anyway, but where they are not, a spiritual relationship is officially inaugurated in a ceremony in which the teacher ties a string to the wrist of the pupil to symbolize the bond between them.

Apart from actual musical form and content, north Indian music has various extra-musical traditions and rituals. These are usually taught orally or by example through distinguished musical families and *gharanas* ("schools"). Traditionally, Indian music is taught on a one-to-one basis, usually from father to son. Nowadays there are many academies and colleges of music in the modern style, but traditionalists still adhere to the gharana system of training, and there remains a great deal of importance attached to membership of a musical family or an impressive lineage.

A gharana, which may be for singing, for any or all kinds of instruments, or for dance, is more a school of thought than an institution. It suggests a particular belief, or a preference for a certain performance style. Gharanas differ from one another not only in broad terms, but also in the minutest of details: how to execute a particular combination of musical notes, or simply the correct way to hold an instrument. They are usually founded by musicians of outstanding ability, and new styles and forms are added by exceptionally talented musicians who may have trained with one particular gharana and then evolved a style of their own.

SCALES OF PURITY AND IMAGINATION

Singing is considered the highest form of classical music, after which instruments are graded according to their similarity to the human voice. The two main vocal traditions are *dhrupad*, the purest of all, devoid of all embellishment and entirely austere in its delivery, and *khayal*, which has a more romantic content and elaborate ornamentation and is the more popular today. Less abstract vocal forms include the so-called light classical *dadra*, *thumri* and *ghazal* as well as *qawwali*, religious music of the Sufi tradition. The degree of musical purity is assigned according to a scale which has music at one extreme and words at the other. As words become more audible and thus the meaning of lyrics more important, so the form is considered to be musically less pure.

Indian musicologists talk about two kinds of sound – one spiritual and inaudible to the human ear, the other physical and audible. The inaudible sound is said to be produced from the ether, and its function is to liberate the soul. But to feel it requires great devotion and concentration which the average person can never really attain. Audible sound, on the other hand, is actually "struck" and is said to have an immediate and pleasurable impact.

Indian music always has a constant drone in the background which serves as a reference point for performer and listener alike. In north Indian music this drone is usually played on the four-stringed *tambura*. The privilege of accompanying a teacher's performance on the tambura is often accorded to advanced students.

Indian music does not describe a mood (as some European music does) so much as help to create that mood, and then explore it to its depths. Where western classical music starts at a particular point and then progresses from it, Indian classical music revolves around the point, probing it from every angle, yet maintaining a dignified restraint. It is this restraint that distinguishes Indian classical music from the carefree abandon of Indian pop and film music.

INDIAN MUSICAL INSTRUMENTS

STRING INSTRUMENTS

The best-known instrument is the **sitar**, invented by Amir Khusrau in the thirteenth century and played with a plectrum. It has six or seven main strings, of which four are played and the other two or three are used to supply a drone or a rhythmic ostinato. In addition there can be any number of sympathetic strings from eleven to nineteen. The two sets of strings are fitted on different bridges. Twenty brass frets fastened to the long hollow neck can be easily moved to conform to the scale of a particular raag, and their curvature allows the player to alter the pitch by pulling the string sideways across the fret to provide the gliding portamento so characteristic of Indian music.

The **surbahar**, whose name means "spring melody", is effectively a bass sitar and is played in the same way. Developed by Sahibdad Khan,

Sultan Khan playing sarangi

the great-grandfather of Vilayat and Imrat Khan, it produces a deep, dignified sound. The neck is wider and longer than that of the sitar but its frets are fixed. Because the instrument is larger and has longer strings, the sound can be sustained for a longer time, and the range of the portamento is wider.

The **sarod** is a descendant of the Afghani *rebab* (no relation to Arab fiddle of that name). Smaller than a sitar, it has two resonating chambers, the larger made of teak and covered with goatskin and the smaller, at the other end of the metal fingerboard, made of metal. There are twenty-five metal strings, ten of which are plucked with a fragment of coconut shell. Four of them carry the melody; the others are used to accentuate the rhythm. The rest are sympathetic strings lying underneath the main strings. The sarod was hugely improved by Ustad

Allaudin Khan. Its best-known exponents today are his pupils Ustad Ali Akbar Khan and Ustad Amjad Ali Khan.

The **sarangi** is a fretless bowed instrument with a very broad fingerboard and a double belly. The entire body of the instrument – belly and fingerboard – is carved out of a single block of wood and the hollow covered with parchment. There are three or four main strings of gut and anything up to forty metal sympathetic strings. Some claim it is the most difficult musical instrument to play in the world. Certainly the technique is highly unusual. While the right hand wields the bow in the normal way, the strings are stopped not by the fingertips of the left hand, but by the nails. The sarangi is capable of a wide range of timbres and its sound is likened to that of the human voice, so it is usually used as an accompanying instrument in vocal recitals. Originally this was its only function, but in recent years it has gained the status of a solo instrument in its own right due mainly to the efforts of Ustad Sultan Khan and Pandit Ram Narayan.

The **santoor** is a hammered zither of trapezoid shape, thought to be Persian in origin, and has only recently been accepted as an instrument for classical music. It has over a hundred strings, pegged and stretched in pairs, parallel to each other. Each pair of strings passes over two bridges, one on each side of the instrument. The strings are struck by two wooden sticks which curve upwards at the end. Its most notable exponent and the man responsible for its recent rise in status is Pandit Shiv Kumar Sharma.

The **surmandal**, sometimes spelt *swarmandal*, resembles a zither and is used by vocalists to accompany themselves in performance. Even though its primary function is to provide the drone, singers sometimes also play the basic melody line on this instrument.

WIND INSTRUMENTS

The **shehnai** is a double-reed, oboe-type instrument with up to nine finger holes, some of which are stopped with wax for fine tuning to the scale of a particular raag. It was associated with grand occasions and in India it remains the traditional instrument for wedding music. A drone accompaniment is always provided by a second shehnai. The instrument demands a mastery of circular breathing and an enormous amount of breath control, particularly for long sustained passages which can be in an extravagantly fast tempo.

Hariprasad Chaurasia on bansuri

The word **bansuri** is used to refer to a wide variety of flutes, all made from bamboo (*banse*). The majority of these are end-blown although some are side-blown – the Hindu god Krishna's famous *murli* was one such. Although the bamboo flute offers a limited range of just under two octaves, it has been developed as a solo instrument on the concert platform. Hariprasad Chaurasia is world famous for his flute-playing.

DRUMS

The **tabla** is a set of two small drums played with the palms and fingertips capable of producing an incredible variety of sounds and timbres, in a range of about one octave. Its name is an abbreviation of *tabla-bayan* – the tabla is on the right and the bayan (meaning "left") on the left. The most popular of the many drums of north India, its invention is attributed to Amir Khusrau, creator of the sitar. Both drum heads are made of skin, with a paste of iron filings and flour in the centre, but while the body of the tabla is all wood, the banya is metal. The tabla is usually turned to the tonic, dominant or subdominant notes of the raag by knocking the tuning-blocks, held by braces on the sides of the instrument, into place.

Pre-dating the tabla, the **pakhavaj** is nearly a metre long and was traditionally made of clay, although nowadays wood is more popular. It has two parchment heads, each tuned to a different pitch. Like the tabla, it is tuned by knocking the side blocks into place. A paste of boiled rice, iron filings and tamarind juice is applied to the smaller head and a wheat flour paste on the larger head helps produce the lower notes. These paste roundels, unlike those of the tabla, have to be removed after each performance. The pakhavaj has a deep mellow sound and is used to accompany dhrupad singing and kathak dancing. A smaller version of the pakhavaj, the **mridangam,** is widely used in south Indian classical music.

RAAGS AND RHYTHMS

The mainstay of all north Indian classical music is the *raag* (or *raga*), an immensely intricate system of scales and associated melodic patterns. There are some 200 main raags, each of which is defined by its unique combination of scale-pattern, dominant notes, specific rules to be obeyed in ascending or descending and certain melodic phrases associated with it. While Indian classical music is renowned for **improvisation**, this only takes place within the strictly defined boundaries of a particular raag. If the improviser wanders away from the main musical form of the raag his or her performance ceases to be regarded as "classical" music. The mark of a good performer is the ability to improvise extensively without abandoning the set of rules defining the raag.

Some raags are linked with particular seasons; there is a raag for rain, and one for spring; raags can be "masculine" or "feminine"; and Indian musicologists may categorize them according to whether they are best suited to a male or female voice. Specifically, each raag is allotted a **time of day**, a time identified with the spiritual and emotional qualities of the raag. Raags are specifically allocated to early morning (either before or after sunrise), mid-morning, early afternoon, late afternoon, early evening, (either before or after sunset), late evening, late night and post-midnight. This system causes a few problems in northern latitudes, for there is some argument as to whether a raag should be heard by clock-time or sun-time. Purists adhere to the archaic tradition of a "raag time-table" even if they're only listening to records.

The **performance** of a raag, whether sung or played on an instrument such as the sitar, sarod or sarangi, follows a set pattern. First comes the alaap, a slow, meditative "mood-setter" in free rhythm which explores the chosen raag, carefully introducing the notes of the scale one by one. The alaap can span several hours in the hands of a distinguished performer, but these days it may only last a matter of minutes; older aficionados allege that the majority of present-day listeners are unable to sustain the attention required to fully appreciate a lengthy and closely argued alaap. As a result,

performers have felt under pressure to abbreviate this section of the raag in order to reach the faster middle and end sections as soon as possible. This became customary in the recording studio, although the advent of the CD, which does not force the music to fit into 25 minutes as the LP did, has initiated a move back to longer performances.

In the next two sections, the *jorh* and the *jhala*, the soloist begins to introduce a rhythmic element, developing the raag further and exploring its more complex variations.

Only in the final section, the *gath*, does the **percussion instrument** – usually the *tabla* or *pakhavaj* – enter. The soloist introduces a short,

Tabla and sarod: Sri Kumar Bose with Ustad Amjad Ali Khan

fixed composition to which he or she returns between flights of improvisation. In this section rhythm is an important structural element and both percussionist and soloist improvise, at times echoing each other and sometimes pursuing their own individual variations of rhythmic counterpoint, regularly punctuated by unison statements of a short melody known as "the composition". The gath itself is sub-divided into three sections: a slow tempo passage known as *vilambit*, increasing to a medium tempo, called *madhya*, and finally the fast tempo, *drut*.

Just as the raag organizes melody, so the **rhythm** is organized by highly sophisticated structures expressed through cycles known as *taals*, which can be clapped out by hand. A taal is made up of a number of beats (*matras*), and each beat is defined by a combination of rhythm pattern and timbre. It is the unique set of patterns (*bols*) available within a particular taal that define it. There are literally hundreds of taals, but most percussionists use the same few favourites over and over again, the most commonly met with being the sixteen-beat *teentaal*.

The most unfamiliar aspect of taal to the western ear is that the end of one cycle comes not on its last beat, but on the first beat of the following one, so that there is a continual overlap. This first beat is known as *sum*, a point of culmination which completes a rhythmic structure, and performers often indicate it by nodding to each other when they arrive at it. Audiences do the same to express satisfaction and appreciation.

Among smaller, more discerning audiences, verbal **applause** such as "Wah!" (Bravo!), or even "Subhan-Allah" (Praise be to God!), is considered the standard form of appreciation. It is only in western-style concert halls, where such exclamations would be inaudible, that hand-clapping has come to replace these traditional gestures of approval.

LIGHT CLASSICAL MUSIC

Many concerts of classical music end with the performance of a piece in one of the styles collectively referred to as "light classical". Although they obey the rules of classical music with respect to raag and taal, they do so less rigorously than is required for a performance of dhrupad, khayal or other pure classical styles. The alaap is short or non-existent, and the composition is frequently derived from a folk-melody. Indeed, it could be said that light classical music is essentially a synthesis of folk and classical practice. The two most important and widespread types are **thumri** and **ghazal**.

The origin of thumri is popularly ascribed to **Nawab Wajid Ali Shah**, who governed Lucknow (Avadh) from 1847 to 1856. Although little interested in matters of state, he was a great patron of the arts and during his reign music, dance, poetry, drama and architecture flourished.

Thumri employs a specific set of raags and is particularly associated with *kathak* dance, as the graceful movements of the dancer are echoed in the lyricism of the musical style. Although classical instrumentalists in concert frequently perform a thumri as a relaxation from the intensity of the pure classical style, most thumri is vocal, and sung in a language known as Braj Bhasha, a literary dialect of Hindi.

The singer is always accompanied by the tabla, but the other accompanying instruments vary: the tambura, the sarangi or the surmandal are frequently used, and sometimes the violin or harmonium.

The lyrics of thumri deal with **romance**. They are love songs, written from a female perspective, which stress such themes as dressing up for a tryst, the heartache of absence and betrayal, quarrels and reconciliation, and the joyful return from a meeting with a husband or lover. Such themes are often expressed metaphorically, with references in the lyrics to the (suggestive) flute-playing of the god Krishna, who is the symbol of young love. Despite the lyrics' concentration on the woman's point of view, some of the greatest singers of thumri have been men, notably **Ustad Bade Ghulam Ali Khan**. As male singers are frequently middle-aged and overweight, there is a certain initial incongruity in the spectacle of this depiction of the gentle and delicate emotions of a beautiful young woman. Yet a fine artist, fat and balding though he may be, can make a song like this one infinitely affecting: "My bracelets keep slipping off/My lover has cast a spell on me/He has struck me with his magic/What can a mere doctor do?" Her bracelets have slipped off because, while pining for her absent lover, she has starved herself to the point of emaciation.

Still more songlike than the thumri is the ghazal. In some ways the Urdu counterpart of thumri, the ghazal was introduced to India by Persian Muslims and is mainly a poetic rather than a musical form. Although some ghazal tunes are based on the raag system, others do not follow any specific mode. The taals are clearly derived from folk music and at times the ghazal shades into the area of sophisticated pop song. Indeed, at the more commercial end of the scale – the so-called **film ghazal** (see the article on the Bombay film music industry) – sophistication gives way to mere charm. The ghazal has played an important part in the cultures of India, Pakistan and Afghanistan since the early eighteenth century, when it was one of the accomplishments required of a courtesan. Ghazal singers of modern times usually come from a more "respectable" background. All the same, Britain's **Najma Akhtar** had to overcome a certain amount of parental concern when she first began singing.

While thumri singers take on a female persona, emotions in the ghazal are almost always expressed from the male point of view.

Star of thumri and ghazal, Shobha Gurtu

Some of the finest performers of ghazals are women – **Begum Akhtar** and **Shobha Gurtu** among them. Many favourite ghazals are drawn from the works of great Urdu poets such as Daagh, Jigar Muradabadi, Faiz Ahmed Faiz and Mirza Ghalib.

A patriotic poem by **Faiz Ahmed Faiz**, "Mujhse Pehli Si Muhabbat Mere Mehboob Na Maang" (Do not ask me my love, to love you the way I used to love you), proved a milestone in the advance of art poetry into the realm of the film ghazal. Sung by the popular Pakistani singer **Noor Jehan** in her inimitable style, her interpretation is said to have so impressed the poet Faiz that he formally relinquished all claims to it in her favour.

TALES OF THE GOLDEN AGE

Ghazals can be heard every day on the radio or on films either in India or Pakistan or in Asian communities abroad. But pure classical music is, for those who don't get invited to a mahfil, most often heard in concert – a far cry from the golden age of Indian classical music, when its chief patrons were *nawabs* (Muslim noblemen), *maharajahs* (Hindu kings) and *zamindars* (feudal landlords). At this time Indian classical music was essentially **court music,** and its forms and practices, perfected within this framework, were clearly aimed at a leisured elite able to appreciate the subtleties that the musicians were developing.

Many traditional tales tell of this period. For instance, the Prince of Mysore would take his court musicians to a neighbouring district, inhabited by deadly snakes. The performers would then play the *poongi*, a kind of wind instrument. As the sounds grew louder, the snakes would venture from their holes and slide towards the musicians. The snakes would encircle the players completely and sway in perfect rhythm, as if intoxicated by the sound. Then, as soon as the music stopped, they would glide away quietly without biting anyone.

Another story is that of **Tan-Sen**, the greatest singer that India has ever produced and court musician to the Moghul Emperor Akbar. Tan-Sen was said to have such extraordinary power over his music that one day, when he began singing a late-night raag at noon, the world was plunged into darkness.

But if another story is to be believed, there was a singer even greater than Tan-Sen. One day, as Tan-Sen sang the fiery "Raag Deepak", the whole palace went up in flames. A young water-carrying maiden who happened to be passing by saw the flames, and taking a deep breath began to sing the **"Raag Megh"** (associated with rain). She sang with such emotion and sincerity that the heavens poured forth torrents and the flames caused by the great Tan-Sen were extinguished. Even in modern times, skilful performers are often credited with averting famine by singing "Raag Megh". But "Raag Deepak" is superstitiously avoided these days.

Nearly every Indian musician has such tales attached to his or her name. Another story relates to **Ustad Imdaad Khan**, court musician at Indore and exponent of the surbahar. One night, as he accompanied the Maharajah's entourage on a tiger hunt, there was concern about a mad elephant on the rampage. As night set in and everyone prepared to settle down and remain quiet for fear of the elephant, Imdaad upset the whole party by getting his surbahar out – for this was his usual practice time. When he had been playing a while, a most unusual sight was seen outside his tent – a huge elephant, swaying to the sound of the surbahar as though hypnotized. From then on, all through the hunt, Imdaad was ordered to play the surbahar each night in order to keep the elephant quiet.

SOUND OF THE SOUTH

Southern India's classical music, *karnatak*, is essentially similar to Hindustani classical music in its general outlook and theoretical background but differs in many details, usually ascribed to the far greater influence of Islamic culture on the north. To the western ear, karnatak music is emotionally direct and impassioned, without

GHAZAL HARMONY

....

British singer Najma Akhtar introduced harmonies to the ghazal, to the consternation of the Indian musical community. She has since toured all over Europe, Japan and America and has released three albums. David Muddyman talked to the rising star of the ghazal.

"The first time I heard a ghazal singer was in London in 1980 or '81. The singer was Baves Mendi from Pakistan, accompanied by a famous tabla player called Tari. The two of them were magnificent. I think my love of the ghazal started then. Later on I saw a husband and wife team, Jagjit and Chitra Singh, who used western instruments instead of the usual combination of tabla and harmonium or tabla, harmonium and sarangi.

"I was sent tapes from Pakistan and I started to copy them. Later, in 1984, I saw a second-hand harmonium which my parents reluctantly bought for me. I learnt one song on it, and when another singer heard me and said I had a good voice and I should try and learn, I started having lessons. It was very difficult at first. I strained so much that I lost my voice for the first two weeks. But I persisted, and in 1984 my teacher wanted me to enter an Asian song competition. My parents were not very happy. They couldn't see the point. I couldn't either, really, but I came first."

"In 1986 I went to India to record an album, but it wasn't publicised well. When I came back here, in 1987, I met Iain Scott of Triple Earth and we did an album, 'Qareeb'. We used vocal harmonies, which are alien to the classical tradition. This was Triple Earth's idea. At the time I was apprehensive, because as Ravi Shankar once said, Indian music is very beautiful and within the raag itself you don't need to harmonize anything, because it's so pure, so perfect, you don't need anything to lift it up. But Iain explained his ideas to me and I began to work them out with the help of a Walkman."

The sound of the album was strange to those used to traditional ghazal, with saxophone, slap bass guitar and synthesized washes added to the more familiar sounds of tabla and violin. At first

the Indian community reacted with consternation, but good reviews followed and gradually the innovations became accepted.

"The original idea was to introduce jazz influences. We spent a lot of time experimenting, because if you can't hear the words, or the words are masked by the instruments, then Asian people won't like it. But I saw Iain's side of it too — we were making a new sound."

"Shortly after 'Qareeb' was released I was invited to perform at the Glastonbury festival. It was the first time I'd ever performed live, apart from the song competition. I remember Iain coming up to me and saying 'Najma, Najma, we've got a spot for you at the Glastonbury

Triple Earth's World Music marketing of Najma Akhtar

pop festival'. I said 'What is that?' A week before the festival we got together with the band, who I'd only met in the studio, and rehearsed three songs. When I think about it, my singing was awful! There was no soundcheck, and so when I got onto the stage I couldn't hear myself properly. After that I learned fast, and toured Holland and Germany. That was fun, but I'd never performed in dives before. I didn't know what clubs were like. After that we got more and more calls for concerts and that's when I really started practising and studying the raags and the rhythms."

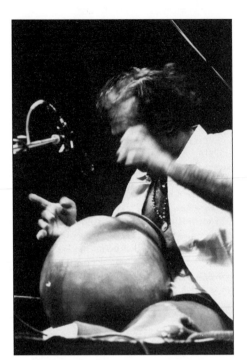

Vikku Vinayakram on the ghatam – a water pot

written by the most influential figure in the development of karnatak music, the singer **Tyagaraja** (1767–1847). He was central to the music, not only for his compositions but also for the development of techniques of rhythmic and melodic variations. Southern India's biggest music festival, held annually near Tanjore on the banks of the Cauvery River, is named after him.

Although the vocal tradition is central to this music, its singers are perhaps less well known in the west than instrumentalists. M S Subbulakshmi and Dr M Balamurali Krishna are among the famous names, but the most celebrated is probably **Ramnad Krishnan**, who has taught in America.

The **instruments** of karnatak music include the *veena*, which resembles the sitar but has no sympathetic strings (karnatak musicians appear not to like the somewhat hollow timbre that they give to the instrument), the *mridangam* double-headed drum, and the enormous *nadasvaram*, a type of oboe nearly four feet long which takes great experience and delicacy to play. The violin is widely used – listen to the playing of **Dr L Subramaniam** or his brother L Shankar, perhaps better known for his fusion experiments with guitarist John McLaughlin than for his classical recordings. The mandolin is growing in popularity and the saxophone has made a strikingly successful appearance in the hands of **Kadri Gopalnath**. Among veena players look out for **S Balachander** and **K S Nayaranaswami**, while flute player **Dr N Ramani** has recorded for Nimbus.

Percussion is very important, perhaps more so than in Hindustani music, and **percussion ensembles** frequently tour abroad. In addition to the mrindangam percussion instruments include the *ghatam*, a clay pot played with tremendous zest and sometimes tossed into the air in a burst of high spirits. **"Vikku" Vinayakram** is its best-known player.

NEW PATHS

In earlier times the job of musician was more or less hereditary: would-be musicians began their musical education at the age of four, and music (as a profession) was considered beneath the dignity of the well-to-do and the academic classes. However, in recent years traditional restrictions have been relaxed, and music is no longer the province of a few families. Many Indians from the educated strata of society are becoming involved in both performance and

the sometimes sombre restraint that characterizes much of the north's music. For instance the alaapaana section, although it introduces and develops the notes of the raag in much the same way as the alaap of north Indian music, interrupts its stately progress with sparkling decorative flourishes. Often, too, the alaapaana is succeeded by a set of increasingly complex elaborations of a basic melody in a way that is more easily grasped than the abstract, sometimes severe improvisations of the Hindustani masters. Compositions, both of "themes" and the set variations upon them, play a much greater role in karnatak musical practice than in Hindustani.

The raags of karnatak music, like those of Hindustani music, are theoretically numbered in the thousands and musicians are expected to be familiar with them all. In practice, however, only a few hundred are ever played, and probably only fifty or sixty are in common use.

Song is at the root of south Indian music, and forms based on song are paramount, even when the performance is purely instrumental. The vast majority of the texts are religious, and the temple is frequently the venue for performance. The most important form is the *kriti*, a devotional song, hundreds of which were

Sarod master Ustad Ali Akbar Khan

composition, and as public performance loses its stigma so too the requirement for musicians to begin their training at a very early age becomes less forceful. **Women instrumentalists** too are beginning to make their mark – a startling innovation in a male-dominated musical culture. Two women with a particularly high reputation

are violinist **Sangeeta Rajan** and tabla player **Anuradha Pal**, both of whom have recorded in India. Several gharanas have been set up abroad, notably the one in California run by sarod player **Ali Akbar Khan**, who is probably Indian music's most influential living figure, and there is a steady trickle of westerners who are willing to subject themselves to the disciplines of study.

However, the importance of the old families is barely diminished. Among the younger generation of players are such names as sarod player **Brij Narayan**, son of Ram Narayan, **Nikil Banerjee**, who studied sitar with his father Jitendra Nath Banerjee, and **Krishna Bhatt**, who studied with Ravi Shankar and also comes from a family of musicians. Other important figures to listen out for are sitarist **Rais Khan** and vocalist **Rashid Khan**. These, like the other names mentioned, bear witness to the remaining vitality and richness of the classical music tradition in India and abroad.

▶ DISCOGRAPHY ◀

A good first choice from the vast quantity of recordings available would be any of the Nimbus releases. All are beautifully recorded and are uninterrupted versions on CD, often over an hour long.

NORTH INDIAN CLASSICAL MUSIC

Amir Khan *Raags Ahir Bhairav and Bageshree* (EMI, India). Just one of a whole string of masterpieces from this singer, born in 1912, who specialized in the Khayal singing of the Indore gharana and was known for his extensive research on tarana and khayal.

ⓒ **Amjad Ali Khan Atma** *Amjad Ali Khan Atma* (Audiorec, UK). Featuring "Raag Bihaag" and "Raag Jhinjhoti". Although a highly trained sarod player in the classical tradition, of which this record is an example, Amjad is best known for his rendering of popular folk tunes.

Begum Akhtar *Thumri, Sawan, Ghazals* (Music India, India). This disc, by a famous ghazal and thumri singer who studied in the Patiala gharana and who still has a large cult following many years after her death, contains one of the best recordings of the famous "Raag Des" song "Chha rahi kari ghata".

Bismillah Khan *Raags Saarang, Chandra Kauns and Kajaree* (EMI, India). Bismillah Khan, who is today's most distinguished exponent of the shehnai, was born in 1916. He trained with his uncle Ali Bux and follows the family's own unique tradition of playing the shehnai with a highly "vocalized" technique.

ⓒ **Dagar Brothers** *Chant Dhrupad* (Auvidis, France). Zahiruddin and Faiyazuddin Dagar perform the raags "Bageshri" and "Bhatiyar". The Dagar brothers are descended from a long line of famous dhrupad singers, and it is largely due to their efforts that this ancient and extremely difficult form has been preserved in a number of beautiful recordings.

ⓒ **Fahimuddin Dagar** *Raga Kedar* (Jecklin Musikhaus, Germany). This CD from a member of the famous family contains a full 80-minute-long performance of this beautiful and sensuous raag.

ⓒ **Hariprasad Chaurasia** *Raag Ahir Bhairav* (Nimbus, UK). One of the finest renditions of this morning raag, beautifully played and recorded. Hariprasad, who was born in 1938, originally trained as a singer and then learnt the flute from Raja Ram. He is as at home in the fields of classical and light classi-

cal music as he is playing for the Bombay film industry. ⓒ *Veru* (Rykodisc, US) is a Mickey Hart-produced disc featuring him together with tabla virtuoso Zakir Hussain.

ⓒ **Imrat and Vajahat Khan** *Raag Jhinjhoti and Raag Pilu* (Nimbus, UK). The great Imrat Khan, born in 1935, performs on the surbahar, the bass sitar invented by his great-grandfather Sahibdad Khan. Here he is accompanied by two of his sons – Vajahat on sarod and Shafaatullah on tabla.

ⓒ **Lakshmi Shankar** *Les Heures Et Les Saisons* (Ocora, France). Put this top of your list. A mixture of khyal, thumri and bhajan devotional songs from this exceptional singer who trained with Ravi Shankar and other distinguished musicians. She sings khayal in the Patiala gharana tradition and has also studied karnatak music.

ⓒ **Pandit Bhimsen Joshi** *Pandit Bhimsen Joshi* (Moment Records, US). Beautifully produced by Zakir Hussain, this recording of a concert by the most popular of today's khayal singers features a stunning performance of the notoriously difficult "Raag Shuddh Kalyaan".

ⓒ **Ravi Shankar** *Pandit Ravi Shankar* (Ocora, France). Ravi Shankar, probably the best-known Indian musician, began his career as a dancer with his brother Uday and, after learning to play a wide variety of instruments, concentrated on the sitar as a pupil of Allaudin Khan. Although he is noted for experimental interests, this record shows him playing in the purest classical style.

ⓒ **Salamat Ali Khan and Sons** *Raags Gunkali, Saraswati and Durga* (Nimbus Records, UK). Salamat Ali Khan, who lives in Pakistan, is a khayal singer of the Sham Chaurasi gharana. Originally teamed up with his late brother Nazakat Ali Khan, Salamat is now always accompanied by his sons Sharafat and Shafqat, as in these deeply felt performances.

ⓒ **Shiv Kumar Sharma and Zakir Hussain** *Raag Madhuvanti and Raag Misra Tilang* (Nimbus, UK). Santoor exponent Pandit Sharma has only recently had his instrument accepted as a concert instrument. Tabla player Zakir Hussain trained with his father Alla Rakha and toured extensively with Ravi Shankar. He founded the fusion group "Shakti" and recently worked with American musician Mickey Hart on his "Planet Drum" project.

THE INDIAN SUBCONTINENT

Sultan Khan *Singing Sarangi* (Chhanda Dhara, Germany). Sarangi performances of raags "Kaunsi Kanada", "Chandra Madhu" and "Mishra Tilang" from a master from a long line of sarangi players, today regarded as one of India's best exponents of it.

Ustad Ali Akbar Khan *Signature Series Vol 1* (AMMP, US). Undoubtedly India's best-known sarod player, he was born in 1922 and from the age of three studied with his father Allauddin Khan, the grand old man of Indian music. Three raags here, one of which, "Chandranandran", was famously invented by the master himself. A reissue of 1960s American recordings, it contrasts strikingly with his latest Californian New Age output.

Ustad Ahmed Jan "Thirakwa" *Rhythms of India* (EMI, India). "Thirakwa", whose nickname is an onomatopoeic description of his playing, was born in 1891 and was one of India's finest ever tabla players. This recording of his solo drumming is hard to find, but repays the effort one-hundred-fold.

Vilayat Khan *Raag Bhairavi* (India Archive Music, US). A fine performance of this favourite raag by Imrat Khan's older brother, renowned for his individual style of "gayaki" playing, in which the sitar emulates the human voice.

KARNATAK MUSIC

Dr N Ramani *Music in the Ragas Kannada, Kalyanavasanta, Natakuranji, Ranjani, Des* (Nimbus, UK). A splendid example of a typical south Indian ensemble of flute, violin, mridangam and ghatam playing five raags of contrasting character. Very attractive.

Ramnad Krishnan *Vidwan – Songs of the Carnatic Tradition* (Nonesuch, US). Well-nigh perfect performances from this important singer and teacher, backed by violin and mridangam. The performances are given plenty of room to breathe, making this a good first choice.

Dr L Subramaniam *Raga Hemavati* (Nimbus, UK). Nimbus' karnatak recordings are as scrupulously well produced and annotated as their Hindustani discs. Highly recommended performance by one of south India's finest musicians.

U Srinivas *Modern Mandolin Maestro* (GlobeStyle, UK). The title says it all; no better introduction to the current sounds of karnatak creativity could be asked for.

Vadya Lahari *South Indian Instrumental Ensemble* (Music of the World, US). This fine ensemble, led by the woman violinist A Kanyakumari makes a thrilling sound and takes the bold step of combining the intimate veena and raucous nadasvaram in the same ensemble. Recommended.

GHAZALS AND THUMRIS

Various *Taadgaar Thumriyan* (EMI, India). The title means "memorable thumris" and no better description could be found for this outstanding collection of songs by the heavyweights of the style: Bhimsen Joshi, Ustad Bade Ghulam Ali Khan, Kishari Amakan and others. Prabha Atre's performance of "Kaun Gali Gayo Shyam" is unforgettable.

Abida Parveen *Super Hit Ghazals Vol 4* (IRH, UK). One from a series of four cassettes released by this Southall label. Soaring vocals over a delicate mix of sarangi, harmonium and tabla.

Asha Bhosle and Hariharan *Aabhaar e Ghazal* (CBS, India). A collection of lightweight but beautiful ghazal, with some wonderfully eccentric arrangements from one of the Queens of Film Music, Ashe Bhosle.

Bade Ghulam Ali Khan *Great Master, Great Music – Thumri Tilak Kamod etc* (EMI, India). First-rate performances in thumri style from the archives of All India Radio by the master born in 1901 who belonged to the Patiala gharana. Although he sang khayal he is best known for light classical music and is probably the best thumri singer ever.

Begum Akhtar *Malika-e-Ghazal* (EMI, Pakistan). A selection of some of the most memorable Urdu ghazals rendered in the unique Begum Akhtar style. The collection features the work of the great poets as well as more recent popular poets like Shakeel Badayuni.

Farida Khanum *Gulistan Farida Khanum Gulistan* (Music Today, India). A truly delightful collection by one of Pakistan's leading female singers. For many ghazal fans Farida Khanum is the ultimate, with a passionate singing style and a uniquely dramatic form of expression.

Iqbal Bano *Iqbal Bano Sings Faiz* (Shalimar Records, US) – 2 vols. Live recording of a concert featuring the revolutionary poems of renowned Pakistani poet Faiz Ahmed Faiz. Tumultuous cheering by the audience adds another dimension to Iqbal Bano's distinctive, haunting voice.

Jagjit and Chitra Singh *Unforgettables Vol 1* (HMV, Pakistan). A moody collection of songs from the husband and wife team. A variety of instruments play behind the guitar and voices. Listen out for the similarities with Najma Akthar's style.

Najma Akhtar *Qareeb* (Triple Earth, UK). Still the best of her albums, this was an inspired recording which crosses many boundaries and yet remains out on its own. Buy it for the harmony vocals alone and you won't be disappointed.

Nusrat Fateh Ali Khan *(Vol 42) Ghazal & Geet* (Star Cassette, UK). An amazingly soulful and soothing album from the "king" of qawwali here playing ghazal. Violins, accordions, synth and guitar play over some inspired tabla.

Nusrat Fateh Ali Khan *Qawwal & Party (Vol 53) Urdu Ghazals* (Star Cassette, UK). More forceful than "Ghazal & Geet" but no less soulful with the usual qawwali instrumentation of harmoniums, drums and handclaps.

Shobha Gurtu *Shobha Gurtu* (CMP, US/Germany). A well-recorded disc of traditional-style light classical songs. Sensitive accompaniment by Sultan Khan on sarangi.

Shobha Gurtu, Begum Akhtar & Chandralekha Devi *Thumriyan* (Music India, India). A splendid collection of three of the best-known women singers of thumri and ghazal performing some of their favourite repertoire.

BOLLYWOOD NIGHTS

THE VOICES BEHIND THE STARS

The Indian film industry is the world's largest and most prolific, churning out endless tales of love and passion, heroic derring-do, vice frustrated and virtue rewarded, and all to the sound of music provided by the playback singers in their hutch-like recording booths. Nasreen Kabir and Rupert Snell introduce the voices belonging to India's best-loved and least-seen singers.

Leave Bombay airport to head into the city and a continuous flow of images stretches before and behind you. Listen to the hum of humanity. Car horns blare, the insistent, ever-present, three-wheeler auto-rickshaws buzz insistently as they weave their way alongside run-down Japanese trucks, seemingly oblivious to safety. Above the road, the melodramatic faces of movie stars loom from giant billboards. And amid the rush of life, you hear in the distance the high-pitched sound of transistorized voices singing out to stir the hearts of millions through every imaginable variation on the theme of love.

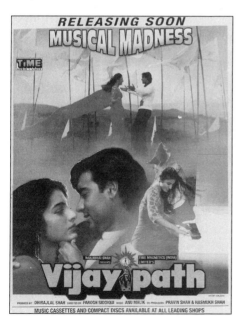

Lights! Camera! Music! Action! Now on video

THE PLAYBACK SINGERS

The popular music of India comes from the cinema screen, out of the mouths of the actors and actresses whose singing voices belong to invisible performers – the **"playback singers"** or dubbing artists – who record a given song which is then "played back" over loudspeakers on the film set. While it is being played, the film or dance director instructs the actor to mime to the words or dance to the music. What results on screen is a cinematic illusion, commonly known in India as "song picturization".

Since the advent of sound in Indian cinema in the 1931 production "Alam Ara", music has been an integral part of popular cinema. Theatrical and folk traditions, in which little distinction is made between drama, music and dance, were the basis of narrative form in film. Some of the early sound productions of the 1930s managed to squeeze over fifty songs into a single film. The studios flourished, aided by the popularity of their music scores and their stars. At this time actors were known as "singing stars", for they were required not only to act but also to sing. But the late 1940s saw the decline of the major studios and the end of the singing star era: the celebrated actor/singer KL Saigal died in 1948 and "Melody Queen" **Noor Jehan** migrated to Pakistan. A new generation of film directors emerged to whom it was clear that a greater variety of talent could be exploited if actors no longer needed a good singing voice. Thus it was that the legends of the popular cinema (Kumar, Kapoor, Anand, Nargis, Kumari and many, many others) won the hearts of their audiences through their screen presence and acting ability, while the singing was left to the playback artist. Many playback singers had studied in the classical tradition of Indian music, and their skill strengthened the music itself and contributed to the widening of the range and quality of Hindi cinema.

THE GOLDEN ERA

The golden era of Indian cinema began in the 1950s and lasted until the early 1960s. Much of the magic of this period is attributable to the immortal melodies of countless films. Although

THE INDIAN SUBCONTINENT

the songs of the Bombay film industry – "Bollywood" – are numbered in the thousands, they are sung by a remarkably small number of playback singers. **Mohammed Rafi** (who died in 1980) and **Mukesh** (who died in 1976) were the most important male artists, while no female singer has to date rivalled the continuing popularity and phenomenal success of **Lata Mangeshkar**, born in 1928, who appears in the Guinness Book of Records as the world's most recorded artist with over 30,000 songs, in

Sizzling Hits of
ASHA BHOSLE

Another day, another fourteen hits for Asha Bhosle

more than 2,000 films to her credit. Other leading playback singers who have given life to memorable duets and solos are Kishore Kumar, Talat Mahmood, Manna Dey, Hemant Kumar and the female vocalists **Asha Bhosle** (Lata Mangeshkar's younger sister) and **Geeta Dutt**.

Each singer has an individual style, but what they all have in common is their ability to sound convincing whether singing for the greatest faces of the Bombay screen or the greenest newcomer among actors. Such is the fusion (or confusion) between actor and singer that – for example – Mukesh's voice seems for audiences to be the voice of actor/director Raj Kapoor, who once said, "Mukesh's voice is the voice of my soul."

Clearly defined genres on the lines of the American romantic comedy, thriller or western are rare in Indian popular cinema. Any film may include any, or all, genres, and nearly every film leads repeatedly to situations where a song becomes unavoidable. The ever-popular "boy-meets-girl" plot with its age-old romantic themes of meetings, partings, rivalry and the pain of star-crossed lovers demands poetic expression.

As in popular music throughout the world, **love songs** deal with certain clichéd situations: the discovery of feelings for the beloved – "Kaun aayaa mere man ke dwaare?" (Who has entered the world of my heart? – Waqt, 1965), or the revelation that one is in love – "Aaaj mere man main sakhi baansuri bajaaye koi" (Today I hear the sweet sound of a flute – Aan, 1952). The awakening of mutual love is expressed in a duet such as "Na ye chaand hogaa, na taare rahenge, magar ham hameshaa tumhaare rahenge" (The moon and the stars may not last, but I shall be yours forever – Shart, 1954). Another common type is the song sung to pacify an angered lover, like *Dekho roothaa na karo, baat nazaron ki suno* ("Don't be angry, listen to what my eyes say" – Tere Ghar Ke Saamne, 1960).

Apart from love songs, **communal songs** involve the entire population of a village in a festive celebration; **songs of friendship** emphasize the virtues of loyalty or sacrifice; and **devotional songs** (an important group which uses *bhajan* and *qawwaali* as its models) implore the divine for grace through a kind of musical prayer.

COMPOSITION A LA CARTE

The music of the film song is written by talented and highly trained composers (invariably men) who specialize in adapting other musical genres for the screen to create a musical form peculiar to the cinema. For example, **Naushad Ali** made use of the folk music of Uttar Pradesh and even Egypt; **SD Burman** based his melodies on Bengali folk songs; **C Ramchandra** blended a Marathi style with Latin American rhythms; and **Shanker Jaikishen** popularized certain classical raags. The innovations of the 1950s' generation of composers have had an immense and enduring influence on their successors, and more recently rock, disco, funk, country and western and Lebanese popular music and even Algerian rai have left their mark.

To western ears the sound of Indian film music takes some getting used to. What is the basis of this sound, a mixture of the familiar and the unfamiliar? To start with, the **vocal timbre**, especially that of the female singers, whose voices sound high-pitched and nasal, is utterly different to that favoured in the west. Secondly, although Indian film composers may use western-style harmony in their compositions, they often don't follow western notions of harmonic progression, and most film songs concentrate on the melody and the rhythm. Often when writing a song a composer uses the western orchestra in much the same way that he would use traditional Indian solo instruments such as the sitar, the bansari or the sarangi – to play a single melodic strand free of the harmonic underpinning central to western practice. Great banks of violins swirl their way through the tune in unison, interrupted by the contrasting sounds of sitar and tabla, or even a banjo break in bluegrass style.

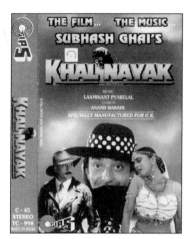

The Singing Detective – Bollywood style

The **lyrics** and their musical setting have always been closely connected. Many music directors worked with only one lyricist. The lyricists of the 1950s excelled in giving depth to the film song and, at that time, established poets often wrote for the cinema. Sahir Ludhianvi, Shailendra, Shakeel Badayuni, Majrooh Sultanpuri, Kaifi Azmi and Hasrat Jaipuri among others raised the level of the film song to a form of poetry.

One of the earliest musical/poetic forms to be coopted by the cinema was the ghazal, which has a thousand ways of expressing the agonies and ecstasies of love, and as a result the songs of the "Hindi" film actually depend quite heavily on the poetic traditions of Hindi's sister language, Urdu. As the film industry grew, a particular development of the ghazal took place, resulting in something quite different to the original. Composers of such **film-ghazals** used western harmonies and inserted lush orchestral interludes. Naturally there was little room for improvisation. There was also a standardized vocal style introduced by film-ghazal's main exponent, **Talat Mahmood.**

This style of ghazal remained popular until the late 1950s, when it temporarily went out of fashion until a new crossover style, the **ghazal-song**, appeared in the 1970s. It was an immediate success, partly owing to the disappearance of the more melodic film songs of the late 1950s and 1960s in favour of a more disco-oriented style required by the new breed of action-packed **masala** ("spice") films. The crossover ghazal with its slow smooth tempo, soothing melodies and sentimental lyrics – these

days often celebrating the joys of alcohol – was first made popular by Pakistan's **Mehdi Hassan** and **Ghulam Ali**. The success of such leading lights of the ghazal-song as Pankaj Udhas, Anup Jalota and Jagjit and Chitra Singh has led to more work for mediocre poets who can turn out simple, comprehensible lyrics in a more everyday register of Urdu than was traditional for ghazals. The decline in quality since the great days of the 1950s has meant that songs and soundtracks are more ephemeral than they used to be, becoming wildly popular for a few weeks and then vanishing without a trace; "Pop goes the ghazal" is now a well-established journalistic cliché.

MAGICAL SYNTHESIS

Unlike some forms of Indian classical music, in which the words of the song are little more than a vehicle for the human voice, the Hindi film song is very much a synthesis of words and music (with the visuals, of course, completing the picture). Individual film directors established their own styles of song picturization. **Guru Dutt**, **Raj Kapoor**, **Bimal Roy**, **Mehboob Khan** and **Vijay Anand** are the masters in this specialized area of Indian film-making. In the work of these directors the song becomes a natural extension of the film dialogue; the dialogue tells the story while the song reveals the characters' inner feelings. To some extent the switch from dialogue to song represents a change of level from reality to fantasy, or from the mundane to the poetic. The dialogue, which must obey the rules of social behaviour, is earth-bound and deals with the specifics of the characters' situations and the development of the plot, whereas the song is expected to be infinitely more daring, romantic and suggestive, breaking the bounds of convention and expressing sentiments that would be frowned upon in everyday life.

When a film song becomes a hit it comes to life in the streets and lanes of India. It is an excuse for interaction between people who may otherwise hardly communicate with each other. A recent hit song, inspired by Gloria Estefan's

"The rhythm is going to get you", starts with a contagious cry of "Oye oye!". At the height of its popularity a young voice calling these words could often be heard in the street of an Indian town, instantly matched by a neighbour's response: an echoed "Oye oye!" floating through the suburban air. It is said that the police imposed fines of fifty rupees on anyone who was heard shouting the famous words, claiming that the song had become a public nuisance. But film music is the real popular music of the sub-continent: unstoppable, irrepressible, unchanging and yet ever new, an unfailing expression of the rawest or the most idealized emotion. Amidst the struggles of everyday life there's always time for a song.

◼ DISCOGRAPHY ◼

N avigating your way around an Indian or Pakistani cassette shop can at first be a daunting task. Most have an enormous stock, and the average current film song, like the average current chart single, has a very short life. Nonetheless, various classic film scores are continually being released, deleted and reissued. The Gramophone Company of India has recently released literally hundreds of CDs, either of original soundtracks or of greatest hits of the playback singers. Lata Mangeshkar, Kishore Kumar, Mohd Rafi, Asha Bhosle and Geeta Dutt all have numerous collections on this label with generic titles such as: Haunting Melodies, Rare Gems, Magic Moments, In a Blue Mood and so on. Among releases of classic soundtracks (the songs of two movies are on each CD), try the two Mangeshkar CDs:

◎ **Vijaya Anand** Dance Raja Dance: the South Indian Film Music of Vijaya Anand (Luaka Bop, US). Vijaya Anand is one of the new wave of Indian film music composers. This is a marvellously eclectic collision of ancient Indian melodies with screaming fuzz guitar, soul strings and Hollywood mambo.

◎ **Lata Mangeshkar** Pakeezah with Razia Sultan (Gramophone Co. of India, UK/India). Music by Ghulam Mohammed, lyrics by Kaifi Azmi and others. "Pakeezah" was a milestone in Indian cinema, directed by Kamal Amrohi, and released in 1971.

◎ **Lata Mangeshkar, Manna Dey** Awaara with Shree 420 (Gramophone Co. of India, UK/India). Music by Shankar Jaikishan, lyrics by Shailendra. The English title of the 1951 "Awaara", directed by Raj Kapoor, was "The Rogue of Bombay". Mangeshkar in stunning form – every song a winner. It was even a huge hit in the USSR.

◎ **Various** Baiju Bawra with Shahab (Gramophone Co. of India, UK/India). "Baiju Bawra" is from 1956, directed by Vijay Bhatt, with music by Naushad and lyrics by Shakeel Badayuni.

◎ **Various** Chori Chori (Gramophone Co. of India, UK/India). "Chori Chori, directed by Anant Thakur, came out in 1958, with music by Shanker Jaikishan and lyrics by Shailendra and Hasrat Jaipuri.

◎ **Various** Golden Voices from the Silver Screen Vols 1–3 (GlobeStyle, UK). Three wonderful compilations produced in conjunction with the UK Channel Four TV series Movie Mahal. A fine choice of material that gives an idea of the astonishing range of styles pressed into service by the industry, and drawn from a range of films produced from the 1950s to the 1970s and with a list of singers that includes Asha Bhosle, Mohammed Rafi, Geeta Dutt and Lata Mangeshkar. Indubitably the best introduction.

SONGS OF PRAISE

SUFI DEVOTIONAL MUSIC OF PAKISTAN

Sufism explores the mystical elements of Islam. Among its ecstatic techniques are dancing, the hypnotic repetition of holy names and music that is literally entrancing. Jameela Siddiqi listens to qawwali and talks to its performers, the qawwals, while Helen Jerome profiles its greatest living exponent, Nusrat Fateh Ali Khan.

Q awwali is the Sufi music of India and Pakistan. Essentially it is religious poetry set to music, sharing certain traits with the light classical music of the subcontinent. But its sound, with its typically sweeping melodies and rhythmic hand-clapping, is quite distinctive and instantly recognizable. Its intensity has made it extremely popular in Indian films as well as in clubs and other gatherings in India and abroad, but the popular filmi qawwali is a far cry from the original – a spiritual song that transports the mystic towards union with the Creator.

The term "qawwali" refers both to the genre itself and its performance. A performer of qawwali is known as a **qawwal**. A group of qawwals can consist of any number of people, but the minimum requirement is a lead singer, one or two secondary singers (who also play the harmonium), and at least one percussionist. Every member of the group joins in the singing, and junior members also clap rhythmically. Under the guidance of a religious leader or *sheikh*, these groups of trained musicians present a vast treasure of poems in song, articulating and evoking a mystical experience for the spiritual benefit of their audience.

RITUALS AND TRANCES

Qawwali gatherings are organized for the purpose of realizing the ideals of **Islamic mysticism** through the ritual of listening to music (*sama*). By enhancing the message of mystical poetry, and by providing a powerful rhythm that suggests the ceaseless repetition of God's name (*zikr*), the music of qawwali has a religious function: to arouse mystical love, even divine ecstasy – the central experience of Sufism.

While Islamic musicologists wrote about the use of music to achieve a trance-like state in order to gain spiritual insight as early as the ninth century, qawwali in its present form is thought to have begun with **Amir Khusrau**, (1253–1325), an exceptionally talented Sufi poet and composer, putative inventor of the sitar and tabla, who was the favourite disciple of the great Sufi saint Nizamuddin Auliya in Delhi. His poems and melodies form the core of the traditional repertoire. Following Khusrau, the Sufi communities of the Indian subcontinent have continued the tradition of the **Mahfil-e-Sama** (Assembly for Listening), which remains the central ritual of Sufism to this day.

Through sama, the Sufi seeks to activate a link with his living spiritual guide, with the departed saints and ultimately with God. The music serves to kindle the flame of mystical love, to intensify his longing for mystical union and to transport him to a state of ecstasy.

THE LANGUAGE OF ECSTASY

The **texture** of qawwali is like that of north Indian song in general. There is a sung melodic line which is always reinforced by an instrument, in this case the harmonium, and supported by the rhythm articulated on the drum – traditionally the *dholak* and more recently tabla. The usual form is one of solo verses punctuated by a choral refrain and instrumental interludes.

The hand-pumped **harmonium** is now well established in qawwali and seems to have permanently replaced its less "satisfactory" predecessors like the sarangi. The sarangi has a subtler sound and is not restricted to a tempered scale, but as it requires extensive retuning between numbers it is considered less amenable in live performance. The tabla is now increasingly used alongside the dholak, but is played using a flat hand technique (*thaap*) as opposed to the normal finger technique (*chutki*) of north Indian music.

Qawwali is sung in many languages but its original repertoire is composed of verses in Persian (Farsi) and an old form of Hindi known as *Braj Bhasha* – the two main languages used by Khusrau. There is also an extensive repertoire in Punjabi, mainly drawn from the verses of **Baba Bulleh Shah**. In recent times there has been a growing tendency to use Urdu (a relatively modern language of northern India and Pakistan), and even Arabic, although the Arabs themselves have no musical affinity with the genre. The arabization of qawwali is largely the doing of present-day Pakistani qawwals.

SCENES FROM A SHRINE

Qawwali music has special features which make it distinct from all other north Indian musical forms. These features are directly linked to the basic raison d'etre of qawwali – its religious function. The performers see themselves as entrusted with a religious duty to evoke the name of Allah, and it is their sense of actively performing a religious function that distinguishes qawwals from other north Indian musicians.

Sama is most splendid in its traditional setting, the occasion of a Sufi saint's *urs* (a commemoration of his death and hence his reunion with God) at the shrine of the saint. This is qawwali performed in its true context, and the experience of attending such a performance is a memorable one. The sound system may not amount to much, various background noises add to the texture of the music, the mosquitoes bring their own buzz to the occasion, but the novelty of listening with the stars shining above and the ants crawling below is magical. The whole atmosphere is charged with an inexplicable energy, a rhythmic ecstasy which has the power to render the more sensitive listener unconscious: "I see you, yet I see you not; O you who are totally secret, I sacrifice myself to you." In the words of another song we are advised to think with our hearts and not let reason dictate our activities: "Taste the pleasure of the ecstacy that lies beyond the rational."

Qawwalis may assemble anywhere, but they do so particularly at **shrines** dedicated to Sufi saints, since saints symbolize that nearness to God which the Sufi seeks to achieve in a sama. Although the prime occasion for a qawwali is the anniversary of a saint's death, they are also held on lesser occasions, such as weekly on Thursdays (the day on which Muslims remember the dead), or on Fridays, the day of congregational prayer. In addition to such regular events, spiritual leaders often convene special qawwalis either for themselves or for visiting pilgrims. The Sufi manner of worship is considered heretical by fundamentalist Muslims, who reject the concept of saints or intermediaries as a way of reaching out to Allah.

SOUNDS AT THE SHRINE

Such lyrics as "I have forsaken all and I stand forlorn at your doorstep/Just one glance from you would fulfil my life's dream/Take one look at me, and I'll never look back on the world I have spurned in order to cling to you", move the devotees to tears. Many come to these shrines, notably the shrine of **Khwaja Mohin-ud-din Chishti** in Ajmer, northern India, because they are vexed with life's problems and it's believed that the wishes of those who visit the shrine and listen to qawwali there will be granted. Childless women hope for children, mothers pray for their

NUSRAT FATEH ALI KHAN

••••••••••••••••••••••

Nusrat Fateh Ali Khan is a qawwali superstar, the greatest qawwal of his generation. A gentle mountain of a man who carries a small handkerchief to mop his brow, much in the manner of that other larger-than-life legend, Luciano Pavarotti, he alone is known as Shahen-Shah, the Brightest Star. Helen Jerome was received by him.

Born on October 13, 1948, in Faisalabad, Pakistan, where he still lives, the young Nusrat could hardly avoid music. His father, **Ustad Fateh Ali Khan**, was a famous classical musician and qawwal who sang with his brothers in a legendary "party", or group. But he had different ambitions for his son. He wanted him to be a professional, a doctor, in fact anything except a performer, because he knew only too well how difficult the profession of music could be.

HOOKED ON CLASSES

Nusrat admits that as a small boy he used to spend hours secretly eavesdropping on the classes his father was giving. One day they found him listening and practising, and realized he was already hooked on singing. He was just nine years old.

In 1965, one year after his father's death, Nusrat started singing properly, initially concentrating on classical music. Then he joined the party led by his uncle, **Ustad Mubarik Ali Khan**, whose son Mujahed now sings with Nusrat. His other uncle, **Ustad Salamat Ali Khan**, had taught the keen teenager the art of qawwali.

The performing partnership ended in 1971 after six fruitful years, when Nusrat's uncle Ustad Mubarik died. But the young man pressed

on undeterred, gradually building up a formidable reputation throughout Pakistan. He listened to recordings by his father and his uncles for inspiration, and then created his own style, increasing the tempo very slightly to make the audience more receptive. In short, he updated qawwali to suit the times.

DREAMING OF THE MASTER

Nusrat's recurring dream of performing at a shrine in which no qawwal had ever sung finally convinced him to become a qawwal and follow in his six-century-old family tradition. Latterly, his father had encouraged him by telling him that one day the dream might come true.

He did not know the shrine in the dream was that of **Hazratja Khwaja Mohin-ud-din Chishti** in Ajmer, India, but both his uncles had recognized it from his descriptions. In 1979 the dream became reality when the party were visiting the shrine as pilgrims and Nusrat was the first visiting qawwal invited to sing there.

family's well-being, the unmarried hope for success in love. For any number of human problems looking for resolution, the sounds of qawwali accentuate the believers' pain, yet provide hope and a mood of joyful exuberance which recalls the days when music was used for healing. As each wish comes true devotees return to the shrine for thanksgiving.

Each shrine has a particular group of performers attached to it. Music in India, whether secular or sacred, is a family profession handed down from generation to generation, and the musicians are quite often direct descendants of the original saint, or of members of their spiritual family of followers and devotees. Distinguished visiting qawwals are permitted to perform at the shrines, particularly if they have claimed an affinity with that particular saint. There is a complicated protocol governing the relations between residents and visitors which

---

Above all, Nusrat loves to perform. He says that if an artist isn't enjoying himself then the audience won't enjoy his performance; and conversely his experience of touring in Europe and North America has shown him that people who don't understand the language can still appreciate the music.

"It doesn't need words," he comments. Even though the poems they sing convey the message of the Sufi and the saints, his music, he says, is not exclusively for Muslims but for anyone who believes in God, for music is an international language.

A hefty stack of books filled with both romantic and religious poetry is on hand for each performance. "Aaj Sik Mitran Dee Vadehre Ay" in praise of the Prophet and dating from the fourteenth century is the oldest song in the set, but the members of the party write new songs all the time.

First they select a poem and choose a suitable raag and taal for it. Then they all sit down together and practise it. The process is democratic. If any member disagrees with the shape the song is taking it can be changed. If they feel particularly inspired they may even start composing in concert. And there is no need for rehearsals, explains Nusrat, because they are constantly performing.

BY POPULAR REQUEST

Many of the songs performed at concerts are **requests** from the audience. Like many western artists, Nusrat finds that people demand the same familiar songs again and again, and admits that he sometimes gets tired of one particular song if it's requested all the time. But if he finds that one particular phrase or section of the composition affects the crowd, he will repeat it over and over in order to raise them to a state of ecstasy.

As a song progresses from its long, still, beginning to its compelling heart, Nusrat's hand flies up and out, turns and delicately conducts his watchful Party, who follow and echo his every nuance. As he improvises with impassioned virtuosity they fall silent until he signals for them to re-enter, which they do in powerful unison.

In Pakistan the Party's performance, geared as it is to an audience more familiar with the music, is slightly different. The evening begins with music from the pure classical tradition; later the group moves to light classical music, where the musical rules are less rigorous and there is a greater emphasis on the words. Those in the crowd may fall into a trance as the repeated lyrics and the melody are driven home by the intense, swaying rhythms.

THOUGHTS OF A MASTER

Members of the gathering are often exclusively male. Nusrat emphasizes that this is required by religious tradition. He himself dotes upon his only child, a daughter, but unless a son is born he will probably pass on his singing secrets to his nephew Rahat, currently his pupil singer.

According to Islam women must be housewives, so there are no female qawwals. Nusrat claims that qawwali is very difficult and he believes that women do not possess the stamina to perform it. Besides, the Sufis would certainly not approve. Women may perform secular music, film songs, folk songs, classical raags and ghazals, but religious music is out of bounds for them.

Always ready to try new ventures, in 1991 he collaborated with the American avant-garde/ambient music composer **Michael Brook** to produce the Real World album "Mustt Mustt". A single version of the title track was then remixed, to the consternation of purists, by dance-floor group **Massive Attack,** while Star's cassette release, "House of Shah", a set of remixes by Mick St Clair, has met with great success.

As well as filling a hectic performance schedule at home and in the west, where his popularity is escalating, Nusrat also records whenever there is time. In Pakistan he releases around four cassettes every year, and in Europe the numerous Oriental Star audio- and videotapes quench the thirst of his fans.

settles the question of seniority between different groups of qawwals.

The **Nizamuddin Auliya shrine** in Delhi is a good example of a place where qawwals perform, and its pilgrims include significant numbers of non-Muslims – Hindus, Parsees, Sikhs and Christians. The hereditary qawwali community at this shrine traces its descent to the original singers supposedly trained by Amir Khusrau himself and who are known as *qawwal bachche*, the qawwal offspring.

INITIATION, TRAINING AND PERFORMANCE

A qawwal receives his **training** from his family. Boys are instructed at an early age by their male elders (for women have no part in qawwali singing at any stage). First they are taught the fundamentals of classical music, after which they must memorize the text and tunes of the basic repertoire. Since qawwali is a group song, the young performer has to be initiated into the skills of group singing and assigned his place in the ensemble. Just who becomes a lead singer, a group singer or an instrumental accompanist is determined by musical talent and ability to recall verses swiftly and tellingly, as well as qualities of leadership.

A pupil is not considered capable of performing on his own until he has gained a full understanding of the purpose of his music. This means a thorough background knowledge of Sufi thought as well as experience of actual performance which every young qawwal gains on the job while supporting his elders' performing group.

With the move in the west towards concert hall performances which cater for mass audiences from the Asian communities, qawwali has begun to abandon its traditional form. Such gatherings tend to be spectacular, glittering occasions, usually held in massive halls where the qawwals perform on a concert stage which separates the audience from the performers. This can cause some difficulties. The singers maintain that they need to gauge the mood of their audience in order to persist with certain themes in their songs and to bring in others as appropriate – an impossible task in a darkened auditorium. Traditionalists even argue that the act of sitting upright in a seat physically prevents the listener from gaining those spiritual heights which set the soul soaring, and which are only attainable when seated on the floor, close to and at the same level as the performers. They are usually quick to single out the handful of real devotees or well-seasoned qawwali listeners in the audience, and quite often direct their whole performance towards these "senior" listeners.

The **dialogue** between the audience and the musicians is central to the performance. The performers will often repeat and dwell on portions which strike the right chord in the audience. The impact of vigorous hand-clapping tends to produce a trance-like state described by those who have experienced it as a feeling of flying. **Flight** is also the image used by Sufis to describe their endeavour to achieve union with the divine. In a famous, traditional, untitled poem Khusrau proclaims:

Each dares to leap and cares not who falls.
One soul transported in his spirit's flights
Yet stays confined within the garden's walls,
While others pass beyond the Heavens' lights.

A VISIT TO A MAHFIL

Genuine aficionados usually avoid concert hall performances. Many of them take it upon themselves to arrange smaller, more intimate gatherings or **mahfils** in their homes for an invited audience of "spiritually aware" listeners. Such gatherings are more musically satisfying for the performers as well as the audience, and it is also argued that the giving of *nazar* (a gift), a small amount of money handed to the performers in appreciation of a particular verse, is more easily and spontaneously done in an intimate chamber atmosphere than when scrambling over rows of seats in a large hall.

The tradition of giving nazar is integral to qawwali and dates from the days before recording contracts and overseas tours when it was the musician's main source of income. A successful qawwal with hundreds of recordings and a healthy bank balance to his credit still displays the humble gratitude of a *fakir* when a five-pound note is pressed into his hand in appreciation of his art. In that one moment of accepting a small gift of cash, a wealthy and sometimes world famous and distinguished musician is reminded of his humble duty.

The sama itself has a strict set of rules governing content and running order. The performance gets underway with an instrumental prelude, usually played on harmonium and accompanied by percussion. Once the last strains of the prelude have died away, it is customary to begin the singing, quietly at first, with "Hamd", a hymn in praise of Allah, followed by "Naat", in praise of the Prophet Muhammad. Only after this is it appropriate to sing the praises of Hazrat Ali, by tradition the first Sufi and son-in-law of the Prophet. The song usually performed at this stage is Khusrau's famous "Man kunto Maula, fa Ali-un-Maula" (Whoever accepts me as Master, Ali too is his Master) in "Raag Yaman". Although relatively short, it is one of the earliest and best known of all qawwali songs and it embodies a central tenet of Sufism: that there is an uninterrupted chain of master-pupil relationships that stretches back to the time of the Prophet.

Once these introductory songs have been performed the singer is free to choose from a huge variety of poems set in various raags. Many of them were written by Khusrau or other great Persian poets like Maulana Jalal-ud-din Rumi and Hafez Shirazi, but there are also a large number of Hindi poems in praise of the Sufi saint Khwaja Mohin-ud-din Chisti. A sama is concluded by singing "Rang" (Colour), composed by Khusrau to celebrate Nizamuddin's agreeing to be his teacher. Qawwals and their audiences usually go into a state of *haal* (or pure ecstasy) during the performance of "Rang" – the song evokes a mood of sheer joy and exuberance and it is easy to picture Khusrau's delight on becoming Nizamuddin's pupil.

The songs are usually extended by inserting additional verses called *girahs*. Qawwals normally have a large stock of verses from which they can draw an appropriate girah, which may be in a language different from the main body of the song. The girah should ideally add a fresh perspective to the main verse, thereby enhancing its original meaning as well as adding a dimension to the main poetic idea in a way that enables more and more girahs to be added.

Singers are judged by their ability to add the right girah at the right moment – the more unexpected the better! It is the flexibility that this practice lends to qawwali that makes each performance of a song unrepeatable, a synthesis of ideas and poetic content that belongs to a particular moment, a synthesis in which both performers and listeners have a part to play.

QAWWALI TODAY

Present-day qawwals, notably **Ustad Nusrat Fateh Ali Khan**, who is considered the music's greatest living exponent, have been quick to diversify their performances to match current trends in east–west fusion. One of qawwali's

The Sabri Brothers at the controls

more important elements, *tarana*, has easily lent itself to the development of a **disco/jazz tarana** which can be heard on many of Nusrat's more popularly oriented recordings. Tarana itself was originally a way of expressing esoteric religious ideas in a secret manner by stringing together Persian syllables which made no overt sense but had been given a private meaning. In this way, ideas that were politically risky could be expressed in a code, and these days, although the mystical sense may not be known even to the singer, it is still known to be present whether understood by the listener or not.

Another qawwali group to have gained a worldwide reputation is the **Sabri Brothers** from Pakistan. **Haji Ghulam Farid Sabri**, who died in 1994, and his younger brother **Maqbool Sabri** were particularly noted for their highly original style of rendering well-known numbers from the traditional qawwali repertoire, as well as their distinctive style of percussion. The older Sabri was renowned for the spirituality he brought to the songs, and his periodic refrain of "Allah" between verses became a signature of the Sabris.

A less well known, but old-established family of qawwals, **Munshi Razi-ud-din Ahmed** and his sons, Farid Ayaz and brothers (now based in Pakistan), recently toured the UK and were eagerly received by "hard-core" traditionalists. As yet relatively new to the world of recorded music, the Farid Ayaz Brothers made their mark at numerous mahfils in the homes of discerning listeners who welcomed this return to classical, even antique qawwali as a breath of fresh air in contrast to recent crude attempts at modernization by better-known performers.

Munshi Razi-ud-din Ahmed with Farid Ayaz and Brothers *Songs of the Sufi Mystics* (Namu Cassette, UK). These recordings made live at various mahfils in the UK include a deeply moving rendering of "Baghdadi Sanya" in praise of the Sufi saint Abdul Qadar Gillani. The cassette may be a little hard to find, but it's well worth searching for.

Ⓒ **Nusrat Fateh Ali Khan Qawwal & Party** *Shahen-Shah* (RealWorld, UK). An interesting selection, concentrating on the more popular aspects of qawwali, including romantic poems in Urdu. Ⓒ *The Last Prophet* is his latest release from Real World, beautifully recorded and performed. Nusrat's cassette of dance-floor versions of old favourites, Although Nusrat's music has often been remixed to the current whim of the producer – reggae, hip-hop etc – Ⓒ **Mustt Musst** (Real World, UK) was the one he always wanted to do: a set of bite-sized qawwals given the mainstream pop treatment.

"Nothing without you" and the club friendly title track stand out. *Volume 58 – House of Shah – The Mick St. Clair remixes* (Star Cassette, UK), is odd but totally addictive.

Ⓒ **Sabri Brothers** *Ya Habib* (Real World, UK). The Sabris are perhaps instrumentally more adventurous than Nusrat's party, a shade rougher and more soulful. Their stature in Pakistan is colossal. "Ya Habib" (Oh Beloved) features four long songs. Their cassette, *Greatest Hits of Sabri Brothers Vol. 2* (EMI, Pakistan), features some of the finest of Amir Khusrau's compositions, including "Rang" and "Zehaal-e-miskeen".

Various *Musique de l'Islam d'Asie* (Inédit, France). An unusual compilation that includes a performance of "Naat" by the Nizami Brothers (qawwals at the shrine of Nizammudin Auliya in Delhi), ghazal singer Abida Parveen singing eighteenth-century Sufi poetry, plus the Sabri Brothers singing a "Naat" by Amir Khusrau.

BHANGRA BANDWAGON

ASIAN MUSIC IN BRITAIN

Bhangra is one of World Music's hidden success stories, a sound that has grown from its beginnings as a drum-and-percussion music of field workers in the Punjab to become a modern British-Asian pop music selling cassettes and CDs in the hundreds of thousands, and pulling huge crowds of young movers into glittering discos and concerts. Yet many people have never heard it. Kim Burton and Sairah Awan examine the hype for signs of truth.

Despite the fact that bhangra's name is bandied about as the "next big thing" by music journalists and fashion correspondents, it never appears in the pop charts and only rarely on TV, and reaches the air waves only on a few radio shows, generally on community stations with a local reach. Even the journalists who hail bhangra as a revitalizing force for British music are usually talking about some other sound altogether: it might be rap, reggae, rave or out-and-out pop music in the western style, but as long as it's performed by Asians, preferably wearing turbans, shades, leathers and big trainers – then it must be "bhangra".

This is a long way from the farming communities of the Punjab, the area in the northwest of the Indian subcontinent that was

divided in 1947 between the newly independent India and the newly created Pakistan. The population is mainly Sikh and Muslim, who, as a result of the population movements at the time of Partition, are mostly divided between the two countries according to religion. Here, bhangra was a dance music that was performed during the festival of *bisakh,* the celebration of the end of harvest. The crop being harvested was frequently hemp (*bhang*) and it is from this word that the music derives its name.

Agricultural bhangra was accompanied only by the *dhol,* a large wooden barrel-drum of the type that is found from Nepal to Albania, one head being beaten by a heavy stick, the other by a light switch and capable of decorating a fairly simple basic rhythm by means of complicated cross-rhythms between the hands. It was here that bhangra developed its characteristic loping swing, which has made the transition from drum to drum machine more or less unchanged. The rhythmic groove answered the needs of a dance derived from the movements of everyday life; in this case the movements of a reaper with a scythe.

The dance and its accompanying rhythm eventually became immensely popular throughout the Punjab, and made the move into the towns and cities. Here, around 200 years ago, it abandoned its original role as a festival dance and became a part of popular

THE INDIAN SUBCONTINENT

entertainment. The biggest change was the substitution of the *dholak* for the dhol. The dholak is the most widespread of north India's folk drums, double headed and tapering at each end, and played with the fingers and palms. It is both quieter than the dhol, and capable of more subtle rhythmic nuances above the solidity of the basic. In the hands of a skilled player the beats can follow one another like a magician riffling a deck of cards. The lyrics were light-hearted and playful, as suited a music that was intended as entertainment after the strenuous work of harvest. The subjects were usually romantic, or contained an element of sly humour, as indicated by the presence of such songs as "Sas Kutni" (Wicked Mother-in-law). As well as drums, melody instruments were added. Some, like the simple *alghoza* duet flute and the *thumbi*, a one-stringed fiddle made from a gourd, were from the village; others, like the *santoori* zither, the Indian harmonium and the violin, came from urban or foreign traditions and were soon joined by mandolin, guitar and saxophone. What remained constant were the rhythmic life of the music and a limited set of melodic patterns combined and recombined to form new songs.

By this time bhangra had altered considerably from its rural origins, but the greatest change was yet to come. The transformation of bhangra from a popular local style, rarely heard outside the Punjab, into a modern mass-produced music for second- and third-generation British Asians who have adopted it as their music (whether or not their origins are Punjabi), took place in the late 1970s, kick-started by the release of an album – **"Teri Chunni De Sitare"** by the group **Alaap**.

Alaap was just one of the bhangra acts that was playing at weddings and other events for the Punjabi community in England, and their sound, with violin, accordion and acoustic guitar backed by dhol and tabla was quite traditional. It's clear that young Asians in Britain were looking for ways to assert their identity as members of a large, economically mixed community with little political power. A shared interest in bhangra was one of the things that aided them. Alaap's album, with the title printed on the cover in English, Punjabi and Urdu, gave something for people from disparate origins to share. **Channi**, the band's lead singer, explained, "I came from India in 1976 and discovered that our youngsters did not have anything to identify themselves with, and that Punjabi was not respected. The boys and girls would go to English discos so I

Alaap lead singer, Channi

thought it would be a good idea to bring them back to their roots."

Whether or not Alaap's popularity and the adoption of bhangra as a badge of ethnic pride was as premeditated as Channi suggests, the album had an immediate impact. Melodically fluent, well recorded and imaginatively arranged (the instrumental lines are particularly lovely), it mixed the feeling of traditional bhangra with a far more pop-oriented approach, and was hailed as "the Southall Sound" (Southall is a predominantly Asian suburb of west London). They heralded a new direction, and precipitated the creation of an array of groups, some good, bad and indifferent, and some merely made up of hasty and unskilled opportunists. Alongside Alaap, other worthwhile bands from this era include **Heera**, **Premi** and **Holle Holle**.

The arena in which the new bhangra developed was a specifically British Asian phenomenon known as the **all-dayer** or **day-timer**. Given the strength of family expectations and duties within the Asian immigrant communities, it was difficult if not impossible for young people, particularly girls, to visit the evening clubs and discos frequented by their white and Afro-Caribbean contemporaries. As a result, young entrepreneurs began to set up their own small daytime clubs in the back rooms of pubs or in school halls. Granted, attendance at these clubs sometimes involved playing truant from school but this was, it seems, a less heinous crime than being caught out in dubious company late at night. At first the clubs were simply discos playing reggae and soul, but soon the audience started to request particular bhangra tracks, and the promoters hit on the idea of booking bands to perform a live set, which eventually led to all-bhangra concerts held in halls for up to 2000 people. It was in this period that bhangra acquired the slightly kitsch image of glittery suits and white shoes which has dogged it ever since.

SPOT THE VEGETABLE

The next step was a thorough-going modernization of the sound of the music. A western-style drum kit and synthesizer became de rigueur, while elements of other western popular musics were added to update the sound.

Moody beat masters Achanak

This was not always as successful as might have been hoped; in comparison with "Theri Chunni De Sitare", Alaap's 1991 "Na Dil Mang Ve" is a bit of a mess of soul clichés and heavy-handed kit-drumming, though the band's undiminished melodic gifts are still evident. A better result was reached by the second generation's **Achanak**, who (in their 1989 release "NACHurally") use some synthesizer sounds that hark back to folk instruments as well as some that conjure up images of the big screen, theatrical snatches of salsa and disco that break up the rhythm, and one very effective slow ballad, "Yaadai Tereha" which shows off the voice of lead singer **Vijay**, one of bhangra's best singers. It was this album that featured a rather good competition:

Electro-bhangra: it started here . . .

"Somewhere in this album, Vijay mentions a vegetable. You must identify the vegetable."

Achanak are closely connected with the Birmingham-based **Nachural** label, set up by their tabla player Ninder Johal and responsible for many of today's most interesting developments. One such was foreshadowed in Arishma Record's 1987 release **"Bhangra Fever"**, a set of remixes of tunes by Heera, Holle Holle and Kalapreet laid out over a sequenced drum track with a heavy backbeat. This was really the ancestor of much of the style best represented by the **Safri Boys**, currently the biggest-selling bhangra act and one known for their use of samples and breakbeats in rave style under predominantly Punjabi lyrics.

PROPER BHANGRA

Since bhangra is essentially teenage music with the kind of energy that responds very quickly to changes in fashion and new ideas, the music is in a process of constant change. Members of the first-generation bands argue that it has changed so much since its first popularity in the UK only fifteen years ago that it's no longer right to call it bhangra. Channi from Alaap claims, "I would not class the music in the bhangra charts as proper bhangra because they have lost the Asian touch. Bhangra is when you have more authentic sounds like the dhol and the alghoza. Although in this country the instruments have become modern like synths, I think that the touch, the beat, must be there, because that's how bhangra came into existence – from the beat of the dhol. Bhangra came as a new form of music to this country with us, and I'm afraid bhangra will totally lose its cultural values."

The other point of view is put by Mikha K from the Midlands-based **K K Kings**, from post-industrial Derby, who named themselves in an ironic swipe at the Ku Klux Klan as well as in homage to the five Ks of the Sikh religion, the *kara, kunga, kesh, kachera* and *kirpan* – comb, bangle, long hair, undergarment and sword. "Traditional bhangra story-telling is in a very basic form and does not deal with subversive issues. Our lyrics are more political in comparison with pure bhangra. In some ways we are purists because we also tell stories, but I wouldn't call what we do bhangra, although we work within that tradition. Safri from the Safri Boys is very traditional, but he still gets a kick out of playing with us because of the computers we use. I find the old bhangra lyrics objectionable. We have three women vocalists in the band and we don't sing in the traditional way because it would offend them."

It is a sign of the rapid change in musical culture and social mores to find women and men working together in a band, when it has only been a few years since they have felt comfortable mixing even on the dance floor. **Kuljit Bhamra**'s 1988 "Rail Khadi" was the first track intended to allow girls and boys to dance together, even if the movements required of the dancers were more Hokey Cokey than passionate embrace.

Where the two "generations" differ is in the value that they put on bhangra. Another pioneer, Kumar from the band **Heera**, believes that "bhangra should be reflected in the right way, allowing people something to identify with. Traditional bhangra music is very light-hearted and talks about love and romance." The very aspects that Mikha K objects to are the ones that Kumar believes are central to the music.

Linked with this disagreement is the nature of bhangra as a popular commercial music. **Teenage rebels** in a consumer society are bound to reject the popular music of the previous few years. Young Asians are much more interested these days in breaking into the mainstream market by producing a sound that appeals outside the Asian community without altogether abandoning an Asian identity. Indeed, dance/rap-oriented pop groups like **Fun-Da-Mental** or indie group Cornershop specifically address the problems of the Asian community in Britain in facing racism and losing touch with their roots. They see their identity as Asians both as a fact and as a useful marketing tool, but have very ambivalent attitudes to bhangra as a source or a basis. Aki Nawaz, leader of Fun-Da-Mental, says: "I love bhangra. Pure bhangra is amazing, it's the ultimate in dance music. Our single, "Countryman", was filmed in Pakistan and has pure classical music running through it. There are so many different forms of bhangra. If you look at rap, it'll be different in America, Africa, the Middle East, or Asia. I find bhangra sexist and patronizing to women. Bhangra these days is a weak and more desperate attempt to be commercial. True bhangra music exists in the Punjab – the bhangra music in England is diluted. It's time for new blood to take over." Nawaz's somewhat contradictory statements seem to suggest that the desire to embrace bhangra as a cultural icon is offset by its irrelevance to everyday life. So it tends to get located in a partly imaginary Punjabi past.

Nevertheless, bhangra continues to be popular among Asian youth, and although the daytimer movement – with its bills jam-packed with bhangra stars playing, miming and making "personal appearances" – has lost some momentum it is compensated for by the appearance of bhangra nights at mainstream clubs. At London's Wag Club **Bombay Jungle** plays bhangra and rap for a predominantly Asian audience, while **Asia**, at Plastic People, another central London venue, concentrates even more on bhangra and bhangra/rave fusion of the type that the Nachural label specializes in (their compilation CD "East 2 West" is a good source for those interested in current experiments). In the Midlands, the true cradle of British bhangra, daytimers are still common, but so are club nights in high-profile venues like The Dome in Birmingham.

BIG AS IT WILL GET

Despite repeated predictions that bhangra is poised to break through and become a mainstream music it has consistently failed to do so. Mikha K seems to be right when he says that "at least three-quarters of the bhangra bands sing the same songs. They may be very big on the underground scene, but they won't be big mainstream. Bhangra is as big as it will get."

But other factors are at play apart from creative stagnation. One of the most important of these is the **distribution network** for bhangra records and cassettes. The record companies are small, and the profit margins on sales so tiny that the only retailers willing to take them are those catering to the Asian community who are assured of large sales – and these shops don't make returns to the chart compilers. As a result, a record like the Safri Boys' "Bomb Thumbi", which achieved sales of 20,000, fails to appear in the charts and remains quite unknown to a wider public. A sign that changes may be on the way is given by several recent deals which Asian record companies have struck with the majors. Multitone is now a subsidiary of BMG, and Keda, run by **Kuljit Bhamra**, has a distribution deal with Polygram that stems from the success of his score for the movie "Bhaji on the Beach". Nevertheless, it's still unclear whether the large companies are interested in finding a wider audience for bhangra or simply in acquiring a slice of the lucrative Asian market.

Another problem that bhangra faces is what happens if it becomes more widely accepted as a contemporary music with mass popularity: would it tend to lose its symbolic function as a rallying point for Asians from different backgrounds? The faint undercurrent of hostility shown by many bhangra and other Asian pop artists towards reggae/rap singer **Apache Indian** is quite instructive. Apache Indian, although of Asian origin, has never claimed to be a bhangra singer but uses Afro-Caribbean ragga (rap/reggae fusion) as a vehicle of social protest. Although many of his lyrics deal directly with the position of Asians in British society he is often accused (for example by Aki Nawaz) of being "the acceptable face of Asian people" and of being "more into reggae".

In continental **Europe**, bhangra, although remaining in the World Music fold, has had a greater impact on the sector of the public that follows non-European music. Although not as popular as African and Latin music, its profile is higher than in Britain.

The future of bhangra in one or more of its forms seems assured, although whether it will ever become a widely accepted music that appeals to a public outside its core audience remains doubtful. One thing seems certain, the beat of the dholak and tabla will be filling dance floors for many years to come.

Thanks to Mustafa Awan and Helen Riris for extra information and Rick Glanvill and Satwinder Sehmi for discography faves.

DISCOGRAPHY

Alaap *Teri Chunni De Tare* (Multitone, UK). The album that started it all – and still one of the most imaginative and melodic. Gentler than today's sound but still important.

Safri Boys *Bomb Thumbi* (Roma Music Bank, UK). The Safri Boys, right now the biggest sellers in the bhangra world, are rooted in tradition, but unafraid of samplers, sequencers and heavy-duty grooves.

Achanak *PaNACHe* (Multitone, UK). Bhangra beats fuse with soul. Lead singer Vijay's voice is one of bhangra's finest: he lends it, in the song "Poll Tax", to a rocking good attack on the tax too far which brought about Margaret Thatcher's downfall.

Bally Sagoo *On the Mix* (Mango, UK). "Wham Bam!" mix-master's finest moments, wedding superb vocals from the likes of Nusrat Fateh Ali Khan to dense, imaginative dub.

Chirag Pehchan *Bhangra's Party* (Multitone, UK). Another group with one foot in the past and one in the future. Features the catchy playground anthem "Rail Gaddi".

DCS *Bhangra's gonna Get You* (Multitone, UK). The best bhangra band to emerge in the late 1980s, with a more decadent rock-star image.

Holle Holle *Holle Holle* (Multitone, UK). Vocalist Manjeet is one of the finest in bhangra, and this set includes two stingers: the "Holle Holle" theme and "Ishkaan De Mamle".

Various *East 2 West* (Nachural/Music Club, UK). A budget-priced monster helping of finest modern bhangra – nearly 80 minutes – from Achanak, Anakhi, TSB Golden Star, Saqi and Johnny Zee, among others. If you're not sure whether you like the music, you will be after this.

Various *Ragga Riddim Bhangra Beat* (Multitone, UK). The cultural cross-fertilization that produced Apache Indian: bhangra and dancehall reggae. Apna Sangeet, DCS and Sonia are among the ragga rebels.

FOLK ROOTS OF INDIA

MOUSETRAP AT THE CENTRE OF THE UNIVERSE

Indian folk music is as rich and varied as classical. Jameela Siddiqi and David Muddyman go rooting about – and also discover some good recordings.

There are very many kinds of **Indian folk**, but the main regional strands are the folk musics of Uttar Pradesh, Rajasthan, the Punjab (spread across both India and Pakistan), and Bengal (including Bangladesh). In the northwest Frontier Province of Pakistan, folk music shows a definite affinity with the music of Afghanistan. Kashmir produces its own distinctive folk sound, and the music of many of India's tribal peoples more closely resembles that of southeast Asia or even Borneo than anything else in the subcontinent. Apart from obvious linguistic differences, the folk songs of each region have their own distinct rhythmic structures and are performed on or accompanied by different musical instruments. Some of the classical instruments are used, but the following are mostly associated with less formal folk occasions.

In Rajasthan, music is always played for weddings and theatre performances, and often at local markets or gatherings. There is a whole caste of professional musicians who perform this function and wonderful variety of earthy-sounding stringed instruments like the *kamayacha* and *ravanhata* that accompany their songs. The ravanhata is a simple, two-stringed fiddle that, skillfully played, can produce a tune of great beauty and depth. Hearing it played by a fine street musician behind the city walls of Jaisalmer, it seems the perfect aural background for this desert citadel.

The *satara* is the traditional instrument of the desert shepherds. A double flute, it has two pipies of different lengths, one of which plays the melody while the other provides the drone – rather like bagpipes without the bag. The bag is the musician himself, who plays with circular breathing. Local **cassettes** of these instruments are readily available in small stores across Rajasthan. Just name the instrument you want to hear and they'll pull out some samples for you to audition.

In Kashmir the *santoor zither* (as used in classical music) and the bowed viol – the

Rajasthan – the bagpipe without the bag

sarang – are favoured for indoor performance, while in the open air, the raucous *surnai* oboe (related to the classical shehnai) and the loud, unsubtle *dhol* drum entertain the festival crowds and wedding gatherings. The dhol is a large instrument, played with a pair of sticks and quite often beaten to attract the attention of a crowd immediately before an announcement.

Another drum, the *dholak*, with a fat waist and tapered ends, is made from a hollowed tree trunk. Its two heads are of skin stretched over hoops, and the pitch can be varied by adjusting rings thorough which pass the interlacing cords linking the heads. The dholak is played with the fingers and usually a second player marks time with a ring or small stone on its body.

The **gardha** or *ghatam* is a large earthenware water cooler. Almost spherical, with a short neck and slight lip, it is played with the fingers, sometimes wearing rings to produce a sharper sound.

As well as drums, India boasts a variety of tuned percussion instruments. The most popular in this category is the *jaltarang* – a water-xylophone – consisting of a series of porcelain bowls of different sizes, each containing a prescribed amount of water. The bowls are usually struck with a pair of small sticks, but sometimes these are abandoned as the player rubs the rims of the bowls with a wet finger.

There are also many kinds of **bells and gongs** of which the small brass, dome-shaped cymbals called *manjira* or *taal* are the best known.

FOLK AND FILM

There are songs for all kinds of work and play. Almost every activity is represented in song, and there is an extensive repertoire of dance music. Inevitably, film music has drawn heavily from this folk tradition, but sadly has also become a relatively effortless substitute for most of it. In some instances, "pop" adaptations of traditional folk music have served to revitalize and add a fresh lease of life to the original form – *bhangra*, the folk music of Punjab, is a very good example of this. British "bhangra-rock" has created a fresh interest in the original bhangra of the Punjabi farmers.

Folk music is now beginning to awaken greater interest, particularly with non-Indian record companies, and largely as a result of the growing western interest in different kinds of Indian music. Perhaps this overseas interest has come just in time, for although it is still practised in the old way in more traditional settings and for particular **rituals** – weddings, births, harvest time and so on – folk music on the whole, if it is to be defined as the "music of the people", has largely been eclipsed by the output of the Indian film industry.

Whereas in the past traditional wedding songs would have been sung by the neighbourhood women all through the festivities, it is now more usual to hear film songs blaring away at Indian weddings. Nonetheless, fears that traditional music is vanishing altogether seem unwarranted: in Pakistan the unique sound of the **sohni bands** – clarinet-led brass bands which play at weddings – fills the air with wild melody, and in Rajasthan members of the traditional musicians' castes still make their living by playing at ceremonies and for entertainment. The radio and cassette player are by no means all-conquering.

DISCOGRAPHY

Khamisu Khan *L'Algoza du Sind* Arion, France). Music played on the double flutes, clay pots and drums by the Pakistani master of the endless breath. Hypnotic stuff.

Various *Music Of The Dance And Theatre Of South India / Unesco Anthology of the Orient Vol. 7* (Bärenreiter Musicaphon, Germany). Heavy beats and soulful, exotic voices, but rather roughly recorded.

Various *Rajastan: Musiciens Du Désert* (Ocora, France). Popular music of the Langas and the Manghanyar castes. The Langas play two types of sarangi and a double-piped clarinet or *murali*. The Manghanyar use a smaller type of viol called *kamayacha* accompanied by dholak and castanets.

Various *Inde – Le Bhakti Yoga: Musiques de l'Asie Traditionelle Vol. 18* (Playasound, France). A strange selection of songs in praise of various deities, accompanied by a mixture of string instruments. Sounds oddly like slowed-down qawwali.

Various *Inde/Rajastan/Musiciens Professionnels Populaires* (Ocora, France). A good and varied selection of folk music including solos for the murali and the satara, Manghanyar mar-

riage songs, love ballads and epics. The playing of the one-stringed bhapang on track 11 is one of the most extraordinary things we've discovered while compiling this book. Fearsome glissandos and percussive snaps.

Various *Kashmir Traditional Songs & Dances Vol. 2* (Nonesuch Explorer, US). A lovely folk collection which includes all the major forms of Kashmiri music from Sufi style to folk opera, dance music and *chalant* (a song form).

Various *Songs of the Madmen* (Le Chant du Monde, France). Poetry sung to the sound of some wicked percussion. Not to everyone's taste, perhaps, but how can you resist titles like "There is a Mousetrap at the Centre of the Universe" and "You Came to This World to Play a Game of Cards"? Essential for budding fakirs.

Various *The Garos of the Madhuphur* (Ocora, France). A mesmeric album of song-stories backed by a trumpet which only plays one note, a horsehair fiddle that sounds as though it were still attached to the horse, and counter-intuitive percussion. Great fun if you don't weaken.

THE HILLS ARE ALIVE

MUSIC FROM THE MOUNTAINS AND VALLEYS OF NEPAL

The music of Nepal, either ceremonial and played on trumpets, cymbals, giant drums and ear-splitting shawms or made at home for an evening's entertainment, is as yet very little known outside the country. Carol Tingey, back from another visit, makes sense of it all and suggests some dates and places for music lovers.

Sandwiched between India and Tibet, Nepal is a kingdom of rich diversity ruled by powerful Indo-Nepalese castes, and with a population comprising more than 36 ethnic groups, each with its own language, traditions and music. Indeed, Nepal is a melting-pot of Hinduism, Buddhism, Tantrism and many local religions, each of which has its own brand of sacred music. Although **Tibetan influences** are noticeable in the music of the Sherpas and other peoples who inhabit the high fastnesses of the northern mountains, the rest of the country has a closer relationship with the musical traditions of north India.

One tradition found throughout the country is that of playing a small barrel-drum (the *madal*) to accompany folk songs. In addition to the many traditions of folk and religious music, there is a classical music tradition related to that of northern India, and a genre of "modern" film and radio music, in which Nepalese folk idioms and elements of Hindi film combine to produce a Nepalese national light music.

DIVISIONS OF LABOUR

For the majority of the population, music-making is regarded as a male activity, and female participation is restricted to specific occasions. **Women** of the Indo-Nepalese castes only sing in public on three occasions: during the arduous work of rice-transplanting; while keeping an all-night vigil at a shrine during the annual women's festival (*teej*); and at the all-female wedding party celebrated at the groom's home whilst the men are away at the bride's. An exception is found at the Royal Court, where female **ritual singers** are employed to sing for various Hindu rituals, rites of passage, coronations and festivals. Among the Tamangs

and other hill-dwelling peoples, pairs of men and women duel with one another by singing improvised duets. The loser, if a woman, risks having her hand offered in marriage to the victor.

The **gaine** are a caste of professional musicians who earn their living by wandering from house to house, singing for patrons in return for food. They accompany themselves on hand-carved four-string bowed fiddles (*sarangi*) and have a vast repertoire of heroic ballads in praise of historical and legendary figures, hymns, folk songs and musical anecdotes. Today, many minstrels have stopped wandering in favour of supplying tourists with (somewhat inferior) home-made fiddles.

TAILOR-MUSICIANS AND BLACKSMITHS

For a **wedding** almost anywhere in Nepal a *panchai baja* – a raucous band of shawms, kettledrums and barrel-drums, cymbals and C-shaped horns – is indispensable, so much so that "they got married without panchai baja" is a euphemism for living together. The band

Tailor-musicians prepare for the wedding

accompanies the groom to the home of the bride, plays during the wedding ceremony, and again for the return procession. Apart from playing popular folk songs and film numbers, the musicians, who belong to an "untouchable" caste restricted to tailoring and playing in such wedding bands, have a traditional repertoire of tunes linked to specific moments in the

Beating the hour-glass drum

The make-up of the wedding band varies from place to place. In the Kathmandu Valley, the traditional band has been replaced by western military-style bands played by uniformed bandsmen, and in western Nepal, the musicians wear ceremonial dress and dance as they drum, in ensembles of up to 36 kettledrums. In this area, the tailor-musicians also sing ballads and trance songs, accompanying themselves on an hour-glass drum.

Tailor-musicians are also employed at shrines to play during daily offerings and sacrifices. Temple ensembles consist of large kettledrum, shawm and one or more trumpets or horns of various shapes and sizes.

Nepalese blacksmiths make and play an iron jews' harp, producing a rich gamut of overtones. They play purely for their own amusement, their repertoire consisting of all the local folk songs and current radio and film songs.

KATHMANDU VALLEY DRUMS

The **Newars** were the earliest inhabitants of the Kathmandu Valley. In a traditional Newar community, most young men undergo a ritual apprenticeship in drumming, dancing or singing, which qualifies them to participate in the nightly music-making at their local shrine and to take part in the musical processions around the town during major festivals. Newars are renowned for their spectacular masked dances which re-enact well-known stories of the gods. These dances are accompanied by bands of drums and cymbals. Newar singing has an extremely nasal quality, and as the emphasis is on devotional ardour rather than consistent intonation, uninitiated outsiders find it rather hard on the ears.

A Newar town is never silent. Strolling around a traditional settlement such as Bhaktapur or Kirtipur, particularly at full moon or on festival evenings, you are serenaded from all quarters. On almost every corner there is a group of singers, fervently praising their local deity and accompanying themselves with resonant drums and the metallic shimmering of little cymbals. No sooner does the sound of one die away than the racket of the next group emerges from the twilight. All this takes place against a backdrop of buzzing cicadas, howling dogs and radios insistently playing the latest film numbers.

Newar music is dominated by drumming, against which shawms or flutes may provide a

ceremony; for instance, a "bride-requesting tune" played when the weeping bride is about to depart from her family home, in which the shawm player mimics the bride's wailing.

This type of music is considered auspicious, and is a necessary accompaniment to processions, Hindu rituals and rites of passage. The musicians (and their instruments) need to be thoroughly doused in rice-wine in order to play well; only then are they considered to have the stamina to play continuously throughout the night.

One of the most atmospheric of the events in which panchai baja participate is an all-night vigil at a shrine situated deep in the mountain forests. The bands, which lead processions of devotees with flower offerings or sacrificial goats, resound far across the dark hillsides and can be heard long before the processions come into view. Eventually, tiny dots of light from the pilgrims' lanterns can be discerned approaching from all directions, wending their way down the steep and convoluted jungle paths, as the music gets louder and louder. Suddenly, they burst into the sacred clearing, and the hidden shrine throbs with life and enjoyment.

melodic accompaniment. Drum ensembles come in a great variety of shapes and sizes. Newar farmers are virtuoso performers on enormous cylindrical drums (*dhimay baja*), played en masse with cymbals during festivals. Another popular processional band combines flutes and barrel-drums. At some shrines, in addition to a group of singers accompanied by one or two large barrel-drums and small cymbals, there is a complement of nine drums (*nava dapha*). Each drum is played in turn throughout the course of the ceremony, accompanied by a band of cymbals and either shawms (for the louder drums) or flutes (for the quieter).

The Newars, both Hindus and Buddhists, have a caste system, and some castes have musical responsibilities. The Newar **jogi**, descendants of medieval Indian Hindu ascetics, are ritual shawm players who can be summoned to accompany the drum bands of other castes. Newar butchers have the duty to play their particular drum (*naykhin*) during funeral processions. Newar **Buddhist priests** sing esoteric hymns (*caca*) which, when accompanied by mystic dances and hand gestures, have immense occult power. The secrets of this tradition are closely guarded by initiated priests.

Today, weakened by the rival attractions of cinema, television and video, and starved of money, Nepalese and Newar musics are in a state of decline. Directly visiting them and attending performances and festivals are the only ways to encourage the maintenance of tradition.

THE FESTIVALS

Musically, the best times to visit Nepal are during the major festivals: Newar New Year in the Kathmandu Valley (March/April), Dasain all around the country, but especially in the Kathmandu Valley and Gorkha (September/October); and the Newar festival season in the Kathmandu Valley (August/September).

If you're interested in the sex lives of the gods as well as music, the **Newar New Year Festival** (*Bisket jatra*) in Bhaktapur is the one for you. A glorious two-week celebration of fertility and renewal, it begins with a massive chariot tug-of-war and continues with the erection of an enormous pole and divine procreation all over town. All the local music groups accompany the sexual activities of the deities, as well as playing for them daily. New Year's morning begins early with a musical procession around the town.

MOTHER SITALA

....

The well-known Newar song "Sitala Maju" (Mother Sitala) is addressed to the Goddess of Smallpox. It relates the story of the smallpox epidemic that gripped the Kathmandu Valley during the reign of Rana Bahdur Shah (1777–1806). His wife, Queen Kantimanti, was a victim of the disease, and following her death, Rana Bahdur ordered the banishment from the valley of all children suffering from smallpox. "Sitala Maju" is the pitiful song of a distressed mother:

How did this miserable thing come to pass, Sitala Maju?

The children who were suffering were not allowed to stay.
The child had much to suffer
First funeral music was played, and the soldiers surrounded the children
They had to cross the Tama Kosi River.
How did this miserable thing come to pass, Sitala Maju?

This is the song of a mother, carrying a child on her back.
The food is carried by someone else.
Tears are wiped away by one corner of the shawl.
How did this miserable thing come to pass, Sitala Maju?

A dead child cannot be cremated and cannot be buried.
They must cross the Tama Kosi River.
How did this miserable thing come to pass, Sitala Maju?

The Goddess of Death is Sitala. The Goddess of Survival is Bachala.
And the Goddess that takes them across the Tama Kosi is Sitala Maju.
How did this miserable thing come to pass, Sitala Maju?

The sole King of Nepal Maharaja Bhimsen.
You must rescue the world and the people.
How did this miserable thing come to pass, Sitala Maju?

Not recommended for vegetarians or animal rights campaigners, **Dasain** is a two-week festival in honour of the Mother Goddess in all her manifestations. Her lust for blood is satisfied by thousands of animal sacrifices intended to keep her well disposed during the coming year. At larger shrines the decapitations are accompanied by special sacrificial music, and throughout the season, the Dasain music (*malasri*) is played and sung everywhere, as well as being broadcast on Radio Nepal.

At the end of the rice-transplanting season in August, the Newars of the Kathmandu Valley celebrate a series of **agricultural festivals** – so many that almost every other day is a public holiday. Each festival has a different purpose – to drive away demons, to honour one's deceased family members, to mark the end of the Newar Buddhist time cycle, to ensure the success of the rice, and to stop the rain. The festivals normally involve musical processions around the towns, and are all extremely lively and colourful.

■ DISCOGRAPHY ■

Various *Castes de musiciens au Népal* (Musée de l'Homme, France). Excellent recordings of *damai*, *gaine* and *hudkiya* music, accompanied by really detailed notes.
Various *Folksongs of Nepal* (Albatros, Italy). A pleasant introduction to Tamang folk song.
Various *Folksongs of Nepal* (Lyrichord, US). Folk songs of Newars and Tamangs of the Newar valley, selected for their social rather than their musical value. Good sleeve notes.
Various *Gaines de Hyangjia* (Musique du Monde, France). Although pleasant to listen to, this record is not representative of the gaines' range of repertoire, as it contains only popular folk songs.
Various *Music of a Sherpa Village* (Folkways, US). Folk songs recorded in Helambu, with a typical Sherpa *damien* (lute) accompaniment.

Various *Musique de fête chez les Newar* (Archives Internationales de Musique Populaire, Switzerland). A good collection of recordings made in 1952 and 1953, before things started changing. The notes are detailed, but not entirely accurate.
Various *Musik der Nevari-Kasten* (Klangdocumente zur Musikwissenschaft, Germany). A cross-section of Newar music. Detailed notes in German.
Various *Songs and Dances of Nepal* (Folkways, US). A wide selection of short extracts of folk music from northwest Nepal recorded during a 1959 expedition. Again, informative sleeve notes.

TEAHOUSE EPICS

FOLK AND CLASSICAL MUSIC OF AFGHANISTAN

Afghani music looks west and east, north and south. The classical tradition of Central Asia rubs shoulders with Persian and Indian *ghazal*, while the music of the countryside sometimes sounds Arabic, sometimes Chinese. David Muddyman explains.

On the road in Afghanistan

Afghanistan is situated at the crossroads of Asia, and the three cultures that surround it – Persian, Indian and Central Asian – have all influenced its society and music. Afghanistan's peoples, too, reflect this mix. The majority of Pashtuns, Tadjiks, Balouchis in the south and Hazaras of central Afghanistan all speak a form of the Persian language, Farsi, while the Uzbeks, Turkmens, Kazakhs and Kirghiz in the north are closely related to the Türkic peoples who live across the

border in the former Soviet republics which bear their names.

Despite all these influences Afghan music has a unique sound which evokes the mountainous terrain from which it comes. This is especially true of the songs and music played on the *rebab*, a short-necked lute with a metal soundboard which gives its sound a distinctive echoing quality that conjures up a sense of great space.

The rebab is only one of a bewildering variety of different **lutes**, bowed and plucked, that are used in Afghanistan. There are so many that confusion can arise because the various ethnic groups may use different names for the same instruments – or, conversely, the same name for different instruments.

Wind instruments of the oboe and flute family and drums are the most common instruments otherwise, but the most unusual instrument, the *vaj* or *waji*, comes from the northeast region of Nuristan. This, an arched harp similar to the type found in southern India and Burma, is rarely met with these days but was formerly used to accompany epic poetry.

MEN, WOMEN AND MUSIC

As in many societies, especially Muslim ones, when it comes to music there is a clear sexual demarcation line. Women, traditionally, are not allowed even to handle most of the instruments, and the only ones they're permitted to play are the tambourine and the jew's harp. They occasionally sing, but generally not in public and they rarely turn professional. Men, on the other hand, may play any instrument but generally shy away from the women's instruments.

Before 1950 a **musician's status** was fairly low. Everybody enjoyed listening to music but nobody wanted their son to be a professional. Such fame as musicians had was restricted to a narrow, local circle, and professional musicians relied on weddings, circumcisions and religious festivals to make a living, perhaps performing in the teahouses where they could make a little extra. With the coming of radio all this changed. A musician who performed on air became a national name and was able to charge a much higher fee than before. It was prestigious to have a well-known singer at your wedding. The introduction of multilingual broadcasting in 1972 also helped the dissemination of regional musics, so that people in the south could, possibly for the first time, hear the epic singing of northern areas such as Nuristan.

UNITY IN DIVERSITY

With such a variety of ethnic groups it is not surprising that the range of traditional folk songs is large. Each group has its own particular sound, but each is part of a wider, recognizably Afghani, whole.

The Pashtuns make up the largest ethnic group in Afghanistan and many of them are still nomadic. They have a bottomless passion for epic songs and campfire tales. These epics often carry a moral or social message directed at young and old alike. Urban Pashtuns also have their epic songs, and in addition a form of folk poetry called *landai*, accompanied by harmonium and *tambur*. Pashtuns are enthusiastic dancers, and they use a variety of instruments in accompaniment. One of the most popular dances is the *attan*, a round dance accompanied by the bowed *sarinda*, which represents the women and evokes their emotions, and by the rebab, which does the same for the men. Other, more energetic dances are accompanied by the raucous sounds of the *surnai* oboe and the large drum, the *dhol*. Pashtun folk music, interacting with other musics heard from abroad, forms the basis for a new blend called *kiliwali*, which has been broadcast on the radio all over the country and which is the closest thing to an Afghani "national" music. Kiliwali is performed by professional musicians, and at one time even had its own bevy of stars. But since the Soviet withdrawal and the intensification of the civil war most have vanished or fled.

The largest of the other ethnic groups are the Tadjiks and their linguistic relations, the Uzbeks. **Uzbeki music** can be split into two categories: folk music and the classical music of the Bukharen style. The **Bukharen** style stems from a tradition with its origins outside Afghanistan, in the central Asian towns of Samarkand and Bukhara. The main instrument is a two-stringed plucked lute, the *dutar*, and the music is usually performed in private houses. Uzbeki **folk music** is mostly performed in teahouses and at larger festivals. A typical teahouse group consists of two singers with players on a *dambura* (a long-necked plucked lute with two strings) and possibly a *ghichak* (two-string bowed lute). The singers compete against one other in a mixture of satirical and religious poetry – a form of singing competition found all over Central Asia.

Tadjik culture and folk music have many links with that of the Uzbeks, and Tadjiks are often bilingual in Farsi, their traditional language, and Uzbek. These languages are often mixed in songs where stanzas alternate Farsi and Uzbek. There is also a more recently developed instrumental genre, a sort of suite or medley made up of Afghani pieces heard over the radio,

Singer in exile Ahmed Wali

songs learned from Indian films and Uzbek or Tadjik folk songs native to the area.

The other important popular song form in Afghan society is the *ghazal* (as in Indian light classical style), although Afghani ghazals are melodically simpler than those from the Indo-Pakistani tradition and, since the arrival of Indian films, the ghazal has taken on a new dimension and the pop-ghazal has emerged. **Ahmed Wali**, arguably the greatest living exponent of ghazal, now lives in Germany.

As long as the various factions of the mujaheddin are fighting among themselves to settle the question of who will have ultimate control over Afghanistan, the prospects for music are grim. Many of the best professionals have left the country, while for those who remain, the freedom to perform is subject to the whims of Islamic interpretation of the factions' leaders.

DISCOGRAPHY

The albums listed below, with the exception of Ahmed Wali's, are field recordings with varying sound quality, but all include music of exceptional beauty.

Ahmed Wali *Wali Bahar* (Mimosed, Germany). Soulful and smooth ghazals with backing from a mixture of traditional and modern/western instruments, beautifully recorded. Although it may be hard to find it's well worth persevering. Wali has also released ⓒ *Zendagi* and ⓒ *Dost.*, both on the same label.

ⓒ **Various** *Afghanistan* (Playasound, France). A well-recorded selection of instrumental solos with drum accompaniment. The rebab pieces are especially pleasing.

Various *Folk Music of Afghanistan Vols 1 & 2* (Lyrichord, US). An outstanding selection recorded in the late 1960s which includes several tracks with a flavour of China or Xinjang. Although older and not as well recorded as some, this selection is still well worth investigating.

Various *Inside Afghanistan* (ASV Records, UK). Three types of music are highlighted on this album: hypnotic dance music performed on the *ghichak* (bowed lute) and *zeir baghali* (gob-

let drum); extremely noisy dance music for surnai and dhol; and beautiful unaccompanied songs from Abdul Kadar. Relatively easily available.

Various *Music of Afghanistan Unesco Anthology of the Orient Vol. 3* (Bärenreiter Musicaphon, Germany). A well-documented choice of music which displays a wide variety of styles.

Various *Music from the Crossroads Of Asia* (Nonesuch Explorer, US). Mainly ensemble music performed by members of the Radio Afghanistan Orchestra, who mix folk songs and ghazals, with religious and folk poetry. A wonderful selection.

Various *Music from Kabul* (Lyrichord, US). A good cross-section of styles from the early 1970s. The recording quality leaves a lot to be desired but a beautiful duet for rebab and dhol makes it worth buying. Also includes ghazals, a wedding song and several other duets.

ⓒ **Various** *Songs of the Pashai* (King, Japan). Folk songs of the Pashai people from the ethnomusicological Japanese label. Japanese notes.

WEST AFRICA

There are few areas of the world that can match the range of rhythms, melodies and musical textures of West Africa. From Senegal's dramatic *mbalax* to the lilting highlife guitar sounds of Ghana, from the soaring Manding music of Mali to the pounding percussion of Nigerian *fuji* and *juju*, the region steams with good sounds. Plenty of fans swear blind that West Africa is the home of the blues, of reggae, even the fundamental spiritual nursery of rock. It's true that the core of much of what's taken for granted as "western" popular music derives at least partly from West Africa through the 500 years of the transatlantic slave trade and its aftermath. If you have the good fortune to travel there, you can hardly fail to come back with a medley of tunes in your head, and probably a pile of tapes in your luggage. It's a World Music hothouse.

The region consists of fifteen countries. Apart from Liberia, which has been technically independent since the early nineteenth century (not that 150 years as an American vassal state has helped the Liberians much), the four anglophone countries – The Gambia, Sierra Leone, Ghana and Nigeria – share a British colonial inheritance. The Cape Verde islands and Guinea-Bissau threw off Portuguese rule in 1975 but socio-economically their links to Paris are now as close as to Lisbon. The rest – Senegal, Mali, Guinea, Burkina Faso, Niger, Togo, Benin and Côte d'Ivoire – were part of France's colonial empire and, culturally, they still tend to look to Paris before their neighbours, viewing the French metropolis as their true capital. The old colonial ties, surprisingly resilient to more politically correct pan-African ideals, divide the music scene predictably into two major spheres of influence, dominated by London and Paris.

Many of the great names of West African music have had a good airing in the last decade and the countries and styles covered in this chapter are those that have had most impact outside West Africa: But where to start?

Manding music, the historically rich repertoire of much of Mali and Guinea, has been enormously successful overseas. Many from the traditional caste of musical storytellers, the *jali*, have become internationally renowned and perhaps a couple of hundred CDs are already available, not to mention countless thousands of locally produced tapes. Salif Keita, from Mali, found a global market for his haunting voice and unforgettable compositions, while Mory Kanté from Guinea took electrified kora to the dance floors of Europe. The special feature on Malian Ali Farka Touré takes account of his unique musical personality and pivotal, cross-over role.

The music of Senegal and The Gambia has produced some of the biggest World Music stars, including the hugely influential and talented singer Youssou N'Dour – now firmly established on the international festival circuit – and the more politicized, conservatoire-trained, Baaba Maal.

Osibisa from Ghana and King Sunny Ade from Nigeria had already prepared the way for their countries' musical exports when the tag "World Music" was devised in the late 1980s. While less has come out of those two countries in the last decade than from French-speaking West Africa, their contribution to the African musical pantheon is a major one. A delightful variety of highly accessible music – and much more on CD than might be imagined – awaits the true explorer.

This chapter also features the little-known island nation of Cape Verde, which has a number of musical styles varying from mournful sentimentality to upbeat danceability. And there are smaller features on the Abidjan music industry, Sierra Leone, Guinea-Bissau, Benin and a profile of the influential producer Ibrahima Sylla.

Throughout West Africa, the areas with strong traditional states – such as Mali, Ashanti and Yoruba-land – tend to be those with the most vigorous output of popular music. In many parts strong Islamic influences run through both lyrics and vocal inflections, while church choirs have been the training ground for countless young singers in Christian areas. Indigenous instruments of all kinds have mixed with imported ones, especially guitars and accordions. Modern state support has been important too: in Mali and Guinea in the 1960s the presidents of the newly independent nations actively encouraged musical achievement and instituted government support for musicians.

A theme which runs right through this chapter is the question of rights and duties as a musical performer. Many, if not most West African cultures have traditionally held ambiguous views about musicianship – a somewhat sleazy, even demeaning, trade on the one hand; an enviable social skill, accompanied by potentially large earnings and huge powers of influence on the other. In some areas, the profession of praise-singer or musician is an inherited one and people with certain names have the right to perform while others are discouraged from doing so. Although this system is breaking down fast, the traditional values which underpin it are still present. West African musicians have the ears of the most powerful men (and they are usually men) in the region. A critical song is highly influential, and any music which brings established values into question can do as much to change society as the rock'n'roll revolution in the west.

NAMES, SPELLINGS AND TONES

None of West Africa's 200-plus languages have indigenous written forms. While many are now written, the rules of spelling reflect the colonial power. The same common, Manding, name can be spelt Jallow in The Gambia or Sierra Leone, Diallo in Mali or Senegal and Djaló in Guinea-Bissau. Diabaté is often seen as Jobarteh, Touré as Touray, and so on. But there is little consistency and artists' names are often spelt in different ways. The French liked to insert apostrophes where their language would disallow two adjoining consonants – hence the confusing N'Dour. In the francophone countries, accents are included or omitted very much at the will of the writer. We've tried here to be consistent with each individual. But there are evidently no rules. The situation is further complicated by the use of a number of letters from the international phonetic alphabet in the anglophone countries (though not in this book). It's worth knowing also that many languages are to some degree tonal – which means that the meaning of a word can depend on the pitch of the voice in pronouncing it – posing interesting challenges for musicians, and leading to the most fantastic talking drum conversations, especially in Yoruba juju music.

WEST AFRICA ✈ GLOSSARY

Agidigbo Yoruba dance rhythm from Nigeria, named after the thumb piano.

Apala Yoruba style of heavy, talking-drum percussion from Nigeria.

Asonko Ghanaian ensemble of large, log xylophones.

Bajourou Style of light, rhythmic and melodious songs from Mali.

Bala/Balafon Eighteen- to 21-key xylophone found widely in West Africa and often written misleadingly "balaphone" (NB *balafo* means "to play the *bala*").

Batuco Traditional Cape Verdean rhythm of slaves.

Berimbau A Cape Verdean plucked bow which uses a separate calabash, or player's mouth, as a soundbox.

Bolon/Bolombata Three- or Four-stringed Manding bass harp.

Cavaquinho Four-stringed Portuguese instrument like a ukulele used in Cape Verde.

Cimbó Cape Verdean single-stringed "spike fiddle" with a small calabash soundbox played with a deep bow.

Coladeira Upbeat Cape Verdean dance rhythm.

Didadi Dance rhythm from Wassoulou in Mali.

Djembe Senegambian single-headed goblet-shaped drum.

Donsongoni Six-stringed hunter's harp from Mali and Guinea.

Dundun Nigerian Yoruba drum.

Finaçon Cape Verdean improvised song style.

Flé Calabash strung with beads from Mali.

Funana Old dance style from Cape Verde.

Funacola Cape Verdean cross between *coladeira* and *funana*.

Fuji Popular Nigerian Yoruba percussion and vocal style.

Gonggong/gangan Nigerian Yoruba talking drum.

Griot Generic term for a West African oral historian-cum-minstrel (the feminine is *griotte*) commonly used in French and probably a corruption of the Fula word *gawulo*.

Gudugudu Small, Yoruba kettledrums from Nigeria.

Highlife Good-time dance music of English-speaking West Africa.

Hoddu Fula lute from Senegambia, like a *ngoni*.

Jali Manding tem for *griot* (see above).

Jalimuso Female *jali* (French spelling: *djelimousso*) (plural: *jalimusolu/djelimoussolou*).

Juju Popular Nigerian Yoruba music style.

Kamalengoni Six-stringed youth's harp from Mali and Guinea.

Konin/Konting Mandinka lute, like a *ngoni*, from Senegambia.

Mbalax Wolof music popularized by Youssou N'Dour.

Morna Mournful Cape Verdean blues-type song.

Ngoni Three- to five-stringed Bamana or Maninka guitar/lute, from Mali and Guinea, precursor of the banjo.

Ndjarka Single-string Songhai fiddle with a calabash soundbox, from Mali.

Osibisaba 1930s Ghanaian dance rythm.

Osode Ghanaian beat based on a traditional, recreational dance.

Palm-wine Acoustic guitar style from English-speaking regions.

Sabar Large, free-standing Senegambian drum.

Sakara Small clay and bamboo drum from Nigeria; also the eponymous music style, precursor of *fuji*.

Tama Senegambian talking or variable-pitch drum.

Tchinkoumé Funereal water-calabash percussion from Benin.

Ventilateur Senegambian Wolof women's dance.

Viola Twelve-stringed Cape Verdean tenor guitar.

Violão Cape Verdean (or Portuguese) term for guitar.

Waka Nigerian Yoruba music style performed by women

Xalam Three- to five-stringed Wolof lute from Senegambia.

MUSIC CREATED BY GOD

THE MANDING JALIS OF MALI, GUINEA AND SENEGAMBIA

Bamako, the capital of Mali, is a dusty town that hugs the bank of the Niger River. There's one small recording studio and precious few venues for live music, yet it is one of West Africa's most musical cities. Music is as much a part of Bamako's scenery as the neo-Sudanic architecture, the haze of red dust and wood smoke, the pervasive smell of incense, and the silvery waters of the Niger. Lucy Duran paints an intricate panorama of one of Africa's oldest and most absorbing musical worlds.

Music wakes the city up. At 5am, the cries of the muezzin from the mosques – "God is great!" – echo through each other across town in a kind of random counterpoint. Women begin the food preparation for the day and the rhythmic beat of millet-pounding thuds out from every compound, mingling with the music on Radio Mali's morning programme – haunting Bamana sounds, soaring Manding voices accompanied on electric guitars, and punchy rhythms from Wassoulou.

Drive through the city on weekends, and you're bound to come across a wedding party – a crowd of vibrantly dressed women sitting in a semicircle under an awning stretched across the street, with, at one end, an ensemble of electric guitars, ngoni lute, and one or more women singers, belting out their latest arrangements of classic Manding tunes through massive amps.

At night, when the dust settles from the pot-holed streets, the fires for cooking are extinguished, and the air is transparent and soft, Bamako resounds to the voices of a host of Malian singers played through a thousand ghetto-blasters and taxi cassette decks. Malians love their own music more than anything, and for sheer beauty of melody, few traditional musics rival it.

LANGUAGE AND MUSICAL CULTURE

The closely related **Manding languages** (part of the big Mande group) are spoken by peoples who trace their ancestry to the Manding Empire, based around the capital of Kaba (Kangaba) in western Mali from the early thirteenth century to the late fifteenth century. It was founded by a warrior prince, Sunjata Keita, who remains one of the most powerful symbols in Manding culture. The epic song "Sunjata" is still today the most important song in every traditional musician's repertoire.

The most important Manding languages are: Maninka, spoken in the Manding heartland of western Mali and eastern Guinea; Bamana (or "Bambara"), spoken in central Mali and also Mali's lingua franca; and Mandinka, spoken in The Gambia, southern Senegal and Guinea-Bissau, which is the most different, being about as close to Bamana as Spanish is to Italian. The terms Maninka, Bamana and Mandinka are often used interchangeably by outsiders. But to the Manding way of thinking, each language also defines a musical style, with different repertoires, vocal delivery, lyrics and tunings and preferences for certain instruments.

Maninka represents the most classical musical style of Manding – the style of Ami Koita and Salif Keita, characterized by a medium tempo, very ornamental melodies over static harmonies, and sweet, long, flowing vocal lines. Dance is an important part of Maninka style, and women are the preferred singers. The *ngoni* lute is the traditional accompanying instrument, along with the *tama* and *doundoun* drums. Maninka is also the style of eastern Guinea, epitomized by the music of singers like Sekouba Bambino Diabaté. In Guinea the rhythms may be a little faster, and the music seems to float, with the vocal lines more "sing-song" and with more harmonic changes, creating a circular, rippling effect. The guitar has been the favourite instrument in Guinea since the late 1940s, and is also widespread in Mali.

Bamana music is noticeably different from other regional styles of Manding music except for Wassoulou, with which it shares many features, especially a five-note (pentatonic) scale. Bamana melodies are stark, and tend to be in slow tempo, linking it more closely to music of the northern desert regions. The best-known traditional singer of Bamana music is Fanta Damba. Bands that have specialized in it include the Super Djata Band and Super Biton de Ségou, Mali's oldest dance band.

The music of the **Mandinka** people of Senegal and The Gambia also has a very distinctive style and a favoured instrument – the *kora*. Mandinka is partly influenced by the music and dances of neighbouring non-Mande peoples like the Wolof and Jola (also spelled Diola and not to be confused with the Jula or Dioula of Côte d'Ivoire). Mandinka music, as performed for example by Dembo Konteh and Kausu Kouyaté, is lively, highly syncopated and hard-driving. Men do most of the singing, and their voices are usually high-pitched and very nasal.

With independence in the 1960s, the new political structures, plus radio, television and the advent of a thriving local cassette industry, as well as the opportunities for performing and recording abroad and exposure to different styles of music, have inevitably brought about many changes in Manding music. The most exciting developments were the creation of **dance bands** like the Rail Band in Mali, Bembeya Jazz in Guinea and Ifang Bondi in The Gambia, who gradually began to draw more and more on their own traditional music.

After two decades of a flourishing home-based industry, the scene in the 1980s began to shift towards the cities with the big recording studios: Abidjan, Dakar and, inevitably, Paris. Consequently, the most successful dance bands, especially from Mali and Guinea – countries that were undergoing severe economic and political difficulties – moved abroad. The involvement of

Mory Kanté – from Rail Band to world stage

international record companies with the music of such artists as Salif Keita and Mory Kanté has given Manding music worldwide exposure. At the same time, it has meant that other Manding musicians have been forced to cultivate a purely local market. But because of the lack of recording studios and an infrastructure to support dance bands, the local market was left open for traditional music.

In the 1990s, the dividing line between acoustic and electric is fine. Increasingly popular in Mali and Guinea are small, **semi-acoustic ensembles** featuring traditional instruments combined with electric guitars and a drum machine. Many musicians play in both acoustic and electric bands. But there is a perceived difference between "modern" (pop or dance-band music) and "traditional" Manding music. The dance bands include horns, and are fronted by men, not women singers, and they play at clubs, restaurants, and hotel foyers; whereas "traditional" music – even if it involves electric instruments – is usually fronted by women and is played at private parties for weddings and naming ceremonies, or at public concerts, but not at clubs.

Common to all Manding music is its virtually exclusive performance by a caste of professional musicians – the *jalis* – whose musical art is called *jaliya*.

THE JALIS

Traditionally, Manding society is hierarchical. At the top are the nobles or freeborn (*horon*), descended from Sunjata Keita and his generals and considered socially superior to the casted professions (*nyamakala*), which include hereditary musicians as well as blacksmiths and leatherworkers. Traditionally, the castes are expected to marry within their caste and even in the 1990s those born into a jali family are regarded as jalis whether or not they have ever touched an instrument or sung a note. The nyamakala are allowed to intermarry within the different castes, but marriages between jalis and horon are rare even today.

All the casted professions have their own **surnames**. For example, the Kantés are blacksmiths (though many are also musicians), and the Kouyatés are exclusively jalis. The surnames Diabaté (spelt Jobarteh in English), Koné, (a variant of Konté), Sissokho or Cissokho (with variants Suso in The Gambia, and Damba and Sakiliba for women), Kamissoko, Soumano, Dambele and Sacko are also commonly though not exclusively found among jalis.

Until the end of the nineteenth century, when the French put an end to traditional kingship, substituting it with chieftancies, the jalis were attached to the royal courts. They entertained the nobility with their epic songs and stories about the major events in Manding history. They guarded the knowledge of genealogies and the complex "praise names" attached to every surname.

Although their status is not as high as the freeborn, jalis are highly respected for their skills, not just as musicians and entertainers, but as trusted messengers and advisors. The jali is considered lower on the social scale because, as the late Gambian kora player Jali Nyama Suso explains, "a member of the nobility will not talk freely to someone of the same class, who might be a rival, whereas musicians can be trusted because they are no threat". They have played a vital role in Manding history: "They're journalists, they interpret events of now and of the past", he remarks. "The art of the jalis lies in their ability to praise, which gave our kings the courage to fight battles." Indeed, battles could be won or lost by the sheer power of the jali's word. Nowadays, they may sing for politicians or businessmen instead of kings, but they function in very similar ways. Their gift of speech has made them ideal "go-betweens" – they patch up quarrels and feuds, arrange marriages, and negotiate the most delicate economic and political matters. In the words of Toumani Diabaté, one of Mali's most brilliant young kora-players, "They are the needle that sows."

The jalis operate like a closed trade union, and guard their profession with jealousy. Until recently it was difficult for a non-jali to take up music as a profession, and in practice very few have done so. One of the best-known exceptions is Salif Keita, a noble by birth who chose, against his parents' wishes, to sing professionally and makes it clear that he is an artist and does not have the specific social obligations of the jali.

Some Wolof musicians trace their ancestry from Manding. In Siné-Saloum, a region in Senegal just north of the Gambia River, most of the older traditional musicians include the classic Manding songs in their repertoire and even sing partly in Maninka. Senegalese superstars Youssou N'Dour, who is Wolof, and Baaba Maal, who is Tukulor, have both recorded versions of many well-known Manding tunes.

There are many versions of how jalis originated. Some musicians recount how a certain Sourakata, while mocking the Prophet Mohammed in disbelief, was frozen in his tracks three times.

THE WOMEN SINGERS

Since independence, the most consistent stars of traditional Manding music have been the **jalimusolu** – the famed women jalis. With their bleached skins, magnificent gowns and gold jewellery, the jalimusolu are the closest thing to superstars in Mali. Their flamboyant personalities and independent life-styles have made them the subjects of intense, often malicious, gossip. "It's brought us many problems from jealousy and intolerance", says **Ami Koita**, "but personally I have had no choice but to go ahead anyway; this is my destiny."

One of the first women singers to become extremely popular after independence was **Fanta Sacko** from Kita, whose only album was released in the 1970 series "Anthology of Malian music". She called her style *jamana kura* (meaning "new age") – light, rhythmic and melodious songs with love lyrics, accompanied on two acoustic guitars in non-standard tunings, with a capo high on the neck, imitating the kora and the insect-like sound of the ngoni. Referred to in Bamana as *bajourou*, this represents the most popular trend of guitar-based music in Guinea and Mali since the 1970s. Her most famous song, "Jarabi", first appeared on the album, and has since been recorded in dozens of cover versions by most of Mali's best-known artists. Apart from being a beautiful minor-key tune, "Jarabi" was a local hit because of its lyrics, which advocate passionate love above all other feelings. They made a huge impact in a society in which most marriages are more or less arranged:

> Love is an illness no doctor can cure.
> Wait for me, my love, for I cannot live without you.
> Loves knows no father, no mother,
> no brother or sister.
> Love is blind and deaf to all this.
> What counts alone is what you have said to me.

In many ways Fanta Sacko paved the way for a whole new generation of Mali's women singers. But she paid bitterly for her fame when in the early 1980s she burned herself with skin bleach (many Malian women singers, still believe that pale skin is a shortcut to success). And she was never paid for her record, still sold on bootleg cassettes.

Probably the most respected of all the jalimusolu was the late **Sira Mory Diabaté** from Kangaba, an imposing, nearly blind woman with a moving alto voice, and composer of several famous songs such as "Bani" and "Sara". Unlike many of today's jalimusolu her voice is low-pitched and leisurely, her lyrics more moralistic than praising. In "Sara", a tune later made famous in a stunning arrangement by the Guinean band Balla et ses Balladins, she sings, "Sara ("popularity") is not sung for those who have money, sara is sung for those who keep their word." Sira Mory had uncompromising principles: she was favoured by President Modibo Keita but neglected by his successor Moussa Traoré because she did not sing praise songs for him.

The first Malian jalimuso to tour Europe as a solo artist, in 1975, was the Bamana singer from Ségou, **Fanta Damba**, who sings in the cool, classic Bamana style of Ségou, accompanied on ngoni, kora and guitar. Her voice became something of a cult, much admired by musicians such as Youssou N'Dour, whose song "Wareff" was a reworking of material from her album "Sidi Mohammed Sacko".

Another of the finest women singers of the 1970s was the Guinean **Kadé Diawara**, "the Archangel of Manding". She has a typically Guinean, open-throated, liquid-sounding voice. In the 1980s she stopped singing after a nervous breakdown – the result, so it was said, of witchcraft directed at her by rival singers – but in 1992 she made a strong comeback with her cassette "Kadé Diawara l'Éternelle", with a semi-acoustic backing ensemble.

Tata Bambo Kouyaté, praise singer extraordinaire

After the third demonstration, he realized the power of the prophet, and his taunts became praises. From then on, the principal role of the jali has been that of "praise singer".

The jalis traditionally make their living on the generosity of patrons (*jatigui* in Bamana and Maninka; *jatio* in Mandinka, literally meaning "host"). In precolonial times, the patrons were kings (*mansa*), or otherwise members of the freeborn including farmers, traders and *marabouts* – Muslim holy men. Until the time of independence (when jalis were first employed as part of government-sponsored ensembles) they were never paid as such but instead received gifts, sometimes of extraordinary generosity, which might include land, animals, a house, cloth, gold, wives and slaves. Still today, the jalis praise their patrons with phrases like "the hundred-giver" (*kemenila*), meaning someone who gives one hundred of something.

Patron and jali have a close, trusting and mutually dependent friendship. In precolonial times, if the jatigui died, the jali might even commit suicide. *Lanaya soro man di* – "It's not easy to find a trustworthy person" – is a constant refrain of Manding songs, reminding both jali and patron of their duty of loyalty to each other. Those who consider themselves patrons rely heavily on the advice and diplomacy of their jali. The presidents of Mali, Guinea, The Gambia and Senegal have had thousands of songs dedicated to them. But while the jalis are praise-singers, their relationship is not based on deference. In the words of Jali Nyama Suso, "I may have patrons, but no-one is my boss."

REPERTOIRE AND STRUCTURE

Despite its different regional styles, Manding music is unified by a basic repertoire of songs that dates back to precolonial days and which is common to all the Manding regions. It serves as the core or "classical" repertoire, performed for special occasions such as the reroofing of the sacred hut in the old capital of the Manding empire, Kangaba, every seven years. The most important songs in this repertoire are "Sunjata Faso" (which has many variants), "Lambang" which is one of the oldest songs in the repertoire, in praise of music (*O, jaliya-o, Allah le ka jaliya da*: "Ah music! God created music"), and "Tutu Jara", a song composed for an eighteenth-century Bamana king of Ségou. The melodies of these songs are used over and over again in different arrangements and with new lyrics. Older singers such as Fanta Damba and even Tata Bambo Kouyaté use "Lambang" and "Tutu Jara" as the basis for virtually all their music.

Other often-played songs which are common to all the Manding regions are "Koulanjan", a song in praise of hunters; "Duga" a slow, minor key song in praise of warriors; "Tara", in honour of the nineteenth-century Muslim Fula leader Cheikh Omar Tall; and "Sori", in honour of the nineteenth-century freedom fighter Almami Samory Touré and his brother Ibrahima (nicknamed Sori) who was a passionate devotee of music.

Younger singers tend to use newer, more specifically regional songs. Many date from this century. Favourites are the Gambian kora song "Alla l'aa ke"; "Kelefa" and "Jula Jekere" (as on Baaba Maal's album "Baayo"); as well as the Malian songs "Kaira", "Jawura" (a song and dance from Kita) and "Apollo" – a song named after the Apollo space missions, and also the name for a style of dress fashionable in the late 1960s. A recent version of this can be heard on Sekouba Bambino Diabaté's beautiful 1992 semi-acoustic album "Le Destin" (on World Circuit) in the opening song "Ka Souma Man", in praise of tailors.

All these songs, whether in purely traditional versions, semi-acoustic, or accompanied by a full electric dance band, tend to follow the same structure. The singing is divided into two sections, a choral refrain or *donkili* which is precomposed and the improvisation.

The vocal improvisations are formulaic, consisting mainly of praising family surnames and reciting their ancestors. Every family name has an epithet or *jammu* which tells something of its origin. The name Musa, for example, is praised by saying "Jealous and able Musa, four-eyed Musa; Bala, the adventure-seeking Musa", which were the praises for Musa Molo, last king of the Mandinka, who died in 1931. The Tourés are "The holy nobles from Manding" and praised with the name Mandjou. There is a small repertoire of songs in praise of specific jali family names – for example "Tessiry Magan" on Kasse Mady Diabaté's album "Kela Tradition" (Stern's) is dedicated to the Kanoutés.

Proverbs and pithy sayings are also important. The lyrics are quite moralistic, warning against betrayal, hypocrisy and obsession. Saws like "Silver and gold cannot buy a good name" litter lyrics as they do conversation. Even Youssou N'Dour, who doesn't speak Bamana, used the well-known jali cliché "Saya Man Nying" (Death is Ugly) as the title for a ballad on his vol. 11 cassette.

Often the songs are directed at a single person. In the opening lines of a song by Kandia Kouyaté, which she recorded in 1986 for Zoumano, one of her main patrons, she sings many of the standard jali phrases:

> *Eh Yammaru [the brother of Sunjata Keita], eh war!*
> *Zoumano, the hundred-giver,*
> *Kandia Kouyaté is singing for you.*
> *Don't force me to become someone else's jali,*
> *The life of a jali patron and that of someone with no jali*
> *Are not to be compared.*
> *Cool down the instruments!*
> *Don't let the music make me lose my head!*
> *Betrayal is bad,*
> *And so is obsessive thinking.*
> *The hundred-givers have not vanished completely,*
> *But there are certainly very few left.*

She then goes on to recite the names of all Zoumano's family as well as his ancestors and all his deeds of generosity towards her and other jalis.

The instrumental accompaniment of the Manding repertoire is a two- or four-bar phrase. This riff, as in jazz or blues, serves as the basis for improvisation and provides the framework for the song. The accompaniment is called "the main way" or "big meeting", and the variations are known in Mandinka as *birimintingo*, an onomatopoeic word imitating the sound of the kora strings, and in Maninka as *teremeli*, meaning "to bargain" – in other words, to take the notes higher and lower.

INSTRUMENTS

By far the most popular of the three traditional instruments of the jalis is the **kora**, which is a cross between a harp and a lute with 21 to 25 strings. Unlike the other Manding instruments, the kora traditionally is not played by any other ethnic group. Although some of the most famous kora players are from Mali, the kora itself is said to come originally from the area which is now Guinea-Bissau.

One of the oldest and most prestigious of the Manding instruments, formerly played to entertain kings, is an oblong lute which has three to five strings, a resonator carved from a single piece of wood, and a skin sound table. In Bamana and Maninka it is called **ngoni**, in Mandinka *konting*. This instrument is also played by griots from other peoples such as the Wolof, who call it *khalam* (*xalam*) and the Fula and Tukulor, who call it *hoddu*. As an instrument type the earliest examples known are from ancient Egypt and it can be found throughout the West African savannah. The Moroccan traveller Ibn Battuta, who visited the court of Mali during the reign of Mansa Musa in 1352, described such an instrument, embedded with gold and silver. West African slaves re-created this instrument in the New World, where it came to be known as the banjo. Today, the ngoni – which is technically quite difficult to play, and also a very quiet instrument – is not often heard in Senegal and The Gambia, though it is still extremely popular in Mali and Guinea, where it is usually played with an electric pick-up as accompaniment alongside acoustic and electric guitars. The electric guitar, played with almost exactly the same technique as the *ngoni*, and often with a variety of unusual tunings, has become the ubiquitous Manding instrument.

Another instrument reported by Ibn Battuta at the fourteenth-century Mali court was the **xylophone**, called *bala* or *balafon* in Maninka. The bala usually has 18 to 21 keys cut from rosewood, suspended on a bamboo frame over gourd resonators of graduated sizes. It is played

ENSEMBLES AND BALLETS

●●●●●●●●●●●●●●●●●●●●●●●

In **Mali's** early days of independence, traditional Manding music was given a major boost through government-sponsored ensembles who performed for state functions. Mali's first president, Modibo Keita, founded the **Ensemble Instrumentale** in 1961, under the directorship of his former classmate Nfa Bourama Sacko (father of the guitarist Bouba Sacko, one of Bamako's leading guitarists in the bajourou style). In its 1970s heyday, the ensemble was a powerhouse of traditional music, the training ground for many of Mali's finest singers including Tata Bambo Kouyaté, Fanta Damba, Ami Koita, Sali Sidibé and Coumba Sidibé. By the late 1980s, lack of funds had forced most of the best musicians to leave, and the ensemble was disbanded in 1991 with the overthrow of the dictatorship.

After **Guinea's** fraught independence in 1958 (the country had said "No" to continued economic links with France), its first leader, Sekou Touré – a Manding of aristocratic ancestry – introduced a nominally Marxist regime and placed major emphasis on indigenous music in his cultural policy. He founded a National Ensemble and encouraged the formation of national and regional orchestras, who were expected to draw on local traditions. In most cases, the music was Manding. Sekou Touré also arranged state backing for soldier-poet Keita Fodeba's dance company, **Les Ballets Africains**, one of West Africa's first and most successful ballet companies.

Keita (in Guinea surnames are usually put first) had studied in Dakar and Paris and his ensemble brought together musicians from other African countries and featured Kanté Facelli, who adapted traditional Manding instrumental styles for the Spanish guitar. The Ballets made a number of popular recordings in the 1950s and went on to do several world tours on a grand scale. But the overseas travel aroused Sekou Touré's paranoia and, in 1969, Keita, who was close to the leadership and by now Minister of the Interior, was arrested and murdered in Camp Boiro, the notorious prison that he himself had built. The incident was a significant marker in Sekou Touré's bloody career and a reminder of the uneasy links between the Manding chauvinism of revolutionary Guinea and Touré's "progressive" support for the arts. The Ballets Africains survived, however, and a decade after the death of the dictator they're still going strong.

---

with two beaters, and often played in pairs, one musician performing the basic riff while the other improvises. The Susu people of western Guinea, who are linguistically part of the Mande family, are experts on this instrument. Even in the story of Sunjata Keita, the bala originally belonged to Sunjata's rival Sumanguru Kanté, king of the Susu people. Once Sunjata's musician heard the sweet sounds of the bala, he was so entranced that he began to play it – hence his nickname "Bala" Fasigi Kouyaté. Still today, the greatest balafon players are from Guinea, such as El Hadj Djeli Sory Kouyaté, leader of Guinea's National Ensemble and a legendary virtuoso. The Guinean superstar Mory Kanté, a blacksmith by birth from a musical family, famous for his hit song "Yeke yeke" (in praise of smiths), started his musical career as a balafon player. Malian singer Salif Keita also recently incorporated the balafon into his otherwise purely electric band, where it is played by the brilliant and versatile musician Keletigui Diabaté.

There are three Manding **drums**: the *tama*, or variable-pitch drum (the "talking drum"); the *djembe*, a single-headed goblet-shaped drum with a high-pitched tone, played with the hands, which is the drum par excellence of the Wassoulou region; and the *doundoun*, a large double-headed drum which is played with a heavy stick, formerly used to announce the arrival of the king.

CUBAN SOUNDS AND THE RISE OF THE GUITAR

After World War II and the return of African conscripts, the **guitar** quickly became a symbol of neotraditional music. In Guinea, Kanté Facelli, his younger cousin Kanté Manfila and Sekou "diamond fingers" Diabaté were the guitarists who were most responsible for developing a **Guinean style** of playing. They introduced love lyrics and a new harmonic element of constantly shifting chords, under strong melodies. Songs like "Tallasa" (Put the light out, my love) and "Lanaya" (The one you trust) came out of this period and remain eternal favourites.

In **Mali**, in the decade before independence, a number of regional towns, in particular Kita (birthplace of many of Mali's best-known musicians) and Ségou, had their own dance bands. Kita's orchestra was led by Boureima "BK" Keita, Mali's first professional saxophonist. Kita was an important colonial centre, and every Saturday people would take the train from Kayes and Bamako to hear the town's modern orchestra.

Another of Mali's earliest bands was Afro-Jazz de Ségou. Founded in 1952, under the leadership of trumpeter Amadu Ba (nicknamed "Armstrong" because of his admiration for Satchmo), their repertoire throughout the 1950s consisted of waltzes, tangos, paso dobles, rumbas, and French chansons. By 1964, they had joined with a rival band under the name "Alliance", and became the official orchestra of the region. They dropped

Jalimadi Tounkara, Rail Band lead guitarist

the ballroom songs and, influenced by Guinean dance bands, cultivated a more Afro-Cuban sound.

As in Guinea, state-subsidized orchestras were a prominent feature of Mali's first years of independence under President Modibo Keita; they were established in Kayes, Ségou, Sikasso, Gao and Mopti, of which the first three were predominantly composed of Manding musicians. Modibo Keita also founded the Orchestre Nationale A, Mali's first national electric dance band. Led by Keletigui Diabaté on guitar and Tidiane Kone on sax, it had a standard Latin/jazz line-up.

In Bamako an orchestra was founded for each *quartier* of the capital. The most popular of these district bands was Pioneer Jazz of Missira. Jalimadi Tounkara (today the lead guitarist of the famous Super Rail Band) was a member of Pioneer Jazz in the early 1960s, his first experience away from purely traditional Manding music: "At that time our bands weren't using folklore, just Latin American music, some jazz, and some rock. I especially liked Chuck Berry and I tried to imitate his style."

Other Malian bands of the time, like the Harmonie Soudanaise, Sinfonia, Fiesta Tropical, and Askia Jazz, were independent, and mainly played cover versions of Latin music learnt from imported records. Like the state regional orchestras, disbanded with the downfall of Modibo Keita, those early independent groups are now mostly forgotten.

Throughout the 1960s the biggest outside influence on Malian pop – as in the rest of Francophone Africa – was Cuban dance music. The rhythms and musical structures of *son* and rumba are remarkably close to those of Manding music: indeed the characteristic "clave" of Cuban music, or "Bo Diddley" rhythm, seems originally to have been brought to Cuba by Manding slaves. Even when dance bands performed Manding tunes they were almost invariably given Latin arrangements, and Latin music remains extremely popular in Mali even today. As Salif Keita has remarked, "I used to sing in Spanish – or at least I think it was Spanish, because I didn't actually speak it. I love Cuban music, but more than that, I consider it a duty for all Malians to love Cuban music, because it's through Cuban music that we were introduced to modern instruments."

The 1960s were the golden years for Guinea's dance bands. More than a dozen first-rate orchestras sprung up around the country: **Keletigui et ses Tambourins**, **Balla et ses Balladins**, **Les Amazones de Guinée** (West Africa's first all-woman dance orchestra, recruited from the police), **Lanaya Jazz**, **Horoya Band**, **Super Boiro** – all immortalized on a series of superb LP records on Syliphone Conakry. The majority of their repertoire was Manding, the lyrics political and exhortatory in true cultural-revolutionary style, but the Cuban influence, especially in the rhythms and arrangements, was strong. It tended to be reinforced by the close political ties between Sekou Touré and Fidel Castro, and by the popularity of Congolese/Zairean rumba; the

Zairean musician Joseph Kabasele – "Le Grand Kalle" – played in Guinea in the early 1960s and made a huge impression.

The most important and famous band of the time was **Bembeya Jazz National**. Specializing in arrangements of Manding classics, with the rolling harmonies of Guinean guitar, they featured a Latin-style horn section and percussion, with Sekou Diabaté on guitar, and the sweet voice of Aboubacar Demba Camara. Founded in 1961 in Beyla (eastern Guinea), they won prizes at Guinea's first two national *Biennale* festivals in 1962 and 1964, where regional bands competed with each other and, in 1966, were awarded the status of "National Orchestra".

Sékou "Diamond Fingers" Diabaté of Bembeya Jazz dispenses with the amp

The year before, Bembeya had made a memorable visit to Cuba. The well-known Cuban singer Abelardo Barroso was reportedly moved to tears by the voice of Bembeya's lead singer, Aboubacar Demba Camara. Tragically, Camara was killed in a car accident while on his way to a concert in Dakar in 1973, an event which plunged Guinea into nationwide mourning. Bembeya subsequently went into a decline, and – combined with increasing political and economic problems in Guinea – never quite recovered their previous popularity. By 1991 they had dispersed completely, though Sekouba Bambino Diabaté (not to be confused with his older, guitarist colleague Sekou Diabaté) has now become Guinea's most popular singer of semi-acoustic Manding music.

RETURN TO ROOTS

Throughout the 1970s in Guinea, Sekou Touré continued to subsidize music, organizing huge concerts for state occasions and awarding medals and "National Orders" to preferred singers and instrumentalists. The kora player Sidiki Diabaté was awarded the National Order, and Salif Keita was given a gold medal for his concert with the Rail Band in Conakry in 1976. In return, Keita dedicated his song **"Mandjou"** to Sekou Touré – a leader now viewed as a despot. Asked two decades later if he regrets having sung a praise song to the dictator, Keita is pragmatic: "I don't have any regrets, it was a different time. From the moment I knew what dictatorship meant, I hated it. And I never criticize someone who is dead."

Mali's second president, Colonel Moussa Traoré, maintained close political links with Guinea and followed their example by initiating, from 1970, a *Biennale* festival, a national youth arts jamboree of competing regional orchestras and musicians. Under the entry rules, each band had to perform music based on local **folklore**. Thus the search for a more traditional idiom began. Gone were the imitation Cuban costumes, now replaced by tunics of tie-dyed damask or the black-and-white patterned mud-dyed cloth of the Bamana.

The **Super Biton de Ségou** (latest incarnation of Alliance and Afro-Jazz, and named after Biton Coulibaly, founder of the Bamana kingdom in Ségou), won first prize twice in a row. The driving dance rhythms of their Bamana music translated powerfully onto guitars and horns, creating a new style, refreshingly different from previous Manding pop. "We made the big changeover in 1970", recalls Amadu Ba, Super Biton's trumpeter and founder member, now retired. "At first we encountered lots of difficulties because above all it involved a change of attitude. It was hard to break with the colonial mentality. Even when we musicians accepted a return to a more indigenous style, we had to struggle to convince our audience. It was a long process but eventually it worked." Super Biton's example was followed by other

THE KORA

· ·

With its striking appearance, beautiful ringing sound, and versatility, the kora has come to symbolize Manding music. No other African instrument has had the same impact on the international scene. The work of Foday Musa Suso with Herbie Hancock and Bill Laswell, the flamenco and classical crossover albums of Toumani Diabaté, and the amplified rock style kora of Mory Kanté, have all helped to establish it as one of the world's great solo instruments.

The Scots explorer Mungo Park reported seeing an 18-string "korri" played for one of the Manding kings in 1796. But the kora only came into its own in this century. Although there have been various innovations, the standard 21-string kora's most distinctive feature is its wide-notched bridge dividing the strings into two parallel rows at right angles to the sound table and a large gourd resonator.

Two main kora-playing **styles** are recognized – eastern, from Mali and Guinea, and western, from Casamance in southern Senegal and The Gambia, where most of the famous players originally came from. The western style is "hotter" and more percussive, with more cross-rhythm, lots of strumming and pinching of the strings, and rhythmic tapping of the handles – players talk about "beating the kora" (*ka kora kosi*). Some use up to 25 strings to increase the bass range and allow for more change of key. Men do the singing – though women may sing the chorus. The eastern style is more vocally oriented with a slower, more linear and staccato "classical" sound, borrowed from the ngoni and balafon. They talk about "speaking the kora" (*ka kora fo*), which is seen more as an instrument of accompaniment. Women do most of the solo singing.

It is said that all great kora players are likely at one point or another to be possessed by *djinns* (much in the way that some blues players are said to have made a pact with the devil), especially if they play late at night. Jali folklore is full of stories of players being bewitched or possessed; too much virtuosity is believed to make a musician vulnerable to illness.

MASTERS OF THE KORA

Some – though by no means all – the great names are here. For a selection of CDs and LPs, see the discographies at the end of this feature and at the end of the Senegambia feature.

Cissoko, Soundioulou (Senegal). From a dynasty of kora players and influential in the

Kora ambassadors Dembo Konteh and Kausu Kouyaté

1960s and '70s. His best-known song, the joyfully melodious "Mariama", exists in many local, dance-band versions and has been covered by Baaba Maal.

Diabaté, Sidiki (The Gambia/Mali). Developed a solo instrumental style where the kora plays both melody and accompaniment – a tradition followed by his son Toumani.

Diabaté, Toumani (Mali). Virtuoso Malian artist, who has made the kora one of the world's great solo instruments and has also shown its enormous crossover potential – for example with flamenco in "Songhai" and "Songhai 2".

Drame, Lalo Keba (The Gambia, died 1974). Prolific composer, whose songs are still played daily on Radio Gambia. His dizzily fast technique remains a model of the Gambian style for young musicians. Pirated tapes circulate endlessly.

Jobarteh, Amadu Bansang (The Gambia). First kora musician to tour Britain, in 1980. His lyrical style and precise technique reflect his Malian heritage.

Jobarteh, Malamini (The Gambia). Adoptive son of Alhaji Bai Konteh, he toured the USA in the 1970s. His eldest son, Ebrima Jobarteh ("Tata Dinding"), follows the Jaliba Kuyateh style of acrobatic kora playing. Pa Jobarteh, another Malamini offspring, toured the UK in the late 1980s when he was barely a teenager.

Jobarteh, Wandifeng (The Gambia; died in the 1950s). A legendary kora-player and composer of some of The Gambia's most oft-played tunes, such as "Nteri Jato".

Kanté, Mory (Guinea). Originally a bala player, he developed a unique, almost linear jazz style on the kora, and introduced his sound to the clubs of Europe, giving a robust new edge to perceptions of roots music.

Konteh, Alhaji Bai (The Gambia; died in 1986). Virtuoso in the Casamance tradition, and the first kora player to tour the USA in the 1970s, appearing at the Woodstock festival.

Konteh, Dembo (The Gambia). Alhaji Bai Konteh's son, he plays in a similar style, usually in duet with his brother-in-law, the brilliant Kausu Kouyaté.

Kouyaté, Batourou Sekou (Mali). Entirely self-taught, he evolved a unique, highly staccato style and made his reputation as the accompanist to singer Fanta Damba. Hear him with Sidiki Diabaté on the first instrumental kora record, "Cordes Anciennes", an all-time classic from 1970.

Kouyaté, Kausu (Senegal). Specialist in a Casamance style called "Yeyengo" (named after a song) with its own tuning and much strumming on a 23-string kora.

Kuyateh, Jaliba (The Gambia). Has built a repuatation as a local entertainer, leading a Wolof/Manding ensemble of percussion, amplified kora and electric bass.

Sissoko, Jali Mori (Senegal; died in the late 1970s). Best-known of the super-strung kora players: his instrument had 25 strings and he played in a very bluesy tuning, with a strummed technique.

Suso, Foday Musa (The Gambia). One of the earliest kora masters to quit Africa in the late 1970s, when he went to the USA and formed the Mandingo Griot Society with Don Cherry. Latest involvement is with the Kronos Quartet.

Suso, Jali Nyama (The Gambia; died in 1991). One of the most influential of Gambian kora players in the 1960s and '70s, he was the first kora player to teach in the USA, was favoured by President Jawara's first wife, and even arranged the Gambian National Anthem. He was shunned after Jawara's divorce and rarely performed in his later years.

bands like **Super Djata** – led by the percussionist and guitarist Zani Diabaté – and **Kené Star** of Sikasso.

Tidiane Kone was another of the major figures in the campaign to "return to folklore". His wizardry on the ngoni was legendary – he was said to play so fast that his fingers disappeared completely from sight. But he also learnt to play most other dance-band instruments, and was the mentor of many musicians. In 1969 Koné set up a new band, the **Rail Band du Buffet Hôtel de la Gare**, which was to launch the careers of two of West Africa's most internationally successful singers: Mory Kanté and Salif Keita.

Salif Keita is a composed, impassive man whose self-image is clearly of enormous importance to him. Being an albino carries a stigma in most African countries and Salif's youth in his native Djoliba, a village west of Bamako, close to the heartland of the old Manding empire, was not easy. On both his mother's and father's side he is a Keita and there was no precedent for someone of such high lineage to take up singing as a profession. Salif's mother had a fine voice, though she never sang in public. His father and he communicated little. Salif trained as a schoolteacher but poor eyesight prevented him from teaching as a profession, so, despite his family's disapproval, he began to sing for a living in the streets and bars of Bamako.

When Salif was first approached by Tidiane Kone to join the Rail Band he refused: "I don't do modern music, and anyway I'm not supposed to sing." But he was persuaded: "My family opposed me, but isn't it true that the evolution of civilization is marked all the time by revolution? It was necessary to mark another century that wasn't the century of the ancestors. So that's why I decided to sing despite the position of my family."

In 1971 another band formed in Bamako, **Les Ambassadeurs du Motel**, the resident band of a small hotel in Bamako with a flourishing nightclub. While the Rail Band was known for its Manding roots repertoire, with songs like "Sunjata", at least half the Ambassadeurs' numbers were foreign-style pop – rumbas, foxtrots, French ballads, Cuban and even Senegalese Wolof songs at which Ousmane Dia, their lead singer, was particularly good. Les Ambassadeurs was one of the few bands who were not government sponsored.

Both groups began to attract big followings. And two Guinean musicians now arrived on the scene, who were to become particularly important: the singer **Mory Kanté**, a bala player from an illustrious musical family from Kissidougou in eastern Guinea; and his cousin **Kanté Manfila**, an innovative guitarist who had learnt to play in Côte d'Ivoire. Manfila was invited to become leader of the Ambassadeurs, while Mory became a second singer in the Rail Band. (During the early 1970s, Mory also studied the kora in Bamako and after he moved to Paris in the 1980s, it was as a kora player that he became famous.)

In the Rail Band, Mory Kanté was immediately seen as a potential rival to Salif. They both had powerful, inspirational voices and were adept at praise lyrics. During 1972 Salif made a brief trip out of the country, and on his return found Mory doing the lead singing. Snubbed, Salif's response was to "defect" to the Ambassadeurs, which created an uproar among his fans and even greater rivalry between the two bands.

Today, he denies any rift: "There's nothing bad between us. He's my brother, Mory. He's my brother. And what's more he's my griot! People spread these rumours, but it's not true. There's no problem between him and me, Mory. Why should there be? Why, we're both part of the same motor and if the different parts of the motor disagree the motor will stop."

CONTEST

The relative merits of each band were soon put to the test. President Traoré – in one of his more enlightened programmes – had launched an adult literacy campaign called *Kibaru* ("News") aimed at the vast majority of rural Malians who were unable to read. In order to attract attention to the campaign, Traoré invited the Rail Band and the Ambassadeurs to perform in a Kibaru concert to be held at the National Sports Stadium.

By the morning of what was immediately billed a contest, a huge crowd had gathered outside the stadium. The atmosphere was as tense as at a major football game. The Rail Band, fronted by Mory Kanté, were first to go on. "Our first piece was 'Soul Makossa' by Manu Dibango", recalls the guitarist Jalimadi Tounkara. "We had really rehearsed well, so from the first note the public went wild. Afterwards we played 'Doundounba', a piece by Mory. At that time, singers didn't dance, they would just stand still. It was Mory Kanté who started to dance in the modern orchestras." Mory was wearing a *grand boubou*, a traditional robe notoriously difficult to dance in; but his performance of the graceful *jalidong* was breathtaking. It drove the audience to a frenzy.

Then it was the Ambassadeurs' turn. The line-up of the band included many of those who have continued to work with Salif Keita even after its break-up – the Guinean guitarist Ousmane Kouyaté; Keletigui Diabaté, the left-handed virtuoso whose main instrument is the bala; Cheikh Tidiane, the keyboard player; and Kanté Manfila on guitar. Salif and Manfila had written a song for the occasion called "Kibaru", starting out with a slow section encouraging farmers and workers to take reading classes, and concluding with a fast, humorous passage where the word "Kibaru" was broken into syllables, as in a spelling lesson. Later, when this song was recorded, it took up the whole side of an LP.

Salif Keita, 23 years old, came on defiantly, not in the expected grand boubou but in the traditional garb of Manding hunters: a rough, undyed, home-spun cotton tunic sewn with all kinds of magic charms. It was a costume that reflected his ancient and noble ancestry, similar to the one he wears on the cover of "Amen". There was uproar: here was an educated albino of noble ancestry, dressed like a hunter, singing – in the style of the jalis – a song about literacy.

Salif Keita rests his vocal chords

Rail Band played at the Buffet Hotel almost every night of the week and it was always full. On Saturday nights you couldn't get in. "But in 1979", recalls lead guitarist Jalimadi Tounkara, "I left for Abidjan with Mory Kanté. We left because we had asked for a pay rise and didn't get it. We were on low wages and our fees always went to the Rail company, so we got discouraged. In Abidjan we formed our own band, the Rail Band International. The atmosphere in Abidjan was hot!"

The Ambassadeurs had also left Bamako for Abidjan in 1978 to record their album "Mandjou". "Mandjou" had almost become the group's signature tune – demanded by their audiences everywhere – (though according to Kanté Manfila, the track on the album that the group itself preferred was "Ntoma", which reappeared on Salif's "Amen" album as "M b'i fe"). "Mandjou" was recorded in the rehearsal room of the Ivoirian TV station, and transformed Salif into a star overnight.

MODERN TIMES

The 1980s saw a shift of the musical scene – at least for the dance bands – away from Conakry and Bamako, initially to Abidjan, and from 1985 onwards, to **Paris**. When Mory Kanté left the Rail Band, he was replaced by Lafia Diabaté (younger brother of Kasse Mady), whose lyrical voice is less classical than that of his brother and was perfectly suited to the band's new lighter repertoire. Renamed the Super Rail Band, they recorded their superb album "Foliba" in Abidjan, subsequently re-released by GlobeStyle as "New Dimensions in Rail Culture".

The original **Rail Band** still survives, but they've not had an easy time. They continued to be sponsored by the Malian rail company through the 1980s, but audiences at the Buffet de la Gare began to decline and by the late 1980s they were only playing once a week, competing with Bamako's discos and video clubs. There are few other dance bands in Bamako. The Super Djata band, one of Mali's hottest groups a decade ago, has now disintegrated. National Badema still rehearse but rarely play. The market is dominated by the traditional musicians.

The Ambassadeurs, renamed the **Ambassadeurs Internationaux**, only survived as a band until the mid-1980s. In 1980, Salif Keita, Kanté Manfila and two other musicians from the Ambassadeurs spent four months in the USA making another of their classic records,

There was no winner – it was considered a draw – but to this day the "contest" is remembered as a showcase event for modern Manding music and a stimulus for other bands to look to tradition for their sources. Meanwhile, the competition between the two bands continued throughout the 1970s, turning Bamako into one of West Africa's most exciting cities for dance music.

Another band had also entered the scene: the National Badema, formerly the **Maravillas de Mali**, composed of a group of musicians including Boncana Maiga, who had been studying music in Cuba for eight years. They were joined in the mid-1970s by the singer **Kasse Mady Diabaté**, a jali from Kela near Kangaba, as part of a drive to introduce traditional Maninka praise-singing to their *charanga*-style arrangements. Their biggest hits were "Nama" and "Fode", a song which, in the late 1980s, Kasse Mady re-recorded in Paris for the Syllart label.

The Rail Band remained the most traditional of the three bands, often inviting guest singers such as Djelimadi Sissoko to join them for special recordings. Throughout the 1970s, the

MALI AND THE RAILERS

· ·

The Rail Band is a unique institution. In 1970 the railway administration and the Ministry of Information decided to sponsor a big band to safeguard and develop Malian music. The idea was that, once in Bamako, weary travellers could tumble off the packed carriages into the Buffet Bar, where the Rail Band was meant to provide a taste of real Manding music, with a full modern orchestra. All the instruments are government-owned and band-members are obliged, as state employees, to troop up the platform occasionally and knock out a few tunes for an arriving ministerial functionary. But on Saturday nights they play in the hotel garden. In its first three years its lead singer was Salif Keita and, over more than two decades, it has featured some of Mali's finest musicians. Andy Kershaw visited while making a series of three programmes for BBC Radio 4, "Now that's what I call Mali".

Bedtime in Bamako was not the restful recharging that nature demanded. In fact so much nature penetrated the mosquito nets, they couldn't have stopped a donkey strolling into my sleeping space if it so wished. The slightest movement in the clattering spring beds made nearly enough noise to drown out the sound of shunting locomotives while, above me, ancient, broken light-fittings hung loose. The night air was moist with the vapours of bug repellent, drains and over-heated engines. And on the end of my bed sat a strange woman eating an orange.

With considerable effort and crashing about – but without knocking – she'd opened the louvred doors of the cavernous room and strolled in for a bit of a chat. The Rail Band were no longer booming and wailing in the garden right outside the room so it must have been about 3am. My producer and I were getting used to this. On other evenings – or rather at the dead of night – we'd been visited by potential guides, dope-peddlars, and members of the Rail Band grumbling about the state of their government-loaned equipment. I'm pretty keen on the work of Mali's legendary group, but I don't want the buggers turning up by my bedside at dawn to talk drum kits.

The Rail Band has been an academy for Malian musical talent. Through its ranks have passed Salif Keita, Guinean guitarist Kanté Manfila, and Mory Kanté, all key names in the recent history of Manding music. The old recordings from the 1970s represent a golden age of modern Malian music. The playing has fantastic lightness and swing; there's the wailing sound of brass and sax and perfect use of wa-wa pedals and '70s trickery. Despite the modern instruments you can hear the link back to traditional Manding instruments like the kora, particularly on their updated versions of ancient epics like "Sunjata".

It's odd how often legendary locations turn out to be unremarkable when you eventually visit them. In our case, imagination lent the Buffet Hôtel de la Gare a grandeur that the reality of a low-rise crumbling plaster-and-concrete annexe to a railway station couldn't live up to. But if the Buffet Hôtel was a bit of a charmless dump, the station was swell – a grand colonial building with arched windows and a mosaic inscription – Chemin de Fer Dakar au Niger. We checked in with a gloomy receptionist. In the fluorescent-lit office an eager bunch of beer-drinkers were watching a Salif Keita documentary about the local boy made good.

Even in the blinding light of noon, it is dark and cool in the bar – a fine place to sit out the heat sharing a huge chilled bottle of excellent Castel beer with a musician or engine driver. The restaurant was not so accommodating. Ordering the chicken (the only thing available

The train keeps rolling

"Prinprin", working with local session musicians. But in 1982, conflict between Salif and Manfila came to a head with Salif leaving the band altogether and moving to Paris. Rumours about his health – always fragile – began to circulate, since he had not recorded for some time. In reality he was working on a fusion album – "Soro" – with French keyboardist Jean-Philippe Rykiel and Senegalese producer Ibrahima Sylla, which was to launch Manding music around the world.

The mid-1980s was an exciting period. In Paris, the scene revolved around a chic Malian restaurant called the Farafina, where Salif and Mory Kanté made regular appearances and often sang to packed audiences. Mory had also been moving towards stardom with his album "10 Cola Nuts" which, allowing for its heavy disco beat, still had a strong Manding flavour, especially in songs like "Teriya", a version of the Rail Band's old number "Balakoninfi". In 1988, Mory's version of the classic old favourite "Yeke Yeke" reached number one in several European charts and, remixed, even became a standard of the early acid house scene. But subsequent albums by Salif and Mory – recorded at great expense in Los Angeles – have not been as successful.

Many of Salif Keita's original group of musicians – some of whom, like Cheikh Tidiane and Ousmane Kouyaté, had been with him since the days of the Ambassadeurs – left him after "Soro" to form their own groups, and a scattering of "Soro-sound" records came and went, often featuring the same group of musicians. **Kasse Mady**'s excellent album "Fode", despite his magnificent voice and some fine arrangements, did not make the impact it might have done had "Soro" not existed.

But the mid-1980s also saw the release of some of the best Manding acoustic albums. The first to receive international attention was the haunting 1983 Abidjan recording "Yasimika", featuring the young Guinean singer and kora player **Jali Musa Jawara** (half-brother of Mory Kanté), accompanied on balafon and guitar and with a chorus of three women including Djenné Doumbia and Djanka Diabaté. **Kanté Manfila**'s acoustic album "Tradition", which includes Mory Kanté on kora, is another all-time classic.

LOVE, NOT PRAISE

In the late 1980s, disillusion with the government and the severe economic crisis of the country resulted in a swing away from praise song with its built-in expentancy of reward (or, more precisely, protection) and its reinforcement of the status quo. Instead there was an upsurge of interest in different styles of Manding music. The strongest development was the rise in popularity of the music from the region of **Wassoulou**, south of Bamako.

The people of Wassoulou are a mixture of Bamana and Fula, with Fula surnames (Sidibé, Sangaré, Diakité and Diallo) although they speak a local dialect of Bamana. They do not have jalis, and their music is based on an ancient tradition of hunters' songs, with pentatonic (five-note) melodies. It has more in common with Bamana than with Maninka music, and traditionally it is accompanied on the *donsongoni* (six-string hunter's harp). The stars of Wassoulou use a smaller version of this harp called *kamalengoni* (the youth's harp), reflecting the fact that this is regarded as music played by people in their teens. Only a few decades ago these songs were regarded as socially subversive, and were forbidden by the elders. The kamalengoni has a nervous, staccato sound which characteristically drives the rhythm on, punctuated by the scraping of the *karinyang* metal scraper. The women play the *fle*, a calabash strung with cowrie shells, which they spin and throw in the air at weddings in time to the music. The best-known Wassoulou dance rhythm is the vigorous *didadi*, performed with a scarf in each hand.

Wassoulou music is also dominated by women singers. In the 1960s, **Kagbé Sidibé** was one of the pioneers of the modern Wassoulou sound, accompanied on electric guitars and percussion, which imitated the sounds and rhythms of the kamalengoni. Another Wassoulou singer, **Coumba Sidibé**, also won a large following in the 1970s and early 1980s with her gritty voice and funky style.

Three young singers, however, brought Wassoulou music to a much wider audience in the late 1980s. **Nahawa Doumbia**, who comes from Bougouni, recorded two electric albums of Wassoulou music for the Syllart label in Paris which did much to promote the genre as a serious rival to Manding praise song. The first, "Didadi", was recorded with many of Salif Keita's musicians as well as Jean-Philippe Rykiel, the blind French keyboardist who has featured as musician and arranger on many albums of Manding music. The second album, "Nyama Toutou", has some memorable songs, but it was clearly "Paris-Wassoulou" in concept.

Sali Sidibé, another successful Wassoulou singer and a former member of the National Ensemble, recorded a series of low-tech but musically very strong cassettes with her own firmly traditional brand of Wassoulou music. Her ensemble includes the large Senufo bala, the four-string *bolon* bass harp, and the single-string Fula horse-hair fiddle, the *soku*.

The Wassoulou singer who has had the biggest hit is **Oumou Sangaré**. Her album, "Moussolou" (Women), recorded in Abidjan in 1989, sold over 200,000 copies. The song which rocketed her to local fame was "Diaraby nene" (Love fever), a sensual piece about the shivers of passion. Oumou's music is mainly traditional with only electric guitars and bass added to a kamalengoni-led ensemble. A lot of her lyrics are about love and the importance of freedom of choice in marriage – an issue on which she feels she has a true mission to fulfill. There is an especially poignant focus on the misery of polygamy in her new album, "Ko Sira".

"Since childhood, I've always hated polygamy. My father had two wives. It was really a catastrophe. From a young age I started to sing, from nursery school, and I said the day that I take a microphone in front of a crowd of people, the first thing I'm going to do is I'm really going to deplore the people who marry four women, who engage in forced marriage. I had a lot of problems at first. At my concerts at the Palais de la Culture, the men used to wait in their cars. Their wives went into the concert and the men stayed outside. But a few men came inside and now more come. Lots of young women understood and really agreed with me. They had all that in their heads and were refusing forced marriages. When their parents tried they refused, but they could not express the pain they felt. So, now they had someone who could help them to cry out what they felt."

Oumou's success has paved the way for a host of other young women singers from Wassoulou, of whom **Dieneba Diakité**, who has a high-pitched and affecting voice, is the best known.

Several male singers have also made names for themselves as Wassoulou stars – such as **Yoro Diallo**, whose style is similar to that of Oumou Sangaré; and **Abdoulaye Diabaté**, the lead singer of Sikasso's regional band Kené Star. His album "Kassikoun", recorded in Abidjan in 1990 with Kené Star and later released in Paris on the Syllart label, features the didadi rhythm on the powerful track "Sissi Kouloun".

Wassoulou music is youth music, a breath of fresh air after the strict conventions of

Oumou Sangaré – loving, not praising

Manding society. "The jalis direct their singing at a particular individual," says Sangaré. "I sing for everyone, about things that concern everyone; not for one person to make them feel superior. At first we had a lot of problems with the jalimusolu, they complained that we were not griottes, so we had no right to sing. Our answer is that all of us in Wassoulou are artists, all our parents are artists. Before, if you weren't a griot you couldn't sing in Mali. It is we the Wassoulonke who have turned all that around." It's a mood that's well attuned to an increasingly confident and democratic Mali.

◄ DISCOGRAPHY ►

MALI

ⓒ **Les Ambassadeurs Internationales** (Rounder, US). A great CD compilation of tracks from the mid-1970s with Salif Keita on vocals and Kanté Manfila on guitar.

ⓒ **Bajourou** *Big String Theory* (GlobeStyle, UK/Green Linnet, US). Top guitarists Jalimadi Tounkara (of Rail Band fame) and Bouba Sacko team up with ex-Rail Band singer Lafia Diabaté for a rare, acoustic set recorded in the heat of the Bamako night. Knocks the dust off you.

ⓒ **Abdoulaye Diabaté & Kéné Star** *Kassikoun* (Syllart, France). Rousing electric Bamana music, plus the didadi dance rhythm from Wassoulou, by one of the best male singers backed by the Kéné Star band from Sikasso. Recorded in Abidjan with Boncana Maiga arrangements.

Sira Mory Diabaté *Sira Mori* (Syllart, France). The only recording of the First Lady of Malian jalimusolu this cassette includes her famous love song "Sara" (covered by Balla and the Balladins). Technically poor, but wonderful none the less.

ⓒ **Toumani Diabaté** *Kaira* (Hannibal, UK). Instrumental solo kora music at its finest, including melodies like "Alla l'aa ke" and "Jarabi". ⓒ *Shake the Whole World* (Ki-oon, Japan) mixes him with string quartets, percussion and programming.

ⓒ **Nahawa Doumbia** *Nyama Toutou* (Stern's, UK). Paris-produced electric Bamana and Wassoulou music featuring one of the best young female artists. A fresh, pure voice.

ⓒ **Salif Keita** *Soro* (Stern's, UK). One of the biggest-selling African recordings ever – outside the continent – and one of the greatest successes of World Music. Seamless hi-tech arrangements make a perfect backdrop for extraordinary vocals. ⓒ *The Mansa of Mali* (Mango, US) features highlights from this and from follow-up releases ⓒ *Ko-Yan* and ⓒ *Amen* plus his 1978 hit "Mandjou". Lastly, listen out for Keita's recent cassette-only release, *SOS Albino*.

ⓒ **Ami Koita** *Tata Sira* (Bolibana, France). Semi-acoustic music in the jali tradition, with powerful renditions of classic tunes, plus her own compositions. ⓒ *Songs of Praise* (Stern's, UK) is also semi-acoustic, but more elaborately produced.

ⓒ **Tata Bambo Kouyaté** *Jatigui* (GlobeStyle, UK). Stunning praise-singing from 1985 by one of Mali's most accomplished female artists. Entirely acoustic accompaniment from the full range of instruments, plus Fulani flute.

ⓒ **Kasse Mady (Diabaté)** *Kela Tradition* (Stern's, UK). Great recording of arguably the best voice in Manding music, the jalis jali of Kela, the famous acoustic village. Features ngoni and balafon plus guitars and Rykiel on keyboards. Long, gorgeous versions of classic songs like "Koulandjan" and "Kaira". ⓒ *Fode* (Stern's, UK) is overproduced but saved by Kasse Mady's spectacular improvisations.

Fanta Sacko *Fanta Sacko* (Bärenreiter Musicaphon, Germany). The first LP of bajourou music, from 1970. Love and praise songs, with moving vocals by a great artist and kora-sound-alike acoustic guitar backing.

ⓒ **Super Biton du Ségou** *Afro-Jazz du Mali* (Bolibana, France). Hard-hitting early 1980s recording of Bamana music by the pioneering roots band.

ⓒ **Le Super Rail Band du Bamako** *New Dimensions in Rail Culture* (GlobeStyle, UK). 1982 recording from Abidjan featuring the mellow voice of Lafia Diabaté and Jalimadi Tounkara's inimitable rocking guitar. Keen rail-spotters will also want to track down the LP/cassette *The Rail Band of Bamako* (Mali Music/Bärenreiter Musicaphon, Germany), which features classic recordings of the band with Salif Keita

ⓒ **Oumou Sangaré** *Ko Sira* (World Circuit, UK). A breath of fresh air from a young woman singer whose impact on traditional musical culture could hardly have been greater, wielding her voice like a weapon, and deploring, as she puts it, the male-dominated status quo. Beautifully produced, this is Wassoulou music at its best.

ⓒ **Boubacar Traoré** *Mariama* and *Kar Kar* (Stern's, UK). Solo voice-and-guitar love songs, in a folky style unique to this non-jali composer from Kayes.

Various *Cordes Anciennes* (Bärenreiter Musicaphon, Germany). Classic 1970 recording by three of Mali's greatest kora players: Sidiki Diabaté, Batourou Sekou Kouyaté and Djelimadi Sissoko.

ⓒ **Various** *The Wassoulou Sound: Women of Mali* and *The Wassoulou Sound: Vol 2* (Stern's, UK). Excellent compilations featuring a range of female voices and Wassoulou styles, including the pioneers of "Wassoulou electric", Kagbe Sidibé and Coumba Sidibé. Buy the CDs as a set as the notes were written for both.

ⓒ **Various** *Electric and Acoustic Mali* (Hemisphere-EMI, UK/US). Ironically the first and last tracks - actually Guinean - are the best on this selection: it kicks off with a blinder of a number from Sekouba Bambino Diabaté. Issa Bagayogo's "Fengué" is also a great swinger of a traditional acoustic song. Altogether highly recommended.

GUINEA

ⓒ **Balla et ses Balladins** *Reminiscin' in Tempo with...* (World Circuit, UK/Popular African Music, Germany). A compilation album of greats by one of Guinea's top regional bands, with the old-time rumba-sound of the 1960s and '70s. Includes two superb examples of the love song "Sara".

ⓒ **Bembeya Jazz National** *Live – 10 Ans de Succès* (Bolibana, France). Atmospheric recording from 1971 of the country's most famous band at the finest hour. Wild solos from "diamond fingers" Diabaté measure up to the unforgettable voice of Aboubacar Demba Camara. ⓒ *Regard sur le Passé* (Bolibana, France) is a re-release of Guinea-rumba-style praise songs about the country's national hero, Samory Touré.

ⓒ **Sekouba Bambino Diabaté** *Le Destin* (World Circuit/Out of Africa, UK). Bembeya's former lead vocalist leads his own semi-acoustic group through the lighter side of the praise song tradition. Beautifully sung, with wonderful arrangements.

Kadé Diawara *L'Archange du Manding* (Bolibana, France/Guinea, cassette only). Simple, classic, 1970s recording of rolling love songs with one acoustic guitar, from Guinea's finest Manding woman singer.

ⓒ **Jali Musa Jawara** *Yasimika* (Hannibal, UK). First prize for the most-released kora recording; formerly issued as *Jali Musa Jawara* by Tangent (France, 1983) and Oval (UK, 1986); then as *Direct from West Africa* (Go Discs, UK) before its current release. Fully justified attention for a superb, ethereal, all-acoustic guitar, kora and balafon set, with luscious choruses and soaring vocals from JMJ. An absolute classic.

CD Kanté Manfila (Manfila Kanté) *Diniya* (Sonodisc, France). Some fine melodies buried beneath a full-blown, hi-tech production. His earlier *Tradition* (Mélodie, France), with its lovely rolling Kankan melodies and kora by cousin Mory, proves what a fine carrier of that tradition he is.

CD Mory Kanté *10 Cola Nuts* (Barclay, France). Heavy on the drum kit and synth, but some fine material, including the beautiful "Teriya". **CD** *Akwaba Beach* (Barclay, France) was his breakthrough album, with his dance floor-shaking version of "Yeke Yeke".

CD Sory Kandia Kouyaté *L'Epopée du Mandingue Vol 1 & 2* (Bolibana, France). Late-lamented epic praise-singer with the high, mezzo-soprano voice – Guinea's top vocalist of the 1970s. Each of his CDs offers a major tranche of deep-Malian oral history. Acoustic kora accompaniment from Sidiki Diabaté.

CD Wandel *Momo Soumah* (Buda, France). A rich voice to complement a strongly flavoured union of jazz and Guinean music. Manding crossover in the best sense.

RIVER SPIRIT BLUES

SONGS OF MALI'S ALI FARKA TOURÉ

Ali Farka Touré, from northern Mali, was born into a family of noble origins, who trace their ancestry back to the sixteenth-century migration from Spain of a Moorish army known as the Armas – part Spanish, part African – who crossed the Sahara to take control of the trade in salt and gold. He plays guitar with a highly distinctive style that's earned him the title "Bluesman of Africa". An absolute individualist, his music is a passion for him, but not a profession in the jali-manner. He plays as if his fingers had a life of their own, and his conversation, in French, can be equally hard to follow. Journalist and broadcaster Andy Kershaw visited Ali Farka Touré while recording three radio programmes for the BBC, "Now that's what I call Mali!".

"It was the spirits who gave me the gift"

I was sent one of Ali Farka's recordings out of the blue. I put it on and was stunned. I wasn't the only one. Of all the records I have ever played on the radio this was the one that elicited the most enquiries. With the rhythmic guitar-picking style and the nasal lonesome vocals, it was the West African version of the delta blues of Lightnin' Hopkins or John Lee Hooker.

Ali's musical roots are firmly in the Songhai and Tuareg cultures of the region between Timbuktu and Gao, although on his recent albums, "The River" and "The Source", he has teamed up with other musicians. While they're superbly recorded and well produced, and give Ali's music refreshing new perspectives, nothing can beat the sparse com-bination on the early Sonodisc recording of voice, guitar and insistent rhythm tapped on the calabash.

Niafounké, Ali Farka's village, has charm if not much else. There's a quay, a shipping office, school, market, flophouse and a couple of thousand people. Life revolves around the Niger, especially when the steamer makes its irregular stops and the riverbank is shrill with the noise of commerce.

From his sporadic earnings, mostly the rewards of European tours, Ali feeds an extended family of more than fifty. His mud-walled compound teems with offspring, second cousins, "petit frères", the elderly, the newborn and Ali's one wife. Ali was proud to have his British chums in town. Very proud, we reckoned, after our walkabout with him on the first day. I'm a friendly bloke, most of the time, but exchanging "Ça va?" "Ça va" for eight hours under the Saharan sun tested my curiosity in my fellow human beings.

Ali Farka didn't touch his guitar once the whole week we were in Niafounké. Ali's mother thinks it's beneath the dignity of her son to play music. "If you want music," she'd say, "go out and hire a musician." Good thing she wasn't on the trip to Timbuktu when he played his ass off, there and back. I'll never forget the searing sound of his voice and guitar, floating into the still spookiness of a night on the Niger.

ALI FARKA ON ALI FARKA

Ali Farka Touré's position in Niafounké society is partly maintained by his fame and comparative fortune. But he also holds sway in local religious circles and his music is inspired by powerful spiritual experiences which continue to this day. His grandfather was a sorcerer and snake-catcher (he used to sell the skins) and Ali is credited with precognitive gifts and a certain responsibility for keeping open the lines of communication between this world and the world of the ancestors.

Richard Trillo first asked him about his time with Britain's best-known popularizer of World Music.

AFT: I'm very proud of my country. My country is very proud of me. Wherever I go in Mali, I'm welcome. I have no problem. So, I went with Andy Kershaw as far as Timbuktu. He saw nearly all the traditions. He can say he has seen a little of Mali. He saw how journeys are made. He saw just how much suffering we have to put up with. I am very proud that he saw that. It's not like here. You can walk out and go by car, or train, or plane. Someone just says, "Let's go" and you go.

I remember he had a small Walkman like yours, but I don't know what he said. I haven't heard the programmes. It's now up to him. He can't say he was badly received, that's all I can say. And nor can he say – well, of course he can say whatever he likes, journalists are journalists, there's so much defamation, I'm only speaking the truth, though it's not like French journalism, when you say it's black they say it's red and blue…

How did you learn to play?

It was the spirits who gave me the gift. I remember that night in Niafounké. A night I'll never forget. I'd been chatting with some friends. I had the monochord (ndjarka) in my hand. I was walking and I was playing just ordinary songs, just like that. It was about 2am, something like that. I got to a place where I saw three little girls like steps of stairs, one higher than the other. I lifted my right foot. The left one wouldn't move. I stood there like

that until 4am. Next day, what happened? I left my family. I didn't have my instrument with me. I went to the dispensary. I walked to the edge of the fields. There's a snake which has a strange mark on its head. One snake. I knew the colour straight away. Black and white. Not yellow, not another colour, black and white. And it wrapped itself around my head. I brushed it off, it fell and went into a hole. I fled. At that point I started having attacks. For some time. In fact, they lasted about two years. I was mad. I was aggressive. I didn't want to see people. They tied me up. This was 1951 and I was about 12. So, they tied me up. I still have the scars of the ropes. They took me to Hombori to stay with a Songhai family who treated me. And when I was cured, I went back to my mother. And then, when I played my monochord, it was very, very well received by all the groups of spirits. And I was normal. But it was very difficult. I was frightened. My maman was frightened too, because I was her tenth boy and if I had died it would have been very serious – very bad luck if the tenth child dies. It was like that.

Anyway, I got into music in about 1956. I had a chance meeting with Keita Fodeba [the director of Guinea's National Ballet] and I took the decision to learn the guitar.

How did your collaboration go with Taj Mahal on "The Source"?

We had every imaginable problem. He couldn't even manage to play or keep up. He was very tiring, very tiring. But I liked him very much, because he really wants to understand. I like that about him a lot, he really wants to learn. It's not that he understands what I sing. He can't. No.

So that's why you would have trouble playing with western musicians and western producers, because they wouldn't understand the music enough?

Yes, but if I say I want to record with European musicians it's not to say I want to learn European music. No, no. I will write the songs and they will play them. If they can play them, fine, if not I'll teach them and they can accompany me. They must stay on the right path, though.

You say you don't understand Salif Keita because European musicians and producers had too much influence on him? Has he left the path?

Oh Salif, he's really left it. To me that's not really African music. I've told him to his face. He gave me his point of view, but that's a secret between us.

Can you tell me about the instrument you're holding [a single-string fiddle with a calabash soundbox that sounds more like a flute when played].

This instrument is called *ndjarka*. I made this one myself this year. These pebbles stay in the calabash. There are rituals you have to do when making it. You never put skin on the calabash without putting fetishes inside to prevent spirits, because when you play to an audience you must prevent spirits getting into people so they can live with music without having an attack. Right, to do that, you have to have a completely red chicken, okay? You sit down. The calabash is empty, nothing inside. Then you take the chicken and you cut its throat over the calabash. All the blood from inside the chicken you pour into the calabash. When it has absorbed the blood, you empty it on the ground, you leave and you get a white kola nut and a red kola nut, and that's the sacrifice. You leave it hanging like that for two days. On the third day you get the piece of skin and stretch it over. And that's it. Then you can play it.

DISCOGRAPHY

Maybe all comparisons are odious (many have said Touré sounds more like the acerbic blues troubadour JB Lenoir than John Lee Hooker) but for a real pre-AFT slice of AFT – one that perhaps points to a genuine roots link – go to Big Joe Williams' recording of "Baby Please Don't Go", a classic 1930s cut complete with acoustic guitar, one-string fiddle and washboard (which sounds strikingly similar to AFT's acoustic guitar, one-string fiddle and calabash). Many of the songs from this session are available on CD on the Austrian RST label.

Ali Farka Touré *Ali Farka Touré*(Shanachie, US). The original Ali Farka sound, nice and simple. Look for the distinctive red cover of the LP.

 Ali Farka Touré *Ali Farka Touré* (World Circuit, UK). Ten, all-acoustic songs from 1987, coinciding with the first rush of Ali Farka fever. Dig the big blues sound on "Amandrai". Essential.

ⓒ *The River* (World Circuit, UK). Ali gets collaborative: guests on a part-electric set include Rory McLeod, Chieftains Sean Keane and Kevin Conneff, and Steve Williamson.

ⓒ *The Source* (World Circuit, UK). Having rated the first World Circuit release "essential", it's hard to know what to say here: except that this one is even more so. Associates this time include Taj Mahal, Nana Tsiboe and Nitin Sawney on tabla. The best of ten great tracks are "Hawa Dolo" and the upbeat loping river sound of "Mahini Me".

ⓒ *Talking Timbuktu* (World Circuit, UK). A miracle of 1994, top of many of the indie charts within days of release. A World Music record out of left field that actually sounds like people playing together in a room. Feel that feel.

OUR CULTURE

SENEGAMBIAN STARS ARE HERE TO STAY

The Gambia and Senegal have produced some of World Music's biggest stars – the mbalax of Youssou N'Dour and the stunning voice and stage presence of Baaba Maal need little introduction. Jenny Cathcart, who has been visiting the region for over a decade, traces the development of some of West Africa's most powerful musical muscles. With thanks to Lucy Duran for input on matters Manding and suggestions for the discography.

I n **Senegal**, appearances count. The Senegalese have taken French chic and made it their own. The first French settlements were established in 1659 and there were small numbers of Senegalese with French citizenship by the end of the eighteenth century. With their traders, teachers and administrators travelling widely abroad, a minority of Senegalese had a cosmopolitan outlook long before most West Africans retrieved their independence in the 1960s.

Society is dominated by the largest language group – the **Wolof** – who are big in business and government and whose musical culture and language are spreading constantly. Small Wolof kingdoms used to cover the heart of the country, an area now largely planted under peanut fields. But much of Senegal has unreliable rainfall and, if you look beyond the glamour of Dakar's fine-robed elite, there is poverty and extreme hardship – and religious devotion. Muslim brotherhoods – not fundamentalist but hugely important – cut across society's ethnic and language divides.

The Senegalese people must be among the most chauvinistic followers of their own music in the whole of Africa. And who can blame them? If you go to Dakar during Christmas and New Year you'll see a people who, whatever their circumstances, really know how to enjoy themselves. Senegalese see the New Year in with a "nuit blanche", an all-night rave. There are house parties; the clubs are full; the police and the army and the firemen turn their barracks into ballrooms and host black-tie dances with top bands –Youssou N'Dour and the Super Étoile, Lemzo Diamono, Thione Seck and the Raam

Daan, Baaba Maal, Super Diamono, Ismael Lô or Kiné Lam. The whole of Dakar dances. At four or five in the morning, the revellers retire to breakfast at local cafés or with friends. Firecrackers explode and the new year is ushered in with a cacophony of klaxoning car horns.

It's not much of an exaggeration to say that only a few years ago, if all the cars in **The Gambia** had hooted together, it wouldn't have made a very loud noise. This tiny sliver of a nation, which was a British colony until 1965, only built its first proper highway in the early 1990s. Visiting the capital, Banjul, even today you're likely to wonder where the city is. Like Senegal, which entirely surrounds The Gambia except on its seaward side (the two countries shared a brief "Senegambia confederation"), the country is one of Africa's most stable and tolerant. Down along the beach, a couple of dozen hotels support the tourist industry which is its most important money-earner. People complain that this isn't the real Africa, that the hustlers are unbearable and the tourist markets tawdry. But the reality is more promising: visitors who take the time to get away from the hotels' immediate environs are rewarded with tranquility and real warmth; musical holidays are easy to arrange; and local Gambian clubs and even bands that visit the hotels can be hot.

Jali Nyama Suso's venture with Bill Laswell

In The Gambia and southern Senegal, traditional **Mandinka music** since independence has revolved around the *kora*. Individual musicians such as Soundiolou Cissoko and Lalo Keba Dramé dominated the scene and influenced younger talents with their particular styles. More significant changes began in the 1980s with the widespread use of amplified koras and an emphasis on dance rhythms rather than praise lyrics. It has not been the "big business" that Maninka music is in Mali and Guinea, but it has its audience. The most popular is a semi-acoustic ensemble lead by an amplified kora and percussion including the traditional Wolof *sabar* and *tama* drums and, where possible, an electric bass. Small ensembles like this go from village to village playing at weddings or other local festivities and are more and more in demand in cities as well. The schoolteacher and kora player Jaliba Kuyateh from Brikama in The Gambia is one of the main people responsible for developing this style, which follows on from the Casamance style of kora. The music is bright and lively and the singing is almost entirely choral, without the traditional improvised solos.

Because of the concentration of the music business in Dakar, where Wolof culture predominates, Mandinka music has not been as important an ingredient as Wolof in the dance bands of The Gambia and Senegal. But the popular Gambian bands, **Super Eagles/Ifang Bondi** and **Guelewar**, of the 1980s, drew on the Mandinka drumming repertoire and other types of song not associated with the kora *jali*. And several Senegalese regional bands of the late 1970s – for example Canari from Kaolack and UCAS Jazz from Casamance – drew heavily on Mandinka music, as in Canari's delightful version of the kora song "Sutukum Kumbusora". UCAS Jazz, one of Senegal's oldest bands formed in the late 1950s, was the first Senegalese band to include a kora in its line-up, and has played host to many well-known musicians over the years. Despite recent political unrest in Casamance, they continue to play regularly in their home town of Sedhiou.

BAOBAB CLUB

Even before World War II, Latin music, particularly **Cuban dance rhythms**, had become extremely popular in Senegal. Dakar was one of West Africa's biggest ports and foreign musicians were not uncommon. By the 1960s, Cuban bands like Orchestra Aragon and Johnny Pacheco were household names who inspired Senegalese musicians to create their own Afro-Cuban music and to sing in Spanish – even if they didn't always understand the words. To celebrate Senegal's Independence in 1960, Ibra Kassé formed the **Star Band de Dakar,** fronted by singers Labah Sosseh and Pape Seck, to play at his club, the Miami Bar. Soon, a number of groups including Orchestre Le Sahel and Kaad Orchestra were playing music with a distinctly Latin flavour in clubs like the Sahel, the Ngalam and the Moulin Rouge.

Orchestre Baobab – luminous performers Seck and Sidibé (right)

In 1970 a new group, **Orchestra Baobab**, was formed to play at the opening of Dakar's Baobab Club. The line-up had vocals by Balla Sidibé, Ndiouga Dieng, Radolphe Gomis and Médoune Diallo (Thione Seck joined the band later), Issa Cissokho on sax, Mountaga Kouyaté on drums, Peter Udo playing clarinet, Papa Ba on rhythm guitar, Barthelemy Attiso playing guitar solo and Charles Ndiaye on bass. It was a creative gathering. They played Afro-Cuban rhythms with languid grace and huge enjoyment and sang mainly in Spanish or Kriolu (Portuguese Creole). But lyrics in Wolof and Mandinka (the natal language of Sidibé and Cissokho) soon crept in, on "On Verra Ça" for example; and one of their finest pieces, re-released on Stern's "Bamba" CD, is "Ndiawolou" (Enemies), a version of the Gambian kora song "Alla l'aa ke". In a conscious effort to indigenize their music, Orchestra Baobab invited Laye Mboup to sing traditional Wolof songs with them, and they added the Wolof word *gouyegui* (meaning "baobab") to their name.

The *ndaga* fusion between salsa and the *tama* talking drum was one of the first moves towards integrating the Wolof drums that later became the hallmark of Senegalese popular music. The talking drum and the *sabars* were vital in urging the Wolof women into wild dances. Like birds, their *boubous* flying and legs and arms flailing the air, the best dancers, like the players, understood the drum's secret language: the resulting dialogue played a key role in shaping the new music.

Thione Seck, whose griot ancestors sang the praises of the king Lat Dior (one of the great nineteenth-century Wolof resistance fighters) is a fine singer with a powerful and true voice. He's highly respected in Senegal – the lyricist's lyricist, a muscian's musician. His band's fast-paced *mbalax* has an almost oriental accent with a Spanish tinge. His pop songs are sympathetically arranged by keyboard player

SUPER EAGLES

· ·

In 1967, The Gambia's top group, the Super Eagles, donned their Chelsea boots and took the second-hand Salvation Army uniforms they had just received from London down to Leman Street in the Half-Die district of Banjul. Here, Modou Peul, the best tailor in town, transformed them into trendy Sergeant Pepper suits complete with gold-stitched epaulettes. Being the only English-speaking state among eight francophone countries, the newly independent, ex-British colony had a head start in getting to know the latest pop songs and kept open a hotline to swinging London. Enterprising young Gambians like Oko Drammeh acquired copies of the London magazine FAB-208, which printed the lyrics of hits by the Beatles, Monkees, Rolling Stones and other top groups and sold them at a decent mark-up to the fans.

Drammeh later became manager of The Super Eagles and today runs an annual African music festival in Holland: "African music was still considered to be 'bush bush' music then," he says. "Salsa and foxtrot were all the rage, and of course soul music from the Beatles to James Brown. The Super Eagles' new album in 1969, which was called 'Viva Super Eagles', was mainly direct imitations of western pop music sung in English with only one or two African numbers. Francis Taylor, who was the keyboard player, was one of the first Africans to really master the synthesizer. And Paps Touray, the lead singer, was idolized even by people like Thione Seck and Youssou N'Dour."

Serekunda – which was a village in those days but is now The Gambia's largest town, close to Banjul – became a popular meeting place for musicians in the early 1970s. Among them were the three Touré brothers (of Touré Kunda) from Casamance in southern Senegal, Bembeya Jazz from Guinea, Les Merry Makers and Psychédélique from Dakar, Salif Keita from Mali,

the Sahano Band from Sierra Leone and Super Mama Jombo from Portuguese Guinea Bissau. Sustained by palm wine, the artists exchanged ideas and, on Sunday afternoons, taxied into Banjul for jam sessions called hawarehs, which Oko Drammeh organized at the Swedish-owned Tropical Nightclub in Clarkson Street.

The Senegalese musicians Majama Fall and Cheikh Tidjiane Tall invited the Super Eagles to Dakar where they lived in a large house in the densely populated Medina district and were joined every day by the brothers Diagne and young Omar Pene of the group Diamono. The Super Eagles played nightly in the Adeane Club and, by the end of their stay, had recorded an LP, "Saraba", described on the sleeve as "authentic music from The Gambia" and to this day their biggest hit. Inspired by the example of the Senegalese group Xalam, who took their name from the traditional lute, the Super Eagles changed their name to Ifang Bondi, a Mandinka phrase meaning "Be Yourself".

Back home in The Gambia the group spent more time in the villages listening to traditional musicians like the late great Jali Nyama Suso and also began experimenting with jazz and different African rhythms, bringing local percussion into use. The attempted coup in The Gambia in July 1981 brought in a state of emergency, prohibiting public gatherings and shutting down clubs. As a result, there was virtually no music for five years and many musicians went abroad. The Super Eagles' singer Moussa Ngom went to Dakar where he joined the group Super Diamono. Ifang Bondi went to Holland in 1984 to record their seminal fusion album of Afro-Manding sounds – bluesy, jazzy horns and African percussion topped by the inimitable voice of Paps Touray. They called it "Mantra", a nostalgic reference to the heady Maharishi-inspired days of the Sixties.

WEST AFRICA

and guitarist Adama Faye, elder brother of Habib and Lamine. Others retain a strong percussive base and remain determinedly authentic. The lyrics are punchy, too, as with this from "Yeen":

Hypocrites, I will take away your masks
Evil Ones, I will nurse you
Racists, I will eradicate you
Murderers, I will neutralize you.

Seck's 1991 cassette includes "Papa" a novel song about the evils of music cassette piracy.

While human beings are God's greatest creation, says Seck, they are also feeble sinners. They have the talent to tame leopards or make elephants play football but they can also go to Sandaga market and pick up a newly released cassette which they will secretly copy and sell. He asks: do they know just how difficult it is to produce such a cassette? and then painstakingly lists the entire production process before finishing his song with the salutary reminder that such ill-gotten gains will in any case be worthless one day.

"We all came into the world with nothing and when God takes us we will leave with nothing except the seven metres of cloth that make up a shroud."

BLUES OF THE RUES

Formed in 1974, the group **Super Diamono** were fronted at different times (and eventually together) by singers Omar Pene, Mamadou Maïga and Moussa Ngom. Each brought distinctive colours to the songs – a rueful blues sound from Pene, wailing jali-esque tones from Maïga and Baye Fall-style *xiin* rhythms from lock-laden Ngom. In its large and influential line-up, Diamono featured the excellent guitar-playing of Lamine Faye and **Ismael Lô**, and the sabar-substitute bass guitar of Bob Sène. Emphasizing imported rather than local instruments, they presented a style they called *mbalax blues* or *afro-feeling*, which appealed to a younger audience that was less rootsy than streetwise – one that tended to be predominantly male and as much interested in substance as style. In albums such as "People" and "Cheikh Anta Diop" (dedicated to the great Senegalese philosopher), Super Diamono tackled social issues head-on – apartheid, polygamy and human rights.

Super Diamono split in 1991; one half, led by Lamine Faye, went to work with the idiosyncratic Moussa Ngom who had quit the band in 1988 (and is still remarkable as much for his sartorial quirkiness as for his original hit songs such as "Africa Teye"), while the others regrouped under Maïga and Omar Pene.

Then a new round of musical chairs re-established the Super Diamono group name under Omar Pene. Following the departure of Moussa Ngom (who now has his own band), Lamine Faye created Lemzo Diamono which is fronted by a trio of singers: Alioune Mbaye Nder, Fallou Dieng and a young lady with a powerful voice, Mada Ba.

EXPERIMENTS

Founded in 1970 by Prosper Niang and his brother Magay, **Xalam** were always intended to be an experimental band. Perhaps because of their penchant for jazz and provocative lyrics, Xalam (the name is Wolof for the traditional guitar or lute) never gained the recognition they deserved at home. In 1973 the group moved to Paris where one of their new recruits was Jean-Philippe Rykiel, who has since figured prominently in many productions – most notably Salif Keita's "Soro" and most recently on Youssou N'Dour's album "The Guide – Wommat". In Europe, Xalam felt free to develop a distinctive fusion which was variously labelled Afro-jazz or *zouk-mbalax*. In 1975,

Afro-feeling with Super Diamono

ISMAEL LÔ: SENEGAL'S ANSWER TO BOB DYLAN?

Ismael Lô's mother was from Niger; his father was a clerk from Senegal. A painter but also a talented guitarist and harmonica player (the "Bob Dylan of Senegal"), he attended the School of Art in Dakar. An early graduate of the Super Diamono band, he then spent time in the Canary Islands before returning home to form his own group playing "New Look" mbalax with sweet melodies, melded with soul and a bit of funk. He talked to Richard Trillo.

Can you tell me about the song "Tajabone"?
It reminds me of my childhood. It's about an annual festival when the children all go round the neighbourhood, knocking on people's doors and stealing anything they fancy. It's the only time the sin of "theft" is allowed. Then the owners come and buy it all back. And the children have a party with the money they get, drums and everything. Tajabone.

You've advised your children not to take up music as a profession – why not?
Well it's very time-consuming. It leaves you no time for your family or yourself. I'm a real perfectionist. Recording takes me forever. And it's easy to fall into bad ways with drugs and women. I wouldn't

forbid them – just advise them against it. It's hard – when I started I didn't realize. I did it for love.

This "Bob Dylan of Senegal" nickname – how did you get that?
My father had given me a harmonica. I used to pin it to the wall while I played the guitar. People kept saying "Bodylan, Bodylan" and then they gave me some cassettes and I realized who Bob Dylan was. Now I begin to wonder if I'm supposed to owe him something!

How did you start playing with Super Diamono?
Well, they were a very big group and I loved them. They were in The Gambia one time and I was booked to play between their sets. It was great for me, alone on the stage in a big stadium. So I did that a few times and then we started jamming and got some keyboards behind me and it was already quite different from my own things. And so Super Diamono's manager asked if I wanted to join them and go with them on tour. I was with them for four years. My pay was a packet of cigarettes a day, and if you wanted something like shoes or something, you asked the boss, like a son to his father.

they toured Africa with Hugh Masekela and Miriam Makeba and, in 1979, they won a major award at the Berlin Jazz Festival.

While mixing their second album, "Gorée", in London in 1983, the group met their teenage idols, the Rolling Stones, and were delighted to accept the Stones' invitation to play percussion on a track for their album "Under Cover of the Night". Xalam's 1988 album, "Xarit", had a more rootsy mbalax base and featured the natural griot gifts of vocalist Souleymane Faye. Xalam toured extensively in Europe, Japan and the US (playing with Dizzie Gillespie and Crosby, Stills and Nash) until the untimely death of drummer Prosper Niang in 1989 left them leaderless for a time. Souleymane Faye returned to Dakar to start a new solo career.

In some ways, the group **Touré Kunda** were a band before their time. They were playing to audiences of 20,000 French fans even before World Music became fashionable. The brothers Ismael, Sixu and Amadou Touré were born in

Casamance in southern Senegal and came as students to Paris in the late 1970s. By 1979, they were combining Mandinka melodies (their father was originally from Mali) with mbalax, highlife, soul, salsa, and a reggae beat they called *djambaadong*, a strong favourite with European audiences. Tragically, in 1983, Amadou collapsed at a performance at the Chapelle des Lombards and died later in hospital. The group was devastated but rallied to produce a memorial concert and a tribute album, "Amadou Tilo". Amadou was immediately replaced by another Touré brother, Ousmane, a very fine singer who added greatly to the group's stage presence. The star attraction in Touré Kunda shows was the energetic dancing of Seynabou Diop, a veritable firebrand who illuminated the stage with her exuberant physicality. Touré Kunda toured extensively in Europe, the US and Japan and notched up two gold discs with sales of over 100,000. One was a double album, "Paris–Ziguinchor Live", recorded when the group hired a truck fitted to carry a mobile stage and set out with technicians and a TV crew to tour Senegal, ending with a triumphant return to Casamance. The other was the 1986 album "Toubab bi". But their most exciting project was the album "Natalia", recorded in hi-tech conditions and produced by Bill Laswell. The album had many critics, perhaps because of its technical innovations, but it has something of the unity of style and concept that marks out classic recordings like the Anglo-Spanish-Malian collaboration, "Songhai", or Salif Keita's "Soro" or that other great Syllart production, "Africando".

GRIOT SON OF GRIOTS

Youssou N'Dour's music has been to places where the country's peanuts and phosphates and even the presidential plane have never been. The boy from the Medina, this griot son of griots became a superstar in Senegal before conquering France and Europe and then travelling the world with Peter Gabriel, Tracy Chapman, Sting and Bruce Springsteen on the "Human Rights Now!" tour in 1988.

Being of the generation born with Independence in 1960, N'Dour felt that Cuban music was rhythmically compatible with Senegalese traditional music but harmonically different. And why not sing in Wolof so that everyone would understand? He began his singing career with the Star Band No. 1 at Ibra Kassé's Miami Club, but in 1977 he formed his own band, the Étoile de Dakar. His new style of music had a Wolof name, *mbalax*, the word the griots used to describe the distinctive rhythm played by the *mbung mbung* drum. "In my group I gave some of the traditional sabar drum parts to the guitars and keyboards while the rhythm guitar took on the role of the mbung mbung".

Retaining what he describes as the "black soul sound" of the Cuban horns, he added new jazz inflections and made full use of traditional singing techniques such as *tasso* (an early kind of rap), *bakou*-trilling (the traditional chant accompanying Wolof wrestlers) and scat. By the early 1980s when the group had grown into their new name, Super Étoile de Dakar, their latest hits – always topical, always relevant – were emanating from every courtyard and market stall and had the dancers on the floor at every club. N'Dour's female following was particularly devoted.

He sang about "Awa Gueye", a Tukulor friend of his mother who sold cotton materials at the market; about "Taaw", the eldest child of the family, responsible for looking after the younger members (N'Dour is a *taaw*); about the "Medina", the densely populated, low-rent quarter of downtown Dakar where he was born; and about larger-than-life characters from Senegalese history, as in "Alboury", the last king of the last independent Wolof kingdom of Jolof.

In 1983 after his first visit to Paris, he wrote "Immigrés", a powerful plea to the hundreds of thousands of emigrant Senegalese to remember their homeland: "Whatever you may have become/Even if you've aquired social status/It's only right that one day/You should return to your homeland." This song proved to be his ticket to the international stage. Peter Gabriel met him in Dakar the following year: "The thing that amazed me was the voice – like liquid silver. I felt the hairs rising on the back of my neck."

"The Lion", N'Dour's first LP for Virgin Records, was a huge flop. Recording in Paris with guest musicians, the band reworked tracks already arranged and produced for release on cassette in Dakar. Many fans preferred the African versions of these songs, and the new album was slated for its lack of toughness and energy. "With the money it took to make that one album they could have built a studio in Dakar where they would have been able to record me and many other artists," said N'Dour later. The second Virgin album, "Set", recorded in a Brussels studio in quasi-live conditions, was much nearer the real thing, but Virgin dropped N'Dour nonetheless. He quickly signed to Spike Lee's American label, Forty Acres and a Mule.

With the experience of hindsight, and with a new confidence in the international appeal of his mbalax fusion, N'Dour declared that future recordings would be the same for Senegal as for the rest of the world. The "Xippi" cassette, recorded in N'Dour's new **Studio Xippi** in Dakar, and produced by himself, Habib Faye and the French musician, Jean-Philippe Rykiel, was followed by the international CD "Eyes Open" – the same tracks as "Xippi" (which means "eyes open"), plus six more. The World Music columns had something to rave about.

NOBLE IDEALS

"Like listening to Muddy Waters for the first time," said British DJ John Peel of **Baaba Maal**'s 1986 acoustic release "Djam Leelii". A member of the Fula ethnic group, Baaba Maal

YOUSSOU N'DOUR: THE GUIDE

T hrough the line of his Tukulor mother, Ndeye Sokhna Mboup, Youssou N'Dour is a *gawlo*, a singing **griot**. Born with a beautiful voice, he has also inherited the knowledge of generations in that singing tradition. Until late in the present century, the great griot families, the Mboups, the Secks, the Fayes, the Kouyatés and the Diabatés, married among themselves and found it difficult to marry out of their serving role to the nobility. This also had the effect of guarding their secrets – thus restricting the oral history record to one social class. Today's griots are less concerned with traditional distinctions of rank and inherited status, but are still remarkable for their natural gifts of speaking, communication and musicianship. Many are broadcasters, journalists, poets, or politicians.

But N'Dour has never forsaken his Senegalese roots, or his family and friends. He paid a tribute to them and all his fans on "Samay Nit" ("My People"), one of the most beautiful tracks on "Wommat – The Guide". He will never forget the friends of his youth in the Medina, he sings, and even if he cannot see as

much of them as he used to and cannot meet his fans individually, they have all contributed to his success. A fair dose of cynicism would seem to be in order – but in Senegalese terms these sorts of sentiments are normal, even expected. The song has the power of a prayer, and an almost perfect simplicity.

"The Guide", as the Sony/Columbia release is entitled, was the first of N'Dour's albums, indeed the first Senegalese album, to be conceived, rehearsed, recorded and mixed entirely in Senegal. A collaborative effort, with contributions from all his musicians, it also had guest appearances by Neneh Cherry, Jacob Desvarieux and Branford Marsalis. "I think Branford was impressed by me", said N'Dour in a recent interview with Jo Shinner for The Wire, "because he used to try and copy my voice on his sax."

Volume twenty in a prolific career, "The Guide" is a rich collection of moods and styles. There's pure mbalax, and there are ballads, and jazzy grooves and intricate dance rhythms hewn from other roots and branches of the African musical tree. As you might expect from a modern-day griot, there is also a leaning towards wise words drawn from African community values – though the lyrics on "How Are You?" ("These times and those times are different/In our ancestors' time nobody starved to death") suggest N'Dour's historical awareness lags a long way behind his vocal skills. There's a new maturity in the singing and a greater sense of structure and presentation in the songs. "Undecided" is a daring, dense composition that echoes traditional improvisations and cuts through to new musical combinations. And "Gorgui" (The Old Man) is the direct descendant of "Wooy", a modern mbalax composition, launched with a new dance, the *xath-bi*, that had Senegalese audiences in ecstatic uproar.

Youssou N'Dour (right) with long-time tama-playing colleague Assane Thiam

has been keen to popularize the music and dances of his native Fouta Toro region which lies along Senegal's northern borders with Mauritania and Mali. Although not a griot by birth, his own family griot, **Mansour Seck**, remains his constant companion and mentor. Maal, who trained at the music conservatoire in Dakar and won a scholarship to study in Paris, is regarded as the intellectual among Senegalese artists.

Moreover, he seems to have inherited the wisdom of the saints, identifying easily with mystic Muslim leaders like Omar Tall whose army waged a jihad to bring Islam to Senegal and who introduced the Tijaniya brotherhood (the confrerie to which Baaba Maal belongs) and Ahmadou Bamba, the leader of the big, mostly Wolof, Mouride brotherhood. Taking on the mantle of entertainer, teacher and messenger, Baaba Maal has a rare gift for expressing in music and words his profound faith in God as well as a sure confidence in the future of humanity. Nowhere is this more evident than in the album "Olel" (Mango/Island, UK) about which Baaba Maal had this to say:

"God is very methodical, respecting order. Just as the world turns regularly on its axis, just as the leaves fall from the tree and bud and break out again with a new season, so everything happens in its own time. Life is an eternal beginning, so we always have the chance to renew and recycle. Up to this point, and especially in the west, there has been too much emphasis on the concrete and not enough on the abstract; too much on the material which rarely brings peace of mind and too little on the development of the spiritual including noble ideals such as friendship and fellowship. I believe that individualism is the greatest obstacle to world harmony. God is one and He wants the world to be one. When humanity begins to work together for new ideals they will succeed."

One of Maal's previous albums, "Nouvelle Génération", was dedicated to young people. "It is the youth who want to break down barriers and we should have confidence in them. Our children and grandchildren will be less weighed down by problems than we are, more intelligent and more keenly aware of the truth."

NEW GENERATION

In a land with few natural resources, Senegal is a fertile garden of musical talent and energy. Music itself is beginning to be viewed as an exportable commodity, like phosphates or fish. But few musicians get the same opportunities as Youssou N'Dour and Baaba Maal and many professionals complain about the lack of structure and low pay.

To try to combat these circumstances, many musicians are working to break the established, Eurocentric focus of the music industry by producing music in Senegal rather than going to overseas studios. The notion that it's preferable to record African music and market it abroad is beginning to make more and more sense. If the counterproductive effects of local piracy can be overcome, Senegal, with an already developing infrastructure, has the potential to create a viable music industry.

A host of younger Senegalese stars, no longer inhibited by the secrecy of the old griot codes – and seemingly less jealous of their reputations – are taking the stage with a new spirit of collaboration. The following run-down sketches over an exciting and diverse field:

Coumba Gawlo Seck, a talented young female singer, **Souleymane Faye**, a former singer with Xalam, and ex-drummer-turned-singer **Cheikh Lô**, have each guested on the albums of the other two. "Seytane", "Teylulen" and "Dohandeem" have all been produced in Dakar by Lebanese producer Robert Lahoud, with accompanying video clips.

The ex-Xalam guitarist and veteran of the Senegambian music scene, **Cheikh Tidiane Tall**, has produced recent albums for two female stars, **Kiné Lam** ("Galass") and **Dial Mbaye** ("Fawade Wele").

Pape Dieng, once a drummer with Youssou N'Dour and the Super Étoile, works from his own midi-studio. His output has included top-quality albums by **Thione Seck** ("Papa") and the veteran

Baaba Maal – "My voice passed a certain level"

BAABA MAAL AT MIDNIGHT: LOOKING AHEAD

The King of Fouta Toro talked to Richard Trillo about his songs, World Music and being Fula.

Is there really something important happening in Senegalese music these days?

Yes, definitely. For example, the arrival of lots of women, who previously didn't have the courage to do modern music, like Kiné Lam and Coumba Gawlo Seck. The message they're putting out in their cassettes is very important for Senegal: they've passed by the praise-song themes, where one sings to people to get money.

How do you see yourself now in comparison with other Senegalese musicians?

Well, I know that the majority of young musicians identify with me in some ways, because, well, I come from far away. I come from the north, so I'm not part of the establishment. The majority of musicians in Senegal do basically Wolof music, which is more about rhythm. So, I turn up with music that's from the Sahel, from the interior, much more related to Malian and Guinean music and the music of the Niger River, much more melodious.

What do you think is the special mark of your vocal style?

Well, I grew up in the Sahel, with a lot of space. My voice was always very loud but very thin. After training, I passed a certain level – what we call the "voice exploding" or *daandé heli* in Fula – when it gets much bigger, much more voluminous. When you arrive at this moment, you can never have a quiet voice. This happens in your development.

How can you explain the dominance of Senegalese musicians in World Music?

It's because Senegalese music is not closed or tight. The first modern group, Orchestra Baobab, came from mixing these Cuban feelings and Cuban rhythms and harmonies with popular traditional music. Senegalese music is evolving all the time. But I'm sometimes afraid to hear about "World Music". I'm afraid to see our music taken like a fish, hooked out of the water. I think it's important for people to have a name. But I don't want people to put African music or other kinds of music in a corner and say after all these *other* kinds of music you have this kind of music, and call it "World Music". No.

Is there any difficulty for your music in competing with Wolof- or Manding-based music?

It's the same in all Africa, when someone is in the minorities, he has a very big problem to show himself. In every country, like Guinea or Senegal, there are Fulanis but they are in the minority. And some people aren't educated enough to know the origin of all these ethnic groups. In Dakar, I meet people who have never been to the north. They hear about it, they think it's two or three countries away, it's so far off in their heads.

Why did you choose the very rock-styled song "Minuit" to end the "Lam Toro" album with?

Yes, it's not too, too, too Baaba Maal. It's more of a commercial track. But the lyrics are very important. Midnight is the time when the spirit takes stock and looks ahead to the new day. It's important for every person to have a midnight in their life – to know what you have done and what you have yet to do.

"Midnight is the moan of the spiritualist
Struggling with the will of the Gods
The sound of distant thunder
Midnight is everything which cries, groans, shudders
Midnight brings hope for a new day
A day of peace and freedom, Free Mandela
Freedom, Liberty, Mandela is free"

---

griotte, **Khar Mbiaye Madiaga** ("Bedentiwo").

A voice from the 1960s – that of blind singer **Pape Niang**, who once sang with the Kaad Orchestra – reappeared on the showcase compilation album "Dakar '92". He describes the song "Diambar" as "soul with a touch of mbalax", and it also retains something of the 1960s Cuban sound.

Also on the CD is **Aminata Fall** from St-Louis in the north, who has been singing and acting at Dakar's Théâtre Sorano for years. Dubbed the "Mahalia Jackson of Senegal" for her lusty jazz style, she has a forceful voice, and the improvisations on "Yaye Boye" are astonishing.

Other tracks on the Revue Noire CD include "Bagn Bagn", on which the rappers Killer B, Dug E Tee and Awadi from Positive Black Soul, join with **Demba Ba**.

Among the top new names of 1993 was **Madou**

Diabaté, whose intriguing "Madame Johnson" came with a comedy video clip that dealt with serious issues – drugs and alcohol.

Wassis Diop, who is based in Paris but returns frequently to Senegal, is a musician and composer who produced a stunning soundtrack for the feature film "Hyènes" directed by his brother Djibril Diop Mambety.

Finally, any mention of new Senegalese stars would be incomplete without referring to the innovative genius of Soriba Kouyaté, a kora player who, apart from being an absolute master of the 21 strings, has extended the repertoire into the realms of jazz and pop. He occasionally teams up with Jean-Philippe Rykiel on keyboard and Leon Sarr (bass) but you can also hear his twinkling tones on several tracks of Youssou N'Dour's new CD

DATE WITH SYLLA – WEST AFRICA'S NUMBER ONE PRODUCER

Ibrahima Sylla has produced some of the most successful African albums in the world. With such an obvious passion for music it's hard to imagine him as just the money man. He admits to being ignorant of musical theory but believes that a good musical ear, a knowledge of African cultures and a long-standing love of many types of music enable him to judge the potential of the demos he receives. Lois Darlington tracked down Africa's most successful producer.

"First I ask the musicians what they want to do. If I want to do something, I tell them how they should work so that we can achieve it. It always works out well because my advice always seems to be in agreement with what they themselves want."

"For example, musicians often lack confidence – you have to tell them, you should record in Paris, you should open your music up. One mustn't confuse 'opened up' with 'distorted' or 'misrepresented' (dénaturé). African music remains African music. But we can make openings so that other ears will accept it."

If he has confidence in them, Sylla generally gives musicians a free hand in the studio. "If not, or if I see they've closed in on themselves, and stayed too rootsy, that's when I intervene."

Sylla is very much behind African-western collaborations in principle. But when the result is too denaturé he blames the artists. "Okay, steal a bit of Weather Report, steal a bit of George Benson or whoever. But the result must become your own!"

Take Ray Lema for example: "His music is completely denaturé. He calls it ouvert but we Africans can't relate to it. It doesn't interest us at all. The problem is over-complex arrangements. Yet Ray Lema is capable! He could work with the Zairean beat and open it up. But the Zairean beat in his music is absent."

The recognizable stamp of Sylla's sound is evident in his most successful production so far, Salif Keita's "Soro", which opened a path to the west for a wealth of African music. Sylla had a feeling this was going to be a special record. "They say that when you work with an albino it brings luck!"

Sylla pushed the barriers as far as he dared with "Soro". But it was a risk. "When I listen to it now I find it was very opened up. Today, I would think twice before making a record like that. I liked Jean-Philippe Rykiel's work very much and, with the three tracks he arranged, I thought it wasn't too dangerous. But with the other tracks that François Bréant arranged ("Soro", "Souareba" and "Sina"), there was really a lot of opening-up. I let him get on with it, but I was adamant that one track, "Sina", had to stay "roots". I really insisted on it. I said they had to use ngoni [the "Mandingo guitar" credited to Ousmane Kouyaté].

With Kasse Mady's "Fode", accessibility-versus-roots was still a major concern but the intention was different. "I wanted to make a good record but not one as open as "Soro". Kasse Mady did not have as much experience as did Salif. He had never left Mali."

For someone who is so aware of the needs of western audiences, it is perhaps surprising to learn that, today, he sees his main market as Africa. His guided tour of Dakar's huge central market goes a long way to explain this. "It's immense. They sell everything you can imagine there and it's the first place to go for new releases. I sold 10,000 copies of "Diawar" (by Ismael Lô) in one hour. Children take twenty cassettes and run around town selling them."

"Diawar" was recorded in Paris, and, in order to outsmart any would-be pirates, the cassettes were sold in Africa before the LP was released in Europe. This has for some years been the dominant practice with Sylla and other big African producers: the artist is hired for the recording sessions on an ad hoc basis. Contracts, promotion, and all the paraphernalia of the recording industry in the west is absent, or has been until very recently. There is a grey area where ownership of works, rights and royalties is often in dispute, which means that plenty of recordings have never been released.

At the moment Wassoulou music is in the ascendant. "Young people want to sing more about social problems. They don't understand why you should praise someone just because he is rich. That's daddies' music." He's producing female artists like Oumou Sangaré, Sali Sidibé, Coumba Sidibé and Dieneba Diakité. Along with their voices he wants to introduce a new sound into Europe: "half-traditional, half-modern – you use acoustic instruments but you add a touch of keyboards, bass guitar, and" – he whispers – "it works!" The new formula has grown partly out of economic constraints, for its spell can be woven in slightly less sophisticated and much cheaper studios in Africa.

In his early teens, Ibrahima travelled throughout West and Central Africa with his father, a renowned marabout, soaking up the different cultures and music. And back at home, life in the Sylla household in Dakar was a constant round of births, naming ceremonies and weddings – and naturally the griots sang for all of them.

Cuban music was at the height of its popularity in Senegal when Sylla was in his teens ("At one time I could tell you the names of all the musicians – I have more than 6,000 Cuban records") and he saw Johnny Pacheco, Orquesta Aragon and Ray Baretto when they visited Africa. He's also mad about soul and has all James Brown's records except two.

Sylla's "Cuban period" brought him into contact with a small label, Salsa Musique, in Paris, who introduced him to record production. After coproducing "Absa Gueye" for Youssou N'Dour's group Étoile de Dakar, Sylla was ready to go it alone. Dakar's Gold Baobab studios were soon kept busy with dozens of Sylla productions. Records were manufactured in the States because it was cheaper, "and it meant I could continue to collect old Cuban records." The Cuban connection has continued until today, with Sylla producing the gathering of New York sessionistos and Senegalese singers that resulted in the acclaimed "Africando" project.

Does he intend to make his fortune and get out fast? Not at all (or rather yes and no). He is happy doing what he's doing, so why try to escape! His ambition? "To produce, produce, produce."

Adapted from an article first published in World Beat magazine.

■ DISCOGRAPHY ■

COMPILATIONS

ⓒ **Various** *Ancient Heart* (Axiom/Mango, UK). Subtitled "Mandinka and Fulani Music of The Gambia", this features rare ensembles of traditional musicians, brought together by Jali Nyama Suso and produced by him and Bill Laswell.
ⓒ **Various** *Dakar '92* (Revue Noire/Insitut Français de Dakar, France). Compilation by the Franco-African journal Revue Noire – featuring everything from rumba to rap: an excellent round-up of new talent on a vibrant music scene.
ⓒ **Various** *Senegal Waaw* (Gandalf Muziektijdshcrift, Belgium). With detailed liner notes, in Flemish and French, this – "Yes, Senegal" – showcases the contemporary scene admirably.

ARTISTS AND BANDS

ⓒ **Africando** *Africando* and *Africando 2* (Stern's, UK). With strong Latin input from a distinguished New York line-up, and sheer charm from the Senegalese singers, these recent releases are languid, lilting nostalgia for the golden age of Cuban dance music in Africa.
ⓒ **Orchestra Baobab** *Pirate's Choice* (World Circuit, UK). Blissfully good 1982 session from the best Senegalese band of the 1970s. How did they come up with these songs? ⓒ *On Verra Ça* (World Circuit, UK) is almost as hot: ⓒ *Bamba* (Stern's, UK) is definitely third choice.
ⓒ **Ifang Bondi** *Sanjo* (D&K, Netherlands). One of the few available CDs of non-kora Gambian music, this is Manding

world-rock in the Mory Kanté mould, with kora-style guitars and much mbalax influence.
ⓒ **Pascal Diatta and Sona Mané** *Simnade* (Rogue, UK). Casamançais songs defying categorization, this matches the amazing acoustic guitar style (thumb and two fingers) of Diatta against the gruff vocals of his cross-looking wife Sona Mané, in a set recorded live in one of Zinguinchor's worst hotels.
ⓒ **Étoile de Dakar** *Vols 1–10* (Stern's, UK). A major series of releases, the collected works of one of Senegal's seminal bands, featuring Youssou N'Dour. Near-essential.
ⓒ **Ismael Lô** *Diawar* (Stern's, UK). Features one of Lô's best tracks, "Sophia", a 1989 interpretation of the song "On Verra Ça" previously recorded by Orchestra Baobab. ⓒ *Tajabone* (Barclay, France) is a soulful and highly accessible excursion into a more commercial sphere. This latest ⓒ *Iso* (Mango, UK) is feeble in comparison.
ⓒⒹ **Baaba Maal** *Djam Leelii* (Rogue, UK). Playing acoustic guitar and singing with childhood friend, Mansour Seck, Baaba Maal interprets the traditional tunes and themes of the Senegal river region where he was born. Music to be transported by. ⓒ *Lam Toro* (Mango, UK), is the most personal of all Maal's albums, dedicated to his mother who died young but who remains the guiding spirit in all his art. Note that the similarly packaged US version is subtitled *The Remix Album* and has the dubious benefit of geography-lesson rapping from Macka B.

Youssou N'Dour *Immigrés* (Earthworks/Virgin, UK). The immigrants in question are Senegalese migrant workers in France. The track and the LP hinted at the international success to come. **Eyes Open** (Sony/Columbia, US) is rich and satisfying, with songs in Wolof, French and English. The new **The Guide** (Sony/Columbia, US) offers Youssou N'Dour and the Super Étoile in mature, innovative mode, with collaborations both successful (Branford Marsalis) and embarrassing (Neneh Cherry). There's also a cut-price introductory compilation , **Hey You!** (Music Club, UK).

Omar Pene and Super Diamono *Sai Sai* (Syllart, France). LP featuring strong mbalax beat with cheeky lyrics and the winning combination of Pene's dulcet tones and the Super Diamono sound. **Thione Seck et le Raam Daan** *Unesco* (local cassette, Senegal). Offering the bravest mbalax in the business with almost hysterically up-tempo rhythms against his robust, measured vocals, Seck is a musician's musician par excellence. The LP-release, *Le Pouvoir d'un Coeur Pur* (Stern's, UK), is a good vehicle for his voice, most emotive on the silky ballad "Yeen", but the rhythms are less to the fore.

Touré Kunda *Natalia* (Celluloid, France). Delightful, moody meander through the Diola world of *djambaadong* with subtle technical assistance from producer Bill Laswell.

Xalam *Gorée* (Celluloid, France). LP of Senegal's super jazz group with excellent ensemble work and vintage performances from all sections.

GAMBIAN KORA ARTISTS

Amadu Bansang Jobarteh *Tabara* (Music of the World, US). The Gambia's senior exponent of the crisp, up-river (tilibo) tradition of kora, with an intimate style, creating a strong sense of music from bygone days.

Alhaji Bai Konteh *Alhaji Bai Konteh* (Rounder, USA). Atmospheric 1972 recordings made at the Konteh home in Brikama. The Gambia's finest exponent of Casamance-style kora, with bluesy tuning and lightning-fast variations.

Dembo Konteh & Kausu Kouyate *Simbomba* (Rogue, UK). Duets and songs in deep, Casamance style. On "Jali Roll" the famed duo go electric with members of 3Mustaphas3.

Dembo Konteh and Malamini Jobarteh *Jaliya* (Stern's, UK). Excellently recorded kora and voice duets from Alhaji Bai Konteh's sons. Includes a powerful rendition of the historical song "Cheddo". LP only.

Jaliba Kuyateh *Jaliba Kuyateh à Paris* (VSSF, France). Kora, voice, bass, percussion and trumpet from The Gambia's most popular young artist. Frenzied, relentless dance music.

Jali Nyama Suso *Kora Manding* (Ocora, France). Tuneful, accessible kora and singing in both upper-river and coastal styles, recorded in 1972 in the US. LP only. *Kora Music from the Gambia* (Free Music, Germany, LP only) contains his famous valedictory song "Jali Nyama Suso".

SWEET SORROW

THE MUSIC OF CAPE VERDE

Two hours flying time west of Dakar lie the Cape Verde islands, a unique archipelago adrift in the Atlantic Ocean. David Peterson explores *morna*, *coladeira* and *funana* – the music from a country most of whose people live overseas.

Many music-lovers will have heard of the jazz pianist Horace Silver, and Tavares, the disco group immortalized on the "Saturday Night Fever" soundtrack. Both are Cape Verdean. But the music of the islands themselves is still largely unknown and, with the exception of **Cesaria Evora**, "the barefoot diva", the attention given to African music in recent years has largely bypassed Cape Verde.

The Republic of Cape Verde is an archipelago 600km off the coast of Senegal, named after Cap Vert, the peninsula of Dakar. Divided into two groups of islands – the windward Barlavento group in the north and the leeward Sotaventos in the south – the Cape Verdes are an Atlantic world apart, an ex-Portuguese colony, independent since 1975, not quite African, but

scarcely European. Although prone to catastrophic drought, only four of the islands are truly barren and several have steep, mountainous interiors with towering peaks and vegetation-choked ravines.

Although uninhabited when the Portuguese first arrived in 1455, the Cape Verdes became an important supply station on the transatlantic trade routes. With the arrival of African slaves and sailors, the islands became quite mixed racially, and most of the population speaks Kriolu, a creole language which blends old-style Portuguese with West African languages. The Kriolu language has subtle differences from island to island: Brava's Kriolu is the most Portuguese, while the most Africanized Kriolu is spoken on Santiago, which is home to the *badius*, who are peasants descended from runaway slaves.

In the 500 years of its occupation, Portugal almost totally ignored the islands' development. Thousands perished in famines, went to São Tomé as plantation workers, or emigrated overseas. Of a million people who

WEST AFRICA

Cesaria Evora: "I only regret my success has taken so long"

call themselves Cape Verdean, only about a third actually live on the islands. The remainder are scattered in the US (mostly New England) and Europe (principally Portugal, France and the Netherlands). On some islands, almost every family has relatives overseas. It's this history of bittersweet separation and longing which has most vividly coloured the Cape Verde's musical culture.

Several outside influences have contributed to the musical life of Cape Verde, but there are a number of native styles, some of which have changed little in centuries. Some styles, such as the *morna*, sound quite European: 500 years in Portugal's forgotten backyard has left a strong Lusitanian imprint on Cape Verdean music. Of course, the West African element is also deeply felt, both in the morna, but more strongly in styles such as the *batuco* and *funana*. Portuguese folk songs, the improvised, rhythmic songs of the badius, and influences from the Caribbean and Brazil have, over the centuries, combined into Kriolu music's easy fusion of African and European sensibilities.

THE MORNA

What the *corrido* is to Mexico or the tango to Argentina, the **morna** is to Cape Verde. This national song form is at least a century and a half old and is part of nearly every Cape Verdean band's repertoire. Almost always written and sung in Kriolu, mornas have minor-key melodies and are slow, often with a beat similar to that of

a Cuban *habanera*. But their lyrics are the heart of the matter. The lyrics of a morna can stand alone as a poetic form, and there have been several published anthologies of morna lyrics. Lyrics usually speak of love and longing for one's distant *cretcheu* – "beloved". The *manija*, which literally meant "verse" or "song", was a form very similar to the morna, but it is rarely heard now.

The origins of the morna are disputed. Some have said that it was influenced by the ballads of sailors from the British Isles picking up coal in Mindelo on the island of São Vicente; others that it was imported from Brazil in the 1800s. It certainly brings to mind a Brazilian *modinha*, such as composer Heitor Villa-Lobos' "Seresata No. 5" and Portuguese *fado*. Indeed it's been suggested that the fado and morna share common (and very mournful) roots in the Gulf of Guinea slave plantation islands of São Tomé and Príncipe where a rhythm called *lundum* originated. Whatever the truth, the morna evokes an unmistakably Cape Verdean feeling of *sodade* – the Kriolu version of the Portuguese *saudade*, meaning yearning, longing, homesickness – especially when sung by an artist such as Bana or the New England-based Vickie Viera. The classic mornas are by the nineteenth-century composer **Eugénio Tavares**, but the genre is not exclusive to dead poets and the form is still actively composed.

The instrumentation of the morna ensemble has changed over the years. Until the advent of electric instruments in the 1960s, mornas were accompanied by string orchestras of different sizes. These consisted of at least one guitar, often a fiddle, an occasional bass or piano, and, less often, an accordian. In addition, the high-pitched strumming that is an identifying feature of many mornas is the cavaquinho, an instrument popular in Portugal and Brazil, from where it was introduced to the islands. The *cavaquinho* is very much like a ukulele, with four strings, either of steel or gut, that are tuned like the top four strings of a guitar. Although they were usually homemade in the early days, there are instrument-makers today in Madeira, Portugal and Brazil who make good cavaquinhos. Another instrument is the twelve-stringed tenor guitar called the *viola*, which is a little shorter than a standard guitar. The viola's rhythmic role was supplanted by the louder sound of the maracas, but it is still used on occasion.

Contemporary mornas make use of a wider range of instruments. A trumpet, sax, clarinet or electric guitar often states the melody or plays an instrumental break, backed by a piano, synths, a string section, or even a few touches from the drum kit. But the cavaquinho is almost always still used in present-day recordings.

Travadinha's "Dark Skinned Temptress" album

For sheer instrumental virtuosity, the like of which may not be heard again, **Travadinha** (Antonio Vicente Lopes) was a stunning example. Part of a large musical family, his skill on the violin, the viola, the cavaquinho and the guitar is legendary. A recent commemorative CD (he died in 1987) has been released by the Portugal–Cape Verde Friendship Society.

OTHER STYLES

At the more African end of the Cape Verdean musical spectrum is the *coladeira*, and, closer still to mainland roots, the *batuco*, *funana* and *finaçon*. These styles are faster in tempo than the morna, and while they are sometimes less involved lyrically and melodically, they are usually more rythmically complex.

In earlier times, the word **coladeira** referred both to a processional dance on feast days and to a group of female singers improvising topical songs, sometimes accompanied by drums (Ana Prócupio was a noted Kriolu female improviser in the early years of this century, of whom it used to be said "Lots of people sing, but Ana Prócupio was a singer"). However, by the 1960s the coladeira had started to denote a style of dancing and music which was fast and light-hearted. Coladeiras often have a strong French Antillean flavour, particularly influenced by such groups as Galaxy Selection and Exile 1, popular in Cape Verde during the 1970s. Although coladeiras sometimes developed from mornas, the result is always quite distinct, with more whimsical, even cynical lyrics, and a tight, sexy rhythm.

The **batuco**, the **funana** and the **finaçon** grew out of the *tabanca* rites, celebrated by the *badius* of Santiago. Tabanca were their mutual aid associations which had their own social organization, from king and queen down. Originally, the batuco (essentially percussion) and the funana (a dance rhythm, later on for couples) were forms improvised by singers, accompanied by hand-clapping, choral responses, the beating of cushions or rolls of cloth (*tchabeta*) held between the legs, and sometimes accordions and scrapers (*ferrinhos*). In earlier times the ancient African stringed instruments, *cimbó* and *berimbau*, were also used. These styles were looked down upon by the Catholic Church and the upper classes of Cape Verde. Since independence, however, all three genres (funana, batuco and finaçon) have been incorporated and revitalized by many of the pop bands of the islands in a movement similar to those in other African countries where traditional music was adapted and sometimes transformed into new sounds.

These days, the more mundane pop-funana recordings have a sound akin to a kind of lopsided *zouk*, often with similar drum-machine and synth programming. But the most distinctive funanas have a nervous, jerky beat, usually propelled by figures played on the snare drum. In some funanas, there is a suspended feeling of time – fast, yet free-floating. And vocals are sung using simple harmonies with an energetic abandon.

Funacola, a melding of coladeira and funana, is a recent development popularized by the Praia/Paris-based group **Finaçon**.

EUGÉNIO TAVARES: COMPOSER OF MORNAS

·······················

Eugénio Tavares, born in 1867, was a native of Brava, and is the best-loved writer of mornas in the islands, as well as a romantacised figure in Cape Verdean lore. Working most of his life as a journalist and civil servant, he was a champion of Kriolu language and culture. Much of his popularity resides in the fact that he was one of the first to compose poetry of a high standard in Kriolu instead of Portuguese.

Most of his mornas dealt with the pain and spirituality of romantic love, as in "Força de Crecheu" and "Vida sem Bo Luz". One of his most popular mornas, "O Mar Eterno", was inspired by his romance with a wealthy young American woman who was visiting Brava by yacht. She was impressed by Tavares' poetry, and the two fell in love. But her disapproving father doused the affair by setting sail one night. Tavares found out the next morning that she had gone, and he set down his sadness

in a morna, that is still often perfomred in the islands today.

A number of his compositions portray the sadness of those emigrating from the islands, such as in "Morna de Nha Santa Ana" and "Hora di Bai" (The Hour of Leaving), which is his most famous. It is a morna that has been traditionally sung at the docks in Brava as people boarded America-bound ships. It is also often sung in both countries to signal the end of an evening's festivities.

Tavares was also a writer of prose, in which he expressed resentment over mainland Portugal's mismanagement of Cape Verde and also attempted to illustrate the hardships of the Cape Verdean people.

On his death in 1930, Tavares' body was accompanied to its resting place by flocks of people singing and playing his mornas. "Mornas e Manijas", by Osório de Oliviera, is a collection in Portuguese of many of Tavares' best known morna lyrics.

CURRENT STARS

There are currently a number of top groups and singers in Cape Verde, who regularly release recordings on labels in Portugal and France, where most of the music is recorded. Many of these artists divide the year between Cape Verde and either Portugal or New England, playing to large audiences at independence festivities held in the Cape Verdean enclaves.

One long-standing group is **Bulimundo**. They combine both acoustic and electric guitars with jazzy trumpet and sax solos to create their own blend of folkloric and modern music.

Another group, with a similar style, based around morna and coladeira, is **Os Tubarões** (The Sharks), a seven-piece outfit fronted by vocalist Ildo Lobo, who have been to Boston several times and are essentially the "house band" of Praia, Cape Verde's capital. A recent album of theirs, "Bote, Broce, e Linha", sold

more than 10,000 copies – pretty successful for a Cape Verdean group. In a recent interview, reprinted in the New Bedford paper Cape Verde News, Lobo described their themes: "We deal with problems faced by women and with emigration. Every house in these islands has some sort of problem linked with emigration. I don't agree with living abroad. People abroad don't experience the day-to-day life here, and so they can't make real Cape Verdean music. Still, we are subject to imported influences. Our people abroad send us all types of music, and we are changing. But what you hear most is Cape Verdean." Os Tubarões play frequently at their open-air nightclub, outside Praia.

A group that has achieved widespread popularity for their dynamic use of Cape Verde's musical heritage (and their abrasive, topical lyrics) is **Finaçon**, formed on Santiago in the late 1980s by brothers Zeca and Zeze di Nha Reinalda. With Finaçon, named after the badiu improvised women's style of that name, the brothers went to Paris and worked with the ground-breaking Zairean musician Ray Lema ("our style was deeply influenced by his advice") to produce their "Funana" CD.

Sax-player and clarinettist **Luis Morais** and multi-instrumentalist **Paulino Vieira** have produced and played on many albums by Cape Verdean artists, and they continue to lend their talents to many recordings. Vieira, in particular,

is a musical explorer who has brought together various overseas influences (reggae, country, R&B) with homegrown rhythmic and instrumental roots.

A long-established group of artists that have achieved big success while misleading novice listeners with their name is **Cabo Verde Show**, a dance music vehicle for Paris-based musicians and singers Manou Lima, Luis da Silva, Serge da Silva and René Cabral (the "Cape Verdean Al

BAREFOOT DIVA IN PARIS

....

Cesaria Evora is the best-known Cape Verdean artist in Europe, a powerful singer of the potently sentimental morna style of nostalgia-laden ballad. The niece of disabled morna composer Francisco Xavier da Cruz, known as "B.Leza" (a cruel pun on *beleza*: beauty), Cesaria Evora began peforming in her late teens in the handful of bars in her native Mindelo, the town of São Vicente island, Cape Verde's most "cultured" island. She was accompanied by the celebrated clarinettist Luis Morais and by the age of twenty was the darling of the local radio station. But only when she was in her mid-forties did she leave the islands and make

her break in Paris, under the tutelage of Bana, who produced her first solo recording, "Distino di Belita". Most of her subsequent output has been produced by Cape Verdean emigré Jose da Silva for his Lusafrica label. With "Mar Azul" and "Miss Perfumado", her most recent releases, she's found her mark – superb, gutsy, acoustic songs telling of her country's hardship and her own heartbreak.

Cesaria Evora's trademark is performing barefoot, always. It's her mark of solidarity with those left behind, with the ragged children of the island interiors for whom even a trip to Praia (the little capital, on Santiago) is just a dream.

Her albums are distinguished by her extraordinary voice and most include one or more morna compositions by Uncle "B. Leza". Her current musical director is pianist Paulino Vieira, and her band includes Morgadinho, the original guitarist from the Holland-based band A Voz de Cabo Verde.

A whiskey-drinking, cigarette-puffing grandmother, married three times, thrice deserted and now scornfully independent, Cesaria Evora is an unlikely diva. At her age she has little interest in the frills and thrills of stardom: "I wasn't astonished by Europe and I was never that impressed by the speed and grandeur of modern America. I only regret my success has taken so long to achieve."

Thanks to Andy Morgan for supplementary material.

SODADE

Quem mostra' bo	Who showed you
Ess caminho longe?	This far journey?
Quem mostra' bo	Who showed you
Ess caminho longe?	This far journey?
Ess caminho	This journey
Pa São Tomé	To São Tomé
Sodade, sodade	Sodade, sodade
Sodade	Sodade
Dess nha terra São Nicolau	For my land of São Nicolau
Si bô 'screvé' me	If you write to me
'M ta 'screvé' be	I'll write to you
Si bô 'squecé' me	If you forget me
'M ta 'squecé' be	I'll forget you
Sodade, sodade	Sodade, sodade
Sodade	Sodade
Dess nha terra São Nicolau	For my land of São Nicolau
Até dia	Until the day
Qui bô voltá	On which you return

By Luis Morais and Amandio Cabral from
"Miss Perfumado" (Mélodie, France), translated by Caroline Shaw

LIVE AT THE BAY OF CATS

· ·

Started in 1984 by a group of young people from a Mindelo cultural centre, the **Baia das Gatas Music festival** on the island of São Vicente had grown by 1993 into Cape Verde's major summer attraction, with 30,000 people attending for the three days in August. Many festival-goers camp out, sleep in lorries or cars on the dunes, or, increasingly, occupy little weekend chalets that are springing up around the bay. A village of wood and sackcloth bars and restaurants comes into existence (it never rains), buzzing with merry-makers every night until 3am. Anything from a dozen to twenty local and visiting acts play, with lengthy pauses for sound checks, from a permanent stone stage on the beach, while festival-goers dance, sunbathe or dive off the long, stone breakwater extending into the bay. National radio and TV cover the event continuously. Many expatriate Cape Verdeans time their summer holidays to coincide with the festival, and the area jostles with reunited families and the noise of long-unseen friends bumping into each other. The quality of the music is variable, with international groups of indifferent quality sometimes booked for local youth appeal, and the top local acts disappointingly absent. But it's nevertheless an event well worth catching and, if any excuse were needed, a great reason to visit Cape Verde. In practical terms, if you want to go, inter-island flights are all heavily booked at this time and hotel rooms are hard to find in Mindelo, the only town on the island. Public transport between town and bay, a roughish twenty-minute taxi ride, may involve some waiting – and sometimes a high price –, but is reasonably plentiful.

Philip Sweeney

Jarreau"). Often labelled as zouk-derivative, they say their music was a precursor of Jacob Desvarieux's Antillean sound, and claim it was he who was influenced by the sounds of the islands, rather than the reverse.

Another popular singer, with many fine albums to his credit, is **Bana**. In Mindelo in the 1950s, he used to transport the disabled composer B.Leza from gig to gig. His popularity, his wide travels (Senegal, Europe) and perhaps even his outstanding physical stature (he is nearly two metres tall) earned him an unjustified reputation as a collaborator with the Portuguese, a slur he has never quite shaken off, despite a reconciliation with the Cape Verdean government. After stints in Rotterdam and Paris he is now based in Lisbon.

Other current popular singers include **Masa Abrantes**, Celina Goncalves, and the Paris-based singer **Nando**. But the most famous name in Cape Verdean music today is that of **Cesaria Evora**.

CAPE VERDEANS IN AMERICA

Throughout the nineteenth century, each year saw a few Cape Verdeans escaping poverty by fleeing to New England with American whaling ships, but islanders began to move to the United States in large numbers from the beginning of this century. Today there are more Cape Verdeans and people of Cape Verdean descent living in America than in the islands themselves. California and Hawaii both have big Cape Verdean communities, but by far the largest concentration is in New England. In fact, with the decline of the whaling era, many of the ships were bought by Cape Verdeans and sailed back and forth between the US and Cape Verde, delivering supplies to the islands and transporting emigrants to America.

The emigrants brought their music with them, playing it at social gatherings and on special

Bana, giant of the morna

occasions. Early Cape Verdean string bands included the **B-29s**, the **Cape Verdean Serenaders**, and groups led by Augusto Abrio and Notias. Cape Verdeans also contributed to the Big Band era, with orchestras such as Duke Oliver's Creole Vagabonds, and the Don Verdi Orchestra. These groups played mostly the swing music of the day, but also included their arrangements of Kriolu songs.

At present, there's a good number of groups and musicians playing in New England, mostly based in Boston. **Rui Pina** grew up making drums and singing in the neighbourhood. He was influenced by Ildo Lobo and Zeca di Nha Reinalda – and later by Prince and Phil Collins. Pina's first album, "Tchika", in 1985, was backed by the group **Tabanka Djazz**. "Nase pa Vive", his first solo album, was released on his own label, Kola Records. The 1992 release, "Irresistible", has contributions from another Boston-based artist, **Norberto Tavares**. A native of Santiago, Tavares and his group Tropical Power play both Cape Verdean and Brazilian music. His latest solo album is "Jornada dum Badiu" (Working Day of a Badiu, though in a more poetic sense *jornada* also means "journey").

Also based in Boston is singer-songwriter **Frank de Pina**. Born in Cape Verde in the 1950s, he and his brothers formed his first group, Os Vulcanicos, in 1971. Later, he left for Portugal and, ultimately, the United States, where he has made four albums:, including the excellent 1990 album, "Ansiedade".

The **Creole Sextet**, who specialize in the older Cape Verdean styles, have been playing parties, benefits, and dances in the New England area for many years. Based in New Bedford, the group consists of Flash Vieira on vocals and electric guitar, Johnny Duarte on violin, Moe Garça on bass, and Vickie Viera, a highly esteemed singer, on vocals.

The hot new names on the US-based Cape Verde scene are the **Mendes Brothers**, João and Ramiro. Ramiro is in fact a veteran strings arranger and producer, having worked on most of Cesaria Evora's releases and those of many other Cape Verdean musicians. Their new label, MB Records, already has a string of interesting releases available of US- and Cape Verde-based artists, including Gardenia Benros, a relatively young singer based in Rhode Island, the very danceable Mirri Lobo and the morna-singer Saozinha, for whom they have released a CD of beautiful old Eugénio Tavares songs. Their own recording, "Palonkon", is an eclectic mixture of everything.

◼ DISCOGRAPHY ◼

COMPILATIONS

◎ **Various** *Cape Verde Islands: the Roots* (Playa Sound, France). Momas, coladeiras, and funanas with cavaquinho, the old-style viola and accordion. There's also a tune for the *cimbó*, a kind of fiddle used to accompany the *batuco*. Intriguing CD, recorded in 1990.

◎ **Various** *Funana Dance* (Mélodie, France). Interesting compilation of eight hi-tech funanas by several different groups.

◎ **Various** *Musiques du Monde: Cap Vert* (Buda, France). A recent collection of traditional Cape Verdean musicians. Includes Kodé di Dóna, Augusto da Pina, Mino de Mama and the group Pai e Filhos.

MODERN RELEASES

◎ **Bana** *...Chante la Magie du Cap Vert* (Lusafrica, France). Bana exercises his vocal chords around a sweet, classic selection of momas and coladeiras, reunited with a band that understands the good old ways. Highly recommended. His LP *Ritmos de Cabo Verde* (Movieplay, Portugal), also good, has the best Cape Verdean attempt at soukous you're likely to hear.

◎ **Gardénia Benros** *Mix 2* (MB Records, US). Most recent release by a young Rhode Island-based singer, encompassing medleys of the whole range of Cape Verdean styles, including B. Leza compositions.

◎ **Bulimundo** *Funana Dance, Vol 2* (Lusafrica/Mélodie, France). Tends, like much modern Cape Verdean music, to hover between bluesy tradition and slushy Euro-pop – most uncomfortably on the faster numbers. But the slower songs work a gradual spell.

◎ **Cesaria Evora** *Miss Perfumado* (Lusafrica/Mélodie, France). Evora's most recent CD has been a major hit, especially in France, thanks to astute marketing – and, of course, her wonderful voice. Earlier recordings include ◎ *Distino di Belita* recorded in Paris, with Luis Morais and Ramiro Mendes – the release that first drew the world's attention to Cape Verdean music – and ◎ *Mar Azul*, another Mendes production. ◎ *La Diva Aux Pieds Nus* shows off Cesaria in particularly fine form. All four are available (Lusafrica/Mélodie, France).

◎ **Mirri Lobo** *Paranoia* (MB Records, US). Sprightly set of coladeiras by one of archipelago's most popular singers.

◎ **Mendes Brothers** *Palonkon* (MB Records, US). Named after their home village on the volcanic island of Fogo, this is a first CD for veteran music-fixer Ramiro and brother João. Unclassifiable, but spends most of its time animatedly on the dance floor.

Frank de Pina *Ansiedade* (own label, US). One of the very best, this recording features two exquisite mornas with a string section and the twelve-string guitar and cavaquinho of Ramiro Mendes, who also produces. The other four cuts are fast dance tunes with fine brass and sax.

Rui Pina *Irresistible* (Kola, US). Pina's third album is in a mostly zouk setting, but darker, with a Cape Verdean approach to melody, featuring unhurried intros, velvety sax, strings, accordion, and even a high-school choir on one cut.

◎ **Saozinha** *Saozinha Canta Eugénio Tavares* (MB Records, US). The mornas of Eugénio Tavares have been overshadowed in recent years by those of B.Leza and his protegés. Here's a CD of classic songs to right the balance.

① Chico Serra *Piano Bar of Mindelo* (Buda, France). Momas in a lounge setting, at the classic venue, backed by two guitars, cavaquinho and bass.

① Norberto Tavares *Jornada di un Badiu* (Lusafrica/Mélodie, France). Tavares is a US-based original, whose output usually has a distinct political overtone. "Day [or "journey"] of a badiu" is a set of, mostly, funanas.

① Travadinha *Le Violon de Cap Vert* (Buda, France). A tribute to the late great fiddler, here displaying a dazzling range of finger skills.

OLDER RELEASES ON LP/CASSETTE

A large number of records were produced in the 1960s and '70s with Cape Verdean artists, especially on the Portuguese CDLS label. Some may still be obtainable if you search in Lisbon or the US. In the US, try Henda Records & Video, 10 Durfee St, PO Box 2537, Fall River, MA 02722; MB Records, 84 Foster St, Brockton MA 02401, ☎ (508) 587-3439, or Qualiton Importers on ☎ (718) 937-8515. For videotapes, try Pimental's in New Bedford, ☎ (508) 997-2854. Noteworthy records include:

Luis Morais e seu Conjunto Broadway (CDLS, Portugal). Instrumentals by the Cape Verdean clarinettist, including coladeiras – and cumbias.

Ima Costa *Folklore de Cabo Verde* (Osiris, France). Female lead singer, male backup, with coladeiras and mornas for guitar, cavaquinho and maracas.

Jovino *African People* (Discos Monte Cara, Portugal). With Luis Morais on tenor sax and Voz de Cabo Verde, this is an unusual album which includes the unlikely "Ballad to Henry K." (yes, that one).

Voz de Sanicolau *Fundo de Maré Palinha* (label unknown, Portugal). One of the better 1970s albums, this features cavaquinho, guitar, organ and drums running through mornas and coladeiras, plus the unlikely bonus of "Viva España" complete with a flamenco intro.

Dani Silva *Lua Vagabunda* (own label, Portugal). A personal favourite, featuring both Paulino Vieira and Portuguese rocker Rui Veloso on guitars and vocals. A morna, a soukous-inflected tune, and some other up-tempo songs with a fine brass section.

NAKA AND KABA

GUITARISTS FROM GUINEA-BISSAU

The small republic of Guinea-Bissau is perhaps the least known of the world's Guineas (the others are Guinea, Equatorial Guinea and Papua New Guinea). A part of Lisbon's suffering overseas empire until 1974 when fifteen years of guerilla war finally kicked the Portuguese out, the government has recently shed most of its Marxist pretensions and the country is on the edge of a new democratic era. Richard Trillo talks to one of the country's most successful musicians.

During the colonial era, Portuguese rules of citizenship were applied ruthlessly (Guiné was governed as an overseas province of Portugal, not a foreign colony), education was limited to a tiny percentage of the population, and full citizen's rights were only extended to those who could pass certain tests – fluency in Portuguese for example. In practice, the majority of such *assimilados* had Portuguese ancestors. It was from the ranks of this educated middle-class that the liberation movement grew.

The Portuguese ruled the province through mixed-race administrators, with the assistance of a few appointed chiefs from the Muslim community. In colonial times, most of the successful bands played musical variations on the big Cuban/Manding themes common to Guinea and Mali. **Kaba Mane**, the first Guinea-Bissauan to release an LP internationally, in 1986, is part of this tradition.

Ramiro Gomés Días (born in 1955 and nicknamed **Naka** by his mother for luck: she kept losing children) came from an assimilado background, and his career followed a different path:

"They thought I had a sporting career ahead of me. I used to be able to do 100m in 12 seconds. But I hadn't got the determination for that." Naka was dismissed from the church choir when he asked why all the saints were white. "I got really into music during my *fanado* [three months' seclusion in the bush leading up to circumcision].

"I participated in Guinea's independence for two years. But I wasn't at all happy with the way the country was going, politically. Cape Verde and Guinea-Bissau joined forces to fight the Portuguese. But after they left, the Cape Verdeans in Guinea-Bissau effectively took power there. I used to get accused of collaborating with the Portuguese, because I didn't fight in the bush. Well, who didn't 'collaborate'? On one occasion I challenged a soldier and they put me in prison for a couple of days. Someone else came along and released me. It was a very disorganized period. And I'm quite an organized man."

Despite his father's disapproval, Naka had formed a band in Bissau, **N'Kassa Cobra**, playing African covers. In 1976 he was sent to Lisbon to study. But his music took over. Although the African community welcomed him, there were barriers to advancement as a musician: "People hadn't really come to terms with the fact that now they had to treat Africans as equals. The Portuguese are racists. And attitudes haven't really changed much. It's beginning to change, because there are quite a few people from the old colonies now and people are getting more used to foreign music, and more tuned in to African music. When the Portuguese were in Guinea they didn't listen to Guinean music at all – *fado* in the evenings sometimes, or Beatles-style imitators like Roberto Carlos from Brazil, but even the more rootsy Brazilian music like Martinho de Villar wasn't popular."

Naka move to Paris, where, after a couple of false starts with other bands, he established himself as a solo artist, adapting one of the traditional rhythms of Guinea-Bissau – the *gumbe* – to his own flamboyant tastes: "Originally, gumbe was a rhythm that was played over generations on all big occasions – marriages, baptisms, funerals. And it can be a kind of praise-singing, or flattery song. It used to be played with old instruments, calabashes and so on. I wanted to add the personalities of the band to it – so I call my music *Afro-gumbe show*."

The *jali* tradition – musicianship as an inherited right or duty – doesn't exist in Guinea-Bissau as strongly as in Mali and Guinea: "The classic idea is that not everyone is allowed to play music. I'm not from that generation. I believe in natural talent – anyone can play if they want to, if they have ability. I'm not sure what really drives me. Just wanting to play, to sing. But also it depresses me to realize how many people don't even know of the existence of Guinea-Bissau. That's a pretty good reason to sing and express our musical culture."

Although the guitar is Naka's instrument, he doesn't always play it in performance: "Let's say I don't like monotony – I like evolution in my musical life. I started by singing solo, then I took up the guitar. It's a big passion. It's an instrument that's helped me a lot. And when we were rehearsing, if the others didn't turn up sometimes, I'd fill in on the drums or other instruments. As my father used to say, 'You can't control something if you don't understand it.' So I thought, well, it's not a bad idea to be able to do everything. But nowadays, while I still play guitar, and I'm still learning, and all my arrangements are made thanks to the guitar, I don't think I really have a good format for my stage show yet. If I just do vocals, I often feel there's something missing."

On stage, Naka flings himself into energetic dancing and whooping. You get the impression he needs a lot of space. "It's true I'm a real performer. I'm not timid. Sometimes I see that things aren't really swinging in the band – it's difficult to find a musician who comes up to my intellectual level, the level I want. It's hard to find a good guitarist who plays well and who can also dance – I've been looking for twenty years. I definitely don't want to do something tacky and commercial. But I can't see how music that has the power to move people doesn't get them dancing!"

DISCOGRAPHY

ⓒ **Kaba Mane** *Best of...* (Mélodie, France). From the broad Manding tradition, Mane learned the kora when young and went on to play electric guitar, kora-style. He was the first musician to dent the overseas charts with his delightfully infectious *Chefo Mae Mae* LP. Tracks from that and the follow-up, *Kunga Kungake*, are on this CD.

ⓒ **Ramiro Naka** *Salvador* (Mango, UK). Showcase album for an exuberant talent, this ranges from upfront rock on the title track to Kriolu/Cape Verdean inflections in "Tchon Tchoma" and "Rabo de Padja" and an appealingly offbeat roots sound in "Nha Indimigo".

ⓒ **Tino Trimó** *Kambalocho* (MB Records, US). A forthcoming album ("Unfaithful") for gumbe fans – traditional songs played "live" in the studio. Strong album, great voice.

PALM-WINE SOUNDS

SIERRA LEONEAN MUSIC FOR THE AFTERNOON

For a country where the recording industry died in the 1970s and hasn't looked back, where the delightful common greeting is "How de body?", to which you reply "Body fine", it's hard to feel anything but sympathy and regret as Sierra Leone toys with economic collapse and its petty civil war. Richard Trillo listens to the cool sounds of Calender, Rogie and others.

O nce one of West Africa's most progressive and wealthy nations, Sierra Leone, thirty years after independence, is going through some bad, bad times. Things could be worse: most people agree that the young army officers who recently threw out the corrupt civilian government are an improvement. But musically, it's a sad day when the birthplace of **palm-wine music** can't field a single exponent for the world stage – unless you count an old-timer who left twenty years ago.

Palm wine is the naturally fermented sap-juice of the oil palm – poor people's booze in a country where a bottle of imported beer costs a

day's wages. The music to accompany the refreshment, palm-wine music, or *maringa* as it's locally known, was first made internationally famous by **Ebenezer Calender and his Maringar Band**. Calender (1912–85) played a soft, breezy, calypsonian, verse-and-chorus style of music which came in part from the Caribbean freed slave immigrants who had given Freetown its name. At root, Trinidadian calypso and Freetown *maringa* may have the same seaborne origins in the Kru-speaking people of Liberia – great sailors and very accomplished guitarists – who, from a very early date, were hiring themselves out to foreign vessels as well as undertaking their own trading expeditions all along the West African coast, spreading their guitar style as they went.

Calender was the son of a soldier from Barbados. He trained as a carpenter and was a well-known coffin-maker, but his music soon took over and by the early years of independence he was a mainstay of the Sierra Leone Broadcasting Service. He recorded dozens of shellac 78rpms in the 1950s and early '60s, mostly in Krio, the creole-English of Freetown. The popular song "Double-Decker Buses" (celebrating their arrival from England, and the party on wheels which ensued), epitomizes this good-time, slightly tipsy, afternoon sound.

The late SE Rogie going easy

In January 1951,
The RTS made a big party.
The boneshaker and the ariya
Preceded the double decker.

Welcome to Sierra Leone double-decker bus,
Welcome to Sierra Leone double-decker bus.

The manager is Mr Stobbart,
His assistant is Mr Garmon.
They are trying to do their level best
By sending the double decker.

Welcome to Sierra Leone double-decker bus,
Welcome to Sierra Leone double-decker bus.

Mr Stobart, Mr Garmon and the citizens
Had a party in east to west.
My grandfather and my grandmother
Refused to go to the top stairs.

Welcome to Sierra Leone double-decker bus,
Welcome to Sierra Leone double-decker bus.

Sierra Leone had a great palm-wine emissary in the venerable shape of **SE Rogie** (Sooliman Rogers), who left in 1973 for the US, and moved to England, where he spent as much time as a cultural ambassador in the schools as on stage with his guitar. His greatest successes were "My Lovely Elizabeth" and "Go Easy With Me", a song with lyrics as irresistibly suggestive as its melody. Sadly, he died in 1994, just after the release of his wonderful new CD on Real World which looks set to gain his music a new popularity.

The biggest overseas exposure for Sierra Leonean music was in the late 1970s, in London, where a tight-knit community of expatriate musicians provided the backbone of many of the London African bands and begun getting radio play. Bands such as **Super Combo** regularly provided spare members for other African, if not necessarily Sierra Leonean, groups.

Many of their recording activities came under the genial aegis of the larger-than-life **Aki Dean** who, in a crossover master-coup, united the "soca-beat" of the time with Sierra Leonean vocalists and guitarists – including the young **Abdul T-Jay** – and Ghanaian jazz saxophonist Ray Allen, to produce a series of hugely popular 12-inch releases – **Bunny Mack**'s "Easy Dancing" for example – which still animate West African parties in the UK.

At home, Sierra Leone's musical heritage is expressed these days through the occasional variety show or "concert party", through the songs that go with life-cycle rituals like initiation for boys and girls, and through the acoustic, percussion-based noise of *milo jazz*, dominated by **Dr Olo**.

DISCOGRAPHY

◎ **SE Rogie** *Dead Men Don't Smoke Marijuana* (Real World, UK). The last outing by the ever-cool Sooliman is a delicious piece of music-cake – so long as you like his one tune, the basis of nearly all the tracks.

◎ **Abdul T-Jay's Rokoto** *Fire Dombolo* and *Kanka Kura* (Rogue, UK). A hard worker on the London scene, with a high profile, Abdul T-Jay's band deliver high-energy dance music with more than a passing nod to Sierra Leone.

◎ **Various** *African Elegant: Sierra Leone's Kru/Krio Calypso Connection* (Original Music, US). A fascinating ethno-muse, but elegant isn't the word that immediately springs to mind.

Indeed some of these artists would surely be embarrassed about these ragged old Decca takes being played on CD decks around the world. There's redemption in most of Ebenezer Calender's numbers. Unfortunately the liner notes and track listing don't quite tie up.

◎ **Various** *Sierra Leone Music* (Zensor, Germany). Wolfgang Bender's lovingly packaged compilation of Krio and up-country tracks, recorded for the radio in Freetown in the 1950s and early '60s, is a real collector's item. Again though, as on *African Elegant*, you sometimes wonder what the musicians would think. Excellent accompanying booklet.

IVORY TOWERS

THE ABIDJAN RECORDING INDUSTRY

Bordering Côte d'Ivoire's Ebrié lagoon lies the city of Abidjan, a modern metropolis with the rough, grey Atlantic on one side and cocoa plantations and savannah on the other. The city's fast, noisy downtown district – Le Plateau – caters to transient business types while the street life of the city happens in the low-rent Treichville district, with its teeming market, cheap bars and seedy hotels. Brooke Wentz went there to check out the heart of the West African music industry (after Paris, of course).

Abidjan's technically sophisticated **studios**, and the diversity of talent attracted by them, have established the city as a hub for musical and cultural exchange. Musicians from all over west and central Africa – Guinea, Mali, Niger, Cameroon and Zaire – come to absorb new rhythms and try out their own native beats in the hope of landing a record deal. Salif Keita, Kanté Manfila and Mory Kanté all refined their talents with the Ambassadeurs, playing the Treichville clubs before venturing on to Paris in the late 1970s. The sax player and "Soul Makossa" man, Manu Dibango, directed the Ivoirian television orchestra in 1975 and four years later another Cameroonian, Moni Bilé, ventured to Abidjan to record his first album. Today, established local artists like **Aicha Koné**, **Alpha Blondy** and **Luckson Padaud** hold international recording contracts and their music is heard over the airwaves throughout Africa and parts of Europe and America.

As one expatriate in the music business commented, "If the Ivoirians say 'No' to your music, then it is 'No'. All over the country everybody – Africans, Europeans – listens to Radio Côte d'Ivoire to hear all the latest sounds. And if your song isn't played you've got little chance of success." In 1993, as if to emphasize Abidjan's preeminent position in the African music industry (a position contested only by Johannesburg), the city hosted the Marché des Arts et Spectacles Africains – a week-long trade fair and showcase event which attracted entertainment executives from around the world.

RADIO COOL

Every day, from 6am to 9am, Souleymane "Cool" Coulibaly presents the morning show on the government-sponsored **Radio Côte d'Ivoire** (RCI), the only station. Cool's tastes are not narrow: he'll play anything from Roy Ayers, Cameo and Michael Jackson to the newest releases of Ismael Lô, Fela Kuti, Youssou N'Dour and Papa Wemba and emerging local talent like reggae artist Waby Spider, soukous star François Lougah and zouk-singer Monique Seka.

On Cool's morning show, in between running giveaways and request spots, he reviews concerts, interviews artists and

highlights new releases. A bit of a local star in his own right, Cool's musical knowledge is encyclopedic and he's constantly on the move, meeting musicians and checking out the newest clubs in town. He also hosts a monthly show for Radio France International, where he comments on current African trends.

Although government funded, RCI is a commercial station and also programmes pretty well whatever it wants. Songs critical of the presidency of the late Houphouët-Boigny may not get an airing, but some singers, **Blissi Tebil**,

for example, are so well known that their songs get played without raising hackles. In his songs "Marche sur Bassam", "Gaba" and "L'Article Sept", which have had airtime on RCI, Tebil condemned Houphouët's corrupt regime and called for democracy.

BUSINESS

One of the largest and most powerful record companies in West Africa is **EMI Pathe Marconi**. Its spacious offices are located in Abidjan's salubrious Cocody hills and its employees are predominantly Europeans engaged in a battle to eradicate the rampant piracy that plagues the local industry. EMI signs local musicians and licenses foreign material from all over Africa and even Europe, the US and the Caribbean. It's a prodigious operation, releasing some 300 recordings a year. For over a decade, their most successful international star has been Alpha Blondy, a reggae singer whose releases are sold all over the world.

Other important players in Abidjan's music industry are the recording studios JBZ and Nefertiti. **JBZ**, also located in lush, palmy Cocody, is one of the oldest studios in West Africa. A one-room facility, this studio has been responsible for some of the best African recordings of recent years, including releases by Kine Lam, Nahawa Doumbia, Pepe Kalle, Super Biton, Djanka Diabaté, Sam Mangwana and Lokassa. They have a 32-track Hollande series 6000 board, top-of-the-line Revox, Sony and Tascam tape decks, Yamaha synthesizers and Roland equipment. American blues guitarist Johnny Copeland discovered JBZ and recorded here while on tour in Abidjan; Youssou N'Dour used it to record some of his early material at a time when no other facilities were available in West Africa; and Toumani Diabaté's successfully eccentric "Shake the Whole World" was put together here too.

The recently established **Nefertiti** studio is also worth a visit. Opened by Stevie Wonder's engineer of fifteen years, Abdoulaye Soumaré, Nefertiti is in the heart of the bustling Plateau district. Soumaré, originally from West Africa, returned to Côte d'Ivoire with two expert engineers to run this state-of-the-art 24-track set-up. Nefertiti caters to Abidjan's growing advertising and video industries, as well as hosting musicians.

The studios may be where all the big money gets spent, but if you're looking for the fruits of their labours, visit the many cassette shops in Treichville where you don't have to buy pirated cassettes – the real thing costs about £2 ($3). Recordings from all over Africa, not to mention Abidjan, can be found here, though CDs are almost unobtainable because of the high import tax – and the distinct lack of consumers. You can avoid pirate recordings by making sure that the tapes you buy are marked *Burida* (Bureau Ivoirien du Droit d'Auteur – the national copyright office).

LIVE AND LOCAL

In the 1960s of newly independent Côte d'Ivoire, the twin vocal sounds of the **Soeurs Comöé** and other Baoulé artists were heard from transistor radios in every bar. Then, in the 1970s, the new dynamism of **Sery Simplice** and his Frères Djatys bubbled up, based around the heavy-duty *gbegbe* rhythm.

Although the excitement of Abidjan's indigenous music scene today seems to be inversely proportional to the energy of its recording industry, **live entertainment** by local artists can be a treat. If you want to keep an eye out for today's local talent, rent a taxi for the evening and check out the smoky bars in Treichville, the home of Ivoirian reggae, or kick up your heals at the ritzier clubs in the Plateau district. Maybe you'll catch singer **Aïcha Koné** (whose style greatly resembles South African diva Miriam Makeba's). Koné's album "Kilimanjaro" expresses the constant struggle many young Ivoirians have growing up in Abidjan, heavily influenced by western culture and modern technology, while members of their families live in rural parts up-country, deeply rooted in old traditions. In a pattern repeated countless times in Africa, Koné's family forbade her to sing in public. Instead, she secretly

Le Zagazougou – unplugged and very, very fast

enroled in the National Institute of the Arts and met her mentor, Boncana Maïga, who landed her an opportunity to sing with the Ivoirian TV orchestra and work with its director Manu Dibango. After recording in Paris with perfomer Deni Keleni and film-maker Yeo Kozola, Koné moved there. Her international reputation now flourishes and she is a star back home.

Other local heroes worth catching live are **Meiway**, who play a new dance beat called *zouglou* or "dance des jeunes" (a communal, conga-like dance), and Gnaoré Djimi, whose fourteen-member band play an amazingly fast version of a traditional beat called *polihet*, a variation of another ethnic rhythm called *ziglibithy*. Both groups have spearheaded new dance movements in Côte d'Ivoire.

Zagazougou, "discovered" by DJ Cool, released a CD on the Piranha label, "Zagazougou Coup". The local cassette copies of this surprised everybody by outselling the slicker, local electric bands.

◢ DISCOGRAPHY ◣

Natari is EMI/Pathe-Marconi's sole agent in the UK and all cassettes – there are many – are available through them. **Natari, 23 Maybridge Sq, Goring, West Sussex BN12 6HL ☎ (01903) 244948.** In the US contact: **Africassette, PO Box 2491, Detroit, MI 48224.**

ⓒ **Alpha Blondy** *Apartheid is Nazism* (Stern's, UK). Surprisingly listenable.
ⓒ **Gnaoré Djimi** *All Polihet Up* (GlobeStyle, UK). Forthcoming special. Suggestions for alternative titles welcomed.

ⓒ **Aïcha Koné** *Mandingo Live from Côte d'Ivoire* (Weltmusik, Germany). Featuring Miriam Makeba's famous paean to pan-Africanism, "Kilimanjaro".
ⓒ **Various** *Super Guitar Soukous* (EMI-Hemisphere, UK/US). Misleading title, as the best tracks are wild Ivoirien Polihet. Just listen to Zoukunion's N'Nanale!
ⓒ **Zagazougou** *Zagazougou Coup* (Piranha, Germany). Ivory Coast unplugged, all accordions and percussion and very, *very* fast.

GOLD COAST

HIGHLIFE AND ROOTS RHYTHMS OF GHANA

Ghanaian music is possibly the best researched on the continent, but, in terms of what you can get in the record stores, it's in shorter supply than at any time during the last fifty years. Ronnie Graham looks into the history of highlife – and at what else has been happening in the country which invented one of Africa's most pervasive dance forms.

Ghana's urban, good-time music is quite well known abroad, but the country has a strong, living tradition of strictly indigenous rural music, which continues to influence urban sounds. Apart from music for its own sake, the main types of folk music to be heard are the court music played for chiefs, the ceremonial music of special occasions and work songs to accompany agriculture and domestic chores. In Ghana, although musicianship tends to be inherited, musical output is not the prerogative of a particular social caste, as it is in the Mande-speaking world to the north and west. However, as in Mali, Senegal and Guinea, a particular ethno-linguistic group does hold cultural sway over other communities – the Akan language group. Akan nationalities include Fante and Asante (also spelled Ashanti) or Asante-Twi. On the coast of Ghana, the main groups are the Ga-Adangme and the Ewe. All are part of a broadly related family of languages.

ROOTS

Northeastern Ghana is home to a cluster of Voltaic-speaking peoples – best known of which are the Dagomba, Mamprusi and Frafra. In this area the instruments are mostly fiddles, lutes and wonderful, hourglass talking-drum ensembles. It's customary for musicians to perform frequently for the local chief – in the Dagomba country each Monday and Friday. Passing through towns like Tamale and Yendi you might find something going on, because professional musicians, although attached to chiefs, regularly perform for the general public. Dagomba drummers are always a great spectacle, their flowing tunics fanning out as, palms flying, they dance the *takai*.

In the northwest, the main instrument of the Lobi, Wala, Dagarti and Sissala is a xylophone – either played alone or with a small group of drums and percussion instruments. Finger bells and ankle bells are often worn by the dancers.

The Ewe are the main people of southeastern Ghana. Their music is closer to the traditions of Togo and Benin than to that of other Ghanaian peoples and, with their enthusiasm for music associations and drum dance clubs, they've developed many different kinds of recreational music, like the *agbadza*, which evolved out of a traditional war dance in the 1920s or '30s, and the *borborbor*, which is a fusion of Ewe music and *konkoma* (or *konkomba*) highlife that was put together in the eastern town of Kpandu in the early 1950s. In the southern part of central Ghana the Akan peoples, notably the Asante and Fante, have an elaborate court music using large drum ensembles and groups of horns. Another great spectacle is huge log xylophones played in *asonko*, a form of recreational music.

HIGHLIFE

Although **highlife** is now recognized in all the English-speaking West African countries and, indeed, across Africa and around the world, its roots are embedded in the clubs and dancehalls of the colonial Gold Coast. By the early years of independence in the late 1950s and early '60s, it had effectively become the national music of Ghana and has proved one of the most popular, enduring, and adaptable African styles.

The story begins in the early years of this century, when various outside influences – including European church music, military brass band music, sea shanties – and other, specifically African, influences from along the coast in Liberia, were introduced to local rhythms and idioms. The forms that went into the mix included *osibisaba* (from Fante country in southwest Ghana); *ashiko*, originally from Sierra Leone; Liberia-originating *mainline*, *fireman* and *dagomba* guitar styles (no relation to the northern Ghanaians of the same name); and *gombe*. Gombe was introduced to Ghana from Sierra Leone, which in turn had acquired it from freed Maroon slaves from Jamaica in the early

Joe "Teacher" Lamptey with his boys' fife band (including ET Mensah) in 1932

waltzes, quicksteps and ragtimes. At the other extreme were the poor, often rural, **guitar bands** playing a neotraditional African style for less westernized audiences (often dubbed, especially when least respectable, as "palm-wine music"). Initially a coastal music of the Fante people, it spread inland after World War I and thereafter focused on Kumasi, Ghana's second town and capital of the Ashanti region. In the early days the instruments were simple acoustic guitars, often homemade, plus a tapped wooden box, a beer bottle hit with a stick or coin and, of course, voices. The vocals were often pitched high and had a nasal quality. Later, the bands acquired electric guitars and more sophisticated percussion.

Although there's plenty of room for argument about which category each Ghanaian artist and band belongs to, the broad dance band/guitar band distinction quickly took hold, and was given official sanction in 1960 when separate musicians' unions were set up for the dance and guitar bands. An important guitar band variation is the **concert party** – a mixture of comic drama, music and dance.

During the 1930s and '40s thousands of 78rpms were released and the highlife style spread to Sierra Leone, Nigeria and even as far south as the Belgian Congo where musicians

nineteenth century – a very complicated picture.

Instrumentation depended on what equipment was available and, out of a welter of neo-traditional variations there gradually emerged a form known generically as "highlife". The term itself, coined some time in the 1920s, is a reference to the kind of European-derived evening of dressing-up and dancing (the "high life"), to which the local elites aspired and to which new immigrants to the towns of West Africa between the wars were quite unaccustomed – but which they soon made their own.

Highlife has emerged in many shapes, but initially there were two key varieties. At one extreme was the high highlife of the **ballroom-dance-band style** favoured by the coastal elite (toppers and tails and much ceremony, according to means). The bands were large-scale string and brass orchestras, playing the full array of foxtrots,

BUY THE MAN A DRINK

· ·

In Ghana, palm-wine music was the forerunner of guitar-band highlife. It remains the popular street or compound music of the Akan people – a relaxed, rural, acoustic guitar style associated with late afternoon drinking sessions at palm-wine bars in the bush – usually simple, outdoor affairs under a big tree, the equivalent of the bantaba of Manding-speaking regions. A musician would turn up with his guitar and play for as long as people wanted to buy him drinks. This is music purely for entertainment, and such palm-winers tend to be comedians as well as parodists of the local scene.

Palm-wine guitar music is fast dying out in Ghana, partly because musicians are enticed into the electric guitar bands and concert party groups (or overseas if they're really good, and lucky), and partly due to the lack of instruments. In many places, still, someone will be able to point you in the direction of a palm-wine musician, but you may have to find an instrument for him to play on. Buy the man a drink and you may well find your name included in the current number.

remember highlife for its simple appeal and attractive, two-finger guitar lines. By the end of World War II, highlife was established in West Africa and the UK as typifying virtually all modern African dance music.

ET AT HOME

The already exuberant dance band style was further enriched during the war by elements of swing and jazz, introduced by servicemen, to produce what many consider to be classic highlife. The big bands flourished during the rapid process of urbanization and social change unleashed by the nationalist struggle of Kwame Nkrumah.

With independence, in 1957, Nkrumah's socialist-aligned government actively encouraged indigenous music. Apart from funding dozens of state bands, the president frequently travelled to neighbouring countries with a full dance band in his retinue. Ghana's music reflected the assertive self-confidence of Ghana at the time – newly independent, reasonably prosperous and widely respected in the pan-African struggle. Showy, dance-band highlife went from strength to stength. The top highlife orchestras composed original material in English, Spanish and all the local languages, incorporating traditional rhythms into new arrangements. The basic highlife framework was augmented by forays into "Congo" music, calypso, and any other style which grabbed the leader's fancy. The result was a lilting, relaxed, sophisticated dance style with enduring appeal.

Emmanuel Tettey "ET" Mensah led the charge with his talented **Tempos** band. A consummate musician, equally at home on sax or trumpet, ET Mensah brought a new level of professionalism to African dance music while finding the energy to popularize it throughout the region. Anyone privileged to see one of his live performances, from a wheelchair, in London or Amsterdam in 1986 couldn't fail to appreciate his contribution.

ET took over the Tempos' leadership and direction from the master drummer **Guy Warren**. The young Warren (known today as Kofi Ghanaba, *ghanaba* meaning "son of Ghana") was a precocious talent, responsible for introducing Afro-Cuban rhythms into the more relaxed highlife groove. After a trip to London where he met a lot of Afro-Caribbeans, Warren was also responsible for the introduction of calypso throughout West Africa, playing it live with the Tempos whilst widening its appeal on

his radio programmes. In 1953 he began to redirect his efforts and moved, via Liberia, to the US where he released a series of radical albums combining modern jazz with African percussion and aiming to reintroduce black Americans to their African roots – legendary recordings now worth their weight in gold.

King Bruce, who came from a musical background, and whose trumpeter's taste was for jazz and swing, established a stable of dance bands to further popularize the style, which included his own, famous Black Beats, the Barbecues, the Barons and five other groups, all beginning with B and mostly playing "copyright", in other words covers.

No money trouble for ET Mensah (right)

Another B, the Broadways, led by the guitarist Stan Plange and not part of the King Bruce stable, went on to become the big-band-jazz Professional Uhuru Band in 1965.

The other big highlife dance band was Jerry Hansen's **Ramblers International Dance Band**, formed in 1962 by Hansen and nine other Black Beat escapees and eventually consisting of a fully professional, fifteen-man line-up. Almost uniquely, they made a living from their shows and records for nearly twenty years (and, in a second-generation, Jerry-Junior incarnation, are still going about it in the 1990s).

Yet fashions were changing and a foretaste of highlife's decline came in 1966 with the CIA-inspired overthrow of Nkrumah and the first in a long line of corrupt, military juntas. By the 1970s, dance-band highlife was on the way out, undermined by new, imported pop styles and the near-impossibility of maintaining large, full-time groups of musicians in a declining economy.

YAA AMPONSAH

•••••••••••••••••••••••

The melody of this famous guitar highlife number, written by Kwame "Sam" Asare in about 1925, was used by Paul Simon for the song "Spirit Voices" on the album "Rhythm of the Saints". Its key elements can be found in most susbequent highlife compositions – hundreds of songs like it have been written. The following Akan lyrics are by Sam's nephew, Kwaa Mensah, translated by AEF Mendi of the Ghana Information Service.

Yaa Amponsah, let's be lovers.
It is more romantic that way.
If we're no longer married, never mind.

Nothing can stop my love for you,
Not even your mum's threats to douche me
with pepper,
And your dad's to give me an enema of boiling
water.
You are so sweet.
If I were a millionaire,
I would give all my wealth to you.
Your silky hair,
Your graceful neck like an adenkum [a long-
necked gourd],
Your black berry eyes charm me most.
I cannot bear our separation.

RETRIEVAL

Guitar-band highlife had first achieved big popularity in the 1930s, when the top guitar band was Sam's Trio, led by Jacob Sam (**Kwame Asare**). His Trio first recorded in 1928 for Zonophone, in London, and put out three versions of his famous song "Yaa Amponsah", the structure of which runs through nearly every great highlife number. Kwame Asare's nephew was **Kwaa Mensah**, the "king" of the palm-wine, two-finger guitar sound. In the 1960s, the guitar bands all went electric and the rootsier, older style vanished for a decade.

Ghana's **"Roots Revival"** of the mid-1970s adopted several guises but it's hard to overstress the importance of the 1971 "Soul To Soul" festival which featured Santana, Wilson Picket and Ike and Tina Turner on the same bill as home-grown highlife, drum and gospel bands. The presence of internationally successful black musicians acted as a kind of stimulus, almost seeming to legitimize Ghanaian musical endeavour. Equally, however, the contrast between the local and the imported, for those who attended, and its subsequent reverberations through the Ghanaian music scene, looked for a while like wiping out indigenous sounds altogether and replacing live music on the dance floor with imported vinyl and glamorous lifestyles.

But the threat acted as a spur. The guitar-band variety of highlife – still a vibrant, popular style in the hands and voices of **Nana Ampadu and the African Brothers**, the Ashanti Brothers, the City Boys, **Alex Konadu**'s Band and dozens of others – seemed to receive a new lease of life. F Kenya, CK Mann and Eddie Donkor, all had big hits with new variations on the highlife theme as they responded to the rising challenge of disco and, sub-sequently, reggae.

In the early 1950s EK Nyame was in the vanguard of the folk guitar scene and developed the guitar band repertoire by adding double bass and Latin percussion. As leader of the Akan Trio, he was also the first to combine acoustic guitar with the kind of vaudeville concert show that had been popular entertainment for several decades. In 1975, Nyame recorded a set of old numbers under the title "Sankofa" (Go back and retrieve) in a conscious effort to keep for posterity what had only been recorded previously on fragile shellac.

The retro approach to evolving new music – rather than merely preserving the old – was

The prolific Kwaa Mensah in regal mode

The African Brothers giving it the grand calabash

groups were characterized by powerful Ga drumming, sweet female harmonies and exciting floor shows, yet they were as comfortable in hotel cabarets as they were in downtown Accra compounds.

The guitarist Daniel **"Koo Nimo"** Amponsah ("koo nimo" means "scapegoat" in Twi, a name inherited from his uncle), absorbed the guts of his style from Kwame Asare, Kwaa Mensah and EK Nyame, and went on to revitalize and popularize the dying, finger-picking guitar style. Taught classical guitar in his late twenties, Koo Nimo has been wide open to European and American jazz and classical influences – among them figures as diverse as Julian Bream, Charlie Byrd and Django Reinhardt – and has been described as an African Segovia. In turn, Koo Nimo has been a source of inspiraton and encouragement for many Ghanaian musicians who are trying to graft new musical stock onto old roots – though a number also credit his "influence" on their work somewhat vainly.

Koo Nimo is experimental, but the traditional palm-wine style is still his natural environment, even as he composes new songs and stresses the importance of formal training. Now in his early sixties, he continues to perform regularly at concerts and festivals with his all-acoustic Adadam band and commands huge respect among Ghanaians at home and abroad. There are two albums available in Ghana: a good place to start is "Odonson Nkoro", though it's almost impossible to get hold of.

adopted by a number of bands promoted by the forward-looking music entrepreneur **Faisal Helwani**. Helwani supported innovative fusion groups like Hedzolleh (which means "Peace-Freedom" in Ga, the language of Accra), Basa-Basa ("Chaos") and the Bunzus, to dig into Ghanaian culture and present it in a sophisticated package much as **Osibisa** had done abroad. At the same time, Helwani tried to repackage giants of the past, promoting ET Mensah, the Uhurus and the acoustic guitarist Kwaa Mensah (who died in 1991, see profile) in a series of weekend variety shows. On one memorable occasion he was able to persuade Fela Kuti and ET to share a stage at the roots revival headquarters – the Napoleon Club in Accra.

Another initiative came in the form of the **Ga cultural revival** spearheaded by the neotraditional cultural troupe Wulomei (Ga for "Fetish Priest") – to encourage pop-minded young people "to forget foreign music and do their own thing", in the words of leader Nii Ashitey. They did a six-week tour accompanied by Kwaa Mensah. Wulomei were soon followed by other Ga bands, most notably Dzadzeloi, Blemabii, Ablade and Suku Troupe. These

Daniel Amponsah (Koo Nimo) finger picking

Economic decline may have compromised their chances of earning a living from music but there was no doubting the ability or imagination of Ghanaian musicians in retrieving the past and charting a fresh course for the future – either at home or overseas.

TRAVEL AND SEE

For almost two decades – the golden era of Nkrumah's Revolution – Ghana was the very heart of African music. However, with his overthrow in 1966 the country began a downward spiral of political instability, corruption and economic collapse. Musicians suffered alongside everyone else but their livelihoods were directly threatened when the clubs and dancehalls began closing, the instruments and equipment finally broke down and the beer dried up. The nucleus of **Osibisa**, for example, had left Ghana shortly after the 1966 coup and throughout the 1970s, many others drifted out of the country – Eddie Quansah, George Lee, Kris Bediako and Tony Mensah to mention just a few. The revolutionary government of Jerry Rawlings, which came to power in 1981, tightened up the copyright laws, severely limiting what most bands could play if covers were outlawed. The final straw came with the imposition of a 10pm curfew, and the migration of musicians grew into a veritable exodus.

While the business of travelling overseas to buy new equipment, make a few recordings and even earn some cash was nothing new to Ghanaian musicians – they often went to London – the choice now confronting the leading artists was simple: either "travel and see" or slip into semi-retirement at home.

Nigeria, just three countries down the coast, was enjoying a period of booming oil prosperity in the late 1970s and early '80s. It was the most obvious first destination for economically challenged artists. Many Ghanaian highlife bands flourished in Lagos and in the eastern, Igbo regions. Okukuseku became the best-known and most successful before returning to Ghana in 1985, but dozens of others – among them the Canadoes, the Opambuas, Odoywewu, the Kuul Strangers, the Beach Scorpions, the Golden Boys and Citystyle – also made their mark in Nigeria, often recording only one album before returning to the relative safety and sanity of Ghana.

The relationship with England was, of course, long established. The folk musician Kwame "Sam" Asare had sailed to England as early as 1928 to make the first-ever highlife recordings. He was soon followed by others and, during the 1930s, all the county's top musicians made the pilgrimage to Decca's London studios.

Ghanaians also started to put down roots in the UK: many arrived as students and seamen and ended up settling as musicians. An early arrival in the 1930s included **Cab Quaye** (father of the noted percussionist Terri Quaye) who joined Billy Cotton's Big Band, to be joined in the 1940s by Guy Warren, who played bongos with Kenny Graham's Afro-Cubists, Eddy Lamptey and the guitarist Rans Boi, who made dozens of recordings on the Melodisc label as part of the celebrated band of Ambrose Campbell. By the 1960s, a new generation was arriving, including Michael Osapanin, Ray Allen, George Lee and the percussionist Speedy Acquaye. UK tours by ET Mensah, Jerry Hansen's Ramblers and even the Gold Coast Police Band served to keep expatriate Ghanaians in touch with home.

In the early 1980s scores of talented individuals arrived to add momentum to the burgeoning interest in African music, making their presence felt as sessionists, teachers and bandleaders. Important contributions were made by Kwabena Oduro-Kwarteng, Kofi Adu, Herman Asafo-Agyei and Sam Ashley, the core members of **Hi-Life International**, a successful London-based band with two albums on Stern's ("Travel and See", 1983, and "Na Wa For You", 1985). Other Ghanaian arrivals became core members of busy touring and recording groups like Orchestra Jazira and Kabbala, while another, Dade Krama, ploughed a lonelier furrow with an innovative, more arty approach. And there were dozens of other Ghanaian musicians on the scene, joining bands on a short-term basis while they struggled with solo recording careers, often with the assistance of leading session figures like guitarist Alfred Bannerman, keyboard specialist Jon K and vocalist Ben Brako. Space alone precludes more than merely mentioning musicians like Rex Gyamfi, Baffour Kyei, Asare Bediako and Nana Budjei, who worked alone to put highlife back on its feet.

Styles varied, from neotraditional to funk and reggae fusions, but behind it all lay a firm foundation of musical expertise and experience. Yet it proved hard to make a living and, despite the growth of interest which was eventually to culminate in "World Music", real success continued to elude everybody – or nearly everybody.

By the mid-1980s, due to changes in British immigration laws, Ghanaians were beginning to focus their attentions on **Germany**. Here, highlife was being fused with funk and rock to produce a new, harder-edged, studio sound. **George Darko** led the way and his song "Akoo Te Brafo" (recorded in Berlin but a big hit in Ghana) gave rise to the term "burgher highlife". He claims Koo Nimo as a major influence, although, in truth, it's hard to hear many traces of the classical/palm-wine guitarist. Such has been Darko's success that he returned to live in Ghana in 1989.

Darko led the way for the band **Kantata**, a Berlin-based combo consisting of breakaway members of Darko's own group. They have released a number of successful albums of dance floor music including "It's High Time", and their single "Slim Lady" was a huge success back in Ghana.

Towards the end of the 1980s, **Canada** – in particular Toronto – started to attract an increasing number of Ghanaian musicians drawn by fresh markets, enthusiastic audiences (including a substantial Ghanaian community) and a more liberal working environment. **Herman Asafo-Agyei**, the bass player, composer and leader of the Afro-funk outfit Native Spirit, led the way and he was later joined by drummer **Kofi Adu** and star vocalists **Pat Thomas**, **AB Crentsil** and **Jewel Ackah**.

Pat Thomas, one of Ghana's premier highlife vocalists, sang with many of the country's great dance bands in the 1970s before going solo in the following decade. He was the first artist to record in Germany, and subsequently gained international recognition with the release of several albums, including the 1986 "Highlife Greats".

AB Crentsil and his **Sweet Talks** were one of Ghana's most successful 1970s highlife bands. Originally based at Tema's Talk of the Town club, the group gained national popularity after a string of hit albums, the first of which was "Adam and Eve". In 1978 they went to the US and recorded their classic "Hollywood Highlife Party". Soon after the group's split, Crentsil formed the new Ahenfo Band. International acclaim came with the Ahenfo's first British release, "Tantie Alaba", in 1984.

Surprisingly, perhaps, foreign-based Ghanaians were highly successful back home: the itinerant producer, "Big Joe" Asiedu, flitted back and forth, bringing home the overseas productions of Pat Thomas and AB Crentsil, as well as those of new "burgher" stars like Kantata and the **Lumba Brothers**.

Apart from Nigeria, Britain, Germany and Canada, the highlife diaspora includes individual artists based in other countries – the **Kumbi Salleh** band in Holland, **Mustapha Tettey Addy** in Germany, Andy Vans in Switzerland and Obo Addy in the US. And everywhere they go, Ghanaians become effective music teachers, planting deep roots in host communities through their work in schools, clubs and social centres.

Alex "One Man Thousand" Konadu

GOSPEL-REGGAE-RAP

At home, Ghanaian music entered the 1980s in much the same shape as the country itself – hungry, revolutionary and weakened by a decade of neglect. The industry itself was in poor shape: massive cassette piracy undermined the motivation to record while only two studios had survived the degradations of the 1970s, forcing ambitious musicians to move abroad. Those remaining at home began to organize and lobby through the musicians' unions for government understanding and support. Despite disagreements, the government has, since 1981, helped to bring about a number of progressive measures to support culture and the right of

THE BIG NAMES
OF GHANAIAN MUSIC

ET Mensah

Emmanuel Tettey "ET" Mensah – the "King of Highlife" – was born into a musical family in Accra in 1919. He learned the fife and played in the huge school band run by the legendary teacher, Joe "Teacher" Lamptey. At secondary school he furthered his musical studies on organ and sax before forming the Accra Rhythmic Orchestra in the 1930s.

But it was World War II which marked the turning point in his career. In 1941 Accra had the busiest airport in the world, as the Alllies mobilized forces for the Middle East campaign. Thousands of European and American soldiers (among them many musicians) passed through Ghana and introduced modern jazz and swing into the indigenous highlife style. ET joined forces with Scottish trumpeter Sergeant Jack Leopard, who encouraged him to notate his music, tighten up the arrangements and accommodate new influences. After the war he joined the famous Tempos, then under the joint leadership of Guy Warren and bassist Joe Kelly. ET, with a more disciplined approach to band management and a masterful touch with arrangements (not to mention several armloads of instruments), gradually assumed control of the band, and by 1952 they were ready for their first studio venture.

Featuring trumpet, trombone, saxes, double bass, drums, congas, clips (claves) and maracas, ET and the Tempos cut a swathe through the competition with hit after hit, including "Schoolgirl", "You Call Me Roko", "All For You" and a variety of calypsos, cha-cha-chas, boleros, charangas and, of course, highlife numbers. The band toured regularly and made an enormous impact in West Africa.

But the days of big-band highlife were numbered and, when the crunch came, ET Mensah went into musical semi-retirement, earning the living he trained for as a government pharmacist. He was called back into action during the mid-1970s roots revival, recording several golden oldie albums for Afrodisia producer Faisal Helwani, and performing regularly in Accra. He made further comebacks in 1982, with a trip to Nigeria and the release of "Highlife Giants of Africa" with Nigerian trumpeter Victor Olaiya and in 1986 when a batch of original recordings from 1956 were reissued on the London-based RetroAfric label.

EK Nyame

A fundamental figure in the history of guitar highlife – the name most often quoted as an influence by later musicians – EK Nyame (1927–1977) led the most popular of all the postwar guitar highlife bands. He added bongos and jazz elements to the existing sound, began to sing in the local language of Kumasi – Twi – and then turned the performance into a complete entertainment – a concert party. As was traditional, EK's group was a threesome, the **Akan Trio**, and they played stock roles from the concert party repertoire – "Bob" (a joker), "the gentleman", and "the woman" (a man dressed in women's clothing). With these characters they would mount quite lengthy, semi-improvised routines and plays (intended to be hilarious as well as topical), breaking to take up their instruments. They were a huge success everywhere they played. Sadly, none of EK Nyame's output has ever been released outside Ghana.

Nana Ampadu and the African Brothers

Nana Ampadu and his African Brothers International Band, formed in 1963, are still one of the country's most innovative and enduring guitar groups. They had their earliest and one of their best-loved hits in 1967 with "Ebi Tie Ye" – a plea for democracy in the dark days following the fall of Nkrumah – and had released over 100 songs on singles before 1970 and the release of their first LP, "Ena Eye A Mane Me". Since then they've made nearly sixty albums and twice as many singles. Always a group to mix street wisdom with thinly veiled political comment, they never let this interfere with good music, and are forever trying something new: unlike many bands who rely on the compositions of others, they haven't played cover versions ("copyright") since 1973. During the 1970s they experimented with a variety of styles including reggae, rumba and what they called *Afro-hili*, a James Brown-inspired beat which was a challenge to Fela Kuti's Afro-Beat and was supposed to embrace all African forms. In recent years they have returned to a more refined highlife with strong rhythms and sparkling guitars.

Alex Konadu

Alex Konadu and his band play music firmly rooted in Ghanaian traditions – he is quite often dubbed a purist – and he is today the uncrowned king of guitar-band highlife, a mantle taken over from EK Nyame. He has enjoyed massive sales throughout anglophone West Africa of his highly personal, reflective songs, mostly sung in Twi, the Asante language. But it's in his charismatic live shows that Konadu's "one man thousand/one man bulldozer/one man army" personality is most clearly released. It's claimed he has played in every town and village in Ghana and his loyalty to the country and to guitar-highlife music are legendary. Konadu has put out about a dozen albums, including the 1989 CD on World Circuit – "One Man Thousand – Live in London".

Kwaa Mensah

Kwaa Mensah (no relation to ET) had a good musical start: he was taught the wonderful two-finger guitar-picking style by his folk musician uncle, "Sam" Kwame Asare, composer of the seminal song "Yaa Amponsah". Mensah's career peaked in the postwar years, and he released some 500 78s in the 1950s. A decade later, as dozens of other bands copied his style and performed his songs, his name was still highly respected, but he had already withdrawn from the limelight. He had a brief spell of fame in the late 1970s, when he toured the US with the Ga roots troupe, Wulomei. He made only one LP – "Wawo Christo" – in 1975. He died in 1991, with the bulk of his lifetime's huge output unavailable.

CK Mann

CK Mann was one of the most influential guitarists of the 1970s. He graduated out of Moses Kweku **"Kakaiku"** Oppong's band (Kakaiku's) in the 1960s and, in his new band, Carousel Seven, started composing songs with a close version of the traditional *osode* beat and a single guitar – his own. The slightly melancholy results were enormously popular and CK more or less had the rootsier end of the Ghanaian highlife market to himself in the mid-'70s, at least along the west coast of Ghana. But, with commercial success came a steady dilution of what made the sound really distinctive and, by the mid-1980s, CK Mann had retired into relative obscurity. He is now based in Canada.

Osibisa

In the UK at the end of the 1960s, nothing had prepared pop audiences for the "criss-cross rhythms which explode with happiness" that were introduced by Osibisa. Formed in London in 1968 by Ghanaians **Teddy Osei, Mac Tontoh** and **Sol Amarfio**, and with an African and Caribbean line-up, Osibisa's "Afro-rock" singles climbed the British charts in the 1970s and three of them – "Dance the Body Music", "Sunshine Day" and "Coffee Song" – made it into the top ten (still an almost unknown experience for African musicians). The name "Osibisa" derived from *osibisaba*, a prewar proto-highlife rhythm, and was chosen to reflect the coming-together in their music of African roots and foreign pop. They were, for many years, the world's best-known African band and they made a lasting impact throughout Africa. As the situation deteriorated back home in Ghana, Osibisa became a beacon of hope to musicians struggling to keep body and soul together.

But they were, perhaps, five years too early. Dismissed by western purists for melding African roots with western rock, but asked repeatedly by record companies to adjust their style and presentation to the needs of America's burgeoning soul and disco markets, Osibisa switched from label to label and steadily lost momentum. And by the early 1980s, at a time when Sunny Ade's undiluted juju was making headlines for Virgin Records, Osibisa's popularity had largely melted away.

Osibisa, possibly regretting all those Roger Dean album sleeves

musicians to make a living from it. For example, in 1985, copyright infringement (ie piracy) was made a crime. Even more effective, but more controversial, was the mid-1980s legislation concerning traditional music, which effectively brought all culture under government control: no longer could someone pick up a traditional melody and register a copyright.

Ghanaian music overseas largely went quiet with the demise of Osibisa, though both Alex Konadu and Nana Ampadu made impressive, short UK tours, thrilling audiences with the rural guitar-band highlife which had largely survived intact as a result of their commitment to arduous, rural touring and top-quality musicianship. But in Ghana itself, gospel and reggae were the new forces on the music scene.

With economic decline came a rise in religious activity. As the African churches grew stronger and secular nightlife took a dive, many musicians were hired by churches to promote the message musically. There was a huge increase in the number, wealth and quality of gospel highlife bands and, while few records were made, cheap cassettes flooded the market (do everything possible to hear something by the wonderful **Genesis Gospel Singers**, one of seven bands of the Christo Asafo mission, an indigenous church). Of course this connection between the church and music was not new – many of Ghana's finest vocalists had received their early training in church choirs – but during the early 1980s, the numbers involved exceeded anything seen before, as pentecostal and evangelical churches

It's all Yaa Amponsah: classic acoustic highlife

gained ground at the expense of more orthodox religious organizations.

Reggae, with its strong appeal for the disenfranchised underclass, resonated heavily throughout Ghana in the late 1970s. By the mid-1980s Côte d'Ivoire's reggae star Alpha Blondy was filling football stadiums. By the early 1990s, Ghana's homegrown **Amekye Dede** had become so successful, he had established his own nightclub in Accra, Abrantie Spot. The reggae boom shows no signs of abating. **Kojo Antwi**, originally a singer with a group called Classique Vibes, is now a solo singer specializing in soft reggae songs sung in Twi. **KK Kabobo** sings a kind of reggae highlife, also in Twi. There are even a few artists beginning to rap in Twi – Ghanaian music comes full-circle.

GHANA'S MUSIC INDUSTRY IN THE 1990S

Over the last two decades, Ghanaian music has been exposed to wide-ranging innovation, exploration and change. Ghanaians are constantly experimenting with crossover and fusion and, as a consequence, overseas audiences are still unsure of what exactly Ghanaian music is – and largely unaware of just how much good highlife is around. Ironically, the desire to pioneer has diluted much of what is best about indigenous Ghanaian music. Now, with a revitalized **musicians' union**, support from Jerry Rawlings' relatively stable government and a renewed entrepreneurial spirit, an atmosphere has been established in which musicians can take stock and look to the future.

Considering the near-fatal experience of the late 1970s when so many musicians left the country, Ghana's music industry in the 1990s is in surprisingly good shape. Accra, has a bustling live music scene with a thriving market for the entire range of contemporary Ghanaian music – from guitar bands and Ga dance troupes to homegrown reggae and imported highlife. Ghanaian music, which so dominated Africa at the time of independence, is drawing breath for what will surely be a long-awaited resurgence at home and abroad.

Many thanks to John Collins for additional information.

The history of recorded music in Ghana began in the late 1920s with the local release of UK-recorded artists. These 78s survived well into the 1950s when they were gradually replaced by 45s, a few EPs and then the first of the vinyl albums. LPs, in turn, lasted until the mid-1980s when the ubiquitous C60 cassette gained a total monopoly. By 1990, CDs were starting to appear but, in the almost total absence of CD players, it's going to be some years before they have much influence on the market inside Ghana. Older material, from the 1960s and 1970s, is now extremely hard to find. British fans and collectors, for obvious historical reasons, still have a better chance of unearthing old Ramblers or George Darko albums than they do of digging up early Franco or Star Band de Dakar.

COMPILATIONS

Various *Akomko* (Decca, re-released by Afrodisia, Nigeria). Rarely available early 1950s items, and, despite the poor pressing still one of the best introductions to dance- and guitar-band highlife. Some of the bands have tracks on the "I've Found My Love" collection (see below).

Various *Guitar and Gun Vol. 1* and *Vol. 2* (Africagram/Cherry Red, UK). Two albums recorded by John Collins in 1984 which show what was really going on in Ghana in the mid-'80s. Mixing highlife with gospel and reggae, these compilations constitute the foundation of any new collection of Ghanaian music.

Various *Highlife Giants of Africa* (Polygram, Nigeria). ET Mensah teams up with the "Evil Genius" (Sir Victor Olaiya) to produce new highlife. Poor recording and slightly dated but still a gem.

ⓓ **Various** *Giants of Danceband Highlife 1950s–1970s* (Original Music, US) A great stack of fine old dancehall numbers from ET Mensah and the Tempos, the Ramblers International and Professional Uhuru. Grand listening, recalling the golden era when the genre reigned supreme – a good place to start any collection.

ⓓ **Various** *I've Found My Love* (Original Music, US). Guitar band highlife from the 1950s and '60s. Relaxed, "Yaa Amponsah"-style shuffles.

HIGHLIFE BANDS AND ARTISTS

Jewel Ackah *Electric Hi-Life* (Asona, UK). A personal favourite from 1986 – mellow, melodic and mature. Jewel, alongside Pat Thomas and AB Crentsil, is one of Ghana's top vocalists.

African Brothers Band *Agatha* (local LP, Ghana). Led by Nana Ampadu, the African Brothers are still the best current highlife outfit. This 1981 hit is an abiding favourite. They record prolifically and tour endlessly.

George Darko *Highlife Time* (Oval, UK). A blend of highlife and funk from the original Burgher King, whose hit song "Akoo Te Brofo" (Parrot speaks European) made an international impact.

ⓓ **Alex Konadu** *One Man Thousand Live in London* (World Circuit, UK). The master of sweaty, good-time music – infectious tunes that come back to you months later.

ⓓ **Koo Nimo** *Osabarima* (Adasa/Stern's, UK). Now acknowledged as one of the masters of palm-wine music, Koo Nimo originally recorded this in 1976, his only commercial recording to date.

ⓓ **ET Mensah and the Tempos** *All For You* and *Day By Day* (RetroAfric, UK). Excellent compilations of 1950s and '60s numbers remastered from original 78s. These songs demonstrate the richness of the dance-band highlife idiom, augmented by forays into various other styles of the era, and featuring the full variety of rhythms and languages for which the Tempos were famous.

EK Nyame *Sankofa* (RAL, Ghana). A pioneering artist equally at home in concert party or guitar band, EK, who died in 1977, was enormously influential and highly respected by colleagues. Considered the "King of Guitar Band Highlife" (a title now inherited by Alex Konadu) his albums are almost impossible to find. The "Sankofa" (Go Back and Retrieve) collection was put together to preserve old songs for posterity.

Okukuseku *Take Time* (Rogers All Stars, Nigeria). Modern highlife guitar band who spent many years in Eastern Nigeria. The Igbo highlife touches are obvious enough on this 1983 record, but this is basically a top-drawer Ghanaian outfit now back home.

Osibisa *Double Album* (Celluloid, France). All the hits are here, from "The Coffee Song" to "Sunshine Day". In terms both of sales and influence, Osibisa's international impact has never been surpassed by any subsequent African band. If you're too young to remember, then don't delay. Move heaven and earth for this collection. A new triple-CD retrospective is also in the offing.

The Ramblers *The Hit Sounds of the Ramblers* (Decca, Nigeria). Classic highlife from one of the best and most resilient of the 1960s orchestras. They finally called it a day in the early 1980s when leader Jerry Hansen moved to the US.

ⓓ **Sweet Talks and AB Crentsil** *Hollywood Highlife Party/Moses* (Adasa/Stern's, UK). Recorded in 1978, this is beyond a doubt the best Ghanaian album of the last twenty years. The Sweet Talks split soon after, spawning a host of solo stars.

FOLK, ROOTS AND OTHER MUSIC

Mustapha Tettey Addy *Mustapha Tettey Addy* (Tangent, France). Ga master drummer from the talented Addy family of drummers. This 1972 recording, still widely available, demonstrates the wide variety of Ga drum styles. A new, still-going-strong CD is out on Weltwunder, Germany.

Dade Krama *Ancestral Music* (own label, UK). London-based neotraditional group, adapting and creating powerful, atmospheric percussion music.

Amekye Dede *Magye me Giri* (KAK, UK). With five albums in the space of three years, Dede is the current star of Ghanaian reggae.

ⓓ **Kakraba Lobi** *The World of Kakraba Lobi* (JVC, Japan). Percussion of northern Ghana from a Lobi-speaking master of the xylophone (two kinds: *kogiri* and *kokore*).

Guy Warren *Africa Speaks – America Answers* (US). Kofi Ghanaba, as he is now known, at his Afro-Cubop best in 1958. No understanding of modern Ghanaian music can be complete without appreciating Guy's singular contribution. A serious collector's item: check archives.

Wulomei *Wulomei in Drum Conference* (Phonogram, Ghana). The best of the 1970s Ga roots revival albums. Difficult to find and perhaps a bit too "sweet" on first hearing. Perseverance is repaid.

LA DIABOLIQUE

BENIN'S WORLD ROCKER ANGELIQUE KIDJO

With a rash of "Ayé Kidjo not" profiles, the rock-and-slightly-interested-in-World-Music press had a field day reviewing Angélique Kidjo's 1994 CD, "Ayé". Richard Trillo looks at her career.

In "Ayé", the Beninoise funk diva more or less dispensed with the quirkier style of songs that made her earlier CDs, "Logozo" and particularly the first, "Parakou", interesting. On "Parakou" the songs range from driving dance numbers to sepia-toned laments and a cappella and there's a huge wealth of dramatic and intriguing percussion. By comparison, "Ayé" is straight funk-rock, slickly packaged by a pop producer and, whichever way you look at it – not necessarily with any purist inflection – the songs on it are less engaging.

Kidjo is aggressively unapologetic about the evolution, as she made plain to Brooke Wentz in *The Beat*, "I won't do my music different to please some people. I'm not going to play traditional drums and dress like bush people. I'm not here for that. I don't tell Americans to play country music." She relishes the "she-devil" label pinned on her by the Paris music press.

How does Kidjo's music go down on the streets of Cotonou and Ouidah? She hasn't performed in Benin for thirteen years. Increasingly, she gets cassette and radio exposure, but the full range of African, European and American sounds is available in the newly opened country – everything from juju to soukous, zouk, C&W and reggae. And as a star, she's strictly international: her fans are the global CD-class.

Born in 1960, as a girl Angélique Kidjo listened to James Brown and the Beatles, and sang her own words, in Fon, to the tunes. When she joined her brothers' band, Simon and Garfunkel and Santana were the favourites. Later she sang with the afro-jazz-weirdness fusioneers Pili Pili, based in Holland and led by Jasper Van t'Hof. Her first record in her own name, "Pretty", used Beninois rhythms like the *gogbahoun*, tapped out with a coin on a bottle. But those direct roots are little in evidence in her more recent work. With her voice, it would have been easy to slip into the traditional approach for musicians from Benin based in Paris, of working with Ivoirian and Gabonese artists, producing something with limited roots appeal. Instead she has put her remarkable vocal talents to work with a loose and eclectic community of French, Caribbean, African and American musicians, commuting between Paris, London and America to include recording sessions with Manu Dibango and Branford Marsalis. She still sings almost exclusively in Fon, a tonal language, like the closely related Yoruba. The tonality of the lyrics imposes restrictions on the melody line, and thus the words very much direct the song.

Angelique Kidjo: a listening experience

Although Kidjo keeps in her groove of sensible lyrics on "Ayé" – hunger, homelessness, AIDS, injustice – she always denies being a political person. In French, especially in Africa, the word *politique*, which also means "policy", often implies a party-political agenda. In the new, multiparty states, most artists are anxious to avoid any suggestion of political ambition. Pan-African idealism is more her marque. She still rates

Miriam Makeba as a role model, and certainly one of Kidjo's best songs, on the "Logozo" album, is her haunting rendition of the love-song, "Malaika" that helped make Miriam Makeba famous.

Angélique Kidjo was brought up in an artistic household in Ouidah (the voodoo capital of Benin) by the kind of parents who helped create a *quartier latin* image for the country, as the seat of Africa's intellectual and creative avant garde. They provided unusual support for her stage-struck ideas. Dahomey, as the country was formerly known, was also the historical home of the Amazon women warriors, the most striking of a number of background factors which make a singing career here more socially acceptable for a woman than in many other parts of West Africa. Her natural asset is a staggeringly powerful voice, coached by jazz training in Paris and the influence of *zilin* – a blues-like vocal technique from Abomey, the Fon heartland in central Benin.

The first African woman since Miriam Makeba to achieve real international stardom, she is irrepressible but realistic. She hates artistic ghettoization and despises purists who would curtail her freedom to record as she likes. But reaching an audience beyond African music fans is one thing: connecting with those who like their songs in English and their stars conventional is another. Her internationalist outlook, flat-top hairdo, unique, strident voice and exhausting on-stage

dynamism may well carry her through. But she's taking success one step at a time: "I am like St Thomas", she said in an interview with The Wire magazine: "What I don't see, I don't believe."

> *Show yourself, priestess of Voodoo,*
> *Show yourself and teach us your wisdom.*
> *Nothing in this world is certain,*
> *And that's the wisdom of life.*
>
> From "Tombo", on "Ayé"

WATER MUSIC

Although Benin has a number of popular stars of *apala*, *fuji* and *juju* (see the Nigeria section) it's hard to come up with Benin-based artists whose output is distinctively Beninois. Perhaps the most influential musician has been Wally Badarou, cofounder of Level 42, but his outside interests are even more catholic than Angélique Kidjo's.

Perhaps the most outstanding representative of Benin in the 1990s is **Gnonnas Pedro**. Pedro, a veteran singer and composer, has a CD – "La Compilation Vol 1: Afro-cubaine" – on the Ledoux/Mélodie label, France.

Stan Tohon is a local cassette star. His *tchink-system* is a musical style that derives from the local funeral music known as *tchinkoumé*, traditionally played with "water percussion" – half-calabashes sitting in water-filled larger half-calabashes and whacked with a sandal or other handy item.

◼ DISCOGRAPHY ◼

Angélique Kidjo *Parakou* (Mango, UK). From 1989, the first and best of her modern output, with stylish arrangements, intriguing percussion and vocals allowed full rein.
Logozo (Mango, UK) is already tearing away from Benin roots, while the 1994 *Ayé* (Mango, UK) is bound for every dance floor and beyond.

Various *No Make Palaver* (Piranha, Germany). Among other good things, this fine African compilation CD features a live slice of Stan Tohon's water-led sound of death – no dirge to be sure.

JUJU GARBAGE

NIGERIA'S GIFTS TO THE WORLD

The Nigerian musical heritage extends from the traditional court drumming of the Hausa emirates to the efforts of Fela Kuti to drum out the military dictators with LPs like "Coffin for Head of State". Ronnie Graham digs into the rich musical stew of Africa's most populous nation.

In many ways, Nigeria is the heart of African music. The industry is well developed here, with numerous recording studios and pressing plants and a huge home market, big enough to sustain artists who sing in regional languages and experiment with indigenous styles. A number of major musicians have their own labels. Drawing from traditional sources and outside influences, three main types of modern music have developed – highlife, *juju* and *fuji*. Both juju and fuji are almost entirely sung in local languages, principally Yoruba, and have praise-song vocals at their heart.

Jazz, rock, soul, reggae, pop and gospel have all played a part in shaping modern Nigerian music but the results are distinctively Nigerian, reflecting the nation's reality with a force and directness few other countries have been able to maintain. **Sunny Ade** and **Fela Kuti** are the most conspicuous figures in the story of contemporary Nigerian music. Both are Yoruba and both have had roller-coasting careers. But while Sunny Ade is very much a society favourite who achieved international success in the mid-1980s, Fela has remained an uncompromising critic of every government Nigerians have suffered since independence in 1960.

The three decades since 1960 have seen several major successes by other Nigerian stars. Prince Nico Mbarga and Rocafil Jazz had a huge hit in 1976 everywhere from Zambia to the Caribbean and throughout West Africa with "Sweet Mother", a musical phenomenon that bulldozed everything in its path. Then there was another pan-African hit in 1978, when

Sonny Okosun released "Fire in Soweto", a moving tribute to the Black Consciousness Movement set against the driving rock-reggae fusion he called *ozzidi*. But once again, while Okosun maintained an impressive output of music (appealing particularly to African-Americans) he could not repeat the success of his first hit. Most Nigerian musicians seem condemned to this one-hit wonder existence – a paradoxical situation for a country with 100 million people, the best musical infrastructure on the continent and at least a dozen popular dance styles ranging from the juju of Obey and Ade, to Igbo highlife, *ikwokirikwo* and the many flowerings of Yoruba musical life, including *agidigbo*, *were*, *apala*, *sakara*, *waka* and fuji.

IK Dairo MBE (on accordion) with his Morning Star Orchestra

Ironically, once the initial excitement over Sunny Ade had worn off, Europe and America both turned their backs on Nigeria. By the late 1980s, at the very height of the World Music phenomenon, Nigerian music had become unjustly ignored. One leading world music magazine (Stern's *Tradewind*) went for over three years without reviewing a single Nigerian release.

Perhaps the plethora of new, independent companies spawned by the World Music boom didn't really know their stuff; perhaps these companies shaped public taste to suit personal preference; and quite possibly Nigerian entrepreneurs were guilty of overselling a product which, at least on vinyl, produced some of the worst pressings around. Whatever the cause, Nigerian music virtually disappeared from the record stores overseas and half a generation of World Music *aficionados* were denied a great deal of pleasure. With a recent spate of fuji CDs and various re-releases, the pendulum may be swinging back.

FOLK ROOTS

The "Giant of Africa" is a country of enormous cultural and musical diversity. With over 400 distinct ethnic groups, even the most esoteric musical styles find some degree of commercial success.

In the north, **Hausa music** traditionally offered a variety of percussion and *goje* (one-string fiddle) music to accompany ritual and recreational activities – weddings, births, circumcisions, wrestling matches. A strong vocal tradition, invariably in the praise-song category, complemented a range of percussion instruments including hundreds of different skin drums, water drums, xylophones, whistles and bells. Furthermore, the ruling Hausa-Fulani elite helped establish a courtly trumpet tradition. Hausa is a lingua franca across a vast swathe of the Sahel belt, which ensures regional as well as local audiences for songs with Hausa lyrics. Hausa music has flourished since the sixteenth century and the fall of the empire of Songhai (in present-day Mali), which previously ruled over much of what is now Hausa-land and with whose music Hausa still has many parallels. Today, travellers are unlikely to find much on disc but there is a flourishing cassette market for the big names, who often appear at state occasions, holding audiences enthralled with lengthy praise songs of traditional and modern rulers.

Moving south through the plateau states of minority language groups, the music becomes more varied in terms of instrumentation and performance. Islamic strictures are slightly looser and the Tiv, Idoma and Jukun all enjoy extensive drum and vocal traditions.

The **Igbo** people of the southeast have always been receptive to cultural change. This ease is reflected in their music (highlife quickly took root in this fertile soil) and in the incredible variety of instruments played in Igbo-land, one of the most pleasing of which is the *obo*, a thirteen-stringed zither, which can be heard at many a nostalgic palm-wine drinking session.

You find musicians at any event associated with the *obi* (chief) and no local occasion would be complete without them. In more traditional communities, royal music is played every day, when the *ufie* slit drum is used to wake the chief and to tell him when meals are ready. A group, known as *egwu ota*, which consists of slit-drums, drums and bells, performs when the obi is leaving the palace and again when he returns. The traditional Igbo musical inventory of drums percussion, flutes, xylophones, lyres and lutes was enriched by the arrival of European instruments (producing an important brass band tradition) and Christian musical traditions – which, conversely, also tended to denigrate the indigenous.

Yoruba instrumental traditions are mostly based on drumming. The most popular form of traditional music today is *dundun*, played on hourglass tension drums of the same name. The usual ensemble consists of tension drums of various sizes together with a small kettledrums called *gudugudu*. The leading drum of the group is the *iyalu* ("mother of the drums"), which "talks" by imitating the strong tonality of Yoruba speech. It's used to play out praise poetry, proverbs and other oral texts. Another important part of Yoruba musical life is music theatre, which mixes traditional music with storytelling or live drama.

European and Christian influence, spreading inland from the coast in the nineteenth century, introduced new melodies and rhythms to Yoruba music, together with new brass instruments and sheet music, early record-players and then, in the 1930s, radio. There was also an important Brazilian contribution, from the influential Brazilian merchant community of the early nineteenth century. Meanwhile, the southward spread of Islam was accompanied by new percussion styles, new vocal styles and a totally different approach to music and culture. During the nineteenth and early twentieth centuries, all three traditions were introduced to the Yoruba and adapted and incorporated to produce a hot-bed of competing rhythms and idioms. Apart from being the country's largest city, Lagos has always been at the forefront of musical expression in Nigeria.

JUJU MUSIC

From the Lagos melting pot, where indigenous **Yoruba** people mixed with the descendants of freed slaves from Sierra Leone and Brazil, came

HAUSA MUSIC

• •

There are two broad categories of Hausa music – rural music and urban music of the court and state. The emirates of Katsina and Kano together with the sultanate of Sokoto, and to a lesser extent Zaria and Bauchi, are the major creative centres.

Ceremonial music – *rokon fada* – of the Hausa states plays a great part (though not a very musical one) in Hausa traditions, even today. The instruments of ceremonial music are largely seen as prestige symbols of authority, and ceremonial musicians tend to be chosen for their family connections rather than any musical ability – in fact quite often that doesn't come into it at all, with painful results.

Court musicians, on the other hand, are always chosen for their musical skills. Exclusively dependent on a single wealthy patron – usually an emir or sultan – the most talented players are rarely seen in public. The greatest praise singer was **Narambad**, who lived and worked in Sokoto: he died in 1960 and it's doubtful if you can still get his recordings.

The most impressive of the Hausa **state instruments** is the elongated state trumpet called *kakakai*, which was originally used by the Songhai cavalry and was taken by the rising Hausa states as a symbol of military power. Kakakai are usually accompanied by *tambura*, large state drums. Lesser instruments include the *farai*, a small double-reed woodwind instrument, the *kafo*, an animal horn, and the *ganga*, a small

snare drum. Ceremonial music can always be heard at the *sara*, the weekly statement of authority which takes place outside the emir's palace on a Thursday evening. The principal instruments accompanying praise songs are percussive – small kettledrums (*banga* and *tabshi*) and talking drums (*jauje* and *kotso*).

Traditional **rural music** appears to be dying out in favour of modern pop which still draws inspiration from the roots. The last expressions of rural music are to be found in traditional dances like the *asauwara*, for young girls, and the *bori*, the dance of the spirit possession cult, which dates back to before the arrival of Islam and continues to thrive in parallel with the teachings of the Koran. Zaria is its main stronghold.

Popular **Hausa folk music** thrives both in town and countryside and although very little seems to be of interest outside Hausa-land, musicians can still make a good living satisfying local needs and, as ever, voicing and sometimes moulding public opinion. The leading Hausa singer, Muhamman Shata, is always accompanied by a troupe of virtuoso drummers who play *kalangu*, small talking drums. There's a fair number of other worthy artists such as Dan Maraya, leading exponent on the *kontigi* one-stringed lute, Ibrahim Na Habu, who popularized a type of small fiddle called the *kukkuma*, and Audo Yaron Goje who plays (not surprisingly) the *goje* or one-string fiddle.

new styles and aesthetics. In the palm-wine shacks of the Yoruba neighbourhoods, where men met to drink and socialize after work, an informal style called palm-wine music emerged, essentially a similar kind of music to what developed under the same name in Sierra Leone and Ghana. Played on guitars, banjos or any other available string instrument – backed up by shakers and tapped drinking calabashes – palm-wine was first and foremost a vocal music relying on the vast liturgy of Yoruba proverbs and metaphors to deal with the issues of the new urban culture.

By the 1920s several individuals were emerging as popular stars of this new music, including **(Baba) Tunde King**, who is credited with coining the term "juju". Though its origin is much disputed, one widely accepted explanation

is that juju music was named for the "ju ju" sound of the small hexagonal tambourine, a popular instrument used by Lagosians of Brazilian descent. The word also works as a mild expression of colonial disparagement – musical mumbo jumbo – taken on by juju musicians themselves to subvert it, just as "queer" and "nigger" have been re-adopted in the 1990s. *Jojo* also happens to be the Yoruba for "dance".

Whatever the truth about its name, British record labels like His Masters Voice sensed a commercial opportunity in the budding city, recording many early juju musicians and pressing 78s for distribution by local traders. Like the pioneers of any music style, juju's early performers achieved little financial success. However, artists like Tunde King, Ojoge Daniel and JO "Speedy" Araba developed a corpus of work which is still drawn upon by today's stars. The first recordings of this dreamy style started coming out in the early 1930s, but juju really took off, establishing itself as one of the premier urban dance music styles, just after World War II with the introduction of amplified sound.

Tunde Nightingale, a fine palm-wine singer, became juju's first big star. He developed a popular stylistic variant, which dominated the clubs and the record industry of postwar Nigeria, called *s'o wa mbe* (literally "is it there?", a reference to the strings of waist beads commonly worn by women beneath their clothes to accentuate dance movements).

In 1957, **IK Dairo** with his band The Morning Star Orchestra (later to become the Blue Spots) launched a career that changed juju music. With the development and availability of new technology, Dairo began to infuse new elements, such as electric guitar and accordion, into his music. And whoever was responsible, this same era also saw the introduction of the *gangan* (Yoruba talking drum) into the ensemble. However, it was IK Dairo's lyrical skills and mastery of short catchy phrases which helped him master the recording technology of the day with a string of hit records still without equal. In 1963, Dairo received an MBE for his achievements – the only African musician ever to

Chief Ebenezer Obey

hold such a title. At the height of his career in 1972, Dairo was in demand not only in Nigeria, but in London, Europe and even Japan. By the mid-1970s, after riding the charts for over 15 years, Dairo's record sales plummeted literally overnight as younger generations of style-conscious Nigerians flocked first to Ebenezer Obey and then Sunny Ade as juju's heirs apparent.

Ebenezer Obey formed his first group, the International Brothers, in 1964. Since then he has released over fifty LPs. The success of his blend of talking drums, percussion and multiple guitars had already caught on by the time he renamed his group the Inter-Reformers in 1970. With the new band he rose quickly to prominence with his exciting bluesy guitar work and lyrics which manged to be steeped in Yoruba tradition and at the same time address issues affecting the new urban elites and impart the conservative Christian values which Obey espoused. "Murtala Muhammed" and "Immortal Songs for Travellers" were among albums he was turning out at a staggering rate in the late 1970s, with guaranteed advance sales of over 100,000 each.

The rivalry between the right-wing man-mountain Ebenezer Obey (now dubbed Chief Commander by his fan club) and the more populist, more Yoruba (and incidentally remarkably slim) **"King" Sunny Ade** led to fast and furious development in juju music. Each struggled to be the first to introduce a new instrument, style or sound, with each new development labelled a "system". The juju ensemble, which had started with four and expanded to over ten musicians with IK Dairo, now pushed beyond thirty people on stage, with as many as four guitars, various keyboards, Hawaiian guitars, trap set, a wide range of traditional and modern percussion and numerous background vocalists. As technological developments allowed, the recording emphasis shifted from short songs to 22-minute long LP-busting tracks. Even in this longer format, juju musicians continued to be prolific in the recording studio, averaging three or four albums each year. And, pulled along in the wake of Ade's and Obey's popularity were several hundred other juju bands scattered throughout southwestern Nigeria.

In 1980 Obey went international with "Current Affairs" followed by the rather weak "Je Ka Jo" on Virgin and the much tougher "Solution" on Stern's. As a result he rose briefly to stardom on the world music scene. But by now, Sunny Ade was already out in the world.

THE LAST OF BIG-TIME JUJU?

As juju fractured into several strands in the late 1980s, Ebenezer Obey concerted his appeal to an older generation of fans, responding to the competition from up-coming fuji in a more traditional manner than Sunny Ade, with an optimistic approach to the vagaries of the music business in his new songs about patience, determination, security and satisfaction.

Then Yoruba "pop music", *Yo-pop*, crashed onto the scene, in the person of **Segun Adewale**. All speed, thunder and lightning, Yo-pop found a huge young audience, especially in Lagos – and two international releases on Stern's.

Starting out as backup singers in the band of Prince Adekunle, a contemporary of IK Dairo's, both Segun Adewale and Shina Peters had split

KING SUNNY ADE

••••••••••••••••••••••

Born Sunday Adeniyi to a branch of the Royal family of Ondo town, Sunny Ade began his musical career playing in various highlife bands in the early 1960s. By 1966 he had formed his first band, the Green Spots, with whom he recorded several modestly successful albums. In 1974 he renamed the band the African Beats and released "Esu Biri Ebo Mi" under his own record label, Sunny Alade, which solidified his support and propelled him into the limelight. Other hit albums included "The Late General Murtala Muhammed" (MM was Nigeria's most popular military dictator, remembered almost with fondness), "Sound Vibration" and "The Royal Sound". In 1977, a group of journalists and music critics named him the King of Juju Music.

Island Records, searching for a replacement for Bob Marley as the standard bearer of tropical music, selected King Sunny Ade in 1982. His guitar line-up, weaving intricate melodic patterns against a back-

ground of thundering percussion, the call-and-response "conversations" of the talking drums, and the infectiously winning, "African-prince" style of the man himself – all gave off strong commercial signals. The 1982 release of "Juju Music", produced by the Frenchman Martin Meissonnier, was a big success – a huge one in terms of the perceived market at that time for African music in Europe and North America (not to mention Japan). Tours linked to heavy promotion – Sunny Ade was in the shops, on the TV, in clubs and theatres – resulted in brisk record sales. His live performances wowed audiences around the world with their complex sound, tight groove and Sunny's delightful stage presence. The band's second Island release, "Synchro System", met with even greater success and there was more touring. But there were looming doubts: Sunny Ade's Yoruba lyrics and complex rhythms were less readily accessible than the English lyrics and regular rhythms of the reggae greats he was supposed to replace. Records one and two had also encouraged a glut of Nigerian imports. The third Sunny Ade release, "Aura", with Stevie Wonder playing harmonica on the title track, bombed. Island dropped him in 1985 and his band subsequently walked out in the middle of a prestigious Japanese tour. It was clear that the international juju boom was over.

Meanwhile, King Sunny's short-lived international stardom had secured his position as juju's frontrunner at home, where he continued a full schedule of performances and recording interrupted only by occasional overseas sorties on the World Music circuit. His lyrics became more pointed: he started to sing of rumours, jealousy, destiny, new directions – and family planning. This latter foray into the world of population politics on the 1989 album "Wait for Me" (clandestinely underwritten by the USAID Office of Population) was not calculated to enhance the domestic reputation of a musician with twelve children.

off to form their own group which they called Shina Adewale. Together they recorded several albums and achieved enormous success, but ultimately private ambitions led to a split and each struck out on his own.

By 1990 many young music fans in Nigeria, raised on Sunny Ade, were turning to a new variant, the music and stage show of **"Sir" Shina Peters**. Now a name in his own right with wealthy Nigerian backers, Shina combined juju with bits of Fela Kuti's Afro-Beat style and the upfront drum sounds of fuji music into a style he dubbed *Afro-juju*. His 1989 release on CBS, "Afro-Juju Series 1", became a multimillion seller in Nigeria and abroad (video release, US tour) and launched a youth craze called Shina Mania. The stunning success of "Afro Juju Series 1" and his powerful live performances secured Shina Nigeria's Juju Musician of the Year award for 1990. His long-awaited follow-up record, "Shinamania", involved blending fuji-style percussive force with Roland and DX7 synthesizers to create a modern juju style with reduced guitar lines, throaty vocals and the synth carrying the frontline melody. Despite healthy sales, the result was widely panned by Nigerian critics, who quickly diminished the force of the two-year craze.

Shina's success did manage to open up the juju market to newcomers and, while he is still very popular, big plaudits have recently been received by relative newcomer **Fabulous Olu Fajemirokun**, who has yet to release anything on CD.

Juju music – like highlife – has a remarkable ability to revitalize and re-create itself within a basic framework, its evolution depending on the development of new "systems". But the hot money in the mid-'90s is on fuji. Check out both styles and make up your own mind.

THE ERUPTION OF FUJI

Although **fuji** has been around in Yoruba-land for nearly three decades, three top names – Sikiru Ayinde Barrister, Ayinla Kollington and Wasiu Barrister – had come totally to dominate the Lagos scene by the early 1990s. Named, somewhat disappointingly, after Mount Fuji, Japanese mountain of love (mostly for the sound of the word, according to originator Sikiru Barrister), the first fuji bands had appeared in the late 1960s. They assimilated elements of *apala* (a style with a praise-song core, named after the talking drum and popularized by Ayinla Omowura and Haruna Ishola), together with *sakara* and *were* into a new recreational dance style.

Sometimes glibly described as juju music without guitars (interestingly, Ebenezer Obey once described juju as mambo music with guitars added), fuji is in fact a far more complex style drawing on Yoruba percussion roots (the small round clay and bamboo *sakara* tambourine-drum and *apala* talking drum) while adding a specifically Muslim feel with wailing vocals. True, there are virtually no stringed instruments involved: apart from the Hawaiian guitar it's an overwhelming wall of sound in percussion and vocals.

From a slow start, fuji steadily gained in popularity, overtaking juju as the main recreational music of the Yoruba by 1986. It was associated loosely with Islam, in the same way that juju tended to be associated with Christianity.

Sikiru Ayinde, better known by his fans as **Barrister**, is the leading Yoruba fuji singer. He started singing Muslim *were*, the singing-alarm-clock songs performed for early breakfast and prayers during Ramadan, at the age of ten. After a brief career in the army, he returned to music and, in the early 1970s, formed the Supreme Fuji Commander, a 25-piece outfit. They soon became one of Nigeria's top bands, firing off a battery of hit records.

Ayinla Kollington is ranked second in the fuji popularity stakes behind Barrister. He's very much the source of social commentary in the Yoruba Muslim music scene. His lyrics can be razor sharp – though he rarely puts himself on the front line alongside Fela Kuti. He released over a dozen albums in the 1980s, including "Motun De Pelu Ara" and "Knock-out Special".

Success spawned success as Kollington and Barristers Sikiru and Wasiu (the latter has done an extraordinary job of copying his illustrious role model, apparently without any recriminations, legal or otherwise) vied with each other to accumulate titles, doctorates and other ciphers of status. But the real action was taking place on vinyl. Each fuji leader continued to add new touches to the basic formula – a drop of Hawaiian guitar here, a lone trumpet there; from a subtle synth in the background to an up-front school bell. Proletarian and relentless, the moving percussive force of fuji swept Lagos off its feet and, by the late 1980s, had become synonymous with dance-floor excitement. Wasiu scored with "Talazo in London" and "Jo Fun Mi"; Kollington with "Megastar" and "Fuji Ropopo"; Sikiru with "Extravaganza" and "Fuji Garbage". "Fuji Garbage" was titled thus to preempt any abusive comments from rivals. They thought it was garbage? Sikiru would call it garbage himself (if

Michael Jackson was *Bad*, Sikiru Ayinde Barrister was *Garbage*!). It also expressed his contempt for the space taken up in the fuji columns of the Nigerian papers over the alleged gossip and feuding between him and Kollington. Like the term "fuji", the epithet has worked – especially as the associated dance style swept through Nigeria's Christian and Muslim communities alike – and the "Garbage" series, which started locally on LP and includes his debut CD on the GlobeStyle label, now numbers many volumes.

Twenty-plus strong (Sikiru Barrister's full line-up, when there's room for all of them on stage, is 34), the fuji percussion orchestras are a sight to behold. They can occasionally be enjoyed in London and New York when they drop over for shows that are vastly underpublicized – outside an ecstatic Nigerian community. At his London gigs in 1993, Sikiru Barrister's stage and line-up resembled a Lagos street scene, as the audience mingled with the orchestra and an organized currency-changing operation was set up on tables and chairs to one side.

A recent departure is the release by all the leading fuji stars of videos mixed from live shows, street theatre and home life. Enormously entertaining and of excellent quality, these fuji videos are now the best way to experience the fuji phenomenon – short of a long weekend in Lagos.

HIGHLIFE RISE AND FALL

While juju and fuji have ruled among the Yoruba, high-quality **highlife** was the norm in the east for well over forty years. Highlife arrived in Nigeria from Ghana in the early 1950s in the shape of guitar bands and dance bands.

Light, flowing and eminently danceable, highlife is one of the few "core" dance rhythms in Africa and it easily took root in Igbo-land. The Igbo have a traditional familiarity with stringed instruments; early "Igbo Blues" is redolent of later guitar-band idioms and Congolese and Cameroonian guitar bands toured the east from 1959 onwards. Highlife, with its western and Christian musical links, slotted well into the Igbo cultural framework – non-Muslim, individualist, outward-looking. And the struggle for independence in Ghana (highlife's heartland) was closely watched in Nigeria, branding the style as the cultural expression of West African nationalism, worthy of emulation. ET Mensah, the king of Ghanaian highlife, toured frequently during the 1950s, and his music struck an immediate chord with southern Nigerians.

Bobby Benson, one of the pioneers of dance band highlife, devoted himself to this style after hearing ET Mensah. In the 1950s, he created Bobby Benson and his Combo, whose early hits went a long way to popularize the style at home.

Rex Lawson began playing trumpet in bands at the age of twelve, and when highlife took off in the 1950s, he worked with many of the greats. In the 1960s, his eleven-piece group, Mayor's Dance Band, produced successive hits including "Jolly Papa" and "Gowon Special". Lawson died suddenly in 1976, at the height of his career. Many of the classics can be heard on his "Greatest Hits" album on Polydor Nigeria – though you'll be hard pressed to find it.

Prince Nico Mbarga and Rocafil Jazz are reckoned to have sold some thirteen million copies of "Sweet Mother", making it the biggest-selling African song of all time. Hundreds of bands copied it; radio stations played it incessantly; vinyl copies could only be had at twenty times the normal price. But why? For a song about not forgetting mum, with its vaguely guilt-ridden undertones, and, on first hearing, unadventurous composition, it's hard to see much beyond an innocent charm. But it is an infectious song and its potent appeal was concocted from Mbarga's use of pidgin English (broadening his audience enormously) and a style he called *panko* – for the first time incorporating sophisticated rumba guitar-phrasing into the highlife idiom. In fact "Sweet Mother" is a highly charged dance number, mid-paced and sensual, with brilliant rhythmic breaks. The use of homely lyrics was a perfect subterfuge, releasing millions onto the dance floor who might otherwise have considered the song too daring.

Sweet mother, I no go forget you,
For the suffer wey you suffer for me, yeah,
Sweet mother, I no go forget you,
For the suffer wey you suffer for me, yeah.

When I de cry, my mother go carry me.
She go say, "My pikin, wetin you de cry?, oh,
Stop, stop, stop, stop, stop, stop
Make you no go cry again, oh".

When I de sick, my mother go cry, cry, cry.
She go say, instant when I go die, make she die, oh.
She go beg God, "God help me,
God help me, my pikin, oh."

But "Sweet Mother" was an outstanding success in a story of general decline. The Nigerian civil war in the late 1960s virtually put an end to highlife in western Nigeria: tribal

PRAISE AND "SPRAYING"

Like all Yoruba music, juju and fuji music is primarily about words. As the Yoruba language is strongly tonal (in other words the pitch of a syllable determines the meaning of spoken words), lyrics and melody have a peculiarly close relationship, unlike anything derived from cultures with non-tonal languages (for example English, French, Wolof). Juju music is steeped in Yoruba oral traditions and its singers draw from the large corpus of proverbs, metaphors and traditional praise poems of the spoken language. While popular juju and fuji musicians play nightclub and theatre shows, the vast majority of performances take place in more traditional contexts such as weddings, naming ceremonies, funeral feasts and other major commemorative events.

The musicians are generally given a guaranteed fee for performing, but the bulk of their earnings come from what is known as "spraying". The lead singer of the band makes sure he collects the names and other pertinent information about prominent individuals attending the event (there is usually a nonperforming band member dedicated to this important task). The singer will then praise these individuals one at a time, invoking their heritage, heaping praises on their relatives and, through formulaic proverbs, establishing their great and worthy credentials for all to hear. In response, the patron whose head has "swelled" with pride will come on stage and slap bank notes onto the forehead of the sweaty musician – quickly collected by a colleague. The more money given, the longer the patron's praises are sung.

At a typical ceremony, the music will begin around 11pm or midnight and the band will play nonstop for two or three hours. It is common for these *inawo* (literally "something to spend money on") to last until eight o'clock the next morning or later. As long as patrons are spraying, the musicians are playing. Artists like Sunny Ade, Ebenezer Obey and Sikiru Barrister, who demand guarantees of around $1000, routinely get sprayed upwards of $10,000 per show.

Barrister trawls in the tips

discrimination forced all Igbo musicians – including Rex Lawson – to leave Lagos, and guitar-band highlife was increasingly identified with the east as "Igbo highlife" (where, with a few honourable exceptions, it gradually withered), while juju, and later fuji, became the staple diet of the Lagos recording industry.

Among the highlife survivors was the Yoruba singer and trumpeter **"Dr" Victor Olaiya** (the "Evil Genius of Highlife") – one of the few top Lagos musicians to continue with the genre and stick to his musical roots throughout the war and after. Two other diehards are the sonorous-voiced, old-timer **Stephen Osita Osadebe**, with almost half a century of traditional Igbo guitar songs behind him in the shape of more than thirty albums, and **Orlando "Dr Ganja" Owoh**, the inveterate king of *toye*, a juju-highlife cross-style which contrives to be both traditional and provocative, by staying acoustic, topical – and stoned.

Old albums from the early highlife stars are rarities these days although it is still possible to lay your hands on 1970s and '80s material by the fabulous **Oriental Brothers** (and off-shoots Dr Sir Warrior and Kabaka) as well as the classic highlife of Ikengas, Oliver de Coque and, of course, Prince Nico Mbarga. And a steady trickle of re-releases continues to refresh the style.

For some details on Nigerian Reggae, see Chapter Ten.

Thanks for extra juju input from Andy Frankel.

FELA KUTI AND THE AFRO-BEAT REVOLUTION

••••••••••••••••••••••••

Of all African musicians Fela Kuti probably needs the least introduction. He's passed his half century with over fifty albums to his credit, and – sweating, naked to the waist, with a massive spliff clenched between his teeth – has become the radiant rallying point for the Nigerian underclass, and for political prisoners everywhere. Controversial, stubborn, outspoken, innovative, and always on a track entirely his own, Fela has maintained a creative momentum unparalleled in West Africa. His career, now spanning three decades, has been repeatedly interrupted by government violence against his musicians, his family and his person. Records have been banned, his extraordinary, extended-family base, the Kalakuta Republic, was destroyed, his mother killed, and the man himself beaten up and imprisoned; yet still he fights on against the corruption, brutality and banal inhumanity of successive regimes.

Fela Anikulapo Ransome-Kuti was born into an elite Yoruba family in Abeokuta, north of Lagos. The town, established by the British in the early 1800s for freed slaves, and the home of Nobel-prize-winning novelist Wole Soyinke, was always a creative and radical hotbed. The Ransome family had a history both of anticolonial, nationalist activity and musical talent. Fela's grandfather was a celebrated composer, his father and mother a piano-playing pastor and a nationalist leader respectively. In the late 1950s Fela moved to London to study music and stayed four years, studying trumpet and musical theory at the Trinity College of Music and forming the **Koola Lobitos** in 1961 with his friend and mentor JK Braimah.

Returning home in 1963 he soon came under the influence of Sierra Leonean soul singer Geraldo Pino's Afro-soul style, itself close to James Brown. Fela combined this innovative style with elements of highlife, jazz, and traditional music

Fela in offstage attire

and dubbed his sound **"Afro-Beat"**. In 1969 he moved to the US where he read about African-American history and was strongly moved by his contact with the Black Panthers. Nigeria was plagued by political instability and military rulers of uncertain calibre. As the plight of the poor in Nigeria worsened, Fela sharpened his wit and honed his musical revolution.

He started slowly with a couple of unmemorable albums before hitting a true purple patch in 1972 with a series of Afro-Beat classics. He then launched into a series of stinging attacks on everything from military governments to skin-bleaching, Lagos traffic, arbitrary arrest and, above all, the political and economic systems which reproduced such grinding poverty. His efforts did not go unnoticed. For him, the 1970s were characterized by police harassment and violence, conflicts with multinational record companies, self-exile in Ghana and a growing international reputation.

Afro-Beat emerged as a powerful musical force featuring the fantastic percussionist **Tony Allen** on the drum kit, brooding brass parts, call-and-response vocals and a spectacularly choreographed, twenty-strong female chorus, and of course Fela himself, alternating between tenor-sax, alto-sax and keyboard – on which he frequently comes out with classical themes. Building to magnificent, thundering climaxes, Afro-Beat carved out a niche in the crowded Lagos musical market with best-seller following best-seller.

In 1985, the military government nailed him on spurious currency charges and locked him away on a five-year sentence. But such was the international outcry and massive protest inside Nigeria that he was eventually released in 1987, weakened but unbowed. Towards the end of the decade he blasted back with classics such as "Army Arrangement" (a stinging indictment of military corruption under the Obasanjo regime),

"Beasts of No Nation" (a lashing for the reactionary conservatism of Reagan, Thatcher and Botha in South Africa), and the standing accusation of all Nigerian governments entitled "Which Head Never Steal?".

Accompanied by his forty-strong band, the **Egypt 80** (formerly the Africa 70), Fela has never been an easy star for western journalists to deal with. He stands accused of racism, extravagant sexism and overweening egoism – all charges which he shrugs off rather than refutes (though he divorced his 28 wives in 1986, announcing "no man has the right to own a woman's vagina"). His penchant for rewriting history deepens with the passage of time – a favourite story of recent years concerns the Scottish explorer Mungo Park, who was killed at Busa in northern Nigeria. According to Fela, Park was sent by George III not to follow the course of the Niger but to steal the sacred Power Pot of the Yoruba from Ife, near Lagos. There isn't a shred of evidence that Park ever got further south than Busa, but the pot, says Fela, has been kept at

Windsor Castle ever since, from where it has caused half the world's ills, not to mention the great fire of 1992. His songs, sung in pidgin English, have wide appeal for their humour and clever use of language, but his music has never been dance-oriented and the lengthy on-stage polemics – haranguing captive audiences through a haze of smoke – are legendary.

During Fela's periods in jail, his bands have carried on, led by his son Femi and others. **Femi Kuti** has now launched a career of his own, to escape from the shadow of Fela. Where his father is ranting and polemical, Femi is less vitriolic, more a musician's musician. If he doesn't have the old man's voice, his positive approach is a suitable complement to Fela Kuti's negativity. Together with the rest of the huge artistic community in Nigeria, they suggest the possibility of a way forward for Africa where "democracy" and "development" are failing – a movement for real progress led by creative people in touch with their own roots.

■ DISCOGRAPHY ■

Traditional music from Nigeria is seldom available on vinyl disc although the old Decca "Native Music" series with a repertoire ranging from early *apala* to Hausa music and Igbo Blues is a treasure trove of mid-century recordings. There are also two excellent records of traditional Hausa music available on Bärenreiter Musicaphon. A great deal of postwar material, including early juju and highlife, is locked away in the warehouses of Phillips, Decca and EMI.

TRADITIONAL AND DRUMMING

ⓓ **Gaspar Lawal** *Kadara* (GlobeStyle, UK). London-based master drummer. Economical with his precocious talent, Gaspar is in a class of his own for neotraditional percussion.
ⓓ **Babatunde Olatunji** *Drums of Passion* (Rykodisc, US). Spritual drumming and chanting, with the help of Mickey Hart, to invoke the Yoruba gods Ajaja, Kori, Ogun and Shango. Two volumes ("The Invocation" and "The Beat"). Ultimately, it gets to you.
Haruna Ishola *Various titles* (Decca, West Africa). One of Nigeria's greatest apala performers, Ishola's music helped pave the way both for juju and fuji. Before he died in 1983, Ishola had produced some 25 LPs and opened his own recording studio. It's still relatively easy to find many of his later records like *Apala Songs* or *Haruna Ishola and his Apala group*.
ⓓ **Various** *Yoruba Street Percussion* (Original Music, US). A rich diversity of short tracks from the 1960s including *agidigbo* by the New Star Orchestra, apala from Haruna Ishola, early fuji, *sakara*, various female *waka* artists and a sound dubbed "natural juju". "Borrowed" from Decca West Africa.

HIGHLIFE

Oliver de Coque *Ogene Super Sounds* (OGRLPS, Nigeria). A classic highlifer, the colourful de Coque occupies a unique

position in the highlife pantheon, incorporating classic Congo guitar into laid-back highlife rhythms.
Ikengas *Late Celestine Ukwu* (Rogers All Stars, Nigeria). A fine Igbo guitar band, ranking alongside the Peacocks and self-exiled Ghanaians, Okukuseku, as serious purveyors of highlife. Difficult to find but worth the search.
ⓓ **Prince Nico Mbarga & Rocafil Jazz** *Aki Special* (Rounder, US). A bumper CD with nearly two LPs' worth on it – including the global hit "Sweet Mother" – which makes as good a starting point as any for a collection of Nigerian music.
Osita Osadebe *Osondi Owendi* (Polygram, Nigeria). Osita, now in his mid-50s, seems to be slowing down a bit. New albums should be bought on sight! This one from 1984 represents the Chief at the height of his powers.
Orlando Owoh *Dance Music* (SOS, Nigeria). The originator of *toye* (ganja/cannabis) music, Owoh is a Lagos rebel who has not only survived but flourished over the last two decades. A rough-and-ready highlife-juju variant.
ⓓ **Oriental Brothers** *Heavy on the Highlife* (Original Music, US). After dozens of Nigeria-only releases, this wonderful burn-up of a guitar-highlife album sets the standard. Relentless, sexy grooves: thank you John Storm Roberts.
Celestine Ukwu *His Philosophies* (Polygram, Nigeria). Classic, gentle and lyrical 1976 Igbo guitar-band highlife from the late master. Ukwu's albums are rarely seen these days so snap up any of his half dozen LPs when you see them. He cannot be replaced.
ⓓ **Various** *Azagas and Archibogs* (Original Music, US). Subtitled "the Sixties Sound of Lagos Highlife", this includes little-known outfits with startling names plucked from Decca's vaults of vinyl obscurity. While East Nigerian guitar highlife prospered after Biafra, the big-band variety disappeared at the end of the 1960s. The best of these cuts are very cool.

WEST AFRICA

NIGERIA **309**

WAKA

Queen Salawah Abeni and her Waka Modernizer (local cassettes, Nigeria). Waka is very similar to fuji – an Islamic style for women. Queen S is to waka what Barrister is to fuji. And she joins in the self-indulgent feuding with the best of them.

Lijadu Sisters *Double Trouble* (Shanachie, US). Identical twin all-rounders, related to Fela Kuti. On this slightly dated (1984) but still available record, they display a modernized version of waka with electric guitars and bass and choral vocals making it much more than a female waka.

JUJU

Sunny Ade *Juju Music* (Island, UK). The record that launched a million passions for African sounds. Still wonderful after all these years, *Juju Music* includes many of Ade's best songs, among them the sweet "365 is My Number", a longer, sharper, and looser version of which takes up a whole side on the 1978 release *Private Line* (Sunny Alade, Nigeria). If the Velvet Underground had been African this is how they might have sounded. On *Bobby* (Sunny Alade, Nigeria) – probably the best juju album of all time – Ade runs through all the classic riffs in a flowing 1983 tribute to legendary band leader Bobby Benson. The classic *Synchro System* (Island, UK) is from the same year as *Bobby* (1983) but a different sound – a more measured approach to the western market.

Segun Adewale *Play For Me* (Stern's, UK). The album on which rests Adewale's reputation as master of the kick-start juju dubbed Yo-Pop, an aggressive, up-beat style.

Ⓒ **IK Dairo** *Juju Master* (Original Music, US). Singer, composer and band leader, Dairo was responsible for the consolidation of juju music among the Yoruba and introduced the accordion to the style. He is still active, both musically and in the church. This is a classic round-up of Decca West Africa 45s. IK's new CD, *Ashiko* (Xenophile/Green Linnet, US), has him in tune, at last. The talking drums are really speaking here.

Ⓒ **Ebenezer Obey** *Get Yer Jujus Out* (Rykodisc, US). Lengthy, live juju. Alternatively, the *Solution* LP (Stern's, UK) is fully representative of Obey at his best and really easy to get hold of.

Sir Shina Peters *Afro-Juju I* (Columbia, Nigeria). Creator of Shina Mania, Shina has over twenty albums to his credit and is still in his early 30s. This album was a landmark in the evolution of juju music, combining it with elements of Afro-beat and fuji.

Ⓒ **Various** *Juju Roots, 1930s-1950s* (Rounder, US). Excellent introduction to the early juju years with comprehensive sleeve notes. Featuring Irewolede Denge, Tunde King and Ojoge Daniel – essential.

FUJI

Ayinla Kollington *Ijoba Ti Tun* (KRLPS, Nigeria). Fuji's "Man of the People". Challenging lyrics, driving percussion and, more recently, a touch of Hawaiian guitar. Of his thirty-plus albums this one is an abiding personal favourite.

Ⓒ **Barrister** *New Fuji Garbage* (GlobeStyle, UK). With the first international outing for fuji, the GlobeStyle team strike gold with a recording which is likely to define the style for western ears for years to come. Barrister's voice here is slightly mellower than usual and the band surround it with a pounding panoply. Not forgetting the Hawaiian guitar.

Ⓒ **Adewale Ayuba** *Mr Johnson Play for Me* (Flame Tree, UK). Quite a recent recording, now reissued. The first international CD release for the young pop pretender of fuji.

AFRO-BEAT/ROCK

Ⓒ **Fela Kuti** *The 69 Los Angeles Sessions* (Stern's, UK). First release for some vintage numbers from Black Panther days – and ten tracks all under seven minutes make it unique in the Fela oeuvre! Ⓒ *Beasts of No Nation* (JDEUR, UK) even the cover makes an unmissable statement and the recording confounded critics who felt Fela was past it, as he entered the 1990s in great shape, howling against Thatcher and Reagan. Of the archive Fela still available on vinyl, *Underground System* (Stern's, UK) is perhaps the most essential – two scornful tracks and many credits.

Sonny Okosun *Fire in Soweto* (Oti, UK). A powerful plea for the victims of apartheid, this rock-reggae-styled album was a huge hit across Africa. Ⓒ *Liberation* (Shanachie, US) is high-quality material, repackaged for the US market, where Okosun has kept a large, devoted following.

CENTRAL AND EAST AFRICA

T he vast region of Central and East Africa has produced some of World Music's most influential and successful musicians and without any shadow of doubt the best guitar music in the world – a theme which runs through many of the articles that follow. Geographically, the chapter covers a swathe of equatorial and tropical Africa, touching or lingering on seven countries – Zaire, Cameroon, Equatorial Guinea, São Tomé, Kenya, Tanzania and Madagascar – of the dozen or so in the region. They're a mixed musical bag of roots and influences, though the former colonial capitals still wield enormous influence over output. Paris, for example, actively encouraged the Europeanization of its territories: now Paris and Brussels have large expatriate populations of Africans, the main market for a thriving music industry based on the former colonies. Conversely, London's mild disinterest in the fate of its colonies has resulted in an extremely limited musical output from Kenya or Tanzania, except on local cassette.

Zaire comes first: this vast zone of rivers and rainforest and savannah is Central Africa's heart, musically and in every other sense. It's the region in which the important Bantu-speaking language groups underwent their first stages of cultural development two to three thousand years ago, before spreading to the east and the south. Musically more significant, Zaire's seething capital Kinshasa is one of Africa's giant cities, a music powerhouse on a par with Cairo and Johannesburg. From Kinshasa and Brussels – the old colonial capital – the upbeat dance musics of rumba, soukous and their variants have emanated for more than three decades and can now be heard worldwide through the records of Franco, Kanda Bongo Man, Papa Wemba and scores of others, perhaps 500 of which are available on CD.

Near-neighbour Cameroon is one of Africa's great meeting places – geographically, linguistically and culturally. The French and the British both ruled parts of the country before independence, and anglophone/francophone issues are the focus of fierce political debate. As musically diverse as anywhere in Africa, Cameroon's folk traditions are many (the Sultan of Bamoun's Musical Theatre to note one of the more elaborate), but its biggest musical export is the hot, dance beat, *makossa*. Recent years have seen the upsurge of another folk style turned electric and international – guitar-based *bikutsi* – but it remains to be heard if the rich horn-led recipe of makossa, flavoured increasingly with Antillean zouk, has really lost its edge to the upstart.

Before crossing to East Africa, this chapter visits two small and almost unknown countries tucked between Cameroon and Zaire. Equatorial Guinea and São Tomé both have interesting indigenous musical traditions and the potential in their modern musicians for global break-out.

Nairobi's music industry has perhaps been more influential than the music of Kenya – having attracted musicians from all over Central and East Africa – but Kenyan guitar-band styles are eloquently developed, and groups play in most of the country's languages as well as Swahili.

Swahili is the language of *taarab*, the remarkable accordion-meets-Bombay-musical-in-Arab-dhow style of the Indian Ocean coast, to which a special feature is devoted. From almost total isolation a decade ago, there is now a good number of CD releases.

Also mostly Swahili-based is the surprisingly thriving dance-band scene of Tanzania with its mighty exponent Remmy Ongala – as much a figure of importance for his lyrics as his musicianship. Formerly socialist Tanzania is one

CENTRAL AND EAST AFRICA

INTRODUCTION **311**

of the few countries in the region to have a tradition of state-sponsored bands, a situation which has created a pool of talent amid a dearth of instruments.

This chapter concludes with a survey of the Madagascar music scene. Like taarab music, the sounds of this extraordinary island were almost unknown abroad until the mid-1980s. Now, with new CDs being released almost monthly, a number of key artists and adventurous music labels are opening Madagascar's musical riches to the world.

How a Chapter was Born

There was no lack of comment from contributing authors on the decision to include various countries in "Central and East Africa". There is certainly some case for including Cameroon in West Africa. Graeme Ewens, a self-confessed Congo-centric, believes the whole Zaire–Congo area holds the key to much of what's vital about all African music and considers it has more in common with the west coast from Senegal to Nigeria than with East Africa. A number of musicologists have suggested that the guitar first made an appearance in Central Africa when West African sailors visited the Congo River: we could have ended up with a West Africa chapter incorporating half of this one... But the overwhelming influence of the Zairean sound on modern popular music in Kenya and Tanzania – the salient fact that so many Congolese artists have forged careers in Nairobi and Dar – meant there was never much doubt about how the division, imperfect as it is, should go.

Unfortunately, while squeezing into the chapter unusual entries like São Tomé and Equatorial Guinea, we've had to leave out contenders of perhaps no less significance such as **Uganda**, which has produced the brooding solo talents of **Geoffrey Oryema** (CDs on RealWorld); **Burundi**, famous for its astonishing royal percussion troupe **The Drummers of Burundi** (CD, again, on RealWorld, but more essentially an unmissable live spectacle); and **Rwanda**, from where a disc of fragile, haunting songs by Brussels exile **Cécile Kayirebwa** has recently been released on the GlobeStyle label. These and more will have to wait until the next edition.

CENTRAL AND EAST AFRICA ✈ GLOSSARY

Benga Dominant indigenous guitar style of Kenya, an adaptation of traditional rhythms and string instruments to guitars.

Bikutsi Fast and furious dance/music from southeast Cameroon; from *biku*, "to thump" and *tsi*, "the ground"

Chakacha Women's and girls' Swahili wedding dance (taarab)

Chemko Faster dance parts of a song or seben (Tanzania)

Danço Congo Spectacular folk music entertainment (São Tomé)

Goma Dance for special occasions (taarab)

Likembe Central African thumb piano, like a sanza or mbira

Lundum Traditional rhythm from São Tomé

Makossa Fast dance and dominant popular music of Cameroon; from *kosa*, "to strip off"

Mchiriku Youth folk-funk revival style of Tanzania

Mtindo (pl. mitindo) Dance/music styles (Tanzania)

Mutuashi Erotic, hip-thrusting dance popularized by Tshala Muana (Zaire)

Ngoma Drums or drumming, singing, dancing (Bantu languages)

Omutibo Acoustic guitar style with fanta bottle percussion (Kenya)

Sapeur "Member" of the Society of Ambienceurs and Persons of Elegance (Zaire)

Seben Guitar-led improvisational section which has become the trademark of soukous (Zaire)

Soukous Folk dance, now the generic name for Congo-Zairean dance music

Tchiloli Traditional musical drama (São Tomé)

Tumba Conga drums (Tanzania)

Vugo Older women's Swahili wedding dance.

HEART OF DANCENESS

THE MUSIC OF ZAIRE

From Roots Rumba to Anti-Choc, Graeme Ewens follows the streams and tributaries of Central African musical culture to trace the sources of the continent's most successful sounds. See the note on spelling in the introduction to Chapter 6, much of which applies here. In Zaire, French accents are not de rigueur: Pépé Kallé is invariably spelt Pepe Kalle.

The rumba of **Zaire**, formerly the Belgian Congo, is one musical form that has hit a nerve throughout Africa, animating dancers of all ages and social classes in a way which no other regional style, not even West African highlife, has come close to matching. With its spiralling guitars and hip-swinging rhythms, soukous, as it's commonly known, has also had a bigger cumulative effect on western dance floors than any other African music. Since colonial times, Kinshasa (then known as Leopoldville) has been the musical heart of the continent, pumping out a regular flow of life-giving "Congolese" music by great dance bands like African Jazz, OK Jazz, and African Fiesta and their descendants from the "new generation" of the Zaiko Langa Langa family, who blended rumba with rock during the 1970s.

Despite social, political and economic difficulties, Zaireans have maintained a reputation for knowing "how to enjoy", and dance has been central to any expression of emotion. The early social dances such as the *maringa* and *agbwaya* were "cool" expressions of physical grace involving subtle hip moves and shifts of balance, rather than fancy footwork and pirouettes. This understated style has remained the basis, while each seasonal variation readjusts the emphasis and adds a few simple gestures or arm movements. Many of the dance crazes which came out of the Congo also made their mark in neighbouring states, and the passing of time can be measured by memories of seductive rhythms such as the *rumba-boucher, kiri-kiri, cavacha,*

kwasa-kwasa, madiaba and *sundama,* rather than the titles of particular songs. The music has developed through specific stages, and many of the new-generation artists who came to prominence at the start of the 1970s, like Zaiko Langa Langa, Papa Wemba, Pepe Kalle and Bozi Boziana, are still very much in their prime and gradually consolidating appreciative audiences in Europe, North America and the Pacific rim as well as across Africa.

But in 1991, Zaire, which had once been the wealthiest country in Africa, was plunged deep into anarchy and economic chaos as it lurched towards democratic reform. Many musicians quit Kinshasa – which had always had a reputation for rumba-round-the-clock – and the vibrant ambience of the Matonge music district was frighteningly muted. Despite the military-inspired mutiny and sacking of Kinshasa's business and residential areas, however, musical activity was not completely stifled and, indeed, the main musical forces, OK Jazz and Zaiko Langa Langa, were still performing there in 1993. Many of the other bands which generated the city's special musical appeal went on extended foreign tours; others had splintered, with individual soukous musicians settling in London and the US as well as Brussels, Paris

Kanda Bongo Man – the sound of Zaire all over Africa

SOUKOUSEMANTICS

∙∙∙∙∙∙∙∙∙∙∙∙∙∙∙∙∙∙∙∙∙∙∙∙

There is really no generic term used by Zaireans themselves to describe their music. People speak of *miziki na biso* ("our music") to distinguish it from imported sounds, but even that phrase relies on the French word *musique* rendered into Lingala. African languages have many words for different dances and song forms but rarely a single term for music. Various styles of Zairean music have been named over the years after the dances from which they sprang, or which they generated, but none of them applies to the whole, expansive genre.

Western recording industry professionals, promoters and marketing people can't stand this sort of thing: they seem unable to function without a brand name with which to label their product. The bland *rumba-rock*, with its suggestion of Cuban accessibility, has rather stuck as one catch-all moniker for Zaire/Congo styles, but to combine a Cuban word with an American word to describe something distinctively African seems doubly inappropriate and it's not a term that any local musician or music fan would ever use. The seemingly more politically correct (and sweet-sounding) *soukous* has been the tag of recent years, even since before the existence of that other dubious handle, World Music, and at least serves to locate the music and to some extent identify it for western ears. But in Zaire *soukous* refers to a particular dance style popular in the late 1960s; and it's currently in vogue as a football term, describing when a player feints and dribbles the ball around an opponent. Using the word *soukous* to describe music as different as Joseph Kabasale's classics and Papa Wemba's latest offering is like referring to everything from "Why Do Fools Fall in Love?" to "Cop Killer" as twist.

Ken Braun,
The Beat

and Geneva. The number of Zairean releases on the market has slumped in recent years, but in December 1993, a showcase event in Kinshasa demonstrated that the music had not been silenced. A major festival at the newly opened Kamanyola stadium brought the remaining big bands together with artists like Kofi Olomide and Papa Wemba, who had been recalled from Europe, to show that soukous was alive and well.

Soukous, which was nurtured in the closed system of Zairean "authenticity" imposed by President Mobutu in the early 1970s, eventually brought a contemporary, urban image of Africa to the dance floors of the west. It also brought a continuity: the sapeurs who strut and flutter their expensive designer gear in western capitals, dancing to the latest Zaiko, **Wenge Musica**, or **Anti-Choc** release, are descendants of the youth cult of the "Yankees" who posed around Kinshasa's Ngiringiri market during the early 1950s, dancing, promenading and showing off their American shoes. And the kind of red-hot, fast-track Parisian soukous of western disco favourites like **Loketo, Matchatcha, Soukous Stars** and **Kanda Bongo Man** has evolved directly from the mellow, Congolese rumba which blossomed in the 1950s.

ROOTS AND BRANCHES

In the aftermath of World War II life was sweet for the new urbanites, attracted to **Kinshasa** by well-paid work, public health and housing — and by its reputation as a "town of joy". Following independence from Belgium, the town quickly grew into the largest French-speaking city outside France with a population now estimated to be over four million. But Zaire, as the second largest country in Africa became known in 1974, was never French; it has its own flamboyant identity.

Zairean music is renowned for the stylish intricacies of electric guitars which combine melody and rhythm in a way that is both mellow and highly charged. But creative excellence apart, soukous had practical advantages which made it an internationally viable popular music. First it was "non-tribal": it used the interethnic trading language of Lingala, a melodic tongue which has been the vehicle for some of the sweetest singing voices in Africa. The distinctive guitar style was an amalgam of influences brought to the lower Congo from the west coast of Africa and from the interior, and therefore struck a chord across the continent.

The dance format which stormed West and Central Africa before and after World War II was the Afro-Cuban rumba. Itself a new-world fusion of Latin and African idioms, the rumba was quickly reappropriated by the Congolese, most notably by adapting the piano part of the son *montuno* to the guitar and playing it in a similar way to the *likembe* or *sanza* – the thumb piano. Although this was not the first fusion dance music with popular pan-African appeal, Congolese music was less influenced by European taste than highlife music and was in many ways more African, even though western instruments were preferred.

The music also appeared in the right place at the right time. The Belgian Congo was booming and astute Greek traders in Kinshasa saw the commercial potential of discs as trade goods to sell alongside textiles, shoes, and household items, including, of course, record players. Inspired by the success of the GV series of Cuban records distributed by EMI, the influential labels Ngoma, Opika, CEFA and Loningisa released a deluge of 78rpm recordings by semiprofessional musicians of local rumba versions alongside releases of folklore music. Radio Congo Belge, which started African music broadcasts in the early 1940s, provided the ideal promotional medium. While live performance remained more informal, the record companies maintained their own house bands to provide backing for individual artists. The CEFA label employed Belgian guitarist and arranger **Bill Alexandre**, who brought the first electric guitars to the Congo and has been credited with introducing a finger-picking style at a time when most guitarists strummed. The rival Loningisa label recruited **Henri Bowane** from the Equatorial region, who injected even more colour into the style.

The forefathers of Congolese popular music included the accordionist Feruzi, often credited with popularizing the rumba during the 1930s, and the guitarists Antoine Wendo, Jhimmy, and Zachery Elenga. These itinerant musicians entertained in the African quarters at funeral wakes, marriages and casual parties. In more bourgeois society, early highlife, swing and Afro-Cuban music were the staples of the first bands to play at formal dances where the few members of the elite "evolués" could mix with Europeans. While many of the pioneers came to Kinshasa from the interior, others turned their sights east. One of the first guitarists to become known in the eastern regions was **Jean Bosco Mwenda** from Katanga, who was recorded in the field by the South African musicologist Hugh Tracey and later made his career in Nairobi.

In the capital, Kinshasa, life was more cosmopolitan: French-style *variété* or cabaret music made its mark, while other ingredients which combined to form the classic Congolese sound included vocal harmonic skills learned at church and, more recently, a tradition of religious fanfares played on brass-band instruments. All these elements can be clearly heard in the last and greatest of the big bands, OK Jazz, while only the horns are missing from the modern variations of the Zaiko generation, sometimes replaced by synthesizer or voices.

THE BELLE ÉPOQUE

The scene really came alive in 1953 with the inauguration of **African Jazz**, the first full-time recording and performing orchestra led by **Joseph "Le Grand Kalle" Kabasele**. In the same year the 15-year-old prodigy "Franco" Luambo Makiadi (see box) first entered the Loningisa studio to play with his guitar mentors Dewayon and Bowane. Three years later Franco and half a dozen colleagues from the studio house band formed Orchestre Kinois Jazz (a Kinois is someone from Kinshasa) which quickly became known as **OK Jazz**.

Joseph "Le Grand Kalle" Kabasele – father figure of modern Zairean music

FRANCOFILE

•••••••••••••••••••••

The continuity of Congolese music was broken in 1989 with the death of **Franco Luambo Makiadi**, leader of **OK Jazz** and the last surviving giant of the Belle Époque. As well as being a stunning guitar stylist with a hard, metallic urgency, Franco had a relationship with his audience that remains unmatched. More than any other public figure Franco accompanied his country's progress from colonial repression of village society through independence and statehood to the constricts of military rule and the first murmurings of democracy.

Born in 1938, Franco had grown up alongside his mother's market stall, among the "Yankees" and "bandits", and he was always more in tune with the street people of Kinshasa who liked their music hard and their songs to deal with day-to-day realities. His first instrument was a home-made, tin-can guitar with stripped electrical wire for strings, but at the age of 11 he was given his first real guitar and came under the tutelage of **Paul Dewayon**, one of the early recording artists who also moved among the market people rather than the intellectual

Franco – Le Grand Maître at his peak

évolués (literally "evolved") classes.

Franco's fancy finger-picking, his street-cred and boyish good looks made him an almost instant success. He was quickly hailed a "boy wonder" and, by the age of 15, was a popular recording star and member of the **Loningisa** label house band, in demand for modelling the latest clothes, and a heart-throb for the women of Kinshasa. In 1956 he helped found OK Jazz and, although he was only third in seniority, his organization and commitment, combined with star quality, made him very much the leader. A couple of spells in prison early in his career – for speeding and riding his Vespa without a licence – only reinforced his reputation.

When independence came unexpectedly to the Belgian Congo in 1960, the founder of the first dance orchestra and acknowledged "father" of Congo-rumba music, **Joseph Kabasele**, set up a recording deal for OK Jazz in Europe, and through the 1960s the band evolved into the biggest, most effective music machine in Africa. By then known as the "Sorcerer of the Guitar", Franco re-Africanized the Afro-Cuban rumba by introducing rhythmic, vocal and guitar elements from Congolese folklore. Although primarily a dance band, OK Jazz was also a vehicle for Franco's observations and criticisms of modernizing society, and his songs had more information and educational value than any other medium. His sternest morality lecture was "Attention Na Sida" (Beware of Aids), in 1987.

Like many African superstars, Franco had an ambivalent relationship with the state. He was a true patriot, but he also felt compelled to speak his mind and, while he was an essential element in Mobutu's *authenticité* ("authenticity") programme, he was also reprimanded and jailed more than once and several of his records were banned. Although he was a stern moralist, he could slip quite easily into obscenity in his declared mission to provoke and tell the truth. The meanings of his songs are often opaque, with layers of allusion covering a subtext or hidden agenda. His own constituents, however, have always known exactly who and what Franco was criticizing. In fact many of his narratives came from ideas suggested by his listeners.

Why do you do so?
You quarrel with everybody with no sense of shame
You quarrel with your wife in the street
And you tell her things you shouldn't
Why are you so uncivilized?
You don't feel ashamed even for your wife?

You go to see people and take off your shirt
Showing sweating armpits.
And you raise up your arms – what a smell!

Why are you so ill-bred?
Why do you do so?
Why are you so uncouth?

You are very impolite,
Very impolite,
Very impolite,
But why?
From "Très Impoli" (1984)

He also pumped out standard African praise and memorial songs, and covered a whole range of topics from football to commercial endorsement. But the theme to which he constantly returned was the conflict between men and women, and he couched many of his messages in a soap-opera style. The format reached a peak in 1986 with the episodic "Mario", about a lazy but educated young man and the older woman he lives with and exploits (until she eventually gets fed up and kicks him out of the home).

The strength of Franco's relationship with his home audience can be gauged from the number of sobriquets and titles he acquired. From the "Crazy Kid" he became known as "Franco My Love", then "The Sorcerer"; later he was formally awarded Zaire's Grand Order of the Leopard and made a Grand Maître – a title normally reserved for judges, professors and sorcerers. The Congolese writer Sylvain Bemba called him the Balzac of African music, after the writer of the Comédie Humaine. To others he was "The Godfather".

More than any other musician, however, Franco's music transcended the boundaries of language, class, nationality and tribal affiliation. His music was as hugely popular in anglophone Africa as in the French-speaking countries, and OK Jazz records have been licensed almost worldwide. He played only once in Britain and once in America, and all subsequent efforts to promote him were thwarted, often because of last-minute obligations to the Zairean ruling party.

During a career which lasted nearly 40 years, Franco released over 150 albums and composed some 1,000 songs, while the band's complete repertoire was closer to 3,000. He had the bulk to match that reputation, weighing around 140 kilos at his peak. The band too was massive, with up to 40 musicians on call and over 100 families dependent on their fortunes.

When Franco died after a long illness in October 1989, Zaire spent four days in national mourning, while the radio played nonstop OK Jazz. His long-time rival, Tabu Ley Rochereau, said at the time he was "like a human god". Sam Mangwana said he was the kind of man who appears only once in a hundred years and compared him with Shakespeare or Mozart, combined with Muhammad Ali or Pele.

A FRANCOPHILE DISCOGRAPHY

As well as the essential "Azda" (see discography), over eighty Franco CDs and cassettes are currently available and a vast amount of Franco and OK Jazz material is being re-released on CD by Sonodisc (France). For a terrific re-release on CD of the very first recordings of OK Jazz, get "Originalité" (RetroAfric, UK). This was the point where classic rumba began the long journey into soukous. You enter OK, you leave very KO'd. Also massively recommended is the long, soap-opera CD "Mario & Réponse de Mario" (Sonodisc, France). Even without understanding the dialogue the man's charisma is almost tangible. Worth getting hold of, although it's not on CD, is "Attention na Sida" (African Sun Music, Franco's own label, Zaire), his famous, beware-of-AIDS sermon – powerful oratory set against a memorable folklore rhythm. With Sam Mangwana, Franco came out in 1982 with "Coopération", an essential album of rich and wonderful dance music – though again not on CD. "Mabele" (African, Zaire) offers a fulsome treatment of folklore dating from 1974, including the classic title track ballad, composed by "vice-president" Simaro Lutumba and sung by Sam Mangwana.

Kalle's African Jazz, which came to include another guitar wizard, **Nicholas "Dr Nico" Kasanda**, alongside singer **Pascal Tabu "Rochereau"** and the Cameroonian saxophonist and keyboard player Manu Dibango, ensured themselves musical immortality with the release in 1960 of "Independence Cha Cha Cha", which celebrated the end of colonial rule in the Belgian Congo and became an anthem for much of Africa. Kalle was a showman as well as composer and arranger, and he created an international-sounding fusion, which gradually re-Africanized the popular Latin rhythms. Franco and the school of OK Jazz also started from the same points of reference but their music was rootsier, drawing on traditional folklore rhythms and instrumental techniques, and the songs were more down to earth.

During the 1950s and '60s there was constant movement between musicians in the French and Belgian colonies where the proliferation of "Congo bars" and a mood of optimism gave the region its good-time reputation. In Brazzaville a founder member of OK Jazz, **Jean Serge Essous**, and fellow sax player **Nino Malapet** soon set up the equivalent Congolese big band institution, **Les Bantous de la Capitale**, with **Papa Noel**, **Brazzos** and a few others who later returned to play with Franco. In the decade following independence both cities spawned hundreds of dance bands, releasing 45 rpm singles on dozens of record labels. By now the music had evolved a stage further and, thanks largely to the extended playing time of the 7-inch discs, more emphasis was placed on the exciting instrumental section known as the *seben*, when the slow rumba breaks, singers stand back and the multiple guitars go to work on the dancers. Franco was a master of the seben and his style was mimicked (though never matched), throughout Africa.

For several years the careers of African Jazz and OK Jazz ran parallel, but African Jazz disbanded in the mid-1960s after recording some 400 compositions. Rochereau, who later took the name **"Tabu Ley"**, set up **African Fiesta** with Dr Nico, whose rich, florid, solo style gained him a huge following of his own. What came out of the relationship was something new and slightly experimental, with a greater diversity of rhythm and melody and occasional hints of western soul and country music. African Fiesta rapidly garnered a rather urbane audience. Regrettably for their many fans, proponents of fusion, they also separated after two years, but Tabu Ley eventually formed **Afrisa**, which maintained the allegiance of a "sophisticated" audience and for some time was the only serious rival to OK Jazz. Both Kalle and Nico faded during the 1970s, Nico dying in 1982, followed a year later by Kalle.

Key figures who emerged from the growing ranks of these great dance bands included the raucous, honking sax player **Kiamanguana Verckys**, who spent six years with OK Jazz before setting up **Orchestre Veve**, and went on to produce some of the hard-core bands of the new wave. Others also found varying levels of solo fame after working in both camps, notably the erstwhile co-president of OK Jazz, **Vicky Longomba**, as well as Ndombe Opetum, Dizzy Mandjeku and **Sam Mangwana**.

Mangwana's smooth, sympathetic vocal style endeared him to followers of both camps and all ages. He started out in the early 1960s with **Vox Africa** and **Festival des Marquisards** before joining Tabu Ley's Afrisa. In 1972 he switched allegiance to OK Jazz for three productive years before returning to Afrisa. Eventually he set up a splinter group in West Africa called **African All Stars**, with whom he developed a pan-African sound with pop and Caribbean rhythmic undertones, which has provided the basis for a successful globe-trotting solo career.

A one-time colleague in OK Jazz, the guitarist **Mose Fan Fan** was Franco's deputy and co-soloist for several years, introducing a tougher, rock inflection to the OK Jazz rumba. In 1974 he took his fate in his hands and moved to East Africa with **Somo Somo**, where he fed the craze for Lingala music, before settling in Britain.

By the 1970s, the Kinshasa scene was getting crowded and many Zairean musicians appeared in other parts of the continent. Among the first wanderers was Ryco Jazz, founded by Bowane, who brought Congo rumba to West Africa and the French Antilles during the 1960s and early 1970s. In East Africa, too, the likes of Baba Gaston, Real Sounds, Orchestra Makassy and Samba Mapangala's Orchestra Virunga have all enjoyed more acclaim outside Zaire than they might have done at home.

RIDING THE NEW WAVE

The classic Congolese sound was a rich tapestry of vocals, guitars and rhythm instruments, embellished with full-blown horn arrangements which became more prominent after the visits of James Brown to Kinshasa in 1969 and 1974. During that time, however, a new stream of pop music had sprung from the students at Gombe High School, who had picked up on the western rock group format and who, independently of the older-generation musicians, started doing their own thing. While some recent graduates were able to experiment and record in Brussels as Los Nickelos, their juniors back home formed **Thu-Zaina**, which influenced a whole generation during its brief existence. The groups which capitalized most on the new wave were **Stukas**, led by the outrageous showman Lita Bembo, who played with a frenetic intensity, and Zaiko Langa Langa, which was to lead the way for the whole post-independence generation.

The new music was raw and energetic, with greater emphasis on spiralling, interactive

LE TÉLÉPHONE SONNE

SOUZY KASSEYA

Waty

Zairean single sleeve

guitars and rattling snare drums during the seben, and not a horn to be heard. Taking elements of the animation (shouting) from raucous forms of shanty-town music, and also from the word play used at Bakongo funerals, the new bands brought an extra vitality to the music, adapting traditional dances like the soukous and inventing new ones such as the *cavacha* to accompany the extended seben.

The core group of the new era was **Zaiko Langa Langa**, founded by conga player DV Moanda with lead singer Nyoka Longo. The name was constructed from "Zaire ya Bakoko" (Zaire of our Ancestors); Langa Langa is the name of a people in the Equator region. They also added the prefix "Tout-Choc-Anti-Choc" (which, roughly translated, means "Shaking but Shock-proof").

Within months the band had expanded to take in a line-up of singers and guitarists who helped to redefine soukous. Among the early members were **Papa Wemba**, who eventually formed **Viva La Musica**, Evoloko Jocker of Langa Langa Stars, Bozi Boziana who joined Choc Stars before setting up the rival Anti-Choc, Pepe Feli Manuaku of Grand Zaiko Wa Wa and dozens more. Unlike other bands, Zaiko was never the personal property of one leader. It has always been a group, totalling over twenty musicians, and even following a serious rupture in 1988, one original drummer and the solo, rhythm and bass guitarists remained with Nyoka Longo, who took up an old ZLL slogan "Nkolo

Mboka" ("Village Headman"). The defectors meanwhile set up Zaiko Langa Langa Familia Dei ("Family of God"), which also splintered soon after. By now Zaiko was a national institution and although the prodigals rarely return to the fold, they can always evoke the Zaiko name.

A host of rival new-wave groups had appeared in the early 1970s, including Lipua Lipua, Bella Bella, Shama Shama, Empire Bakuba and Victoria. The music had a rough, sweaty feel, while most of the singers, with the exception of husky-throated "elephant" Pepe Kalle, compensated with honey-toned vocals. Many of the new-wave bands were promoted by Verckys, who turned to record production and created a kind of Kinshasa "garage-band" sound. From the ranks of these bands and their subsequent offshoots came Kanda Bongo Man, Nyboma, Pepe Kalle and Emeneya.

Soukous really took hold in international markets during the mid-1980s when musicians began recording in Europe, and the cleaner Paris sound edged out the less polished Kinshasa variants. Among the early successes were the **Four Stars (Quatres Etoiles)**, whose smooth arrangements and streamlined presentation offered a direct challenge to the more ornate big bands – although the top two orchestras were still thriving, with Franco and Tabu Ley releasing international albums at a prolific rate.

During the mid-1980s Tabu Ley boosted the effectiveness of Afrisa with the introduction of **Mbilia Bel**, a young singer with a dreamy, rich voice who became the continent's first female superstar. Bel had started her career as a dancer with **Abeti Masekini** who had paved the way for female singers a decade before, along with **Vonga Aye**. While the male bands were obliged to stick to their winning dance formulas, women artists were able to experiment with European-style ballads and a variety of regional rhythms. One of the most versatile and charming was **M'Pongo Love**. Until her untimely death in 1990, Love, "La Voix Limpide du Zaire", enjoyed a glittering career. The women's contribution has been maintained by **Tshala Mwana**, who debuted as a dancer in M'Pongo Love's band Tsheke Tsheke before finding fame as the Queen of *mutuashi*, the funk-folk rhythm of the Baluba people. A whole string of young women singers has been introduced more recently through Anti-Choc, notably Jollie Detta and the angel-voiced **Deyess Mukangi**. Kinshasa is also home to TAZ Bolingo, one of Africa's rare all-female bands, who play a particularly languid, smoochy soukous under the slogan "self-control".

Deyess – a new wave of women singers

An aspect of the new-wave phenomenon which brought soukous to international attention was the **fashion** ingredient. Inspired by Papa Wemba, the cult of kitende celebrated cloth and cut and promoted style consciousness to the rank of a religion. The sapeurs took their name from an informal but highly competitive group of poseurs who called themselves the "Société des Ambianceurs et des Personnes Elegants" (the Society of Cool and Elegant People). Reminiscent of eighteenth-century dandyism and of the 1960s British mod scene, the sapeur movement was viewed as the antithesis of hippiedom. Although any new-rumba music provided the soundtrack for sapeurs' fashion battles, the main style icons were individuals such as Wemba, Emeneya and Kofi Olomide, while the deities were Japanese and European designers – above all, at least in the early years, Yohji Yamamoto and Jean-Paul Gaultier. Like the mods, the sapeurs' look was adapted by mainstream culture while the main proponents toned down their flamboyance. The hippest sapeurs have long since publicly claimed "Sape is dead", but true believers can still be identified by the way they wear their gear.

PAPA WEMBA: LE SAPEUR

"We are not a fashion! We're a whole continent".
Papa Wemba, at a WOMAD press conference, expounds his views in French on soukous, the Japanese, and the importance of being nicely turned-out.

How did the interest from Japan come about?
There was a big surge of Japanese tourists in Kinshasa who were interested in Zairean music. This was in 1984. They lived with the ordinary people in La Cité and that's where they found the music of Papa Wemba. I got to know a Japanese diplomat and I've been to Japan every year since 1986. I think the Japanese are very intelligent. The next century will be spectacular for the Japanese. Did you know the richest man in the world is Japanese? The French discover African singers… but they don't provide the means to promote the artists. Even the English, they discover an African singer but they don't promote properly. And we're at the mercy of show business. I wanted to sign with Chris Blackwell of Island Records, but when I

realized that Island was a reggae label to begin with, I said to myself, Island has a plethora of artists while the Japanese welcomed me with open arms. So I thought, better to sign with the Japs because they'll put up whatever's necessary to promote me.

What is it about Zairean music that appeals particularly to the Japanese?
I don't know, but I'll tell you something, there are Japanese groups who play Zairean music…who sing in Zairean…in Lingala. If you closed your eyes you'd think you were in front of a Zairean band, really. Even on stage. We were at Osaka and saw a group who played at the Nelson Mandela festival, the Yoka-Shock festival. They were a clone-group, there was a Papa Wemba double and doubles of all the young singers. They dress like us, they do their hair like we do, they follow the repertoire of a typical Zairean group, they compose their own things, everything. We even jammed with them! It was great.

How important a role do your clothes and appearance play?
There's no special significance to the gear I wear.

You can see what I'm wearing now, it's a traditional robe with a T-shirt. On stage, true, I love to dress up but I'm not a slave to *le sape* [fashion]. I started as a singer and I still feel more of a singer than a *sapeur*.

But sapeurs are important in modern African society, aren't they? You're the origin of a clothing fashion, surely?
No, not really. Our parents and grandparents knew how to dress, you know…they dressed really well. Especially on Sundays when they went to mass. For me it was around 1979, when I discovered the Japanese designer Takio Kikuchi, that was when I started to get into high fashion. I suppose my current favourites are Matsuda and Comme des Garçons. I'm not so keen on Gaultier – he does much more "sexy" stuff. I don't like to look feminine. When I say "well-coiffed, well-shaven, well-perfumed" I'm simply encouraging youngsters to be clean and neat. When one is nicely turned-out one is well received everywhere.

Your soukous music…
Wait. It's not soukous. What we play is not soukous. That's just one of the dance styles. There are very many others and they change every six months. And so you see, we choose not to play soukous, otherwise we'd have to do an album every six months!

How do you feel about the rise in interest in African music abroad?
You sometimes get the impression that Africa is a trend – somebody was saying that it's a sort of fashion that will pass. We are not a fashion! We're a whole continent which lives and which has ancient traditions. The traditions have always existed, it's just that the means of communications have evolved – and it's just happening faster here. We've had the impression that people perceive the "fashion" is on the rise and by the same token that it will pass in time. But we're here, okay? We're not just "soukous" – we're a whole continent with a multitude of musical forms.

Can you see a future for a proper career in Kinshasa?
I think that rich Africans must provide the incentive to stay. We saw Tamla Motown in the 1950s and '60s in the USA. Why can't we Africans build our own recording industry, directly in Africa, with all the structures necessary to promote African music? We come to Europe because in Africa we don't have the infrastructure.

What do you think about Franco and his relationship with the new generation of musicians?
Franco had a tremendous impact on Africa first of all, and in Zaire. He was really the master.

Franco was the only African musician who could say anything, who denounced and opinionated on everything. For me, Franco's death was terrible. Even if OK Jazz still exists it exists for the simple reason of existing – people can't go without work – but, bluntly you feel there's something missing.

Between you all, between OK Jazz and Zaiko Langa Langa and all these groups, is there a bonhomie and much contact?
Well there are informal contacts but there aren't many professional links. Zairean music has been divided in the sense that the competition has been unfair – and open. Even if your own brother is in another group, you're professional enemies.

When you were a kid, what were your first musical influences?
It was Cuban music. But when I started my career in the 1960s, it was the era of rhythm and blues. That gave me a huge shock – you know that rhythm comes from Africa – my singer was Otis Redding. When I listened really carefully I felt close to that rhythm. I said to myself, there's a bit of me in that. To make this music was not at all difficult for me. We just didn't have a word, in Africa, to express that kind of music. The Americans took it and called it rhythm and blues…we just didn't have a name for it.

Did President Mobutu's "authenticity" movement in the 1970s have much impact on Zairean music?
Oh yes. A number of Zairean musicians realized we had to plunge back into traditional music. I realized it myself. But too few understood.

How did you do that? Out to the countryside?
No, we didn't have to go into the bush. Even in the big towns you could hear traditional music. Sometimes when I heard a traditional song in town I would record it and then I would reinterpret it later as part of my repertoire.

And are the songs you sing now traditional? What about the words?
My music is basically dance music, but I don't do things that are simple and straightforward. Everything has a traditional source, and I take my themes and rhythms from that. It's a mixture, traditionally based. I try to mix the traditional with my own ideas. After all I am modern myself!

And what do you see as your goal now?
My goal is to explode everywhere, internationally!

NEW SHOOTS

By the end of the 1980s the "classic" era was over, and the Zairean music business had fragmented. Of the big three, Franco was dead, Tabu Ley was semidormant (with Afrisa having partially disintegrated), and Verckys' business influence was waning. The Zaiko generation still appealed to Zaireans who weren't even born when they started, but international listeners favoured the more minimal studio sounds coming out of Paris.

Spearhead of the Parisian soukous of the 1980s was **Kanda Bongo Man**. Kanda, with commercial foresight, cut back on the fancy choral parts and architectural quality of regular arrangements to create fast-track party music which he has brought to audiences around the world. **Pepe Kalle**, who started out in Bella Bella, developed his career with the rowdy Empire Bakuba band – although like Kanda, he found greater album success with sparser Paris sessions. One of the most crucial Paris-based musicians has been the guitarist **Rigo Star** who came out of Wemba's Viva la Musica in the early 1980s. Rigo Star, with his clean, crisp guitar contribution, accompanied Kanda Bongo Man on his first UK visits from 1983, and then appeared on countless records, often as arranger, with a galaxy of star names including Wemba, the camp crooner **Kofi Olomide**, OK Jazz vocalists Madilu and Evoloko, and Mbilia Bel, with whom he teamed up when Bel quit Tabu Ley's band. Another guitarist in Kanda's first touring group was **Diblo Dibala** who went on to form Loketo, whose crossover sound, packaged for young, pop-wise western audiences, made them the darlings of the dance floor. In 1991, Diblo regrouped with **Matchatcha** in which his devilish licks featured even more prominently. Lokassa Ya Mbongo's Soukous Stars offer a similar fast-food version of Zaire's musical haute cuisine.

At home in Kinshasa, the continuity maintained by young bands such as Wenge Musica, Rumba Ray, and Zaiko veterans Bimi Ombale and Dindo Yogo has been threatened by recent social upheavals. With Verckys' Studio

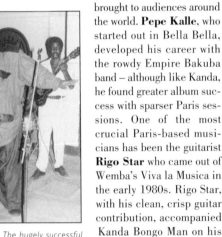

The hugely successful Pepe Kalle

Veve inactive, only the 16-track Bobougo studio was still operational in Africa's music city during 1993. Some artists like OK Jazz, now under the leadership of Simaro Lutumba and the Choc Stars' offshoot Big Stars, led by Defao, were using the recently revamped 48-track IAD studio in Brazzaville. For many years, IAD has been the best studio in Central Africa (though most musicians still prefer to record in Europe). While the prolific flow of Zairean records has recently abated, the market in video releases has expanded. Apart from some dire "playback" sessions, the best of these videos show bands like Zaiko and OK Jazz performing on Zairean TV to receptive, dancing crowds.

No country could be totally monocultural – especially not one as vast as Zaire – and, although rumba is the musical equivalent of the Zaire River, there are many interesting tributaries which have been explored over the years. Just as the rumba rhythms can be claimed as Congo originals, so too can many other musical genres from funk to reggae. Artists such as the now-defunct funkers **Trio Madjesi**, **Bobongo Stars**, or individual stylists like **Kalamu Soul** and the World Music fusionist **Ray Lema** could hold their own in any contemporary music forum.

One of the most interesting departures of recent years from the established guitar-based line-up has been **Swede Swede**. Swede Swede – whose name is cryptically translated by them as "mouse hole", but which it's also been suggested is the sound of sex – were a rhythm revelation. Using a variety of drums, percussion, vocals and harmonicas, they created a sound both postmodern and neotraditional, which recalled the raw, rhythmic charge of pre-electric music. Their smart dress, rowdy performance and local cult following paralleled the street theatre of the "Yankees", who flourished forty years earlier. But to most ears, Zairean music should be all about guitars, and while they are heroes at home in Kinshasa, they have had a tough time breaking into the international markets. Like many of the great bands of Zaire, Swede Swede confused foreign listeners by splitting into two – then three, then four – different line-ups. The main movers are "Classic" Swede Swede, led by **Boketshu Premier**. For their 1994 album recording they have added marimba and bass guitar and expanded their repertoire with rhythms from all over the country, demonstrating that there is still a place in the modern world for raw folklore.

Classic Swede Swede – raw folk, electrified

DISCOGRAPHY

Bantous de la Capitale *El Manicero* (Soul Posters, France). Subtitled the "Best Saxes in Central Africa", this is a showcase for Essous and Malapet, from across the river in the Congo Republic. Mellow, big-band backing and some actual "Latin" rumba, dating from 1970.

Bozi Boziana, Deyess and Anti-Choc *La Sirène* (Bade Stars Music, France). Bubbling guitars, skippy rhythms and Deyess in fine form, in 1988. The title track is a classic and production on the whole album clear as a bell. There's also the Sylla-produced ⓒ *Little Goddess* (Stern's, UK) .

Mbilia Bel *Keyna* (Genidia, Zaire/France). At the peak of her career with Tabu Ley – great songs, creamy vocals and fine dance action.

ⓒ **Choc Stars du Zaire** *Celio Déclarant* (FDB, France). Bumper value from the late 1980s. The song "Celio" is mellow yet passionate. Cool seduction by soukous, with just the right touch of studio tech.

ⓒ **Evoloko Jocker** *Mingelina* (FDB, France). A vocal curiosity so sweet it sticks to you, from one of the true eccentrics of the ZLL family. A classy singer with a taste for camping it up.

ⓒ **Franco et le TPOK Jazz** *Azda* (Sonodisc, France). Re-release with a lovely title song, actually a "record ad" for the local VW distributor, hence the unambiguous chorus (and every member of the band got a VW Passat). The complete big-band treatment with wonderful horn arrangements. For more selections, see the Franco profile.

ⓒ **Pepe Kalle** *Gigantafrique* (GlobeStyle, UK). A collection that packs a double ration of Kalle dance tracks, including the kwassa kwassa hit "Pon Moun Paka Bougé".

Emeneya Kester *Nzinzi* (KL04LP, France). A major breakthrough from one of the original new-wave singers. A "Zulu" bass beat and hi-tech production made it a big East African hit.

Joseph Kabasele *Merveilles du Passé 1957–75* (Sonodisc, France). A comprehensive selection of hits from the "father" of the music.

ⓒ **Sam Mangwana** *Rumba Music* (Celluloid/Mélodie, France). All-star action from the international Sam, including New York salseros.

ⓒ **Nouvelle Génération** *Porokondo* (FDB, France). Hot debut from ex-Wemba musicians, keeping the new wave rolling on.

ⓒ **Kofi Olomide** *Pas de Faux Pas* (Sonodisc, France). A fulsome production in which the new-wave crooner cranks up the excitement with dynamic arrangement and tasty sebens.

ⓒ **Swede Swede** *Toleki Bango* (Cramworld, Belgium). Their first CD is still widely available, though the new release (forthcoming) adds melodic sampled marimba xylophone to their usual percussion in a less raucous, more mature development.

Tabu Ley *En Amour y a pas de Calcul* (Genidia, Zaire/France). First release on his own label – a career highspot for a breathtaking singer and a great bandleader.

ⓒ **Various** *Roots of Rumba Rock – Zaire Classics, Vol. I* (Crammed Discs, Belgium). A compilation of Loningisa label singles from the mid-1950s. Early rumba and traditional (folklore) music.

ⓒ **Papa Wemba** *Papa Wemba* (Stern's, UK). Wemba's unique, yearning, almost hymnal voice is the first asset of his music. On this, still one of his best albums, made in 1988, Rigo Star's guitar work bursts through. You might also sample his mellow foray with Stervos Niarchos – the king and crown prince of sapeurs together – on *Dernier coup de sifflet* (LP/cassette only). Niarchos composed a couple of tasty rumba ballads on this for his sartorial hero. Recommended.

ⓒ **Wenge Musica** *Bouger Bouger* (Natari, UK). Their original release now available again, this is high-grade Kinshasa soukous with classy segues, synths and a nice line in shouting.

ⓒ **Zaiko Langa Langa** *Zaire–Ghana* (RetroAfric, UK). Recorded in Ghana back in 1976, this includes "Zaiko Wa Wa", the band's theme song. Raw and sweaty, it was produced by Bowane with the only example of horns on a ZLL recording. Nyoka Longo bounced back from the Zaiko split-up with ⓒ *Jetez L'Éponge* (Carerre, France). A Kinshasa classic from the madiaba era, 1989, this is probably their strongest album yet, with hard guitars, thoughtful arrangement and powerful ambience.

MAKOSSSA: 1 BIKUTSI: 1

CAMEROON: MUSIC OF A SMALL CONTINENT

"As the Archbishop entered the President's living room to ask for the banning of 'The Lift', he heard Biya himself asking his wife to 'play that song again'. Katino Ateba's songs are pornographic and anti-clerical. But this is only bikutsi...." Jean-Victor Nkolo describes the latest sounds from his homeland.

If you ever happen to travel to Cameroon on Cameroon Airlines from Paris, the on-board airwaves will certainly be filled with horn-flavoured *makossa* music, one of the best cultural exports of this bilingual country, propelled worldwide by **Manu Dibango**. Flight attendants serve you in the language of your choice, French or English. However, on any flight, each of the 250 seats of the 747 could well be occupied by a Cameroonian citizen speaking a different language. This linguistic diversity suggests a cultural salad which may partly explain why Cameroonian music is so rich. There are not just many tongues, but also innumerable dances, a huge number of traditional instruments, a mixed German, French and British colonial heritage, and a variety of religions including many indigenous belief systems and more recently imported Christianity and Islam.

Cameroonians love to say that their country symbolizes the whole of Africa. At least as far as music is concerned, this is true. In Cameroon, you find "thumb piano" music; the talking drum; the *balafon* (xylophone); the accordion; music inspired by Islam; huge religious choirs; a cappella; traditional trumpeters in the Bamoun country; and various urban pop styles, from the makossa of Douala to the *bikutsi* of the Yaoundé district, via the *ashiko* of the coastal region, *ambassebe* guitar-based street music with fast rhythms and *mangambe* of the Bamiléké highlands. Then a lot of Cameroonian musicians play highlife, soukous, juju music... just name it.

Cameroon Airlines managers have doubtless renewed their Cameroon music track on the on-board entertainment channels as planes now also land at the new international airport at Yaoundé, deep in the equatorial forest. This is not the country of the urban makossa. Yaoundé, despite being the capital, is more "bush" and at the heart of the bikutsi, the frenetic, punching rhythm and dance of the Beti group of peoples which is proving a serious challenge to makossa. Welcome to Cameroon.

BIKUTSI'S ESSENTIAL THRUST

Despite the great variety of homegrown sounds, music from Cameroon tends to imply "makossa" to the rest of the world. But the preeminence of makossa on the international scene has been threatened in the last few years by the more self-consciously avant-garde bikutsi, a "confrontation" which has taken on political overtones. It's a fact that bikutsi musicians are becoming more provocative, if not any more inventive. Musically, too, bikutsi has more rhythmic scope than the relatively limited variations of makossa.

Thanks to the rule of President Paul Biya – himself a Bulu Beti and a great bikutsi aficionado and dancer – the style has flourished on the otherwise heavily censored state-run radio and TV. A story that hit the drinking parlours of Yaoundé a couple of years back – part-joke, part-rumour – went like this: the archbishop of Douala, Monseigneur Jean Zoa, goes to the president's palace, hoping to get the latest bikutsi song banned. The piece in question was "The Lift", in the Ewondo language. It comes from the raunchy Catherine Ateba, known as **Katino Ateba**, a young woman who fears no man, not even an archbishop.

According to the story, as the archbishop entered the president's living room to ask for the banning of "The Lift", he heard Biya himself asking his wife to "play that song again". The Monseigneur had to change his tune and his subject, throwing in the towel before uttering a word. Katino Ateba's songs are indeed crude, pornographic and anticlerical. But such themes are the essential thrust of bikutsi, a style whose origins go far back.

Originally, bikutsi was a blood-stirring war rhythm – the music of vengeance and summoning to arms, sounding through the forest. It used rattles and drum and the *njang* xylophone or balafon. Then, for decades, if not centuries, Beti women tricked the Christian church, as well as their own men, by singing in the Beti tongue and by using complex slang phrases reserved for women. While clapping out the same rapid-fire rhythm, they sang about the trials and tribulations of everyday life; they discussed sexuality, both theirs and their men's; and they talked about sexual fantasies and taboos. In the middle of the song, a woman would start a chorus leading to a frenzied dance of rhythmic foot-stamping and harmonious shaking of the shoulders, the back and the bottom in that order: shoulders-back-bottom-clap-clap-clap-clap-clap. The whole thing was accompanied by strident screams and whistles. These, in short, are the origins of bikutsi. The bellicose themes are no longer significant, but many women still perform the old folk dances, across the sprawling hills of Yaoundé city and beyond to the south.

Later in the development of bikutsi, whole balafon orchestras were brought in as accompaniment, for example in the historic **Richard Band de Zoetele** – whose fame unfortunately did not survive the technical difficulties of electrifying their six-to-eight piece balafon band.

Ascenseur: Le Secret de l'Homme
Action 69!
The lift, every male's secret
I like men who are no fools
Those who know how to press my sensitive button
The lift, that's every male's secret
I like a man who is no fool
I like a man who will suck me downstairs
I like a man who will suck me upstairs too
I like men who sin on earth
I like men who sin in heaven too
Even the parish priest loves that
Instead of giving me a private service
He comes home to sin downstairs
And I like the priest who sins upstairs too
And his mass will not be sad as a funeral ceremony
Because, every male is a boss
Even in his pyjamas
But only when he's strong and big
With his prick as solid as a man's gun
Solid as a church's big candle
And I'll lick him up and down
And then, and only then, I'll ask him
To press the button in my lift
Every male's secret...
Katino Ateba

FIRED-UP

The inventor of "modern bikutsi", as a staple of the Cameroonian pop mainstream, is probably **Messi Me Nkonda Martin**, founder of the band **Los Camaroes**. His tunes were played incessantly on provincial radio stations in the 1960s and '70s. Messi Martin was heavily influenced by a Spanish-language radio station broadcasting from neighbouring Equatorial Guinea with a very powerful transmitter: "You are listening to Santa Isabel radio from the country of Fernando Pó." This Spanish influence gave the young Martin an enduring love for the acoustic guitar. However, the author of "Bekono Nga N'konda" (a tribute to his mother) and "Mengalla Maurice" – two landmarks in the bikutsi evolution – wanted to translate the sound and magic of Richard Band de Zoetele into his music. Since he only played guitar, Messi Martin was the first musician to accomplish what later synthesizers and other hardware would do at the touch of a button – create the sound of a traditional instrument, the balafon, by using a modern, electrified instrument, the electric guitar. He managed it by linking together some of the strings with lengths of cotton cord to give a damper tone, with a slight buzz. Since then, bikutsi performers have all followed Messi Martin's example in trying to imitate the balafon sound. One of the earliest electrifiers was the singer **Maurice "Elamau" Elanga** – whose 1989 cassette release "Elamau 89 – Grand Retour" is a golden reminder.

If bikutsi's sound is characterized by a lot of screaming, clapping, stamping, and balafon-playing (or bala-style guitar-playing), the real superiority of bikutsi over makossa lies in its heavily charged content: where there's bikutsi, there must be dance, controversy, social debate and always sex, either implied or explicit. Messi Martin has been a master of all that, with his mellow voice, liberal doses of social commentary and his, to say the least hectic, private life. He was once the focus of a fight, thanks to his eternal womanizing, in the Mango Bar – a popular drinking and dancing "mecca" in Yaoundé's Elig Efa district. Just days after the brawl, the song he wrote as a result, entitled simply "Elig Efa", was already on sale. In it he bitterly criticized the local community. They, in turn, took revenge and banned him from ever setting foot in Elig Efa again. (If you ever go to the Mango, be very careful if you're trying to win over an apparently lonely heart.) Since Messi

Martin has almost completely stopped composing and performing – the man is chased by devils other than music – his younger brother **Beti Joseph** has taken over. Joseph's latest release, "N'Son Anyu", is a rant against local journalists, whose style makes London's tabloid reporters look like angels.

Bikutsi musicians have recently been trying hard to improve the technical quality of their music and their sales and distribution – areas where makossa remains far superior. Elanga Maurice, a bikutsi singer of the 1970s, shrewdly added brass to bikutsi. **Nkondo Si Tony** has been working at electronic keyboards and synthesizers, and bringing state-of-the-art production to bear on acoustic traditions of balafon and slit-log drums. His output on the local cassette market is impressive and he's acquired something of a cult status among Yaoundé youth.

But of all the artists that Cameroon has produced in recent years, **Les Têtes Brulées** have made the biggest impact. To be sure, this has had more to do with industrious public relations, and an image that matched the jaded requirements of European africaphiles, than with musical talent. Their overseas gigs have been well attended and the response to a newly fired-up, world-credible, roots African music, very enthusiastic.

If the Têtes have been criticized – and particularly Jean-Marie Ahanda – for having made the world believe that this was bikutsi, one thing is certain: other, more experienced musicians didn't wait to turn the impression on its head. **Uta Bella, Marilou & Georges Seba** and **Jimmy Mvondo Mvelé** – who grew up in the Yaoundé area, and who now work as producers, session and concert musicians in Paris and New York – have been trying hard to counterbalance the relatively easy-listening "Têtes Brulées Bikutsi" made for European consumption.

In the longer term, too, **Sabbal Lecco** and **Vincent Nguini** are very promising musically. Thanks to their huge and undervalued contribution on Paul Simon's "Rhythm of the Saints", they have demonstrated to the world the forcefulness of the new bikutsi – and its marketability.

Possibly the best example of bikutsi is the track "Bikutsi Hit" on **Sissi Dipoko's** album "Munam" (cassette only). In Cameroon's musical-political mix, Sissi Dipoko, a woman from Douala (makossa-land) would not have been expected to perform bikutsi – or at least she was not expected to be this good at it. It signals an easing of the clash between bikutsi and makossa – Dipoko's music "by right". Mainly arranged by Justin Bowen, a top Paris-based session player, "Bikutsi Hit" was made possible by a complicated combination of the Têtes Brulées themselves: Atebas, their charismatic bass player who left them to form **Les Martiens** (a band which quickly flopped, spoiled by heavy commercial input); **Les Vétérans**, a long-established bikutsi band from Yaoundé; Têtes-style singer **Gibraltar Drakus**; and the hot guitarist Georges Seba. Guest stars on the album include Manu Dibango and the ubiquitous producer **Aladji Touré**.

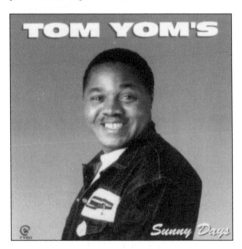

Other bikutsi names to listen out for, either of whom could be taken up by a World Music label, include the strikingly gifted singer **Tom Yom's** and **Sala Bekono**.

JULES ET MAMBO LA LA LA

The new interest around bikutsi is certainly justified. However, makossa, thanks very largely to Manu Dibango, has not yet given way, and it's still the main representative of Cameroon's pop. A style with a cosmopolitan swing in its modern variant, makossa developed in Douala out of the contact between local people and the foreign influences arriving by steamship at the port. Originally a folk dance and music, once it had escaped the mission school environment where it was given extra vigour by new instruments such as guitars and accordions, it became an urban, electric style, with a dance rhythm precisely cut for the nightclubs.

BURNT-OUT HEADS

••••••••••••••••••••••••

Les Têtes Brulées, the first bikutsi band to appear on CD, brought a dramatic new global awareness to Cameroonian music. On stage, their wild, cross-cultural appearance – body paint, sculpted hair, layers of clothing and clumpy trainers – comes over as a kind of tribal pantomime. Their initial gigs abroad whipped up a whirlwind of media attention and earned them equal measures of censure and adulation at home. The name was provocative enough – what could they mean by "Burnt Heads"? It implied hyperactive self-indulgence, burnt-out, blown minds.... They didn't sit comfortably in the pantheon of African music stars.

The Têtes' publicity files filled up early on after the release of the well-made "Man No Run" film of their first French tour, directed by the Cameroon-born maker of "Chocolat", Claire Denis. And an interesting and relatively young Cameroonian cinéaste, Jean-Marie Teno, made a rather good docudrama on the politics of water in Cameroon, starring Théodore

Epémé – aka Zanzibar, founder member of the Têtes – entitled "Bikutsi Water Blues". The sensitive young lead guitarist (the song of the same title is a fresh composition, brilliantly played) committed suicide shortly afterwards, either because of a disastrous love affair or because of the pressures of stardom. He is said to have died in the arms of Jean-Marie Ahanda, at the time a journalist from the daily "Cameroon Tribune" who turned musician overnight, and who shortly afterwards became the manager and leader of the band. More suspicious circles in Yaoundé alleged sorcery.

Even before the death and replacement of Zanzibar, bikutsi purists were claiming that, despite their imagination and status, the Têtes Brulées were not a good bikutsi band. They insist, with some justification, that their music is rather limited, their singing poor, their lyrics empty, and the frenzy and screaming not all it's got up to be.

Les Têtes Brulées in characteristic low-key stage make-up

In the 1930s, various record companies such as Pathé imported primitive equipment and persuaded historic figures like **Thimothé Essombé** to have a go at the gramophone: they had to sing in one take, after saying very briefly who they were and where they came from. The first recordings of those early years are so bad it's difficult to know the composition of the band or the lyrics, or even exactly what type of instrument is being played. You hear something like:

It's me, Thimothé Essombé, from Yabassi, near Douala, and I am happy, today, in the year nineteen-something or other, to sing this song for my loved one. La la la Jules et Mambo...Thimothé...Chérie...Maria...

Jules et Mambo la la la: it was all over in less than two minutes! The makossa movers have moved a long way since then.

Another early, though musically modern artist, **Ekambi Brilliant**, had the same relationship with makossa (before embarking on his international career) as Messi Martin had with bikutsi. Brilliant's single "N'Gon Abo" was such a hit that, to this day in Cameroon, just play it at any party and you'll have everyone on the dance floor in seconds, shaking their waists.

In those days, music was not as politicized or as tribalized as it is today. Just as Ekambi Brillant did a song in the Ewondo language (the language of the Beti people from the Yaoundé district), so Messi Martin also made attempts to sing, quite beautifully in fact, in the Douala language, thanks to the collaboration of **Nellé Éyoum**, himself from Douala and one of the fathers of modern makossa.

RELATIVELY STRANGE

It might be provocative to claim that **Manu Dibango**, whose 1972 album "Soul Makossa" made him one of the world's best-known African

MANU DIBANGO: SAX AND SOUL

•••••••••••••••••••••••••••

Sax-player, composer, singer, pianist and arranger, **Emmanuel "Manu" Dibango's** inspirations are diverse. He has performed and recorded in Brussels, Paris, Zaire, the United States, Jamaica and Côte d'Ivoire and has lived in Europe, mostly Paris, since 1949, when he was fifteen. He came into contact with American sailors in his early years and was much affected by the jazz they brought with them. Graduate of Francis Bebey's jazz instruction and then of the Brussels jazz-club scene in the early 1950s, he has since busied his alto-sax and other talents with everything from reggae to rock and collaborated across the music world with everyone from Johnny Pacheco to Fela Kuti, Fania All-Stars and Don Cherry. But it was the release of "Soul Makossa" in 1973 that made his name. Picked up by a New York radio station, it was a startling, instant hit worldwide. Dibango even won a case against Michael Jackson, who "borrowed" 77 seconds of "Soul Makossa" on "Wanna Be Starting Something" on his "Thriller" album (a rather bigger seller...). Back home, "Soul Makossa" paved the way for a new generation of artists who now rely on a combination of traditional inspiration and hi-tech recording facilities to produce the highly exportable dance music that has turned Douala into one of the dynamos of African music.

Now in the superstar class – more than thirty years after his first single – Manu Dibango is one of the few African artists guaranteed to draw a full house virtually anywhere in the world.

musicians, was never on the musical map of Cameroon, never even on the map of makossa. But the fact remains that, with the exception of his bold venture (this is not his territory, say purists) into bikutsi with "Mouvement Ewondo" on his "Seventies" album, and maybe another exception, "Idiba" (composed by Francis Bebey), Dibango, who is primarily a jazz musician, has never been the cup of tea of Cameroon's DJs, nor popular in the drinking parlours, nor has he cut any kind of figure in the clubs or on the dance floors.

Cameroonians generally consider "Soul Makossa" to be a hybrid – funky music with lashings of brass and a relatively strange rhythm that's good for signature tunes and other uses abroad, but is rarely played at home – and certainly not makossa. Anyone who listens will have difficulty finding any makossa in Cameroon that has a beat even close to that of "Soul Makossa" – or vice versa! The only "makossa" thing about the hugely successful track is the name, and Cameroonians are always lost when they have to dance to it. But while not a single Dibango track has been a dance success in Cameroon, his career has followed a very different path abroad, where he has been a figure of real importance.

If you want to find genuinely good makossa, riches abound. Just look at the discography. Start with CDs by the sophisticated **Moni Bilé** and anything you can find by **Moundy Claude** (known as "Petit Pays"). Or seek out cassettes of some of the musical ancestors of the makossa genre. There are dozens – historic fathers, like **Eboa Lotin**, the "enfant terrible" of makossa

from Douala – and forefathers, like Ebanda Manfred & Villa Vienne. If you can get something of theirs, there's no need to bother with "Ami", the international success by Bébé Manga. Then listen to Ben Decca and try the elegant makossa mix of the group Esa.

Other "must hears" for the full Cam treatment are: **Sam Fan Thomas**, probably the biggest Cameroonian name abroad after Manu Dibango and Roger Milla; **Toto Guillaume**, who has backed just about everyone who ever recorded in Paris and is now one of the main engineers of the explosive affair between Antillean zouk and African music; **Lapiro de Mbanga**, who achieved fame with his anti-ruling-party pidgin-English vitriol in song, then, to the bafflement of all, turned against the people and started praising President Biya's regime. Overnight, he became Cameroon's Salman Rushdie, under government protection at the Yaoundé Sofitel. But the story of Cameroonian politics is another, longer one.

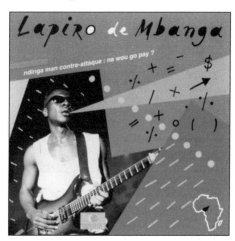

CAMEROON DIARY

Jane Hayter-Hames fills in the Cameroon story with a diary of visits to secret societies and bikutsi clubs (adapted from an article in Folk Roots magazine).

Heavy clouds hang over Douala airport, symptomatic of the mood of the nation. Every conversation quickly comes round to the corruption of the government and the bleakness of the future. I take a bush-taxi to Oku in the Bamenda Highlands, to visit the Mount Kilum Forest Project, which is working with local people to save what's left of their forest. All-male secret societies still perform the **traditional ceremonies** of Oku (they often call themselves juju – a widely used term in West Africa for such groups and activities). The core instrument is the *njang*, a huge log xylophone which takes four men to play it. It's accompanied by a simple flute, formerly of bamboo, but now made from plastic tubing, though retaining its traditional cowrie-shell decoration. The only metal instrument is a double gong. Carving is an integral part of this forest-based culture, and the carvers make the drums, but the forest can sustain no more felling and the carvers are banned from cutting wild timber.

The performances involve troupes of masked dancers whose thick anklets of large seed pods, also from the forest, clash in massive percussion as they dance. The groups' principle function is to perform at funeral ceremonies but it is also intimately associated with the use of medicinal herbs, still the major form of medicine in Oku. "It is believed", says Tamfu Wambeng, a village elder, "that some of the jujus still have magical powers. Certain people, predisposed to have these powers, can fully develop them within the society. Maybe they also use some leaves to become magicians. There is a controlling power, the Kwi-Fon, the traditional council."

Mkong Philip Yunji, a society member, tells me "Each family has its own dance. The group walks far to perform at ceremonies. Most of the dancers here are groups that use a lot of medicines. For instance, certain groups go out with mixtures of leaves and spread the mixture on all road junctions and just in front of bridges. When a stranger comes with evil intentions and passes such a place, the evil is changed to good. There are also some juju artists who go out during wars, and any enemy seen will just die. This artist is known in Oku as Ntak. People are frightened of that. Young people are warned that they should never see this part of the artist." Even if the practices are dying out, the beliefs persist.

HEAT OF THE MYSTIC NIGHT

Yaoundé. Pierre Tchana, middle-aged, softly spoken and suave, is a senior figure in Cameroonian music. "I play a variety of music – salsa, highlife and rumba. People call it imported music, but it's music which left Africa through the slave trade. It's coming back now, and it's important that we make it sound more African than it was before. When I was young, I

listened to jazz, merengue and salsa. In the 1940s and '50s African music was principally merengue. Rumba was played all over West Africa. Kinshasa had a recording studio in colonial times so it had an advantage.

"If you listen to my music you hear a lot of religion in the background – my mother was very strong in the church. I sang in the choir and from there I drew my inspiration." He plays me a recording of *mankamba*, the traditional music of his western region. But I detect no trace of it in his own music. Indeed, the most prominent records in his collection are by Franco and Celia Cruz.

Mystic Djim, backbone of the music industry in Cameroon

I fall in with **Mystic Djim**, an important figure in local music production circles, a reggae-singer and the owner and engineer of "Mystic Djim's Mobile Studio". His woolly hat hides no dreadlocks. Cameroonians equate dreadlocks with drugs, while he is a respectable family man and works at Cameroon TV.

The cassette market in Yaoundé turns out to consist of wall-to-wall drum machines. I ask Mystic why he uses one. "Because people today are no longer interested in using the traditional instruments. The drum machine is more perfect. Today on the local market you would scarcely find very good drums, let alone someone who could play them. The scarcity is a glaring fact. The drum machine is purer, closer to my conception. In bikutsi, of ten cassettes on the market, I am behind seven.

"I play reggae because in Africa we have a lot to do for our children. We have to work for our children because our fathers didn't do it for us. People use reggae to fight. When the music is from black men, the roots are here. I'm Bamileke.

We have rastas. When we say *kamsi* or *jussi*, we mean what we call 'godwives'. God talks to women who then cure diseases, and they are original rastas. They have the same philosophy, they believe in God, in love, in peace. Leaders are the oppressors. When someone has power, they will try to remove all the things the previous leader did. So we don't have history."

Modern congas and drum kits are expensive, while drum machines are small, cheap and portable. Using a machine avoids the tendency of human drummers to dominate, so the melody can come to the fore – attractive to many singers and guitarists.

Mystic takes me round the Yaoundé nightclubs to meet the young bikutsi and makossa stars. Despite its comparative wealth, Cameroon has not invested in musical equipment and when Sala Bekono sings, I can hardly hear his voice above the painful screams of over-amplified electric guitars.

Sala Bekono started singing in the village church choir. I ask about the development of bikutsi: "Messi Martin had the inspiration to merge the xylophone with the guitar. Since then many musicians have brought to life what bikutsi is today. The *mvet* was part and parcel of original bikutsi. It's music which was handed down to us from our parents. When I was young my mother used to sing me a lullaby in bikutsi."

What was the song he just sang? "I was singing about going back home, not to live in the village but to get more inspiration so that my music, bikutsi, gets a wider audience, gets international."

Who are his influences? "In Cameroon there is no-one great apart from Messi Martin. In makossa there is Ndedi Eyango. In Zaire there was Franco, and Loketo. I still love them."

TRAPPING ATEBAS

Trapping **Atebas** is hard work. He appears like an electric pixie in the pulsating night outside the Escalier club and immediately disappears again, but Mystic gets him into the back of the car for a quick chat. Atebas is the singer and bass guitarist with Les Têtes Brulées.

"I started music in my home. My mother was very particular about music. Then I started in a xylophone group. My first teacher was Endo Kraman in a group called Titanes and before that I used to play in the quartiers. After Les Titanes I went to Nigeria and met a Zairean called Soukalo George, he was my godfather in music.

I played with Têtes Brulées and we had a problem and I left the group but I came back. I play many other instruments but I think that the bass guitar was a treasure handed down to me. I can't say how but I love it particularly."

At 3am we lurch off to another club to find Emil Kangué, a makossa singer. He turns out to be a charming flirt. He doesn't think there is much difference between makossa and bikutsi. "What we should do as Cameroonians is try to conquer the outside world. Thank God, we have outside influences like modern instruments. Makossa you dance with the whole body, bikutsi more with the trunk and upper body, it makes it look difficult to dance. There is about ten percent similarity between makossa and Zairean music, both are danceable. Makossa is message-carrying, it uses a dialect particular to the people. In Zairean music you don't get typical Zairean dialect. I sing in Douala, in French and I try a little in English. Zairean music is more a noise than message-carrying."

I fall into bed at 4.30am – quite early.

ANNE-MARIE NZIE

At 9am I have an appointment at Cameroon Radio to meet **Anne-Marie Nzie**. The studio is the only place we can play her record, "Liberté". It is scratched and filthy; and when it won't play properly the engineer adjusts the weight so the arm ploughs through the dirt more firmly. But I can hear her voice, rich and sure, rising into pure high notes and dropping with perfect timing into those deep wells that vibrate in your stomach.

Anne-Marie Nzie, "La voix d'or du Cameroun", is small, pretty, more than 70 years old and full of life. She started singing at the age of eight and was a national star by the 1950s. Though no longer a chart-topper, she remains one of the most respected and popular female singers in the country. She still performs and wants to come to Britain, a country she has never visited. Some tracks on "Liberté" are pure Africa and really exciting; others sound like they owe more to Edith Piaf than to Cameroon. She takes a big shine to me, holding a generous breast up towards me in both hands and announcing "You are my daughter, everything in here is for you." Joseph, my interpreter, gets slightly choked translating this.

Anne-Marie's father was a minister and she too started in a choral group. She sings all kinds of music, but "I have never interpreted someone else's song. When God gives you something, you have it. At first my orchestra was mvet zither, drum and talking drum. There were no European instruments, that's why I started with mvet and those drums, that is the rhythm instruments in my orchestra. Now I also use guitar, we try to mix up everything. I bought an electric guitar. I want to mix the black and white cultures."

What does she think of the young people's music? "I'm not happy about the music. In fact I can say I don't like it. It's not that it's not danceable, but it has too much foreign influence, they try to play more like Zaireans. I think they should draw inspiration from within themselves, they want to do things in an easier way so they copy. The youth of today play music because they want to make money. When I was young, I sang because I really loved singing. They go to Zaire to get music which is danceable and easy to sell. You must first of all love it, give all your heart to it, then it will succeed. The young people are not interested in what we have from here. But I will stay with my drum until I die. I cannot lose that because that is what really makes me feel like I'm African."

BEND SKIN

As in Zaire, the richness of Cameroon's musical talents and potential is awe-inspiring: for such a small country (population only 12 million) the future holds a lot. **Bend-skin** is a new kind of street-credible percussion-led folk music. Kouchoum Mbada are the main protagonists, the Swede Swede of Cameroon perhaps. On their album "Bend Skin" (cassette only) they have Sam Fan Thomas on keyboards.

Lastly, listen out for **Gibraltar Drakus**, currently "Le Roi du Bantowbol". This is a style which owes something to folk roots and something to bol – from "bal" accordion-playing. He plays quite often in the Nkono suburb of Douala, sometimes with Nkondo Si Tony. There's a good cassette out, distributed, in France at least, by Mélodie, "N. Owona-Jojo: Roi du Bantowbol".

◀ DISCOGRAPHY ▶

BIKUTSI AND "FOLK" STYLES

◎ **Francis Bebey** *Akwaaba: Music for Sanza* (Original Music, US). Unusual and varied album of songs majoring on thumb-piano and percussion, from an artist who defies categorization. The useful liner notes, as usual on this label, indicate lyrics of substance.

Javis et les Idoles *Opérateur* (local release). This is the type of music that you'll rarely hear abroad, but only in Cameroon. Cassette only.

Georges Seba *Dédicace*s. Flourishing his superb voice, Seba is an all-round musical performer. The song "Oncle Medjo" is dedicated to one of the fathers of Cameroonian pop, Medjo'o Me N'Som Jacob, who played ashiko for decades, before recording. Great people, who'll not die rich on local cassettes like this.

◎ **Les Têtes Brulées** *Les Têtes Brulées (*Stern's, UK). First and so far only CD from the band that broke bikutsi to the world in 1990. Lots of energy but no depth.

◎ **Various** *Baka Forest People: Heart of the Forest* and *Baka Beyond: Spirit of the Forest* (Hannibal, UK). The result of a 1993 field trip by Martin Cradick. The first CD is straight recordings, the polyphonie quite captivating in parts; the second something less pure – a heavily produced sound spectacle.

◎ **Tom Yom's and the Star's Collection** *Sunny Days* (TJR, France). A revolutionary part-bikutsi artist with an exceptional, high, clear voice, singing compositions by, among others, Eboa Lotin. Ignore the naff packaging and a few duff numbers: Yom's is a singer and musician of real power and range. Watch this space.

MAKOSSA

◎ **Moni Bilé** *10th Anniversary: Best of ...* (MAD Productions/Sonodisc, France). Bilé really maximized the excitement potential of makossa. This includes his great, dance-floor stirrers, "Bijou" and "O Si Tapa Lambo Lam".

Guy Bilong et les Camerlogs (local release). A trained percussionist and arranger, and a very gifted musician and now programmer, Bilong produced this superb compilation of makossa artists, including Ben Decca and Douleur, in 1990.

◎ **Grace Decca** *Doi la Mulema* (Sonodisc, France). Produced by guitar wizard Toto Guillaume, six satisfying portions of stimulating modern makossa for dancing feet. Brother Ben Decca is a gifted and committed artist: almost everything he does – local cassettes only – is beautiful.

◎ **Manu Dibango** *Live '91* (Stern's, UK). The output of Africa's foremost jazz sax-player is so vast, it's hard to know where to begin. If you find nothing to please among the variety on this CD you can be sure you don't like him.

◉ **Lapiro de Mbanga** *Ndinga Man Contre-Attaque: na wou go pay?* (Label Bleu, France). A master of political rap, Lapiro is hugely controversial – a tough blend of politics, rhythm and language and a big name in Cameroon. Here – with a hard mix of makossa, zouk, soukous and Afro-beat – he rebuts the criticism that he sold out to the powers that be. Recommended.

◎ **Charlotte Mbango** *Konkai Makossa* (Makossa New Form) (Touré Jim, France). A serious makossa asset with fifteen years of recording under her belt. Behind Mbango you hear Sissi Dipoko, Aladji Touré and Toto Guillaume. If you want to know what hi-tech, 1990s makossa means, venture no further.

Petit Pays (Moundy Claude) *Ça Fait Mal* (local release). A young artist, who has given to the makossa scene one of its best successes so far, and who should deliver more. First work, great record. Local cassette only.

◎ **Sam Fan Thomas** *Si Tcha* (MST Productions, France). SFT's makassi style is virtually indistinguishable from zouk on this brief (30 minutes), bouncy release.

Ⓒ **Sam Fan Thomas & Charlotte Mbango** *African Typic Collection* (Virgin Earthworks, UK). Four Cameroonian songs (and one stray Cape Verdean number via Paris) built around the big-hit dance number "African Typic Collection".
Various *Fleurs Musicales du Cameroun* (FMC, Cameroon). An authoritative and comprehensive collection in a three-album set (LP/cassette only), produced for the government by

Manu Dibango to showcase the country's musical vitality. One disc of folk songs and two of makossa, mangambe, bikutsi and ashiko.
Ⓒ **Various** *Makossa Connection Vols 1–4* (TJR, France). Four-hour makossa celebration, with everyone you can think of and many you won't – Guy Lobé, Emile Kangué, Manulo, Moni Bilé, Ben Decca, Salle Jean, Lapiro de Mbanga, Hoigen Ekwalle, Epée et Koum, Ndedy Dibango and Gilly Doumbé.

EQUATORIAL GUINEA BOYS

MUSIC OF BIOKO ISLAND

Broadcasters Paul Lashmar and Andy Kershaw visited Equatorial Guinea in search of music and beer. As Paul Lashmar describes, their efforts to find local musicians were aided, and encumbered, by the presence of a minder from the Ministry of Tourism and Culture.

Of all African countries, the music and culture of **Equatorial Guinea** is perhaps the least known to the rest of the world. Always a remote backwater, the country has been virtually isolated for over twenty years by dictatorship and poverty. Its notable features are rainforest, gorillas and corruption. Tourists have only recently been admitted.

Yet because of the Spanish heritage Equatorial Guinea has a rich musical culture unique in Africa: the Guineos ease the pain of a repressive regime with a thriving culture based around beer and music. The Paris-based group Loketo have been great favourites recently, but you're as likely to hear salsa from Juan Luis Guerra or makossa from Manu Dibango of neighbouring Cameroon. Any night after 10pm it all thumps out from **Malabo**'s only nightlife street, Calle Nigeria, which throngs with bars, cafés and street vendors.

In comparison with its power and influence in South America, Spain's grip on Africa was slight. Equatorial Guinea consists of all its former territories in sub-Saharan Africa. Fernando Pó, now known as **Bioko**, is a lush little volcanic island, just 800 square kilometres, off the coast of Cameroon. The mainland part, Rio Muni, is sandwiched between Cameroon and Gabon, and the third part is the tiny island of Annabon, far out in the Atlantic. EG has a population of 370,000. Malabo, with its neo-Gothic cathedral and the president's "People's Palace", is on the north edge of Bioko island. For the most part the country is thick rainforest. On Bioko and the coastal plain there are stretches of cocoa plantations, many so neglected that they are rapidly returning to nature.

In 1968 the Spanish handed power over to Macias Nguema, a seemingly mild-mannered civil servant. His rule rapidly deteriorated into a dictatorship with few equals. By the late 1970s, a third of the population had disappeared, fled the country or been killed. After a coup in 1979, Nguema senior was replaced by his nephew Lt-Col Obiang Nguema, who, while not exhibiting the same genocidal tendencies, has starred in a number of Amnesty International reports.

With the exception of the local radio station Africa 2000, there are no proper recording facilities. The owner of Herbo Music, Malabo's only record store, is planning to build the country's first recording studio. His shop is basically a small shack where tapes are recorded for customers from a limited stock of LPs.

FANG

The Fang, Equatorial Guinea's largest ethnic group, have a vigorous oral tradition conveyed through songs. The main local instrument is the *mvet*, a harp-zither fashioned from a gourd, the stem of a palm leaf and strings woven from plant fibre. Mvet-players have evolved a musical notation disclosed only to initiates of the **Bebom-Mvet** society, a kind of fraternity who are the griots responsible for maintaining folk traditions. In Fang culture, the mvet plays a similar role to that of the kora in Mali, used for accompanying epic songs of history. Like the kora, too, it has a two-sided bridge with the string plucked with both hands. The Fang also use other instruments, like the wooden xylophone, the *ngombi*, an eight-stringed harp, and the *nlakh*, a horn.

Most villages, plantations and barrios have one of these traditional **chorus and drum groups**, the dominant form of traditional music. One of the largest is in Basupa, a plantation village 20km outside Malabo, where the inhabitants describe themselves as Creole – mixed race. This group consists of twenty singers, mostly women, supported by five male percussionists. The government minder – who accompanies visitors to such groups – riles them by insisting they sing the praises of President Obiang, and their unease and resentment often inhibit the performance.

One of the finest vocal groups in Malabo is the **Bisilia De Malabo**, a four-woman ensemble from the Bubi ethnic group, the indigenous inhabitants of Bioko island. When performing they wear traditional, two-piece straw dresses. Their choral style has an almost medieval religious quality and is uncannily similar to that of the Trio Balkana from Bulgaria. The call-and-answer format often starts with Rosa's high, melancholic, girlish voice, answered by the eerie minor-chord harmonies of Isabel, Immaculada and Pulqueria. On some numbers they accompany themselves with cowbells carved from wood. They give a marvellous, exuberant performance – yet you wonder how much more they might enjoy themselves without the presence of the man from the ministry.

MARVELS OF SALVAGE

Equatorial Guinea's colonial heritage has spawned an engaging acoustic music that blends Spanish folk styles and guitar music with the local fondness for stringed instruments. Like Sierra Leone's **palm wine music**, this is played mainly in bars. Typically musicians sing in a mixture of languages. The Remigio Brothers, for example, a Malabo bar trio with more enthusiasm than ability, sing one in Spanish, one in Bubi and one in Creole.

In a small bar in Basupa, the **Guinea Boys** play for afternoon beers. Their three guitars are

a marvel of salvage, held together with packing tape, nails and bits of wire, the fretboard of one so warped it's been converted into a bass. The insistent shuffle rhythm is supplied by a makeshift cymbal and beer bottle tapped with a piece of metal. They launch into some virtuoso playing. In a fairer world – and given an electric guitar – the lead guitarist, Antonio, would be a Paris recording star.

The finest of these bands is **Desmali y su Grupo Dambo de la Costa**. They come from the remote island of Annabon and are legendary throughout EG. The musicians and their families

Guinea Boys - making do on Bioko Island

have been forced to move to Malabo for economic survival. Desmali's voice is full of delightful contradiction, sweet, but with a ragged edge echoing the pain of exile – especially on songs like "Lament for our Village". He's also a great acoustic guitar player. The accompanying group percussion and harmonies sung in thirds elegantly complement and fill the songs. Dambo de La Costa use a square frame drum brought from Annabon, called the *pandero*. Originally a North African instrument established in Spain during the Moorish occupation, it is now only commonly found in Portugal.

It is hard to categorize the music of Desmali and friends: the influences are too diverse to pin down. But they are most immediately comparable with the Congolese acoustic scene of the early 1950s. There's also a related Latin influence, probably from the Cuban 78s that were common along the coast during the 1940s and '50s.

Despite the difficulty in obtaining and using electric guitars and musical equipment (phenomenally expensive and hindered by power cuts) there are one or two electric bands based in Malabo. The dominant style is Cameroonian makossa, though rock and soukous can also be heard. Several bands made albums in Paris in the mid-1980s: Maele recorded "Evom Nguan"; Baltasa Baltsar Nsue ("Le Grand Bessoso") came out with "Tan Solo Si, Tan Solo No"; and Victoriano Bibang ("Efamba") recorded "Mamba Ane Mot Duma". Some of Cameroon's makossa artists, including Toto Guillaume, Ebeny Wesley and members of Manu Dibango's band, are featured on these albums.

Live shows are rare and usually take place in Malabo at the Hispano-Guinean Cultural Centre, a large colonial building in the town centre. A recent concert – "To celebrate the Feast of the Immaculate Conception" – was presented by local musician and impresario David Bass, and featured Efamba, Mastho Ribocho, Lily Afro, Cocal Bass, Samuelin and Wanto.

Lastly, there's a small group of rappers of surprisingly high quality. Elvis Romero, DJ Savao, and Homegirl Vanessa have put out "Buenos Dias Africa", a powerful anthem for the continent.

LAND OF LUNDUM

MUSIC OF SÃO TOMÉ AND PRÍNCIPE

The republic of São Tomé and Príncipe consists of two small equatorial islands lying in the Gulf of Guinea about 270km from the coast of Gabon. Lusophone expert Caroline Shaw takes a look at the music of a tiny African island republic.

Uninhabited when the Portuguese discovered them in 1471, the islands were soon settled by a mixture of **Portuguese** adventurers and West Africans brought over as slaves to work on sugar plantations. In the nineteenth century cocoa became the principal crop. Slavery was abolished in 1875 but plantation owners circumvented the letter of the law by bringing in labourers under contracts from other Portuguese African colonies, mainly Angola and later Cape Verde. Conditions were so terrible on the plantations that in 1909 chocolate manufacturers, led by Cadbury's, boycotted São Tomé cocoa. At the time the islands were the world's biggest producer of the crop, and although profitability has since declined, cocoa is still the main source of foreign currency. The plantations were nationalized when the islands achieved independence from Portugal in 1975. The Marxist ruling party lost power after one of sub-Saharan Africa's first multiparty elections in 1991.

The elections took place with a musical accompaniment. Competing parties hired local bands to lure the public to open-air hustings, and for several weeks the roads were full of sound as the parties' trucks blared out their bands' latest tapes from ramshackle PA systems. For the bands themselves, such involvement seems to be just another day's work, not necessarily an act of political commitment.

The Brazilian-style danço congo

Music is an important part of the culture created by the various peoples brought to the islands and plays a major role in various **traditional art forms**. Drumming, for example, is a vital part of the *danço congo*, in which twenty to thirty dancers, in elaborate and brightly coloured costumes reminiscent of a Brazilian samba school, represent masters, servants, jesters, angels, magicians and devils. The danço congo is the vehicle for so many old folk tales – including the saving of someone from a dragon by the Virgin Mary, the defence of a plantation inherited by four clown-brothers, and the arrival of a Congolese prince, as a slave – that sorting out the interpretations is impossible.

The spectacular *tchiloli*, which consists of a sixteenth-century Portuguese play about the Emperor Charlemagne, interrupted and extended by a courtroom drama heavily satirical of Portuguese colonial government, has a continual accompaniment of bamboo flute, guitar and drum. The actors, all masked and mostly in nineteenth-century European costume, dance to this music as they move across the forest clearing used as a stage.

There are many types of dance in São Toméan traditional culture. The *lundum*, for example – which, by the end of the nineteenth century, seems to have ceased being performed – was as important for its singing as its dancing. The steps were very similar to the rumba, but dance partners had to keep a modest arm's length apart. The music was provided by three instruments: the *dunfa*, the *caixa media* and the *caixa requinta*, each made of hide, a hoop and a wooden cask and having

specific diameters of 20cm, 23cm and 30cm respectively. A member of the chorus beats out a rhythm on the caixa media with his palms, as in the Angolan *batuque*. The stars of the show were a pair of singers known as "Senhor Gatela" and "Senhora Gatela". Accompanying themselves with the caixa requinta and dunfa, they took it in turns to challenge each other in improvised verses. The refrain in the chorus of "Ah Deçu muê mula vôlô muê" ("Oh my God, the woman insults me!") gives an idea of the content of some of these songs, although they could contain declarations of love as well as such lively criticism. In one of the last known performances of the lundum, things became unusually heated between the Senhor and Senhora. When Senhor Gatela's song reached a peak of offensiveness, Senhora Gatela replied by hitting him over the head with her dunfa.

Today, a number of well-established electric bands produce music closely related to the Congolese sound, with an insistent beat conducive to extended evenings of dance. The musicians – all men it seems – sing in Forro, the most widely spoken of the three Creole languages of the islands. Brass instruments are sometimes included alongside the standard guitar and percussion accompaniment. Names to look out for are **Agrupamento Sangazuza São Tomé** and the brilliant **Africa Negra**. Both have released cassettes which you might come upon in the local tape stores of quiet São Tomé city. Many of these tapes have been produced and copied with a minimum of technology: copyright is an issue which is only just beginning to be addressed.

DISCOGRAPHY

ⒸⒹ **Gilberto Gil Umbelina** *Vôa, Papagaio Vôa* (Celuloid, France). The only CD available of São Tomé and Príncipe dance rhythms, produced by this Paris-based multi instumentalist.

Africa Negra *San Lena* (local cassette). Congolese-style tunes.
Agrupamento Sangazuza São Tomé *Various releases* (local cassette).

UNTIL MORNING

THE LIFE AND TIMES OF KENYAN POP

It's 9.30 on a Friday night. Early. Doug Paterson jumps in a matatu, a shared pick-up taxi, in Nairobi's central business district and heads for Eastleigh, the start of a musical tour of Africa's number-one tourist destination – and not a safari suit in sight.

Only a ten-minute ride away, it's a different world. Unlike Nairobi's near-deserted business centre, Eastleigh's streets are crowded and the shops and street vendors in full swing. Off the main thoroughfare, the half-kilometre dirt road to the club is pitch dark but for the kerosene lamps of the all-night kiosks.

As you approach, the music comes floating out from behind a corrugated iron sheet fence. This is Muungano Point – "Get Together Place". On payment of a small entry fee the gate is opened to a lively scene of dance, boozing, and hustling. The house band, Muungano All-Stars, are warming up with some golden oldies that everyone ignores. It's difficult to say which are the older, their battered instruments or these African hits from the past. As the crowd concentrates on getting the few beers down and placing their orders for roast meat, an old Luo busker sits in the open courtyard vigorously strumming his *nyatiti* (a traditional lyre) for a few shillings from passers-by.

This scene is repeated at scores of bars and clubs across the country. Some are fancier, like the Carnivore Restaurant's "Simba Grill" or the JKA Resort Club on the outskirts of Nairobi. Others, like the downtown Althusi Bar, are basically combination dancehall-butcheries, and have no more than the bare essentials: a barman dispensing beer from a wire mesh security cage, overworked barmaids squeezing round a few school-issue tables and chairs, and a cramped kitchen, white-tiled in classic Kenyan butchery style, with meat on the grill.

As the club fills the band eases into its repertoire of original songs: by midnight the floor is packed and table space is at a premium. Nairobi audiences and club-owners demand a lot from their musicians. At many clubs, the band will continue playing until 3 or 4am, or, as fly-posters boldly advertise in Swahili slang, *Mpaka Cheeeeeee* – "Until Morning!".

EVEN BEFORE 1900

Even before 1900, guitars were being played among the freed slave population at Frere Town on the mainland near Mombasa island. It wasn't long before other mission communities in rural areas outside Mombasa had produced a number of well-known guitarists. Sometimes referred to as Kenya's "first generation" of guitarists, this group, born between 1915 and 1925, includes Lukas Tututu, Paul Mwachupa and **Fundi Konde**. Their songs dealt with secular topics but in form and harmony were similar to church music – several verses and perhaps a refrain.

From the mid 1920s into the 1930s there were several dance clubs in the Mombasa area playing music for Christian Africans to do European dancing. **The Nyika Club Band**, for example, had guitars, bass, banjo, mandolin, violin and a sax/clarinet player. There's little in the historical record of this period about what was happening musically in other parts of Kenya apart from singing and drumming – and a bit of accordion playing among the Kikuyu.

During World War II, many African soliders were sent to fight in Ethiopia, India and Burma. Some of the coastal musicians were drafted into the Entertainment Unit of the Education Corps of the King's African Rifles. With a couple of Ugandan recruits, the group comprised guitars, mandolin, accordion and drums, and after the war they continued as the Rhino Band. Based at first in Kampala, they soon worked their way

Early Kenyan recording artists, Fadhili William (left) and Fundi Konde

down to Mombasa. The Rhinos split in 1948, but some of the members formed themselves into the distinguished **Kiko Kids**, while Fundi Konde, Daniel Katuga, singer Ester John and her husband sax player Ben Nicholas made a very successful collaboration – they have some tracks on Original Music's "Before Benga, Vol. 1" CD.

From the early 1950s, the spread of radio and a proliferation of recording studios pushed genuinely "popular music" across a wide spectrum of Kenyan society. Konde and Katuga were prominent broadcasters and also recorded on HMV's Blue Label series (run by Peter Colmore, who had been behind the wartime Entertainment Unit). Konde's early songs, especially his chord sequences, were closely allied to those of contemporary European dance bands, and it's a fair guess that if Konde's songs had been in English rather than Swahili, much of his tight, melodic and very rhythmic output would have found favour with Euro-American, pre-rock-'n'-roll tastes of the time.

FINGER-PICKIN' GOOD

While Fundi Konde's urbane style was much in demand, the "second generation" of Kenyan guitarists were making their names, often with a different playing techinque – the thumb and forefinger **finger style** first heard in the music of eastern Congolese players like **Jean-Bosco Mwenda**, Losta Abelo and Edouard Massengo.

Bosco's recordings were available in Kenya from 1952 and by the end of the decade he and Massengo had moved to Nairobi. Finger-style music has a lively, fast-paced bounce, especially where a second guitar follows the lead guitar with syncopated bass lines. The Kenyan finger-pickers sometimes pursued solo careers, but more usually they formed small guitar-based groups, with two-part vocal harmony and simple percussion using maracas, a tambourine, wood-blocks or even soda bottles. From the mid-1950s, this "new sound" – a scene dominated by Luhya-speakers from the west – gained a huge following and produced spectacular record sales. AGS, the African Gramophone Store, one of the bigger labels, claims to have sold 300,000 copies of **John Mwale's** "Kuwaza Sera" 78 rpm.

By the mid-1960s, finger-style acoustic guitar bands were losing ground to other electric guitar styles The rhythms of the new urban Swahili music were also influenced by Congolese rumba and South African kwela, or what was locally called **"twist"**. Twist's underlying rhythm is the beat of "Mbube" (The Lion), better known internationally as "Wimoweh" but played faster. Original Music's fine compilation "Before Benga Vol. II: the Nairobi Sound" has some superb twist examples.

Although the old styles had lost favour, they were not entirely discarded. On the contrary, they had been absorbed in part into the new music, and many ideas taken up by the electric

BASICS OF KENYAN MUSIC

••••••••••••••••••••••••

It isn't very meaningful to speak of Kenyan pop as a genre. There are really a number of styles that borrow freely and influence each other in a cross-fertilization that gives the music its unifying Kenyan flavour. What is fundamental, though, is the prominent role of guitars and guitar solos. The Earthworks compilations "Guitar Paradise of East Africa" and "Kenya Dance Mania", along with Rounder Records' "The Nairobi Beat", provide ample evidence, with an excellent cross section of Kenyan pop spanning the last twenty years. Another ingredient in the Kenyan mix is the *cavacha* rhythm popularized in the mid-1970s by Zairean groups such as Zaiko Langa Langa and Orchestra Shama Shama. A sense of this rhythm is conveyed by Bo Diddley's distinctive beat, the "shave-and-a-hair-cut, six-bits" rhythm which closely approximates cavacha. This rapid-fire percussion, usually on the snare or high hat, quickly took hold in Kenya and continues to underlie a great sweep of Kenyan music from the Kalambya Sisters to Les Wanyika and Orchestre Virunga. Many Kenyan musicians direct their efforts towards their own linguistic groups and perform most of their songs in one of Kenya's indigenous languages. Alongside this regional/ethnic orientation – often simply referred to as "tribal" in Kenya itself – are two other local pop music varieties: one consisting of songs with lyrics in Swahili or the Zairean language Lingala, aimed at a national and largely urban audience, and the other pro-pelled by foreign tourism and Kenyans with a taste for international pop.

bands were based on the finger-picking and soda bottle percussion of the preceding period. One of the most important groups of the new electric era of the 1960s was the **Equator Sound Band**, first formed in 1959 as the Jambo Boys, a studio and performing combo for the East African Records company. Led by **Fadhili William**, they took their famous name in 1962 and went on into the 1970s as African Eagles and Eagles Lupopo. Some of the most famous names of the period – Daudi Kabaka, Gabriel Omolo, Sylvester Odhiambo and the Zambian emigrés Nashil Pichen and Peter Tsotsi – distinguished the line-up. Typical Equator elements were the two-part vocal harmony, a steady, often "walking" bass and a bright, clean lead guitar. There's often a strikingly American feel in the guitar solos and chord formations, suggesting the rock and country influences that were so pervasive. A string of songs with their musical support can be heard on Original Music's "The Kampala Sound" CD.

BENGA WIZARDS

The end of the 1960s and early '70s was a time of transition in Kenyan music. While the African Eagles and others continued to play their brands of Swahili music, many top Kenyan groups, such as the Ashantis, Air Fiesta and the Hodi Boys, were playing Congolese covers and international pop, especially soul music, in the Nairobi clubs. But it was also at this time that a number of musicians were beginning to define the direction of the emerging *benga* style, which, perhaps more than anything else, became Kenya's most characteristic pop music.

Although the word and what it represents originated with the Luo people of western Kenya, benga's transition to a popular style has been so pervasive that practically all the local bands, Luo or otherwise, play variants of it and today most of the regional or ethnic pop groups refer generally to their music as benga. As a pop style, benga dates back to the 1950s when musicians began adapting traditional dance rhythms and the string sounds of the nyatiti and orutu to the acoustic guitar and later to electric instruments. During its heyday much of the early benga was exported to west and southern Africa where it was very popular.

Throughout the 1970s and into the 1980s, benga music dominated Kenya's recording industry and, although the whole industry is in serious decline, it remains an important force.

By any measure, the most famous benga group is **Shirati Jazz** led by **D. O. (Daniel Owino) Misiani**. Born in Shirati, Tanzania, just south of the Kenyan border, he has been playing benga since the mid-1960s. His style is characterized by soft, flowing and melodic two-part vocal harmonies, a very active, pulsating bass line that derives at least in part from traditional nyatiti and drum rhythms, and stacks of invigorating guitar work, the lead alternating with the vocal.

Misiani may be a "benga wizard", but benga is not his exclusive property and, contrary to the impression you might receive in a London or New York record shop, there are many other important benga artists. Pioneering Luo names include Colella Mazee and Ochieng Nelly – either together or separately in various incarnations of **Victoria Jazz** and the **Victoria Kings** – as well as George Ramogi and his Continental Luo Sweet Band. All are still active in Kenya although Misiani's Shirati is one of the few full-time Luo groups. Other current Luo groups are Migori Super Stars, Omore Kings, Ambira Boys Band, Sega-Sega, and Sega Matata Band. The Ambira Boys and Sega groups have done very well as storytellers of the trials and tribulations of modern life and they have set off a trend that has spread to other language groups.

One Luo name which doesn't fit neatly into any of these stylistic categories is Ochieng Kabaselleh and his Luna Kidi Band. There are some typical examples of his music (as it was in 1985) on the Earthworks compilations. His songs are mostly in Luo, but sometimes with a liberal seasoning of Swahili and English. Likewise, the melodies and harmonies are from the Luo benga realm but the rhythm, guitar work, and horns suggest influences from the Zairean/Swahili-dominated sound. Kabaselleh, who languished in prison for several years (for "subversion"), is back in the music world with a flood of new releases.

NURSERY BOYS

The Luhya highlands to the north of Luo-land are home to many of Kenya's most famous guitarists and vocalists. Daudi Kabaka, despite his renowned early career, struggles today with only the occasional hotel gig and few recording opportunities. The humorous social commentary of **Sukuma bin Ongaro** has made him a giant of the current scene, although mainly among his fellow Luhya-speakers. **Shem Tube**, however, is an artist who straddles both past and

D.O. MISIANI:
MASTER OF THE FASTER BEAT

For Kenyans, and especially western Kenyans, Daniel Owino ("D.O.") Misiani is the king of benga music. Born in 1940 in Shirati Location in northwestern Tanganyika (later Tanzania), he moved to Kenya in the early 1960s to try his luck on the Nairobi recording scene. After a few acoustic recordings he got an electric guitar and, in 1967, formed his Orchestra D.O. 7 Shirati Jazz. They achieved unprecedented popularity in the 1970s benga boom. In the early 1990s they are still at the helm of Luo music and are the only purely Kenyan band to have had success on the international scene. Werner Graebner talked to D.O. Misiani about sources and inspiration.

What does "benga" mean?
Benga is the style of music we play. In this context the word has no special meaning. You might use the word to refer to a beautiful person, especially to a very beautiful girl; you have to call her *obengo*.

What kind of music did you play in your youth?
I played Swahili music [i.e. rumba] and other songs in Luo [the main language of western Kenya]. This was my life. It was at that time that I began to play benga. There were other people who played a style called *ubele*, but we experimented with it until it had a contemporary feel, until it was a modern beat. In those days many people, even musicians, put me down for playing that way. They said I had done a very bad thing to play that fast beat. I also introduced the foot drum. At first people were sceptical, but soon everybody liked it.

This ubele, what kind of music was it?
It resembled benga. But we took it out of its relationship with these *ngoma* [traditional dances]. It used to be played at funerals or other social functions. People danced very energetically to go with the fast beat of the drums. We took this, what they played on the drums, and introduced it to the guitar.

Do you remember some of the early guitar players?
The first I saw playing the guitar was one Raphael Oro who came out of the military [i.e. World War II] with a guitar. But he played rumba, you know, this slow-walk thing. I was still in school back then. He taught me a bit, but even back then I liked a faster beat.

Did you hear any other musicians at the time, maybe on records?
Jean Bosco Mwenda, Losta Abelo, and locals like Ben Blastus, John Mwale, Isaya Muinamo were top at the time [the late 1950s and early 1960s]. But when we came with the benga, you know, the people who played this style – let's say it came from the French-speaking countries, the label was "Ngoma" [from Kinshasa] – they had this style from outside; when we came with the benga, it had more "power" than their style. They became weak and we woke up.

You often sing about religious topics. Is that because you have become a religious man?
No, it is because it is my trade. In general up to 1975 I sang about love, then I got into history and also taking sayings from the Bible as a lead. You know, when I sing about love, the records sell; but they have a fast turnover; they don't get old. That's why I got into these more serious topics. They sell for a longer time; that is why I like them. The same with the historical songs. It also helps to build my name, my reputation. Your rank is higher than when you only sing about love.

How do you see the developments in today's benga?
Sure there are changes. You know we introduced this fast beat and people liked it everywhere – in the neighbouring countries as well. We played fast, but there was a development in our songs, and we knew what to do when it came to the "climax" [i.e. the faster, second part of the song]. Now these people from outside, bands from Zaire resident here, and South African imports, they start with the climax, fast from the beginning. It is only speed, and they have enough instruments, and all this modern stuff. They have changed the Kenyan music.

You know, the people here in the government they don't know; they don't consider music to be work. We try our best, but we can only trust in God.

present in his music, though it's his musical past which has given him a popular following in the UK and Europe.

In 1989 GlobeStyle Records released "Abana ba Nasery" (the Nursery Boys), a compilation of songs by Tube and his group in the *omutibo* style. With two acoustic guitars (playing high and low), and rhythm played on a Fanta bottle, the Abana ba Nasery collection offers a glimpse of a musical era of the 1960s and early 1970s which has largely vanished. Coming together as a trio in the early 1960s, Abana ba Nasery were innovators, blazing a path for Kenyan pop to follow. While using traditional Luhya rhythms and melody lines, their two-guitar line-up and three-part vocal harmonies (and the Fanta bottle) were a hint of things to come. Abana's style from the 1960s contains the major elements of today's contemporary pop sound in Kenya: the central position of the solo guitar in Kenya's electric groups is anticipated in Shem Tube's solos of 25 years ago. Justo Osala's guitar parts in the lower ranges are like the rhythm and bass parts in today's electric bands. Even Enos Okola's Fanta rhythms are a precursor of the modern drum kit.

While Abana's first CD release created tremendous interest – a rootsy but very accessible African sound – the compatibility

Abana Ba Nasery (Nursery Boys) strike that Fanta!

of their music with strands of European folk tradition is clear in their second CD release, recorded by Globestyle in London: "Nursery Boys Go Ahead!" Guest artists included members of the Oyster Band and Mustaphas as well as Ron Kavana and Tomás Lynch. Although it's an all-acoustic recording, several songs on this collaborative effort are true rockers – which is not out of character with the group on their home turf. Although they've never earned enough money to buy their own electric guitars and amps, Abana ba Nasery have had a string of local hits as an electric band under the stage names Mwilonje Jazz and Super Bunyore Band (listen, for example, to Super Bunyore's "Bibi Joys" on the "Nairobi Beat" compilation). If the Nursery Boys have their way, it won't be long before audiences outside Kenya get a taste of their electric music too.

PRAYERS FOR THE COUNTRY

As Kenya's largest ethnic group, the **Kikuyu**-speaking people of Central Province and Nairobi are a major market force in Kenya's music industry. Perhaps because of this large "built-in" audience, few Kikuyu musicians have tried to cross over into the national Swahili or English-language markets. On the international scene, Kikuyu-language music is conspicuously absent but for the few songs that have made it onto some of the compilation CDs. Kikuyu melodies are quite distinct from those of the Luo and Luhya of western Kenya and their pop manifestations also differ significantly in harmonies and rhythm guitar parts. In contrast to Luo and Luhya pop, women vocalists play major roles as lead and backing singers for Kikuyu groups. Many of the top groups have women's auxiliaries – duos and trios invariably called the something-or-other sisters. While Kikuyu pop music has a traditional melodic structure, there is a good deal of stylistic variety and innovation. Most often, Kikuyu pop takes the form of the benga/cavacha style, but popular alternatives are also based on country and western, reggae, and Zairean soukous.

The king of Kikuyu pop is **Joseph Kamaru**, who has been making hit records since the release of "Celina" in 1967, performed, on one guitar and maracas, with his sister Catherine Muthoni. Since then he has carved a small empire – which includes his **Njung'wa Stars** band and the Kamarulets dancers – two music shops and a recording studio. He sees himself as a teacher, expressing the traditional values of his culture, as well as contemporary social commentary, in song. One recent number, "Mahoya ma Bururi" ("Prayers for the Country"), that gently criticized the government, resulted in his shop being raided and the banning of the song from the airwaves. Kamaru takes pride in his lyrics for going beyond trivial matters. "My songs are not like other peoples'… 'I love you, I love you,' they keep on singing…No, no, no! My songs are not that way. I can compose a love song but very deep, a grown-up loving."

Joseph Kamaru's raunchy pop – he's giving it up for gospel!

Since "Mahoya ma Bururi" in 1990, Kamaru's popularity has only increased, giving him a full schedule playing his regular and "X-rated, Adults Only" shows to packed nightclub crowds. Thus his announcement in 1993 that he had been "born again" was a bombshell for his fans. He declared an end to his "Adult" concerts, suggested that his band might want to carry on without him, and said he might form a gospel group.

Kamaru may not write songs for teenage lovers but someone who does, and who has become famous in the process, is hit-maker **Daniel "Councillor" Kamau** ("DK"). Kamau released his first three records in 1967 while still at school and continued with a highly successful career through the 1970s. He is regarded as having brought Kikuyu music into the benga mainstream, but it was not until 1990 that he returned to the stage with a new **Lulus Band**. In Kenya's rapidly changing political climate, the councillor has found a responsive chord in his fans and the population at large with his recent Top Ten hit, "FORD Fever", about one of the new political parties. DK has continued to address political and human rights issues: in partnership with singer-composer Albert Gacheru, his 1993 cassette, "Clashes – Mbara ya Molo na Narok", denounces the ethnic violence in the highlands of western Kenya.

MERRY-GO-ROUND STYLE

East and southeast of Nairobi is a vast, semi-arid plateau, the home of the **Kamba** people,

linguistically close relations of the Kikuyu. Kamba pop music is firmly entrenched in the benga/cavacha camp. Although distinctive melodies distinguish Kamba pop from other styles of benga, there are other special Kamba features. One is the delicate, flowing, merry-go-round-like rhythm guitar that underlies many Kamba arrangements. While the primary guitar plays chords in the lower range, the second guitar plays a fast pattern of notes that mesh with the rest of the instrumentation to fill in the holes. This gentle presence is discernible in many of the recordings of the three most famous Kamba groups; the **Kalambya Boys & Kalambya Sisters**, Peter Mwambi and his Kyanganga Boys and Les Kilimambogo Brothers Band, led, until 1987, by Kakai Kilonzo.

These groups have dominated Kamba music since the mid-1970s. Mwambi, although he can get into some great guitar solos, has a following that comes largely from within the Kamba community: his musically simple, "pound 'em-out", pulsing-bass drum style may not have enough musical variation to keep non-Kamba speakers interested.

The Kalambya Sisters are a different story. Backed by Onesmus Musyoki's Kalambya Boys Band, the Sisters (now disbanded) are famous, even notorious, throughout Kenya and they even had a minor hit in Europe with "Katelina". This relates the comic plight of a young woman, Katelina, who likes to drink the home-brew *uki*, but gets pregnant with annual regularity in the process. The soft, high-pitched, feline voices of the Sisters whine engagingly in unison over the delightfully sweet guitar work of Musyoki and the Boys (check out their style in "Kopulo Onesi" on "The Nairobi Beat" CD). After a ten-year absence from the studio, Musyoki returned to record "Sweet Sofia" in 1993, while founding Sister Mary Nduku now leads the Mitaboni Sisters.

To reach a larger audience, a number of local-language artists have turned to Swahili, which is widely spoken throughout east and central Africa. Kakai Kilonzo and Les Kilimambogo Brothers band were always identified as a "Kamba" band, but once Kakai started recording in Swahili, the group enjoyed widespread popularity in Kenya. With socially relevant lyrics, a good dose of "merry-go-round" guitar and a solid dance-beat backing, Les Kilimambogo were national favourites until Kakai's death in 1987.

These days, a new generation of musicians, relative newcomers to the Kamba hall of fame, is drawing most of the limelight away from the old guard. The Katitu Boys Band have come to dominate the Kamba cassette market. Leader David Kasyoki, a former guitarist with Mwambi's Kyanganga Boys, won the 1992 Singer of the Year award for "Cheza na Katitu". Other groups of the new Kamba generation include the Kimangu Band and Katitu offshoots Ukambani Original Sound Stars.

BIG-NAME BANDS

The big-name bands in Kenya can usually muster sufficiently large audiences for shows in sprawling, ethnically diverse towns like Nairobi, Nakuru or Mombasa. Unlike the groups with a particular ethnic leaning, the national performers can appeal to a broad cross-section of the population with music which tends to be either

a local variant of the **Zairean** sound or **Swahili music**, a Kenyan-Tanzanian hybrid sound, unique to Kenya.

In both Zairean and Swahili popular music, rumba has always been a major ingredient. Songs typically open with a slow-to-medium rumba which ambles through the verses, backed by a light percussion of gentle congas, snare and high hat. Then, three or four minutes into the song there's a transition – or more often a hiatus. It's goodbye to verses and rolling rumba as the song shifts into high gear. A much faster rhythm, highlighting the instrumental parts, especially solo guitar and brass, takes over with a vengeance.

There are some significant points of divergence in Swahili and Zairean styles. The tempo of Swahili music is generally slower, even in the fast section. Swahili music over the last twenty years

KOPULO ONESI
(CORPORAL ONESI)

....

The story of Onesi and his lover Kaluki highlights a number of big issues in modern Kenya without really saying who is right and who wrong.

Kaluki:
I chased Onesi until my shoes wore out.
Because we made a plan to marry and when I got pregnant you left me.
Onesi mine, my dear,
Why do you hate me, my dear?

Observer addressing Kaluki:
Why have you been following him?
You can't force him to marry you.
Girls, your behaviour is very bad so no one will marry you.
Girls, your behaviour is very bad and men are angry about it.

Onesi:
You girls have bad manners, my love.
You have abused your parents and drank beer, and drinking alcohol is very bad.

Kaluki:
I met Onesi in a bar.
And he knows even when I drink I have good manners.
Why do you hate me, my dear?

Why when you are responsible for my pregnancy, my dear?
Men you are liars.

Onesi:
Kaluki, that was just sex, find a man to marry you.
Because I have my own wife and I cannot be a corporal for a woman [two stripes: two wives].
Why are you following me and you are a spare woman?
It's going to be hard for you to marry because you drink so much, you have become a completely bad person.

Kaluki:
My husband is you Onesi because I'm carrying your child.
My husband is you Onesi and to marry anyone else would be difficult.
I will follow you to your home.
I will follow you to your wife.
Because the pregnancy is from you, my dear
You will be a corporal my dear.
Like it or not, that's the way it will be.

Onesmus Musyoki and the Kalambya Sisters, on "The Nairobi Beat" (Rounder, US).

has been particularly faithful to this two-part structure although, today, both Swahili and Zairean musicians often dispense with the slow rumba portion altogether. While the Zaireans are famous for their vocals and their intricate harmonies, Swahili groups are renowned for their demon guitarists and crisp, clear guitar interplay.

While Swahili music is usually associated with Swahili lyrics, it isn't distinguished by the language. In fact one of the greatest Swahili hits of all time, "Charonyi Ni Wasi" is not in Swahili but in the closely related Taita language. Similarly, Nairobi's Zairean scene has become less Zairean as it has moved from the near-exclusive use of Lingala twenty years ago to a preponderance of Swahili lyrics. Nearly all the songs on the recent "Feet on Fire" CD from the immensely popular Orchestra Virunga are in Swahili, helping to guarantee popularity with a mass audience. As for Lingala songs, while few Kenyans understand the lyrics, their mysterious incomprehensibility and a veneer of Gallic sophistication gives them a certain sex appeal.

Most of the Swahili and Zairean music produced in Kenya comes from giants like Polygram and Sony (formerly CBS) or is put out by independent labels run by British or Asian Kenyans. When European and American interest in African music began to emerge in the early 1980s, it was these companies with their international connections that put out the first, tantalizing sounds from Nairobi. Although they were also involved in the vernacular language scene, the early Kenyan recordings released in London were drawn from the big names and featured artists such as Super Mazembe, Orchestra Makassy, Orchestre Virunga, Lessa Lassan, Issa Juma, and Lovy Longomba. Of these, all but the Tanzanian-born Issa Juma come from Zaire – there's not a Kenyan among them – and it was not until several years later, after Shirati Jazz had done their first British tour, that Kenya achieved an international reputation for its indigenous benga dance music.

IMMIGRATION DEPARTMENT

Zaireans (or Congolese as they were previously known) have been making musical waves in Kenya since the late 1950s. It was the Congolese OS Africa Band that opened Nairobi's famous Starlight Club back in 1964. But it wasn't until the mid-1970s, after the passing of the American soul craze, that music from Zaire began to dominate the city nightclubs. One of the first musicians to settle in Kenya during this period was **Baba Gaston**. The rotund Gaston had already been in the business for twenty years when he arrived in Nairobi with his group Baba National in 1975. A prolific musician and father

One of Africa's all-time best voices: Samba Mapangala

(he has twelve children), he stole the scene until his retirement as a performer and recording artist in 1989.

In the mid-1970s, at about the same time Baba Gaston was just getting settled in Nairobi, the Zairean group Boma Liwanza was already on the scene at the Starlight Club and the popular Bana Ngenge were about to leave Nairobi for a year in Tanzania. Super Mazembe had just completed their migration from Zaire to Kenya by way of Zambia and Tanzania. And soon to follow were **Samba Mapangala and Les Kinois**, though they stopped along the way in Uganda for a couple of years – and had a near-fatal encounter with the army, before moving to Nairobi in 1977. With the break-up of Les Kinois in 1980, some members moved to Mazembe while Samba began putting together his first version of **Orchestre Virunga**. The famous "Malako" recordings included several members of Bana Ngenge, including vocalist Fataki Lokassa and the late Lawi Somana, who went on to lead Tabu Ley's Afrisa.

Meanwhile, despite their rising popularity in 1982–83, Super Mazembe began to fragment. The group's versatile lead singers Lovy Longomba and Kasongo wa Kanema (of "Kasongo" and "Shauri Yako" fame) quit the band – Kasongo to team up with Virunga and Lovy to front his own group, Super Lovy, and later Bana Likasi.

By 1984, Samba Mapangala's line-up had experienced a number of changes in personnel but was still going strong. It wasn't long, however, before Virunga also ran into the Kenya Immigration Department. With extensions to their work permits refused, Virunga were soon out of money and falling apart.

Out of Virunga's misfortune came **Ibeba System**. It was led by ex-Virunga guitarist Sammy Mansita and other Virunga/Kinois alumni including Siama Matuzungidi on guitar, Johnny-Ko Walengo on bass, and vocalists Kasongo wa Kanema and Coco Zigo Mike. Lovy Longomba also did a spell with Ibeba System before setting off to Dar es Salaam to join Afriso Ngoma. When Ibeba first took over from Virunga at the Starlight, the group was a virtual clone of the Virunga sound. Over several years performing at the JKA Resort Club they became one of Nairobi's most accomplished club acts with a good mix of their own soukous and covers of African pop.

The ultimate Zairean crossover band in Nairobi, and darlings of Kenya's young elite, were **Vundumuna**. The group formed in 1984 with guitarist **Tabu Frantal** of Boma Liwanza

and Shika Shika, Ugandan vocalist Sammy Kasule, and bassist Nsilu wa Bansilu of Bana Ngenge and Virunga. Vundumuna quickly gained institutional status at the Carnivore packing in the crowds with their Wednesday and Saturday night performances. With the best equipment in the city, they presented a clean, hi-tech sound fusing Zairean soukous, benga rhythms, and elements of western jazz. Their flawless horn arrangements blended beautifully with leader **Botango Bedjil's** keyboards and Frantal's guitar. After three LPs and riding a crest of popularity, the future was looking bright until, once again, the Immigration Department struck. The group played its farewell concert at the Carnivore in late 1986 and, since then, they have worked abroad in places as far afield as Japan and Oman. In between jobs, they return to Kenya – several band members have Kenyan wives and children – and they have been allowed to play short stints as guest performers.

By the 1990s, Nairobi's status as an island of opportunity for Zairean musicians had fallen flat. With harder economic times, a declining record industry, fewer live music venues and restrictive work rules for foreign musicians, Nairobi has become a departure point for greener pastures.

When Virunga returned to the Garden Square club in Nairobi in 1988 they had no trouble recapturing the abundant enthusiasm they left behind after their untimely departure from the music scene three years before. With a captivating stage show, they played dazzling renditions of all their familiar hits. New compositions like "Safari" and "Miaka Kumi ya Enzi ya Nyayo" (Ten Years of the Nyayo Era) joined the list of favourites. Although the musicians continue to change, nothing has altered Samba Mapangala's formula for brilliant music – a catchy, not over-complex melody, faultless vocal harmonies, innovative, interlocking guitar lines and superbly crafted horns floating over light, high-tensile percussion.

WANYIKA DYNASTY

Songs with **Swahili lyrics** are part of the common currency of East African musical culture. Kenya's own brand of Swahili pop music has its origin in the Tanzanian pop styles of the 1970s but, since that time, the Kenyan variety has followed a separate evolutionary path from the Tanzanian mainstream.

In addition to the stylistic features it shares with the Zairean sound (light, high-hat-and-conga percussion and a delicate two/three-guitar interweave), the Kenyan Swahili sound is instrumentally sparse, allowing the bass to fill in gaps, often in syncopated rhythms. Trumpets and saxes are common in recorded arrangements but usually omitted in club performances because of the extra expense.

One of the first groups to migrate to Kenya was Arusha Jazz, the predecessor of what is now the legendary **Simba Wanyika Original** ("Simba Wanyika" means "Lion of the Savanna"). Founded by Wilson Peter Kinyonga and his brothers George and William, the group began performing in Mombasa in 1971. The following year, they began recording for Phonogram (Polygram), making a name for themselves with single releases such as "Eliza Wangu" (My Eliza), "Jose Twende Zaire" (Jose Let's Go to Zaire) and "Mama Suzie". In 1975, the three brothers, along with Tanzanian recruit Omar Shabani on rhythm and Kenyan Tom Malanga on bass, shifted their base to Nairobi and released their first album, "Jiburudisheni na Simba Wanyika" (Chill Out with Simba Wanyika). Ever since, the group have been Nairobi favourites, performing regularly in clubs and making scores of recordings.

Despite their great local popularity, Simba Wanyika's fame in Kenya produced few monetary rewards and little international recognition. It was not until 1989 that the group finally got its first break with a trip to Holland. Their warm reception led to more European tours and the release of their first CD, "Pepea", in 1992. Just as it looked like many of leader Wilson Peter's ambitions for the band were going to be realized, the death of his brother George cast a cloud of uncertainty over Simba Wanyika's future. He died of tuberculosis at the age of 42 and will be sadly missed, not only for his fine guitar-playing and vocals, but as the composer of the band's best songs.

Over Simba Wanyika's twenty-plus years, the Kinyonga brothers maintained a remarkably consistent style despite several major changes in personnel. However, their most widely circulated recordings outside Kenya present a rather different sound from their typical recordings for Polygram in Nairobi. In both their international releases, "Simba Wanyika Original: Kenya Vol. I" and "Pepea", the group has taken a page from the benga handbook and quickened the pace considerably – though the vocal and instrumental parts are indeed "original" Simba Wanyika of great guitars, classic sax (on "Vol. I") and

pleasing, listener-friendly vocal lines. For purists interested in Simba Wanyika's Polygram sound, the albums "Haleluya" and "Mapenzi Ni Damu", recorded before and after "Kenya Vol. I", are more representative of what you might hear in Nairobi. George Peter's "Pole" cassette, released under the name of his own band Orchestra Jobiso, features alternative versions of several of their most famous songs, with the rougher Nairobi versions sounding quite different from the more polished, Dutch-produced "Pepea". There's a striking contrast in the vocals, for example, placed distinctly out at the front on "Pepea" but further back and with a ton of echo in the "Pole" mix. The Kenyan version also has stronger congas and high hat and the luxury of a pair of saxophones. But like the differences between various Mazembe and Makassy productions of a decade before, it's hard to say if either the Kenyan or European version is superior.

The Wanyika name is famous in East Africa not only for Simba Wanyika, but for several other related bands that emerged from the Wanyika line. The first big split occurred in 1978 when the core of supporting musicians around the Kinyonga brothers left Simba Wanyika to form **Les Wanyika**. Among those who made the move were rhythm guitarist "Professor" Omari Shabani, bass player Tom Malanga, drummer Rashid Juma, and vocalist Issa Juma, who had only joined Simba Wanyika the month before. The group added another crucial member in Tanzanian lead guitar player John Ngereza, who had been playing in Kenya with the Zairean group Bwambe Bwambe. After six months' practice, Les Wanyika began performing at Garden Square and soon found fame across Kenya with their massive hit "Sina Makosa" (It's not my Fault) which was quickly followed by singles such as "Paulina", "Pamela", and "Kajituliza Kasuku".

Under Ngereza's leadership, Les Wanyika have remained one of Nairobi's top bands. While cut from the same mould as the Simbas, Les Wanyika have distinguished themselves with imaginative compositions and arrangements, a typically lean, clean sound and the delicious blend of Professor Omari's rhythm guitar mastery with Tom Malanga's bass. The sparse percussion majors on the high hat and a muted, pulsing kick drum. This lean instrumentation provides the backing for vocalist and lead guitar player Ngereza, who alternates between the two roles. During vocal choruses, there's solid vocal backing in multipart harmonies from Mohamed Tika and other Swahili session vocalists. The finest example of their work is on the "Dunia Kigeu-geu" compilation, released in Kenya in 1985.

Some of Les Wanyika's most recent recordings have attempted to cash in on the popularity of disco music in Kenya. The remake of their greatest hits into two disco medleys (on "Les Les Non-Stop '90") was locally quite successful and carried over into their next album ,"Kabibi" – an unfortunate departure into the dismal realm of international disco crossover. Mercifully, Ngereza's most recent cassette has returned with the classic Wanyika sound to a welcoming audience. "Weekend na Les Wanyika" spent nearly the whole of 1993 and much of 1994 in Kenya's Top Ten.

WHAT KIND OF BUSINESS?

An important figure in the Wanyika story is Tan-zania-born **Issa Juma**, who quickly established a name for himself in Kenya as a premier vocalist in the early days of Les Wanyika. Mention his name today and many Kenyans will immediately think of "Sigalame", a character from his 1983 single of the same name and now a part of Kenyan vocabulary. "Sigalame" is Issa Juma's most famous song, not because of the music, which is generic cavacha, but because of its entertaining lyrics. Sigalame is a mysterious character who has disappeared from family and friends but is rumoured to be living in Bungoma doing "business". What kind of business? ("Biashara gani?") With so many illegal activities to choose from, it was up to the listener to answer.

Following five years' experience with Tan-zanian and Ugandan bands, Issa Juma had been recruited to sing in Kericho Jazz, in Kenya's tea country, in 1971. That band didn't last but Issa stayed, working with the Chandarana recording studio in Kericho until 1977. Barely a year after moving to Nairobi, he linked up with Les Wanyika for two years, then, when he quit, got together with former members of Simba Wanyika

and Orchestra Jobiso as well as Issa Bendera of Super Volcano and Les Volcano fame to form Super Wanyika in 1981.

Despite numerous personnel changes and splits in the line-up, Issa Juma continued into the mid-1980s with a long series of hits on at least four different labels featuring half a dozen variations on the Wanyika name – Super Wanyika Stars, Wanyika Stars, Waa-Nyika, L'Orchestra Waanyika and Wanyika Super Les Les.

As one of the most productive recording artists of the 1980s, Issa Juma released many numbers in the style of Swahili-benga fusion heard in "Sigalame". Yet, he has been perhaps the most versatile and creative of the Swahili artists in his willingness to take his music in different directions. With producer Babu Shah, some of his songs sound very much like the Zairean music of the time. Others are more in the old rumba style of Simba Wanyika. On the Earthworks CD "Kenya Dance Mania", there's a rough-sounding mix of "Si Mimi" (Not Me) with crashing, out-of-tune guitars and tom-toms that sound like someone banging on dustbins. As much as this side of Super Wanyika is enjoyable, there's a lot of cleaner and more delicate material produced by Felix Njakumu and others. Even the Kenyan album release of "Si Mimi" is softer edged, with excellent solos on lead, a lighter vocal mix and a consummate rhythm guitar virtually absent on the Earthworks release.

Although the Wanyika bands have been dominant in Swahili music, it is not their exclusive domain. Foremost among other

Malaika

Malaika, nakupenda malaika	Angel, I love you angel
Malaika, nakupenda malaika	Angel, I love you angel
Nami nifanyeje? kijana mwenzio	And me, your boyfriend, what should I do?
Nashindwa na mali sina wee	If I weren't struggling for money
Ningekuowa malaika	I would marry you angel
Nashindwa na mali sina wee	If I weren't struggling for money
Ningekuowa malaika	I would marry you angel
Pesa zasumbuwa roho yangu	Money is troubling my soul
Pesa zasumbuwa roho yangu	Money is troubling my soul
Nami nifanyeje?...	What else could I do? ...
Kidege, ukuwaza kidege	Little bird, I'm always dreaming of you, little bird
Kidege, ukuwaza kidege	
Nami nifanyeje?...	Little bird, I always think of you, little bird
	What else could I do? ...

Authorship disputed

Tanzanians and Kenyans performing in the Swahili style are the **Maroon Commandos**. Still members of the Kenya Army, the Commandos are one of the oldest performing groups in the country. They first came together in 1970, although they had a serious setback with deaths of several band members in a road accident in 1972. In the mid-1970s, the group was mainly a "covers band" playing the current hits of Zaire. But by 1977 they had come out as a strong force in the Swahili style with the huge Taita-language hit "Charonyi Ni Wasi". Within their genre, the Commandos do not limit themselves to any sort of rigid formula. Like many of the Swahili groups, they use trumpets and sax liberally but they're also quite experimental and have at various times added a keyboard and innovative guitar effects and, at their most creative, mingle Swahili and benga styles.

MUSHROOM SOUP

Down on the coast, north and south of earthy Mombasa, are the tourist resorts, where a successful band can make a living just playing hotel gigs. **Tourist pop bands** typically have highly competent musicians, relatively good equipment and, overall, a fairly polished sound. In live performances, they play a schizophrenic mixture of old Congolese rumba tunes as warm-ups, popular international covers, a few Zairean favourites of the day, greatest hits from Kenya's past, and then some original material that leans heavily towards the American/Euro pop sound but with lyrics relating to local topics.

The most successful Kenyan group in this realm is a perennial favourite, the excruciatingly named **Them Mushrooms**, followed by **Safari Sound**, teen sensations **The Pressmen**, **African Vibration** and relative newcomers **Tausi Five**. Them Mushrooms are without doubt Kenya's most active band today, with at least a dozen albums to their credit. Over the years, they have produced a series of highly successful collaborations, highlighting quite diverse artists, including pioneering musician Fundi Konde, taarab star Malika and the Kikuyu singer Jane Nyambura. Despite TMs' wide popularity, it is Safari Sound which has Kenya's best-selling album ever in "The Best of African Songs" cassette.

Foreign visitors on the tourist circuit are seduced by the music of both groups, but in particular one catchy little tune has permeated every tourist haunt for nearly two decades. While not exactly advancing the cause of African pop as an artform, "Jambo Bwana (Hakuna Matata)" seems to capture the essence of what a Kenyan holiday is all about – a tremendous singalong-Swahili ditty that goes down a storm in the package hotel discos (even if its "no-problems-in-Kenya" lyrics sound unintentionally ironic these days). The composition has been around for some time: for a twist-style precursor listen to "Jane Umrongo" on "Before Benga: Vol. 2".

Another regular tourist number is "Malaika" (see p.347), a beautiful old composition about ill-starred love first popularized by Fadhili William, taken up by Miriam Makeba and most recently given a stirringly soulful treatment by the Paris-based Béninoise singer Angélique Kidjo – who unfortunately mangled the Swahili lyrics.

DISCOGRAPHY

COMPILATIONS

Various *Guitar Paradise of East Africa* and *Kenya Dance Mania* (Earthworks, UK). Companion CDs providing an excellent introduction to Kenya's various styles, although not always the best or most representative material from the artists. Still, the intros are a joy; "Shauri Yako" on the first volume is worth the price of the CD; while "Dance Mania" has two all-time Swahili classics – "Sina Makosa" by Les Wanyika and the Maroon Commandos' fantastic "Charonyi Ni Wasi".

Various: "Wanyika" *Dunia Kigeu-geu* (Polydor, Kenya). Four of Les Wanyika's best with solid tunes from Simba Wanyika and Orchestra Jobiso.

Various *Before Benga, Vol. I: Kenya Dry* and *Before Benga, Vol. 2: The Nairobi Sound* (Original Music, US). Both the acoustic collection on "Kenya Dry" and the electric "Nairobi Sound" provide an excellent cross-section of guitar music from the 1950s to the 1970s. These are styles which have largely disappeared in Kenya

Various *The Nairobi Beat: Kenyan Pop Music Today* (Rounder, US). Some of Doug Paterson's selected favourites from the mid-1980s, with an emphasis on regional styles. Includes the Kalambya Sisters' "Kopulo Onesi" (see p.343)

Various *The Kampala Sound: 1960s Ugandan Dance Music* (Original Music, US). Delightful collection of lazy dance numbers evoking a lost world of weekend afternoons. Although all the songs are in the Luganda language, most were recorded in Nairobi and no less than five have the backing of the famous Equator Sound Band.

ARTISTS AND BANDS

Abana Ba Nasery *Abana Ba Nasery Classic Acoustic Recordings From Western Kenya* (GlobeStyle, UK). As it says, "classic acoustic" guitar and Fanta bottle in the omutibo style. On **Nursery Boys Go Ahead! The Guitar and Bottle Kings of Kenya** (GlobeStyle, UK/Xenophile, US) you get further omutibo in new recordings with some interesting guest collaborations.

Tabu Frantal *Frantal* (African Music Gallery, US). This is the Zairean equivalent of "soft rock" with an international crossover. For more than two years, Frantal's band Vundumuna packed the Carnivore in Nairobi with this sound.

Orchestra Jobiso *Pole* (Polydor, Kenya). Interesting alternative versions of some of Simba Wanyika's best-known tunes, by the late George Peter Kinyonga and his own band.

Issa Juma & Orchestra Super Wanyika Stars *Mpita-Njia* (Editions FrancAfrique/AI Records, Kenya). If you come across this Nairobi release, it has the alternative version to "Si Mimi" on "Kenya Dance Mania".

ⓒ **Kapere Jazz Band & Others** *Luo Roots: Musical Currents from Western Kenya* (Globestyle, UK). Today's versions of the traditional music of the Luo people, suggesting the foundations of benga.

Les Kilimambogo Brothers Band *Simba Africa* (African Music, Germany). A fine Kamba collection – the late Kakai Kilonzo's best.

ⓒ **Henry Makobi** *New Memories: Guitar Music from Kenya* (Music & Words, Holland). Recorded in 1991 in a Nyahururu hotel room, Makobi brings the 1950s finger-picking era alive with his superb renditions of old George Mukabi, Losta Abelo, Ben Blastus, John Mwale and Jean Bosco songs.

ⓒ **Samba Mapangala & Orchestra Virunga** *Virunga Volcano*, (Earthworks, UK/US). A perfect album of beautifully crafted songs that are as fresh and enticing today as they were in the early 1980s. Includes their most famous song, "Malako". ⓒ *Feet On Fire* (Stern's Africa, UK) offers first-rate Mapangala in his most recent recordings. Also check out ⓒ *Paris-Nairobi* (Sasa

Music, UK). One of the appealing things about Samba is that he doesn't sound just like every other Parisian soukous star. The Paris tracks with the Quatres Étoiles are an interesting diversion but the Nairobi recordings score over them easily.

ⓒ **DO Misiani & Shirati Jazz** *Piny Ose Mer/The World Upside Down* (GlobeStyle, UK). Recent Shirati recorded in Kenya. There's old Shirati, but a nice collection of songs, on the *Benga Blast!* LP-and-cassette release (Earthworks, UK).

ⓒ **Shirati Jazz** *Benga Beat* (World Circuit, UK). Personal favourite, with great guitars, but some critics say it's got no soul. It's got no DO Misiani, that's certain.

ⓒ **Simba Wanyika** *Pepea* (Kameleon, Netherlands). Recorded in Holland, this superb 1992 release is probably the best representation of the current SWO sound. The Kameleon label's name is a pun on the Kinyonga brothers' name, which means "chameleon" in Swahili. The LP-and-cassette release *Kenya Vol. 1* (African Music Gallery, US) is an excellent recording of some of the band's best music (but compare the Nairobi release of "Baba Asiya" by the late George Peter Kinyonga's Orchestra Jobiso for an interesting contrast).

Super Mazembe *Kaivaska* (Virgin, UK). One of the fine early 1980s releases from Nairobi that put Kenyan music on the map.

ⓒ **Victoria Kings** *The Mighty Kings of Benga* (GlobeStyle, UK). A different perspective on benga (i.e. not Shirati Jazz) from one of the other great Luo groups from western Kenya. Features two of benga's most renowned artists, Ochieng Nelly and Collela Mazee, playing some of their energy-packed hits of the late 1970s and early 1980s.

SWAHILI MUSICAL PARTY

ISLAMIC TAARAB MUSIC OF EAST AFRICA

Taarab is the popular music of the Islamic Swahili people of the East African coast and islands. Distributed via cassettes and the radio, this music is a general feature of the aural landscape of the coast. Werner Graebner looks into a unique East African style.

For outsiders, the first impression may be an Arabic sound, especially when hearing the Zanzibar variety of orchestral *taarab* with its Egyptian film orchestra-style line-up. If you're listening to taarab in Mombasa it's the Indian film music links that impress. Yet the lyrics are invariably Swahili and the distinct Swahili voice quality and the rhythms of the various *ngoma* characterize it as essentially African. The combination of Africa, India and Arabia in the intricate Indian Ocean musical culture perfectly expresses the complex identity of the Swahili people.

Once heard, the **sound of taarab** is never forgotten. Taarab is sung poetry, so the vocals are especially important. The voice quality is definitely Islamic, yet it's as far from the standards of Cairo as is Youssou N'Dour. Vocals that cut through the instrumentation are the most popular among the Swahili and there's a distinct preference for high, clear female voices like that of **Shakila**, or Sharmila, or, back in the 1920s and '30s, that of **Siti bint Saad**.

Siti Bint Saad and her group in the 1930s

Rhythm retains a special importance and there is no band that features less than three percussion players. Various small drums are played, most often *dumbak*, *tabla* and *rika* (a tambourine). Taarab is generally based on the rhythms of local ngoma, the *kumbwaya* being the most prominent. Others are *chakacha*, *goma* and *vugo*. The use of some Latin American rhythms goes back to the popularity of Cuban records in the 1940s.

While some of the other **instruments** used in taarab are oriental in origin, like the Arabian *oud* and *kanun* and the Japanese *taishokoto* (a sort of banjo/typewriter-key hybrid), most instruments today are of western provenance: organs and electric keyboards often substitute for accordions and harmoniums, while guitar and bass guitar are found in almost every band. European stringed instruments like violin, viola and cello are a feature of the Zanzibar and Dar Es Salaam orchestras.

TAARAB HISTORY

After a period of stressing the African elements, current cultural values now favour a stronger link to Islamic roots. For example, recent writing from Zanzibar attributes the origin of the taarab to Arabic or, more specifically, Egyptian roots.

The name *taarab* derives, in fact, from the Arabic *tariba*, "to be moved or agitated", yet the meaning in Swahili has broadened to cover the whole music and its context. The name itself became currency only in the 1950s. The Egyptian attribution comes from the chronicles of the **Ikhwani Safaa Musical Club** founded in 1905, which has come to be viewed in some circles as the history of taarab. Yet this view of history does not account for the rise and fame of **Siti bint Saad**, the most famous of all Swahili singers and a woman, in the otherwise exclusively male world of Zanzibar music clubs. Siti and her musicians were the first East African musicians to make commercial recordings, recording more than a hundred songs from 1928 onwards. Many other female voices, from Zanzibar and elsewhere, were popular at the time.

Members of the **Culture Musical Club**, the second largest club in Zanzibar, contest the Ikhwani Safaa story and point instead to the African roots of taarab and the influence of African music on the music of the Arabian Peninsula. Instruments, music styles and musicians from east and northeast Africa are common in Yemen, and as far afield as Kuwait and Iraq.

Musicians and local historians from Lamu and Mombasa add to these views by bringing

The Culture Musical Group in performance in Zanzibar

in the older Lamu traditions of Swahili poetry. This poetry was always meant to be sung, and there are descriptions (dating from the nineteenth and early twentieth centuries) of performances called *gungu* and *kinanda* showcasing this poetry, accompanied by gongs, small drums and the *kibangala*, a stringed instrument also called *kinanda* or *gambusi* by the Swahili. These days this type of instrument is obsolete on the East African coast, but similar instruments may still be found on the Comoros Islands and in Malaysia and Indonesia.

More interesting pointers in this web of opinions are provided by the social occasions on which taarab is played. Like the gungu and kinanda, which it has supplanted, taarab is well integrated with the festive life of the Swahili: weddings are the main outlet for performances.

SWAHILI WEDDINGS

• •

Normally the streets and lanes of Mombasa's Old Town are almost empty by 10pm, just a few men sitting outside to get a breath of fresh air in the sultry climate. The Swahili wedding season reaches its peak in the month before Ramadhan and then the atmosphere is completely different. There is a bustling of activities and the Old Town seems to be exclusively populated by women and girls, with women clad in the black, *buibui* cloaks and veils, rushing to a wedding ngoma or the taarab which crowns a wedding on its last day.

Swahili weddings are community affairs. They involve the extended family and friends as well as the neighbourhood. Celebrations take place in the streets, lanes and small squares between the buildings. The square or street is simply fenced, mats spread, and some tented roofs erected as a sunshade or umbrella and for privacy. A wedding lasts between four and seven days and takes in the preparation and decoration of the place by the women, all the cooking and a good deal of fun, especially during the vugo and chakacha – dances accompanied by ribald songs – which are performed through some of the nights. All these festivities – vugo, chakacha and the taarab ya Kiswahili – are strictly women's affairs; the musicians are the only men allowed to participate.

Festivities culminate in the taarab given on the last day, the *kutoleza nje*, the ceremonial first presentation of the bride in public after the consummation of the marriage. On this night the bride is placed prominently under one of the tented roofs, clad in the best clothes the family can afford, adorned with jewellery, and with her hands, arms, and feet decorated with henna patterns. Unmoving, she has to sit like this for hours for all to admire.

The guests arrive in groups, all clad in buibui, soon to be opened to show off new dresses and henna-decorated limbs. Perfumes fill the air and mix with the cooking aromas.

The band is positioned under one of the tented roofs opposite the bride's parents' house. Heavily amplified, the instruments – organ, accordion, and various drums and percussion – start their romp through the thumping rhythms, some borrowed from the ngoma of preceding days. Melodies from the latest Indian films mix with Swahili poetry. After a short warm-up, the lead singer takes her or his place at the microphone. The taarab may now last until the following morning.

As the evening unfolds, the band and wedding guests get more and more involved with the songs and the music: the women join the refrain of current hits or get up to display their dancing skills and new clothes. Song requests scribbled on scraps of paper are handed to the musicians. Appreciative *tuzo*, or tips, are given to the musicians and especially to the lead singer for unusually clever lyrics. Giving tuzo for a certain song, or at a certain passage in the lyrics, is also used as a not-so-subtle public agreement with whatever is being sung – for example as a warning to a jealous neighbour to back off, or to a friend for meddling in one's affairs. Men have their own celebrations at the house of the husband-to-be, but on a much smaller scale.

There is also a kind of men's taarab, which the Mombasans call *taarab ya kiarabu* (Arab-style taarab). In this type of taarab men and women celebrate together, though the men's and women's sections are divided by curtains. The band plays on the male side and the men, including the groom, also dance. This is a type of taarab favoured more by families who consider themselves rather "Arab" in background and lifestyle: the Zein type of taarab is kiarabu.

TAARAB CENTRES AND ARTISTS

On **Lamu** island, the old centre of Swahili culture and literature on the north Kenya coast, most weddings are served by a few amateur groups. There are no active professional taarab groups these days, and groups are bused up from Mombasa for well-to-do marriage ceremonies. The **Zein Musical Party**, based in **Mombasa**, is the heir of Lamu's taarab tradition. Zein l'Abdin Alamoody was born in Lamu and hails from a family in which the Swahili arts were highly valued. Together with the Swahili poet Sheikh Nabhany he has unearthed many old poems which now form part of his repertoire.

Mombasa's main favourites at weddings are **Maulidi Musical Party** and **Malika**. Maulidi

Zuhura Swaleh from Mombasa

are at ease both with traditional Swahili wedding songs and the Hindi-style songs which are so characteristic of Mombasa taarab. Often Swahili words are set to tunes from the latest Bombay movie success. Maulidi's band used to back Malika when she was visiting from Somalia where she lived for a while. Recently she decided to return home to Mombasa and now leads her own group. Though her voice has suffered as a result of a health problem, hers is still the female voice most in demand in today's taarab. Mombasa's other female star is the enchanting **Zuhura Swaleh**, whose energetic songs have a firm base in chakacha rhythms and lyrics. The

taishokoto is a prominent sound in her group. As for the men, "golden voiced" **Juma Bhalo** used to be the hero of Indian-style taarab, but he's no longer very active. **Matano Juma** and his **Morning Star Orchestra** are all-time favourites and Matano is highly praised by fellow musicians as one of taarab's leading composers. He has one of the most outstanding voices in taarab and he also practices a most idiosyncratic ensemble style which, besides his heavy organ-playing, features a drum set and violin.

Club life was one of the main features of taarab from its beginnings. In Kenya most clubs have faded away, like Mombasa's **Jauharah Orchestra**, a big orchestra similar to the big ones of Zanzibar today. Club life seems to be still intact in **Zanzibar**, however. Besides the big orchestras, **Ikhwani Safaa** and **Culture**, which are organized along club lines, but which are also linked to official organizations like the ruling party and the Ministry of Culture, a number of smaller clubs have flourished for decades. Two of the best known are **Sahib El-Ahri**, which features the doyenne of Zanzibar taarab, **Bi Kidude**, and **Royal Air Force**, which incorporates elements of various ngoma, parades, theatricals, and long raps into a rather iconoclastic taarab style.

Until the early 1960s and the advent of the **Black Star Musical Club, Tanga** town, on the northern Tanzanian coast, had little influence on the taarab scene. Taarab was also a music almost exclusively enjoyed by the Islamic Swahili proper – people who claimed long Swahili ancestry and often overseas origins. With their new style, introducing elements of dance music, local ngoma, and instruments like guitar and bass guitar, the Tanga groups revolutionized taarab, crossing national boundaries and winning new audiences as far away as Burundi and Zaire. Today most of the taarab groups active in Tanzania as well as in Burundi and Kenya are modelled on the style and instrumentation of the **Black Star Musical Club**, its offspring **Lucky Star** and their star female singer **Shakila**. A new voice has recently emerged out of Tanga – that of **Mwanahela**, whose clear, powerful tones are close

to Shakila's. Together with her group **Golden Star**, Mwanahala has become one of the favourites on the Mombasa cassette market. Golden Star's hit "Vidonge" was copied by taarab goups up and down the coast (including Malika) and was even covered by Zairean/Kenyan Samba Mapangala and his Orchestra Virunga.

As with Tanzania's dance band scene so the taarab scene focuses increasingly on **Dar Es Salaam**. Dar has had small taarab clubs since early this century. But the big revival came in the 1930s with the foundation of the **Egyptian** and **Al-Watan Musical Clubs**, which soon grew to the size of today's orchestras. Both clubs are still going strong, but are outshone by various state-run taarab orchestras. The most prominent of these is **JKT Taarab** – the biggest taarab orchestra in East Africa: JKT stands for Jeshi la Kujenga Taifa, the "Army for the Construction of the Nation" (the compulsory national youth service). In contrast to the rather restrained Zanzibar style, JKT creates a lot of rhythmic excitement, and performances usually wind up with most of the women in the audience dancing the chakacha. Led by violinist and singer **Issa Matona**, the band features many fine female vocalists. Recently **Shakila**, of Black Star and Lucky Star fame, joined them as a featured voice. JKT's rhythm section is outstanding in that it features a twin double bass/bass guitar team. Most of the other bands active in Dar Es Salaam today are modelled along the lines of the Tanga bands, with guitar, bass guitar and keyboard or accordion. **Bima Taarab, Muungano Taarab** and **All Stars Modern Taarab** are some of the busier Dar groups.

In 1993 the formation of a new taarab orchestra by the name of **TOT** (Tanzania One Theatre) created quite a stir on the Tanzanian scene. At the moment the interest of the public and the media for this group even outshines that for dance music. TOT is the flashiest taarab ever heard in East Africa, featuring lots of synthesizers and a hot rhythm team including two bass guitars. But it is not really the instrumentation that creates all that excitement, but the sometimes offensive song lyrics. When one of their featured singers, Hadija Kopa, crossed over to Muungano Taarab this resulted in a heated song exchange between the two groups.

Many Tanga musicians have moved to Dar, like Asmahan who is now a member of **Bima**, and Mohamed Mrisho who sings with **Muungano**. Dar Es Salaam's taarab groups, besides playing the usual wedding gigs, play the regular Dar performing circuit, in dance and entertainment halls, throughout the week, and most prominently on Saturday afternoons. As taarab is otherwise almost exclusively performed privately, and public performances are limited to the big Islamic and state holidays, the dance-hall concerts are the only way for most visitors to enjoy live taarab. From an atmospheric point of view these dancehall shows are way superior to the tourist hotel gigs on the beaches north and south of Mombasa. In Zanzibar the Bwawani Hotel usually features taarab performances, including invitees like **Malika** or **Zuhura Swaleh**, on public holidays.

TAARAB AND THE MUSIC INDUSTRY

From 1928 to 1931 all the major record companies, including HMV and Columbia, recorded taarab. While brisk business was done in those days, in postwar years the activities were left to local, mostly Asian-owned music stores. The Mombasa-based **Mzuri label** recorded and released hundreds of taarab records from the 1950s to the mid-1970s, and scored a big hit with Tanga taarab. Mzuri regularly featured Mombasa taarab by the likes of Bhalo, Maulidi, Zein and Zuhura. Meanwhile the industry has completely shifted to cassettes and the big dubbing centres in the Old Town quarters of Mombasa and Zanzibar do good business. In Zanzibar they usually bid for the right to record performances where new songs are played for the first time, thus keeping up with demand for the latest songs.

TAARAB LYRICS

· ·

Taarab songs form part of the long tradition of Swahili poetry: a song's excellence is judged by the selection of words and on adherence to the rules of metre and rhyme in the lyric. Contrary to the songs sung at ngoma or in dance music, the story of a taarab song is of minor importance.

Taarab's main themes are love and sexual relationships. But there are also songs that deal with social or political issues. Taarab songs use a language of metaphor and allegory that only those familiar with Swahili poetry can understand. The lyrics are pregnant with hidden meanings and double entendres and they may relate to people or events only known to the writer. A lyric which an outsider takes to be a simple love song may in reality comment on a happening in the local community or concern national politics. This allegorical nature of taarab poetry makes it a perfect tool for social criticism. There have been some good examples of this in recent hits. The first is "Kitanda" (The Bed) by **Shakila and JKT Taarab**:

> You elders explain to me, so that my head
> may get rest,
> (Even you men of God, may you open your
> books);
> The bed always to be in a corner, is it a
> custom or law?
>
> I have travelled all over the country, and from
> Europe to Asia;
> I have gone into the houses, looking carefully
> for the beds;
> The bed was in the corner wherever I went in.

In an allegorical way, the song asks why, throughout the world, love is something to be hidden, relegated to the corner of society. This is the song's first meaning, and the one that made it so popular. But some have given it a political gloss: the Tanzanian president Ali Hassan Mwinyi repeatedly quoted from the song in connection with the transition to a multiparty democracy: in modern society, the value of cherished customs is always open to question and the one-party system – the basis of modern Tanzania – should not be taken for granted.

The life of the Swahili is closely related to the sea, so maritime images often appear in poetry and songs, as in the story-line of "Manahodha" (The Captains) by **Malika**:

> I encountered something amazing, a war on
> the sea,
> A shoving and pushing has ocurred, and me
> I'm in the boat,
> The captains have a war, they fight for the
> rudder.
>
> They show strength to each other, the fighting
> captains,
> And their rudder is rotten, and they have
> already cut the sail,
> But with all their might, they are fighting
> the wheel.
>
> Me I leave the sea, I cannot stand their fighting,
> Whenever I think I can see their end,
> It will be that the nails will come to be far
> from the boards.

The story is not about two real captains fighting over the course of a boat, but really, as Malika explains, about the "captains of the house" – two women fighting over rights in a polygamous household and over the best of their husband.

DISCOGRAPHY

Black and Lucky Star Musical Clubs *Nyota: Classic Taarab from Tanga* (GlobeStyle, UK). The all-time greatest taarab recordings – originally on Mzuri singles in the early 1970s – you can't fail to fall in love with this sound: voices of Sharmila, Shakila and Asmahan, nice guitar work and wonderful bass.

Culture Musical Club *Taarab 4: the Music of Zanzibar* (GlobeStyle, UK). Typical orchestral taarab from one of the leading Zanzibar clubs, featuring Bakari Abeid's classic "Sabalkheri Mpenzi" and the fine chakacha of "Mwiko".

Golden Star *Cassette No. 5* (Mbwana Radio Service, Mombasa, Kenya). Mwanahela is the new voice from Tanga, hailed as a likely successor to Shakila and Sharmila. Great tunes, great voice, and that fat Tanga bass. Available in most cassette stores along the coast.

Ikhwani Safaa Musical Club *Taarab 2: the Music of Zanzibar* (GlobeStyle, UK). Orchestral taarab from the island's oldest club, featuring the voices of Rukia Ramadhan, Mohamed Ilyas and Seif Saleh. The latter's "Nipepee" is a highlight.

JKT Taarab *Cassette No. 2* (Mbwana Radio Service, Mombasa, Kenya). Includes Shakila's big hit "Kitanda", the popular "Nahodha", and some of Issa Matona's favourites. Orchestral taarab with a punch. Locally available cassette.

Malika *Cassette No. 8* (Mbwana Radio Service, Mombasa). Malika is one of the best-loved taarab singers. Her voice was better on some of the older recordings, but this one has her version of the smash hits "Vidonge" and "Sitaki sitaki" to recommend it. Again, widely available locally.

Issa Matona *Kimasomaso* (Tanzania Film Company, Tanzania). Recorded live at a Dar Es Salaam wedding, this is very strong on atmosphere with lots of audience interaction. "Kimasomaso" is a half-hour rap on marriage, wifely duties and the pleasures of love. Cassette copies are available in Dar, though the record is out of print. But buyers beware: vendors call almost all Matona's cassettes "Kimasomaso".

ⓒ **Maulidi Musical Party** *Mombasa Wedding Special* (GlobeStyle, UK). Mombasa's premier musical party with a selection of songs from their Swahili-wedding repertoire. Favourites are "Mume ni Moshi wa koko" and the mwanzele dance "Mkufu" featuring the organ-cum-nzumari (oboe) playing of Adio Shigoo.

Muungano Taarab *Limbukeni* (Mamu Stores, Tanzania). New-style taarab from Dar Es Salaam featuring the most talked-about singer, Hadija Kopa. Locally available cassette.

TOT Taarab *Cassette Vol. 5 and Vol. 7* (Space Recording, Tanzania). Rhythmically infectious hi-tech taarab featuring two bass guitars and lots of synthesizer. A fashionable style from Dar with lots of tough lyrics, including "Ameumbuka", a song attacking ex-lead-singer Hadija Kopa, now with Muungano.

ⓒ **Zein Musical Party** *Mtindo wa Mombasa: the Style of Mombasa* (GlobeStyle, UK). Some great tunes from this often overlooked master of the oud. A personal favourite on this CD is the tour-de-force on "Wanawake wa Kiamu"; just oud, dumbak and vocals.

ⓒ **Zuhura and Party** *Jino la Pembe* (GlobeStyle, UK). A compendium of Zuhura's most popular chakacha songs, most notably "Parare" and the title tune "Jino la Pembe". Recorded on her European tour with the Maulidi Musical Party, this is one of the best introductions to taarab music.

Zuhura and Party *Singe Tema* (Polygram, Kenya). Early 1980s recording of this great voice, with taishokoto and nicely distorted organ. Out-of-print, but watch out for cassette copies eventually becoming available on the Kenyan market.

MARASHI YA DAR ES SALAAM

DANCE WITH STYLE: THE FLAVOUR OF DAR ES SALAAM

"A bicycle has no say in front of a motorbike / A motorbike has no say in front of a car / A motorcar has no say in front of a train." The lyrics of Remmy Ongala - "The Doctor" - have always been trenchant. Werner Graeber stays up late in Dar to listen and learn.

Open Uhuru, the Swahili daily newspaper of **Dar Es Salaam**, and you'll find several pages of advertisements for live music. A dozen or more ads bill the big names – DDC Mlimani Park, International Safari Sound, Juwata, Maquis Original, Super Matimila and Vijana Jazz; add to this list the lesser names and the various groups combining ngoma, taarab and theatre and you've got a live music scene hardly equalled anywhere else in Africa.

But Dar city centre is dead. Almost all the live music bars and dancehalls are located in the suburbs, anything up to twenty kilometres from town. Throughout the week the orchestras rotate through the different districts. Transport is difficult, especially at night, and this arrangement gives everybody a chance to have their favourite band within walking distance once a week, or at least every couple of weeks. On Saturday nights and Sunday afternoons the bands play their home base.

Performances usually warm up from around 10pm. The band starts out on an instrumental or two, then moves into old favourites as the place slowly fills. Meanwhile, spare musicians circulate around the hall greeting friends or organizing drinks for the hours to come. Only once the full band is on stage to perform the more recent songs does the floor fill with dancers. Songs then segue into each other almost without interruption, as musicians who have paused mid-song smoothly take over the instruments from their colleagues. And as the night heats up, the songs get longer while the *chemko* – the fast second part of each song featuring the tight interplay of three or four guitars plus occasional riffs, and question and answer games by the horns – comes to a boil. By midnight the band will be in full swing, revving in top gear to deliver their best for a good three hours more. Most bands have a team of between twenty and thirty musicians, of whom maybe fifteen will be on stage at any one time. The basic line-up is three guitars, bass guitar, drum set, tumba, two or three trumpets, two or three saxophones and three to five singers. The extra members allow the bands to play at least five days a week for up to six hours – an energetic schedule by any standards.

TANZANIAN NEW WAVE

* *

Mchiriku is back in Tanzania – official. A variant of the popular Swahili chakacha style, *mchiriku* was first heard in the 1970s before being banned by the government for its lewd lyrics and erotic dance style. Twenty years on, it has resurfaced as the cult music of the young generation in the Tanga-Mombasa area. Denied access to imported instruments, the new mchiriku groups make do with three or four local drums, a tambourine and a cheap Casio keyboard. The bands, usually featuring seven or eight teenagers (sometimes even younger kids) produce a steady rhythmic backdrop of drums punctuated by wild raucous Swahili vocals and swooping keyboards in a style not entirely unlike that of the legendary Swede Swede from Kinshasa and probably fuelled by some of the same frustrations and pent-up musical talent. Dozens of these mchiriku groups now exist, working under names such as Night Star Musical Club, New Fadhila Musical Club and Hisani Musical Club. They may not represent the last word in musical sophistication but mchiriku looks like it's here to stay. It is sufficiently popular to have recorded cassettes for the local market and may even lay the basis for a distinctly Tanzanian sound.

Ronnie Graham

PUBLIC AND PRIVATE

Opportunities to perform in Dar are not lacking, but Tanzanian musicians have much to grumble about. The industry in Tanzania tends to keep personal ambitions in check and has done so since the wholesale nationalization of the economy in the early 1960s. The privately run music and dance clubs that dominated the scene after World War II became obsolete within a few years of independence in 1961. With the restructuring of the economy, most Tanzanian bands operated under the umbrella of state organizations, a common system even today. The organization owns the instruments and employs the musicians, who draw more or less regular salaries plus some percentage of the gate. The wage system for musicians doesn't favour stardom or easy money but it has its advantages. At least it offers a kind of security and, considering the situation in neighbouring countries, like Kenya where musicians barely manage to make a living, the Tanzanian dance band scene is a healthy one.

Today almost all bands work along these lines, even privately owned orchestras like Maquis or International Orchestra Safari Sound. Although band members' income is high above the Tanzanian average, they all aspire to the status of those few African musicians who have made it internationally by selling recordings rather than endless live shows. After ten or twenty years of bashing from one performance to another over pot-holed roads, most of their sound equipment and instruments are close to ruin.

At the root of the music industry's problems in Tanzania is the lack of proper **recording facilities**. For a long time now, Radio Tanzania Dar Es Salaam (RTD) has had the only working recording facilities in the country. The radio gets music for its programmes at a negligible sum and the bands get publicity for their live performances. The direct financial gain may be low but the role of Radio Tanzania in fostering the local music scene cannot be overemphasized. Since the late 1960s the radio has consistently sponsored and exclusively featured Tanzanian bands on its Swahili programmes, contributing to the development of a specific Tanzanian musical style. On the other hand the quasi-monopoly of the radio also poses its problems. The officials' main interest is with "clean" songs and didactic works in support of government policies. There are accusations of censorship, but the radio songs can often be surprisingly frank.

The big problem for Tanzanian music is copyright. Tanzania has not signed any of the international copyright conventions and songs recorded for Radio Tanzania, are regularly pirated across the border in Kenya: the musicians hardly see a shilling. Piracy is also rife at home, with so-called "recording houses" doing brisk business: bring in your blank cassette and for 200 Tanzanian shillings (about 30p or 50¢) you can walk away with the latest hits.

TUMULTUOUS CLIMAXES

Ever since their formation in 1978 **Orchestra Mlimani Park** have been Tanzania's most popular band, easily verified by their audience turnouts and the amount of radio play they get. Mlimani have cooed their way into the hearts of Tanzanians with an endless string of hits sung and composed by the likes of Hassani Bitchuka, Cosmas Tobias and Max Bushoke. In Tanzania the first and foremost way of appreciating a song is through its lyrics. Mlimani are famous for their themes and the intricate poetry delivered by their lead singers. Today, Hassani Bitchuka is Tanzania's top songwriter and singer, compared with the first star of Tanzanian pop music, **Salum Abdallah**, active in the 1950s and early '60s, and the late **Mbaraka Mwinshehe**, the most popular musician in East Africa in the 1970s.

Good, topical lyrics are a general feature of Tanzanian music, however, and it is really Mlimani's instrumental sounds – the interplay of the guitars and the finely honed horn arrangements – that are their trademark, qualifying them as one of Africa's outstanding bands. Though composition and arrangement are usually group processes in Tanzanian dance music, the final authority in Mlimani is "King" **Michael Enoch**, whose knowledge and experience is the force behind the development of the distinct Mlimani sound. Enoch has been a legend since he joined the **Dar Es Salaam Jazz Band** in 1960 as a solo guitarist. He soon became the bandleader and developed into one of Tanzania's leading solo players and composers, a multi-instrumentalist who has taught many Tanzanian musicians including the late Mbaraka Mwinshehe.

Mlimani's performances are tumultuous affairs, with dancers going wild and the audience all over the stage slapping appreciative tuzo (tips, banknotes) onto the musicians' heads. The performance reaches its peak as the solo guitar, second solo and rhythm guitars work into each other in the chemko climax section, while the young bass player Abdallah Ramadhani "DogoDogo" adds yet more rhythmic excitement for the dancers to follow.

NO SWEAT

Compared to Mlimani, performances of **Orchestra Maquis Original** are genteel affairs. Their image, ever since they popularized their

THE MOROGORO JAZZ BAND

························

Formed in 1944, Morogoro was one of the first jazz bands in what was then Tanganyika (a break-off group, the **Cuban Marimba Band** led by Salum Abdallah, was one of East Africa's most popular bands in the 1950s and early '60s). At the time this photo was taken, the young Mbaraka Mwinshehe had recently joined. He became one of the region's outstanding guitarists, singers and composers and his songs ruled the airwaves until his death in a car crash in 1979. His last song, "Shida" (Trouble), was the biggest-ever-selling record in East Africa.

Kulwa Salum is still active in the 1990s, back on stage again after nearly seventeen years, fronting the veteran's outfit **Shikamoo**, sometimes alongside Juma Kalaza who took over the reins at Cuban Marimba following the death of Salum Abdallah in 1964.

The picture below shows the band in 1968 (right to left), Kulwa Salum (sax, vocals, bandleader), Choka Mzee (drums), Mbaraka Mwinshehe (solo guitar, vocals), Peter (bass), Issa Khalfani (rhythm guitar, 2nd solo), Shaban Nyamwela (vocals, bass), Rajab Bilali (bongos) and Abdallah Hassani (maracas).

Kamanyola bila jasho – "dance Kamanyola without sweating" – style in the late 1970s, has been laid-back and easy-going. Originally from the Lubumbashi area of southeastern Zaire, Maquis' founder members settled in Dar in the early 1970s. It is quite common for musicians from that area to tour East Africa: Nairobi's recording studios have always attracted numerous musicians from Zaire. Yet in Tanzania foreign musicians are a lot more integrated into the local scene and they usually sing their songs in Swahili. For an outsider, Orchestra Maquis' style (especially their vocal harmonies) may sometimes sound close to Kinshasa soukous. But it's really the other way round: even their Lingala numbers show Maquis' roots in a specifically East African music culture. Before the advent of colonialism, and even to this day, the eastern parts of Zaire have always had closer cultural and economic ties to East Africa than to the Congo basin.

Maquis have always managed to cause a stir with each new dance style (*mtindo*) they invent: one of their latest, *zembwela*, introduced through their 1985 hit "Karubandika", has been so pervasive that the name is still commonly used as a synonym for dancing per se. Orchestra Maquis' latest mtindo is called *sendema*, featuring guitar prodigy Dekula Kahanga (known as "Vumbi" – Dust – after his high-pitched guitar licks). Vumbi was the outstanding discovery of the late 1980s dance scene. Maquis' second featured member throughout the decade was singer Tshimanga Assosa (he sang "Mambo Bado" on Orchestra Makassy's "Agwaya" release for Virgin). He composed and sang most of their recent favourites including "Ngalula", which won Maquis the first prize in the 1990 national band contest.

BRASSY VETERANS

What is most remarkable about Tanzanian bands is their collective strength. Musicians come and go all the time, yet the band's musical character remains recognizably the same. The **Juwata Jazz Band**, for example, formed in 1965 under the wings of the National Union of Tanzania (hence their original acronymic Nuta Jazz Band), is the oldest band in the country and provided the model for many of the groups that emerged in the 1970s and 1980s. A number of prominent band members – Muhiddin Maalim, Abel Balthazar and Hassani Bitchuka among them – left the Nuta Jazz Band to form Dar International and later Mlimani Park Orchestra, and the original name Nuta Jazz was changed to Juwata Jazz Band in 1977 to mark a new beginning (Juwata is the Swahili equivalent of Nuta). The musical style of Juwata is mainstream Tanzanian, with their brassy horn section sometimes evoking the times when Cuban records, distributed on HMV's "GV" label, were the rage all over Africa. Recently they acquired a new set of instruments and PA equipment and signed contracts to welcome back singing stars Hassani Bitchuka and Muhiddin Maalim. As it completes its third decade the band is stronger than ever and there is no doubt that Juwata will be a force to reckon with as one of the top Tanzanian bands of the 1990s.

A band similar in outline and organization to Juwata Jazz and Mlimani Park, though with a slightly different sound, is **Vijana Jazz**, the band of the youth organization of the ruling party CCM (Chama cha Mapinduzi). Long one of the country's most consistent bands, with a large following, they have lost some of their focus since the death in 1990 of their bandleader of more than a decade, Hemedi Maneti. Vijana was the first band to get foreign exchange clearance to buy new equipment in 1987, hence they differ somewhat from the norm in having the sounds of synthesizer and electronic drums added to the standard guitar, trumpet and sax line-up.

The strongest band to emerge on the Tanzanian scene in the last decade is the **Tancut Alimasi Orchestra**, the band of the national diamond mining company. Their fans also call them "Mabush Stars" because they are based in the town of Iringa deep in the interior, literally in the "bush", and in the wastelands of the Tanzanian music business. Despite this, with their new instruments and good rates of pay, the band has been able to lure several leading musicians away from Dar, among them the twins Kasaloo Kyanga and Kyanga Songa, former stars on the Maquis vocal line-up. Not surprisingly, Tancut's sound can get close to that of Maquis, yet they inject local colour by basing some songs on local Iringa rhythms and melodies.

REMMY'S WORLD OF MUSIC

One of Tanzania's most enduring musicians is **Remmy Ongala** (see box). Born in the Kivu region of Eastern Zaire, Remmy Ongala came to Dar Es Salaam in 1978 to join **Orchestra Makassy** – his Uncle Makassy's band. When Makassy disbanded his Dar-based orchestra and moved to Nairobi in the early 1980s (there's more about their time in Nairobi and the various recordings they made in the Kenya section), Remmy Ongala joined Orchestra Matimila. He soon became the bandleader and his personality

and the punch and outspokenness of his lyrics quickly became the band's most magnetic appeal.

Unfortunately, the local reputation of Remmy's band, now **Super Matimila**, suffered from their WOMAD tours and Remmy's long absences from Dar Es Salaam. While the tours and recordings have helped to buy much-needed equipment, and to make Remmy for the first time independent of a band-owner, the demands of touring, having only a few and less prominent musicians, and Womad's insistence on a more mainstream Zairean sound, have destroyed the original line-up of the band. The Remmy magic – his compositions and stage presence – is still there but aside from solo guitarist Osenga Batii, none of the other band members has the ability to sustain a five- to six-hour performance. Yet changes and improvements are on the way. After experiments with a second lead singer (Cosmas Tobias of Mlimani fame), Remmy recently re-formed his whole band. A featured member of the new line-up is bass player Banza Mchafu, formerly one of the pillars of Orchestra Maquis. And some of Remmy's new lyrics have stirred considerable interest.

MTINDO: DANCE WITH STYLE
••••••••••••••••••••••••

Let's move ahead – Sendema
Now go backwards – Sendema
Left and right – Sendema

"**S**endema is a dance. We musicians dance it, and our fans may follow the way we dance on stage. We have taken it from one of the ngoma that was danced here in Tanzania in the past: it used to be danced with bells on your ankles, you had a bare chest and you were balancing a kind of spear – dancing back and forth, left and right. We are not strictly imitating, we just try to project an image. It is something we invented and even most of the dancers need not strictly follow what we do. Still they like it, sendema."

Kaumba Kalemba, Orchestra Maquis Original

In Dar Es Salaam every band has its own mtindo or style, a trademark that describes the music and characteristic performance of a band, as well as the dance associated with it. The mtindo is really a kind of nickname for the band used by fans to express their affection for that type of music. In

everyday speech, the names of the various mitin-do (the plural) are used as synonyms for dancing.

Many mitindo refer to the musical traditions of Tanzania. Mlimani Park's *sikinde* or IOSS's *ndekule*, for example, take their name and inspiration from the ngoma (song-and-dance events accompanied by drums) of the Zaramo people who come from the Dar Es Salaam area. Juwata Jazz Band's *msondo* is the name of a particular drum as well as of a dance. Some mitindo are descriptive of a certain way of dancing – like Maquis' mtindo of the early 1980s, *ogelea piga mbizi*, which describes the swimming and diving motions which were a feature of the dance – while others refer to the lyrics or contain non-musical references.

Some of the bands, Mlimani for example, stick to their mtindo over extended periods of time; in fact the catch-phrase *ngoma ya ukae*, as featured in the band's emblem, means "the ngoma you'll stay with". Other bands change it every so often, to mark a new beginning after a change in personnel, or just to create new excitement with their followers.

THE ROOTS OF MUSIC

....

Tanzanian songs tend to be long and in some cases would run to several pages if transcribed. Much of the highly valued poetic quality of the songs, including the word play and allusions to which Swahili lends itself so remarkably, gets lost in translation, but the following excerpts from the songs of **Remmy Ongala** convey a general impression. His songs, with their strong social themes, are an easy universe to enter.

In "Asili ya Muziki" (The Roots of Music) Ongala sings about the ambiguous position of musicians – the tension between the musician as champion and outcast.

> Where are the roots of music?
> Whose is the music?
> Music has no owner
> Music is a calling
> Music is learning
> Music is prayer and mourning
> You won't see me sing when I am happy
> I sing when I have sorrow in my heart.

Musicians tend to be considered vagabonds, alcoholics and drug addicts. Yet their music and particularly their songs are liked by many people. The government and official media place a high educative value on song lyrics. This is how the song concludes:

> Musicians are not bandits
> Or, if we are – why do you buy cassettes?
> If we're vagabonds – why do you request songs on the radio?
> If we're crooks – why do you buy records?
> If we're outcasts – why do you dance to the music?

Remmy Ongala's fans hanging on his every word

In many of his songs Remmy Ongala takes the position of a spokesman for the urban poor, describing himself as *mnyonge* (humble, debased person) or *sura mbaya* (ugly-face), as in the song "Mnyonge hana haki" (The poor person has no rights):

> A bicycle has no say in front of a motorbike
> A motorbike has no say in front of a car
> A motorcar has no say in front of a train
> The poor person has no rights
> I am poor, I have no right to speak
> Poor and weak before the powerful
> Weak as long as the powerful likes.

This sounds like a hymn to fatalism, but possibilities for action and change are already apparent in the imagery and rhetoric in the original Swahili. The following excerpt from "Dunia" (This World) gets right to the point:

> It is not the world as such that's bad
> Its inhabitants are the bad ones
> It's the people who don't listen to each other
> It's the people who don't like each other
> The earth's inhabitants are no good, I am sad, oh this world
> Today you beat me, tomorrow you'll be beaten
> When you insult me, you too will be insulted.

Not all Remmy Ongala's songs are as pessimistic. There's room for anecdotes and songs about particular people – "sugar daddies", mothers and girlfriends. He gets most poetic in his love songs, though Tanzanian songs in general seldom wallow in the theme of unrequited love so dear to western pop:

> The one who loves will eat raw food
> Will neither hear nor see
> Love doesn't distinguish between insects and animals
> Even fish reproduce
> Love does not discriminate.

There's also a new turn, in relation to gender, money and AIDS, which Ongala took up most recently in the mammoth rap "Mambo kwa soksi", a short course on the use of condoms. The song, which alarmed some people with the frankness of the debate, warns against the delusion that Aids can only affect others, the "beautiful ones":

> We "bad ones" strut proudly these days, thinking we don't have AIDS

MUSICIANS ON THE MOVE

While it's their collective image and the resulting fantastic dance entertainment that count most, all the Tanzanian bands feature fine individual musicians who have their own followings. The conflicts arising from individualism and personal expression are rife in a musical culture where the average outfit has twenty or more members. People are forever moving between bands in search of greener pastures.

These moves occasionally generate quite chaotic conditions and disturb a delicate balance. A classic example happened in 1985 when businessman Hugo Kisima disbanded Orchestra Safari Sound (OSS) and lured away six of Orchestra Mlimani Park's leading musicians to form the new **International Orchestra Safari Sound** (IOSS). The reshuffle left the former OSS leader, twelve-string stylist Ndala Kasheba, without a band to lead and Ochestra Mlimani Park in serious trouble.

For a time IOSS, led by former Mlimani singer Muhiddin Maalim and guitarist Abel Balthazar, were contenders for their old band's position as number-one outfit. Since then, many musicians (Maalim and Hassani Bitchuka among them), have rejoined their former bands; and other musicians have left to join the newly established bands made possible after the mid-1980s economic liberalization programme which allows musical instruments to be privately imported. Within the last two years Safari Sound have been through a series of less successful editions. The situation changed when **Nguza Viking**, solo guitarist extraordinaire and former leader of Maquis, was offered the job of leading Safari Sound. The band came back to high acclaim with a new mtindo called "Rashikanda Wasaa":

meaning enjoy the freedom of Rashikanda (a ngoma from Nguza's home town in eastern Zaire). And then Nguza landed an instant hit with "Mageuzi" (Changes), a song on the political changes underway in Tanzania – the transition to a multiparty system. In spring 1992, inexplicably, the owner of the instruments disbanded the orchestra yet again.

A number of former IOSS musicians followed erstwhile bandleader Abel Balthazar and joined the newly formed Magereza Jazz. Some others are still with Nguza and a new band called Achigo Stars. Another new band which has attracted attention in Dar music circles is MCA

Hukwe Zawose of the National Musical Ensemble, with thumb piano

International, currently featuring top composer-singers Zahir Ally and Cosmas Tobias. A number of new bands have cropped up in the last few years, but few survive the competition with the big names in the long run. The year 1993 also saw the formation of two temporary All-Star groups which have performed on special occasions: One, **Shikamoo**, is an oldie band uniting some of the leading musicians of days gone by like Salum Zahoro and Juma Mrisho (see box on p.357). The other, Stua, is a celebratory band of musicians of Zairean origin, performing old songs from the Maquis and OSS repertoires.

DISCOGRAPHY

Tanzania has no record industry and those recordings available in the so-called "recording houses" in Dar, or pirated for the Kenyan market, are all tapes from Radio Tanzania. Most cassettes are terrible quality – but fear not, the music still kicks. Look out for the Kenyan Ahadi label. They have about 50 cassettes of Tanzanian dance band material, from the latest Radio Tanzania recordings to oldies. The quality is often very poor, so check before you buy. Polygram Nairobi has also re-released cassette compilations of Tanzanian songs from the late 1960s and '70s.

ARTISTS AND BANDS

⓪ **Mlimani Park Orchestra** *Sikinde* (Africassette, US). Mlimani Park is the greatest Tanzanian dance band and these are some of their best tunes. Enjoy the voices of Cosmas Tobias and Hassani Bitchuka, Michael Enoch's horn arrangements, and the skills of recording engineer James Mhilu. More Mlimani goodies from the mid-1980s can be found on the Kenyan LP-release of Radio Tanzania material, *Best of…Vol. I, Vol .2* (Ahadi, Kenya). If it's out of print, local cassettes should still be available.

Orchestra Makassy *Agwaya* (Virgin, UK). Absolutely perfect, and difficult to find, this was one of the best European releases of African music in the early 1980s – a sweet record by the Nairobi-based Tanzanian outfit, long overdue for re-release.

Orchestra Maquis Original *Karubandika* (Ahadi, Kenya). One of Dar's leading bands in recordings from the early 1980s, featuring lavish horns, the voices of Kasaloo Kyanga and Kyanga Songa, and Nguza Viking's outstanding solo guitar. It's out-of-print, but cassette copies should still be available. *Sendema ya Moto* (Maquis Original, Kenya) is a locally available cassette – a recent Maquis recording featuring Tshimanga Assosa on all songs and including a remake of his mid-1980s hit "Uba".

Mbaraka Mwinshehe Mwaruka *Ukumbusho Vol. I, Vol. 3*, and *Pesa No.I* (Polygram, Kenya). Mbaraka Mwinshehe (with either Morogoro Jazz or Super Volcanoes) ruled the East African music scene in the 1970s, recording many songs which are constantly being re-released. About ten cassettes of these Ukumbusho (Remembrances) are available at the moment. *Pesa No.I* and *Vol. 3* feature some of the nice early 1970s recordings with the typical Morogoro Jazz horn sound. *Vol.I* has Mwinshehe's voice at its best on the 1979 hit "Shida" (Trouble), posthumously released, and the biggest-ever seller on the East African market.

Nuta Jazz Band *Old is Gold* (Polygram, Kenya). Early 1970s recording of this longest-surviving Tanzanian band, with early samples of Muhiddin's voice and the typical Nuta/Juwata horn sound.

⓪ **Remmy Ongala** *Songs for the Poor Man* (Real World, UK). Features the hard drive of "Kipenda Roho" and Remmy's own all-time favourite "Mariamu Wangu", which is based on the popular mdunkiko ngoma from Dar Es Salaam. ⓪ *Mambo* (Real World, UK) is not as highly recommended, but features a studio version of the political rap "Mrema" and the voice of former Mlimani singing star Cosmas Tobias**.**

Vijana Jazz Band *Usichezee Bahari* (Remanco, Kenya). An LP release (the cassette has two extra songs) of Vijana hits recorded in Nairobi. This one stands for the new sound in Tanzanian music with lots of electronic drums and synthesizer. Their latest cassette, "Kumbu Kumbu ya Marehemu Maneti", is a compilation of classic Vijana tracks dedicated to the late Hemedi Maneti and featuring such classics as "Mary Maria", "Vicky" and "Ngoma".

⓪ **Hukwe Zawose/Master Musicians of Tanzania** *Tanzania Yetu and Mateso* (Triple Earth, UK) and *The Art of Hukwe Zawose* (JVC/Victor, Japan). This is Tanzania's National Music Ensemble. They combine songs and instruments of the various ethnic groups with (mostly) Swahili political lyrics, which makes it kind of a "national folklore". Recommended for the giant thumb-piano sound of Hukwe Zawose.

COMPILATIONS

⓪ **Various Artists** *Tanzania Dance Bands Volume 2* (Line-Monsun, Germany). Includes highlights from the Orchestra Maquis repertoire – Tshimanga Assosa's "Ngalula", and old favourites "Mabruki" and "Mpenzi Luta" – plus Juwata Jazz's brass sound, notably the killer bass on "Tupa Tupa", and selections from International Orchestra Safari Sound featuring the voices of old master Muhiddin Maalim and Hassani Bitchuka, especially "Homa imenizidia" – "This fever is too much for me".

⓪ **Various Artists** *The Tanzania Sound* (Original Music, US). The 1960s sound of Tanzania, originally released as singles in East Africa, here pirated for an international public. Recommended, despite the tracks' status, because of the good moments from Salum Abdallah circa 1964 and various favourites from the Western, Dar Es Salaam and Kilwa "Jazz Bands".

MAD ABOUT MADAGASCAR

INDIAN OCEAN MUSIC FROM SOUTHEAST AFRICA

When the island of Madagascar broke away from East Africa many millions of years ago to exist in relative isolation in the Indian Ocean, it prepared the way not only for separate evolution of its unique fauna and flora, but eventually for a distinct cultural development as well. Just as the geography of this huge "island continent" (it's 1600km long, two-and-a-half times the area of Britain, half as big again as California) can vary from rain forest to cactus desert, from high, barren, mountains to palm-fringed beaches, so the culture is multifaceted with around 18 distinct tribes. The music sounds like everywhere and nowhere else at the same time, and Ian Anderson ("I could have sworn I'd been kidnapped by Hawaiians") is rather attached to it.

Madagascar was happily free of humans until around the third century AD. The first inhabitants, the Vazimba, were of Malayo-Polynesian origin (as is the consonant-rich Malagasy language), arriving both directly across the Indian Ocean and via southeast Asia and East Africa: there are still some distant cultural connections with parts of Indonesia, like Sulawesi for example. Arabs and Swahili-speaking Africans later mixed with the population. The Portuguese were the first Europeans to arrive, followed later by British – mainly Welsh – missionaries and eventually the French as a colonizing power. Slaves were brought to Madagascar as well as being taken from there, especially to the sugar plantations of Mauritius but also to the Americas. Independence came in 1960, but after a military coup in the mid-1970s the country was run in almost complete isolation by the socialist government of President Ratsiraka until he was forced from office in 1992. It's only in the last four or five years that the country has opened up again to the west: many more imported goods are now coming into the shops, the capital Antananarivo (Tana) is clogged with traffic, and there are new radio stations, French satellite TV, and increasing numbers of tourists from Europe, America and South Africa. The first

elections under a new constitution in 1993 were won by the opposition. Allowing for the occasional drought or severe hurricane, prospects are perhaps as good as anywhere in nearby Africa.

Blind accordionist Martin Rakotoarimanana with offspring on shaker

Madagascar is an island of puzzles and surprises. Even around the capital, the varied landscape and architecture could convince you that you were in central Europe, or West Africa, or the high Andes, or maybe Asia with its terraced rice fields. You look at the people and they could possibly be Indonesian, or Asian, or African, or South American. Then you hear the music, which contains little clues, passing sounds, harmonies, riffs, playing styles and instruments that all seem to be related to other parts of the world. But it is audibly unique.

The proximity of East Africa – or East African airwaves – explains why there's a coastal style of electric guitar band dance music called *watcha watcha* that's a dead ringer for Kenyan benga.

TRADITIONAL INSTRUMENTS

....

Madagascar's most famous instrument is the *valiha*, a tubular zither made from bamboo with around 21 strings running lengthways all around the circumference, lifted and tuned by small, moveable pieces of bamboo or calabash. Traditionally the strings were strands of bamboo skin lifted from the surface, but nowadays they tend to be steel, giving a sound similar to a harp or the West African kora. Leading players include Sylvestre Randafison, an almost-classical virtuoso who once led a celebrated traditional music ensemble called Ny Antsaly, and dazzling younger musicians like Zeze (Ravelonandro – who, sadly, died in 1992), Tovo, Rajery and Paris-based Justin Rakotondrasoa (aka Justin Vali). Although it's typically a highland plateau instrument, nevertheless all over the island you will find remarkable traditional valiha players such as Mama Sana, an incredible septuagenarian singer from the west coast near Morondava who wears coins braided into her hair and attacks her instrument with the ferocity of a Mississippi blues guitarist.

Madagascar's other zither is the *marovany*, a suitcase-like wooden box with two sets of strings on opposing sides. One of the best players was the late, legendary Rakotozafy (the Robert Johnson of Madagascar) but once again it's a common traditional instrument, particularly in the south. Current virtuosos include Matrimbala, from the Antandroy tribe, now living in Antananarivo, and a woman player, Masy, who is based in Tulear in the southwest and, unusually, is exclusively a professional musician.

The traditional, end-blown flute is the *sodina*, and the undisputed master is Rakoto Frah. A charming old man with an impish twinkle in his eye, he has represented Madagascar all over the world and his picture appears on the F1,000 note, but he still lives in a tiny house in Isotry, the capital's poorest area.

The *kabosy* is a small guitar with four to six strings and partial frets. It's a relatively easily made instrument – the body is often just a slim, rectangular box and the strings unbraided bicycle brake cables – but it's played to a high standard. It's not uncommon to encounter small groups of boys on street corners in provincial towns playing with the drive of electric guitar bands, sometimes even including a larger, bass version. The best player is probably Jean Emilien.

The *jejy voatavo*, mostly used by the Betsileo tribe, has a large calabash resonator, a neck with huge block frets and two courses of strings on ninety-degree opposed sides. Its sound can be reminiscent of the Appalachian dulcimer, and a singer will sometimes add echo effects to his voice by directing it into the back of the calabash. The best known player is Zafy Lahy Edouard from Fianarantsoa.

Finally, the *lokanga* is a three-string fiddle, once again often with a simply made box-style body, played mainly by Bara and Antandroy tribes from the south.

"Tourist" instruments, especially valiha and jejy voatavo, are offered for sale in the markets, hotels and on the street. But if you're visiting Madagascar, and in the market for music, beware. They look pretty hanging on the wall but they are rarely very playable (and often harbour fearsome Malagasy woodworm). It's better to seek out and buy from a good musician or instrument-maker.

Imported instruments have also been adapted for local use. The accordion is found all over, if less so these days because of difficulties in getting spare parts for repairs. Martin Rakotoarimanana and his father, from a hereditarily blind family of accordion players, appear regularly at the beautiful old palace at Ambohimanga. The most famous young player, Regis, now works in Europe, recording with Manu Dibango and many others. The piano has also long been a favourite for accompanying choral singing, and guitars are found everywhere. Along with fiddle and accordion, brass and woodwind instruments are the characteristic sounds for the hiragasy, the popular mixture of street theatre, oration, opera and dance. The same brass players make the joyful noise for Madagascar's extraordinary *famadihana* or re-burial ceremonies.

Traditional flautist in the money

The racial origins of the Malagasy would certainly explain the almost Polynesian harmonies that are found in the music of the Merina, the highland people. I've sat on a car journey with a singing family and could have sworn I'd been kidnapped by a vehicle full of genial Hawaiians. And a lot more can be traced back to the slave trade, those Welsh missionaries and French colonialists. But that still doesn't explain why the musicians who accompany the travelling players called *hiragasy* – the most popular being the **Ramilison** troupe and **Sahondra Finina Zandriny** – so stunningly resemble Mexican street bands, or a myriad other connections to anywhere and everywhere. Has all the music in the world bumped into Madagascar at some time in history? Or did it all start here and wander off somewhere else? This is the island enigma.

ROSSY, RICKY, TOTY

The first major modern group in Madagascar were unquestionably **Mahaleo**. Emerging at a time of student unrest in the early 1970s, they fused western soft-rock with typical Malagasy harmonies, rhythms and traditional instruments like the *kabosy*. Combined with complex, meaningful lyrics addressing many aspects of the lives of Malagasy people, their music became enormously popular and their songs known by everybody. Though no longer a full-time band, they occasionally reform for big concerts and their leader, Dama, is still a strong musical force, though his music career is somewhat restricted by his election as a deputy in the new government. Mahaleo have a good "live" CD available in Europe, whilst Dama has a solo release.

Following Mahaleo's lead was the multi-instrumentalist Paul Bert Rahasimanana, otherwise known as **Rossy**, who formed the group that bears his nickname. They became the most successful band of the 1980s, touring in Europe, and evolved a dynamic, hi-tech stage act that mixed roots styles from the island's varied regions with the latest trends in the world's music. Rossy is very skilled at tailoring things to the audience – European pop, Johnny Clegg and zouk influences for the home crowd, where they have a following from all echelons of society, and conversely a more Malagasy roots repertoire abroad.

Tarika ("the group") began as the well-respected folk revival band called **Tarika**

Sammy, who mixed instruments and styles from other areas and tribes with the distinctive, melodic vocal harmonies of the Merina. Although selected for inclusion on a number of western compilations, real success eluded Tarika Sammy until 1992 when a new line-up considerably tightened and upped the musicality, energy and visual impact of their act. Their two subsequent albums were among Madagascar's most acclaimed musical exports. In 1994, the singer-writers **Hanitra** and **Noro** assembled fresh musicians for future touring and recording under the new, shorter name, while instrumentalist Sammy went on to follow other projects with a family band.

Rossy – modern and multi-talented

Jean Emilien, a Betsileo musician originally from Fianarantsoa, plays an amplified kabosy, blows harmonica on a rack, sings in a high, energetic voice and, in live performance, leaps around the stage in leather trousers. He started out playing covers of western music, but at some point in his travels around the island realized that he was in danger of losing his Malagasy musical roots and set about learning and modernizing the *vako-drazana*, the ancient traditional songs, and mixing them with dance music. So far he's only released three superb tracks on a compilation for Germany's Feuer & Eis label, and a very dodgy album for Mélodie in France that, sadly, can't be recommended because of poor production and a general out-of-tuneness.

D'Gary is a stunning guitarist from the Bara tribe, who has evolved a complex style based on the sound of the marovany. Easily rivalling other African acoustic guitar greats such as Ali Farka

FAMADIHANA: WAKEY-WAKEY!!

·······················

The Malagasy people give enormous respect to their ancestors, who are considered to exist still on a spiritual level. This is reflected in the huge amount of money that an extended family will invest in their tomb, sometimes a far more substantial dwelling than the house for the living, on the logical theory that the amount of time to be spent there will eventually be far greater than the insignificant period of passage through the mortal world. A man is traditionally entombed in the village from which he came, whilst a woman will be stashed with her in-laws.

Equally large amounts of money, sometimes stretching a family's resources to the limits, are spent on the traditional Malagasy famadihana or re-burial parties. These are not held at fixed intervals: perhaps a person may have expressed a wish as to frequency before their death, or a living relative may receive a hint from the ancestor that the tomb is cold and they need new clothes.

The event will last a whole day and involves much feasting, drinking, dancing and merry-making by the entire extended family and local village. Musicians, usually a hiragasy troupe playing instruments like trumpets, clarinets and drums that can be heard above a rowdy crowd outdoors, will be hired to play nonstop to drive the affair on. The party will process to the tomb, disinter the remains of the loved one, rewrap them in fresh cloth (traditionally known as *lamba mena* – red cloth – even though it is rarely red these days), carry them around the area on their shoulders to see the new local sights, provide them with food and drink, and finally put them back to rest, resealing the tomb.

The whole affair is totally joyous, not the least bit macabre, and the music is wild and glorious. Outsiders – officially invited – can be made very welcome. The best time of the year for maximum famadihana yield is September.

Touré or Jean Mwenda, his first solo album was released by Shanachie in 1993.

With local newspaper headlines like "Rickymania!", **Ricky** (Randimbiarison) is a name to watch. Malagasy singing is usually at its strongest in harmony: Ricky is the best solo vocalist to emerge to date. He's toured with marovany player Matrimbala and is to record with the acappella group Salala, but mainly he works with an electric band who include the best musicians in town, particularly **Toty**, who plays extraordinary bass guitar in marovany style. They call their music *vakojazzana* (a mixture of vako-drazana folk and jazz).

Solo Miral are the other renowned vakojazzana outfit, a quintet of brothers among whom electric guitarist **Haja** and bassist **Fanaiky** are truly outstanding marovany-style players. The hardworking members of Solo Miral are also often seen in other bands: Haja with Ricky, and Ny Ony with Tarika, for example. There are no recordings yet, though they've already toured in France.

Tsimihole are a powerful group playing the music of their Antandroy people from the far south, and very influential – often copied, but rarely bettered. They are one of the few Malagasy acts to have released an independent tape,

though it's hard to find, and have one track on a Malagasy compilation CD issued by the Mélodie label in France.

Salala are another Antandroy group. Usually an acappella trio with strong vocal harmonies, including a lead singer who could be ranked with Aaron Neville, they also sometimes appear as part of an eight-piece band. So far unrecorded, other than on local bootleg cassettes, a German CD is promised for late 1994.

HALF-GREEN AND SALEGY

The electric dance band music called watcha watcha, similar to Kenyan benga, comes from the northwestern coastal region (which receives the clearest mainland African radio signals). It is popular in places like Mahajanga, pronounced Majunga, the home town of the Paris-based guitarist **Freddy de Majunga** (who everybody used to assume was Zairean because he played with Loketo, Diblo and co). But there are a number of other modern dance styles, including the lilting *sega* (also common in nearby Mauritius) and most characteristic and omnipresent of all, the driving *6/8 salegy* rhythm.

Back in the 1970s, there was a thriving record industry in Madagascar, in the course of which hundreds of salegy and watcha watcha seven-inch singles of vibrant dance music were produced, some of which reputedly sold over 60,000 copies. But the last local singles were pressed by DiscoMad in the mid-1980s. The record plants closed in the deteriorating economic climate, and masters have been lost or destroyed. Now, even in the capital, you can barely find a few very scratchy, secondhand copies on market stalls. Yet singles by **Orchestre Liberty, Jaojoby, Jean Fredy** or **Abdallah** rival the recordings of famous bands from mainland Africa. Many have a distinct Malagasy style, a few directly absorbing East African and South African sounds (particularly those produced by the influential **Charles Maurin Poty**). This is a real shame. A whole genre of music – known colloquially as *tapany maintso* ("half-green") because of the half-green labels of the old, long-defunct Kaiamba label which produced the wildest of these discs – is in danger of vanishing into undocumented history.

But if the old salegy records do disappear altogether, at least there's now a new generation of recordings coming onto the market – oddly a result in part of interest from outside. For ages, all you could find in the market were multi-generation bootlegged cassettes of a not very inspiring French-released salegy compilation from the 1980s. However, in 1992 Rogue managed to record Jaojoby in Madagascar for a complete album. Freddy de Majunga made a hi-tech version in Paris, and Rossy contributed a few tracks to a Shanachie compilation with ex-Smokers singer **Roger Georges**. On the local front, **Tianjama** (ex-Orchestre Liberty) made the first successful new salegy cassettes in the classic style for Mars (DiscoMad's successor), and a couple of impressive hit tracks from them found their way to Europe on a Buda compilation. Now there are more and

Kaiamba label, "half-green" singles

more regular local cassette releases by names like **Mily Clement**, **Jean Rigo**, **Cactus**, the heavily soukous-influenced **Dedesse** and the stunning **Lazan'i Maroantsetra**.

POOPY POP

What recently happened with music in Madagascar was a mirror on the whole culture. With the opening up of the economy, French TV beamed western styles into bourgeois homes and the rich few, making their consumerist pilgrimages to Paris, brought back synthesizers, drum machines and European fashion. A new breed emerged of rich-kid pop stars and artists with wealthy patrons. There are Euro-pop chanteuses with names like **Bodo, Poopy, Landy, Liva** and **Plibiche** – bubble-gum salegy (all Mickey Mouse synths and drum machines) and embarrassing heavy metal bands like **Apostol Rock** and **Kadradraka 2000** ("Cockroach 2000"). After years of national isolation, it became the height of chic to ape all things European and American.

Only a few had the talent to do it well: the group **Njila** made American-style soft rock with superb harmony vocals that could only be Malagasy, but they've now dissolved. Paris-based singer and songwriter **Rakoto** recently released the first really well-crafted international rock-styled album in the Malagasy language. Charles Maurin Poty's proteges **Feon'ala** and regional groups like **Zaza Club** from Tulear and **Clo Mahajanga** have all released better-than-average tapes through Mars (though, once again, beware the drum synth syndrome). But, largely, the contemporary pop phenomenon consists of the rich elite paying to get on television. And as TV spreads, it's the Malagasy roots that get marginalized. In Tana, you hardly see women wearing the

LIVE MUSIC

·····················

traditional lamba cloth wrap any more. What affects the capital spreads to the rest of the country, albeit slowly given the handicapped transport system and poor communications.

A couple of years ago it looked like curtains for Malagasy roots. However, outside influence has had a surprisingly beneficial effect. The real catalyst was GlobeStyle Records' 1985 recording trip which produced two classic compilations that set the stylistic and artistic agenda for other western producers. Things came to a head in 1992 with a flurry of releases, including a project instigated by American musicians David Lindley and Henry Kaiser. The "World Out Of Time" album, which featured them playing with many of the leading roots musicians (Rakoto Frah, Rossy, Tarika Sammy, Sylvestre Randafison, Dama Mahaleo, D'Gary,

Malagasy roots quintet, Tarika

Mama Sana, etc) was a World Music hit in America, where they toured with Rakoto Frah and Rossy. Simultaneously came Tarika Sammy's rapid ascent via two albums and long tours of Europe and North America. Back home, the message that the west liked all this music helped to reinvest pride in traditional culture. Traditionally rooted musicians could, suddenly, not only aim to make a living from music (something almost unheard of before) but travel abroad as well. So the musical climate has changed again: at the end of the long national strike in early 1992, one local newspaper pointed out that while Madagascar was in desperate straits, at least Malagasy musicians were achieving something in the wider world.

Madagascar's musical individuality is not so much at risk any more. As artists go out and enjoy success in the west playing Malagasy roots music, the rich (who, as in all rapidly developing countries, are getting richer while the poor get poorer) are beginning to think that Malagasy culture is okay after all. Even some westernized pop stars have begun looking to their roots: the latest Poopy tape has a distinctly Tsimihole-influenced track.

The Malagasy haven't yet got their equivalent of Youssou N'Dour or Thomas Mapfumo, a national superstar making a radical new music for the 1990s out of traditional styles and values (though keep eyes and ears on Ricky). But surely on a huge island where the most important people are your ancestors, it can't be impossible to preserve your very roots?

Thanks especially to Hanitrarivo Rasoanaivo, without whom writing most of this article would have been impossible.

DISCOGRAPHY

Author's disclaimer: with the knowledge that Rogue Records is my own company, you can adjust the influence of those particular recommendations accordingly! Unless mentioned otherwise, all releases are 1990s.

COMPILATIONS

Ⓓ **Various** *Madagasikara One – Current Traditional Music* and *Madagasikara Two – Current Popular Music* (GlobeStyle, UK). GlobeStyle's two anthologies, recorded by Ben Mandelson and Roger Armstrong in 1985, led the way for most other western recordists' activities later on. Featured names included Rossy, the original Tarika Sammy, Mahaleo, Rakoto Frah, Zeze, and salegy band Les Smokers. Both sets sound just as good today, and have excellent notes.

Ⓓ **Various** *Madagaskar 1: Music from Antananarivo, Madagaskar 2: Music of the South, Madagaskar 3: Valiha – Sounding Bamboo* (Feuer & Eis, Germany). After GlobeStyle, next to hit the recent field were these three fine thematic acoustic sets from Birger Gesthuisen's label released from 1989 to 1992. Vol. 1 introduces the remarkable Jean Emilien to the world, and features more Rossy, Sammy, and Rakoto Frah & Zeze together as Kalaza. Vol. 2 showcases the intriguing southern traditions – currently a hot roots influence on local revival styles – which GlobeStyle hadn't been able to reach. Vol. 3 collects together the very best players of the valiha, notably Sylvestre Randafison, the excellent Tovo and the last recordings of Zeze.

Ⓓ **Various** *Musiques de Madagascar* (Buda, France). An interesting mix of acoustic and electric roots-based styles from 1992. Worth buying for the two local hit tracks by salegy master Tianjama alone, it also has five pieces by guitar king D'Gary and a couple by veteran songwriter Levelo.

Ⓓ **Various** *World Beat Vol. 7 – Madagascar* (Celluloid, France) Malagasy roots-pop licensed in 1993 from local label Mars, this one is probably the most accurate reflection of what the Malagasy themselves enjoy – your chance to check out the likes of Tsimihole, Clo Mahajanga, Feon'ala and Zaza Club.

Ⓓ **Various** *A World out of Time – Kaiser & Lindley in Madagascar* (Shanachie, US). Two American musicians play with all the greats – the by-now familiar (Rossy, Tarika Sammy, Rakoto Frah, Mahaleo) and some fine new introductions to the world stage such as Mama Sana, D'Gary and Voninavoko. While the American twosome give themselves top billing, musically they stay tastefully in the back seat. Dates from 1992.

Ⓓ **Various** *Vol. 18: Music of Madagascar* (WDR/World Network, Germany). A stunning set of live recordings made by German radio from artists touring there in the 1980s and early '90s, including marovany players Matrimbala, with Ricky, the Justin Vali trio and some particularly good takes on Mahaleo and Rossy.

Ⓓ **Various** *Madagascar – Musique Traditionnelle du Sud-Ouest* (Pithys, France). Released in 1991, this has some upbeat 1982 location recordings of musicians from the Antandroy, Sakalava and Vezo peoples of the south, including lots of seriously wild marovany, percussion, accordion, partying and call-and-response singing.

Various *Valiha Madagascar* (Ocora, France). A 1964 release, repackaged in 1983, this features Rakotozafy and Sylvestre Randafison.

ARTISTS AND BANDS

Ⓓ **Bemiray** *Polyphonies des Hauts-Plateaux* (Silex, France). A really lively recent set of the kind of music made by the hira-gasy troupes, including some stunning a cappella singing. Notice the inexplicable echoes of Mexico…

Ⓓ **Dama** *Malagasy* (Anima Music, Japan). Also recent, and also released as *Mélodies of Madagascar* (Playasound, France). Beautiful contemporary acoustic singer/songwriter music from the leader of the legendary band Mahaleo.

Ⓓ **D'Gary** *Malagasy Guitar Music from Madagascar* (Shanachie, US). 1993 debut CD of a man with a dazzling acoustic guitar style, based on the playing of those traditional Malagasy zithers.

Rakoto Frah *Flute Master of Madagascar* (GlobeStyle, UK). Rakoto Frah, represented on some of the compilations, does impossible things with his simple end-blown flute on this 1986 release.

Ⓓ **Jaojoby** *Salegy!* (Rogue, UK). The only western-released CD to date (1992) by any of the great local salegy bands. The subtitle "Hot dance music from Madagascar" will suffice for description.

Ⓓ **Mahaleo** *En Concert* (AAFM/WDR, France). The Beatles of Madagascar, well recorded here, live in concert in Germany some time in the 1980s, featuring most of their hit songs. A guaranteed sing-along success for any Malagasy house party!

Ⓓ **Freddy de Majunga** *Tsinjaka* (Rogue, UK). Spirited salegy in hi-tech Paris fashion, the way they make soukous records.

Ⓓ **Malgache Connexion** *Bilo* (Silex, France). Paris-based valiha master Justin Vali with an excellent group who push at the boundaries of acoustic roots music with a jazz influence.

Ny Antsaly *Folklore de Madagascar* (Vogue, France). From the early 1960s, but Randafison's group, just about the only Malagasy traditional group to tour internationally at that time, still sound fine today.

Ⓓ **Rakoto** *ZandryKely* (Carrere Music/East-West, France). Well-crafted international adult-oriented rock, sung in Malagasy; big in France.

Rakotozafy *Valiha Malaza – Famous Valiha* (GlobeStyle, UK). The legendary and hugely influential marovany player lovingly re-issued in 1986 from surviving Malagasy master tapes.

Ⓓ **Rossy** *Island of Ghosts* (Real World, UK). Although in fact a film soundtrack, of the four Rossy CDs available this one gives probably the most enjoyable across-the-board representation of their music.

ⒸⒹ **Tarika Sammy** *Balance* (Rogue, UK/Green Linnet, US). Second album by the group who enjoyed the most concentrated international success in the early 1990s, mixing pan-Malagasy roots influences into a new brew. Detailed sleeve notes and lyrics.

SOUTHERN AFRICA

The Republic of South Africa has had such a long and dominant role in the musical life of southern Africa that the styles of other countries seem quite overshadowed and insignificant in comparison. The South African record industry speaks for itself. Without much exaggeration, it's fair to say that it has trailed close behind the music industries of Europe and America for the last fifty years, producing tens of thousands of 78s, seven-inch singles, LPs, cassettes and now CDs. Although the licensing of foreign recordings has always been important, the home market has also fed on South Africa's own musical output, from the early days of "swing", *marabi* and "African Jazz", through pennywhistle and sax jive, to the development of the tougher, township style of *mbaqanga* as performed by Mahlathini and the Mahotella Queens, and modern soul and pop. Alongside these developments, the vocal and choral traditions of the country have been moving out of purely church-oriented styles to *mbube*, and the apogee of Zula a cappella singing, *iscathamiya*, as performed by Ladysmith Black Mambazo. And, at the same time, there's been a continuous evolution in the sounds collectively called "neo-traditional" and known as Zulu-Trad, Sotho-Trad and so on. Little of this huge range owes much to influences from other African countries.

The first article in this chapter charts a course through the sweep of South Africa's musical history, touching along the way on studio issues and recording techniques, gospel, the music of white South Africa and the story of "Graceland". This is followed by a shorter account of South African jazz, placing the key figures and setting them in the context of a country tearing itself apart in the wake of the apartheid policies instituted in 1948.

Zimbabwe is the second great musical powerhouse of southen Africa. Zairean guitar music has been very influential here, and many bands play what is essentially a Kinshasa sound, but artists like the Bhundu Boys and Thomas Mapfumo have had a major impact on the World Music scene with their own, different but distinctively Zimbabwean, sounds, while the *mbira*-playing of Stella Chiweshe and others – and its influence on local guitar styles – has had a knock-on effect across the region.

The music of Zambia and Malawi – there's a short article on each – is much less known abroad. Zambia found a flurry of fame in the late 1980s for its *kalindula* artists, who emerged with an indigenous style from a Congo-saturated environment, but Malawi is still a musical mystery, only slowly being revealed by the Scottish-Malawian recording initiative, Pamtondo. There's every hope that, with the optimism engendered by the newly elected government, Malawi will become a new musical focus in the region.

The war-torn countries of Angola and Mozambique have a rich musical heritage – one which peace in the latter is once again allowing expression. Centuries of Portuguese rule, enslavement, settlement and intermarriage have left both countries with a musical legacy similar to Brazil's – though the African part is provided by indigenous styles, while Brazil's was furnished by slaves largely from West Africa.

Apart from civil war, the other great scourge of central and southern Africa is AIDS. Sadly, and perhaps not surprisingly, the HIV virus has ripped through the musical communities of Zambia, Malawi and Zimbabwe like nowhere else in Africa. Many well-known performers have died in recent years and a number of bands – the Bhundu Boys for example – have effectively ceased to exist as a result.

A cappella Singing without instrumental accompaniment

African Jazz Post-World War II style based on marabi, and incorporating American "swing".

Bira Traditional Zimbabwean (Shona) ceremony, featuring the mbira and dancing.

Bubblegum Modern South African township pop music featuring synthesizers, disco beats from a drum box, and glittery personalities.

Chimurenga Shona word meaning "struggle", used to describe the protest music Thomas Mapfumo pioneered during the fight for independence in Zimbabwe.

Cothoza mfana Smooth style of South African harmony singing which preceded iscathamiya.

Harepa Music style of the Pedi-speaking people from South Africa, named after the German instrument, the autoharp.

Hosho Gourd rattle from Zimbabwe used to accompany the mbira.

Iscathamiya Traditional Zulu call-and-response a cappella choral music from South Africa.

Ishikwela jo Strident, Zulu harmony singing popular in South Africa in the 1950s.

Jit/Jit jive Hard, fast percussive Zimbabwean dance music, influenced by mbira-guitar styles (jit-jive was a name coined by the Bhundu Boys).

Jive Generic South African term for popular music.

Kalindula Very fast, Zambian "electric-roots" style derived from a bass instrument of the same name.

Kizomba Angolan music derived from traditional marimba-playing.

Kwela South African pennywhistle music.

Marabi South African three-chord township music of the 1930s–1960s, which evolved into "African jazz".

Marimba Xylophone from Zimbabwe and neighbouring countries.

Marrabenta Mozambique's most popular roots-based urban rhythm, a very distinctive dance sound.

Maskanda Zulu "traditional" music, derived from the Afrikaans word *musikant* meaning musician.

Mbaqanga South African township music (literally "dumpling", meaning "homemade"), a mixture of traditional and urban styles which came to be characterized by heavy bass, clipped guitars and choral vocals.

Mbila Xylophone of the Chopi people from Mozambique (plural: *timbila*).

Mbira Hand or thumb piano from Zimbabwe and neighbouring countries – plucked metal strips on a wooden base with a resonator, usually a calabash.

Mbube Zulu a cappella singing style from South Africa, with a high lead vocal and bass-rich four-part harmonies (named after the song, "Mbube" "The Lion" – later "The Lion Sleeps Tonight".

Mbumba Malawian women's music, performed on special occasions.

Mohabelo Urbanized Sotho a cappella style derived from traditional notes.

Mqashiyo Literally "to bounce", a tougher version of mbaqanga, with groaning male vocals, popularized by Mahlathini.

Pennywhistle Tin flute, very popular in South Africa in the 1950s and early '60s.

Pungwe All-night Zimbabwean music and dance session where the villagers met with the freedom fighters during the war.

Trane trekker Literally "tear puller" – a South African Afrikaner style popular from the 1930s to the 1960s, derived from US country music.

Tufo Mozambiquan women's choral group, originally Islamic, now secularized.

Ukupika Zulu guitar-picking style popularized by John Bhengu (aka "Phuzushukela") in the 1950s.

TOWNSHIP JIVE

FROM PENNYWHISTLE TO BUBBLEGUM:
THE MUSIC OF SOUTH AFRICA

South Africa is distinguished by the most complex musical history, the greatest profusion of styles and the most intensely developed recording industry anywhere in Africa. Despite many regional and stylistic variations, its music – vocal-based and long and deeply influenced by Europe and America – is different from what you'll hear anywhere else on the continent, even from nearby parts of central Africa. Rob Allingham treks across the musical veldt, follows the historical courses of the styles, and highlights the careers of some outstanding musicians.

The earliest known musical activity in southern Africa originated about 4000 years ago with a stone-age group of hunter-gatherers called the **San** – or Bushmen – who sang in a strange click language (the "!" clicks in modern Bantu languages are a San inheritance), fashioned a variety of instruments – rattles, drums and simple flutes – and exploited the musical properties of their hunting bows. Present-day San music still sounds quite otherworldly to a Western ear. Then, some 2000 years ago, another group called the **Khoi** filtered down from the north with their herds and pushed out the San. Known perjoratively as Hottentots, the Khoi are now extinct as a group, though their mixed race, or "coloured", descendants are an important part of South African society. Khoi music seems to have been more complex than San: Vasco da Gama noted in 1497 that his Khoi hosts greeted his arrival with a five-man ensemble of reed flutes.

About 200 AD, the first **Bantu-speaking peoples** arrived in the region, and by the beginning of the seventeenth century various Bantu linguistic groups – the most important of whom spoke early forms of **Sotho**, **Xhosa** and **Zulu** – had completely occupied what is now South Africa. Their musical glory was their vocal tradition, with songs to accompany every routine, ritual and rite of passage from birth to death. Each tribe had its distinct and characteristic songs, tonalities and harmonies, but the underlying musical structure always remained the same – two or more linked melodic phrases repeated ad infinitum, often resulting in a kind of hypnotic warp. These parts were not played or sung in unison; instead each was staggered in relation to the others, thus producing a simultaneous polyphony. This arrangement may well have been a Bantu invention – it was certainly an African one – and it underlies the basic "call and response" structure of many African-American styles including gospel and its later derivatives, doo-wop and soul.

In the hinterland, the first contact with Western music usually coincided with the arrival of Christian missionaries, who made their first visits in the early nineteenth century. Once the mission school system was established, it provided most of the few educational opportunities available to Africans, and always included a musical training. Out of this system came Enoch Sontonga – who composed the

Earthworks' landmark compilation of township music

national anthem, "Nkosi Sikelel' i Africa" at the turn of the century – and later, nearly every prominent black composer and performer right up until the 1960s.

But the most important catalyst for musical evolution was urbanization – Cape Town was visited by American musicians in the 1840s and Johannesburg grew rapidly in the 1880s after the discovery of gold. Among the many professional musicians who travelled to South Africa before World War I were African-American minstrels, vaudevillians and ragtime piano players. A remarkable series of tours was undertaken in the 1890s by **Orpheus McAdoo's Jubilee Singers** who introduced black spiritual singing to great acclaim from all sections of the South African public, black and white alike.

MARABI

By the 1920s, Africans had established a secure foothold in the cities despite increasing government restrictions. Out of the necessity of coping with the nightly curfew that applied to all Africans, an entertainment institution, the "Concert and Dance", developed in **Johannesburg** – the largest African city south of the Sahara. Vocal groups and comedians held the stage until curfew at 11pm. Then, after midnight, dance bands with names like the Merry Blackbirds and the Jazz Maniacs played until 4am, when it was once again legal to go on the streets. The Jazz Maniacs were a rough-and-tumble outfit, and while they played dance music for black middle-class audiences, they also incorporated elements of a style from Johannesburg's black slumyards called *marabi*.

Originally, marabi was banged out on battered pianos to the percussive accompaniment of pebble-filled cans in countless township shebeens – illicit drinking centres (alcohol was illegal to Africans until 1962 unless sold in government "beer halls"). Structurally, marabi consisted of a single phrase built around a three-chord progression repeated endlessly in the indigenous fashion, while melodically it was a highly syncretic form, providing enough space for improvisation to incorporate snatches of anything from traditional melodies to hymns or current popular fare from Tin Pan Alley.

Some time later, perhaps by the mid-1930s, marabi was being played on guitars, banjos, and concertinas but the underlying structure remained the same. By the post-war years and into the 1950s, a number of related popular urban styles based on three chord marabi patterns were being played and sung in different languages and on a variety of instruments in townships throughout southern Africa. By this time, the music was often referred to as **"jive"** (as in "violin jive" or "Ndebele jive".) Meanwhile, in Johannesburg and other South African cities, marabi and American swing were combining to create "African Jazz" – for more on which see the article that follows this.

THE RECORDING INDUSTRY

By the late 1940s, southern Africa boasted a remarkable collection of black musical styles. These not only included the distinctive African-Western crossovers of the cities but also a variety of tribally-diffentiated styles. The latter in turn varied in their make-up from the almost purely indigenous to others which exhibited varying degrees of western influence. Most of these styles existed outside any commercial infrastructure, and thus constituted a genuine "folk music" in the broadest sense of the term.

The occasional local **commercial recordings** tended to document the music passively, without affecting its style or substance. The UK-based Gramophone Company Ltd, producer of the HMV and Zonophone labels, was responsible for most of the early innovations. They initiated the first recording sessions in Africa by dispatching a portable field unit to Cape Town and Johannesburg in 1912. Later sessions in the company's London studio produced the first recorded version of "Nkosi Sikelel' i Afrika" by ANC co-founder Sol Plaatjie in 1923, and the 150 landmark recordings by composer Reuben Caluza's Double Quartet in 1930.

Eric Gallo's Brunswick Gramophone House sent a few Afrikaans and African musicians to London in 1930 and 1931 to record for their new Singer label. And Gallo went on to build a local studio – the first in sub-Saharan Africa – which produced its first satisfactory masters in 1934, effectively marking the inauguration of the South African music industry.

By the mid-1950s, a number of other recording operations had been established – Trutone; a local branch of EMI and an EMI subsidiary, Teal, which later separated and grew into a formidable industry presence; and Troubador Records. Meanwhile, Gallo Africa and its subsidiary, Gramophone Record Company, were producing over a million discs a year by 1952.

THE PRODUCERS

In the 1950s, urban Africans were an enormous untapped audience for commercial music. But how were white-run companies to determine what they wanted to buy? The dilemma was resolved by hiring African "talent scouts", later referred to as "producers", though many of them in fact wielded far more power than any conventional record producer. The most powerful producers ran virtual African fiefdoms within the companies and five in particular loom as major figures.

Strike Vilakazi ran Trutone's black division from 1952 to 1970. A vocalist, trumpeter, drummer and composer, he directly influenced the course of popular black music by recording pennywhistler Spokes Mashiyane in 1954, touching off the "kwela" craze. Four years later in an even shrewder move, he persuaded Mashiyane that his pennywhistle music would be even more popular when played on a saxophone. The earliest *mbaqanga* style, "sax jive", resulted, a sound that would dominate South African black popular music for many years.

Cuthbert Matumba singlehandedly developed Troubadour Records from a fledgling concern into a giant that at times controlled much of the African market. In addition to a multitude of hits, Matumba's catalogue included practically every urban and urban-rural crossover style from the Cape up through central Africa. He had a gift for composing simple, catchy melodies and possessed a uniquely topical lyrical sense. Matumba permanently employed a large contingent of singers and musicians who spent eight hours a day recording among themselves (under an endless variety of names) or providing backing. Despite this assembly-line approach, the innovative spirit remained high thanks to a studio policy which encouraged moonlighting by musicians from other companies. Early most mornings the producer himself would be out playing test pressings on the Troubadour "mobile" (a van fitted with turntables and speakers) gauging public reaction to the previous day's studio output. A promising record was available in the shops 24 hours after it was recorded. Troubadour's decline was as abrupt as its rise. Within four years of Matumba's death in 1965, the label's few remaining assets had been swallowed up by Gallo.

Rupert Bopape joined EMI as a producer in 1952 and quickly built up the industry's most successful African Jazz catalogue by carefully employing a few key figures like Zacks Nkosi, Elijah Nkwanyane and Ellison Temba (see the Jazz article) on a permanent basis. But his real talents lay in developing vocal groups. In the early 1960s, his most successful pennywhistler band, the Black Mambazo, evolved an all-male vocal style featuring the leader and principal composer, Zeph Nkabinde, and occasionally, Nkabinde's younger brother Simon, known as "Mahlathini". The Black Mambazo's all-female counterpart were the Dark City Sisters, probably the single-most popular vocal group in South Africa in the first half of the 1960s. In 1964, Bopape left EMI and joined Gallo to run a new African operation called **Mavuthela**, bringing a number of his EMI musicians with him. Within two years, the label dominated the market with a mbaqanga vocal style called *mqashiyo*, the most famous exponent of which was Mahlathini and the Mahotella Queens, backed by the Makgona Tsohle Band. In the early 1970s, Bopape began to farm out some production duties to a number of his talented understudies, including Marks Mankwane, Lucky Monama, and **West Nkosi**.

David Thekwane (who died in 1984) was the last of the old-style producers to carve out a significant niche in the music industry. He began producing for Teal in 1972 after following a fairly successful career as a saxophone jive artist under Strike Vilakazi. Thekwane had a violent personality and often intimidated his musicians physically. Nonetheless, throughout the 1970s, his Teal artists – especially the Movers, a group of consistent hit-makers who evolved a winning mixture of marabi and local "soul" – regularly accounted for a substantial percentage of all African record sales. His mbaqanga stars included sax jivers Thomas Phale and Lulu Masilela, accordionist Johnson Mkhalali, and vocal group, the Boyoyo Boys.

Hamilton Nzimande is the only one of the "big five" producers active in the business today. In a thirty-year career he has overseen a remarkably broad cross-section of commercial African music, from the last sessions of African Jazz great, Zacks Nkosi, to the earliest bubblegum pop with some of today's biggest names. He began his career as a singer, going on to handle promotion for Rupert Bopape at EMI (often driving the mobile). He finally got his break as a producer in 1966 when he went to help run the Gallo subsidiary Gramophone Record Company. By the mid 1970s, Nzimande's mbaqanga catalogue almost rivaled Mavuthela's under Rupert Bopape. And he was the first producer to take local "soul" music seriously and make it massively successful, with bands like the Inn-Lawes. The Beaters, another group from his soul roster, spawned solo star Sipho "Hotstix" Mabuse. And it was at Nzimande's suggestion that the hugely successful Soul Brothers copied

In The Studio: Nkosi and Lindemann

West Nkosi has participated in the South African music scene from the streets to the boardroom. Best known internationally for his productions of Ladysmith Black Mambazo, he took over producing and managing Mahlathini and the Mahotella Queens in the early 1980s, and continued to play sax with their backing band until a few years ago. John Lindemann has been in the music scene since hotel band days in the early 1960s and started working with West Nkosi as a sound engineer in 1983. They talked to Louise Meintjes.

Saxophonist and producer West Nkosi

WEST NKOSI

How did you get into producing?

WN: We used to get good musicians coming for audition and Rupert Bopape turned some of them down. I could feel the potential in those groups and I got a part-time job to produce. For instance Ladysmith Black Mambazo – nobody wanted to record that type of music, without guitars. But I took it up and it worked out good. I had others, like Mparanyana, one of our top soul singers.

When you started producing Mahlathini and the Queens how did you change their sound?

WN: The overseas market, they don't like the disco type of material that we are having here now. They like the real ethnic South African music. I knew we have got that and I changed a little bit. I added more instruments. I used the keyboards plus our guitars to keep the natural feel. And I changed the arrangements as well. Some of the songs are wedding songs, so they are sung by a lot of people, and I doubletrack the three girls to sound like they are about six or ten – sort of like when you walk in the sun there's your shadow. I put the shadow in.

Why the addition of the keyboards?

WN: If you play acoustic guitar alone, it doesn't appeal to the young people. They are now used to the big sound – bang bang bang! So we put those keyboards in to cover the sound, to make it a little bit stronger. But the guitar is there to keep the originality of the South African sound. If you take that guitar out, it is no longer a local sound and people will easily pick that up.

JOHN LINDEMANN

What would you say is the biggest change in recording techniques over the years?

JL: Well, black music really started evolving technically with disco. Everything started becoming electronic. What's been happening a lot, an inexperienced band comes in. They'll play live and the producer copies what the drummer is playing onto the drum box. Same with a bass line – if he's battling to play it himself, it's just cheaper and quicker to use a keyboard player copying his things onto a synth bass. It's a matter of economics.

And how has the recording of Mahlathini changed since they've hit it internationally?

JL: Basically the technique didn't really change, except we used the drum box, just to get a tighter feel on the bass drum. But all the bass, saxes, the guitars, particularly that double guitar sound – the typical mbaqanga guitar which people love overseas – we kept all of that. West still tried to keep that live feel.

And is that something that Mahlathini himself requested?

JL: No, no, that's West. Mahlathini is an incredible guy. He's a simple, very simple man. He hasn't changed in all these years. He's just a singer and just so dynamic on stage. But the direction of the music was in West's hands, in the producer's hands – totally, totally. West is the guy that believed in bringing them back. The record companies didn't believe it.

It's interesting to consider what it is about the South African sound that Europeans love.

JL: I think it's the rawness. It's a very unique style, that's what people love. That mbaqanga guitar – like Ray Phiri on Graceland – it's all played up at the top, very high. It's a bit of a rip-off of the East African guitar style. But our guys made it harsher. They wanted it bright. It had to bite. As an engineer I had to get it so bright that it hurt.

When you mix an album for an international audience as opposed to a local audience how do things change?

JL: I think the most successful way is to still mix it the way we mix it. Americans and Europeans like it that way because it's different – because of the bass. The mbaqanga bass is right up there. And it's melodic, you can sing along to it. And it's not your normal 2/4 bass line. In a lot of cases it's a cross rhythm. You know if I got a mbaqanga bass player to play a bass line without anything else, a white drummer would pick up the rhythm but would be on the wrong side of the beat – always.

The bass guitar in mbaqanga music is one of the most important parts. Blacks used to buy mbaqanga just for the bass riff. It still works today. For instance there's a guy Thomas Motshwane who produced Thomas Chauke, who is Shangaan traditional – one of the biggest sellers. He gave me such a hard time. I mean I just couldn't believe how much bottom he wanted, and yet he still wanted to hear everything else! I had to push more bass and push more bass. All the elements were fighting with each other. But it was a fantastically big seller. It's all very well to sound great on big hi-fi speakers, but you've got to somehow get some drive into that thing so that when the average person listens through their little ghetto blaster it works. It used to give the cutting engineers endless problems because the records jumped. But if a record jumped, it was a sure-fire seller.

---

their vocal harmony style from Zimbabwean Shona township music. Nzimande also encouraged the trend in religious recordings, popularizing the Zula a cappella style, *cothoza mfana*, which anticipated the sound that was to make Ladysmith Black Mambazo so famous.

The age of the producer is over – musicians today flog their demos around the cost-conscious companies like everywhere else – but many suspect that the artistic result has been a less adventurous musical culture which discriminates against the poor but talented.

RADIO APARTHEID

Very little radio reached Africans until after World War II. And only in 1962, after much government consideration, was a development programme for **"Bantu Radio"** implemented. The government's plans constituted a cynical exercise in apartheid wish-fulfilment: broadcasting was to be harnessed as a propaganda tool to foster "separate development". In the cities, monolingual programming would encourage ethnic identity while in the rural "bantustans", radio would provide the voice of incipient nationhood. It was intended that the rural stations would feature exclusively the traditional music of their regions, in order to encourage ethnic separatism.

In practice, even the bantustan stations were forced to play a mixture of styles just to gain a listenership. The failure of the traditionalism policy reflected the government's ignorance of rural people. Music and culture in the rural areas hadn't remained suspended in a traditional time warp, and economic development had thoroughly diluted the indigenous character of the hinterland. But Bantu radio handed the record companies a powerful marketing tool and revolutionized the way in which black music was promoted. Whereas previously the companies had relied on mobiles to advertise their newest records directly to potential customers, they could now reach a mass market immediately. Radio also opened up new rural markets for record companies, encouraging them to focus more attention on areas outside the cities where individual rural traditions were being combined with modern, urban-based influences.

After the advent of radio the lyrical content of African recordings became more conservative. In the 1950s and before, black musicians often recorded material that commented openly on the social and political issues of the day ("Sobadubula Ngembayimbayi" by the Alexandra Swing Liners, released in 1955, contained the chorus "We will shoot the whites with bazookas"). The new African radio services instituted a draconian censorship code and mobiles were banned as a "public hazard". Purely commercial considerations inevitably led to a great deal of self-censorship on the part of labels and their artists.

FROM PENNYWHISTLES TO SAXOPHONES

Pennywhistle jive, focussed as usual on Johannesburg, was one of the first musical styles to become a commercial phenomenon and the very first to win a measure of international renown. The indigenous predecessor to the pennywhistle was the reed flute of cattle-herders, with three finger holes. When the herd boys came to the cities, they bought similar "tin" whistles with six finger holes, made in Germany.

Willard Cele, a disabled teenage musician living in Alexandra Township, is credited with the discovery that by placing the flute's mouthpiece at an angle between the teeth to one side of the mouth with the soundhole slanting outwards, its tone was not only thickened but it was possible to vary the pitch of each note and vastly extend the instrument's melodic capabilities. Although Cele himself was to die young, his new style quickly inspired a legion of imitators, especially following his appearance in a 1951 movie, "The Magic Garden". Soon, groups of three and four **pennywhistlers** were working out elaborate arrangements where a lead flute would extemporize a melodic line over chords provided by backing flutes.

After a short period in the early 1950s as an exclusive township phenomenon, pennywhistlers moved into the suburbs and city centres where they were part of the urban environment for another decade. In the white areas, the potential financial rewards were greater but so were the hazards. Flute musicians, some of them not even into their teens, would travel out of the townships to perform on street corners and in parks, playing a cat-and-mouse game with the police who would arrest them for creating a "public disturbance". Eventually this musical presence attracted a white following, particularly from rebellious suburban teenagers referred to as "ducktails" (the equivalent of "teddy boys" in the UK or "delinquents" in the US). It was the ducktails that renamed pennywhistle jive *kwela* (meaning "climb up", the command barked out to Africans

being arrested and ordered into the police van) and the term eventually became generic among white fans.

It took several years for the record companies to wake up to the commercial potential of the pennywhistle. Little flute material was released until 1954, when **Spokes Mashiyane**'s "Ace Blues" backed with the "Kwela Spokes" became the biggest African hit of the year. Only then did record producers begin to take flute jive seriously, and in the following decade around a thousand 78rpm pennywhistle discs were issued.

After his initial success, Spokes Mashiyane remained the single most famous pennywhistler, although another flute star, **Abia Temba** was also very popular throughout the 1950s. Troubadour's two biggest pennywhistle artists were Sparks Nyembe and Jerry Mlotshwa, whose material was released using an endless number of pseudonyms. The **Black Mambazo** from Alexandra Township recorded for EMI; they too appeared under different names. In 1957 they recorded a popular local hit called "Tom Hark", which featured on British TV and promptly caught the public's fancy, perhaps because of its slight similarity to the "skiffle" music that was popular at the time. It was issued as a UK single and promptly rose to number two in the charts.

Gallo's pennywhistle catalogue eventually cornered the largest share of the market and featured the greatest number of top-notch players, especially after the company lured Spokes Mashiyane away from Trutone in 1958 (he became the first African musician to receive royalties rather than the standard flat fee). The label's pennywhistle productions often featured quite elaborate arrangements by Gallo musical director Dan Hill, a fine clarinetist and band leader.

Among the company's principal pennywhistle artists were the **Solven Whistlers** from Jabavu-Soweto, instantly recognizable by their jazz-influenced harmonies and sophisticated compositions, largely the work of **Peter Mokonotela**. The Solven's lead flute, **Ben Nkosi**, was probably the single greatest pennywhistle soloist, his best work exhibiting a level of technique and improvisational dexterity that belied its execution on such a simple instrument.

The beginning of the end of the pennywhistle craze can be precisely pinpointed with the song "Big Joe Special", Spokes Mashiyane's first recording on the **saxophone**. Much as his "Ace Blues" had created a sales sensation and inspired a legion of imitators four years before, "Big Joe Special" proved to be the trendsetting hit of 1958. In its wake, every black producer now wanted material by similar-style sax players and most pennywhistlers, assuming they could get a saxophone, were happy to provide it.

The sax was obviously a more versatile instrument than the pennywhistle and even in the hands of an unschooled musician offered a far greater range of music. Even more importantly from the standpoint of both the players and their audience, it connoted an urbane, pan-tribal sophistication that was satisfyingly contrary to the prevailing apartheid image of the heathen tribalist. Only the white kwela fans were disaffected: it proved virtually impossible for African street musicians to perform with a saxophone at their former city and suburban haunts. Now they were limited to playing in the townships, a world beyond the ken of even the most rebellious white teenager.

After the success of "Big Joe Special", sax jives overtook pennywhistle recordings in popularity to become the most popular black musical genre, a development which didn't meet with universal approval. One jazz saxophonist, Michael Xaba, disdainfully referred to the new style as **mbaqanga** – literally a "dumpling" in Zulu but in this instance connoting "homemade" – because most of its practitioners were musically illiterate. Ironically, the name soon gained a common currency as a term of endearment and indeed, the public's taste for instrumental mbaqanga went on to last for almost another two decades.

Sax jives were usually built around very simple repeated melodic fragments, so much of their appeal and interest depended on their instrumental accompaniment. Initially, the sax was backed with the same marabi-derived acoustic 2/4 rhythm of most flute jives. Then, beginning in the early 1960s, the rhythms became discernibly heavier, more elastic and more African. The **electric bass**, in particular, with its higher volume and unprecedented sustaining and attack capabilities, provided the foundation for the new style. The pioneer African bass player whose innovations played such a major role in shaping this evolution was **Joseph Makwela**.

His bass guitar, the first one imported into South Africa, was purchased from a local white session musician who had seen an example of the newly developed instrument when Cliff Richard and The Shadows played Johannesburg in 1960. Makwela and Marks Mankwane, another influential figure who was the first African musician to fully exploit the electric guitar, formed the nucleus of the famous Makhona Tsohle Band, which backed the Gallo studio's mbaqanga saxophonists like West Nkosi but also accompanied their vocal groups. The band's electric sound became an integral part of a new vocal genre developing in the mid-1960s which also went under the name of mbaqanga and then later *mqashiyo*.

MAHLATHINI'S "HOMEMADE" MUSIC

The vocal component of mbaqanga developed directly from the 1950s township vocal styles made famous by groups such as the Manhattan Brothers and the Skylarks. These styles had at first been copied directly from African-American models but local musicians increasingly Africanized their sound to create a distinctively South African synthesis.

Simon "Mahlathini" Nkabinde – groaning superstar

One of the crucial developments leading towards mbaqanga's characteristic harmonies was the use of five vocal parts rather than the four part harmonies common in African-American vocal styles. Female studio vocalists at Troubadour discovered that if the single tenor line was divided into a high and low tenor part,

The Mahotella Queens on a roll

the resulting harmonies took on a breadth that was reminiscent of traditional vocal styles. A group of session vocalists at EMI, the **Dark City Sisters**, usually featuring the sweet-voiced lead of Joyce Mogatusi, became the best known African vocal group of the early 1960s using this technique, which rapidly became a distinctively South African sound. Their style was still described as "vocal jive" but the formative harmonies of mbaqanga were already evident.

Another element which defined much of the classic vocal mbaqanga output was **"groaning"**: bellowing, ultra-bass male vocals that contrasted dramatically with softer, all-female harmonizing. At first this was a commercial "gimmick" invented by Aaron Jack Lerole of EMI's Black Mambazo in the early 1960s. Lerole subsequently gained a measure of groaning fame as Big Voice Jack, and in the process managed to permanently strip his vocal chords. His efforts were soon overtaken by **Simon "Mahlathini" Nkabinde**. As a teenager, Mahlathini secured a considerable reputation as a singer of traditional wedding songs in Alexandra Township where he led a large female group in a typically African, polyphonic fashion. His magnificent bass voice was naturally suited to the groaning style and Rupert Bopape began to utilize it in conjunction with varying combinations of EMI session vocalists. At the same time, Nkabinde developed an aggressive and dramatic stage persona as "Mahlathini The Bull", greatly enhancing his growing reputation.

When Rupert Bopape left EMI for Gallo in 1964 he brought Mahlathini along with him. All the essential mbaqanga elements now coalesced under the Mavuthela production facility: the male groaner roaring in counterpoint to intricately arranged five-part female harmonies, underpinned – thanks to the Makhona Tsohle Band – with the new-style, totally electric instrumental backup. After several years of growing popularity vocal mbaqanga began to be referred to as **mqashiyo**, from the Zulu word meaning "bounce" – though mqashiyo was actually the name of a popular dance style; no musical characteristic distinguished it from vocal mbaqanga in general.

As was the case at EMI, Bopape's regular roster of female session singers was nominally divided into several distinct groups. These line-ups maintained a degree of regularity for live performances, but in the studio vocalists were fairly interchangeable, and in any event the output of each group was simultaneously released using a number of different names. For example, the vocalists who performed "live" as the **Mahotella Queens** were also the Dima Sisters, the Soweto Stars and Izintombi Zo Mqashiyo on several different Gallo record labels.

Rival producers attempted to emulate Mavuthela's success with mqashiyo. Only one, however, Hamilton Nzimande at GRC, managed to build a strong roster. His two best known groups were **Amatshitshi** and **Inzintombi Zesi Manje Manje** (literally "The Modern Girls"), but Nzimande's crew also included two wonderful

groaners, the brothers **Saul and Bhekitshe Tshabalala**, as well as a great instrumental backing band, **Abafana Bentutuko**. All of which provided stiff competition for Bopape's Mahlathini/Mahotella Queens/Makhona Tsohle steamroller.

In the 1970s, the female chorus-plus-groaner formula retained its popularity when practiced by old favourites like the Mahotella Queens, but

SOUTH AFRICAN GOSPEL

....

South Africa's most popular gospel choir is a group of portly male Methodists called **Amadodana Ase Wesile** (motto: One Heart, One Way). Dressed in blue blazers and red waistcoats, these men eschew their church's celebrated English hymns for a distinctive brand of stirring multi-part harmonies and passionate solos, all to the solid thud of a Bible, beaten with one hand. There is a whole network of such choirs throughout the country's black Methodist churches, but Amadodana have reigned supreme for some time. Recorded on local cassette or vinyl, they're a take-it-or-leave-it sound. Live, however, they are fantastic. Their ponderous musical pace contrasts with some agile dance routines, making full use of versatile faces and substantial stomachs.

The Holy Brothers

By far the bulk of recorded gospel, however, comes from members of the country's non-established churches – everyone from white-robed Zionists with a penchant for extreme ecstasy to Pentecostal-style churches, with well-groomed preachers, frequent Praise-the-

Lording from the congregation, and a portable keyboard with a built-in drum machine for musical accompaniment.

The South African music industry records an enormous quantity of choirs and groups from right across this spectrum. Gospel has long been considered a very safe bet. The artists are often naive, and will comply with any demand and sign (or not) any contract in order to get their break; recording and packaging costs are minimal; lyrics never posed any political problems for the companies during apartheid; and the product sells very well indeed. Fortunately, none of this has prevented the release of gospel music of great fervour and power.

There are many noteworthy groups. One of the best is **Pure Gold**, a ten member male choir, all brothers or cousins, who are backed by the talented African Youth Band, making their sound danceable and lively. The **Holy Spirits** have been mega-sellers in South Africa for some years, but are currently out of favour, though this need not deter any new listeners, who will be treated to some epic and stirring singing. The **Holy Brothers** and **Hosana Hosana Hosana** are more formulaic successes, doing what most South African Gospel groups do, only superbly well. Their backing tracks aren't great but they can, and do, rise above them to produce some compelling music.

Despite the enormous number of recordings, most gospel goes unrecorded for lack of opportunity. Yet every township and rural area has countless choirs, groups, and soloists, many of whom are powerful and moving beyond belief. If the recorded article often seems a travesty, the live version, in church, at a funeral, or simply in someone's back yard, is unforgettable.

Gregory Salter

almost every successful new mbaqanga group had an exclusively male line-up. At the forefront were the Gallo label's **Abafana Baseqhudeni** (literally the "Cockeral Boys", so named after Gallo's rooster trademark), an extremely popular five-man lineup featuring the bass leads of Potatoes Zuma and Elphas Mkize as well as groaner Robert "Mbazo" Mkhize.

In the mid-1970s, David Thekwane produced a string of hits at Teal with the **Boyoyo Boys**. Originally assembled as a studio backing band for sax jive artist **Thomas Phale**, the same musicians later accompanied and lent their collective name to a male vocal group led by principal composer Petrus Maneli. Their half-chanted harmonies and loping rhythms gave the Boyoyos a totally unique sound. One of their biggest successes, "Puleng", later caught the ear of British producer Malcolm McClaren who subsequently transformed it into the 1981 British number one hit "Double Dutch".

Beam us up Scotty – Ladysmith Black Mambazo in Zulu Trekkies gear

ZULU A CAPPELLA: THE RISE OF ISCATHAMIYA

In the years following World War I, as an industrial economy began to develop in Natal, a cappella vocal styles became closely identified with the area's emerging **Zulu working class**, newly forged as rural migrants found employment in mines and factories. Forced in most cases to leave their families behind and live in all-male hostels, they developed a weekend social life based on vocal and dance group competitions, staged within and between hostels, and judged by elaborate rules and standards. By the late 1930s a cappella competitions were a characteristic of Zulu hostels throughout industrialized Natal and had also spread to Zulus working in Johannesburg.

In 1939, **Solomon Linda**'s Original Evening Birds, a group from Pomeroy in northwestern Natal, began recording for Gallo's Singer label in Johannesburg. Their evocative rendering of Linda's song "Mbube" ("The Lion") proved to be a commercial milestone. "Mbube" was the first recording in Africa to sell 100,000 copies and it later provided the basis for two American number one hit records, "Wimoweh" by the Weavers in 1950 and "The Lion Sleeps Tonight" by the Tokens in 1961.

The Original Evening Birds exerted a vast stylistic influence as dozens of imitators sprang up in the wake of their success, thus setting the scene for the next stage in the long history of western-influenced Zulu music. *Mbube* became the generic term for a new vocal style that incorporated Linda's main innovations: uniforms for the group, highly polished but softly executed dance routines and – perhaps most importantly – the use of a high-voiced lead set against four-part harmony where the ratio of the bass voices to the other parts was increased to two or three. These characteristics remained at the heart of the music through the late 1940s when mbube evolved into the *isikhwela jo* or "bombing" style – so named because of its strident, almost shouted harmonies – and on into the 1960s, when a far smoother approach became popular.

By the mid-1950s, the pan-tribal audience that had once purchased substantial quantities of mbube and isikhwela jo recordings by groups such as the Morning Stars and the Natal Champions had largely disappeared, and interest in Zulu a cappella reverted to the hostels. Then, in the 1960s, the audience broadened once again following the establishment of **Radio Zulu** which gave extensive exposure to Zulu a cappella and could be heard throughout Natal as well as in large areas of the Transvaal and Orange Free State. One Radio Zulu programme was particularly influential: "Cothoza Mfana", hosted by Alexius Buthelezi, featured a cappella vocal material exclusively. Indeed for a time, the newer, smoother style which superseded bombing came to be known generically as *cothoza mfana*.

The architects of the Bantu Radio system, and especially its administrative director Evonne Huskinson, were keen to promote cothoza mfana because the style incorporated the secular lyrics that had characterized most Zulu a cappella since at least World War I. With a judicious application of influence and suggestion, cothoza mfana lyrics could be easily tailored to promote the twin pillars of apartheid: tribal identity and ruralism. A typical example was a radio recording by the New Hanover Brothers subtitled "Hurrying of People In Durban So Disturbed Him, He Caught Train Back Home".

When the record industry at first showed only a minimal interest in cothoza mfana, Bantu Radio bridged the gap by recording their own transcription discs, and for many groups these provided a first step before graduating to commercially issued recordings. This was the case with Enock Masina's King Star Brothers, the most influential a cappella group of the late 1960s and early 70s, who featured on Radio Zulu for at least four years before they finally landed a contract with Hamilton Nzimande at GRC in 1970. By this time the King Stars' style was called *iscathamiya*, a term derived from the Zulu word meaning "to stalk or step softly", which described the dance routines that the group invented to match their swelling, polished harmonies.

But it was Gallo-Mavuthela producer West Nkosi's signing of another group of Radio Zulu veterans, Joseph Shabalala's **Ladysmith Black Mambazo**, ("Black Mambazo" signifying the "Black Axe" that would defeat all opponents in group competitions), that transformed the status

GRACELAND

·

There was a rash of copycat imitators when Ladysmith Black Mambazo caught success — at least eight of whom managed to incorporate "Ladysmith" into their names. But by the mid-1980s the boom was over, and except for the still numerous fans of LBM the audience for Zulu a cappella was again reduced to its original migrant-proletarian core. At this juncture, in 1986 Paul Simon discovered iscathamiya. He recorded with Ladysmith Black Mambazo on two tracks co-composed with Joseph Shabalala which appeared on "Graceland", one of the best selling albums of the decade (seven million copies) and one of the most critically acclaimed. While reviving Simon's flagging career, "Graceland" also provided unprecedented exposure for a South African act in the international arena. A Black Mambazo album recorded in the US and produced by Simon called "Shaka Zulu" also won a Grammy for the best World Music Recording of 1988, and sold 100,000 around the world.

Not everyone was pleased with this success. The most vociferous complaints were voiced by anti-apartheid organizations who claimed that Simon's album and tour violated the cultural boycott, a crucial component of the sanctions programme then in effect against South Africa. Even after the UN Anti-Apartheid Committee called the objections "misconceived", many idealogues continued to label Simon an imperialist, accusing him of appropriating local culture.

In fact, Paul Simon's role and methods, although obviously self-serving to a degree, appear largely exemplary. The artist went out of his way to credit his collaborators and then used all the commercial clout and prestige he could muster to establish the Black Mambazo in the international arena. The contrast between Simon's behaviour and that of British pop producer Malcolm McClaren a few years earlier could not have been clearer. McClaren hired South African musicians and composers to create the substance of a series of recordings which produced the hit "Double Dutch", then refused to pay any of the promised royalties, only grudgingly capitulating after the case reached the British High Court.

Thanks to the platform provided by Paul Simon, Ladysmith Black Mambazo launched themselves as international artists and today the group tours the world. Iscathamiya is now almost certainly the most widely recognized form of South African music and the Black Mambazo are the country's single most famous musical ambassadors.

of Zulu a cappella. Initially at least the Mambazo's popularity owed more to the quality of Shabalala's lyrics than to any remarkable musical innovations, but his seven-man group was ambitious, disciplined and willing to soldier on through an endless number of appearances arranged by Alexius Buthelezi of Radio Zulu.

In 1973, Ladysmith Black Mambazo released their initial album, "Amabutho", the first African LP to achieve Gold Record status (sales of 25,000 – and it later went on to sell many times that figure). The group has now recorded over thirty records all of which have gone gold – even the recent more religious ones. The lineup on each album has varied from seven to thirteen voices while the increasingly rich harmonies have been combined with ever more softly modulated dynamics, but the underlying framework remains much the same as originated by Solomon Linda back in the 1930s. Only Zulu speakers, however, are able to appreciate the subtle, metaphorical, and deeply evocative words of Shabalala's songs.

THE NEO-TRADITIONAL STYLES

While most South African styles evolved against a backdrop of migration to the towns and – with the exception of mbube-iscathamiya – have assumed a pan-tribal character, the traditionally-based music of the Sotho, Zulu, Pedi and Shangaan rural areas, adapted to imported instruments, is an important element in South Africa's musical range. Interestingly, too, these **neo-traditional** music styles – which are usually labelled "Sotho-Traditional", "Zulu-Traditional" and so on – don't always use the western seven-note scale.

The Zulu, Sotho and Xhosa vocal/concertina records produced by several companies in the late 1930s and 40s consisted of a basic call-and-response structure with a **concertina** counterpoint to the lead vocal instead of the former group voices. The concertina became popular after World War I following the large scale import of cheap foreign models known as "bastari" after a popular Italian brand.

Sotho melodies and harmonizations are based on a six-note scale, with the lead, the call, a characteristic, half-sung, half-shouted vocal, usually of praise lyrics, delivered in a rapid, staccato fashion. The actual melody is often most strongly suggested by the response from the chorus voices or instruments. **Tshwatla Makala** was the first Sotho neo-traditional musician of any commercial significance. He used deftly-fingered runs on a concertina to counterpoint his vocals and became a mentor to numerous other concertina artists. The next Sotho-Traditional development was a pure a cappella style called *mohabelo*; frenetically intoned lead vocals and chanted response choruses, first popularized by the group **Basotho Dihoba**, led by Latsema Matsela, who was born in Lesotho, the source for his music. The most recent evolutionary stage of Sotho-Traditional has seen the concertina replaced by an accordion leading an electric backing band. Propelled by pounding bass lines and often including multivoice response choruses, these combinations produce a powerful and distinctive sound. The first LPs appeared in the late 1970s and **Tau Oa Matsheha** were the first famous group of this type.

The European influence in the principal neo-tradional style of the **Pedi** (related to the Sotho) is suggested by its name, *harepa*. In the nineteenth century, Lutheran missionaries were the first to proselytize among the Pedi, bringing with them the German **autoharp**. Local musicians soon adapted the instrument to indigenous musical forms (hence *harepa* from "harp"), plucking its strings in a single-note fashion to accompany their vocal music. The African call-and-response structure has remained, as have the Sotho-style harmonies – but the characteristic descending melodic lines of *harepa* strike most uninitiated listeners as alien and astringent. The most prolific and successful artist from the 1970s, when there was a little Pedi-Traditional harp boom, is probably the Gallo label's **Johannes Mohlala**.

The **Zulu** neo-traditional style followed a unique course by embracing the **guitar**, which had first been introduced by the Portuguese in the sixteenth century. It was compatible with indigenous harmonic practice and became popular among Zulus after cheap locally-made instruments became available in the 1930s. For several decades the sight of a Zulu man with a guitar, picking out a melody while walking along a rural road, was a familiar sight. Among all the different southern African cultures, only Zulus, the related Ndebeles of Zimbabwe, and the Shangaan, took up the instrument.

The father figure of Zulu-Traditional performance and recording is **John Bhengu**, born in central Zululand in 1930. As a street musician in Durban in the early 1950s, he had already earned a formidable reputation through his skill in adapting indigenous melodies to the guitar and particularly for his unique fingerpicking style called *ukupika* (before Bhengu, the guitar was always strummed). His records on the Troubadour

Zulu-Traditional musicians

label helped establish a standard Zulu-Traditional structure that became the model for several generations of performers, each song beginning with the *izihlabo* – an instrumental flourish – followed by the main melody, then interrupted once by the *ukubonga*, a spoken declamation of praise for clan, family, chief, or even the singer himself. In the late 1960s Bhengu switched from acoustic to electric guitar and adopted a new persona as the sensationally successful **Phuzushukela** ("Sugar Drinker"). Backed with a full mbaqanga production package that included an electrified rhythm section and backing vocals, this led to a golden era for Zulu-Trad music in the 1970s. Hundreds of recordings were produced by dozens of bands, constituting some of the most easily assimilable performances in any neo-traditional style.

In the last decade or so, Zulu traditional music has undergone a further evolution. Today it is usually referred to as *maskanda*, a Zulu derivation from the Afrikaans word *musikant* meaning musician. The influence of urban pop/bubblegum is discernible in the increasing use of electronic instrumentation while the now-standard bass and drum rhythm appears to be a modified pattern borrowed from local disco. After suffering a long standing decline in popularity, the concertina has mounted a surprising comeback and, as a counterfoil to

the guitar, it is now a mandatory part of any group. But much of the music has lately shed that roughness which formerly generated its energy and appeal.

The biggest selling maskanda album in many years – and one of the most unusual – was **Vusi Ximba**'s "Siyakudumisa", a maskanda comedy album which married the musical style and lyrics of staple African humour – for instance older woman chasing the much younger man. A subsequent, somewhat racier Ximba album was unsuccessful – a conservative Zulu audience rejected it as exceeding the bounds of decency.

The first neo-traditional **Shangaan** recordings (a language group of the region bordering Mozambique) were those made by **Francisco Baloyi** in the early 1950s for Gallo. These contained call-and-response vocals and a circular structure, descending melodic lines and harmonies which sound more African than European together with a distinctly Latin rhythm section made up of a guitar and several percussion instruments. In the 1950s and '60s Alexander Jafete and Fani Pfumo, two versatile Mozambiquans who played guitar and mandolin with equal facility, made hundreds of recordings for every studio in Johannesburg. Their work included contributions to many jive/mbaqanga sessions but they also recorded a large number of "Portuguese Shangaan" items that mixed those two elements. After 1975, with Mozambique's independence and revolution, and the opening of a Shangaan station by Radio Bantu, Shangaan-Traditional style was largely stripped of its overtly Portuguese component.

The typical modern Shangaan band features a male vocalist leading a female response chorus, an upfront lead guitar, and an electric keyboard or synth, with a bass-and-drums rhythm section pounding out a disco beat. The first prominent group with this new sound was **General MD Shirinda & the Gaza Sisters** in the mid-1970s (one of their songs later became "I Know What You Know" on Paul Simon's "Graceland"). Today, the hottest group in Shangaan pop/disco (as it is now labelled) is Tusk Records' **Thomas Chauke & the Shinyori Sisters** – probably the best-selling group in any neo-traditional genre.

SOUL AND THE RESISTANCE OF YOUTH

In the late 1960s, American soul music gained an enthusiastic following among black and coloured township teenagers – Wilson Pickett, Booker T and the MGs and Percy Sledge were especially popular. The record industry eventually issued hundreds of 45 rpm "seven singles" by **local soul** outfits sporting names like the Question Marks and the Hurricanes.

Most of it – typically featuring a Farfisa organ, a spare melodic outline on an electric guitar and a dance rhythm from bass and drums – does not make for inspiring listening. Instrumental performances predominated and where there were vocals English lyrics were generally preferred to African languages, though they usually sounded awkward.

A few years later, in the mid-1970s when imported US disco music became popular, local soul was easily modified to effect its transformation into local **disco**. Recording techniques, and in some instances the level of musicianship, had improved and more sophisticated keyboards came in. The characteristic disco bass lines and drum beat were grafted onto the bottom end but otherwise the other elements of the soul formula remained much the same. All these developments heralded a revolution in taste which profoundly affected every subsequent township music style.

There was also a generation cleavage (the older township residents disliked soul) which the political events of 1976 widened into an abyss. The spontaneous **uprising** of school children against government authority that marked the beginning of the end of apartheid was soon also directed at township parents and grandparents who were accused of "selling out" to the system. This political judgement was extended to matters of style and taste, including music. Virtually every pre-soul genre was now regarded by the young with suspicion, not merely for being old-fashioned but indicted as a government-sponsored, tribal opiate. The local audience for marabi, sax jives and mqashiyo-style mbaqanga vanished overnight, never to return. It's perhaps surprising to learn that an internationally renowned band like Mahlathini and the Mahotella Queens are now almost forgotten in their own country.

The relatively small percentage of soul and disco bands that achieved more than ephemeral popularity did so by tampering with the standard musical formulae in some trademark fashion. The most commercially successful band of all was undoubtedly the **Movers**. Discovered and first recorded by Hamilton Nzimande they only gained real fame under the tutelage of David Thekwane. Their secret was to temper soul with a healthy dose of marabi. The organ remained a prominent part of the foundation, but in addition to the usual chord patterns keyboardist Sankie Chounyane played intelligent, jazzy solos. More importantly, the Movers' sound featured prominent saxophones, either grouped as a section or playing extended solo lines. And they had writing ability: their hundreds of recordings included many strong original compositions, as well as covers.

The second important soul band was the **Soul Brothers**, also "discovered" by Nzimande, in 1975. The band's single most distinguishing characteristic was their two-part, almost quavering vocal harmonies, inspired by certain Shona vocal groups popular in Zimbabwe in the early 1970s. Otherwise, the band's saxophones and their rhythm section were more reminiscent of the later type of electric bass mbaqanga than of archetypal soul.

The Movers' complicated style defied easy imitation and in any event David Thekwane's violent reputation was enough to make any would-be close copyists somewhat wary. In contrast, the Soul Brothers spawned literally dozens of epheïeral clones, most of whom contented themselves with attempting their vocal style and organ accompaniment. Today the Soul Brothers are regarded as one of the country's "oldest" groups (although only two remain from the original line-up) and they are active both in the studio and on tour. Despite a high level of synthesizer saturation, their style is now referred

WHITE SOUTH AFRICAN MUSIC

The major influences on **Afrikaans music** since World War I have been American. While Afrikaans musical roots lie with Dutch and French sources, **hillbilly string bands** added the final ingredients to a concertina-led brand of dance music which began to be recorded in the early 1930s. Today this style has been revived as "traditional" but its antiquarian pretensions far exceed the historical reality. Traditional *boeremusiek* is now closely associated with Afrikaner right-wing politics but the music produced by an all-acoustic, traditional Afrikaans "orkes" can nonetheless be exhilarating. One of the best traditional groups is the **Oudag Boereorkes** who have recorded several albums and occasionally appear in European festivals.

Within the Afrikaner community there was also a decided predilection for imitating the most mawkish and maudlin elements of American **country music**. In the 1930s a legion of melancholic duos and trios specialized in *trane trekkers* ("tear jerkers") and the same sentimental tendency was still very much in evidence among a later generation of artists influenced by Jim Reeves (massively popular amongst Afrikaners). There are, of course, clear parallels between the experiences of Afrikaners and whites in the American south.

The growing nationalist fervor of Afrikanderdom after World War I revealed a class-based musical fault line. The audience that preferred concertina dances and trane trekkers was agrarian or urban working class. In contrast, most Afrikaner nationalists came from a more educated, middle-class background, with musical prejudices fashioned by the elitist European cultural establishment. Traditional melodies were championed as the true voice of the "volk" but were acceptable only if rendered in "serious" performance. Most nationalists detested the truly popular Afrikaans styles of the day and complained at length when labels began committing them to disc. Radio stations promoted a gradual "upgrading" of mainstream Afrikaans music at the expense of rural sounds.

The musician who dominated the 1950s was accordionist **Nico Carstens** whose lightly swinging, slightly jazz-inflected dance music was extremely successful. The trend thereafter was to incorporate MOR sounds, then later in the 1970s, Eurobeat. Afrikaans music lost much of its distinctiveness in the process. Today the state of the music is exemplified by the most – indeed almost the only – commercially successful Afrikaans entertainer, **Bles Bridges**, a Wayne Newton imitator whose trademark is throwing plastic roses at his predominantly middle-aged female audiences.

Only two artists or groups have made an international impression as English-speaking South Africans. **Johnny Clegg** began performing Zulu-Traditional material with **Sipho Mchunu** in the early 1970s, then later expanded into a full electric band format as **Juluka.** The increasingly westernized sound eventually led to Mchunu's departure and the band dissolved to be replaced by a new lineup called **Savuka.** Clegg has enjoyed major success in France (as "Le Zoulou Blanc") and a more limited popularity in the UK and America. While much of his music sounds predominantly Western, and his group's image remains highly dependent on their energetic Zulu dance routines, there's no denying Clegg's commitment to freedom during the darkest days of apartheid, when his open embrace of African culture was an audacious statement.

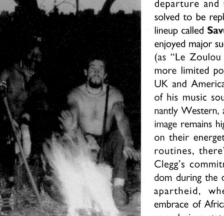
Sipho Mchunu and Johnny Clegg

There is an even more marked contrast between image and musical content in **Mango Groove**, the latest South African crossover export who have experienced some success in the UK, France and Australia. While they are advertised as having achieved a synthesis of white pop and township style, the core sound is not really African but a slickly arranged orchestral pop – the kind of thing that was popularized three decades ago by German bands like Bert Kaempfert and Horst Wende. More recently, Mango Groove's material has downplayed the African element even further to concentrate on raising the profile of their white female lead singer.

to as mbaqanga, proof positive of the all-encompassing elasticity of that label.

The Cannibals, starring the young guitarist **Ray Phiri** (now famous through his recording and performing with Paul Simon), achieved recognition playing instrumentals under their own name and backing various Gallo mqashiyo artists such as Irene Mawela and the Mahotella Queens. In 1975, the band was paired with Jacob "Mparanyana" Radebe, probably the single finest male vocalist of the entire soul-disco era. Four years of recordings followed (until Radebe's death in 1979) under the name **Mparanyana and the Cannibals**, and the best of these, featuring Radebe's impassioned vocals and monologues together with a sharply produced backing of hot guitar, saxes and female choruses, invite favourable comparisons with Otis Redding's similar-sounding Stax material. The Cannibals eventually evolved into **Stimela** in the 1980s, updating their style with more contemporary Afro-jazz influences.

One hugely successful soul band of the early 1970s, the **Flames**, exclusively covered American soul and mainstream pop. The Flames were something of an anomaly and not only because of their multi-racial following. The band members were coloured, not African, based in Durban instead of Johannesburg, and generally recorded albums rather than singles. Two members, Steve Fataar and Blondie Chaplin, emigrated to the USA and joined the Beach Boys in 1972.

The demise of the Flames created an opening for another local band that could convincingly interpret American-style funk, soul and pop music for a young African-to-white audience. Selby Ntuli, Sipho Mabuse and Alec Khaoli joined together as the Beaters, then renamed the band **Harari** after a successful tour of Zimbabwe. After returning to South Africa, they began to draw almost exclusively on overseas rock influences. In fact, the only distinctively South African element was linguistic, as they featured lyrics in Zulu and Sotho as well as English. It all proved very successful and, together with the band's ethnic designer-chic, attracted a big multi-racial following. After Ntuli's death in 1979, the Mabuse-Khaoli partnership dissolved and both musicians persued separate careers. **Sipho "Hotstix" Mabuse** reached local superstar status in the later 1980s with huge hits like "Burnout" and "Jive Soweto" (the latter featuring West Nkosi on sax) which finally achieved a seamless, totally South African, synthesis of mbaqanga, pop and soul.

BUBBLEGUM

The latest development in township music took place in the mid 1980s with the ascendency of a slickly produced brand of African pop referred to by fans and detractors alike as **bubblegum**. In certain respects, bubblegum is basically an indigenous style – more vocal than instrumental, with the vocals arranged as overlapping call-and-response patterns where one short melodic phrase is repeated in traditional fashion. In other respects, however, bubblegum reflects the culmination of more contemporary tendencies. The modern love affair with electronic keyboards has now triumphed completely. Bubblegum is awash with synthesizers – as many as four in one band – and even the modified disco beat which propels the music is usually now produced by an electronic drum box. Saxophones are rarely heard while the guitar has fallen completely out of favour.

Four musicians can rightfully claim to be the most popular and enduring figures in bubblegum. The group **Splash** is in reality almost entirely the creation of vocalist **Dan Tshanda**, who composes and produces all the music and has retained control over the careers of the band's spin-off artists.

Sello "Chicco" Twala, like Tshanda, is an all-round vocalist, instrumentalist, arranger, composer and producer. One of his biggest hits, "We Miss You Manelo", was a coded tribute to the then-imprisoned Nelson Mandela. A later piece of political commentary which also became a hit, "Papa Stop The War" from 1990, resulted from an interesting collaboration with **Mzwakhe Mbuli**, where the almost hypnotic spoken cadences of the "people's poet" were set against Chicco's collage of synth textures and backing vocals.

Chicco contributed in the late 1980s to the career of "The Princess Of Africa" **Yvonne Chaka Chaka**. "I'm in Love with a DJ", her first single in 1984, was a massive hit and immediately launched a career that has produced a string of gold and platinum successes. Her belting alto voice with its distinctive timbre accounts for much of her popularity, but her success is partly down to the unusually high standard of her well-crafted and arranged material. Chaka Chaka's songs are usually built on two catchy interlocking melodies, and the lyrics – which are almost always in English – are nicely phrased and convey real meaning. She has become South Africa's most successful export to the rest of Africa since Ladysmith Black Mambazo in the 1970s. While cassette piracy makes sales figures an unreliable gauge, the wildly enthusiastic reception she has received in countries as far afield as Zaire and Uganda testifies to a large and dedicated following.

Brenda Fassi is Chaka Chaka's big rival. Like Chaka Chaka, she had an immediate hit with her first single, "Weekend Special", and she has remained a prominent bubblegum artist ever since. Fassi's real appeal is difficult to pin down, but she has a talent for self-promotion that would do credit to Madonna (a figure with whom she's frequently compared) and she still lives close to her audience in the lower-middle-class area between Soweto and Johannesburg, while Chaka Chaka has moved off to the affluent and mostly white suburbs north of the city. Lyrically, Fassi's songs are a mish-mash of the latest township lingo, sometimes barely comprehensible even to locals, but they stick in the minds of her listeners. Her most recent release, "Amagents", was the biggest local album of 1993.

THE FUTURE

Sales of South African music in South Africa have dropped sharply in recent years, from a third of total sales in 1990 to a mere 17 percent in 1993. While the recent recession has been disastrous, radio programming shares the blame. For years, locally recorded music has been receiving less and less radio exposure, even on the former Radio Bantu ethnic stations of the SABC. And when Radio Metro, an SABC station that targets the urban African audience with a largely African-American playlist, suddenly expanded their reception area from Johannesburg-Pretoria to cover the rest of the country, local music sales began to drop within weeks while those of Metro's international fare rose accordingly, even in traditional "ethnic" areas. The local recording industry is now lobbying the broadcasting authority to implement a minimum local content quota similar to those in force in Australia, Canada and France. But lack of radio exposure is only part of the problem. While people are bored with bubblegum, the record industry has neither the ability nor the interest to develop a replacement and nor will new broadcasting policies alter the perceived value of almost any US import. An expensive American CD is going to continue to bring its owner more credibility than any home-dubbed cassette of the latest local sounds. And slick commercial fare from the US will continue to provide many of the models which South African musicians will want to emulate. Music from the rest of Africa might help to temper American influence. It's been tried before, but usually without success because most African music just sounds foreign to local ears.

Ironically, some of South Africa's musical riches can be attributed to the colonial mission education of the early part of this century, in which music theory and practice played a major role. When it was replaced with the stultifying banalities of Bantu Education under apartheid, children's musical talent was allowed to wither. It's to be hoped that the schools in the new South Africa don't regard a musical education as a frivolity.

South African reggae and ragga is covered in the Reggae feature in Chapter Ten.

DISCOGRAPHY

Many of these releases are Gallo recordings (either on the Gallo label, or their subsidiary Teal). However, most, if not all the CD releases are available on the labels of overseas licensees – usually Kaz (UK), Celluloid (France), Conversation (Japan) or Shanachie (US). A discography of South African jazz can be found at the end of the next article.

TRADITIONAL & NEO-TRADITIONAL

Ⓒ **Various** *The Heartbeat of Soweto* (Shanachie, US). Misleading title for a collection of fairly recent examples of Zulu- Shangaan- and Tsonga-Traditional styles.
Various *Music of the !Kung Bushmen* (Folkways, US). The most accessible example of this music.
Ⓒ **Various** *Singing in an Open Space* (Rounder, US). The only neo-traditional historical survey, which charts two decades of development of Zulu-Trad from simple acoustic guitar accompaniment to a full band format.

Ⓒ **Various** *Songs from the Roadside Vol I* (Rounder, US). Forthcoming re-release of recordings by Hugh Tracey of Bantu-language music with minimal external influences.
Various *Siyahlabelela Kwazulu – Songs Of Zululand* (Gallo, South Africa). Well worth searching for, though sadly out of print.

MARABI

Ⓒ **Various** *Township Swing Jazz* (Harlequin, UK). A good overview of the marabi/swing bands of the 1950s and early 60s.

PENNYWHISTLE AND SAX JIVE

Ⓒ **Spokes Mashiyane** *King Kwela* (Celluloid, France). A reissue of Mashiyane's classic 1958 Trutone release.
Ⓒ **West Nkosi** *Sixteen Original Sax Jive Hits* (Gallo, South Africa). The single best collection of the genre.
Ⓒ **Various** *Jackpot 15,000* (Gallo, South Africa). A compilation of classic cuts from producer Nzimande's stable.

○ **Various** *Best of Pennywhistle* (Gallo, South Africa). In a field with very little available, this forthcoming 2-CD set with some 50 tracks is worth looking out for.

MBAQANGA

○ **The Boyoyo Boys** *Back in Town* (Rounder, US). The vocal mbaqanga group whose song "Puleng" inspired Malcolm McLaren's "Double Dutch" – though this recording was made long after that time.

Izintombi Zezi Manje Manje *Isitha Sami Nguwe* (Gallo, South Africa). One of seven compilations of recordings by the biggest rivals to Mahlathini & the Mahotella Queens. The other six have their moments, but this is the one to go for first.

○ **Mahlathini** *The Lion of Soweto* (Earthworks, UK). Simon Nkabinde in the 1970s, after his bust-up with Bopape. Not tops, but available.

○ **Mahlathini & the Mahotella Queens** *The Lion Roars* (Shanachie, USA). Classic recordings from the 1960s and early 70s. For a taste of the current edition of the band, get the ○ *Best of…* (Kaz, UK), ○ *Thokozile* (Earthworks, UK) or ○ *Mbaqanga* (Kaz, UK/Shanachie, US), which is perhaps the strongest of the available CD releases.

○ **Mahotella Queens** *Marriage is a Problem* (Shanachie, US). Classic Queens sound, *sans* Mahlathini, from the late 1960s and early 1970s.

○ **Various** *Zulu Jive: Umbaqanga* (Earthworks, UK/Carthage, US). Pacey selection of cuts re-released from 1983 of urban soul-style mbaqanga from Joshua Sithole, more traditional pounding from Aaron Mbambo and Shoba, and accordion/guitar jive from Sithole's backing band The Rainbows.

MBUBE/ISCATHAMIYA

○ **Reuben Caluza's Double Quartet** *1930s – African Ragtime* (Heritage, UK). Featuring the work of composer Reuben Caluza, this offers a good selection of the group's landmark 1930 recordings which contributed to the development of both urban styles and mbube-ischathamiya.

○ **Ladysmith Black Mambazo** *Favourites* (Gallo, South Africa). ○ *Classic Tracks* and ○ *The Best of…* (Shanachie, USA). First-class ports of entry into a vast back catalogue, most of which is still available. Once smitten, try ○ *Shaka Zula* (Warners, US), the album produced by Paul Simon, which best captures the group's sound as it has evolved after many years of development.

○ **Various** *Mbube Roots* (Rounder, US). A wonderful survey covering the history of mbube and early iscathamiya.

SOUL

The Movers *The Best of the Best Vol 1* and *Vol 2* (Gallo, South Africa). If not actually "the best", still the first to be released, and huge sellers. Vol 2 is worth getting just for the wonderful track "Soweto Inn".

○ **Sipho "Hotstix" Mabuse** *The Best of Sipho Mabuse* (Gallo, South Africa). Mabuse's two essential hits "Jive Soweto" and "Burn Out" nicely packaged on this ten-track compilation.

Jacob "Mpharanyana" Radebe *Burning Soul* (Teal, South Africa). All the greatest hits of the most influential South African soul vocalist.

○ **Soul Brothers** *Soul Mbaqanga: the Dance Remixes* (Riverboat, UK). The brothers reggae-fied by producer Chris Birkett of Sinéad O'Connor and Mango Groove fame. For something more representative, try ○ *Jive Explosion* (Earthworks, UK). Their classic, early sound, culled from the Nzimande glory days in the 1970s is *Mantombanzane*, on cassette only.

BUBBLEGUM

○ **Yvonne Chaka Chaka** *The Best of…* (Teal, South Africa). An excellent introduction to the genre – contemporary township pop – with contents that are a cut above 98% of the rest in this category.

○ **Sello "Chicco" Twala** *The Best of Chicco* (Teal, South Africa). Along with Chaka Chaka, Chicco's songs are well made, and stand out above the bubblegum crowd.

COMPILATIONS

○ **Various** *From Marabi to Disco* (Gallo, South Africa). Lovingly compiled by Rob Allingham, this comprises a one-stop compendium of the history of the urban township style over a period of four decades. Twenty-eight tracks and every one a classic!

○ **Various** *Siya Hamba! 1950s South African Country & Small Town Sounds* (Original Music, US). A mix of neo-traditional (even a Pedi autoharp!) and early township jive, recorded by musicologist Hugh Tracey.

○ **Various** *The Indestructible Beat of Soweto Vols 1-4* (Earthworks, UK). If not for a new Gallo release, this series would have to take star billing – over fifty great tracks from the 1980s mixing later-phase mbaqanga, some soul and even the more urbanized of the neo-traditional genres. A prequel compilation ○ *The Kings and Queens of Township Jive* showcases some of the big names from the 1970, while a best of the best ○ *A Taste of the Indestructible Beat of Soweto* is just that… As Trevor Herman writes, "best heard loud and standing up".

CROSSOVER

○ **Paul Simon** *Graceland* (Warner, UK/US). Simply too good, after all these years, and musically too interesting, to omit. Features, alongside large measures of Simon, the Boyoyo Boys, Baghiti Khumalo, General Shirinda and the Gaza Sisters, Ray Phiri and of course Ladysmith Black Mambazo. If you missed out on your own copy during cultural boycott days, it's not about to go out of print…

HIP KINGS, HIP QUEENS

THE STORY OF SOUTH AFRICAN JAZZ,
AT HOME AND OVERSEAS

The decade between World War II and the late 1950s was the great Age of Jazz in South Africa. Rob Allingham charts the connections that led up to it, visits the major figures and listens to the current state of play.

The postwar era was a time of tremendous growth and innovation for Africans in all the arts, and corresponded to a substantial population increase in the townships as migrants poured in from the rural areas to take jobs in a rapidly expanding industrial economy. Living conditions remained sub-standard or desperate for many, but before the draconian structures of the new apartheid system were fully implemented, township residents indulged themselves with a certain reckless optimism and even an illusion of permanency and belonging.

The acknowledged connection between jazz and the cultural and political ferment of the times is largely due to a talented group of journalists and writers associated with "Drum", the black illustrated magazine that documented the era. Much of the jazz audience and most jazz musicians came from similar urban backgrounds and were products of mission school educations. At least some of their enthusiasm for jazz had more to do with attitude, style and aspirations than any attributes of the music itself. Tribalism, traditionalism and ruralism – the values extolled by apartheid policy – were rejected in favour of the apparent success and sophistication of the African-American lifestyle, of which jazz was perceived to be an integral component. Ironically, at the very time that jazz was being embraced by African urbanites, it had already been abandoned by most of their American role models for more accessible genres like rhythm and blues. In fact, the predominent type of jazz being incorporated into the South African variety was swing, already regarded as passé in the USA by the late 1940s.

Unlike earlier African-American music, transmitted directly by visiting performers, there wasn't a single early example of an American jazz or swing player, black or white,

touring South Africa (the first, Tony Scott, arrived much later in 1956). Instead, printed orchestrations, films and recordings provided the sole source of inspiration. American jazz records were being sold in South Africa as early as the late 1920s but only became a common commodity during World War II. Visiting Allied soldiers brought the latest swing band hits into the country and heightened local awareness of contemporary jazz and swing developments in Britain and the US.

By 1950, most towns supported at least one or two local jazz bands. The cities of Cape Province – East London, Port Elizabeth and Cape Town – were particularly jazz-oriented, perhaps because of their predominently Xhosa populations: the complex harmonies and structures of traditional Xhosa music helped to foster an intuitive understanding of jazz harmony and improvisation.

But, as usual, it was Johannesburg where the cutting edge of innovation was sharpest and which hosted the greatest number of bands and the biggest audience. The city's "Concert and Dance" circuit spawned Solomon "Zulu Boy" Cele's **Jazz Maniacs**, the archetypal "African Jazz" band of the late 1930s. After World War II, the equally influential **Harlem Swingsters** were active for several years. Alumni from both bands went on to create other groups, some of which remained popular for another two decades. Alto saxophonist-composer **Isaac "Zacks" Nkosi** from the Jazz Maniacs, led bands under various names, like the Country Jazz Band and the City Jazz Nine, supported by stalwarts like tenor man **Ellison Temba** and trumpeter **Elijah Nkwanyane**. Another ex-Maniac, tenor saxophonist **Wilson "King Force" Silgee**, led the Jazz Forces. **Ntemi Piliso** left the Harlem Swingsters to form the Alexandra All Stars, thus initiating an important career as a tenor soloist, composer and band leader.

Unless they happened to be reading from an imported score (most jazz musicians could read music), township jazz bands played in a dynamic, original style that mixed elements of American swing with the basic structure of **marabi** – the name by which African Jazz continued to be known. The songs consisted of one or two repeated melodic phrases constructed over two or three chords. Although they were less complicated in structure than a typical American jazz composition, these essentially African melodies were then performed with the instrumentation of an overseas swing band. This permitted the complex voicings and arranged alternation between sections – usually brass against saxophones – that had typified American big-band jazz since the 1920s.

Frequently, there was considerable space available for solos. Sometimes these consisted of a straight restatement of the melody; at other times, a considerable degree of improvisation was involved. In the case of the most imaginative and technically advanced players like clarinetist-altoist **Kippie Moeketsi**, there were touches of bop and cool jazz, styles which otherwise largely by-passed South Africa.

THE JAZZ SINGERS

This was also the great era of female African Jazz vocalists, many of whom modelled their style on the likes of Ella Fitzgerald or Sarah Vaughan, but like their instrumentalist counterparts, sang what were essentially marabi-structured melodies. **Dolly Rathebe** was the first to come to prominence as the leading actress-singer in the first African feature film, "Jim Comes To Jo'burg" (1948). She also starred in the superb "Magic Garden" in 1951, and as "The Queen Of The Blues" retained her fame and popularity for another decade. Next in the spotlight was Zimbabwean **Dorothy Masuka** (interviewed in the article following this) who began her sensational career as a vocalist and recording artist in 1951. Like Dolly Rathebe, Masuka was also a famous "cover girl" in the black picture press.

Male solo jazz singers were a far less common breed but there were a number of male vocal quartets. The best known of these was the **Manhattan Brothers** led by Nathan "Dambuza" Mdledle, whose celebrity in the late 1940s and early 50s was matched only by Rathebe and Masuka. Although regarded as part of the local jazz firmament, the Manhattans' roots lay in a slightly different African-American tradition: the secular-pop branch of close-harmony singing that antedated jazz and later developed alongside it in a parallel fashion, eventually producing groups like the Mills Brothers and the Inkspots and then later still,

doo-wop. Philemon Mokgotsi's **African Inkspots** offered the Manhattans some stiff competition until the mid-50s when the **Woody Woodpeckers** led by **Victor Ndlazilwane** eclipsed both groups with their striking mixture of Xhosa-Traditional and American jazz-influenced melodies and harmonies.

Miriam Makeba, the last singing star to come out of the Jazz Era, was perhaps the most significant. She first came to public attention as a featured vocalist with the Manhattan Brothers in 1954, then left to record with her own all-female **Skylarks** vocal group while touring the country with impressario Alf Herberts' African Jazz & Variety, a talent vehicle which launched the careers of many black artists. In 1959, Makeba took on the female lead in **"King Kong"**, a South African-Broadway musical crossover billed as a "jazz opera" with a fine score by pianist-composer Todd Matshikiza. Sharing the top billing was Nathan Mdledle of the Manhattans playing the part of the boxer, King Kong, who murders his girlfriend and dies in prison. This slice of township life electrified its audiences, black and white alike. To circumvent apartheid regulations which rigidly segregated public entertainment, it was often staged at universities.

Miriam Makeba – now back home from exile

At the very apogee of this success, Makeba left the country for the United States. There she quickly re-established her career with "The Click Song" and "Phatha Phatha" and transferred her celebrity status to the international stage, the first South African to do so. She also fired an opening salvo in the external battle against apartheid with her impassioned testimonial before the United Nations in 1963. The South African government, irritated by the glare of adverse publicity, responded by revoking her citizenship and right of return. After her marriage to Stokeley

Carmichael, one of the leaders of the Black Panthers, she was also harassed by the American authorities and, despite the support of the likes of Marlon Brando and Nina Simone, fled again to exile in Guinea.

Makeba was only the first exile of many. In 1961, "King Kong" was staged in London where it enjoyed a successful run. And after the show closed, many of the cast – including the four Manhattan Brothers – chose not to return. The outward rush of South Africa's artistic talent had begun.

PROGRESSIVE JAZZ
IN THE 1960S

In the 1960s South African jazz divided into two distinct strains, similar to the dichotomy affecting American jazz in the immediate postwar years. On the one hand, the marabi-style dance bands still commanded a large following and a new "African Jazz" band, the **Elite Swingsters**, began a long and distinguished career by recording "Phalafala", probably South Africa's biggest selling jazz disc ever. On the other, a new type of jazz was evolving that emulated the American avant garde led by Thelonious Monk, Sonny Rollins and John Coltrane and which strove for a more self-conscious artistry. It also incorporated an overtly political dimension as protest music, a wordless assault on apartheid and all that it symbolized.

Despite the fact that it was essentially elitist and indeed less "African" than its marabi-based counterpart, this jazz on the American model became, indeed remains, inexorably identified with the people's struggle.

Trumpeter **Hugh Masekela**, trombonist **Jonas Gwangwa**, pianist **Dollar Brand** and that most forward-thinking of the older generation jazzmen, **Kippie Moeketsi**,

Hugh Masekela

Dudu Pukwana blowing for freedom

constituted the core of the progressive first wave. Masekela and Gwangwa played together as teenagers in the **Father Huddleston Band** (named after their mentor, the famed English anti-apartheid Anglican priest) before graduating to the Jazz Dazzlers, a small band that included Moeketsi and provided the instrumental accompaniment to "King Kong".

In 1959 **John Mehegan**, a visiting American pianist, organized the "Jazz In Africa" recording session, featuring Masekela, Gwangwa and Moeketsi. This produced the first two LPs by African jazzmen and the first opportunity to overcome the time restraints imposed by the three minute-a-side 78 rpm format. After Mehegan's departure, Capetonian Dollar Brand arrived to take over the piano. The resulting formation, now called the **Jazz Epistles**, recorded another album and garnered a great deal of critical acclaim for its performance at the first Cold Castle National Jazz Festival in 1960. Then, rather suddenly, Brand left for Switzerland – and international jazz renown – followed quickly by Masekela and Gwangwa, both of whom remained in exile in the United States for another three decades.

The departure of three of the principal Epistles left a large gap in the local jazz scene, but the

1962 Cold Castle Jazz Festival demonstrated that a new generation of jazzmen had been inspired by their example. Pianist-composer **Chris McGregor** and tenor saxophonist **Dudu Pukwana** were probably the most famous and influential musicians in this new wave. Kippie Moeketsi remained an inspiration and **Gideon Nxumalo**, an older pianist-composer who like Moeketsi had grown up in the Harlem Swingsters, blossomed into a particularly original talent.

The best players from several different bands which had performed at the 1963 Cold Castle Festival were gathered together under the direction of Chris McGregor and produced a classic LP, "Jazz The African Sound", perhaps the finest single product of a brilliant era. Sadly, it also proved to be a swansong. A general wave of oppression had followed the Sharpville massacre of 1960 and, as the government dug in with its new order, many of South Africa's best minds and talents fled the country into exile.

The progressive jazzers were badly affected as apartheid regulations designed to separate mixed-race bands and audiences became increasingly onerous. In the face of this dispiriting onslaught, McGregor, Pukwana and their entire band, the **Blue Notes**, including Louis Moholothe, left the country for good in 1964. The Blue Notes, and their later manifestation the Brotherhood of Breath, added a distinctive touch to the rather moribund European jazz scene but, as was the case with other exiles, their influence on musical development in South Africa ceased at that point.

AFTER THE DIASPORA

The exile of so many talents left South African jazz fans and historians forever pondering "what if ..." but there were still some fine and interesting moments to come. The **Malombo Jazz Men** featuring Abbey Cinde on flute, Philip Tabane on guitar and Julian Bahula on African drums, won first prize at the final Cold Castle Festival in 1964 with an intriguing mixture of jazz harmony and improvisation crossed with indigenous Venda music.

In the 1970s a further stylistic refinement prolonged the popularity of the old **marabi-based bands**. The Elite Swingsters, Zacks Nkosi, and two Ntemi Piliso studio bands, the Alexandra All Stars and The Members, wedded the electric instrumentation of mbaqanga – guitar, bass and keyboards – to a jazz-style front line with brass and saxophones. Long, leisurely

performances which often took up an entire LP side (as in the case of the Elite's hit "Now Or Never" or the Members' equally popular "Way Back Riverside") were constructed from simple chord progressions with no shortage of space provided for the solos. This was township good-time music for dancing, drinking and partying, and it remained popular with all age groups until the late 1970s when local soul and disco finally displaced it.

The **progressive jazz** strain produced a few more classics before it also dried up for lack of an audience. Saxophonist **Winston "Mankunku" Ngozi** scored a substantial hit in 1968 with his Coltrane-influenced "Yakal Nkomo". In 1974, Dollar Brand returned to South Africa for the first time in over a decade and recorded his classic "Mannenburg" with Cape alto saxophonist **Basil Coetzee**. "Mannenburg", a dramatically slowed version of an old Zacks Nkosi tune called "Jackpot", reaffirmed Brand's marabi roots and contrasted dramatically with the Americanized style which had given him a measure of international fame. The **Jazz Ministers**, led by composer, vocalist and tenor sax man **Victor Ndlazilwane**, mixed touches of marabi and mainstream and underlaid both with a distinctive Xhosan essence. The Ministers performed at the 1976 Newport Jazz Festival – the first all-South African lineup to appear there – and Ndlazilwane's early death a few years later deprived local jazz of one of its finest voices.

JAZZ TODAY

Jazz had virtually disappeared in South Africa by the end of the 1980s, but has staged a dramatic comeback in the last few years. A promising **new generation** of young artists has grown up – a sure sign of musical health and renewal – and the jazz scene today seems more vibrant than at any time since the relatively halcyon days of the early 1970s. Musicians such as saxophonist **Zim Ngqawana** and keyboard player **Khaya Mahlangu** have swelled the ranks of the faithful few, including saxophonists **Mike Makhalemele** and **Barney Rachabane** and pianist **Tete Mbambisa**, who kept the spirit going during the bad years.

Many of the jazz exiles who survived the experience of dislocation have now returned home to revitalize the music. Miriam Makeba, the first major figure to leave, is once again a South African resident while her old friend and rival, Dorothy Masuka, persona non grata with the authorities since 1961, is also back and

Abdullah Ibrahim – aka pianist Dollar Brand

(formerly Dollar Brand), lives in New York but occasionally performs in South Africa. His current style retains a degree of local flavour but adheres more closely to a pure jazz idiom.

Representing an even older tradition, two bands derived directly from the late-marabi style with an electric rhythm section are now performing and recording regularly once again. The Elite Swingsters' sax-dominated ensembles feature the added attraction of Dolly Rathebe, still in fine form as a vocalist. Ntemi Piliso's **African Jazz Pioneers** enjoy a measure of renown in France and Japan that probably exceeds their reputation at home, pointing up the continuing contradiction that the jazz style which is most purely South African is precisely the one least favoured by those who embrace jazz as Afro-chic.

Revival or no, it's perhaps not surprising that jazz still means very little from the South African commercial standpoint. Indeed, the largest single music-buying audience, the township youth, continue to ignore it in favour of their own bubblegum pop.

determined to rebuild her once formidable reputation. Singer **Letta Mbulu** and her producer-arranger husband Caiphus Semenya have returned after two decades' success in the American music industry, bringing back skills to further develop their own local jazz roots. Hugh Masekela and Jonas Gwangwa now regularly gig in and around Johannesburg but their current repertoire is a far cry from the modernist approach of the old Jazz Epistles. During three decades in exile their music gradually expanded to include a measure of homestyle marabi and mbaqanga as well as African-American funk and soul. The result is an exciting and totally South African mixture, albeit one with considerable jazz overtones. The other prominent ex-Epistle, **Abdullah Ibrahim**

DISCOGRAPHY

A s in the main South Africa discography, most of the following released on South African labels are available overseas through licensees.

JAZZ VOCAL

Miriam Makeba & the Skylarks *Miriam Makeba & the Skylarks* (Teal, South Africa). A 2-CD set of thirty-two wonderful recordings from the 50s featuring a wide variety of accompanists. Kaz (UK) has done an inferior single-CD *Best Of. . .* release from these.

Various *King Kong: Original Cast* (Celluloid, France). The South African soundtrack of the 1959 musical with Kippie Moeketsi, the Manhattan Brothers, Miriam Makeba and Hugh Masakela among others.

INSTRUMENTAL JAZZ

African Jazz Pioneers *Live at the Montreux Jazz Festival* (Kaz, UK). Ntemi Piliso and his current band in fine form in 1991.

Jazz Espistles *Verse One* (Celluloid, France). Dollar Brand, with Hugh Masakela, Kippie Moeketsi and Jonas Gwangwa. The South African version of US mainstream.

Jonas Gwangwa *Flowers of the Nation* (Tusk Kariba, South Africa). Recorded in the UK before his recent return to South Africa, a contemporary mixture of jazz and South African urban influences.

Dollar Brand *African Sun* (Kaz, UK). Just one of a series of Kaz releases of South African jazz, featuring Ibrahim (Dollar

Brand) and a raft of other luminaries. ⓒ *Blues for a Hip King* is dedicated to the cool monarch of Swaziland. Superb.

ⓒ **Hugh Masekela** *Hope* (Triloka, US). Recent live recording of greatest hits with a newly assembled, young band.

ⓒ **Chris McGregor** *Live in Willisau* (Ogun, UK). Recorded in 1974 in Switzerland. This features all the Blue Notes originals.

ⓒ *Jazz The African Sound* (Teal, South Africa). Finest of any South African contemporary jazz, from the white-South African pianist. All-star line-up.

ⓒ **Zacks Nkosi** *Tribute* (Celluloid, France) and *Our Kind of Jazz* (Conversation, Japan). In Gallo's African Classics series, valedictory recordings by one of the major African Jazz performers and composers.

ⓒ **Gideon Nxumalo** *Jazz Fantasia* (Teal, South Africa). Fronted by the pianist and compser Nxumalo, this is the only recording featuring both Kippie Moeketsi and Dudu Pukwana. Fine stuff.

ⓒ **Various** *Jazz in Africa Vol. 1* and *Vol. 2* (Kazuk). Major icons of the 1960s reinstated after an absence of over two decades, including American John Mehegan, Moeketsi, Masekela and Gwangwa; basically the Jazz Espistles before they were called such (and before Ibrahim).

PUT MORE ZESA!

JIT, MBIRA AND CHIMURENGA: MUSIC OF ZIMBABWE

Zimbabweans like their music loud – a problem in a country where equipment is scarce and public address systems often poor. But that doesn't deter the punters, who throng to have their ears blasted and their hips bumped. Wherever you go, the distorted thump from straining speakers driven beyond their full capacity is part of the experience and makes for an electric atmosphere. Judy Kendall goes out dancing and talks to musicians through the din.

Zesa! Zesa! Put more Zesa! Harare's nightclubs reverberate with this cry at the end of the month when payday brings out the crowds. Zesa is the national electricity board, struggling, as everywhere in Africa, to meet the needs of its consumers. On payday they want to go out to hear Oliver Mtukudzi's experiments with traditional beats at Club Hide Out, or the rumba swing of The Real Sounds at The Playboy, or Thomas Mapfumo with his *chimurenga* music at Queens Garden – a popular haunt of tourists and pickpockets.

Harare, the capital of Zimbabwe, means "don't stop". It's a good name for a city where the bands go on forever, many of them dependent on their venues for equipment and practice time, and forced to play sometimes until dawn in all-night *pungwe* style. Before independence the pungwe was a dedication to the struggle. Now these herculean performances are dedicated more to beerhall profits. More hours means more drinking time and more bucks. Musically, it is not an enriching environment, and complaints of maltreatment and hardship abound. A member of the Black Spirits band

sighed: "We just promote in hotels to get enough money to live, and as for equipment, we have two guitars at the studio, but those are for recording only". And a sound engineer matter-of-factly asked: "Can you marry me so I can move to a studio in London – things are better there technically."

Because of the demand, there is a real need for stamina in both audience and band – and the music reflects this: songs are long and complex. There is time to build up a repetition that familiarizes the audience with a song and then to play around with the complex and intricate rhythms that have been set up by the guitars and the voice.

The gig scene in downtown Harare

When these bands, groomed to marathon performances, start performing elsewhere, they find it undemanding. The husband-manager of Stella Chiweshe, traditional *mbira* player, complains about squeezing her programme into a one hour show. "We have to limit her to 25 songs when she goes overseas".

But those who do make it "outside" (overseas) are often reluctant to return to the gruelling way of life as a Zimbabwean musician. As Dorothy Masuka, the veteran jazz singer from Bulawayo, explains, "I know that if I want money I must go out – a concert here will give you about enough to buy a bag of mealie meal [staple of ground corn]. I wouldn't do what the youngsters are doing these days – Kambuzuma today, Highfield tomorrow – it's too much hard work. You play in the bar and people come to drink. They don't appreciate your music. I'd rather do thirty minutes, work once and stay for a year not working – a big concert will give me enough money and is better than working three nights a week!"

COMING UP

The conservatism and chauvinism of Zimbabwe society has meant that **women musicians** have had a difficult time, and some brilliant musicians are unable to make their way. "I have been going around looking for girls", says Oliver Mtukudzi, "but when I find one she can't come to the stage and perform because she's scared of what people will say about her."

Thandeka Ngono, singer with Southern Freeway, explains: "It's a lot to do with the attitude that women in show business are whores – that they're cheap and loose. Zimbabwe really does not want to cater for women musicians, but since we are there, there's nothing they can do about it." Thandeka says that in her experience this is a problem unique to Zimbabwe. "I performed a lot in South Africa, and there were no problems about being a woman musician. When I tried to infiltrate here, I had problems. In order to get into a group I would first jam with them so that they could hear that I could sing, but that made it worse! Maybe they thought I was going to take their jobs!"

"There are plenty of women singing" says Amai Muchena, "but they have problems with the money – the band takes the money and you get nothing." Sexual harassment is also a problem, as Thandeka Ngono has found: "These guys seem to think that a female singer is a cheap person and it's easier to get at you than the other women around because you're prepared to go on stage."

In 1990, a Women Musicians' Advisory Group was set up, with the aim of advising and educating about rights and discrimination. Its members include all the top female performers. Stella Chiweshe is confident: "We are slow but we are coming up – you will see us."

I KNOW WHAT I LIKE

The essential in the manic mix of Harare nightlife is **beer**: people are fiercely loyal to their brand, whether it be Castle, Lion, Zambezi, or the cheaper cartoned *chibuku*. Booze flows liberally during and between sets, and there's a real art to dancing to that intricate weave of Zimbabwean beats among the packed crowd on the floor, while keeping your upper body steady enough to preserve every precious drop of the brew in your hand. Dancing is a communal affair and no-one need feel left out. If the band is good, people of all ages come on the floor – men with men, women with women, children with adults, groups and loners.

The public tend to be as fanatically loyal to their chosen band as they are to their favourite beer – a conservativeness of taste that new, or more experimental groups frequently bewail. People like to know the songs. Even Thomas Mapfumo is obliged to churn out the old favourites in his shows, and a new band needs to have a very big hit to persuade people to see them

Getting on down at Queens Garden

live (a relatively important source of income). Musicians who are successful overseas, such as Stella Chiweshe, cannot draw the crowds in Zimbabwe if people are not used to seeing them. John Chibadura, who has a hugely successful group in Zimbabwe and has also broken through in the UK, is concerned that his sales in the country will drop as live shows give way to touring overseas. His record company, ZMC, acutely conscious of the need to keep the Zimbabwean link going, has jokingly threatened "We will kill him if he changes his music." As a result, some of the more popular musicians in Zimbabwe are not musically the best: among these are Solomon Skuza and Simon Chimbetu – sentimental and predictable, but eminently danceable.

MBIRA: A MAN'S INSTRUMENT

Home-brewed beer plays an essential role in the **bira**, a ceremony of traditional music, chanting and dancing that brings Zimbabweans into contact with the spiritual world. Traditional instruments used include the **mbira** (thumb

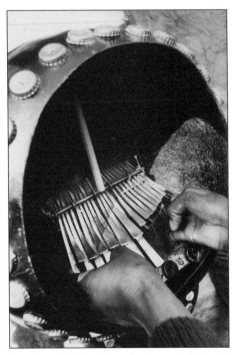

Every key a spirit: the mbira

piano), *marimba* (xylophone), and the *hosho* (rattles). They play an important part, even today, in the spiritual life of Zimbabwean communities. The mbira plays a crucial part in the bira ceremony, which can last all night. It is a powerful instrument, best heard outside, producing a reverberating sound and usually accompanied by high-pitched singing, hosho (rattles) and drum.

Together they can produce a hypnotic elevating effect. You can dance to them for hours. The mbira is traditionally used to summon the ancestors, those who are nearest to God.

Although it is traditionally a man's instrument, there are now a number of women mbira players in Zimbabwe. One of them, **Amai Muchena**, a well known traditional mbira player with Muri ko Muchena (The Muchena Family), has been playing since she was five. She explains how she uses the mbira to contact the spirits: "To get a message to the spirits you have to make an appointment and then speak to the spirit. If you have a problem, you must buy some clothes and beads and cook beer and then have a party and play mbira then everything will be okay. If someone is suffering and sick from a spirit I will play mbira until the spirit comes up and then talk to it. It might say 'buy a gun or spear to keep in your house'."

Muchena views the instrument as a sacred thing: "I don't play in beerhalls, because the spirit is like a God to go to if there are problems, but I can play in the Sheraton – there are no drunks there."

In contrast, **Beulah Diago**, a serene woman who believes strongly in the message of her music, plays in beerhalls in Chitungwiza, a satellite town of Harare. "Some people don't know mbira, like youths in bars, so I take mbira to them."

Stella Chiweshe, the Mbira Queen and perhaps the best-known player of the instrument outside Zimbabwe, has provoked some criticism for her avant-garde mixture of sacred and commercial music, a controversial issue in a country where music is so close to the spiritual centre of life. She certainly uses the mystique of the instrument in her shows to good effect, sometimes going into a trance on the stage. With her penetrating eyes, habitual snuff-taking, ankle charms, and dreadlocks, she can be a frightening presence when she chooses. She is partly based in Germany and more often performs overseas than in Zimbabwe.

Ephat Mujuru and the Spirit of The People are one of the best electric mbira groups around. Their music borders on the **chimurenga** beat, and they cite a variety of other influences, including afro-jazz, soca and reggae. Simon Bright's film, "The Spirit of the People" (Zimmedia, 1990), examines the links between traditional mbira music and modern electric *jit*. The film starts with Ephat Mujuru playing traditional mbira music with fireside singing

STELLA CHIWESHE ON THE MBIRA

David Muddyman spoke to Stella Chiweshe about playing and teaching the mbira.

What led you to learn to play mbira?

It was the music – the music is just so sweet, it didn't leave me when I heard it, so I wanted to hear it again and again. And so I had to learn, it was a must. It's like when you are so sad, there is something which is inside your heart which needs to come out. When I learned, then I felt soothed – that feeling left. I learnt to play it key by key until I could play the whole tune, and I knew the song fully. It was in 1963 or 64. I was taught by my mother's uncle. After that, other people taught me.

With mbira–playing being a man's world, did you find any problems in being taken seriously in wanting to learn?

Yes, a lot of problems, from both men and women, because it was strange for them that a woman would like to play mbira. And so they would say a lot of irritating things. But that gave me a lot of courage. I wanted to prove them wrong. The women were suspicious because they saw that I was without a man, and they thought it was a way of getting close to men. For men, they thought that I was really stubborn and some people thought I'd lost my mind.

Do you teach the mbira?

Yes, but I really want to teach people who seriously want to learn, because it is painful to teach. There are three types of people. The first is the one that has the pain and really wants to play. The second is the person who really likes to hear mbira, and think that they want to be able to play just to be able to hear that sound – and these are really the people I should play mbira for. And the third are the people who really just want to find a way of talking to me. The first two types of people are very close in a lot of ways, but when I see that they are the second kind, I say "OK, let me just play for you".

The keys of the mbira are each said to contain a spirit – mother, father, first child, and so on. Is this true?

This is how it comes in his head to the one who is playing. He explains it like that. When I'm playing I can really feel the spirit of a person plucking the keys and then I know that this one is for this spirit and this one is for that spirit. It feels like the spirits are waking up, and sometimes they are shocked and you look away, you just look down – you must not show that you know what you are doing.

Do you mean the spirit enters you?

No, but it's like the spirit stays with us. You know, it's very different when you hear mbira on the radio or on record, to hearing mbira live because the keys get warmer and get hot, and they get sweeter and sweeter. And when the keys get hot, it sounds like the music is coming from somewhere else and not from me, and I think I'm listening. But it's me who's playing.

What kind of mbira do you play?

Where I grew up we knew the mbira as "Dzama Komwhe" – the spirit that makes the rain. It's the spirit that we call if there's a drought. Mbira is music of the water. The music that comes out of water is mbira, that's why when you hear mbira it's familiar because you know water. It is like tuned raindrops.

When you play in a bira (religious ceremony), do you need to know what you are called for?

No, I am called for playing, they want the music. It could be because someone is ill, not because they are sick in their body, but something mental. It could be somebody from the person's past who has come back and is tormenting their body. So when he enters, it's like something gets into your flesh, you don't feel good and you need to get it out. He enters into your soul and you feel sickened. And so the remedy is mbira.

Do you feel differently, playing in Europe where they like your music but don't understand the words?

It did worry me at first, but then I crossed that barrier and found that it was okay. I went to China in 1984 and I really got to love Chinese music but there wasn't even an explanation to explain what the song meant and again the same in Korea. I loved the music even if I didn't understand what the song meant. Now I don't put it in mind that I'm playing for this kind of people, or that kind of people.

and dancing in the rural areas. It ends with Thomas Mapfumo on stage in an urban, commercial show, with lighter, electrified instruments and microphones. The differences in setting are vast, but the mbira strains in Mapfumo's music are unmistakeable and directly echo Mujuru's work.

CHIMURENGA MAN

As with anything Zimbabwean, it is impossible to ignore the effects of colonialism, which for Zimbabwe began in 1890. The situation worsened after prime minister Ian Smith's unilateral declaration of independence from Britain in 1964 and only ended with the establishmnet of the Mugabe government in 1980, after a prolonged liberation struggle in which music played an important part.

From the first missionaries onwards the tendency of the white population was to undermine and devalue local people's traditional culture, and this extended to the music, presenting it as primitive and worthless. Because so little local music was recorded the country was awash with imported sounds from South Africa, the USA (country music especially), European pop and central African rumba, all of which have had an influence on today's Zimbabwean music.

Thomas Mapfumo – TM to everyone – is perhaps the most famous Zimbabwean musician, the proverbial Lion of Zimbabwe, the majestic dreadlocked exponent of electric mbira music. Like most Zimbabwean musicians, Mapfumo started his career playing "copyright" music; cover versions of western hits. "I don't regret playing copyright music because it taught me a lot of things I didn't know." In the 1970s, Mapfumo began playing his own music. "I had become matured. I was looking for my identity. Today I am a man so I must be called Thomas Mapfumo. I can't be called Elvis Presley."

He began to experiment with traditional sounds and beats, adapting the mbira by bringing mbira players into his band and translating its rhythms and sound into guitar riffs. The result was a hypnotic, almost trance-like music, guitars splattering out their individual mbira lines, held together by a complicated set of drum beats. For the vocals, he drew on an incredible wealth of traditional songs and chants and also began to use Shona rather than English lyrics. It was a brave and crucial step for a generation that had been taught to look down on their cultural traditions as primitive. Initially his experiments were viewed

Thomas Mapfumo: Lion of Zimbabwe

with bemusement, but they soon caught on and he was rapidly followed by other musicians, who openly acknowledge his influence – notably Oliver Mtukudzi and Comrade Chinx.

Just as the mbira itself had a firm place in the strong spiritual world, so this modern electric mbira music rapidly became a tool of the liberation struggle. Chimurenga music (chimurenga means "liberation war") was used to good effect during the *pungwes* – all-night meetings of villagers with the liberation fighters. The irresistible beat provided an opportunity for community dance and affirmation that was vitally necessary to a society split by secrecy, repression, guerrilla warfare and counter-terrorist activities. Shona and Ndebele lyrics could not be understood by the majority of the white population and so were a valuable means of communication for the liberation movement.

Some of the lyrics of Thomas Mapfumo's chimurenga songs were overtly political, while others made use of the Shona tradition of "deep proverbs" to conceal messages of resistance: "Oh grandmothers/Oh mothers, oh boys/There's a snake in the forest/Mothers take hoes/Grandmothers take hoes/Boys take axes." (from "The Chimurenga Singles").

THOMAS MAPFUMO

David Muddyman and Richard Trillo talked to the big man of chimurenga about bad timing, the liberation war – and his favourite Elvis song.

Can you tell us about your first gig?

I think that was in in late 1958, that's when I played first and I was singing rock 'n' roll music. I remember I was playing with these guys who were older than I was. They usually played what we call African Jazz, like what the Mills Brothers used to do, or the Crewcuts. Music done by quartets. People loved it, they thought I was just a good rock 'n' roller. Later, at school, I joined a singing contest and this white band, the Bob Cyclones, backed me. It was very exciting. I went in with a song by Elvis Presley, "A Mess of Blues" – my favourite tune. People went wild about it. I was on the front page of the paper. After that I joined a group called The Cosmic Four Dots. They were a quartet, but this time they were modern youngsters. One time we were doing our practice at a house belonging to an old musician, called Mr Mataga. He and all his family were musicians. He had a young son called Edison, seven years younger than me, who was a very good pianist. I was not very good when it came to timing. He would play piano and he'd stop the song and say "Look here brother, that's not the way to do it – when I get here, that's where you come in". He taught me a lot. He mastered my timing. He could play any type of music. He was a genius, Edison, even though he was young, but sadly now he's died.

What made you bring in mbira patterns played on the guitar?

We wanted to separate ourselves from the colonial era. Playing this type of music actually gave us enough moral support to fight the struggle. And to feel that this is my culture and that I am supposed to be someone with a country, someone with a home, someone who is not called a second citizen in his own country. Well, this made me feel very bitter and I composed a lot of militant songs. As you know, before, a lot of our youngsters were playing copyright music – soul music, funky, the Beatles, the Rolling Stones. When my music came in, with Shona lyrics, it changed everything.

How did you start to bring the mbira into you music?

It had been on my mind for a while, ever since I started playing this kind of music, but I was never able to find the really good mbira players. You know most of them were living in the communal lands [the countryside], it was very hard to communicate with them.

And then you joined the Acid Band. Slightly strange name?

I don't know how they got this name. We used not to associate with these people. I was playing at a nearby nightclub and they were just next door. So one night I went there to listen and they were playing a lot of rumba music, but they had a few mbira tunes and I said "Wah, these guys are good, man." I said I must talk to them. We had a chat, me and Charlie, the leader of the band. I spoke to him, I said we could practice a song or two. They agreed to do some practice with me. I went there one morning and we finished one song. The next day we did another song. So we went into the studio to record this music and it was an instant success. That was 1976, the time when Ian Smith said that he wasn't going to see a black government. There were three guys playing lead, rhythm and bass guitar, and the drums and then came the saxophone. We only had one horn and then myself. After a long spell with the Acid Band we decided to make some changes. We saw that some of the musicians we were playing with were not real professionals so we had to bring in some better musicians. That's when I brought in Jonah Sithole on guitar, and then my band was the Blacks Unlimited. This is when we brought in two horn players from the Salvation church. We thought we could just talk to them and bring them into the band. They accepted, after we had had some serious talks with them. The sound was different after that. I arranged everything from the lead to the bass to the drum.

Where were you able to perform at that time?

In the African townships, playing for our own people. That was in the heat of the war and it was very dangerous to travel. Sometimes you had to line up in convoy. But we didn't worry too much because we knew that the people fighting the war supported us.

With your album, "Chamunorwa", you went almost wholly traditional and seem to be using a different kind of rhythm.

The style is a deep traditional form of Zimbabwian music. It is really traditional mbira but then when you listen to it, it appeals to the younger generation as well as the older generation. It has very strong bass lines. In fact if you take away the instruments

These days Mapfumo is a legend in Harare, a BMW owner, but a firm believer in the political relevance of his work. A recent album ("Chamunorwa") dealt with corruption, a problem in Zimbabwe as elsewhere, and it lost airplay because of this. "Even if you insult me I know you fear me/Even if you insult me I know you hate me/The newspapers say bad things, but they are afraid/Those who read about me know the damage I can do/You plan to kill me but I know you fear me."

Mapfumo declares that "Chimurenga means justice so justice must be seen to be done in the rest of the world. We have a duty as musicians to sing about what is really happening in the lives of our people." The fine line between catering for the international market while still remaining true to your background is a battle that many Zimbabwean bands are conscious of these days. As Mapfumo has remarked, "You've really got to be yourself and come up with something that has never been heard before which still reflects our own culture."

SHORTWAVE LOVE

Comrade Chinx is a strange mixture – mystic hippy cum social critic – and his name brings a smile to the lips of Shona music fans. Originally a choirmaster for liberation troops in the war, he realized the power of traditional chanting and used it as the basis for his music. After independence he developed the chants and accompaniment with his backing group, the Mazana Movement, to become a real force in Zimbabwe, singing of peace and reconciliation, and also providing a firm voice of social criticism: "For love, with love only, I walked in my father's land/ in my mother's land, in my grandmother's land/You can see for yourself love is enough/Mugabe said this and so did the comrades/Only love, love is enough."

Chinx broke into synthesizer pop with the help of his backing group, Ilanga, with his biggest-selling record "Roger Confirm" about love through a shortwave radio.

Paul Matavire is the blind singer, songwriter and front man for the **Jairos Jiri Sunshine Band**, originating from a welfare organization founded to assist the re-integration of disabled Zimbabweans into society. Their 1980 song "Take Cover", about a guerilla group's journey through the war zone, mirrors the rattle of a machine gun as Matavire sings "At home there's war and nowhere to live." Today, their songs

often incorporate acute social observations: "Our music differs from overseas music. It has moral lessons telling you how to behave. Songs from overseas are only for entertainment."

"Love First" was written as a result of a request by a group of women to explain what happens if they go for a job:

I've got a job for a beautiful woman
A portable juicy young woman.
Before I start, just one comment,
You are killingly beautiful.
I am attracted by your front side,
But I want someone who is beautiful back and front,
Turn around.
Electric plus solar power.
Here is lunch and transport money from the boss's pocket.
Now we go for entertainment.
Love your husband at home,
But love me more at work.

HELLO TUKU

Oliver Mtukudzi (Tuku) easily outsells Thomas Mapfumo in Zimbabwe and is a definite contender for the title of giant of Zimbabwean music – having produced more than two dozen LPs, as well as "Hello", the biggest-selling single in Zimbabwe in recent years. He is very much influenced by Mapfumo's chimurenga, as well as by mbaqanga and rumba beats, and is a strong traditionalist. Although a true innovator, he remains deeply commited to his roots. For example, a recent album, "Kuvaira", is typical Shona: "It's not fused to any other kind of music. I did it for the older people of Zimbabwe, for those who want pure pure Zimbabwe music, straight straight deep deep deep deep traditional sounds." But Tuku is not afraid to experiment, switching from mbaqanga and jazz fusion in one album to "ancient deep traditional beats" in the next: "Recently I composed a deep deep traditional song – with an ancient beat that no one believed could be sung in English – but the English lyrics fitted very well – they enjoyed it."

Tuku's blatantly swinging renditions of the rootsiest beats, accompanied by his soulful voice and husky laugh, is irresistible. Tall, slim and handsome, with real stage presence, an easy manner and a slick line in dance moves, his performances with the Black Spirits are captivating.

Mtukudzi is very conscious of the importance of his lyrics, as are all

Zimbabwean musicians: "When it hasn't got meaning then that song is likely to be a flop." He is a deeply moral man – he sang the first AIDS song in a Zimbabwean film that was later banned by the government. His lyrics place an emphasis on discipline. "If one is disciplined then one is less likely to be corrupt. I believe in who we are, so my songs – though some might be in a different beat or a fusion of western beats – don't run away from our tradition and customs. Mostly I use proverbs and idioms that we use from long long back – when I sing in Shona. In English my lyrics change but I'm an African so I record my English as I speak it. That's me, that's Oliver Mtukudzi – that's how I am."

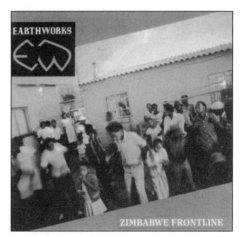

Hot Zimbabwean dance cats – a top-rated CD

JIT HITS THE FANS

"Jit Jive" was a term coined by the **Bhundu Boys** to describe their energetic dance music that hit the scene in Britain in the mid 1980s, what British DJ John Peel called "the most flowing natural music I can remember hearing." Their "popcorn" style of guitar-playing and fast, hard rhythms quickly earned them a name in the UK. But they were never as popular in Zimbabwe, and their music suffered dangerously from over-exposure to western pop, culminating in the disastrous release of the unfortunately named "True Jit" in 1987, which they remedied in part with a prolonged period back in Zimbabwe to regain that initial flow of sound.

Since "True Jit", a series of sad blows has resulted in a significant drop in their popularity. First, there was an acrimonious split with charismatic frontman **Biggie Tembo**, who now plays with the **Ocean City Band**. And then one

Biggie Tembo in happier days with Mark Knopfler

after another the bass guitarists died of AIDS. A subdued and less bubbly Bhundu Boys still play to a posse of faithful fans in Zimbabwe and overseas, but the quality of their music in no way compares with their formidable achievements of nearly a decade ago.

DON'T LOSE IT

The **Four Brothers** are a straightforward fast Shona band, their vocals dancing above rippling guitar riffs, and, once again, strongly influenced by Mapfumo (one of them, Marshall Munhunumwe, is Thomas's uncle, and learned drums and singing from him). Their first hit, "Makoro" (Congratulations), was dedicated to the freedom fighters at independence, and they became one of the top Zimbabwean bands during the 1980s.

They called themselves the Four Brothers in order to remain equal, so that no brother would become "big" – a fate that has shattered too many Zimbabwean bands in the past. And despite their prolonged exposure in the West they stick firmly to their traditional roots, claiming to have learnt the Bhundu Boys' lesson. They deliberately choose to record in Harare rather than in technically superior UK studios. As their songwriter, drummer and singer, Marshall Munhunumwe, says "We mustn't lose our touch as an African band. We are known for our traditional music. If we go out of that line then we are lost."

The **Runn Family** come from Mutare in Manicaland in the northeast

The Runn Family – reggae, rumba and mbira beats

Zimbabwe. They formed in the early 1980s and have an amazing brass section. Their first big hit was "Hachina Wekutamba Naye", a song about the death of Mozambique's charismatic president, Samora Machel. They have also released two albums, "Ndoita Wekudiniko", and a compilation of old songs. "Our music is traditional," explains drummer Anselm Mboka, "based on the mbira. It is Zimbabwe hybrid music. It has been an upward battle, a hard struggle. We try to make music through whatever comes out, we experiment with that. Our grandfather is a mbira player and he is our inspiration. He is now in his seventies, but he still helps us with traditional sounds." The Runns also play reggae and rumba, and are excellent cover artists.

RUMBA-RUMBIRA

Zimbabwean **rumba** is unmistakable and forms an essential part of most bands' repertoires. While the influence is from Zaire, the fast, mbira-style playing can only be Zimbabwean.

The **Real Sounds** are adoptive Zimbabweans, originally from Zaire, and expert proponents of Zimbabwe rumba, mixing the Zairean beat with the Zimbabwean mbira to produce a sound which they have christened **rumbira**. This 11-piece band combines a rolling, soukous-style rumba beat, the frenetic performance of a steaming cohort of brass and an exuberant drummer. It makes for compulsive dancing and an unmissable live show. They have an enthusiastic following both at home and overseas.

Jonah Moyo and the Devera Ngwena Jazz Band were formed just before independence, with singer/song writer Moyo on lead guitar. Their music is a highly infectious form of rumba and, although they haven't achieved much recognition outside Zimbabwe, locally they're a very popular band.

John Chibadura, with his **Tembo Brothers**, however, has been a real triumph, and one of Zimbabwe's biggest-selling artists. Posing as shy, introverted "anti-star", he has had amazing success, winning the following of young Zimbabweans with the result that all his records routinely sell in vast numbers. He combines fast-moving Zimbabwean dance music and rumba.

To non-speakers of Shona, the songs sound relentlessly happy, but the lyrics often describe grim social conditions and deep-rooted fears, which, with typical Zimbabwean stoicism, are sung over a defiantly good-time beat: "My mother, my uncle, my grandmother and my father all died when I was small/Now I'm ill and my children are dying of witchcraft/When I think of my problems I break down and cry" ("Hupenyu Wangu"/"My Life").

BULAWAYO JAZZ

Compared with Harare, Bulawayo in Matabeleland – the southwestern part of Zimbabwe near the South African border where the majority speak the Zulu-related language **Ndebele** – is a sleepy one-horse town. Music venues are often empty and rarely draw Harare-sized crowds. But this has not always been the case, as Bulawayan musicians feel acutely that the dominant positions in Zimbabwe are occupied by Harare and the culture of the peoples of Manicaland and Mashonaland.

"Before the 1980s," remarked Dorothy Masuka, "even blacks and whites played together in Bulawayo and there was a good music scene – but somehow after independence there was a split between Shona and Ndebele – things got moved to Harare and it has never recovered. If there are musicians from Matabeland in Harare then they are playing the Harare music – since this is Mashonaland – they [the Shona] are actually the owners of this country."

Lovemore Majaivana is a flamboyant, if uneven, performer with a rich powerful voice and a penchant for brilliantly coloured, skin-tight lurex suits. He is one of the few Bulawayo names to have made it big in Harare as well as overseas. The Zulu influence is very strong in some of his

DOROTHY MASUKA

Dorothy Masuka has recently returned to South Africa, where she lived during her school days – and where she picked up her jazz-inflected musical style, marabi. Prior to the move, she talked to Judy Kendall in Bulawayo.

Dorothy Masuka's jazz-inflected musical style, *marabi*, is steeped in the South African jazz and Zulu rhythms she was immersed in at an early age. She spent her formative musical years in South Africa and stayed there after school, making her way as a professional singer.

"I was in a show called African Jazz and Variety, which was a group of all kinds of singers. We were imitating American singers, like Ella Fitzgerald. We would all sit on the stage and then one by one go to the microphone and do our turn and then go and sit. Every one of us: me, Miriam Makeba, Hugh Masekela – all big names in African music today. In South Africa I started recording and touring the country. We had concerts for whites only. Then came King Kong – a very big show that came to UK in the late 1950s, again with Miriam and Hugh.

"Then it was politics – some of us musicians took off and went to London and some people to the USA. Miriam Makeba went to the US and met up with Harry Belafonte and she really put up the African music on top of the world. That's when everyone started knowing about southern African talent – she broke the ice.

"I went to London and stayed in Kensington for many years, but people were not very interested in African music at that time. There was a a fund-raising concert for the anti-apartheid movement that I played at the London Paladium. And there was that campaign for that Labour man Wilson somebody. I performed in Wimbledon during one of their campaigns. But still in 1964 people were not aware of African music.

"In those days young people never dreamt of coming to England on their own. They would look at us and say 'You've been to London!' It was like you'd been to heaven. In 1965, though, I came back to Rhodesia, as it was then. I played in a nightclub that was strictly for whites only and I stayed in a hotel that was for whites only. We used to have white strippers and I think this was the reason they did not want blacks there."

Dorothy Masuka's music at this period reflected the political turmoil of the time. Her song "Kutheni Zulu" warned against Africans taking sides and pleading for everyone to calm down.

"Then I was away from home for a long time and I couldn't go back till 1980. I used to sing songs that were no good according to the government. That feeling of seeing wrong never changes. Now we are independent I still see a lot of wrong, though I've grown to keep quiet and let things happen.

"When a Western audience listens to African music they will understand the music but they won't know the suffering – it will be understood by a very few people in the audience. I'm out of that now – a few years back I would cry in my singing but now I'm not looking for sympathy. We are lucky in Zimbabwe. Now we are like any other country and people in Zimbabwe are out to work for themselves – each person is working for himself which is good. That's why now if you are singing on stage you can't start singing 'We are suffering'. People will just look. We sing about joy."

Dorothy Masuka's view of music is almost sacred: "Music has to be respected. There's no any other thing in the world like music. There's no king above music. The only thing above music is God himself. When you finish performing the king will clap his hands."

She is determined to be successful in the 1990s: "I would like to give my two grandchildren what I never had, because as an African child there are certain things you wished to have and couldn't have – a beautiful doll, toys, nice shoes – because your parents never earned enough money. A good home, a tricycle – black children thought that was for white children. After that I'm going to sing once or twice a year then I'm going to sit down and rest. I'm giving what I have to the youngsters."

Black Umfolosi – whirling a cappella

music, though he also plays mbira melodies.

Southern Freeway are a new group with members from Bulawayo, South Africa and Harare – including the talented session guitarist, Louis Mhlanga. They back the South African Steve Dyer, a versatile musician who has spent much time in Botswana, and Bulawayan singer Thandeka Ngono. Their music ranges from mbaqanga and jazz to more Shona-influenced guitar playing and they sing in six languages – Zulu, Xhosa, Ndebele, Shona, Tswana and English. In their first album, emphasis is on the South African penny whistle, but more recent music has acquired a Shona sound.

Black Umfolosi are an a cappella group of singers and dancers from Bulawayo – an amazing live experience with their precise and acrobatic singing and dancing to a strong Zulu beat – and clearly reminiscent in style and content to Ladysmith Black Mambazo. They are regular fixtures on the international World Music festival circuit, where they can be seen performing their version of a South African miners' gumboot dance.

Dorothy Masuka (see interview box on the previous page) is the "mama" of African Jazz from Bulawayo, with a musical career that spans over forty years. She sang with Miriam Makeba and Hugh Masekela in South Africa in her early days, later fleeing to London to escape from the white minority ruled Rhodesia, and then campaigning for a free Zimbabwe all over Southern Africa.

After independence her music changed as she explains: "I still see a lot of wrong but people are tired of politics – they want to be happy, drive nice cars, live in good homes – they are really tired. So I sing about joy, funny little songs, nice events that are happening, things that people can get up and dance to."

Like many Bulawayan musicians, Masuka draws a lot on South African influences, playing a mixture of swing and local melodies in a style known as marabi. "The Ndebele-speaking people who live in Matabeleland and Bulawayo are Zulus. They came into this country and settled in Matabeleland. My grandfather for example comes from a village in South Africa in Natal. He married a woman from this part of the world. This is why the traditional kind of music down south is South African."

A glamorous and dominating personality, Dorothy Masuka is one of Zimbabwe's strongest female performers. "To tour with me is a serious thing." She dresses in vibrant colours and, with her amazingly powerful voice, sweeps up South African jazz and links it to more traditional beats.

NEW BANDS, LOCAL IDIOMS, WESTERN POP

New bands make their mark with difficulty in Zimbabwe. Venue-owners are reluctant to take them and with no contracts will drop them at a moment's notice if they can book someone better known. To find a venue a new band needs to play in the "growth points" (developing commercial centres in the rural areas). Here a band can guarantee full houses every night as the people are desperate for entertainment, but transport is necessary and with the high price of fuel in Zimbabwe, this becomes very expensive. Indeed, most of the big bands keep to the towns, instead of touring in the rural areas, making it even more difficult for less well-known groups with more limited means of transport to make a living.

Sometimes more established musicians help them out. Mtukudzi acts as a talent scout in this way. "There's a lot of talent lying around. I help them write their songs – if they're accurate I take them to the studio to produce them." **Penga Udozoke**, a very danceable band with a fast rhythm borrowing from rumba as well as chanting traditions, is Mtukudzi's top group. "Their album is competing with us – people thought they wouldn't go far but I could sense they had a unique touch in their music. Though they play Zimbabwean music they are different from the others and when I released their music people just went and bought the record because it's a new line. "

The **Frontline Kids**, a fast young band, whip the crowd up into frenzies with their energetic and aerobic dancing. At times this can have catastrophic results – when they were performing at the "Chico and Chinamora" concert in Harare in 1991 the crowd twice broke down the gates.

Robson Banda is another musician who draws on Mapfumo-influenced electric mbira music, as well as on strains of South African mbaqanga. Banda is a professional with a powerful voice, and plays instantly infectious music with **The New Black Eagles**.

Other, established bands to listen out for are the prolific **Pied Pipers**; **Harare Mambos**; **The Marxist Brothers**; **Leonard Dembo**; **Zexie Manatsa and the Green Arrows**; and **Nyami Nyami Sounds**.

The rate of early death of musicians in Zimbabwe – through illness including AIDS, or motor accidents – is high. **James Chimombe**, who died in 1990, was a very talented musician, vocalist and songwriter with the Ocean City Band, with a touch of country in his music, and a great influence on younger Zimbabwean groups.

Tobias Areketa, who also died in 1990, initially worked with Mapfumo. His music with the **Shazi Band** is remarkable for its haunting, mournful melodies with words packed in over a relentlessly poignant beat. Unfortunately he left only two albums.

■ DISCOGRAPHY ►

Ⓓ **Various** *Zimbabwe Frontline Vol 1* (Earthworks, UK). A taste of some of the best in Zimbabwean Shona music from Mapfumo to Mtukudzi, including the breathtakingly speedy dance music of Devera Ngwena and a rare chance to hear the talented Susan Mapfumo (no relation).
Ⓓ **Various** *Spirit of the Eagle: Zimbabwe Frontline Vol 2* (Earthworks, UK). An overview of some of the greats of Zimbabwean music, from Thomas Mapfumo to the Four Brothers, though the emphasis is very much on Shona, rather than Ndebele music.
Ⓓ **Various** *Viva! Zimbabwe* (Hannibal, UK/Carthage, US). Good collection with some unusual names – Elijah Madzikatire & the Brave Sun, Patrick Mukwamba, James Chimombe & OK Success, the Super Sounds and the New Black Montana, plus Mapfumo, Four Brothers, Devera Ngwena and Nyami Nyami.
Ⓓ **Black Umfolosi** *Festival – Umdlalo* (World Circuit, UK). Showcase for the group's mellow a cappella talents.
Ⓓ **Bhundu Boys** *Shabini* (DisqueAfrique, UK). For many, especially in Britain, this album was the first port of entry into Zimbabwean music when it hit the world by storm in the mid-80s. Exquisitely speedy and irresistible.
John Chibadura and the Tembo Brothers *More of the Essential...* (CSA, UK). Essential indeed if you want to know what's slapping the boards in Zimbabwe these days. An expert demonstrates how to do tight dance numbers.

Ⓓ **Stella Chiweshe** *Kumusha: Pure Mbira Music from Zimbabwe* (Piranha, Germany). No complaints here: if you like mbira you'll soon be in a trance. Ⓓ *Ambuya?* (GlobeStyle, UK/Shanachie USA) is a super experiment, only troubling purists with its lively 3 Mustaphas 3 participation on bass and drums.
Ⓓ **The Four Brothers** *Bros* (Cooking Vinyl, UK). A good introduction to the four, with solid dancing tunes. Ⓓ *Makorokoto: the Best of...* (Cooking Vinyl, UK) is joyful, exuberant, seductive – uncompromising Shona music.

Ⓓ **Thomas Mapfumo** *Shumba* (Earthworks, UK). A compilation of early work when his use of traditional songs and beats for political and protest purposes was at its height. Ⓓ *The Chimurenga Singles: 1976–80* (Shanachie, US) is a bit of a classic – a re-release of a wonderful Earthworks LP (love the cock-a-doodle). Ⓓ *Chamunorwa* (Mango, UK) is a 1990 outing for a more traditional, heavy bass rhythm.
Ⓓ **Dorothy Masuka** *Pata Pata* (Mango, UK). One of the big singing stars of the African Jazz swing sound, Masuka's career goes back to the 50s. Here she demonstrates the continued range and fire of her voice.
Ⓓ **Oliver Mtukudzi** *Shoko* (Piranha, Germany). A giant of an artist in Zimbabwe, Tuku hasn't received the recognition he deserves elsewhere.
Ⓓ **Real Sounds** *Vende Zoko* (Cooking Vinyl, UK). Close your eyes and you could be in Zaire. But listen harder for that characteristic nippy Zim guitar style.

KALINDULA BANDWAGON

A ROUGH GUIDE TO ZAMBIAN POP

Kalindula has been a long time coming. Just 25 years ago you could have passed through Zambia without hearing any music which could even vaguely have been considered Zambian. Today, as Ronnie Graham was delighted to discover, all that has changed.

In the 1960s, kwela from South Africa, rumba tunes from the Congo and western pop dominated the few airwaves buzzing through the Zambian bush. Lusaka nightlife consisted of a few up-market hotels frequented by ruling party heavies and the remains of the colonial set, relaxing to the Broadway Quintet, the Crooners and De Black Evening Follies rendering straight "copyright" (cover) versions of foreign hits.

Up north, in the copperbelt, things were considerably tougher. In the hard-drinking mining camps an evening's entertainment might consist of a drunken brawl and a visit to a strip joint. There was local music here: the likes of **Stephen Tsotsi Kasumali**, **William Mapulanga** and **John Lushi** walked with their guitars from camp to camp, picking out morality songs to the wry amusement of all.

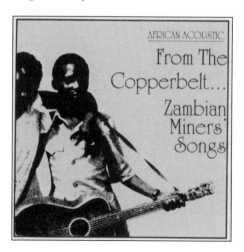

But mostly Zambia was a country of importers and imitators. The musician and sound engineer **Alick Nkhata**, the electic guitarist **Nasil Pinchen Kazembe**, and guitarist/composer

Emmanuel Mulemena were the only musicians even interested in tapping into the rich and varied seams of local musical culture.

During the 1970s there was some progress, but two unsteady steps forward were usually followed by one back. President **Kenneth Kaunda**, himself an enthusiastic amateur guitarist, took an unguarded leap in a speech in 1976 when he declared that henceforth no less than 95 percent of music on the radio was to be of Zambian origin – nineteen songs in every Top 20. The result was not quite the cultural roots revival he had intended. Instead, every Zambian teenager with a box guitar and a singing voice tried their hand at being a pop star. Hundreds of bands were established, often by opportunistic entrepeneurs with a truck-load of instruments, to play note-perfect renditions of other African styles. True, some original material emerged, from the Afro-Rock bands like **Musi-O-Tunya**, **The Witch**, the **Ngozi Family**, the **Fire Family Band** and the literally-named army group, the **Machine Gunners**, all of whom took to Osibisa (the London-based Ghanaian combo who visited Zambia in 1972) like fish to water.

During the 1970s, Lusaka rocked with a lively night-club scene and plenty of live music. The industry responded with a flood of hot singles and a flurry of impressive albums. Yet it still wasn't really Zambian music. **Zam-rumba** ruled the roost with **Bumba Massa**, **Super Mazembe** and **Nguashi N'timbo** leading the way, while traditional culture languished in the villages.

But pan-African currents could not be ignored and the general trend across the continent towards roots soon had Zambian musicians looking for their own. Several key performers and industry figures – notably **Peter Musungilo**, **Gideon Mulenga**, **Herman Striedl** and **Graham Skinner** – led the way and, by the mid-1980s, the combined efforts of musicians, producers and companies had produced a specifically Zambian urban dance style, *kalindula*, which took its inspiration from the northwestern province of Luapula and was named after a one-string bass instrument of the area.

Alick Nkhata (left) recording in the countryside in the 1960s

feed ideas. For the second time in a decade, Zambia was enjoying a musical renaissance as new outfits like **Mashabe, Makishi, Bwaluka Founders, Majoza** and the **Junior Mulemena Boys** packed the compound bars and suburban hotel dance floors. The city centre hotels still preferred Zairean bands covering the latest Kinshasa styles, but for the majority of Zambians a good night out revolved around copious quantities of *Mosi* beer and kalindula action on the dance floor.

Brasher than soukous, and funkier, kalindula is characterized by rumba-style guitars and a solid, rapid-fire bass line. The drums set off at a frantic pace (just check Amayenge's contribution to the "Zambiance" collection on GlobeStyle) with the guitarists seemingly struggling to find the rhythm. But 30 seconds into the song, a cooler inside groove emerges to provide dance floor satisfaction.

The first wave of kalindula comprised five bands – **Amayenge, Shalawambe, Zambezi, Masasu Band, Julizya** – and two outstanding soloists – **PK Chisala** and **Akeem Simukonda** – which stimulated sufficient interest for British tours. By the late 1980s, there were half a dozen albums out on World Music labels.

Others soon followed as kalindula moved away from its origins and became a generic Zambian style into which each tradition could

Today, Zambia offers a lively variety of bands, styles and venues. **Mike's Car Wash**, on the outskirts of Lusaka, opens at lunchtime on weekends and warms up with variety acts before Amayenge take the stage late in the afternoon (clear the buckets). Livingstone, the Victoria Falls capital of Zambian tourism, starts to move at weekends to the **Freedom Justice Rockers** at the Fairmount Hotel – a cute courtyard venue with the usual barbecue and beer.

Everything revolves around **beer**: no Mosi, no show. Even the superstar Tabu Ley from Zaire couldn't convince anyone to stay at his gig when the taps ran dry. But despite deep recession and rocketing inflation, the beer rarely runs out, even in the smallest rural hostelry.

DISCOGRAPHY

Various *Zambiance* (GlobeStyle, UK). Terrific collection of contemporary Zambian dance music, mostly in the kalindula mould, including the speedy Amayenge, Shalawambe, the Fire Family and sublime guitar on the late Alfred Chisala Kalusha Jnr's, "Ni Maggie" (two sides of a single).

Various *From the Copperbelt... Zambian Miners' Songs* (Original Music, US). In the "African Acoustic" series, eighteen interesting-to-beautiful songs by the mine camp entertainers of the copper-belt that straddles Zambia and southeastern Zaire, field-recorded by ethno-musicologist Hugh Tracey in 1957.

Alick Nkhata *Shalapo* (RetroAfric, UK). There's no knowing how far Nkhata's talents would have taken him if he had not been killed by Rhodesian soldiers during a cross-border raid on a Zimbabwean guerilla camp next to his farm in 1974 at the age of 52. This re-issue is a selection from his large output of guitar songs – perhaps 100 compositions all told.

MUSICAL YOUTH

AS HEARD ON MALAWI BROADCASTING CORPORATION

It was the country where visiting gentlemen were asked to shave off beards, ladies to keep their skirts below the knee and everyone to measure their jeans for signs of illegal flare. Until 1994. A newly elected government has at last booted out the sagging dictatorship of Hastings Banda, and Malawi is a happy place to be once more. But even in the dark days of hair-length rules and affiliation with apartheid, ask anyone who had been there what they remembered and two features stood out: Malawians' love of music and their friendliness. John Lwanda introduces the sounds of "the warm heart of Africa" – much more than a tourist board cliché (though it really is a tourist board cliché).

Long before the first CDs, in 1859 in fact, David Livingstone heard the xylophone music of southern Malawi and, with typically Scottish enthusiasm described it as "wild and not unpleasant" – one of the first World Music reviews. This little country has had an underrated influence on southern and East African music. You can hear Malawian strands in musicians as diverse as Jairos Jiri, Robson Banda, Dorothy Masuka and Devera Ngwena from Zimbabwe; Ray Phiri from South Africa; Sam Mangwana from Zaire; and Alick Nkhata from Zambia, to name just a few.

Malawians are great travellers and have taken their music to every city from Nairobi to the Cape. Malawian soldiers served in central and East African British battalions during World War II and a number brought back guitars. From the late 1940s to the early '60s Malawian **banjo artists** (Thailo & Kapiye, Maganga, Barton Harry and Nyerere) and **guitarists** (Wilson Makawa and Ndiche) were very popular. The commonest dance format was to have the banjo leading and the guitar playing rhythm.

This banjo/guitar style was followed by a kwela craze (Donald Kachamba) and then, in the 1970s, by a jazz band boom (including Alan Namoko and his Chimvu Band, Mulanje Mountain Band and Linengwe River Band). Gospel music using traditional rhythms and instruments became popular after independence and reggae has been a popular influence for twenty years or more.

As in Zimbabwe and Zambia, the 1960s saw musicians electrifying various traditional rhythms, resulting in the **afroma** (afro-rock-Malawi) beat. In amongst all this there have been folk, pop and gospel guitar-and-banjo singer-songwriters (Stonnard Lungu, Snodden Ibu, Michael Yekha), a clutch of mainstream jazz groups, and big bands like the **army and police string bands**, both of which are well-equipped and would give the increasingly techno-dependent Zairean bands a run for their money in a live show.

The **MBC Band** (the national broadcasting corporation's house band), has been a training ground for many musicians and plays everything from South African mbaqanga to afroma, cabaret jazz and Lucky Dube-style reggae. The Malawi Broadcasting Corporation and its predecessors have been very important to popular musicians for mass exposure. "As heard on radio" is the Malawian equivalent of "As seen on TV".

ETHNOGRAPHER'S CORNER

Malawi is a small landlocked country dominated by the beautiful Lake Malawi. The country's eight million inhabitants are at present host to over a million refugees from neighbouring Mozambique, all packed into a largely rural 94,000 square kilometres – an area little larger than Scotland or Maine. Malawi has nine main tribal/linguistic groups: Chewa, the largest, which is also the national lingua franca, Nyanja, Lomwe, Yao, Tumbuka, Sena, Tonga, Ngoni and Nkonde.

This ethnic diversity means that there are numerous **traditional dances and rhythms** such as the Chewa masked *gule wa mkulu* (the big dance), the Ngoni's *ingoma* war dance, *beni* marching bands among the Yao, and so on. There are also dances for women only such as *chimtali* and *chioda*. Popular musicians are influenced primarily by these longstanding traditions. Most of the songs recorded in the 1940s and '50s, for example by **Alick Nkhata** and **Hugh Tracey**, can still be heard in the villages today. The predominantly rural nature of life in Malawi – despite the strong influence of radio – and the shortage of electric instruments, have led to a stronger "jazz band" tradition (rural or semi-rural popular musicians using acoustic instruments: imagine an acoustic Devera Ngwena or Shirati Jazz) than in, say, Zimbabwe. Musicians take a pragmatic attitude to instruments, using homemade or imported ones as need or affordability determines.

Because of the lack of exposure, however, the Malawian bands, though influential, lost out from the commercial point of view. Perhaps this is one of the factors that has kept the music closer to its folk roots and why the **syncopation** is more marked than in Zimbabwe or Zambia.

A common source of rhythms and songs is women at the mortar. As they pound the staple maize the thumping produces various rhythms by which they accompany their songs of lament, blues, gossip, celebration or what have you. Young musicians like Mitoche and the Kasambwe Brothers show this influence clearly. The most popular non-commercial music in Malawi is also by women, the *mbumba* ("women") music sung by them at ruling party and state occasions – songs of celebration and praise with drum accompaniment, based on traditional dances.

The Kasambwe Brothers Band

The **Kasambwe Brothers** are Isaac and Frank Chikwata, in their late teens, from Thyolo district in southern Malawi. They started in 1987, and they play homemade instruments, lead and bass guitar respectively. They were joined in 1989 by their (then) nine-year old cousin, Kennedy Nagopa backing them on

vocals, drums and percussion. Their folk-based material is startlingly original and they have strong lyrics, too, about matters like family life, separation and survival, marriage and duty in a matrilineal society – and of course love and alcohol. This is a song called Nidlibe Ambuye ("I have no uncle") from their highly recommended Pamtondo CD:

I went to old Rodgers' place
With matrimonial matters on my mind.
Rodgers asked: hey kid,
what is it you want here?
I replied: the hand of one of your daughters, sir.
Rodgers sneered: away with you!
And next time bring your uncle!
Now, my uncle is far away
And I'm all the poorer for it.
For I can't get my marriage arranged,
For what shall I, a lad with no uncle, do?

BEFORE THE POPE

Morson Phuka, who died in 1991, was the leader of the **Jazz Giants** and the **New Scene**, seminal jazz and afroma groups. A father figure for Malawian electric music, and a talented vocalist, composer and arranger, Phuka trained countless musicians who passed through his band. The late **Dr Daniel Kachamba** was an influential folk guitarist. His brother Donald is a kwela flute musician. **Alan Namoko** is a blind bluesman and a major musical personality whose band, **Chimvu Jazz**, are still turning out the type of roots blues you could die for on acoustic banjo, guitar and percussion. Sadly, **Samangaya**, a veteran police orchestra band leader and composer, and **Malekula**, the MBC's long-serving lead vocalist, both died in 1991.

On the **gospel** scene, the current conventional leaders of the pack are the **Katawa Singers** of Katawa Presbyterian church. But the electric gospel band that's really sizzling them in the pews at the moment is the **Alleluya Band**, formed at the Roman Catholic Church at Balaka with Italian instruments and studio laid on. They've gone from strength to strength since performing before the Pope during his 1989 visit. But they're not exclusively popey: they're poppy too, and play everything from reggae to soukous and jazz.

Thanks to George Mgoola for additional information

There is very little recorded Malawian music available overseas. The best current source is a pioneering small Malawian label called Pamtondo, with a branch at Airdrie Health Centre (c/o Dr John Lwanda), Airdrie, Scotland, ML6 0JU, UK. Virtually all their releases are good.

Kasambwe Brothers, Jivacourt Kathumba and Alan Namoko *Ndilibe Ambuye* (Pamtondo, UK). Like a cold shower on a hot afternoon, a refreshing acoustic set from some very talented musicians. Gravel-voiced Jivacourt Kathumba is billed as Malawi's Mahlathini. The Kasambwe

tracks are 7–13, presented in a vigorous, confident manner, with brisk guitar work and snappy percussion belying the fact that their combined ages when they recorded this was only 47. Rather scrambled liner notes.

Various *Pamtondo cassettes PAM001–PAM006* (Pamtondo, UK). Six cassettes of assorted Malawian good stuff, the best of which is on the above CD.

Various *Sounds Eastern and Southern* (Original Music, US). In their "African Acoustic" series, this has two tracks from Malawi: "Ndiza Fera Chuma" by Sitero Mbewe & Frank Mukweza and "Elube" by SR Chitalo & the De Ndirande Pitch Crooners. Fantastic name: delightful song.

A LUTA CONTINUA

MUSIC IN LUSOPHONE AFRICA: ANGOLA AND MOZAMBIQUE

Portuguese-speaking southern Africa has been late arriving on the World Music scene. Not that the sounds haven't been evolving in various directions for centuries, as everywhere. But the peculiarly Portuguese approach to imperial conquest and settlement – and the long and bitter wars which this imperialism fuelled – have kept Mozambique and Angola isolated and economically hamstrung for all of the two decades since they won back their independence. Nevertheless, as Richard Trillo discovers, they both have powerful and engaging musical cultures, including various versions of the modern guitar band sound and other strands derived from folk music.

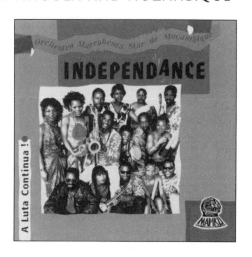

P ortugal itself was a dictatorship until 1974. Its overseas "provinces" were ruled by mixed-race *asimilados* – people whose Portuguese blood and educational good fortune assured them the citizenship status accorded to a tiny fraction of the population. It is largely these same people who form the elite in both countries.

ANGOLA

In Angola, while the democratically elected MPLA government of Eduardo Dos Santos continues to be besieged by the Jonas Savimbi's right-wing UNITA rebel group – and atrocities and the mass suffering of malnutrition and

disease are still commonplace – there's slim chance for music to move and prosper, either in the relative calm of Luanda or the miserable conditions of the countryside. Since independence in 1975, the government has had a virtual monopoly on music production - operator of the only studio, licenser of all performances, but also the sponsor of dozens of folklore groups and a number of town-based guitar bands.

The first musicians to make much of an impression in Europe were the **Kafala Brothers**, who toured in 1988 and 1990. Their CD, "Ngola", sold modestly well, but enthusiasm for their mournful acoustic guitar duets didn't endure much beyond the brothers' departure.

More promising (indeed the promise was fulfilled decades ago) is the upbeat, tropical dance splatter of the **Orquestra os Jovens do Prenda** (the "Prenda Boys Band" – Prenda is a poor suburb of Luanda), a large guitar band who were formed in the mid-60s, peaked in 1971, then disbanded in 1975, until being re-formed by two original members in 1981. With a large team of musicians, including four guitarists, two trumpets and a sax, and half a dozen percussionists and drummers, they produce a generous, fast-paced wall of sound, whistled along at key moments. The core of their style, which has much in common with Brazilian samba (though the direction of influence is more the reverse), is a sound they call **kizomba**, rooted in the two-person *marimba* xylophone: the four guitars ("solo", "contra-solo", rhythm and bass) play the parts of the marimba to achieve the sound of a single instrument. Meanwhile, the trumpets and sax interrupt in fanfare unison and the pile of drums – *tumba*, bongo, *buita*, *bate-bate* – punches out more rhythms than you can keep up with. Orchestra os Jovens' lyrics became increasingly politicized in Portuguese times, but with the sour background of civil war at the time of their re-formation, the band's second-incarnation lyrics are now the conventional staples of love and fortune – often forcefully expressed, as in the sulky "Manuela":

Abdul Remane Gino and Zena Bakar of Eyuphuro

> "*You Manuela*
> *You are very old-fashioned.*
> *Manuela, if you have a good heart,*
> *Let's go home and talk about it*
> *And if you don't like good advice*
> *Then get the fuck out of here.*"

> *Nowadays Manuela has changed.*
> *She passes and she doesn't greet me anymore.*

Other Angolan artists to look out for are the politically committed **Kuenda Bonga**, based in Paris; **Teta Lando**; and **Eduardo Paim**.

MOZAMBIQUE

No less than Angola, newly independent Mozambique was comprehensively wrecked and deserted by the Portuguese when they left. It was further damaged by years of futile terrorist activities at the hands of the South African military stooge organization RENAMO at the cost of at least a million lives (out of a population of sixteen million) and millions more orphaned, displaced or merely traumatized. But since 1992, the country has been relatively peaceful and an active return to "normal" civilian life is currently underway, making visits and travel increasingly feasible.

None of the turmoil seems to have much harmed the quality of what little music is available. **Marrabenta Star**, the national radio station's house band, is an outfit of enormous guts and sparkle. Their name is taken from the marrabenta rhythm of the capital Lourenço Marques – now Maputo – which is itself based on the older, more sedate and rural *marika*, spiced and heated during decades of colonial rule in the city. Marrabenta was mistrusted by the Portuguese: it was a medium of revolution and a cultural form they had no way of controlling, with lyrics often in local languages rather than

Portuguese. Marrabenta Star are a big company, with bass, rhythm and lead guitar, three vocalists, two trumpets and a sax, a drummer, a percussionist and four dancers from the national dance troupe, whose performance makes every Marrabenta show a memorable event.

Two other bands have come to prominence outside Mozambique through the RealWorld label associated with the WOMAD organization. Zena Bakar and Abdul Remane Gino's **Eyuphuro** come from Ilha de Moçambique on the northeast coast, a partly Swahili area and very much an Indian Ocean cultural crossroads. The big band **Ghorwane**, led by Tchika Fernando, (who have the usual three guitars, trumpet, sax and percussion line-up) come from the drought-prone province of Gaza and name themselves after a lake that remains a permanent water-source.

Traditional music has recently become available overseas as well: the *timbila* xylophones of the **Chopi** people, with their idiosyncratic tuning, and the *tufo* women's **choral groups** accompanied by percussionists, have been recorded by GlobeStyle.

Ghorwane percussionist

DISCOGRAPHY

MOZAMBIQUE

ⓒ **Eduardo Durão** *Timbila* (GlobeStyle, UK). First modern (and modernized) recordings of the bittersweet sound of Mozambiquan mbila: some tracks are incorporated into a modern African guitar and drums groove.

ⓒ **Eyuphoro** *Mama Mosambiki* (RealWorld, UK). Gentle songs in a folk tradition, best when Zena Bakar's voice is allowed full rein, as on her beautiful composition, "Kihiyeny".

ⓒ **Ghorwane** *Majurugenta* (RealWorld, UK). More in the Marrabenta Star mould – a big sound, though heavily coloured in this CD by the breezy sax of the late Zeca Alage.

ⓒ **Orquestra Marrabenta Star de Moçambique** *Independance* (Piranha, Germany). What's so wonderful about Marrabenta Star is the joyous variety of their music – everything from loping dance grooves to brooding songs like the closing track, "Nwahulwana".

ⓒ **Various** *¡Saba Saba!* (GlobeStyle, UK). Acoustic dance music from Nyampula in the northeast interior, an exuberant kind of afro-skiffle with multi-layered vocals.

ⓒ **Various** *Music from Mozambique Vols 1* and **2** (GlobeStyle, UK). Down home in Mozambique, this is mostly acoustic field recordings, partly set up from regional folk bands, partly stumbled across. Exhaustive liner notes.

ⓒ **Various** *Sounds Eastern & Southern* (Original Music, US). In the "African Acoustic" series, this has three tracks from Mozambique, recorded by ethnomusicologist Hugh Tracey in 1957.

ANGOLA

ⓒ **Kuenda Bonga** *Paz em Angola* (Rounder, US). A plaintive, rootsy voice with the political credentials of Zimbabwe's Thomas Mapfumo or South Africa's Miriam Makeba.

ⓒ **Orquesta os Jovens do Prenda** *Berlin Fiesta* (Piranha, Germany). Bounces along happily, but doesn't leave much trace in the ear of the listener.

ⓒ **The Kafala Brothers** *Ngola* (Anti-Apartheid Enterprises, UK). Acoustic guitars back heavy, poetic lyrics, somewhat after the manner of Agostinho Neto, Angola's first (poet-) president.

THE FAR EAST

C overing a range of countries and cultures from Indonesia to Japan, this chapter must surely be the most heterogeneous in the book. There are so many civilizations, each with its own rich and diverse musical traditions, that we can only sketch a region that is still little known in the west, even to World Music aficionados.

Part of the difficulty is that many of these forms are so far removed from western musical traditions, not just in the sounds themselves, but in the philosophy behind them. A great deal of the music is allied to religious ceremonies, traditional epics like the Ramayana and Mahabharata, or royal court ritual, and calls for an awareness of the meaning and context of the performance. But it is usually worth making the effort – music that can seem strange at first just takes a bit of time to appreciate and then you find yourself in a whole new world of extraordinary sounds. And much of the music covered in the following articles is stunningly beautiful and instantly appealing.

For those wanting to make their first explorations into Far Eastern music, Indonesia is perhaps the place to start. Here there is music that is contemporary and distinctively Indonesian, set alongside a classical and traditional music, gamelan, with its seductive tones and multi-layered structure. Javanese and Balinese gamelan groups perform quite often in Europe and North America, while playing the music is becoming increasingly popular among westerners, too. The sounds of modern Indonesian pop, like dangdut and jaipongan, are equally amazing – exotic, wild and a lot of fun, especially if you get the chance to see them live in cocnert.

The percussion-based classical music of Thailand is not much known beyond the borders but is scarcely less accessible than gamelan, as played by modern ensembles like Fong Naam. Thailand also embraces a diversity of traditional and regional folk musics, some of which, as in Indonesia, have emerged in fusion experiments with rock and pop.

Laos and Vietnam, too, have some interesting – and often unexpected – musical forms, ranging from folk opera to crooners.

The traditional music of China has suffered the onslaughts of the Cultural Revolution and a continuous pressure from the authorities to "modernize", but in the provinces some village ensembles are still hanging on. Their music has a wonderful raw quality and a tradition stretching back thousands of years. The sounds of neighbouring Mongolia are surprisingly accessible, closely related, as they are, to the Tuvan throat singers, across the Russian Federation border. Several excellent recordings of "overtone" singing and the equally distinctive horse-head fiddle have recently appeared.

Japan is, of course, the economic powerhouse of the region. World Music has become very popular there and since 1991 WOMAD has held regular festivals in Yokohama. Meanwhile, Tokyo has become one of the centres of the Asian pop music industry. The idea, as espoused by a group of north Asian musicians and producers, led by producer Makoto Kubota, is to combine Japanese production with Asian talent to produce a "local" pop industry. It's happening already, in fact, as witnessed by the Japanese success of Singapore singer Dick Lee and of some of the Indonesian pop bands, so it is perhaps only a matter of time before the pop music of Thailand – luk thung and mor lam – breaks through, too.

Whether Far East pop gets a hearing in the west, though, is a rather more moot question. Much of it is dynamic and fun, but a great deal more of it is dire mimicry of western pop and rock bands – and not very good ones at that. This book is interested in the indigenous styles that co-exist alongside the westernised music or which share Asian and western roots. Right now the most interesting names in this new music sphere are coming from Japan (and in particular the islands of Okinawa), Thailand and Indoniesia: musicians like Rinken Teruya and Nenes in Okinawa, Pimpa Pornsiri in Thailand, and Rhoma Irama in Indonesia. In China the rock star Ciu Jian represents a successful east–west synthesis and, more importantly, a protesting voice.

The appearance in the west of recordings by Asian artists like Detty Kurnia, the Rinkenband, Shoukichi Kina (recently profiled by David Byrne's Luaka Bop label) and others suggests that their music may, at last, be breaking through. This is a trend that is likely to become more widespread as the region's own fascination with the west wears off and a rediscovery of local music takes place. Successful syntheses are sure to be found. After all, many of the local pop styles covered throughout this book had their genesis in similar conditions during the 1940s, '50s and '60s, when imported styles were blended with local ones to create an original music. Let's hope this is one case where history will repeat itself.

FAR EAST ✈ GLOSSARY

Biwa Japanese lute with 4, 5 strings like the Chinese pipa.

Bon odori Old Japanese Buddhist festival celebrated in summer.

Bonang Set of Indonesian knobbed gongs.

Cai Luong Popular Vietnamese opera.

Dangdut The most popular form of contemporary Indonesian pop music.

Degung Sundanese popular song form.

Enka Sentimental Japanese ballad style.

Gagaku Ancient Japanese court music.

Gamelan Indonesian ensemble mainly of tuned percussion.

Gendèr Indonesian bronze xylophone with resonating tubes beneath the bars.

Jaipongan Sundanese popular music style with gamelan.

Kabuki Popular traditional theatre form in Japan.

Kantrum Thai-Cambodian pop.

Kayagum 12-stringed Korean zither.

Kayakyoku Japanese popular music, usually a fusion of Japanese and western styles.

Kebyar Distinctive dramatic style of Balinese gamelan.

Kecak Balinese monkey dance.

Khaen Thai mouth organ with reed pipes, like the Chinese sheng.

Khöömi Mongolian singing producing two notes at the same time to give a melody and bass.

Kobushi Japanese vocal style with heavy vibrato.

Koto Large 13-stringed zither used in Japanese classical music.

Kroncong European-influenced Indonesian urban folk.

Lakorn Thai classical dance drama.

Luk grung Sentimental Thai ballad music.

Luk thung Popular Thai country music.

Min'yo Japanese regional folk song.

Mor lam Folk music from the Isaan region of northeast Thailand.

Mor lam sing Popular modernized form of mor lam.

Morin khuur Mongolian horse-head fiddle.

Muay Thai kick-boxing.

Noh Ancient stylized Japanese drama.

Ondo Japanese festival music.

Oud Middle Eastern lute.

Pi-phat Classical Thai ensemble of tuned percussion.

Pipa Chinese lute with 4 silk strings.

Qasidah Modern Indonesian pop with Middle Eastern sound.

Qin 7-stringed Chinese zither.

Rebab 2-stringed spike fiddle of Arabic origin, widespread in Asia.

Samulnori 4-man drum ensemble from Korea.

Sanshin 3-stringed banjo with snakeskin soundbox from Okinawa.

Saron Indonesian bronze xylophone without resonators.

Senggak Vocal percussion noises in Indonesian music.

Shakuhachi Japanese bamboo flute.

Shamisen 3-stringed Japanese banjo played with a plectrum.

Sheng Traditional Chinese mouth organ with reed pipes. Its sound is supposed to imitate the cry of the phoenix.

Silk-and-bamboo Instrumental music from the teahouses of Shanghai.

Siteran Javanese street ensemble.

String Mainstream westernized Thai pop.

Taiko Large Japanese barrel drum.

Zheng (or cheng) 13-stringed Chinese zither.

Zikir birat Malaysian song.

A STORM OF BRONZE

GAMELAN: THE ENCHANTED MUSIC OF JAVA AND BALI

The sound of the gamelan has delighted and perplexed western visitors to Indonesia for half a millennium. Sir Francis Drake, who visited Java in 1580, recounted hearing music "of a very strange kind, pleasant and delightful": a description that sums up most people's initial reaction. Gamelan, as Jenny Heaton explains, is quite unlike any other music: a dance, a ritual, a state of enchantment, which in this century has inspired composers as diverse as Debussy, Messiaen, Britten and John Cage.

T he Mangkunagaran Palace, Surakarta, central Java. A cool, gentle breeze wafts through the spacious entrance hall. Birds flutter in and out. Inside it is still and peaceful in contrast to the noise and activity outside. Across the cool expanse of the marble dance floor sit musicians, sipping tea, chatting and smoking clove cigarettes. Two dancers appear wearing long, brightly coloured sashes and armed with shields and daggers. The musicians start playing, and the whole hall is filled with the captivating sonorities of a piece known as "Kyai Kanyut Mesem" (Swept Away by a Smile). Welcome to the world of gamelan.

WHAT IS A GAMELAN?

A **gamelan** is an ensemble of tuned percussion, consisting mainly of **gongs**, **metallophones** (similar to xylophones, but with metal instead of wooden bars) and **drums**. Ensembles of gongs and drums are common throughout Indonesia, but the gamelan tradition is unique to Java, Bali and Lombok.

Larger gamelans are generally made of bronze, but iron and brass are also common, especially in the villages of Java. The wooden frames of the instruments are usually carved and painted in red and gold. On top of the gong-stand, in a Javanese gamelan, sit two serpents, tails entwined.

The Javanese say the first gamelan was created by the god-king Sang Hyang Guru, who ruled his kingdom in the third century from a mountaintop. He named his gamelan – which consisted of a few gongs and drums – "okonanta" (King of the World), after himself.

The historical origins of gamelan instruments are something of a mystery as there are few written records. But from temple reliefs and ancient bronze drums we know that cultural influences came from China, mainland southeast Asia and, in particular, India. Hinduism came to Java from India in the first century AD and along with Buddhism was the predominant religion in Java up until the fifteenth century, when Islam spread inland from the north coast.

The last great Javan Hindu kingdom, Majapahit, fell to Muslim rulers around 1500. Today, nearly ninety percent of Java's population is Muslim, but the traditional arts of gamelan, dance, theatre and batik have their roots in the older Hindu-Buddhist culture.

INSTRUMENTS OF THE GAMELAN

A gamelan is often described as "one large instrument sounded by many players". Every gamelan musician learns all the instruments and so develops a deep awareness and understanding of the whole ensemble. During the all-night shadow play, *wayang kulit*, it is common for musicians to change places and for special guests to be invited to play.

A complete gamelan is made up of two sets of instruments in the two Javanese **scales**, the five-note *laras slendro* and the seven-note *laras pelog*. The two sets are laid out with the

Bali's Heavenly Orchestra

corresponding instruments at right angles to each other. No two gamelans are tuned exactly alike and a Javanese musician will often prefer the sound and feeling of a piece played on one gamelan to another. Larger court gamelans are traditionally given a name; that of Yogyakarta, for example, is known as "The Venerable Invitation to Beauty".

All the instruments in the gamelan have a clear role to play and this is reflected in the layout of the ensemble. Simply speaking, the musical texture is made up of three elements: a central melody played on the instruments in the middle of the gamelan; an elaboration of the melody, played on instruments at the front; and "punctuation" of the melody by various gongs at the back.

Each **gong** has an onomatopoeic name evoking its sound: *kenong, ketuk* and *kempul*, for example. The word "gong" is Javanese and the highly skilled gongsmiths of central Java are famous throughout Indonesia. No piece of music can begin or end without a stroke on the large gong (*gong ageng*), while the smaller kenong, ketuk and kempul mark off shorter sections of the melody. The gong ageng is the most important instrument in the gamelan and it is believed that the soul or spirit of the gamelan resides within it.

In the middle of the gamelan are the **metallophones**. There are two main types: the *saron*, which has no resonators and is played with hard mallets, and the *gendèr*, which has resonators and is played with soft mallets. These instruments are used to play the *balungan*, the "skeleton melody".

This **melody** is fleshed out by the various instruments at the front of the gamelan, which include the *bonangs* (small kettle gongs mounted in a frame), and a collection of soft-toned instruments: *gendèr, gambang* (xylophone), *rebab* (fiddle), *suling* (bamboo flute) and *siter* or *celempung* (zither). These embellishment instruments have a larger range than the balungan instruments and it is said that they realize an unplayed melody, a hidden melody "sung by the musicians in their hearts".

Although a large gamelan may be played by as many as forty musicians, there is no conductor nor any visual cues, as the players all sit facing the same way. The whole gamelan is coordinated by the drummer in the centre of the ensemble, playing a selection of double-headed drums. Musical notation, although now used extensively in teaching, is never used in performance. When learning to play in a gamelan, musicians usually start with the simpler instruments at the back and work their way forward.

The full ensemble also includes **vocalists** – a male chorus and solo female singers. Nowadays the female singers often use microphones, but traditionally all the layers of the musical texture were perfectly balanced. There are no soloists in the gamelan tradition – it is a communal form of music-making – and there is little improvisation, either.

THE COURT GAMELANS OF JAVA

In central Java, the arts of gamelan and dance reached the peak of refinement at the royal courts of **Surakarta** (Solo) and **Yogyakarta** (Yogya). In the nineteenth century, the heyday of the courts, the sultans owned the finest gamelans and employed the best musicians and dancers. Distinct styles of dance and gamelan music developed at each of the courts. The Solonese are still known for the subtlety and refinement of their music and dance while the Yogyanese style is bold and strong in character.

Since independence in 1945, the importance of the courts as artistic centres has diminished and the new generations of musicians and dancers are trained at the state academies. However, some of Java's finest gamelans are still housed in the courts, including a number of special **ceremonial gamelans.** The largest and loudest, the **Gamelan Sekaten**, is still played once a year. This extraordinary gamelan is said to have been created by Java's first Muslim prince in the early sixteenth century. He built two enormous gamelans in the hope of drawing the largely Hindu population to the new Islamic faith, and had the gamelans played continuously for a week in the newly built court mosque during the celebration of Mohammed's birth, the **Sekaten festival**. This festival still takes place every year with the gamelans at the Great Mosques of Solo and Yogyakarta.

Some of the ceremonial court gamelans are believed to be magically charged. The most sacred instruments are the gongs, which are given ritual offerings of flowers and incense before performances. In the past, at the royal courts of central Java, different gamelans were played on different occasions. For outdoor ceremonies loud ensembles were played in

specially built pavilions. For indoor entertainment, such as the all-night shadow plays, an ensemble of gentle, soft-toned instruments was used. The modern gamelan has developed from a combination of these loud and soft ensembles.

It is within the palace walls that gamelan playing is traditionally regarded as a spiritual discipline, a way of reaching the ideal state of *iklas*, emotional detachment. The Javanese hero in theatre and dance is always in control of his emotions and dispenses with his raging enemies – giants, ogres and demons – with a graceful flick of a dagger. The refined austerity of the court compositions best conveys this sense of calm and contemplative detachment.

GAMELAN MUSIC IN PERFORMANCE

The repertoire of gamelan music is astonishingly versatile. It may be played on a large palace gamelan for an official ceremony; on a small collection of soft-toned instruments at a wedding reception; on an iron gamelan at weekly sessions in the village hall; on a bamboo ensemble accompanying a village dance; or by a group of street performers busking on homemade instruments.

In Yogya there are frequent performances by **siteran groups**, made up of zithers, vocals, a drum and a large end-blown bamboo tube that is used like a gong. Unlike the large bronze gamelans, these instruments are cheap, portable and often homemade. The siteran ensemble plays pieces from the gamelan repertoire and, with as few as four musicians, recreates with great resourcefulness the musical texture of the gamelan. In the quieter residential streets a lone siter player may perform of an evening, accompanying his traditional songs on a homemade instrument.

In both Java and Bali gamelan music is inseparable from the arts of **poetry, dance and drama.** A gamelan player will be familiar with dance movements and poetry and many dancers are quite at home sitting in the gamelan. The gamelan is rarely played on its own; like many other southeast Asian ensembles, it is closely linked to the theatre. Although the gamelan may on occasion be played purely for entertainment, as background music at a wedding reception, for example, it is rare for anyone to sit and listen and there are no concerts in the western sense.

One of the most popular forms of theatre in Java is the all-night shadow play, **wayang kulit**. The wayang was originally associated with ancestor worship in the pre-Hindu era, but later adopted the Hindu stories of the Ramayana and Mahabharata, which have formed the basis of Javanese dance and theatre for over a thousand years.

A wayang performance is a social occasion. Stalls selling hot roasted peanuts, clove cigarettes and hot drinks are open through the night and the audience will include invited guests and locals, young and old alike. From an early age children learn to recognize the wayang characters by the shape of the head-dress and the size of the nose, eyes and body of the delicate carved-leather puppets silhouetted against the screen. During the night the attention of the audience comes and goes and often the gamelan players fall asleep, too.

The wayang used to be accompanied by a small ensemble of soft-toned instruments in the slendro tuning, but these days it is usually accompanied by a full gamelan using both tunings. The gamelan music here is an integral part of the performance. The musicians take their cues from the puppeteer (*dalang*), who in turn needs a deep knowledge of the music as he or she controls the gamelan throughout the performance. The gamelan players have to respond quickly and accurately to the dalang's signals, which often include riddles or jokes from the clowns requesting a particular piece of music.

As well as accompanying dance and theatre, the gamelan is played at traditional rituals and ceremonies. In Java there is an old saying: "It's not official until the gong is hung". No **wedding ceremony** is complete without gamelan music – whether live or recorded – and specific pieces accompany important parts of the ceremony. There are welcoming and leaving pieces, many of which were originally composed for the arrival and departure of the sultan at palace ceremonies. As soon as guests at a reception hear the opening notes of a "leaving" piece they know the occasion is drawing to a close and will leave while the piece is being played. There are a few pieces, too, that are believed to release magical power when they are played and can ward off evil spirits.

In **Sunda** (west Java) the **gamelan salendro**, similar to a small central Javanese gamelan, is used to accompany dance and the rod-puppet

---

GAMELAN PERFORMANCES

. . . .

If you are going to a performance, it is polite and considerate to respect local attitudes to dress: avoid shorts, vests and sleeveless dresses. Tourist information centres will be able to provide further information, details of festivals and ceremonies and times of performances. Below, however, are a few highlights.

CENTRAL JAVA

YOGYAKARTA (YOGYA)
Kraton Yogyarkarta (Royal Palace). Dance performances are open to the public on Sundays; gamelan rehearsals take place on Mondays and Wednesdays.
Siswa Among Beksa (Kraton Dance School). Dance performances in the evenings.
Romo Sas. Dance performances in the evenings.
Pura Paku Alaman. Every 35 days, on a Sunday named Minggu Pon, there is a live radio broadcast of the court gamelan.
ISI (Institut Seni Indonesia). The Institute of Performing Arts.
Jalan Malioboro. The main shopping street of Yogyakarta, where siteran groups may gather to play in the evenings.

Prambanan Temple (outside Yogyakarta). Ramayana ballet, performed in the open air at full moon during the dry season (March–August).

SURAKARTA (SOLO)
Mangkunagaran Palace. Regular dance rehearsals Wednesday mornings.
Sriwedari Amusement Park. Nightly performances of wayang orang (dance drama based on Mahabharata).
STSI (Sekolah Tinggi Seni Indonesia). The Academy of Performing Arts.

BALI

Major temple festivals such as **Galungan and Kuningan** (every 210 days), and the more frequent **odalan** ceremonies (celebrating the anniversary of the village temple at full moon), are dependent on the Balinese calendar. Check out the dates in Bali. A temple sash must be worn when visiting a festival in Bali.

There are also a large number of tourist performances of gamelan and dance, particularly in **Ubud**, **Peliatan** and **Bona** (*kecak*). The setting won't be traditional Balinese, but the standard of performance is generally high.

Siter player, Surakarta, Java

theatre (*wayang golek*). The more exuberant character and culture of the Sundanese is mirrored in the music which, although sharing the same roots as the central Javanese tradition, has developed quite independently.

Other Sundanese ensembles are unique to the area: the hauntingly beautiful **cianjuran**, epic poems sung with flute and zithers, and the popular *gamelan degung*. There is also a rich tradition of folk music, which includes *angklung*, an ensemble of bamboo rattles. (See the Indonesian pop article, following, for more on Sundanese music.)

GAMELAN IN JAVA TODAY

Life is changing in Java. For many young people the gamelan represents the values of the past. In search of a better future young people are moving away from the villages – and they listen to western rock and Indonesian pop rather than the gamelan. At wedding ceremonies cassette recordings are increasingly used as a cheap alternative to live musicians. In the towns and cities, short, two-hour wayangs are becoming popular. Older dalangs complain that their young pupils no longer understand the spiritual teachings and philosophy of the wayang.

But for many the gamelan tradition is alive and well. In the towns of Yogya and Solo most neighbourhoods have a gamelan in the local hall and music-making continues to play an important part in community life. In Solo the annual contest at the radio station draws a huge number of enthusiastic gamelan groups from the town and surrounding area. Men and women generally play in separate

groups with the exception of the *pesindhen*, female singers. Some of the larger batik shops have a gamelan upstairs for the employees to play after work, and a number of schools also have their own gamelan.

In the major towns the state **radio stations** (RRI, Radio Republik Indonesia) employ professional studio musicians and actors. Programmes include a wide range of gamelan music: live broadcasts from the courts, *wayang orang* (dance dramas), wayang kulit, and more lighthearted "listeners' requests" programmes, which often feature popular pieces and lively arrangements of traditional pieces by the late **Ki Nartosabdho**, a greatly respected gamelan musician and dalang.

In Yogya the music and dance of **Bagong Kussudiardja** is well known; his fame as both composer and choreographer has spread throughout Indonesia. For most composers and choreographers, however, financial support and sponsorship is a perennial problem and for this reason many new works are performed only once.

Nonetheless, the gamelan tradition is constantly evolving, with a lot of artistic experimentation and innovation going on at the **academies of performing arts** (STSI in Solo, ISI in Yogya, ASTI in Bandung, etc). At

Rebab player from Gamelan Sekar Tunjung

these academies, which were set up in the 1950s, after independence, musicians and dancers from Java, Bali and Sumatra work together on new choreography, new storytelling methods, new sounds, instruments and styles of playing. A series of recordings of experimental music by such composers has recently been released by Lyrichord and gives a sense of the scope of contemporary Indonesian gamelan music.

While musicians from different regions work happily together at the academies, outside them the Javanese and Balinese are not too keen on each others' music. To the Balinese, Javanese music is too soft, too slow and lacking in vitality, while the Javanese dismiss Balinese music as harsh, unrefined and too loud . . .

BALINESE GAMELAN

It is late evening. In the main courtyard of the temple a hundred men sit in circles. Only the sound of the crickets breaks the silence. There is a feeling of suspense. Suddenly, with several short cries the men rise up, then sink down again, making a hissing sound. A single short shout follows and the men break into a rhythmic chant, "Uchak-a-chak-a-chak . . . ", swaying from side to side, hands waving in the air. A solitary voice rises above the rhythmic chattering of the chorus, singing a quivering, wailing melody. Another short cry and the men sink down again.

This is the famous and spectacular **kecak** or monkey-chant of Bali. In the kecak, the chorus of men imitates the chattering and jabbering of the monkeys (there are several monkey forests in Bali), while the complex rhythms are taken from the gamelan.

The Balinese love to take something from elsewhere, incorporate it into their art and make it uniquely Balinese. In the stone temple carvings of north Bali, in among the ornate mythical beasts and flowers there may be a Dutchman in colonial uniform on a bicycle, or in the middle of a traditional painting by a young artist you may find a car.

In a similar way, the kecak was adopted this century from an ancient trance dance into a dramatic form using the Hindu Ramayana story. The chorus represents the monkey army helping King Rama rescue his queen, Sinta, from Rahwana, the ogre-king. The kecak is performed as a spectacle rather than as part of a ceremony and new versions are commissioned

for festivals and television. However, much of Bali's abundance of music, dance and theatre continues to play an essential role in the elaborate temple ceremonies central to life on the island.

HINDU BALI

In the late fifteenth century the Hindu-Javanese Majapahit Empire fell to Muslim rulers and many of the Javanese princes fled eastwards across the narrow strait to Bali, taking with them their priests, dancers and musicians. To this day the Balinese practise their own **Hindu-Balinese** religion, a unique blend of Hinduism and traditional Balinese beliefs.

Gamelan Angklung Procession in Bali

The village temple is at the heart of Balinese life and culture. Hardly a week passes without several **temple festivals** happening all over the island. Important island-wide festivals, such as **Galungan**, which comes once every 210 days (a Balinese year), call for ten days of prayer and festivities. At Galungan the spirits of the ancestors visit the island and they must be greeted with offerings, prayers, music and dance.

GAMELAN WORKSHOPS

•••••••••••••••••••••••

Over the past decade, Gamelan workshops have become quite a passion in European and American schools, universities and arts centres. It's a highly social form of music-making, with everyone involved in an ensemble that is capable of accommodating a wide range of abilities in a non-hierarchical way – there are, anyway, no virtuosos or soloists.

"I'm not really a musician", someone said to me, nervously arriving at a gamelan workshop. In a group learning to play the gamelan for the first time, this person may be at an advantage over the professional musician, who has far more to "unlearn". For the music system of the gamelan is totally different to anything in the western musical tradition, and the learning process is quicker for those able to approach the music with an open mind. The techniques of playing the main instruments are, in any case, pretty simple, although the soft-toned elaborating instruments (gendèr, gambang, rebab, etc) require a high level of technique and understanding of the music.

What is it that draws people to the gamelan? "It calms me down after a day's work", says one person at my workshop; "the music reaches a part of me that nothing else does", reveals another; and one says, simply, "I just love being around the instruments".

The gamelan is also making a strong impact in special education, where its aspects of coordination and control are important. A child with learning difficulties can easily play the large gong, the instrument that begins, ends and punctuates the music. It is easy to accomplish, but central to the music and gives a great feeling of satisfaction.

The different instruments of the gamelan invite exploration yet also present challenges for coordination, control and restraint. The visual impact of the gamelan, too, and its etiquette – removing shoes, not stepping over instruments – as well as the range of sounds of the instruments, combine to create a unique and stimulating experience in group music-making.

Gamelan music is primarily an oral tradition. For western players, learning by ear bypasses the obstacles of western musical theory and challenges us to listen, observe and imitate rather than analyze. Above all, the gamelan develops listening skills, flexibility and sensitive ensemble playing. The concepts of "right" and "wrong" take on a new light in gamelan music, where there is always more than one way of doing things.

Check it out – there may be a gamelan near you!

In the larger villages all the different gamelans are brought out for Galungan. The four-tone gamelan angklung is played by the older boys of the village, as part of the long procession of women bringing the family offerings to the temple. Further down there are the clashing cymbals of the processional *gamelan bebonangan*. Within the open-air temple itself several different gamelans are played all at once in separate pavilions. Only the gods and spirits are listening. Like the carefully arranged fruit and rice, like the flowers and incense, the music is an offering.

Later on, though, in the cool air of early evening, crowds will gather to watch a dance drama or the ancient **gambuh** theatre, accompanied by flutes and percussion. At night there may be a wayang kulit, accompanied by the intricate music of a quartet of gendèrs.

Most villages in Bali boast several gamelans owned by the local **music club.** The club members, all men, meet there in the evenings to rehearse. They are almost all amateurs, earning their living as farmers, craftsmen or civil servants. Gamelan playing is traditionally considered a part of every man's education, like learning the art of rice growing or cooking ceremonial food.

The village gamelan is kept in a public place and rehearsals usually draw an interested audience of onlookers who offer comments and suggestions. Many villages have a distinctive style or speciality: Peliatan is known for the refinement of its courtly *legong* dance and music, Sukawati for the complexity and brilliance of its gendèr playing. It's said that people can find their way around the island in the dark by recognizing the distinctive tones of the local gamelans in the night air.

KEBYAR STYLE GAMELAN

When the Dutch took control of Bali, the island courts all but disappeared, as many royal families sacrificed themselves in the cannon-fire to die an honourable death rather than submit to Dutch rule. This had an enormous impact on the musical life of the island. The court gamelans had no function outside the palace walls and were sold or taken to the villages where they were melted down to make new gamelans for the latest style that was taking Bali by storm: **kebyar**.

The word literally means "like the bursting open of a flower". Kebyar originated in north Bali and replaced the slow, stately court playing with fast, dynamic music, full of dramatic contrasts, changes of tempo and sudden loud outbursts. It was not long before Bali's most famous dancer of all time, **I Mario**, choreographed the first kebyar dance, in which the intricate and beautiful movements of the dancer's eyes, head and hands mirror the dazzling display of the music. It is this dynamic virtuosic new style that makes much Balinese gamelan music today sound so different from the Javanese.

The kebyar style has influenced other repertoires in Bali, as well as that of the bronze gamelan. The most stunning example is the all-bamboo *joged bumbung*. In this ensemble, even the gong is made of bamboo, making it a cheap alternative to a bronze gamelan. Joged bumbung is most popular in west Bali, where the style originated in the 1950s, growing out of a lively folk dance accompaniment.

The **older court ensembles** still remaining in Bali include the stately **Gamelan Gong Gedé** and the delicate **Gamelan Semar Pegulingan** (Gamelan of the Love God). The semar pegulingan includes bamboo flutes and a pair of genders, played with hard mallets. Originally played near the sleeping chambers in the palace, this beautiful ensemble is now often played for the legong dance. Sacred gamelans in Bali include the **Bamboo Gambang** ensemble, which is played for cremations, and the ethereal **Gamelan Selunding** from the ancient village of Tenganan in east Bali. Excellent recordings are available of these various ensembles.

BALINESE RHYTHMS

Where Javanese music is quiet, contemplative and restrained, Balinese is loud, sparkling and extrovert. It is, after all, outdoor music. Like the elaborate temple carvings and paintings, the music is intricately detailed. Just as the harmony of village life depends on the delicate balance of opposing forces of good and evil, night and day, so in the gamelan the instruments appear in pairs, even the drums, which are called male and female.

The rhythmic vitality of Balinese music comes from lively interlocking patterns played on various pairs of instruments. These patterns, called **kotekan**, are played on the bronze *gangsas* (similar to the Javanese gendèr, but struck with bare wooden mallets), the two drums and the *reong* (a set of little knobbed gongs in a frame, played by four men).

The Canadian composer Colin McPhee, who lived and studied in Bali in the 1930s, writes in his delightful book *A House in Bali* of the stir his Steinway grand caused in the village where he lived for ten years. When he played a waltz his Balinese friends were dismayed. "Where's the beat?" they asked, "There's no beat! Like a bird with a broken wing!"

Apart from the rhythm, there's another kind of beat in Balinese gamelan music. The various pairs of instruments are tuned slightly "out" with each other, so that when two instruments are played together, there is a "harmonic beating". This gives the Balinese gamelan its characteristic shimmering quality.

Benjamin Britten, who was introduced to Balinese music by Colin McPhee, visited Bali in 1956 and was captivated by the music he heard there: "The music is fantastically rich melodically, rhythmically, texturally (such orchestration!!) and above all formally. It's a remarkable culture . . ."

The island has changed a lot since the 1950s, of course. Bali is now one of Indonesia's top tourist attractions and draws around a million people each year (more than a third of Bali's population). The roads buzz with motorbikes, *bemos* (local transport) and huge tourist buses. Some parts of the island have been swamped by tourism. But the arts continue to flourish and grow, the traditional temple festivals go on and more modern festivals, such as the annual **Bali Arts Festival** in Denpasar, have become an important feature of cultural life on the island. On any night of the week, if you're lucky you can hear a number of different gamelans in a temple, a festival, at a wedding, a tooth-filing ceremony or a cremation. Go there – and keep your ears open!

DISCOGRAPHY

JAVA

⊚ **Gamelan of Kraton Surakarta** *Court Music of Kraton Surakarta* (King, Japan). A complete recording of a palace dance, including sections of unaccompanied vocals.

⊚ **Gamelan of Kraton Yogyakarta** *The Sultan's Pleasure: Javanese Gamelan and Vocal Music* (Music of the World, US). A very fine recording from the Royal Palace in Yogyakarta, with the majestic loud-style playing for which the Yogyanese are famous.

⊚ **Gamelan of Pura Pakualaman** *Javanese Court Gamelan* (Elektra Nonesuch, US). An equally good recording of the other main palace gamelan in Yogyakarta.

Gamelan of Pura Mangkunagaran *Javanese Court Gamelan* (Elektra Nonesuch, US). Yet to appear on CD, this recording from Solo is perhaps the best gamelan court recording, capturing beautifully the space of the *pendopo* (entrance hall) in which the gamelan is played.

⊚ **Imas Permas and Asep Kosasih** *Tembang Sunda* (Nimbus, UK). Not gamelan music, but the classical songs of Sunda. Beautiful mellow performances accompanied by zither and flute. Text translations are included.

⊚ **Various** *Chamber Music of Central Java* (King, Japan). A gadon – a chamber gamelan of soft-toned instruments – featuring top musicians from Solo.

Various *Street Music of Central Java* (Lyrichord, US). Recording of a siteran ensemble from Yogya with singers.

BALI

⊚ **Bamboo Ensemble of Sangkar Agung Village** *Jegog* (JVC, Japan). A wonderful recording of a jegog – bamboo – gamelan ensemble. An unusual lively and sonorous sound, enlivened further by audience reaction.

⊚ **Gamelan Batel Wayang Ramayana** (CMP, Germany) Village gamelan from Sading performing music from the shadow puppet play. Excellent recording.

⊚ **Gamelan Eka Cita** *Gamelan Gong Kebyar* (King, Japan). A terrific example of the lively new kebyar style. The gamelan is from a small village near Denpasar. Excellent.

⊚ **Gamelan Semar Pegulingan** *The Heavenly Orchestra of Bali* (CMP, Germany). A beautifully sonorous recording of the gentle, refined gamelan from the village of Kamasan in eastern Bali. Not as wild and frenetic as much Balinese music.

⊚ **Music of the Wayang Kulit** *A Shadow Play from the Mahabharata* (JVC, Japan). Sung narration and percussion accompaniment to a shadow puppet play.

⊚ **Kecak** *The Choral Dramas of Peliatan Village* (JVC, Japan). A choral incantation of the Hindu epic saga of Ramayana by a cast of 300. An amazing sound – though devotees only will last the course.

⊚ **Various** *Bali: Gamelan and Kecak* (Elektra Nonesuch, US). An excellent selection of different ensembles giving a good cross section of gamelan and other music from Bali, including the ancient gamelan salunding.

⊚ **Various** *Bali: Musique pour le Gong Gedé* (Ocora, France). Another recording of the older, gentler style of Balinese gamelan, played by two ensembles from Batur and Tampaksiring.

NEW MUSIC

⊚ **Sekar Jaya Gamelan** *American Works for Balinese Gamelan Ensemble* (New World Records, US). An interesting disc of music by three American composers, played by this Californian-based gamelan. Evan Ziporyn's "Kekembangan" is a fine piece for gamelan and saxophone quartet.

⊚ **Various** *Asmat Dream* (Lyrichord, US). Contemporary pieces in the gamelan tradition composed for concert performance with extra solo instruments and overdubbing. This disc features four composers from Sunda, and there are two more volumes featuring Javanese and Balinese composers.

BEYOND THE GAMELAN

THE WILD WORLD OF INDONESIAN POP

No question about it, the popular music scene in Indonesia is the most exciting in southeast Asia and the Far East. From the vast range of music throughout the islands, Colin Bass, in Java, introduces the shimmering and seductive, the raunchy and vivacious – the astonishing world of kroncong, dangdut, jaipongan and more.

Indonesia's archipelago of 13,600 islands spans from west to east a distance equal to that between Glasgow and Baghdad. The islands are home to nearly 180 million people, 360 ethnic groups, and about 250 different languages: an amazing mix of cultures that is reflected in quite a diversity of pop music.

To take a look below the tip of this tropical iceberg, it's still necessary to buy an air ticket or stow away on a steamer, destination Java. Having arrived in Jakarta, a good place to start would be the downtown street called Jalaan Agus Salim. Enjoy the ubiquitous smell of clove cigarettes mingled with the exhaust fumes of the turbulent traffic as you acknowledge the constant greetings from passers-by.

You may feel slightly disappointed as you walk past the *Burger King* and *Dunkin' Donuts*, so as an antidote stop by the *Sumatran Padang* restaurant. If you're going to perspire you might as well sweat. Okay, a little further, past the man

THE FAR EAST

INDONESIAN POP   **425**

selling posters of President Suharto and Samantha Fox (er, that's two separate posters) and the fruit seller (that's not the drains you can smell but a durian fruit – make a mental note to try one later), and enter the portals of the *Duta Suara* cassette shop. The ground floor is unpromising, stocking cassettes of western rock and pop, which are big business in all the Indonesian cities. But head upstairs and it's quite another story, as you enter a room of music-loving Javanese of all ages seated along the rows of cassette players, listening on headphones to their choices. And the choices along the walls cover a bewildering range. Kroncong, dangdut, jaipongan, degung, pop-sunda, mandarin, pop-batak and qasidah modern are just a few of the stops on a musical tour of the archipelago, so fill up a basket, find a vacant player and don the headphones.

KRONCONG

For a historical perspective you could start under the sign for **kroncong** (pronounced ker-ong-chong), a music that actually predates the cassette era, tracing its roots back several centuries to when the Portuguese were establishing trade links with Africa and south Asia. The arrival of European instruments laid the basis for what later became the first major urban-folk style, gaining national popularity in the 1930s through its use by the new Indonesian film industry.

Rhoma Irama giving it some reverb

Then, a typical ensemble consisted of one or two *kroncong* (ukeleles), guitars, violins, a flute, and sometimes a cello and percussion,

accompanying a singer, usually female. The mid-tempo rhythms and the languid, sentimental vocals of this period are reminiscent of the east African taarab style and Madagascan valiha music, and many of the melody lines show similar roots in Portuguese fado singing. Whatever the origins, the polyrhythmic patterns created by the orchestra set against the lilting vocals make for a unique and exciting sound.

In the 1980s the popular singer **Hetty Koes Endang** revived the kroncong form, but for the most part kroncong appeals today to a mainly middle-aged audience and many of the different styles you'll find on the shelves are rather tepid Mantovani-type string arrangements of western pop songs. Look for "Kroncong asli" (original kroncong), and when you get home, find a copy of the CD "Street Music of Java" on the US Original Music label, which contains some fine examples of "authentic" kroncong as played by street musicians. Also on this record you will find some street-level versions of what occupies by far the biggest shelf-space in the shop – dangdut.

DANGDUT

Dang-dut-dang-dut-dang-dut-dang-dut-dang-dut-dang-dang. This is what you're most likely to hear spilling onto the street from shops and passing minibuses and taxis. **Dangdut**, Indonesia's equivalent of danceable Latin music, has been thriving since the mid-1970s. It grew out of kroncong but its most obvious influence is that of Indian film song.

As with many Indonesian musical terms, dangdut is an onomatopoeic word derived from the rhythm usually played on a *tabla* drum (so that you know your dang from your dut, count in fours and hear the low dang note struck on the fourth beat and the high dut note struck on the first beat of the following bar). Alongside the tabla, a typical group consists of electric guitar, bass, mandolin, percussion and synthesizer. But of course it is the singers that are the stars: glamorous men and women singing of love – falling in it, falling out of it, losing it – or of moral issues such as family matters, being poor, getting rich, staying honest, etc.

Dangdut draws its audience largely from Muslim youth of the lower and lower-middle classes. And it speaks for them, expressing their resentment at inequalities in Indonesian society. Most of these protest songs are composed and performed by the pre-eminent superstar of dangdut, **Rhoma Irama**. It was Irama who led

Jakarta night. Tourists are rare in this neck of the woods, so your entrance will have heads turning – but don't be intimidated. Once you've watched how to dance dangdut-style – a sort of slow jogging – dive onto the dance floor, where your efforts will be much appreciated by all.

There are also several larger dangdut dance halls in the area known as Mangga Dua, just off the Gayah Madah, the main street running from the central Menteng area to the old Dutch colonial capital, Batavia. On many records, the constant marking of the upbeat with a piano chord gives dangdut a reggae feel and the dancehall DJs may well feature a local cover version of a current reggae hit.

Dangdut star Elvy Sukaesih

the way in the dangdut explosion of the mid-1970s, with a famously outrageous stage show. He also turned to producing dangdut films, starting a new wave in the Indonesian cinema. Designed to inspire the poorer classes, these semi-autobiographical rags-to-riches stories set new trends not only in music and film but in dress, behaviour and attitudes.

Rhoma Irama is still immensely popular today, and still breaking new ground, as with his recent collaborations with Indian film-song legend Lata Mangeshkar. But of course there are a host of younger stars championing various new strains of dangdut. Look for current favourites like the beautiful women singers **Detty Kurnia**, **Maryam Mustafa**, and the current queen of dangdut, **Elvy Sukaesih**.

If this whets the appetite, then a visit later in the evening to Jalan Halimun on the east side of town is recommended. On a short stretch of this street, seemingly in the middle of nowhere, are a dozen ramshackle saloons, festooned with coloured lights, blasting out dangdut into the hot

Qur'an dan Koran

From age to age
Man's civilization develops
By now everywhere
Man is changing the world
Tall buildings scrape the sky
They adorn almost every country
In fact technology in this day and age
Can reach into outer space
But it's sad to say
Men have forgotten who they are
And become arrogant
They think they're even taller
Than those skyscrapers

As progress marches on
People get so busy
That they forget their duty
To pray to God five times a day
They are so drunk with progress
They think the computer is God (you're kidding!)
When they talk about the world
They're wonderfully clever
But talk to them about religion
And suddenly they're allergic
Reading the newspaper is a necessity
The Qur'an is just there for decoration
Everybody's crazy to learn English
Arabic is considered backward (they're wrong!)

What good is success in this world
If it brings disaster in the next?
Let us try to be happy
Not only for today but for eternity.

Rhoma Irama
(from "Indonesian Popular Music 2",
Smithsonian Folkways).

JAIPONGAN: IT'S NOT ROCK'N'ROLL . . .

Just occasionally in the dangdut dancehalls, the drum machines and bendy guitars may be interrupted by a percussion-based style whose unpredictable tempo changes fail to deter some inventive dancing from those left on the floor. This will be **jaipongan**, a style that has no detectable western influence, using only instruments from the Sundanese gamelan tradition.

In jaipongan songs, the *rebab*, a two-stringed bowed fiddle, plays the introduction as the *kendang*, a large two-headed barrel drum, improvises in free time underneath; then, with whooping cries, the rest of the orchestra enters.

Blak-ting-pong-blak-ting-pong-blak-ting-pong. The kendang sets to, building and releasing tension through a 16- or 32-beat pattern marked by a single stroke on a large gong, while a smaller damped gong, a *kempul*, beats out one-note bass lines. The mellow sounds of the *bonang rincik* and the *panerus*, sets of ten and seven pot-shaped gongs, play stately, cyclical melodies, as the *saron*, a row of seven bronze keys set over a resonating box, hammers out faster arpeggios. The rebab anticipates, accompanies and answers the singer, or *sinden*, as she floats like a butterfly through tales of love, money and agriculture, while throughout various members of the orchestra indulge in more whooping, wailing and rhythmic grunting, known as *senggak*.

JAIPONGAN: WORSE THAN THE TWIST!

. . . .

Colin Bass met **Dr. Gugum Gumbira Tirasondjaja**, the Bandung-based producer, composer, arranger, choreographer, and the creator of jaipongan.

Gugum lives in an imposing Dutch-style residence surrounded by smaller buildings containing his recording studio and the premises of his music and dance school. Now in his mid-forties, he began his music career as a college student in the early 1960s, listening to rock'n'roll and practising the twist and jive. These studies, however, were interrupted by President Sukarno's new Indonesian identity drive, which saw rock'n'roll banned.

Hard times for a young rebel! In front of me on his opulent sofa, Gugum laughs and shakes his head as he describes his dilemma at the time: "The government wanted us to create new art forms based on our old traditions. I thought for a long time how. . . ? how . . . ?" He re-enacts his despair, sinking his head into his hands. "I remembered when I was a boy everybody dancing and singing Sundanese but in my school we preferred Elvis Presley and Chubby Checker. My father and mother were traditional artists so I asked them to teach me the old songs and dances. Then my father asked me to travel round west Java to see all kinds of Sundanese culture."

This started what was to be twelve years of such journeys, observing and participating in vil-lage dances and festivities. Gugum described a trip to the north of Java where he encountered a village ensemble. "I felt the music was too slow, so I asked the musicians to play faster". Gugum jumps to his feet and demonstrates again how he wanted to liven things up. "They said I must pay, OK I will pay"; he mimes expansive money distributing gestures. "But I will arrange the gamelan and the terbang (drum). So they played an old song, "Botol Kecap", with my new arrangement. The people copied my dance steps. Everybody liked it." Encouraged, Gugum went back to Bandung and started recruiting musicians and dancers.

The basis of his new style he took from a village dance called *ketuk tilu*, named after its main instrument, a set of three pot-gongs. Small groups consisting of ketuk, rebab (two-stringed fiddle), kendang (double-headed drum), gong, and a female singer-dancer, the ronggeng, had long played in the streets for payment but the style had fallen into disrepute among modern urban Javanese, due to its associations with prostitution. Gugum choreographed a more active but respectable role for the ronggeng, brought in a solo female singer, and replaced the ketuk with the bonang (a large set of pot-shaped gongs) and other instruments from the gamelan. He made the singer's role clear in the lyrics, too:

Many people don't respect me
Other women say I steal their husbands
I am not like that
I am just a singer.

Musically, the most striking innovation was in the drumming. "The songs are divided into sections, with certain counts between the strokes on the large gong, as in old-style gamelan. I kept this as the link with the traditional, but introduced a more dynamic drumming style." This owed much to Gugum's first drummer, Suwanda. "I found him playing in a *topeng banjet* [masked dance] group. He was very young, still wearing short trousers, but he was the best kendang player I had seen. I took him back to Bandung and changed his trousers to long ones. He brought the topeng banjet drumming, and also the senggak, its vocal percussion noises. In fact we took the name jaipongan from a combination of senggak noises. They imitate the sounds of the instruments – like "blak-ting-pong" or "jai-i-pong" – and thus we hit on "jai-i-pong-an"'.

Gugum and his troupe achieved their first local fame in a 1974 festival to showcase new Sundanese music sponsored by the government. "There were a thousand people in the audience and when we played – waah!", Gugum waves his hands in the air, 'Lagi!, Lagi!' [more! more!], and the young ones joined in the dancing. Afterwards, though, there was a seminar, common at that time, and some people were angry about the sensual movements in the dance."

It seems that the enthusiastic interpretations of the young people in the audience had shocked the guardians of public morals and attempts were made to nip the thing in the bud. Why, this was worse than the twist! Gugum was called before the governor. "I was a big problem!" he cheerfully admits, clearly relishing the irony of offending the defenders of Indonesian culture with a traditional dance. "They asked me to stop it, but it was already too late, it was not in my control." Thanks to the controversy, his dances chool was oversubscribed and he opened branches in several other towns. "I was not interested in money, I just wanted to spread my creation," insists Gugum.

In 1976 Gugum released the first cassette on his own label, Jugala, featuring jaipongan and other genres performed by his **Jugala Group**. Thereafter his creation indeed began to spread. Other companies started producing their own jaipongan recordings and regional variations appeared throughout Java and Sumatra. By 1980 the Jugala Group had made it to national television (an event denoting official approval – in itself).

These days, the jaipongan dance craze is over, though it has evolved, with constant reinterpretation by Gugum, into a "Modern Classic" concert style, which the Jugala Group have performed both at home and in Europe and the US.

Dr. Gugum Gumbira Tirasondjaja with Euis Komariah and the Jugala Orchestra

Jaipongan is part of the rich culture of the Sundanese people. Sunda covers a large area of southwest Java and its regional capital, Bandung, is home to many universities and colleges. It was in Bandung that jaipongan first appeared in the mid-1970s and by the end of the decade it had become the first Sundanese music to inspire a national dance craze, and all without an electric guitar in sight.

It is possible that jaipongan would not have happened had it not been for a piece of repressive legislation introduced over a decade previously by President Sukarno. Concerned that the young republic was suffering from a cultural invasion, he launched his Indonesian identity drive, calling on artists and musicians to shun western influences and revitalize indigenous art forms. Severe restrictions were placed on the importation and broadcast of foreign music, particularly the dreaded rock'n'roll. These were all rescinded after Suharto seized power in 1965 but the seeds had been sown for the Sundanese roots revival, led by Gugum Gumbira (see box on previous page).

Jaipongan is a music that sounds tunefully exotic to western ears and there are a couple of excellent recordings, by **Euis Komariah** (GlobeStyle) and **Idjah Hadidjah** (Elektra Nonesuch), now available in the west. You can also find the music cropping up on dangdut releases. In much the same way that bhangra music has mixed Indian pop with ragga and hip-hop beats, many new dangdut releases combine jaipongan percussion with rock and rap rhythms. One good example among many is **Canelia Malik**'s "Rindu Berat", which categorizes itself as disco-dangdut-jaipong.

Detty Kurnia

DEGUNG

Meanwhile, back in the cassette shop, if the gongs and bonangs of jaipongan have worked their magic, let's get really relaxed and investigate the soothing sounds of **degung** music.

Wistful, melancholic, meditative, the sound of degung evokes the calm atmosphere of warm Javanese evenings, when harmony and repose are re-established after the travails of the heat of the day. The haunting melodies often carry stories of love – sometimes found but usually lost – sung in Sundanese. Here are a couple of examples by Euis Komariah and Yus Wiradiredja:

Salam Sono
When you are away I miss you
Yes, I haven't seen you for a long time
But when our hearts come together
it is very beautiful.

Ramalan Asih (Horoscope of Love)
Don't return on Sunday
It will rain all day on Monday
Tuesday is a floating day, be careful
On Wednesday neighbours will gossip,
love can be broken
Someone could make you unhappy on Thursday
Friday there is danger of flooding, be careful
Saturday is an unfortunate day
And the next week looks just the same.

The roots of modern degung lie in a centuries-old Sundanese variation of the even older Javanese gamelan tradition. It takes its name from the scale played on a set of hanging gongs whose presence in any orchestra denotes it as a *gamelan degung*. References to degung orchestras can be found in records of the courts of Sundanese kings dating back to the sixteenth century.

The degung scale and accompanying modes were deemed the most suitable for playing while guests were arriving at social functions: peaceful, harmonious background music characterized by gentle percussion, delicate improvising on the *suling* (an end-blown bamboo flute), and soft arpeggios played on the bonang (a set of pot-gongs), and sometimes a *kecapi* (a plucked zither).

Variations of this style can still be heard in rural areas, performed by village ensembles at weddings, religious festivals, circumcision ceremonies and so on. The social changes following independence led to a decline in interest in such traditional arts among the new generation of urban youth, who perceived them as archaic remnants of the feudal era (an era Indonesian historians cite as ending with the declaration of independence in 1945) and who were more excited by western pop music. However, the success of jaipongan stimulated new interest in degung and, while it has never achieved comparable popularity, it now looks like outliving its fading cousin, its more "accessible" quality finding increasing favour among tourists in Bali.

A mark of quality to look out for is the name of **Nano S** on the cover. This amazingly prolific songwriter is also responsible for the best examples of the **pop-sunda** style. Those suffering electric-guitar withdrawal symptoms may care to take a brief listen.

Pop-sunda is the ubiquitous sound on the streets of Sunda. At its worst (which is all too frequent), it's a bland mix of sickly sweet western-style pop ballads with plodding drum machines and cheesy synthesizer sounds. But occasionally a gem is thrown up that makes it worth a mention. Two of my own favourites are "Cinta" (Love) by **Hetty Koes Endang**, and "Kalangkang" by **Nining Meida**, which were the biggest selling cassettes of the late 1980s. Both were Nano S compositions, with degung-style melodies for voice and traditional flute set against a pleasant soft-rock backdrop. The dangdut star **Detty Kurnia**, who has been working with producer Makoto Kubota in Japan, is another name worth looking out for.

QASIDAH MODERN

Ready for a change of scene on the cassette shelves? Then move away from the Sunda racks and on to central Java and the Islamic pop of **qasidah modern**.

Qasidah is a classical Arabic word for epic religious poetry, traditionally performed by a storyteller-singer, accompanied by percussion and chanting. Indonesian Muslims practise their own versions of this, improvising lyrics in local languages that address contemporary concerns and moral issues.

Qasidah modern presents this in a pop-song form, adding electric guitars, mandolin, keyboards, violins and flutes. Dangdut-style rhythms and melodies are used, often borrowed from Arabic pop songs, while the lyrics, in Bahasa Indonesia, tend to give moral advice to young lovers (don't do it!), extolling a virtuous

life and warning against corruption and other temptations of the Devil. Recently, they've been joined by a "new wave" of qasidah songs tackling environmental issues such as pollution, nuclear power and cigarette smoking.

The most popular of all the qasidah modern artists is the **Nasida Ria Group**, a nine-woman orchestra from Semarang, with some 25 successful albums to their credit. The music sounds much more like that of the Middle East than Indonesia. One of their albums, "Keadilan", is available on the Berlin-based Piranha label.

SUMATRA

Quite different musical styles are to be found among the Muslim Minangkabau people and the Batak of west Sumatra. The **Batak**, concentrated in the area around Lake Toba, have a long tradition of percussion-based music, with additional flutes, *seruling* and *serunai* (reed-trumpets), to accompany healing and other ceremonial occasions. Sometimes lasting for days on end and designed to induce trance states in the participants, this is exciting stuff. Not much of this excitement transfers itself onto the **pop-batak** you may find on the shelves in our cassette shop, so a flight to Medan and an expedition inland is recommended.

The **Minangkabau** are one of the few surviving matrilineal societies in the world and to check out their music it's necessary to visit Bukittinggi, a charming hill town north of the sea port capital of Padang. Far removed from the haunting pentatonic scales of Java, the music here has startling similarities with Madagascan dance music. It features brash and joyful tunes on flute, kecapi and percussion, sometimes combined with choral singing of a discernable Polynesian flavour. Both pop and traditional *minang* music display influences assimilated from centuries of trade and integration with Arabic, Indian and east African cultures.

DISCOGRAPHY

Thanks to Smithsonian Folkways (see below), you can sample Indonesian pop in most of its manifestations. If this just whets your appetite, you'll want either to visit Indonesia (and why not?), or write off for a catalogue from The Far Side Music Co (205 Sun City Hikawadai, Hikawadai, Nerima-ku, Tokyo T179, Japan ☎/fax 813/3936 9464). Far Side offer a good range of Indonesian discs, including many on the enterprising Japanese label, Wave Records.

THE FOLKWAYS SERIES

◎ **Indonesian Popular Music** (Smithsonian Folkways, US) is an ambitious series of CDs – six to date – that aims to present Indonesian music in its fullest variety. The discs so far released are well on that road, and, with their extensive notes, are the definitive western survey of Indonesian music.
Volume 1: Songs Before Dawn: Gandrung Banyuwangi presents the music of a night-long entertainment from eastern Java. The gandrung is a young, unmarried dancer and singer who entices men into her highly charged sexual dances. She is backed by a group of musicians, playing violins, drums, triangle and gongs, who will also protect her if any of the dancing men get over-amorous. Without the live drama, it's a bit hard-going.
Volume 2: Kroncong, Dangdut and Langgam Jawa is likely to appeal to a much wider audience with its enticing fusion of rock, Indian and Middle Eastern elements. The dangdut tracks include several by Rhoma Irama and Elvy Sukaesih.
Volume 3: Music from the Outskirts of Jakarta: Gambang Kromong showcases the music of the Peranakan (Indonesian Chinese) and other ethnic groups, combining Chinese, Indonesian and western instruments. While the old repertoire (*lagu lama*) material is an acquired taste, the contemporary style (*lagu sayur*) is marvellous and highly accessible, like a surreal dream of familar but strange musical cultures, sounding at times like a sort of Dixieland-gamelan.
Volume 4: Music of Nias & North Sumatra: Hoho, gendang karo, gondang toba is another delight, especially the instrumental Gendang Karo music that opens the disc, with its web of interlocking drum taps and gongs, and reedy oboe melodies. This is followed by Hoho, choral singing from the island of Nias, which sounds a bit like Georgian polyphonic song – a little of this goes a long way. The real glory, however, is the gondang toba: a stunning ensemble of tuned drums that play complete melodies in their own right.
Volume 5: Betawi and Sundanese Music of the North Coast of Java includes theatre music, wild village gamelans, and a typical Indonesian fusion of European brass and eastern gongs and drums.
Volume 6: Night Music of West Sumatra. Intimate chamber-like music of vocals, flute and lute.

KRONCONG AND DANGDUT

◎ **Detty Kurnia** *Coyor Panon* (Flame Tree, UK/Wave, Japan). Kurnia has made over 30 albums but this is the first to make it onto a western label. It is fabulous and recommended no end: a highly successful mix of traditional Sundanese sounds with modern production values.
◎ **Elvy Sukaesih** *Elvy Sukaesih* and *Return of Diva* (Wave, Japan). Some of the best from the current queen of dangdut. Melodic and tightly arranged.

◎ **Maryam Mustafa** *Kau Mulai Tak Jujur* (Sony, Japan). Another of the current dangdut stars. A more electric and synthesized sound than that of Elvy Sukaesih.
◎ **Bengawan Solo** *Kroncong Instrumental* (Omagatoki, Japan). Very melodic, rhapsodic and quite enchanting instrumental kroncong on flute, violin, ukeleles and bass. A real discovery.
◎ **Various** *Betawi Songs from Old Jakarta* (Bomba, Japan). Old style kroncong 1940s-style. Flute-and-violin led instrumental ensemble with two female vocalists, Rita Zahara and Sumiati.
◎ **Various** *Street Music of Java* (Original Music, US). Good recordings of kroncong and dangdut made in Yogyakarta in the late 70s.
◎ **Campur DKI** *Dangdut or not?* and *Funky Dangdut* (Wave, Japan). *Dangdut or not?* is state of the art dancefloor dangdut. *Funky Dangdut* is one for the oddity enthusiasts – dangdut arrangements of 1970s disco hits.

DEGUNG

◎ **Original Degung Instrumentalia** *Seuri* and *Sorban Palid* (Flame Tree, UK). Two volumes of instrumental degung. Soft, wistful sounds assumed by many visitors to Bali to be local music due to its ubiquity in tourist restaurants, but which in fact comes from Sunda in west Java. Beautiful.

JAIPONGAN AND SUNDANESE

◎ **Euis Komariah and the Jugala Orchestra** *Jaipongan Java* (GlobeStyle, UK). Gugum Gumbira's greatest hits specially recorded for GlobeStyle. Essential jaipongan.
◎ **Euis Komariah** *The Sound of Sunda* (GlobeStyle, UK). A cross section of Sundanese degung and other popular music. To be played "after 6pm in a peaceful environment, while your guests are arriving for dinner or when your love-object has left you". Strongly recommended.
◎ **Imas Permas and Asep Kosasih** *Tembang Sunda* (Nimbus, UK). The classical songs of Sunda and the roots of the Komariah disc above. Beautiful mellow performances accompanied by *kacapi* (zither) and *suling* (flute). Very helpfully, translations of the texts are included.
◎ **Idjah Hadidjah** *Tonggeret* (Nonesuch Explorer, US). Hadidjah was a singer in a wayang golek puppet theatre before turning to jaipongan. The title track is stunning and the album includes music for listening as well as dancing.

OTHERS

◎ **Sabar Habas** *Denpasar Moon* (Piranha, Germany/Wave, Japan). This is a very wonderful and addictive oddity: dangdut styles, mixed with global rhythms and English lyrics, from the singer/bassist with Britain's greatly adored 3 Mustaphas 3. Some suspect Habas to be none other than Colin Bass, author of the article you've just read.
◎ **Moluccan Moods Orchestra** *Moluccan Moods Orchestra* (Piranha, Germany). If you haven't heard of the Moluccans since they held up Dutch trains in the 1970s, give this disc a listen. Traditional songs arranged in an exotic and laid-back style with exciting percussion, keyboards, saxophone and flute.
◎ **Nasida Ria Group** *Keadilan* (Piranha, Germany). Sounding more like Middle Eastern pop than anything Indonesian, this all-female group presents some bouncy moralistic numbers.

AT THE CROSSROADS

MALAYSIAN MUSIC FIGHTS FOR SURVIVAL

Malaysia is one of the Muslim nations of southeast Asia and much of its music has Islamic origins, although its geographical position makes it essentially a country of cultural fusions. Like many places in the region, it is rapidly westernizing at the expense of its own traditions, and it lacks the dynamic indigenous music scene of its neighbour Indonesia. However, as Charles de Ledesma discovered, local music is still worth the effort to seek out.

Malaysia has been a cultural crossroads for centuries and the richness of Malaysian music results from the peculiar blend of ethnic influences brought by the Arab and Chinese traders, the Indian workers, and colonizers from Portugal, Holland and Britain. The Malays adopted Arabic instruments such as the *gendang* (double-headed drum) and *rebana* (frame drum), the harmonium from India, and the *tawak* gong from China, to make their own folk styles. The most prominent melodic instrument is the *rebab*, the spiked fiddle of Middle Eastern origin, found also in Thailand and Indonesia. A lot of contemporary musicians also use the western violin, brought to Malaya by the Portuguese, which they play in rebab style, in the lap.

The creation of the Malaysian nation in 1963, from a trio of ancient colonized territories, had the obvious effect on music of pushing the traditional styles, like the court gamelan music, **nobat**, and traditional folk music, **asli**, into the background. Now such music tends to be heard only at festivals or in the Islamic heartland of Kelantan state, in the northeast corner of Peninsular Malaysia. In its place are the pan-Asian pop styles that have more in common with western pop music than Malaysian traditions.

Nonetheless, there are survivals, notably the **pantum** style of Malaysian singing – centuries old and still very popular. This consists of vocal duets, sometimes with drums, but more often a capella, which are nearly always improvised. Pantums developed from Islamic devotional song, where sections of the Koran would be sung. Nowadays even adverts can be sung in pantum and can often be witty or slapstick. Pantum has become quite an informal style with its loose-metreed dialogue offering opportunities for the singers to be topical and satirical and still occasionally devotional.

KELANTAN: SILAT AND ZIKIR BARAT

Kelantan, in the north of Malaysia, is the heart of the country's folk culture and the place to start a musical tour of the archipelago. The capital of the state is Kota Bharu, a sleepy town just a few kilometres inland from the glittering South China Sea. It is a flat, hot town where bicycle rickshaws, ridden mostly by Indians, are the main mode of taxi transport, and the calls of muezzins ring out loudly from the mosques.

THE BEST OF
SHEILA MAJID
VOL ►II

Featuring LEGENDA & SINARAN

EMI

Three times a week, Malay music and dance is performed at the cultural centre. A small ensemble of *aderams* (long drums), *serunai* (a cross between a clarinet and an oboe) and tawaks generate a loose set of cross rhythms while two Malay gents in baggy costumes perform **silat** – an ancient dance of self-defence – in a sandpit. As the music intensifies, their flowing Tai Chi-like movements change and they grip each other. The first to throw the other onto the ground is the winner. The music rises to a crescendo as the wrestling intensifies, the serunai screeching

Blind street musicians in Kuala Lumpur. The sign reads "Enjoy the music while you donate".

atonally while the drums and gongs quicken the loose rhythm.

Alongside the silat band are twelve men sitting in another sandpit with small, brightly coloured wooden xylophones in front of them. The rhythm they hammer out in unison is fast and jolly and the idea is for all the players to end each piece at precisely the same time. Though a recreational activity more than an art form, this is an interesting communal music, known as **kertok**, which originated with the natives of the region, the Orang Asli ("original people").

Later in the day there is a **wayang kulit** (shadow puppet) performance. This artistic tradition occurs across southeast Asia and presents tales from the Hindu epic, the Ramayana. In Malaysia, however, the sound is very different to the gamelan that accompanies Indonesian wayang kulit. A larger version of the silat band, now including a xylophone, hammers out the fanfare. The puppeteer sits beside the musicians on the stage behind a screen, and while he chants the epic he illustrates the story with dozens of wooden shadow puppets.

Wayang kulit is a fascinating example of the interfusing of cultures in Malaysia: the Hindu story was brought from India, the craftsmanship of the puppets is Indonesian and Malay, while the core of the music is Arabic refracted through the Malaysian prism.

An altogether different side of Malaysian music emerges at night in Kota Bharu, as people meet after evening prayers for supper at the market's outdoor wok stalls. Here, along the paths bordered by hundreds of brightly coloured stalls, you can hear the distinct refrains of **zikir birat**. Singers chant rhythmically in the Malay language, Bahasa Malay, over a dense bed of percussion. Each player takes turns to chant a verse, and these can be elaborated, allowing the performance to go on for many hours.

The form is basically a version of Islamic ritual and particularly Sufic singing (known as zikir). In its most traditional form, two singers perform on the street outside mosques or in markets, alternating verses in praise of Allah to the rhythm of a single tambourine. As it took on a secular branch, however, teams of men would chant newly composed texts about anything of topical interest. Zikir birat now has its pop stars, like **Draman**, **Dollah** and **Mat Yeh**, and is beginning to be recorded by Indian and Chinese singers, too.

Elsewhere on the Malaysian peninsula, other east coast towns have odd performances of silat and wayang kulit, but they are hard to catch other than at festival time, and very few recordings of this music are made. Sadly, another traditional form of Malay music, *rebana ubi*, played on groups of huge drums for weddings and harvest celebrations, seems to have disappeared altogether, as has the nobat court music, which dates from feudal times and relates to the elaborate formal ensembles of Thai and Khmer music.

KUALA LUMPUR: GHAZAL AND DONDANG

Go south on the peninsula to **Kuala Lumpur** (KL) and you find music doesn't seem to play the same integral part in everyday life. That's because KL has become such a modern commercial centre that cultural expression doesn't often get a look-in, festivals excepted.

Most of the music you hear in the city, pounding from the cassette bars, is homegrown pop and rock. In addition to these, however, wandering the streets you hear snatches of Islamic love songs, not unlike *ghazals*, performed by blind buskers, who accompany themselves on tinny keyboards.

More professional (and more strictly) ghazal artists are to be heard on cassette or in concert. The great star of this genre was the lamented **Kamariah Noor**, who died recently. She had a voice both intense and languid, bending and holding notes to squeeze maximum emotion.

Kamariah often sang with her husband, **Hamzah Dolmat**, Malaysia's greatest rebab player, whose slow, rather mournful style is characterized by a wonderful melodic creativity.

Other recent Malay stars include the ensemble **Kumpulum Sri Maharani**, who play **dondang sayang**, a slow, intense, majestic music led by sharp percussive drum rolls, which trigger a shift in melody or a change in the pace of the rhythm. This is a quintessentially Malaysian style, bringing together Indian, Arabic, Chinese and Portuguese instruments to create a mood of gentle intensity. *Tabla* and harmonium from India and the double-headed drum (the gendang) and tambourine from Arabia mark out the rhythms, while the violin and the *oud* provide the melodies.

Dondang traditionally accompanies classical singing – usually duets whose lyrics like in ghazal, are often romantic epics. Maharani's band integrate electric keyboard and snippets of guitar into the traditional framework. Songs these days are short, starting with fast, expressive drumming. When the singers begin, the rhythm slows down, only to accelerate for dramatic emphasis towards the finale.

MALACCA: RONGGENG

Heading south from KL you get to the old Portuguese town of **Malacca**, the main port in the sixteenth century for the southeast Asian trade in spices. It is a beautiful town of narrow, café-strewn streets, and a good musical stop, to hear the old **fiddle music** of the rebab.

Village musicians

KENANGAN ABADI
P. RAMLEE A.M.N.

ASSALAMUALAIKOM   TOLONG LAH KAMI
SABAR   BARANG YANG LEPAS JANGAN DI KENANG
HANCOR BADAN DI KANDONG TANAH   RUKUN ISLAM
GETARAN JIWA   PUTUS SUDAH KASEH SAYANG
JANGAN TINGGAL DAKU   ADUH SAYANG
SEPANJANG RIWAYAT KU   DI PINGGIRAN
MENGAPA DERITA   DEWI ILHAM KU
MENCHECHEH BUJANG LAPOK   ENTAH DI MANA
TING TARA TILALLA   MALAM KU BERMIMPI

Vol.1

P. Ramlee: the Harry Belafonte of Malaysia

This has been adapted here to the European instrument: a Malaysian style of playing that is the base for the main folk dance music across the country, **ronggeng**. Other instruments in the ronggeng unit include two (frame drums)rebana and a brass gong to mark the time.

Ronggeng fiddlers play a wide range of melodies, which, perhaps due to the music's Portuguese heritage, sound a trifle Romany or Moorish. Performances revolve around dozens of tunes that locals know instinctively. When the singers join in, the rhythm slows and the violinist switches from ebullient fiddler to plaintive accompanist.

One of the most popular dances is the **joget**. Other percussive instruments are added to the basic ronggeng format and most joget tunes end with a "chinchang passage" – the point where the drums and violin quicken and the dancers hop from one leg to another like dancing cockerels.

And then there is **zapin**, yet another of those World Music styles led by the accordion. Like in so much Malaysian folk music, Arab, European and Indian elements come together here to form something new. The zapin tempos start out slow

but will often quicken abruptly as the accordion provides the cue for the dancers to improvise around their steps.

CROONERS AND POP SINGERS

Malaysian pop music was born in the 1950s when a young singer called **P. Ramlee** rose to fame. Very much the Harry Belafonte of Malaysian music, Ramlee set romantic lyrics to Malay melodies, bringing the dondang sayang style up to date in duets with his wife Saloma. Musically, he expanded the folk instrument reportoire, often recording with an orchestra, and reflecting the influence of Cuban mambos and chachachás in the immediate postwar period. His singing style is a European version of classical dondang – an Arabic-inflected purring baritone, romantically lush but vulnerable. His great duets with Salome are Malaysian pop music's finest hour.

Ramlee launched a new movement in modernizing classical singing, shortening the songs and using western instruments. Singers like **Zaleha Hamid** continue the tradition, singing in a more upbeat but still orthodox style, backed by kit drums, keyboards, bass and flute. Along with other stars like **Sharifah Aini** and **Herman Tino**, Hamid's material is the most popular of the older-style Malaysian music.

The younger generation have, however, firmly turned their back on this kind of Malay music. In the 1960s and '70s they looked to Indonesian pop, which was adapting western rock ideas. These days, Malay rock and pop cassettes outnumber dondang, ronggang and zikir twenty to one in the stores and there is little to be said in its favour as it is so completely derivative. The only Malaysian element is the lyrics which, due to legislation, have to be sung in Bahasa Malaysia rather than English.

The brightest light at the soft-rock end of the spectrum is **Sheila Majid**. She has become Malaysia's first international pop star, filling halls in Indonesia and Japan. Her singing style is a kind of mellow Asian soul, with a synthesized backdrop and George Benson-style guitar rhythms. Her producer and husband Roslan Aziz is keen to introduce more traditional instrumental sounds but the market at present wants things western. Nonetheless, Majid has provided a link between the traditional and the modern in her album "Legenda", where she covers songs by P. Ramlee.

NEW DIRECTIONS

Although western-style pop and rock dominate the Malaysian charts and media, over the past few years a few musicians have started looking back to their roots and traditional melodies, while still working within a western context. It's perhaps not enough to talk of as a movement, though it does have a name ready – **musica nusantara** (music of the archipelago).

The two main artists involved are **Shequal** and **Zainal Abidin**, both of whom use acoustic instruments like accordions, tabla, sitar and flute. They write their songs and melodies themselves, rather than updating classics, and they both come from rock backgrounds. Abidin used to sing with soft-rock band Headwind before leaving to search for a more indigenous direction.

He found this in what he called *kampong* (village) music, and began to write lyrics concerned with the erosion of the old ways of life. His song "Baba" warns of the threat to the Baba culture, the Malay-speaking Chinese community in Malacca. More recently, however, he has started playing what he calls "World Music", mixing rock and traditional styles with those of the African musicians, Youssou N'Dour and Papa Wemba, whom he met at a WOMAD festival in Japan.

Shequal is well worth checking out, too. His best-known song, "Balada Nusantara", is a beautiful melody led by a lovely accordion line. The mood is upbeat but relaxed, evoking the atmosphere of the coast with its slow pace of life and traditions.

Another interesting direction is evident in the releases by a fusion group called **Asiabeat**, who are causing a stir around KL with an intriguing blend of east and west, fusing traditional eastern instruments like the *shakuhachi* (Japanese bamboo flute), played by an American, John Kaiser Neptune, with saxophones and guitars.

Other musicians pursuing individual destinies include **Kit Leee**, who records way-out electronic pieces, most recently with a talented Brazilian singer, Marilia, and his friend and some-time collaborator **Rafique**, who produces KL's only music with a political edge. He gets away with criticizing the government, he says, because he is the only person doing it. His songs include "Shut Up", about the mid-1980s Internal Security Act, and "Khalwat", about the Muslim law that forbids courting couples from getting too close before marriage.

Thanks to Jak Kilby for additional research.

DISCOGRAPHY

Malaysian music has yet to make the jump to western labels and much good music is available on cassette only, through local labels.

TRADITIONAL

ⓒ **Kumpulum Sri Maharani** *Dondang Sayang Mambo* (EMI, Malaysia). Slow, intense music with the lovely voice of veteran singer Fadzil Ahmed and some hopping ronggeng.

ⓒ **Orkes Maharani** *Ghazal Parti* (EMI, Malaysia). Lively ghazal singing over harmonium, violin and guitar.

ⓒ **Various** *Album Melayu Deli* (EMI, Malaysia). Zaleha Hamid and other singers use traditional melodies in a popular context.

Mat Yeh and Dollah To'deh *Modern Zikir* (Suara, Malaysia). Leading exponents of zikir barat.

Keluaran Syarikat *Irama* (Irama, Malaysia). Music of the indigenous Kayan people from Sarawak: yodelling voice, drums and gongs.

Taboh Kajat Iban *Iban Music* (MSP, Malaysia). Music of the Iban people from Sarawak, singing over a variety of gongs.

POP

ⓒ **P. Ramlee** *Kenangan Abadi Vols 1 & 2* (EMI, Malaysia). The great crooner's best-of, with lush orchestral arrangements and slushy melodies.

ⓒ **P. Ramlee and Saloma** *Di Mana Kan Ku Cari Ganti* (EMI Malaysia). These duets were perhaps Malaysian pop's finest hour – although there is some dross, too! Not even P. Ramlee can get away with singing with kids.

ⓒ **Sheila Majid** *Legenda* (EMI, Malaysia). Best-selling singer's classic album of Ramlee covers. Lightweight musically but with a persuasively sweet voice.

ⓒ **Zainal Abidin** *Zainal Abidin* (WEA, Malaysia). Kampong singer blending old styles and some traditional instruments with pop.

NOT ALL THE WORLD
IS AMERICA

FREDDY AGUILAR AND FILIPINO FOLK ROCK

A group of islands north of Indonesia on the far reaches of the South China Sea, the Philippines are symptomatic of the fate of much indigenous music on the rapidly developing Pacific rim. As John Clewley reports, the overwhelming popular taste is for western models, but in the person of Freddie Aguilar there is an important ambassador and figurehead for Filipino music.

Not all the world is America, the world is where you are, sing the Filipino teenybopper band, Smokey Mountain. The band, impish but safe in trendy denims, sing in English; the song sounds like a cross between a Miss World-type theme tune and easy-listening US rock/pop. Ironically, the name of the band is taken from Manila's infamous garbage dump and shantytown, a place where the slum dwellers' atrocious living conditions leave an indelible impression upon the visitor. There's something obscene about a band using such a name, but that's par for the course in the world of Filipino pop music.

Of all the southeast Asian countries, the Philippines has the least developed indigenous popular music. This is no reflection on the ability of the country's musicians, for Filipinos are legendary for their musical talents; you'll find Filipino bands all over the world, in hotel lobbies, clubs and bars. But you won't find them playing Filipino songs, for all of these bands play cover music, usually British or American pop.

The successive colonial administrations of Spain and the United States seem to have buried local and ethnic music. Unlike Indonesia, Thailand or Malaysia, there is little recorded local folk music available and musicians don't seem to be aware of their own very strong local traditions. Musicologist José Maseda, who has spent the last thirty years researching Filipino folk music, says that there are many similarities between indigenous Filipino music and that found in other southeast Asian countries. "Fundamental to the local music are gongs and all kinds of instruments made from local materials like bamboo," he says. "And music is social, related to ritual, agriculture, harvest and thanksgiving ceremonies."

Sadly, you'll be hard pushed to find one cassette in Manila relating to any traditional music, but if you're travelling around the country, check out local events, as the archipelago contains many different ethnic groups, each with its own music.

Because so many Filipino musicians are unaware of their own cultural roots, they do not have a solid base from which to develop their own popular music. Most draw on western sources, either Spanish or American. "It's a big problem," explains the nation's top singer **Freddie Aguilar**, one night in the Hobbit Bar in downtown Manila. As he speaks, a local band gives an accent-perfect imitation of Glenn Campbell. "Right now, everyone is doing covers of Michael Jackson and the like. But the only way is to create your own music. Originals always stay. We have so much traditional music we can revive. We can take it on . . ."

Aguilar is an influential musician, one of the few Asian popular musicians to have made a significant impact abroad. He burst onto the scene in 1978 with the folk-rock ballad "Anak", which not only became the most successful Filipino song ever recorded but also sold four million copies in Europe and has so far generated 54 cover versions in 14 languages. Aguilar's folk-rock developed out of the Pinoy rock movement that started in the mid-1970s, a genre based around western folk styles, social activist concerns, and sung, most importantly, with lyrics in tagalog (the national language). Aguilar rose to fame along with **Heber Bartolome and the Banyuhay**, the **Asin group** and **Coritha**, and was later followed by the "street-conscious" group **Inang Laya**.

The early days of Filipino folk-rock were hard for the performers, says Aguilar. "We were stuck during the mid-70s doing cover songs, we couldn't do our own music. And if we did, we got fired!" Aguilar continued undaunted, and moved to Olangapo City where he played to US servicemen. Their response was so enthusiastic that Aguilar knew he was on the right track.

His debut performance at the 1978 Metro Manila Popular Song Festival, where he won a place in the finals with "Anak", stunned the audience. Here was someone without the trappings of stardom, playing a simple, moving song about a child growing up, and not in English, but in his own language. As the folk-rock movement took off, so mainstream pop artists started to compose songs either in tagalog or a mixture of tagalog and English – taglish, as some called it.

Aguilar's success inspired other Asian musicians, notably Japanese singer-songwriters. He remembers, too, that in the early days one of the members of the Thai rock band Carabou (the name comes from the tagalog word for water buffalo) used to regularly attend his shows. The current importance of folk-rock in the entire southeast Asian region owes more than a little to his work over the past fifteen years.

The future of indigenous popular music in the Philippines looks bleak. The chaotic economic and political situation, and the virtual civil war that has existed for too long, both work against the musicians. Until more artists like Freddie Aguilar come along, with the will and the talent to try new things, the Filipino popular music scene will remain the Far East's musical backwater.

Freddie Aguilar

DISCOGRAPHY

 **Freddie Aguilar** *Greatest Hits* (Ugat/Vicor, Philippines). A good compilation of Aguilar's work.  *Hala Bira* (Alpha, Philippines), one of Aguilar's most recent releases, includes the excellent "Ipaglalaban Ko".
 **Inang Laya** *Atsay Ng Mundo* (Dypro, Philippines). Lilting singing and hard lyrics from one of the most popular and "street credible" folk-rock bands.

 **Asin** *Asin* (Ugat/Vicor, Phillipines). Tight harmonies and haunting flute dominate one of the original folk-rockers' best selections.
 **Various** *Handog Ng Pilipino sa Mundo* (WEA, Phillipines). Compilation of artists including Inang Laya, Coritha, and Apo Hiking Society, with high spirits that relate to the "Peoples' Power" resistance to the Marcos dictatorship.

THE MANY SOUNDS OF SIAM

THAI MUSIC RANGES FROM CLASSICAL TO BIKERS' ROCK

Thailand is one of those countries where indigenous music – in the form of luk thung and mor lam   – is a truly popular force, and it exists alongside a sophisticated classical tradition, too. John Clewley, introduces the dynamic Thai music scene in its numerous (and ever-changing) incarnations.

S ituated at the confluence of two of Asia's great civilizations, India and China, Thailand is unique among the southeast Asian countries. The Thais are canny assimilators, having absorbed many influences from the Chinese and Indians, as well as other neighbouring peoples – Khmer, Lao, Burmese, Mon, Malay and Indonesian. They are less Indianized than the Malays and Indonesians, and less Sinicized than the Vietnamese, but they retain elements from both civilizations. The result is a distinct culture based on a strong sense of identity and independence, bolstered by the fact that Thailand, unlike its neighbours, was never colonized by European countries.

Music is an important part of Thai culture, whether related to Buddhist activities in the local temple (still a focal point for many communities), animist rituals, Brahmin ceremonies, or the wide range of popular song styles. The most interesting types of Thai music, *luk thung* and *mor lam*, are incredibly popular and distinctively Thai in character. But they – and Thai popular music in general – are largely ignored by visitors to the country. The little that tourists do tend to hear are classical or court ensembles at restaurants or the National Theatre, or the discordant pipes and drums that accompany Thai boxing (*muay*).

Make your own way and you'll have a lot more fun, and remember, always, that the Thais have a deserved reputation as a fun-loving, laid-back people. Delving into the music with a *sanuk* (fun) attitude will guarantee you'll have a good time, be it buying cassettes or checking out a local act.

THE CLASSICAL TRADITION

Thai classical dance and music can be traced back to stone engravings during the Sukhothai period (c. 1283 AD), which show ensembles of musicians playing traditional instruments, called **pi-phat**. The pi-phat ensembles include a large array of percussion instruments, rather like the Indonesian gamelan – gong circles, xylophones and drums – plus a raucous oboe called the *pi-nai*. The music was developed to accompany classical dance-drama (*khon* or *lakorn*) or shadow puppet theatre (*nang*), and you can see an ensemble playing for a shadow-puppet show depicted in the magnificent Ramakien murals in the Grand Palace complex in Bangkok.

Pi-phat music sounds strange to western ears as the seven equal notes of the Thai scale fall between the cracks of the piano keyboard. But heard in the right environment – in a temple, at a funeral or a dance performance – it can be entrancing. As there is no notation, everything is memorized. And, as in all Thai music, elements have been assimilated over the years from diverse sources, and then synthesized into something new.

Bong lang music, with a cute young potbanger to front the band.

Despite the country's rapid westernization, Thai classical music has been undergoing something of a revival in the past few years, partly as a result of royal patronage. There have been recent experiments, too, that attempt to blend Thai classical and western styles – often jazz or rock; led by avant garde groups like **Kangsadan** and **Fong Naam** (see box), they have been quite a success. There has even been a return to using Thai classical music as backing for popular singers: **Ood Oh-pah Tossaporn** had the luk thung hit of the year in 1990 with classical backing, and other singers have followed his lead.

There are regular dance and classical music performances in Bangkok at the National Theatre and daily shows at the Vimanmek Palace. Look out, especially, for concerts by the veteran flautist and pi-player **Chamnian Srithaiphan**, recently made a National Artist. Somewhat lacklustre **temple dancing** can usually be seen at the Erawan shrine on Rama 1 road and the Lak Muang Temple behind the Grand Palace. People pay for the temple musicians and dancers to go through a routine in thanks for their good fortune. A number of restaurants also mount music and dance shows for tourists.

FOLK MUSIC

Thailand's folk musics are often referred to as **pleng phua bahn**, which encompasses styles from any of the country's four distinct regions (central, north, northeast and south), with their 61 languages and dialects. Despite the rapid social change of the past decade, numerous folk styles are still enthusiastically played, from the hilltribe New Year dances in the far north to the all-night singing jousts of northeastern *mor lam glawn*, to the haunting Muslim vocals of *likay wolou* in the deep south.

The most notable folk style to have grown in popularity in recent years is the up-tempo and danceable northeastern instrumental style known as **bong lang** (the name comes from a wooden xylophone that is attached vertically to a tree). Bong lang is thought to predate Indian-Thai culture, and while it is clearly an ancient music, the style continues to be refined; as recently as the late 1970s, the *phin hai*, a jar with rubber stretched across the mouth, was introduced, though often only to put a cute young woman at the front of the band. The sound, made by plucking the rubber, is similar to that of a double bass.

The best place to see bong lang is upcountry, especially in Kalasin province between November and March. In the major cities – Khon Kaen, Ubon Ratchathani and Udon Thani – check with the tourist authorities for details of **festivals** like Loy Kratong (Nov) and Songkran (April).

HAPPY, NO PROBLEM: THAI POP

For the last decade or so, the Thai popular music industry has developed at an unprecedented rate, reflecting the high economic growth rates and rapid industrialization, the wider availability of cheap cassette players, and the introduction of the 1979 Copyright Act (which has helped local artists, even if it has had little effect on the piracy of top western acts). "Happy, No Problem", as the hit song by Asanee & Wasan put it.

The most popular genre to emerge during this period has been **string**, a westernized form of Thai pop. String artists like the nation's top singer, **Thongchai "Bird" Macintyre**, sell hundreds of thousands of cassettes and feature in nationwide advertising campaigns for consumer products. The range of styles within this genre goes from ballads to rock to hard rock to disco and rap; whatever is popular in the US or Britain gets picked up quickly and is reassembled with Thai lyrics, plus a particular local flavour that often favours sweet melodies.

Assimilation of western styles has been boosted by performances in Thailand by top western acts like Michael Jackson and INXS. Often these shows are supported by local upcoming national favourites, like new reggae band **T-Bone**, or the "blues" singer **Mama Blues**. Currently popular are lead female singers backed by cute toy-boy dancers, à la Madonna. Nearly every southeast Asian country has its own version of Madonna or Michael Jackson: in Thailand it's the vampy **Honey** and Jackson soundalike **Tik Shiro**.

SONGS FOR LIFE

Another big genre is **pleng phua chiwit**, or "songs for life", which started as a kind of progressive rock in the early 1970s, with bands like **Caravan** (no relation to the Canterbury songsters) blending *pleng phua bahn* (folk songs) with western folk and rock. Caravan were at the forefront of the left-wing campaign for democracy with songs like "Khon Gap Kwai" (Human with Buffalos):

> Greed eats our labour and divides people into classes
> The rice farmers fall to the bottom
> Insulted as backward and ignorant brutes
> With one important and sure thing: death.

Although an elected government survived from 1973 to 1976, the military returned soon after and Caravan, like many of the student activists, went into hiding in the jungle. There they performed to villagers, hilltribe people and gave the occasional concert. In 1979 the government offered an amnesty and most of the students, and Caravan too, disillusioned with the Communist Party's support for the Khmer Rouge in Cambodia, returned to normal life. The military's predilection for coups, however, continues. The bloody street riots of 1992 (in protest at the then military-installed government) once again brought some "songs for life" artists out to support the pro-democracy protests.

More generally, in the 1980s, the strong social activist stance was replaced by more individual and personal themes, as can be heard in the music of Thailand's most successful rock band, **Carabou**. The band has since splintered into smaller groups and its position as top rock act has been taken by **Zuzu**, one of the more interesting rock groups, who often use regional music and instruments. Individual singer-songwriters in this genre are mostly earnest young men like the hugely popular **Pongsit Kamphee**, reputedly a former stagehand for Caravan. Interestingly, Caravan often reform for Japanese tours. In May 1990 the band led a "Woodstock-style" benefit gig in Pnom Penh and Angkor Wat, Cambodia, dubbed "Music for Peace: Encore Caravan".

But what is significant is that the generation that has grown up in the 1980s has done so on a diet of mainly Thai pop, in contrast to the 1970s generation, who followed western pop. This is particularly the case with the growing middle class in Bangkok. Similarly, rural youngsters have also caught on to string music, while at the same time enjoying a much wider selection of Thai country music: luk thung and mor lam.

THAI COUNTRY MUSIC

Go to one of the huge **luk thung** shows held in a temple or local stadium on the outskirts of Bangkok, or to any temple fair in the countryside, and you'll hear one of the great undiscovered popular musics of Asia. The shows, amidst the bright lights, food stalls and fairground games, last several hours and involve dozens of dancers and costume changes.

Like modern Thai pop, luk thung has its roots in the development of radio and the influence of the west in the 1940s. Western orchestration for Thai melodies had been introduced in the 1930s and this led to the development of *dontree sakol*, or modern music, in the form of big band and swing, country and western, Hollywood film music, rock'n'roll, and so on. In the early days, two distinctive Thai genres developed: *luk grung*, a schmaltzy romantic ballad form; and luk thung, country music. Currently the popular music market divides into 40 percent luk thung, 30 percent string and 20 percent luk grung.

Luk grung, with its clearly enunciated singing style and romantic fantasies, has long been associated with the rich stratas of Bangkok society; it's the kind of music played by state organs like Radio Thailand. However, it was largely transformed during the 1960s by the popularity of western stars like Cliff Richard; as musicians started to mimic the new western music, a new term was coined, *wong shadow* (wong means group, and shadow came from the British group, The Shadows). This trend led to the development of string in the 1980s.

In contrast, **luk thung** (literally, "child of the field") has always been associated with the rural and urban poor, and because of this has gained nationwide popularity over the past forty years. According to luk thung DJ Jenpope Jobkrabunwan, the term was first coined by Jamnong Rangsitkuhn in 1962, but he says the first song was "Oh Jow Sow Chao Rai" (Oh, the Vegetable Grower's Bride), recorded in 1937, and the first big singer, **Kamrot Samboonanon**, emerged in the mid-40s. Originally called *pleng talad* (market songs) or pleng chiwit (songs of life), the style blended together folk songs (pleng pua bahn), central Thai classical music and Thai folk dances (*ram wong*).

In 1952, a new singer, **Suraphon Sombatjalern**, made his debut with a song entitled "Nam Da Sow Vienne" (Tears of the Laotian [Vientiane] Girl) and became the undisputed king of the style until his untimely murder (for serious womanizing, rumour has it) in 1967. Along with female singer **Pongsri Woranut**, Sombatjalern helped to develop the music into a mature form.

FONG NAAM

Fong Naam are one of the leading classical ensembles of Thailand. They are a captivating sight in performance and can be heard on two stunning CDs produced by the British record company, Nimbus.

The founders of the group were **Boonyong Ketkhong**, one of the great masters of the renat (Thai xylophone), and **Bruce Gaston**, an American who went to Thailand in the late 1960s as an alternative to military service, immersed himself in the music and stayed. He is among the best *khong wong* (gong circle) players in the country.

A Thai pi-phat ensemble is made up of a larger and smaller gong circle (*khong wong yai and khong wong lek*), two xylophones (*renat ek* and *renat thum*) plus different kinds of drum (*klong*). This percussion ensemble is supplemented by oboe, flute and fiddle, and is capable of high-speed virtuosity, with sticks and hammers flying, as well as beautiful moments of delicacy and repose.

The repertoire Fong Naam plays comes essentially from the last 200 years, but as this is a constantly developing oral tradition with an element of improvisation, every generation of musicians can add something new to the piece, and Fong Naam are no exception. Each of the instruments improvises in its own way around the shared melody, which is not played aloud by any of the instruments but sung in the hearts of the musicians.

"Thai music is very tactile," says Gaston, "the pi-phat orchestra is divided up on the basis of actions. It's a very Buddhist way of doing things. The oneness of what's going on in your mind and what your body is doing. *Fong Naam* itself is the title of an ancient melody and can be translated as "bubbles". It is a unique insight of Thai Buddhist culture to think of art as a bubble, the transparent beauty of which is most clearly identified with a short, fleeting moment of existence – beauty which points towards impermanence as the condition of all things."

The two Nimbus discs, "The Sleeping Angel" and "The Nang Hong Suite", are a great introduction to Thai classical music and make compelling listening – particularly the second, which consists of Siamese funeral music. Rather than being sorrowful, it is extremely happy and considered an antidote to the grieving of the mourners. "Of course, Buddhism views happiness and sorrow as essentially the same," says Gaston. "By using this joyful music in the sad context of a funeral, the traditional intention was not to create a new mood of mirth to replace the tears, but rather to jolt the consciousness of the listeners onto a higher level – the Middle Path which lies between joy and sorrow."

Simon Broughton

Fong Naam in action with Bruce Gaston fourth from left

There was initially, says Jenpope, a folk sound but external influences soon changed the music. Malay string-band sounds were added in the 1950s, as were Latin brass and rhythms like the chachachá and mambo (Asian tours by Xavier Cugat influenced many Asian pop styles during the 50s), as well as elements from Hollywood movie music and "yodelling" country and western vocal styles from the likes of Gene Autry and Hank Williams.

Luk thung megastar Pompuang Duangjan

Today, luk thung is a mix of Thai folk music and traditional entertainment forms like *likay* (travelling popular theatre), as well as a range of western styles. There are certainly some strong musical affinities with other regional pop styles like Indonesian dangdut and Japanese enka, but what is distinctly Thai – quite apart from the spectacular live shows that include upwards of fifty dancers in amazing costumes – are the singing styles and the content of the lyrics.

Vocal styles are full of glissando, wavering grace notes and wailing ornamentation. A singer must have a wide vocal range, as luk thung megastar **Pompuang Duangjan** explained: "Making the luk thung sound is difficult, you must handle well the high and low notes. And because the emotional content is stronger than in luk grung, you must also be able to create a strongly charged atmosphere."

Duangjan had the kind of voice that turns the spine to jelly. She rose to prominence during the late 1970s, joining sweet-voiced **Sayan Sanya**

as the biggest male and female names in the business. Like Sombatjalern, both came from the rural peasantry, making identification with themes and stories that related directly to the audience much easier. Songs narrate mini-novellas, based around typical characters like the lorry driver, peasant lad or girl, poor farmer, prostitute or maid; and the themes are those of going away to the big city, infidelity, grief, tragedy and sexual pleasure.

Interestingly, it is not always the lyrics that carry the sexual charge of the song (and if lyrics are deemed too risqué by the authorities the song will be strictly censored) but rather the vocal style and the stage presentation, which can be very bawdy indeed.

With the advent of TV and the rise in popularity of string, the number of large up-country luk thung shows has declined. It's not easy, said Duangjan, to travel with over a hundred staff, including some fifty dancers in the *hang kruang* (chorus). "We play for over four hours," she said, "but string bands, with only a few staff members, play a paltry two hours!" Her response to the advent of string and the increasing importance of promotional videos was to develop a dancefloor-oriented sound – **electronic luk thung**. Few luk thung singers are capable of this, but Duangjan had the vocal range to tackle both ballad forms and the up-tempo dance numbers. Her musical diversification increased her popularity enormously.

She died in 1992, aged only 31, and up to 200,000 people, from the country's royalty and elite to the rural poor, made their way to her funeral in her home town of Suphanburi. A massive tribute was staged at the temple with everyone in the luk thung business performing her songs. As top TV broadcaster Somkiet Onwimon said: "She was certainly a role model for many poor, rural people. She always had time for everyone and, despite her obvious educational handicap [she was illiterate], she made something of her short life."

MOR LAM

Luk thung has also faced a strong challenge from another area: **mor lam**. This is the folk style from the poor, dry northeastern region of **Isaan**, an area famed for droughts, hot spicy food, good boxers and great music. Over the last ten years, the modern pop form of this style has risen dramatically, at luk thung's expense.

Mor Lam musicians from the northeast

khaen (bamboo mouth organ), the *phin* (2–4-string guitar) and *ching* (small temple bells).

Modern mor lam developed from *mor lam glawn*, a narrative form where all-night singing jousts are held between male and female singers, and from *mor lam soeng*, the group dance form. Both still play an important part in many social events like weddings, births and deaths, festivals and temple fairs. A mor lam may sing intricate fixed-metre Laotian epic poems or may relate current affairs in a spontaneous rap. In the large groups, western instruments like guitar (replacing the phin) and synthesizer (for the khaen) are used.

The style came to national prominence some fifteen to twenty years ago, when a female mor lam singer, **Banyen Rakgan**, appeared on national TV. In the early 1980s the music was heard not only in Isaan but also in the growing slums of Bangkok, as rural migrants poured into the capital – and continue to do so – in search of

Traditionally, a mor lam is a master of the *lam* singing style (sung in the Isaan dialect, which is actually Laotian), and is accompanied by the

THE HILLTRIBES

• •

Much of the Thai tourist industry is focused in the north, encouraging treks, rafting, and visits to hilltribe villages. Hilltribe music has been exposed as a result, and many craft stores, as well as cassette shops, sell hilltribe recordings with titles like "The Sounds of The Golden Triangle".

Hilltribe music may be a new strand in Thai folk but it is as old as the mountains in which tribes like the Lahu, Lisu, Mon and Karen have settled, to escape persecution or to find new agricultural lands. It can be seen at its best at festivals, which are spectacular throughout the region, especially over the New Year (Dec 1–7) celebrations. If you can't make it to one of these, then you can get an idea of the music at folklore performances in the regional centre of Chiangmai.

Possibly the best hilltribe performance in Chiangmai is that put on by Andalay Sempa, from the Lahu hilltribe who, like the Karen, have fled poverty and ethnic persecution in Burma. Andalay is the main *naw* (pronounced "lenor") player in Chiangmai and lives in a hilltribe village on the edge of the city, which tourists visit to see folk dancing. The naw is very similar to the Isaan khaen but is lighter and has fewer bamboo reeds sticking up from the mouthpiece that Andalay blows into like a mouth organ. During the show he leads five Lahu around the stage,

the others playing *jae-ku* (long drum), *buluku* (gong) and *chae* (cymbals).

When I met Andalay later in his hut in his village, he talked about the festival music. In Lahu villages in Burma and Thailand the first inkling that festival time has come around again is when men put away their bamboo flutes (*talula*), which they play on their way to and from the fields, and bring out the jew's harp (*at-ta*). They play traditional courting tunes outside a prospective partner's house for as long as it takes for the girl to come out and meet her boyfriend. On New Year's Day, December 1, the musicians "take the percussion instruments out and go to a bamboo pole erected in the forest. As the music plays and gets faster, so people in turn run round the pole. On the last night, the 7th, we have theatrical performances, stage plays where we play all our instruments, flutes, jew's harps, gongs, naw as accompaniment."

The most important moment in the celebrations comes when an ancient custom is enacted. Seven people each hold a piece of wood which they tie together. Then each person tries to break the clump of wood. They cannot. The simple symbol of the triumph of nature over man signifies the unity of the Lahu people and the enacting of the custom ensures the survival of the people through the many trials they will encounter.

Charles de Ledesma

work. By the end of the decade stars like **Jintara Poonlarp** (with her hit song "Isaan Woman Far From Home") and **Pornsak Songsaeng** could command the same sell-out concerts as their luk thung counterparts.

A show by rising star **Chalermphol Malaikham** is typical of those of the bigger artists and the format is similar to luk thung shows – lots of dancers in wild costumes, comedy skits, and a large backing orchestra. Malaikham sings both styles, thus appealing to as wide a group of people as possible. The subject matter is similar in both, but musically they are very different. Mor lam has a much faster, relentless rhythm and the vocal delivery is rapid-fire, rather like a rap; it's also sung in Laotian.

Pimpa Pornsiri: the new sound of luk thung

You'll immediately recognize a mor lam song with its introductory wailing moan "Oh la naw", which means "fortune". Mor lam artists, brought up bilingually, can easily switch from luk thung to mor lam, but luk thung artists, who speak only the national central Thai dialect (Siamese), cannot branch out so easily. This is another reason why Pompuang Duangjan moved into a dancefloor sound. Some years ago, Sayan Sanya tried his hand at mor lam with Banyen Rakgan and bombed.

LUK THUNG PRAYUK AND MOR LAM SING

One way producers have tried to revitalize luk thung has been with **luk thung prayuk** ("applied" luk thung), which mixes the two country styles in one song. At the forefront of this innovation is **Pimpa Pornsiri**. She came to prominence in 1985 with the nationwide hit "Nam Da Mia Saud" (Tears of Mrs Saudi), a song about a lonely wife left in Isaan by her husband who is away working in the Middle East.

Pimpa tours throughout the country for as many as forty weeks a year, supported by 133 people and nine trucks. Her band features western instruments like a drum kit, bass, guitars and a three-horn brass section, in addition to Thai instruments like the *ching* (small cymbals) and *glong kaek* (a pair of barrel drums played with sticks). The latter instruments provide much of the basic rhythmic pulse to Thai music.

Another new and exciting development has been **mor lam sing** (see box), a turbo-charged modern version of mor lam glawn, pumped out by the small electric combos that are becoming an increasingly common sight in Isaan. The number of large travelling luk thung or mor lam shows has declined in recent years, due to high overheads, TV entertainment and the popularity of string bands, so mor lam sing satisfies the need for local music with a modern edge.

Mor lam sing is clearly a development of traditional mor lam glawn; maybe this is a case of traditions being kept alive, albeit in a racier, more contemporary format. Rural life in Isaan is changing, and mor lam sing seems to mirror the times. As motorbikes replace bicycles and the pace of life speeds up, it's interesting to note that the *sing* in mor lam sing comes from the Thai slang for a wayward "biker" teenager – *dek sing* (sing is short for the English word, racing), literally, a "racing kid". Many of the cassettes featuring this music, which come from places like Khon Kaen and Ubon Ratchatani, have a subtitlesomething like, "Sing Pet Pet" (Hot, Hot Sing) or "Sing Saeb Saeb" (Spicy Hot Sing).

The music is definitely hot, especially if you see it live, when bands will often play through the night, never missing the groove for a minute, driven on by the relentless phin and khaen playing. To some people, the fast plucking style of the phin gives a West African or Celtic tinge; the khaen has a rich sound – over a bass drone players improvise around the melody, while at the same time vamping the basic rhythm. Male and female singers rotate or duet humorous love songs, which often start with one of the mor khaens setting up the beat. They sing about topical issues, bits of news, crack lewd jokes or make fun of the audience. All very tongue-in-cheek.

KANTRUM: THAI-CAMBODIAN POP

"Isaan nua [north] has mor lam, Isaan dai [south] as *kantrum*," sings **Darkie**, the first, and so far only star of **kantrum**, Thai-Cambodian pop, in his song, "Isaan Dai Sah Muk Kee" (Southern Isaan Unity). His music is a very specific offshoot, from the southern part of Isaan, where Thai-Cambodians mix with ethnic Laotians and Thais.

At a recent festival in the town of Buriram, organizers explained that the local kantrum talent contest was held to try to find a new group to challenge Darkie's position as the style's top singer. The winning group, **Saw In Concert**, combine both kantrum and mor lam in their show. For the kantrum numbers, the music is based around the plaintive melody of the *tro* (a two-stringed homemade fiddle, known in Thai as a *saw duan*) and the thumping rhythm of the conga-like *sko* drums. The rhythm seems harder, faster than mor lam, and one band member suggests that this is what people like about the music. A male-female lead vocal team fronts the band – opening songs with a wavering wail, dancing and alternating lead singing – and is supported by a five-woman dancing group, wearing, as is now customary, very short skirts.

Modern kantrum has developed from Cambodian folk and classical music, played in a small group consisting of fiddle, small hand drums and *krab* (pieces of hardwood bashed together rather like claves). This traditional style is now quite hard to find in Thailand; some ten or so years ago, musicians started to electrify the music, using both traditional and western instruments. So far kantrum is only popular in Isaan, and that seems unlikely to change, as few people outside the region speak either Cambodian or the Thai-Cambodian dialect, Suay.

◣ DISCOGRAPHY ◢

CDs are now produced in Thailand but feature mainly string artists and a few luk thung bands. There are, however, a few excellent discs on western labels.

There are a lot more variety on local Thai cassettes – which comprise all the non-CD recommendations below. Buying them can be fun. In Bangkok, check out day and night markets, or the tape stores on Charoen Road, and tell the sellers the name of an artist you'd like to hear. Most major luk thung or mor lam artists release a cassette every three months, which is often given an artists' series number. Old-style recordings of Suraphon Sombatjalern and the like can be found on the ground floor of the Mah Boon Krong Centre near Siam Square.

CLASSICAL

Fong Naam *The Hang Hong Suite* (Nimbus, UK). This is the best introduction to the vivacious and glittering sound of classical Thai music, from one of Thailand's very best ensemble. The disc includes some very upbeat funeral music and a series of parodies of the musical languages of neighbouring cultures: Chinese, Cambodian, Laotian, Vietnamese and Burmese. The group's Ⓓ *The Sleeping Angel* (Nimbus, UK) is also a splendid recording while their most recent Thai cassette is a great collaboration with Isaan mor lam musicians, notably khaen player Sombat Simlao, and US bass player Abraham Laboriel.

Ⓓ **Musicians of the National Dance Company of Cambodia** *Homrong* (Real World, UK). Some tracks on this disc are strikingly similar to Thai classical music; others are more folk-based and are clearly at the root of present-day Thai-Cambodian pop, kantrum. The story of the National Dance Company reviving the traditions of classical Cambodian music after the horrific destruction of the Pol Pot regime is inspiring.

Ⓓ **Various** *The Music of Cambodia Vol I* (Celestial Harmonies, US). An atmospheric recording of classical Khmer music performed in the temple of Angkor Wat, Cambodia.

Ⓓ **Various** *Thailande* (Auvidis/UNESCO, France). An atmospheric disc of three contrasting ensembles from Chiangmai. Intricate textures that draw you in.

HILLTRIBE MUSIC

Ⓓ **Various** *Thailand: Musiques et chants des peuples du Triangle d'Or* (Globe Music, France). Recordings of the traditional music of Thailand's main hilltribe groups: Meo, Lisu, Shan, Lahu, Yao, Akha and Karen.

LUK THUNG

Ⓓ **Pompuang Duangjan** *Greatest Hits Vol 2* (BKP, Thailand). A representative selection of luk thung hits from the late star of popular country music with a full, rich voice unlike anyone else in the business. In Thailand, the best of many cassettes to go for is called *Pompuang Lai Por Sor* [Pompuang's Many Eras] (Topline, Thailand).

Pimpa Pornsiri *Tee Sud Khong Pimpa* [The Biggest of Pimpa]. (Rota, Thailand). All the hits of luk thung prayuk's biggest name.

Suranee Ratchasima *Jeep Dor* [Returning Courtship] (Sure, Thailand). Rising luk thung singer from Korat shows off her pipes on this set of standards.

Ood Oh-pah Tossaporn *Pleng Wan* [Sweet Songs] (Onpa, Thailand). Rock singer Tossaporn made a stunning luk thung debut with this 1990 recording, with catchy Thai classical backing.

THE FAR EAST

Sayan Sanya *Luk Thung Talap Thong* [Luk Thung from the Golden Tape] (Onpa, Thailand). Heir to Sombatjalern's throne, sweet-voiced Sanya has never sounded better than on this greatest hits collection.

Suraphon Sombatjalern *Mere Mai Pleng Thai* [Mother of Thai Song] (Crown, Thailand). Greatest hits by the King of luk thung.

MOR LAM/NORTHEASTERN MUSIC

Ⓒ **Isan Slété** *Songs and Music from North East Thailand* (GlobeStyle, UK). Excellent selection of traditional mor lam. Vocal and instrumental numbers, played by a band of master musicians.

Ⓒ **Various** *Instrumental Music of Northeast Thailand* (King, Japan). Wonderful collection of bong lang and related instrumental northeastern styles. Lively and fun. Unmissable.

Ⓒ **Various** *Mo Lam Singing of Northeast Thailand* (King, Japan). Most mor lam gawn narrative and dance styles, even spirit possession rituals, are included on this, one of the best Thai CDs available.

Banyen Rakgan *Luk Thung, Mor Lam Sood Hit* [Luk Thung, Mor Lam Top Hits] (Rota, Thailand). Sixteen scorchers from the first national mor lam star. Rakgan's voice is a standout. Good example of the big-band mor lam sound

Pornsak Songsaeng *Gaud Mawn Nawn Pur* [Holding the Pillow in My Delirium] (Onpa, Thailand). Selection from mor lam's top male act, a fine singer with a deep, distinctive voice.

Jintara Poonlarp *Dam Jai Nam Da* [Depends on the Tears] (MGA, Thailand). Poonlarp has conquered mor lam over the past few years with her powerful voice and fast delivery.

Sarm Tone *Pong Pong Chung* [Sound of the Drum] (Kita, Thailand). An interesting group, founded in 1990, who mix mor lam and luk thung in a humorous urban pop style. good fun live, too.

KANTRUM

Darkie *Kantrum Rock Vols I & II* (available on separate cassettes). Benchmark recordings by kantrum's only major star. Darkie's fine wailing voice is featured in rock-kantrum, kantrum and kantrum luk thung. Unfortunatley, this cassette is only available in southern Isaan at present!

OLD STYLE INDOCHINA

THE SOUNDS OF LAOS

Tourism is largely undeveloped in Laos, and the country still has a vibrant and intact folk culture in which music, weaving, herbal medicine and festivals all remain important. A visit offers a fascinating glimpse of old-style life in southeast Asia and the chance to hear music in a traditional and everyday context. John Clewley gets down to the cassette stalls.

Vientiane must be one of the sleepiest capitals in Asia, though there are signs that it is beginning to wake up. The opening of the Mitraphab (Friendship) Bridge across the Mekong river in spring 1994, for example, has provided the landlocked Laotians with their first real land route to the rest of southeast Asia. But so far, the pace of development matches the pace of life, which is leisurely. The government of the People's Democratic Republic, wary of the problems caused by too rapid development in neighbouring Thailand, has wisely chosen to move step by step.

A population of four million, spread over a mainly mountainous country slightly larger than Britain, means that population density is the lowest in the region. Being one of the world's least developed countries also means that music (ie cassette) production is rudimentary; indeed, some of the local stars record cassettes in northeastern Thailand, where facilities are better. Nonetheless, wander around the capital's Talat Sow (morning market), where several cassette stalls are located, and you can find excellent hilltribe music, as well as mor lam, the national music of Laos and northeast Thailand (see above).

As in Thailand, the bamboo reed pipe, the *khaen*, is the basic instrument of mor lam, and different versions of it are used in many hilltribe music styles. Traditional Laotian mor lam, involving jousting pairs of singers backed by the khaen, or colourful troupes, can be easily found on cassette. For live performances, check out a local *boun* or temple fair (usually held on Buddhist holidays), where mor lam is sure to be found.

National mor lam stars include the woman singer **Malawan Duengpoomee** and the male **Acharn (Professor) Sanaan**. Each region of the country, however, has its own style of mor lam. **Lam saravane** (from the southern town of Saravane) is widely popular and can be heard in Thailand as well. In fact, there are more ethnic Laotians in Thailand than in Laos – around 18 million – and a visit to northeastern Thailand, prior to a Laos trip, will definitely help in getting a handle on this pulsating style.

There is a good deal of cultural exchange between mor lam musicians of both countries. Generally speaking, Thailand has the newer, racier styles, like the electric mor lam sing, while in Laos there is more of an emphasis on traditional styles (though several key players left Laos after the Pathet Lao takeover in the mid-70s). Sometimes accordions have been used in place of the khaen (an influence from the former eastern bloc countries), whereas in Thailand electronic keyboards take the same role.

Laos also has the equivalent of Thai luk thung, as well as **sakorn**, a sugary modern mix of western melodies and Laotian lyrics. **Taoboangern (Silver Lily) Chapoowong** is the leading modern singer in Laos. Classically trained in Hanoi and Moscow, he had an enormous hit in Thailand and Laos in 1992 with "Kookhwan Fang Khong", a series of duets of old Thai and Laotian luk thung plus modern hits with Thailand's leading luk thung singer, **Sunaree Ratchasima** (Laotians enjoy hits from many Thai acts).

Despite being a star in his own country, Chapoowong says he has to market his own tapes, as well as compose songs, arrange and produce. If there is a gig, he has to organize it all; all this in addition to being a radio DJ. "We play everything," he says, "from Laotian farmers' songs to mor lam to sakorn to western hits." He has led his band on tours to eastern Europe, Indochina and Cuba, where he recognized similarities between Latin rhythms and mor lam. A trip to Vientiane's hottest nightspot, the Vienglaty mai, confirms this Latin tinge: locals

Taoboangern Chapoowong

love to dance – as in Vietnam and Cambodia – to mambo, chachachá, tango and other Latin styles.

The Laotian artist who is best known internationally, however, is Laos-born but California-resident **Swanthong Chaisombat**. This singer is enormously popular in the US among expats and former refugees from Thailand and Indochina, especially in Los Angeles. Each of her nine stateside releases has sold in excess of 20,000 copies and they regularly get bootlegged and sold in Laos. Two years ago Chaisombat released a mor lam and rock mix in Thailand, "Isaan Lam Rock", which was only marginally successful. In the future it's likely that she'll be sticking to those audiences that know her best.

DISCOGRAPHY

As with Thai music, there's a choice of western label CDs and local cassettes. For the latter, try Vientiane's Talat Sow (morning market), and check tapes before you buy them as their quality can be crude.

TRADITIONAL

Molam Lao *Music from Southern Laos* (Nimbus, UK). Traditional *mor lam saravane* from the south. The ensemble is composed of a number of the country's finest musicians who have lived in France since the 70s.
various *Lam Saravane/Musique pour Le Khene* (Ocora, France). Again, this is a recording by Laotian artists in Paris; breathtaking khaen playing and a long traditional mor lam narrative song sung in the southern Saravane style.

Various *Laos* (Musicaphon, Germany). Splendid introduction to various folk, mor lam and classical styles.

CONTEMPORARY

Taoboangern Chapoowong and Sunaree Ratchasima *Kookhwan Fang Khong* [A Couple Sings from Both Sides of the Mekhong] (Sure, Thailand). Commercially successful fusion of mor lam and luk thung.
Swanthong Chaisombat *Long Kham Loke* [Singing Songs Across the World] (MCA, Thailand; also pirated in Laos). Popular American-based Laotian singer.
Malawan Deungpoomee and Acharn Sanaan *Sud Yort lam Lao* [Greatest Hits of Lao Mor Lam] (no label). Fine up-country Laotian mor lam.

SATURDAY NIGHT IN SAIGON

CHACHACHÁ, OPERA AND
JOAN JETT: VIETNAM HAS THE LOT

Vietnam in the 1990s is southeast Asia's hippest travel destination – and with the end of the US boycott, every business and its dog is piling in. Which is good news, on the whole, and perhaps even for the musicians, as John Clewley discovers.

The locals come out at the weekend in **Ho Chi Minh City**, driving for hours around a circuit downtown. Mopeds and bicycles, for there are few cars yet, snake past Uncle Ho's statue, down Dong Khoi street and past the Hotel Continental and the Municipal Opera House. Families, out for a walk, have portraits taken in front of Uncle Ho; there's a carnival atmosphere. Outside the impressive Opera House building, rich kids decked out in jeans and shades lounge on their motorbikes. Someone is playing Joan Jett's "I Hate Myself For Loving You" (this song has been hugely popular right across Asia). And yet the sound that catches the attention on the noisy streets is not Joan but the clapping of *hu tieu* sticks by noodle sellers, rather like Latin claves.

Cai Luong – Vietnamese opera

Saigon, as everyone (except government officials) calls it, is bustling these days. Business is booming, as in many other major southeast Asian cities, but so far without awful pollution,

traffic snarls or construction. It still retains an elegance, a charm that has disappeared from other cities in the region. But Saigon's young people share the same kind of tastes as their Thai, Indonesian or Singaporean peers: they want to listen to western pop or the local version of it. One day I'm in Ban Than market, searching for tapes by the legendary *cai luong* (a popular opera style) singer Le Thuy, and up pushes a young guy who buys a bootleg of Michael Jackson's "Bad", making a big show of it. Very hip.

Saturday night down at the **Hoa Binh** open-air theatre offers an interesting glimpse at what's top of the pops in Saigon. Backstage, as singers hurriedly get changed, the musical director and veteran composer Tran Huu Bich tells me "There are two main trends in pop music here right now: western songs, or *nhac ngoai*, sung as covers or Vietnamese-language versions, and slow ballads, *nhac tru tinh*. These ballads; old songs from before 1975, are coming back now that things seem to be more relaxed."

Hoa Binh is packed – mums and kids, couples and students – for the start of the show. Each singer gets up for one or two songs (depending on how famous they are) and for the next two hours an amazing array of music is pumped out by the house band, from "La Bamba" to chachachá to rock'n'roll (in Vietnamese) to screaming hard rock. There are several lingering, melancholic ballads. A joker launches into a kung fu parody of Chinese songs (in Cantonese). He's followed by a slight lady in a lime green mini-skirt singing the Joan Jett number, complete with Madonna-style male dancers, before unleashing the surprise of the night: lambada-reggae (in English), with her toy-boys dancing with huge black rag-dolls, since this infamous dance is banned for couples!

The country's most popular singer, **Thai Chau**, gets the biggest hand for his emotive old ballads. His style of delivery bears a striking resemblance to both Thai luk thung and Japanese enka, and the subject matter seems similar too, with themes of parting, grief and forlorn love predominating.

Thai Chau: Vietnam's answer to Frank Sinatra

With the night still young, the next stop is a **soirée dansantes** – a dancehall. These places are found in most hotels and some nightclubs, and they cater to those with money; there's usually a live band, playing a mixture of western pop, tango, chachachá and waltz – and, of course, the Joan Jett song. The standard of ballroom dancing, even among the young, is very high. But the places that many young people prefer to go are the less well-known discos and coffeeshops, where they listen and groove to western pop, or watch rock videos.

The availability of cheap cassettes of pirated western pop – mostly imported from Thailand – has had a drastic effect on both traditional and older popular forms. Local folk singer **Miss T. Vi** explains that "young people like modern music and ballads – they want to be different." She says that Vietnam has a rich folk tradition, **dân ca**, with strong regional variations. But she adds, "people still like the southern style of singing, because of its sentimentality and sweetness of melody."

That "sweetness" is at the heart of one of Vietnam's unique popular forms, **cai luong**.

You can find this kind of opera behind the daytime electronics market in Saigon, in an old, fading theatre. Company director and author of the night's scenario, **Thanh Cao** has been in the business for over fifty years. Cai luong, he explains, started in the 1920s as the "reformed theatre" from *hat boi*, or classical theatre. The show they are presenting is based on the sixteenth-century life of General Nguyan Trai and the murder of his family. It's a lavish production on a shoestring budget. The action looks quite Chinese: stylized movements, great sword fights, humorous interludes, lingering deaths and good versus bad narrative. The baddies are in black, the goodies in white.

But what really makes cai luong fascinating is the music, for at least seventy percent of the action takes place in song. The link between the stage action and the music is provided by guitarist **Van Vi**, who leads a small orchestra, divided into western and Vietnamese sections. He binds the narrative together with his virtuoso playing – dissonance, harmonic percussion, vamping, lightning runs. Vi has achieved that extra bend on notes by scalloping out a concave shape between each fret on the neck of the guitar. The "new" instrument is called an *octaviana*.

Vi propels a vicious story of skullduggery with his eerie guitar, helping the cast to break out into song every few minutes. The climax is a rendition of "Vong Co" (Nostalgia for the Past), and there's not a dry eye in the house as the lead singers trill the high notes. The melodies are truly sweet, the costumes sumptuous and the action fast and furious. It seems a shame that this lively style is slowly fading away. As Cao says, "Cai Luong is not as popular as it was in the 50s and 60s. There are too many videos, cassettes and coffeeshops these days."

While Saigon shows the fast, commercial side of Vietnam, **Hanoi** in the north still has an old French colonial elegance and a far slower pace of life. In Hanoi and the area of the Red river delta there is an extraordinary tradition of **water puppetry**, unique in southeast Asia. This is a fine musical experience but an even more thrilling visual one.

The puppet shows tell stories of everyday life and tales of mythical animals and gods. Fire-breathing dragons burst from the water, heralding a selection of rural and mythical scenes. Two phoenix dance and fall in love, boys swim in the river, men fish for frogs, and mysterious goddesses dance out of smoke on the water. It is all the magic of southeast Asia in microcosm.

The puppets are operated by rods under the water, but exactly how it is done is a seriously guarded secret. The puppeteers are hidden from view behind a sort of pavilion or screen and are standing up to their waists in water. The musical accompaniment comes from a band of half a dozen musicians playing various drums, percussion instruments, two-stringed fiddle and

flute. It alternates between the fast and percussive and the soft and lyrical.

Performances are still given on festival days on village ponds and this is the most exciting way to see the art form, but there are also regular shows (Tuesdays, Thursdays and Sundays at 7.30pm) by the Hanoi Water Puppets, 32 Truong Chinh Road, Hanoi. Essential viewing.

◆ DISCOGRAPHY ◆

Various *Mùn Hè* (Lido, US). Produced in California for the Vietnamese expatriate market, this is an excellent compilation, ranging from traditional music to the latest club sounds, and including most of the major stars of contemporary Vietnamese pop.

Various *Vietnam: Tradition du Sud* (Ocora, France). Fine recordings of a duo on Vietnamese banjo and two-string fiddle.

Various *String Instruments of Vietnam* (King, Japan). Classical music from north Vietnam for zither, banjo, fiddle, etc, performed by members of the Hanoi University of Music.

Quy Bon Family Vietnamese Folk Theatre: *Hat Cheo* (King, Japan). An acquired taste but a good recording made in Hanoi.

SWAN SONG

THE PRECARIOUS TRADITIONS OF CHINESE MUSIC

The casual visitor to Beijing or other Chinese cities could be forgiven for thinking that Chinese music consists entirely of muzak, Richard Clayderman arrangements, and schmaltzy Hong Kong pop, blasted out on the ubiquitous loudspeakers. But the cities are only a small part of Chinese life. There's a large gap between urban and rural culture, which has increased since the Communist "Liberation" of 1949. Just as misleading is the gulf between the official sanitized, and secular, image of Chinese culture, and the realities of traditional life. Stephen Jones examines the survival of Chinese traditional music, while Stephen Hallet tells the remarkable story of leading rock star Cui Jian.

Chinese music dates back millennia but many of its modern forms had their beginnings in the "decadent" early years of this century and the long-delayed meeting of east and west. After the Opium Wars of the mid-nineteenth century, China was continually humiliated at the hands of the imperial powers, and in the turbulent years after 1911, when the last imperial dynasty, the Qing, was overthrown,

western ideas became widely popular, at least in the towns.

Musically, some exciting urban forms sprang up, such as new genres of **narrative singing** and the wonderful **Cantonese music** of the 1920s and 30s, which fused the local traditional music with western elements, notably jazz, played on Chinese instruments, saxophone, violin and xylophone. Musicians like the composer **Lü Wenzheng**, the violinist **Yi Zizhong** (who played in London in 1924) and **He Dasha** ("Thicko He") made many wonderful commercial 78s during this period, which richly deserve to be reissued.

If they are, however, it's likely to be on western labels. The official Chinese line castigates colonial Canton (Guangzhou) before 1945 as a place of extreme decadence, and much of its music as "unhealthy" and "pornographic". After the Communist victory of 1949, this kind of music more or less disappeared; indeed, the whole ethos of traditional musical performance was challenged. Anything "feudal" – including a lot of traditional folk customs and music – or religious was severely restricted, while Chinese melodies were "cleaned up" with the addition of rudimentary harmonies and bass lines. New **"revolutionary" music**, composed from the

Tale of the Red Lantern cassette sleeve – one of eight model operas permitted during the Cultural Revolution

1930s on, was generally march-like and optimistic. During the Cultural Revolution (1966–76) musical life effectively ceased, with only eight model operas and ballets permitted on stage.

Since the end of the Cultural Revolution, however, and spurred on by the economic liberalization of the 1980s and 90s, Chinese classical and popular music has revived, while western classical and pop sounds have entered the scene in a big way. Western pop has actually begun to dominate in places like Guangzhou, where you get much the same bland, escapist lyrics as across the (temporary) border in Hong Kong. Alongside it, though, a few more interesting (and more Chinese) aspects have found their way into rock, especially in the fusion of Xibei Feng (northwest folk music) and in the work of Cui Jian. There has been some adventurous film music, too, notably the soundtrack to *Swan Song*, directed by Zhang Zeming, which focuses on an old Cantonese musician and his son's rejection of the old folk tradition, and Chen Kaige's *Yellow Earth*, which uses traditional music to strong effect.

Traditional music, can also still be heard in rituals and ceremonies, in the opera houses, and in teahouses, both in the villages and towns. Travel around for a while and you should catch a fair range. You might even run into Chinese musical fieldworkers, who for the last fifteen years have been compiling an exhaustive "Anthology of Chinese Folk Music", a national project involving field recordings in each of the provinces.

OPERA AND QIN CLASSICS

On the classical Chinese music scene, vocal and dramatic music is dominant. There are several hundred types of regional opera, of which **Beijing Opera**, and the more classical but now rare **Kunqu** are the most widely known. There are also some beautiful **puppet operas**. If you visit China, you should be able to find an opera going on anywhere in the country, any time. Even in Beijing you will see groups of old men meeting in parks or, incongruously, at spaghetti junctions where the old gateways used to be, going through their favourite Beijing Opera excerpts.

There are also many forms of **narrative singing**, often long classical stories accompanied by a single drum or Chinese banjo. You may find a teahouse full of old people following the story avidly. There is also **xiangsheng**, a comic dialogue with a know-all and a straight man, though its subtle parodies of traditional opera may elude the outsider.

Solo traditions of plucked instruments live on, too, in the conservatoires, with musicians trained as soloists on the pear-shaped **pipa** lute and the **zheng** and **qin** zithers. Of these, the most exalted – and possibly the oldest – is the qin (also known as a *guqin* – ancient qin). This seven-string plucked zither has been a favourite subject of poets and painters for over a thousand years, and it is the most delicate instrument in the Chinese repertoire. It is the most accessible, too, producing expressive slides and ethereal harmonics. In the classic compositions, contemplative melodies give way to dramatic arpeggios in a texture in which silence is as important as sound.

Village ceremonial shawm band

Despite its status, the qin is not a well-known instrument outside the conservatoires. Few Chinese have heard its sound, or even heard of the instrument, and there may be only about two hundred qin players in the whole of China. Fortunately, there are some excellent recordings available and if you ask around at the conservatoires you may get to hear a private recital. In Beijing, I was fortunate enough to hear some of the great elders such as **Zhang Zijian**, **Wu Jinglue** and **Wu Zhaoji**. There is an accomplished middle generation of qin players, too, including **Li Xiangting**, currently resident in London, **Wu Wen'guang**, **Lin Youren** and **Gong Yi**.

Strangely enough, the art of the qin was protected during the Cultural Revolution. Through incongruous personal connections with the notorious Kang Sheng, chief of Mao's secret police, and Yu Huiyong, the leftist composer of the revolutionary opera "Taking Tiger Mountain by Strategy", the qin masters managed to keep working in peace through most of the period. There are many ancient instruments around, too. I've played on a Tang qin, over a thousand years old, and Ming instruments (fifteenth- to seventeenth-century) are common.

The poetic titles of many Chinese classical pieces – like "Autumn Moon in the Han Palace" or "Flowing Streams" – seem a bit programmatic. In practice, though, these are largely irrelevant to the content of a piece and serve only as identification for the musicians. The titles were only ever significant in the music of the literate classes, for solo instruments such as the qin and pipa.

RITUAL MUSIC

If you can, visit the villages, since that is where the traditional music has best survived. If you are lucky you may come across a **wedding** or **funeral**, where you'll hear the most lively forms of music other than opera, sometimes performed by lay Daoist priests. The ritual is operatic, entertaining both gods and mortals. At a funeral in a remote village a couple of years back, I saw the Daoists solemnly present offerings to the deities to ensure the path of the deceased to heaven, and then break into a bawdy routine with one of them pretending to smear the snot from the head Daoist's nose over the face of a straight-man who continued playing the *sheng* (the traditional Chinese mouth organ).

Long and deafening strings of fire-crackers are an inescapable part of much village ceremony,

Suzhou Daoist group

too. You may even find a procession led by a western-style brass band with a *shawm*-and-percussion band behind, competing in volume, oblivious of key.

A little more formally, you could go and watch a daily **temple ritual** at one of the major Buddhist or Daoist temples. Many of these temples have been restored since 1980, particularly in the south of China, where religious practice has been more resilient. Temple building has also been sustained by money from the commercial enterprise of the south and by overseas Chinese who have roots in the region.

The ritual temple music of the south of China is raucous and earthy, with a strong percussive element, and it is surprisingly accessible, even to ears unaccustomed to Chinese music. The Daoist monks from the **Temple of Sublime Mysteries** in **Suzhou**, for example, play a wonderful and wide-ranging music, including pieces for silk-and-bamboo instruments, flutes and oboes, some spectacularly long trumpets and a battery of percussion. The Suzhou monks left China for the first time in spring 1994 for a tour of Britain.

In recent years some traditional genres have found their way into the concert hall, though all too often they suffer from the deadening hand of state control. The **Xi'an Conservatoire** has commercialized the local tradition of ceremonial music, but the real thing is much better and can still be heard in the surrounding area. A more successful exchange has been brought about by the teachers and students of the **Beijing Central Conservatoire**, who have studied the exquisite instrumental music of the Zhihua temple in Beijing its with former monks and performed it on stage with them.

Another genuine folk music tradition is that of the ritual music association of **Qujiaying** village, south of Beijing. This peasants' music was probably learned in imperial times from monks trained in Beijing and, in an interesting initiative, the village has recently sent six teenagers to study at the Zhihua temple.

SILK-AND-BAMBOO AND FOLK ENSEMBLES

Perhaps the most accessible "folk music" in China, however, is the mellifluous **"silk-and-bamboo" ensembles**. It can be heard at its best on any afternoon, played by old-timers in Shanghai's teahouses. The players are all amateur, and turn up for their own pleasure, sitting round a table and taking it in turns to play a set with Chinese fiddles, flutes and banjos. It's a little like an Irish session, only with Chinese tea instead of Guinness. Even better are the Monday afternoon gatherings at the "pavilion in the heart of the lake", where you can listen to the long unravelling of a piece called "Sanliu", or watch the exhilaration of the dash to the finish of "Street Parade", with its breathless syncopations

The music is also arranged for professional folk orchestras. While in China, I attended a "contest" of some forty ensembles from all over the country and southeast Asia. Most were professional or conservatoire-based and even the groups from the home province of Jiangsu were quite far removed in style from the local folk music. In place of the undemonstrative style of the teahouse musicians, they employed Tchaikovsky-esque expressive effects, swaying about on stage, and edited brutally, removing the repeats "in case people got bored". The contest wasn't a rewarding listening experience but it showed just how good and how complex the real teahouse music is, with its captivating dovetailing of phrases. And it showed, too, how Chinese music is being bulldozed by half-baked western romantic misconceptions.

Other good folk music is to be heard around Quanzhou and Xiamen, on the coast of Fujian province, in the form of haunting **nan'guan** ballads. In these songs, popular all along the coast of Fujian, as in Taiwan across the strait, a female singer is accompanied by end-blown flute and plucked and bowed lutes.

THE LONG MARCH OF CHINESE ROCK

Rock music is a very recent phenomenon in China, and, unlike the pop music that the authorities had (after a while) happily allowed to drift in from Hong Kong, it was regarded at first with considerable official suspicion.

It was introduced largely by foreign students in the mid-1980s. They lent cassettes to Chinese friends, set up bands with them in the universities, and first performed in the clubs and underground venues of Beijing, Shanghai and Canton. To begin with, the music was almost entirely derivative, going little further than covers of easy-chord numbers by the Rolling Stones, Led Zeppelin, Status Quo and the like. However, by the end of the 80s, Chinese bands and musicians were beginning to get their own identity, and composing original music and lyrics.

Foremost among them was **Cui Jian**, a trumpeter by training, who had played with the Beijing Song and Dance Troupe in Cultural Revolution days, and in the early 80s recorded an album of Hong Kong-style pop. By 1989, however, he had absorbed the new rock influences in the clubs – The Police and Talking Heads in particular – and released the first significant Chinese rock album, "Rock on the New Long March". It was quite a shock to the older generation – not just in the way it took liberties with history in its title but in its whole posture. Although Cui Jian was never directly critical of the state, his lyrics were double-edged, subverting a lot of the conventions of official ideology.

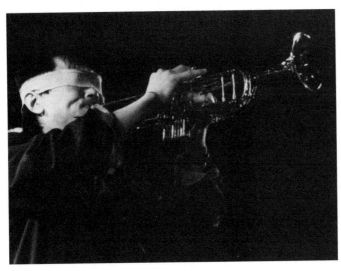

Cui Jian

Predictably, he was accused by the authorities of having a negative influence on public morality. However, in these pre-Tiananmen days, that didn't do a rocker any harm, and the album was an immediate success, selling widely in mainland China, southeast Asia and Taiwan. Cui Jian, meanwhile, played concerts in Paris and London, and continued developing – almost single-handed – a distinctive form of Chinese rock, making use, for example, of traditional instruments such as the zheng and oboe-like *suona*.

It was politics, though, rather than music that catapulted Ciu Jian to national and international fame, through his 1986 song

"Nothing To My Name" (Yi wu suo you). Like many of his lyrics, this is a love song on the surface, though the "you" could just as well be "China" or "the state":

For a long time I kept on asking
When will you come with me
But all you do is laugh at me
For I have nothing to my name
I want to give you all my dreams
To give you my liberty too
But all you do is laugh at me
For I have nothing to my name.

The song became an anthem of student demonstrations at the end of 1986 and again during the Tiananmen student demonstrations of 1989. Its popularity evoked a memorable complaint from General Wang Zhen, a veteran of the Long March. "What do you mean, you have nothing to your name? You've got the Communist Party, haven't you?" The authorities were unhappy, too, with Cui Jian's perfor-mance theatrics, which included wearing a blind-fold during a song called "The Red Cloth Blinds My Eyes".

After the Tiananmen Square massacre of June 4, 1989, Chinese youth culture went into the deep-freeze for a while and Cui Jian was forced to lie low. In January 1990, however, he was allowed to launch a concert tour of China to help raise funds for the Asian Olympics (held in Beijing that September). This was a huge success but, midway through, the authorities had second thoughts and banned any further concerts due to "dangerous disorder". For a year or so, Cui Jian was unable to perform in public, his records were withdrawn from sale, and his lyrics "investigated". Since 1991, however, he has been back on the scene, performing again in China and abroad, and recording. His recordings are widely available in China and other groups frequently cover his songs.

Cui Jian's band includes a drummer who trained in Spain and a Japanese guitarist. Among China's small rock community, they are acknowledged as the pioneers of Chinese rock. However, through the 1990s a number of new bands have emerged, including **1989** (an experimental rock group), **Tang Dynasty** (heavy metal) and **Cobra** (an all-women band). **Wei Hua**, formerly a broadcaster on Chinese TV's English-language service, has emerged as China's leading female rock singer.

Future trends in Chinese rock could go two ways. On the one hand, there's an unhealthy respect for US and British rock output. On the other, Chinese **folk traditions** are getting a look-in, following the success of the gutsy, north-west-style singing in films like *Yellow Earth* and *Red Sorghum*. The **xibei feng** ("north-west wind") style has strongly influenced Cui Jian, with its staccato vocals and vaguely reggae-like rhythms, and has also been adopted by other rock bands, notably the Cantonese songwriter **Xie Chengchang**. Perhaps the fusion will continue, for, as Cui Jian puts it: "Chinese culture is like a river without an outlet. We need to unblock this river so that it can flow freely into the sea and mingle with the world."

DISCOGRAPHY

Conservatoire recordings of souped-up arrangements dominate the Chinese music that's available on CD. Even the better examples like the Saydisc recordings of the Jing Ying soloists are sadly lacking in spirit. The selection below highlights the best authentic recordings of Chinese instrumental and religious music and opera.

CONTEMPORARY

Cui Jian *I Have Nothing* (EMI, Hong Kong). Powerful songs and good arrangements from China's outstanding contemporary musician.

Ⓒ **Tan Dun** *Ritual Opera – Nine Songs* (CRI, US). A wonderfully odd composition for choir and instrumental group from one of China's most interesting young composers. Heavily influenced by the traditional music of his home village in Hunan province.

TRADITIONAL FOLK

Ⓒ **Various** *China: Chuida Wind & Percussive Instrumental Ensembles* (UNESCO, France). Three traditional ensembles from southern China recorded in 1987, including silk-and-bamboo from Shanghai and ceremonial music for weddings and funerals.

Ⓒ **Various** *A Happy Miao Family* (Pan, Netherlands). The first in a projected series of recordings of minority musics in China. Lively recordings of songs and dances from the Miao people of the southwest, with reed organ, lute and tree leaf!

Various *Sizhu zhi xiang* and *mingqu huicui* (Yunnan yinxiang gongsi, China). These two cassettes are authentic Shanghai silk-and-bamboo music. Available, with a bit of luck, in Shanghai.

Ⓒ **Various** *Chine: Xinjiang, the Silk Road* (Playasound, France). A taste of the Turkic vocal and instrumental music of Xinjiang and the western regions of China towards central Asia.

Ⓒ **Various** *Chinese Turkestan: Uighur Music* (Ocora, France). A pretty scholarly two-CD set of classical and popular music traditions from Xinjiang.

RITUAL MUSIC

Ⓒ **Monks of the Zhihua temple, Beijing** *Beijing Zhihua si yinyue* (Wind Records, Hong Kong). These are volumes 8 and 9 from an otherwise dubious series of Chinese ritual music. They feature exquisite ancient music, recorded in 1990, played on double-reed pipes, flutes, Chinese mouth organs, a frame of pitched gongs and percussion.

Ⓒ **Tianjin Buddhist Music Ensemble** (Nimbus, UK). Ancient and evocative music with mouth organs, flute, chimes and percussion, but above all some wonderful oboe playing.

CLASSICAL

Ⓒ **Various** *Chine: musique classique* (Ocora, France). A selection of solo pieces featuring the qin, pipa, sheng, guanzi (oboe) and dizi (flute), played by outstanding instrumentalists of the 1950s.

Ⓒ **Various** *Nan-kouan: chant courtois de la Chine du sud* (Ocora, France; 6 vols). Haunting chamber ballads with a female singer accompanied by end-blown flute and plucked and bowed lutes.

Ⓒ **Wu Man** *Chinese Music for the Pipa* (Nimbus, UK). A fine recording from this brilliant young musician featuring traditional and contemporary works for the solo plucked lute.

Ⓒ **Li Xiangting** *Chine: l'art du qin* (Ocora, France). Refined meditations on the qin. A good and easily available recording.

CHINESE OPERA

Ⓒ **Various** *An Introduction to Chinese Opera* (Hong Kong Records, Hong Kong). A series of four CDs illustrating different styles, including Beijing, Cantonese, Huangmei and Qin Qiang operas.

Ⓒ **Various** *Opera du Sichuan: la legende de serpent blanc* (Musique du Monde, France). A double CD of traditional opera from the spicy southwest province of Sichuan.

HERDSMEN AND HORSE-HEAD FIDDLES

THE SOUNDS OF THE MONGOLIAN STEPPE

Outer Mongolia is the home of nomadic horsemen living on the vast steppes of central Asia. There are two million Mongols and twenty-eight million cattle. Sean Hinton has spent many months in Mongolian yurts enjoying a surprisingly beautiful music.

A Mongol prince traversed the skies on a wondrous winged horse to visit his beloved each night. One morning, determined to keep him from leaving, she secretly clipped the animal's wings. The prince mounted his steed and they rose into the sky, but after a distance they crashed to earth, killing the horse. In his grief the prince gathered up the remains of the animal and fashioned a fiddle-like instrument – the horse's head formed the body and its thigh bone made the fingerboard, while from the hair of its tail he made strings and a bow. With this instrument he played and sang of his grief and love for his lost steed, his beloved and his distant homeland.

Thus the Mongols tell of the mythical origin of their most typical instrument, the **morin khuur** (literally "horse fiddle"). Nowadays it is built of wood, but in place of the scroll on a modern violin, a horse's head is carved as a reminder of the instrument's origin.

The Mongols are traditionally nomadic herdsmen and for millennia they have traversed the steppes of central Asia. With the Gobi desert to the south and Siberia to the north, the Mongolian Republic is a vast, harsh, sparsely populated land – three times the size of France. On the plains, living in their tiny felt tents (*yurts*), the Mongols sit out the perishing -40°C winters – and sing!

The Mongols state that every human being must sing or play on the morin khuur. In the old days a person who refused to sing or play at a feast would be ritually beaten and punished. Because everyone sings, the relationship between singer and audience is very close – everyone is a performer and everyone is a listener. Music is a form of communication and a language that every Mongol speaks.

But singing is much more than just performing. The famous technique of **khöömii**, where one singer produces both melody and bass at the same time, was born from the nomads imitating the sound of the wind whistling around Jargalant mountain, in the west of Mongolia. By imitating nature you can understand and communicate with it. The same technique is found among the Tuvans, a closely related people in the Russian federation to the north of Mongolia (see p.103).

Of the many types of traditional Mongolian songs – satirical, epic, praise-songs and the like – the most highly regarded is the **urtyn duu**, the Long song, held by the Mongols to be one of the greatest flowerings of their culture. Long songs are named not for their duration, but because their melodies are said to represent the land in which they were created. Their drawn-out, free, chant-like melodies evoke the

Ulan Bator ensemble

endless plains, occasionally rising steeply to a great peak, but always returning to the timeless steppe. This is one of the few examples where it is not too fanciful to relate music directly to the landscape that gives birth to it. The songs are richly ornamented and sung passionately, in full voice, but are performed in almost total stillness – not even the singer's jaw moves more than a fraction.

Mongolian music is one of the great undiscovered treasures of central Asia and khöömii singing and melodies on the morin khuur are surprisingly accessible to the unaccustomed ear. They have lyrical beauty and a sense of timeless space that is very powerful. The country is still remote and inaccessible, but less so than ever before. As everywhere, the question is how resistant the traditional music will be to the inevitable western influence.

People living in such a harsh environment do not display their emotions easily. "Keep your hardness on the outside and hide your love within", one Mongol proverb admonishes. The granite-like strength of a Mongol face is as flat, hard and impassive as the land, but occasionally that facade masking human sentiment slips. When a Mongol sings it is like a spring of pure water gushing up from a subterranean cave. In the words of one song:

Like a beautiful long song
Lifting the mind and heart
Clear and tranquil in the distance . . .

DISCOGRAPHY

For more discs of khöömii singing and morin khuur from Tuva, see also the Russian discography in Chapter two.

Various *Enchanting Mongolia* (Nebelhorn, Germany). Traditional vocal and instrumental pieces plus some more modern material including a morin khuur quartet.

Various *Inedit Mongolie* (Inedit/Auvidis, France). The best introduction to traditional vocal and instrumental music. Spectacular khöömii singing and beautiful melodies on the morin khuur.

Various *Mongolian Folk Music* (Hungaroton, Hungary). A 2-CD Hungaroton-UNESCO collaboration featuring recordings made in Ulan Bator in the late 1960s. A more comprehensive survey than the above discs, beginning with a song telling the legendary origins of the morin khuur.

ENKA, OKINAWA AND THE MASTERS OF CLONE

THE JAPANESE ARE COMING!!

Japan is, after America, the world's largest market for recorded music – and its appetite is voracious. The Japanese are into just about every kind of rock music, not to mention bluegrass, reggae and salsa, and in each genre they have top-class bands of their own. World Music is a passion here, too, and the WOMAD festival in Yokahama has become an established part of the scene. But as John Clewley reports, there are strong Japanese indigenous musics, too, from the sentimental enka ballads to the astonishing contemporary roots music of Okinawa. Deservedly, these are beginning to make an impact on the international scene.

Exploring Japanese music, you might, in good Japanese fashion, take three musical snapshots of a typical summer's Saturday in Tokyo:

• Picture One. The teenage fashion haunts of Harajuku and Shibuya, on *hokosha tengoku* (Paradise Walk). Every five yards or so on Route 23, a kaleidoscope of bands pound out everything from punk, thrash and hard rock to hip-hop and reggae, to teen idol copycats, dancing and singing on roller skates.

• Picture Two. The annual summer *bon odori* festival on Fuji TV avenue, downtown. In the hot Japanese summers these old Buddhist festivals are held all over the country, when folks return to their hometowns to pay respects to their ancestors' graves. Tonight scratched old popular songs like "Tokyo Ondo" are spun by old ladies on aged gramophones. As the music booms out, people form a circle around a huge *taiko* drum and dance. Tradition still runs strongly through high-tech Japan.

• Picture Three. The editorial offices of the rock magazine *Takarajima*. Work is disrupted by the arrival of two youths dressed as chickens! It's a record company promotion.

These are snapshots of the world's most enthusiastic music consumers. Over 325 million CDs, tapes and records were sold in 1991, valued at over £2.3 billion ($305 billion). The market is roughly 75 percent domestic and 25 percent international. Two things stand out: the staggering speed with which musical trends are picked up and dropped; and the fact that this is one product the Japanese haven't seemed able to export.

Shang Shang Typhoon

The situation as the 1990s progress, however, is changing. For the first time, Japanese bands, playing what is clearly Japanese pop music, are poised to make waves overseas. Led by Shang Shang Typhoon (SST), and Okinawans like the Rinkenband and Nenes, these bands give rise to some optimism for the future of Japanese popular music.

SST leader and composer Koryu explains: "The current Japanese pop scene is like junk food – idol singers are easily accessible but ultimately not satisfying. People are tired of rock and pop, they used to have meaning but not any more." He sees the answer not in copying the latest western trends but in returning to Japanese roots. "What we want to do is to take those things that the Japanese have forgotten in the culture and bring it out in a new way."

KAYOKYOKU

Ten years in the making, that "new way" has turned **Shang Shang Typhoon**'s music into an eclectic mix of Okinawan, Latin, reggae, Chinese and southeast Asian pop. You get sassy mambos, plaintive Chinese ballads and Japanese folk styles. The band also draws heavily on many popular entertainment forms: *rokyoku* (storytelling), *ondo* (festival music) and *min'yo* (folk). Koryu even introduces members of the band while singing a song made famous by the 1960s comedy act, Crazy Cats.

This kind of musical blending is typical of a **kayokyoku** (fusion) band, says Koryu, and SST songs further illustrate the process. "Let It Be", for example, isn't just a cover. In SST hands it's a wild festival reggae song, complete with kazoos. "I imagined I was on a desert island with only one LP, by The Beatles. What would it sound like as a cross between a *bon odori* dance and reggae?" Lyrics to SST songs adopt phrases from everyday life, whether it be a parody of a child's song on "Cha Cha Bitter Tea" or Buddhist proverbs in "Buddha".

The term kayokyoku came into widespread usage just after World War II, when it was applied to a whole range of local popular styles that emerged from the fusion between Japanese music and imported styles like jazz, R&B and country and western. Musical synthesis has had a long and fruitful history in Japan. "What used to be great about kayokyoku was that it combined so many elements – Japanese music, Latin, Hawaiian, black American and the like," Koruyu explains. "But right now it's disappearing because the whole music market is geared towards a very young audience."

Koryu's band perform, though, in a very different Japan to that of the immediate postwar period, which was characterized by famine and devastation. In 1945, "Ringo No Uta" (The

Postwar heart-throb Misora Hibari

It was during this time that **Japanese Latin** music really developed, though its roots go back to the 1920s and 30s, particularly for tango. In the 50s and early 60s tango and Cuban-style bands were formed; the **Tokyo Cuban Boys** became well known in Cuba, while tango singer **Ranko Fujisawa** toured Latin America and recorded in Buenos Aires. Japan, incidentally, produces more tango records a year than any other country. There is even one original Japanese Latin rhythm from the time, the *dodompa*, which can be heard on "Tokyo Dodompa Musume" by Mari Watanabe. SST use the rhythm on their song "Kibun Wa Sento".

Today, there are many Latin bands in Japan. This newer generation got a shot in the arm in the early 80s from visits by Tito Puente and the Fania All Stars, and the upshot is that Japan has developed one world-class salsa band, **Orquesta De La Luz**, who recently topped Billboard's Latin dance charts in the US with "Salsa caliente del Japon". La Luz are well known in Central and South America.

GROUP SOUNDS

The arrival of British pop groups like The Beatles and The Animals in the mid-1960s provided a new direction for popular music, and saw the decline of genres like Hawaiian music. **"Group Sounds"** developed, with musicians forming bands with keyboards, mop-top haircuts and heavy beats. Bands took on names like The Tigers or The Blue Comets. By the end of the decade rock, folk, folk-rock and even psychedelia were enthusiastically received. And the music played wasn't just a translation of western songs – there were serious attempts to create Japanese forms.

An important aspect in the development of Japanese rock music was the issue of whether the Japanese language was suited to the style. Some bands preferred to sing in English, but a significant number of underground bands experimented with Japanese lyrics; often song themes reflected the situation of conflict that existed during the late 60s between young people, mainly students, and the authorities.

Perhaps the most influential band to experiment with Japanese lyrics was **Happy End** (1970–73), led by composer **Haruomi Hosono** and lyricist **Takashi Matsumoto**. While Matsumoto explored themes of love and politics, Hosono tried to mesh folk-rock with Japanese melodies. The band signalled a period

Apple Song), sung by Michiko Namiki and Noburo Kirishima, was released. The optimism of the song struck a chord with people suffering from great hardship. It set the tone for the future. Then in 1949, at the tender age of twelve, the greatest of all Japanese popular singers, **Misora Hibari**, made her debut; from that day until her death in 1989 her popularity never waned, and her records still sell by the hundreds of thousands. Hibari's vocal versatility – including the sobbing *kobushi* style – enabled her to handle mambo, jazz, *min'yo* and, above all, *enka* (see box overleaf), the sentimental ballad form of kayokyoku that is often referred to as the "soul of the Japanese".

At the same time as Hibari was making her debut, western popular music was being fused with local styles. Shizuko Kasagi's "Tokyo Boogie Woogie" brought a Japanese vocal style together with American shuffle rhythms. Composer Ryoichi Hattori even managed to link folk music with shuffle rhythms on "Shamisen Boogie Woogie". At the same time, rockabilly started in Japan, alongside bluegrass experiments, doo-wop, a (second) Hawaiian boom (in colleges) and, later, the growth of jazz coffeeshops. Electrified instruments were enthusiastically taken up as the economy started to pick up in the 1960s.

of classic Japanese rock, during which interest in local and foreign styles blossomed; the popularity of rock even affected kayokyoku and enka, which became slanted towards the middle-aged. But the biggest shock came from an unknown artist in Okinawa (which had been returned to Japanese sovereignty in 1972) called **Shoukichi Kina**, with his band **Champloose** (see the Okinawa feature), and a song called "Haisai Oji-san" (Hello Uncle). Kina had been

---

ENKA - THE SOUL OF JAPAN

Harbours, tears, rain, saké, broken hearts and longing for home: these are the recurrent themes of **enka**, Japan's unique ballad form. All a singer needs is a kimono, a sobbing *kobushi* vocal and plenty of tears. Enka may have changed over the long time it has been in existence, but the one thing that remains consistent about the sound is the sobbing vibrato-like quality of the singing; whether it's Latin-tinged, schmaltzy strings or melancholic min'yo doesn't matter, the highly charged singing style is what counts.

The term enka was originally associated with political dissent during Japan's rapid westernization in the late nineteenth century ("en" from "enzetsu" for a public speech, and "ka" meaning a song). However, by the early 1920s enka had become the first popular style to successfully synthesize western scales with Japanese minor modes. The breakthrough came with a song called "Sendo Kouta" (Boatman's Song) by **Shimpei Nakayama**.

Enka's enduring popularity since then owes much to the ability of legendary composers like Nakayama and **Masao Koga** to accurately reflect the mood of the times. Koga's first hit, "Kage Wo Shitaite" (Longing For Your Memory), remains one of the all-time classics; the song is often cited as an example of the "Koga melody" – another essential element in enka. The music, too, seems to have been able to absorb other native and non-native elements, from min'yo to Latin to Korean melodies to old narrative folk songs (*rokyoku*).

But enka will forever be associated with one singer, **Misora Hibari**, the undisputed queen of the genre, with over 500 records to her credit before she died aged 52 in 1989. From her debut, aged twelve, in the late 1940s, she was a cultural icon, reflecting the shifting moods of the times. Her image is forever associated with the unforgettable song "Kanashii Saké", during which she would always cry.

Currently the big enka star is **Miyako Harumi**, a singer with a wide vocal range, growling voice and the essential ability to create an intense emotional atmosphere. She has recently played sets with a rock backing group.

Enka star Miyako Harumi rocking out

experimenting with a mixture of Okinawan min'yo and rock, and the resultant song became a major hit – today it is even used as a drill song for high-school baseball teams.

Kina and Hosono were a big influence on young musicians, and a lot of bands started out in the mid- to late 1970s, trying to forge an Asian rock sound. Successes included **Carol**, **RC Succession** and, later, **Shinji Harada** and **The Southern All Stars** (who became the biggest-selling band in Japan in 1990).

The seminal Haruomi Hosono

Pioneers like Hosono, however, had already moved on, developing a new music – known in Japan as **technopop** – based around synthesizers and electronic instruments. The **Yellow Magic Orchestra** led the way with their computer/video game-inspired ditties, becoming the most successful Japanese band at home, and overseas. They were the creation of Hosono, along with two other highly influential Japanese musicians, Ryuichi Sakamoto, and Yukihiro Takahashi. A couple of other bands,

The Plastics and **Melon**, also made some inroads overseas.

Many of these musicians later became involved in writing for **idol singers**; for example, Hosono wrote "Pink Mozart" for top idol **Matsuda Seiko**. Japan's idol singers are plucked by the record industry, packaged into safe roller-skating bands like **Hikaru Genji** or, if they're girls, dressed like **Miho Nakayama** or **Wink** as cutesie Christmas decorations. Idols have a brief half-life and then as their careers falter, they are picked up as *talentos* (which is just what most of them lack) for TV game shows.

However, over the past few years there has been a marked decline in the popularity of idols, mainly due to the rise of small live-venue bands and TV shows like *Ikaten*. This talent show for amateur rock bands became an overnight success and has launched the careers of several new Japanese rock and **indie-type** bands, like **Tama** and **Little Creatures**. The show is the TV equivalent of the popular weekend bands on Paradise Walk and marks a shift from over-produced bubble-gum pop to post-punk rock, heavy metal and thrash, mirroring a worldwide trend.

WORLD SOUNDS AND MIN'YO

During the last decade the massive power of the Japanese economy started pulling in music from around the globe. World Music artists have started to arrive in increasing numbers and, as mentioned earlier, the **WOMAD festival** made its Japanese debut in 1991.

Just as the influx of foreign artists and music in the 1940s, '50s and '60s led to the development of new and distinct styles of popular music, so the invasion of new World sounds in the '80s and '90s will affect future styles. Initially this means that bands tend to replicate music they hear. Reggae, for example, is a solid fixture and there are many good **reggae** and **ska** bands, like the wacky Madness-like **Tokyo Ska Paradise Orchestra**, singer **PJ** and dancehall toaster **Rankin' Taxi** (who toasts in Japanese). Visits by Zaireans like the dapper Papa Wemba have spawned local **lingala** (soukous) bands, some of whom sing in Japanese. Many of these kind of bands try to take a foreign style and then slowly turn it Japanese, initially by singing in their native tongue. Sometimes it can partially work, as with "underground" bands like Jagatara or S. Ken and the Hot Bom Boms, but ultimately

OKINAWA: RHYTHMS FROM FIRE ISLAND

· · · · · · · · · · · · · · · · · · · ·

Each year towards the end of August, under a balmy subtropical full moon, the Okinawans pay respect to their ancestors. This festival is known as **Ei-sa**, the Okinawan version of the Japanese bon odori. Groups of *sanshin* (three-string Okinawan banjo) players, *taiko* drummers and a massed chorus of *paranku* hand drummers and dancers take to the streets or perform around local shrines, often through the night. The women dance, the men drum in harmony, and the distinctive Okinawan melodies seem to match the excitement in the air. It's an event quite unlike any other in Asia, blending as it does traditions from mainland Asia and the Pacific.

Okinawa lies some 500km south of mainland Japan, and is the largest group in the Ryukyu chain of islands between the East China Sea and the Pacific. It has a long history of foreign domination: first China, then Japan, the Americans after World War II and then the Japanese again in 1972. Its isolation has helped preserve a thriving traditional culture, which is just as exotic to the Japanese as to anybody else.

Okinawans need little excuse to get out their sanshins, *sanbas* (castanets) and drums and sing. In an increasingly homogenized Japan, this is one of the few places where people spontaneously play music, and a distinct min'yo song culture survives. Each island has its own min'yo style and dances, and the locals call their music **shima uta**, which means "songs of the islands". Okinawan folk culture is the bedrock for modern Okinawan popular music.

The main island of Okinawa is an unusual place, having both a big US military presence and a Japanese administration. Ironically, this mirrors times in the past when Ryukyu kings paid tribute to both China and Japan. It has a tragic history, as Teruya Rinken, leader of the Rinkenband, explains: "Three hundred years ago we came under Japanese rule and culture. We became gloomy. I imagine our music was a lot brighter before that, as the people must've been. It was the same after the Second World War, this gloominess got into our hearts. You must remember that until recently teachers discouraged students from speaking our own language."

But throughout periods of colonial rule, the Okinawans have determinedly kept their identity. Koryu, leader of the Japanese band Shang Shang Typhoon, says that he was originally inspired by his visits there. "They have a strong sense of identity and a solid spiritual basis for their music. I've learned from that to look for the same things in my own culture."

What inspired Koryu and others like him was the stunning debut by **Shoukichi Kina** and his band **Champloose** (the name comes from an Okinawan mixed stir-fry) in the mid-1970s. Kina wrote a song in high school, "Haisai Oji-San" (Hello Uncle), which he recorded partly with his father Shouei's min'yo group (Shouei Kina is Okinawa's most famous postwar min'yo singer), partly with mandolin and other western instruments. The song sold 300,000 copies in Okinawa (a third of the population), and Kina's fusion of min'yo with rock and electric instruments opened a whole new vista not only for Okinawan rock musicians but also for the Japanese. "I created a new style, I opened the way," explains Kina. "But it was natural really, because we were a new generation, in a different world to our fathers."

you wonder if it's worth it. In contrast, the very best of Japanese pop seems to come from a strong **Japanese tradition** that is then synthesized with outside influences, as with SST, Takio Ito, the Rinkenband and the diverse collaborations of Haruomi "Harry" Hosono.

Haruomi Hosono, following his success with the technopop Yellow Magic Orchestra, has moved on to a whole host of experiments. He characterizes himself as a "cultural half-breed", caught, like many of his generation, between Japanese and American pop cultures, and perhaps that's why he has spent so much of his career searching for identity both within Japan and overseas. His work includes collaboration with southern Indian, Okinawan, traditional Japanese and Korean, Hawaiian, Arabic and western musicians. He's made documentaries on Bulgarian and Arabic music; he's worked with James Brown, Ry Cooder and the Tunisian vocalist Amina Annabi. He has

The Rinkenband demonstrate the famous Okinawa whistle

ting, and they caused an immediate stir in Japan. Plaintive min'yo ballads, featuring the haunting voice and soaring grace notes of Tomoko Uehara, are followed by *katcharshee* dance numbers, with the graceful hand movements found all over southeast Asia. The rhythm is incessant, "like a tropical hurricane pounding on a sandy shore, with syncopation imbedded in syncopation, jangling and chanting, swirling colours, hot dance numbers", reported the *Daily Yomiuri*.

The band's leader, Teruya Rinken, explains: "On katcharsee songs, the sanshin plays both the rhythm and melody. The various drums like paranku [hand drums] and the shima daiko [big drum] lay down the melody." That infectious rhythm, adds Kina, catches the listener so easily because it comes at the beginning of the bar. There's no escape.

The third artist of note to emerge from Okinawa is **Sadao China**, who records solo and produces other artists. Apart from his own excellent min'yo releases, he produced a fine 1991 album, **"Ikaw˘u"**, by a female quartet of traditional singers and musicians, **Nenes** ("sisters" in Okinawan). China blended the women's high-pitched vocals with music from islands around the world – reggae, calypso, even Greek music – with great success. Nenes have proved themselves to be one of the most interesting new groups on the Asian scene.

Kina went on to record several albums, including "Bloodline" with Ry Cooder and Yellow Magic Orchestra's Haruomi Hosono. One of his songs, "Subete No Hito No Kokoro Ni Hana O" (Flowers For Your Heart), has been recorded by many overseas artists, including Indonesia's Detty Kurnia and Thailand's Caravan. Since his comeback in 1990, his new work has included reggae and the chic Parisian sound of a François Breant production, but he still retains his charisma and outspokenness. "Now I play punk-min'yo." he says with a laugh.

Kina seemed to fade away during the 1980s. His experiments were considered unusual at home, and it was not until the appearance of the **Rinkenband** in Tokyo in January 1990 that Okinawan pop music again hit the limelight. Rinkenband fused min'yo and ei-sa festival music into bright pop songs, in an almost musichall set-

The Rinkenband have also been experimenting, notably with some members of the British eclectics **3 Mustaphas 3** on the "Rikka" mini-LP. Their addition of tighter drumming and bass works very well, though it remains to be seen whether this kind of approach will be incorporated fully in the future.

Whatever the future, it looks assuredly Okinawan. The issue of authenticity, of being true to your roots, crops up again and again in conversations with Okinawan musicians, and, as Kina puts it, "Whatever we do, the Okinawan feeling comes through. We play Okinawan music, period."

had a huge influence on the new generation of Japanese "roots" bands, and his work often anticipates future directions. Once settled into a new direction, however, he will pick up and move off on another tangent. "There's a cultural chaos here in Japan. We're bombarded with music from everywhere, so we're spoilt for choice. And we don't know what to do if we don't know who we are. The problem of identity is always there . . . it's always a search."

For **Takio Ito**, the enfant terrible of the min'yo world, the search was a little more focused. Born on the northern island of Hokkaido, he was brought up on **min'yo**, a highly conservative style of song, dating back centuries to singing geishas, but developed into virtuoso instrumental music early this century. It is played on the banjo-like *shamisen*, which when it gets up-tempo has an almost metallic clapping sound. In its conventional form, min'yo is probably at its best on the island of Tsugaru, home of a well-known itinerant and blind master player, **Chikuzan Takahashi**.

Ito, however, had no intention of staying within conventions, leaving his archly conservative min'yo school after three months, declaring that his teachers could tell him nothing. Since that time he has tirelessly searched for new approaches to the music, and his current band, **Tryin' Times**, features western electric instruments as well as traditional min'yo instruments like shamisen, shakuhachi (bamboo flute) and taiko (the huge barrel drum made famous by the Kodo drummers). The result, led by Ito's powerful voice and shamisen played by Shinichi Kinoshita, is superb: a tradition refreshed and made new. (And for the scale of this achievement, keep in mind that there are min'yo societies in Japan that specialize in singing only one song, in its original form).

Min'yo, however, is by no means the only traditional style to influence contemporary pop, for prior to westernization in the mid-nineteenth century Japan had a sophisticated urban culture that featured many varieties of popular entertainment. These included **zokuyo** (Japanese popular songs, often performed in entertainment revues), **ondo** (festival music), and Kansai region narrative forms like **kawachi ondo** and **rokyoku**.

All of these styles have had an impact on Japanese popular music from the late 1980s on, often in distinctly bizarre fusions. Who would have guessed that one of Japan's oldest folk narrative styles, kawachi ondo, mixed with reggae and with lyrics about "freeters" (young people who scorn joining corporations and instead work part-time at any job), would be a runaway hit in the summer of 1991? "Kakin Ondo", however, sung for a TV commercial by Osaka's **Kikusuimaru Kawachiya**, was just that – and at the same time put the spotlight on those Kansai region singers who perform their songs at local bon odori festivals. A new-found popularity helped *goshu ondo* singer **Tadamaru** ("Musical Anarchist") **Sakuragawa** and his wonderful band **Spiritual Unity** break out of the summer festival circuit.

Kawachiya has also been working with **Asian pop and rock** musicians, a combination that is looking almost like a trend. Young music fans,

A THUMBNAIL GUIDE TO JAPANESE CLASSICAL MUSIC

. . . .

Gagaku court music, established some 1200 years ago, is the oldest surviving music in Japan. It is now mainly preserved at the Imperial Court and a few temples. There are four main genres: *kangen* (instrumental ensembles), *bugaku* (dance music), and songs and ritual music for *shintô* ceremonies. There are nearly twenty instruments used in gagaku, ranging from *shô* (the Japanese equivalent of the Chinese sheng, or reed-pipe mouth organ) to drums, gongs, flutes and chimes. Except for kangen, most of the music is monophonic. Sometimes it sounds like cats being tortured, sometimes it is melodic and meditative.

Of the two main theatrical forms, *noh* is very much high art, said to be the ultimate synthesis of literature, theatre, dancing and music, while **kabuki** is more energetic and popular. Noh began over six hundred years ago and was particularly popular among the samurai. The music consists of solo and unison singing by male actors and chorus with an ensemble of four instruments – flute and drums. The music and drama are highly stylized and ritualistic, based on simple materials and a slow dramatic form. While noh is aristocratic, kabuki is a more popular folk form. A little over two hundred years old, it developed in the Edo period and mixes dancing and melodrama, accompanied by ensembles of flute, drums and shamisen.

These musical genres are very compartmentalized in Japan and the classical forms have had very little influence on popular folk traditions or on contemporary popular music.

The most important classical **instruments** are the *shakuhachi*, a bamboo flute with a very beautiful ethereal quality; the *koto*, a large 13-stringed zither related to the Chinese *zheng* and the Korean *kayagum;* and the *biwa*, or lute.

perhaps looking for something different, have been turning increasingly to Asian pop music, particularly Indonesian dangdut and Hong Kong balladeers, and with the strength of the Japanese recording industry, coproductions are burgeoning. **Makoto Kubota**, for example, has been very busy producing Indonesians like Sundanese singer Detty Kurnia and dancefloor youngster Mellyana, and remixing CDs of Sumatran Elli Kasim.

His biggest success though, has been Singaporean **Dick Lee**, with his "Don't forget

your Asian roots" message, catchy lyrics and easily accessible music. Famous for songs like "Fried Rice Paradise", Lee embraces an eclectic range of Asian musical styles and, despite his years, enjoys a large following from young Asian audiences.

Says producer Kubota, "I have a lot of fun, mixing east and west, east and east, or whatever. It's like alchemy. But it has to be an Asian thing. I want to make Asian pop music into a mix, in the same way that rock'n'roll or R&B came about."

Big in Japan: Singapore singer Dick Lee and his band

DISCOGRAPHY

Recordings from Japan, Okinawa, Indonesia, Thailand, Korea and elsewhere can be ordered from Paul Fisher at The Far Side Music Company, 205 Sun City Hikawadai, 4-40-10 Hikawadai, Nerima-ku, Tokyo T179, Japan (☎ and fax: 813/3936 9464).

TRADITIONAL MUSIC

Ⓒ **Ono Gagaku Kaï** *Japan: Gagaku* (Ocora, France). One of the oldest musical forms in the world, gagaku is an acquired taste. The music is slow and ritualistic. Excellent recording, nonetheless.

Ⓒ **Japanese Koto Consort** *Japanese Koto Consort* (Lyrichord, US). Fine recordings of the stately Japanese plucked zither and shamisen banjo with shakuhachi flute.

Ⓒ **Kohachiro Miyata** *Shakuhachi – The Japanese Flute* (Elektra Nonesuch, US). One of the most important solo instruments in Japanese traditional music. The music has an abstract meditative quality.

ENKA

Ⓒ **Misora Hibari** *Greatest Hits* (Nippon Columbia, Japan). It's either this or the 20-volume CD set, since we're talking about the greatest Japanese popular singer of the twentieth century.

Contains a fair sample of Hibari-chan's astonishing output, including the tearjerking "Kanashii Saké".

Ⓒ **Miyako Harumi** *Greatest Hits* (Nippon Columbia, Japan). Japan's number-two enka singer has a harder vocal attack than Hibari, with a trademark growl. This collection features her famous tune, "Sayonara".

CONTEMPORARY

Ⓒ **Haruomi Hosono** *Tropical Dandy, Omni Sight Seeing* and *Tale of the Genji* (Epic-Sony, Japan). If you can find it, *Tropical Dandy* is one of Hosono's earliest solo efforts; *Omni* sees Hosono on a trip with various World Musics (eg Amina/Arabic) and Japanese folk singing. *Genji* is a superb classically inspired soundtrack for the cartoon version of the Japanese classic tale.

Ⓒ **Takio Ito** *Takio* (CBS-Sony, Japan) and *Takio Spirit* (FDX, Japan). The enfant terrible of the min'yo world, Ito's powerful voice dominates as does the virtuoso shamisen playing of Shinichi Kinoshita. *Takio Spirit* offers a better sound mix than the first release, *Takio*, and a more powerful, better balanced band, Tryin' Times.

Ⓒ **Kikusuimaru Kawachiya** *Happy* (Rackyo/Pony Canyon, Japan). Mercurial kawachi ondo singer Kawachiya raps away on this unusual mix of standards plus his TV CM hit "Kakin Ondo" and a splendid cover of Kina's "Hana". Reggae, dang-dut and hip-hop also make appearances as does Singaporean Dick Lee, who produced "Hana".

⚆ **Kikusimaru Kawachiya and Brave Combo** *Ondo Saves the World* (Teledisc, Japan). The first in an exciting new series in which leading Japanese folk musicians team up with artists round the world. Here Kawachiya mixes it with Texans Brave Combo – and to stunning effect.

⚆ **Orquesta De La Luz** *De La Luz* (BMG/Victor, Japan). Close your eyes and you won't believe that this outstanding Latin band is Japanese. Contains the American smash hit "Salsa caliente del Japón", a song now covered by several Latin singers.

⚆ **Tadamaru Sakuragawa** *Ullambana* (Wave, Japan). Debut album from "musical anarchist" and goshu ondo singer Tademaru, set to the wondrous backing band Spiritual Unity which features electric guitar played shamisen-style.

⚆ **Sandii and The Sunsetz** *One Love* and *Rhythm Chemistry* (Toshiba/EMI, Japan) and *Airmata* (Sony, Japan). *One Love* is a fine 80s album of reggae, dancefloor and the odd Indonesian tune. *Airmata* turns to Indonesian dangdut.

⚆ **Shang Shang Typhoon** *Shang Shang Typhoon* (Epic-Sony, Japan). There are now five SST albums but this debut release still somehow seems the freshest from perhaps the most interesting Asian band to emerge on the rock scene. To explore further, try their latest album ⚆ *Ai ga aru kara dai-jobu*, which incorporates ska and high-powered African pop.

OKINAWA

⚆ **Sadao China** *Shima Uta* (Akabana, Okinawa). Classy tradi-tional min'yo singing and a surprisingly soft sanshin playing style.
⚆ **Shoukichi Kina** *The Music Power from Okinawa* (Japan

Records, Japan/GlobeStyle, UK), *Bloodline* (Polydor, Japan), and *Rainbow Movement* (Nippon Phonogram, Japan). Kina's semi-nal first album, *Music Power,* contains "Haisai Ojisan", which caused a sensation in the late 70s. *Bloodline* includes Ry Cooder and Haruomi Hosono on selected tracks. The recent *Rainbow Movement* is quite a departure, featuring some of Japan's hippest young bands. The recent ⚆ *Peppermint Tea House* (Lunka Bop, US) is an idiosyncratic compilation.

⚆ **Nenes** *Ikaw̆u* (Akabana, Okinawa), *Ashibi* and *Dabasa* (Sony, Japan). *Ikaw̆u* was produced by Sadao China, who guided this Okinawan women's band around various World Music stations, including Greece and the Caribbean. *Ashibi*, recorded in Japan and Brazil, include Indonesian guitar licks and a version of "No Woman No Cry". The latest disc, *Dabasa*, was recorded in LA with Ry Cooder, David Lindley and David Hidalgo of Los Lobos guesting.

⚆ **Rinkenband** *Rinken Band*, *Rikka* and *Ajima* (Wave/Sony, Japan). *Rinken Band* is an early 1990s "best of" collection, introducing the blend of katcharsee dance songs, ei-sa festival music, bright pop tunes and the haunting voice of Tomoko Uehara. *Rikka* is a mini-CD produced by Hijaz Mustapha and featuring several 3 Mustapha 3 luminaries. *Ajima*, pick of their recent releases, is a fusion with Indonesian music.

⚆ **Rinsho Katagaru** *Rinsho Katagaru* (Marufuku/Victor, Okinawa). One of the great postwar Okinawan singer/ sanshin players, veteran Katagaru doesn't sing a dud on this unmissable collection of straight Okinwan min'yo. A personal favourite.

⚆ **Various** *Shichigwachi-Eisa* (Marufuku, Okinawa). Massive drum ensembles, sanshins and singers, chorus singers, dancers and whistlers are all featured on this wonderful ei-sa festival compilation.

EASTERN BARBARIANS

THE ANCIENT SOUNDS OF KOREA

Korea, the "land of morning calm", has a rich musical history that can be traced back some five thousand years. The books of ancient China, such as The Legend of the Eastern Barbarians, described a people who enjoyed lavish musical festivities. And so it continues, according to Hideo Kawakami and Paul Fisher.

Modern research into the culture of the three ancient Korean kingdoms of Silla, Paekche and Koguryo indicates that many styles of court and folk music had already evolved to something like their present-day form even before the unification of Korea under the Shilla kingdom in the seventh century. Subsequently, the greatest period of cultural and musical development was during the reign of King Sejong (1418–50), himself a musicologist

and composer, when the Korean alphabet was created and an advanced form of musical notation developed. Although there were close contacts in this era with China, from where many Korean instruments developed, Korean music has an identity distinct from Chinese or Japanese music and it retains a pervasive triple metre not found in the neighbouring countries.

It is thought that the lively folk traditions of *nongak* (farmers' music), *samulnori* drumming and the ritual shamanistic music, all of which are still performed, go back to agricultural and religious festivities described in the Chinese annals. In short, Korean folk and classical music has one of the world's most ancient ancestries.

Today, the National Classical Music Institute is active in promoting young musicians to carry on these traditions. The state views its traditional culture in a serious, if perhaps also stultifying way, and recognizes its leading craftspersons, artists and musicians as "living national treasures".

CLASSICAL MUSIC

Korean classical traditions are undeniably ancient, though it is impossible to say that any particular piece was created at any specific date. The repertoire has evolved and developed over centuries. In fact, the best way to get a grasp on the slow, formalized style of the classical music ensembles is to think of the music as the aural equivalent of an oriental garden, with the juxtaposition of different sounds and textures and the ornamentation of melodic phrases coming together in an almost organic way.

The distinguished *kayagum* (zither) player **Hwang Byung-ki** expounded on this theme: "The pieces have the beauty of ages, like old and grand trees. There is no feeling of structure or climax, it is like the placing of rocks or trees. What you hear in this music is a natural rather than artificial beauty. What is essential when playing a melody on the kayagum is the vibrato and the microtonal shadings on the notes. If a melody makes a leap down you can think of it like a waterfall, and the bottom note needs to vibrate in the way that water bubbles at the bottom of a waterfall. This is what gives Korean music its special character."

In Seoul there are regular performances of classical and folk music at the National Classical Music Institute. However, while these are easily accessible and present a digestible selection of folk and classical pieces, by far the best occasions to catch the ceremonial music are at the ritual performances twice a year in spring and autumn at the **Confucian Shrine** (on the campus of the Songgyun'gwan University) and once a year on the first Sunday in May at the **Ancestral Shrine** (Chongmyo) in downtown Seoul.

The music for both ceremonies is over five hundred years old. The large orchestra of flutes and oboes and bronze and stone chimes is set out in the court and terrace of the temples. The frames of the chimes are richly decorated with colourful dragons and birds, and the costumes of the dancers and musicians are equally bold and bright. There are no other ancient court ensembles like these playing anywhere in the

Ensemble playing at Ancestors Temple in Seoul

world and the music certainly has a mysterious, timeless quality. The pieces are concluded by striking a wooden tiger three times and then scraping the beater along its serrated back.

Traditionally, other court music was played for banquets, with a wide assortment of string, wind and percussion instruments. These pieces are now performed as concert repertoire. There are various types of vocal music: *kagok*, accompanied by a chamber ensemble; and *sijo* and *kasa*, which are usually accompanied by the hourglass drum and perhaps a flute.

SAMULNORI AND FOLK MUSIC

The most exuberant and widely known Korean music is the **samulnori**, played on drums and gongs by a quartet of musicians. Its repertoire comes from rural farmers' dances, which are performed wearing spectacular hats with long ribbons swirling into complex shapes with the movements of the head. Samulnori ensembles also perform some of the shamanistic music of rural Korea. They have toured quite widely in the west and groups have collaborated with jazz musicians Bill Laswell and Jamaladeen Tacuma. The energy and dynamism of the performances are thrilling.

The spectacle that is samulnori

The **kayagum** also plays an important part in the folk repertoire, providing the accompaniment to vocal music in *kayagum pyongch'ang* and playing the improvised solos in *kayagum sanjo*, accompanied by *changgo*, the hourglass drum. These *sanjo* instrumental suites are also played on the *taegum*, the wooden flute, once again to the rhythmic patterns of the changgo.

The **vocal forms** of folk music are perhaps harder for outsiders to penetrate, and none more so than **p'ansouri**, the operatic singing of dramatic songs by a solo voice accompanied by a drum. A complete performance can last from four to eight hours, with a fan and a handkerchief the only props. Among current p'ansori performers, Kim Sohi has been designated a "living national treasure".

PONCHAK ROCK

Korea may be a country with one of the most remarkable musical cultures in Asia, but walking the streets of downtown Seoul it's a well-kept secret. The country has developed economically at a staggering pace, but in terms of popular music there is nothing to match the remarkable contemporary sounds of Indonesia, Okinawa or Japan.

Korea remains the last divided nation in the world, cut in half by the 38th parallel. The music of North Korea is still something of a mystery outside political propaganda and occasional folk music. And the popular music of the south betrays the continued American presence in the country since the cessation of hostilities in 1953, along with the respectable conformity induced by the military government.

But central to postwar Korean cultural thinking has been a statement of identity, to counter the 36 years of Japanese occupation until 1945. During those years Korean language, history and culture were severely attacked and the popular music legacy was **torotto**, the sentimental Korean equivalent of Japanese enka.

Leading the movement in popular music to create a distinctive Korean style are **Kim Su-chol** and **Lee Sun-hee**. Also active in the classical field, Kim Su-chol has been a prominent singer-songwriter over the last decade, producing a stream of hits with titles such as "A Handful of Flowers that Missed Their Bloom". His experimental work was chosen to be the official music of the 1988

Olympics, which enhanced his reputation at home and abroad. He has consciously tried to bring indigenous Korean melodies and rhythms (based on the typical triple metre) into his work and has used Korean percussion instruments, kayagum and *komun'go* (small six-stringed kayagum) alongside western instruments and synthesizers.

Lee Sun-hee took the Grand Prix at the First Kanpyon Song Festival in 1984 and, despite her persona of the chaste girl-next-door, has brought issues of real importance into her songs. Typically these often refer back to the period of Japanese occupation, as in her 1992 album, featuring songs recounting the misery of women forced to work in camps as prostitutes under the occupation – currently a significant political issue between Korea and Japan.

Lee Mi-ja has rarely been out of the Korean charts since 1960, when she released a song called "Tombaek" (Winter Oak Maiden). She is so highly regarded as the archetypal voice of the Korean spirit that when the influential *Korea Daily* published a special feature on New Year's Day 1985, entitled "The hundred people who have shaped the Republic of Korea", she was the sole representative of the entertainment world. What she performs is a music that Koreans call **ponchak rock**, a Korean combination of sentimental song and danceable beat.

Another, younger ponchak rock musician is **Cho Yong-pil**, a squeaky clean teen idol, guaranteed to favour a cup of hot ginseng tea over anything steamier. His relentlessly banal hits, glutinous versions of traditional Korean songs, highlight the problems popular musicians run into when they try to synthesize western and traditional styles. Korean melodies are typically slowly paced and rhythmically flexible, whereas rock is up-tempo with a steady beat. The essence of Korean traditional music lies in the subtle variations and microtonal shadings – not a rock characteristic.

In short, there is a basic incompatibility between Korean traditional music and the international language of western pop and rock. Yet those who have attempted to bridge the divide in their various ways are among the most interesting musicians in a bland and western-dominated scene.

MINJUNG

In the 1970s and '80s Korean students led **protests** against the military regime, demanding a return to democracy. The riots culminated in an insurrection in Kwangju in 1980 which was savagely repressed with about 190 people killed. Protests continued sporadically throughout the 80s, with hopes for a sustained peace only coming with the election of the new civilian president, Kim Young-sam, in December 1992.

Hand in hand with the student protests was an art movement called **minjung**, which criticized not only the Korean government but the American presence that was seen to be supporting it.

While the students were all in favour of indigenous Korean traditions, they chose not the fine art or music styles supported by the government, but looked instead towards the shamanistic culture of the rural dispossessed. Minjung art consisted of bold prints, often bearing agit-prop messages about re-unification with the north, while minjung music took the form of popular songs for community singing at student demonstrations. The government strongly disapproved of the minjung movement, condemning the urge for re-unification as communist propaganda.

There was one minjung singer, **Kim Min-gi**, who wrote some fine songs and had some major successes beyond the agit-prop market. However, with the return to civilian rule it seems likely that the minjung movement has now run its course.

ROCK, RAP AND FUSION

Rock bands started to spring up on the student campuses of Korea in the 1970s, basically following American models. The latter half of the 80s was a golden age for heavy metal bands such as **Sanulim**, **Sinawe** and **Baekdoosan**.

As in the west, the 1990s have seen the rise of house and dance music. Korea's most successful exponents are **Sotaeji-wa-idol**, a three-piece rap group with a passionate following. They are rare in Korea in expressing life's frus-trations in their songs, though, unlike minjung bands, they don't have a particular political motive.

Musically, a perhaps more fruitful direction is pursued by the rock-fusion group, **015B** (Kong-il-O-B), fronted by the brothers Chung Ho-il and Chung Sok-won. Their music is simple and largely acoustic, with a Korean poetry in its melodies. They emerged at the end of the 1980s and have been in the charts most of the time since, notably with their last album, "Love of New Generations".

DISCOGRAPHY

TRADITIONAL

⊙ **Hwang Byung-ki** *Kayagurn masterpieces* (Seoul Records, Korea). A fine introduction to kayagum zither playing, including pieces from the modern and traditional repertoire.

⊙ **Various** *Samulnori: Record of Changes* (CMP, Germany). Samulnori is best witnessed live, though drumming fans might go for it on disc.

⊙ **Seoul Ensemble of Traditional Music** *Korea* (World Network, Germany). This excellent cross section of classical Korean music for various traditional instrument ensembles is the best introduction to traditional Korean music.

⊙ **Various** *Korean Traditional Music Vol 1* (SKC, Korea). Highlights from the Korean court tradition. Music for the Ancestral and Confucian shrines, plus ensemble music and songs. The sound is strange at first, but captivating.

⊙ **Various** *Korean Traditional Music Vol 2* (SKC, Korea). A similar but less accessible compilation from the folk repertoire. Includes kayagum sanjo, p'ansouri and samulnori.

⊙ **Various** *Music of the Kayagum* (JVC World, Japan). The refined art of kayagum zither playing, performed by Soung Gumnyon and Shi Sounja.

CONTEMPORARY

⊙ **Kim Su-chol** *Sorrow, Human Life, Living & Death* (Seoul Records, Korea). Contemporary compositions making use of traditional percussion and folk instruments.

⊙ **Lee Mi-ja** *30 Years of her Songs* (Jigu Records, Korea). An impassioned live performance at the Sejong Cultural Centre in Seoul.

⊙ **Lee Sun-hee** *Where the Love Falls* (Seoul Records, Korea). A taste of one of Korea's new voices.

⊙ **Sinawe** *Sinawe Toy's* (Factory Records, Japan). Korea's foremost heavy metal band making their international debut.

⊙ **015B** *Love of New Generations* (Seoul Records, Korea). Korea's best new fusion band offer some hope for the future.

THE CARIBBEAN

Viewed from a global perspective, the world's most vibrant and fruitful musical regions are those where different nationalities, cultures and traditions are juxtaposed and combined. Richness comes from diversity rather than purity and nowhere makes this point clearer than the Caribbean. The many musical styles that have been propagated in these island cultures are among the most dynamic and influential in the world, and their artists – names like Mighty Sparrow, Kassav, Celia Cruz, Ruben Blades, Juan Luís Guerra, and the late, great Bob Marley – have a truly global following.

The roots of modern Caribbean music date from the islands' colonization by Europeans. The culture of the indigenous inhabitants was comprehensively destroyed by the colonizers, leaving, in the musical sphere, just a couple of native percussion instruments – the maracas (shakers) and guiro (scraper) – which crop up frequently in Caribbean bands. The Europeans brought with them their own particular musical instruments and styles and, crucial to subsequent development, imported slaves from Africa. So the basic musical ingredients of today's styles are a fusion of African and colonial sounds.

Essentially, then, the islands' diversity of musical forms is based on a combination of rhythmic elements derived from Africa and melodies and verse forms from Europe. This applies to calypso in Trinidad, the biguine and cadence in Martinique and Guadaloupe, plena in Puerto Rico, merengue in the Dominican Republic and the slower méringue in Haiti, mento and reggae in Jamaica, and son and many more in Cuba. These various styles comprise different ingredients depending on the colonial power – Spanish, Portugese, French, British or sometimes a combination – and the region of Africa from which the slaves were drawn. Alongside the music, syncretic religions grew out of the African cults brought by the slaves and the European Catholicism imposed by the colonizers. Afro-Cuban Santería is the best known of these, but it has its equivalents on most of the Caribbean islands and the percussive rhythms of these cults and their deities are a potent force behind the region's music.

As an expression of island cultures, the Caribbean musical styles developed along relatively independent lines, grafting on new influences and sprouting distinctive shoots according to their own particular historical circumstances. In Jamaica, for instance, the African-based percussion styles were repressed by the British and are far less apparent than on nearby Cuba or Haiti – the most "African" islands of them all. By contrast, in the Dominican Republic merengue was given deliberate and political promotion in the postwar years by the dictator Rafael Trujillo, who saw in it a nationalist symbol in tune with his humble roots.

But the Caribbean is also a region of cross-fertilization and change. The music might have started out as a product of African and European roots on individual islands, but the soil has been continually mixed and enriched by further transplants from within the Caribbean and beyond. Around 1800, during the Haitian revolution, thousands of refugees fled to Cuba; after the abolition of slavery many colonial governments invited Asians from India and China to work on the land; people left their islands to settle in Europe or America – and returned with more cultural baggage; the French colonial ties between Haiti and the French Antilles have made zouk from Martinique and Guadaloupe a powerful force in Haiti; and other contacts have been forged between Caribbean and contemporary African bands. As well as all this, the more recent influences of jazz, rock and other international styles have been brought by radio, disc and cassette.

The western world has long been interested in the hothouse musical world of the Caribbean. In calypso and reggae it has proved its capacity for satire and social protest, but it is first and foremost good-time music for dancing and partying. More recently, with the growth of interest in roots and current popularity of dance music, salsa – the bottom-wiggling, pelvic-

10

thrusting development of Cuban son – has become an international force. Meanwhile soca, the party offshoot of calypso, and zouk, the exuberant music of Guadeloupe and Martinique, are not far behind, having taken the dancefloors of Paris, London and New York. And merengue, from the backwaters of the Dominican Republic, has recently propelled itself to the top of the Latin charts through the music of Jean Luís Guerra. The power and fertility of the Caribbean continues in the rhythm and in the change.

THE CARIBBEAN ✈ GLOSSARY

Bajan Barbadian.

Biguine Martiniquan dance music, popular in the 1920s.

Cadence Antillean pop music, popular from the 1940s on.

Calypso Traditional form of song and comment in Trinidad.

Campesino Peasant or rural.

Chachahá Mid-tempo Cuban dance popular in the 1940s and 50s.

Changó Afro-Cuban deity.

Changui Form of son from eastern Cuba.

Charanga Cuban ensemble with distinctive mix of violins and flute.

Chouval bwa Carnival music from Martinique.

Clave Repeated rhythmic pattern, played on the claves (wooden sticks), which underlies and structures Cuban music.

Compas Haitian pop music.

Conjunto Cuban or salsa band, consisting of brass, congas, bongó, bass and piano.

Cuatro Small Puerto Rican folk guitar, with four strings arranged in four courses.

Danzón European-style Cuban dance, also very popular in Mexico.

Deejay (DJ) Jamaican DJ music is a talk-over, rapping style (toasting), often using a dub backing track.

Dub Jamaican (reggae) studio remix technique characterized by inventive use of track muting, delay/reverb and sound effects.

Gwo ka Drum- and voice-based carnival music from Guadaloupe.

Kaiso West African shout of encouragement used in Trinidadian calypso; also refers to early calypso with a line-up similar to that of New Orleans jazz bands.

Mambo Up-tempo Latin dance music that originated in Cuba and was developed by New York big bands.

Maracas Pair of gourd rattles of indigenous Caribbean origin.

Mento Calypso-influenced Jamaican roots music.

Merengue Dance music originating in the Dominican Republic.

Montuno The call-and-response section of a song.

Pans Drums in a steelband.

Ragga (Ragamuffin) Dancehall reggae of the 1980s and 90s with rap-style DJs, often characterized by "slack" or obscene lyrics.

Ra-ra Haitian carnival music.

Rastafarianism Jamaican millenarian religious sect.

Rock steady Jamaican music of the "rude'" boys – a precursor to reggae in the 1960s.

Rumba Afro-Cuban dance music for percussion and voices.

Salsa Latin dance music developed from the Cuban son; singers, players and dancers are known as *salseros*.

Santería Afro-Cuban religion.

Ska Primarily instrumental Jamaican music, with jazz and R&B influences.

Soca Modern dance-led fusion of soul and calypso.

Son The main dance and song form of Cuba – and the root of salsa; a *sonero* is the improvising lead singer.

Tambora Double-headed drum used in traditional merengue bands.

Timbales Mid-size Afro-Cuban drums played with sticks.

Tres Small Cuban guitar with three sets of double strings.

Trova Vieja Trova is the old Cuban song tradition; Nueva Trova, the Cuban branch of the Latin New Song movement.

Voodoo Afro-Haitian religion.

Zouk Modern dance music from the French Antilles.

¡QUE RICO BAILO YO!

"HOW WELL I DANCE!": THE CUBAN MUSIC SCENE

Jan Fairley explores Cuban riches – rumba, mambo and son, the collective roots of salsa – and explores an island music industry shaped by revolution.

The title of a song by Orquesta Ritmo Oriental pretty much sums up the Cuban music scene – "¡Que rico bailo yo!" – "How well I dance!" For this is the island that gave the world the rumba, the mambo, the chachachá, the danzón and the habanera: dances that have travelled all over the new world, the old world, and even gone back to their roots in Africa thanks to the strong influence of Cuban music on West African bands. Forget sugar, cigars and rum – music is Cuba's greatest export. This island is one of the musical powerhouses of the world.

You've only got to go to Havana's outdoor dancehall, the Tropical (known locally as the "salon rosada" because of its pink-washed walls), and join the thousands of mostly black Cuban teenagers swivelling hips and bottoms to bands like Orquesta Revé to feel the vitality and driving physicality inherent in the island's music. For all the teasing sexuality between musicians and audience (and audience and audience), however, this is never just vapid dance music. In Cuba the words of many songs enter everyday currency precisely because they capture (often with a mocking sense of irony) the very situations people are living through. A few years back Los Van Van's "¡L'Habana no aguanta más!" (Havana Can Take No More) commented on the shortage of housing in the capital, while more recently Orquesta Revé's "El ron pa'despué" (Save The Rum For Later) exploited a double meaning – referring to a chronic shortage of beer while rum remained plentiful, and to a classic seduction technique. Song lyrics, like jokes, can provide a more acute insight than newspapers into what Cuban people are thinking.

This immediate topicality of Cuban music, its inseparability from daily life, goes right back to its African roots, to a culture of survival, resistance and ritual in the sugar cane plantations. Nowhere in the Caribbean is the African influence on music so pronounced – a fact due, as much as anything, to the island's

deeply conservative history prior to the revolution of 1959. African slaves were imported to Cuba long after the slave trade was illegal elsewhere; the island was one of the last in the Americas to liberate itself from the Spanish; and the feudal plantation economy endured right up until the revolution.

AFRICAN ROOTS

Little survives of pre-Hispanic Cuban music save the maracas and the adoption of the name of one of the tribes, Siboney, by the recording studio in Santiago de Cuba. Indian culture was effectively obliterated by the **Spanish colonization**, which started in 1511, and it was not until the mid-eighteenth century, with a major immigration of slaves to work in the sugar plantations, that another culture took its place.

Cuban music at the crossroads

The slaves came mostly from the West African coast – Nigeria, Cameroon, Benin and Congo – and by the 1840s they constituted nearly half the population. They preserved their identity in associations called *cabildos*, from which emerged the four main Afro-Cuban religions of Lucumi, Abakua, Congo and Arare. **Santería**, the dominant Afro-Cuban religion today, drew on various of these, revering a panoply of African deities or *orishas*, which after emancipation were fused with Catholic saints to give them a veneer of respectability.

In Cuba today a fair section of the population maintains a faith based on Santería and you can see dances and music performed in honour of the various orishas. Each orisha has its own colour:

Changó, the spirit of war and fire (associated with Santa Barbara) has red, and Oshún, the goddess of love and water (twinned with the Virgen de las Caridad del Cobre, the patron saint of Cuba) has yellow. As well as a colour and an element, each has his or her own characteristic set of rhythms or toques played by the hourglass-shaped *batá* drums and *shekere* rattles that provide the music for religious rituals.

Rumba band Los Muñequitos de Matanzas

These complex rhythms are the heartbeat of Cuban music, working away beneath the Latin layers on top. The batás and shekere of the ceremonies crop up regularly in contemporary Cuban bands, and the physical and emotional intensity of musical performance in Cuba emanates in part from the power and potency of African ritual and its participatory nature. Celina González, for example, Cuba's "Queen of Country Music", pays homage to Changó in her wonderful song "Santa Barbara" (brilliantly covered by the queen of New York salsa, Cuban exile Celia Cruz). The links between Afro-Cuban religions like Santería and music-making remain close.

essentially secular and divides into three traditional types: the *yambú*, the *guaguancó* and the *columbia*, each with its own dance. The yambú is a slow dance for couples, popular with older people, the guaguancó a faster, modern one; in both the couple dance provocatively without touching. The columbia is a solo male dance and the fastest and most acrobatic of the three.

Accompanying these dances are interlocking cross rhythms from a whole range of percussion instruments: the *claves* (a pair of sticks struck against one another, which always start the rumba by playing the pattern called "the clave" – which means "key", in the sense of a key to a code – to which all the other rhythms relate); the *cata* or *guagua* (a wooden tube played with sticks); the *maruga* (an iron shaker); conga drums of various pitches; and wooden packing-cases, dating from the days when drums were unobtainable. For religious occasions, batà drums (three double-skinned drums of Yoruba origin) are added.

Santa Barbara (aka Que Viva Changó)

¡Que viva Changó!	Long live Changó!
¡Que viva Changó Señores!	Long live Changó, gentlemen!
Santa Barbara Bendita	Blessed Santa Barbara,
para ti surge mi vida	My life springs forth
y con emoción se inspira	Inspired with emotion
ante tu imagen bonita.	in front of your beautiful image.
¡Que viva Changó!	Long live Changó!
¡Que viva Changó Señores!	Long live Changó, gentlemen!

(Chorus and opening verse only) **Celina González**

RUMBA

Forget the glitzy ballroom-dancing image of **rumba**. The genuine article, heard in Cuba itself, is pure Afro-Cuban music for voices and percussion. Rumba music has its roots in religious ritual but the modern repertoire is

The description of the shape of rumba holds true for most Afro-Cuban music. A long lyrical vocal melody sung by a soloist or a duet unfolds above the muttering drums, then suddenly, on a cue from the leader, the rhythm tightens up, the chorus joins in, and the call and response section steams off, the *quinto* (lead drum) improvising wildly under the singer's *inspiraciones*. This was to become the famous *montuno* section of son montuno and salsa, when the band really gets going and the dancing starts to heat up.

Top rumba is to be heard today in Havana and notably in Matanzas, on Cuba's north coast, where slaves of Yoruba, Calabar and Congo descent were brought. The town's famous rumba band, **Los Muñequitos de Matanzas**, have been going for some forty years, their members now embracing three generations.

DANZÓN

While the rumba in Matanzas represents the essential Afro-Cuban tradition, just a short walk away from the Casa de la Trova, where the Muñequitos perform, you can hear **danzón**, one of the most European styles of traditional Cuban music. Here on the main square, every Saturday night, in a once opulent, now shabby, mirror-lined ballroom, predominantly elderly couples enact their sedate and dignified dances. The typical *orquesta*, comprising cornets, saxophones and clarinets, plus percussion, plays melodies descended from the European contradanzas. The majority of today's clientele are black and creole, but the atmosphere couldn't be further removed from the rumba down the road. This is music adopted from the colonial masters by domestic servants, rather than the music of rural labourers, and its petty-bourgeois flavour is about as "respectable" as Cuban music gets.

Listen carefully, though, and sometimes you'll hear that insistent, tell-tale percussion break through from under the European dances, just to remind you where you are. In part, this is a legacy of the 1930s, when **Arcaño y sus Maravillos** introduced a final *montuno* section and incorporated elements from son, a style that caught on like wildfire, replacing danzón as the most popular dance.

THE SOUND OF SON

Son is the predominant musical force in Cuban song and dance and the most influential element in popular Latin dance music. It originated in Oriente province at the eastern end of the island but has now become universal. It takes many forms, from simple, rustic bands to the brassy arrangements of New York salsa, a style which it underpins.

In the last century, **Oriente** boasted a very mixed population and a correspondingly rich musical culture. Thousands of refugees, black and white, had arrived around 1800 in flight from Haiti's revolutionary wars; as francophone immigrants, they brought new elements to Cuba's African and Spanish mix. Son itself was forged in the 1880s, by black and mulatto musicians, during the struggle for the abolition of slavery. Its fusion of African and Spanish elements is a real microcosm of Cuba's history and its constant ability to absorb and adapt ensures its continued popularity.

As in the rumba, the clave rhythm is central, whether or not it is actually played by anyone, and the percussion – bongó, maracas and *guiro* – adds a complex improvisatory rhythmic counterpoint. On top of this "African" base, the Latin layer provides harmonic and melodic elements. A combination of guitars will include the Cuban *tres* (so-called for its triple sets of double strings), plus a plucked bass. The lyrics, originally improvised, follow the old Spanish décima verse form with rhymed octosyllabic lines.

In Baracoa, at the southern tip of the island, **Kiriba y Nengon**, a band of *aficionados* ("enthusiasts" – they all have full-time day jobs), play local variants of son. A straight Spanish-African blend, they are possibly the closest to an early rural ensemble still in existence. As well as bongó, guiro and tres, they play the *marimbula*, a primitive bass made out of a wooden box with five metal keys riveted to the front and tuned to various pitches – a large Caribbean descendent of the African thumb piano.

Son reached Havana from Oriente through the forces liberating the island from slavery. A great turning point was the development of the **Sexteto Habanero**, a group that evolved from the **Trio Oriental**, who came to Havana in the early years of this century. By 1920 they had established what was to become the classic *sexteto* format: tres, guitar, bongó, string bass and a pair of vocalists who also played claves and maracas. In the late 1920s, with the addition of a cornet, the sexteto became a *septeto* – and the son swung!

Part of the grass-roots appeal of son came from the bongo players' adoption of rhythmic elements from various of the island's African sects and cults. At the same time, son was brought into the repertoire of the society danzón orchestras and the music was diffused through the higher levels of Cuban society. From 1912

CELINA GONZÁLEZ

••••••••••••••••••••••

With its layers of pulsating African percussion and Latin melodies on guitar and tres there's no mistaking Cuban country music for its American namesake. **Musica campesina** is a kind of roots salsa and its queen is **Celina González**. Her music ranges from just voice, percussion and guitar, to more of a big-band sound with punchy brass and strings. But whatever the line-up, her style is rooted in the music of the Cuban countryside – various types of son as performed by rural bands fusing Afro-Cuban rhythmic patterns and Spanish verse forms and melodies.

Celina González was born in 1928 in Jovellanos, a small town in Matanzas province, east of Havana. This region is at the heart of the old sugar plantations where rural traditions have remained the strongest – and with them the African religious and musical elements brought by the slaves. When young, Celina moved to Santiago de Cuba at the eastern tip of the island, another powerhouse of Cuban music. There, as a sixteen-year-old, she met **Reutilio Dominguez**, who became her singing partner and husband – a collaboration that lasted until Reutilio's death in 1971.

Before the revolution Celina and Reutilio made a name for themselves performing with the basic resources of a guitar, bongó and powerful vocal harmony. "We had a radio programme in Santiago," Celina recalls of the time, "where we used to sing songs denouncing the government and praising the Cuban people, and this caused us a lot of problems. But we were lucky to get a contract with Saurito, one of our most famous radio stations in Havana, and since then I've worked regularly on radio and TV." Celina has worked, too, with a huge range of Cuban musicians, singing as easily with a full orchestra as with a small acoustic group.

Celina is a staunch supporter of the Cuban revolution and continues to live in a suburb of Havana. In her house is a large statue – almost an altar, decorated with fairy lights and plastic flowers – of Santa Barbara, the saint for whom she wrote her first and most famous song. Her early songs were in fact largely religious, reflecting her interest and belief in Santería; despite being white herself, the Afro-Cuban religion had been part of her upbringing. The Santa Barbara song expresses devotion to the Catholic saint and at the same time is a song for the Yoruba god Changó, mirroring the way the two deities are twinned in the Santería pantheon. Beneath it runs a pulsating dance rhythm.

In the 1970s, after the death of her husband, their son Reutilio Junior joined Celina as her singing partner, and, with the band **Campo Alegre**, helped update the music by incorporating the trumpet, bass, congas and marimba from the urban septetos of Havana. Although for top artists in Cuba the music business is often frustrating – the opportunities to release records can be few – Celina has done all right. Her kind of music was looked down on and discriminated against before the revolution, but in the years since she has developed and revitalized its rural charm with a power that never fails to captivate urban audiences both at home and abroad. In Cuba itself every single national radio station has at least one daily programme devoted to country music, while Celina has her own daily programme on Radio Taino.

Abroad, Celina and Reutilio gained a reputation in the early 1950s, singing with Beny Moré in New York, and touring the Caribbean. The years of Cuban isolation meant a long break from the international scene but over the past decade Celina has again toured extensively outside the island, attracting huge crowds at music festivals in Latin America – she is a huge star in Colombia and Venezuela – and playing, too, in Europe and North America, where compilations of her hits have gained a new audience.

"The true folklore of Cuba" is how Celia describes the music she plays. "Even though I now incorporate modern elements, it still remains firmly rooted in the campesina tradition. Because our young people listen to a lot of foreign music, it's important for country music to grow with the times. I myself sing with the group Campo Alegre which has a lot of modern instruments in it. We have to make our music as danceable and as tasty as salsa."

American companies recorded and distributed the music of son groups like the Sexteto Habanero and **Sexteto Boloña**, but it was the advent of Cuban radio in 1922 and the regular broadcasting of live bands that consolidated its success.

The very wonderful and enduring Orquesta Ritmo Oriental

Two leading instrumentalists furthered the son sound: the trumpeter **Félix Chapotín**, who joined the Sexteto Habanero in 1927, and the blind tres player **Arsenio Rodríguez**, who added more horns, extra percussion and piano to his ensemble, which became the most influential band of the 1940s and 50s. The two musicians played together until Rodríguez moved to New York in 1951 and Chapotín took over Sexteto Habanero in Cuba. Perhaps their most significant innovation was to use tight arrangements for the horn section, in the style of American swing bands of the period.

Another Cuban bandleader, **Beny Moré**, further developed this style, moving it towards mambo (of which more on p.487). Known as the "Barbarian of Rhythm", Moré started his trailblazing band in 1953, adding Cuban drums to the regular big band line-up and using his vocal skills to move effortlessly from romantic *boleros* to punchy up-tempo grooves.

Also popular were the larger charanga bands, which expanded the instrumentation with violins and flutes. **Orquesta Aragon** set the model for this style, which is most closely associated today with **Ritmo Oriental**, a band formed in the 1950s that retains an original charanga line-up – including three violins – and still plays the "típica" Cuban sound; their wonderful 30th anniversary compilation is available on the Globestyle label.

Many other Cuban dance forms were played by the son, danzón and charanga ensembles, with the bolero (slow), chachachá (mid-tempo) and mambo (up-tempo) becoming particularly popular. In the 1940s and 50s these dances entered the repertoire of the American big bands and caught on all over the world. Chachachá – developed by band leader **Enrique Jorrín** – and mambo were immensely popular in New York, where Cuban music was proving dominant among the Hispanic communities and beginning to flirt with jazz.

Son also began to take off internationally, though it was misnamed rumba in the US. There, mixed in with mambo, the Latin rhythms of Puerto Rico, Colombia and Dominican Republic, and an injection of hi-tech instrumentation and rhythm, it was eventually to transmute into salsa (for more on which, see the article following).

The most popular themes in son **lyrics** are love and romance. Songs are invariably written by men about women and they tend to burden their subjects with all the stereotypes around – beauty, faithlessness, ungratefulness, and so on. The language often has a second, deeply sexual level, which can be extremely crude and deeply chauvinistic. Male chauvinism is actually pretty endemic to Cuba. The island is always referred to as a woman and the revolution, too, is often described in mother/lover terms.

Son to Cuban Women

From all the Cuban men worthy of a
Cuban woman
Of noble and sound spirit and of
pleasant demeanor
Music, sunlight and gaiety, contentment
and satisfaction
Cuba, its women and the son sing in my soul.

Listen! Look at my joy!
The cadence of my song and its sweet
inspiration.

Sexteto Matancero (1930s).

SON TODAY

All the best-known bands that play today in Havana and abroad have evolved from the son tradition. The **Septeto Nacional de Ignacio Piñero** was founded in 1927 but the current group was re-established in 1985 to perform classic son. **Celina González** (see box) made her reputation singing **musica campesina** – son from the rural tradition – and has successfully updated the sound. The **Orquesta Ritmo Oriental**, with a traditional flute and violin charanga line-up, play a music with elements of musica campesina, while **Orquesta Original de Manzanillo**, in turn, have imaginatively adapted the charanga sound. An excellent younger band, following the classic sexteto traditions, is **Sierra Maestra**. They remain firmly Cuban-based but tour frequently in Latin America and Europe: catch them if you can.

Elio Revé (right) gets on down

The most successful contemporary son band is **Los Van Van**, led by Juan Formell. Basically a charanga band with a strong jazz influence, they are one of the few island-based bands that have been able to record outside Cuba. The Paris-recorded "Songo" album and the rootsier "Sandunguera" illustrate the extremely complex rhythmical structures (even for the Caribbean) of contemporary Cuban salsa bands.

Irakere, led by composer-pianist Jesus "Chucho" Valdez, have moved even further into jazz and combined it with Afro-Cuban cult music. Their name is Yoruba for "forest", and refers to a region where the best African drummers lived and contests were regularly held. Their album "Misa negra" (Black Mass) is a big-band composition recreating a Yoruba ceremony – highly sophisticated concept-salsa-jazz. Many of Cuba's modern bands emphasize their African inheritance in their names and their music.

One of the most enduring Cuban bands, from whose ranks Juan Formell emerged, is **Orquesta Revé**, who perform *son-changui*. Changui is a form of countryside son from Guantánamo at the eastern end of the island, and the potency of group leader Elio Revé's music comes from the fusion of this strong regional form with urban son and the use of the batá drums from Santería ceremonies. His lyrics are imaginative, too, reflecting popular opinions on social and political issues besides the traditional themes.

As to a new generation, perhaps the future is indicated by the band whose name implies just that: **NG La Banda** (New Generation – The Band). Founded in 1988, they are currently one of Cuba's most popular groups, following their 1993 hit, "Echale limon" – literally, "Put a Lemon in it", the Cuban slang for when things go wrong. The lyrics – a witty response to the situation (when things go wrong, there's nothing you can do about it anyway), couched in uncompromising barrio slang – caught the mood of the country, and the music is as powerful as anything in the past, mixing in elements of rap and jazz, along with complex arrangements by *los metales de terror* – the horns of terror!

TROUBADOURS OLD AND NEW

As in son, the Spanish décima verse form is central to Cuba's **trova** (ballad) or **canción** (song) tradition. This remains an active part of the Cuban scene, to be heard throughout the island in *casas de la trova* (see box), though originally the *trovadores* were true troubadours, roving the island, singing and accompanying themselves on guitar.

The early songs were typically concerned with love and patriotism, often with Cuba itself personified as a woman. One of the island's most popular singers of all time was the diminutive **Sindo Garay**, from Santiago de Cuba, the creator of unforgettable boleros such as "La Bayamesa" (Girl from Bayamo), written in 1909 and still a part of the trova repertoire. The town of Bayamo was the cradle of the independence movement and the Girl in question was thus the love of all Cuban patriots. Other major figures of this early canción world included **Joseito Fernandez**, who wrote "Guantanamera" (a tribute to the women of Guantanamo and including lines from Cuba's national poet, José Martí), one of the most covered songs of all time; **Nico Saquito** from Santiago de Cuba, who composed over five

hundred songs in the trova tradition; and **Carlos Puebla**, whose quartet sang witty songs of the revolution's achievements, including such classics as "Y en eso llegó Fidel" (And Then Fidel Arrived) and "El son de la alfebetización" (The Son of Literacy).

Puebla was Cuba's only notable political singer until the **Nueva Trova** movement of the early 1970s – the one significant musical tradition to emerge on the island since the revolution. The nueva trova – "New Ballad" – had obvious links with the nueva canción (new song) composers appearing in this period throughout much of Latin America, and its lyrics replaced the old love

CASAS DE LA TROVA

T he best place to hear music in Cuba is in a **Casa de la Trova**. Most towns have at least one of these clubs, which are a communist-era update of an old Cuban institution – a place where trovas or ballads are sung by trovadores. Nowadays the performances are more diverse and often completely spontaneous, with people joining in and getting up to play whenever they feel like it. You can hear anything from a single trovador with a guitar to a traditional Cuban sexteto or septeto.

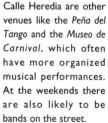

The casas range from grand old colonial buildings with courtyards and palm trees to small, impromptu performing

Saturday night at the Santiago Casa de la Trova

spaces with a few chairs off the street. In practice they are like informal clubs or bars (although often there are no drinks on offer) where musicians gather to play, people gather to listen and everybody exchanges opinions and reminiscences.

The most celebrated Casa de la Trova is in **Santiago**, on Calle Heredia, and there is music here virtually all day and night on Saturdays and Sundays. It's just one room with wide windows and doors open onto the street and a small platform at the end for the performers. The walls are lined with photographs and posters of local musicians going back the best part of a century.

Next to the "stage" is a sort of stable door leading into a back room where an old man guards the musicians' instrument cases and serves rum begrudgingly from a battered tin measuring cup: in a setting like this, those Cuban rhythms are irresistible. Further up Calle Heredia are other venues like the *Peña del Tango* and the *Museo de Carnival*, which often have more organized musical performances. At the weekends there are also likely to be bands on the street.

In **Havana** there are two Casas de la Trova, the *Cerro* (c/Panchito Gómez 265 & c/Perfecto Lacoste y Néstor Sardiñas) and the *10 de Octubre* (Calzada de Luyanó & c/Reforma y Guasabacoa). The latter is a little out of the way, in the Lujana area, but worth finding: a small local hall in a line of severely peeling colonial terraces, it possesses all the charm of old Havana, and appropriately enough features regular performances by the historic Sexteto Habanero.

There are other good Casas de la Trova in **Baracoa, Sancti Spiritus, Matanzas, Pinar del Río** and **Guanabacoa.**

Also worth checking out for concerts are the **Casas de Cultura** around the island, another revolutionary Cuban institution.

and nationalism formula with personal experience, relating the contradictions and anxieties of growing up in a revolutionary society. They are usually literate and sophisticated, belonging on much the same wavelength as contemporary Latin American poets like Neruda and Vallejo. The music drew on the French chanson style and on folk guitar traditions known in the Spanish-speaking world as *canto-autores*, a more political and philosophical version of the American and British "singer-songwriters" of the age. South American influences, especially from Brazil, sometimes creep in, too, as the musicians pay their respects to their nueva canción counterparts.

Many of the movement's musicians, the nuevos trovadores, came together at Havana's ICAIC film school, where they worked with Cuba's leading composer and guitarist, **Leo Brouwer**. Among them were **Pablo Milanés** and **Silvio Rodríguez**, arguably the most influential nueva canción singers in the Spanish-speaking world. Musically, the main ingredients are vocals and solo acoustic guitar, though both artists lead bands of varying size, their music easily adapting itself to big arrangements without losing its sense of reflection and vulnerability – a hallmark of their songs. With both composers, the Cuban experience is pre-eminent in the lyrics. Indeed, Silvio Rodríguez seems to have followed in the steps of José Martí and taken on the mantle of national poet in the eyes of his public and the Cuban press.

A new voice is that of **Carlos Varela**, currently the most popular singer in Cuba. He is a highly articulate songwriter, expressing the troubles of Cuban society and the frustrations of the island's youth, and delving, too, into global politics, commenting on the collapse of communism in Eastern Europe, for example. Political commentators often quote his song "Guillermo Tell" (William Tell), with its warning to the old generation of politicians: "William Tell, your son has grown up/And now he wants to shoot the arrow/It's his turn now to prove his valour/Using your very own bow!" Musically, Varela fluctuates between the old-style acoustic treatment of Milanés and Rodríguez and a rock (often heavy rock) backing. Despite his popularity, he remains unreleased in Cuba; his first (and, as yet, sole) album was recorded in Venezuela and issued on the New York-based Qbadisc label.

For more on nueva trova – and an interview with Silvio Rodríguez – see the nueva canción article on p.573.

MUSIC AND THE REVOLUTION

Prior to the **revolution of 1959**, Havana was a favourite nightclub and cabaret playground for American tourists evading the prohibition laws. Beneath the gloss it had some fairly ugly elements, with its mob connections, prostitution and gambling, but musically it was fertile ground as the close links with New York gave rise to superbly stylish and inventive big bands.

This tradition didn't entirely disappear with the revolution. However, the island's music business changed radically under communism, with nightclubs, radio stations and record companies being replaced by state institutions, and many of the major stars going into self-imposed exile in Florida and New York. The US economic boycott, meanwhile, meant (and means) a struggle for island-based Cuban musicians to acquire equipment and record.

Nonetheless, the Castro government's cultural policies were (and are) highly active and included great efforts to establish music as a viable profession. **Musicians** are categorized either as *aficionados* or *profesionales*; the former have daytime jobs and play music the rest of the time, while the latter draw a state salary. Currently, there are something over five hundred professional groups registered with the Ministry of Culture. Most of the younger profesionales have had Conservatoire training – a university musical education that draws on both classical and popular island traditions – and to earn their salaries they play a wide variety of styles at events throughout the island.

This has ensured that Cuban music continues to find its natural habitat in live performance – and a band's creative inspiration comes from close, regular contact with a wide public. Interaction between musicians and audience can be exceptional and a band will often be surrounded onstage by dancers from the audience: a vital inspiration for the improvisation that exists in so many different kinds of Cuban music.

On the negative side, many Cuban musicians feel restricted by the state's interference with what they do, and by the **severe shortages of equipment**. EGREM, Cuba's one and only recording company, is state-owned and has to function in an economy that has priorities over importing vinyl, tape or even paper for record sleeves. Starved of supplies and with a production policy that tries to cover all genres of island music – rural, Afro-Cuban music was revalued after the revolution – the company ensures that some interesting non-commercial music gets released but also creates terminal frustration for musicians unable to record albums as they wish. Popular albums get sold out instantly on release, the shortage of vinyl means there is no re-pressing, and with the lack of hard currency, cassette technology has not taken off, although EGREM have started releasing CDs for an overseas market. Resources in the 1990s have become so scarce that those musicians who have international careers and travel abroad are now also recording almost exclusively abroad, too.

The 1990 defection of the leading jazz musician **Arturo Sandoval**, once one of the revolution's great supporters, brought into focus the pressures on musical life in Castro's Cuba, although his motivation probably owed as much to a desire to explore projects abroad with world-class jazz players as a desire to join the large community of Cuban musicians in exile. For musicians who haven't made it on international tours, the US blockade frustrates any direct contact with Latin fusions developing in places like New York, although conversely, perhaps, it also means that Cubans continue to develop an identifiably national sound – and to experiment without total regard for commercial sales.

When Cuba really opens up, though, as it one day inevitably must, there will surely be a transformation of the music along with the economy. Till then the attitude to music in Cuba is essentially patriotic, or, as one popular classic puts it: "¡Cuba, que linda es Cuba, quien la defiende la quiere más!" (Cuba, how beautiful Cuba is, whoever defends her loves her most!).

DISCOGRAPHY

Cuban nueva trova albums are featured in the nueva canción discography on p.576. For Cuban (and especially exile-Cuban) salsa, see the salsa discography on p.494.

GENERAL COMPILATIONS

⊕ **Various** *A Carnival of Cuban Music* and *Cuban Dance Party* (both Rounder, US). These two volumes make a superb introduction to Cuban music. *Carnival* ranges from Afro-Cuban music, through some of the classic sounds of the 1940s and 50s, to contemporary bands like Irakere and Los Van Van. *Dance Party* is a similar selection with a more modern slant.
⊕ **Various** *Cuba Classics 2: Dancing with the Enemy* and *Cuba Classics 3: ¡Diablo al Infierno!* (both Luaka Bop/Warner, US). These two volumes in David Byrne's Cuban series (*Cuba Classics 1* is devoted to Silvio Rodríguez – see p.573) are fabulous selections, mixing the big names with some truly obscure bands and recordings. Volume 2 covers the "typical" Cuban sound of the 1960s and 70s; Volume 3 delves into the more eclectic 80s and 90s, with salsa, charanga, even Cuban ska.
⊕ **Various** *Cuban Gold: Que se sepa ¡Yo soy de La Habana!* (Qbadisc, US). New York-based Qbadisc have an ear to the ground in Havana and if you're interested in contemporary Cuban bands, they're the label to watch. This is a great compilation including bands such as Los Van Van and Irakere, along with much less- known names like Grupo Manguare and Orquesta Original de Manzanillo.
⊕ **Various** *Cuba Fully Charged* and *¡Sabroso!* (both Earthworks, UK). A duo of lively compilations featuring many of the best dance bands now playing in Cuba, including NG La Banda, Sierra Maestra, Irakere, Los Van Van and Orquesta Revé. *Fully Charged* is basically a son collection while *¡Sabroso!* tilts more towards salsa.
⊕ **Various** *¡Pinareño!* (Piranha, Germany). A fine collection devoted to ensembles from Pinar del Río in the west of Cuba. The opening track has an invigorating Cuban country sound and the disc continues with sones, canciónes, and the famous Grupo el Organo Pinareño, who feature a huge mechanical organ.

SON AND CHARANGA

⊕ **Dan** *Den Viejo Lazaro y otros exitos* (Qbadisc, US). One of Cuba's most popular contemporary bands, founded by Juan Carlos Alfonso from Orquesta Revé. Great dance tunes and rhythms and very funny lyrics, printed in Spanish and English in the CD booklet.
⊕ **Irakere** *Misa negra* and *Homenaje a Beny Moré* (both Messidor, Germany). Son/salsa given a contemporary jazz treatment by Cuba's most successful modern group; *Homenaje* features the fabulous "Bacalao con Pan".
⊕ **Los Van Van** *Dancing Wet* (World Pacific, US) and *Songo* (Mango, US). Two fine albums from Cuba's most successful modern son/charanga group – more rock- than jazz-influenced, compared to Irakere – and featuring knock-out piano.
⊕ **NG La Banda** *En La Calle* (Qbadisc, US). The Young Turks of Cuban dance play flat out; brilliant arrangements and virtuoso performances make up for the occasional lapse of taste.
⊕ **Orquesta Revé** *La Explosion del Momento* (Real World, UK). Led by veteran timbales player Elio Revé, this is Afro-Cuban son-changui: dance music a-go-go, quirky, rhythmic and infectious.
⊕ **Orquesta Ritmo** *Oriental Historia de la Ritmo Volumes 1 and 2* (Qbadisc, US) and *La Ritmo Oriental te esta llamando* (GlobeStyle, UK). The sharp, punchy sound of a traditional charanga band founded over thirty years ago, with violins, wooden flute, piano, bass, singers and percussion. There is little overlap between the Qbadisc and GlobeStyle albums, so, if you like what you hear, go for the lot!
⊕ **Pupy** *Pupy y su charanga* (Tumi, UK). First disc from Felix Lagaretta (aka Pupy) and his charanga band. Splendid flute, strings, percussion and piano evoke a world of clubs and dancefloors, fresh yet familiar.
⊕ **Sierra Maestra** *Son Highlights from Cuba* (Wergo, Germany). Sierra Maestra are perhaps the best contemporary son band – the true heirs of Piñeiro, fusing sensual rhythms with witty lyrics, all with a wonderful, caressing mellowness.
⊕ **Various** *Cuban Counterpoint: History of the Son Montuno* (Rounder, US). A wonderful romp through the development of son, from its rural beginnings to the popular mainstream. Includes Sextetos Habanero and Boloña, Septeto Nacional, Arsenio Rodríguez, Celia Cruz and Beny Moré.
⊕ **Various** *Septetos Cubanos/Sones de Cuba* (Corason, Mexico). Recorded in 1986 in Santiago de Cuba, Colon in Matanzas, and Havana, this is a magical double CD selection of rural son and changui.
⊕ **Various** *Cuba – El son es lo más sublime* (Aspic, France). More from the classic son bands, including some excellent tracks from the Septetos Nacional and Habanero.

THE CARIBBEAN

MUSICA CAMPESINA

ⓒ **Celina González** *Fiesta Guajira* (World Circuit, UK) and *¡Que viva Chango!* (Qbadisc, US). These two superb discs overlap somewhat. Both are drawn from Celina's 1980s albums, recorded on the Havana-based Egrem label, and show the Queen of Cuban country music – musica campesina – at her very best.

ⓒ **Various** *Cuba Musica Campesina* (Auvidis, France). Great collection of rural Cuban bands, capturing the country style in all its freshness. It even has a decent version of the most over-played Cuban song, "Guantanamera".

RUMBA

ⓒ **Los Muñequitos de Matanzas** *Rumba Caliente* (Qbadisc, US). This is classic Cuban rumba – rich in African elements, using percussion and vocals only, and brilliantly melodic. The Qbadisc release combines two Cuban albums, recorded eleven years apart, and is a better buy than *Cantar maravilloso* (GlobeStyle, UK), a quickie recorded while on tour in London.

AFRO-CUBAN CULT MUSIC

ⓒ **Sintesis** *Ancestros* (Qbadisc, US). Afro-Cuban ritual melodies given soulful modern arrangements by a great song-leader, Lazaro Ros, who closes the album with passionate solo vocals.

ⓒ **Various** *Cuba: Les Dance des Dieux. Musiques de cultes et fêtes Afro-Cubains* (Ocora, France). A good, though rather unfocused selection of ritual music from Cuba's African-based cults.

ⓒ **Various** *Afro-Cuba: A Musical Anthology* (Rounder, US). Field and studio recordings from the main Santería cults.

ⓒ **Various** *Africa in America* (Corason, Mexico). This comprehensive 3-CD set goes way beyond Cuba, exploring Afro-American music in 19 countries around the Caribbean and Central America. If the subject interests you at all, this is an absolutely essential release, full of material you will never hear elsewhere.

TROVADOR

ⓒ **Cuarteto Patria** *A una coqueta* (Corason, Mexico). Cuarteto Patria emerged in 1940 in Santiago de Cuba. A string-based band, they are improvising troubadours with immaculate pace and balance.

ⓒ **Carlos Puebla** *Carlos Puebla y sus Tradicionales* (Egrem-Artex, Canada). Puebla was the hero of Cuban revolutionary song. This anthology presents some of his most stirring material, accompanied by guitar, close harmonies and percussion.

ⓒ **Nico Saquito** *Goodbye Mr Cat* (World Circuit, UK). Gentle, sensuous, shuffling songs from a vintage performer (born 1901); a fine set, even if there are a few too many mentions of henpecked and bewitched men.

See p.577 for Cuban nueva trova recommendations.

VINTAGE BANDS

The last few years have seen some terrific re-releases of Cuban and Cuban-American bands of the 1920s to 50s. The discs below include son, chachachá, mambo and charanga and could as easily fit into the salsa section – of which they are the predecessors – as here. Whatever, they are wonderful music, and immediate investment is highly recommended!

ⓒ **Machito and his Afro Cuban Orchestra** *Tremendo Cubano* and *Cuarteto Caney featuring Machito: 1939–40* (both Tumbao, Spain). Machito's big-band sound is to be heard to fine effect on these CDs, though the man is at his all-time best on the album *Cha Cha Cha at the Palladium* (Palladium, Spain), recorded live at the Palladium Club in New York.

ⓒ **Orquesta Aragon, Beny Moré and Perez Prado** *Orquesta Riverside Years* (RCA International, US). Orquesta Aragon were the seminal charanga band, and their sweeping strings and trilling flute inspired New York mambo. They're featured here with the golden voice of Beny Moré and stunning piano solos from Prado. For the band's 1950s chachachá sound, check out ⓒ *That Cuban Cha-Cha-Cha* (BMG Tropical Series, US).

ⓒ **Orquesta Aragon** *Danzones* (Discuba/Casino, US). Danzón at its most witty, with incisive playing from Aragon at their most European. Elegant and infectious.

ⓒ **Orquesta Casino de la Playa** *Memories of Cuba: 1937–44* (Tumbao, Spain). Earlier classics from Prado's first band, which included a trio of great vocalists – Cascarito, Miguelito Valdés and Antonio de la Cruz.

ⓒ **Perez Prado** *Havana 3 a.m./Mambo Mania* (2-album CD, Bear Family Records, Germany). Sublime mambo from the man who claimed to invent the form in the late 1940s, and including the biggest Latin hit of the 50s, "Cherry Pink and Apple Blossom White".

ⓒ **Sexteto Habanero/Sexteto Boloña** *The Roots Of Salsa* (Arhoolie, US). Two of the most influential Cuban son bands from their early years in the 1920s; raw and utterly charming.

ⓒ **Various** *Hot Cuban Dance Music 1909–37* (Harlequin, UK). Son in its earliest acoustic form from the sextets and septets who laid the foundations. Still some of the most timeless and appealing Latin music recorded – and the sleeve notes (including lyrics) perfectly evoke the era.

ⓒ **Various** *Sextetos Cubanos* (Arhoolie, US). A wonderful archive compilation of 1930s son bands, including Sexteto Matancero and Sexteto Nacional.

DANCING WITH THE SAINTS

THE INTERNATIONAL SOUND OF SALSA

Salsa was born out of the encounter of Cuban and Puerto Rican music with big-band jazz in the Latin barrios of New York. Today it is a global music, massively popular across the Caribbean, Latin and North America, and with established outposts, too, in Europe and Japan. Sue Steward charts the stations of the salsa world, along with the music's roots and transformations.

Salsa is a word with vivid associations but no absolute definitions, a tag that encompasses a rainbow assortment of Latin rhythms and styles, taking on a different hue wherever you stand in the Spanish-speaking world. In her own definition, the Queen of salsa, Afro-Cuban singer Celia Cruz, says: "Salsa is Cuban music with another name. It's mambo, chachachá, rumba, son . . . all the Cuban rhythms under one name."

Literally the word salsa means "sauce" or "juice" and in Latin American musical circles it takes its origins from a cry of appreciation for a particularly piquant or flashy solo. It was first used to describe a style of music in the mid-1970s, when a group of **New York-based Latin musicians** overhauled the classic Cuban big-band arrangements popular since the mambo era of the 1940s and 50s. They set about reworking them into something tougher and more appropriate to their modern, integrated, bicultural lifestyles. The salsa tag was coined by a Venezuelan radio DJ, so myth has it, and it caught on.

The powerhouse for New York's salsa innovations was the Manhattan studio of **Fania Records**, under the direction of musician-producer **Johnny Pacheco**. The Fania team went beyond the Cuban templates, introducing Puerto Rican classics into the son repertoire, which endeared them to the vast numbers of "New Yoricans" and other exiles in the US. The trombonist and producer **Willie Colon** brought in Yomo Toro's *cuatro* guitar, a lead instrument in Puerto Rican country music, added Brazilian songs to the repertoire, and persuaded **Celia Cruz** to sing a Brazilian composition, "Berimbau", on an early collaboration.

Salsa was soon imitated throughout Latin America and the Caribbean, and put New York at the epicentre of the Latin music world, where it stayed, the focus and envy of the continent, for the next two decades. No one, however, no matter how anti-communist their stance, would deny that salsa is essentially **Cuban music**. Even the Cubans themselves acknowledge the fact these days, their government having tactically abandoned its original line that the term was an American imperialist cover-up for poaching their music.

THE DIASPORA AND THE SAINTS

Vague though the term may be, salsa is today instantly identifiable: an up-tempo dance music blasting from jukeboxes, radios and stages the length and breadth of the vast Latin American diaspora, from Peruvian villages of the Andes to the cities of Medellin and Caracas, from the nightclubs of Mexico, Puerto Rico and the Dominican Republic to North America's long-established barrios in New York, Miami and Los Angeles, Boston and Chicago.

In most of these territories, there's a local salsa star, and a particular flavour or *sabor*. The music's celebrities have the status in Latin America of football players in England or the USA, and salsa lyrics unite exiles and generations. They also contain subtle clues to **national identity**. Targeting the older exiled Cubans, the regal Celia Cruz goes straight to the heart in songs like the epic "Bemba Colora" (thick red lips), which closes all her shows, and sings yearningly of landmarks and beauty spots in the Cuban countryside. For Colombians in Miami, New York or London, a song like Grupo Niche's "Cali Pachanguero" (about a party-animal from the city of Cali), or any number of praise-songs to Cali or Baranquilla, will always bring the house down.

One unifying theme in salsa is the reference to the syncretic **Afro-Catholic religions**. Afro-Cuban Santería (see p.475) and Afro-Brazilian Candomblé have equivalents throughout Latin America, some involving the same saints and

WILLIE COLON

••••••••••••••••••••••••

Trombonist and singer **Willie Colon** has been demolishing salsa's clichés ever since he had his first hit, "El Malo", at the age of sixteen: a song he recorded with a lean two-trombone octet that blasted forth the tough sound of teenage Brooklyn's salsa-jazz-bugalú.

Colon was responsible for more innovations in New York's salsa heyday than any other producer. He incorporated Brazilian music and paid tribute to Puerto Rican styles. His lavish brass arrangements backed the era's greatest singers, including Celia Cruz and the evocative voice of Hector Lavoe. The compilation "Exitos de Willie Colon" (Fania) illustrates that breadth and variety and showcases the great vocalists for whom he worked his musical magic.

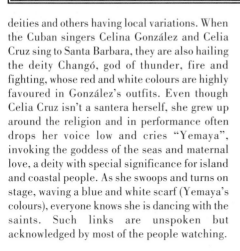

Colon's potent, late 1970s, socio-political vignettes with Ruben Blades are still best-sellers. Blades became a mouthpiece for oppressed Latin America and while Colon's own political contributions are sometimes overlooked, songs like "Era Nuclear" and "El General" (from the 1984 album "Criollo") are no less significant.

What he calls his "Latin-Jazzbo" single, "Set Fire to Me", a kind of jazzy house tune with a fiery piano solo from Charlie Palmieri and thunderous timbales solo from Tito Puente, brought Colon unexpected crossover dance chart success in 1986. A new Willie Colon album is still guaranteed to surprise. Starting with the rich musical cultures on his Latin American doorstep, he moves ever outwards.

---

deities and others having local variations. When the Cuban singers Celina González and Celia Cruz sing to Santa Barbara, they are also hailing the deity Changó, god of thunder, fire and fighting, whose red and white colours are highly favoured in González's outfits. Even though Celia Cruz isn't a santera herself, she grew up around the religion and in performance often drops her voice low and cries "Yemaya", invoking the goddess of the seas and maternal love, a deity with special significance for island and coastal people. As she swoops and turns on stage, waving a blue and white scarf (Yemaya's colours), everyone knows she is dancing with the saints. Such links are unspoken but acknowledged by most of the people watching.

TAPPING THE ROOTS

The variations in modern salsa are directly linked to the various Caribbean island cultures and, in particular, to the influence or dominance of their immigrant African slaves. On **Puerto Rico**, for example, relatively few slaves were brought in, and as a result the island's music bears a greater **Spanish** flavour. This is most evident in the high, plaintive singing style of the hill farmers, backed by the cuatro and other

guitars: a style epitomized by the venerated 1930s and 40s singer **Ramito**, "El Cantor de la montana" (The Singer of the Mountains). The pure, high, nasal voice is still essential for soneros from Puerto Rico – and for Cubans, too, where colonial sounds stayed late. The plaintive tone of singers like Frankie Ruiz, Lalo Rodríguez and Marvin Santiago, or Gilbert Santo Rosa, Andy Montanez, Hector Lavoe and Willie Colon from the earlier generation, all recall the Caribbean's Spanish history.

Salsa in addition encompasses a whole range of **Afro-Cuban** dance rhythms and styles, in particular son, salsa's most direct ancestor. Son was wildly popular in Cuba in the first decades of this century, when the original sextetos and septetos were formed, and its songs, timelessly sweet and lyrical, were carried by one or two male voices, singing a call-and-response, verse-to-chorus format. The son coalesces the dual African and Spanish ancestry of Cuban music: in the African percussion and rhythms, the relationship between the vocalists, and in the unmistakeably Spanish flavour of the guitar. Hit songs like "Suavecito" and "Loma de Belen", by Sextetos Habanero and Nacional, have been endlessly updated and revamped in modern salsa recordings.

The son bands eventually metamorphosed into larger line-ups, better suited to the grander scale of Havana's clubs than the septets and sextets, which were primarily outdoor and street bands for the poor black community. The immediate forerunners of today's salsa bands were the world famous Cuban mambo and charanga orchestras of the 1940s and 50s, orchestras like **Aragon**, **Riverside** and **Chapotín**, who played in Havana's casinos and nightclubs to free-spending Americans.

Meanwhile, over in New York, at the mecca of the chachachá and the mambo, the **Palladium Dancehall** on 52nd Street, energetic new musical arrangements were being created by the bands – led by Cuban musicians like **Pérez Prado**, **Machito** and **Tito Rodríguez**, and the Puerto Rican **Tito Puente**. This was the era of razor-sharp arrangements, swinging horn sections based on the great swing bands of the day (Kenton, Basie, Miller), and a line of formidably inventive percussionists. Accompanying them were a roomful of dancers, riveting acrobatic soloists whose moves were imitated all around the US. As bandleader Tito Puente put it, "Everyone was an exhibitionist at the Palladium".

The basic unit of salsa has changed little since the mambo era. The **orquesta** is a big band divided into horn and rhythm sections, plus piano and bass, which act as a bridge between the two. It is fronted by one or more lead vocalists while the all-important *coro*, the chorus that answers the sonero's vocal improvisations, is usually sung by band members. The crucial percussion section regulates a complex mesh of rhythms and powers along the music, while the other sections are ranged around it. Of paramount influence on the individual sound of a salsa band is the taste and skill of the **arranger**, who choreographs the sections and gives the band its "feel". The sections work with and against each other, in a way that draws on 1940s big-band riffing as much as the African call-and-response format.

The **sound** is determined particularly by the balance between the horns and the rhythm section, and by the choice of lead instruments. The latter is affected strongly by fashion: in the 1950s and 60s, when charanga bands were all the rage, the sweet flute-and-violins combination was essential; shortly after came conjuntos, trumpet-led groups with a hard, steely edge. The Puerto Rican band **La Sonora Ponceña**, with its original line-up of five trumpets and no

saxophones, has consolidated this sound. In the 1960s, **Eddie Palmieri** sparked a craze for trombones, which continues today in **Oscar D'Leon's** trombone-led sound, while in Cuba, **Los Van Van** have broken all the rules by pitting three violins (as employed by charanga groups) against three trombones, creating an exquisite rough-tough-sweet effect. The rich deep tones of a single baritone saxophone, epitomized by **José Alberto's** band, are a current flavouring.

SINGERS AND SONGS

Salsa **singers**, like their son and mambo predecessors, are expected to be improvisers, ad-libbing during verses and sometimes over the instrumental solos, chatting and scatting to the rhythms. Reputations used to hang on that skill: the great Cuban soneros **Ignacio Piñero**, **Beny Moré** and **Celia Cruz** all developed formidable technique, never missing a beat. Celia Cruz's way of racing through the complexities of a song is stunning. In the 1980s, when salsa slumped into rather formulaic doldrums, improvisation

Fania's fattest hits (album cover detail)

ceased to be desirable, until a new wave of soneros, particularly **José Alberto** and the Colombian **Joe Arroyo**, spurned a reliance on sexually explicit lyrics as a route to success, and returned to free form.

Most salseros avoid politics but a few serve as commentators and provide symbolic inspiration.

The most notable example is lawyer, performer and movie star **Ruben Blades**, who for the past two decades has been a spokesperson for North American Hispanics, and in 1994 narrowly missed election as president of Panama. Blades' parables and allegories, resist the nationalism that pervades salsa and divides its audiences, and on stage he reinforces his songs with short speeches, telling his audiences, "We are all Americans – Latin Americans". Almost uniquely, he sees his audience as stretching beyond the traditional Latin market and has actively sought crossovers with American and British rock musicians. In the 1980s, for example, he recorded an album called "Nothing but the Truth", featuring songs in English by Lou Reed, Elvis Costello and Sting.

A handful of other songwriters, including Willie Colon (who translates his lyrics into English on the sleeves), **Omar Alfanno**, merengue artist **Cuco Valoy**, Colombian singer Joe Arroyo, and veteran Puerto Rican songwriter **Tito Curet Alonso**, also deal with issues. In Cuba, Los Van Van's songs are broadsheets, airing local issues and passing advice that becomes catchphrases in Havana, carried on a wave of sophisticated salsa, while the younger band **Mezcla** employ a musical fusion of salsa, rock and jazz to carry their (mild) messages of criticism. **Juan Luís Guerra**, the hugely successful merengue star from the Dominican Republic (see merengue feature, following), also has a political agenda in his lyrics.

The majority of salsa songs, however, are pure escapism, with the same function as the soap operas that fill Latin American TV channels, musing on love and sex, dance and romance, and scornful of commenting on the awful realities of everyday life.

CELIA CRUZ: QUEEN OF SALSA

• •

They call **Celia Cruz** the Queen of Salsa, the greatest female singer to emerge from Cuba, and a living legend. Her rich contralto voice has thrilled audiences for over half a century, first as the toast of 1950s Havana, then in a series of films through the 1950s and 60s, and more recently in the movie of Oscar Hijuelos's book, *The Mambo Kings Play Songs of Love*, in which she performed with her regular touring partner Tito Puente – the King of Mambo. As witnessed by this film, and her duet with David Byrne, "Loco de Amor", in his movie, *Something Wild*, she is one of the few Latin stars to have acquired an all-American audience.

Celia left Cuba after the 1959 revolution, along with Cuba's most popular band, Sonora Matancera, and has since recorded with all the Latin greats. The salsa song "La Dicha Mia" (My Luck), written for her by Johnny Pacheco, tells of this move and her subsequent musical career. "I left Cuba and headed for New York, looking for another atmosphere" and recorded with "the great Tito Puente", she sings. Next comes "the great Dominican, Johnny Pacheco" ("We caused a sensation"), and collaborations with Willie Colon, Papo Lucca and his Sonora Ponceña, and the singer Pete "El Conde" Rodríguez. The chorus chants, "It's the luck of the Great Lady", to which she responds: "I thank God and the saints every day for my luck".

The greatness of Celia Cruz is immediately apparent in performance. On stage, even approaching seventy, she has dazzling energy, sensuality and rapport with the audience, chatting and joking with them, dancing throughout a two-hour set. In the songs, she ad-libs and improvises with extraordinary style and speed. When Johnny Pacheco first worked with Cruz, he was amazed by her reaction to the song "Caramelo", in which she needed to improvise a few lines about fruit: "It was like watching a computer: she listed every tropical fruit you can imagine at a speed I couldn't believe".

SALSA STATIONS

Leaving aside Brazil – whose traditions are very much its own – virtually every major Latin American (and US) city has its own self-contained salsa scene. Bands incorporate traditional ideas and instruments to give their music a local piquancy, which appeals to the fans, and also gives clues about the country's older music. The Colombian bandleader Joe Arroyo, for example, will drop in a clarinet line to recall the traditional lead instrument of the *cumbia* – the country's other dominant music. In the Dominican Republic's salsa-influenced development of merengue, Wilfrido Vargas and Bonny Cepeda have both inserted synthesized accordion lines into their high-speed tunes, evoking the rural, hillbilly sounds they grew up with.

Trade winds and economics have shaped salsa, too. The most obvious turning-point was the **Cuban revolution** of 1959, which relocated vast numbers of Cubans, including musicians – and their fans – in New York and Miami. A disastrous economic **recession in the Dominican Republic** in the late 1980s prompted a huge migration to New York, which became merengue-mad for a couple of years, the style becoming a major influence in salsa. In the same decade, the **Colombian drug industry** launched new communities of exiles, including musicians, in New York and particularly Miami, while in Colombia itself an increasingly affluent record industry began to promote its artists beyond the home crowd.

There are salsa stations, too, in **London**, where Colombian bands often crop up in the clubs, or mix it with local musicians, and a notable scene in **Japan**, whose home-grown **Orquesta de la Luz** has become one of the hottest acts on the international salsa circuit.

CUBA

In **Cuba**, the cauldron of salsa, the post-revolutionary years were spent re-evaluating and incorporating Afro-Cuban music into a distinctly new sound. The island was effectively sealed off from the world by the American boycott and left to develop in a virtual musical vacuum – a state that was reinforced, after hints of openness, by Castro's expulsion of 125,000 Cubans in 1981.

This, the so-called "Mariel Exodus", created deep ripples in the international music scene, particularly in Latin jazz, with the arrival in North America of conga player **Daniel Ponce**, drummer **Ignacio Berroa** and (through defection) saxophonist **Paquito D'Rivera**. All injected a crucial new vitality into Latin jazz and salsa, introducing ideas from post-revolutionary Cuba, particularly along Afro-Cuban lines.

In the 1990s, **Cuban influences** are creeping into salsa again, with cover versions of Cuban songs by Willie Chirino and Sonora Ponceña, and the Puerto Rican Roberto Roena. Island-based bands like **Los Van Van**, Ritmo Oriental and Adalberto Alvarez are making inroads into the scene as well, with original versions of salsa. And of course the Cuban expatriate **Celia Cruz**, who left the island after the revolution, remains the biggest star salsa has yet produced, providing a link with the homeland for all generations of Cuban Americans (see feature box).

COLOMBIA

Although salsa is not native to Colombia it has become immensely popular there in the last couple of decades. As in many other Latin American countries the local bands began by copying what they heard on the radio and records, but they very soon started to incorporate elements of local music. Cumbia, which can be very close to the salsa sound in its modern style, was the most obvious fusion, but other bands began working in the *vallenato* accordion sound, or incorporating dance rhythms from the Caribbean coast.

One of the earliest Colombian groups to carry out such experiments was **Peregoyo y su Combo Vacano**, who had begun in the 1960s playing cumbia mixed with Cuban son. However, it was **Joe Arroyo** and his band **La Verdad** (see box) that really put Colombian salsa on the international map. Arroyo is a true salsa superstar – although hard to box closely into any defined style. His "tropical" sound is largely salsa-based but draws on a whole range of Caribbean and Latin musical styles, especially merengue and calypso. **Clan Caribe**, too, have had massive success throughout the continent, adding elements of soca and reggae to the mix.

Joe Arroyo got his break working with the record label **Discos Fuentes** (for more on which, see p.555) and its king, the bassplayer, singer, composer and producer Ernesto Estrada, better known as **Fruko**. Fruko is himself a key player on the Colombian salsa scene, with his long-established band **Los Tesos**, but it is as an arranger that he is best known, consistently producing the catchiest and freshest in tropical music. He has been called, and aptly, the "Quincy Jones of Latin music".

Other big names in Colombian salsa include Diego and Jaime Galé and their band **Grupo Galé** from Medellin, and the Cuban emigré violinist **Alfredo de la Fé**, who has made his home in the same town. There are also a clutch of bands based in the old sugar town of Cali, which is fast rivalling Medellin with its recording studios and clubs. These include the **Latin Brothers**, **Guayacan** and **Grupo Niche**. The last have recently made it big in New York, with the slightly odd consequence that many of their hits now exist in two recorded versions: the original Colombian recording and a later one reworked by New York-based arrangers to conform with the international rules of salsa. These rules are mainly concerned with the treatment of the clave, the rhythmic

framework on which all aspects of the music depend, and to which Colombians have a typically cavalier attitude.

PUERTO RICO

Puerto Rico is a less publicized capital of salsa but has long been home to some of the classic, and classiest bands. Its expatriates, too, are among the greatest soneros to be heard. They include **Cheo Feliciano**, **Hector Lavoe** and **Andy Montanez**, the young Cuban-style sonero **Cano Estremera**, and two anti-heroes who sing like a dream when they're out of prison – **Frankie Ruiz** and **Marvin Santiago**.

On the island itself, Puerto Rican music is dominated by two great bands of around thirty years' standing, **El Gran Combo** and **La Sonora Ponceña**. Together, these two epitomize the island's sound, producing smooth,

JOE ARROYO

• •

Colombia's music scene is exceptionally rich, but one artist shines above all others – the singer, composer and bandleader **Alvaro José Arroyo Gonzalez**, the country's most popular singer and most exalted salsa export. Colombian salsa is flavoured heavily by cumbia, the national music (see p.549), as well as Cuban son, and to this mix Joe Arroyo has welded a myriad Caribbean influences: the rocking rhythms of Haitian compas, the dazzling Dominican merengue, splashes of reggae and Trinidadian soca. The emergent style is unique – as its name, **Joe-son**, infers – and has influenced salsa everywhere in the 1980s and 90s.

Miraculously, although it draws on just about every style going, and appeals to audiences across Latin America and the Caribbean, it does not have a hint of homogenization.

Arroyo started singing professionally at the age of eight, in a strip joint in the port of

Cartagena, and joined the illustrious band of **Fruko y sus Tesos** at sixteen. His distinctively abrasive tenor voice, darting and leaping around the rhythms and melodies, has been part of Colombia's soundscape ever since. He founded his own group, **La Verdad** (The Truth), in 1981, with whom he sings songs of praise to his country and its cities ("En Baraquilla me quedo" – I'm sticking around in Baraquilla) and of historical events that unite the people.

The band had their first international break a couple of years later at the New York Labor Day Fiesta, and from there they went from strength to strength – despite a drugs overdose that nearly killed Arroyo in the early 80s. Today, La Verdad's live stage show, with their split-second precision playing, and Arroyo's magnetic voice and inimitable dancing style, is one of the most exhilarating in Latin music.

polished arrangements that are far less syncopated and African than the Cuban variety, and danced in a glide rather than in the angular, funky Cuban manner. The bands' longevity guarantees an unrivalled tightness and cohesion and a repertoire of songs that every islander can recite. Both are driven from the keyboards, El Gran Combo by Rafael Ithier, whose style is florid and bright, and Sonora Ponceña's four-trumpet line-up by the jazz-influenced maestro, Papo Lucca.

A visit to the Puerto Rican capital, **San Juan**, can be disappointing: the salsa is concealed and the tourist joints ignore the local music. Visit the island in July, however, when every sizeable town celebrates its Saint's Day, and you can travel around on a spree of *fiestas patronales*, with all-night drinking, eating, dancing, and music from the island's great and small salsa bands.

The sporadic African presence in Puerto Rican music is most evident in the towns of **Loiza Aldea**, close to the capital, and **Ponce** in the south of the island, both of which retained large populations of slave descendants along with their African cultures. They are known these days for *bomba*, an African-based music that is the Puerto Rican equivalent of Cuban rumba, played on drums, sung and danced. It was incorporated into a salsa-type sound in the 1950s and 60s by the singer **Ismael Rivera** and percussionist **Rafael Cortijo**, who had earlier perfected a commercial, big-band version of the music, a style still played by island bands like ABC.

The most Spanish – and the most melodious – variety of Puerto Rican salsa is the *plena*, a repertoire of songs accompanied by guitar and the related cuatro. Plenas are long, emotional and anecdotal, and were originally sung by groups of farmers sitting around after a day's work in the fields. **Willie Colon**, faithful to his family tradition, has revamped some classic numbers, including "Wolo" by Rafael Hernandez (on his "Tiempo pa'matar" album), complete with Andrews Sisters-type female chorus. In New York, **Los Pleneros de la 21** call themselves after the bus stop in San Juan's Santurce district, where many musicians work and live, and self-consciously keep the flame of plena burning, reviving songs unsung at home, while the cuatrista **Yomo Toro** brought the flavour of the Puerto Rican countryside into New York salsa in the Fania records of the 1970s and his own later solo work.

VENEZUELA

For **Venezuela**, salsa is almost a national music, and in its capital, **Caracas**, a city in a bowl between mountains, a city where cars never stop, horns puncture the hazy air and salsa explodes from every street corner. Venezuela's proximity to Brazil has resulted in a strong samba and bossa nova influence, evident in the smooth, sweet, apparently effortless sound of bands like **Daiquiri**. There are some very long-established bands, too, such as **Billo y su Caracas Boys** and **Los Melodicos**, both of which seem to get ever better with age, and have proved launching pads for most of the leading singers, like the hugely popular José Luís Rodríguez, aka **El Puma**.

In global terms, the big name, of course, is **Oscar D'Leon**, these days to be seen as often in New York or Miami as in his home country. His brand of salsa is in fact rooted in Cuban rather than Venezuelan sounds, and he is heavily influenced by the Cuban swing bands with their horn phrasing and son-rhythm piano solos. His singing, too, which leaps from croon to falsetto, owes much to the Cubans, and, above all, his idol Beny Moré. He maintains a spectacular nineteen-piece orchestra, a showcase for incredibly tight musicianship, while he dances, sings and duets with his teenage sons, all the while lugging his trademark white baby-upright bass across stage. This is one of the most exciting shows in salsa today.

Oscar D'Leon – without the bass for once

Other Venezuelan bands, such as **Nelson Pueblo** and **Un Solo Pueblo**, play salsa mixed in with *llanera* – the country's national music (similar to the Colombian variety) – and merengue. The singer **Natusha** has gone even further, adding lambada to the brew.

MIAMI

Miami sits like a lighthouse, radiating and receiving music from the Caribbean and Latin America. It is a rich city, where sponsorship still pays, music is the greatest lure, and summer festivals and street parties fill the weekends with music. America's biggest street party plugs Little Havana's main street, Calle Ocho, every March as the Cuban Carnival draws over a million people to fifty stages hosting the best music in Latin America.

The Miami Sound, with its weave of imported strands and threads, reflects the city's geographical importance and, above all, the presence of **Cubans** and, in patches, Colombians. Miami was known as "Old Cubans' Town" until the early 1980s, when the drugs trade brought in the first wave of **Colombians**, and an economic miracle transformed the city. Castro's ejection of 125,000 Cubans in the so-called "Mariel Exodus" in 1981 changed the population again, while subsequent events in Central America have brought in a substantial Nicaraguan and Salvadorean population. There are scatterings of Puerto Ricans and Dominicans, too, each maintaining their own separate, exile-music scene.

Miami is home to a league of Cuban legends, whose youthful, glamorous images you'll find on record sleeves in the nostalgia stores of Little Havana, and whose deep-lined faces pop up at special nights in the city's hotels and nightclubs, and at outdoor gigs. The ubiquitous Cuban singer **Roberto Torres**, who created his own Cuban-Colombian hybrid, Charanga Vallenata, in the 1980s, is a local hero, singing crisp and clear behind radio ads, opening shows in the hotel nightclubs, and running the **Guajiro record label**, which is dedicated to keeping the pre-revolution tradition alive, and local musicians in work.

Miami's other Cuban forty-somethings include **Emilio Estefan** of **Miami Sound Machine** (MSM), **Joe Galdo** (ex-MSM), **Willie Chirino**, and **Carlos Oliva** (of Clouds). Together they constitute the Beatles-and-salsa generation that created the **Miami Sound**, a variable blend of salsa with rock and pop. Chirino favours a vibrant percussion section, a salsa-Caribbean base and rock fantasies. **Emilio** and **Gloria Estefan** – the most successful Latin artist of the 1980s – started with Spanish ballads, moved through Spanish- and samba-flavoured rock, and then hit the salsa groove and both Latin and Anglo charts with hits like "Doctor Beat" and "Oyé mi canto". These days Gloria Estefan is firmly in the American pop mainstream, sings mainly in English, and the salsa is subdued to the point of middle-of-the-road, yet she continues to command an immense Latin following. In 1993, however, she returned somewhat to her roots, recording traditional Cuban son to fine effect on the album "Ay mi tierra" – a huge success among North American Cubans (and, surprisingly, a non-Latin audience) with its fervent anti-Castro message.

NEW YORK

The 1990 success of Gloria Estefan's "Oyé mi canto" was a testimony to the arrival of Latin Americans as Americans; David Byrne's album, "Rei Momo", recorded in the same year, was a gesture in the opposite direction. Hitherto, salsa had been a bit of a secret for non-Hispanics, even in **New York**, where Hispanics are by far the largest ethnic group. As throughout the US, nightclubs tend to be partisan in their musical policy, catering to the traditional tastes of the local community, and it still requires a little detective work to dance the night away as if in a different country.

New York certainly has the riches, if you go looking. Check the Spanish press, especially the Friday edition of *El Diário*, or the weekly *Village Voice*, and you will be directed to some fabulous salsa crossovers and occasionally lavish all-star extravaganzas. The neighbourhoods divide fairly neatly into nationalities, each with their own musical identities.

High up in Manhattan, for example, is **Washington Heights**, with a population that is about eighty percent **Dominican**. The heavy merengue beat (see p.495) rumbles through clubs like *Studio 84* and *Club 2000*, where the island's top bands play alongside New York's even more frenetic local outfits and couples blur in a spin, their hips matching the impossibly fast scraped 2/4 pulse of the metal grater-like guiro, essential for hissing out the propulsive rhythm. Out in the streets, shockwaves radiate from massive speakers in the back of cruising cars, leaving saxophone jags and guiro scratches in their wake.

Over in Queens, the flavour switches: **Jackson Heights**, here, is overwhelmingly **Colombian** – it's known as "Little Medellin". Inside clubs like *La Discotueqa*, *Illusiones* or *Juan Pachanga*,

Afro-Cuban salsa is overshadowed by the light, bright cumbias and accordion-led vallenatos, and couples kick their heels and dance facing each other with arms outstretched.

In the mirrored glitz of Club Broadway, meanwhile, just a few blocks from **Spanish Harlem**, the crowd is almost entirely **Puerto Rican**, as are the bands they dance to – El Gran Combo, Andy Montanez, Gilberto Santarosa and Sonora Ponceña all regularly jet in. To unfamiliar non-Latin ears, their particular kind of salsa – and the merengue popular at the younger clubs – can sound too smooth, but this audience barely sits all night, the men in pastel suits and big-lapelled satin shirts dancing with women in tight, frilled dresses. The dance style is courtly and

RUBEN BLADES

....

"I write about people, not ideology. But in Latin America it's impossible to live without being affected by politics and so a song about people becomes political. But I've never sat down to write a political song".

Ruben Blades, dubbed the "Latin Bruce Springsteen", is one of the few salsa stars to give his music a political edge. In addition to his involvement in salsa, he's considered to have much in common with the nueva canción movement (see p.569), addressing the realities of life in Latin America under the influence of writers like Gabriel García Marquez and Carlos Fuentes. At the same time, Blades' music is incredibly popular and grows directly from the dance tradition: his 1978 album "Siembra", made in the salsa hothouse of Fania Records with Willie Colon, was the most successful Latin album ever.

Blades ascribes his success to having widened the audience for the music, breaking the stereotypes of most salsa lyrics. "My criticism of salsa is that its songs are stuck physically and mentally in a ghetto. Instead of just looking at the street corner for my subjects, I looked down the neighbouring street, then at the city and the whole world. Suddenly the sales jumped. The middle classes that didn't feel any connection with salsa before were suddenly hearing stories that affected them as part of the city and they started buying the records."

Blades was born in Panama in 1948 and trained as a lawyer in Panama City before moving to New York and doing a masters degree in international

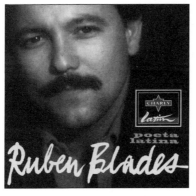

law at Harvard. He has been an outspoken critic of American interference in Latin America, trying to articulate a voice for the Latin community and dent the stereotypes. "The Americans are so insulated, you have to explain to them that the Latin stereotypes – Carmen Miranda with fruit in her hair, or the sleeping Mexican with a cactus – are gone. We can't allow them to persist, so you have to compete in their own arena. That's why I went to Harvard to study law. They can no longer say you aren't smart enough."

After his stint in the Willie Colon band, Blades left to record in his own right, making what remains perhaps his best album, "Buscando America" (Searching for America), in 1984. This features songs about the murder of El Salvadorean priest Oscar Romero, and the "disappeared" of Latin American dictatorships. Musically, the move from Willie Colon's band meant replacing the traditional brass section with a newer synthesized sound. This was a crucial innovation, introducing elements from pop and rock, though losing salsa's immediate danceability.

As part of Blades' proselytizing mission, the lyrics to his songs are printed on the albums in both Spanish and English. With his strong beliefs and fusion of diverse tropical dance forms he's salsa's most original voice. He also has considerable political aspirations and in 1994 stood in the election to become president of Panama; he came second, as it turned out, which is perhaps music's gain, and Panama's loss.

restrained, subtly sexy – a heavily syncopated foxtrot or quadrille rather than a lambada.

Downtown, Americans and Latins mingle on Monday nights at *SOB's*, which replaced the two-decade stint of "Salsa meets Jazz" at the *Village Gate*, a club which drew visitors from all around the globe, including Japanese salsaholics, trailing in the wake of their homegrown Orquesta de la Luz. DJ Anna Arais promotes nights of jazz-tinged salsa, soloists fronting one of the legendary local salsa bands like Eddie Palmieri's.

Midtown offers the Copacabana, another ritzy haven with live bands, popular for an after-work cocktail and spin on the dancefloor.

Way downtown, in the traditional Puerto Rican **Lower East Side**, is the resurrected New Yorican Poets Café, named in tribute to the original 1960s venue. Latin bohemia rules here, with poets, politicians and jazz-type jams, or *descargas*, from a new generation of Hispanic artists.

Finally, a New York institution is Ralph Mercado's **Labor Day Fiesta** at Madison Square Gardens. This is a festival to end them all, uniting on stage ten of the top international salsa bands. The singers duck into each others' bands, clamouring for mike space in the unison numbers, or pushing instrumentalists front stage for a solo. The crowd, too, is amazing, singing, dancing and edging its way to delirium.

DISCOGRAPHY

INTERNATIONAL

Various *¡Oye Listen!* (GlobeStyle, UK). An irresistible collection of songs by island- and American-based Cubans, Colombians and Panamanians: salsa with splashes of son, cumbia, mambo and rumba.

Various *Viva Salsa!* (4-CD set, Fania, US/Charly, UK). An anthology featuring all the Fania team – lots of Ray Barretto and Johnny Pacheco – along with a whole disc of Tito Puente.

Super Salsa Hits, (Charly, UK) featuring Ray Barreto, Willie Colon and Tito Puente , is a slimmed down, single-CD version.

COLOMBIA

Joe Arroyo y La Verdad *Rebellion* (World Circuit, UK) and *Fire in My Mind* (Mango, UK). *Rebellion* is a compilation, showcasing Arroyo's flawless arrangements, impassioned singing, and infectious fusion of styles and idioms. It's a perfect introduction. If you want more (and you will), move on to his 1991 album, *Fire in my Mind,* which shows him at his best to date in the 90s and features some wonderful Afro-Caribbean tracks.

Alfredo de la Fé *¡Salsa!* (Discos Fuentes, Colombia/Mango, UK). This is really Cuban music, but produced in Colombia, featuring an updated charanga sound. With his computerized violin, Fé is another one of the voracious experimenters in Latin American music.

Fruko y sus Tesos *The Godfather of Salsa* (Discos Fuentes /Mango, UK). Fruko picked up much of his salsa style in New York and it shows. This music is much closer to the North American sound than Peregoyo or Joe Arroyo. Good stuff all the same.

Grupo Niche *Grandes Exitos* (Globo, US). Full of sumptuous melodies and tight arrangements, this is closer to the New York mould than the tropical coastal sound. The exitos include their rhythmically stunning "Cali Pachanguero".

Guayacan Orquesta *Cinco años aferrados al Sabor* (FM, Colombia). One of the new generation of Colombian salsa outfits, and more support for the assault that Latin American countries are mounting on the hegemony of New York.

CUBA

Adalberto Alvarez *La Salsa Caliente* (Sonido/Vogue, France). Alvarez is one of the hot properties in Cuban salsa, with a highly commercial sound – making the odd nod to son – that goes down a storm on his regular festival tours.

La Sonora Matancera and Guests *65th Anniversary* (TH-Rodven, US). A historic record of the band that gave Celia Cruz her break. In addition to Cruz, these 1950s tracks fea-ture Bobby Capo and Ismael Rivera, the great voices of Puerto Rico and the Dominican Republic.

Various *¡Sabroso!* (Earthworks, UK). Modern Cuban salsa that's immediately distinct from the smooth Latin American style. Features all the great modern Cuban bands: Los Van Van, Orquesta Revé, Irakere, Chepin and Conjunto Casino, Sierra Maestra, and to complete the collection, Celina González, singing guajira.

Various *Demasiado Caliente – Hot!* (Coco, US). Top-grade 1960s Latin jazz in all its permutations: Machito and Mario Bauza, founders of Afro-Cuban jazz; pianists Eddie and Charlie Palmieri; bomba-jazz from Puerto Rico's Cortijo; and Tito Puente in his prime.

See also the Cuban Music discography for Cuban salsa precursors – son, chachachá, mambo and charango.

NEW YORK/MIAMI

Fania All Stars *Live at Yankee Stadium Vols I and II* and *Los Hits Gordos de Fania* (all Fania, US). Classic numbers and the greatest names from the powerhouse of New York salsa. On the live albums, the band are joined by cuatro player Yomo Toro and Camerounian saxophonist Manu Dibango. Other CD re-issues of the Fania classics, solos and compilations from Celia Cruz, Ruben Blades, Ray Barretto and Eddie Palmieri have appeared on the UK-based Charly label, and this magical era is vividly recreated in the video *Celia Cruz and the Fania All Stars Live in Kinshasa, Zaire* (BMG, 1974), which features every illustrious soloist from the Fania stable, performing to an incredulous African crowd.

Celia Cruz *Introducing Celia Cruz* (Charly, UK). Her greatest Greatest Hits collection, including the sublime "Cucala" and, of course, "Santa Barbara".

Willie Colon *Grandes Exitos* (Fania, US). A fine selection of Colon's eclectic repertoire, spanning two decades of recordings with Celia Cruz, and Hector Lavoe – who possesses the original, harrowing, jibaro, countryman voice. Colon's trombone passion infuses every track.

Ruben Blades *Siembra* (Fania, US). Produced by Willie Colon, this is Blades at his very best, with the Fania crew in tow. Other recommended Blades albums include **Ruben Blades y Son del Solar . . . Live!** (Electra, US) and **Buscando America** (Electra, US), the latter a political "salsa concept album" which gets away with it.

Willie Chirino *Amandote* (CBS, US). Miami salsa, tropically flavoured with a splash of Beatles; guest saxophonist Paquito D'Rivera toughens one track while Chirino's Cuban drum corps keeps the ancestral flame alight.

Eddie Palmieri *History of Eddie Palmieri* (Tico, Venezuela). No Latin music collection is complete without at least one Palmieri LP. This album is essential, if only for the most sensual track of all time, "Café", a slow Cuban guajira that creeps up on you. Also recommended are **Salsa Brava** (Charly, UK) and **Sun of Latin Music** (Coco, US).

Henry Fiol *Sonero* (Earthworks, UK). A New York reversion to rustic Cuban sound with tres, saxophone, searing trumpet and superb piano. Fiol calls it corazón – heart music – and it scores a direct hit on physical emotions.

PUERTO RICO

La Sonora Ponceña *Soul of Puerto Rico* (Charly, UK). Puerto Rican salsa as no-one else plays it. The smooth arrangements and trumpet-led brass section are instantly recognizable.

Rafael Cortijo and Ismael Rivera *Los Dos Grandes de Siempre: sus 16 exitos* (AF Records, Puerto Rico). A musical marriage made in heaven: the strong, deep roots of Afro-Rican culture combine with Rivera's husky voice and the percussion-heavy arrangements of Cortijo.

Various *The Music of Puerto Rico 1929–46* (Harlequin, UK). Culled from the era of guitar trios, imported from Puerto Rico into New York: sweet high voices straight from the countryside and the nostalgic Spanish flavour of the island with wry comment on everyday life in the new home,

Nueva York. Some tremendously emotive voices, including the fabulous Canario.

VENEZUELA

Oscar D'Leon *Riquiti* (TH-Rodven, US). D'Leon, from Venezuela, was born with his soul in Cuba and has adapted Cuban classics as his own. He has constructed a unique line-up with a backline of trombonists who give his songs their recognizable flavour.

JAPAN

Orquesta de la Luz *La Aventura* (BMG Ariola, Japan). Slot this into your CD drive, close your eyes, and you really won't believe you're listening to a Japanese band. This is contemporary salsa as hot as it comes – and a huge success even in Latin America and New York.

AFRICA

Africando *Trovador* and *Tierra Tradicional* (both Sterns, UK). The original *Trovador* was an intriguing album put together by Boncana Maiga, a Malian flautist who had toured with Fania All Stars in the early 1980s. He brought in Papa Seck and other Senegalese vocalists to rework salsa classics with top Cuban New York session players. *Volume 2: Tierra Tradicional,* produced by Ibrahima Sylla, follows in the same vein. (For more on the Senegalese side of things, see Chapter Six).

MERENGUE MANIA

THE BURGEONING BEAT OF THE DOMINICAN REPUBLIC

Merengue is synonymous with the Dominican Republic, the country that shares the island of Hispañola with Haiti. Sue Steward looks at the music that has spawned Latin music's newest superstar, Juan Luís Guerra.

In its traditional form, **merengue** is played on accordion, saxophone, box bass with metal plucked keys, a *guayo* (a metal scraper – transformed from a kitchen implement), and a two-ended *tambora* drum, struck with hand and stick. It is a rural music with close affinities to Haitian *méringue* – though the latter, sung in Creole, tends to have a slower, more nostalgic sound, based on guitar rather than accordion.

In the Dominican Republic, merengue experienced something of a golden age during the dictatorship of Rafael Trujillo, who held power from the 1930s until his assassination in 1961. Trujillo was from peasant roots and he promoted the music as a symbol of national expression and the culture of the former underclass. He constrained its traditional role as a music of

social commentary but provided a forum for the musicians in the dancehalls. Larger merengue orchestras were developed, with piano and brass to cater for these new urban audiences.

Merengue is still to be heard at times in a simple, acoustic form – innovatively so in recordings by the virtuoso accordionist **Francisco Ulloa**. His band is distinguished by frantic arpeggios from both accordion and saxophone, free-sounding, triple-time bass, and a driving throb from the tambora. Ulloa's lyrics, too, look back to the old social commentary: "I'm not political," he says, "but I do sing about what my people can't take – la situación."

More often, though, these days, merengue comes as **big-band**, salsa-cousin dance music, employing hi-tech instruments. This sound was developed from the 1960s on, notably by **Johnny Ventura**, as the country opened its ears to North American influences – and to the salsa that was being forged all across the Caribbean.

The biggest change to the sound came through boosting the saxophone's role, either overdubbing in the studio or lining up players on

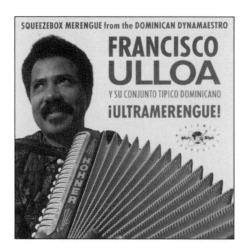

SQUEEZEBOX MERENGUE from the DOMINICAN DYNAMAESTRO

FRANCISCO ULLOA

Y SU CONJUNTO TIPICO DOMINICANO

¡ULTRAMERENGUE!

stage, which gives the music a sharp, stuttering momentum that the old style only hinted at. The other significant break has been in replacing the accordion with electric guitar, keyboards and synthesizers, or occasionally sampling it, like a ghost memory.

Despite the change of instruments, the **rhythym** of merengue has changed very little, and remains unmistakable, even in the radical versions by singer-songwriter **Juan Luís Guerra**, the star of the moment. The tambora keeps a fast pulse going, working around conga patterns, while a bass drum, operated with a foot pedal, provides a monotonous thumping 1–2–3–4 beat.

Merengue **vocalists** tend to come in threes, swapping the lead part, dancing in split-second formation routines like The Temptations on speed, and maintaining an impossibly fast hand-jive. Classic singers like **Johnny Ventura** keep audiences primed with their thrusting hip-swivelling routines, while **Wilfrido Vargas** leaves the erotic foreplay to his singers, conducting them from the edge of the stage, where he plays trumpet. At the other extreme, the popular all-girl group **Las Chicas del Can** perform a sexy floor show where the music is less important than the ambience.

Modern merengue **composers** tend to be less narrow-minded than their salsa counterparts: Wilfrido Vargas, Johnny Ventura and **Cuco Valoy**, to mention but few of many, have long trawled the Caribbean for inspiration.

Valoy's passion is Cuban music and calypso, given a political slant; Ventura wanted to be the Dominican Elvis and succeeded in bringing merengue into the rock'n'roll era with his 1960s Combo Show; while Vargas, a musical magpie, has drawn in music from all over the Caribbean – Haitian compas, Martiniquan zouk, Jamaican reggae, and more recently a hint of rap.

Dominican musical developments and merengue attitudes take on slightly different forms in Santo Domingo and New York. In the latter, **Millie y Los Vecinos**, the teenage, poppy **New York Band**, and **Victor Roque's Gran Manzana** (big apple) rarely perform with salsa acts; their music is maintained quite separately, even though the same audiences thrill to both. The Latin American merengue boom of the late 1980s has been superseded in New York by a fresh upsurge in salsa, particularly with the arrival in the US of Joe Arroyo and Oscar D'Leon. Back in the Dominican Republic, the recession hit so hard that there is now hardly any live music in the capital city, and it's only the tourist towns that can afford to pay the big-name bands, who spend most of their time abroad.

For all these problems, merengue is currently undergoing yet another lease of life, with the neo-merengue composer, **Juan Luís Guerra** – with his **Grupo 4:40** – established as the world's top-selling Latin artist. He began

Ojala que llueva café	I hope it rains coffee in the fields
Ojala que llueva café en el campo	that there falls a shower
que caiga un aguacero de yuca y té	of yuca and tea
del cielo una jarina de queso blanco	from the sky a tub of white cheeese
y al sur, un montaña	and to the south, a mountain
de berro y miel	of butter and honey
oh, oh, oh, oh	oh, oh, oh, oh
Ojala que llueva café	I hope it rains coffee in the fields

Juan Luís Guerra (from the album "Ojalá que llueva café")

breaking records in 1991 by having albums at numbers one and two of the Billboard Latin charts, outselling even Julio Iglesias, and has since captivated dancers and listeners in every corner of Latin America – and much of Europe and the US.

Guerra's trick has been chiefly to slow down the merengue, softening it with harmonies inspired by Manhattan Transfer, and to introduce a poetic gentility, in the manner of nueva canción songwriters like Silvio Rodríguez, that had never before seen seen in the music.

JUAN LUÍS GUERRA

Juan Luís Guerra tells Jan Fairley how he and his band 4:40 have changed the traditional merengue sound into the hottest Latin music of the moment.

Merengue – along with *bacháta* – is the traditional folk music of the Dominican Republic: it's the national music, popular in local bars and dancehalls. But we've changed it: both the sound and the lyrics, which with us have a different perspective, so they're not just about love but include social and political themes. I studied literature in Santo Domingo and the lyrics reflect my enthusiasm for poets like Neruda and Vallejo. Although I grew up with merengue my musical heroes were The Beatles. I didn't speak much English at the time but I loved their melodies and the way they harmonized the chorus. "Till There Was You", for example, is a kind of bolero, a bacháta without bongós or maracas. I was influenced, too, by the Rolling Stones, Pink Floyd, Jethro Tull – a lot of rock. But essentially I write what I call Caribbean music.

And the songs – where do they come from?
"Ojala que llueva café en el campo" (Let's Hope it Rains Coffee in the Fields) comes from an anonymous poem I found when I went to the village of Santiago los Caballeros. It's probably the work of a campesino – a peasant – and it was such a beautiful metaphor I had to develope it.
"El costo de la vida" (The Cost of Living) deals with political and social issues. The tune belongs to the Zairean guitarist Diblo, who I first heard playing in New York at *SOB's*. It's an example of how our music is not only danceable but makes you think while you do so. It's not that we think songs have a tremendous effect – it's people who struggle, not songs, who make things happen. But songs can raise consciousness. Dominicans have a wry sense of humour, and this is what makes "Cost of Living". Irony works better than heavy messages and it's more fun!

So are the songs essentially written for a Dominican audience or do you have a broader message in mind?
I certainly write for a home audience: my songs have expressions that are purely Dominican and that's part of their originality. But they seem to travel well.

It's difficult to transmit a message through a danceable music but I think that's something we've done. Ruben Blades was one of the first to do that with salsa, which showed you can do it with any genre. He's very political, of course, a real maestro. I am also influenced by nueva canción – new song – especially Silvio Rodríguez. For me he's one of the greatest songwriters – he's influenced everyone throughout the Caribbean. He's one of the masters, along with Pablo Milanés and Joan Manuel Serrat.

How about the musical side of the songs? You have quite a jazz sound in your kind of merengue – and your singing is pretty distinctive, too.
I studied jazz at Berklee College, Boston, learning composition, harmony and arrangement through the whole evolution of jazz – from ragtime through all the greats to Pat Metheny and Chick Corea.
I have a very nasal voice which a lot of people like, others don't! Luckily it's a very popular timbre in the Americas: it has an *aguardiente* (a firewater) inside it that other voices don't. It's natural for bacháta and merengue.

How do you write?
I compose alone, just voice and guitar – usually the chorus first. I put it on tape. I develop fragments of songs – it depends on my mood and inspiration. Then I sing them to my wife, my family, my friends. If they like them that normally means they'll be a success. A record is like a pregnancy – nine months minimum – because a lot of songs need time to mature. You have to let the story gel, that's the essential thing for a songwriter, the story. I don't think you should make a new album each year or even two years.

How about the role of your band, 4:40?
4:40 are the key to my music – we've worked together for the last fifteen years. We began as a kind of Caribbean Manhattan Transfer. That was when I had just returned from Boston and was into sophisticated arrangements. After we had some success with that, on our first album, we decided to shift back towards our roots – to merengue. We felt, in a way, we were playing a music that seemed elite, and we wanted to play a music that appealed to everyone at home, a music that seemed more natural and intuitive.

Juan Luís Guerra y 4:40 *Bachâta Rosa* (RCA, US). The sound of magical realist merengue with discreetly erotic lyrics and mildly critical socio-political themes. Musically, Guerra springs surprises with delicately African guitar work, South African choruses and delightfully mellow Cuban son. Hugely recommended, as are all Guerra's albums, especially ℗ *Ojalá que llueva café* (RCA, US) and his latest, the sublime and huge-selling ℗ *Areito* (RCA, US/Arista, UK).

Francisco Ulloa *¡Merengue!* and *¡Ultramerengue!* (GlobeStyle, UK). Never has the accordion sounded like this.

Wild music from a man who must have more than his natural quota of fingers to bring it off.

℗ **Various** *Aquí esta merengue* (Karen/BMG, US). A roundup of Dominican merengue featuring Wilfrido Vargas, creator of the 1980s merengue-fusions with zouk and soca; his former protege, Sergio Vargas, one of the sweetest voices in salsa today; plus Las Chicas del Can and more.

℗ **Various** *Haiti Chérie Mérengue* (Corason, Mexico). Wonderful street bands playing Haiti's rougher but closely related version of merengue.

COMPAS, CARNIVAL AND VOODOO

HAITI'S JOYFUL DANCE MUSIC
TRANSCENDS THE ISLAND'S TROUBLES

Sue Steward traces dance, carnival and voodoo in Haiti's unique mix of African and French Caribbean music and magic.

To the outside world, **Haiti** is a troubled tropical island whose most ready associations are voodoo, violence, and the **tyrannical regimes** of Papa and Baby Doc Duvalier. The Duvaliers' brutal rule saw the island decline from a prosperous colony to the poorest territory in the Caribbean. Their loyal thugs, the Tontons Macoutes (Creole for "Bogeymen"), hired voodoo priests, or *houngans*, to terrify their opponents, confirming the universal image of voodoo as evil black magic and Haiti as a barbaric place. After a few brief months of optimism in 1991, when Father Aristide was elected president, a military coup took place, supported by Haiti's wealthy elite, and injustice and uncertainty returned.

However, there's no starker contrast in the Caribbean today than between Haiti's poverty and horrific history, and the joyful, melodic dance music that has existed here since the early decades of the century. Like Cuba, Haiti in the 1940s and 50s was a magnet for American tourists with Port-au-Prince, its capital city, rivalling Havana in its nightclubs and bars, where some of the greatest musicians of the day were employed. This scene collapsed during Papa Doc's reign of terror, though there were respites under the Baby Doc regime at the end of the 1970s, when the island became a hip resort for rock aristocrats like Mick Jagger and Iggy Pop, and at the end of the 1980s, when film-maker Jonathan Demme put together "Konbit", a wonderful compilation of Haitian music.

If the troubles are resolved, then Haiti's music, based on the wonderful rhythms of *compas* and as rich as any in the Caribbean, could be ripe for exploration again on its home ground. For the present, only the brave would venture beyond a discovery on disc or in the Haitian outposts of New York and Miami.

AFRICA, CREOLE AND VOODOO

Haiti occupies the western third of the island of Hispañola, which it shares with the Dominican Republic. Like all Caribbean islands, the character of the country was shaped by its colonial history. The original colonizers, the **Spanish**, handed Haiti over to the **French** in 1697, but held on to the east of the island until it won its own independence in 1865, six decades after Haiti.

It's hard to believe today, but at the height of French colonization Haiti was the richest colony in the world, the "Pearl of the Antilles", exporting more sugar, coffee and tobacco than the other islands put together. These industries were sustained by African slaves, who by 1800 numbered over half a million: eight times as many as the whites and mulattos, a ratio that precipitated the country's liberation and shaped the island's strong African identity.

Haiti was the first colony to achieve independence. An initial slave revolution was headed by a voodoo priest called Boukman, who was executed by the Spanish. Then, after years of bloody wars, the legendary saviour, **Toussaint L'Ouverture** led the country to freedom. In 1804, when Africa itself was still waiting to be carved up by the colonial powers, Haiti declared itself the first independent black nation.

The island's strong African character is still obvious today – in the food, the Creole language, the voodoo and the music. **Creole** (*Kreyol*), a phonetic fusion of various African languages and French, was scorned and banned during Papa Doc's time but is enjoying a revival today. This campaign for Creole pride is endorsed by a number of popular dance bands, including the radical **Boukman Eksperyans**, who sing mainly in Creole. Their catchy hit, "Se Kreyo'l Nou Ye" (We Speak Creole), on the album "Vodou Adje", has become something of an anthem for the young generation.

The word **voodoo** is Dahomeyan, from West Africa, and means "spirit" – both good and evil. Voodoo practices unite many African religions and effectively brought together slaves from different countries. The drummers conveyed coded messages and gave psychological and spiritual sustenance to the slaves. Voodoo still has that function in the stricken island today: there's an old saying that "Haitians are 80 percent Catholic and 100 percent Voodoo".

The Africans merged the Catholicism imposed by the Spanish and French with their own animistic religions to create the new hybrid. In a voodoo ceremony, held at an outdoor temple, the houngan prepares his congregation with drumming and chanting, calling the gods (*loas*) down to inhabit a chosen living or inanimate object. The loas, who speak through the "possessed" person, are identified with Catholic saints who have similar personalities or attributes. If anything like safety returns to Haiti, and you visit, you can, if you're lucky, get to see one of the secret ceremonies in a temple, or in one of the hotels which, in the days when Haiti had tourists, used to offer voodoo evenings with drumming, dancing and chanting. The records of the neo-traditional **Grupo Mackandal**, an acoustic drums-and-voices ensemble, offer a taste of many of the roots rhythms of Haiti.

COMPAS

Compas, the popular music of Haiti, has little in common with voodoo and owes more to colonial dance rhythms. Typically, it is played by a big band or **orchestre** and is divided into sections that change abruptly in mood, texture and key. The overall sound is sweet and smooth and the melodies are carried on

flowing guitar lines, regulated by a characteristic rocking beat that pivots between the hi-hat and a bass drum on the floor.

Like most Caribbean music, compas is a compôte of musical styles, with a base in traditional rhythms like méringue – a slower, Haitian variant of the Dominican merengue, retaining the guitar that has been supplanted over the border by the accordion. It also absorbed many other Caribbean influences, especially salsa, soca and zouk, and later jazz, funk and rap from North America. A further strain was Central African *soukous*, whose intricate guitar patterns were imported by Haitian teachers who went to work in Zaire after that country's independence.

Haiti's proximity to Cuba, just fifty miles away, and to Puerto Rico and the adjoining Dominican Republic, has meant that **Latin music** has always played the most important part in shaping the local sound. In addition to the Dominican merengues, Cuban dance bands from the 1930s onwards have brought the most popular music of the day: boleros, rumbas and mambos. **Calypso** too has left a permanent mark in the form of the huge orchestras like **Septentrional** and **Tropicana d'Haiti**, both of whom still release regular "Anniversaire" albums, swinging with the sensuous lilt of old-style calypso.

The foundations of modern compas were laid early in the century. With the US occupation of the island (1915–1934) came **Swing Band** music, and suddenly the horn sections of the sedate orchestras playing Cuban or European dance styles "swung". The most influential was **Les Jazz des Jeunes**, founded in the early 1940s by René St-Aude, a saxophonist who now runs a record shop and label in Brooklyn. Les Jazz des Jeunes's blend of Afro-Cuban and Afro-Haitian music with swing dominated the scene until the arrival of a pair of flamboyant young saxophonists who, in the 1960s, created two new strands of popular music.

These men were **Nemours Jean Baptiste**, who invented *compas direct*, the basis of today's compas sound, a big-band mix of mambo and compas with a steady bass drum and cowbell beat, and **Webert Sicot**, who came up with *cadence rampa*, which stuck closer to the Cuban line. For nearly a decade the two were bitter rivals, taunting each other's fans with confrontational lyrics, until Sicot wrote the truce song, "Polemic Fini" in 1965, proclaiming in its chorus, "Oh yes, the polemic is over".

Truce or not, **rivalry** – often of a pretty vicious nature – is a perennial feature on the Haitian

CARNIVAL IN PORT-AU-PRINCE

••••••••••••••••••••••••

The **carnival** in Port-au-Prince represents a route of six to eight kilometres through the city. Groups, mounted on trucks disguised as floats, covered with loudspeakers and microphones, move forward at a tortuous pace in the middle of a veritable human sea that sweats, dances and pushes. Throughout the entire trajectory, lasting from six to seven hours, each group plays only a single composition, and when they arrive back at the Place de l'Hôtel de Ville for the popular dance (which lasts another two hours) they continue playing the same piece! Perhaps the director of the orchestra has also contracted for a nightclub engagement on the same evening, where they have to play from midnight until three o'clock in the morning, taking care to open and close the dance with a long version of that same carnival méringue.

After three days of these bachanals, one can deduce that the compas musicians have played intermittently for nearly fifty hours, under appalling conditions, while consuming a good amount of alcohol and an overdose of decibels. Moreover, the musical core of their repertoire is a hit of energy, designed to excite the crowd, and its execution at an exaggeratedly quick tempo requires superhuman quantities of energy. So, they have to hold their rhythm for three days, under the sun, and three nights in insufferable heat, even when they can't hear what they're playing. The golden rule is: Never Fade. On the hundred and one stops of this competitive route, they have to win one-on-one on the applause meter before being able to stake a claim as heroes of the evening.

From **Ralph Boncy's** La Chanson d'Haïti: 1965–85, translated by Gage Averill for The Beat magazine. If you can read French, this book – a collection of articles on all facets of Haitian music – is a must. The book and an accompanying CD (see Discography) can be ordered through Editions CIDIHCA, 417 rue St-Pierre, Suite 408, Montréal, Québec, Canada (☎514/845-6218).

music scene. It encompasses the big established orchestras, Septentrional and Tropicana, and seeps into relationships, too, among the exiles in New York, Miami and Montréal.

MINI-JAZZ, ZOUK AND AMERICAN FUSIONS

The 1960s were in all respects a critical decade in Haiti. Papa Doc installed his oppressive state machinery, prompting the flight of hundreds of thousands of Haitians to the United States and Canada.

For the musicians back home, or in these new communities, influences came from beyond the Caribbean, as The Beatles and American and French pop singers spawned a generation of **"mini-jazz" bands** who performed at house and school parties. With electric guitar, bass, saxophone, drums and percussion they played covers of imported pop and Haitian classics, and original teen-oriented songs. They included some great groups: **Ibo Combo**, **Les Freres de Jean**, **Les Fantasistes de Carrefour**, **Shleu Shleu** and **Los Incognitos de Petionville**. It was a formative era and the starting point for most of today's influential musicians.

Most of the mini-jazz bands mutated into larger formations and moved to the US in the early 1970s. Los Incognitos metamorphosed into the most famous of all Haitian bands, **Tabou Combo**, who put compas on the international map. Their 1969 debut album, "Haiti", launched a new era for the music, while "8eme Sacrement", recorded in 1984, after their move to New York, sold millions – and reached number one in Paris. The latter includes the group's big performance song, "New York City", a high-speed swirl of funfair accordion, electric guitars and sizzling hi-hats, amid which the singer switches from French to Spanish to English. It sounds as fresh and modern as anything produced today and still sends audiences into ecstasy.

In recent years, compas has undergone radical changes, especially among Haitians living in the USA. In New York – Brooklyn has the largest Haitian community after Haiti's capital, Port-au-Prince – and Miami, access to hi-tech equipment and to other musics have made changes inevitable. Throughout the 1970s, influences filtered into compas, particularly in New York, and above all from salsa. The group **Skah Shah**, for instance, employed a salsa-style backing

Tabou Combo

section of trumpets and trombones to create a delicious new combination with the compas rhythm section and shifting guitars.

From the mid-1980s, **French Antillean** zouk was another major force in the Caribbean, and a three-way trade developed between merengue, zouk and compas, with their respective bands producing a rush of sparkling covers of each others' songs. The song "Vacances", for instance, captivated Haiti in the early 1970s, on its release by merengue and compas bands Les Fantasistes de Carrefour and Shleu Shleu, and then re-emerged as a monster zouk hit for the Guadeloupian band **Kassav** in the 1980s. Kassav and the other disco-oriented zouk bands continue to be hugely popular in Haiti.

Many of Haiti's so-called **Nouvel Jenerayshun** (New Generation), who came through on the island and in the USA in the 1980s, have the typically bright, electronic sound associated with both merengue and zouk bands. Exponents like **Sakad** – a funk-based outfit – featured sharp synthesizers, themes borrowed from American dance music, the intricate horn arrangements of merengue, and breathy female choruses (women singers were a radical step for Haitians). **The Phantoms** and the **System Band** are typical new generation, combining live horns and the compas style with synthesizers and every electronic device, while, even more radically, bands like **Zin** in New York and Miami's **Top Vice** have introduced rapping over a compas backing. Another recent arrival is a spate of female bands, most notably **Karesse** and **Risque**, a new generation of women who attach loosely feminist lyrics to the compas beat.

Tabou Combo's catalogue parallels the recent history of compas, from the accordion and guitar drive of the "New York City" era, to

N ew York's Haitian community is centred around **Nostrand Avenue, Brooklyn**: a street where every other storefront is a church, and there are more record stores and barber's shops than tropical food outlets. Here JD's Records, run by record producer Jerome Donfred, sells the entire history of Haitian music. There are racks of classics from big orchestras like Septentrional, the whole range of Tabou Combo, local zouk and rap-influenced bands like Zin, and political records like Fedia Laguerre's "Operashun Dechoukaj" (Operation Uprooting – a reference to the uprooting of the Tonton Macoutes after the Duvaliers left), which can't be sold in Haiti. Around the shop are Haitian newspapers, such as *Haiti Culture* and the music magazine *Nouvelaute*, and fliers for bands at local clubs like Le rendez-vous and Château d'Or. Another record store at the centre of the scene is Nouvel Jenerayshun, on the same street.

Miami's "Little Haiti" is closer geographically, and also in looks, to Port-au-Prince, with its Creole shop signs and graffiti, although the restaurants and record shops indicate a higher standard of living than on the island. Elegant nightclubs like Le Limekey and Obsession heave with couples dancing cheek-to-cheek (*cole cole*), in their finest silks, until dawn. This is an uneasy bicultural ghetto, with regular run-ins with both the police and the neighbouring Afro-Americans of Liberty City. But here, as in New York, the population pulses with a vitality and optimism that is impossible to conceive of back home. The top local Haitian band here at present is **Top Vice**.

its 1980s electronic, zouk-influenced entry into the rap age. Their live album, "Aux Antilles", reveals how they've adapted compas to the synthesized format and reworked their own history through new versions of earlier hits. Their offshoot, **New York Superstars**, have moved onto straight rap over a compas beat: the sound of 1990s Brooklyn.

A RETURN TO ROOTS: RA-RA

Back on Haiti, with no chance of access to hi-tech zouk gear, many Port-au-Prince bands and musicians have turned to the island's roots, particularly voodoo and the Easter carnival music, **ra-ra**, for inspiration.

Ra-ra, although a secular music, has close connections with the ritual practices of voodoo. The music is made up of interlocking rhythmic figures played on a variety of percussion instruments and simple bamboo trumpets, with saxophones and trumpets sometimes brought in as well. You can hear it in its raw form on "Caribbean Revels", a Smithsonian Folkways CD recorded in situ in Haiti and among Haitian cane cutters in the Dominican Republic.

The ra-ra beat is also a trademark of the band **Boukman Eksperyans**, who have pioneered a blend of Afro-Haitian religious music, sung in

Boukman Eksperyans

Creole. They feature prolonged percussion workouts on a set of traditional instruments, while weaving in rock guitar, funk and reggae bass lines. In "Nou pap sa bliye" (We're Not Going to Forget This) the band chant out ra-ra and the other rhythms they use: "Petro, Congo, Rada, Ibo, Nago: our ancestors were there." The two female singers dip and swoop, mimicking the street dancers in the ra-ra processions; Haitian audiences go wild in recognition of their street culture in this context. Lolo Beaubrun, the group's leader, explains their use of voodoo elements as an attempt "to reinstate our culture, which had been despised and rejected for years. Even Boukman himself was written out of history because he was a voodoo priest."

While Boukman Eksperyans pioneered this style and maintain it, their career has been punctuated by periods of silence in the face of threats and danger. Their 1992 carnival entry, "Kalfou Denjere", for example, was banned in the wake of the military coup as "too violent", and the authorities also prohibited broadcast of their 1990 anthem "Kèm Pa Sote", with its chorus "My heart doesn't leap – You don't scare me". Other ra-ra bands, like **Bouka Guinee**, were forced to leave Haiti altogether for the safety of New York.

The artist considered most subversive – and thus the most persecuted musician on Haiti – is singer-songwriter **Manno Charlemagne**. He sings guardedly metaphoric lyrics backed by a big band that employs the traditional tall upright drums. Seen as a kind of Haitian Bob Marley, and drawing vast crowds in concert, he openly opposed Duvalier and then the Generals, and gave very public backing to Aristide. He remains a key figure of the Haitian music scene, both on the island and in Miami, where he has spent periods of exile.

Other contemporary island-based bands include **Sanba-Yo**, who occupy a similar rock-roots territory to Boukman Eksperyans, with a ra-ra beat and other rural rhythms and choruses, and **Coupé Cloué**, led on electric guitar by grandmaster Gesner Henry, who still play true compas. They have an ambivalent reputation on Haiti, as one of the only surviving mini-jazz bands, and one that has played at Tontons Macoutes parties (not that bands can exactly refuse to play for the Macoutes, if invited). Their music has updated itself over the years but still bears the sensual languor of the tropics rather than the brash speed of the new US-based sounds.

Younger bands on the island include **Mizik**, and **Tropicana**, both of whom play a safe, old-fashioned line; **Foula**, who have developed a voodoo-jazz-funk sound with a range of traditional rhythms; and **Ram**, led by Richard Morse, who contributed a track to the soundtrack of Hollywood's first AIDS movie, *Philadelphia*. Morse is the owner of the Olaffson Hotel, which is as close as anything on Haiti gets to being a centre of the music scene. It's here that most media visitors stay, and in outhouses behind the hotel workshop space is offered to musicians, dancers and artists.

La Vie en Exile

Si ou se yon lidè	If you are a leader
Se pou w panse a pèp-ou	You have to think of your people
Yon pèp ki fè w konfyans	A people that gives you their trust
Ki gen dwa a yon chans . . .	Who have a right to opportunity . . .
Kapten bato-a, wa koule	Captain of the boat, you'll sink
Si w pa ban la men.	If you don't give me your hand.

Tabou Combo (from the album "Aux Antilles").

DISCOGRAPHY

COMPILATIONS

Various *Konbit: Burning Rhythms of Haiti* (A&M, US). A superb compilation by film-maker Jonathan Demme, with the collaboration of compas fans The Neville Brothers, who play on a couple of tracks. The selection perfectly illustrates the trends of the past forty years, opening with Nemours Jean Baptiste and compas direct, then moving through mini-jazz units and big-band synth-era sounds, and on to ra-ra beat from Sanba-Yo, the salsa-influenced Magnum Band (led by former Tabou Combo guitarist Dadou Pasquet) and the funk of Sakad.

Various *Caribbean Revels* (Smithsonian Folkways, US). A remarkable disc capturing the rough and ready sound of authentic ra-ra, recorded in cemeteries and streets in Haiti in the late 1970s.

Various *Haïti Chérie: Méringue* (Corason, Mexico). Street bands playing Haiti's rougher version of merengue.

ARTISTS

Boukman Eksperyans *Vodou Adje* and *Kalfou Danjere* (Mango, UK). New directions: compas spurned for other rhythms, especially ra-ra music, and with plenty of American influences in the guitar and neighbouring Jamaica in the bass lines. Notable, too, for the brave political edge of the lyrics. Both albums – and especially *Kalfou Danjere* (Dangerous Crossroads) – are highly recommended.

Coupé Cloué *Maximum Compas from Haiti* (Earthworks, UK). Traditional compas from a band who have stayed in Haiti and, under composer Gesner Henry, developed a lush, languorous guitar-led style.

ⓓ Ensemble Nemours Jean Baptiste *Musical Tour of Haiti* (Ansonia Records, US). Great collection of tracks from the creator of Haitian compas. Punchy and rhythmic saxophone, accordion and brass.

Orchestre Septentrional *La Boule de Feu Internationale "40th Anniversaire"* (Marc Records, Haiti). The pre-compas sound of the 1940s and 50s, with duelling trumpets and saxophones, wild guitar, and masses of swing.

Orchestre Tropicana d'Haiti *La Fusée d'Or* (Geronimo, US). Longstanding rivals to Septentrional, who claim on their sleeve notes to be "for 15 years the only big Haitian orchestra of an international quality". Whatever, the vocals are sublime and the rhythm mixed, retaining roots elements in the compas.

Shleu Shleu *Haiti mon Pays* (Ibo Records, Haiti). The epitome of the 1960s mini-jazz era – the "uptown Port-au-Prince" sound, featuring topical songs about Haiti, baseball, fishing and girls.

Ra-Ra Machine *Break the Chain* (Shanachie, US). The sound of the future: rap and ra-ra fused by Brooklyn Haitians into dance music. Okay if you dig a hi-tech beat.

ⓓ Skah Shah *Forever* (Mini Records, US). One of the best products of New York Haitian fusion.

ⓓ Tabou Combo *8eme Sacrement* and *Zap!* (Mini Records, US). Compas dropped into Brooklyn's Caribbean cauldron and brought out with meandering accordion and Cuban-style conga.

ⓓ Zèklè *San Mele* (Nouvel Jenerayson Records, US). This is a welcome 1994 return from a band at the heart of the 80s Nouvel Jenerayshun scene. It's a gem with sharp songs from Ralph Boncy and Joël Widmaier and a neat pop sensibility.

ⓓ Zin *Lage'M* (Zin, US). A Nouvel Jenerayshun band from New York, Zin produce a blend of zouk, compas and soul.

OUT OF THE ORCHID HOUSE

CALYPSO AND SOCA FROM TRINIDAD AND BEYOND

Charles de Ledesma and Simon Broughton on the legendary calypso music of Trinidad – and the development of its modern offshoot, soca.

Calypso is a music with a long and distinguished history. It began in Trinidad in the nineteenth century and crossed over to New York and London in the 1930s, following an exodus of emigrants from the island. As a partying, carnival music, it developed a huge international appeal, and remained a dominant sound of the Caribbean right through to the 1970s, when salsa and reggae took over the headlines. Calypso, however, mounted a spirited rearguard action, as the island and exile musicians responded to the new zest for dance music by combining calypso with soul music and hi-tech production techniques to produce a new form of Caribbean popular music – soca.

> "I have faith in the vigour and nourishing climate of this little orchid house that will accept all things and turn them around and change them. In this little island much of the trash of western culture is taken, adapted and reborn in forms that are unique and original."
> **Peter Minshall**, Trinidadian carnival costume designer.

Like reggae, and more so reggae's predecessor, *mento* (see p.523), calypso is rooted in social and political comment, and peppered with patois and slang. However, calypso places much more emphasis on the lyrics, which are characterized by topical, satirical comments, and calypsonians also employ an art known as *picong* – impromptu versifying, teasing a public figure or even a member of the audience. Musically, calypso has an airborne spring to its rhythm – very different to reggae's earthy bass beat.

Soca, being that much more of a dance form, and produced for a wider, international market, is in some respects a blander offspring. As **Chalkdust**, one of the current calypsonians concerned about the problem, put it: "Are we to put water in the brandy and compose for the international market, singing just two or three words you can understand and dance to? Or are we to keep to the traditions of calypso and compose for the home market and tell the story as it was? Many calypsonians today are suffering from that dilemma." Right now it seems that the traditionalists are losing. But musical development never stands still – particularly in the Caribbean.

CALYPSO ORIGINS

The legendary calypsonian **Roaring Lion** has compared his art to that of the jongleurs and troubadours who travelled medieval Europe telling stories and spreading the news.

Traditionally calypsonians were the newspapers of Trinidad and the whole history of the island has been told in calypso lyrics.

Musically, though, its origins go back to the **gayup**, a communal work song the West African slaves brought with them to the plantations. In call-and-response style, the gayup often had two sections and referred to a particular competition or event. The slaves sang the first part to celebrate victory, then the second to pour scorn on the losers. You can still hear work songs in Trinidad today from the fishermen pulling in nets on the shore, who use the music to help coordinate their movements and ease their task. In the plantations each work group was led by a *chantwell*, a sort of lead singer who would sing one line which the others would answer in chorus as they worked. There was a legendary slave and chantwell called **Elephant**, because of his thunderous voice, who was something like a forerunner of today's calypsonians.

The word calypso is thought to be a corruption of the West African word **"kaiso"**, a cry of encouragement or satisfaction akin to "olé" or "bravo". In fact you can still hear it shouted in the calypso tents today after a particularly fine performance, in praise of a finely crafted or skilful calypso. Chalkdust sees calypso as a peculiar hybrid springing from African roots: "The origins – the melodic patterns and rhythmic structure – are African. But culture changes and we have pulled from the French – in the mas [carnival masquerade]; we have pulled from the English – we speak English; we have pulled from the Spanish – in the melodies; and we have pulled from jazz and the Americans. They have all influenced the calypso."

This variety of influences reflects Trinidad's particular colonial history. It was originally settled by the Spanish in 1532, subsequently came under French rule, and in 1802, along with its sister island, Tobago, became a British colony. The French planters had brought with them the Catholic tradition of celebrating Lent with masquerade balls and processions, and although the African slaves could not take part, they set up alternative **"canboulay" processions** based on West African celebrations for the end of harvest. (The word comes from the French "cannes brûlées" – burning sticks – because the marchers carried flaming torches.) With emancipation in 1834 these two forms of carnival merged. The gayup song was adapted to create calypso and masquerades became satirical street pantomime.

CARNIVAL

Carnival was the time for letting off steam and featured bands of drummers and stick-fighters with chantwells egging them into action. Both the drumming and the stick-fights were banned by the British after carnival riots in 1880 and the Sunday-night Canboulay procession was replaced by the Kalenda March and Dance on Monday morning. But the connection between carnival and music remained and developed.

These days, the carnival season stretches from New Year to the pre-Lent celebrations (on the two days preceding Ash Wednesday) in March, and throughout this period calypso and calypsonians are everywhere. In the run-up, the calypsos are rehearsed and aired in so-called **calypso tents**, originally bamboo tents, but now cinemas or halls, often capable of holding an audience of thousands. In the old days the chantwells engaged in picong contests in the tents, trading insults with their rivals, and this continued in the calypso competition. Now official prizes are given: the **Calypso Monarch**, awarded for the best calypso of the year, is chosen by a panel of judges and the **Road March** – the peoples' choice – is for the most-played calypso; generally speaking the Monarch is chosen for its lyrics and the Road March for melody. Prizes aside, the tents serve as vital ground for apprentice singers and bands and it is here, almost without exception, that calypsonians first make their reputations.

The steel drums, known as **pans**, are one of the most evocative sounds of carnival, and like calypso their roots go back to popular forms of protest. After stick-fighting was banned, tambour-bamboo bands would bang bamboo sticks together as an accompaniment to carnival songs. These too were eventually banned but they reappeared, once again transformed, in 1937, when a carnival band performed with an orchestra of frying pans, dustbin lids and oil drums. Aftr the war this makeshift battery was replaced by a carefully tempered orchestra of oil drums, finely tuned by beating with a hammer and chisel (see box).

Trinidad, Land of Calypso

People are interested to know where
calypso originated:
Some say it came from Cuba, some say
British Guyana
Some contend seriously it was sung by
Moses crossing the Red Sea
But I told them no, no, oh no
Trinidad is the Land of Calypso
No, no, oh no
Trinidad is the Land of Calypso.

It was a serious contention that was
causing some real confusion
Some said it's Japanese or the folksong of
ancient Chinese
A fellow said, yes certainly, like I used to
sing calypso to Samson
One said he heard when Nero was burning
Rome he sang calypso
One said that in India they sang calypso
when charming cobra
Another said that Elijah sang a calypso in the
chariot of fire
They argued with one another, trying
to find out the owner
They mentioned every country, all but
the land of la Trinity!

The Roaring Lion

ORATORICAL CALYPSO

From abolition to ninety-eight
Calypso was still sung in its crude state
From French to English it was then translated
By Norman Le Blanc who became celebrated
Then it was rendered grammatically
In oration, poetry and history.

The lines above, from a calypso by Lord Invader, provide a potted history of the form's progression and its role in recording the events of the island. As Roaring Lion, one of the last of the great calypsonians, observed: "The whole history of Trinidad is in calypso voices."

These voices were evident by the late nineteenth century, when chantwells like Hannibal and Boadicea entertained at carnival time and struck out at the repressive policies of the colonial government. The above-mentioned **Norman Le Blanc** sang about the British threat to abolish the Port of Spain City Council in 1898 and he and other early bards regularly lampooned the colonial government as well as rival bands. They forged out of African communal song a distinctive style combining Cuban melodies, Spanish guitar and the patois words absorbed into everyday usage.

Calypso was first recorded in 1914 and in the 1930s entered something of a golden age, with calypsonians improvising with great wit and dexterity on issues of the day. The early stars included **Lord Executor**, commonly considered the greatest extemporizer, **Lord Invader**, **Roaring Lion**, **Mighty Destroyer** and **Attila the Hun**. The names calypsonians sing under are almost always Lord This or Mighty That – a reminder of the competitive nature of the music and of its use in Trinidad as a political weapon. In these prewar years, with government-suppressed media, the so-called oratorical calypso had an almost broadsheet role, expressing popular discontent.

Calypsonians often ran into trouble with the police over songs that were considered politically unsuitable or obscene, and there was a period in the 1930s when the government attempted to license the songs. The idea was soon dropped due to public opposition and the censorship itself became a ripe subject for calypso in this lyric by Attila the Hun:

To say these songs are sacrilegious, obscene or profane
Is only a lie and a dirty shame
If the calypso is indecent, then I must insist
So is Shakespeare's Venus and Adonis

The young Roaring Lion (centre)

Boccaccio's tales, Voltaire's Candide
The Martyrdom of Man by Winwood Reid
Yet over these authors they make no fuss
But they want to take advantage of us.

POSTWAR CALYPSO AND
MIGHTY SPARROW

World War II and the arrival of American troops in Trinidad brought about a new wave of political calypso. Musicians like the **Saga Boys** and **Mighty Sparrow** – the island's rising star – camouflaged their invective against US influence by singing about local girls who had been whisked away by the Yankee dollar. Lord Invader's hilarious "Lieutenant Joe" told of a man so concerned to keep his girlfriend that he didn't mind when she gave birth to a coloured baby, offspring of a brief liasion with GI Joe. Sparrow's "Jean and Dinah", which won him the calypso crown in 1956, was about the postwar mess the Americans left behind them.

Well the girls in town feeling bad
No more Yankees in Trinidad
They going to close down the base for good
Them girls have to make out how they could

Is now they park up in town
In for a penny, in for a pound
Yes, is competition for so
Trouble in town when the price drop low.

The other effect of American presence on the island was a wider market for calypso. Calypso artists like Roaring Lion and Attila the Hun had recorded in the US in the 1930s, but it was in the war years that recordings from the island found a significant market in America, as the songs and rhythms were adopted by American bandleaders and singers. **The Andrews Sisters** had an enormous hit with Lord Invader's "Rum and Coca-Cola" (itself based on the Cuban "Son de la Loma"), which they virtually stole, giving cause for a copyright suit. Their plundering of the song (which was about prostitution) gave the words an added irony:

Rum and Coca-Cola
Go down Point Cumana
Both mother and daughter
Working for the Yankee dollar.

The American recording industry took due note of this success, and RCA-Victor (Elvis Presley's label) signed up Sparrow, as well as the American-born **Harry Belafonte**, who in the 1950s had worldwide success with his album "Calypso", the first ever LP to sell a million copies. Belafonte was hardly the real McCoy, as he sung in standard American English and lacked the Trini linguistic inventiveness and political message. However, his songs – the best of which were written by **Lord Melody** – undoubtedly put calypso on the world map, and primed an American audience for calypso's greatest postwar stars, Lord Kitchener and the Mighty Sparrow.

Lord Kitchener (Aldwyn Roberts) represented a new generation of calypsonians – dubbed the Young Brigade – who broadened the subject matter of calypso from its somewhat parochial island concerns. He dipped into world events, lived for a while in London, and, back home, notched up a record series of eleven Road March victories at the Port of Spain carnival. These triumphs stretched from 1946 to 1976, when he retired from competition, devoting most of his musical energies to compositions for steelbands. Enormously technically accomplished, he has delved into jazz territory and even had a soca hit, "Sugar Bum Bum", in 1978. His most famous song, "Give Me the Ting", is still a dancehall classic.

Although actually born on Grenada, **Mighty Sparrow** (Francisco Slinger) moved to Trinidad as a child and the island claims him as its own.

THE CARIBBEAN

A brilliant singer and arranger, he is – even more than Kitchener – the dominant figure of postwar calypso, both on the island and in America, where in the 1950s and 60s he would often fill New York's Madison Square Gardens. He got his name, he says, because he hopped around so much on stage, whereas other calypsonians got their message across by standing on the spot and pointing accusingly at the audience. In an attempt to marginalize the young buck, his elders called him Sparrow – unlike Lion, Tiger or Executor, hardly a name to instill respect. Sparrow added the prefix Mighty as a form of damage limitation.

Sparrow's musical success brought political influence, which he lent, enthusiastically, to Eric Williams' People's National Movement, after it came to power in 1956. Sparrow wrote a string of calypsos in their support:

> Praise little Eric, rejoice and be glad
> We have a better future here in Trinidad
> P.N.M. it ain't got nobody like them
> For they have a champion leader
> William the Conqueror.

For many Trinidadians, particularly the lower classes, the nationalist government had come as a breath of fresh air, though disillusion with Eric Williams and his party set in during the mid-1960s. Sparrow articulated this, too, in his song, "Get To Hell Outa Here". And he continued doing it: "If you really know the true role of the calypsonian," he explained recently, "then you should understand that somewhere along the line you gonna be treading on the corns of the people in power."

Sparrow remains an important figure in the Caribbean and his music was in some ways a first step towards soca, which he has warmly embraced, much to the disgust of the traditionalist **Roaring Lion**, another key figure of postwar (and even prewar) calypso. Lion – his real name is Hubert Raphael de Leon – is a Trinidad institution, well into his eighties now, and resident again on the island after a long spell in Britain (see box). He has total contempt for soca's lack of wit and narrative lyrics. As he put it: "Fellows just yelling "Party! Party!" all the time; where's the story in that?"

While on the subject of wit and lyrics, it has to be noted that – although one of the most famous nineteenth-century calypsonians, **Boadicea**, was a woman – calypso is very male-dominated and a great many songs are shockingly sexist. One of the commonest themes is the calypsonian's great sexual prowess and Sparrow's "Village Ram" is typical:

> Not a woman ever complain yet with me
> I ain't boasting but I got durability
> And if a woman ever tell you that I
> Ever left her dissatisfy
> She lie, she lie, I say she lie.

Double standards for men and women are the norm. Men boast of sleeping around while women are supposed to be faithful and obedient. Many calypsos are simply smutty or hide their obscenity in double-entendres to get round radio bans.

Female calypsonians didn't really reappear till the 1960s with the emergence of **Calypso Rose** (Linda Lewis). A one-time singing partner of Kitchener, Rose is the only woman to have won the title of Calypso King, in 1978, which was thereafter changed to Calypso Monarch, in her honour. In the last decade, female calypsonians like **Singing Francine** and **Singing Diane** have written calypsos reflecting the concerns of the women's movement, Singing Francine, for example, advising women to leave men who mistreat them in her hit song "Run Away":

> Cat does run away, dog does run away
> Fowl does run away when you treating
> them bad
> What happen to you?
> Woman, you can run away too.

HOT! HOT! HOT! – SOCA TAKES HOLD

In the mid-1970s calypso began to change under the influence of soul and dance music, new technology and – once again – America. Calypso musicians were increasingly recording in

STEEL PANS

The **steel pan** is a fitting symbol for Trinidad and the carnival. The Trinis put something cheap and abundant to extraordinary good use and created one of the few acoustic instruments to be invented this century. At carnival time a steelband can have up to 100 players and 300 pans. The sound – like a crashing wave – is overwhelming.

To make your steel pan you need a 45-gallon oil drum, a sledgehammer, small hammer, metal punch, ruler, compasses and chalk. The unopened end of the oil drum is "sunk" with the sledgehammer – deeper for the higher drums and shallower for the cello and bass pans. The position of the notes (around the perimeter and in the centre) is outlined with compasses and chalk and then beaten out with a hammer and tempered with fire and water. The final tuning is carefully done with a small hammer and rubber-tipped playing stick.

In a steelband the melodies are played on the **tenor pans**, and at that pitch a complete range of notes can be fitted onto one drum. A **double tenor** is a lower melody instrument and has the notes distributed on two drums. A **double second** is a pair of drums for accompanying chords and a **treble guitar** a trio of pans for lower harmonies. The lower the note required, the more space it takes up on the drum, so the bass might need a range of four or six pans with just a few notes on each.

The steelbands really got going after 1941 when the US Navy had bases on the island. Although Carnival was officially suspended for the duration of the war, it was celebrated secretly in the slums of Port of Spain and the "panmen" acquired a dangerous and disreputable reputation, their name synonymous with trouble. In the 1956 carnival, two steelbands, Tokyo and the Invaders, had a street battle that lasted for hours.

Now, young troublemakers are actively encouraged by the government to join steelbands to keep them out of trouble. The pans have become respectable and they even play Mozart and Tchaikovsky ("bomb tunes", as they are known). But nothing can beat the sensation of a band on the streets and you can sense its history in the high-octane physical thrill of those hammers on steel.

As Earl Lovelace described it, in his wonderful evocation of Carnival, *The Dragon Can't Dance* (Longman, UK), the panmen "troop off street corners, desert their battlefield and territory, and turn up the hill to the steelband tent to assemble the drums . . . The tent becomes a cathedral, and these young men priests. They will draw from back pockets those rubber-tipped sticks, which they had carried around all year, as the one link to the music that is their life, their soul, and touch them to the cracked faces of the drums. Hours, days; hours, days; for weeks they beat these drums, beat these drums, hammering out from them a cry, the cry, the sound, stroking them more gently than they will ever caress a woman; and then they have it. At last they have it. They have the tune that will sing their person and their pose, that will soar over the hill, ring over the valley of shacks, and laugh the hard tears of their living when, for Carnival, they enter Port of Spain".

Brooklyn rather than Trinidad and there they encountered hi-tech production techniques and powerful arrangers, who began shaping the sound to a dance formula, introducing drum machines and the like. Disco culture was at a peak in New York and beyond – this was the era of John Travolta – and there was money to be made from a hot "Latin" sound that satisfied the dancefloor's cravings for grooves closer to James Brown, Isaac Hayes and Tamla Motown.

The first of these new songs to be recorded was **Lord Shorty**'s "Soul Calypso", whose abbreviated name coined the term **soca**. Built around a soulful bass hook and a disco drum beat, it was a ground-breaking mixture of funk, mid-tempo ska and calypso. In fact, Shorty's free movement in foreign forms was a kind of Trinidad equivalent of the way Toots Hibbert (of Toots and the Maytals) shifted Jamaican music from a countrified insularity into the dangerous world of rock guitars and loud, soulful vocals. On the downside, soca lost the unique vocal inflections that had characterized calypso, substituting them with a flatter, less distinctive soul-soaked purr. The rhythm rather than the voice led the songs, which clearly addressed the body rather than the mind, with lyrics – "Paartiee tonite, paartiee all nite!" – often barely audible and trivial in content.

These new developments weren't due only to international influence – Trinidad itself was enjoying new-found oil wealth and a party atmosphere – and nor were they completely dominant, at least back home. The calypsonians' preoccupation with controversial lyrics remained and in 1986, when a drop in the oil price triggered a financial crisis, **Gypsy**'s "The Sinking Ship" caught the mood of the nation. It was in the classic calypso tradition of sustaining a satirical metaphor over numerous verses and was credited as the final blow in bringing down the government.

> The Trinidad, a luxury liner
> Is sailing the Caribbean sea
> With an old captain named Eric Williams
> For years sailed smooth and free.
> But sadly Eric Williams passed away
> The ship hit rough water that day
> And someone turned the bridge over
> To a captain named Chambers
> Made blood crawl, things start to fall
> Hold me head when a sailor fall.
> Captain, the ship is sinking,
> Captain, the seas are rough.
> Shall we abandon ship?
> Or shall we stay on it
> And perish slow? We don't know
> Captain, you tell me what to do.

Clearly, however, soca represents a crossroads in the calypso story and a dilemma for musicians, which is encapsulated in the careers of two artists, Mighty Chalkdust (Hollis Liverpool) and Arrow (Alphonsus Cassell). As commercial soca has pushed clever calypso backstage, **Chalkdust** (his name comes from his job as a schoolteacher) brilliantly maintains the tradition of calypso as comment. He won the Monarch prize twice in the 1970s but in 1983 put on his soca hat and produced the magnificent album "Kaiso with Dignity", which included the funk-soca "Drunk Monk" with a cracking dance break. But he's best known for his sharp observations about the developments affecting calypso's traditional role. This is from "Man Want to Dance":

> Long ago, when you hear kaiso, it was protest
> and commentary
> The things the government didn't want you
> to know
> They were sung in the tent likely, you see?

> But today, when the kaiso play, all the lyrics
> describing fête
> And the philosophy of yesterday has suffered a
> musical death.
> Man used to live in poverty so he liked social
> commentary
> But now my pockets have money, man want to
> fête and scream
> Man want to kaiso tell, to hear about government
> But now he have finance, man want to dance.
> No more protesting song, sarcasm and picong
> Lyrics don't stand a chance, man want
> to dance.

By contrast, **Arrow** wrote and recorded the anthem of party soca, "Hot, Hot, Hot", an incredibly successful and catchy song with virtually no lyrics to worry about. Born outside the island, Arrow is not entitled to enter the annual calypso March competitions and thus is perhaps more radical in his innovations, adding salsa and merengue to the mix. He says he never really went along with the idea of calypso as social protest and makes records to please as

David Rudder

many people in as many ways as he can. On stage, he plays a dancehall-reggae-soca, "Bills", a zouk-soca, "Zouk-Me", and a latin-tinged soca, "Limbo Calypso". He believes in intermingling Caribbean musics, bringing all cultures together, and has undeniably done

ARROW PLEADS GUILTY

Arrow spoke to Simon Broughton about the transition from calypso to soca – and the loss of the old traditions.

In the past calypso has been strongly political in its lyrics. Now you've placed the emphasis on dance. Do you feel any need to address issues in your songs and reflect the history of the music?

A lot of my earlier music up to 1979 was message-oriented, because I was trying to be Calypso King of Montserrat and Calypso King of the Caribbean. But even my new material touches on issues in songs like "Pressure", "Life" and "Budget Love". Of course, my primary goal is dance music, and to unite through my music all people, all races – to have everyone singing and dancing together. I leave it more to the news media to tell the people of the problems of the world. I'm taking the message of hope and happiness.

There's something about soca music which gives you the feeling that you want to get up and dance. Forget whatever problems you have, let's take you into some temporary utopia, let's forget the bills and just enjoy yourself! Even people who have never heard the music before, after one or two songs everybody is into the rhythm and the beat.

You've been accused of being the man responsible for destroying the old calypso. How do you feel about that?

I think I might be guilty of that, but for good results. I've been able to put a more commercial appeal onto soca and calypso. I think that the calypsonian or soca artist of the Caribbean can no longer be burdened with being the mouthpiece of the people. We are now in an age when Caribbean people are a lot more outspoken and we have opposition parties. It's no longer one-party rule and as musicians we should do what we have to do – make people happy.

Trinidad calypso was good, but now it's a new age and we need to move on. We need to take this music beyond the people of the Caribbean and show that the world can dance to it. This is what soca music has done.

---

much to introduce soca to a wider audience with his superbly adept backing band, The International Force.

Between the two extremes is **David Rudder**, an artist rooted in the calypso tradition but wide open to new ideas and fusions, and a proselytizer for soca's international dimension. "Calypso was very insular at one time," he claims. "It was what was happening on the block. I see the music going beyond the boundary of our islandness. I see it as a world statement, not an island statement."

Rudder sings alongside the equally celebrated **Chris "Tambu" Herbert** in the band **Charlie's Roots** but is best known for his 1986 solo hit, "The Hammer", which revelled in the sound of the steelband in a tribute to the great pan player Rudolph Charles – "the man with the hammer gone" – who had died the previous year. While "The Hammer" won Rudder the

Road March title, "Bahia Girl" later gained him the Monarch prize. It took the theme of cross-cultural sexual attraction and used it as a metaphor for the unity of all the people of African origin in Trinidad and Brazil. In a more directly political vein, on the anthemic title track from his "1990" album, he played on the initials IMF to read "Islands Must Fail": classic old school calypso yet accompanied by music just as iconoclastic as Shorty's or Arrow's.

The Rasta calypsonian **Black Stalin** (Leroy Calliste), too, never fails to deliver a strong message in his electrifying stage performances. Sometimes he acts the true oratorical calypsonian, standing and wagging his finger confrontationally at the audience – he did his apprenticeship in Kitchener's carnival tent – and other times leaps around with locks swaying wildly to make the point. His 1986 song "Bun Dem" begged Saint Peter to be

CALYPSO IN LONDON

••••••••••••••••••••••

Bill Rogers will stay
As a resident in the UK
Tell them how I am living so fine
Nothing at all to disturb my mind
Tell them I give lung to you
Blasting out mission, too.
Bill Rogers "Sightseeing in the UK".

Bill Rogers from Guyana was one of thousands of emigrants from the Caribbean who settled in Britain after World War II and made London a second capital of calypso. Others included **Lord Kitchener** and **Lord Beginner**, two of Trinidad's greatest calypsonians, who disembarked from the Empire Windrush at Tilbury on June 21, 1948 and by 1950 were recording sessions for EMI. **Lord Invader**, too, who had written "Rum and Coca-Cola", the song that The Andrews Sisters appropriated back in 1944, spent part of the 1950s in Britain.

A valuable selection of this British West Indian music was released on the UK Charly label in the 1980s as "Port Of Spain Shuffle" and "Caribbean Connections": they're no longer on catalogue but well worth tracking down. As well as tracks from Kitchener and Beginner, there are some great numbers from **Roaring Lion**, who came to London to play at the 1951 Festival of Britain and stayed on through most of the decade, running a cosmetics company and an immigrants' accommodation agency, as well as singing calypsos.

In their new environment, the calypsonians combined the roles of cultural ambassadors for Trinidadian music and nostalgists for life back home. But they also brought their tradition of calypso as social observation to the immigrants' experience of Britain. Beginner, for example, wrote a calypso about waiting for the results of the 1950 General Election to be posted on the lights in Piccadilly Circus:

Names went up in rotation
Some said we'll get more employment
Others said better house rent
Balloon went up too
I saw red and blue
For Attlee supporters roar
And for Churchill who won the war

One of the most popular records of the 1950s, as much with British as Caribbean audiences, was Lord Melody's "Cricket, Lovely Cricket", which celebrated the West Indies' first victory over England on British soil. Roaring Lion's calypsos were more concerned with island culture, though he had something of an obsession with the Royal Family, and he also got a name for sauciness. A classic example of this is the lyric to "Tick! Tick! (The Story of the Lost Watch)", a double-entendre number about a girl who steals a watch and hides it in her vagina – the police an hear it ticking but can't find it. There are still Roaring Lion records in the BBC library with old stickers saying "Do not play this track!".

Thirty years on, calypso retains a presence in London through the annual **Notting Hill Carnival** – the biggest carnival in Europe – which features steelbands and road march calypso on floats and on stage.

---

prepared to cast into the fire world leaders like Thatcher, Reagan and Botha.

Musically, the blending of soca and other styles has led to some great **cross-fertilizations**, drawing on styles from the Carribean and beyond. Two of the most interesting developments came from **Nelson**, who created **soca funk** in songs like "Black Gold", "Disco Daddy" and "Shango", and **Shadow**, who introduced a deep bass sound and swooping, manic violin melodies – heard to breathtaking effect, with his quavering baritone vocals, on his classic "De Hardis". **Arrow**, too, broke new

ground, with a rolling drum beat almost like Zairean soukous, while **Super Blue** (aka Blue Boy – Austin Lyons), another multiple Road March winner, drew on the spiritual tradition with his first and biggest hit, "Soca Baptiste". Meanwhile Lord Shorty, soca's originator, had become a Rastafarian, changing his name to Ras Shorty I and forming a gospel-soca band, **Love Circle**.

These innovations were at their peak during the late 1970s and early 80s, when the calypso constraints had gone out the window and the more restrained **Brooklyn sound** was still in germination. Some of the best Kitchener and Sparrow songs also emerged in these years, when Trinidad's greatest arranger, **Art de Couteau**, ruled the roost on the island. It's hard to overstate the influence of arrangers, and, over the past decade, **Pelham Goddard**, who works with Dave Rudder and Tambu, has fulfilled a similar role in soca calypso. Songwriters, too, are crucial: in particular **Winsford Devine**, who has penned lyrics for Sparrow and, more recently, **Baron**, the hugely popular, sweet-voiced exponent of 1990s **"lovers' soca"**.

Over the last few years, the most consistent winners of the Road March and Monarch prizes have been **Super Blue**, **Crazy** and **Tambu**. All of them seem to have the knack of coming up with surefire soca dance hits with appealing lyrics, combining wit and parody with sexual teasing – a formula that always goes down well. Tambu, David Rudder's singing partner, is perhaps the most successful of them all, having won the Road March three years in succession, from 1988 to 1990, when he recorded the soca anthem par excellence, "No, No, We Eh Going Home".

Through the 1980s and 90s, though, Trinidad's neighbouring islands have played an ever-increasing role. Soca has come of age on the **smaller islands** of Barbados, Grenada and St Vincent. Bajan (Barbados) singers like Gabby, Grynner, Archie Miller and Ray Iley, and bands like Red Plastic Bag, Spice, Chocolate Affaire and Positive Vibes turn out speedy, highly melodic soca. **Spice**'s "De Congaline" was much

TRINIDAD & TOBAGO
Land of Calypso

Aldwyn Roberts
Kitchener **50**c

copied in Trinidad and in 1990 **Chocolate Affaire's** "Massive Bam Bam" was a smash hit on many of the islands. **Gabby**, interestingly, has written some of the most political calypsos of the last decade. One of his biggest hits, "Jack", was a critique of the tourist hotel industry on Barbados, kicking out the locals from the beaches they had annexed. It caught the attention of Eddie Grant, who subsequently became his producer, introducing another vein of sound and turning Gabby into a Caribbean-wide star.

These bands from outside Trinidad were perhaps readier to absorb **new musical influences** than the island's soca and calypso artists. **Red Plastic Bag** incorporated Spanish guitar on "Sweet Rosita", while **Positive Vibes** blend soca with *spouge*, the up-country folk music of Barbados, played on guitars, mandolins and hand drums. Reggae, too, made an appearance, through St Vincent's **Burning Flames**, whose "Workie Workie" has been one of the 1990s best-selling soca tunes. Meanwhile, various Indo-Caribbean musicians on Trinidad have forged their own variety of calypso, which they've dubbed, succinctly, "chutney music".

Importantly, too, soca and calypso have found new audiences, eager for novelty, in Europe and North America. Trini and other island immigrants keep a scene going year-round, and the carnivals – London's Notting Hill, Brooklyn's Mas, Toronto's Caribana, and Miami carnival – provide a focus for others to get into the music and party.

DISCOGRAPHY

VINTAGE CALYPSO

⊙ **Various** *Trinidad Loves to Play Carnival: 1914–1939* (Matchbox, UK). A wonderful archive jaunt through the history of street marches and early carnival calypsos. Excellent sleeve notes and lyrics.

⊙ **Various** *History of Carnival 1933–39* (Matchbox, UK). More golden-era calypsos from carnival and Christmas celebrations, including Attila the Hun's "History of Carnival". Again, good sleeve notes and lyrics.

⊙ **Various** *Calypso Breakaway: 1927–41* (Rounder, US). A splendid collection from the golden era, featuring songs by King Radio, The Lion, Lord Beginner and Attila the Hun.

⊙ **Various** *Calypso War: Black Music in Britain 1956–58* (Sequel, UK). A fine collection of calypsos from Lord

Invader, The Mighty Terror, Lord Ivanhoe and Jamaican-born Ben Bowers.

⊙ **Various** *West Indies – An Island Carnival* (Elektra Nonesuch, US). Fascinating anthology of rustic groups from various islands of the Lesser Antilles – Trinidad, St Lucia, St Vincent, etc. In addition to calypso, there are examples of religious music: Hindu, Muslim and Afro-Trinidadian Shango.

MORE CALYPSO THAN SOCA

⊙ **Calypso Rose** *Soca Diva* (Ice, UK). Cracking numbers with vicious wit and winning melody from the island's top female calypsonian.

Chalkdust *Port of Spain Gone Insane* (Ebony Records, UK). A tuneful, danceable album including "Too Much Quacks"

and "Man Want to Dance", about the decline of calypso standards.

℗ **Gypsy** *Natural High* (Hot Vinyl, UK). The essential Gypsy compilation in calypso and soca mode, including "Sinking Ship" and "Party and Fire Jump".

℗ **Lord Kitchener** *Klassic Kitchener Volume One* (Ice/RAS, US). AS good a place to start as any is this collection of Kitch's classic songs, dating back to the 1940s. ℗ *Longevity* (JW, US) is a superb 1993 release, showing him still to be up there with the new dance rhythms.

Mighty Sparrow *Calypso Carnival* (La Records, Trinidad). One of Sparrow's greatest carnival releases, showing his lyricism at its peak, plus wonderful melodies, especially on the opening number, "Mr Walker". *Party Classics Volumes 1 & 2* (Charlie, US) comprise Sparrow's greatest hits from the 1950s on.

℗ **Mighty Sparrow and Lord Kitchener** *Carnival Hits* (Ice, UK). Sixteen hits from the two veterans – as fine an introduction as they come.

℗ **Roaring Lion** *Standing Proud* (Ice, UK). An essential anthology of octagenarian Lion's finest work. Includes his best known song, "Never Make a Pretty Woman your Wife (Always Marry a Woman Uglier than You)".

MORE SOCA THAN CALYPSO

℗ **Arrow** *Soca Dance Party* (Mango, UK) and *King of Soca* (Arrow, US; 2 vols). The best Arrow collections on CD. *Dance Party* is a faultless selection, including the pan-Caribbean classic "Zouk Me" and the mid-tempo "Easy Dancing"; *King of Soca* has the works from the late 80s and early 90s, including, of course, "Hot, Hot, Hot".

℗ **Black Stalin** *Rebellion* (Ice, UK). A fine introduction to Black Stalin, featuring his massive hit "One Tune Pan Man". For earlier Stalin, check out the compilation *Roots Rock Soca* (Rounder, US), issued under his previous Mighty Stalin alias.

℗ **Burning Flames** *Dig* (Mango, UK). Reggae meets soca in this release from the St Vincent band; includes their monster hit "Workey Workey".

℗ **Crazy Jump** *Leh We Jump* (DY, US). Crazy is a versatile new-generation voice: a dreadlocked calypsonian as much at home with mid-tempo calypso as roll-your-belly soca.

℗ **Gabby, Grynner and Bert "Panta" Brown** *Soca Trinity* (Ice, UK). A lively, witty set from the satirical calypsonians; includes Grynner's most famous song, "Best Brown".

℗ **Rootsman and Bally** *The Best of Rootsman and Bally* (JW, US). An enormously enjoyable album from these leading soca artists, including Rootsie's irresistible "Soca In De Palace".

Red Plastic Bag *Red Alert* (Rohit, US). Soca from Barbados, with one of the most progressive fusions – "Sweet Rosita" – introducing flamenco guitar to a slightly slower beat. ℗ *Happiness* (World Records, US) is their best recent outing.

David Rudder and Charlie's Roots *The Hammer* (Lypsoland, Trinidad/London Records, UK). Rudder's greatest set includes "The Hammer" and "Bahia Girl", which won him both Monarch and Road March titles. ℗ *Here Comes the West Indies* (Lypsoland, Trinidad/JW, US), Rudder's latest album, shows him once again in top form.

℗ **Singing Francine** *This is Singing Francine* (Red Bullet, Netherlands). One of the strongest women socalypsonians.

℗ **Super Blue** *Flag Party* (Ice, UK). The latest outing from one of the current soca stars in top form.

Tambu (Chris Herbert) *Culture* (Lypsoland, Trinidad/Sire, US). The classic carnival record of 1988, including Road March winner "This Party Is It".

℗ **Various** *Soca Carnival 93* (Ice, UK). Top cuts from Super Blue, Crazy, Kitchener and Roaring Lion.

℗ **Various** *Soca Gold* (Hot Vinyl, UK). There are currently four volumes of these Soca compilations, collecting the best output over the last ten years from artists such as Sparrow, Invader, Merchant, etc.

Various *Soca Music From Trinidad* (Rounder, US; 2 vols). A soca compilation that puts the emphasis on lyrical content. Thoroughbred wit from top calypsonians Chalkdust, Plainclothes, Shadow and Rio.

℗ **Various** *Wind Your Waist* (Shanachie, US). A superlative collection of soca hits from Arrow, Shadow, Burning Flames, Drupatee and Spice.

STEELBANDS

℗ **Various** *Panorama – Steelbands of Trinidad and Tobago* (Delos, US). A good recording of steelbands on the street with all the atmosphere of carnival.

ZOUK TAKEOVER

THE MUSIC OF THE FRENCH ANTILLES

Charles de Ledesma on the dance-funk music of the French Antilles – the islands of Guadeloupe and Martinique and their outlying colonies in Paris.

Until Brazilian lambada and house music hit the international pop scene, **zouk** – the music of the **French Antilles** – had been the 1980s' most copied new rhythm. A blend of African styles, Caribbean pop and American funk, this was the Caribbean's first really hi-tech dance music. It in fact owes much

of its sound to developments in Paris, where French Antillean expatriates set about forging a hot new style that would set the pulses of Europeans as well as Caribbean people racing.

Zouk is a Creole word that used to be slang for a "party"; the sound systems that replaced live music in the 1960s in the French Antilles were called zouks. The music you heard at them tended in those days to be *cadence*, the Antillean pop that preceded zouk, but with the rise of **Kassav** – the style's frontline band – going to a zouk was one and the same as dancing to Kassav.

Consequently, around 1980, the music took on the new tag and the accompanying infinitive, *zouker*, came into being.

THE ZOUK MESSAGE SPREADS

Zouk has always had two homes – the islands and Paris – but it travels prodigiously. Its influence has been keenly felt in Brazilian lambada and other Caribbean styles like merengue and soca. It's in **Paris**, though, where Caribbean and African styles mesh most smoothly, that its impact has been greatest. Cameroonian *makossa* and Zairois and Congolese *soukous* haven't been the same since zouk founders **Jacob Desvarieux** and **Pierre Eduard Decimus** took root in the French capital.

Kassav founder Jacob Desvarieux

It may seem odd that a style coming from islands whose music previously hadn't had much influence made such an impact. However, crossbreeding now characterizes much of the music from the Caribbean, Latin America and Africa, and zouk is very much a generic and tropical music. Records on sale in Paris with names like makozouk and soukouzouk indicate that in France and Africa zouk has been absorbed as if it were another branch of the gigantic African pop tree.

That, in fact, is pretty much what zouk is. Like many Caribbean styles it owes much to Africa, and especially to the music that West African slaves brought with them to the islands. But the zouk story is shaped by bizarrely eclectic influences. Although native Antillean influences form the music's base, the style's self-proclaimed founder, **Jacob Desvarieux**, was actually a heavy metal guitarist on the European studio circuit and had previously spent little time in the French Caribbean. His rock background is perhaps the main reason why zouk – as he forged it – has proved so appealing to a Western market.

ROOTS: GWO KA AND CHOUVAL BWA

Paradoxically, the most striking elements in zouk's musical mixture are not the new, hi-tech innovations but the basic African elements. These come from a traditional drum and vocal music called **gwo ka**, performed in the hills of **Guadeloupe** at festival times.

The various drums of the gwo ka range from the knee-high *ka make* to the waist-high *ka boule*. They are made of local wood to a West African design and a gwo ka "unit" can consist of up to ten drums: in full stride, island musicians like **Ti Celeste** and **Marcel Magnat** play intricate improvisations around a basic rhythm. Gwo ka drumming is often heard alone but sometimes accompanies song. A fine example is **Ti Celeste's** "Ban Mwen", from the soundtrack to the film *Coeurs de Couleur*. While three ka boula and a ka make drummer set up fast, interlocking rhythm, two singers cut across the beat with a tense, beautiful melody.

At carnival time on Guadeloupe, dozens of gwo ka units tour the island, playing endless improvisations on a basic theme, much like the samba schools in Brazil. It is a participatory type of music with people grabbing any percussive instrument they can find and joining in. The additional, year-round presence of the music on the radio and on discs – plus mega-concerts by Ti Celeste and others on the island, around the Latin world and in Paris – is largely down to Kassav, who pulled gwo ka out of the hills and into the urban recording studio, thereby popularizing the traditional style.

The vocal side of gwo ka is rather like the South African township gospel of Ladysmith Black Mambazo: deeply layered singing, at times grainy and guttural, then smooth and light. This vocal form has survived from slavery days in the hills of Guadaloupe, where Esnard Boisdur and Eugene Mona are famous exponents of the style.

Esnard Boisdur, although singing in Creole, has a texture of voice and sense of phrasing that sounds West African. Listening to his rendition of "Devenn" in the film *Coeurs de Couleur*, you could easily imagine the uplifting pattern of melodies and complex harmonies (provided by a trio of backing singers) to be some kind of French Antillean gospel.

While Boisdur is essentially a traditional gwo ka singer, **Eugene Mona** has a more populist delivery, performing his own compositions with great drama over a deeply textured gwo ka drum line. Like Ti Celeste, he is an established favourite in Paris.

The roots music from Martinique, **chouval bwa** (or *chouval bois*), also fed into Kassav's zouk developments. Like gwo ka, it is performed at carnival time and traditionally at fairs, where it would provide music for the merry-go-round and the party that gathered around it. These days, chouval bwa groups and parties take to the road on floats, the orchestra hammering out a rhythm to awaken dancers and spirits alike.

The rhythmic centre of the chouval bwa orchestra is provided by the *tambour* **drums**. The lead drum is a huge instrument called the *bel-air*, ridden like a horse with the player dampening the skin with his heel; smaller tambours are played from the waist. Other musicians play *timbales* and *chachas* – gourds or tins filled with

stones – or strike large chunks of bamboo known as *ti bois* ("little – *petit* – wood"). The players also sing the chorus, responding to the calls of the leader, often the bel-air percussionist.

The most famous chouval bwa orchestra around these days is **Marcé et Tumpak**. Their album "Zouk Chouv" (released on GlobeStyle) is a fine example of roots zouk, packed with exciting multi-rhythmic drumming and flute, accordion and brass. **Pago Bernard**, alias Marcé, plays in a highly original way, adding synthesizer, electric guitar and bass to create a refreshing, punchy sound: zouk- and biguine-influenced, while staying true to the original forms of chouval bwa.

THE MARTINIQUANS BEGUN THE BIGUINE

Martinique has its own form of folk jazz, too – the **biguine** – and this again contributed to the sound of zouk. The biguine had evolved over the past three hundred years, first as string band music formed around guitar or banjo chords, with percussion borrowed from chouval bwa, and latterly by absorbing clarinets and violins. The biguine dances were a fusion of African style with French ballroom steps.

Alexandre Stellio's biguine band

In the 1920s and 30s there was a biguine craze in Europe, when Martiniquans shipped to France to fight in World War I settled there with their music. Their Creole tunes were the staple of the popular Parisian dancehall, Le Bal Nègre, and the Martiniquan clarinettist **Alexandre Stellio** became a major figure in the jazz world. Stellio's fusion of biguine with New Orleans jazz – and his international success – foreshadow the recent spread of zouk.

The **Orchestre Antillais** – led by Stellio and later by another clarinettist, **Sam Castandet** – remained a presence on the Paris nightclub scene into the 1950s, playing biguines, boleros and tangos. They – and other Antillais biguine bands – played back on Martinique, too, in shack-nightclubs known as *paillotes*, and, of course, at carnival.

CADENCE

It was **cadence** that led most directly to zouk. Cadence was the first pop music the French Antilles could call their own – and the first to become a dominant force in the Caribbean, where it was picked up by the Haitians. The style was an amalgam of all the earlier Antillean sounds: the strings and reeds central to the biguine, the percussion of chouval bwa and gwo ka. It emerged in the 1950s and 60s and was most exploited by the Haitian orchestras, who made it a truly pan-Caribbean sound, adding a swing from other island rhythms like their own compas and the Trinidadian calypso.

Haitian orchestras frequently toured Guadaloupe and Martinique in this period and came to dominate the local music scene. In the 1970s, however, Antillean cadence bands once again proved their innovation as the music began to metamorphose into zouk. The way this happened followed a rather odd route. In the 1960s a band called **Exile One**, from the small Caribbean island of Dominica, settled in Guadaloupe and built up a repertoire that layered onto the cadence rhythm elements of soul, rock, Latin and the Afro-funk of Manu Dibango. Song titles like "Lotsa Music Onboard" and "Instant Funk", at a time when almost all the local lyrics were in French Creole, got the point across.

Exile One's lead singer, **Gordon Henderson**, went on to found a highly original cadence band, the **Vikings of Guadaloupe**. The Vikings' style was very much a precursor of Kassav, whose own co-founder, Pierre Eduard Decimus, was a member of the group. Onto the lilt of cadence was forged a crash of hot violins, jazzy sax, loping bass and full chorus.

The Vikings' name soon became a generic term for their kind of "progressive" cadence, and was borrowed by bands on both Martinique and Haiti. The **Martiniquan Vikings** released a scorcher of an LP in the late 1970s, "Djouk Djouk". Like soca from Trinidad, this new cadence had a wonderfully open and unpretentious feel, with its collision of horn improvisations, rich vocal melodies, funky bass and jazz keyboard.

KASSAV PULLS TOGETHER THE THREADS

Kassav was formed in Paris in 1978 by **Pierre Eduard Decimus** and **Jacob Desvarieux**. Their first two records were a bit of a wobbly balance of American funk and traditional styles but – crucially for zouk – they introduced an eleven-piece gwo ka drum unit. These percussive rhythms – the equivalent of Cuba's rumba and Brazil's samba – were usually only heard at carnival time in Guadaloupe. Now they were being fused with rock guitar, cadence rhythms and harder, more flattened horns.

The original Kassav line-up was all-Guadaloupian but early on the two founders were joined by Martiniquans **Jean Claude Naimro**, **Claude Vamur**, **Jean Philippe Martheny** and **Patrick Saint-Eloi**. Martheny and Saint-Eloi were singers, who grafted on elements of American soul, just as the band's drummers were turning for inspiration to African percussion. The mature Kassav style – choppy and sparse but closely melodic – sounded like nothing that had come before, and put the Antilles once and for all on the Caribbean music map.

Kassav's appeal also had a political dimension. Their most famous song, "Zouk-La-Se Sel Medikaman Nou Ni" (Zouk is the Only Medicine We Have), implied that zouk was a banner for the cultural and economic unity of Guadaloupe and Martinique. This was an explosive message for Guadaloupians in particular, as for the past century they had received second-class treatment from the French, who still govern both islands. It was a political message, however, that wasn't taken up by other zouk songwriters, and indeed Kassav themselves shied away from discussing the key issue of independence from France.

Through the 1980s, Kassav went from strength to strength, acting as a reservoir for Antillean styles and absorbing elements like the chamber ensembles held over from the French grand bals. The swooping violins on songs like "Mwin Devue" bring a classical touch that sits with startling originality alongside Desvarieux's heavy metal guitar and Jean Claude Naimro's synthesizer-accordion. Gwo ka was less in evidence than before but still put to ingenious use for links in medleys. Kassav's singers would do wild things, like launching into Creole raps – a sound uncannily like the commands in French country dancing – which had been popular on the islands up until the 1950s.

Kassav added West African guitar to the cadence beat as well. This wasn't the first time contemporary African pop had found its way into French Caribbean music. The **Orchestre Rico Jazz** from Zaire had spent some years in the Antilles in the 1970s and opened a few ears to polyphonic guitar playing. From then on, African guitar licks would creep onto French Antillean records, sounding as though they had always been there; after all, not only did the two musics spring from the same root, but zouk musicians living in Paris increasingly played and recorded with African musicians – throughout the 1980s influences travelled both ways.

Kassav themselves began to lose their dominance and, some would have it, their touch towards the end of the 80s, despite a deal with CBS International. There were brilliant songs on the **"Desvarieux and Decimus (GD)"** album, but the overall sound was increasingly formulaic and the most exciting developments came on solo projects – especially singer **Jocelyne Beroard**'s brilliant "Siwo".

Now Kassav have broken up, the zouk mantle is being carried by two main groups, **West Indies Attitude (WIA)** and **Kwak**. Both follow in Kassav's footsteps by applying razor-sharp production to melodic, mostly mid-tempo songs. However, they have added a new element to the mix, incorporating the rhythms of Haitian compas: a move which, in turn, has seen zouk's influence extend further across the Caribbean.

MARTINIQUE

The rebirth of Antillean music, through Kassav, had two sides. The first was the launching of a sophisticated music with a sound modern enough to hold its own on dancefloors the world over, which has been much imitated by Antillean musicians. The second was the reawakening of interest in the **roots** of the music, not only the neo-African chouval bwa and gwo ka, but also the biguine and the European waltz, all of which have received inspired treatment by multi-instrumentalist **Kali** on his album "Racines".

Kali, who lives in the hills of Martinique and espouses a philosophy that has parallels with Rastafarianism, is the moving force behind **Pakatak**, a band that unites a number of

Dédé Saint Prix

important musicians in an attempt to forge an alliance between zouk and modern jazz. Their "Chouval Bwa 87" album, an intriguing collage of Latin jazz and traditional percussion, featured Marcé, pianist **Vasco**, singers **Thimothy Herelle** and **Max Ramsay**, as well as Kali, himself playing banjo as though it were a Cuban tres.

Yet more evidence of the symbiosis of zouk and the folk music of the islands was provided by developments in Martinique's important tradition of flute playing, especially by **Max Cilla** and **Dédé Saint Prix**. These two exponents have followed very different routes. Whereas Saint Prix has followed Ramsay and Kali in casting his net wide to pull in a huge range of dance-oriented styles to update traditional music, Cilla's haunting playing is reflective and gentle, drawing on classical music and rich in Latin-tinged melodies. His band includes the extraordinary pianist **Georges-Edouard Nouel**, whose improvisational and rhythmic abilities recall the late New Yorican maestro Charlie Palmieri.

Another approach is followed by fiery ranter **Joby Bernade**, who represents a radical black nationalist tradition opposed to French economic domination. His Creole includes fewer French words than most singers use and is peppered with phrases from African dialects. Although you might expect him to use gwo ka to accompany his broadsides, he prefers sophisticated studio electronics; nonetheless, his work does not make for comfortable listening.

The guttural, expressive elements in gwo ka singing have been absorbed into zouk by many singers, the best-known of whom are **Sartana** and **Franky Vincent**. Sartana, with a large following on the islands, prefers to remain a big fish in a small pond rather than compete for attention in the wider Paris scene. His dramatic vocal style and sense of theatre make his recordings some of the most musically satisfying zouk has produced.

Vincent began his career in 1983 with a scorching track, "Licette", in which his deep husky voice rattles across a mid-tempo drum and bass rhythm complemented by jazz horns. But in recent years success as the islands' number-one male pin-up has distracted him and reduced his music to a pale commercial shadow of its former self, though one that fills the island's dancefloors.

THE NEO-CLASSICISTS: MALAVOI

One intriguing offshoot of zouk is the work of a group of classically trained musicians centred around the band **Malavoi**. Like Kali they reinterpret the biguine, mazurka and waltz, but more radically, giving them a spicy Latin feel. Their classic song, "Bona", is an astonishingly innovative piece of music, starting with some virtuoso writing for violin and ending with a haunting drum and vocal workout very close to Cuban rumba.

Malavoi have been recording since the 1960s, honing their fusion, mixing in Cuban charanga-style violins, horn sections, percussion from Dedé Saint-Prix, and top-class singing from Edith Lefel and other guest Antillean vocalists. With each successive album, they have continued to reinvent their sound, combining European dance forms like the quadrille, gwo ka drums, zouk beats, bossa nova, and rural melodies and rhythms from the French Antilles. They seem most assured, however, in their big, spirited string arrangements, where lead singer Pipo Gertrude (who replaced Ralph Thamar in 1987) duets with his guests. Like Kassav, they are produced by Georges Debs.

Michel Godzom is another Caribbean neo-classicist, whose flute weaves and ducks through electronic bubblings, up-tempo zouk and soft,

sentimental passages of his "Horizon" album. Though the mood is subtle and fluid, very much in the classical-folk-jazz mould of Malavoi, Godzom is in fact interpreting seven traditional folk rhythms, including the gwo ka; the results, however, are very different from the polyrhythmic improvisations that have previously characterized these styles.

Malavoi and their string section

THE ZOUK MACHINE

With Kassav taking a backseat, a host of new names have taken over the zouk scene in the past few years, some of them with considerable commercial success in France. **Zouk Machine**, founded by Kassav's Jocelyn Beroard, and fronted, spectacularly, by three women singers, had some massive hits at the end of the 1980s, and one of the trio, **Joelle Ursull**, went on to make one of France's biggest-selling pop records, "Black French", in 1990. Ursull remains a big name on the Paris scene. She strips down the polyrhythmic complexities of zouk, blends in house rhythms and uses synthesizers to back her wonderful voice, clear and cool and erotically charged.

The influence of Kassav is also heard in the work of another fine woman singer, **Edith Lefel**. Her biggest hits, "Poutch" and "La Vie Trop Kout", are perfectly crafted mid-tempo pop tunes where the taut textures of Kassav-style zouk have made way for a less tense backdrop of synthesizers, horns and strong vocals. Her most beautiful song, "Yche Man Man", an island number one in 1986, forged a popular, gentler variant of zouk – **zouk-love**. It was recorded with the highly innovative guitarist **Dominque Gengoul** and singer **Jean-Luc Alger** of **Lazair**, who play a particularly Gallic brand of zouk, a long way from Kassav in mood despite its Caribbean guitar rhythms and soca-style horns.

More than a decade after zouk's inception it seems that it has joined reggae and salsa as a Caribbean music with worldwide influence. There are zouk bands all over the Caribbean and Central America, in the Dominican Republic and on the Atlantic coast of Colombia.

Although zouk's international profile has waned since the height of the craze in the late 1980s, back home in the Antilles the music's success has led to a vigorous re-exploration of local roots music and new fusions.

DISCOGRAPHY

ZOUK AND CADENCE

Jocelyne Beroard *Siwo* (Georges Debs, Guadeloupe). Zouk-love from Kassav's lead singer, backed by the band.
Max Cilla *Des Flutes des Mornes* (GD, France). Flautist Cilla blends Latin, African and indigenous rhythms and melodies, alongside wild improvised piano, in this magical acoustic set.
Jacob Desvarieux *Yelélé* (Georges Debs, Guadeloupe). A 1984 release with Kassav's founding musician on finest solo form, with contributions from the rest of the band.
Kassav *Zouk Is The Only Medicine We Have* (Greensleeves, UK). Kassav's greatest hits, including their most famous number – the title track – and the wonderful "Kaye Manman" by lead singer Jocelyne Beroard.
Lazair *Yche Man Man* (Kadence, France). One of the top female singers in the French Antilles, Edith Lefel, excels on this sumptuous slice of zouk-love: a late-night party treat.
Malavoi *Live au Zenith* (Blue Silver, France). A sublime 1987 concert, featuring Edith Lefel on vocals. If you're hooked, the band have over a dozen albums on catalogue, though their most recent outings border on bland easy listening.
Sartana and Gordon Henderson *Ostilité* (Fiso, France). Expressive vocals from Sartana, backed by Henderson from top cadence band Exile One.
Sex Machine *Mwen Peche* (GD, France). Golden period up-tempo zouk. Keyboards sound like West African kora, horns like the best soca, and the band's scorching vocals pin you to the condensation-drenched walls.
Soukoué Kô *Ou Vacances* (NR, France). This is actually Kassav under another name and includes the number-one French West Indies disco track of all time, "New York City Ambience", written by Haitians Tabou Combo – fifteen minutes of joyous melody.
Joelle Ursull *Miyel* (CBS, US). The best solo outing to date from this former Zouk Machine singer.
Vikings of Guadeloupe *Les Précurseurs du Zouk* (Cocosound, France). The Vikings were the top cadence band of the 70s and this is a great run through their hits.
Zouk Machine *Maldon* (Henri Debs, Guadeloupe). A fine album from this female trio, who were a big hit in Paris in the late 80s.

Various *Dance Cadence* (GlobeStyle, UK). An inspired compilation which introduced pop-style cadence to the World Music market. Also includes up-country flute and cracking early zouk dance numbers.
Various *Zouk Attack* (Rounder, US). A fine introduction to 1980s and early 90s zouk.

BIGUINE

Michel Godzom *Hôtel Diamant des Bains* (Georges Debs, Guadeloupe). Arguably the best contemporary biguine to come out of the island.
Alexandre Stellio *Et son Orchestre Créole* (CBS, France). Classic biguine from the 1920s and 30s from the great clarinettist.
Various *Au Bal Antillais* (Folklyric, US). A great collection of biguines, recorded in 1920s and 30s Paris, including several tracks from the great clarinettist Alexandre Stellio.

CHOUVAL BWA AND GWO KA

Kali *Roots* (Philips, France). Superb compilation drawn from Kali's first three albums.
Marcé et Tumpak *Zouk Chouv'* (GlobeStyle, UK). Martinique's top band play old chouval bwa music but fuse the percussive style with bright electric instrumentation. A folk-jazz-dance World Music of the highest order.
Eugene Mona *Volumes 1 and 2* (Hibiscus, Guadeloupe). Exquisite 2-CD set of flute, drum and vocal tracks.
Dédé Saint Prix *Mi Se Sa* (Mango, UK). Flautist Saint Prix includes acoustic and electric work here on this enjoyable percussion-heavy set of cadence and chouval bwa-flavoured zouk.
Ti Celeste *Ses Plus Grands Succes* (Henri Debs, Guadeloupe). Gwo ka drums and singing given a contemporary, zoukish treatment.
Various *Coeurs de Couleur* (Atoll Music, France). Movie soundtrack featuring gwo ka singing from the hills of Guadeloupe by Esnard Boisdur and drumming from Ti Celeste.
Various *Guadeloupe: Gwoka. Soirée lewoz a Jabrun* (Ocora, France). Live recording from an evening's partying in the hills. Drums and voices only.

THE LOUDEST
ISLAND IN THE WORLD

JAMAICA, HOME OF THE REGGAE BEAT

Jamaican music has been a global force for the last thirty years – a remarkable feat, considering the island's tiny size and population – yet many of its diverse strands are hardly known. Gregory Salter dives into the island's roots – maroon, religious and carnival music, mento, ska and rock steady – that underlie the great Caribbean powerhouse that is reggae music.

Jamaica is a serious contender for the title "loudest island in the world". On any night, and especially at week-ends, it shakes to the musical vibrations of thousands of sound systems, revival sessions, *nyabinghis*, Maroon and Kumina possession ceremonies, and old-time *mento* dances. Tens of thousands of radios, cranked up to full volume, add to the hubbub. Inevitably, the sounds with the most wattage grab the limelight, but the other musical styles have proved enduring – some have been around on the island for four hundred years.

TELL IT TO THE MAROONS

In 1492, the history books tell us, Jamaica was discovered by Christopher Columbus. "Christopher Columbus was a dyam liar," reply Jamaicans, "The Arawaks was here first." And so they were. The Spanish who followed Columbus, however, saw fit to carry out the genocide of the island's original population. By the time Oliver Cromwell's navy wrested the island from the Spanish in 1670, they had been wiped out. In their place were small numbers of African slaves, mostly from Ghana, who had been armed by the Spaniards and instructed to defend the island from the British while they themselves escaped.

Most took to the hills instead, to remote parts with names like Me No Sen, You No Come, where their descendants, the **Maroons**, live in their own secluded communities to this day. They forged a percussive style of music – still played today – at "possession ceremonies", religious rituals in which the musicians and dancers get increasingly frenzied as they become possessed by whichever type of spirit – ancestor or god – they have invited to the occasion. The music is available on a couple of well-annotated discs (see Discography), which point to the roots that nourished reggae.

With colonization came **plantations**, which were thrown into turmoil by the Abolition of Slavery in 1838. Despite prolonged advance warnings, few plantation owners had bothered to restructure their operations, and more slaves continued to die than be born on their estates. Faced with a diminishing workforce, planters resorted to devious devices. A number of Angolans were brought over in the ensuing decades under the guise of "indentured servants". These people seem to have been the main constituents of the **Bongo Nation**, which is responsible for the religion and music of **Kumina**. The music, again available on a couple of ethnographical recordings, takes a similar form to Maroon music.

Maroons and the Bongo Nation make up a tiny proportion of Jamaica's population. Few others were able to preserve their African cultural identities in such an undisturbed fashion. Most Jamaicans, as song after song remind us, were the sons and daughters of slaves, from families and peoples systematically broken up on the plantations. Although this repressive system severely curtailed music-making, an extremely rich **folk tradition** emerged on the island, and one drawn from an amazing range of creative sources. In the enormous canon of Jamaican folk music, there are traces of African, British, Irish and Spanish musical and vocal traditions, and heavy doses of Nonconformist hymns, arrangements and singing styles. Each of these influences is blended with characteristic Jamaican wit, irreverence and creativity. There are songs for courting, marrying, digging, drinking, playing ring games, burying – and just for singing, too. One of the all-time classics is "Hill and Gully Rider", a timeless ode to transport on an island strong on hills and weak on roads.

Unfortunately, none of the available recordings of this folk music is of much value. They all seem to have been made by earnest ethnomusicologists in the 1950s, using people plainly embarrassed to have a huge microphone put in front of them while all their family watched on. When in Jamaica, however, you can hear examples of it all the time, particularly in the country areas, and it has recently emerged as an element in the stark, minimalist modern **dancehall music**. As DJ Admiral Bailey says, "Old time someting come back again".

GIMME THAT OLD TIME RELIGION

As well as being extremely loud, Jamaica is also extremely religious. If you get up early on the island on a Sunday morning, and walk from town into the ghettos, or into the hills, you pass by an incredible variety of **religious ceremonies and musics**. From the graceful plantation-era buildings of the Anglican Church come the thin, reedy voices of middle-class Jamaica, struggling with turgid Victorian hymns. From smaller churches further along emanate the more boisterous melodies of the Nonconformist churches, and, further still, the tambourine-shaking sounds of the Pentecostal denominations. But up in the hills, and down in the ghettos, can also be found the jumping sounds of **Pocomania** and **Revival Zion**.

Both these Churches date from the early 1860s, when a great religious revival swept through Jamaica. Both draw on Christian and African traditions, with more Christianity in Revival Zion, and more Africa in Pocomania. As in the Pentecostal churches, both types of service feature much Bible-reading, tambourine-rattling, and foot-stamping, but unlike the Pentecostal churches, they also use persistent and hypnotic percussion, and **trumping**. Trumping is the process that leads to possession, and involves moving in a circle, often around a symbolic object, like a glass of rum, and breathing very deeply. Worshippers grunt as they rotate, faster and faster as the spirit possesses them. The combination of trumping and drumming is unforgettable and recordings – though available – don't do it justice. However, the poco sound, with its powerful, rolling side-drum patterns, has, like Jamaican folk, turned up in a dancehall mode.

Most Jamaicans are Christians. As is well known, however, a sizeable minority are not, including, most notably (at least in music circles), the Rastafarians – of whom more below.

Often ignored are Jamaica's **Hindus** – people of Indian origin who, like the Angolans of the Bongo Nation, were "indentured" to the plantations after Abolition. Though most intermarried, there is still a distinctive Jamaican Indian culture and associated music, though not on the scale of Trinidsad, where Indians settled in far greater numbers. Again, Jamaican roots discs include intriguing examples of their **baccra** music – Hindustan compositions often referred to by Jamaicans as "coolie music".

RASTAFARI FOR I AND FOR I

Rastafarians make up only around thirteen percent of the island's population but their influence on Jamaican music is out of all proportion. Bob Marley is only the most famous of an enormous number of Rasta musicians. In the late 1960s and 70s, virtually every reggae artist seemed to have adopted or emerged from the religion.

Rastafari is non-doctrinal, in the sense that no one church is powerful enough to impose its version of religious purity and heresy, and that one person's version of it is as valid as another's, as long as he or she is possessed of the Spirit of Jah (God). Certain themes, however, do recur. Among them is the belief that Jah is a living force on earth, and not a mere otherworldly palliative. Jah enables otherwise disparate humanity to unite. To embody this in speech, Rastas refer to each other as "I". Thus I am I, you are I, and we are I and I. Such is the Rasta emphasis on the importance of the spoken word that many other words are similarly altered: "Unity" becomes "Inity", "brethren" becomes "Idren", and so on. Unity, or Inity, is essential if Rastas are to stand strong against the wicked forces of Babylon – the oppressive (or downpressive) system.

Marcus Garvey, a forceful campaigner, in the 1920s and 30s for black unity, pan-Africanism, and a return to Africa, is of great importance to many Rastas, who revere him as a prophet, and even as the reincarnation of John the Baptist. In one of his pamphlets, he urges Africans of the New World to look to Africa for a Prince to emerge. This was taken by many to mean the then Emperor of Ethiopia, **Haile Selassie I**. His claimed descent from Solomon, and his battles in 1937 with the wicked forces of Rome (Mussolini), were taken as fulfilling the prophecies of the Book of Revelation, and Selassie was worshipped as Christ come again. Selassie was deposed in 1974, and died a few years later, although to Rastas "Selassie cyaan dead" and is living still. Rastas believe that they are awaiting repatriation to Africa – Zion – and regard themselves, and all New World black people, as living "slavery days" in bondage.

From time to time Rastas hold reasoning sessions. Larger and more protracted reasonings are called **nyabinghis**. Like their Revival Zion and Pocomaniac counterparts, nyabinghis feature Bible-reading, hymns, foot-stamping, and drumming. Rasta drumming, though, is much slower, with a beat more or less the speed of a human pulse. Other differences include the reasoning itself, in which matters religious, social, political and livital (about life) are discussed collectively, aided and abetted by copious consumption of *ganja* – Jamaican colly weed, the good herb, the *Irie*. Rastas adore ganja and lovingly cultivate it, cure it, smoke it, brew it (non-alcoholically), use it for medicines of all sorts, and, above all, talk about it. For this, Babylon brutalizes them no end, but to little avail. As Jah Lion sings, "When the Dread flash him locks, a colly seed drops."

There are some good recordings of traditional Rasta music, though, inevitably, they fail to capture the Dread atmosphere and significance of the real thing, which is recommended to anyone interested. Nyabinghis occur quite frequently in Jamaica, are generally well advertised and easy to find. By far the best Rasta sounds on record are the extraordinary "Grounation" sessions, performed by the late, great **Count Ossie and his Mystic Revealers of Rastafari**. Count Ossie was a master Rasta "repeater" drummer from the Kingston ghetto. In the early 1960s, a number of very talented

musicians came under his influence, including most of the subsequently legendary Skatalites. Listen to "Grounation" (copies turn up on various obscure labels) and you will find astonishing Rasta drumming and chanting, bebop and cool jazz horn lines, and apocalyptic poems.

THE PARTY LINE: MENTO

Religious music has left Jamaican Sundays fairly well covered, but what of its Saturday nights? Most plantation owners conceded Saturday nights to their slaves, as well as the various feast days: crop-over, the yam festival, Christmas and the New Year. Plantation owners' diaries abound with complaints of splitting headaches in the middle of the night, and even references to what seem like the forerunners of today's sound systems. One eighteenth-century plantation owner wrote: "I am just informed that at the dance last night, the Eboes obtained a decided triumph, for they roared and thumped their drums with so much effect that the Creoles were obliged to leave off singing altogether."

The main surviving elements from all of this are **mento** – Jamaica's most popular folk music – and the Christmas carnival sounds of **Jonkonnu**. The latter, like all the carnivals of the Americas, is a time of display, finery and revelry. Its music is traditionally played on fife and drums, and can still be heard in that form today, though calypso and mento, and whatever reggae sounds are in vogue, regularly slip in too.

Mento is greatly influenced by Trinidadian calypso. The recent promotion of the **Jolly Boys** from Portland has extended its audience, previously almost exclusively Jamaican. Mento contains many of the elements that have made its famous relative, reggae, so successful. It is witty, topical, rebellious, and unafraid to "wind and grind". Actually, most mentos seem to come round to the subject of sex sooner or later – usually sooner. Musically, the mento contains that essential shuffling strum – the "kerchanga, kerchanga" – that marked out reggae from its more metronomic predecessor, the rock steady.

Mento was Jamaica's dominant sound until the late 1940s. It was in that period that radios finally became both affordable and available to most Jamaicans. The new radio owners soon discovered that American radio stations were a good deal more lively than the stuffy local ones and before long a whole generation was going crazy over American R&B. People started flying over to the States, scouring

THE JOLLY BOYS

· ·

When Bob Marley's mother, Cedella, was asked in a BBC TV documentary about his musical beginnings, she burst into a lilting, saucy song, "Touch me Tomato", with which the young Bob had entertained the neighbourhood.

> Please mister don't you touch me tommy at all
> Please don't touch me tommy at all
> Touch me on my pumpkin potato
> For goodness sake don't touch me tommy at all
> Touch me this, touch me that
> Touch me everything I've got
> Touch me plum and apples too
> But here's one thing you must not do. . .

The song was mento: a music as sweet as sugar cane, as rude as a bunch of bananas and, surprising as it may seem, the principal root of reggae. Hugely popular in the 1930s and 40s, until it was swamped by the new styles of ska and reggae, it has now been rediscovered with the revival of interest in roots music.

The **Jolly Boys** have been playing the music regardless of fashion at the Trident Hotel, Port Antonio, Jamaica, for years. There are four of them, although only one, **Moses Deans**, is a founder member of the group; in the good old days they played for Hollywood parties at Errol Flynn's villa in Port

Joseph Bennet on kalimba

Antonio. Moses plays banjo and sings, Allan Swymmer sings lead and plays the bongos, Noel Howard fills out the texture and rhythm on guitar, and Joseph Bennett plays the *kalimba*, a large thumb piano that provides the bass. It's a beautifully balanced acoustic sound, perfectly in keeping with a languorous life in the sun.

"We sing what the old people used to sing," says Moses. "A lot of them dead and gone. The younger generation don't know the old-time songs. They take some of the sound and make reggae. Reggae come right down from there." The music is relaxed and unmistakeably good-time with an infectious lilt like Trinidadian calypso. It's underpinned by rhythmic patterns on the bongos and interspersed with instrumental solos on the banjo. The lyrics are rarely deep and often bawdy: at least half the songs are about sex. But they have the richness of colour, rhythm and dialect that marks out the best of Caribbean poetry.

The Jolly Boys see themselves as a living archive of Jamaica's roots music. "What you don't use, you surely lose. It's part of our heritage so you don't want to throw it to one side. Someone's got to be there to present it to the new world. It's good to have a museum and I think we're one!"

---

record shops for exclusive pressings, rushing back, and playing them through homemade box speakers at parties in people's yards. Thus were sound systems born.

SOUND SYSTEMS, SKA AND ROCK STEADY

Sound systems were a crucial development in Jamaican music and were to reverberate right through the next five decades, giving rise to the Jamaican record industry – the first local discs were produced for the sound systems – and to

a whole host of styles. As early as the 1950s, the sound-system DJs would talk over the records they played, attracting custom, and the technique slowly developed into the tradition of toasting or chatting, of which more later.

Another key event was the emergence of a handful of producers – the sound-system chiefs – who struggled for supremacy amid an atmosphere of intense, often violent competition that was to become permanently associated with the Jamaican music scene. Three men soon began to dominate: **"Sir" Coxsone Dodd**, **"Duke" Reid**, and **"Prince" Buster** – their names an ironic tilt at the old plantation chiefs. Meanwhile, Stanley Motta established the island's first recording studio, and future prime minister Edward Seaga set up WIRL (West Indies Records Ltd) to record local mento artists like Lord Flea and Lord Fly. Soon the studios were also being used to record local R&B. The sound-system chiefs, at first in order to feed their own sounds, and later to supply the general (and especially expatriate) public, set up their own studios and thus began some important careers.

By the early 1960s, Coxsone Dodd, and local Jamaican musicians, notably the innovatory Skatalites, had come up with something new. Using fast R&B as their music's basis, they cut out half the shuffle, leaving an abrupt series of off-beats. They called it **ska**, and it quickly took off in the dancehalls of Jamaica and Britain, where Jamaicans had begun to settle in large numbers (see Reggae in Britain feature). Its bands employed much the same line-up as R&B groups, with a piano, electric guitar, drums and a couple or more brass instruments. Most of the musicians came from a jazz background – swing bands were popular in wartime Jamaica – and they could solo and improvise at will.

From this point on, the availability of Jamaican music improves dramatically: there are masses of ska records. The **Skatalites** were the masters, particularly when their phenomenal trombonist Don Drummond was alive. Nonetheless, their Rastafarianism counted against them, and radio stations gave more time to the blander sounds of bands like **Byron Lee and the Dragonnaires**, who were patronized by Edward Seaga's studio.

Meanwhile, in 1964, another local entrepreneur, **Chris Blackwell**, founded **Island Records**, which kicked off with a phenomenal British and Jamaican pop-ska hit, "My Boy Lollipop" by Millie Small.

Ska is primarily an instrumental music, perfect for sound-system dancing, but its rhythms can be difficult to sing over and sound-system operators needed something to spice up their dances. Many brought in **DJs** to do just that, developing the old act of talking over records to draw custom into an art of its own. The greatest of the early DJs were Count Matchuki, King Stitt and Sir Lord Comic. Sadly, they were rarely recorded, but some of their efforts can be found on old Trojan records.

Jamaica became independent in 1962 and for a period the whole of society seemed infected by euphoria and optimism. You can hear it in the music – joyous, up-tempo ska tunes that seem now not to express a care in the world. People were flocking into Kingston every day, seeking work, money, and a better life. Some found it. Thousands never did, and settled in fast-growing shantytowns like Dungle, and badly built housing schemes, like Trenchtown, Riverton City and, later on, Tivoli Gardens. From this community of the underemployed and the abused, those whom Jamaicans call "sufferers", came the infamous rudeboys.

Rudeboys were young men who gave voice to their disaffection, establishing a reputation for ruthlessly defending their corner, and hustling their way to their next meal or dance entrance fee. The island's two main political parties, the Jamaican Labour Party (JLP) and People's National Party (PNP), soon recognized their vote-garnering value, and both began distributing weapons, patronage and, if in government, inviolable protection to their "dons", in return for bringing in the votes at election time. It was a recipe for the violence that has plagued every election to date, and particularly in 1976 and 1980.

Although the last years of ska, and particularly the music of the Skatalites, reflected the sombre mood of the rudeboys, it was **rock steady**, ska's successor, that became their sound. Over the rock-steady beat, rudeboys sang of their problems, fears, and their "rude" attitude. Typical was the song "Dreader than Dread," by Honeyboy Martin and the Voices: if you were foolish enough not to believe them, "you'll wind up in the cemet'ry, because you'll be dead." Musically, ska's jazzy horn lines faded from prominence, while the bass grew more important and the rhythm guitar played a steady off-beat – the rhythm that was to become reggae.

The gentler pace of rock steady provided the perfect opportunity to express tender emotions, too. Vast numbers of love songs poured out of the studios, often with sensuous American soul tunes for their inspiration, and close harmony execution. Duke Reid's **Treasure Isle** studio was probably the top studio for rock steady, with Sir Coxsone's Studio One a close second. Bands and singers to look out for from this period – which is well represented on modern compilations – include **Tommy McCook and the Supersonics**, the **Techniques**, the **Ethiopians**, the **Paragons**, the **Heptones**, the **Melodians**, and the champion lover, **Alton Ellis**. It was Ellis who had given the name to this new movement, with his song "Get Ready to Rock Steady".

TOUGHER THAN TOUGH: REGGAE TAKES OVER

As the 1970s beckoned, Jamaican music changed once more when a new, lolloping dance called the **reggae** hit Kingston. Producers and musicians searched around for a beat to suit it and hit upon the idea of incorporating the old-time mento shuffle with the rock steady, thus bringing Jamaican pop that much closer to its roots.

This purely musical shift would have meant little, however, had it not been for other, more profound shifts that were taking place in society. Politically, there was a growing mistrust on the part

The original Wailers: Bunny Wailer, Marley and Peter Tosh

of the "sufferers" of the ability of the system to provide for them – and the size of their communities was growing fast. The visit of the Ethiopian Emperor Haile Selassie to Jamaica in 1968 had also encouraged a huge growth in Rastafari, which dismissed politics as "politricks", and looked instead for the return to Africa, when the captives would be set free. Rastafarian singers and musicians were increasingly asserting their right to preach their message, and to be heard.

Despite considerable misgivings, ex-policeman Duke Reid and Coxsone Dodd, the studio chiefs, had little option but to oblige. For one thing, there was the first real competition to theirs and Prince Buster's cozy triumvirate. Former employees, fed up with their situation, set up their own labels, with themselves as **producers**. Derrick Harriott, Bunny Lee, Clancy Eccles, Winston "Niney" Holness, Joe Gibbs, Sonia Pottinger, and the legendary **Lee Perry** (see box), all emerged as producers in this period, a genuine golden era for Jamaican music.

The list of notable artists, already lengthy, expands hugely at this point. Those who started out at this time, and are still famous, include **Burning Spear**, who has arguably never bettered his early recordings for Studio One, **Dennis Brown**, **Gregory Isaacs**, **John Holt**, **Horace Andy**, **Delroy Wilson**, **Toots and the Maytals**, and the **Wailers**.

> "There is a greater output of recorded music in Jamaica than in any other country in the world. This is because right from the beginning the different manufacturing and distribution companies in Jamaica opened their facilities for individual producers. So anybody who has enough money to go into a studio and make a record and then go to a pressing plant and order five hundred records to be pressed can start a label. So a lot of people have tried their luck."
> **Chris Blackwell**, founder of Island Records.

"I PLAY THE FOOL CATCHWISE": LEE PERRY

•••••••••••••••••••••••••

Lee Perry, otherwise known as "Scratch", or "The Upsetter", has played a critical role in the development of Jamaican music since the late 1950s. Though he is a fine and distinctive vocalist, he is best known as one of the island's most innovative producers.

His career began in 1959, when he worked as a bouncer with Prince Buster, for Sir Coxsone Dodd's mighty Downbeat sound system. Within a short time, both of them were producing records, usually uncredited, at Dodd's Studio One. Perry left Dodd in 1967, worked briefly for Joe Gibbs, then established his famous Upsetter label in 1968.

Even in his early releases, like the classic "People Funny Boy", Perry showed a genius for the use of the bizarre sound effect – in this case, glass breaking and a baby crying – and the scathing personal attacks against the many he deems to have crossed his path. It was in this period that he concocted many of his best rhythms, to which he (and countless imitators) returned again and again: "Return of Django" (a British hit), "French Connection", "Cold Sweat", and many others.

The late 1960s also saw Perry in immensely fruitful partnership with the **Wailers**. Of all the many producers they worked with, he alone seemed best to have understood the sparse arrangements that offset so perfectly their quaver-ing harmonies. Perry was also one of the first pro-ducers, in the early 70s, to recognize and encour-age the phenomenal talents of dub maestro **King Tubby**. Perry excelled with dub, and, though many Jamaican producers have produced great dub music, none have touched the eccentric, ganja-soaked brilliance of the Upsetter's Black Ark offer-ings. The Black Ark was Perry's studio, until he burned it down in 1980 – a true mecca for dub fiends from all over the world.

Though all the major singers and DJs of the 1970s, like U Roy, Big Youth, the Meditations and the Congoes, recorded at Black Ark, it was never the hits factory that some studios became. Perry did score a huge and deserved hit with **Junior Murvin's "Police and Thieves"** in 1976, but, for the most part, his releases were steady, low-key sellers that were greatly respected by the industry, and by reggae lovers everywhere.

Though Perry has been involved in every important Jamaican musical development from the late 1950s to the late 1970s, and has in many cases pioneered them, it is the quirky and unique nature of his output that makes him memorable. He has frequently been accused of madness, and has spent periods in the sanatorium. Tales abound of his peculiar habits: planting records in his garden, performing whirling dervish dances at the mixing desk, declining interviews but granting outer-views . . . Certainly, the burn-ing of his studio, and the increasingly inpenetrable mysti-cism and silliness of his records since do seem to be the acts of a madman, but Perry plays the fool "catchwise" – to catch you out.

Perry has contributed little to the dancehall and ragga styles that dominate reggae today, and shows little interest in doing so. Though some of his recent albums are interest-ing, his earlier material will never be bettered.

WAILING AND GROANING

The Wailers – Bob Marley, Peter Tosh and
Bunny Wailer – started life as the Wailin Wailers,
one of many rock steady groups competing for
attention in the mid-1960s. It was producer Lee
Perry, the "Phil Spector of the Caribbean", who
recognized their potential. He put them
together with the unrivalled drum and
bass duo of Carlton and Aston
"Family Man" Barrett from his
studio band, The Upsetters, with
whom they recorded two of the
great early reggae albums,
"Soul Rebels" and "African
Herbsman".

Musically, Marley matured
fast in this period working with
Perry, and he already had an
incredible songbook, including
classics like "Lively up Yourself",
"Trenchtown Rock" and "Kaya", which were to
resurface in later years under Island Records,
to which the band signed in 1972. Island
relaunched the group in 1974 as **Bob Marley
and the Wailers** (see box), with Peter Tosh
and Bunny Wailer leaving to pursue successful
solo careers. Marley, meanwhile, went from
strength to strength. Purists might argue that
his new female backing singers, the **I-Threes**,
were a poor substitute for the beautiful close

harmonies of the original Wailers, and that
the arrangements of his Island records
conceded too much to the unsubtle demands of
rock, but no one could deny the power of his
lyrics, nor the magnetism of his performances.

No one could deny the phenomenon of his
success, either, which placed reggae and
Jamaica on the world map. Thanks to his
powerful persona, and some shrewd
marketing, Marley became a
symbol of rebellion all over the
world. This brought him
enormous fame abroad –
especially in Africa, where he
had superstar status from
Morocco to South Africa – and
a very high profile at home. In
such a politicized society as
Jamaica, it also made him a target,
and sure enough, he was nearly
assassinated in the violent election year
of 1976. Bravely, Marley decided to try to use his
prominence to encourage peace on the island,
bringing together the two party leaders at the
famous One Love Concert in 1978.

Marley died of cancer in 1981. Peter Tosh was
shot dead six years later, in circumstances that
have yet to be properly explained, after a
turbulent career that had earned him many
enemies, thanks to his uncompromising stances,
particularly on the issue of ganja. And so only the

Toots Hibbert – Reggae Got Soul

BOB MARLEY

••••••••••••••••••••••

Robert **Nesta Marley** was born in Nine Miles, Jamaica, in 1945. His mother, Cedella, was 19 and black, and his father, whom he hardly met, was 51 and white, an ex-British army officer from Liverpool. Bob Marley spent his youth in the tough Trenchtown ghetto of West Kingston immortalized in his rudeboy songs, but his roots up-country – where he listened to the Jamaican popular music mento – and his mother's gospel singing were also important in his musical development. Nine Miles was also, appropriately enough, in the heart of so-called "ganja parish"; in mid-career, Marley was said to smoke a pound of the herb each week.

In Kingston Marley joined up with childhood friends Peter Tosh and Bunny Wailer to form the Wailin' Wailers, and their first song, "Simmer Down", a reaction to the street violence of rival gangs, was a big hit in 1964. The rude-boy image of the Trenchtown ghetto was central to their early Jamaican hits and the ghetto experience remained a crucial part of the Marley songbook.

From 1972, when the Wailers were signed up by Chris Blackwell of Island Records, Marley began to move onto the world stage. His messages of strength and social unity were potent and the time was ripe. By the mid-70s rock had lost its sense of rebellion and Marley's was the revolutionary voice to shock the complacency of Anglo-American music. With Tosh and Wailer, he recorded the wonderful "Catch A Fire" and "Burnin" albums – the first reggae records conceived as albums rather than songs – though his commercial breakthrough came in 1975 with the "Natty Dread" album and its anthemic single, "No Woman No Cry". Bob Marley was finally up there with the big-name rock stars in Britain and the US, and around the world, especially in Africa, his was the biggest name of all.

In 1976 Marley won the dubious distinction of being the first music star subject to an assassina-

tion attempt. Seven armed men broke into his home at 56 Hope Road, Kingston, on the eve of an electioneering concert organized by Prime Minister Michael Manley and the ruling PNP party. He sang at the concert all the same, with a bandaged arm, and then left for the safety of Miami for a while. As Jamaica headed for civil war, Marley returned for a historical performance in 1978 that symbolically linked the arms of opposing leaders Manley and Edward Seaga on stage in the song **"One Love"**, a hymn to peace and brotherhood.

Marley's Rastafarian belief was central to his music and his message: the "One Love" concert was to commemorate the visit of Haile Selassie to Jamaica twelve years earlier. Selassie's myth – a promised land in Africa – had reverberations, too, on Marley's second most famous concert, celebrating the independence of Zimbabwe in 1980. The new Zimbabwean flag shared the Rasta colours – yellow, red, green and black, representing the sunshine, the bloodshed, the jungle and the people. Marley gave the performance of his life at the celebrations to mark the new nation's freedom.

Marley died of cancer just thirteen months after this triumphal performance. His funeral brought ten thousand people onto the streets and Jamaica to a standstill for two days. His body lies in a mausoleum and Ethiopian Orthodox shrine attended by dreadlocked guards in Nine Miles, his home village.

mystic man, Bunny Wailer, survives. He has been seen around more frequently lately, castigating the youth for abandoning their roots and their principles, and receiving precious little respect for doing so.

After Marley, the other key musician in forging the reggae sound was **Toots Hibbert**, together with his band, the Maytals. Toots' mother was a Revival Zion preacher, and he inherited from her his legendary impassioned groaning, which is clearly derived from Revival's trumping tradition. He had been around since ska and rock-steady days, shaping the sound with Otis Redding and American soul, but was then jailed (a stay immortalized in his classic "54-46 Was my Number"), before emerging to blast into reggae, with songs like "Pressure Drop", "African Doctor" and "Monkey Man". These remain some of Jamaica's greatest ever songs.

DJS, DUB AND SINGERS

By the early 1970s, a pattern had emerged, whereby the singers ruled the studios, and **DJs** continued to whip crowds into a frenzy in the dancehall. This arrangement was broken up as a result of master engineer **King Tubby**'s musical experimentations. He began by removing vocal tracks from hit tunes, leaving only the instrumentation. This too was pared down, until often only the drum and bass remained. The tune could then be rebuilt to taste: the old vocals could be made to float in and out, with an echo attached, guitar riffs and strange noises could be dropped in at random, and so on. Here lay the origins of dub, the innovation at the heart of much of the subsequent music from the island, and the cornerstone of sampling and hip-hop.

Tubby's other innovation, which was also crucial to hip-hop, was to add the extraordinary vocals of the DJs U Roy to the mix. **U Roy** evolved a unique, rambling, **talk-over** or **toasting** style, and the results of their collaboration proved hugely successful. As a sad postscript to this immensely creative partnership, however, King Tubby was shot dead in 1989, becoming yet another of Jamaica's murdered musical heroes.

As dub sounds took hold, scores of DJs poured into the studios, reworking old hits and making new ones. Most of them, then as now, were instantly forgettable, but a number emerged as stars. Cream of the early crop were **Dennis Alcapone**, **I Roy**, **Scotty**, **Prince Fari**, and **Prince Jazzbo**, with "daddy" U Roy holding his

Winston Rodney – Burning Spear

own as the master of the art. As the 1970s progressed, new generations included **Big Youth** – acknowledged as the "Don" (champion), **Dillinger** (of "Cocaine Running Around my Brain" fame), **Dr. Alimantado**, **Mikey Dread** and the versatile **Sugar Minott**. All of these produced some brilliant material.

Dub music also developed in its own right. Its spacey, trance-like nature attracts the mystic, and few have been more mystical than **Augustus Pablo**, famous both for his production and his eerie melodica playing. Also important in dub developments were **Scientist**, **King Jammy**, and London's **Jah Shaka** (see Reggae in Britain). Dub and DJ art added a further branch with the "dub poetry" of Briton **Linton Kwesi Johnson** and Jamaicans **Mutabaruka** and **Mikey Smith**; Smith, a wonderful and radical artist, was another casualty of political violence, murdered by JLP gunmen in 1982.

In the mid-1970s, the music changed once more. At the forefront of this evolution was Channel One studio, whose house band were the **Revolutionaries**, built around the powerhouse of drummer and bassist, **Sly Dunbar** and **Robbie Shakespeare**. Together, Sly and Robbie developed the **rockers** sound, shifting and shuffling the reggae beat to great and popular effect. They have been players and producers on many of the top reggae albums over the past twenty years.

The rockers sound gave a fresh lease of life to the vocal trio – an enduring feature of Jamaican music – that had been a perfect vehicle in the rock-steady and early reggae periods. Groups such as the **Mighty Diamonds** and the **Gladiators** scored a number of hits with rockers songs like "Right Time" and "Chatty Chatty Mouth". Out of rockers, too, emerged a new, dread sound, produced principally by **Joe Gibbs** and **Henry "Jungo" Lawes**. This music was a major beneficiary of Marley's success, with groups like Joseph Hill's **Culture** and the **Wailing Souls** touring all over the world.

Among the singers, **Burning Spear** (Winston Rodney) stood head and dread above the competition. Originally from the Studio One stable, he achieved roots prominence in 1976 with two astonishing albums, "Marcus Garvey" and "Man in the Hills", produced by Jack Ruby at Joe Gibbs' studio, with the Wailers doing the musical honours. At a time when Bob Marley was losing the purists as fast as he was gathering an international rock audience, Spear's rootsier sound gained a massive following. His performances, too, were stunning, whirling away into trance-like heights. A staunch advocate of Rastafari, he is particularly vocal about Marcus Garvey and the necessity of repatriation.

SLACKNESS AND RAGGA

Despite the international prominence of these dread singers, in Jamaica the centre of action and innovation remained the dancehall. Sound-system operators continued to hire outside venues, or just set up on the beach, playing records with DJs toasting over them; intense competition ensured constant musical change. The use of the word "**dancehall**" to describe the music they were playing came about in the late 1970s, associated at first with producer Lincoln "Sugar" Minott and his "Youth Promotion" sound, which drew on the burgeoning youth DJ talent of the Kingston ghettos.

By 1980, the Jamaican top ten, for the first time featured more DJs than singers. Led by the outrageous **Yellowman** and **General Echo**, many made their name on the "slackness" (obscenity) of their lyrics – a far cry from the spirituality of Marley and Burning Spear, or the previous generation of DJ toasters, come to that. Jamaican dub-poet Linton Kwesi Johnson saw the change as "a reflection of the serious decline

in the moral standards of Jamaica . . . and in itself a reflection of the decline in the economic welfare of Jamaicans, and the whole dog-eat-dog ethos of the prevailing ruling party."

Certainly, the programme of IMF-sponsored monetarism of the JLP (Jamaican Labour Party), which won the election in 1980, was much harsher than the non-aligned socialism of the previous incumbents, the PNP (People's National Party), and the 1980s recession hit Jamaica hard. However, not everyone chanted slackness. Rasta DJs, like **Cocoa Tea**, **Half Pint**, **Tony Rebel** and **Garnett Silk**, were a prominent part of the scene, as were those who just observed things with a sharp eye and quick tongue, like **Frankie Paul**, **Lt. Stitchie** and **Admiral Bailey**.

Jamaican music is a faddish beast, and before long things changed again. As happened so often before, the initial changes were technological. Digital technology meant you could make tunes without musicians, which made versions even easier. Versions are reworkings of an original tune, with new arrangements, but often just with a fresh DJ on the top. The first digital tune was **King Jammy**'s "Sleng Teng" rhythm, produced in 1985, which has been used endlessly since. Jammy's sound was the dominant one of the 80s, with DJs like **Josey Wales**, **ChakaDemus**, and **Shabba Ranks**, and singers like **Pinchers**, available and on call.

Most producers saw the digi technology as the route to a quick buck but some have used it to make some very serious tunes indeed. Foremost among them is **Augustus "Gussie" Clarke**, who set the standard with his production of Gregory Isaacs' "Rumours" in 1988. Equally crucial sounds came from **Bobby Digital**, **Mikey Bennett**, **Steelie and Cleevie** and the Penthouse Studio maestro **Donovan Herman**. Their new music was generally up-tempo, with heavy, rumbling bass lines that are admirably catered for by the vast bass speakers sported by the modern sound system.

The digital 1990s DJ is characteristically **ragga** – ragamuffin in style and attitude. Ragamuffin is to today what rudeboy was to the late 1960s – the essence of a bad attitude, which operates on the street, and whose proudest boast is that "we run tings, and tings nuh run we". Hot lyrical themes were "crack" and guns, a reflection of the current state of Kingston.

As the decade has progressed, however, the lyrics have broadened in range. Even **Shabba**

AFRICAN REGGAE

· ·

Reggae is everywhere in Africa. Hotel bands all over the continent can manage "One Love" and other cover versions, and a number of local styles are evolving, most notably in West Africa. Here, Nigeria's **Sonny Okusuns** produced some intriguing efforts in the 1970s, while in the 80s and 90s the mantle moved to **The Mandators**, a fine and enduring band, as is that of **Majek Fashek**, their former lead guitarist.

Somewhat better known in the west, however, are the most confident releases of **Alpha Blondy**, from the Ivory Coast. His "Apartheid is Nazism" album was a rich blend of reggae and West African rhythms, while his follow-up, "Jerusalem", recorded in Kingston with Jamaican musicians, showed he could do orthodox roots reggae with the best of them.

Moving south, Zimbabwe is also very into reggae, with memories of Bob Marley's 1980 Independence concert still fresh for many. **John Chibadura** has recorded some brilliant reggae tunes, although jit remains his staple.

A more committed reggae voice is that of South Africa's **Lucky Dube** – Africa's most phe-

South African dread, Lucky Dube

nomenal reggae artist, who proved his worth by triumphing at the Jamaican Sunsplash, in front of the most critical audience in the world. He began singing Zulu *mbaqanga* music at the end of the 70s but switched to reggae in 1984, adopting a style modelled closely on his hero, Peter Tosh. "Slave" and "Prisoner", his most prominent releases, have each sold over 500,000 copies in South Africa alone, making him the country's most successful ever recording artist. He has toured worldwide, to ecstatic response, perfecting his performance choreography in the process, and frequently unleashing a Smokey Robinson-style falsetto.

Ragga music has been making inroads into Africa recently, too. Shabba Ranks toured Nigeria, Ghana, Zimbabwe and South Africa in 1994, and received adulation everywhere he went. It thus won't be long before African ragga emerges. Indeed, there are signs that it is already doing so. Johannesburg's **Umkhonte keShaka** combines Zulu and ragga sounds to great effect, though he's yet to tour outside the country.

Ranks, famous for his slack (or X-rated, as he prefers it) hit "Wicked in Bed", could be heard quoting the Bible. "Gold teeth, front teeth, Don Gorgon" **Ninjaman** not only quoted the Bible, but delivered very detailed advice to the prime minister and the leader of the opposition.

Sex – mainstay of ragga songs – also received some radical treatment as **women singers** like **Sister Charmaine** and **Lady G** threw an independent anti-sexism into the mix. It was a surprising shift considering how curtailed women's roles had been in the Jamaican scene. There has only ever been one female producer, Sonia Pottinger, who had her heyday in the rock-steady era, and female singers have either sung love songs – lovers' rock, dominated by British

reggae singers – or, like Bob Marley's I-Threes, sturdy Rasta lyrics.

These days, however, women assert themselves on the **dancefloors**. No dance is complete without a women's posse dressed to kill (the current style is bare-as-you-dare plus platinum-blonde wig), winding and grinding with whoever dares take them on. There is even a dancehall queen and numerous princesses, who often have day jobs as models, and who have become as much in demand as the DJs themselves. Male fashion remains more cautious, but behaviour from both sexes on the dancefloor is ever more extrovert. People started out carrying lighters to the dance, flashing them for any particularly wicked selection. Now some use gas canisters, igniting the spray to produce six-foot jets of flame in time to the beat.

Back, though, to the music, where reggae's internationalism has resulted in a huge global influence. **Versions**, **remixes** and **raps** – staples of the modern music industry – all stem from Jamaica. American **hip-hop** and rap have had some reverse influence, too, showing up in tunes like the Sly and Robbie production "Murder She Wrote" sung by **ChakaDemus and Pliers**. Artists like them and **Shaggy** have been experimenting with R&B, too, and have scored big hits with tunes like "Oh Carolina" and "Twist and Shout", and for ChakaDemus and Pliers a mega-hit with a ragga-rap over Curtis Mayfield's soulful "She Don't Let Nobody".

Nonetheless, the music remains predominantly its own. Jamaican sound systems might warm up with soul, but after that, it's reggae all the way – no hip-hop, house or anything. There isn't even a trace on the island of "jungle", the reggae-house music that is gripping many a British dancehall. The one "outside" form that is heard on the island is soca, which has had a resurgence in the 1990s, attracting a mainly middle class audience who regard dancehall as too crude.

Reggae has been helped greatly in Jamaica by the recent arrival of **Irie FM** on the nation's airwaves. Previously, you could only get reggae

Ragga sound of the 90s: ChakaDemus and Pliers

on the radio at night, but now it's on all day, every day, everywhere. Move around the island, particularly at weekends, and you could be forgiven for thinking that the whole place is tuned in. Even in the hills, away from human habitation, you can still hear it, and very wicked it is too. An Irie FM jingle had a man confessing "Mi radio dial stuck 'pon Irie FM, and guess wha? Mi nah go bodder fix it". Go there and you'll probably agree.

KEEPING UP

Jamaican music is totally **singles oriented**, and, with a few notable exceptions, the best albums are compilations. Jamaican music lovers are indebted to the work of Steve Barrow, formerly of Trojan records, who has compiled dozens of impeccably researched, selected and presented albums, among them Island's wonderful "Story of Jamaican Music". In a similar vein, the American label Heartbeat are currently releasing vintage Studio One material, including welcome doses of the likes of Slim Smith, and the Cables. The CD takeover, too, has resulted in a major programme of re-releases of old albums, often imaginatively combined.

Modern reggae output is phenomenal. Most singles are pressed on 7" once, and then deleted. Hits usually make it to 12", and last longer, but even then you have to move fast. The only

way to follow it is to go to the dances, or listen to pirate radio, or buy reggae magazines (*Echoes* is the best in Britain; *The Beat* has good coverage in the US). If none of those is available, your best bets are the Jetstar "Reggae Hits" series, that come out every quarter, or the Greensleeves Samplers.

Alternatively, go to Jamaica. The five-day **Reggae Sunsplash** takes place every year in July at St Catherine's, 20 miles out of Kingston. Virtually all the stars appear, with tourists tending to flock to the old ones, and locals to the DJ night. Apart from maybe getting your pockets picked at some point, you should have a great time. And once you know what tunes you like, head for a **record shack** – there's a whole host around Orange Street, and up around Half-Way Tree, in Kingston – make your selection, and Go Deh!

DISCOGRAPHY

COMPILATIONS

Various *Tougher than Tough: the Story of Jamaican Music* (Island, UK; 4-CD set). This is quite an investment but it would be hard to imagine a better compilation of Jamaican music. The discs cover just about every phase of the Jamaican musical story, from 1958 to 1993, beginning with a superb selection of pre-ska R&B, then moving through the ska and rock steady hits of the 1950s and 60s to an overview of reggae's manifold styles and sub-genres. The songs are gathered from a wide variety of labels – not just from the Island catalogue – and there are superb, virtually book-sized sleeve notes from Steve Barrow.

Various *This is Reggae Music Volumes 1–5* (Mango, UK). More crucial anthologies, if you prefer to pick your reggae years.

ROOTS AND MENTO

Count Ossie and his Mystic Revealers of Rastafari *Grounation* (various labels). Traditional Rasta drumming accompanied by bebop and cool jazz horn lines, apocalyptic poems, and much chanting.

The Jolly Boys *Pop'n'Mento* (Cooking Vinyl, UK/First Warning, US) and *Sunshine'n'Water* (Rykodisc, US). Sunny and lewd, this is classic good-time mento from a band who have been playing it for decades. Strongly recommended.

Various *Drums of Defiance* (Smithsonian Folkways, US) and *The Roots of Reggae* (Lyrichord, US). Two excellent, well-annotated anthologies of the deepest roots music of Jamaica from the Maroon communities.

Various *From Kongo to Zion* and *Churchical Chants of the Nyabinghi* (Heartbeat, US). Traditional rasta music from nyabinghi ceremonies.

Various *Jamaican Roots: Bongo, Baccra and Coolie, Volumes 1 & 2* (Folkways, US). The first volume includes more or less the only kumina music on record, plus Indian Hindu (baccra) music; the second has Revival Zion plus carnival music.

SKA AND ROCK STEADY

Alton Ellis *Cry Tough* (Heartbeat, US). Alton invented the sound of rock steady, and the name – with his song "Get Ready to Rock Steady".

Ethiopians *The World Goes Ska* (Jetstar, UK). Classic 1960s ska, with songs full of ghetto life in Kingston.

Skatalites *Music is my Occupation* (Trojan, UK) and *Hog in a Cocoa* (Esoldun, France). Led by trombonist Don Drummond, the Skatalites had an all-star musical cast, and produced simply the greatest ska sounds. The first disc here is a showcase for Drummond, Tommy McCook and Baba Brooks; the second has them backing the best singers of the 60s at Duke Reid's studio.

The Techniques *Run Come Celebrate* (Heartbeat, US). Classic rock steady from one of the great vocal trios.

Various *Duke Reid's Treasure Chest* (Heartbeat, US). Rock steady gems from the producer who ruled the sound.

JAMAICAN REGGAE

Abyssinians *Satta Massagana* (Heartbeat, US). A legendary dread album.

Big Youth *Hit the Road Jack* (Trojan, UK). This was one of the great toaster records of the 1970s.

Dennis Brown *The Dennis Brown Collection* (Jetstar, UK). A fine, wide-ranging hits compilation from 1993.

Burning Spear *Marcus Garvey* and *Garvey's Ghost* (Mango, UK). Spear's 1976 Marcus Garvey tribute was full of exquisite vocals and horns, and given a sublime dub treatment on *Garvey's Ghost*, packaged with it on this bumper CD. Spear's 1990 album, **Mek We Dweet** (Mango, UK), marked a return to form, updating his sound with heavy guitar hooks.

Jimmy Cliff *The Harder they Come* (Mango, UK). No reggae collection is complete without this 1972 movie soundtrack, combining early reggae standards with Cliff songs like the title track and "Many Rivers to Cross".

Culture *Two Sevens Clash* (Blue Moon, UK/Shanachie, US). The band never equalled this debut with its gorgeous vocals.

Eek-a-Mouse *Wa Do Dem* (Greensleeves, UK/Shanachie, US). One of the wittiest, most imitated 80s toasting discs.

Marcia Griffiths *Naturally* (Sky Note, Jamaica). Greatest hits compilation from Jamaica's top woman singer, and former leader of the I-Threes, Bob Marley's backing trio.

Ijahman *Haile I Hymn* (Mango, UK). Ijahman Levi's unique, soulful, meditative brand of reggae at its (1978) best

Gregory Isaacs *Nightnurse* (Mango, UK). Isaacs has been releasing Jamaica's best love songs for the past thirty years. This set, from 1983, is the finest of the lot to date.

King Tubby and Yabby You *Time to Remember* (Yabby You, Jamaica). Ethereal and heavy dub – just as it should be.

Bob Marley and the Wailers highlights include:
Songs of Freedom: the Complete Bob Marley Collection (Tuff Gong/Island, UK). The definitive Bob anthology: four CDs and 78 songs, dating from 1962 to his death in 1980, including virtually all the classics, plus lots of rare treasures.

Legend (Island, UK). If you want just a single disc, this is a near-faultless "best of" selection.

Burnin' (Island, UK). The sound of the original Wailers in 1973 with Marley and Tosh at their songwriting best on "Get Up, Stand Up" and "I Shot the Sheriff".

The Lee Perry Sessions (Charly, UK). Many consider these the greatest of all Bob's recordings: songs include "Lively up Yourself", "Sun is Shining" and "Kaya".

Mighty Diamonds *Mighty Diamonds* (Mango, UK). Fine selection from one of reggae's best vocal harmony groups.

Junior Murvin *Police and Thieves* (Mango, UK). The title song, inspired by election violence in Jamaica, was a massive hit on the island and in Britain in 1977. Lee Perry produced and shared writing credits.

Augustus Pablo *King Tubby Meets Rockers Uptown* (Jetstar, UK). Pablo and producer King Tubby (the Upsetters' keyboard player, Glen Adams) invented dub in the early 70s and perfected things on this wonderful and innovative album.

Frankie Paul *20 Massive Hits* (Sonic Sounds, UK). One of the best – of innumerable – Frankie Paul compilations.

Lee "Scratch" Perry and the Upsetters *Reggae Greats* (Mango, UK). Jamaica's greatest and craziest producer is responsible for too many classic reggae albums to mention. This compilation has generous doses of his 70s "Super Ape" outings, with wild dub. For true devotees, Greensleeves have released three triple-CD sets which pull in most of Perry's greatest moments, with the Upsetters and as a producer. These are titled: *The Upsetter Compact Set, Open the Gate,* and *Build the Ark.*

Sly and Robbie *Reggae Greats* (Mango, UK). This drums and bass duo are even more prodigious producers than Lee Perry. This is their own stuff – dub at its most sophisticated.

Mikey Smith *Mi C-yaan Believe It* (Island, UK). An album of powerful dub poetry from a radical exponent, Mikey Smith, murdered by JLP gunmen shortly after its release.

Third World *Reggae Greats* (Island, UK). Third World were often too slick for their own good, but their late 70s songs like "96 Degrees in the Shade" and "Now That we Found Love" are pop reggae at its sweetest.

Toots and the Maytals *Reggae Got Soul* (Mango, UK). The title says it all – Toots Hibbert is the man who put soul together with reggae.

Twinkle Brothers *Twinkle Inna Poland Style* (Twinkle, UK). And if Toots put soul into reggae, the Twinkles' Norman Grant was the man who put Polish folk into the genre, on this, the latest of a series of recordings with the Trebunia family. Strangely enough, it works brilliantly.

⊕ **Peter Tosh** *Legalise It* and *Equal Rights* (Virgin Frontline, UK). These two records were recorded after Tosh split from the Wailers, with most of the band along. They're militant songs with razor-sharp backing.

⊕ **Yellowman** *Reggae on the Move* (Ras, US). Yellowman was the biggest toaster of the 1980s, and his slack lyrics, full of crudity and anti-feminist and anti-gay raps, were a precursor of contemporary ragga habits. This is one of his better outings.

⊕ **Various** *Chatty Chatty Mouth Versions* (Greensleeves, UK). Twelve cuts of this hugely popular rhythm.

⊕ **Various** *If deejay was your trade: the Dreads at King Tubby's 1974–77* (Blood & Fire, UK). Sixteen dynamite tracks from Kingston's premier DJs of the 1970s – U Roy, Dr Alimantado, Dillinger, Tapper Zukie and others – produced by Bunny Lee.

⊕ **Various** *Solid Gold, Coxsone Style* (Heartbeat, US). The likes of John Holt, the Abyssinians and Dennis Brown singing their hearts out for Studio One.

DANCEHALL AND RAGGA

⊕ **Buju Banton** *Voice of Jamaica* (Polygram, UK). Bad-boy Buju at his baddest.

⊕ **Cocoa Tea** *Kingston Hot* (Ras, US). A silky-smooth dancehall voice, produced by Henry "Junjo" Lawes.

⊕ **ChakaDemus and Pliers** *Tease Me* (Mango, UK). Mid-90s ragga, mixing in Curtis Mayfield soul and hip-hop rhythms, and produced by the ever-inventive Sly and Robbie.

⊕ **Lovindeer** *One Day Christian* (TSOJ, UK). Dancehall, poco-style, from its finest exponent.

⊕ **Sugar Minott** *Slice of the Cake* (Heartbeat, US). Sweet sounds from "Sugar Sugar", including the great "No Vacancy".

⊕ **Shabba Ranks** *As Raw as Ever* (CBS, US). Hip-hop meets reggae in this pioneering ragga album from 1991.

⊕ **Various** *Reggae Hits – Volumes 1–16* (Jetstar, UK). Essential dancehall and lovers' rock compilations from 1984 to the present.

AFRICAN REGGAE

⊕ **Alpha Blondy** *Best of Alpha Blondy* (Shanachie, US). Like the title claims, this 1990 compilation is classic Blondy, featuring militant songs like "Jerusalem" and "Apartheid is Nazism".

⊕ **Lucky Dube** *Prisoner* (Shanachie, US). Dube's best outing to date, from 1991, is South Africa's all-time bestselling album.

⊕ **The Mandators** *Power of the People: Nigerian Reggae* (Heartbeat, US). A "greatest hits" set from Nigeria's top reggae band – and it even includes a cover of Dolly Parton's "Coat of Many Colours". What more could you ask for?

⊕ **Various** *Reggae Africa* (Hemisphere-EMI, UK). A good compilation featuring most of the above – and more.

SKA AND REGGAE DEVELOPMENTS IN BRITAIN

Gregory Salter completes the Jamaican musical story with a look through the history of West Indian music in Britain, whre it has ploughed an often independent furrow for the last five decades.

Anywhere you find two or more Jamaicans, any country, on a Saturday night, you must have a blues dance. This handy maxim, from Junior Lincoln of the **Royal Rasses**, has been true of Britain since 1948. For 1948, with the arrival of four hundred and ninety-two Jamaicans on the Empire Windrush, saw the beginning of a process of large-scale economic migration from the English-speaking Caribbean to Britain that was to last twenty years.

Today, Britain has a West Indian community of around 700,000, most of whom were born there. Their predominant experience is one of neglect by the system, which once used them as a labour pool, but when the work dried up cast them as a scapegoat for all urban ills. The community, however, has been vocal in its rejection of these roles, and in its articulation of its own evolving identity. This articulation has come in every form, but perhaps most powerfully in music. As the King-David style dub warrior, South London reggae maestro Jah Shaka, has said, "We've had

to do our speaking on sound systems".

It wasn't long after the first Jamaicans arrived that **record labels** to cater for them established themselves in the UK. The names of these pioneers are the stuff of the many obsessively collated lists that aficionados exchange joyfully whenever they come together – Melodisc, Bluebeat, Orbitone, and, the longer-lasting, Island and Trojan. The sheer newness of what was going on lends a kind of epic quality to the many stories that surround the Jamaican music scene in the early 1960s: Daddy Peckins of West London getting fresh releases of pure, wicked ska, straight from Sir Coxsone's backyard, and passing them on to Duke Vin, for use on his sound system in Ladbroke Grove; Mod posses scouring small record shops for copies of Prince Buster's "Madness", the latest killer of a music they called bluebeat, after the label, because the main shops didn't stock it; homemade speakers mashing it at the dance, disturbing the midnight peace in the inner-city badlands of Britain.

Some artists came from Jamaica to stay, notably **Errol Dunkley**, **Owen Gray**, **Alton Ellis** and **Desmond Dekker**, the skinheads' darling. Occasionally, too, Jamaican hits made the UK charts: novelty items like Millie's "My Boy Lollipop"; ska and rock-steady killers like

Desmond Dekker's "Israelites"; Lee Perry specials like "Return of Django"; reggae with strings like "Young, Gifted and Black" (mainly from Trojan); and, later, Marley anthems like "One Love". But generally reggae was ignored by mainstream radio. It still is these days – with the shining exceptions of DJs Ranking Miss P, John Peel, Andy Kershaw and David Rodigan – which explains why reggae pirate stations have done so well. The first prominent pirate, DBC, the Dread Broadcasting Corporation, whose slogan was "Tune In If Yu Rankin", began broadcasting in London in 1981. Most major British cities now host at least one pirate, in between government-enforced breaks in transmission.

British reggae band Aswad

British-based reggae did not develop as a recognizable force until the 1970s. The first major band was **Matumbi**, founded in 1972 by **Dennis Bovell**. Matumbi drew upon soul as well as reggae for its inspiration, in common with many Bovell-led projects. Most of the other stalwarts, who came a little later, adopted a heavier, more roots style, that epitomized their status as conscious, militant, urban dreads. The prime example is Ladbroke Grove's **Aswad**. They were formed in 1975 and released a succession of brilliant records, loved by a reggae audience but not quite making a pop/rock one. In the 1980s, however, they began (often embarrassing) attempts at "crossover" and finally got what they wanted with a number one in the UK charts – a first for a British reggae band.

The late 1970s was a vibrant time for British reggae and spawned a succession of bands in London, Birmingham, Bristol, and other West Indian strongholds. **Steel Pulse**, from Handsworth, Birmingham, were perhaps the strongest, releasing the classic "Handsworth Revolution", an album that caused a stir with its stark proclamation that "Babylon is Burning" – a prediction that came all too true with riots on the streets of St Paul's, Toxteth, Moss Side, Handsworth and Brixton. Other notables included London's **Misty in Roots**, Bristol's **Black Roots** and **Talisman**, the **Naturalites** from Nottingham, and Reading's **Aqua Levi**. Singers of the era, most of whom are still singing, included **Bim Sherman**, now often with the **On-U sound** (see below) and **Dandy Livingstone**.

Equally significant was the emergence of British producers with a distinctive sound. **Dennis Bovell** was one, producing the first British dub album, "Brain Damage", in 1972. Another important British-based producer is the **Mad Professor**. After working on sound systems for most of the 1970s, he established his Ariwa label in 1979. Inspired by King Tubby, Joe Gibbs and, of course, Lee Perry (with whom he has worked), he has produced some of Britain's finest dub, most notably with his "Dub Me Crazy" series, currently up to part eleven. He has also developed what many see as the definitive British lovers' rock sound, of which more later.

Two producers uninterested in the lovers' sound are **Jah Shaka** and **Adrian Sherwood**. Shaka is predominantly a sound system man, specializing in extraordinarily heavy dub, and crazed sound effects, with the strictly spiritual intent of giving praise to the Creator, Jah Rastafari. He produces many of his own dub plates, in the form of "The Commandments of Dub". Though they lose something when not blaring out through ten-foot speakers, they can transform any living room into a place of dread. Adrian Sherwood is also a Lee Perry fan, and produces the kind of heavy dub Perry perfected in the late 1970s. He has often worked with **Gary Clail** on the **On-U** and **Tackhead** sound systems, and has released a number of albums with them.

An innovation of British dub reggae were the **dub poets**, who delivered rhythmic readings of their charged and usually political verse over dub tracks. There are a number of these poets scattered throughout the country, but the ones to have gained most prominence are **Sister Netifa**, **Benjamin Zephaniah** and, especially, **Linton Kwesi Johnson**. Johnson, an astute commentator on the West Indian experience in Britain, in fact invented the dub poetry term, with reference to DJs generally. In collaboration with the ubiquitous Dennis Bovell, he has produced a number of fine albums.

The alliance of reggae and punk at the end of the 1970s, which were brought together as outlaw club music and as part of the "Rock against Racism" movement, also produced a number of multiracial reggae bands. **The Specials**, **The Beat** and **The Selecter** were all formed in the Midlands in the late 70s by young black and white men – and one white woman, Pauline Black, lead singer of the Selecter. **Two-tone**, as their music was known, borrowed heavily from ska and rock steady, and particularly Prince Buster, with the encouragement of two of the original Skatalites, **Rico Rodriguez** and **Vin Gordon**. It added its own lyrical concerns, displaying a vigorous anti-racist commitment.

The Mad Professor in dub action

The pop group **Madness** also started out as two-toners, with a highly marketable brand of "nuttiness", at much the same time as Birmingham's **UB40** who showcased a new kind of pop-reggae – highly effective, for a while, though latterly they have contented themselves with wishy-washy covers of Jamaican classics. Both bands, like Aswad, have had considerable success in the national charts.

Such groups deserved, and received, considerable coverage in the mainstream music press. Meanwhile, Britain's other unique, and far longer-lasting reggae innovation, **lovers' rock**, was virtually ignored outside the black music

papers. Lovers' rock was invented by Dennis Bovell, who made a reggae version of Donnie Elbert's soul tune "Caught You In A Lie", with Louisa Mark, then thirteen years old. Nothing revolutionary about that – Jamaicans had been doing that since rock steady. What was different was the style, which had enough female sensuality, and enough of the modern soul sound for it to appeal to those to whom heavy, roots reggae was anathema. Bovell held auditions every Sunday, and went on to record a number of female artists on his newly formed Lovers Rock label, named after an Augustus Pablo tune.

The songs continually top the UK reggae charts, and have thus found their way onto Jetstar's "Reggae Hits" series. As well as Bovell's label, many of the stars recorded on the Mad Professor's Ariwa label, characterized by a heavier bass sound, a more rootsy feel, and, at times, rare social comment. Most of the lyrics on "Roots Daughters", for instance, concern the social and cultural position of black women in Britain, rather than their boyfriend problems.

Although bands have played a more central role in the development of British than Jamaican reggae, their bedrock is the same: the sound system. It is on the sound systems that the DJs cut their teeth, it is the sound systems that promote, and play at reggae dances, and it is the sound systems that provide the DJs who play reggae on the pirates. Today, there are hundreds, possibly thousands all over Britain. The most famous, aside from the **Shaka** sound, are two London sounds that take their name from Jamaican ones: **Sir Coxsone Outernational** and **King Tubby's**. Every DJ is of course champion in his or her own view, but the most successful to date include gravel-voiced **Sweetie Irie**, one of the few British DJs to arouse much interest back on Jamaica; **Tippa Irie**, who had a big hit with "Hello Darling"; and **Smiley Culture**, who gained deserved attention with his 1984 hit "Cockney Translation", which moves smoothly from Cockney to Yardie, showing him to be fluent in both – and, in fact, to be both.

Another highly original DJ is **Macka B**, a Rastafarian from Birmingham who sings on the Wasifa sound and has teamed up with the Mad Professor. The latter relates the partnership thus: "He just phoned me up out of the blue, "Ah Professor, me name Macka B, an me have some lyrics." He sent a tape, I liked it, and we did the album "Sign of the Times" right off in two days." Since then Macka B has made his name with some of the most articulate, witty and conscious lyrics around.

Almost inevitably, the next big thing was **hip-hop reggae**. Linton Kwesi Johnson saw this as part of an historical process of black musical fusion: "Jamaican DJs were originally influenced by American jive talkers. Hip-hop appropriated the studio techniques of Jamaican dub, so it's entirely natural . . ." First off with this fusion were the **London Posse**, who, with a number of others like them, can be found on Mango's two "Ragga Hip-Hop" compilations, complete with seriously militant songs. Reggae crossing cultures like it does, ragga also has an Indian star, **Apache Indian** from Birmingham, who raps on the Indian caste system and AIDS and has topped both the British reggae and bhangra charts. Another recent innovation is **jungle** – hardcore reggae-house fusion – which has established itself as a mainstay of large chunks of the rave scene.

Midway through the 1990s, we can be certain that reggae will continue to be a dynamic, yet undervalued part of Britain's cultural heritage, castigating the oppressor, and nicing up the dance.

DISCOGRAPHY

SKA

ⓓ **Desmond Dekker** *Black and Dekker* (Stiff, UK). "Israelites", "007" and all the old favourites, recorded with various Pioneers and Equators.

REGGAE/RAGGA

ⓓ **Aswad** *Crucial Tracks* (Mango, UK) and *Live and Direct* (Island, UK). *Crucial* is a hits collection charting the band's career through the rootsy mid-70s sound to their more poppy crossover material. *Live and Direct*, recorded at the Notting Hill Carnival in 1983, is the band at their very best.
ⓓ **Linton Kwesi Johnson** *Forces of Victory* (Mango, UK). An album of highly charged political poems, brilliantly supported by Dennis Bovell's musical arrangements.
ⓓ **The Mad Professor** *Dub me crazy series* (Ariwa, UK). The series is into double figures now: the most innovative British dub on record.

ⓓ **Misty in Roots** *Live At The Counter Eurovision* (Kaz, UK). One of the best British bands, recorded at the end of the 1970s.
ⓓ **Steel Pulse** *Handsworth Revolution* (Mango, UK). This tough, original 1978 debut album by a Birmingham band was the strongest British reggae album of the decade.
ⓓ **UB40** *Signing Off* (Graduate, UK) and *Present Arms* (DEP, UK). The band's earliest and best recordings.

LOVERS' ROCK

ⓓ **Louisa Marks** *Breakout* (Bushay, UK). Classic and stylish lovers' rock, including "6, Six St" and "Moving Target" from the late 70s.
ⓓ **Various** *Pure Lovers* (Jetstar, UK). All the lovers' rock hits of recent years. Currently there are seven volumes but more are added every few months.

LATIN AMERICA

Alongside Africa and the Caribbean, Latin America is a leading force on the global music scene. It shares with the Caribbean a steamy mix of various European styles alongside an implanted African culture, plus a surprising diversity of indigenous Indian styles that have survived not only the conquistadores but also poverty and continued marginalization at the hands of the present century's governments. The sounds are rich and varied – supremely danceable and melodic, enjoyable in their own right. But perhaps more than anywhere else in the world, as well as being an antidote to life's problems, they are also a reverberation of the turbulent past and present of the continent and an aid to understanding it.

Of course, it is Latin dance music that dominates clubs and dancehalls around the world. Salsa, that Cuban-American fusion, may be the slick market leader, but Brazilian samba and Colombian cumbia are not far behind and represent some of the most colourful and exuberant sounds to be heard anywhere in the world. Argentinian tango, on the other hand, is both dark and sophisticated and reeks of the underworld, yet it was probably the first international success of World Music, taking Paris and Europe by storm as early as 1907.

Brazil, by far the largest country in Latin America, is a whole world in itself. Its popular dance forms – samba, bossa nova and lambada – are now part of an international vocabulary, and everyone has an image of the infamous carnivals of Rio, São Paulo or Salvador, when the people go crazy for a few days to frenetic samba drumming. Musically, though, the riches are much more disparate. The Bahia region is home to an ever fruitful Afro-Brazilian ethnic mix, stamped out by percussion-based groups like Olodum, the group that carried Paul Simon's "Rhythms of the Saints". Northeast Brazil boasts forró, an accordion-led dance music that is one of the little-known gems of Latin music. Meanwhile, at the forefront of the scene are the stars of Brazilian popular music – Caetano Veloso, Milton Nascimento, Jorge

Ben and Gilberto Gil, and many others. Their infectious, ever-inventive music makes them some of the most successful performing artists in the Latin world.

Colombia, closer to the Caribbean, is also closer to the Latin mainstream of salsa, which it propagates through the great Discos Fuentes record label, and through one of the acknowledged kings of the music, Joe Arroyo. The country offers a whole lot more than salsa, however, with its big-band cumbia rhythms and the crazy and addictive vallenato – another of those accordion-led styles that pop up where the conditions are right all around the world.

Cumbia is popular, too, these days in Mexico, where it took over from mariachi as the country's dominant style, before being supplanted by the latest craze – brass ensemble banda music. Other Mexican mixes include norteño ballads – the troubador music that has developed in the US as Tex-Mex – and the rural huapango, one of the loveliest Latin sounds, with falsetto singing backed by violin and guitar. All of them prove the remarkable resilience of musical culture, given such proximity to the US.

Latin America's bitter politics have found expression in many of the continent's musics, and never more directly than in nueva canción. This "new song" emerged at the end of the 1960s in Chile, coming to international attention through the wonderful, poetic Víctor Jara, and over the subsequent three decades has played an important role in countries from Uruguay to Nicaragua, and across the Caribbean in Cuba. Its biggest star, these days, is the Argentinian Mercedes Sosa, "the voice of Latin America", as her followers call her.

The other great Argentinian musician of the postwar years has been Astor Piazzolla, who did more than anyone to revive and rework the nation's traditional dance music, tango. This is another of Latin America's seductive accordion-based sounds, and it's alive and kicking, these days, in Buenos Aires.

Finally, this chapter takes a look inland, at the music of the indigenous Indians of the

11

Andes. This is probably the most and least familiar music of the Latin world. Huddles of musicians in llama-wool ponchos clutching panpipes and drums seem to pop up in squares and piazzas the whole world over. But there's a lot more to this music than "El condor pasa", and at the many village fiestas in Bolivia and Peru, where the music is strongest, there is a real contact with the pre-Columbian world. And there are completely different Andean styles, too – among them Peru's hugely popular huaynos, played by small swing orchestras, and chicha, a true local pop music – that are scarcely known abroad.

LATIN AMERICA ✈ GLOSSARY

Antaras Andean panpipes.

Bandola/Bandolim Small Colombian and Venezuelan/Brazilian mandolin.

Bandoneón Type of accordion used for tango.

Barrio (**Bairro** in Portuguese) Urban district.

Bolero Slow sentimental dance or song, originally Cuban but now international. Equivalent of the jazz ballad.

Bossa nova The name, "new wave", referred to a sophisticated new style of Brazilian music in the 1950s; now an international rhythm.

Caja "Box" drum used in vallenato.

Campesino Country dweller or peasant.

Candomblé Afro-Brazilian religion.

Cavaquinho Small four-stringed Brazilian guitar.

Charango Ten-stringed Andean mandolin traditionally made from armadillo or tortoise shell.

Chicha Andean alcoholic drink and an intoxicating music fusing local and modern sounds.

Choro Brazilian instrumental music with roots in European salon music and Portuguese urban folk.

Conjunto Group.

Corridos Mexican ballads, typically about the revolution, heroes and villains.

Cuatro Rustic guitar with four double strings.

Cumbia Colombia's most popular dance music.

Danzón European-style Cuban dance, also very popular in Mexico.

Décima Verse form of Spanish origin with ten lines of eight syllables, used all over the Caribbean and Central America, often for improvised poetry.

Estrabillo Instrumental passage between improvized verses.

Forró Jaunty accordion-led dance music from northeast Brazil.

Gaita Traditional Colombian flute.

Hocket Technique in which two or more people perform a single tune by playing or singing its notes in alternation.

Huapango Dance from central and eastern Mexico – and a general term for music from these areas.

Huayno Popular Andean dance music.

Huayla Another popular Andean dance music, from Peru.

Lambada A humble dance rhythm from northern Brazil that became an international craze in the early 1990s.

Mejoranas Music of the Panamanian mestizos.

Mestizo Person of mixed indigenous and Spanish blood.

Mariachi Mexican band dominated by trumpets and strings.

Merengue Roots dance music from the Dominican Republic, now popular all over Latin America and the Caribbean.

Milónga Traditional song of Argentinian gauchos (cowboys).

Norteño Accordion-led music from the north of Mexico, known as Tex-Mex in its US incarnation.

Nueva canción "New song", the popular political song movement of Latin America.

Porro Fiesta music played by brass bands in Colombia.

Quena Peruvian bamboo flute.

Ranchera Mexican urban song, frequently melodramatic and sentimental.

Samba The most famous dance of Brazil, existing in many forms, based on heavy syncopation above an easy 2/4 beat.

Son Cuban precursor of salsa and also a generic term for various Mexican styles.

Típica Literally "typical"; used of traditional music or line-up of a group.

Tropicalismo Politically oriented blend of Brazilian traditional music and rock.

Vallenato Accordion-led music from Colombia's Atlantic coast.

Yaravi Slow Andean song.

Zampoñas Andean bamboo panpipes.

OVER THE BORDER

MEXICO IS A WHOLE LOT MORE THAN MARIACHI

Mariachis – those extravagantly passionate bands, with their sly rhythms and natty hats – have been shorthand symbols for Mexico in a thousand low-budget films and television episodes. However, they are only the best-known example from a country rich in traditional musics. Mary Farquharson introduces the sound of bandas, cumbia Mexicana, norteño ballads, and huapango – the music that gave the world "La Bamba".

When foreigners run away to Mexico, they tend to bury themselves in bars and – to the sound of local ballads – weep over the hopelessness of love. Mexicans who run away to the United States tend to take their music with them. They complain that gringos (non-Latins) don't know how to throw a party, they indulge in nostalgia through their ranchera songs, and they finance extravagant tours so that they can see their favourite stars in person.

Considering that its border with the US stretches for two thousand miles, Mexico has put up a remarkable resistance to American rock. Yet Mexico's own music is very hard to define. As well as American sounds, musics from Spain, Argentina, Colombia and Britain have all arrived in Mexico and been assimilated and reworked to local taste. All of them are given a treatment that is more romantic, more emotional and more danceable. Thus recycled, they are sold as Mexican music and dispersed by satellite all over the Americas from Alaska to Patagonia.

Mexican versions don't respect their sources and nor are they much bothered by international music fashions. Rap songs become love songs

with a bit of cumbia thrown in. Danzones and boleros are now far removed from the original versions from Cuba, where both styles have almost died out, but are still the most popular requests at barrio parties in Mexico City. Young Mexicans still dance the chachachá, too, along with a Mexican variant of mambo. And in the 1990s, the country has seen an extraordinary craze for brass bands – bandas – playing everything from salsa to ballads.

CUMBIA MEXICANA

Cumbia is now more popular in Mexico than in its native Colombia. In its new home it has become simpler, more direct and danceable. For a long time, a national radio station used to call out "¡Tropi. . .Q!" – the last letter a "cooooooh" that could unblock traffic jams – and then launch into the latest cumbia hit, which was played without reprieve for a month and then forgotten. A song about cellular telephones

Los Leones de Xichu stirring up the dance

replaced "No te metes con mi cucu" (Don't Mess With My Toot Toot), which in turn had taken over from a song about fried chicken and chips – a thinly disguised treatise on how a macho likes his bird.

The flirtatious, addictive cumbia was the most popular music in Mexico in the 1980s, until bandas came along, and it remains a force throughout the country. Outside the capital it tends to take on a more mellow, romantic tone: a sound closely associated with the band **Los Bukis**, whose album "Me volvi a acordar de ti" sold 1.5 million legal copies and an estimated four million more in bootleg cassettes.

Although Los Bukis come from Michoacan in central Mexico, their biggest market – like that of other Mexican bands – is north of the border in California and Texas, among the new Mexican immigrant communities. These are ever-expanding. Each night around four thousand Mexicans risk bandits and immigration officers to cross from Tijuana into California and about half of them get through. Thousands more enter nightly at strategic points between Tijuana and Matamoros.

Most of these migrants come from rural Mexico where the agricultural crisis has left young men with little option but to head north. Wives and children are now beginning to join them and, facing racism and alienation, the communities hold firmly onto the music that they identify with back home. This means principally cumbia and norteño.

NORTEÑO

Norteño, which is known north of the border as Tex-Mex, has its roots in the *corrido* ballads that retold the battles between Anglos and Meskins in the early nineteenth century. The war turned out badly for Mexico, which lost half of its territory, and Mexicans living in what is now California, Arizona, New Mexico and Texas found themselves with a new nationality.

The late 1920s was the golden age of the corrido, when songs of the recent Revolution were recorded in the hotels of San Antonio, Texas, and distributed on both sides of the border. The accordion, which had arrived with Bohemian immigrants who came to work in the mines in the late nineteenth century, was introduced into the originally guitar-based groups by **Narciso Martinez** and **Santiago Jimenez** (father of the famous **Flaco**) in the 1930s, and the sound that they developed

became the essence of corrido ensembles on both sides of the border.

When the accordion appeared, it brought the polka with it, and by the 1950s this had blended with the traditional duet singing of northern Mexico and with salon dances like the waltz, mazurka and the *chotis* (the central European schottische that travelled to Spain and France before arriving in northern Mexico) to produce the definitive norteño style. The accordion had already pepped up the songs with lead runs and flourishes between the verses, but the *conjuntos norteños* needed to round out their sound to keep up with the big bands and so added bass and rolling drums – the basis of today's conjuntos.

> **Cruce el Rio Grande**
> **(I Crossed the Rio Grande)**
>
> I crossed the Rio Grande
> Swimming, not giving a damn!
> The Border Patrol threw me back . . .
> I disguised myself as a gringo
> And tinted my hair blonde
> But since I didn't know English
> Back I go again
>
> **Popular norteño ballad**

Unlike most other regional styles, norteño is popular throughout the country. At a party in an isolated mountain community in central Mexico, the host takes out his accordion and plays norteño corridos until the dawn breaks. In an ice-cream parlour on the Pacific coast, the piped music is a norteño waltz. And waiting for darkness to cross the border at Tijuana, norteños are again the musical backdrop.

This country-wide popularity is most likely due to the lyrics. Norteño songs speak to people in words more real and interesting than the cozy pseudo-sophistication of Mexican pop music. The ballads tell of antiheroes: small-time drug runners; illegal "wet-back" immigrants; a small-time thief with one blond eyebrow who defied the law. Norteño reflects the mood of a country that generally considers the government to be big-time thieves and hence has a certain respect for everyday people with the courage to stand up to a crooked system.

Groups like **Los Tigres del Norte** and **Los Cadetes del Norte** take stories from the local papers and convert them into ballads that usually begin "Voy a cantarles un corrido" (I'm going to sing you a corrido)" before launching into a gruesome tale sung in a deadpan style as if it were nothing to go to a local dance and get yourself killed. One of the most famous corridos, "Rosita Alvírez", tells the story of a young girl who struck lucky: only one of the three bullets fired by her boyfriend hit and killed her.

Los Tigres are by far the most successful of all norteño groups – superstars, in fact – having won a Grammy and subsequently been adopted by the (generally bland) Mexican TV company, Televisa. They recorded their last album in Miami – a sign of the power of the US Mexican market. Quite early in their career, the band modified the traditional line-up by adding a sax and mixed the familiar rhythms with cumbias; however, their nasal singing style and the combination of instruments identifies the music very clearly as norteño.

Los Tigres del Norte in serenading mode

RANCHERA

There is absolutely nothing deadpan about **ranchera** music: a style that is again hugely popular. Ranchera songs are loaded with melodramatic passion and characterized by cries of "¡ay ay ay ay ay!" – joyous exclamations that come from singer and audience alike.

Ranchera is essentially nostalgic and pessimistic – the lament of a people who have left their land and are lost in a strange city or in a different country. The American singer **Linda Ronstadt**, who recorded a fine album of ranchera songs, said she was simply following what her father, a Mexican immigrant, used to sing in their home in Tucson, Arizona. The late **José Alfredo Jimenez**, the greatest ranchera singer of all time, raised pessimism to a high art, and wrote his own epitaph in his much-loved song, "La vida no vale nada" (Life is worth

---

El Gato Felix (Felix the Cat)

I'm going to sing a corrido
About someone who I knew
A distinguished journalist
Feared for his pen
From Tijuana to Madrid

They called him Felix the Cat
Because the story goes that
He was like those felines
He had seven lives
And he had to see them through

He came from Choi, Sinaloa
That was the place he was born
He stayed in Tijuana
Because it took his fancy
And he wanted to help in some way
With what he wrote in the paper

He made the government tremble
He went right through the alphabet
A whole rosary of threats
He made his paper Zeta popular
With his valiant pen

He pointed to corruption
He always helped the people
And more than two presidents
Had their eyes on him

In a treacherous way
the Cat met his end
Death, mounted on a racehorse
A real beast
Rode him down

Now Felix the Cat is dead
They are carrying him to his grave
He will be another one on the list
Of brave journalists
That they've wanted to silence

Candles burn for Felix Miranda
To you I dedicate my song
But don't you worry
There will be other brave people
To take your place

**Enrique Franco
(Los Tigres del Norte)**

Linda Ronstadt and Daniel Valdez

star **Vicente Fernandez**, most of the top singers are women: **María de Lourdes, Lola Beltran, Lucha Villa,** and – the hottest property – **Chavela Vargas**. Vargas has found an audience among Mexico's radical chic, who pay a vast cover charge to hear the same songs that were once the favourites of their mothers' maids.

MARIACHI

The regional style that has contributed most to ranchera is *son jaliscience*, the traditional music of Jalisco, in western Mexico. As in Cuba, the son is the musical form that grew out of the mestizo mix of Spanish and indigenous cultures. The style was popularized by the **mariachi bands** who came originally from Jalisco state.

Mariachi bands were popular at wedding ceremonies around the turn of the century and some say their name is a corruption of the French word *mariage*. One version of mariachi history tells how, in 1907, Mexico's last dictator, General Porfirio Díaz, organized a garden party for a visiting US secretary of state. Since he wanted to include Mexican music, a quartet from Jalisco were contracted – and told to change their white cotton trousers for the charro suits worn by the men who owned the haciendas where they worked as servants. A quartet, even in their fancy dress, still seemed too poor for the occasion, so eight musicians and two dancers

Nothing). His was a world where only the tequila bottle is faithful, where love is violent and jealous and where a man who dies in a duel is a man who has lived.

The music calls heavily on various regional styles but is essentially an urban phenomenon. The songs began life at the beginning of this century and – as well as their unconcealed emotion – are distinguished by the way that singers stretch out the final note of the line and add a glissando. Today, with the exception of TV

Mariachi Coculense "Rodriguez", 1935

were contracted. The Jaliscan son was never the same again, and mariachi, along with its costume, was born.

The early mariachis played violins, guitars, a harp and the enormous *guitarrón*, an acoustic bass guitar; trumpets were added later while the harp has generally been dropped. From the 1920s on, when the legendary (and still flourishing) Cantina Tenampa opened with a resident band in Mexico City, mariachi bands have played mainly in taverns. They are employed today all over Mexico, as well as across the border, where they make better money playing to homesick field workers.

Since most bands are paid by the song, the leader identifies likely customers in a seedy Texas or California bar and the trumpeter grabs a seat at their table, launching himself into a classic piece from the badly missed home country. As the drinkers indulge their sadness, the singer utters the cry, the violins wail and the trumpeter prepares to slide straight into the next song so that, by the end of the evening, a week's wages can easily have been spent on music.

Although mariachis began with a repertoire of sones from Jalisco, today they play cumbias, polkas, waltzes, ballads and an incredible range of popular songs on request. With only two hundred songs, you might as well stay at home in the village, one mariachi told me. Like most of his colleagues, he could play around fifteen hundred pieces on demand.

The golden age of mariachi was the 1950s, when the ranchera music they played accompanied a series of Hollywood films, with Mexican matinee idols serenading their lovers. Many of the greatest films featured **Mariachi Vargas**, a group that was founded in the 1930s and is still considered to be the best in Mexico. Virtually all the original members have died but the band replaces old stars with the pick of the younger generations and they remain very hot. It was Mariachi Vargas, notably, who Linda Ronstadt chose as backing on her "Canciones" album of ranchera classics.

Most of the mariachi songs are old-established classics, although some of the more adventurous and technically accomplished bands will perform songs by the remarkable **Juan Gabriel**. Gabriel is a rare phenomenon in Mexico, an enormously talented composer, arranger, singer and TV star with an excellent understanding of Mexican regional music. He writes and performs canciones norteñas and sones as well as commercial ballads and soft rock. He plays with mariachis and with a symphony orchestra and his concert seasons all over the country sell out months in advance. For years he was excluded from radio and TV on account of being gay – but his talent eventually won through.

THE BANDA BOOM

The enormous success of Los Tigres del Norte and their updated norteño sound resulted in a phenomenon that has changed the face of

Banda del Recodo

Mexican music in the 1990s: **banda** music. This is a fusion of the norteño style with the brass bands that have played at village fiestas all over the country for the last century. There are now hundreds of bandas in Mexico – ranging from four to twenty musicians, and all playing brass and percussion, with just an occasional guitar. Their repertoire includes norteño polkas, ranchera ballads, cumbia, merengue and salsa – all arranged for brass.

The most exciting of these groups is a fiery orchestra from Mazatlán, Sinaloa – the **Banda del Recodo**. This is not a new band. Indeed, its leader, Don Cruz Lizárraga, has been in the business for half a century, starting out in a traditional *tambora* marching band (the tambora is the huge carried side drum) that played a straight repertoire of brass-band numbers. However, Don Cruz has always had an eye for musical fashions, adapting his material to merengue, ranchera – whatever anyone wanted to hear. His great banda hit was a version of Cuban bandleader Beny Moré's classic "La culebra".

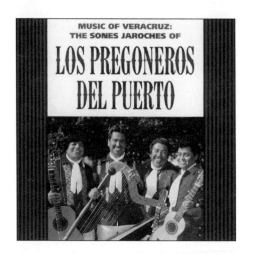

MUSIC OF VERACRUZ:
THE SONES JAROCHES OF

LOS PREGONEROS DEL PUERTO

The banda boom currently dominates the TV music programmes and more or less all points of the country, except for Mexico City, where cumbia and salsa stay top of the bill. Elsewhere, it is the bandas that fill the stadiums and village halls, and it is their names you'll see painted in enormous multicoloured letters on any patch of white wall along the roads. The craze has brought with it a series of new dances, too, including the *quebradita* – a gymnastic combination of lambada, polka, rock'n'roll, rap and cumbia, which is danced with particular skill in all points north of Guadalajara.

HUAPANGOS AND HARPS

In the central Bajío region and along the Gulf coast of eastern Mexico, **huapangos** give banda a run for its money. These are basically variants on son and divide into three main regional types: the *huapango huasteco, arribeño* and *veracruzano*.

The **huapango huasteco** is played on violin with a guitar and small *jarana* guitar and is usually sung in falsetto. Although its repertoire is limited, it requires improvised lyrics that change according to the occasion,

A NEW YEAR'S HUAPANGO DUEL

. . . .

"¡Xichu!" shouted the boy and the old school bus rattled off across the mountains to this small village, more or less at the meeting place of the states of Guanajuato, Queretaro and San Luis Potosí in central Mexico.

We arrived to find the small plaza packed out, and red-lipped carnival figures announcing that a fiesta was about to begin. It was New Year's Eve and, on a temporary wooden stage, old men, the guests of honour, sat in a line. They were troubadours: the current generation of reporters, analysts, prophets, historians and gossips, who have, over the centuries, kept this isolated region in touch with the world. To do so they use music – the huapango arribeño, which, up here, still gets an airing at weddings, baptisms and saints' days, in tandem with local pop groups.

The fiesta we had come to, however, was a special occasion in the huapango calendar: a duel and test of skills. Through the night, two bands, two singers, would hurl improvised verse at each other in turn, showing their skills. Shortly before dawn, the public would decide the winner. There was no prize to be won save for prestige – and of course future party bookings.

Guillermo Velazquez who, with his younger brother Eliazar, had organized this annual tribute to the old troubadours, was first to climb up onto the platform that stood, like scaffolding, on one side of the square. In the crowd, his rival, Cándido Martinez, feigned confidence, greeting the friends and acquaintances who would judge him with applause or derision when it was time for him to mount the scaffolding on the other side of the square.

Guillermo opened with a verse familiar to the crowd that gathers wherever he is playing:
"I'm Guillermo Velazquez
and I've never lost my roots.
I was born in Xichu, Guanajuato
and there I will go to rest one day."
This was the *poesía* that traditionally opens these encounters, the singer introducing himself and his pedigree. Once done, he launches into the *vallena*, improvised verse which must suit the occasion.

It was the end of a troubled year. Guillermo began an analysis of events in the Gulf and in eastern Europe. In décima verse – each line with eight syllables organized in an intimidating rhythmic structure – he prepared an argument that would be developed over the coming hours. When he recited, the public stood and listened. When he paused, closing his eyes for inspiration, the crowd danced, the *zapateado* of their feet tapping out a counter rhythm to the instrumental *estribillo* led by two violins.

Guillermo is recognized as the most talented young troubadour in the region but the more experienced Cándido knew his weak points. After reciting his own greetings to the crowd, he paid profound respects to Guillermo as a man and a poet and then accused him of losing touch with his campesino roots. According to Cándido's improvisation, Guillermo's interest in international politics was not shared by the crowd at the fiesta. Guillermo has travelled, he has taken the huapango arribeño to Africa and Europe: Cándido accused him of having fallen for the seduction of another world.

The duel in progress, around 3am

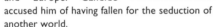

Cándido represents an older generation of troubadours, whose role was to inform rather than analyze. Tonight he was filling heads with technical information about the year that was about to end. In rhyming verse, he counted the days, hours and seconds that were slipping past; it was a lesson in arithmetic from a carpenter who'd never gone to school.

Although by midnight a few drunks had collapsed under the scaffolding and babies were asleep under their grandmothers' shawls, the square was still crowded with men and women dancing: a sea of cowboy hats, brims almost touching, while feet stamped upon wooden boards laid specially for the purpose. A group recently returned from the fields of California held up their ghetto-blasters in front of the platform, recording the festival for their return to the North.

The concert was now entering the *bravata*; the tone became less serious as the two musicians began to take personal digs at each other. Guillermo, who as a child was selected to study in an American seminary, was accused by his rival of having been expelled for stealing the silver chalice. He replied that, had he been expelled, it would have been for stealing Cándido's daughter. As dawn approached, the troubadours moved on to sones or *jarabes*, which give more of a leading role to the music and to the dancers still with the energy to show off complicated footwork.

Cándido and Guillermo refused to give up. At ten in the morning they were still playing and the crowd still dancing between verses. The sun was shining but no one wanted to go home.

Finally, Cándido admitted defeat. The home crowd cheered. Both groups of musicians climbed unsteadily down from the scaffolding, greeted each other warmly and wandered towards Guillermo's house, where mutton had been cooking all night.

There, while Guillermo drank black coffee, Cándido caught the eye of a woman and began to serenade her. It was New Year's Day; he was down, but definitely not out.

---

and it is distinguished by musical flourishes that mean no son sounds the same twice over. There are dozens of huapango huasteco bands, appearing at the fiestas, weddings and parties, bars and brothels of states from Tamaulipas to Hidalgo and Puebla. Several of them feature on locally produced cassettes, where they often add rancheras, paso dobles and corridos, which are given a fiery violin treatment but no falsettos. One of the best groups – who have made it onto CD and the World Music festival circuit – are **Los Camperos de Valles**, a trio from Ciudad Valles in San Luis Potosí.

Further inland, the **huapango arribeño** places more emphasis on the verse, which is improvised in décimas, the old Spanish form. A top group here – for more on which see the feature box – are Guillermo Velazquez's **Los Leones de Xichu**.

The third of the huapangos, **veracruzano**, is instantly recognizable due to Ritchie Valens' rearrangement of a famous local number, "La Bamba". The traditional huapango veracruzano – or *son jarocho* as it is better known – is played on guitars, harp and percussion. To hear it you need to head for Veracruz, where bands vie for business under the arches in the central square and down at the port's seafood restaurants. Outstanding musicians among them include the legendary Don Nicolás Sosa, now in his nineties; Graciana Silva, who plays solo harp and sings in a style inherited from generations past; and the bands **Boca del Rio** and **Mandinga**.

Other **regional styles** of son thrive to the blissful ignorance of just about everyone who lives outside their patch. They include the *sones calentanos* of the hot lands of western Mexico; the big harp music of Apatzingán; the less frantic *sones istmeños* from Oaxaca; and the Purépecha Indian dance music from Michoacán, itself heavily influenced by the calentanos. A recent compilation CD, "Anthology of Mexican Sones", provides an excellent introduction to these styles, all of which have an intensity that sets them apart from their commercial counterparts, modified for radio and cassettes.

▶ DISCOGRAPHY ◀

Mexican recordings are widely available in the US – less so in Europe. A label to look out for is Corason, who are recording and releasing consistently excellent CDs and cassettes of traditional sounds from all over the country. They are distributed in the US by Rounder and by Topic in Britain.

For more Mexican music recommendations, see the Tex-Mex discography in Chapter Twelve.

COMPILATIONS

ⓒ **Various** *Anthology of Mexican Sones* (Corason, Mexico). This 3-CD set is the definitive survey of Mexican traditional music, featuring wonderful recordings of rural bands. Excellent accompanying notes plus lyrics in Spanish and English.

ⓒ **Various** *Mexico – Fiestas of Chiapas & Oaxaca* (Nonesuch Explorer, US). Atmospheric recordings from village festivities in southern Mexico. Marimba conjuntos, brass bands, some eccentric ensembles and great fireworks on the opening track. The next best thing to being there.

Various *Mexique – Musiques Traditionnelles* (Ocora, France). For the more folklorically inclined, music from the many little-known indigenous Indian communities of Mexico.

SONES AND MARIACHI

ⓒ **Conjunto Alma Jarochos** *Sones Jarochos* (Arhoolie, US). A fine disc, the first in a series of regional Mexican releases, featuring sones from Veracruz with harps and jaranguitas.

ⓒ **Los Camperos de Valles** *Sones de la Huasteca* and *El Triumfo* (Corason, Mexico). The Huasteca sones are considered by many to be the most beautiful music in Mexico. Played on violin, guitar and the small vihuela guitar, an important element is the falsetto singing of love songs that are both rowdy and romantic.

ⓒ **Mariachi Coculense de Cirilo Marmolejo** *Mexico's Pioneer Mariachis Vol I* (Arhoolie, US). Wonderful archive recordings from the 20s and 30s of one of the seminal groups. The disc also includes the first ever mariachi recording, from 1908.

ⓒ **Mariachi Reyes del Aserradero** *Sones from Jalisco* (Corason, Mexico). An excellent mariachi band from Jalisco state play the original sones from this region where mariachi was born.

ⓒ **Mariachi Tapatió de José Marmolejo** *The Earliest Mariachi Recordings: 1906–36* (Arhoolie, US). Archive recordings of a pioneer mariachi band, featuring the great trumpet playing of Jesús Salazar.

ⓒ **Mariachi Vargas** *20 exitos* (Orfeon, Mexico). Big-band style mariachi from Silvestre Vargas, who has managed to stay at the top of his field for over 50 years. Always flexible, his band released one disastrous album of mariachi-rock but have otherwise had hits all the way. They work much of the year in the US.

ⓒ **Los Pregoneros del Puerto** *Music of Veracruz* (Rounder, US). Rippling sones jaroches from the Veracruz coast, where harp and jarana guitars still dominate. An enchanting album.

RANCHERA

ⓒ **José Alfredo Jimenez** *Homenaje a José Alfredo Jimenez* (Sony Discos, US). Jimenez.was the king of ranchera and embodied the best and worst of Mexican machismo. As he predicted in one of his songs, everyone in Mexico missed him when he died.

ⓒ **Linda Ronstadt** *Canciones de mi Padre* and *Más Canciones* (Asylum, US). Ranchera classics sung very convincingly by the Mexican-American rocker, accompanied by Mariachi Vargas.

NORTEÑO

ⓒ **Los Pingüinos del Norte** *Conjuntos norteños* (Arhoolie, US). This album pairs up Tex and Mex conjuntos: Los Pingüinos singing corridos live in a cantina in northern Mexico, and Fred Zimmerle's Trio from San Antonio, Texas, performing typical polkas and rancheras.

ⓒ **Los Tigres del Norte** *Corridos Prohibidos* (Fonovisa, US). A collection of corridos about Mexican low life and heroism from one of the best norteño groups in the business.

CUMBIA

Los Bukis *Me volvi a acordar de ti* (Melody, Mexico). The sound of soft cumbia – and the most popular Mexican record ever.

ⓒ **Sonora Dinamita** *Mi Cucu* (Discos Fuentes, Colombia). Mexican cumbia performed by a breakaway group of artists who took the name of the Colombian originals. Their lyrics, full of double meanings, are performed with a zest that has brought huge success in Mexico.

OTHERS

Agustin Lara *Agustin Lara* (Orfeon, Mexico). The legendary crooner, the man who idolized prostitutes and married for love twelve times. One of Mexico's greatest composers of popular music, specializing in bolero ballads and music from Veracruz.

ⓒ **Juan Reynoso** *The Paganini of the Mexican Hotlands* (Corason, Mexico). The title is fair dues: Reynoso is Mexico's greatest country violinist, eighty years old now, but still in fine form on this recording, backed by vocal, guitars and drum.

ⓒ **Various** *Pure Purépecha* (Corason, Mexico). A gem that brings together three duets of Purépecha Indians from Michoacán, singing sweet pirecua love songs, and some rowdy abajeño sones from Conjunto Atardecer.

ⓒ **Various** *New Mexico: Hispanic Traditions* (Smithsonian Folkways, US). A good ethnographic recording from the Mexican diaspora in the US. Dances, songs, corridos and religious music in rustic style.

¡CUMBIA! ¡CUMBIA!

COLOMBIA'S GOLD INCLUDES HOT CUMBIA AND CRAZED VALLENATO ACCORDIONS

Colombia is one of the powerhouses of Latin music, with its highly influential national music, cumbia, one of the great Latin rhythms, and its major role in the salsa world through the label Discos Fuentes and the country's great star, Joe Arroyo (a strand that is covered in the salsa section in Chapter Ten). But that's only half the story, as Kim Burton – with a nod from Dave Hucker – explains.

Colombia is a big country – almost 2000 km north to south and over 1000 km east to west – and encompasses a tropical coast, rolling savannah, icy Andean highlands, and, on the Pacific coast, dense rain forest. In the veins of its people runs the blood of native Indians, Spanish settlers, African slaves and English freebooters. All have left their mark on the tapestry of music that fills the streets, buses, bars and cafés – a tapestry as varied as any on the South American continent.

Colombians have left their imprint, too, throughout the Latin music world and beyond – and not just through salsa. New York, London and Madrid each have a network of clubs where Colombian music is performed by visiting bands or emigré musicians and their local colleagues. At home with the musics of two continents, these new groups conduct their own experiments with rhythm and melody, letting cumbia, paseo, puya and joropo take their place in the New World's musical conquest of the Old.

ROOTS OF CUMBIA

The music that is most closely identified with Colombia is the **cumbia** – a typically Latin mixture of solidly grounded yet very hot rhythm with an airily syncopated melody. This has acquired the status of the national dance – indeed, one famous song, "La Pollera Colora", is practically a national anthem. Colombians will swear to you that it has been played at state occasions in place of the anthem to the general satisfaction of all concerned – musicians, guests, the president himself.

The first cumbia ensembles were made up of percussion and vocals only, but they have developed into much larger bands boasting trumpets, trombones and saxophones, electric keyboards and other modern refinements. For the roots of the music, you need to look to the **Atlantic coast**, where cumbia was originally just one of a whole set of rhythms and dances. Its distinctive shuffling steps are reputedly survivals from the days when the black slaves in their barracks would attempt to dance while restrained by their fetters and leg-irons.

Some of the Atlantic region's folkloric groups still play a roots cumbia using a **drum choir**. A deep *bombo*, played with sticks, calls the other instruments at the start of the song: the conga-like *tambor macho*, which holds down the basic groove with its strong offbeat, and the *tambor hembra*, which is the lead drum, improvising freely and responding to the inventions of the singer. Above these the maracas and *guache*, gourds or metal tubes filled with seeds, rattle away, and sometimes a bassline, is provided by the *marimbula*, a low-pitched thumb-piano.

All these instruments are purely **African** in origin and in the part they play within the ensemble. The **European** part of Colombia's heritage is heard in the shape of the melodies and the forms of the verses, which often follow the

Dancing in the street, cumbia style

Toto La Momposina with a haircut to rival Valderrama's

rules of medieval Spanish poetry, while two rather more unusual instruments reflect the influence of the **indigenous Indian** populations. These are a wild-sounding clarinet called the *flauto de millo* – a piece of cane with a tongue cut in one end to act as a reed, and four finger holes – and a shrill recorder-like flute, the *gaita*.

All of these instruments are used by **Toto La Momposina** and her Bogotá-based troupe of percussionists, singers and dancers, and it is in her work that you are most likely to hear cumbia in something approaching its original form. Toto performs widely in her native land and the group has toured abroad, as well as recording for Real World. A similar group is run by a woman calling herself **La Negra Grande de Colombia**. At one time such drum bands were always booked to play at parties or celebrations, though these days they are presented as part of Colombia's cultural heritage.

CUMBIA MEETS MAMBO AND SALSA

It was in the 1940s that cumbia started to leave the countryside and to become a dance of the urban middle and upper classes, where its interpretation changed radically. It was in this period that cumbia's regular foursquare rhythm, with a distinctive loping beat, likened to riding a horse at a trot, became established.

The first bandleader to begin this process, under the influence of North American big-band music and Cuban-American mambo, was the clarinettist **Lucho Bermudez**, from the town of Carmen de Bolivar. Bermudez's style of

cumbia – he and his band are still very much in demand – lost some of the polyrhythmic complexities of the original cumbia beat, as the arrangements became more urbane. However, the songs invariably stayed close to the old folkloric melodies, albeit somewhat simplified and smoothed out to give a sophisticated big-city sound.

Some of the bands that followed stayed closer to the original spirit of the cumbia, more rural in sound, and often featuring clarinet solos influenced by the tone and melodic shape of the flauto de millo. One of the most interesting was **Peregoyo y su Combo Vacana**, an orchestra that appeared in the 1960s, playing compositions based around the folk dances of the Buenaventura area, as well as slightly distorted versions of Cuban music. Part of their unusual charm – they, too, are still active – comes from their use of guitar instead of the more common piano and from their rough and ready sound, which occasionally threatens to collapse entirely. Nonetheless, once the listener has adjusted to the band's idiosyncratic approach to tuning, its dark-hued swing is very attractive.

From the 1970s on, a new influence hit cumbia in the form of salsa. This showed particularly in the use of repeated rhythmic piano patterns instead of the traditional offbeat chords of earlier times. Both **La Sonora de Baru** and **La Sonora Dinamita** – two of the best modern cumbia bands – make frequent use of this technique. The tune "La Colegiala" (familiar to many in Europe from its use in coffee commercials) changes rhythm from cumbia to salsa for its chorus, a device that is becoming

Peregoyo and his combo

La Sonora Dinamita, with Fruko front left

more and more common. **Joe Arroyo**, of course, Colombia's top musician, merges cumbia seamlessly into his "joe-son" salsa mix (for more on which, see the Salsa section).

Many of today's great cumbia bands were established in the early 1960s, foremost among them **Los Corraleros de Majagual**, on the north coast. A big band with a large brass section, percussion and accordion, they have been a training ground for a catalogue of top cumbia musicians, including Lisandro Meza, Calixto Ochoa, Amando Hernandez, Alfredo Gutierrez, and the great Julio Estrada Rincon, better known as **Fruko** – "The Godfather of Salsa" (see Discos Fuentes box overpage and our Salsa article). The number of hits Los Corraleros have produced over their thirty years of recording is prodigious. The most famous of them all was "Caballo Viejo" (Old Horse), composed by their Venezuelan guitarist Simon Diaz in the 1960s. A decade on it was given the Cuban charanga treatment by Roberto Torres – and then revamped by France's Gypsy Kings into **"Bamboleo"**, one of the biggest (and most annoying!) hits of the 1980s.

La Sonora Dinamita were formed around the same time as Los Corraleros by composer Lucho Argain and the ever-present Fruko. Their unashamedly popular style, mixing cumbia with Central American, Mexican and Caribbean music, has made them huge stars with a long list of instantly memorable hits like "A mover la

colita", "Café con ron", "La Bamba" and "Tu Cucu". The last – in a transition reminiscent of "Bamboleo" – was actually a Colombian version of Rockin' Sidney's zydeco hit, "My Toot Toot".

Among the top younger artists is Melida Yara Yanguma, better known as **La India Meliyara**. She was the first female soloist with La Sonora Dinamita, but now heads her own group, **La Sonora Meliyara**, updating cumbia with distinctive new songs and a glorious voice. Many of the songs she plays put a woman's twist on the typical macho traditions of cumbia – although, strangely enough, they're actually written by male collaborators. They can also be very sexually upfront – enough to get the sticker treatment in the US if Tipper Gore were to happen upon them, as witness the lyrics of "Las Cosquillitas", below.

Cumbia has brought good money to many of its big stars – and especially those who have moved across into the US salsa market – but life has not always been easy for its exponents. One of the most famous of all Colombian musicians was the eccentric **Crecencio Salcedo**, a virtuoso of the flauto de millo and an immensely prolific composer who was said never to wear shoes. Despite writing a host of songs in various Colombian styles, many of which have become standards, he had a poor head for business and died in the early 1980s, eighty years old and scraping a living from busking. Given the poverty and instability of Colombian society throughout this century, this has not been an uncommon fate for musicians.

SMUGGLERS' FAVOURITES: VALLENATO

The sweet, hot accordion-led music called **vallenato** takes its name from its origins in Valledupar on the Atlantic coast. It is a pretty old form, supposedly invented by the legendary **Francisco el Hombre** (see the Accordionist from Hell box, opposite). However, it has only recently become popular beyond its homeland, spreading throughout the country mainly through the patronage of **cocaine traders**. Many of Colombia's new coca rich came from the Valledupar area, where there had been a tradition of smuggling long before cocaine, and vallenato was the music they loved most. One coca baron is even said to have bought up an entire radio station in order to flood the airwaves with 24-hour vallenato, while others showered their favourites with extravagant gifts. Cash, jewellery, cars, houses, even aeroplanes have all been acquired by good players who happened to be in the right place at the right time to tap the generosity of the barons.

In its simplest form a vallenato band or conjunto needs only three musicians. The accordionist (normally playing a three-row button model) is usually the singer and bandleader, while the other essential instruments are the *caja vallenata* (literally the vallenato box), which is a small, fairly high-pitched single-headed drum, and the *guacharaca* scraper.

It was with such a conjunto that the great **Alejo Duran**, "El Rey Negro del Vallenato", began his career. Despite working as a cowboy most of his life, he found the time to write and record a collection of songs that became instant classics. He died in 1989 at the age of 71, having played the accordion for over sixty of those years.

Modern bands such as those of **Lisandro Meza** or the brilliant virtuoso **Alfredo Gutierrez** add an electric bass and maybe extra percussion in the shape of conga and cowbell. These days, too, the skin of the caja is no longer from a goat, but made of X-ray film, more reliable in the heat and humidity of the tropics, and less likely to wear out. The accordions are German-made but are specially adjusted in the factory before export to provide the warm yet penetratingly reedy sound that Colombian performers favour.

It's in the tuneful energy of the music and the virtuosity of the performers that the appeal of vallenato lies. In this, the outstanding feature is the role of the accordion, playing virtuoso introductions and interludes, making sly comment between the lines of the verses, improvising melodic solos and pumping out vigorous riffs to heighten the excitement. Idiosyncratic bass lines notch up the tension still further, and the whole gains much of its appeal from the interplay of African-derived rhythms with sweet, wide-ranging melody.

Las Cosquillitas*

My love . . .
I would like you to . . .
If you wanted to . . .
If you could . . .
Wow! That's something I like!
But, it's that I . . . I . . . I . . . aaagh!

What do you want darling?
What do you like?
What do you want?

That you kiss me and hug me
That you spoil me
That you please me
Every time I ask!
That whenever I need you
Don't let me down for a moment
If you don't please me
I will die (of emotion)

That you whisper in my ear
Sweet and pretty nonsense
That you squeeze me hard
And kiss my sweet lips
That you kiss me wherever you will
From head to toe
But what I ask the most
Is that you give me cosquillitas

And do you like it here? Yes gently!
And over here? Yes, like that!
And over there too? Yes, that's good!
Carry on, go on, don't stop, it's too good.
Meliyara and her orchestra invite you all to dance!

Lucho Campillo, La Sonora Meliyara.
*[*las cosquillitas means teasing or foreplay]*

LATIN AMERICA

THE ACCORDIONIST FROM HELL

....

Once upon a time **Francisco el Hombre** was travelling through Alta Guajira when strange news met his ears. Some villagers came to tell him that an extraordinary new accordionist had arrived in the area, a musician so fine that he outclassed even Francisco himself! Intrigued and perhaps a little worried by the news, Francisco set off to find the stranger.

One day, mounted on his faithful burro, he found himself in a barren and lonely region. Suddenly he heard, far off in the distance, the sound of an accordion – but somehow he could not tell what direction the music was coming from. The music grew louder and louder until it seemed to fill the air around him and in the midst of his astonishment he saw an elegantly dressed man mounted on a black horse, who seemed to have sprung from nowhere. "I am your rival", said the horseman, and he began to play all the dances of vallenato with such skill and finesse that Francisco was left open-mouthed with awe.

Then, of course, he suddenly realized that such perfection could not be attained by a creature of this world and that the horseman must be a creature of the other world – none other than the Devil himself! Muttering a prayer to himself, he strapped on his own accordion and, taking advantage of a moment's silence as the stranger ended one of his tunes, began to play the melody of the Creed – in reverse. As the first notes filled the air, the stranger was seized with panic and disappeared, leaving behind a huge cloud of smoke and the reek of sulphur.

Francisco's victory over the Devil, soon known throughout the villages of la Guajira, is still talked of even today, and confirmed for all time the fame of the greatest accordionist who ever lived, the only man to outplay the Prince of Hell – Francisco el Hombre.

The energetically syncopated, tumbling style of the bass is one of the great glories of modern vallenato; it is said to have been introduced in the mid-1960s by the bass player **Caliya** in his work with Los Corraleros de Majagual. Rhythmically, it is far freer than the functional, rather foursquare bass parts of the cumbia bands and earlier vallenato, and occasionally sounds as if it's on the verge of entirely uprooting the music altogether. Another modern innovation is the singers' use of a high, almost strained vocal register, reminiscent of flamenco singing.

Vallenato lyrics are generally of little interest, dealing with love in the usual sentimental fashion (torment and false promises), sometimes throwing in a line in praise of a wealthy man in the hope of some financial return. In earlier times the songs would sometimes reflect more everyday life, and these days the writers occasionally approach more serious subjects. There is actually a subgenre, *vallenato-protesta*, though this hasn't gained much of a hold with popular audiences – or drug barons.

Cardón Guajiro (Cactus from Guajira)

I met up with grief and neglect.
After a quarrel, grief lost the battle.
I'm the cactus from Guajira
That doesn't wilt in the sun.
Anyone who tries to defeat me
is wasting his time!

In poor soil the cactus survives any weather,
But in damp soil it doesn't live long.
That's why in Guajira the cactus
will never die out.

I'm like the cactus, I have the same strength.
I live cheerfully amid grief and troubles.
I'm the cactus from Guajira,
I belong to my land.

A typical vallenato lyric from Diomedes Díaz and Nicolas "Colacho" Mendoza.

Top contemporary vallenato musicians include Meza and Gutierrez, who mix the music with cumbia; the duo of **Diomedes Díaz and Nicolas Colacho Mendoza** and the **Meriño Brothers**. Your best opportunity to hear these players live is the Valledupar Fiesta de Vallenato, held in April or May each year; it is part competition, with the winner crowned "El Rey Vallenato".

Vallenato has a US-based stepchild in the form of the **charanga vallenata**, invented by Cuban exile **Roberto Torres**. His innovation was to add to the vallenato accordion a charanga-style ensemble of flute, violins and percussion. The result was a totally fresh and highly successful approach to vallenato classics, which has, so far, filled three albums. Others have followed the lead, notably New York Cuban **Jorge Cabrera**, who added slick brass arrangements. Although it's never really taken root in Colombia itself, charanga vallenata is now a distinct strand in the international web of Latin music.

PORROS

Another lively rural tradition are the **porros** – village fiesta bands from the provinces of Savanna de Bolivar, Cordoba and Sucre. Porro is the name both of the bands and of the rhythm they most often play, although most will also throw in other local dances. Their chief characteristic is a wild enthusiasm enhanced by festive spirit, which is perhaps best summed up by an apocryphal tale of an orchestra hired by a well-to-do young man to serenade his girlfriend. The lover suggested a fee of fifty pesos and two bottles of rum to be shared by the

band members while they were playing. After a huddled discussion the leaders returned with a counter-proposition: the band would prefer two pesos and fifty bottles of rum . . .

Porros are normally **brass bands** with a clarinet lead, saxophone, trumpet, tuba (or sousaphone), a euphonium-like *bombardino*, and a three-man rhythm section of bass drum, snare drum and a pair of cymbals. Such a line-up derives from the European-style military bands that were introduced early into Latin America and whose descendants are also found in Guatemala and Mexico.

Most porros have only a local reputation- although a few with greater ambitions have achieved wider renown. **Pedro Lanza y sus Pelayeros** and, more recently, **Orchesta Climaco Sarmiento** have become well-known recording stars. There are quite a few cassette compilations of porros on sale in Colombia and there's an annual festival of the bands in the village of San Pelayo, near Montería.

LLANERA

Both vallenato and cumbia come from the coastal area of the country, on the Caribbean shore. Los Llanos, the vast plains of savannah and scrub that stretch across much of Colombia and into Venezuela, have their own music – **llanera**. This is a music with tremendous drive and swing, intensely rhythmic yet relaxed and with a considerable sentimental streak. Since it's bounded by physical rather than political geography, nearly everything that can be said about Colombian llanera music is also true of its Venezuelan equivalent.

To western ears the most unexpected member of the ensemble is the one that leads it – the **harp**. This is supported by a small group of stringed instruments like the cuatro, the mandolin-like *bandola* and its larger sibling the *bandolón*, and a small guitar called the *tiple*. Above their pounding cross-rhythms the *capachos* (maracas) rattle cheerfully away, while some of the more countrified bands might include a rather scrappily played violin. It seems that these instruments first arrived in Colombia during the eighteenth century, intended for use in church, although a harp seems as out of place by an altar as tied to the saddle of a horse.

As in all other Colombian music, there is a rich variety of rhythms, harmonic patterns and traditional melodic shapes, each with its own name and associated dance. Often the word *joropo*, originally a celebration of birthdays, baptisms or saints' days, is used as a blanket term for llanera dance music (usually songs), while *coplas*, *romances* and *tonadas* are sung to be listened to rather than danced to. The words are usually accounts of local life and habits and often speak of the charms and delights of one particular town or province. Barranquilla, Buenaventura, Carmen de Bolivar and Valledupar all get their praises sung in llanera.

Although the majority of lyrics are less than inspired, there is one type where verbal skill and wit are highly prized. This is the **contrapunteo**, an improvised verbal duel between two contestants striving to outdo one another in their treatment of a prearranged subject. The music and the verse metre, as well as the melody, are fixed by tradition in a form well-adapted to its purpose, as it gives the singer the option of repeating a couplet while awaiting inspiration, and to pause a little for thought during the

instrumental interludes. The shape of the melody itself assists the singer: beginning with a sustained high note, it descends via a short intonation on one note, leading to a sudden low swoop at the end, helping him (rarely her) excite laughter and applause with a telling final phrase.

There is a tremendous number of musicians who play such music, mostly little known outside their own area. Names to watch out for are the groups of harpist **Carlos Rojas** (also a well-known composer) and Venezuelan **Luis Ariel Rey**, singer **Orlando Valdemarra** and the **conjuntos Sabor Llanero** and **Alma Llanera**.

ANDEAN GROUPS

The Colombian Andes still hold a large Indian population, and the music of the area, usually referred to by Colombians as *musica de la interior*, shares some characteristics with the

DISCOS FUENTES

....

Crucial to the development of Colombian music has been the **Discos Fuentes** label, originally based in Cartagena and now in the industrial centre of Medellín.

The company was started by electrical engineer **Don Antonio Fuentes** in 1934, after he'd set up Cartagena's first radio station and wanted local music to play on it. The recordings were financed by the Tropical Oil Company, whose jingles featured on the records. For the first decade the discs were pressed in North America, an expensive and time-consuming operation, until in 1945 Fuentes built his own pressing and production plant in Colombia.

After that, Fuentes did everything in-house – the recording, the pressing, cassette manufacturing, printing and distribution. This has given them a distinct identity, style and sound. They are the oldest and biggest label in Colombia, with a catalogue of over 1800 titles covering the whole history and range of Colombian music. They have also bought up some smaller independent labels like Tropical and Folklor, thereby adding to their comprehensive list. They work their back catalogue hard and consider it the backbone of the company, bringing out new compilations all the time. The signing of a deal with **Mango** (Island Records'

tropical music division) has meant that some of the best Fuentes releases are now easily available internationally.

One of the leading lights of the Fuentes stable is the ubiquitous **Fruko**, who came to work at Discos Fuentes when aged twelve. While serving his apprenticeship in the Fuentes studios he played timbales with Los Corraleros de Majagual and formed his own band, **Fruko y sus Tesos**, who are still in the top league of Colombian salsa. He is now Fuentes' leading arranger and producer, handling his own band, the salsa Latin Brothers, and cumbia's La Sonora Dinamita. The other big arranger is **Alberto Barros**, who represents Fuentes' youth wing and plays trombone in his modern salsa group **Los Titanes**. His music is frequently jazzy and sophisticated with sweet doo-wop vocals.

But the importance of the founder, Don Antonio Fuentes, cannot be overstated. He has been directly involved in the formation of all the major groups on the label and deeply involved in the creation of cumbia as we know it today. Fuentes' patriarchal style, and that of his company director Isaac Villanueva, has created a friendly empire that truly represents all facets of Colombian music.

LATIN AMERICA

better-known Andean music of Peru and Bolivia. Generally, though, it is gentler and mellower in sound, with a harmonic content more typical of the rest of Colombia, and attention given to melody rather than rhythmic complexity.

The traditional Andean group is a trio of tiple, bandola and violin; harps are occasionally found, too, and often a guitar. The movement of the bass lines, played by the guitarist on the lower strings of the instrument, is far freer than in any of the tropical musics and is given to bursting into delightfully complicated runs and arpeggios that complement the melancholy movement of the melodies. The **Morales Pino Trio** represents this style at a very traditional level, while the popular **Estudiantina**, a larger band using similar instrumentation, is more contemporary in its approach.

AFRO-COLOMBIAN MUSIC

The vast majority of Colombian musical styles reflect the nation's intermingling of peoples and cultures. In cumbia, for example, Indian, African and European elements have met and interacted to form an entirely new, purely Colombian music from which the separate strands can no longer be disentangled. However, on the Pacific coast, in the area known as **El Choco**, where there is a large black population, African music survives in something close to its original form. The vast majority of this music is connected in one way or another with the syncretic rites and rituals fusing African spirit cults with Catholicism that are found throughout the New World.

A group of musicians and singers performing a *currulao* from this area sounds quite astonishingly West African. The loping beat of the drums, the interlocking patterns of the marimbas and complex layerings of vocals: all could as easily be traditional music from Mali, the country from which the majority of slaves on the Pacific coast were brought. In the area's secular or semi-religious music, sung at fiestas and other holiday gatherings, the Spanish tinge is much stronger, and traces of Iberian folk melody peep out now and again.

This music is not well known, even within Colombia, but in the area around Buenaventura a small-scale local recording industry serves the immediate neighbourhood.

DISCOGRAPHY

For more Colombian discs, including Joe Arroyo and Fruko, see the salsa discography in Chapter Ten.

COMPILATIONS

CD **Various** *Sueño Colombiano* (Mango, UK). A compilation showing the diversity of Colombian music: the classic Corraleros de Majagual and Sonora Cienguera, plus lots of salsa from Joe Arroyo, Fruko y sus Tesos, Alfredo de la Fé, the Latin Brothers, Los Titanes and more.

CD **Various** *Musique Tropique* (Sonodisc, France). A superb Discos Fuentes anthology of cumbia, vallenato and porro from Los Corraleros de Majagual, La Sonora Dinamita, Lisandro Meza, and others.

CUMBIA

CD **Various** *Cumbia Cumbia* and *Cumbia Cumbia 2* (World Circuit, UK). Two splendid selections of hits from the Discos Fuentes stable. The first volume contains the cumbia that everyone knows, "La Colegiala", and several more that everyone ought to know. Volume 2 is more adventurous and even more interesting, focusing on the great hits of the 1960s.

Los Correleros de Majagual *14 Exitos* (Discos Fuentes, Colombia). The greatest hits of one of the country's most important cumbia/vallenato bands.

CD **La India Meliyara** *La Sonora Meliyara* (Riverboat, UK). Subversive messages and a very sexy, danceable sound from one of the best younger artists.

CD **Alfredo Gutierrez** *El Palito* (Tumi, UK). A mix of cumbia and merengue from this veteran cumbia accordionist, who began his career thirty years ago with Los Corraleros.

CD **Peregoyo y su Combo** *Vacana Tropicalismo* (World Circuit, UK). Recordings from the mid-1970s by one of Colombia's pioneering bands. Rough but rocking.

CD **La Sonora Dinamita** *Cumbia Explosion* (Mango, UK). Features most of the hits from one of Colombia's most commercial groups, led by the ubiquitous Fruko.

VALLENATO

Jorge Cabrera *Charanga Vallenata* (GlobeStyle, UK). This is the best product of charanga-vallenata, the music's Cuban New York offspring. Cabrera's Cuban tres-playing and slick brass arrangements get hot with accordionist Alfredo Gutierrez.

CD **Diomedes Díaz & Nicolas Mendoza** *¡Cantando!* (GlobeStyle, UK). One of the best vallenato records of the last 10 years. Sweeter and fuller-sounding than is usual, with an emphasis on limpid melodies and rich harmonies above the jogging vallenato rhythm section.

CD **Lisandro Meza** *Lisandro's Cumbia* (World Circuit, UK) and *Amor lindo* (Tumi, UK). The unique sound of Lisandro's accordion leads these two great selections of vallenato hits.

CD **Roberto Torres** *Al fin . . . lo mejor de* (Song Discos, US). Charanga meets vallenato in this successful fusion by an exiled Cuban singer. There are now at least three volumes.

CD **Various** *Fiesta Vallenata* (Shanachie, US). A great compilation of the more local-sounding vallenata bands. Listen to the typically wild bass on Julio de la Ossa's "Puno Molio".

OTHERS

Pedro Laza y sus Pelayeros *Porros Vols 1 & 2* (Discos Fuentes, Colombia). This is a far more polished sound than most of the village-based porro outfits, but hot and danceable stuff nonetheless, from an old master.

Various *Afro-Hispanic Music from Colombia and Ecuador* (Smithsonian/Folkways, US). A very well-chosen introduction to the sounds of El Choco.

MEU BRASIL BRASILEIRO

IF THEY HAD A WORLD CUP FOR MUSIC, BRAZIL WOULD GIVE ANYONE A GAME

Brazilian music is a whole world of its own. It may be best known for samba – the irrepressible rhythm of carnival – but that's only a fraction of a story that takes in everything from the drum groups of Bahia (where Paul Simon got his inspiration for "Rhythms of the Saints"), to forró, an accordion-led dance music that's a little like zydeco. David Cleary gets down to the roots and ramifications.

Meu Brasil brasileiro – My Brazilian Brazil, a line from an Ary Barroso song, "Aquarela do Brasil", sums up the way Brazilian music has long since burst its national boundaries while remaining true to its roots. In the 1940s it was translated into English and sung by Carmen Miranda in one of her first Hollywood films; in the 1980s it gave Terry Gilliam the idea for the film *Brazil*, where it served as the basis for the soundtrack. Words that were once Portuguese – samba, bossa nova, lambada – have entered the international vocabulary. Brazilian music is World Music in its most literal sense, played across the world, recognized globally, its influence noticeable in the musical output of many other countries from the US to Nigeria.

"Who hasn't been influenced by Brazil?" said Sérgio Mendes, when asked about Brazil's impact on American jazz. The top Brazilian stars, like Milton Nascimento and Gilberto Gil, sell out Montreux or Madison Square Gardens as easily as the Canecão in Rio, while luminaries like Paul Simon and David Byrne – and an entire generation of American jazz musicians before them – have made musical pilgrimages to Brazil. And yet, funnily enough, Brazilian music on the World Music scene is like an iceberg: a highly visible tip, but an enormous mass of music and musicians lurking beneath the surface, unknown abroad.

A NATIONAL GENIUS

The same rich ethnic cocktail that formed Brazilian society from African, European and Indian ingredients underlies a national genius

for music, and a bewildering variety of rhythms, melodies and regional genres. Everyone's seen clips of the orgiastic music-making of Carnaval (along with other forms of orgiastic activity), but music is an all-year backdrop to life in Brazil.

Carmen Miranda

Hop into a taxi in any Brazilian city and you weave your way through the traffic to the sound of distorted but foot-tapping music pounding through tattered speakers – the beat will be different, depending on the city. Walk into a bar at the weekend, or head for the beach, and you'll run into ordinary Brazilians making often extraordinary music.

Instruments help but aren't essential: match-boxes shake to a syncopated beat, forks tap against glasses, and palms slap on thighs or tabletops – and that's all that's required. This is a country that has had a significant recording industry since the 1920s, where musicians are called *artistas* and draw audiences from the whole population rather than mainly the young, and where some of the most innovative writing in the language occurs in song lyrics: **Caetano**

Veloso and **Chico Buarque** are known throughout the Portuguese-speaking world as great writers as well as musicians.

SOME MPB GEOGRAPHY

Música popular brasileira, habitually shortened to **MPB**, is the catch-all term Brazilians use for Brazilian music in general. It first cropped up in the 1930s, when the growth of a national radio network made it possible for musicians to build up a national audience, and it still refers to the elite corps of nationally – and often internationally – famous *artistas* whose records are available everywhere. But underlying modern MPB, as it has done ever since the term was coined, is a rich tradition of regional music-making, and it's in these regional musical centres that musicians cut their teeth and start to experiment with other musical influences, from elsewhere in Brazil and abroad. It's the regional

variety of Brazilian music that explains its remarkable capacity to produce exciting new sounds, since there are so many genres to pick and mix with outside influences that the permutations are almost endless.

On any musical map of Brazil, **Rio** figures large, especially historically: it was here that *choro*, the precursor to samba, developed in the nineteenth century, and in the city's *favela* slums that samba began to develop around the time of World War I. But viewed from inside Brazil, Rio is only one of a number of musical centres. The city of **Salvador de Bahia**, six hundred kilometres north, has produced as many MPB stars as Rio, and with its unique blend of African and Brazilian influences – not to mention the most musically inventive Carnaval of any Brazilian city – it now has a strong claim to be the music capital of the country. Then there is **Recife**, which lies at the centre of another hotbed of regional genres that Brazilians lump together under the heading of *música nordestina*, northeastern music.

Further north and you hit **eastern Amazonia**, famous for burning rain forests but also – and not a lot of people know this – for lambada, which started out as a souped-up variant of *carimbó*, the dance music of **Belém**, a city with its own regional genres but also strongly influenced by the Guyanese and French Guianan rhythms available on the radio dial. Even **São Paulo**, long derided by non-Paulistanos as a musical desert, has in recent years become home to a thriving rock and punk scene.

But, as for most tourists, any guide to Brazilian music has to start in Rio . . .

RIO ROOTS

If you go on a walking tour of **Rio** to see where it all began, you're unlikely to be impressed. "Little Africa", the area where ex-slaves and the few black bourgeois lived in the centre of town, was where **samba** began in the early years of the century, with the bairro's residents reinforced by contingents from the hillside favelas that were already a feature of Rio's landscape. It started as Carnaval music, and horrified Rio's established (and white) society: it was lewd, loud, the drums were too African, and so the police regularly raided the area to arrest *sambistas*.

There's nothing of it left today: it was swept away by the skyscrapers of Rio's central business district. The beaches from where poor blacks set out on Sundays for day trips to the islands in

---

Aquarela do Brasil (Watercolour of Brazil)

Brazil, my Brazilian Brazil
My courtly mulatto, I will sing you in these verses
Oh the samba it makes, the sinuous dances
The Brazil I love, land of Our Father
Brazil for me, for me, for me.

Ah, open the curtain on our past
Sing praises to the cerrado
Put the Recôncavo in the congado
Brazil for me
Let me sing again about the glory of the moonlight
Every song my love song
I want to see this Lady walking proud
Sweeping her lace dresses through the ballrooms
Brazil for me, for me, for me.

Ah, this palm which gives us coconuts
Where I string up my hammock
In the clear moonlit nights
Brazil for me
And where there are murmuring fountains
Where I quench my thirst
And where the moon comes to play
Ah, this Brazil, so lovely, so richly favoured
And my Brazilian Brazil
Land of samba and tambourines
Brazil for me, for me, for me . . .

Ary Barroso

[*Reconcavo* – Salvador hinterland; *cerrado* – table-lands; *congado* – Afro-Brazilian dance].

Guanabara Bay are long since filled in and turned to docks: where the wharfs stand is where Carnaval as we know it today began, as the returning day-trippers, well-oiled, danced and sang and formed the embryonic, informal music groups that a couple of decades later would evolve into *Escolas de samba* (samba schools), the highly organized neighbourhood associations that parade in the modern Carnaval.

Why "schools"? Before he died in 1975, **Ismael Silva**, a great sambista who was born at the same time as samba, explained: "The sambistas used to rehearse in an empty lot near a teachers' college, and people always said, that's where the professors come from. But nobody knew more about samba than us. People started joking, no, *this* is where the professors come from. That's how the idea of a samba school came about."

Choro band Os Ingênuos

CHORO

Even before samba there was **choro**, literally "crying, sobbing". The original Carnaval music, it still survives today as live music, not just on dusty records, some 120 years after it surfaced. It is mainly instrumental, played by a small combo that might include a flute, a guitar, a *cavaquinho* – a miniature guitar introduced to Brazil by the Portuguese – and a clarinet.

With its roots in European salon music and Portuguese *fado*, choro is generally through-composed with little space for improvisation in its original form. Probably the most influential composer of choros was **Pixinguinho**, (1898–1973), whose classic "Lamento" is still played. Choro was one of the primary inspirations of the great Brazilian composer Heitor Villa-Lobos (1887–1959), who spent his formative years playing cello and guitar in choro bands in Rio's cafés, on street corners and at parties.

Choro is in some ways the opposite of samba, as quiet and private as samba is loud and public. You come across it most often these days as background music in stylish bars in the big cities of southern Brazil. It is currently undergoing something of a revival after decades of neglect, largely thanks to the well-known sambista **Paulinho da Viola**, who has been arguing for a return to Brazilian roots and including a choro or two on all his recent records, most notably the self-explanatory "Chorando".

One of the best choro groups, **Os Ingênuos** from Salvador de Bahia, has recently been recorded by Nimbus and gives a good introduction to the choro style and its diverse solo instruments: the seven-string guitar (an extra bass string brings out the highly mobile bass lines), cavaquinho, trumpet, trombone and soprano sax.

The basic rhythms of choro come from the dances favoured by European immigrants in the last century, especially polkas and waltzes, but overlaid by Afro-Brazilian syncopation to produce a jazzy Brazilian sound, like tropical Dixieland played on string and wind instruments rather than brass. With the clarinet wailing and cavaquinho notes sliding all over the place, you can hear how choro got its name.

SAMBA

It was this choro syncopation that carried over into **samba**, a versatile rhythm that can assume many different forms. Heated up, with a shouted call-and-response verse backed by literally thousands of samba-school drums on parade, it becomes *samba de enredo*, the mass Carnaval music famous the world over. Quite apart from the spectacle, a *desfile* – the formal parade of samba schools that is the centrepiece of Rio's Carnaval – is the loudest music you will ever hear: the drums up close are a physical force as much as music, enveloping and vibrating every part of your body – transfixing, but not the sort of thing that makes the transition to record very effectively.

Slowed down and broken up a little, the samba becomes *samba-canção*, literally "song samba",

¡CARNAVAL!

In Brazil, somehow, **Carnaval** got out of control. All countries colonised at some stage by Catholics have festivities in the days leading up to Ash Wednesday, but in Brazil it goes further – in every sense – than anywhere else. From the Friday the country shuts down for five days, and practically the whole population gets down to the most serious partying in the world.

And Carnaval wouldn't be Carnaval without music: it still plays the crucial role in the development of Brazilian music that it did a century ago, when black revellers in Rio started adding rhythm to European melodies and gave birth to samba. One of the driving forces of Brazilian music is that each year the Carnaval songs have to be new, so the runup to Carnaval sees an outpouring of new music on radio and TV, as musicians compete to supply Carnaval hits. A Carnaval hit – determined by what people start singing on the streets,

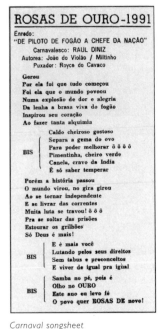

Carnaval songsheet

which is then picked up by radio and TV – is a direct route to national exposure, and every year Carnaval breaks new acts to a national audience.

Carnaval comes in different shapes and sizes; all cities and towns have one, but there are three major events that attract hundreds of thousands of participants from out of town as well. Rio's is the best known, revolving around samba and the parade of the samba schools in a spectacle beyond even Cecil B de Mille. But the idea of having the public in the grandstands watching is utterly foreign to the other two great Brazilian Carnavals in Salvador and Olinda. There the idea is to not have any spectators at all, only participants. Salvador's entire population jams itself into the colonial streets of the centre and gets down to the best Carnaval music in the country, dancing to trios elétricos, bands playing precariously balanced on top of lorries with speakers bolted on, or with the afoxés, Salvador's Africanized answer to Rio's samba schools. It's different again in Olinda, the beautiful colonial district of Recife, where the Carnaval beat is frevo, faster even than samba and even more impossible for foreigners to dance to.

where a lead singer is backed by a group that varies in size but is always built around guitar and percussion. Samba-canção is the staple of Rio's clubs and *dancetarías*, and itself breaks down into several varieties, ranging from the quiet, delicate plucking of a single guitar to frenetic dance numbers played by a large combo. These samba styles include *samba breque*, "break samba", a choppy, almost reggae rhythm, and the most recent, *samba do pagode*, a goodtime soaring dance rhythm exemplified by artistas like **Agepê**, **Clara Nunes** and **Alcione**, and bands like **Raa Negra**, which swept Rio and the country from north to south and first hooked David Byrne, like many others, on Brazilian music. For Brazil's urban poor samba is, like football, an obsession and, for the lucky ones, a route to international celebrity.

BOSSA NOVA

Rio's other great contribution to World Music was **bossa nova**, "new wave", which began in the chic beach neighbourhood of Ipanema by day, and moved to the Copacabana clubs by night, before being discovered by American jazz musicians and going on to become an international craze in the early 1960s. Outside Brazil it often sank under the massed strings and tuxedos of mainly American record producers, leaving most people with the misleading impression that bossa nova is muzak best-suited to elevators and airports. **Tom (Antonio Carlos) Jobim**, the man who penned "A Garota de Ipanema" (The Girl from Ipanema), would later talk of being haunted by innumerable cover versions murdering what in its original form is still one of the most beautiful Brazilian songs ever recorded.

Bossa nova is one of the few brands of popular music that was invented single-handed: the rhythm was devised by Jobim, a classically trained conservatory musician given to hanging out in bars at night, but first sung by Bahian **João Gilberto**, who in July 1957 released the first bossa nova record, a Jobim number ironically titled "Desafinado" (Out of Tune). It was an instant smash in Brazil, where bossa nova, gently crooned to the accompaniment of a single guitar, always had a much more delicate, individual touch than in its later North American distortions.

For a couple of glorious years Jobim, Gilberto, and a small group of other musicians, notably **Vinícius de Morães**, were able to mount a serious challenge to samba's dominance within Rio's music scene, and in 1959 bossa nova took off abroad as well: Astrud Gilberto's quavering English version of "The Girl from Ipanema" became Brazil's biggest ever international hit. There were several reasons behind this success. One was the increasing development of the Brazilian record industry, which by now was exporting to the US and allowing bossa nova to come to the attention of influential jazz musicians like Stan Getz and Charlie Byrd. But underlying that was the large market for a sleek, sophisticated urban sound (bossa nova is lounge-bar rather than dance floor music) among the burgeoning middle classes in Rio, who found Jobim's slowing down and breaking up of what was still a samba rhythm an exciting departure.

Although the bossa craze abroad was eclipsed by the arrival of The Beatles, in Rio bossa nova still survives in its natural habitats of Ipanema and the other middle-class areas of the Zona Sul, while Jobim went on to become one of the elder statesmen of MPB.

BAHIA: DANCING TO A DIFFERENT DRUM

Salvador, capital of the huge northeastern state of Bahia, is like no other city in Brazil. Almost everyone you see on the streets is black, and **African** influences are everywhere. You can taste it in the food, with sauces based on palm oil, peanuts and coconut milk, you can see it in the hundreds of cult houses of *candomblé* and *umbanda*, the Afro-Brazilian religions with millions of devotees across Brazil, and most of all you can hear it in the music. An outrageously high proportion of the major **MPB stars** comes from Salvador and around: a partial list includes

Olodum

Caetano Veloso, **Gilberto Gil**, **Gal Costa**, **Maria Bethânia**, **Dorival Caymmi** and **Vinícius de Morães**.

What makes Salvador's music special is its rhythm, reflected in the importance of drumming and percussion, which in Salvador reaches a peak unmatched elsewhere. No other Brazilian city, not even Rio, can boast such a range of cosmopolitan influences on its local music, with rhythms from the Caribbean, Africa and North America finding their way to the city, being absorbed somewhere in the bewildering range of local genres, and resurfacing as something new and very Brazilian.

The 1980s were an especially good decade for Salvador, building on the achievements of the 1970s, when a wave of black consciousness partly inspired by American soul music transformed the city's Carnaval. A number of new black **Carnaval groups** were set up, playing African-influenced music with heavier, more complicated rhythms than the frenetic Carnaval styles popular elsewhere in the northeast. In the 1980s reggae was absorbed into the city's music in a similar way, and the result was a new Salvador sound that by the late 1980s was vying with samba and MPB for national attention. It mixed up reggae, salsa and samba, added percussion and lyrics that often had an African theme, and came up with a highly danceable style called **fricote**, or **deboche**.

Underlying this success was a thriving network of independent labels and studios based in the city, and the fact that every Carnaval seemed to break a new Bahian singer or group nationally. The new generation of **young stars** from the city, joining the old MPB veterans, include singers like **Margareth Menezes**, **Daniela Mercury**, **Luiz Caldas** and **Abel Duere**, and groups like **Banda Mel**, **Reflexu's**, **Ara Ketú** and **Olodum**.

It was **Olodum** who Paul Simon heard playing on the streets while on a trip with Milton Nascimento and went on to record as the inspired base for much of his album "Rhythms of the Saints". The band began life as part of the rising black consciousness movement, reflected in a rootsy, back-to-Africa sound based entirely around drumming and chanted lyrics about Africa, slavery and racism. **Reflexu's** are in a similar vein, though they have lightened the percussion with synthesizers and a honeyed female voice. Both are excellent in their own way, and especially good live – they were spawned by Carnaval; political correctness can rarely have been more enjoyable.

Two women singers from Salvador have recently made it big. The best-known abroad is **Margareth Menezes**, spotted by David Byrne and plucked from the Salvador club scene directly in to supporting him on tour in the US, where, as Byrne happily admits in the sleeve notes to her album "Illegibô", she often blew him off the stage. She has a beautiful voice and is electrifying when singing native Bahian rhythms. Unfortunately, like many young Brazilian stars who make it big, she insists on cluttering up her records and live act with thrash-rock that would have sounded outdated in 1975.

Margareth Menezes blowing David Byrne off stage

Less well-known abroad, but rapidly becoming a major star inside Brazil, is **Daniela Mercury**. She has everything – a fantastic voice, writes her own music, sticks to Bahian sounds, is remarkably beautiful and, to cap it all, is a quite superb dancer even by Brazilian standards. Expect to hear a lot more of her.

FORRÓ AND NORDESTINA

Northeastern Brazil has a deceptive coastline, lush green with coconut palms framing the best beaches in Brazil, fertile soils and large plantations. But drive directly inland, and in most places it takes less than an hour before you hit the *sertão*, the rocky, arid hinterland where droughts can last for years and periodic waves of migrants – *flagelados*, "the scourged" – give up the unequal struggle with the land and head for the coastal cities. It looks unpromising, but music seems to flourish here, even if little else does.

BRAZIL:FORRÓ

MUSIC FOR MAIDS AND TAXI DRIVERS

One reason is the peculiar delight the region takes in wordplay and poetry: most markets have stalls selling *literatura de cordel*, "string literature", printed ballads by regional poets, and in music this poetic tradition is reflected by **repentismo**, where balladeers pair off against each other with guitar in hand, and improvise verses in a variety of complicated metres on themes shouted out by the audience. A historical impulse was the popularity of dances as social gatherings, especially in rural areas, where prospective marriage partners could look each other over. Since slaves were imported mainly to work on the coastal plantations, most black nordestinos now live in the coastal strip. The main influence on the music of the sertão was Portugal: old Portuguese folk melodies lurk beneath the surface of much *música nordestina*.

Música nordestina has many different forms, but all are instantly recognizable as northeastern: the rhythms are very strong but slower than in other parts of the country, the beat often comes from accordion and/or guitar rather than percussion, and the lyrics are sung in a gravelly, nasal nordestino accent, which you can tell apart even if you don't speak a word of Portuguese.

The varieties of nordestino music include *frevo*, Recife's Carnaval beat; *maracatú*, a blend of African rhythms with Portuguese melodies, most popular among blacks around Recife; and *baião*, a thumping dance style built around a trio of accordion, bass drum and triangle. However, by far the most popular form is a jaunty, danceable style called *forró* – a word that's allegedly a corruption of the English "for all", the name of the dances British companies laid on for their employees in nineteenth-century Recife.

Forró can be played fast, slow or somewhere in between, but whichever it's one of the most enjoyable – and danceable – forms of Brazilian music. Like Louisiana zydeco, the music is accordion-led with a robust and frenetic sound. In its traditional form, forró is played by a trio of *sanfona* (accordion), triangle and drum, with a singer crooning out over the strongest, most foot-tapping rhythm Brazil has to offer. Only danced by couples, it's from forró that the more athletic dances associated with lambada developed. Essentially, the couple swivel round the dance floor, joined only at the pelvis, and nobody in Brazil looks twice at a display that would clear the dance floor most places in the First World.

The accordionist and singer **Luiz Gonzaga** (1912–89) is considered the first big name of forró, popularizing the music – and other nordestino styles – outside his native region

---

Danado de Bom (Damn Good)

It's damn good, it's damn good
My friend, it's damn good
Pretty, kicking, delicious forró music
It's damn good

Check out Camilla on the bass drum
Joe Cupid on the triangle
And Mariano on the bell
There's my brother on the guitar
My nephew on the strings
And Chippy in the middle of the mess
Check out the kids on the spoons
There's more than enough juice
There's enough drunks to irk you
Guys are sticking to their partners like fleas
Girls are winking
And asking me to dance

What a first-class gig!
The place is already packed
And folks just keep on coming
From the kitchen to the backyard
The accordion player and drummer
Back and forth
Damian, my good friend
You can put out the lamp
Because it's almost dawn
Hang tough on your squeezebox, chief
Because a forró like this
Can go on forever.

Luiz Gonzaga and João Silva

and becoming an idol among the northeastern migrants in São Paulo and Rio. He moved to Rio in the 1940s and had an enormous hit with a simple but very moving song about a farmer forced to migrate; called "Asa Branca" (White Wing), after a bird traditionally said to be the last to leave the sertão in a drought, it became a regional anthem and one of the best-loved of all Brazilian tunes, a national standard.

Gonzaga blazed a trail for a number of other northeastern musicians, who became major MPB stars from the 1960s onwards without ever abandoning their regional roots. They included Gonzaga's son, **Gonzaguinho**, tragically killed in a car crash in 1991; **Elba Ramalho**, who looks uncannily like Bette Midler and has a remarkable voice to match; accordionist/singer **Dominguinhos**; **Morães Moreira**; **Alceu Valença**; **Geraldo Azevedo**; and **Fagner**. Most of these musicians bring in additional instruments – including electric guitar and brass – while keeping the accordion to the fore.

AMAZONIA: ¡LAMBADA!

Eastern Amazonia is yet another distinctive musical region: it has its own rhythms and dances, most notably **carimbó**, a lilting, enjoyable dance style that was electrified in the 1960s and became the basis of Belém's nightlife. From around the mid-70s, Belém's DJs and musicians started playing around with carimbó rhythms, adding elements of the merengue, salsa and reggae constantly played on the radio stations of the Guianas only a few hundred kilometres north, and produced a new dance music they started to call **lambada**.

Lambada made its way to Salvador in the 1980s, where it was absorbed and transformed like so many other musical imports, and by the mid-1980s a Bahian version, lighter, even boppier and based around synthesizers, was hitting local radio stations. There it was heard by French record producers on holiday, who were equally interested in the spectacular dance that Bahia developed to go with it: they signed up Bahian lambada dancers and musicians, took them back to Paris in 1988 and the rest, as they say, is history.

The Belém musicians who had played such a critical role in the development of lambada hastily put out records called things like "The Original Lambada" but it was too late: the Bahians had sewn up the market, and added insult to injury by rushing out all kinds of Bahian pop, labelling it lambada, and selling it in Europe, where the market was more interested in dancing than musical roots. Hence the fact that lambada as known internationally refers more to a dance than a distinct style of music. The word had become a marketing category first and foremost, and no longer bore any relation to the original music or the region it came from.

MPB AND THE MILITARY

Modern MPB, like so much else, really began in the 1960s. The impulse was the military coup of 1964, which initiated over twenty years of military rule. In a backhanded tribute to the special importance of music in Brazil, one of the regime's first acts was to impose direct censorship of song lyrics and radio and TV playlists, which they followed up by persecuting musicians thought to be critical of the military; most of the MPB stars of the 1960s spent a year or two in exile in the 1970s.

These strict controls on musical output, which were not relaxed until 1985, had the opposite effect to that intended: they proved a creative spur, forcing musicians to use oblique, subtle images that could make it past the censor, and at the same time gave MPB a coherence it would not otherwise have managed, uniting practically all serious musicians against the military and compelling them to deal with politics as well as the eternal preoccupations of sex and drugs and rock'n'roll. You can get an idea of the depth this gave MPB by listening to a song like Chico Buarque's "Tanto Mar" (So Much Sea), which is ostensibly about a party although all Brazilians of the time – 1973 – recognized as a salute to the Portuguese Revolution of that year, "The Revolution of the Carnations" as it's known in Portuguese.

It was a fine party
I had a great time
I've kept an old carnation to remind me
And even though the party's over
They're certain to have overlooked a seed
In some corner of the garden
So much sea between us,
So much sea between us.

The first sign that the military would find it impossible to keep the musical lid on was **tropicalismo**, a musical movement that erupted in the late 1960s and marked the arrival of a new and extravagantly talented generation of musicians who are still among the leading lights of MPB, most notably **Caetano**

Veloso (see box overpage) and **Gilberto Gil**. Tropicalismo was the most controversial twist MPB ever came up with, since it consisted of mixing a large number of regional genres together, stirring in rock influences like electric guitars and elaborate studio production, and topping everything off with extraordinarily dense, oblique lyrics.

Caetano and Gil were booed off stage and violently attacked in the press at first, accused of being unpatriotic for turning to foreign rock for

Tropicalismo founder Gilberto Gil

inspiration and using electric instruments – a stupid criticism, since música nordestina was as important an influence on tropicalismo as rock. However, the young, thoroughly alienated as Brazil lurched into dictatorship, loved tropicalismo's iconoclasm and rejection of convention. At its worst tropicalismo reproduced the self-importance and studio excesses of much North American and British rock of the period, but at its best, as in Caetano's song "Tropicália", which became the movement's anthem, it was the most successful blend to date of Brazilian musical imagination with rock music. Although tropicalismo only lasted a couple of years, and more or less ended when Caetano and Gil were forced into exile in London in 1971, it left a lasting mark – not least because it inspired many more far less successful attempts to blend rock from abroad with elements of MPB.

Both the founders of tropicalismo went on to greater fame, Gil as the leading Salvador artista and an increasingly successful politician, and Caetano to become, along with Chico Buarque, the most admired and productive MPB star, now in his fourth decade of recording and if anything getting better with age.

CHICO, MILTON AND ELIS

The 1960s also saw the emergence of two stars who were never part of the tropicalismo wave but who have remained at the forefront of MPB ever since. Chico Buarque and Milton Nascimento remained within Brazilian musical styles for the most part, but took them to new heights.

Chico Buarque shot to stardom in the 1960s first as a sambista, singing beautifully crafted sambas alone with only his guitar. What marks him out is the superb quality of his lyrics; excerpts do him little justice, since his trademark is the intricate building up of themes over the course of a song. At first there was little love lost between Chico and the *tropicalistas*, who suspected that the conservatism of his music reflected his politics as well, but Chico soon earned his political street-cred by writing what became the most famous anti-military songs, "Apesar de Você" (In Spite of You) and "Vai Passar" (It Will Pass), and spending a year in exile. His dense lyrics and haunting tunes are still flowing, and along with Caetano, who has similar lyrical gifts and is equally in love with the Portuguese language, Chico has become one of the select band of MPB figures with whom the entire country is on first-name terms.

Chiclete com Banana (Chewing Gum with Banana)

I'll only put be-bop in my samba
When Uncle Sam grabs the drum
When he grabs the tambourine and the zabumba
When he understands that samba isn't rumba.
Then I'll mix Miami with Copacabana
Chewing gum with banana
And that's how my samba will go.
I want to see it all mixed together
Samba-rock, brother
But, on the other hand
I want to see the boogie-woogie played
On tambourine and guitar
I want to see Uncle Sam cooling out
In a Brazilian drumming session.

Gilberto Gil

CAETANO VELOSO

· ·

Since he first burst onto the national music scene in the early 1960s **Caetano Veloso** has been at the centre of Brazilian music, but there is more to him than that: he sometimes seems a kind of Leonardo da Vinci of Brazilian popular culture. His books of poetry and his song lyrics have made him, along with Chico Buarque, into one of the most respected poets in the Portuguese-speaking world. He paints, directs innovative videos for his own songs, and, at just over fifty, is still making great records.

In the mid-1960s Brazilian music split down the middle between the eclectic, innovative tropicalismo style pioneered mainly by Caetano, and the more musically conservative brilliance of Chico Buarque. Of all the singers of that time, Caetano was best able to absorb all the influences of the 60s and blend them with his Bahian roots, and several of his songs sum up the period for a generation of Brazilians in the same way as The Beatles or Tamla Motown did elsewhere.

One of his most popular songs from that period, "Alegria, Alegria", has had a second life. It was used as the theme tune to a smash-hit TV series in 1992 called *Años Rebeldes* (The Rebel Years). The series followed a group of students who graduated in 1964, the year of the military coup, through the military years as they joined guerrilla groups, became hippies, got shot, sold out, fell in and out of love with each other, etc. It served as a rediscovery of the period for a new generation of Brazilian youth born after the worst of the military years were over.

The series happened to be shown as a **corruption scandal** involving President Collor gathered pace and "Alegria, Alegria" became the theme tune of the enormous – and successful – demonstrations calling for his impeachment. Tens and then hundreds of thousands of people were clapping and singing along with the song, culminating in the line "Porquê não, porquê não?" (Why not?): ie why not throw the rascal out?

Today, when Caetano could easily be resting on his laurels, he continues to produce the most innovative and challenging Brazilian music. His records in the 1980s and '90s have the same volatile mixture of Brazilian and foreign influences that characterized tropicalismo, but have acquired a new maturity and depth in both music and lyrics.

Another is **Milton Nascimento**, who came up at the same time and via the same route as Chico, but is musically poles apart. Where Chico was comfortable with what lay musically to hand in his native Rio, Milton's music has returned again and again to the reflective, spiritual music of his native state of Minas Gerais, to the north of Rio, whose people have a reputation for introversion and whose music is heavily influenced by the Catholic church. When you add to this Milton's extraordinary, soaring voice, and his songwriting genius, the result is a dense, compelling sound that has made Milton one of the best-known Brazilian musicians abroad, especially in North America. Since he speaks little English, he is less known abroad for his politics, but he has become the most prominent public spokesperson for black Brazilians and involved himself in the struggle for Indian land rights years before it became fashionable.

Were she still alive, a third star in this MPB trinity would be **Elis Regina**, whom few would argue is the woman who has made the greatest contribution to Brazilian musical history. Elis burst onto the music scene after winning a nationally televized song competition in 1965, when she was only eighteen, and it was immediately obvious that she had the finest voice of her time. She went on to release a series of records that made her the undisputed

musicians have tried to blend rock with Brazilian music; tropicalismo did it with some success, but most attempts to do so since have been embarrassing failures.

The basic problem is musical incompatibility: Brazilian music is built around complicated melodies and rhythms and the Brazilian musical imagination is versatile and subtle – not the ideal cultural recipe for good rock'n'roll, in other words. There is a Brazilian rock scene, centred around São Paulo, but it's very tame and derivative compared to that of London or New York. Brazil has been much more successful in absorbing non-rock influences from abroad, as the music scene in Salvador shows, and we can look forward to more productive plundering of Caribbean and African music in the years to come (a traffic that goes both ways, as people like King Sunny Ade will tell you).

And for all that people say Brazilian music isn't what it was, a foreigner finds it difficult to understand what they're worried about. Long-established genres like samba are still breaking up into new variants, and new music, like the Salvador sound, is being produced at a more than healthy rate. There are more studios and independent labels now than ever before, and the regional music that is the bed rock of MPB is doing as well as ever. If there were a World Cup for music, *meu Brasil brasileiro* could still give anyone a game.

queen of MPB. Her voice was a unique blend of technique and soul: she could put an extraordinary depth of emotion into a song, keeping perfect control at the same time. Tragically, she became something of an Edith Piaf figure: she struggled with drugs and alcohol for most of her career, and died alone in 1982, when she was at the height of her powers, from an overdose that may or may not have been suicide.

LOOKING AHEAD

Brazil, like most places, is full of people eager to argue that things aren't what they used to be, and while they have a point when talking about modern Brazilian football, they're on less sure ground when they express the argument – surprisingly common within Brazil – that Brazilian music is in decline. That's not to say there aren't justified criticisms to be made. The most obvious is that no one of similar stature has come up in MPB to replace the towering figures of the 1960s, most of whom are still producing very high-quality music. But they are also all in their late fifties by now, and they don't have a direct line to Brazilian youth the way they did. There's also the problem of the relationship between Brazilian music and the international music scene. This has a positive side, as David Byrne's repeated trips to Brazil have shown, but it has a downside as well. Many Brazilian

DISCOGRAPHY

GENERAL COMPILATIONS

Various *Brasil: the Ultimate Collection* (Phonogram, France/Philips, UK). An extravagant four-CD boxed set: one each for nordeste, samba, bossa nova and afro. There is so much good material here that it seems wrong to gripe – but there's more joy in the regional compilations by David Byrne and others below. Nonetheless, the bossa nova disc is faultless.

MPB STARS

Various *Beleza Tropical: Brazil Classics 1* (Luaka Bop-WEA, US). The first of David Byrne's excellent Brazilian compilations concentrates on a selection of top MPB stars, including Jorge Ben, Gilberto Gil, Caetano Veloso, Chico Buarque, Milton Nascimento and Maria Bethânia (Caetano's sister). A fine introduction.

Maria Bethânia *Alibi* (Polygram, Brazil). A terrific album of ballads by Barque, Gil, and of course Maria's brother Caetano Veloso.

Chico Buarque *Vida* (Philips, Brazil). One of the masters of MPB in top form: dense, haunting songs picking apart life, love and politics.

Gilberto Gil *Personalidade* (Polygram, Brazil). Selection of Gil's accoustic hits. Beautiful tunes sung by one of MPB's most internationally famous stars.

Gal Costa *Aquarela do Brasil* (Polygram, US). One of the finest voices in the history of MPB lets her chords loose on the songs of Ary Barroso: an inspired combination.

Daniela Mercury *O Canto da Cidade* (Columbia, Brazil). Brazil's brightest new talent. Strong tunes, Bahian rhythms perfectly blended with reggae, salsa and a dash of rock, topped by Daniela's soaring voice make this an instant classic. Possibly the next Brazilian megastar, catch her while she's still singing in Portuguese.

Milton Nascimento *A Arte de Milton Nascimento* (Verve, Brazil). A generous 20-track compilation of Milton, live and in the studio, solo and alongside Veloso, Costa and others.

Elis Regina *Essa Mulher* (Tropical Storm, US). Brazil's finest ever woman vocalist performs songs by key 1960s and 70s composers.

Caetano Veloso *Circuladô Vivo* (Philips, Brazil). This live recording from Veloso's magnificent 1993 tour is perhaps the best introduction to the MPB superstar. *Estrangeiro* (Elektra, US/Island, UK). is his best recent album, showing that, at almost 50, he is still the most original and creative star in the MPB firmament, with a breathtakingly mature tropicalista mixture of Brazilian and outside influences. The title track is the best Brazilian song of recent years.

Caetano Veloso & Gilberto Gil *Tropicalia 2* (Philips, Brazil). An excellent reunion album by two of the tropicalismo originals, thirty years on.

Tom Zé *Return of Tom Zé: Brazil Classics 5* (Luaka Bop/WEA, US). Zé was one of the original tropicalismo stars, with Gil and Veloso, but his subsequent career lapsed into obscurity, due in part, perhaps, to his relentless experimentation, which can be pretty bizarre. Here he is, though, superbly reassessed in a compilation by David Byrne and the Luaka Bop crew.

SAMBA AND CHORO

Various *O Samba: Brazil Classics 2* (Luaka Bop-WEA, US). This David Byrne compilation is music to die for: one of the all-time great compilation albums, perfectly paced, and packed with gorgeous tracks from Clara Nunes, Agepê, Alcione (including the stunning "Sufoco"), Martinho da Vila and others.

Various *Brazil Roots Samba* (Rounder, US). The less slick, more rootsy side of samba from the favelas of Mangueira and Portela. Music from the samba old guard: Monarco, Wilson Moreira and Nelson Sargento.

Agepê *Os Grandes Sucessos de Agepê* (Philips, Brazil). Great samba-canção by one of the kings of the Brazilian dance floor.

Alcione *Romántica* (Philips, Brazil). Another utterly seductive album of samba-canção.

Jorge Ben *Personalidade* (Polygram, Brazil). A fine "best of" collection – including his song "Taj Mahal", which was later hornbly transmuted into Rod Stewart's "Do You Think I'm Sexy?".

Os Ingênuos *Choros from Brazil* (Nimbus, UK). An excellent release from this tuneful Bahian choro group. It is the only choro easily obtainable outside Brazil, which on this evidence suggests a shameful neglect.

Clara Nunes *The Best of Clara Nunes* (World Pacific, US). Greatest hits of the queen of samba, tragically killed in 1989, but immortal in every other sense.

Martinho da Vila *O Canto das lavaderias* (RCA-Victor, Brazil). Listen to Vila's tracks on *O Samba* and you'll almost certainly want more. This is the one to go for.

Paulinho da Viola *Eu canto samba* (Columbia, Brazil). Proof that samba can be quiet and intimate as well. Arguably the greatest living sambista serves up a rich stew of jazzy, laid-back sambas spiced with the odd choro.

BAHIA

Margareth Menezes *Ellegibo* (Polydor, US). The singer who stole the show on tour with David Byrne. This is a mixed set but brilliant in parts, and with the bonus of a poppy duet with soca star David Rudder.

Olodum *Revolution in Motion* (World Circuit, UK). The name Olodum is derived from the Yoruban word for God, in keeping with the group's percussive African sound. An excellent compilation of their powerful and complex music.

Reflexú's *Da Mãe África* (Mango, US). A more commercial but equally magical record from the Salvador group that shot to national stardom with their cover version of Olodum's "Egito-Madagascar".

BOSSA NOVA

Luiz Bonfa *Bonfa Magic* (Milestone, US). A 1991 recording of Bonfa's bossa classics.

João Gilberto *João Gilberto* (Polygram, US). Immaculate compilation with notes by Arto Lindsay – a rock artist who can bossa with the best of them.

Astrud Gilberto *The Astrud Gilberto Album* (Charlie, UK). There are dozens of Astrud compilations, almost all featuring "The Girl from Ipanema". This one is as good as any.

Tom (Antonio Carlos) Jobim *The Art of Tom Jobim* (Polygram, US). Classic songs from the inventor of bossa nova. You may not understand the words of "Desafinado" or "Isaura", but you'll certainly recognize the melodies.

FORRÓ/NORDESTINA

Various *Forró, etc – Music of the Brazilian Northeast: Brazil Classics 3* (Luaka Bop-WEA, USA). A great compilation of nordestina music – one of Brazil's most infectious sounds – including tracks from Luiz Gonzaga, and most of the bigger, more commercial artists.

Various *Music for Maids and Taxi Drivers* (GlobeStyle, UK/Rounder, US). Another superb compilation, with inspired music to match the inspired title. It's more rootsy than the *Brazil Classics* selection and has even more energy.

Luiz Gonzaga *Asa Branca* (RCA, Brazil). Greatest hits of the grand old man of música nordestina. The title song is a national standard, one of the best-loved of all Brazilian tunes.

⊙ **Gonzaguinha** *Luizinho de Gonzaga* (Tropical, US). A funky forró tribute by Gonzaguinha to his father.
⊙ **Oficina de Cordas** *Pernambuco's Music* (Nimbus, UK). Infectious and ebullient string band music.
⊙ **Pé de Serra Forró Band** (Wergo, Germany). This complements the other available recordings of forró music, featuring a really downhome band of five musicians. English lyrics included.

ARCHIVES

Various *Revivendo* (EMI-Odeon, Brazil). A series of budget vinyl reissues of hits from the 1930s and 40s, superbly sung by radio stars like Trio de Ouro, Joel e Gaúcho and Ataúlfo Alves.
⊙ **Carmen Miranda** *Carmen Miranda* (Harlequin, UK). All you could hope for in a Miranda compilation: 25 original sambas, choros and marchas, backed by a restrained combo.

NUEVA CANCIÓN

THE GUITAR IS A GUN; THE SONG A BULLET.

Nueva canción – the "new song" developed in the 1960s in Chile and Argentina, and known as "nueva trova" in Cuba – is a political music, which can be love song, chronicle and weapon, in turn or together. Jan Fairley guides us through a delicate labyrinth.

N ueva canción is more than a music. Indeed, bound up with the politics of a continent, it is perhaps best introduced by events.

First, then, a memory of **Chile**. It is Santiago, July 1969, and the first festival of nueva canción is taking place in a downtown basketball stadium. On the stage are dozens of performers who had campaigned through their music for the election of the Popular Unity government of Salvador Allende. After his election, Allende had appeared surrounded by musicians under a banner saying "There can be no revolution without songs".

Four years later, on September 11, 1973, the winner of that festival, 35-year-old **Víctor Jara**, is arrested by the military and taken to the same stadium, along with hundreds of others on the Chilean left. Tortured, his hands and wrists broken, Jara is murdered, and his body, riddled with machine-gun bullets, dumped outside the Metropolitan Cemetery.

Another eighteen years: April 1991, and Chilean artists, dancers, actors, actresses, street musicians and traditional payadores are back in that same stadium for a wake – a purge – a day-long celebration of the end of dictatorship. This act of celebration and renewal is called "Canto libre" (Free Song) after one of Jara's last songs.

Next, a shift of scene, to Cuba, 1981. **Silvio Rodríguez**, a slight man with a fragile, reedy voice, is singing of a lost blue unicorn, dedicating

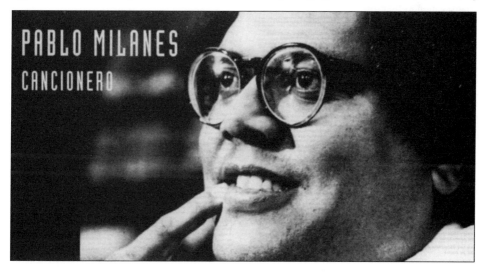

MERCEDES SOSA

········ · · · · · · · · ·

ercedes Sosa is not a songwriter but has won a huge international reputation by interpreting the songs of others. She shows an uncanny ability to choose songs of the moment, drawing material from diverse sources for their emotion, poetry and melody, and singing them for "mi gente, mi pueblo" (my people, my country).

Her infectious singing style ranges from the gentle to the formidable. It can be joyful and

caressing, as in Perteco Carabajal's "Las manos de mi madre" (The hands of my mother ... are like birds in the air), which paints a picture of mothers kneading bread on the verandah, just as they knead life. It can voice the epic, as in Petrocelli's "Cuando tengo la tierra" (When I have the Land) with her wild declamation of the lines "Campesino, when you have the land ... you will have the moon in your pocket." It can portray outrage, too, as in her astonishing version of rock singer Leon Gieco's "Sólo le pido a Dios": "I only ask God not to make me indifferent to war. It is a great monster that tramples on the poor innocence of the people."

Sosa was exiled from Argentina in 1978 after the military arrested both her and much of her audience at a concert. In exile, her voice was a constant of political commitment, particularly during the "dirty war" fought by the military against Argentine youth, and again during the Anglo-Argentine war. Her own views embody both strength and tenderness: "An artist isn't political in the party political sense – they have a constituency which is their public – it is the poetry which matters most of all."

his song to those then fighting with the *guerrilleros* in El Salvador. A continent's youth reported unicorn sightings and embroidered the beast on their T-shirts, symbol of a continual struggle to realize thwarted ideals.

A second Cuban episode. It is midnight on January 27, 1989 and Rodríguez is about to begin a concert tour of the island, playing in the town squares, to celebrate thirty years of the revolution. He starts with an overnight climb of Pico Turquino, the highest peak of the Sierra Maestra. Arriving at the summit at dawn, and surrounded by a crowd of several hundred, he sings some of Cuba's oldest ballads, dedicating them to the memory of national poet José Martí, who had fought in those same mountains for the liberation of Cuba from Spanish colonial rule.

This is the larger-than-life world of Latin America and its nueva canción – music and politics firmly linked in two very different Latin American countries.

PITY THE SINGER...

"Pity the singer who doesn't risk his guitar and himself . . . who never knew that we were the seed that today is life."
Pablo Milanés "Pobre del cantor"

Amid contemporary tastes for "tropical" Latin dance music – both across the continent and further afield – **nueva canción** is sometimes dismissed as an outdated dinosaur. Its rejection of materialistic and financial objectives in favour of human ones, its revolutionary past, of guitar as gun and song as bullet: these are hardly in key with the politics or music of the 1990s. However, "new song" has an uncanny knack of resurfacing and renewing its appeal. In Cuba, for example, the old-guard stars like Silvio Rodríguez and Pablo Milanés have been joined by a young hero, Carlos Varela, who sings rocked-up nueva trova that expresses the frustrations of a new generation. And the old songs – poems, really – are such classic expressions of struggle, nurturing those suffering under dictatorship and their fellow-citizens in exile, that they are still known by heart by audiences throughout the continent.

So what is nueva canción? It is not so much protest song as an expression of politics (in its widest sense) in music. The musicians involved are not necessarily card-carrying members of some international organization or even of political parties. They worked – and work – separately, in different countries with different histories. What links them is a common attitude, a commitment to improve living conditions for the majority of people in Latin America, a reluctance to accept inequality as inevitable, and a desire to see everyone share in the wealth and potential of their country and continent. "La guitarra Americana peleando aprendio a cantar" (The American guitar learnt to sing by fighting), as Uruguayan Daniel Viglietti put it.

The roots of the movement lie in the work of three key figures whose music bridged rural and urban life and culture in the 1950s: Argentine **Atahualpa Yupanqui** (1908–1992), Cuban **Carlos Puebla** (born 1917) and Chilean **Violeta Parra** (1917–1967). Yupanqui and Parra collected and performed songs from old musicians, while Puebla (for more on whom, see p.481) lived within a still thriving rural song tradition. Each of them went on to compose new material based on these songs, creating a primary repertoire for what was to become the nueva canción generation. They celebrated the rural and regional, the music of the peasant and of the economically marginalized migrant.

Nueva canción emerged as a real force in the 1960s when various governments on the continent, supported by the US, were trying to effect democratic social change, extending suffrage and reforming education and agriculture in the hope of preventing the spread of the 1959 Cuban Revolution. These changes released a creative vitality but also fuelled nationalistic movements opposed to US influence. The search for a Latin American cultural identity became part of a wider struggle for self-determination.

The first crystallization of a nueva canción ideal came from Argentina. In 1962 at the Circulo de Periodistas (Journalists' Circle), the singers **Mercedes Sosa**, **Armando Tejado Gomez** and others unveiled the "nuevo canciónero", a musical manifesto that aimed to respond to "new agreements and chords in the air" and to rehabilitate indigenous Argentinian song forms like the *chacarera*, *zamba* and *chamame*. Mercedes Sosa (see box) has gone on to forge an international reputation, with her inspiring voice, well-chosen repertoire and tight arrangements appealing on a musical level, even without the lyrics. Sosa aside, however, nueva canción has been less popular in Argentina than elsewhere in Latin America, with rock nacional taking on its role of political comment.

It was in Chile that the music really forged its identity and it owed this in the greatest part to Violeta Parra and Víctor Jara. As noted above, **Violeta Parra** played a major role in drawing on the traditions of the *payadores*, the often illiterate, rural, popular poets, and she was largely responsible for the introduction of **Andean Indian instruments** to Santiago, learning bamboo flute, panpipes and armadillo-backed charango. She drew also on French chanson traditions, having spent time in Paris, where she met both Yupanqui and Edith Piaf.

All these influences came to fruition in the *peña* (club) that she ran in Santiago, along with Víctor Jara, from 1965 until her suicide in 1967. Her legacy was a repertoire of exquisite songs, many of them with a wry sense of humour, which were taken up all over the continent. Although many are love songs, they are informed by an acute awareness of poverty and injustice. As she wrote (in décimas) in her autobiography, "I sing to the Chilean people/if I have something to say/I don't take up the guitar/to win applause/I sing of the difference there is between what is certain and what is false/otherwise I don't sing."

The work of singer-songwriter and theatre director **Víctor Jara** took the nueva canción onto an even larger stage, and his songs – and his life – reverberated for many years after his murder in 1973. His career charted the history of the Popular Unity period in Chile. A peasant boy from a migrant family who made it despite enormous obstacles, his life is the stuff of Hollywood bio-pics. His mother kept her family by working in the Santiago vegetable market, also singing as a *cantora* for births, marriages and deaths. Jara learnt much from her, including the focused clarity of his gentle singing style and the close relationship between his distinctive guitar style and voice.

Many of Jara's songs caused a furore in Chile in the 1960s. His playful version of a traditional piece, "La Beata", a send-up of the desires of a nun, was banned, as was his accusatory "Preguntas por Puerto Montt" (You ask for Puerto Montt), which named the Minister of the Interior responsible for the massacre of poor landless peasants.

Incendiary, too, was his "Plegaria a un labrador" (Prayer to a Labourer), a reworking of

---

Plegaria a un labrador
(Prayer to a Labourer)

Stand up and look at the mountain
From where the wind comes, the sun and the water
You who direct the courses of the rivers
You who have sown the flight of your soul
Stand up and look at your hands
So as to grow
Clasp your brother's, in your own
Together we will move united by blood
Today is the time that can become tomorrow

Deliver us from the one who dominates us
through misery
Bring to us your reign of justice and equality
Blow like the wind the flower of the canyon
Clean like fire the barrel of my gun

Let your will at last come about here on earth
Give to us your strength and valour so as to fight
Blow like the wind the flower of the canyon
Clean like fire the barrel of my gun

Stand up and look at your hands
So as to grow
Clasp your brother's in your own
Together we will move united by blood
Now and in the hour of our death
Amen

Víctor Jara

---

the Lord's Prayer, which won the first nueva canción festival prize and the hearts of his people. His best-loved canción, however, is "Te recuerdo Amanda", a beautiful, intense, aching love song, which he himself sung superbly and which the British musician Robert Wyatt reworked to wonderful effect in the 1980s.

Quilapayún poster from "the longest tour in history"

Jara's influence on other nueva canción groups, encouraging them to incorporate sounds from all over the continent, was immense. He saw the role of the singer unequivocally: "The authentic revolutionary should be behind the guitar, so that the guitar becomes an instrument of struggle, so that it can also shoot like a gun."

One of the first "new songs" to have an impact outside its own country was "Canción para mi América" (Song for my America) by Uruguayan singer-songwriter **Daniel Viglietti**. Its lyrics – "Give your hand to the Indian, it will do you good; he will show you the roads to follow, and where the blood must be spilled" – set the tone for the nueva canción movement, which soon involved musicians from practically every country in Latin America, and from Spain, too, which was still enduring the Franco years.

Viglietti went on to write a series of classic songs, including the much-covered "Milonga de andar lejos" (Milonga from far away), with its lines "I want to break life, how I want to change it". In 1969 his song "A desalambrar" (Take the Fences Down), calling for the redistribution of land to those who worked it, was banned by the authorities, and in 1972 he was imprisoned. Worldwide protest, including a telegram sent by Jean Paul Sartre, secured his release.

The nueva canción movement grew as many of those involved met one another at festivals in Nicaragua, Peru, Argentina and Brazil in the 1970s and early 1980s, visited each others' countries and sang each others' songs. It crossed languages into Brazil, as well, through its adoption by singers like Caetano Veloso and Chico Buarque. Musically, the most important new influences came from adopting indigenous Indian elements and drawing on the guitar-based music of the peasantry and rural poor. Chilean groups like **Quilapayún** and **Inti Illimani**, clad in the ponchos of the working class, added Indian instruments like panpipes, bamboo flutes, shakers and rattles: a consciously political tribute to those communities who had managed somehow to resist colonialism and its aftermath. Quilapayún also experimented with classical music, working with composer Sergio Ortega to create the "Cantata Santa María de Iquique", about a 1907 strike of nitrate miners.

Both these groups set out on a European tour in 1973, as official cultural ambassadors of the Allende government, during which time Pinochet enacted his coup. The tour ("the longest in history", as they put it) turned into an exile and European residency, where they put nueva canción and Andean Indian music on Europe's agenda of Latin American music. They were the heart and soul of a worldwide Chilean (and Latin

SILVIO RODRÍGUEZ

. . . .

"**B**efore, Silvio was prohibited – now he is obliga-tory!" So runs the Cuban joke, jibing that the man who was questioned in the early days of the reolution is now presented as its mouthpiece. In fact his songs are very far from that and Rodríguez is quick to deny it himself:

"I have never tried to be the voice of the Revolution – that is Fidel. It doesn't appeal to me to be something official because there hasn't been anything more anti-official than my songs, which are critical a lot of the time, show contradictions, doubts and reservations. But yes, I am someone who feels for the Revolution, who believes in it, who believes in Fidel.

"I feel it is necessary to have a sense of unity in terms of feelings for the country and the will to overcome all the problems we have. Even though I think it will always be like this, there will always be things to overcome and we are going to be in disagreement with a whole lot of things because that is life. One does things for human reasons not for ideological ones."

It's the human quality of Rodríguez's songs and their inherent ambiguity that makes them interesting. Even for those unable to follow the words, they have a ballad-like lyricism, sometimes accompanied simply by a guitar, sometimes by a stylish band. With best-selling albums like "Días y flores" (Days and Flowers), he has remained one of Cuba's top songwriters for thirty years, and still holds an appeal for the younger generation.

"In the beginning people didn't understand us. Our songs were self-critical and there was no tradition of that, but they were songs full of commitment. The 1960s were the hot soup of what was happening – new things – and there was a moment when the nueva trova was in the front line of the ideological fight. Now we see clearly that it was and is a privilege that before us no other generation of trovadores could be real protagonists.

"I think that one of the things that most motivates me is the inaccessible, what you cannot do, what you aspire to and desire. This is a constant presence in my songs: it's a little like the line of the horizon. It seems there is always a place further away and the hope of finding that place is, I think, the desire of all human beings."

LATIN AMERICA

American) solidarity movement, for which they performed almost daily for a decade or longer. These days, they are back home, again supporting various political campaigns.

The Andean instruments and rhythms used by Quilapayún and Inti Illimani have also been skilfully incorporated in the 1980s and 90s by a younger Bolivian singer, **Emma Junaro**. One of the most popular singers in the country, she draws heavily on Andean folklore in her songs, while keeping a light jazzy feel to the music.

THE CUBAN CONNECTION

The nascent strands of nueva canción were first brought together at Cuba's 1967 **Protest Song Festival**. This was the first time that nuevo canción musicians from all over the Americas and further afield were able to meet each other and many important links developed. But it was this festival that introduced the erroneous tag of "protest song", a tag decisively rejected by all those involved (including the Cubans, who could hardly protest against their "popular revolution"). It had come from the Cuban government, who were looking in some way to ally themselves with the "protest singers" of the time in the US – those like Bob Dylan, Joan Baez, Pete Seeger and others in the Civil Rights Movement and opposed to the Vietnam War.

Pablo Milanés and **Silvio Rodríguez**, both present at that festival, are the two major figures of **nueva trova** – as nueva canción is known in Cuba. There is a strong empathy between them, as they have followed parallel political and artistic tracks. Both, for example, sing Milanés' "El breve espacio en que tú no estás" (The Brief Space Where You Are Not), and speak of it as a song either could have written. Both are also complex writers, and even in songs of struggle, dedicated to Angola, Nicaragua and Chile, they weave texts with layers of ambiguity, while remaining wholeheartedly revolutionary. Musically, Milanés adopts more jazzy tones in his revisitings of the songs of the vieja trovadores (old black balladeers) or his settings of Cuba's national poet José Martí or the black poet Nicolas Guillén. He is also well known for his love songs, such as the exquisite "Yolanda", which avoid sentimentality by their unusual use of images and language.

**El breve espacio en que tú no estás
(The Brief Space Where You Are Not)**

A trace of dampness still remains
Your perfume fills my solitude
In the bed your outline remains like a promise
To fill the brief space where you are not.

I still don't know if she'll come back
No one knows what the next day will bring
She breaks all my preconceptions
She never admits sadness
She asks for nothing in return for what she gives
She's often violent and tender
And never speaks of unions for life
And yet gives herself
As if there were only one day to love

She won't share a meeting
Yet she likes the songs
That capture what she thinks
Still I didn't ask: will you stay?
I feared her answer might be – never!
I would rather share
Than live my life without her
She's not perfect
But it's close to what, till now,
I had only dreamed about.

Pablo Milanés

The consistent popularity of Milanés and Rodríguez comes from their ability to capture a questioning note, a vulnerability in the relationship between voice, melody and text, even when they are asserting something. This gives enormous depth to their music and perfectly complements the lyrics, in which nothing is straightforward or literal. The Rodríguez song "En busca de un sueño" (In Search of a Dream) speaks of "generations in

CARLOS VARELA
MONEDAS AL AIRE

search of a dream . . . that they win and lose . . . a beautiful madness", while in "La prisión" (The Prison), dedicated to Fidel, he sings "The prison is over, the prison of iron, but the prison of dreams continues."

When Cuba's revolutionary history is re-written it is the songs of Milanés and Rodríguez – and more recently Carlos Varela – that will provide a means of mapping the emotional life of a people "en busca de un sueño y cuántas ilusiones" (in search of a dream and so many illusions), in Rodríguez's words. As the Cuban press has written, "we have here the great epic poems of our days".

Carlos Varela is the best-known voice of the "new generation" of Cuban trova – and currently Cuba's most popular singer. A superbly articulate lyricist, he says what he feels and, for all the frustrations of Cuban musical life (his only record was recorded in Venezuela and released on New York label Qbadisc), he has no plans whatsoever to leave Havana for exile in the US. He is not alone. There are many younger,

---

Circulo de tiza (Circle of chalk)

I used to draw on the sidewalk with chalk
In my dirty barrio in dark Havana
"Cuba declares war against . . . "
My religion is not of the cross, nor the altar
But I'm going to pray that one day
The fog will lift

I lost a friend in the war in Africa
And another who escaping was swallowed by the sea
"Cuba declares war against . . . "
My religion is not of the cross, nor the altar
But I'm going to pray that one day
The fog will lift

I don't believe in newspapers with the picture of Saddam
Nor in ideologies, nor in what will come
The world declares war against . . .
My religion is not of the cross, nor the altar
But I'm going to pray that one day
The fog will lift

They're drawing on the sidewalk with chalk
The children of dark Havana
I don't know against whom, nor against . . .
But I'm going to pray that one day
The fog will lift

Carlos Varela

---

unrecorded Cuban songwriters, who are adapting the old forms to contemporary music and concerns – a new wave that has already been dubbed *novissima trova*. One of its best exponents, a woman singer, **Niyurka** (alas, still unrecorded), explained the continuity: "Nueva trova won't die in Cuba because it's part of us, we carry this music inside. However, we say things straight from the heart, rather than dressing them up like the older generation."

BROTHERS IN ARMS

The Cuban experience that has produced the songs of Milanés and Rodríguez is unique in the Americas. Elsewhere in the continent, nueva canción was at times to play a much more direct and oppositional propaganda role.

In **Nicaragua**, before the Sandinistas' 1979 victory over the Somoza dictatorship, brothers **Carlos** and **Luis Enrique Mejía Godoy** composed "Carabina – M1" and other instructional songs. Broadcast on clandestine guerrilla radio, they enabled an isolated population, many of them illiterate, to assemble their weapons and participate in the armed uprising. Their songs were important as much for their direct advice on how to make Molotov cocktails as for the feeling of solidarity and contact they gave to isolated groups of fighters.

During the Sandinistas' period in power, the "Volcanto" (a fusion of "volcano" and "song") movement was launched to bring musicians together. Song was involved in literacy campaigns and even in encouraging people to eat maize products when the American embargo caused a wheat shortage. In fact, the whole story of the Nicaraguan Revolution, from the guerrillas fighting behind the lines to the Sandinistas in power and their defeat at the ballot box, is tracked in the work of Luis Enrique, who has recently turned his attention to working with indigenous Indian motifs. Nuevo canción was used in a similar revolutionary fashion by the guerrillas in **El Salvador**, and in any number of protests up and down the continent in the 1970s and early 80s, before the collapse of so many of the dictatorships.

Nuevo canción, perhaps, has less of a role in the new centre-right democracies. However, the use of Caetano Veloso's classic song "Alegria, Alegria" by demonstrators calling for the impeachment of the Brazilian president in 1992 suggests that song has in no way lost its political force in contemporary Latin America.

Forward ever: Sandinistas carrying the "guitar as gun" concept into the battlefield

There are signs, too, that nueva canción may move away from its previously somewhat circumscribed musical accompaniment. On **Carlos Varela**'s first album – the vinyl shortage and his controversial lyrics meant a long wait until this eventually emerged on the New York label Qbadisc – there are songs that stay true to the old acoustic roots while on others a heavy rock backing is employed; he even dubs the voice of Lenin onto the opening track. The younger novissima trova Cuban artists, meanwhile, delve into reggae, jazz and blues, while an adventurous fusion is employed on the recent album by the Costa Rican **Adrian Goizueta y el Grupo Experimental**, mixing a Central American sound with influences from all over the continent.

Musical influences, however, have for many years gone both ways, and it is hard to overstate the importance of nueva canción and nueva trova songwriters like Jara, Rodríguez and Milanés in Latin America and the Caribbean over the past thirty years. As Juan Luís Guerra, star of the favourite Latin music of the moment, merengue, put it, "they are the master songwriters – they've influenced everyone".

For more on Cuban trovadores – the precursors of nueva trova – see the Cuban music article in Chapter Ten.

DISCOGRAPHY

NUEVA CANCIÓN

Luis Enrique & Carlos Mejía Godoy *Guitarra Armada: Music of the Sandinista Guerillas* (Rounder, US). The songs of armed struggle, notable for their encouragement to make Molotov cocktails and assemble an M1 carbine.

Adrian Goizueta y el Grupo Experimental *Vienen llegando New Song from Costa Rica* (Aural Tradition Records, Canada). A new, more classical approach for the 1990s, marred by an occasionally patronizing attitude towards women.

⊙ **Inti Illimani** *La nueva canción Chilena* (Monitor, UK). A fine set by the long-exiled Chileans, including several songs by Víctor Jara and Violeta Parra.

⊙ **Víctor Jara** *Vientos del Pueblo* (Monitor, US). A generous 22-song compilation that includes most of the Jara milestones, including "Te recuerdo Amanda" and "Preguntas por Puerto Montt", plus the wonderful revolutionary romp of "A Cochabamba me voy". Quilapayún provide backing on half the album.

⊙ **Emma Junaro** *Mi corazón en la ciudad* (Riverboat, UK) and *Si de amor se trata* (Tumi, UK). A great contemporary singer from Bolivia, with a voice of beautiful purity, imbued with nostalgia. Songs by Matilde Casazola and brilliant arrangements by Uruguay's Fernando Cabrera, featuring Andean instruments plus piano, violin and percussion.

⊙ **Violeta Parra** *Canto a mi America* (Auvidis, France). This CD release is an excellent introduction to Parra. If you want more, look out for *Las últimas composiciones de Violeta Parra* (RCA Víctor, Chile), a 1965 release which turned out to be her last as well as latest ("últimas" means both in Spanish) recording.

Mercedes Sosa *Gracias a la vida* (Phillips, Spain). This is perhaps the greatest of Sosa's many albums, with inspired arrangements for guitar, piano and drum that employ a range of Argentine regional rhythms. Two other fine Sosa albums are ⓒ *Vivir* and ⓒ *Todavía Cantamos* (both re-released on Tropical Music, Germany).

ⓒ Mercedes Sosa, León Gieco, Milton Nascimento *Corazón americano* (Tropical Music, Germany). A remarkable live recording from a 1984 Argentina end of dictatorship concert, with Sosa joined by local rock nacional star León Gieco and Brazil's golden-voiced Milton Nascimento.

Lilia Vera and Pablo Milanés *Lilia Vera y Pablo Milanés* (Areito, Cuba). Venezuelan singer Vera and Milanés exchange songs, voices blending infectiously. An enchanting disc filled with love songs and compelling rhythms.

ⓒ Atahualpa Yupanqui *30 ans de chansons* (Chant du Monde, France). A fine retrospective released after Yupanqui's death in May 1992, featuring the best of his repertoire, including the classic "Basta ya" ("Enough of the Yankee telling us what to do").

Various *April in Managua* (Varagram, Netherlands). The line-up for this Peace Concert, held at a time when the energies of the US military were focused on Nicaragua, is extraordinary: Uruguay's Viglietti, Mexico's Amparo Ochoa and Gabino Palomares, Cuba's Rodríguez, Brazil's Chico Buarque, Argentina's Mercedes Sosa, as well as Nicaragua's own Luis Enrique and Carlos Mejía Godoy.

NUEVA TROVA

ⓒ Pablo Milanés *Cancionero* (World Pacific, US). A fine compilation of the great Cuban songwriter.

Luis Peña/Pablo Milanés *Años Vols 1 & 2* (Egrem, Cuba). Two beautiful discs bringing together Milanés, one of the main nueva trova singer-songwriters, with blind trovador Peña, then in his late sixties. The joy is in the blend of voices and in Peña's playing of the Cuban tres.

ⓒ Carlos Puebla *Carlos Puebla y sus Tradicionales* (Egrem-Artex, Canada). Puebla is the hero of Cuban political song. This anthology presents some of his greatest revolutionary songs, with guitar, close harmonies and percussion.

ⓒ Silvio Rodríguez *Días y Flores* (Hannibal, UK Carthage, US) and *Cuban Classics 1: Canciones Urgentes* (Luaka Bop/Warner). Two compilations showing the man at his best; the latter is part of David Byrne's *Cuban Classics* series and includes good accompanying notes.

Silvio Rodríguez and Pablo Milanés *Silvio Rodríguez y Pablo Milanés en vivo en Argentina* (Cubartista, Argentina). This superb concert, arranged to celebrate the end of dictatorship, brought together the two Cubans with musicians who had sustained the spirit of the country through the dark times.

ⓒ Carlos Varela *Monedas al Aire* (Qbadisc, US). The first album by Cuba's most popular singer is a revelation, rocking up the familiar guitar and voice of nueva canción, but with the lyrics (which are superb – and included on the sleeve notes in Spanish and English) always to the fore.

TANGO ARGENTINO

THE ACCORDION THAT CROSSED FROM CHURCH TO BORDELLO TO BALLROOM

It's been said that Argentina has two national anthems – the official hymn and the tango. Forget the mannered ballroom-dancing image, tango – as Teddy Peiro explains – is a real roots music: sometimes sleazy, sometimes elegant, but always sensuous, rhythmic and passionate – the vertical expression of a horizontal desire!

M y informants all agree on one fact", wrote the Argentinian writer and tango enthusiast Jorge Luis Bórges, "The Tango was born in the brothels".

The informants were a little presumptuous, perhaps, for nobody can actually pinpoint tango's birthplace, but it certainly found its foster parents among the pimps and prostitutes of the bordellos and bars of the *arrabal* and *orillas* (slum districts) on the outskirts of Buenos Aires. It was an urban music: a product of the melting pot of European immigrants (Italians, Spaniards, east Europeans and Jews), local Criollos (of Spanish descent), blacks and natives, drawn together when the city became the capital of Argentina in 1880. Its roots rambled through the musics of all the peoples struggling for a living around Buenos Aires, Montevideo and the Río de la Plata ports: Andalucían flamenco, southern Italian melodies, Cuban habanera, African candomblé percussion,

and – above all – the milónga, the song of the Argentine *gaucho*. It was a music imbued from its inception with history.

In this early form, tango became associated with the unruly world of bordello brawls and *compadrítos* – knife-wielding, womanizing thugs. Machismo and violence were part of the culture and men would dance together in the corner bars to practise new steps, keep in shape and then show off later with the *minas* of the bordellos. These dances tended to have a threatening, predatory quality. In their symbolism, the woman is commonly seen as the country – Argentina – and the man as the arriving immigrant. The conflicts between male dancers over the woman can represent the fights of the immigrants for territory as well as the more literal shortage of women in immigrant society.

El Chóclo (The Ear of Corn)

This cheeky, blustery tango
Gave wings to the ambitions
Of the streets where I grew up.
The tango was born with this tango,
And like a shrieking sound
It fled the stench and scum
In search of the sky.
Strange alchemy, love in cadence,
It opened up new roads
With only hope as a guide.
A mixture of rage, sorrow, faith, absence,
Lamenting with the innocence
of a catchy rhythm.

And in a flash the tarts and chicks were here,
The moon in puddles, hips rolling,
And loving with savage longing. . .

When I recall you, beloved tango,
I feel the earth moving under our feet
As we danced, and hear the rumbling of the past.
Mother is no longer here now
But when your song begins on the bandoneón
I hear her creep in on tip toe to kiss me.

Enrique Sántos Discépolo

The first **tango ensembles** were trios of violin, guitar and flute, but around the end of the nineteenth century the **bandoneón**, the tango accordion, arrived from Germany, and the classic tango orchestra was born. The box-shaped button accordion, which is now inextricably linked with Argentine tango, was invented around 1860 in Germany to play religious music in organless churches. One Heinrich Band reworked an older portable instrument nicknamed the "asthmatic worm", which was used for funeral processions as well as lively regional dances, and gave his new instrument the name "Band-Union", a combination of his and his company's names. Mispronounced as it travelled the world, it became the bandoneón.

In Argentina, an early pioneer of the instrument was **Eduardo Arólas** – a man remembered as the "Tiger of the Bandoneón". He recognized its immediate affinity with the tango – indeed, he claimed it was an instrument made to play tango, with its deep melancholy feeling that suited the immigrants who enjoyed a sentimental tinge in their hard lives. It is not, however, an easy instrument, demanding a great deal of skill, with its seventy-odd buttons each producing one of two notes depending on whether the bellows are being compressed or expanded.

Vicente Gréco (1888–1924) is credited as the first bandleader to standardize the form of a tango group, with his Orquesta Típica Criolla of two violins and two bandoneóns. There were some larger bands but basically the instrumentation remained unchanged until the 1940s.

FIRST TANGO IN PARIS

The tango's association with the whorehouse and low-down *portéño* (port worker) lifestyle, plus its saucy and sometimes obscene lyrics, didn't endear it to the aristocratic families of Buenos Aires. They did their best to protect their children from the corrupting new dance. But because it was sinful and supremely popular it was just the forbidden fruit that most young Adam and Eves wanted to taste! And they did, surreptitiously, in remote rooms of their houses while papá and mamá were enjoying their siesta.

Before long the tango was heard in every area of Buenos Aires, played on the streets by organ grinders and fairground carousels, and was being danced in tenement courtyards, to become the popular culture of the metropolis. It was still looked down on by the upper classes, however, until it was taken to **Paris** – where it proved a sensation. Despite the local archbishop's admonition that Christians should not in good conscience tango, they did, and in very large numbers. Tango was thus the first of the many Latin dance crazes to conquer Europe. And

LATIN AMERICA

BORGÉS AT A BORDELLO

. . . .

Our gang was there at Júlia's fairly early. Her dance hall, between the Gaóna road and the river, was really a big shed built of corrugated sheet iron. You could spot the place from several blocks off by the noise or by the red lamp hanging out front. Júlia was a darky, but she was careful to see that things ran well. There were always plenty of musicians and good booze, not to mention dancing partners who were ready to go all night. But La Lujanéra, who was Roséndo's woman, had the rest beat by a mile. She's dead now, and I can tell you that years go by when I don't give her a thought anymore, but you should have seen her in her day – what eyes! One look at her could cause a man to lose sleep.

The rum, the music, the women, Roséndo talking tough and slapping each of us on the back, which to me was a sign of real friendship – well, I was as happy as could be. I had a good partner, too, who was having an easy time following my steps. The tango took hold of us, driving us along, splitting us up, then bringing us together again. All at once, in the middle of this, I seemed to feel the music growing louder. It turned out that the two guitar players riding in the buggy were coming closer and closer, and their music was mixing with ours. Then the breeze shifted, you couldn't hear them anymore, and my thoughts went back to myself and my partner and to the involutions of the dance.

A half-hour or so later there were blows at the door, and a big voice called out. Since it might have been the police, everything went silent. The next thing we knew, somebody began shouldering the door, and a moment later a man burst in. Oddly enough, he looked exactly like his voice.

From *A Man From the Slums* by Jorge Luis Bórges (included in *Bórges: A Reader*, published by Dutton, US).

---

once the tango had been embraced in the salons of France it was free to take off at home. Back in Argentina, from bordello to ballroom, everyone was dancing the tango.

And then came **Rudolph Valentino**. The tango fitted his image to a T and Hollywood wasted no time in capitalizing on the charisma of the superstar, the magnetism of the tango and the hold they both had on the masses. Valentino and Tango! Tango and Valentino!! The combination was irresistible to the moguls, who swiftly added a tango scene to the latest Valentino film, *The Four Horsemen of the Apocalypse* (1926). The fact that in the film Valentino was playing a gaucho (Argentinian cowboy) son of a rancher – and gauchos don't dance the tango – didn't deter for them a moment. Valentino was a special gaucho and this gaucho could dance the tango. And why not? The scene really was incredible: Valentino, dressed as a gaucho in the middle of the Pampas, holding a carnation between his lips, and a whip in his hand; his partner, a Spanish señorita, kitted out with headscarf and hair comb plus the strongest pair of heels this side of the Río de la Plata.

Predictably enough, the tango scene was the hit of the film and, travesty though it was, it meant the dance was now known all over the world. Tango classes and competitions were held in Paris, and tango teas in England, with young devotees togged up as Argentine gauchos. Even the greatest tango singer of all time, Carlos Gardél, when he became the darling of Parisian society, and later starred in films in Hollywood, was forced to perform his tangos dressed as a gaucho. I say it again – GAUCHOS DON'T DANCE THE TANGO!

GARDÉL AND THE GOLDEN AGE

Back in Argentina, in the period after World War I, the tango moved out of the cantinas and bordellos into cabarets and theatres and entered a classic era under bandleaders like **Roberto Fírpo** and **Julio de Cáro**. It was during this period that some of the most famous of all tangos were written, including Uruguayan Gerárdo Mattos Rodríguez's "La cumparsíta" – the most familiar of them all. In its dance, tango consolidated its contradictory mix of earthy sensuality and middle-class kitsch. A glittering respectability hid darker undercurrents in the obvious macho domination of the male over the female in a series of intricate steps and in the close embraces, which were highly suggestive of the sexual act.

The extraordinary figure of **Carlos Gardél** (1887–1935) was – and still is – a legend in Argentina, and was particularly influential in spreading the popularity of the tango round the world. He was actually born in Toulouse, France, but was taken to Buenos Aires at the age of four by his unmarried mother. He became a real product of arrabal culture, and in his success came to symbolize the fulfilment of the dreams of the poor porteño workers.

In Argentina, it was Gardél above all who transformed tango from an essentially low-down dance form to a song style popular among Argentines of widely differing social classes. The advent of radio, recording and film all helped his career, but nothing helped him more than his own voice – a voice that was born to sing tango. Everything about Gardél, his voice, his suavity, his posture, his arrogance and his natural machismo spelled tango.

During the course of his career, Gardél recorded some nine hundred songs and starred in numerous films, notably *The Tango on Broadway* in 1934. He was killed in an aircrash in Colombia, at the height of his career, and his legendary status was confirmed. His image is still everywhere in Buenos Aires, on plaques and huge murals, and in record store windows, while admirers pay homage to his life-sized, bronze statue in the Chacarita cemetery, placing a lighted cigarette between his fingers or a red carnation in his buttonhole.

TANGO POLITICS

As a mouthpiece of the working classes, the fortunes of the tango have inevitably been linked with social and political developments in Argentina. The music declined in the 1930s as the army took power and suppressed what was seen as a potentially subversive force. Even so, the figure of **Juan D'Arienzo**, violinist and bandleader, looms large from the 1930s on. With a sharp, staccato rhythm, and prominent piano, the Juan D'Arienzo orchestra was the flavour of those years. His recording of "La cumparsíta" at the end of 1937 is a classic and one of the greatest of all time.

Tango fortunes revived again in the 1940s when a certain political freedom returned, and the music enjoyed another golden age with the rise of Peron in 1946 and his play on nationalism and popular culture to win mass support. This was the era of a new generation of bandleaders. At the top, alongside Juan D'Arienzo were

Osváldo Puglíese, **Hector Varéla** and the innovative **Anibal Tróilo**. The last was, of all the bandoneón players, the one who expressed most vividly, deeply and powerfully and at the same time so tenderly the nostalgic sound of this noble instrument. When he died a few years ago half a million people followed the funeral procession to the cemetery.

Buenos Aires in the late 1940s was a city of five or six million and each barrio would have ten or fifteen orchestras – amateurs or semi-amateurs – while the established orchestras would play in the cabarets and nightclubs in the centre of the city. Somehow in this era, however, the music moved away from the province of the working class to that of the intellectuals. Tango became a sort of collective reminiscence of a world that no longer existed – essentially an expression of nostalgia. As a popular lyric, "Tango de otros tiempos" (Tango of Other Times), put it:

Tango, you were the king
In one word, a friend
Blossoming from the bandoneón music
of Arólas
Tango, the rot set in
When you became sophisticated
And with your airs and graces
You quit the suburbs where you were born
Tango, it saddens me to see
How you've deserted the mean dirt-streets
For a carpeted drawing-room
In my soul I carry a small piece
Of that happy past!
But the good old times are over
In Paris you've become Frenchified
And today, thinking of what's happened
A tear mars your song.

In the 1950s, with the end of Peronism and the coming of rock'n'roll, tango slipped into the shadows once again.

PIAZZOLLA AND TANGO NUEVO

Astor Piazzolla (see box overpage) dominates the recent history of tango, much as Carlos Gardél was the key figure of its classic era. Born in Mar de Plata in 1921, Piazzolla spent his childhood in the Bronx, New York, where he was hired at age thirteen by Carlos Gardél to play in the film *El dia que me quieras* and booked for his Latin American tour. Luckily for Piazzolla he hadn't taken up the offer when the fatal aircrash occurred. Back in Argentina, from 1937, Piazzolla played second bandoneón in the orchestra of Anibal Tróilo. While the first bandoneón takes the melody, it is the second bandoneón that gives the music its particular harmony and flavour.

Tróilo left Piazzolla his bandoneón when he died and Piazzolla went on to ensure that tango would never be the same again. In the 1950s he won a government subsidy to study with Nadia Boulanger (one of the most celebrated teachers of composition, who included Aaron Copland and Elliott Carter among her pupils) in Paris, and it was she who encouraged him to develop the popular music of his heritage.

His idea was that tango could be a serious music to listen to, not just music for dancing, but for many of the old guard it was a step too far. As he explained: "Musicians hated me. I was taking the old tango away from them. The old tango, the one they loved, was dying. And they hated me, they threatened my life hundreds of times. They

Tango songsheet cover

waited for me outside my house, two or three of them, and gave me a good beating. They even put a gun at my head once. I was in a radio station doing an interview, and all of a sudden the door opens and in comes this tango singer with a gun. That's how it was."

In the 1970s Piazzolla was out of favour with Argentina's military regime and he and his family moved to Paris for their own safety, returning to Argentina only after the fall of the junta. His influence, however, had spread, and his experiments – and international success – opened the way for other radical transformations.

Chief among these, in 1970s Buenos Aires, was the fusion of **tango rokéro** – tango rock. This replaced the flexible combination of bandoneón, bass and no drums, as favoured by Piazzolla, with a rock-style rhythm section, electric guitars and synthesizers. It was pioneered by **Litto Nébbia**, whose own recent album , "Homage to Gardél and Le Péra", is one of the most successful products of this fusion, retaining the melancholy of the traditional form in a rock format. Tango moved across to jazz, too, through groups such as the trio **Siglo XXX** – Osvaldo Belmónte on piano, Narciso Saúl on guitars and Néstor Tomasini on saxophone, clarinet and percussion.

These days in Argentina, the tango scene is a pretty broad one, with rock and jazz important elements, along with the more traditional sound of acoustic groups. There is no shortage of good tangueros and they know each other so well they don't need to rehearse. They just get together and play and nobody would think they had not been playing together for years.

The big tango orchestras, however, are a thing of the past, and economic considerations mean that this is the era of trios, quartets and quintets, and even a sextet is already serious business. Two of the best sextets, the **Sextéto Mayór** and **Sextéto Berlingieri**, joined together to play for the show **"Tango Argentino"**, which revived an interest in tango across Europe and the USA, but in Buenos Aires each group goes its own way.

The Sextéto Mayór, founded in 1973 and starring the virtuoso *bandoneónistas* **José Libertélla** and **Juis Stázo**, is the best tango ensemble playing in Argentina today. They can be seen periodically at El Viejo Almacén, Casa Blanca, and other tango places in Buenos Aires, when they are not elsewhere on tour.

ASTOR PIAZZOLLA

Astor Piazzolla (1921–1992) brought the tango a long way from when it was first danced in Buenos Aires a century ago by two pimps on a street corner. In his hands this backstreet dance acquired a modernist gloss.

Piazzolla's controversial innovation came from studying classical music, first with Argentine composer Alberto Ginastéra, then in Paris with Nadia Boulanger, who apparently thought his classical compositions lacked feeling – but upon hearing his tango "Triunfal" caught him by the hands and said, "Don't ever abandon this. This is your music. This is Piazzolla."

Piazzolla experimented audaciously, turning tango inside out and upside down, introducing unexpected chords and a sense of dissonance and openness. Traditional tango captures the dislocation of the immigrant porteño, the disillusionment with the dream of a new life, transmuting these deep and raw emotions onto a personal plane of betrayal and triangular relationships. Piazzolla's genius comes from the fact that, within the many layers and changing moods and pace of his pieces, he never betrays this essence of tango – its sense of fate, its core of hopeless misery, its desperate sense of loss.

Piazzolla translated the philosophy expounded by tango poets like Enrique Sántos Discépelo, who, in "El cambalache" (The Junkshop), concludes the twentieth-century world is a filthy place, an insolent display of blatant wickedness, onto the musical plane. A piece can shift from the personal to the epic so that a seeming cry from a cello becomes a wailing city siren as if following a shift in landscape from personal misery and nostalgia to a larger, more menacing urban canvas.

In Piazzolla's tangos, passion and sensuality still walk side by side with sadness, but emotions, often drawn out to a level of almost unbearable intensity, are suddenly subsumed in a menacing, larger disquieting sense of inevitability. If you close your eyes while listening to his work, you can exploit the filmic dimension of the music: create your own movie, walk Buenos Aires alone at Zero Hour, visit clubs and bars, pass through empty streets shadowed by the ghosts of a turbulent history. Piazzolla always said that he composed for the new generations of porteños, offering a music that allowed them to live an often dark and difficult present while absorbing their past.

Piazzolla's own ensembles turned tango into concert music. "For me," he said, "tango was always for the ear rather than the feet." A musicians' musician, his last 1980s appearances attracted an increasingly famous audience, and the performances (like his Vienna concert of 1983 on the Messidor CD) could be thrilling.

Latterly he also composed for films and turned his hand to some atmospheric "classical" pieces, including a 1979 concerto for bandoneón and orchestra, which combines the flavour of tango with a homage to Bach, and, in 1989, "Five Tango Sensations", a series of moody pieces for bandoneón and string quartet, commissioned by the Kronos Quartet.

Jan Fairley

WHERE TO FIND
TANGO IN BUENOS AIRES

•••••••••••••••••••

Buenos Aires is enjoying something of a tango revival right now. There are several dozen **clubs**, and a national radio station, **FM Tango** (95.6m), which transmits 24-hour tango. When you arrive in the city, check listings in the tabloid *Clarin*, which devotes two pages every Tuesday to tango clubs and tango revues at the theatres.

Leading clubs include **El Viejo Almacén** (Av Independéncia & Balcárce), a large salon oriented towards tourists but also popular with Argentines, where chances are the Sextéto Mayór will be playing if they are in town. For a more authentic experience – and a great spectator sport if you don't feel up to dancing – try the **Salon La Argentina** (c/Rodríguez Pena 345), a cavernous dancehall, packed at weekends; the tiny **La Cumparsita** on Balcárce, where you can hear tearful songs from the street; or the large and fashionable **Paladium**, on c/Reconquista near c/Paraguay, where the weekend dances come complete with old newsreels of Carlos Gardél flashed onto the walls!

To get a flavour of the arrabal districts where tango was born, try the Caminíto blocks down by the port in the neighbourhood of La Boca. **Caminíto** was named after the famous tango of the same name written by Juan de Dios Filibérto,

who was born here around the turn of the century. The painted houses with balconies retain the air of the old tango districts, with bars and restaurants frequented by Italian immigrants.

Tango aficionados might also want to visit the **Casa de Tango**, Guardia Viéja 4049, a cultural centre dedicated to tango. Its president is **Osváldo Puglíese**, one of the last remaining tango giants, who occasionally still performs with his orchestra for special events. And if you want to know everything there is to know about tango, you should call the **Academia Portéña del Lunfárdo** (Academy of Buenos Aires Slang; Estados Unidos 1379, 1101 Buenos Aires; ☎383 2393) and arrange an appointment to meet José Gobéllo, its founder. If there is a man who knows about the tango, it is José Gobéllo. He can tell you who wrote what, the date, the place, the kind of manuscript – the lot. His *Crónica general del tango* is the most comprehensive work on the tango and its history and to hear him recite tango poems is entertaining and thrilling.

The best **bandoneóns** are still made in Germany, but Buenos Aires has one high-quality artesan, Duilio Maríni, an Argentine of Italian descent. Each instrument takes nine months. "It's like delivering a baby, he says, and each time I cry!" He has a waiting list of three years.

◣ DISCOGRAPHY ◥

Enthusiasts should check the catalogue of the Spanish El Bandoneon label, which is devoted to CD re-releases of classic tango, including the complete works of Carlos Gardél – a series already into fifteen volumes.

ⓓ **Haydée Alba** *Tango Argentin* (Ocora, France). The deep voice of Haydée Alba, sometimes velvety, sometimes gravelly, with an excellent selection of tangos. Accompanied on bandoneón, violin and piano by a distinguished trio of musicians. Translations of lyrics included.

ⓓ **Carlos Gardél** *The Collection* (BMG, Germany). The best beginner's Gardél album, this contains twenty classic tracks including "La cumparsíta", "Volver" and "Mi Buenos Aires querido".

ⓓ **Osváldo Puglíese** *Osváldo Puglíese y su orquesta típica* (El Bandoneon, Spain). A 1949 recording from the greatest tango pianist of the Peron era, accompanied by three swooning violins, five punching bandoneóns, and the vocalist Jorge Vidal.

ⓓ **Sextéto Mayór and Sextéto Berlingieri** *Tango Argentino* (Atlantic, US). The album of the highly successful stage show and a great introduction to the history of the tango.

ⓓ **Sextéto Mayór** *Quejas de Bandonéon* (World Network, Germany). Classic tangos from Argentina's premiere ensemble, in the studio and live.

ⓓ **Anibal Tróilo** *El inmortal "Pichuco"* (El Bandoneon, Spain). After Piazzolla, Tróilo was the most inventive of bandoneón players. This album features some of his earlier tracks from 1941.

ⓒⓓ **Astor Piazzolla** *Zero Hour* (American Clave, US). The man himself thought this disc, recorded in 1986, was the greatest record he ever made. Also highly recommended is ⓓ *The Vienna Concert* (Messidor, Germany), is a live 1983 recording with some really fiery playing, not least by Fernando Paz on the violin.

ⓓ **Astor Piazzolla with the Kronos Quartet** *Five Tango Sensations* (Elektra, US). Piazzolla composed these pieces for the innovative Kronos string quartet in 1989, and leads them through on bandoneón.

ⓓ **Various** *Buenos Aires by Night* (EMI, UK). Twenty tracks by some of the all-time tango greats: Carlos Gardél, Héctor Varela, Anibal Tróilo, Osváldo Puglíese, and more.

LATIN AMERICA

ANDEAN MUSIC

BEYOND THE PANPIPES AND PONCHOS

Latin America's oldest musical traditions are those of the Andean Indians, the indigenous population spread across the modern states of Ecuador, Peru, Bolivia, Argentina and Chile. Their music is best known in the west through the characteristic panpipes of poncho-clad folklore groups. However, there's a multitude of rhythms and popular musics that deserve a lot more recognition. Below, Charles B. Wolff treks round Peru, while Jan Fairley and Margaret Bullen detail some of the other rich Andean sounds, like Huayno and Chicha, still little known outside the region.

W hen the Spanish arrived on the west coast of South America in the early sixteenth century, they found a highly organized empire ruled by the Inca people. Encompassing the present countries of Ecuador, Peru, Bolivia, parts of southern Colombia, and northern Argentina and Chile, Inca control extended over the towering Andes to the edge of the tropical lowlands on the eastern slopes.

The drink is chicha – source and namesake of Peru's finest and most popular music

To the discerning ear, the old boundaries of the Inca empire still represent a **united musical tradition**, although with regional variation. The Indians of the area spoke an unwritten language, making it difficult to know what they sang about in those days. It's equally difficult to guess what their music sounded like. We do know that drums and flutes set a background for a vocal display which, during some festivals, could last an entire day, and that string instruments were unknown until the arrival of the conquistadores. What followed over the next several hundred years was a blending of musical traditions that is not easily separated. Although this process continues today, many of the rhythmically based song and dance forms can be traced back to pre-conquest times. As these original themes get dragged into smoother-sounding modern performances, the indigenous element fades away, eventually resulting in Latin jazz with a hint of Andean flavour.

THE CUZCO SCENE

Music explodes from every direction in the Inca lands, but nowhere more so than the Peruvian city of **Cuzco**, the old religious and political capital of the Inca state. For at least six hundred years people from all over the highlands have converged on the city, and if you're travelling in the region, it's a good first base for getting to grips with Andean music. Stay a week or two and you will hear just about every variety of Andean folk music that is still performed.

The streets are the best place to start. Most street musicians are highly talented performers and will play for hours on end. Bring along plenty of small coins, for the muscians prefer constant small donations to a single large payment.

Not very early in the morning, perhaps just before noon, you might see **Leandro Apaza** making his way down the great hill of Avenida Tullumayo. Carrying an Andean harp on his shoulder, he is led down the street by a small boy because, like many accomplished regional musicians, he is blind. He will turn right onto Hatun Rumiyoq, the narrow alley that every visitor to Cuzco visits at some time to see the large stone perfectly fitted into place in the side wall of

PANPIPES AND THEIR WINDY BRETHREN

······················

Ask anyone about Andean wind instruments and they will most likely mention **panpipes**. Known locally as the *antaras* or *zampoñas*, these are a very ancient instrument, dating from pre-conquest times, although similar types have developed independently in other parts of the world. Archeologists have found panpipes in ancient sites tuned to a diversity of scales. Played by blowing (or breathing hard) across the top of a tube sealed at one end, panpipes come in many sizes, those with a deep bass having very long tubes. The tubes are made of bamboo and are bound in rows of two or three. The sound is a jaunty one, often described as "breathy" as it includes a lot of air noise.

Modern panpipes may offer a complete scale allowing solo performances, but traditional models have only a partial scale, so that two or more players are needed to pick out a single tune in a kind of hocket technique. Large marching bands of drums and panpipes, playing in the cooperative "back-and-forth" style, captivated the Spanish in the 1500s, and they can still be seen and heard today. Such orchestras exist in the regions surrounding the Peruvian–Bolivian frontier around Lake Titicaca, where they always take part in parades at traditional fiestas. At festivals throughout the Andean highlands, however, you'll find panpipe bands of some description, usually involving most of the men of the community. A fifty-man panpipe band can be quite a sound, especially when they're well inebriated!

Simple notched-end flutes, or **quenas**, were another independent innovation of the Andean highlands. Traditionally made of wood, modern varieties are often manufactured out of PVC water pipe. In ensembles, several players will choose instruments that harmonize and the resulting chorus provides a soothing otherworldly sound. Quenas are often wiggled against the lip when played to create a pleasing vibrato.

The Andean panpipe sound was also very much at the heart of Chilean nueva canción (see p.000), when groups like Inti Illimani and Quilapayún took up this music in the 1960s and 1970s, adding extra percussion and other instruments. Apart from their love of the sound of this music, it effectively embodied collective values and an unmistakable Latin American identity.

Inca Roca's palace. Leandro sets up his harp directly across from the great stone. **Benjamin Clara**, who sometimes accompanies him on mandolin, may already be there waiting. Benjamin cannot always meet Leandro downtown as he is lame as well as sightless and needs to be carried.

The two are there to earn their living by playing the traditional music of the **Quechua** people, the descendants of the Inca. Their repertoire includes a host of styles, the most recognizable being the *huayno*, an unmistakable dance rhythm reminiscent of a hopped-up waltz, which once heard is not easily forgotten. It is musically cheerful, though the lyrics can be sorrowful, and sometimes highly sexually explicit – a fact often not realized by those who cannot understand Quechua, the language in which most songs are written. You can listen to Leandro play for hours on end; he will sit, play his harp and sing in a nasal voice, stopping to retune his instrument in different scales. He will take requests, but he may not know them all. I once stumped him by asking for "Wakcha Urpi", the lament of the "orphaned dove". After struggling through a few bars, he revealed that he didn't know the song. But when I stopped by to listen two days later, he recognized my voice when I greeted him and performed it flawlessly.

Leandro and Benjamin, as street performers, are members of the lowest class of professional musicians. Although probably the most poorly paid, they are among the most talented, perhaps because they are not distracted from their craft by the ability to do more "respectable" work. Very few of them achieve any kind of fame. If they do, it usually means the chance to perform in small clubs or restaurants for a meagre guaranteed wage plus whatever they receive in tips.

One such lucky individual is **Gabriel Aragón**. Another blind musician – due to smallpox contracted when young – he is a huge man, obviously mestizo (mixed-blood), big-boned with a strapping frame but possessed of a gentle voice and a soft touch on his harp. His greater fame means that he will often travel for an engagement, which may be a club date, a wedding or a traditional festival. At his restaurant gigs, he serves up some of the finest traditional folk melodies, ballads and dance tunes – a nostalgic repertoire greatly appreciated by older members of the community, who listen, drink, cry, sing, and dance the night away.

CONJUNTOS AND CONCERTS

Cuzco's tavern scene, like that of any urban region, also plays host to young *cholo* (Indian) and mestizo groups. They are constantly on the move throughout the evening, playing one set in each of the available venues in town during the tourist season. You can pick the club with your favourite ambience and settle in – most of the groups will pass through in the course of an evening, offering a smorgasbord of fresh entertainment all night long.

This kind of "one-night tour" is limited only by the size of a city. In Lima, for example, a group of this type might confine itself to a specific area of town. The smaller mountain villages, by contrast, might have only one nightspot – and if they are lucky a local band. In regions of heavy tourism, such as Cuzco or Ollantaytambo, there is usually a proliferation of groups. If you end up

at one of these mini-fiestas, you will probably be forced to dance, especially if you are a woman, and definitely be forced to drink. Follow along, do your best, and don't mind being the butt of the odd joke. It will be worth it. If you like them, fetch your Walkman. There are no commercially available recordings of these guys.

The ensembles typically consist of five to seven members. Their **instrumentation** includes one or two guitars, a *charango* (the Andean mandolin, traditionally made out of a tortoise or armadillo shell), *quenas* (end-blown notched flutes), other flutes, panpipes and simple percussion. Harps, considered something of a dying art, are very rare these days.

Most of the musicians are adept at more than one instrument and they are likely to switch roles during their set. Their performing is for the most part a social event rather than a serious pursuit of art; their tour is a rolling party and they are usually accompanied on their rounds by friends (you are welcome to join them). As these musicians grow older most of them end up in the backup band of a veteran professional, rather than in a group of traditional musicians.

This latter type of conjunto is made up of upper-middle-class urbanites, usually serious

Rumillatja playing at home

students of music since early in life. They normally have some type of classical training, can write and arrange, and, although emotionally tied to their ancestral heritage, the bulk of their repertoire is newly composed using the traditional idiom and is played on both modern and traditional instruments. They are also able to play a variety of standards, more than likely classic pieces of traditional highland folk. These ensembles are usually highly paid (although, of course, they will accept tips) and do not normally move about throughout the evening. They play at the more elite nightclubs, hotel lounges and arts centres, and often tour abroad.

Although not staunch traditionalists, these bands are promoted as such by those in charge of international cultural exchange. They do play well-known traditional pieces, and often accompany **folkloric dance groups** and the like, while another part of their repertoire is a kind of **Andean New Age** music, a pleasant blend of traditionalism with modern jazz. Because of their broad appeal, they are easier to introduce to a cosmopolitan audience than blind street performers, and their vocal presentation is generally more accessible to foreign ears than the piercing falsetto whine of the traditional vocalist.

The groups usually have recording contracts and are considered professional as they rely mostly on their music for income. Among the best-known – and long established on the international circuit – are **Inti Illimani**, **Uakti** and **El Grupo Expresión** (see box on Panpipes and Ponchos in Europe, on p.590).

Although jacket blurbs hype their stuff as "music of the Inca", it really isn't. What it is, however, is good. It's smooth, professionally executed, carefully recorded and mixed in state-of-the-art studios. But if the traditional stuff is what you're after, stick to the folkloric collections offered by labels like Folkways, Lyrichord and Nonesuch.

PERU'S NATIONAL PERFORMERS

There are also performers who have achieved mass appeal and recording contracts in Peru, and who can support themselves solely by their work as musicians. Nationally celebrated performers include **Florcita de Pisaq** (a huayno vocalist), **Pastorita Huaracina** (a singer of both cholo and mestizo varieties),

Jaime Guardía (a virtuoso of the charango), and the great blind harpist of Ayacucho, **Don Antonio Sulca** (see box overpage).

These performers take pride in being bearers of tradition, play at most traditional festivals and hire themselves out to wealthier villages to provide music for those festive events that require it (just about all of them). Although they hold little attraction for the wealthy urban population (who tend to deny their roots), they often appear at large venues in major urban areas. Enterprising promoters recognize their appeal to the displaced campesinos who live in the *pueblos jóvenes*, "young towns" or squatter settlements that have sprung up on the outskirts of the large coastal cities. These artists travel a circuit of major urban centres, including Cuzco, on local concert tours.

Recordings of these artists are generally only available locally, but they can sometimes be found in shops catering for Latin American immigrants. Occasionally, an artist of this type will end up on an album collection.

FRONT ROOMS AND FESTIVALS

There is, of course, a large contingent of non-professional musicians, and, in the cities, the middle class often perform in impromptu ensembles **at home** in their living rooms. They tend to play huaynos or *chicha* (see below), styles accompanied by falsetto singing in Spanish or Quechua, and often a mixture of both.

The only way to hear a performance in someone's living room is, of course, to get yourself invited. Fortunately, this isn't difficult to do in the Andes, where only a committed sociopath could avoid making friends. To speed the process, bring alcohol with you, accept every drink offered, be sure to encourage others to drink from your bottle, eat everything served to you, and ask to learn the words and sing along. You'll quickly pick up the dance steps.

For the less gregarious, **festivals** are an equally rewarding source of traditional music. One of the best I've encountered takes place in January on the **Isla Amantaní** in Lake Titicaca, its exact date, as is often the case in the Andean highlands, determined by astronomical events. This particular festival is related to the cleansing of the pasturage and water sources; stone fences are repaired, walking paths repaved, and the stone effigies and crosses that guard the planting fields replaced or repaired. Ceremonial areas, public access paths and the like are attended to

AYLLU SULCA AND PERUVIAN HARP MUSIC

· · · · · · · · · · · · · · · · · · ·

The **harp** may be a dying art in Peru but in the blind musician **Don Antonio "Ayllu" Sulca**, of Ayacucho, the country has one of the great masters of the instrument. His huge harp is characteristically Andean, with a soundbox built like a boat and a siren's head decoration. Its form is thought to have evolved from the harp brought from Spain in the sixteenth century and the Celtic harp brought by the Jesuits. It has 36 strings spanning five octaves and including resonant bass notes. In processions in the Andes, harpists often sling their instruments upside down across their shoulders, plucking with a remarkable backhanded technique.

Sulca plays solo and also along with members of his *ayllu*, his extended family, on fiddles and mandolins. His songs are mostly huaynos sung in Quechua, and the most familiar, "Huerfano pajarillo" (Little Orphan Bird), about a bird which has strayed too far from home, is often interpreted as telling the story of the plight of the Indians forced to migrate to earn a living. His most extraordinary song is the tragic and dramatic "Helme", which vividly recounts a story of infidelity that leads to murder.

Sulca's stately style of playing *yaravis* – slow sad tunes, also thought to date from pre-conquest times – is unmatched. Their doleful, introspective character was acquired perhaps during the colonial period, when at least 80 percent of the Indian population perished and the survivors witnessed the destruction of a highly organized ritual world. The yaravi composed at the death of the last member of the Inca royal family, Tupac Amaru, in 1781, became the best-known of all Peruvian tunes – "El Condor Pasa" (Flight of the Condor).

Sulca also plays **dance music** from the early twentieth century, when forms like the foxtrot, waltz and tango were given the Inca touch to produce hybrid forms like the sublime waltz *incaico* "Nube Gris" (Grey Cloud). His version of his city's unofficial hymn, "Adios pueblo Ayacucho" (Farewell, People of Ayacucho), celebrates emotional ties to the place where the Indians beat back the Spanish at the time of the conquest.

on a particular day as part of a general and communal ceremony. A single-file "parade" of individuals covers the entire island, stopping to appease the deities and provide necessary maintenance at each site. At the front are local non-professional musicians, all male, playing drums and flutes of various types.

There are, of course, festivals that are celebrated on a larger scale. On the day of the June solstice (midwinter in the Andes) the Inca would ceremonially tie the sun to a stone and coax it to return south, bringing warmer weather and the new planting season. **Inti Raymi**, the Festival of the Sun, is still observed in every nook and cranny in the Andean republics, from the capital city to the most isolated hamlet. The celebration, following a solemn ritual that includes a llama sacrifice, is more of a carnival than anything else. Parades of musicians, both professional bands and thrown-together collages of amateurs, fill the streets. You will be expected to drink and dance until you drop, or hide in your room. This kind of party can run several days, so be prepared.

Anyone spending more than two weeks in the Andes is almost bound to witness a festival of some sort. Any excuse for a party is valid. The street fills with mildly inebriated men in colourful handwoven clothing, carrying instruments of every conceivable type. Guitars, mandolins, panpipes, quenas, charangos, violins, drums, saxophones, trumpets, trombones, tubas . . . a couple of guys show up carrying large harps hoisted high on one shoulder, which they reach up to play in a backhanded style. Everybody is playing, and they are all playing something different and loud. After what seems like an eternal cacophony, things slowly calm down, but before silence reigns, someone strikes up another tune and everyone joins in. Fortunately, they are all playing the same song. Unfortunately, they are all playing in different keys, at different tempos. Ever so slowly, the noise coalesces into a beautiful symphony as they adjust to one another. The effect is dramatic; the contrast of fine performance growing from a backdrop of sheer pandemonium is nothing short of magical.

CHICHA

Once upon a time in the Andes, **chicha** meant the fermented maize beer made by people of Indian descent and drunk in great quantities on festive occasions. Nowadays, if you request chicha, Peruvians are more likely to point you towards a cassette stall, as the beer has given its name to a new and hugely popular brew of Andean tropical music – a fusion of urban cumbia (local versions of the original Colombian dance), traditional highland huayno, and rock.

Demonios de Mantaro (The Devils of Mantaro), who hailed from the central highlands of Junin. The most famous band today are **Los Shapis**, another provincial group established by their 1981 hit "El aguajal" (The Swamp), a version of a traditional huayno. **Pastorita Huaracina** is one of the more well-known female singers. Another good band – and the first to get a western CD release – are **Belem**, based in Lima.

While most lyrics are about love in all its aspects, their hidden agenda is the Indian experience – displacement, hardship, loneliness and exploitation. Many songs relate to the great majority of people who have to make a living selling their labour and goods in the unofficial "informal economy", ever threatened by the

Top chicha band, Belem

The music's origins lie in the massive migration of Indians from the inner mountain areas to the shantytowns around cities such as Arequipa and Lima. Chicha emerged in Lima in the early 1960s and by the mid-80s had become the most widespread urban music in Peru. Most bands have lead and rhythm guitars, electric bass, electric organ, a timbales and conga player, one or more vocalists (who may play percussion) and, if they've got the money, a synthesizer.

The first chicha hit, and the song from which the movement has taken its name, was "La Chichera" (The Chicha Seller) by **Los**

police. Los Shapis' "El ambulante" (The Street Seller) opens with a reference to the rainbow colours of the Inca flag and the colour of the ponchos the people use to keep warm and transport their wares. "My flag is of the colours and the stamp of the rainbow/For Peru and America/Watch out or the police will take your bundle off you!/Ay, ay, ay, how sad it is to live/How sad it is to dream/I'm a street seller, I'm a proletarian/Selling shoes, selling food, selling jackets/I support my home."

Chicha has effectively become a youth movement, an expression of social frustration for the mass of people suffering racial discrimination in Peruvian society.

HUAYNOS – PERUVIAN MOUNTAIN MUSIC

Europe may know the Andes through the sound of bamboo panpipes and quenas, but visit the Peruvian central sierra and you find a music as lively and energetic as the busy market towns it comes from – a music largely unknown outside the country. These songs and dances are **huaynos** one of the few musical forms that reaches back to pre-conquest times, although the **orquestas típicas** that play them, from sierra towns like Huancayo, Ayacucho and Pucará, include saxophones, clarinets and trumpets alongside traditional instruments like violins, charangos and the large Indian harp.

The music is spirited and infectious, although harmonically very static. The voices are piercing but warm, and the names of the singers express the passion of the people for the flora and fauna of their homeland – like **Flor Pucariña** (The Flower of Pucará) and **Picaflor de los Andes** (Hummingbird of the Andes), two of those represented on GlobeStyle's huayno compilation. Another western CD of this music, released by Arhoolie, features the most celebrated huayno singer of all time – El Jilguero de Huascarán. When he died in 1988 thousands of people packed the streets of Lima to attend his funeral, and recordings he made over thirty years ago are still sold on the streets today.

PANPIPES AND PONCHOS IN EUROPE

. . . .

In the market square of any European town from Dublin to Budapest, in the summer months you're likely to find a band of musicians clad in ponchos and knitted hats, busking on bamboo quenas and panpipes and little charangos from Bolivia and Peru. Their music ranges from the mestizo traditions of the towns and the roots music of the villages to the blander Andean tunes played internationally. Typical of the entrepreneurial culture they come from, they'll probably have their own cassettes to sell.

Andean music in this popular form found its way to Europe sometime in the 1950s and by the mid-60s it had become tremendously popular in Paris through the work of groups like **Los Calchakis**. In Paris today, **Bolivia Manta**, a co-operative community of Andean migrants, have kept the flame alive.

Back in Bolivia, after the 1952 revolution against the military junta led to a period of social reform, one of the pioneering models for the future was **Los Jairas** – *charanguista* Ernesto Cavour, guitarist Alfredo Dominguez and quena player Gilbert Favre (a Swiss flautist) – who played at the Peña Naira in La Paz. While in the mountain villages each instrument has its time and place (the charango is a dry-season instrument which might, if played during rains, cause frosts and hailstorms), Los Jairas and the other popular bands that have followed them play them all together.

In the 1980s and 90s the most familiar groups playing this highly professional, well-arranged and extremely beautiful music are **Rumillajta** (City of Stone in Quecha) and the Aymara Indian **Awatinas** (Shepherds), members of the Condé family and friends. Both groups tour regularly in Europe.

Awatinas were brought up as Aymara speakers and a good half of their performance is traditional Aymara music, including festive and circle dances that form part of the regular rituals associated with the land. This can be a demanding challenge to western ears. Awatinas often appear with a banner saying "awatkipasipxananakasataki" ("let our integrity shine") and they are keen ambassadors of their culture. They compose much of the remainder of their repertoire themselves in the style of urban mestizo music.

Rumillajta stay clearly within this mestizo style and perform it in very beautiful arrangements, although more recently they have included songs from other countries of the continent, including some nueva canción. They have taken their music to remote communities in the Scottish highlands, have been involved in a cooperative music workshop in La Paz and make many of their own instruments. Their album "Hoja de coca" (Coca Leaf) is a good example of the rich textures of their music with deep breathy pipes, both melodic and percussive, over a rippling strum.

Awatinas – the familiar face of Andean panpipe and poncho music

The buoyant, swinging rhythms of huayno songs are deceptive, for the lyrics fuse joy and sorrow. Sung in a mixture of Spanish and Quechua, they tell of unhappy love and betrayal, and celebrate passion. As Picaflor sings in "Un pasajero en tu camino" "on the road of romance, I'm only a passenger without a destination".

As well as in their sierra home, huaynos can be heard in Lima and other coastal towns, where they were brought by Andean migrants in the 1950s. Before then the music of the coastal towns and cities was *musica criolla*, heavily influenced by music from other parts of Latin America, Spain and Europe – a bourgeois music including everything from foxtrot to tango, which filtered down to the working class, often as strange hybrids called, for example, Inca-Fox. Migrants often found themselves living in desperate poverty in the shantytowns, scraping a living as maids, labourers or street-traders, but

would meet up at the Lima *coliseo* (stadium) on a Sunday to dance to their music and recover their identity and pride.

Urban huaynos are performed and recorded by orquestas típicas and enjoy enormous popularity. In the rural areas the style is more rustic. Andean highland settlements are isolated by deep river valleys, making communication difficult in the past. Because of this, students of Quechua are tormented by the extreme variation in language sometimes found between two relatively close villages. One would expect a similar variation between song styles; this is somewhat the case, but the huayno beat is pan-Andean. Each district does add its own peculiar flavour, but as the saying goes, a huayno is a huayno, at least until you listen closely. During daylight hours, some forty Lima radio stations broad-cast nothing but huaynos. Shortwave radio fans, or visitors to Peru, can tune in for a quick education.

DISCOGRAPHY

There is a fair range of Andean music on CD but a lot more on cassette – especially in Peru. If you know what you want, write (in Spanish) to Guillermo Zorra, owner of the Libreria Minishop, Plaza de Armas, Cuzco, Peru); he'll respond with a price, generally less than you'd expect, and will tape a rare find for you on his very high-quality system if he cannot find a copy.

FIELD RECORDINGS

⊙ **Various** *Mountain Music of Peru* (Smithsonian Folkways, US). John Cohen's selection, including a song that went up in the Voyager spacecraft, is a must. Music from remote corners where music is integral to daily life and urban songs tell of tragedies at football matches. Good sleeve notes, too.

⊙ **Various** *Flutes and Strings of the Andes* (Music of the World, US). Superbly atmospheric recordings of amateur musicians from Peru – harpists, charanguistas, fiddlers, flautists and percussionists – recorded in 1983–4 on the streets and at festivals. As close to being there as you can get.
⊙ **Various** *Bolivia – Calendar Music of the Central Valley* (Chant du Monde, France). Ancient music played on pan-pipes, flutes and drums for rituals and ceremonies of Quechua-speaking Indians. Sounds "from the depths of the earth" and a real contact with the pre-Colombian world. Good notes.
⊙ **Various** *Kingdom of the Sun* (Nonesuch Explorer, US). A mix of Peru's Inca heritage and religious festivals recorded in Ayacucho, Chuschi and Paucartambo. Very atmospheric.

CONCERT BANDS

Awatinas *Kullakita* (Awatinas Records, France). One of the pioneering Aymara-speaking groups who have won success at home and abroad with their mixed repertoire of ritual music and urban mestizo styles. Most tracks are new compositions in traditional style.

Ⓒ **K'Jarkas** *Canto a la mujer de mi pueblo* (Tumi, UK). This top Bolivian band took their Andean folk tunes on tour to Brazil in 1976, where, so the band claim, the locals took a liking to a song they called "Llorando se fue" which later resurfaced, on a spectacularly global scale, as the Lambada. The story is apocryphal (we have a quite different account in our Brasil article!) but the track does have a Lambada rhythm and the disc is good stuff whatever!

Ⓒ **Mallku de los Andes** *On the Wings of the Condor* (Tumi, UK). One of the most popular Andean albums ever: the enduring and engaging traditional sound of the panpipes and charangos, arranged by Rumillajta founder Victor Torrico, and his talented Bolivian quartet.

Ⓒ **Rumillajta** *Hoja de coca* (Tumi, UK). A beautifully produced and arranged album of Andean music in its professional concert form. Some great flute and panpipe playing.

Ⓒ **Various** *Music of the Andes* (Hemisphere/EMI, UK). A strong collection of panpipe pieces – plus nueva canción – from Quilapayun, Inti Illimani and others.

HUAYNOS

Ⓒ **Various** *Huaynos and Huaylas: The Real Music of Peru* (GlobeStyle, UK). A tremendous selection of urban orquestas típicas, who replace traditional instruments with saxophones, clarinets and violins. Includes Picaflor de los Andes, Flor Pucariña, and a host of songs expressing loss and love rooted in the astonishing Peruvian countryside.

Ⓒ **Various** *Huayno Music of Peru Vols 1 & 2* (Arhoolie, US). Excellent collections of huayno music from the 1950s to the 1980s in a slightly more local style. Volume 1 includes the master, Jilguero del Huascarán. Volume 2 is drawn from the recordings of Discos Smith, a small label that released huayno and criolla music in the late 50s and 60s.

MESTIZO

Ayllu Sulca *Music of the Incas* (Lyrichord, US). The blind harpist of Ayacucho encapsulates everything that is mestizo music. Accompanied by violin, mandolin and quenas he plays ancient Inca melodies with a pace and swing which owes much to salon music.

CHICHA

Ⓒ **Belem** *Chicha* (Tumi, UK). A pioneering release of Peru's hot fusion music. Belem's mix of huayno, salsa, cumbia, and a touch of rock, deserves a listening. Andean pipe music, it ain't.

NORTH AMERICA

As this book chooses to exclude Anglo-American rock, jazz, blues and country from its remit, it might seem that there is precious little left in North America to write about. Yet with its five hundred years of immigration from every corner of the globe, America is host to every sort of World Music – much of it highly resistant to Americanization – as well as being the natural birthplace of fusion. For many strands of Latin and Caribbean music, America is home to some of the greatest musicians and the largest audiences. The most important of these – like salsa – are covered elsewhere in this book.

The most thriving regional styles in contemporary America owe much of their strength and popularity to the way they are seen as a statement of ethnic identity, away from the Anglo-American mainstream. Cajun, zydeco, Tex-Mex and gospel music all grew out of deep roots in French, Spanish and black American culture, although these days they all have increasingly wide popular followings beyond their local roots. Gospel music is the most notable example, having developed from the negro spiritual music of slaves into a multi-million-dollar industry, with names like Aretha Franklin and the Rev. Al Green at its head. Not that this is a music limited to the stars. With hundreds of inspirational church choirs packing them into the pews every Sunday, gospel is by far the most popular music dealt with in this chapter – and, of course, it has fed directly into R&B, Motown and Soul.

American roots music is also, in large part, linked to the movement of peoples. The early European settlers brought with them their own local sounds, which developed into the distinctive styles of regional music – one of the glories of American folk. The heartlands of this hillbilly or old-time music were the Appalachian mountains and the surrounding states of North and South Carolina, Virginia and West Virginia, Tennessee and Kentucky. It is no exaggeration to say that Irish music, the key ingredient in Appalachian music, is also the ancestor of mainstream country music and (combined with Afro-American music) even rock 'n' roll. This is traditional music transformed by the American experience and it remains a vibrant sound in the bluegrass, and its more contemporary offshoot, newgrass, music played at any number of American festivals.

A very different musical vein runs through Texas, New Mexico and California, which were part of Mexico until the mid-nineteenth century – and are being recolonized fast by new waves of immigrants. The accordion-based conjunto groups of Tex-Mex music are essentially the North American overspill of Mexican norteño, and its greatest exponents, like Narciso Martinez and Flaco Jimenez, have redefined the style in its new North American home. It too has a new offspring, in the youthful and more urban-based Tejano music.

The accordion is also at the heart of Cajun and zydeco music, from neighbouring Louisiana, although this has French and Creole, rather than Mexican, culture for its roots. Great players of old include Iry LeJeune and Nathan Abshire, Clifton Chenier and Rockin' Dopsie, and they have many worthy successors. Cajun, zydeco and Tex-Mex music come from a social fabric that maintains a good network of local dancehalls and nightspots. Like the best "traditional" sounds around the world, this music thrives on being an integral part of everyday life.

Jewish klezmer music also had its beginnings in an everyday culture, being played at the weddings and parties of the *shtetls* of eastern Europe. Its arrival in the New World came towards the end of the nineteenth century with the emigration of a third of the Jews of eastern Europe to the USA. And its revival in the past fifteen years or so has been spectacular, giving klezmer a small but significant part in the American world music scene.

While millions of people arrived in the States, the US was doing its own colonizing and the Pacific islands of Hawaii were annexed in 1898. In the first decades of this century the island sounds, in the form of slack key and steel guitar, reconquered the continent and reached deep into popular music. Hawaiian music is currently undergoing quite a revival, and its distinctive guitar sounds have been widely adopted, too, in rock and blues.

The American music that tends to get forgotten or ignored is that of the two million indigenous Americans. Their traditional music, with its strong spiritual and ecological message, is musically an acquired taste, and almost entirely confined to the Native Americans themselves, who perform it at rituals, *powwows* and festivals. Alongside it, however, there is a wide range of Native American popular music, including protest-song folk music, rap, country, and a New Age variant based on Indian flute traditions, which has crossed over to a more mainstream music market.

NORTH AMERICA ✈ GLOSSARY

A cappella Unaccompanied singing, popular in gospel music.

Appalachian The rustic old-time fiddle and banjo-based hillbilly or old-time music centred on the Appalachian mountains that gave birth to bluegrass.

Bajo sexto 12-string bass guitar common in Tex-Mex or conjunto music.

Bluegrass The more commercial offshoot of Appalachian music.

Bolero Spanish dance in triple time or Cuban song form.

Cajun French-speaking settlers of Louisiana – and their accordion-led music.

Chicken scratch Popular Native American dance music. inspired by Spanish-American polkas.

Conjunto Accordion-led style of Tex-Mex music; the name means "group" and also refers to any Latin ensemble.

Corrido Tex-Mex ballad.

Dobro Electric guitar with a metal resonator found in some bluegrass and new country bands.

Gospel Black American religious and church music, descended from negro spirituals, and the roots of soul and R&B. Gospel also has a white southern cousin that was a major strand in the development of country music.

Gumbo A Louisiana stew with a diverse mixture of ingredients.

Hapa Haole Hawaiian music sung in English.

Hillbilly Appallachian country music, also known as old-time.

Hula Hawaiian traditional dance.

Klezmer Music of the east European Ashkenazi Jews played weddings and celebrations and transplanted with the diaspora.

La-La Old-time creole music from Louisiana.

Mariachi Popular Mexican ensemble.

Newgrass Contemporary or "progressive" bluegrass.

Old-time Appalachian country music, also known as hillbilly.

Polka Dance of Bohemian origin common in Texan music.

Powwow Native American ceremonial and musical gathering.

Race records Music industry term for 78s released in the US, pre-World War II, for the black and immigrant markets.

Redowa Dance of Bohemian origin common in the Texas and New Mexico area.

Ranchera Mexican or Tex-Mex equivalent of country music.

Sashay Texan side-step or shuffle dance.

Slack key guitar Hawaiian style of tuning and playing guitar.

Southern Gospel White gospel music from the southern evangelical churches.

Steel guitar Guitar played horizontally with a characteristic sliding sound. It originated in Hawaii, but soon became widely used in country music.

Swamp pop Louisiana/cajun renditions of American rock'n'roll and pop songs.

Swing Early country music featuring string bands that had a strong influence on various regional folk styles in North America.

Tejano A modern, urban version of conjunto, using synthesizers and other electric instruments.

Tex-Mex Accordion-led music developed by Mexicans in Texas.

Toloche Double bass played in conjunto music.

Ukelele Plucked string instrument with four strings,

Vocables Untranslatable sounds and syllables common in Native American music.

Zydeco Accordion-led music of the black and creole communities of Louisiana.

FOLKWAYS: AMERICA'S MUSIC GUARDIANS

•••••••••••••••••••

American roots music is enjoying a revival in the 1990s but, in a country as dynamic as the US, many of the old regional styles have inevitably disappeared. They are still to be heard, however, thanks to the enterprise of Folkways Records, set up in 1947 to preserve this heritage. Anthony Seeger, heir to the huge Folkways archive, gives the background.

Where else can you find, side by side, regional traditions from every corner of the United States; the greatest exponents of jazz and blues; poetry and political speeches; traditional music from almost every country in the world; recordings of frogs, trains, junkyards and car races; piano music; electronic music; language and instrument instruction and more? All of these are on Folkways, and the sheer size of the catalogue is daunting: over two thousand titles, including 150 blues recordings, 100 bluegrass and old-time country, 50 titles by Pete Seeger, and over 600 ethnographic recordings from outside the United States. Many have extensive notes, often including song texts and analyses of the recordings.

The enthusiast **Moses Asch** founded Folkways Records with Marian Distler in 1947. Asch wanted to capture the whole sonic world, to sell it to the public, and to keep it available as a kind of public archive. He chose the name "Folkways" because he considered everyone to be "folk", no matter where they lived or the kind of music they performed: Beethoven was folk, and so was a South American Indian singer. In the forty years that he ran the label, Asch issued albums ranging from the music of remote Amazonian villages to New York avant-garde poetry, from unaccompanied ballad singers to bluegrass and urban music forms, from Greek literature read in ancient Greek to modern Soviet poetry read in Russian. And he documented not only sounds, but human aspirations – struggles for liberation and justice in Africa, Ireland, Poland, the United States and elsewhere.

The success of Folkways was due to the work and enthusiasm of a large number of compilers and artists, and to Moses Asch's dedication to his ideal. The compilers travelled around the world recording music and writing notes for Asch, in return for just fifty or a hundred dollars; artists often sold him their recordings outright and sometimes had to make do with minimal royalties while Asch struggled to keep the company from bankruptcy. Folkways was driven not by a quest for hits, but by the desire to continue presenting fine artists in a diversity of genres. Sometimes the artists themselves were compilers. Mike Seeger, for example, was given $100 to make the banjo music recordings that would be released as the remarkable compilation "American Banjo, Three Finger and Scruggs Style". Mike travelled around for months with a carryall and a heavy portable recorder, sleeping in his car and occasionally stopping in motels for showers.

The Folkways catalogue was so packed with riches that in 1987 the **Smithsonian Institution** acquired the rights to it from the Asch family, on the understanding that the recordings would be preserved and made available to the public for the foreseeable future: they are now released on high-quality cassette and, increasingly, on CD. Since 1988, the Smithsonian have also been adding material to the catalogue themselves, issuing new releases alongside reissues under the label Smithsonian/Folkways Recordings.

For the music of the United States, Folkways represents a particularly important collection, running to fifteen pages of the label's catalogue. Field recordings from Texas to Maine, and from Massachusetts to Oregon, capture and preserve the variety and beauty of speech and song throughout the country. Pretty much unique in the record industry, no Folkways recording was ever deleted; if you couldn't find a copy in the record store, you could search for it in the library or order directly from Folkways. Even today, all titles are still available from the Smithsonian Institution, which means that a recording that influenced your parents or even grandparents is easy to hear.

Folkways albums appear in discographies throughout this book but the label is especially crucial to old-time, bluegrass and other Appalachian music.

DANCES WITH COYOTES

THE RESILIENT TRADITIONS OF NATIVE AMERICA

From the earliest of ceremonial functions, through the rise of popular powwow dances, to its more recent mergings with country, gospel and New Age, Native American music has adapted to changing circumstances without ever letting go of its roots. David P. McAllester explores a range of sounds.

Native American music, whether traditional or popular, is virtually unknown to the general public of the United States and Canada. Other aspects of Native culture, such as dance, graphic arts, the traditional lifestyle and even religious philosophies, have provoked widespread interest, both serious and romantic – witness the success of Kevin Costner and the spate of "New Western" movies. Which makes it all the more puzzling that the market for this music, live or on hundreds of available recordings, is still almost entirely restricted to the two million or so Native Americans who live on the reservations (about 75 percent) or in communities in the big cities.

Perhaps the main reason for this indifference is that most Native American music is markedly different from that of Euro-America, in both sound and function. The **traditional music** is very hard work for the casual listener – even Native Americans themselves may hear little of it, since it's often confined to very specific geographical areas and tribes. Native American popular music, though, which dominates the communities' airwaves, could easily be better known, especially some of the more recent chicken scratch, country and rock'n'roll music, consumed in vast quantities by American Indians.

However, at present, the only form of Native American music that has had a wider hearing is the **New Age crossover** music developed by artists like the flute player R. Carlos Nakai. This has found quite a following in California

recently, where New Agers have taken it up as a meditative and inspirational sound.

A LIVE TRADITION

On the reservations, especially, traditional music continues to serve its ancient purposes, both ceremonial and secular. Much of it is kept from outsiders, which has prevented any folkloristic popularization, and even at powwows and Indian fairs the music for competition and social dancing is kept "traditional" by the observance of strict stylistic standards.

The music is incredibly ancient, dating back millennia rather than centuries. The European invaders of the Americas encountered a land already occupied by immigrants from Asia (so the anthropological evidence suggests), whose ancestors had arrived some 30,000 years earlier. They had perfected a way of life that recognized no private ownership of land and hence no aristocracy; there was an overwhelming respect for the rights of the individual, and religious persecution was unknown. It is hardly surprising that some Europeans wrote home that they had come upon a paradise where every man was a nobleman and the "trees provided honey [maple syrup] without the intervention of bees".

The philosophic basis for this paradise was, and is, the concept of a harmonious relationship between humankind and nature. All the many forms of Native American religion consider the cosmos, the elements and the living creatures and plants of the earth to be sentient, wise and more powerful than humans, but willing to teach the way to this relationship. A common mythological theme is of the powers bestowing through visions and dreams the ceremonial prayers, songs, arts and theatre that help maintain the fertility of the earth, heal the sick and bring rain to all growing things. The Sun Dance, the Deer Dance, the Snake Dance, the Corn Dance, the Nightway and the Peyote Road are still used for these purposes, on what are often deeply religious occasions attended almost exclusively by Indians.

Music, learnt from deities such as the Sun, the Stars, the Corn and the Coyote, is paramount to the ceremonies. The sounds and the ideas behind them – both utterly un-European – have persisted vigorously in most Native American communities today. Native American rituals have also been combined with elements of Christianity by the pan-tribal Native American Church, which developed in the late nineteenth century and now boasts many thousands of members.

The vehicle of traditional Native American music is the **human voice**, often accompanied by rattles or drums. The voice is raw and robust, suited to the outdoors, and ranges from the piercing falsetto of the plains to the measured bass of the pueblos in the southwest. Ceremonial music is usually sung in unison by a male chorus, and involves much repetition to make for easy learning and a group feeling. Songs of love, child care and personal visions are usually reserved for the male or female solo voice without accompaniment. Much of the music starts high and moves downward, ending with a strong iteration of the key note. Song texts range from **vocables** – untranslatable sounds conveying pure feeling – to epic verses based on creation myths, though most often these too are essentially vocabalie, built around a few phrases of spare, haiku-like text.

An example of traditional music that has maintained its popularity is the **peyote song** – a night-long singing, hymn-like in intensity. The texts are mostly if not entirely vocabale, with a few brief phrases on peyote themes such as the sacred waterbird or the dawn, likened to the red flower of the peyote cactus:

Na he ne nai, he ne,
Whinai haweyo-hinai yeya,
Daylight, kaci yowena,
Heyo nana, red flower,
Yave kici yowena.

The peyote cactus (lophophora williamsii) used as a sacrament in the service is an hallucinogen, and songs like the Comanche one above may refer to the visions given by "Father Peyote". The immense popularity of peyote songs across the continent has seen them come into social as well as religious use, and there are several hundred recordings available.

Native American music was, in fact, the first folk music to be recorded on wax cylinders, by anthropologists such as J. Walter Fewkes and Washington Matthews, a hundred years ago. But their interest was confined to ceremonial music and it was only in the 1930s and 40s that outsiders began to notice the existence of popular

forms – jocular dance songs and sacred clowns, evidence that the impassive, stoic Indian had a sense of humour.

Canyon Records founder Raymond Boley with Navajo singer Ed Lee Natay

POWWOW MUSIC AND DANCE

As the Native Americans lost their land and means of livelihood they were increasingly absorbed into Euro-American mercantile culture, a process that began at the end of the seventeenth century, when the beaver hat industry turned the Indians of the northeast into commercial hunters. The traditional Native American world-view became a nostalgic means of maintaining group identity. Then, in the latter part of the nineteenth century, after a few heady years of besting the US cavalry, the plains Indians were subdued and the last overt resistance came to an end.

The **war dance**, a religious celebration of victory, was subsequently converted to secular use. At a time when former war chiefs were being exhibited at court assemblies, this stately dance, with its bravura singing and exotic costumes, became the *pièce de résistance* at Indian shows and outdoor theatricals like Buffalo Bill's Wild West Show.

Indian fairs and other intertribal gatherings served to relieve the monotony of reservation life and revive old memories, and culminated in the birth of the **powwow**, its name taken from the Algonkian word for a priest or ceremonial practitioner. These pan-tribal festivals, which still take place, provided an opportunity for visiting, feasting, trading, and celebrating Indianness. The war dance was the climactic event, with prizes awarded for the best dancers and costumes. War dance songs, along with similar powwow dance songs like the Rabbit Dance, the Round Dance and the Forty-niner (named after the gold rush of 1849), thus constituted the first intertribal Native American popular music. Eventually some songs began to incorporate English words for humorous effect:

O-wo-wowo, wo-wowo, wo-wowo, weye heye yanja!
You might know, you might know,
How I love you, wowo wo-wo weya, heye neye yanja!
I don't care if you marry sixteen times,
I'll get you yet, wowo wo-wo weya, heye neye yanja!

The popularity of the powwows has hardly waned and in recent years these events have thrown up their own star performers, such as the **Black Lodge**, **Mandaree** and **Blackstone Singers**, whose repertoires range from traditional honour songs to more recent compositions with patriotic American themes – "Operation Desert Storm", for example. Powwows are monthly events in New York, Chicago and other big cities, and take place annually, often on the Fourth of July, on reservations all across the country.

The best-known festivals are the **Crow Fair** at Lame Deer, Montana, and the **Gallup Ceremonial** in Gallup, New Mexico. The professional **Native American Dance Theater**, based in New York City, carries the spirit of powwow and other dancing on domestic and international tours.

POPULAR DANCES

Although it is now a feature at powwows throughout the northeast and southeast, the **stomp dance** and its music originated in the southeast among such tribes as the Cherokee, Chocktaw and Chickasaw. Though this heavy-footed, single-file "snake dance" is undoubtedly Native, its music may owe its call-and-response style and some of its rhythms to the African influence of black slaves in the area. The melodies are somewhat deliberate, rising and falling, often with falsetto calls at the beginning and end, while the straightforward, unemotional delivery is not dissimilar to European folk singing. In the stomp dance, too, there are jocular texts, sometimes in English and often concerning women and courtship.

Squaw dance is another early form of popular music still in vogue. It was developed among the Navajo, the largest tribe in North America, with around 200,000 members. The dance is the focus of the Enemy-way ceremony, the only traditional occasion when men and women dance together socially. It commemorates the triumphant return of Navajo warriors from a mythic war, to be met by young women who danced with them and were rewarded with some of the war booty. Money is still jokily referred to in a number of today's songs, since men are required to pay their partners after a dance.

Heye yeye yeye yanja
Girlfriend, buy me a car,
Then we'll go home together in style!
Yippie yai yay, yai yeye yeye,
Yippie yai yay, yai yeye yanja!

Side by side, the couples step along in a huge circle. The singing is tense, loud and nasal and sometimes soars up into the falsetto range, like plains melodies. The squaw dance style is currently being adapted by some musicians to accommodate modern concepts (see below).

In the Pima and Papago communities of Southern Arizona, early Spanish-American polkas inspired another popular dance form, called **chicken scratch** because of the way the dancers move their feet on the dirt floors. The bands are composed of guitar, bass guitar, saxophones, accordion and drums – there are no vocals. Apart from the fact that it is performed exclusively by Native Americans, there's nothing particularly Indian about the music: still, this is real social music with a distinctive rural charm.

Today a dozen or more popular bands perform and issue chicken scratch recordings, their vigorous playing always heavily amplified. One of the best is **Southern Scratch**, a Pima group based at the Salt River Reservation in Mesa. However, the scene isn't really about stars. There are no featured soloists, and at festivals the musicians move from one band to another in just about every possible permutation. "Chicken

Chicken scratch practitioners Southern Scratch

scratch is the ultimate ensemble music", as John Morthland, writing in *The Village Voice*, put it, "the musical consequence of the traditional Indian belief that the individual matters primarily for his contributions to the group".

COUNTRY, GOSPEL AND ROCK

From the requests that come into radio stations serving the Indian reservations, and sales at the main outlet for Native American music, Canyon Records (see box), it is possible to get an idea of the music most popular with Native audiences.

In the 1970s **country and western** replaced powwow songs as the top choice. Ironically, the cowboy image appeals to Indians just as it does to the colonizers, and in the western US the Indian rodeo has become a major event. Alongside the roping, steer-riding and bronco-busting, there naturally developed an interest in "cowboy music".

Dozens of Native American country and western composers and performers have become well known within their own communities and among other tribes, while **Johnny Cash**, part-Cherokee, has achieved international fame. Although Indian subjects are the focus of just one of his albums, Native American groups frequently cover his regular western songs and those of famous non-Native singers. Among other top Native country and western artists are **Buddy Redbow** and **Floyd Westerman** (Lakota), **Bill Miller** (Mahican), **The Fenders** and **The Sundowners** (Navajo).

Some of these artists have added their own elements to the established format, such as vocables, a departure from the strict 4/4 beat, and messages about their own world-view. The despoilation of the environment is a common theme, examined in the light of traditional Native American values. **Floyd Westerman** (who appeared as Ten Bears in the movie Dances with Wolves) is often more overt in their criticism. This, for example, is his "B.I.A. (Bureau of Indian Affairs) Blues":

> B.I.A. don't you blame me for
> your problems,
> I'm not your Indian any more.
> You belong to Whiteman, weya,
> ha-ya-ya
> B.I.A. you can't change me,
> don't you try,

We don't want your Whiteman rules no more.
We can live our own way, ha-ya-ya, weya ha-ya-ya!

In the early 1980s, **gospel music** pushed country and western into second place among Native Americans. Gospel hymns picked up from Christian missionaries had developed in their own way in different communities, but when they were combined with country and western a hugely popular new musical style, **country gospel**, came into being. Performed in English and usually accompanied by electric guitars, country gospel retains Native American features through local tribal accents and some melodic and rhythmic peculiarities.

It was inevitable that **rock** should also find its way into Native American popular music. This comparatively hi-tech phenomenon holds most appeal for those Indians in the big cities. Minastream hard rock music is the domain of both **XIT**, based in Albuquerque, New Mexico,

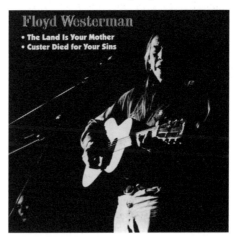

NATIVE AMERICA   **599**

CANYON RECORDS

· · · · · · · · · · · · · · · · · · ·

Canyon Records, based in Phoenix, Arizona, is the largest recorder, producer and distributor of traditional and modern Native American music. It began almost by accident in 1951, when Ray Boley, who had recently set up a studio, was asked by the Phoenix Little Theater to record a few songs by Navajo singer Ed Lee Natay for use in a play. The singing and drum accompaniment so impressed Boley that he decided to put out an album: "Natay – Navajo Singer" was Canyon's first release. More than forty years later, that part-time hobby has become a major business, with over 500 titles in the Canyon catalogue.

Boley has no Native American blood (he is of Lithuanian descent), but a surplus of enthusiasm. In the beginning he travelled around recording the traditional chants and songs of Indians across the continent, from the Yakima and Blackfoots of the northwest and western Canada to the Sioux of the northern plains and the Yaqui of Mexico, from the Iroquois and Mohawks of the northeast to the Pima, Navajo and the Tohono O'odham in his own backyard.

Canyon's principal market is the Indian people themselves and the catalogue has expanded accordingly to include Indian country and western, gospel, chicken scratch, and contemporary singers and musicians like R. Carlos Nakai. And while many Canyon recordings sell no more than 500 copies, the extraordinary range and size of Boley's catalogue gives him an annual turnover of about 160,000 units – small-scale, but very respectable for such a specialized business. The philosophy of the company is organic and supportive, and the artists respond in kind. The big-selling Nakai, for example, despite offers from the majors, prefers to stick with a label that has Native American music at its heart.

Long may it all continue.

---

and **Redbone**, a San Francisco band who have had some chart success, and whose Native members wear elements of traditional costume. XIT are responsible for perhaps the first Native American rock concept album, "Plight of the Redman", whose first part portrays the idyllic aboriginal life before Columbus, while the second protests at what has happened since.

OUT OF THE RESERVATIONS

The small number of Native American musicians who have achieved wider popularity highlights the gulf between Indian culture and the world of showbusiness. Pleasing the ear was not one of the necessary functions of traditional Native American music, and Indians who stay true to the tradition inevitably create music of interest only to their own people. It's no accident that the most successful musicians have grown up largely outside these traditions, especially since those who remain on the reservations, where traditional culture is strongest, must obtain approval from elders whose own tastes may be conservative.

Since the 1970s, however, an increasing number of Native American composers have been adapting the old traditional forms, or developing idiosyncratic styles, thereby creating some highly original popular music. **A. Paul Ortega** (Mescalero Apache) uses flutes, bird calls, guitar and voice in song and narration to promote Indian values.

Buffy Sainte-Marie (Cree), the best-known Native American folk singer, adopted the style of English folk songs for her love ballads and protest songs, such as "My Country 'Tis of Thy People You're Dying" and "When the Buffalo Are Gone". **Kay Bennet**, **Danny Whitefeather Begay** and **Cindy Yazzie** (Navajos) have returned to traditional squaw dance forms to sing about new themes like living in Los Angeles or falling in love with a rodeo cowboy. **Arliene Nofchissey Williams'** spiritual messages are composed in a lilting style of her own, part Mormon hymnody, part American ballad, with a trace of Native drumbeat and a few vocables, along with Nashville orchestration.

Sharon Burch and **Shenandoah** are two contemporary acoustic folk artists. Half-Navajo Burch performs original songs in the Navajo language, often incorporating traditional chants, which she accompanies on guitar. Shenandoah, whose Iroquois chief father was a jazz guitarist, plays countrified folk and enjoys a significant following among Anglos beyond the reservation.

A more modern and politicized native sound comes from **Robby Vee and the Boys from the Rez**, self-proclaimed "electric warriors" who put the message of oppression across with a rap delivery and some wicked sampling (JFK's "pass the torch to the next generation" – seen through Indian eyes), and from the poet **John Trudell (Santee Sioux)**. Trudell, a former chairman of the American Indian Movement, writes superb lyrics which he recites over a backing of Native American drumming and song. He uses electric guitars, too, "the drum of the civilized world", as he puts it, to continue the rhythm. He has toured with the Australian Aboriginal group Yothu Yindi, with whom he shares similar preoccupations.

Bob Dylan declared Trudell's 1986 album, "AKA Graffiti Man", his record of the year. However, the Native American music that has really broken through to a larger US audience is that of the **cedarwood flute**. The plains tribes' tradition of young men serenading their prospective brides by flute was already dying out by the end of the last century, although the music always remained popular at Indian shows. In the 1970s, however, a flute renaissance began to take shape, starting in Oklahoma with **"Doc Tate" Nevaquayah** (Comanche). The mellow, haunting plains flute has rendered such Native favourites as the "Zuni Sunrise Song" well known to schoolchildren and Boy Scouts across the country, along with traditional courtship songs and Christian hymns. "Amazing Grace" often concludes flute albums.

The flute revival entered a new phase in Arizona in the 1980s with the innovations introduced by **R. Carlos Nakai** (Navajo-Ute). To his own meditative New Age flute improvisations he adds synthesizer, piano, harp, guitar, natural sound effects and the tones of newly invented instruments. Traditional melodies from various tribes are woven into rambling impressionistic pieces. He has released a dozen albums since 1983, notably "Earth Spirit", which sold over 100,000 copies, and "Spirit Horses", featuring compositions for Native American flute and chamber orchestra. His music has even inspired a ballet, "Nightchant", by the Martha Graham Company.

Now gaining wide popularity in Europe and Japan, as well as North and South America, Nakai's music also serves a purpose for his dedicated New Age fans – they swear by it as an aid to meditation, massage therapy and giving birth. And that's presumably fine by him. He celebrates sacred places throughout his work and employs the deepest notes of a synthesizer to represent Mother Earth, telling his audience, "I want to teach you how to live in my land!" Confirmation, if any were needed, that Native Americans are taking their place in world culture and making their own contribution to it.

DISCOGRAPHY

Two of the best labels for Native American music are the aforementioned Canyon (4143 N 16th St, Phoenix, AZ 85016, ☎602/279-5941) and, specialising in more ethnographic recordings, New World (701 7th Ave, New York, NY 10036; ☎212/302-0460).

COMPILATIONS

Various *Plains Chippewa/Metis Music from Turtle Mountain* (Smithsonian/Folkways, US). Drums, fiddles, chansons and rock'n'roll from the reservation in North Dakota. Not just traditional stuff, but a cross section of music from ritual chants and drumming to the fiddle dance tune "Red Wing" and contemporary country and rock.

RITUAL AND TRADITIONAL

ⓒ **Various** *Honour the Earth Powwow* (Rykodisc, US). Songs and dances with drumming from a Great Lakes Indian powwow in Wisconsin. Produced by Grateful Dead drummer Mickey Hart.
ⓒ **Various** *Music of New Mexico – Native American Traditions* (Smithsonian/Folkways, US). A scholarly cross section of Native American music in New Mexico. The traditional pieces are hard-going but there are also popular flute pieces and songs by A. Paul Ortega, Sharon Burch and others. Extensive notes.
ⓒ **Various** *Navajo Songs* (Smithsonian/Folkways, US). Archive recordings from 1933 and 1940, originally recorded on 78s by Laura Boulton. A fascinating document of Native American culture half a century ago.

ⓒ **Various** *Songs of Earth, Water, Fire & Sky* (New World, US). Traditional dances – singing and drums only – from nine tribes across America, recorded on various reservations.
ⓒ **The Ashland Singers** *Northern Cheyenne War Dance* (Indian House, US). Northern Cheyenne singers who have performed widely at the principal powwows on the northern plains.
Kaulaity, D. Kozad & J. Kozad *Kiowa Peyote Songs* (Canyon, US). The quiet, hymn-like songs accompanied by the rapid beat of the rattle and water-drum are similar in sound from tribe to tribe. Native American gospel.

SQUAW AND CHICKEN SCRATCH

Gu Achi Fiddlers *Old Time Chicken Scratch* (Canyon, US). Rustic dance music from southern Arizona. One of some fifty releases by Canyon in this popular genre.
Navajo Centennial Dance Team *Navajo Squaw Dance Songs* (Canyon, US). Contemporary examples of one of the older forms of Native American popular music.
ⓒ **Various** *Borderlands: From Conjunto to Chicken Scratch* (Smithsonian/Folkways, US). This is the only chicken scratch on CD and even then it has to share the disc with Tex-Mex conjunto groups. Which, in fact, ain't a bad idea, as the fiddles and accordions merge pretty painlessly.

COUNTRY, GOSPEL & FOLK

ⓒ **Sharon Burch** *Yazzie Girl* (Canyon, US). Pleasant, slightly bland, acoustic folk sung in Navajo with guitar accompaniment. Translations included.

Johnny **Cash** *Ballads of the American Indian* (Columbia, US). One of the-best known country and western singers with ballads on the plight of the Indian by several different composers.

Johnny **Curtis** *Johnny Curtis and Apache Gospel Sounds* (Canyon, US). An Apache version of the country gospel sounds heard across the country.

John **Trudell** *AKA Graffiti Man* (Ryko, US). A superb album from the poet of the Native American experience. Produced by Jackson Browne and hailed by no less than Dylan.

Floyd **Westerman** *The Land is Your Mother/Custer Died for Your Sins* (Trikont, Germany). Simple but haunting songs, powerfully performed. His two best albums on one CD.

NEW AGE AND ROCK

Robby **Bee and the Boyz from the Rez** *Reservation of Education* (Mushroom, US). Native rap and sampling.

R. **Carlos Nakai** *Cycles* (Canyon, US). Perhaps the best-known of his many recordings since it has been used by the Martha Graham Dance Company. The mellow, breathy plains flute and the rumbling synthesizer suggest life energy and the vibrations of the earth. Very New Age.

A. **Paul Ortega** *The Three Worlds* (Waltiska, US). Ortega's narration, something like "talking blues" is the setting for highly original songs, many of which are largely vocable.

XIT *Plight of the Redman* (Rare Earth, US/ Spalax, France). A rock album with good playing and a strong message.

APPALACHIAN SWING

OLD-TIME AND BLUEGRASS

Hillbilly or old-time music, from the Appalachian mountains, has long been a symbol of rural America, and it was from these fiddle and banjo tunes that country music developed. Nick Barraclough traces the old-time roots and charts the course of its more commercial offshoot, bluegrass.

Old-time mountain music shares much the same roots as blues. It was brought about by a world without electricity and instant entertainment, and it came from the pain of poverty and isolation. Its homelands were the mountains of Appalachia, spread across the states of Virginia, West Virginia, Kentucky and North Carolina, where, after the abolition of slavery, the black man was all but driven out, and those who were left fared little better.

When these poor whites came from the hills to search for work in the cities, they were given a name, "hillbillies". They brought with them a music handed down from family to family. Biographies of country singers often begin with a reference to hearing father, uncle or grandpa playing the fiddle while mother or sister played the piano or the organ . . . and all of them sang. It was invariably the men, however, who came to the forefront, as in the interwar years it was not seen as fitting for a woman to be an entertainer.

The early hillbilly singers, then, were white and male. Romantic lyricists of the time would characterize them as Anglo-Saxon, though most probably came from a Celtic background or a combination of European origins. They were Protestants though not devoted churchgoers, and had deeply held, ingrained beliefs in salvation, hell and damnation, all of which were reflected in the music.

FIRST RECORDINGS

Although records had been around since before the turn of the century, only in the 1920s did the industry take an interest in hillbilly music. When they did, however, it took off fast, and the best regional performers suddenly found themselves in showbusiness – radio, movies and the theatre.

In 1927, the first southeastern country music stars, **The Carter Family**, were recorded. The Carters were the archetypal old-time family band – Alvin Pleasant "A.P." Carter, his wife Sara, and his brother's wife Maybelle. What caught the ear of RCA's talent scout, Ralph Peer, was that, unlike other hillbilly bands, whose instruments thrashed around and all but drowned out the singing, the Carters combined clear vocals with complementary instrumentation.

They made famous many of the classic hillbilly songs, such as "Shall the Circle Be Unbroken", "Bury Me Beneath the Willow" and "Keep On the Sunny Side", and set a standard for future instrumentalists with Maybelle's considered and confident pick/strum guitar style and Sara's autoharp, a zither-like instrument with felted wooden bars that formed chords . . . and of course the mainstay of any old-time band, the fiddle.

At the same time as the Carter Family were making their first recording, so was **Jimmie**

Rodgers – and for the same recording executive, Ralph Peer. If the Carters' legacy to country music was instrumentation, Jimmie Rodgers' was his songs. In fact his contribution to popular music has turned out to be greater than just old-time and bluegrass. Artists from the worlds of rock, pop, country, swing and big band all have cause to acknowledge his influence.

There was a lot of blues in Rodgers' songs, many of which followed the twelve-bar format, though with a two-to-the-bar feel. He sang of his life on the railroad, of lost loves, and of tuberculosis, the disease that hampered his life. By 1933 he had sold upward of 20 million records. The story goes that farmers all across the US would visit the general store and order "a loaf of bread, a pound of butter and the latest Jimmie Rodgers record".

PATHOS AND FUN

The success of Jimmie Rodgers and the Carter Family encouraged others to make more of what had been just a way of entertaining the folks at home. Musicians became businessmen and would often sell tonics and laxatives from the

Old-time legends, The Carter Family – currently on the US 39c stamp

stage and on air. The popular musical base was expanding, too: the fiddle was ubiquitous and the guitar was coming into fashion, while the Carter Family brought great popularity to the autoharp, too, an instrument that could be played with relative ease (as long as you could get it in tune). Other newly available instruments were also much in demand, including the mandolin and the Hawaiian guitar.

These original hillbilly songs ranged between pathos, disappointment, tragedy, train imitations and blues. Not a lot of fun, you could be forgiven for thinking, and indeed much of it was pretty maudlin. But there was a joyously raucous side, too, especially in the music of Gid Tanner and the Skillet Lickers and Charlie Poole and the North Carolina Ramblers.

Gid Tanner and the Skillet Lickers were one of several North Georgia hard-driving bands with a riotous style, largely through Tanner's own antics: he sang in a falsetto, played an unrestrained hoe-down fiddle style and generally assumed the part of a rustic fool, often to the chagrin of the other band members. It was quite a band. The revered blind guitarist Doc Watson recently told me his first influence was the Skillet Lickers' own blind guitarist **George Riley Puckett**, famous for his adventurous guitar runs. The band also featured banjoist Fate Norris and seminal fiddler **Clayton McMichen**, whose formidable skill allowed him to play in many other styles as well as simple old-time music.

The Skillet Lickers deliberately projected an image of hard-drinking rough-living young men whose business was to make and drink whisky, and who played a bit of music on the side. **Charlie Poole and the North Carolina Ramblers** were only slightly more ordered. Indeed Poole was one of the first examples of the Hank Williams syndrome – a hard-living country singer doomed to burn himself out at an early age.

Poole died of a heart attack at the age of 39. The music he'd made was a joy: good-time, irresistibly infectious. Songs like "Moving Day", "Goodbye Little Liza Jane" and "Don't Let Your Deal Go Down" owed as much to vaudeville and ragtime as they did to the mountains. And the sound was equally distinctive: a trio featuring Charlie playing fingerstyle banjo, a bluesy fiddle lead, backed up by long, flowing melodic guitar runs.

BROTHER DUETS

Old-time music achieved a level of purity and simplicity with the development of **brother duets**. It was generally held, and generally true, that those of the same blood would naturally empathize musically. With the brother duets the effect was close to the later recording technique of "double tracking", where the same voice is recorded twice singing the same part or a harmony.

The singing was high-pitched, with one voice carrying the melody and the other a third or a fifth above. Instrumentation was a strummed guitar and a mandolin playing rhythm on the off-beat, with the occasional punctuating riff or "turnaround".

The finest and most commercially successful of the early brother duets was the **Louvin Brothers**, Ira and Charlie. Many of the songs they wrote and recorded during the 1940s and '50s. such as "I Don't Believe You've Met My Baby" and "When I Stop Dreaming", became big country hits and part of the repertoires of singers such as Emmylou Harris and Gram Parsons two decades later.

Other brother duets who had gone before, such as **Bill and Earl Bolick**, the **"Blue Sky Boys"**, the **Delmore Brothers** and the **Monroe Brothers**, also had great success. They were seen by reluctant radio and theatre managers as being the acceptable face of an otherwise despised musical genre; where much "hillbilly music" was considered to be coarse,

vulgar and badly presented, brother duets were more acceptably clean and precise.

The brother duet form went on to influence considerably the way popular music was to develop. Ricky Skaggs claims that the Monroe Brothers, Charlie and Bill (Bill who was to become the "father of bluegrass"), had "the greatest influence on twentieth-century music". This bold statement starts to hold some water when he goes on to explain "The Monroe Brothers influenced the Louvin Brothers, The Louvin Brothers influenced the Everly Brothers, the Everly Brothers influenced John Lennon and Paul McCartney . . . "

HILLBILLY TURNS OLD-TIME

Had it not been for the folk boom of the late 1950s and early '60s, old-time music might well have died out as it evolved into bluegrass, country and rock'n'roll, but the tradition was kept alive, mainly by **The New Lost City Ramblers**, a group formed by **Mike Seeger**, brother of the folk singer, Pete. Ironically the music so closely identified with southeastern hillbillies, regarded by many as being of almost moronic simplicity, was now being played by Seeger, a New Yorker; **John Cohen**, a photographer also from New York; and **Tom Paley**, a Yale doctor of Mathematics.

The Ramblers, however, played with absolute, studied fidelity to the original hillbilly sound, with the explicit intention of performing American folk music as it had been before radio and TV had begun to homogenize the regional sounds. They gleaned their material from recordings reissued from the Library of Congress by John Lomax: material which involved a diversity of sounds, all of which they sought to reproduce on stage, requiring large numbers of instruments and long pauses for retuning. Though occasionally they lacked some of the fun side of old-time music, they made a lot of young Americans, dipping into folk music for the first time, aware of the tradition.

With the Ramblers' success came confusion over how to describe their music. The folk-song magazine *Sing Out* called it bluegrass, but their readers soon corrected them. The word hillbilly was studiously avoided, however, and **old-time** or old-timey was settled on.

Touring widely, the Ramblers inspired many other musicians to turn to old-time music, both through archive recordings and up in the mountains, where they sought out the real old-

New York City Ramblers John Cohen and Tom Paley with Jody Stecher (right)

time boys. One such musician who was rediscovered was **Clarence Ashley**, a singer and banjo picker, who had toured the southern Appalachians with a travelling show in the early years of the century, and had recorded several 78s for Columbia and Victor. He came back out of retirement and onto the circuit, where he played, notably, with Arthel "Doc" Watson.

"Doc" Watson, a blind guitarist and singer, was the real star of this old-time revival. He was himself "discovered" by bluegrass musician and folklorist Ralph Rinzler, who was introduced to him in Deep Gap, North Carolina, by Ashley. The breadth and quality of Watson's repertoire and his ability as a banjoist and harmonica player impressed Rinzler enormously, but his outstanding feature was his guitar style. Using a flat-pick (or plectrum) he could play the most complicated fiddle tunes with absolute accuracy and at quite a pace, and he would also sing an upbeat country song such as "The Tennessee Stud", punctuating each line with a flurry of notes.

Rinzler got Doc and most of his family together for recording sessions, where they sang a mix of ballads, church songs, instrumentals learnt from other family members, and commercial releases. The vibrant recordings (on Folkways) represent a good cross section of the local, family-centred music played in small communities throughout the region.

Watson's career took off in earnest at the 1961 Newport Folk Festival and continues today with a repertoire that has broadened from the folk songs of the mountains like "Matty Groves" to encompass more modern country songs and blues such as "Sitting On Top of the World". He is quick to acknowledge his influences – Riley Puckett, Merle Travis and Don Reno; he told me, "I don't think there's one guitarist with a good lick I didn't profit by." He, though, in turn, has influenced just about every young guitarist coming onto the old-time and bluegrass scene, and his version of "Black Mountain Rag" is a classic that every self-respecting player has to master.

BLUEGRASS

It goes against every instinct held by a folklorist to assert that a music has been "invented", but bluegrass comes the closest. In 1938 Bill Monroe split with his brother Charlie and formed a group of musicians whom he named the **Bluegrass Boys**. Monroe was born in Kentucky and named the group after the region of the state known for tobacco growing.

It's tempting to bang on about a natural coalescence of musical styles from all over the world converging in this one band. Indeed, one can spot very obvious traces of Scottish and

Shetland fiddle, east European polkas, much Irish folk music, blues and jazz and gospel. But as far as Monroe was concerned, he just took what was available: an old-time fiddle player, a fingerstyle banjo player, a rhythm guitar player, himself playing the mandolin, and, when he could get one, a double bass player. The difference was that instead of the easy-going, shambolic, ragged-but-right sound any other band of that line-up would have had at that time, Monroe injected into it a discipline of tempo and a fire born of competition among the players.

The old-time influence was still strong, especially in the repertoire of songs, but in a short space of time the music had evolved dramatically, as had the presentation. This is a personal view, but I have always thought that bluegrass came almost from a need to give old-time music respectability. Bill Monroe's Bluegrass Boys wore suits and ties on stage; Monroe eschewed the hillbilly image. He made them play in keys no old-timer would have ventured into – B flat, B. The higher the better. Vocal harmonies were formularized, the melody, baritone (below the melody) and tenor (above), strictly in thirds and fifths, invariably moving in synchronized parallel.

Monroe had four roles in his band: leader, mandolin player, songwriter and singer – though he often preferred to take the tenor or high baritone part in a piercing falsetto that swooped and soared, often overshadowing the poor lead singer. He played mandolin by default – the more obvious instruments, fiddle and guitar, had been taken by his elder brothers – but he did more with the mandolin than had ever been done before. He played it fast and hard, driving the band along with a percussive off-beat and taking solos with flashy runs at breakneck speed.

Over the last five or six decades, the band has been a training ground for young bluegrass musicians. Almost every bluegrass musician of note (excepting, obviously, mandolin-players) has either been a Bluegrass Boy or has played alongside the great man. Monroe has always seen himself as the teacher, and speaks of his life and his music as a mission.

Monroe's songwriting has also been prolific. His work ranges from instrumental tunes such as "Roanoake" and "Wheelhoss" to songs of his young life like "Uncle Pen", written about his fiddle-playing uncle Pen Vanderver, and "Blue Moon of Kentucky", which was to be Elvis Presley's first recording in 1954

Sixty years on the rules set down by Bill Monroe are adhered to by the latest generation of bluegrass musicians, as the music finds itself alongside and, to a great degree incorporated into the huge commercial success of new country music.

FLATT, SCRUGGS AND THE STANLEYS

The most distinguished of Monroe's alumna were **Lester Flatt** and **Earl Scruggs**, the Bluegrass Boys' guitarist and banjoist respectively from 1944 to 1948. Flatt had a strong baritone voice and solid guitar style, but the star was Scruggs, whose banjo style revolutionized the instrument and became the distinguishing sound of bluegrass.

Banjoists had hitherto played in a variety of styles: "frailing", a combination of downstrokes where the fingernails brush the strings and up-picking by the thumb and first finger; and the "clawhammer", using the thumb to lay down a rhythm and picking out notes with the first and second fingers – more like a guitar style. Instead Scruggs rolled. His secret was never to play the same string with the same finger twice consecutively. He constructed a set of "licks" or clichés that he could play at speed with unerring accuracy.

Flatt and Scruggs left Monroe in 1948 to form the **Foggy Mountain Boys**, who became the most successful commercial bluegrass band. Flatt's voice was more appealing to a wider audience than Monroe's because it was a little

Bill Monroe was born into a musical family on a farm near Rosine, Kentucky. His father was a noted stepdancer and his mother played fiddle, accordion and harmonica, and sang old-time songs. His brothers and sisters were also musicians and they were all influenced by their uncle, Pendleton Vanderver, a notable fiddler at local events and immortalized in Monroe's "Uncle Pen": "Late in the evening about sundown/ High on the hill above the town/ Uncle Pen played the fiddle, oh, how it would ring/ You can hear it talk, you can hear it sing."

As a child Bill was teased about his squint and became awkward and shy. His interpersonal skills were never well developed. The reverence he had for his music, however, which he considered to be a gift from God, was total. It was not to be trivialized.

As a bandleader he was notorious. On one famous occasion when the Bluegrass Boys had stopped for a break on a long journey across Tennessee, the guitarist had his thumb badly crushed when the boot lid was slammed shut. While other band members commiserated, Monroe wandered over, saw the problem, said "well, you can't play with your thumb all mashed up", and left him there, with his bag, at the side of the road.

Bluegrass Boys were expected to work for Monroe, body and soul. If there were no shows, they worked on his farm. In the early days he had a baseball team in which band members were also expected to play. Howard Akeman, known as "Stringbean", was hired ostensibly as a banjo player, but also because Bill considered him "a fine short-stop".

---

deeper, more resonant. Songs like "Jimmy Brown the Newsboy" and "Let Those Brown Eyes Smile at Me" almost crossed over with mainstream country. The song that brought most fame to Flatt and Scruggs, though, was a rather poor composition called "The Ballad of Jed Clampett", written for the TV series *The Beverly Hillbillies*. Regular nationwide exposure meant that for the first time bluegrass became recognizable all across the United States.

A decade later came the use of banjo (Flatt and Scruggs' instrumental "Foggy Mountain Breakdown") as aural backing to a fast car chase in the 1967 film *Bonnie and Clyde*. For many second-and third-generation bluegrass musicians the *Beverly Hillbillies* theme and "Foggy Mountain Breakdown" were their introduction to the music. Banjoist Doug Dillard told me, "I was driving down an old dirt track in a Chevy pick-up when "Foggy Mountain Breakdown" came on the radio and I drove straight into a ditch . . . had to get a man to come and pull me out with a tractor!"

The other big commercial boost given to the music was the use of "Duelling Banjos" in the 1972 film *Deliverance*, where city man on an adventure holiday meets banjo-playing hillbilly. They play an apparently improvised duet on guitar and banjo. The tune in fact goes back some decades to Arthur "Guitar Boogie" Smith, and had already been popularized to some extent by west coast bluegrass band the Dillards.

The proliferation of bluegrass through the 1950s was slow, but there was one other band who stood alongside the Bluegrass Boys and the Foggy Mountain Boys: the **Stanley Brothers**. Where Flatt and Scruggs had readily embraced opportunities presented by TV, radio and cinema and were travelling all over the US, the Stanley Brothers in many ways never moved out of the mountains. Their sound is still bluegrass at its purest, with Carter Stanley's mournful baritone and Ralph's clear, rasping tenor.

The brothers played guitar and banjo respectively. Ralph's banjo-playing, though simpler than Scruggs', was as hard-driving and clear as his voice. When Carter died of a liver ailment in 1966, the band polarized to Ralph's uncompromising style, and like Monroe and Flatt and Scruggs, became a training ground for future bluegrass stars such as Ricky Skaggs and Keith Whitley. The legacy of their songs is considerable, too: "How Mountain Girls Can Love", "Little Maggie" and "I am a Man of Constant Sorrow" have all become classics.

For many the best lead singer Bill Monroe ever used was **Jimmy Martin**, a high, reedy singer with a strong rhythm guitar style. Just as uncompromising as Monroe himself, with his own band, the **Sunny Mountain Boys**, he could be very abrasive. He insisted that his musicians played virtually flat-out, up against the microphones; in fact one of his banjo players,

Mark Pruett, once told me Martin would pinch his backside if he ever drifted away from the mike.

The Jimmy Martin sound was at its best when banjoist J.D. Crowe was in the band. The definitive driving, clear, fluffless style of his playing complemented perfectly Martin's more commercial bluegrass songs, such as "On the Sunny Side of the Mountain" and "You Don't Know My Mind".

Another band to achieve a good deal of commercial success were the **Osborne Brothers**. After Jimmy Martin left Bill Monroe in 1954, he had teamed up with the Osbornes, who played mandolin and banjo. The Brothers later struck out on their own to become heretics in the opinion of many bluegrass purists. Sonny and Bobby Osborne broke the rules. Every now and again they used electric instruments, even drums. Their extraordinary vocal harmonies, often with the lead part at the top and the two other parts below, would move in parallel, then, at the end of a phrase, swoop around and exchange parts.

They were just as controversial in their selection of material, which often ignored traditional bluegrass tunes, instead including songs such as "Hey Joe, All I Have to Do is Dream" and their theme song, written by Felice and Boudleaux Bryant, "Rocky-Top".

The Dillards

BLUEGRASS AND THE FOLK REVIVAL

With the folk revival of the late 1950s and '60s, bluegrass took off, initially with concerts and college gigs, then the beginnings of the festival circuit that now fills any bluegrass band's calendar from April to September each year.

Not only was bluegrass heard in all of the United States, it was beginning to be played by those who lived there. The southeastern bands were now recruiting from as far afield as upstate New York, New England and California. The hillbilly stigma, though it lives on to this day, was receding. College kids, new to the music, brought a new approach in terms of worldliness and more academic techniques. The work of banjoist **Bill Keith**, fiddle player **Richard Green**, mandolinist **David Grisman**, and guitarists like **Clarence White** and **Tony Rice**, was, through the 1960s and '70s, to give bluegrass more sophistication, versatility and credibility.

The band who broke through in terms of sheer entertainment was the **Dillards**. Their pivotal figure was **Doug Dillard**, a banjo player from Salem, Missouri, who formed the band with his brother Rodney. The Dillards went to California to seek their fortune in 1962 and for once it worked. Within a couple of weeks they had secured a recording contract with Elektra, residencies in the best clubs and regular appearances on the Andy Griffith TV show.

Their appeal stemmed from an ability not only to play and sing brilliantly, but also to entertain. Where most other bluegrass bands of the time, and many since, presented from the stage in an almost taciturn fashion, the Dillards included comedy in a slick, almost cabaret-style show. **Mitch Jayne** fronted the band and as can be heard on their excellent "Live-Almost" album, begins the show by saying "We're the Dillards and we're hillbillies. Thought I'd better tell you that in case you thought we were the Budapest String Quartet!"

The band eventually progressed from their first bluegrass line-up and material like "The Old Home-Place" and "Never See My Home Again" to include drums and electric instruments in the late 1960s, when they were vying for the same market as the Byrds and the Flying Burrito Brothers.

One of the clubs in Los Angeles where the Dillards made their name was the *Ash Grove*.

Another Californian band to establish their reputation there was the Three Little Country Boys, who eventually became the **Kentucky Colonels**, featuring guitarist **Clarence White** and his brother Roland on mandolin. Their distinguishing feature was Clarence's guitar playing – it was the first time that the guitar was regularly used as a lead instrument. His style was influenced by Doc Watson. It was fast and flowing and set a challenging standard for other guitarists to come.

The Kentucky Colonels were hardly a driving band, but typified the Californian approach to bluegrass, which was, well, laid-back. Clarence went on to join the Byrds and was about to form his own band and no doubt go on to great stardom had he not been hit by a drunk driver and killed as he loaded his car after a gig in July 1973.

A much more "authentic" or "rootsy" sounding band of the time was based in Washington DC. **The Country Gentlemen** – Charlie Waller, John Duffey, Eddie Adcock and Jim Cox – were so called because their roots were more in folk, developing gradually into a bluegrass band. They emanated a studious approach to the music, with carefully constructed vocal harmonies, using instrumentation to complement the song as opposed to the Jimmy Martin "hell for leather" approach. This was the first band to arrange for the song, to sell it lyrically as well as melodically, a good example being the sensitivity with which they performed songs like "Bringing Mary Home" and compositions from contemporary writers like Gordon Lightfoot and Duffey himself.

After he left the Country Gentlemen in 1969, **John Duffey** formed **Seldom Scene**, a prime example of the way bluegrass had been taken on by a new social culture: Ben Eldridge (banjo, guitar) was a mathematician, Tom Gray (bass) a cartographer, Mike Auldridge (dobro) a comm-ercial artist, and John Starling (guitar) a surgeon.

The music was as precise as the muscians' backgrounds would suggest. Duffey stressed that the band was "very choosy" about the songs they recorded, claiming they only ever recorded two songs he was unhappy about. The band picked up a large, educated, middle-class following, including some rising country stars, notably Emmylou Harris, who became a great bluegrass fan, and Linda Ronstadt. Their material ranged wide – from "The Muleskinner Blues" to Steve Goodman's "City of New Orleans" – but was always played with sensitivity, dynamism and flashes of brilliance.

NEWGRASS

Bands like the Country Gentlemen and Seldom Scene, who introduced electric instruments into bluegrass, were the pioneers of what's become known as **"newgrass"**, a more progressive form that emerged to serve the large urban audience that bluegrass was beginning to attract. And, of course, towards the end of the 1960s, the lure of fame and fortune offered by rock'n'roll proved too much for many young bluegrass musicians. Highly skilled singers and instrumentalists, they were much in demand, though since few could write particularly well, long-term success generally eluded them and they found themselves drifting back to bluegrass.

One such bunch of musicians was **Muleskinner**, formed after Bill Monroe failed to make it to a recording for a TV show in New England. The rest of the band, pulled together for the occasion, decided to carry on without him. The band – Peter Rowan (lead singer, guitar), Clarence White (guitar), Bill Keith (banjo), Richard Green (fiddle) and David Grisman (mandolin) – were one of bluegrass's first supergroups. **Peter Rowan** had been one of Bill Monroe's favourite lead singers and **Richard Green** one of his most innovative fiddle players. These two had left bluegrass in the late 1960s for the world of rock in the moderately successful Seatrain.

Bill Keith, another ex-Bluegrass Boy, had breathed new life into the banjo by his introduction of a melodic flowing style. Instead of the old Scruggs technique of stringing together a series of licks or clichés, Keith could play complete tunes by a complicated system that involved rarely playing two consecutive notes on the same string or with the same finger, instead crossing alternately from string to string, often playing a higher note on a lower string. **David Grisman** had done as much for the mandolin as Keith had for the banjo. He was as influenced by swing and jazz as he was by bluegrass. The performance of his composition "Opus 57" showed the way he was set to go with his own David Grisman quartet later in the1970s.

The group only made one album, but the inclusion of songs like "Muleskinner Blues", which featured drums and Clarence on electric guitar, and the more traditional "Dark Hollow", showed that even though they were a generation on from the original bluegrass bands and some of the edges had been rounded off, the passion was still there.

Another supergroup worth mentioning is **Old And In The Way**. This band also involved Rowan and Grisman, but this time included the eccentric banjoist **Jerry Garcia**, better known as guitarist in the Grateful Dead, and **Vassar Clements** from Florida, an inspired bluesy player who had performed in Monroe's band in 1950 when a teenager. Their live album "Old And In The Way" pulled away from many of the traditions of bluegrass. The band was scruffy and long-haired. Mistakes were made, and left in, and though they played hoary old hillbilly favourites like "Pig In a Pen", they also included Rowan's personal tribute to a South American substance in "Panama Red".

Where these bluegrass musicians' excursions into rock were invariably ill-fated, more success was to come as they jumped on and, to a great extent built, the new country bandwagon of the early to mid-1980s. The best-known of these musicians was **Ricky Skaggs**. A prodigious mandolin player, fiddler and guitarist, he cut his teeth as a member of Ralph Stanley's band. He went on to join ex-Sunny Mountain Boys banjoist

---

FIDDLING CONTESTS AND FESTIVALS

· ·

Fiddle festivals are an integral part of the bluegrass and newgrass scene – and, oddly enough, owe some of their success to Henry Ford, the pioneer of the American car industry. Ford was a big fan of Appalachian music and in an attempt to preserve the American moral fibre from erosion by jazz, would often donate prize money for old-time fiddle contests. One winner of Maine's Champion Fiddler Contest, Melle Dunham, was even invited to play at the industrialist's house amid a welter of publicity.

Contests, in fact, had been held in America since the early eighteenth century. In 1736 the *Virginia Gazette* published notice of a fiddle competition to be held as part of celebrations for St Andrew's Day, the prize being – a fiddle! These competitions grew from strength to strength and there are now over twenty such festivals in the USA today. Four of the best include:

World Of Bluegrass, Owensboro', Kentucky (Sept). Run by the International Bluegrass Music Association, this is the bluegrass event of the year. Six days with dozens of top-line artists, some of whom are booked to play, many who just turn up for the event. Concerts, workshops, seminars and trade stands, mean this is a must for the professional or amateur performer, those involved in the business and fans alike. If you can only afford one trip, make it this one. Details from: I.B.M.A., 207 E 2nd Street, Owensboro', KY 42303 USA (☎502/684-9025).

Adirondacks Old-Time Fiddlers Contest (June). Fiddle contests are now basically folk festivals where musicians go to show off and this is one of the biggest and best. Prizes are competed for in all instruments, but there are also shows by professional artists booked for the occasion; plenty for the fan as well as the participant. Details from: Adirondack Lakes Centre For The Arts, Box 101, Blue Mountain Lake, NY 12812.

West Virginia State Folk Festival (June). Another fine fiddlers' contest/festival. Details from: Mack Samples, Glenville State College, Box 362, Glenville, WV 26351.

Grayson County Fiddlers Convention (June). And another. Details from: Jack Rudolph, Box 5, Independence, VA 24348.

Red-hot bluegrass fiddler Alison Krauss

been **Sam Bush** from Bowling Green, Kentucky. He formed the group in 1972 and with many personnel changes it survived until the end of the 1980s. They were progressive from the outset: their debut album featured a breakneck version of "Great Balls Of Fire", which went on to become a bluegrass standard for other bands.

The New Grass Revival's sound was made even more distinctive when they were joined by **John Cowan** on bass. Cowan knew virtually nothing of bluegrass, being a pop and rock fan, but he soon became a convert and the band subsequently developed a sound tinged with rock, particularly in their vocal style. This appealed to a younger audience. In their 1980s recordings, after they had been joined by a phenomenal New York banjoist, **Bela Fleck**, they signed major record deals and songs like "Hold On to a Dream" and "Can't Stop Now" looked at one point like becoming the first real bluegrass hits since Flatt and Scruggs.

THE SCENE TODAY

The scene today is one of a thriving music anticipating even wider popularity. The annual **Owensboro' International Bluegrass Music Festival** plays host to some thousands of fans and musicians, in the home state of bluegrass, Kentucky, each autumn.

Bluegrass has always been a participatory music. At the many festivals held in the United States each year the campsite is filled with musicians of all abilities meeting for the first time or reuniting to play standards from the enormous repertoire of bluegrass songs and tunes. The atmosphere can be very much like a sports meeting or a county fair; the word will get round that there is a brilliant young mandolin player in that session over there, and people will go and look and judge, very much as they would a prize animal or vegetable. Unlike the worlds of country, rock or even, these days, jazz, the stars of bluegrass are still accessible to their fans, and indeed are often to be seen jamming along with the campers.

The music is even changing in terms of its political correctness. Notably, there are many more **women in bands** now. In the past, the only woman you'd see would be when the bandleader wanted his girlfriend or wife playing bass (Bill Monroe, known for his fondness for female company, often did this). These days, however,

J.D. Crowe in **The New South**, where he met Jerry Douglas, the player who has done more for the dobro than anyone since Mike Auldridge of the Country Gentlemen.

Skaggs and Douglas went on to form **Boone Creek**. Whereas a lot of progressive bluegrass in the late 1960s and early '70s was coming out of California and the northern states, this was a band of young players all from the southeast. As a result they sounded more like the real thing; the fire was still there, the competitiveness. They also broke the rules, though, including drums and piano on their recordings.

Skaggs left Boone Creek when bluegrass aficionado **Emmylou Harris** invited him to join her Hot Band. His career then blossomed as he formed his own band and became a driving force in country music's renaissance in the early 1980s. It may have seemed to some that bluegrass lost an enormous talent with Skaggs' entry into Nashville, but in fact he took and used many elements of bluegrass in his music, which inspired subsequent new country artists to do the same.

While Skaggs left bluegrass and became part of new country, the **New Grass Revival** came closest to making bluegrass itself a mainstream, commercially viable music, no longer a sub-culture. The main figure in this band has always

NORTH AMERICA

fiddle-player and singer **Alison Krauss** is currently the biggest album-seller in bluegrass. Still in her twenties, she is recognized as the top player of her generation, guesting on numerous albums by classic bluegrass names. Another woman instrumentalist, banjoist **Alison Brown**, is pretty hot, too.

That said, you'd have to look a long way to find a black bluegrass musician. The argument that the music is too culturally removed hardly holds water when bluegrass has been so readily embraced by the Japanese, who play to extraordinary degrees of excellence. The truth is probably that much of the bluegrass audience, particularly in the south, still lacks that sort of racial tolerance.

Today's bluegrass scene nonetheless offers a rich and broad combination of old-timers and brilliant youngsters. Bill Monroe, at the time of writing, is 82 and still playing concerts and festivals, as are Jimmy Martin, the Osborne Brothers and Ralph Stanley. Meanwhile, the **Nashville Bluegrass Band** are setting new standards, particularly in their selection of material – less obvious songs for a bluegrass band, songs picked for their intrinsic worth, not just a handy chord structure with which to show off.

It is still, however, hard to find a new young band who have the fire, the drive and the competitiveness of the first- and second-generation players. The music was born so directly out of hard times that with the increasingly middle-class background of so many young musicians, it will perhaps never return. As Bela Fleck of the New Grass Revival told me, "It's hard to sing about "My Little Cabin Home On the Hill" when you live on the eighteenth floor of a high-rise in Washington DC".

DISCOGRAPHY

OLD-TIME

ⓒ **The Carter Family** *Anchored in Love, 1927–28* and *My Clinch Mountain Home, 1928–29* (Rounder, US). These are the first two in a projected nine-CD reissue of the Carters' seminal recordings. History aside, they're a delight – pure harmonies and simple, affecting tunes.

Charlie Poole *Charlie Poole 1926–1930* (Historica, US). Fiddle, banjo and guitar full of quirks and oddities. Eminently listenable throughout.

ⓒ **The Louvin Brothers** *Radio Favourites 51–57* (CMF, US). A collection of radio recordings made at the Grand Ol' Opry and put together by the Country Music Foundation. Chet Atkins plays lead electric guitar on a couple of tracks. Audience sounds like it's at a football match.

ⓒ **Gid Tanner etc** *Early Mandolin Classics Vol I* (Rounder, US). Some riotous hoedowning from Gid Tanner's Skillet Lickers, and others.

OLD-TIME REVIVAL

ⓒ **Clarence Ashley** *Old Time Music at Clarence Ashley's Vol.s I & 2* (Smithsonian/Folkways, US). Clarence Ashley recorded on 78 in the 1930s and was sought out by Ralph Rinzler in the 60s to record these splendid sessions of local Appalachian music.

ⓒ **New Lost City Ramblers** *1963–1973* (Smithsonian/Folkways, US). Wonderful evocation of old-time music from this band of faithful revivalists. Includes such classics as "Cat's Got The Measles, Dog's Got The Whooping Cough" and "The Little Girl and the Dreadful Snake".

ⓒ **Doc Watson** *The Doc Watson Family* (Smithsonian/Folkways, US). The classic recordings by Ralph Rinzler that launch into a down-home atmosphere from the very first song, "Ground Hog". Wonderful.

CLASSIC BLUEGRASS

ⓒⓓ **Bill Monroe** *The Country Music Hall Of Fame* (MCA, US). A perfect introduction to the master: 16 of the best versions of his best songs from 1950 to 1988, among them "Walking in Jerusalem", "Blue Moon of Kentucky", the breakneck "Whitehouse Blues", and a duet with Ricky Skaggs.

Also highly recommended are a couple of recent live compilations ⓒ **Bill Monroe and the Bluegrass Boys** *Live Recordings, 1956–69* and ⓒ **Bill Monroe and Doc Watson** *Live Duet Recordings, 1963–1980* (Smithsonian/Folkways, US).

ⓒ **The Dillards** *There Is A Time* (Vanguard, US). The Dillards' best-known tracks from 1963 to 1970. Includes Doug Dillards' scintillating banjo on tracks such as "Banjo in the Hollow" and "The Old Home Place", before moving on to their country/pop of later years.

ⓒ **The Country Gentlemen** *Country Songs, Old and New* and *Folk Songs And Bluegrass* (Rounder, US). Dry, no-nonsense recordings made at the beginning of the folk revival in 1960 and 1961. *Country Songs* is probably the best as a starter.

ⓒ **Lester Flatt and Earl Scruggs** *The Golden Era* (Rounder, US). Crystal-clear recordings of the greatest guitar and banjo players, including "Earl's Breakdown", "Randy Lynn Rag" and "Jimmy Brown the Newsboy".

ⓒ **Various** *Mountain Music Bluegrass Style* (Smithsonian/Folkways, US). The fiddle playing by Tex Logan that opens this disc saws and swoops, and it continues in cracking style. Various local bluegrass bands recorded in living rooms and kitchens. Wonderful.

CONTEMPORARY BLUEGRASS

ⓒ **Alison Brown** *Twilight Motel* (Vanguard, US). Brown is one of the leading lights of progressive bluegrass, pushing out the boundaries with her banjo playing. Guests include Tony Rice on guitar and Jerry Douglas on dobro.

ⓒ **Alison Krauss** *I've Got That Old Feeling* (Rounder, US). The hottest property in contemporary bluegrass. Clear mountain singing and fine fiddle playing – the finest introduction to the modern sound and a Grammy award winner in 1991. She has recently recorded an album of gospel songs.

ⓒ **Nashville Bluegrass Band** *The Boys Are Back in Town* (Sugar Hill, US). The I.B.M.A. band of the year in 1993, featuring ace fiddle-player Stuart Duncan, and Roland White on mandolin. Beautifully recorded and arranged, this is state of the art bluegrass that could do with a couple of thousand volts putting through it but is very easy on the ear. An ideal introduction to bluegrass.

Here are some of the best:

⊕ **The Nitty Gritty Dirt Band** *Will the Circle be Unbroken* (Capitol, US). This country rock band were George Bush's favourites – though he never managed to get their name right. This double CD is a 1972 studio jam session with old-time, bluegrass and country stars of the day, including Jimmy Martin, Earl Scruggs and Doc Watson.

⊕ **Run C&W** *Into the Twangy-First Century* (MCA, US). "Soul music the way God intended – bluegrass style" is the claim from this band, featuring ex-Eagles banjoist Bernie Leadon. Includes "Stop in the Name of Love" and "Sweet Soul Music".

⊕ **Peter Schickele** *Black Forest Bluegrass* (Vanguard, US). Schickele (aka P.D.Q. Bach) mixes a bluegrass band with a chamber orchestra – and it works pretty well. "The Cantata: Blaues Gras" is hysterical.

⊕ **Various** *The Long Journey Home* (IBMA, US). A collection of bluegrass bands from round the world – British, Czech, French, Italian, Dutch, Finnish, Australian and Japanese!

ULTIMATE GUMBO

CAJUN, ZYDECO AND SWAMP : THE SOUNDS OF LOUISIANA

Head out of New Orleans along Highway 10 to Lafayette, a mess of gas stations and advertising hoardings, and you find yourself in the heart of Cajun and zydeco country. The music tends to be sold with images of alligators, swamps and spreading cypress trees draped with Spanish moss, but its home is not really the bayous, but the flat Louisiana prairies where farmers grow rice and cotton and farm crawfish. Simon Broughton lets the good times roll on some of the most thriving regional music in the United States: Cajun, zydeco, la-la and swamp pop.

Louisiana has always been one of the poorest states in the Union. The work is hard, the food is spicy – and the music is hard, spicy and relentless, with high, searing vocals backed by a belching accordion and a violin. The countless waltzes and two-steps often have a surface gaiety that masks an underlying bleakness and tragedy. Such is the essence of Cajun and zydeco music.

Lafayette, and the names of the surrounding towns and villages – Eunice, Mamou, Lawtell, Lacassine, Kaplan – resonate through the history of Cajun music in the titles of countless tunes that have rung out every weekend in southwest Louisiana longer than anyone can remember. Despite periods of repression and neglect, Cajun and zydeco music are currently enjoying enormous popularity at home and around the world. Even Paul Simon – a man who knows a music that can transform – has cashed in, enlisting the super-charged backing of Rockin' Dopsie on his "Graceland" album.

LES BONS TEMPS ROULER

The French ancestors of the Cajuns were settled at the other end of North America in the place they called Acadia (now Nova Scotia, Canada) until they were kicked out by the British as a result of colonial squabbling in 1755. Some Acadians were repatriated to France, others made their way to the French West Indies, but many of them, after years of wandering, found their way to Louisiana, where they established themselves as the dominant clique among the other European and Afro-Caribbean groups in the region.

The culture of the Louisiana Acadians, corrupted to "Cajuns", arose out of this multicultural gumbo. Many of the old Cajun folk songs have French equivalents, while others are based on European contradanses or incorporate elements from Anglo-American or Caribbean traditions. Arhoolie have released a collection of eighteenth- and nineteenth-century songs ("Folksongs of the Louisiana Acadians"), in a revealing cross section of styles, recorded in Mamou in the late 1950s.

Along with Acadian traditions, the Cajuns brought with them the celebrated ideology of "laissez les bons temps rouler". And today they are still letting the good times roll in bars and dancehalls right across southwest Louisiana, to the sound of melancholy waltzes and driving two-steps. "The people are not interested in music for the sake of music," says accordionist Marc Savoy. "They're interested in the atmosphere this music creates, so that they can socialize, so they can drink and relate to one another. Music is the glue that holds the whole culture and society together."

Language plays a part, too. Although many of the more commercial Cajun and zydeco bands sing in English, many do not, and the French language – resurgent after years of marginalization – remains central to a region that stubbornly resists assimilation into the American mainstream.

FIDDLES AND ACCORDIONS

Before the advent of the accordion it was the fiddle that played at Louisiana *bals du maison* – house parties and dances. Cajun fiddlers adopted a double-string bowing technique, playing a drone beneath the melody to be better heard over the dancing feet.

Some performed in pairs, playing a lead and rhythmic backing, a style continued by the famous duo of **Dennis McGee and Sady Courville**, until McGee's death, aged 96, in 1989. McGee was really the last of the old-time Cajun fiddlers, with a repertoire and style established in those days before the accordion took over. His wonderful fiddle recordings are a window on another era, as are those of **Varise Connor** and **Wade Frugé**.

What we now think of as the typical Cajun ensemble, however, arrived with the introduction of the accordion as prime instrument, with fiddle and guitar or triangle for rhythmic backing, in the 1920s. The accordion owed part of its rise to its more durable aspect in the hot and humid Louisiana air, but it could also play both melody and accompaniment, and its volume was a great asset in the packed and noisy dancehalls.

With this new instrument came a new style of Cajun music, since the accordion wasn't appropriate for the old-style fiddle tunes with their idiosyncratic harmonies, complex half-tones and ornaments. With it, too, came the first Cajun **recordings**, by accordionist **Joseph Falcon** and his guitarist wife **Cleoma**. Their first record, "Allons à Lafayette", was recorded in a hotel room in New Orleans in 1928 and released as a Columbia 78, with "La valse qui ma portin" (The Waltz That Carried Me To My Grave) on the B-side. It sold thousands in Louisiana, Texas, and across the USA. Soon after, **Amédée Breaux**, Falcon's brother-in-law, recorded the most famous Cajun song of all time, **"Jolie Blonde"**.

Many of the songs from this period are classics that have retained a place in the popular repertoire for over sixty years. Listen to the recordings of "Jolie Blonde" – the string band versions of the Hackberry Ramblers in the 1930s and Harry Choates in the 1940s; the return of the accordion in the 1950s with Iry LeJeune's soulful recording of "La fitte la vove" (same tune, different lyrics); Vin Bruce's 1960s country-style version with slide-guitar and fiddle; Willie Green's zydeco recording with a heavy tinge of blues; right up to 1989's modern Cajun pop version from Jo-El Sonnier, and Eddie LeJeune's blistering old-style rendering – and you have a thumbnail sketch of half a century's development in Cajun music.

The other key musician in these early recordings was **Amédée Ardoin**, a black

Joseph and Cleoma Falcon: the first ever Cajun recording artists

accordionist. It was rare in those days for a black musician to play at white gigs (and not common even today) but Amédée was respected and hugely popular at house parties and dancehalls. The band could make $2.50 playing at a white dance, whereas at black dances they'd pass a hat around. Amédée was renowned not only for his accordion style but for his immense vocal power and range and his ability to perform for hours on end. The recordings he made with Dennis McGee on fiddle were to be an inspiration to the next generation of accordionists like Iry LeJeune and Nathan Abshire. Amédée died tragically in 1941 after what seems to have been some sort of racial attack. Ironically what his music demonstrates is the common roots of white Cajun and black zydeco music (of which more below), and their rich cross-fertilization over the years.

SWINGS AND LEJEUNES

Oil was discovered in Louisiana early this century, and its effects were soon felt with an influx of new money and a strong Anglo-American presence. French was banned in the schools established by the Americans and before long upwardly mobile Cajuns were regarding French culture as backward and embarrassing, and a widespread "acculturation" took place. Musically this resulted in the new-style Cajun sound of the 1930s: **string bands** influenced by hillbilly music and western swing. The **Hackberry Ramblers** were the leaders of the new trend; their fiddler, Luderin Darbone, had learned to play through a correspondence course and by listening to hillbilly fiddlers in Texas.

Along with lilting versions of Cajun classics, the Ramblers recorded new songs like "Une piastre ici, une piastre là-bas", which reflected life in recession-torn America:

When I was twenty-one years old
My father told me it was time
Time to stop spending
A dollar here, a dollar there.

The Hackberrys and other new bands were fiddle- and guitar-led and boasted drum kits and electric steel guitars. With amplification the fiddlers could be heard in the noisiest dancehalls and they adopted a smoother, lighter touch, abandoning the soulful intensity of the earlier styles. The most popular Cajun fiddler of this period was **Harry Choates**, of "Port Arthur Blues" fame, who brought some English lyrics into the Cajun gumbo and recorded his share of western swing standards. Other notables were **Leo Soileau** and **J.B. Fuselier**.

Probably the greatest Cajun accordionist of all time, **Iry LeJeune** is recognized as the musician who brought the soul back into Cajun music with his piercing vocals and poignant playing style. After 1755, the seminal date in the history of Cajun music is the release of his "La valse du pont d'amour" (The Lovebridge Waltz) in 1948. LeJeune was the son of a tenant farmer, but being nearly blind he couldn't help out in the fields and spent his time practising the accordion. Inspired by the old recordings of Amédée Ardoin, he eventually went out to play his rustic-sounding music, carrying his accordion in a flour-sack.

The release of "The Lovebridge Waltz" and other Iry LeJeune recordings has earned Eddie Shuler's **Goldband Records** a distinguished place in Cajun history. Quite why these records were so popular after years of slick Americanized music is unclear – perhaps people craved the security of their homegrown culture after World War II – but Iry LeJeune certainly gave the identity of Cajun music a much-needed boost. He died at the height of his career, hit by a car on October 8, 1955 (one of a disquieting number of Cajun musicians to have met unfortunate deaths), but his work is continued by his son Eddie LeJeune, and Iry's old recordings, despite their poor quality, are still enjoyed by new generations.

The other great accordionist of this period was **Nathan Abshire**, whose "Pinegrove Blues" has become a Cajun classic. His style was much more exuberant and bluesy than LeJeune's, and he lived long enough to enjoy the international interest that Cajun music began to receive from the 1960s on. Abshire created some of the greatest Cajun music and, though he remained poor and illiterate, was one of the most celebrated representatives of Cajun culture until his death in 1981.

While this old-style revival was in progress, popular music in America continued to develop apace and Cajun musicians like **Laurence Walker** and **Doug Kershaw** recorded songs in English, embracing the new sounds of rock'n'roll and Nashville. Such music is often considered a dilution of the Cajun patrimony, but it was merely the start of the broadening out of the tradition into the range of voices in evidence today. The 1960s Cajun rock'n'roll recordings of Laurence Walker and **Aldus Roger** have these days achieved quite a revered status, in recognition of its distinctive hybrid form.

In the early 1960s the growth of the **national folk revival** movement drew attention to the unassimilated cultures of the United States, and from 1964 Cajun musicians were regularly invited to play at the **National Folk Festival** in Newport, Rhode Island. Their rapturous reception meant that musicians like the Balfa Brothers, Nathan Abshire, Canray Fontenot and Clifton Chenier began to enjoy a national reputation and increased respect at home. Then in 1968 the Council for the Development of French in Louisiana (CoDoFiL) was created, reversing the official policy of the previous decades, and French-language education was established at all levels. The Council has since been responsible for promoting French culture on a musical level through events like the annual **Festivals Acadiens** in Lafayette and the **Zydeco Festival** in Plaisance, the largest annual Cajun and zydeco music gatherings.

THE CAJUN AMBASSADORS

If there's one group that represents the quintessential Cajun sound it must be the **Balfa Brothers**. The sons of a sharecropper in Grand Louis, brothers Will and Dewey played the fiddle and Rodney the guitar, alongside accordionists like Hadley Fontenot and Nathan Abshire. Their repertoire is a glossary of Cajun's all-time greats, played in a pure acoustic style, renowned for its intense vocals and wonderful fiddle duets.

The Balfa Brothers were Cajun music's greatest ambassadors, playing at festivals throughout America and abroad, while at home Will's regular job was driving a bulldozer and Dewey's the school bus. All of this came to an end when Will and Rodney were killed in a road accident in 1978, but Dewey continued to play, making an appearance with Marc Savoy among a bunch of threatening bayou musicians in Walter Hill's film *Southern Comfort*. Highly regarded as a teacher, he had Cajun music introduced into the school curriculum and was considered the grand old man of Cajun music until his death in 1992.

Iry LeJeune taking a cigarette break with Wilson Granger (fiddle) and Alfred "Duckhead" Cormier (guitar)

Two of today's best Cajun musicians were part of the close circle around Dewey Balfa. Accordionist **Marc Savoy** runs the Savoy Music Center in Eunice, where he makes Acadian accordions that are considered the finest in the business. He fights a personal crusade against the "coonass" Cajuns who have debased their culture under the influence of cheap American values. His workshop and store are dotted with placards announcing "No one ever went broke underestimating the taste of the American public!" and "An imitation of something is always more popular than that which is being imitated". The latter is a reference to the Cajun musicians who rushed to pick up their forgotten accordions as soon as Cajun music began to attract international attention, and who play with none of the artistry and understanding of the truly dedicated Cajun musician.

Cajun purists Michael Doucet, Marc and Ann Savoy

Born in 1940 on a rice farm near Eunice, Savoy was captivated early on by his grandfather's fiddle playing. "Sometimes, I would arrive at my grandfather's farm and be fortunate enough to hear a jam session between Dennis McGee, who was at one time a tenant farmer on my grandfather's farm, and my grandfather. But I knew that times were changing. A new lifestyle, and one that was less meaningful, was being grafted onto the old ways. To me it was as though the younger folks were giving up a delicious bowl of gumbo for a cold and tasteless hot dog."

Marc plays accordion in the excellent **Savoy-Doucet Cajun band**, with his wife Ann on guitar and Michael Doucet on fiddle. Ann has also published a book, "Cajun Music – A Reflection of People", collecting song lyrics and interviews with some of the best Cajun musicians. The band don't play local dances, but do perform at festivals and on tour – when you can't keep people in their seats. On Saturday mornings the music store showroom plays host to Cajun jam sessions for talented local musicians and visitors.

Alongside Marc Savoy, the other leader of the Cajun renaissance is **Michael Doucet**, whose own group **Beausoleil** has gone through various configurations – with drums, electric guitars and even saxophone in the line-up – but now concentrates on high-quality traditional Cajun music with a repertoire that goes well beyond the standards. The group takes its name from the Acadian resistance leader Joseph Broussard, aka Beausoleil, who founded the town in Louisiana that bears his name. Doucet only took up the fiddle in 1974, but lists among his teachers some of the most distinguished names in Cajun music – Varise Connor, Dewey Balfa, Canray Fontenot, and especially Dennis McGee.

While Marc Savoy and Michael Doucet are the intellectual leaders of the traditional Cajun revival, the accordionist **Eddie LeJeune**, a worthy heir to his father's legacy, and songwriter and guitarist **D.L. Menard** (see boxes), author of the all-time favourite "La porte en arrière" (The Back Door), are two of its most instinctive exponents.

COMMERCIALIZED CAJUN

At the other end of the scale there are many commercially successful groups and musicians who have introduced elements of blues, rock and country into the Cajun sound. Which begs the question – how soon does it stop being Cajun music? Marc Savoy, from his purist viewpoint, sees this development as a shallow manifestation of coonass culture: "The sad thing is that the good groups are unrecognized and the people who know the recipe of the music are not understood by outsiders. It's not so much the melodies as that elusive thing that comes from living in this heat and this

D.L. MENARD

....

DL Menard's house in Erath is like everybody's dream of rural living in Louisiana – a spacious front and back porch furnished with the rockers he makes in his cottage-industry rocking-chair factory next door. He and his wife Louella are two of the most warm and generous-hearted people you could hope to meet.

When he sings, D.L. has a nasal voice that you might imagine coming out of some furry swamp mammal. He started playing the guitar and singing in the late 1940s when country music was in vogue and his most distinctive songs with the Louisiana Aces have a country feel to them, with accordion, violin and steel guitar.

"I bought me my first guitar when I was sixteen and a half years old. I found it in the Montgomery Ward catalogue and I had to pay eleven dollars for it. That was a mail order guitar and it came to the post office in Erath. At seventeen I played my first dance and I've been playing ever since."

D.L. wrote his most popular song, "The Back Door", in 1961 and it has become the second Cajun national anthem, alongside "Jolie Blonde". "When I wrote that song I had no idea it was going to be a hit, but every time I picked up my guitar my kids asked me to sing that song. I recorded it mainly so that the kids would have a souvenir of the song after I'd passed away. I had

to pay for recording it because we were an unknown group. But it made a hit and still every Cajun band is playing it."

D.L.'s chief musical influence was Hank Williams, whom he met when playing at the Teche Club in New Iberia in 1951. "Everybody calls me the Cajun Hank Williams, but I know better that there was only one Hank Williams and nobody will replace him. But I have a lot of Hank Williams' style and every time I write a song it's not pure Cajun – there's that country flavour in it. He's the one responsible for me being on stage today, so I feel I owe it to him to sing a couple of Hank Williams songs in every show I make. And when I met him he told me something important about songwriting. He said, "it's the feelings that make a song. When you write and when you sing a song, just pretend that it's happening to you and then it's going to come out right.""

The Back Door
Me and my girl had gone to the dance
We went to all the Honky-Tonks
We came back the next morning
The day was breaking
I came in by the back door.

Eddie Le Jeune and D. L. Menard hanging out by the back door

EDDIE LEJEUNE

....

As the son of Iry LeJeune, the greatest Cajun accordionist of all time, Eddie LeJeune had an awful lot to live up to. However, he is cut it and is without doubt the most honest and soulful accordionist and singer in Cajun music today.

"Pure and traditional Cajun music is not only performing on stage, but anywhere you perform – at a house dance or a party. Your feelings and the expression you give out must come straight from the heart, not just from the lyrics. And your feelings are expressed also in the way you play your instrument.

"The way I am playing and recording today with just three instruments – an accordion, fiddle and guitar – is the way my father played and peo-ple even before my father. When you have more people in a band it takes out your personal feelings in the music. When you're playing three musicians you can control the music and just go for it as the mood takes you and express yourself better.

"I feel very proud when I play my father's songs because although I'll never be the musician my father was, at least I have the ability to carry on good, clean, pure, traditional Cajun music. And there are times when I have gotten into it so much that I don't even see the crowd in front of me, because when I sing I close my eyes and this true feeling comes from my heart and the audience captures it as well. These feelings are very emotional and it does penetrate."

---

environment. But for outsiders it's foreign and they can't relate to it. It's like pizza – you don't like Italian pizza because you're used to American pizza. What sells these bands are not the distinctive differences in the music, but the assimilation into mainstream American music. The real masters are not getting the recognition and people who know a hundredth of what they know are becoming instantly famous. Of course music must change, but when you add coconuts to gumbo it stops being gumbo."

For those who would like to try some coconut in their gumbo, accordionist **Zachary Richard** plays a rock-inspired hybrid of Cajun and zydeco; **Filé** stick much closer to mainstream rock'n'roll while keeping the accordion centre-stage. **Jo-El Sonnier**'s music has a distinct country feel, and apart from "Cajun Life" (Rounder), an album of laid-back Cajun classics, he has recorded most of his songs in English. **Wayne Toups** and **Zydecajun** probably set the Balfas spinning in their graves and will send Marc Savoy to an early one.

The best of the bunch, perhaps, are **Steve Riley and the Mamou Playboys**, whose line-up of accordion, fiddle, guitar, drums and triangle is pretty traditional, although their mission is to "perpetuate the styles and repertoires" of their mentors while "recharging the songs of the past with the vitality of the present".

LA-LA: OLD-STYLE CREOLE

Zydeco, the music of the blacks of Louisiana, is if anything a more dynamic force than Cajun right now and enjoying significant international success. According to Rockin' Dopsie's definition, zydeco is "a little jazz, a little blues, a little French and a little rhythm 'n' blues, all mixed together". Whereas many of these influences have upset the delicate balance of Cajun music, they have been easily assimilated by the more robust zydeco.

Cajun country was never a major slave region and the black population often came to Louisiana from other parts of the New World and the Caribbean to work as tenant farmers. The earliest Creole music was made in the fields, without instruments, the singing backed up by clapping and stomping. Creole musicians rarely had enough money to buy instruments, but the few black accordionists that did were formidable players. **Amédée Ardoin**'s influence on Cajun music was huge, and recordings from the 1920s and 30s reveal that black and white music had much in common at that time. Other big names include the accordionists **Sidney Babineaux** and **Adam Fontenot**; and in the next generation, his violinist son **Canray Fontenot**, accordionist **Alphonse Ardoin** (cousin of Amédée) and the **Carrière Brothers**.

The old-style music these guys played – and in some cases still do – is the forerunner to zydeco, called **la-la**. Less melodic than Cajun music, its sound was a combination of accordion and fiddle, backed up by washboard, with a definite spring in the rhythm and a marked R&B influence.

Greatest of the old-style Creole musicians active today is the fiddler **Canray Fontenot**. At the age of nine he made his first fiddle, out of a wooden cigarbox strung with wire, and played it for two years until his uncle bought him a real violin. Canray's songs are highly personal, reflecting the hardships and joys of his life, and he has at last received due recognition, making dozens of recordings and appearing at festivals around the world. His most celebrated partnership has been with accordionist **Alphonse "Bois Sec" Ardoin** and the pair of

them are responsible for some of the best la-la recordings around. They often perform at the club run by Bois Sec's son, next to the Ardoin family house in Duralde, and if you're lucky enough to catch a performance, you're in for the ultimate old-time Creole experience.

Practically the only other group still playing the old-style repertoire are the the **Lawtell Playboys**, featuring the renowned fiddler Calvin Carrière, who perform around the Opelousas area.

CLIFTON CHENIER'S ZYDECO

What we now call zydeco music dates from the postwar years and is largely the creation of one man, **Clifton Chenier**. Born in 1925 on a farm

---

SWAMP POP

· ·

The local record companies of south Louisiana produce another sort of music that sells in much greater quantities than either Cajun or zydeco: **swamp pop**. These are most often cover versions of popular rock'n'roll hits, aimed at the local market, but to put it in these terms is to seriously understate the music's charm and energy.

"Swamp pop is just our old south Louisiana sound," says Floyd Soileau of Swallow Records, searching for a definition. "Sometimes it's bluesy, sometimes it's country and sometimes it has a heavy Cajun accent. It's that gumbo, that mixture of all those influences," he adds, falling back on the usual analogy. "When you hear something that was cut down here, you'll always be able to say "Aha, that was cut in south Louisiana!" If you're after a slick sound, you're not going to come down here to cut it! Just as we have an accent, our music will also have that little accent." The fact that they sound as if they were made thirty years ago gives the records something of a timeless quality. An accordion often features in the mix, and they can be guaranteed to end with a steep, inelegant fade.

A surprising number of swamp pop releases climbed into the Billboard Top 100 in the 1960s and **Tommy McLain's** rendition of "Sweet Dreams" even made the Top 10 in 1966, giving it the bizarre distinction of being the biggest hit to come out of Ville Platte. But it's not their national success that makes these records interesting, but their characteristic local eccen-

tricity. Alongside Tommy McLain, whose recording of "Before I Grow Too Old" is another classic, the other big names of the 1960s were **Johnnie Allan**, **Phil Phillips**, **Cleveland Crochet**, **Belton Richard** (also a notable Cajun singer and accordionist) and **Cookie and the Cupcakes**, a black group from Lake Charles who are still performing.

Floyd Soileau recalls as one of his studio's proudest moments the recording of Johnnie Allan's "Promised Land". This cover of Chuck Berry's song, reinforced with driving accordion breaks, has become the swamp pop anthem. "I was working with Johnny on the song and he thought we should throw a little seasoning in and get Belton Richard to do the accordion. He came in, heard it through and just put the accordion in on the first take. The rest is history!"

In lounges and studios across south Louisiana, swamp pop is still being played and recorded. One of the best releases of recent years is the **Charles Mann** version of Dire Straits' "Walk of Life", supercharged with accordion, which was recorded in the "studio" (a converted bar) of Lanor Records in Church Point. Charles Mann can be seen performing in dancehalls across the region, though much of the rest of his repertoire is cloyingly sentimental. Should you need any persuading to set foot inside Louisiana's drinking establishments, however, the best way to hear the current swamp pop hits is to frequent the bars and feed the jukeboxes.

near Opelousas – still the centre of zydeco territory – Chenier grew up working in the fields of cotton, rice, sugar and corn. It wasn't until the late 1940s, when he was employed at the oil refinery in Lake Charles, that he picked up the accordion and began playing at dances. Signed up by Speciality Records, an R&B label, in 1955, he went on to record over a hundred albums for numerous labels until his death in 1987. Over his forty years of performing, Clifton's repertoire included everything from simple rustic zydeco to major hits with the **Red Hot Louisiana Band**. Nobody questions his title "King of Zydeco".

Chenier transformed the old-style la-la music into the bluesy and rock-based zydeco sound of today, which is led by the accordion and backed by heavy drums, guitar, electric bass, and sometimes saxophone or brass. Adding its unmistakable rasp to the sound is the *frottoir*, the old washboard reincarnated as a more versatile corrugated steel vest, played with spoons or bottle openers. Frottoir playing was developed into a real art form by Clifton's brother, **Cleveland Chenier**, who played with blues singer Lightnin' Hopkins as well as in his brother's band. Like many zydeco musicians, Clifton favoured the triple-row or piano-key accordions, with their wider range of chromatic "bluesy" notes than the simpler double-row accordions preferred by Cajun musicians.

While the word "Cajun" comes from a diminution of Acadian, "zydeco" is, oddly, a corruption of *les haricots* – runner beans. Taken from the old Creole song "Les haricots sont pas salés" (The Beans Aren't Salty), recorded and popularized by Clifton Chenier as "Zydeco sont pas salé", the term somehow came to represent the musical style.

ZYDECO TODAY

The zydeco sound begun by Clifton Chenier has gone from strength to strength, and nowadays over a weekend in Lafayette, or at Richard's and Slim's Y-Ki-Ki, two famous zydeco clubs near Opelousas, it's virtually guaranteed that you'll hear some top-class players. Despite the number of recordings now available, zydeco is really a music that demands to be heard live – to feel that relentless beat on the floor of the dancehall, to hear the wild accordion and get swept up in the action and the sweat of the dance.

The elder statesman of zydeco today is **Boozoo Chavis**, a contemporary of Clifton

Zydeco godfather Clifton Chenier

Chenier, who had his first big hit, "Paper in My Shoe", on Eddie Shuler's Goldband Records in 1954. Several unsatisfactory takes of the song were recorded over three days, until Shuler struck on the idea of loosening up the band with whisky. The story goes that at the end of the take that was finally released, Boozoo fell out of his chair but carried on playing nonetheless; Shuler had to fade the track out (a technique that was new at the time) to hide the crash. After a brief career in the 1950s, Boozoo retired to concentrate on breeding racehorses, only to make an acclaimed comeback in the mid-1980s. He has played gigs right across the US – although he's still best heard on his home territory.

After Clifton Chenier's death, the "King of Zydeco" title had fallen to **Rockin' Dopsie**, who was crowned in 1988 by the Mayor of Lafayette. He died in 1993, however, and the crown is again up for grabs. Contenders among today's leading lights must include Boozoo Chavis, and **Rockin' Sidney**, author of zydeco's biggest hit, "My Toot Toot". Meanwhile, the undisputed "Queen of Zydeco" is **Queen Ida**, a singer and accordion player with a modern rootsy sound.

Without doubt, today's most successful group is **Buckwheat Zydeco**, led by Stanley Dural Jnr, who played for two and a half years in Clifton Chenier's Red Hot Louisiana Band. The band are signed to Island – one of the few zydeco acts on a major label – and featured in the Hollywood film *The Big Easy*. Possibly the best group, however, is **John Delafose and the Eunice Playboys**, who play highly rhythmic zydeco with an Afro-Caribbean flavour. John Delafose is a veteran accordionist of the same generation as Boozoo Chavis and Rockin' Dopsie, who has been performing at dances in the Eunice area for years; his sons Geno and Tony are now in the band. Their album "Père et Garçon" is the best zydeco release in years, containing dances

Queen Ida giving it some wellie

deeply rooted in Louisiana tradition from the likes of Amédée Ardoin and Clifton Chenier, as well as their own material. On stage they bring a violin into the line-up for the more rootsy stuff before launching into their own funky repertoire.

Another musical family to look out for are **Roy and "Chubby" Carrier**, a pair of terrific accordion players based at the delightfully out-of-the-way Offshore Lounge in Lawtell. Family, says "Chubby", is the key ingredient in traditional zydeco music. "Families is what's happening. We played zydeco music; it wasn't played nowhere else but in our homes. We keep ourselves together. When we come back from mass on Sundays, we have cookouts – then we have our music. Mom would actually move her coffee table – that was our dancefloor, in our living room."

"Chubby" Carrier and **Beau Jocque**, another accordion player now making waves, are part of the new generation of Creole musicians who have grown up with the mainstream acceptance of zydeco music. They are both up and coming names on the thumping zydeco map of south Louisiana and on the international scene.

DANCEHALLS AND FESTIVALS

· ·

The best way to hear both Cajun and zydeco is live and in situ, and there are any number of clubs in and around Lafayette to choose from, as well as two great festivals. Beware, though, that the region's predominantly Catholic faith means that dances often stop for Lent – after the big Mardi Gras celebration everything quietens down till Easter.

FESTIVALS

Festivals Acadiens, Lafayette (☎318/232-3808). A celebration of regional music, food and crafts in the third week of September. Girard Park hosts the music festival on Saturday and Sunday and there's an expanded Downtown Alive! Dance in Jefferson St on Friday night.

Zydeco Festival, Plaisance (between Opelousas and Ville Platte; ☎318/942-2392). Louisiana's main zydeco festival, held the Saturday before Labor Day (the first Mon in Sept), with music from 11am to midnight.

DANCEHALLS

Borque's, Lewisburg (☎318/948-9904). The most picturesque of dancehalls, 9 miles south of Opelousas. Saturday and Sunday evenings.

Dup's Lounge, Rt 13 N, Eunice (☎318/457-9162). Four miles north of Eunice, Dup's is a run-down cabin with sawdust on the floor – perfect. The Saturday afternoon dance makes it the ideal stop after Fred's Lounge.

El Sido's, 1523 Martin Luther King Dr, Lafayette (☎318/235-0647). Large dancefloor with zydeco dances on Friday and Saturday nights. Nathan and the zydeco Cha-Chas are regulars.

Fred's Lounge, Sixth St, Mamou (☎318/468-5411). The Saturday morning live radio broadcast has made this a place of pilgrimage for Cajun music fans. The current band is Don Thibodeaux and Cajun Fever.

Gilton's Lounge, US-190 E and Rt 95, Eunice (☎318/457-1241). Cavernous zydeco dancehall that sees some of the big names – and was immortalized in song by Boozoo Chavis.

Grant Street Dancehall, 1113 W Grant St, Lafayette (☎318/237-8513). Premier Lafayette nightclub for Cajun, zydeco and other bands.

Hamilton's, 1808 Verot School Rd, Lafayette (☎318/984-5583). Wooden-frame zydeco dancehall on the southern fringe of Lafayette.

Mulate's, 325 Mills Ave (Rt 94), Breaux Bridge (☎318/332-4648). The world's most famous Cajun restaurant with live Cajun music, generally of superior quality.

Offshore Lounge, off US-190, Lawtell (☎318/543-9996). Set back behind the railtracks in Lawtell, next to some fine wooden houses (a landmark you'll need), this is a fine zydeco dancehall run by accordionist Roy Carrier.

Papa Paul's, Poinciana (Rt 1160) and 2nd St, Mamou (☎318/468-5538). A first-rate old-style zydeco dancehall with dances virtually every weekend.

Rainbeaux Club, 1373 Rt 182 W, New Iberia (☎318/367-6731). Large old-fashioned dancehall with Saturday night Cajun dances.

Richard's Club, US-190 W, Lawtell (☎318/543-6596). A premier zydeco venue in the Opelousas area. Weekend dances in a wooden building with a homely atmosphere.

Slim's Y-Ki-Ki, Rt 167 N, Opelousas (☎318/942-9980). One of Louisiana's top zydeco dancehalls since 1947. Hot, crowded and highly recommended.

LABELS AND RADIO STATIONS

C rucial to the survival and development of Cajun music has been the symbiotic relationship between the local record producers, the regional radio stations broadcasting French music and the jukeboxes that are an essential feature of every south Louisiana bar and lounge.

The small independent record labels first started to appear around the late 1950s. Based in the tiny towns of Lake Charles, Crowley, Ville Platte and Church Point respectively, Eddie Shuler's **Goldband Records**, Jay Miller's **Modern Music**, Floyd Soileau's **Swallow Records** and Lee Lavergne's **Lanor Records** have all been integral to the success of Louisiana's music. Each label has had its share of hits, but for the most part it has been a matter of steering a precarious course through the economic swamps and bayous, to produce records on archaic-looking steam presses inside sheds that open directly onto the prairies.

Dotted across the same area are a dozen or so local **radio stations** that regularly broadcast Cajun and zydeco music. Indicative of Louisiana's

hard-working agricultural life are the early-morning Cajun music programmes, scheduled to give a quick blast of accordion before a day in the rice fields.

The most famous Cajun radio show is the weekly live broadcast from Fred's Lounge in Mamou on KVPI (1050 AM), a station that has been broadcasting French music since 1957. At 9am on Saturday morning **Fred's Lounge**, an ugly brick building that looks from the outside like a toilet, is packed to bursting with revellers swigging beer, waltzing and two-stepping within the ropes that mark the dancefloor.

Illuminated beer signs share the walls with stern notices from Fred – "Please do not stand on the tables, chairs, cigarette machine, booths, jukebox and chairs" and "This is not a dance hall. If you get hurt dancing we are not responsible" – which make letting the good times roll seem rather perilous. The radio show is MC'd by Martel Ardoin, his basic broadcasting gear set up on a wooden table, who reads ads in French for local feed mills, a filling station and Jack Miller's Barbecue Sauce.

John Delafose and the Eunice Playboys

DISCOGRAPHY

GENERAL COMPILATIONS

ⓒ **Various** *J'ai été au bal Vols 1 & 2* (Arhoolie, US). These two
CDs are the most comprehensive introduction to Cajun and
Zydeco music, although the emphasis is more on Cajun. From
early recordings of Joseph Falcon, Amédée Ardoin and Dennis
McGee to Clifton Chenier, Michael Doucet and Wayne Toups.

CLASSIC CAJUN

ⓒ **Nathan Abshire** *French Blues* (Arhoolie, US). The classic
"Pine Grove Blues" and othe 1940s and 50s recordings.

ⓒ **The Balfa Brothers** *Traditional Cajun Music* (Swallow,
US/Ace, UK). Two albums on one CD containing some of the
all-time great Cajun songs. Definitive performances.

ⓒ **Hackberry Ramblers** *Jolie Blonde* (Arhoolie, US). The
Hackberry Ramblers made a hit with their swing version of
"Jolie Blonde" in 1935 and two of them are still playing today.
These are their best recordings from the 1960s.

ⓒ **Iry LeJeune** *Cajun's Greatest* (Goldband, US/Ace, UK). The
collected legacy of the legendary Cajun accordionist. Not hi-fi

recordings, but essential. Listen out for LeJeune's dog on the
"Duraldo Waltz".

Dennis McGee *La Vieille Musique Acadienne* (Swallow,
US). The celebrated Cajun fiddler, playing with his partner Sady Courville. A CD is in the works from Shanachie.

ⓒ **D. L. Menard and Austin Pitre** *The Swallow Recordings*
(Swallow, US/Ace,UK). A first-class compilation of two of
Louisiana's greatest – singer, songwriter and guitarist D. L. and
wild accordionist Austin Pitre. Popular Cajun honky-tonk from
the 1960s. Includes D.L.'s classic, "The Back Door".

ⓒ **Wallace "Cheese" Reed** *Cajun House Party* (Arhoolie, US).
A real cracker of down-home music with Cheese on fiddle
and vocal duty and Marc Savoy on accordion.

ⓒ **Various** *Allons Cajun Rock 'n' Roll* (Ace, UK). Aldus Roger,
Laurence Walker and other exponents of 1960s Cajun meets
rock. Close your eyes and imagine the jukebox in Louisiana.

ⓒ **Various** *Folksongs of the Louisiana Acadians* (Arhoolie, US).
This collection of 1950s recordings amounts to a social history
of the Cajun people. Excellent sleevenotes, too.

CONTEMPORARY CAJUN

Eddie LeJeune *Cajun Soul* (Rounder, US/Hannibal, UK). One of the very best of recent Cajun albums. Eddie on accordion includes a few of his father's classic songs, with D. L. Menard on guitar and Ken Smith on fiddle.

Michael Doucet *Beau solo* (Arhoolie, US). Some old favourites and more unusual choices from one of the leaders of the Cajun revival.

Steve Riley and the Mamou Playboys *'Tit Galop pour Mamou* (Rounder, US). One of the best of the young bands.

Various *Louisiana Chanky-Chank* (Zane Records, UK). A quirky selection of releases on Lanor Records from the 1980s, plus the wonderful Shirley Bergeron (a man) from the '60s.

CLASSIC ZYDECO

Various *Zydeco – The Early Years* (Arhoolie, US). Live recordings of small Zydeco bands in the early 1960s including Clifton Chenier's first cuts.

Clifton Chenier *60 Minutes with the King of Zydeco* (Arhoolie, US). A good compilation of Clifton's recordings throughout his career, including "Zydeco sont pas salé".

Canray Fontenot *Louisiana Hot Sauce, Creole Style* (Arhoolie, US). A wonderful compilation highlighting the earthy music of Louisiana's veteran Creole fiddler.

CONTEMPORARY ZYDECO

Buckwheat Zydeco *Waitin' For My Ya Ya* (Rounder, US). Stanley "Buckwheat" Dural is among the most commercially successful of today's zydeco musician, with a strong Soul and R&B influence.

Roy "Chubby" Carrier *Boogie Woogie Zydeco* (Flying Fish, US). One of Zydeco's liveliest up and coming names.

Boozoo Chavis and Nathan and the Zydeco Cha-Chas *Zydeco Live!* (Rounder, US). While Boozoo Chavis is one of the legendary elder statesmen of zydeco, Nathan Williams represents its youthful wing. Live recordings in Richard's Club.

John Delafose and the Eunice Playboys *Père et garçon* (Rounder, US). Two generations of first-class zydeco musicians playing great music.

Beau Jocque and the Zydeco Hi-Rollers *Pick up on This!* (Rounder, US). The funkiest sound on the zydeco scene: high energy, heavy on the bass, and hugely enjoyable. As Beau Jocque sings, "the Hi-Rollers play a little harder".

Rockin' Sidney *My Toot Toot* (Ace, UK). A great cross section of Sidney's output from the early 1960s and mid-80s, including, of course "My Toot Toot", his most successful cut.

Various *Zydeco Blues 'n' Boogie* (Cooking Vinyl, UK). A great collection of zydeco meets swamp pop from the Lanor label in Church Point. The sort of music you discover with a well-placed dime on the local jukeboxes.

SWAMP POP

Various *Another Saturday Night* (Ace, UK). The essential swamp pop compilation. Tommy McLain's "Before I Grow Too Old", Belton Richard's "Another Sleepless Night" and Johnnie Allan's "Promised Land" and more.

Various *Louisiana Saturday Night* (Ace, UK). A splendid follow-up to the disc above. More Johnnie Allan plus Rusty and Doug Kershaw, Cookie and The Cupcakes and the swamp pop version of "Jolie Blonde" with Rod Bernard and Clifton Chenier sounding like a barrel organ gone wild.

Various *Eddie's House of Hits* (Ace, UK). A jiving collection of swamp pop hits from Eddie Shuler's Goldband Records. Phil Phillips, Cleveland Crochet and the teenage Dolly Parton.

Charles Mann *Walk of Life* (Cooking Vinyl, UK). Mann's version of the Mark Knopfler song is ripping, but the rest of the stuff on this album is bland and disappointing.

¡TEJANO CONJUNTO!

TEX-MEX IS ONE OF THE USA'S GREAT HYBRIDS

The accordion was long maligned as uncool and unhip but in the 1980s it underwent a huge image change in the US, with Rolling Stone pronouncing it the hottest instrument in rock music. And the reason? Tex-Mex, of course: the hybrid music of Mexican norteño and all sorts of American influences, which locals call Tejano Conjunto. Ramiro Burr reports from San Antonio, the music's capital.

Every year the biggest conjunto festival in the world is celebrated in San Antonio, organized by the Guadalupe Cultural Arts Center. It's neat and it's funky, the very essence of roots music. Conjunto (pronounced con-hoon-toe) features the reedy sound of the accordion, leading the melody, set against the percolating "oompah oompah" backbeat of classic polka.

It used to be a regional sound, based here in Texas and, of course, in its Mexican incarnation, over the border. However, the past few years have seen the conjunto sound making an appearance all across the USA, in roots and rock music alike, in a similar way to the accordion-led Cajun and zydeco music of neighbouring Louisiana. Paul Simon, once again, was a prime mover, enlisting Los Lobos, a leading Tex-Mex band, on his 1986 "Graceland" album. Los Lobos went on to subsequent mainstream success; meanwhile the roll-call of rock artists adopting a conjunto-style accordion continues to grow. The accordion is very hot indeed.

It wasn't always so, as Texan DJ Guero Polkas observed: "If we had a school talent show and some dude came out with an accordion everyone would make fun of him. Now you have guys like Flaco Jimenez laughing all the way to the bank." Apart from the money, what's the appeal? Guero Polkas sees several reasons for conjunto's rising popularity, from the music's sheer originality to the Hispanic pride of the younger generation rediscovering its roots. "The bajo sexto [12-string bass guitar] and accordion is *nuestra musica folklorica* – our folk music. This is to us what zydeco is to blacks in lower Louisiana. It's like bluegrass music in Kentucky. We're in an era where it's cool to be Mexicano, cool to be a conjunto musician and cool to squeeze a box."

THE CONJUNTO MIX

Tex-Mex **conjunto** music, for those unfamiliar with the genre, is indigenous to south Texas – and in the finest American tradition it blends the best of several cultures. It has many similarities with Mexican norteño (see Chapter Eleven). Both come from rural backgrounds and, like American country music, deal with the traditional subjects of drinking, lying and cheating. The emphasis in conjunto music, however, is on the danceable 2/4 polka beat, rather than the nasal singing of norteño ballads.

Conjunto developed from a very broad mix of musics: the polkas and other dances of German, Polish and Czech immigrants, stewed in the cultural melting pot with Mexican forms like mariachi and ranchera.

Various recipes of this brew were being tried and tested in the rural communities of the southwest at the turn of the century. At the time, the most common form of Mexican music featured a singer accompanied by guitar, although the mariachi troupes (then considered high-class music) might have had three or four wind instruments alongside violins and guitarrons. German immigrants in Mexico and the USA, though, had **accordions** which, with their versatility, were the synthesizers of their day. They played mainly at weddings and other celebrations in the *haciendas* (ranch houses), and the accordion sound fast became very popular, especially among the proletarian folk.

The earliest accordion – and, in essence, conjunto – recording was made by Bruno Villarreal in 1928. However, the two men regarded as the real pioneers of conjunto were Narciso Martínez and Santiago Jimenez.

MARTÍNEZ, JIMENEZ, AND THE PIONEERS

Narciso Martínez was born in 1911, in Reynosa, Mexico, but his family moved into the Rio Grande Valley the same year and, like most Mexican-Americans in the region, followed the migrant work in the tiny settlements around Texas. Martínez gathered an early reputation

Narciso Martinez

as one of the most accomplished accordion players in Texas and was instrumental in establishing the basic conjunto unit, together with bajo sexto player **Santiago Almeida**.

His career stretched from the early 1930s right through to his death in 1992. In the early years he supported his family through work as a trucker and zoo-keeper, while recording – at $30 a time – for the San Benito label, Ideal Records. As well as playing his own music, he was a leading accompanist to popular singers like **Carmen and Laura** and **Lydia Mendoza**. Out of the hundreds of his recordings, the best-known are "La Chicharronera" (Cracklin Maker) and "La Polvadera" (The Dustcloud). He was awarded, in 1983, a National Heritage Fellowship Award for his contribution to American musical heritage but, interestingly, has never chosen to become a naturalized US citizen, stressing his allegiance to his Mexican heritage.

While Martínez came from a rural background, **Don Santiago Jimenez** emerged from the city of San Antonio, Texas. Known as "El Flaco" (The Skinny One), Jimenez is noted by historians for his introduction of the *tololoche* (double bass) into the conjunto ensemble. Like Martínez, Jimenez also began recording in the mid-1930s, as a part-time musician, working by day as a janitor and in other low-paid jobs. Classic numbers, among his again numerous recordings, include "Viva Seguin" and "La Piedrera". His legacy, however, also includes the First Family of Conjunto, in the form of his two sons, the traditionalist Santiago Jimenez Jnr, and Leonardo "Flaco" Jimenez, a progressive accordion player who fuses rock and country into conjunto. More on these later.

Other pioneers in the conjunto canon include **Valerio Longoria**, also of San Antonio, who was a favourite in the booming postwar years. His first button accordion cost $10 and he remembers, in the early years, being paid $4 for playing at an all-night street party. He is noted for introducing bolero melodies onto the accordion and drums into the conjunto. He got his National Heritage award in 1986.

In a music heavily dominated by men, the name of **Lydia Mendoza** stands out as one of the important women on the scene. She started singing and playing the mandolin in 1927 and her songs with mandolin or guitar are classics in the sentimental or melancholy style.

After World War II female *duetos* became particularly popular with the success of, duos like **Carmen and Laura**, and Lydia's sisters,

Flaco Jimenez on bajo sexto with his brother, Santiago Jnr, taking the customary Jimenez accordion role

Las Hermanas Mendoza. Almost all their lyrics were written from the male point of view, about women's faithlessness and suchlike, which audiences enjoyed hearing sung by sweet female voices. A few of them, however, such as "Mal Hombre", sung by Lydia Mendoza, broke the mould:

I was still a young girl
When, by chance, you found me
And with your worldly charm
You took away my innocence
It was then that you did to me
What all of your kind do to women
So don't be surprised now
If I tell you to your face
What you really are
Cold-hearted man!
Your soul is so vile, it has no name
You are despicable, you are evil
You are a cold-hearted man.

MODERN CONJUNTO

After Narciso Martínez and Don Santiago Jimenez, the next important name in conjunto was **Tony De La Rosa**. From his rural home in Sarita, De La Rosa began a career in the late 1950s that was not only phenomenally successful but also had a big stylistic influence on the music. His most significant development was to establish the use of drums in the conjunto ensemble, and, alongside this, to amplify the bajo sexto and introduce the electric bass. In effect, he pushed the conjunto out of the acoustic era into the electronic age: a move which

NORTH AMERICA

traditionalists dismissed as little more than a circus act.

As an accomplished accordionist, however, De La Rosa also emphasized the melodic side of the instrument and thrilled audiences with his lengthy and intricate accordion runs in his choppy, staccato style. By the early 1960s he dominated the conjunto music scene, attracting packed houses wherever he played, and, over the course of a lengthy career, he recorded more than 75 albums. His repertoire included many polka instrumentals but also a number of tunes that have become standards, including "La Periodista", "Palomo Negra", "El Circo", "El Sube y Baja", and his instrumental adaptation of "Atotonilco", an old Mexican standard. Today he is semi-retired but still makes occasional appearances.

Lydia Mendoza in the 1930s – and she's still singing

The other key band of the 1960s and early 70s was **El Conjunto Bernal**, led by Paulino Bernal and his brother Eloy. Like De La Rosa, they enjoyed great commercial success, selling thousands of records and filling dancehalls and ballrooms across the southwest, and they originated a new sound. This featured faster, more upbeat polka rhythms, and close two- and three-part harmonies – an art developed from their pivotal recording of "Mi Unico Camino",

which featured Ruben Perez on lead vocals with the brothers on second and third.

Although the group disbanded in the late 1970s, the Bernal legacy continues today with ex-members heading some of the biggest modern groups, including **Tonka y Libre, Gary Guajardo and Pleasure, Bobby Naranjo y Superband**, and **Oscar Hernandez and the Tuff Band**.

A third great player, still very active, who rose to fame in the 1960s, was **Steve Jordan**, perhaps the most radical accordion player of them all. He started out playing relatively conventional conjunto, along with his brothers, with whom he recorded as Los Hermanos Jordan. However, as the decade rolled, Jordan's accordion style grew ever wilder, and he would improvise solos like a rock guitarist: no surprise, then, that critics compared his treatment of the accordion to that of Jerry Lee Lewis on piano or Jimi Hendrix on guitar. Again, it introduced a new sound to conjunto, and one immortalized in a Hohner accordion range marketed as the "Steve Jordan Tex-Mex Rockordion".

CONJUNTO STYLES

The predominant rhythm in Tejano conjunto is the polka, with its German oom-pah-oompah beat. However, conjunto is a flexible, still-evolving music and modern groups play a bewildering range of styles and rhythms. These include a variety of European and Mexican dance styles, like the schottische, vals (French waltz), huapango and jaranas, and – a big favourite – the **bolero**, a lively Spanish dance in triple metre.

Many bands also interpret Mexican **ranchera** – songs that idealized hacienda and rural life – in something like a Mexican counterpart to US country music. This itself has all sorts of variants, the most popular of which is **norteño**, a fairly rudimentary music based on the norteño sound of northern Mexico.

Corridos are the mainstays of most Tex-Mex bands. These are essentially ballads, mostly sad or poignant stories of struggle or controversy, usually played at a slow or moderate pace. They may be based on historical incidents, like Anglo-Mexican conflicts, or tell the life stories of notorious criminals, often highly embellished. Alternatively, like rancheras, they may be lyrical songs about bad women, alcohol, lost love, or other struggles reflecting the social conditions of the time.

Another variant of Tex-Mex are **cumbias** – simpler working-class variants of the Colombian dance form, characterized by aggressive syncopation, percussion and the sound of flutes and saxophones.

If Jordan gave conjunto the rockordion, however, it was **Flaco Jimenez** who introduced a conspicuously rock style. Although he learned traditional conjunto accordion from his father, the late Santiago Jimenez Snr, Flaco soon developed a much faster and flashier style, incorporating elements of rock and country. He is perhaps the most eclectic of all conjunto players, equally at ease with all kinds of musicians, as shown by his recent album "Partners", featuring guest appearances by Ry Cooder, Dwight Yoakam, Emmylou Harris, Linda Ronstadt and Los Lobos.

Flaco currently tours on his own and as an accordionist with **The Texas Tornados**, a band he formed in the early 1990s with veteran rock players Doug Sahm and Augie Meyers, and Tex-Mex singer Freddy Fender. They are currently one of the biggest groups on the circuit, with a cross-generational appeal. While Meyer and Sahm bring with them fans of late 1960s Tex-Mex rock from their days in the Sir Douglas Quintet, Jimenez and Fender attract their counterparts from conjunto and Tejano music. Their popularity has been such that Warner Bros released their debut album in both English and Spanish versions.

Tejano music is a younger offshoot of conjunto, urban-based and incorporating instruments like synthesizers and electric guitars. The bands tend to have a glitzy appearance, with leather, glitter and big hair, and their repertoire includes elements from rock, country and pop, as well as the traditional polka-based, accordion-laced conjunto style. Among the current names are **Mazz** from Brownsville, Houston's **La Mafia** and San Antonio-based **Emilio Navaira**. Alongside them, however, are quite a few young bands, like the **Hometown Boys**, **Estrella del Norte**, and **Los Palominos**, who stick to the country shirts and blue jeans, and knock out the old conjunto style.

Tex-Mex supergroup, The Texas Tornados

The biggest of all the rock-conjunto bands right now, however, is undoubtedly **Los Lobos**, who are actually from California. They play basically conjunto-norteño music but their broad-based appeal comes from mixing it with a rock sound and from their unfailing instinct for a hit song – demonstrated most notably by their hugely successful remake of Ritchie Valens'

"La Bamba" in 1988. Despite mainstream success, they have not forsaken their Mexican roots nor the polka-based conjunto rhythms in their music.

This is a characteristic of conjunto music. Despite the modern groups pulling in new directions, conjunto has never lost its link with its humble roots and musical simplicity. Most of the early pioneers had little or no education and suffered economic and family hardships, and anti-Mexican racism, often woven into poignant song lyrics. Such elements gave conjunto solid roots in folk culture and – certainly in its rural forms – an affinity with "la gente pobre", the poor.

In recent times, particularly with the emergence of the Tejano Conjunto Festival, conjunto has taken its place in the fabric of

Los Lobos: the wolves who took "La Bamba" to the world

American culture, winning the respect it deserves but seldom received in the past. Today, it is hailed for its passion, conviction and authenticity, and for remaining a vital musical force.

WHERE TO HEAR CONJUNTO IN SAN ANTONIO

• •

It is stating the obvious, of course, but to hear conjunto and Tejano at its best, you really must get down to Texas – and, more particularly, **San Antonio**. There you can be entertained by some great radio stations, dozens of clubs, and a wonderful annual festival, while in the spring and summer there are weekly concerts and dances in Rosedale Park.

For those interested in learning how to play the accordion, the Guadalupe Cultural Arts Center, on Guadalupe, west of Downtown, offers classes with such luminaries as Valerio Longoria and Santiago Jimenez Jnr.

TEJANO CONJUNTO FESTIVAL

For the last ten years the Guadalupe Cultural Arts Center has saluted the music, its pioneers, and current performers, in an annual festival attracting more than 40,000 people. It is held in mid-May, for four days, and encompasses films, workshops, and inductions into the Conjunto Hall of Fame.

If you'd been at the 1994 festival, you would have caught bands across the whole spectrum, from legends like Valerio Longoria, Santiago

Jimenez Jnr, and Ruben Naranjo, to new turks such as Emilio Navaira, Mazz, and the Hometown Boys.

RADIO

KEDA-AM (1540m) is the undisputed king of the conjunto radio waves, and the show to listen out for is that of Guero Polkas.

KXTN-FM (107) and **KRIO-FM** (94.1) also play conjunto, along with a lot of the more urban Tejano.

DANCEHALLS

Country Road, US-281, 3.5 miles south of loop 410.
El Ranchito, 7167 Somerset.
Eva's Cozy Spot, 2217 Blanco.
Hacienda Salas Party House, 3127 Mission.
King Armadillo, 1619 Malone.
Lerma's Nite Club, 1602 N Zarzamora.
Randy's Ballroom, 1534 Bandera.

RECORD STORES

Janie's Record Shop, 129 Bandera. Janie Esparza stocks over 5000 titles, and can often get new or used copies of rare and deleted recordings.

A NIGHT OUT AT EVA'S

• •

Aaaahoooah! comes the rebel yell from across the dancefloor as Los Cyclones del Norte kick into "Paloma Negra", an old conjunto music standard. The bassist and drummer are thumping a steady backbeat, the singer is belting out another plaintive tale of unrequited love, and the accordionist is weaving his familiar high-pitched sound.

It's a typical Saturday night at **Eva's Cozy Spot** on Blanco Road, San Antonio, and the regulars have packed the dancefloor. Couples half sashay, half twirl to the music, maintaining a steady two- or three-step dance style similar to that of country and western music. Patrons are an eclectic mix: elderly, well-dressed gentlemen, young secretarial types, the garage mechanic still in overalls, grey-haired widows, and street dudes.

The dancefloor is uneven in some spots, but Eva's has a friendly, homely atmosphere. All the patrons know each other – the majority are all regulars here, hard-working types who come in on Fridays and Saturdays to relax, dance and drink some cold beers with their friends. The really fancy dancers spin their partners while circling them in fluid and graceful movements. Cowboy hats, jeans and boots are the norm for men, while women generally dance in either jeans or print dresses.

DISCOGRAPHY

CLASSIC

Conjunto Bernal *Mi Unico Camino* (Arhoolie, US). Many consider this the best conjunto of all time – and it is superbly showcased on this album of 1950s recordings, packed with jazzy chords and switches of rhythm.

Tony De La Rosa *Atotonilco* (Arhoolie, US). A compilation of one of the legends of conjunto music that stretches from his rural recordings of the early 1950s to the modern conjunto line-up with drums, electric bass and horns.

Santiago Jimenez Snr *Santiago Jimenez Snr* (Arhoolie, US). Another of the great conjunto accordion players, recorded in 1979 with his son "Flaco" on bajo sexto. An earthy, authentic sound.

Narciso Martínez *Father of the Tex-Mex Conjunto* (Arhoolie, US). The title says it all: a collection of 1940s and 50s numbers, some instrumental, others with vocals from Lydia Mendoza and the like, from the first great name in conjunto music.

Various *Tejano Roots* (Arhoolie, US). An excellent compilation from the Texas Ideal label, including Narciso Martínez, Conjunto Bernal, Tony De La Rosa and Freddy Fender. A perfect cross section of conjunto history.

Various *Tejano Roots: The Women* (Arhoolie, US). Recordings from the late 1940s and 50s of the celebrated female vocalists – Lydia Mendoza, Carmen and Laura, Hermanas Guerrero, etc.

CONTEMPORARY

Various *¡Conjunto! Texas-Mexican Border Music Vols 1 and 2* (Rounder, US). Two exemplary surveys of conjunto music. Volume 1 is especially wonderful, including Tony De La Rosa, Conjunto Bernal, Steve Jordan and Flaco Jimenez among others.

Various *Conjuntos Norteños* (Arhoolie, US). Real conjunto music as played in bars and cantinas in northern Mexico and San Antonio. A great collection of popular corridos featuring Los Pingüinos Del Norte and Fred Zimmerle and the Trio San Antonio. Lyrics included.

Flaco Jimenez *Ay te dejo en San Antonio* (Arhoolie, US). The best of Flaco's many recordings, here in a traditional vein. Note the polka "El Barrelito" – none other than "Roll out the Barrel" Tejano-style.

Valerio Longoria *Caballo Viejo* (Arhoolie, US). An excellent 1989 recording of the Longoria family conjunto, with Valerio's sons and grandson helping out on the cumbias.

Steve Jordan *The Many Sounds of Steve Jordan* (Arhoolie, US). An essential collection from one of the great innovators of conjunto. Ranges through raw traditional music from the early 1960s to his best recordings from the 80s.

Los Lobos *La Pistola y El Corazon* (Warner, US). The band's excellent 1991 tribute to their Mexican roots, with David Hidalgo pumping the accordion on their blend of conjunto and rock'n' roll.

Mazz *¿Que esperabas?* (EMI Latin, US). Perhaps the best Tejano polka-cumbia outfit on the market, directed by the creative genius of guitarist Jimmy Gonzalez.

Emilio Navaira *Southern Exposure* (EMI Latin, US). One of the new players pushing the frontiers of Tejano. with dance and country influences. His accordionist, Pete Ybarra, is one of the best in the business.

Texas Tornados *Texas Tornados* (Warner, US). The Tex-Mex supergroup's debut album is their best to date – and available in both English and Spanish versions.

DEVIL STOLE THE BEAT

THE INSPIRATIONAL SOUND OF GOSPEL –
THE ROOTS OF R&B AND SOUL

Gospel had its beginnings in "negro spirituals" and has itself constantly fed into other streams of American music. But while many of the music's teenage prodigies, from Aretha to Elvis, have crossed over to become rock'n'roll, soul and dancefloor stars, gospel itself has remained vibrant in the churches and on the radio, keeping its roots and re-importing a little funk from soul and R&B along the way. James Attlee puts on his Sunday best.

A merican gospel music in the 1990s is both a multi-million-dollar industry and a grass-roots folk art that has never lost touch with its powerbase of fanatically loyal devotees. For every crossover act that tops the R&B or soul charts there are hundreds of more traditional artists working the gospel circuit, thrilling primarily black church audiences with a musical style that has changed little in three decades.

Added to these must be the countless thousands who sing in gospel choirs, both well-known and obscure, and those who simply stand up on a Sunday and pour all the faith, the frustration, the anguish and the defiant hope that make up their daily lives into a solo that brings an ecstatic response of "Amens" and "Hallelujahs" from the rest of the congre-gation. To experience the raw power of gospel at its purest, music lovers are advised to be brave and find a place on the pew.

Gospel singers have a saying that has been passed down from generation to generation. "The Devil stole the beat," they will tell you, meaning that far from the aforementioned gentleman having all the best tunes, much of the so-called "Devil's music" has borrowed its style from the black church. There's some truth to this. Many of rock music's charac-teristics, from rhythms to vocal styles, from dance steps to stage-diving, were first conceived on the gospel circuit – and it's perhaps no surprise that it started early, with Elvis Presley, Little Richard and Jerry Lee Lewis (among many other American rock'n'roll singers) getting their training in gospel choirs.

On the soul and R&B front, meanwhile, black music, from the earliest days of recording to the present, has had two parallel streams, the sacred and the secular, each feeding off the other. Performers, even superstars like Al Green and Aretha Franklin, switch camp in both directions, braving the disapproval and misunderstanding of their peers. And for all the mutual mistrust, one would not survive without the other.

SPIRITUAL ROOTS

The style of music we now know as gospel was born a mere sixty years ago in Chicago, in the depths of the Depression. A piano player and ex-blues musician by the name of **Thomas A. Dorsey** ("Georgia Tom") began composing songs based on familiar spirituals and hymns, fused to blues and jazz rhythms. He called them "Gospel Songs" and began hawking them around the churches of America, bringing a much-needed message of hope in hard times. Singers like **Sallie Martin** and the young **Mahalia Jackson** travelled the length and breadth of the country with Dorsey, familiarizing audiences with the new songs, which articulated the faith and the troubles of ordinary people in language they could understand.

Of course the roots of gospel stretch much further back than this. Two centuries before Dorsey was knocking on doors with his briefcase full of tunes, America was in the grip of a religious revival – the Great Awakening. Fiery preachers drew huge crowds to open-air gatherings in the woods, termed "camp meetings", where new hymns and "camp songs" were sung with abandon into the small hours. At the fringes of these meetings, African slaves listened to the music and were enthralled, music being an integral part of the tribal religions banned by slave-masters in the New World (many also proscribed Christianity, which they feared might incite rebellion). Slaves who converted gave new life to the hymns and religious songs with a transfusion of West African rhythms and vocal stylings, producing an entirely new song form. The first true folk music of America, this came to be known as the **"negro spiritual"**.

The spiritual survived and continued to mature well into the twentieth century. As the

and European homes. A black university singing group called **The Fisk Jubilee Singers** appeared before the crowned heads of Europe and were reputed to have brought tears to the eyes of Queen Victoria on a visit to Britain in 1871. The all-male jubilee groups were meanwhile developing a style that was to provide another of the important threads in gospel music: the **gospel quartet**.

GOSPEL'S GOLDEN AGE

In the 1920s and '30s the recordings of religious music on "race records" – the industry euphemism for black music – fell into three main categories. Jubilee quartets like **The**

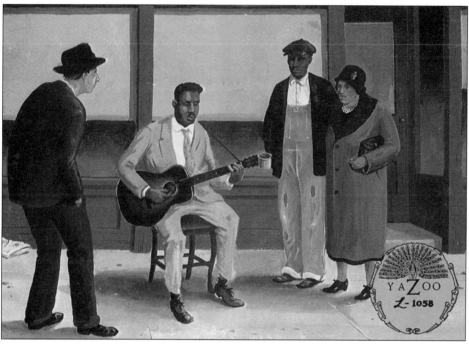

Blind Willie Johnson

form developed and new songs were composed, it became a vehicle for political as well as religious sentiment. Certain songs were coded demands for freedom couched in biblical allegory ("Go Down Moses, Let My People Go"), while others served on occasion as messages of impending escape ("Stealin' Away to Jesus"). Freedom, when it came, brought its own problems, and the songs lost none of their power to express the faith and the frustrations of black Americans.

In a sanitized and expurgated form the spirituals became drawing-room favourites in white American

Golden Gate Quartet and **The Norfolk Jubilee Quartet** were among the first black recording stars, their sophisticated vocal stylings and close harmony arrangements of old spirituals selling discs in the thousands.

In an effort to capitalize on the untapped "race" market, white-owned companies like Capitol and Paramount scoured the south for religious artists. The so-called "jackleg preachers" – itinerant evangelists like **Blind Willie Johnson** and **Washington Phillips** – were the next unlikely stars of the genre. Used to playing for pennies on the street, the immensely influential Johnson, whose unique slide-guitar style and growled vocals made his records eagerly sought after by jazz and blues collectors, received little more in royalties than he had as a busker. He died in poverty with pneumonia in 1949, having been refused entry to hospital because he was blind. Phillips, who made a single record in Dallas, had an achingly beautiful sound, accompanying himself on songs like "I Had a Good Father and Mother" with an obscure and hauntingly melodious string instrument, the dulceola.

The most successful religious artists of all were the **"singing preachers"**. These fervent reverends, guaranteed to turn a sinner's knees to jelly at fifty paces, regularly outsold the blues stars of their day. Leader of the pack was the **Reverend J.M. Gates**, whose hair-raising warnings about the consequences of a life of infamy had colourful titles like "God's Wrath in the St Louis Cyclone", "Hitler and Hell", "Death's Black Train is Coming" and "Will Death be your Santa Claus?"

The end of World War II ushered in an era generally acknowledged to be a golden age for gospel music. Over the next twenty years, thousands of gospel artists packed churches and concert halls across America, often selling records in huge quantities. The first stars of the gospel boom were the quartets. Stylistically, quartet singing had taken a leap: the smooth

harmonies of the jubilee groups was now being joined by one or two lead voices that were not afraid to make use of all the range and histrionic emotion at their disposal.

Powerhouse singing was coupled with stage performances that left audiences in a pandemonium of excitement. One of the hardest quartets of all time was the **Five Blind Boys of Mississippi** – their blind lead singer, Archie Brownlee, was known on occasion to jump off the balcony of auditoriums during performances. The group had such a reputation for laying out their audience that the City of New Orleans required them to pay out special insurance

---

SOUTHERN GOSPEL

••••••••••••••••••••••

Soul and R&B are not the only musics to bear the stamp of gospel influence. The **white churches** of the rural south shared hymns, spirituals and rhythms with their African American counterparts. They too knew about grinding poverty; they too longed for a better deal on the other side of Jordan, and expressed their longing in song. And, of course, many future luminaries of country music cut their teeth on gospel.

For white rural Baptists and Pentecostalists, anything but gospel was the Devil's music, and the church was often the only place for a country boy to learn the trade of a musician. By the 1930s, vocal groups were touring church halls and radio stations in the south, with a slightly sanitized version of the music that was laying out black audiences. Some made it to Nashville and

country stardom, and many of these, finding redemption at the bottom of the bottle, later returned to the fold, cutting gospel albums after they had made it big in the country or bluegrass worlds.

Hank Williams, The Carter Family, Bill Monroe, Boz Scaggs and Tennessee Ernie Ford have all sung gospel, and it was the music that Elvis Presley sang when he was relaxing with his friends. Even the wildest rocker of them all, Jerry Lee Lewis, is prone to bouts of remorse and periodic returns to church.

Today, southern (white) gospel is now a fully fledged sub-genre within country music, with its own charts and award ceremonies. While much of it strays a little too near the white fundamentalism of the TV preachers for most tastes, the best recordings run gospel a close second.

because they were sending so many people to hospital in comas that could last for days. Generating this sort of hysteria, known as "wrecking the house", was something the quartets did on a regular basis throughout the era.

The quartets produced many of the greatest voices in soul music – **Sam Cooke** cut his teeth in the Soul Stirrers, **Wilson Pickett** in the Violinaires, and **Johnny Taylor** followed in Cooke's footsteps, both in the Soul Stirrers and later into soul stardom. The influence of the quartets extended beyond the singers who actually crossed over, however. Many of the vocal stylings and stage antics of soul and rock artists of the past three or four decades originated in the frenetic performances of these pioneers. Of all the frontmen in quartet music, the lead voices of **The Reverend Claude Jeter** of the **Swan Silvertones** and **Julius Cheeks** of the **Sensational Nightingales** have been the most influential. Claude Jeter's falsetto has left its mark on the voices of generations of singers, whether they've known it or not; and as for the screamers, they were born out of Julius Cheek's storming lead performances. The hard men of 1960s soul like James Brown and Wilson Pickett would never have torn it up the way they did if it hadn't been for the Nightingales.

Not all the great voices of the golden age were male. Many female groups travelled the gospel highway through this period, including **The Roberta Martin Singers**, **The Clara Ward Singers**, **The Caravans** and **The Davis Sisters**, to name but a few.

And then, of course, there were **The Staple Singers**, a Chicago family band – "Pop" plus two daughters and a son – who began recording in the mid-1950s and had a series of hits in the gospel, R&B and soul charts over the next three decades. Their sound was the most bluesy gospel has ever been – not surprising, perhaps, as it was built around the echoey guitar of Roebuck "Pop" Staples, originally a Delta bluesman, and backed by session men on bass and drums.

Aretha Franklin

THE BIG TIME

Mahalia Jackson, who had cut her teeth in the Thomas Dorsey roadshow in the 1930s, was the first gospel artist to cross over to an international audience when in 1946 she recorded "Move On Up a Little Higher" for Apollo Records – gospel music's first million-seller. The receipt of a prestigious French award in the early 1950s launched Mahalia into a new phase of her career and she embarked on the first of many tours of Europe, gaining a rapturous reception from a new, non-gospel audience. Back in the States she made the decision to switch to a mainstream label, signing to Columbia in 1954. Inevitably, as she became more and more of a success with white audiences she lost touch with her grass-roots gospel following, but whatever the financial temptations to shift into jazz or pop, she never abandoned the music she loved. Much of the fortune she earned was put to good use in the community, particularly in support of her friend Martin Luther King's Civil Rights Movement, and she was a mother figure and an inspiration to a generation of singers who followed in her footsteps.

Among those influenced by Mahalia was the young **Aretha Franklin**. A preacher's daughter from Detroit, Aretha grew up in a house where gospel stars like Mahalia, Clara Ward, Sam Cooke and James Cleveland would regularly drop in and hold all-night singing sessions. She made her debut at the age of twelve at her father, the Reverend C.L. Franklin's New Bethel Baptist Church, and gained experience travelling the country with the family roadshow – her father was a recording star in the style of the "singing preachers" of the 1920s and '30s. Her first recording was made "live" at New Bethel when she was a mere fifteen years old; it's hard to believe her age, listening to her powerfully moving rendition of the old Dorsey standard "Precious Lord".

By the time Aretha was eighteen she felt ready to follow the likes of Sam Cooke into the pop arena. After a false start at Columbia, she finally hit at Atlantic Records, where producer Jerry Wexler "took her to church", letting her sit

down at a piano and be herself. Her first record to take off was "I Never Loved a Man the Way I Loved You", and it sold a million within a matter of weeks. The gospel-soaked backing vocals on those early hits were provided by a group of singers known as **The Sweet Inspirations**, directed by Cissy Houston, herself a gospel artist and choir director, as well as a soul singer in her own right.

Cissy's daughter **Whitney Houston**, schooled in the twin arts of gospel and soul singing, would go on to join another generation of singers from within the black church to find pop success. Other notable female gospel defectors have included **Dionne Warwick**, who started out singing with the Drinkard Singers, and "Queen of Rhythm and Blues" **Dinah Washington**, who began her career as plain Ruth Jones in the Sallie Martin Singers.

HEAVENLY VOICES

The emergence of **choirs** as major performing and recording artists in gospel is mainly a postwar phenomenon and owes much to the man they called the "Godfather of Gospel", **James Cleveland**. An early signing to Savoy Records, Cleveland generated unprecedented excitement when his hoarse holler was combined with the red-hot harmonies of The Angelic Choir of Nutley, New Jersey. Their second album together, "Peace Be Still", sold

an astounding million copies. Cleveland went on to record literally hundreds of albums, but his greatest contribution was probably the founding of the annual **Gospel Music Workshop of America** in 1968. These Workshops have spawned Mass and Community choirs across the nation and beyond – notably in South Africa and Britain – and have inspired countless singers down the years. Today every US state has its Mass Choir and every city from New York to London its own Community Choir.

There's nothing quite like a gospel choir in action – it's something to do with the tension between the choir's practised split-second timing and the breathtaking improvisations of the soloists, often urged on by shouts of encouragement from brothers and sisters in the ranks. Among the **current hot choirs**, The Florida Mass Choir, The New Jersey Mass Choir, The Southern California Community Choir and The Mississippi Mass Choir are always worth seeing, while The West Angeles Church Of God In Christ is the leading COGIC choir in the country. Still active on the circuit is **Edwin Hawkins**, who introduced much of the world to the gospel choir in 1968, when his group the Edward Hawkins Singers had an international hit with "Oh Happy Day". His brother Walter's Love Center Choir also remains a top attraction.

Most radical of the modern choirs must be the thirty-member **Sounds of Blackness** from Minnnesota. Their debut album "The Evolution of Gospel", co-produced by the mega-platinum team of Jimmy Jam and Terry Lewis, crossed over in a massive way on both sides of the Atlantic. Work songs, spirituals and African choral interludes are all included in the choir's powerfully theatrical live set, which combines the scorching lead vocals of Ann Bennett-Nesby with some of the hardest dance rhythms around.

Other choirs have made forays into the rock world, notably **The New Jersey Mass Choir**, who provided vocal support on the 1985 million-selling album "I Want To Know What Love Is", by rock band Foreigner. The NJMC subsequently issued their own version of the title song and have gone on to achieve a high US media profile, putting out a number of albums that blend traditional gospel values with state of the art recording techniques. The trend in rock's adoption of gospel has continued, with artists as diverse as U2, MC

Hammer, Prince, George Michael and Madness collaborating with choirs over recent years.

THE DETROIT SOUND

Gospel music today is crossing over as it has never done before, mainly thanks to a crop of musicians who have combined the gospel-singing prowess of their parents' generation with today's urban R&B. Various cities have taken their turn under the spotlight in gospel's development, but the 1980s and early 1990s have belonged to the city that at one time (B.M. – Before Motown) was more famous for its automobiles than its music: Detroit.

The premier exponents of the **"Detroit Sound"** all come from the same family. **Delores and David Winans** brought up their ten kids in traditional strict Pentecostal fashion, and no "secular" music was even allowed in the house. Ironically, it is the Winans children who have spearheaded gospel's move into the mainstream of contemporary music. The four eldest offspring, twins **Marvin** and **Carvin** along with brothers **Michael** and **Ronald**, made their debut in the early 1980s with "Introducing The Winans", produced by Andrae Crouch – a man who had more than an eye towards the pop market. The Winans had their first big hit outside the gospel market with "Let My People Go", from the 1986 album of the same name. The song struck a chord in the black community

and beyond by comparing black South Africans caught in the apartheid system with the Children of Israel imprisoned by Pharaoh in ancient Egypt. They were doing what the composers of spirituals like "Go Down Moses" had done a century or so earlier, when they used the tribulations of the Israelites as a metaphor for the evils of slavery.

From that time on The Winans have remained firmly plugged into the pulse of contemporary music, regularly hitting the top of the dance and R&B as well as black gospel charts. They've also earned their share of flak from within the gospel community for collaborations with a variety of non-gospel artists: they sang on Michael Jackson's "Bad" album, and their latest releases have featured guests like Michael McDonald, Stevie Wonder, Kenny Loggins and rapper and swingbeat supremo Teddy Riley. At their best The Winans exemplify the new, hard gospel coming out of the States. At their worst they can turn out a ballad as slushy as they come.

The rest of the Winans family have not been slow to follow in the boys' footsteps. Rivals to their success in the contemporary field have been seventh son **BeBe** and his sister **CeCe** (real name Priscilla), whose big breakthrough came with their third album, "Heaven", in 1988. The single "Celebrate" crossed over into R&B, soul and pop formats and received heavy club and radio play,

BRITISH GOSPEL

• •

Gospel has been a burgeoning force in Britain over the past couple of decades, with enthusiastic audiences for the big American singers and choirs, and a flourishing local scene. The choir with the highest profile is **The London Community Gospel Choir**, better known as the LCGC. Many of Britain's best singers have risen through its ranks and, as in the US, some have stayed with gospel, like Lavine Hudson, The Escofferys, Bryan Powell and the group Nu Colors, while others, like Mica Paris and Paul Johnson, have moved across to soul and R&B.

Other powerful London-based choirs include **The Inspirational Choir** (based in The Pentecostal Church of the Firstborn Living God, 71 Whitelion

St, Islington, London N1), who had a hit with the pop band Madness on "Wings of a Dove", and **The Angelical Voice Choir**, while further north **The Manchester Mass Choir** are building up a large following. Other British artists to look out for include **The Wades** and **Dawn Thomas** from London, and **Divine** from Birmingham.

Since 1991, London has also had its own gospel festival, albeit on a somewhat smaller scale to that of Chicago. **Gos Fest**, held on the third weekend in August, features a two-day programme of American, British and African gospel artists. Information from Gosfest International (First Floor, 50 Hans Crescent, Knightsbridge, London SW1X ONA; ☎071/581 1805).

The Five Blind Boys of Alabama – still a thriving quartet

eventually earning the duo Grammies, Dove and Soul Train awards. Brother **Daniel Winans**' career has remained more rooted in the church tradition and his periodic releases are fiery choir albums. Not to be outdone, the youngest siblings, Debbie and Angela, record as **The Winans Sisters**; sister-in-law **Vickie** has a solo career; and even the previous generation have a stake in the industry in their own right, recording as **Mom and Pops Winans** – which just leaves the family dog unsigned.

Other big names on the Detroit scene include **The Clark Sisters**, who had a dance-crossover hit with "You Bring the Sunshine" in 1983. The Clarks are the five supremely soulful daughters of singer and choir-director Mattie Moss Clark, and their success, alongside the expert advice and tutelage of their formidable mother, has encouraged generations of aspiring singers.

Vanessa Bell Armstrong, who attended McKenzie High School with both The Winans and The Clark Sisters, grew up singing in front of the mirror, pretending to be another long-time Detroit resident, Aretha Franklin. Although she recorded with choirs when in her teens, Vanessa didn't release her first solo album, "Peace Be Still", until she had raised five kids. She has since dropped the traditional material that had many comparing her to her childhood idol, in favour of an "inspirational" style that has

seen her duetting with soul star Jonathan Butler and being cited by Luther Vandross as his favourite singer.

Outside the Detroit mafia, too, gospel has expanded into the dance market, and gospel artists regularly show up on the playlists of urban radio stations across the US – and in Britain, too. Queens of the gospel-disco scene include **Mavis Staples** (from The Staple Singers) and **Helen Baylor** (a former backing singer with Aretha Franklin and Chaka Khan). Another direction has been taken by the extremely popular **Amy Grant**, who has recorded gospel with a soft rock- and even a country-tinged sound.

OLD-TIME RELIGION

Not all the best-selling gospel artists of recent years have been in a contemporary mould. There is still a massive market in America for traditional-style gospel performers among a black church audience that has little interest in the latest club sounds. Some gospel-watchers claim that a reaction against the crossover acts is underway, which could certainly be the case given the huge sales some of the more traditional artists are achieving.

Tramaine Hawkins, who attracted much criticism from her gospel peers for the crossover dancefloor hit "Fall Down" in 1985, has returned to her roots with a vengeance. Her

1990 traditional-style album "Tramaine – Live" became one of the hottest movers in gospel. Though Tramaine first tasted the big time when she sang on the Edwin Hawkins Singers' 1968 smash hit "Oh Happy Day", she remains a relative newcomer compared to the veterans of the circuit.

The undisputed Queen of Gospel is still **Shirley Caesar**, who began her recording career at the age of ten and rose to stardom during her time with The Caravans in the 1950s and 60s. A dynamic and much-loved performer, her "Live in Chicago" choir album, released in 1988, sold over a quarter of a million copies. Shirley is not the only link back to that era, however: many of her contemporaries are still on the gospel highway, and **Dorothy Norwood**, **Inez Andrews** and **Albertina Walker** from The Caravans have all recorded in recent years. A new generation of performers, too, – like **John P. Kee** and **Billy and Sarah Gaines** – are mixing traditional fiery performance styles with modern studio techniques for an audience who prefer their gospel uncut with pop.

Some of the great quartets from the golden age of gospel are still out there performing, too, albeit with a touch less frenzied power than in their youth. **The Mighty Clouds of Joy** made their debut in 1959 and have been on the road ever since, appearing at gospel shows, jazz festivals and rock concerts all over the world. Lead singer Joe Ligon is often cited as the greatest living male gospel singer and when you hear him scream you don't doubt it. Slick they may be, but after over thirty years of performing The Mighty Clouds of Joy are still an unmissable live experience.

The original a cappella style of quartet gospel singing is undergoing something of a revival in the 1990s. One group in particular, **Take 6** from New York, are enjoying great success with material that infuses the harmonies of groups like the Sensational Nightingales with a modern sensibility, drawing on elements of jazz, soul and hip-hop. Meanwhile their success has brought some of the earliest quartets out of retirement, such is the interest in their singing style. **The Fairfield Four**, whose heyday came in the 1940s and 50s, started out in 1921 as a jubilee group. Today they still make occasional appearances around their hometown of Nashville. Another quartet, **The Five Blind Boys of Alabama**, one-time rivals to the Tennessee Blind Boys, who had their first hit in 1949, are still touring the gospel circuit as well as branching out to win new converts at World Music and rock events.

Thanks to Viv Broughton for additional research and information.

GOSPEL: WHERE TO WITNESS

• •

I f you have some time to travel around the US, you can get to hear an astonishing array of gospel: at festivals, conventions and workshops, as well as in churches, and, of course, on the radio.

CHICAGO GOSPEL FESTIVAL

Sponsored by the City of Chicago, this is the premier showcase for gospel acts. It takes place each year on the second weekend in June, when an average of 70,000 to 80,000 gospel fans gather at the Petrillo Music Shell in Grant Park, downtown. Acts range across the board from traditional choirs and quartets to the most modern contemporary sounds. The music programme runs on both days from midday to 10pm – and it's all for free. For information, phone the Festival Office on ☎312/744-3315.

COGIC

Conventions play a vital part in the life of the black church and they inevitably feature performances by both well-known and undiscovered artists. The largest, attracting up to 100,000 people, is the annual **COGIC Convention**, held at the Cook's Convention Center, Memphis, at the beginning of November. Delegations travel from as far afield as Africa, Haiti and London, and the United Choir put together is often several thousand strong. Much of the music happens during the night at "midnight musicals", which often last until dawn and can develop into thrilling contests as singers from all over America and beyond vie with each other for ovations. Needless to say, gospel record company A&R people are always in attendance, on the lookout for new talent.

Non-COGIC visitors will find themselves welcome at these events – the only real problem is finding accommodation, as reasonably priced rooms tend to be booked up months in advance. For further information, contact The Church Of God In Christ, 272 S Main St, Memphis, TN 38101 (☎901/527-1422).

WORKSHOPS

Gospel workshops also have a major role in American gospel. At these gatherings often attended by thousands, aspiring singers can sign up for tuition from top artists and at the end of the workshop give a public performance in front of a large audience.

The biggest event of the year is the **Gospel Music Workshop of America**, founded by James Cleveland, which is held for a week every August at a different location around the US. On payment of a flat fee visitors can wander around the workshops all week – an unforgettable musical experience. For information, write to Ed Smith at The Gospel Music Workshop of America, PO Box 34635, Detroit, MI 48234 (☎313/898-2340).

CHURCHES

Searching out gospel at grass-roots level in the churches is obviously a hit-and-miss affair, but the rewards are great. Much of the music's power and excitement lies in its spontaneity and, of course, "making a joyful noise" to proclaim faith and move the spirit. Which is the reason you so often hear gospel performers trying to re-create that excitement in concert, exhorting their audience "come on people – let's have CHURCH tonight!"

The hospitality of the gospel community is proverbial. However, beyond church walls, the realities of urban America remain. Church buildings are often in the poorer parts of town and it goes without saying that such areas are not the safest place for non-streetwise visitors to wander. It would probably pay to give the church office a call beforehand to say that you are planning to attend and to ask directions – someone may even offer to meet you.

Listed below are some suggested churches to visit; check local phone books for addresses.

Berkeley, CA Ephesians Church Of God In Christ (pastor is Tramaine Hawkins' grandfather, Bishop E.E. Cleveland).

Chicago, IL Christ Tabernacle Baptist Church (has hosted recording sessions with Reverend Milton Brunson and Reverend Maceo Woods).

Cleveland, OH Christian Tabernacle Evangelistic Church.

Detroit, MI The Perfecting Church (pastor Marvin Winans); Mount Everett Church Of God In Christ (pastor is Vanessa Bell Armstrong's father); New Bethel Baptist Church (attended by Aretha Franklin).

Houston, TX Church Of Jesus Christ (pastor former heavyweight boxing champion, Reverend George Foreman).

Jackson, MS Blair Metropolitan A.M.E. Church (The Mississippi Mass Choir powerbase).

Los Angeles, CA Faith United Methodist Church; Testimonial Cathedral Church Of God In Christ; West Angeles Church Of God In Christ.

Memphis, TN Full Gospel Tabernacle (pastor the legendary soul and gospel artist, Al Green); Church Of God In Christ (headquarters of COGIC).

Nashville, TN The Born Again Church (local church for many gospel artists resident in or visiting Music City).

New York, NY Brooklyn Tabernacle (the excellent Brooklyn Tabernacle Choir's home).

◼ DISCOGRAPHY ◼

COMPILATIONS

Various *Jubilation Volume 1: Great Gospel Performances* (Rhino, US). The title is not kidding: this is the business, featuring tracks from Aretha Franklin, Mahalia Jackson, The Soul Stirrers, Shirley Caesar, and more. Volume 2 in this Rhino series is pretty good, too, continuing in the same vein, while Volume 3 introduces gospel's southern white country cousin, with devotional songs from the likes of Hank Williams, Bill Monroe and The Carter Family.

◐ **Various** *All of My Appointed Time* (Stash, US/Jass, UK). Forty years of the best a cappella gospel from male groups such as the Golden Gate Jubilee Quartet and The Soul Stirrers, and female vocalists like The Georgia Peach and Marion Williams.

◐ **Various** *Oh Happy Day* (New Cross, US). Four-CD compilation with 80 tracks from the golden age of gospel. All good stuff from the Chess and VeeJay vaults, including The Five Blind Boys, Staple Singers etc.

SINGERS AND GROUPS

◐ **Vanessa Bell Armstrong** *Peace Be Still* (Benson, US). A flawless album of contemporary American gospel – superlative performance, production and songwriting.

◐ **Shirley Caesar** *He's Working it Out For You* (Sony, US). The First Lady of gospel music, evangelist Shirley is one of the unmissable voices of black music. One of the few veterans who still produce great work, as this recent outing confirms.

Elbernita "Twinkie" Clark *Power* (Sound of Gospel, US). The creative heart of The Clark Sisters in rare solo mode. This hard-to-find mid-80s album is perhaps the most original and moving compositional gospel work of the past decade.

ⓒ **Rev James Cleveland** *Gospel Music Workshop of America* (Savoy, US). The big sound of Cleveland's choir at its best.

ⓒ **Five Blind Boys of Alabama** *Oh Lord Stand by Me/Marching up to Zion* (Specialty, US). Classic 1950s cuts from the Boys.

ⓒ **Five Blind Boys of Mississippi** *Great Lost Blind Boys Album* (Veejay, US). Archie Brownlee and the Mississippi Boys were perhaps the best ever gospel "quartet". This reissue is hugely recommended.

ⓒ **Aretha Franklin** *Amazing Grace* (Atlantic, US). Aretha's definitive, mesmerizing church performances, recorded live in LA with the King of Gospel Rev James Cleveland and the Southern California Community Choir. Double CD.

ⓒ **Al Green** *One in a Million* (Epic, US). A wonderful anthology of the Rev Green's finest spiritual outings.

ⓒ **Mahalia Jackson** *Gospels, Spirituals and Hymns* (CBS, US). Beware of Mahalia re-issues – many are of dubious quality. This, however, is the very best available: the all-time Queen of Gospel at her peak in the 1950s and 60s.

ⓒ **Blind Willie Johnson** *The Complete Blind Willie Johnson* (Columbia/Epic, US). Double CD of the greatest gospel blues artist. Stunning bottleneck guitar and fearsomely gruff vocals infuse gospel classics such as "Bye Bye" and "I'm Going to See the King" with a glorious intensity.

ⓒ **The Mighty Clouds of Joy** *Best of The Almighty Clouds of Joy* (MCA, US). The recordings don't quite catch the Mighty ones' live passion, but an essential part of any gospel collection nonetheless.

ⓒ **Washington Phillips** *I am Born to Preach* (Yazoo, US). The sole testament to the unique talent of Phillips, recorded in Dallas in the 1920s.

ⓒ **The Sensational Nightingales** *Heart and Soul/You Know Not the . . .* (Mobile, US). Two fine albums from the Nightingales post-Julius Cheeks, with Charles Johnson on lead vocals.

ⓒ **Soul Stirrers & Sam Cooke** *In the Beginning* (Ace, UK). This is as fine an example of a 1950s gospel quartet as any on record, with the added bonus of hearing Sam Cooke's best performances – bar none. For more wonderful archive material in the same groove, check out the four volumes entitled *The Gospel Soul of Sam Cooke* (Specialty, US), all of which feature the Soul Stirrers.

ⓒ **The Staples Singers** *Great Day* (Milestone, US). A fine, remastered selection of the Staples' early 1960s recordings.

ⓒ **BeBe and CeCe Winans** *BeBe and CeCe Winans* (Sparrow, US). Brother and sister from the famous first family of modern gospel. The debut and best of their three albums.

UK GOSPEL

ⓒ **Various** *Soul Stirrings: The Nu Inspirational* (Fourth and Broadway, UK). A compilation of the best of contemporary British gospel.

RHYTHM AND JEWS

KLEZMER WAS BORN IN THE SHTETLS OF EASTERN EUROPE – AND REBORN IN THE USA

Klezmer music came to the USA with Jewish immigrants from Poland, Romania, Russia and the Ukraine. It was the essence of "Fiddler on the Roof" – all soulful roots and frenzied dance. And then, as Simon Broughton explains, a new generation got in on the act . . .

The image of itinerant klezmer musicians shlepping their way from shtetl to shtetl in eastern Europe is part of the popular mythology of prewar Jewish life, as typified in *Fiddler on the Roof*, the writings of Sholom Aleichem, or the paintings of Marc Chagall. With the mass emigration to the United States early this century and post-Holocaust, the music became even more itinerant, resurfacing among the diaspora throughout the world.

Although first and foremost an expression of Jewish identity, klezmer has broken out from the confines of the cultural ghetto and can today be heard in Carnegie Hall and other mainstream venues across America. There are now over a dozen ensembles in New York alone, and 130 across the USA, from Seattle to New Mexico, ranging from the quaint and traditional to the experimental and ultra-hip.

Despite years of residence in the New World, however, its roots remain clear. Klezmer music developed in the Jewish communities and shtetls of Poland, Romania, Russia and Ukraine – and it sounds that way, even in its most modern versions. At times soulful and contemplative, at times wild and frenetic, it absorbed much from local east European folk music and combined

Old-world klezmer band

this with an expressive character that was quintessentially Jewish.

In addition to being a hugely enjoyable music, klezmer is an example of a traditional form still developing and interacting successfully with modern sounds. However contemporary their treatment, the new wave of klezmer bands are the legitimate heirs of the tradition, absorbing all the music around them to forge their style.

A KINGDOM WITHOUT BORDERS

In prewar eastern Europe, Ashkenazi Jews were settled across a huge territory stretching from the Baltic to the Black Sea. They maintained communities in small country shtetls and in urban centres like Vilna, Minsk, Warsaw, Białystok, Łodz, Krakow (Kazimierz), Kiev, Bucharest, Kishinev and Odessa. Across this diverse patchwork of groups was a unifying bond of customs and, in Yiddish, a common language.

The word "klezmer" comes from two Hebrew words – *kley* and *zemer*, meaning "instrument of song" – and the name originally referred to the instruments themselves, then later to the men who played them. According to the klezmer clarinettist Giora Feidman: "We are all born singers, this is a natural force. To express this natural force we need one instrument. We are the instrument of song. My father always tried to explain to me the role of what we call an artist or a musician in society. Serve society. You are a channel for sound, for music, for love."

In eastern Europe a klezmer was the sort of man you didn't want your daughter to marry, a musician with a precarious hand-to-mouth existence. The klezmorim served their communities by playing at Jewish weddings. However, like the other professional musicians of eastern Europe, the gypsies, the klezmorim also performed at markets, fairs and taverns, at Christian weddings, where they played the local peasant dance music, and at the houses of landowners and nobility, where waltzes, quadrilles and light classical pieces were also required.

It was a rich repertoire, which was often passed on from father to son, and the *kapelyes* or ensembles often came from dynasties of musical families. These groups were traditionally string ensembles with the **violin** as principal instrument – as in the popular 1936 Yiddish film

about klezmorim, *Yidl mitn Fidl* (Yiddle with his Fiddle). One of the earliest instrumentations was violin, *tsimbl* (cimbalom) and string bass. In

Polish klezmer violinist in the 1930s

the larger bands y u might have got an additional viola, cello, and perhaps a flute.

During the nineteenth century, though, due to the proliferation of military bands, the **clarinet** – which is considered the essential klezmer instrument today – began to take the place of the violin. Old photographs of klezmer ensembles from the early years of this century also show the trumpets, trombones and tubas that became popular once Jews were eligible to serve in the European armies. What the violin and the clarinet share, of course, is their fundamentally expressive quality, almost akin to the human voice, which is an essential part of klezmer music. As the Yiddish writer Sholom Aleichem said: "You can compare the heart in general and the Jewish heart in particular to a violin with several strings."

Although klezmer is essentially a secular music, it flourished in a religious society, and it draws some of its distinctive quality from the particular ornamentation and expression of cantorial chant. The "crying" and "bending" of notes suggests the emotive style of the synagogue. It also recalls an older music that doesn't fit too comfortably into western scale patterns, and the oriental-sounding augmented second that often crops up in klezmer melodies points to Semitic origins in the Middle East. The more "oriental" klezmer melodies actually have much in common with the early *rembetiko* music played by Greeks in Asia Minor, too, and the exchange likely went both ways. Many tunes in eastern Europe were shared by Jewish and non-Jewish musicians, while one of the most celebrated Constantinople rembetiko singers, Róza Eskenázi, was Jewish and included klezmer music in her repertoire.

On top of this were the rhythms and intonations of eastern Europe, as certain of the dance names carried across to America still suggest. Among the most popular are the *bulgar* and the *freylekh*, fast circle dances with syncopated rhythms, and a trio of Romanian styles – the *hora*, the *sîrba*, and the slow, rhapsodic *doina*.

THE NEW WORLD

At the end of the nineteenth century the Jews of eastern Europe were suffering economic hardship, persecution and pogroms, and started to leave in large numbers. Between 1880 and 1924 a third of them, around three million, emigrated to the United States. The legendary klezmer clarinettist Dave Tarras was one of those who came through Ellis Island in 1921. His bag was fumigated and his clarinet broken but, like many of the newly arrived immigrants, he wasn't expecting to make music his living.

It wasn't too long, however, before American record companies saw the potential of releasing 78s for the Jewish market. The violinist and bandleader **Abe Schwartz** was taken up by Columbia and the clarinettist Harry Kandel signed to Victor in 1917. **Kandel's Orchestra** became one of the most popular of all American klezmer bands and, while there were still violins in the band, it was Kandel's clarinet that led and established the American klezmer style. Between 1905 and 1942 around 700 titles were released by klezmer musicians.

The most celebrated players of this generation were **Naftule Brandwein** (1889–1963) and **Dave Tarras** (1897–1989). Brandwein, who was unable to read music, is remembered for the energy and fire of his playing and his eccentric performances. He was likely to turn up at Bar Mitzvahs dressed in a plug-in neon Uncle Sam suit and perform with his back to the audience

so they couldn't learn his tricks. A 1924 press release didn't hold back: "Here's speed for you! Observe the swiftness of this remarkable music, the clarity and ingeniousness of the melodies that come so rapidly from Naftule Brandwein's musicians, and you will be thrilled." Dave Tarras, on the other hand, was a highly trained musician famed for his smooth and elegant style. Tarras glides and swoops where Brandwein rips and tears.

Tarras lived long enough to witness the revival of interest in klezmer and to take his place as the grand old man. But the old 78 recordings of both these guys have become source material for the new generation: "three-minute musical Rosetta Stones", as Henry Sapoznik, one of the leading lights of the American klezmer revival, calls them. The period of mass Jewish emigration to America coincided exactly with the development of the recording industry, and the

The Young Dave Tarras

78s are snapshots of a tradition in transition, as it moved from a pre- to a post-industrial society.

Once in America klezmer started to draw again on the traditions that surrounded it. In New York, Jewish musicians were playing more fox-trots than freylekhs, although there were orchestras that specialized in a specifically Jewish-American sound. In the 1920s, **Joseph Cherniavsky's "Yiddish American Jazz Band"**, featuring players such as Brandwein and Tarras, performed in Yiddish theatres and on the vaudeville circuit.

And despite everything there were definitely elements of klezmer rising to the surface in mainstream **American jazz** music. You can't hear the opening clarinet solo from Gershwin's "Rhapsody in Blue" without being reminded that he, like many of America's popular musicians, was Jewish. The jazz clarinettist Benny Goodman, the "King of Swing", was the son of Jewish immigrants, too, from Poland. He was not a klezmer, and didn't play klezmer melodies, but his 1920s recordings like "That's a-Plenty" certainly have something of the klezmer style. A decade later, the trumpeter Ziggy Elman (Harry Finkleman) brought Jewish tunes to Goodman's band: "And the Angels Sing" and "Bay mir bistu sheyn" became immensely popular. Yiddish music made the big time. Some years on, after World War II, the clarinettist and saxophonist **Sam Musiker**, who was (as his name implies) from a klezmer family, led a band that achieved a real klezmer and jazz fusion.

Making it in America, however, meant moving up and out of the ghetto, so American music had a much stronger influence on Yiddish music than the other way round. The truth is that most immigrants preferred to forget their life in the old country and were even ashamed of it. The demand for Jewish music dwindled to a few tunes trundled out at weddings. Meanwhile Hitler put an end to the Jewish communities of eastern Europe and their culture forever. Klezmer, it seemed, was a music of the archives.

THE KLEZMER REVIVAL

Over the past twenty years, however, a new generation of Jewish musicians, free from the stigma attached to the old country, have taken a fresh look at klezmer. This move was spearheaded by The Klezmorim in Berkeley, California, and then by **Henry Sapoznik**, who created an Archive of Recorded Sound at the YIVO (Institute for Jewish Research) in New York. There he explored and catalogued all those old 78s and re-issued the best on a series of compilations.

These were picked up on by an entirely new generation of Jewish (and some non-Jewish) musicians, with a new interest in roots music. They set up revival groups to play klezmer, and

it wasn't long before there was a festival, too, **KlezKamp**, in the Catskill Mountains, where classes, workshops and concerts brought young musicians together with the surviving old-timers.

In recent years, the veteran stars at KlezKamp have been **Sid Beckerman**, **Howie Lees** and **Max Epstein**, all American-born and thus inheritors of both the European klezmer tradition and the American dance band experience. The revival has given them a new lease of life. "It's a wonderful thing," says Epstein, "I lived this music all my life practically and I've finally come into my own. Retirement is not for me, 'cause if I stop playing I'll die. So I'm sticking with it. I'm eighty years old, I've still got a few notes left and I'm going to peddle them off before I die."

The best-known klezmer clarinettist of today, however, is **Giora Feidman**. A fourth-generation klezmer born in Argentina, he played for a time with the Israel Philharmonic Orchestra before devoting himself to klezmer music and its revival. He is not one of the klezmer purists and his repertoire is as much Israeli as Yiddish,

Giora Feidman

but he is simply one of the best clarinettists around, with the ability to speak, laugh and cry through his instrument.

Among America's pioneering – and leading – revival bands are **The Klezmorim**, the **Andy Statman Orchestra** and **Kapelye**. All of these play traditionally based material, and they get to do so these days at major venues. As Henry Sapoznik, who plays with Kapelye, noted: "We gave this concert in the sculpture court of the Metropolitan Museum of Art, surrounded by classical nudes in heroic poses. There we were playing

Yiddish music right in front of this Hercules with a huge great "shlong" that wasn't even circumcized!"

The **Klezmer Conservatory Band**, based in Boston, is a bigger ensemble. Listening to them you can hear how American big-band music has fed back into the Jewish repertoire – hardly surprising as many klezmer musicians play in jazz, rock and salsa bands as well.

Most of the revival bands also include songs in their repertoires that come from outside the strict klezmer tradition.

NEW DIRECTIONS

The rediscovery of the old music was only the first step and these days a number of groups are trying to develop it further. **Brave Old World**, led by **Michael Alpert**, stick to traditional forms but "strive to take klezmer music to its next stage: away from imitating the past and towards creating a living music for the future". They have recorded some striking new compositions, including the startling song "Chernobyl", with lyrics in Yiddish, about the site of the nuclear disaster, which was once a thriving shtetl.

The clarinettist **Joel Rubin**, a former member of Brave Old World and currently based in Berlin, is one of the leading researchers into the history and development of klezmer and is doing interesting work in Europe. His recording, with Joshua Horowitz, of clarinet tunes and historical button accordion and tsimbl duos is one of the best examples of simple yet soulful klezmer musicianship around.

Another group worth looking out for is the **Flying Bulgar Klezmer Band** from Toronto, Canada. Under the leadership of trumpeter David Buchbinder, they play danceable and witty arrangements of classic tunes plus some new compositions of their own.

The Klezmatics represent the cutting edge of klezmer. They are up to the minute yet deeply rooted in the tradition – klezmer meets the 90s. Their leader, the eclectic trumpeter Frank London, explained: "The Jewish music tradition has always been one of reacting to the place where they were living, whether they were in Odessa or Romania. Klezmer was this Jewish take on the east European music. They came to America and again they started reacting to the American music.

"The Klezmatics started playing the old tunes off 78 records, but we couldn't keep our own personal music history out of it, nor did we

want to. Alicia Svigals, our violinist, who grew up listening to Led Zeppelin records, would scream guitar licks on top of it, and I would bring in the experience of working with people like David Byrne and the Art Ensemble of Chicago. The Klezmatics can't help it. We're Jews. We're in the 1990s. This is New York City. And this is our music!"

To see what he means, take a listen to the opening track of their album "Rhythm + Jews", a tune called "Fun Tashlikh". An old number from Naftule Brandwein's repertoire, it is yanked right up to date with improvisatory bass clarinet, wailing brass, and an underpinning Nubian drum rhythm showing some of the old links between klezmer and Arabic music. It is a sensational sound and the band are even better if you get a chance to see them live.

Another surprise appearance on the New York klezmer scene has been the black American jazz clarinettist **Don Byron**. He's taken to performing the music of Mickey Katz, written in the 1940s and 50s. "Mickey Katz was not among the klezmer purists," he explains, "his music kinda skips around. It's kinda schizophrenic. He has a little bit of klezmer stuff and then a parody of a pop tune. He and Spike Jones' band parodied everything." The Mickey Katz repertoire tends to be a bit kitsch and rather thickly orchestrated, but Byron cuts a cool figure while playing it – bouncing around with his dreadlocks swinging. He's done the traditional klezmer apprenticeship, too, playing for several years with the Klezmer Conservatory Band. For him it's a musical fascination rather than an ethnic one: "When I first started playing the music, what I saw was a lotta clarinet players really expressing themselves in tiny little spaces as they varied a melody, as opposed to just trying to play something really cool over the 2-5-1 progression!"

KLEZMER IN ISRAEL

Alongside the klezmer explosion in the United States, there has been a similar but separate revival in **Israel**. The State of Israel has always been uneasy about Yiddish culture and has chosen to emphasize instead the Hebraic links with the Semitic culture of the Holy Land. So too in the music. Where the American klezmer revival is often nostalgic, the Israeli is mystical, bringing to the fore the music's roots in Hassidic *nigunim* or religious songs. There is an annual klezmer festival in the town of Safed in northern Galilee, but there has been virtually no connection between the American and the Israeli klezmer scene.

Obviously, given their geographical location, Israeli bands have explored more of the connections between the oriental ingredients of klezmer and the traditions of the Middle East. The **Akiva Ben Horin** ensemble, for example, bring in a lot of Turkish and Druze elements.

Sulam, led by clarinettist Moshe Berlin, is perhaps the best-known klezmer band on the current Israeli scene. Their line-up includes a number of Soviet emigrés and they play a powerful mixture of east European nigunim and secular melodies.

Klezmer music, as it has evolved in Israel, is exclusively a product of Hassidic and Orthodox communities, and many of the best musicians are unknown to the general public, since they perform only for their own people.

THE NEW OLD WORLD

The recent changes in eastern Europe have re-focused attention on the original homeland of klezmer music.

In the old **Soviet Union**, where Jewish culture was effectively forbidden, the music gained an underground strength. The hugely popular singer and bandleader **Leonid Utyosov**, a Jew from Odessa, adapted Jewish songs and klezmer tunes and took them into the mainstream of Russian light music. His song "Uncle Alef", for example, a massive hit among Russians, was simply a reworking of a Yiddish song, "The Rabbi Elimelakh". Dissident music in the 1970s flirted with the Jewish music of the Odessa underworld, extolling Chicago-style crime, the black market and prostitution.

Now that Jewish culture is freer in Russia and the Ukraine, albeit subject to widespread anti-Semitism,

klezmer bands can be heard in Odessa, Moscow and other cities. And there are less conscious survivals, too. In the town of Vinnitsa in western Ukraine, Michael Alpert heard a local Ukrainian brass band with dozens of Jewish tunes in their repertoire playing at village celebrations. They had learnt the tunes from those who remembered them from the pre-Holocaust period. They are one of several groups in the area being documented by Professor Izaly Zemtsovski from St Petersburg, and recordings are due to be released.

However, with Russian Jews leaving in huge numbers for Israel, America and elsewhere in the west, the future of Jewish music there seems precarious. The musicians, however, are likely to provide a fresh injection in their new communities. The Russian element in Sulam has been noted above. In London, there is Russian emigré Gregori Schechter's ensemble, the **Klezmer Festival Band**, who play material with a Russian tinge and a glitzy finish.

Another interesting consequence of the changes in Russia has been the rediscovery of some of the klezmer and Yiddish recordings made between 1927 and 1948 by **Moshe Beregovsky**, the leading scholar and ethnographer of Soviet Jewish music. His written collections have long been a source of material for klezmer revival groups, but these cylinder recordings will be a unique insight into klezmer music in Russia and are likely to be fascinating in their own right as well as helping to rejuvenate the current repertoire.

Elsewhere in eastern Europe, the Jewish communities simply no longer exist following the Holocaust. However, the music, as in Russia, still seems to resurface. In the Szatmár region of **Hungary** there's a gypsy band who have recorded Jewish tunes they learned before the war, while playing alongside real klezmorim. The songs now have a strong gypsy flavour but are possibly the closest we can get to the living klezmer style.

Always there are shadows left behind. Another was discovered by the Hungarian group **Muzsikás**, who have recorded an album with some wonderful old gypsy musicians from **Transylvania** who still know the old Jewish tunes. The music is exquisite, with a genuine, old-time rural feel, and the musicians, Gheorghe Covaci on fiddle and Árpád Toni on cimbalom, like those klezmorim of old, are real "fiddlers on the hoof", the last heirs to a tradition of playing functional music for a rural community that has taken on a new life and a cosmopolitan aesthetic with groups like The Klezmatics on the streets of New York.

ARCHIVE ALBUMS

⦿ **Various** YIKHES: *Klezmer recordings from 1907–1939* (Trikont, Germany). The best compilation of remastered 78s, including a couple of 1910 tracks from Belf's Romanian Orchestra, virtually the only European band to have been recorded on disc, plus some great tracks from Naftule Brandwein, Dave Tarras and others. Excellent notes, text is available in both English and German versions.

⦿ **Various** *Klezmer Pioneers: 1905–52* (Rounder, US). Another excellent compilation of old masters, including Abe Schwartz, Harry Kandel, Sam Musiker, Naftule Brandwein and Dave Tarras.

⦿ **Dave Tarras** *Yiddish-American Klezmer Music 1925–1956* (Shanachie, US). An amazing collection of popular Yiddish music, with clarinettist Tarras playing with various bands for radio, theatre and commercials.

CONTEMPORARY US KLEZMER

⦿ **Various** *Doyres 1 and Doyres 2* (Trikont, Germany). Doyres means "generations" and these are terrific compilations of the new and old names of the klezmer revival.

⦿ **Brave Old World** *Klezmer Music* (Flying Fish, US) and *Beyond the Pale* (Pinorrekk, Germany). One of the best contemporary ensembles. *Klezmer Music* has some fine instrumental tracks and the "Chernobyl" song; the more recent *Beyond the Pale* is mixed but includes fantastic rustic-style playing and the "Bobover Wedding March" – worth the cost of the album alone.

⦿ **Don Byron** *Plays the Music of Mickey Katz* (Elektra Nonesuch, US). A most convincing – and fun – performance of the rather kitsch repertoire of this arch parodist.

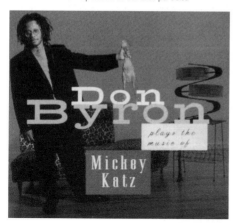

⦿ **Epstein Brothers** *Zeydes un Eyniklekh (Grandfathers and Grandsons)* (Wergo, Germany). The Epstein brothers are surely the last of the great old-time klezmer musicians. They play here with the young clarinettist Joel Rubin. A very fine disc.

⦿ **Giora Feidman** *The Magic of Klezmer* (Delos, USA). Many of Feidman's recordings are a bit kitsch. This is one of the better ones. He has a fantastic tone.

⦿ **Kapelye** *Chicken* (Shanachie, USA). New York's leading band in the more traditional style. "Der Yid in Yerusholayim", a great instrumental dance number, plus a series of pieces for a traditional Yiddish wedding.

⦿ **The Klezmatics** *Rhythm + Jews* (Piranha, Germany). The cutting edge of contemporary klezmer. Fantastic instrumental solos on clarinet, violin and trumpet. Listen out for "Fun Tashlikh" and "Bulgar a la Klezmatics". Their earlier disc ⦿ *Shvaygn = Toyt* is also highly recommended.

⦿ **Klezmer Plus!** *Klezmer Plus!* (Flying Fish, US). Yiddish dance music featuring old-time musicians Sid Beckerman and Howie Less. Klezmer born of the American popular tradition.

⦿ **Klezmorim** *Metropolis* (Flying Fish, US). Good performances from one of the leading bands of the klezmer revival.

KLEZMER FROM ELSEWHERE

⦿ **Flying Bulgar Klezmer Band** *Flying Bulgar Klezmer Band* (Dorian, US/Flying Bulgar, Canada). Fine debut album from a ground-breaking Canadian ensemble. Their followup, *Agada*, also has some evocative new compositions.

⦿ **Salomon Klezmorim** *First Klez* (SYNCOOP, Holland). Over the past few years there has been a huge growth in the number of klezmer bands in Europe. This group, led by clarinettist Marcel Salomon, is among the best, with a sharp, incisive sound.

⦿ **Muzsikás** *Máramaros* (Hannibal, UK). Another essential disc for those interested in the roots of klezmer in east European folk. Marvellous performances accompanied by old-time Transylvanian gypsies.

⦿ **Rubin & Horowitz** *Bessarabian Symphony: Early Jewish Instrumental Music* (Wergo, Germany). First-class clarinet, accordion and tsimbl playing from two of the best young exponents of traditional klezmer music. Good east European repertoire.

⦿ **Sulam** *Klezmer Music from Tel Aviv* (Wergo, Germany). A good example of Israeli klezmer music.

⦿ **Various** *Chansons Yiddish – Tendresses et Rage* (Ocora, France). Not exactly klezmer but the closely related tradition of Yiddish song. Pieces with a real atmosphere and excellent musicianship on violin, accordion and guitar, performed by Moshe Leiser, Ami Flammer and Gerard Barreaux.

⦿ **Various** *Hungarian Folk Music from Szatmár Region* (Hungaroton, Hungary). Earthy playing from real gypsy village bands, including some old Hungarian Jewish tunes.

HAWAIIAN HULA BALOOS

AMERICA'S PACIFIC SOUND OF STEEL AND SLIDE GUITARS

Hawaii rode a World Music wave as early as the 1920s, with its distinctive slide-guitar sound and hula dances. And for all the islands' postwar immersion in tourism, the music has continued to pursue a highly individual path. Mike Cooper, who plays a mean slack key himself, surveys the scene.

Although the Hawaiians are of Polynesian origin and the exotic paradise islands lie deep in the Pacific nearly 4000 km west of San Francisco, the links with American history and culture are strong. The islands were formally annexed by the United States in 1898, and since 1959 they have been the 50th state – and a hugely popular tourist destination – of the USA.

Hawaii's musical roots, however, belong to another world, with their bedrock of traditional Polynesian chants and drum dances. The *hula* (dance) and the *mele* (chant) were the simple indigenous forms, as everywhere in Oceania, and the music was essentially vocal with accompanying drums. The *pahu* (shark-skin drum) is both the oldest instrument on the islands and a symbol of the ancient links of present-day Hawaiians to their Polynesian ancestors.

The mele chants were addressed to the gods, to chiefs, and to families, and they recorded the genealogy, history and sacred attributes of their subjects. The *mele hula pahu* (chants accompanied by dance and drums) are formal, sacred and (still) treated with great respect. Not so by the missionaries, though, who arrived in the 1820s and set about destroying this "heathen" culture. It has only been revived in the last few decades.

With the first colonists and settlers, the island was exposed to a somewhat bizarre array of musical influences. Missionaries from New England introduced vocal harmonies and hymns, while cowboys from Mexico brought guitars, and Portuguese sailors an early form of ukelele. The population also experienced a drastic shift, as western and eastern diseases, imported with the new immigrants from Japan, the Philippines and China, as well as Europe and America, devastated the indigenous Hawaiian peoples.

Later, however, towards the close of the nineteenth century, a new kind of Hawaiian music emerged, under the patronage of the Hawaiian royal family, who set up the Royal Hawaiian Band, headed by an illustrious bandleader, Henry Berger, recruited from the Prussian army. Berger became a great lover of Hawaiian music and performed arrangements of Hawaiian songs as well as marches and ragtime compositions of the day. It was in the early twentieth century, however, that modern Hawaiian music saw its most significant innovations, with the invention of the slack and steel guitar, and the emergence of *hapa haole* songs, written in English but drawing on the traditions of hula.

Hula Blues
Oh oh oh, those hula blues!
Tell me, have you heard those hula blues?
You can't imagine what you're feeling blue about
You simply glide and take a slide
and you want to shout
You wiggle, you giggle, you wiggle to the hula blues.

'Neath swaying palm trees
And friendly sea breeze
Where you hear the mellow steel guitars
Moaning softly under tropic stars.

Pale land of flowers
And golden showers
Where the hula girlies swing and sway
On the ukelele hear them play.

The Genial Hawaiians, 1934.

SLACK AND STEEL GUITAR AND HAPA HAOLE

The guitar had been introduced to the Hawaiian islands by Spanish, Mexican and Portuguese sailors and cowboys. In conventional guitar tuning, strumming the open strings produces a dischord. The Hawaiians, however, retuned the strings to create a harmonious chord and developed a whole range of open tunings – a new style that they called **Ki Ho'alu** or **slack key**.

That was just the first innovation, for around the turn of the century one Joseph Kekuku, a school student on Oahu Island, left his mark on guitar history. He discovered that if you slid a solid object up or down the strings after you had plucked or strummed them, you got the chord sliding up and down in a glissando. Hawaiian **steel guitar** was born: a new guitar sound and a new guitar posture, with the instrument played on the lap or on a stand.

At more or less the same time the **hapa haole** ("half white") style of song was also invented. This was a form of songwriting that merged traditional Hawaiian music forms with English lyrics, reflecting the increased contact between the islands and the American mainland. Ragtime also appeared as another influence on Hawaiian music.

But the influence was to work both ways. At the San Francisco Panama-Pacific Expo in 1915, which celebrated the opening of the Panama Canal, the new Territory of Hawaii invested heavily in its pavilion, and with this exposure to the sounds of Hawaiian string bands, the American mainland was launched into a new craze.

Aloha . . .
A stands for dear aloha,
L for the laughter and the smiles,
O is for out in the Pacific, where the angels
built those tropic isles.
H is for dear old Honolulu, far across the
ocean blue, and
A just means aloha, and aloha means I love
you.

By 1916 more Hawaiian records were being sold in the US than any other type of music. It was one of the first World Music crazes, outdoing even the tango in popularity, and gave birth to some amazing virtuoso steel-guitar recordings. Groups such as the **Kalama Quartet** introduced four-part falsetto harmony singing with two steel guitars playing counterpoint. And another cultural collision occurred as Hawaiian musicians like Sol Ho'opii and Bennie Nawahi discovered jazz.

Bennie Nawahi was a key figure in the music of this time – a steel-guitar wizard who performed with equal dexterity on mandolin and ukelele. He had started out as a busker, then worked a cruise ship with his brothers, and developed along the way an extraordinary showmanship, playing the steel guitar with

his feet and the ukelele behind his head with one hand. With America in the grip of a ukelele craze, Nawahi played the vaudeville circuit with huge success in the 1920s, being dubbed "King of the Ukelele", and launching a recording career that was to stretch nearly fifty years, until he suffered a stroke in the late 1970s.

During his early busking days Nawahi had worked with **Sol Ho'opii**, another musician who has become a legend among steel-guitar players. Ho'opii played a synthesis of American jazz and traditional Hawaiian music and had a profound and lasting effect on a whole generation of musicians, who played not only jazz and Hawaiian music, but western swing and country as well. His playing was technically brilliant and advanced in the use of chords, harmony and phrasing. Early in his career he developed the tuning that led to the development of the pedal steel guitar and the modern country music/Nashville sound we know today. He too recorded extensively, from 1925 up until the early 50s.

Inspired by figures like these, musicians the world over explored the Hawaiian sound. From the late 1930s on Hawaiian-style bands and steel-guitar players started to appear all round the world. There were English Hawaiians, German Hawaiians, Japanese Hawaiians, even Indian and Indonesian Hawaiians. In London, for example, the **Felix Mendelssohn Hawaiian Serenaders** were a hugely popular radio, recording and dancehall act, performing a mix of traditional Hawaiian, hapa haole, jazz and popular songs.

ROCK'N'ROLL, TOURISM AND SLACK KEY

From the 1950s on tourists began to flock to the islands from all over the world and "Hawaiian music" became a part of the experience, with grass-skirts revues to match the travel agents' packaged paradise. The music in these places was, and still is, cheap Americanized cocktail jazz. Hawaiians, meanwhile, discovered rock 'n' roll. Throughout the 1950s and '60s, interest in the steel guitar fell away, and young Hawaiians dreamed of becoming The Beatles.

Older styles were never completely lost, and in the 1970s ecological and political awareness grew, as in many parts of the world, and a new-found sense of identity led to a renewed interest in Hawaiian sounds. The islanders rediscovered slack-key guitar playing, and local record labels put out songs again in the Hawaiian language.

One of the great musicians of this revival was **Gabby Pahinui**. By the 1970s he was already a legend on the islands, though utterly unknown on the American mainland until Ry Cooder happened to buy one of his records in Honolulu. What Ry heard interested him so much that he went searching for the musician and found

The Pahinui Brothers

not only Gabby, but a whole family of Pahinui musicians. They recorded together with Cooder, whose music was a fine match for the slack-key style, and, although Gabby himself died in 1980, the **Pahinui Brothers Band** continue to play slack-key music in the style that Gabby taught them, as well as developing their own mixture of Hawaiian, soul, country and reggae slack-key music.

SLACK KEY AND STEEL GUITAR

••••••••••••••••••••••••

The **slack key guitar** is unique to Hawaiian music and, as its name suggests, the guitar's retuning involves slackening the strings to achieve an open chord. For instance, if you take the standard guitar tuning (from high to low – EBGDAE) and slacken the first string from E to D, the fifth from A to G and the sixth from E to D, you get a tuning of DBGDGD. This is an open chord of G when strummed, and placing a finger (or steel bar) across the strings at the fifth and seventh frets will give you the other two chords you'll need for any three-chord song, like a blues.

This is one of the simplest tunings, but the Hawaiians made an art out of different tunings and some were closely guarded secrets. They also developed two ways of playing with open tunings. One involves the fretting of the strings with a metal bar – the classic steel-guitar technique. The other technique, slack key, is less

known. It involves picking the strings, with the thumb providing a constant bass while the other fingers play a melody on the upper strings – often a slightly altered version of the sung melody. These styles have been so widely adopted that many think they were developed by blues musicians. Not true – they are Hawaiian inventions.

The **steel guitar** developed from the slack key and is played horizontally with the strings facing upward. The steel rod is pressed on the strings with the left hand to produce a harmonious sliding sound. The first electric guitar, a Richenbacher nicknamed the "frying pan", was actually a Hawaiian lap steel guitar made in 1931. The pedal steel guitar, with its mechanical devices to change tunings and volume, is less favoured by Hawaiian musicians and used more often in country music.

FESTIVALS

Big Island Slack Key Guitar Festival. Third Sunday in July on Hilo.

Gabby Pahinui/Atta Issacs Slack Key Festival. Third Sunday in August in Honolulu.

Steel Guitar Association Festival. First week in May on Oahu.

CLUBS, BARS AND HOTELS

IN HONOLULU

Elsie's, Downtown. A salt-of-the-earth bar in the red-light district, with funky Hawaiian music. Not for the faint of heart.

Halekulani Hotel. Music 4–7pm every day on the veranda, from a classic ensemble of steel, slack key and bass, plus a hula dancer. Barney Isaacs and Alan Akaka alternate on steel.

Jubilee's, Kalihi. Hawaiian music every night with "name groups" on Fridays and Saturdays.

Kahala Hilton. Old-time Hawaiian music from 4–7pm with Barney Isaacs on steel. One of the nicest, genteel spots for Hawaiian music.

Keyhole Lounge, Kalihi. A blue-collar bar in the industrial area that often has live Hawaiian music, and sometimes puts on slack-key guitarist Sonny Chillingworth.

Waikikian Hotel, Waikiki. The Tahitian Lanai here has unbelievable community singing on Fridays and Saturdays, from 1950s high-school alumni.

The Willows, Manoa. Old-style strolling Hawaiian musicians. Thursday to Saturday nights.

ELSEWHERE

Big Island. Musicians play regularly at the Mauna Kea Beach Hotel in Kona.

Lanai Island. Slack-key guitarists sometimes play at the Manele Bay Hotel, Manele Bay.

Maui island. Slack-key guitarists sometimes play at the Maui Lu Resort, Kihei.

RADIO STATIONS

KCCN (1420 AM). Honolulu's full-time Hawaiian music station.

KAHU (1060 AM). Big Island's Hawaiian music station.

The Pahinuis are a string band, typical of the best Hawaiian groups today – who have settled into a regular format of guitars, ukelele, steel guitar, bass and vocals. The music rarely makes it out of the islands, even in recorded form, so you really have to go to Hawaii to hear it and to buy it. Among the best local bands are the **Genoa Keawe Group**, the **Ho'opii Brothers Band** and the **Sam Bernard Trio**.

Look out, too, for solo artists like the slack-key masters **Ray Kane** and **Sonny Chillingworth**, both of whom have recorded for US labels. Kane is one of the great living slack-key players, playing something like Hawaiian country blues, with slower, more meditative rhythms. Chillingworth has a more contemporary style, influenced by Gabby Pahinui, in whose band he used to play. He has also brought in a few new influences of his own, including a touch of Portuguese fado.

There are, too, some great veteran players on the island, such as **Tau Moe**, who was rediscovered by the American steel-guitarist Bob Brozman in the mid-1980s. His re-emergence is a good story. Brozman got a letter from Moe ordering a couple of his records, and the name set bells ringing, for it was that of a

Slack key master Ray Kane

steel-guitar player on some legendary 1929 recordings of a band called Mme Riviere's Hawaiians. He called him up and discovered to his amazement that it was the very same man, who had returned to Hawaii in the 1970s after fifty years of touring with Mme Riviere's band, across Asia, the Middle East and Europe. After Brozman met Moe and his wife Rose, the band's singer, he suggested that they re-record the songs from those old 78s. They did so, and the resulting release on Rounder Records, with Brozman on steel guitar, is one of the great collections of Hawaiian music.

DISCOGRAPHY

The best source for Hawaiian music, outside the islands, is Dancing Cat Records (Box 639, Santa Cruz, CA 95061), who specialize in slack-key records and are distributing and releasing some fine contemporary and historic recordings. In Hawaii, look out for recordings on the Hula, Tradewinds and Music of Polynesia labels, and check the Honolulu record stores – Harry's Music (3457 Wai'alae Ave) and House of Music (1365 Colburn St).

ROOTS

CD **Various** *Hawaiian Drum Chants: Sounds of Power in Time* (Smithsonian/Folkways, US). A record of the earliest known forms of Hawaiian music, some of it from old cylinder recordings. As close as we can get to the stuff Captain Cook would have heard when he first arrived.

Rose Moe

CLASSIC STEEL AND SLACK

CD **Various** *Vintage Hawaiian Music: The Great Singers 1928–34* (Rounder, US). A first-class collection compiled by Bob Brozman. Includes tracks by Mme Riviere's Hawaiians, Kalama's Quartet and the Sol Ho'opii Trio.

CD **Various** *Vintage Hawaiian Music: Steel Guitar Masters 1928–34* (Rounder, US). A companion volume of golden age recordings, including King Bennie Nawahi, Sol Ho'opii and Tau Moe.

CD **Various** *Tickling the Strings* (Harlequin, UK). A compilation of steel-guitar tracks from 1929 to 1952, featuring Tau Moe, Sol K. Bright and Andy Iona, and including a lot of electric steel tracks.

CD **The Kalama Quartet** *Early Hawaiian Classics* (Arhoolie, US). A gem of Hawaiian falsetto harmony accompanied by two steel guitars.

King Bennie Nawahi *Hot Hawaiian Guitar 1928–49* (Yazoo, US). This and the Sol Ho'opii collection below are the best real hot Hawaiian guitar available.

CD **Sol Ho'opii** *Master of Hawaiian Guitar* (Rounder, US). Probably the most influential of all Hawaiian guitarists.

CD **Tau Moe Family** *Remembering the Songs of Our Youth* (Rounder, US). The veteran Tau Moe family rework classic 1920s cuts with Bob Brozman. A great collection.

CONTEMPORARY

CD **The Gabby Pahinui Hawaiian Band** *The Gabby Pahinui Hawaiian Band* (Panini/Warner Bros, US). A must for any Hawaiian music collection. The great Gabby Pahinui with Ry Cooder.

CD **The Pahinui Brothers Band** *The Pahinui Brothers Band* (RCA/Private Music, US). The best album of contemporary Hawaiian music internationally available, from a band led by Gabby's sons.

CD **Sonny Chillingworth** *Sonny Solo* (Dancing Cat/Wyndham Hill, US). Slack-key guitar and vocals, including a couple of fado-style songs in Portuguese, from a former Gabby Pahinui Band guitarist.

CD **Ray Kane** *Punahele* (Dancing Cat/Wyndham Hill, US). Wonderful country blues – mainly instrumentals – from another of the great living slack-key players.

AUSTRALIA AND THE PACIFIC

This small chapter deals with Pacific island music – the thousands of tiny little atolls and islands that comprise Polynesia, Melanesia and Micronesia, and the very large islands of Papua New Guinea and New Zealand as well. Covered here, too, is the largest island of them all, Australia, a continent in itself with 50,000 years of indigenous history.

Australian Aboriginal music is both the newest and most ancient phenomenon on the globe. Australia's indigenous people can boast the oldest intact culture on earth and the resonant sounds of the didgeridoo evoke a sacred mythological world that demands respect.

Sadly, that is what the Aborigines did not get. From 1788, as Australia was developed as a penal colony for white settlers, the indigenous people were driven off their ancestral land and resettled, or hunted and killed like animals. Such practices persisted until well into this century, and discrimination has continued, with the recognition of Aboriginal rights a relatively recent phenomenon.

The sudden growth of modern Aboriginal music has been a consciousness-raising accompaniment to this political movement. In that way it shares many qualities with Native American music, particularly the mystical and sacred attachment to the land that is so much a part of Aboriginal belief. As an expression of that solidarity Aboriginal and Native American performers – notably the Australian group Yothu Yindi and the Indian singer John Trudell – have supported each other on concert tours. Bob Marley, too, has been a huge influence on Aboriginal musicians with his espousal of black power and the struggle for rights.

In the fusion of these musical and spiritual influences with their own black, but not African, traditions the contemporary Aborigines have forged a distinctive new musical voice which is reminding the world that they are, after all, the first Australians. The voice is to be heard in all manner of forms, from the roots sounds of ceremonial playing to the powerful Aboriginal rock of bands like Yothu Yindi.

While the destruction of Aboriginal culture was essentially a spiritual one, by breaking the ancestral contact with the land, it was a much more physical process in the Pacific islands, where missionaries arrived and burnt ceremonial houses, musical instruments and anything connected with "heathen" customs. If there's one thing that links the thousands of Polynesian islands scattered through the Pacific it is the destructive legacy of captains Cook, Bligh, Fletcher Christian and the rest of Spanish and French seafarers at the end of the eighteenth century and the missionaries in their wake.

Many of the Pacific islanders' indigenous cultures suffered near fatal blows at that time, and what survives in Polynesia today are, for the most part, fusions of European secular and religious music with those indigenous elements that managed to survive the colonizers' onslaught – or which have been painstakingly resurrected in recent years. In Melanesia and Micronesia Europeans arrived somewhat later and the indigenous traditions of those islands are fractionally more intact.

Most of the music of the Pacific has yet to make a real impact on the world scene, but perhaps our article, compiled with the help of roving composer and ethnomusicologist David Fanshawe, will help steer people towards some of the exciting discoveries to be made: in the rich choral singing of Tahitian choirs, for example, or the crazed relentlessness of Solomon Island and Papuan "flip flop" and bamboo bands.

Atoll A circular coral reef or string of coral islands surrounding a lagoon.

Balanda An Aboriginal word for whites.

Bilma Clapsticks used in Aboriginal music.

Contact The arrival of Europeans in the Pacific.

Corroboree Ceremonial or festive gathering of Aboriginal clans.

Didgeridoo Traditional Aboriginal instrument made from hollowed eucalyptus and blown with circular breathing.

Garamut Slit-log drum of Papua New Guinea.

Haka Maori welcome chant of New Zealand.

Hoko Easter Island war dance.

Himene (or Imene) Polynesian hymns and chants.

Kundu Hour-glass drum of Papua New Guinea.

Lali Slit-log drum of Polynesia.

Moai Easter Island monolithic statues.

Pahu Polynesian drum.

Singsing Festival in the highlands of Papua New Guinea.

Tiurai Tahitian July Festival.

Yidaki An Aboriginal term for didgeridoo.

Yolgnu Aboriginals.

Australian Aboriginal dancers

I HAVE A DREAMTIME

ABORIGINAL MUSIC AND BLACK RIGHTS IN AUSTRALIA

Five years ago, when people talked of Aboriginal music the picture that came into the minds of the Australian public would probably have been an ethnographic one – a group of people in the bush with a didgeridoo. As Marcus Breen reports, all that's now changed and Aboriginal groups have arrived as a powerful force in contemporary music and one bound up with the struggle for land rights and an end to discrimination.

Politics is always on the agenda in the world of contemporary Aboriginal music, but so, too, is an element of spirituality which invariably takes the music beyond simple agit prop.

The singer **Ruby Hunter** – one of the best new names on the Aboriginal scene and the first woman artist to record solo – is typical in this respect. On her 1994 debut album, "Thoughts Within", there is a song called "Kurongk Boy, Kurongk Girl" about a south Australian Aboriginal clan. Ruby has an incredibly deep voice and her first utterances seem like indecipherable sounds coming from the earth itself. Only gradually do the words come into focus:

Kurongk boy, Kurongk girl
Living in a brand new world
Drawing in the sand we did
Ran barefoot when we were kids
Light a candle, stormy nights
Open fires, Family nights
Oh! I go back
Yeah! I go back
In time, in time.

For those who have been following the arrival of Aboriginal music on the Australian popular music scene, here once again is proof that previously unheard voices are challenging white Australia's preconceptions with a knowledge that is both new and ancient. Through this music, non-Aboriginal listeners discover an unfamiliar perspective in which they are the outsiders and no longer dominant.

The members of **Yothu Yindi**, Australia's best-known Aboriginal group, have decisively put this music on the map. They, like most other Aboriginal artists right now, perform songs that

Singer-songwriter Ruby Hunter

remind European settlers of their shameful history in respect to the Aborigines – a history that has only been documented and acknowledged relatively recently. Theirs are songs that make contact with a culture that has 50,000 years of history – the oldest intact civilization on the planet – and they carry their own musical rewards.

SOME BACKGROUND

Since European settlers and convicts arrived in 1788 the story of the Aboriginals and the white settlers has been a one-sided one. It involves the dispossession of land, suppression of language and culture, denial of identity, dispersion and resettlement, the poisoning of water supplies, and as recently as the 1930s systematic massacres. The indigenous population of Tasmania was virtually eliminated in this unholy process.

In the late nineteenth century Protestant and Roman Catholic missionaries moved into remote parts of Australia to establish mission stations. They rejected the "heathen" music and culture of the

Aborigines and taught them the hymns of Europe. The strong influence of gospel singing can still be heard in Aboriginal women's choirs and in the work of some of the Aboriginal singer-songwriters.

In Australia today there are around 250,000 Aboriginals (about 1.3 percent of the population) and some 200 surviving languages. As well as the mainland Aborigines there are also the Torres Strait Islanders, of Melanesian descent, inhabiting the islands between the coast of Queensland and Papua New Guinea (with which they share their cultural and musical heritage).

The vast majority of Aboriginals are scattered across the continent in country towns and settlements, with large concentrations in the urban centres of Alice Springs, Darwin, Broome and the Redfern suburb of Sydney. In suburban areas Aboriginals are pretty well integrated into Australian society, although elsewhere there is deprivation, unemployment and alcoholism.

SONGLINES

An important modern cultural development for Aboriginals was the establishment in 1964 of the **Institute of Aboriginal Studies** in Canberra, now known as the **Australian Institute of Aboriginal and Torres Strait Islander**

THE DIDGERIDOO

• •

The **didgeridoo** (*didjeridu* is the more scholarly spelling and *yidaki, yiraki, magu, kanbi* and *ihambilbilg* are some of its Aboriginal names) is the traditional instrument unique to Australia's Aborigines. It is made from the limb of a eucalyptus tree, naturally hollowed out by termites to form a long tube, and is often finely decorated with carvings and symbols. Originally found amongst the Aboriginal clans of northern Australia, the didgeridoo is now used all over the country – and often by non-Aboriginal performers.

Traditionally the didgeridoo was played only by initiated men, selected by tribal elders, and for strictly structured sequences of totems and rhythms at ceremonies. To learn the didgeridoo, players are encouraged to spend time listening to the sounds and spirit of the bush so as to imitate and respect insects, animals and nature. The instrument itself is, of course, a part of nature.

In keeping with its ceremonial role, the didgeridoo was used with utmost respect by these initiates. Recently there has been debate in the Aboriginal community about its use by women musicians and – to a greater degree – white Australians.

Bearing such sensibilities in mind, Mandawuy Yunupingu of Yothu Yindi consulted elders of the Yirrkala tribe in Arnhem land before the instrument was used in their hit single "Treaty".

Foremost among today's Aboriginal didgeridoo players is **Joe Geia**, whose repertoire ranges from traditional to folk rock. A noted white player of the instrument is **Charlie McMahon**, who worked as adviser to the Kintor people for two years. There he was given access to some of their secret knowledge and, combining this with his own sensibility, he has brought the music to white audiences with his band **Gondwanaland**.

As the deep vibratory sound of the instrument has become internationally recognized, some of the aura it has carried and the resonances of its continent may disappear. Yet the didgeridoo will never lose its place as the instrument that best reflects the Aboriginals' 50,000 years of tradition and experience.

Young didgeridoo players on Mornington Island

Studies (AIATSIS). This has sponsored work in all aspects of traditional Aboriginal life, including, on the music side, an archive of over 7000 hours of indigenous music, gathered from across the country and collected from 1898 to the present. Selections from the archive have been issued on cassette.

Many Aboriginals have themselves only recently started to appreciate their own music, having grown up on a diet of western pop and rock. But as their musicians have moved into rock and "singer-songwriter" formats and gained a universal audience, more and more have wanted to listen to their own people sing about their situation. To Aboriginals this should come as no real surprise for the implicit power of traditional music is recognized as a binding cultural and creative force in their culture.

Aboriginal creation myths tell of legendary totemic beings who wandered over the continent in the **Dreamtime**, singing out the name of everything that crossed their path – birds, animals, plants, rocks, waterholes – and so singing the world into existence. The **songlines** are paths which can be traced across the continent linking these totemic emblems: sacred objects that have returned to the land – perhaps a lizard, a kangeroo or an outcrop of rocks. Each Aboriginal clan takes one of these totemic beings as ancestor and will have maybe a lizard-Dreaming or a kangeroo-Dreaming or a rain-Dreaming.

According to Bruce Chatwin's book *Songlines*, the totemic ancestors are thought to have scattered a trail of words and musical notes along the lines of their Dreaming-tracks. An ancestral song is both a map and direction-finder: "Regardless of the words, it seems the melodic contour of the song describes the nature of the land over which the song passes. One phrase would say, 'Salt-pan'; another 'Creek-bed', 'Spinifex', 'Sandhill', 'Mulga-scrub', 'Rock-face' and so forth. An expert song man, by listening to their order of succession, would count how many times his hero crossed a river, or scaled a ridge – and be able to calculate where, and how far along, a Songline he was."

As the songlines suggest, music and song are central to Aboriginal identity. Through singing, dancing, painting and ceremony, people become coparticipants in the ongoing creation and re-animation of life. Songs can contain the history and mythology of a clan, the practical instructions for the care of land or advice about dangerous foods or animals; and, of course, there are songs for fun and entertainment.

Traditional Aboriginal music is strongly rhythmical with a dependence on "natural" sounds – clapping hands, body slapping, the stamping of bare feet on the ground or the clapping together of *bilma* (sticks) or boomerangs. The best-known instrument is, of course, the **didgeridoo** (see box), a hollowed-out trunk which is blown with circular breathing to give either a rhythmic or sustained accompaniment to a dance, sacred ceremony or *corroboree* – a meeting of neighbouring tribes with singing and dancing. The instrument's deep, resonant sound is instantly recognizable and it has become the most popular and distinctive addition to contemporary Aboriginal bands.

ROCK-DREAMING

For white Australians, traditional music has long been a primary, but marginal, experience of black Australia. Its otherworldliness helped maintain the image of Aboriginal issues as being on the periphery of "Australian" life, and it received very little attention outside anthropology or ethnomusicology circles.

The first significant change in perceptions came with the 1979 documentary-drama film **"Wrong Side of the Road"**, which told the story of racist oppression and denial of land rights denied through the eyes of young Aboriginal musicians. The idea of Aboriginal music was seen to encompass a contemporary scene, as well as its purely traditional forms.

The film showed the Aboriginal bands **No Fixed Address** and **Us Mob** struggling to get exposure playing their reggae-influenced songs, and marked the beginning of a public recognition of music as a tool in the fight to communicate the Aboriginal story. In particular the No Fixed Address song "We Have Survived" made the point that the Aboriginals would not disappear into the background:

We have survived the white man's world
And the torment and the horror of it all
We have survived the white man's world
And you know, you can't change that!

The influence of Bob Marley was marked in the early days of this Aboriginal contemporary music scene. Marley had toured the country in 1979 and left many admirers in his wake. As throughout Africa, Marley's socially conscious music – the "Get Up, Stand Up" assertions – created an instant bond for Aboriginal artists, and a number of Aboriginal-based bands set up, or began using, reggae and rock formats and expressing their connections with the other black peoples of the world. They included Bart Willoughby of No Fixed Address, a former student of the Centre of Aboriginal Studies (CASM) in Adelaide, and, in particular, Yothu Yindi, whose founder Mandawuy Yunupingu cites Marley as a crucial model:

Multi-culti Australian group Yothu Yindi

"His philosophy and knowledge was very appealing. He's been a big influence on my songwriting, with his freedom themes, although my songs aren't necessarily like his. But some of the things I feel about my life, our country, are the same as Marley would have felt. I usually centre my melodies around a traditional song. I might then add a reggae beat or whatever, but the whole concept and idea is derived from my understanding of Aboriginal song."

Of course, the contemporary path cannot be isolated from the traditional one. Indeed, if there is one element of Aboriginal music that is increasingly recognized throughout Australia it is that the music speaks primarily of the experience of the people and tells of a spiritual connection with the land.

YOTHU YINDI

Yothu Yindi, hailed by *Billboard* magazine as "the flagship of Australian music", are far and away the most successful exponents of distinctively Aboriginal rock, and they are integrally linked to the struggle for Aboriginal rights. Mandawuy Yunupingu and his fellow band member, Witiyana Marika, are sons of leaders of the Gumatj and Rirratjingu clans in Northeast Arnhem land. Both fathers were involved in the early days of the Aboriginal land rights movement in the 1960s, and in addition to Mandawuy and Witiyana several members of both families appear in the band.

Yothu Yindi's first album, "Homeland Movement", was released in 1988 – Australia's "bicentennial year", and an event which provided a focus for their protest. On the follow-up albums, "Tribal Voice" and "Freedom", and in concert, the band have continued to address social injustice and land rights as well as the wish for harmony and reconciliation between black and white.

The band itself symbolizes this with a mixture of Aboriginal and white musicians. Yothu Yindi means "Mother Child", and their music consistently emphasizes the relationship between Australia's original inhabitants and white Australians. Mandawuy Yunupingu was declared "Australian of the Year" in 1992 for his work in promoting Aboriginal culture and interracial harmony.

Yothu Yindi are quite an experience live, with their body-painted dancers. Musically the main ingredients are guitar, drums and keyboard, plus yidaki (didgeridoo) and bilma (clapsticks). Their repertoire includes arrangements of

Freedom

We've been working on a course for change, trying to work out a balance Sometimes I feel I'm so alone and I wish you were here Making money can be one thing, building bridges can be the other one All it takes is understanding now, to make that dream come true You and me bayma, we can make it happen "freedom" You and me liya-wayma, we can see it through "freedom".

Yothu Yindi

traditional and sacred songs giving a strong spiritual ingredient to their music beyond the political sloganizing. Here, for example, is their song "Timeless Land":

I feel the spirit of the great sisters calling on me to sing
This is the learning of the great story I'll tell you about this place
From the edge of the mountains fly down the valley, down where the Snowy River flows
Follow the water down to the ocean, bring back the memory
This is a timeless land. This is our land.

LAND

Land is the primary issue addressed by Aboriginal artists and it's a political question that has been recognized by Australia's major political parties since the mid-1970s.

Yothu Yindi's album "Tribal Voice" includes the "Treaty" song which calls for land rights and reconciliation through a treaty which was drawn up but never signed between the white invaders and the continent's original inhabitants:

Well I heard it on the radio
And I saw it on the television
Back in 1988
All those talking politicians
Words are easy, words are cheap
Much cheaper than our priceless land
But promises can disappear
Just like writing in the sand.
Treaty Yeh, Treaty Now,
Treaty Yeh, Treaty Now.

Interestingly enough, the original version of "Treaty" flopped as a single and only took off

once it had been remixed for the dance floor – the "filthy lucre mix" the band dubbed it.

Since then the "Mabo decision" has brought cause for optimism. In a celebrated 1992 case, the Australian High Court overturned the so-called *terra nullius* doctrine which regarded the continent as unowned land (meaning that no other colonial power had laid claim to it). Eddie Mabo, a Torres Strait Islander, argued that the Aboriginal community on Murray Island were the legitimate owners and this is what was finally recognized in the historic Mabo decision. Yothu Yindi celebrated it in song:

Terra nullius, terra nullius,
Terra nullius is dead and gone
We were right, that we were here
They were wrong, that we weren't there . . .

While the verdict has set a precedent and the song is an exuberant statement of vindication, it is no easy task, given the resettlement policies, for Aboriginal groups to prove they have had the continuous relationship with the land they are claiming that the law requires. At least the Mabo legislation that has followed the court case means that in principal the return of land to Aboriginal people has become a nationally recognized priority.

ASSIMILATION

"Assimilation" was the euphemistic term for a policy practised in the 1950s and '60s of taking children of mixed race from their parents and raising them in white foster homes or institutions. Many of these children were literally kidnapped and told that their parents were dead. In an astonishing feat of "doublespeak" the institution responsible was called the "Aborigines Protection Board". The theory was that children reared away from traditional influences would choose to become like whites.

In fact a good many children went on to try and track down their families and rediscover their roots. Over the last decade, three of them – Kev Carmody, Archie Roach and (his partner) Ruby Hunter – have become major Aboriginal singer-songwriters and are today among the most powerful indigenous voices of Australia.

Kev Carmody, who was taken from his family when he was ten, has become the leading balladeer of Aboriginal concerns and has been dubbed Australia's Dylan. The angry lyrics of his 1990 album "Pillars of Society" were well informed by his research work as a doctoral candidate examining the white's treatment of Aborigines. He is especially contemptuous of the materialistic non-spiritual European society which had used Christianity as a tool in its genocide – a theme brilliantly developed in "Thou Shalt Not Steal".

Carmody's most recent album, "Bloodlines" (1993), sustains his strong vocal style with hard-strummed electric guitar and didgeridoo. Some of the material is linked to a community project he was involved with in Brisbane. His is an influential voice which has found an audience at a wide level, including, notably, the schools. "The positive part", he says, "is that we get so many requests from kids who want to quote the songs for school projects. It's so important to make the kids aware. The older generation are set in their ways, but it is great that the schools can use the oral tradition, because the curriculum still tells lies about what happened."

Thou Shalt Not Steal (First verse only)

1789 down Sydney Cove the first boat people land
And they said sorry boys our gain's your loss we're gonna steal your land
And if you break our new British laws for sure you're gonna hang
Or work your life like our convicts with a chain on your neck and hands
They taught us Oh Black woman thou shalt not steal
Hey Black man thou shalt not steal
We're gonna change your Black barbaric lives and teach you how to kneel
But your history couldn't hide the genocide, the hypocrisy to us was real
'cause your Jesus said you're supposed to give the oppressed a better deal
We say to you yes our land thou shalt not steal, Oh our land you better heal
Oh white man thou shalt not steal, Oh our land you better heal.

Kev Carmody

Archie Roach

Archie Roach was taken from his parents at the age of three and told that his family had perished in a fire. It was only as a teenager that he discovered that his mother had just died, and the shock was devastating. Dispossessed and rootless, like thousands of Aborigines he resorted to drink and spent the next ten years in an alcoholic haze. "I went from city to city, living on hand-outs. Playing music was my way of getting money to drink. Finally I stopped drinking and music seemed the natural thing to fill up the void. It was therapeutic. Still is."

Roach's songs, often simply written for voice and guitar, sound confessional and many come directly from his own experience. His song "Took the Children Away" made his name and appeared on his 1990 album, "Charcoal Lane":

Told us what to do and say
Told us all the white man's ways
Then they split us up again
And gave us gifts to ease the pain
sent us off to foster homes
As we grew up we felt alone
Cause we were acting white
Yet feeling black

The recognition that some of the evils committed against Aboriginal people are at last being overturned is an important theme in Roach's second album, "Jamu Dreaming". The title track, for instance, celebrates the rediscovery of lost ancestral values by urban-dwelling Aborigines.

ALCOHOL AND EDUCATION

Crawled out of bushes early morn
Used newspapers to keep me warm
Then I'd have to score a drink
Start me up, help me to think.

Archie Roach, "Down City Streets"

The rootlessness and alienation felt by so many Aboriginals has led to a chronic alcohol problem. Music has been used as a tool in publicly funded campaigns to stop alcohol abuse. The Central Australian Aboriginal Media Association (CAAMA – see overpage)

Blek Bela Mujik – a long way from Rolf Harris (see below)

released a cassette in 1988 titled "Wama Wanti: Drink Little Bit". It featured singer-songwriters, choirs and bands from Central Australia who developed music as part of the 1986 "Beat the Grog" campaign. The limited contemporary musical experience of people in the desert regions has meant that the music features either choirs of women and children with simple drum beats to maintain the rhythm, or four- and five-piece rock bands featuring a lead singer. The production values are quaint, but with message-music communication is everything.

Another campaign for Aboriginal education was launched in 1989 to fight AIDS. The cassette entitled **"AIDS! How Could I Know?"** drew on a broader range of styles, mostly in the country-rock tradition. "Aids: It's a Killer" sounds like a roughly recorded version of a Sun Studios single released in the early 1950s with rock'n'roll attitude in the guitars, drum kit and hand claps.

These campaigns have recently been complemented by the decisions in communities and missions in remote parts of Australia to ban the sale and consumption of alcohol within the settlements. In Broome, the musicians developed a community centre and alcohol rehabilitation programme as an extension of their activities.

CAAMA AND THE MEDIA

The Central Australian Aboriginal Media Association (CAAMA) was created in Alice Springs in 1980 with three volunteers and little more than a typewriter and a second-hand car. Today CAAMA broadcasts to all of Central Australia, runs a TV company, and owns a recording and publishing label – the only one run by and for Aboriginal and Torres Strait Islander people.

The Association has been particularly active in recording and releasing music from the remote desert areas, and their recent sampler CD, "From the Bush", is a brilliant introduction to the exciting range of music that is stirring in the dusty heart of Australia. Among the bands that have emerged under CAAMA's auspices, the current stars are **Blek Bela Mujik** – a powerful group featuring, on lead guitar, Johnny Ngarritj Blanasi, the son of the didgeridoo player who taught Rolf Harris! They mix a straight, heavy rock sound with didgeridoo and bilma rhythms, and a singing style that uses the nasal intonation of traditional Aboriginal song. Like Yothu Yindi, they seem on the verge of crossover success with dates supporting Tina Turner on her recent Australian tour.

The CAAMA model is being translated to other bush areas and indigenous broadcasters are already set in the regions of Townsville, Brisbane, Warringarri, Cunnunarra and West Australia. These radio stations have a strong link to music creation and production, as too do the network of nearly 200 urban community radio stations. Aboriginal music is used extensively on their specialist programmes and it is making waves, too, on national stations such as ABC's Radio National, where on a weekday afternoon it is now possible to hear exclusively Aboriginal tracks played over a couple of hours between interviews. Having tried special Aboriginal programmes on radio and TV which were felt to be patronizing, ABC seems now to favour a more integrated approach. It is remarkable that five years ago there simply would not have been enough Aboriginal music of high enough quality for this to happen.

Festivals, too, are mushrooming, following on from the success of the 1988 "grog-free" Festival of Aboriginal Rock Music in Darwin.

THE ROCK CIRCUIT

The number of **Aboriginal rock bands** formed over the past decade is nothing short of phenomenal, and is on a scale similar to that of the punk explosion of the late 1970s in Britain or America. In the sparsely populated Northern Territory alone there are now over fifty Aboriginal bands, and there are perhaps a hundred others in the rest of Australia.

Most exist well outside the mainstream of the major record labels – who are yet to show a real commitment for Aboriginal music – and in alliance with CAAMA-style outfits. In Broome, Central Western Australia, for example, local bands have developed the Broome Musicians Cooperative, largely on the efforts of **Jimmy Chi**, whose song "Bran Nu Dae" was turned into a musical and broadcast on national television, raising public consciousness about racism. Broome has had a modest success in the rock field, too, with the band **Scrap Metal**. This included musicians of mixed descent – Aboriginal and French, Filipino, Japanese and Indonesian – and made a couple of good albums at the end of the 1980s.

Elsewhere, notable bands include the desert-bred rock'n'roll **Warumpi Band**, who attracted attention as the first mixed Aboriginal and white band, singing in a mix of tribal language and English, and **Coloured Stone**, one of the longest-established groups. Formed in 1978, they are still a major presence on the scene and did much to update the Aboriginal sound with their 1991 album "Unma Juju - Dance Music", a remix of earlier material that brought a disco beat and the backing of a major label, BMG.

DISCOGRAPHY

TRADITIONAL

Various *Budal Lardil* (Larrikin, Australia). Songs and didgeridoo material from the Lardil people of Mornington Island. Includes dreaming songs from an ancient and contemporary perspective. Fascinating.

Various *Dawn Until Dusk: Tribal Song and Didgeridoo* (Australian Music International, US). A wonderful and atmospheric recording with vivid sounds of the Australian outback integrated with didgeridoo and songs. Not entirely authentic, but not as New Age as the admirable CD Eco-pak, made from recyclable materials, might suggest.

Various *Songs of Aboriginal Australia* (AIATSIS, Australia). An overview of Aboriginal music which offers a variety of sounds from many regions. An excellent introduction with accompanying notes. Cassette only.

Various *Traditional Music of Torres Strait* (AIATSIS, Australia). Dance songs and funeral chants from Murray Island with drum accompaniment and many Papuan influences. Cassette only.

CONTEMPORARY

Blek Bela Mujik *Blek Bela Mujik* (CAAMA/Mushroom, Australia). Rock and didgeridoo rhythms from a tight band set to follow along Yothu's trailblazing path.

Kev Carmody *Pillars of Society* (Larrikin, Australia). Unrelenting critique of white Australian society from this powerful singer-songwriter.

Ruby Hunter *Thoughts Within* (White Records, Australia). Evocative personal perspectives from the first woman to engage with these issues as a solo recording artist.

Charlie McMahon *Gondwanaland Wide Skies* (Warner, Australia). White Australian musician McMahon rocks along with synthesizer backing while maintaining the integrity of the didgeridoo.

Archie Roach *Charcoal Lane* (Aurora/Festival, Australia). A detailed account of the Aboriginal experience from the troubadour's perspective with moving songs about childhood experiences. Mainly voice and guitar.

Tiddas *Thing About Life* (Id/Phonogram, Australia). A trio of young Aboriginal women singing a cappella in acoustic folk style to address the urban experience. Sweet Honey in the Ayer's Rock!

Yothu Yindi *Tribal Voice and Freedom* (Mushroom, Australia). Tribal Voice is the landmark album in Aboriginal music history and the first to really cross over to a mainstream audience. Freedom follows it up with more fine Aboriginal rock fusion.

Various *From the Bush: CAAMA Sampler* (Polygram, Australia). A fine introduction to the contemporary music of central Australia's desert regions.

Various *Winds of Warning* (Australian Music International, US). Multi-instrumentalist Adam Plack and didgeridoo master Johnny "White Ant" Soames in a percussive and dynamic evocation of the outback. Traditional music reworked in a contemporary form.

A PACIFIC ODYSSEY

THE MUSIC OF OCEANIA

The Pacific Ocean covers a third of the earth's surface and contains the deepest waters in the world. It's a region with deep musical traditions, too, buffeted by the regular currents of colonists and explorers and now undergoing dramatic changes. You can hear music ranging from ancestral navigational chants and glorious polyphonic singing to laments about nuclear testing. Since 1978 David Fanshawe has spent ten years on a Pacific Odyssey, exploring and recording the traditional music of Polynesia, Melanesia and Micronesia. Simon Broughton met him for a musical tour around Oceania.

T he South Pacific is one of the last-to-be-explored regions of the globe with its thousands of volcanic islands and coral atolls scattered over 38 million square kilometres. Ethnically the territory is divided into three areas – Melanesia, lying mostly south of the equator, Micronesia, north of the equator, above it, and Polynesia, spread over a huge area to the east.

The people of **Melanesia** (from the Greek word *melas* – black, and *nesos* – island), which includes Papua New Guinea, the Solomon Islands, Vanuatu and Fiji, are very dark skinned with Afro hair and are thought in the very distant past to have migrated by canoe from East Africa across the Indian Ocean by way of Indonesia.

Fanshawe detects that ancestry still in their music and dancing: "Many of the dances of Oceania are sitting dances – people perform sitting down and it's the upper body that moves. Maybe this is something to do with the canoe culture, I don't know, but the island choreography is principally the movement of the arms, so different from Africa which is movement of the feet – you don't see a sitting-down dance in Africa. The ancestral relationship between east Africa and Melanesia is manifest in the fact that much of the music in Papua New Guinea, especially, is standing, not sitting. And Melanesia also has the widest diversity of instruments in the region – all sorts of drums and slit-log gongs, a great variety of flutes and pipes – but no stringed instruments apart from the guitar and ukelele brought by the Europeans."

David Fanshawe laying down some Pacific tracks

Micronesia (from *mikros* – small) is a group of small islands – including Yap, Truk, and the Marshall and Gilbert islands (Kiribati) – east of the Philippines and north of Melanesia. The inhabitants are thought to be of southeast Asian descent and Fanshawe feels the music shares some elements with that region:

"It is thin, wiry and taut – like the rigging of an outrigger canoe, with a single line, tough and defined. It's like the music of southeast Asia but without the instruments – you don't find drum bands at all. Perhaps in the far distant past the Micronesians travelled down the Mekong River and then set sail across the ocean from there. Their music is very voice-oriented with chanting, stamping and body-percussion. In the stick dances of Micronesia I've heard the best examples of pre-contact music, telling the legendary histories, genealogies and navigational tales of the islands."

The **Polynesians** are taller, lighter skinned and – it is believed – originated in southeast Asia and migrated down to Fuji and then fanned out over a vast territory from there. Polynesia (from the Greek *poly* – many) – stretches in a huge triangle from New Zealand in the southwest to Easter Island 8,000 kilometres away in the southeast and as far again to Hawaii (covered in our America chapter) at its northern apex.

"As you go east into Polynesia," Fanshawe explains, " the Melanesian flutes disappear and the instruments become more sparse, but the passion of the music becomes greater – particularly in the harmonic content which comes straight from the heart. The **"gospel" choirs** of **Tahiti** are simply astonishing. This is the 'sweet scent of the flower of Polynesia' that intoxicates everybody who witnesses it. You have the strum of guitars and ukeleles backed up with slit-log gongs and perhaps a bass drum or a 'cabin-tin' drum.

"Music is a reflection of topography and people reflect the landscape they are living in.

You must remember that these people came by canoe; they only carried what they needed for a voyage and when they arrived there often wasn't the wood or the material to make instruments. Very broadly speaking, highland people will have more instruments because they have wood; atoll people have shells and, if they're lucky, what they can make out of a coconut tree. That's why traditionally there are so few instruments in the Pacific. They didn't carry them on their canoes and the canoes were sacred and they weren't going to break them up to make instruments when they arrived."

COMPETITIONS

Even with such a bewildering number of islands and peoples, Fanshawe believes it is possible to find common features that define a Pacific-island style and mind-set: "Just think of what

TAHITI'S FÊTE TIURAI

. . . .

Without doubt, the Fête "Tiurai", held each July on Tahiti, is the most thrilling experience I have ever had in my career as a musician. Nothing could have prepared me for its magnitude. It is the greatest competitive event in the Pacific.

It was originally a Bastille Day (14th July) celebration but that's only an excuse really. The fête has grown into an event lasting a whole four weeks and groups come to Papeete, the Tahitian capital, from throughout the islands of French Polynesia. They compete for prize money in professional and amateur categories and participate in competitions for best overall group, best choreographer, best costume, best drummer, best female dancer and so on.

It's all really one glorified dance, which takes place on Vai'ete Place in the heart of downtown Papeete. It starts around seven or eight each night with dancers energizing the crowds and it will go on till one in the morning. So you've got five or six hours of nonstop performance every night. The dances are extremely sensual. They show the love between a man and a woman and they connect with the universe. Although there are solo dances, in essence Tahitian dancing is a group activity. The dancer and choreographer Jean "Coco" Hotahota, the grand old man of Tahitian dance, has always stressed that moving as an ensemble is the most important element of the dance. Coco's group, Te Maeva, is probably Tahiti's most celebrated.

The Tiurai is Tahiti performing not for tourists, but for Tahiti itself in a truly competitive festival of music, dance and culture.

David Fanshawe

Tahitian drummer at the Fête Tiurai

The Tahitian Gospel Choir tell it like it is

they all have in common – the ocean. They talk about the singing reef, which is like a background to all the music of the islands, in both a physical sense and an historical one. It has led to a great competitive spirit.

"The fact that the islanders originally came thousands of miles by canoe in many hundreds of years of migration to find their home atoll or island meant that they had to be competitive to survive. The Pacific islanders have a great desire to tell everybody how good they are. If it's fishing, it is how they catch the best catch, how they have the best rod, line and hook. It comes back to that basic principle of arriving on an isolated island, finding your tract of land and deciding that it's better than anybody else's and, in a friendly way, saying "Yahoo" to your cousins on the next island or on the other side of the fence.

"Everything is organized by competition – from building to music and it's that morale-boosting spirit of competition that I think has kept the islands' individuality through the centuries. And it has also helped them survive the onslaught of the outside world – first the missionaries and now the pressures of development and tourism – because they are coming through all that with their own identities, even now.

"Musically the competitiveness ranges from the smallest events, like village choirs competing at the Sunday service, to the vast inter-island events like the **Tiurai** – the July Tahiti Fête (see box) – and the **South Pacific Festival of Arts**. This latter is a sort of Olympiad of Pacific music

and takes place every four years in a different location." The last was held in 1992 on Rarotonga in the Cook Islands, and the 1996 festival will be in Samoa.

Fanshawe has also, at times, promoted his own contests, such as on a 1982 trip to Puka Puka in the northernmost Cook Islands. "I was going to the island on a *copra* (coconut) boat and my bed was a trunkload of videos – the first videos to go to Puka Puka. I was going to make music recordings, but the islanders were eagerly awaiting the videos – old Presley films like *Blue Hawaii* which are hot property in the northern Cooks. So I had to negotiate with the island council to hold back the videos while I sponsored a music competition to be held.

"There were all the categories – from *mako*, the old chants, and *imenetuki*, gospel singing, to *popo* and *deesco*. I was lucky to have a patient president of the island council who saw the wisdom of recording all this knowledge which is threatened with extinction. I think that this special music competition was probably the last to be held on Puka Puka. As I left everyone was watching the videos in the courthouse."

THE TAHITIAN CHOIR

One of those sudden and surprising discoveries of World Music came with a disc of the **Tahitian Choir**, released in 1992 by the French musicologist Pascal Nabet-Meyer. This recording was a huge international success and was most people's first introduction to Polynesian music. It includes religious hymns, ancestral legends and untranslatable lyrics sung by a mixed choir of 120 people on the island of Rapa Iti, a thousand miles south of Tahiti.

The Polynesians have always had a musical reputation and, according to missionary reports, singing was the most effective route to conversion. The local **himene** (songs) represent a typical Polynesian fusion of ancient music with the hymns brought by the missionaries in the early nineteenth century. Sometimes it is possible to hear distinct echoes of western hymns – "All Creatures of Our God and King", for example, on one of the Tahitian Choir tracks – and at other times it has a complex and distinctive form all its own. One of the most extraordinary features is the way it suddenly lurches down in tone, almost like a record player running slow.

This choral tradition is one of the highlights of Polynesian music and it was David Fanshawe's initial introduction to the Pacific: "I had never heard singing before like the unaccompanied chanting of the Cook Islands and Tahiti, and when I arrived there I found myself in seventh heaven.

"I went first to Rapa, on the Cook Islands, in 1982 and stayed for a while in the villages of Ahurei and Area, a very competitive duo set across the bay from each other. I made my recordings of the choir singing in Ahurei village – the same choir Mr. Nabet-Meyer recorded a decade later. 'The choir that sings flat', they've been called, but they don't hear it like that. They like the sound and it works like a sort of cadence at the end of a phrase.

"I'm sure that the choir music performed these days is pretty much what it would have been 150 years ago. The interesting and debatable question is whether they sang in harmony before the missionaries got there. Most authorities reckon that there was always some sort of polyphonic choral singing in Polynesia, long before white men arrived on the islands. If you listen to the *imenetuki* of the Cook Islands or the *imenetarava* of Tahiti, the singing is so far removed from western church music that it must have soaked up something indigenous.

"However, for the last 250 years people have been arriving on these islands with something new and the islanders have liked the new thing – they've taken it and adapted it to their own island tradition. Thus the Pacific islands have the music they have today through that transformation. The music is unlike anything else in the world, it is unique to Polynesia. The message, though, is the Christian one, let's make no mistake about that. They are not praising ancient chiefs and warriors or long-forgotten battles; they are praising God, a Christian God."

THE MISSIONARIES

Despite these choral fusions, the arrival of the missionaries in the nineteenth century was essentially destructive. As far as the missionaries were concerned, all aspects of native music were pagan and had to be eliminated – not only the rituals, but the instruments as well. The islanders were taught to praise a new God through the Bible and no longer needed the discipline of the old chants to the ancient gods. Gradually even the languages of the old chants became unintelligible.

Satawal stick dancers doing one of their sitting numbers

"The effect on the whole of the Pacific was so profound that in the space of about fifty years, from around 1790 – just after Captain Cook's time – to 1840, just about all the rituals that would have taken place had been replaced by Christian services. Take Tonga in Polynesia, for example. Once the king had been converted he himself decreed that all the old 'heathen' artefacts should be destroyed. The canoe sheds, the nose-flutes, the idols were all burnt. Anything made of thatch was deemed to be of pagan origin and so even houses were burnt. The old rituals were replaced by new ones – the Sunday service, Christmas and Easter.

"In Micronesia – on Yap, Truk and the Marshall Islands, where the missionaries didn't arrive until much later – there are still ancient **stick dances** that relate to precontact customs. These include both standing and sitting dances where lines of performers beat sticks and recount their legendary history, genealogies and, most notably, the patterns of the stars and navigational stories of how they reached their islands. These are all in forgotten languages and when I asked what the chants meant they would understand only a few isolated words and no more than that. I spent six months there recording anything I could of navigational knowledge, starpath chants, names and so on and then going into the canoe sheds to see them practising the stick dances."

HAKAS AND HOKOS

New Zealand is the biggest landmass of Polynesia and its indigenous inhabitants, the **Maoris**, are a large tribe who arrived from the Cook Islands between the tenth and fourteenth centuries. They now, however, only represent about a tenth of the New Zealand population.

"Musically the Maoris are cousins of the Cook Islanders, the Samoans and Tahitians, and you can hear how these old ritual Polynesian chants can be brought up to date and serve a new purpose", Fanshawe enthuses.

"The Maoris have a great gift for language and oration is the key to this music – just as it was 200 years ago or 500 years ago. That's why when Prince Charles visits a tribe in northern New Zealand a new **haka** (welcoming chant or war dance) is composed which mentions the Prince and the event they are celebrating."

Hakas generally have a call-and-response form with vigorous stamping, thrusting and flourishing movements plus facial grimaces and sticking out of the tongue. Although it has doubtless changed over the years, the haka is an example of a pre-contact form that has somehow endured.

Emphasizing an underlying unity beneath this vast scattering of islands, the haka of New Zealand is surely related to the **hoko** (war chant)

of Easter Island, far distant at the other corner of Polynesia. A group of Easter Islanders re-enacted a hoko specially for Fanshawe in a subterranean cavern – and it could be done once only – no retakes.

"It was the most difficult recording I have ever made. The chants hark back to the days when warriors paid allegiance to their tribe, boasting about their strength and solidarity. A rough translation would be:

What is your tribe?
Who are your leaders?
Where are your canoes?

At the end of the recording you can hear the warriors backing out of the cave bearing flickering torches, like ghosts vanishing into the sea."

Easter Island (*Rapa Nui* in Polynesian) is only twenty kilometres long and incredibly remote – its nearest neighbours are Tahiti and Chile, each 3,500 kilometres distant. The ancient inhabitants of what the islanders call *Te Pito o Te Henua* (the navel of the world) felt that the closest land to them was the moon. They erected the famous moai monolithic statues and had the only ancient form of writing known in Oceania. The island's discovery by Europeans in 1772 was the most tragic of all Pacific histories. In 1862 Peruvian slave ships kidnapped a thousand of the inhabitants (a third of the population) and, after protests, returned the survivors – a mere fifteen people – who brought with them a smallpox epidemic which devastated the rest of the islanders. The population sunk to a little over a hundred people.

The island's musical traditions, obviously, perished alongside. Fanshawe relates that "According to legend the moai statues are said to have danced to their final resting places with the help of supernatural powers. But it is very hard to hear any music on the island at all, these days. There are close contacts with French Polynesia, so that is what you will hear for the most part. There are probably no more than half a dozen pure Easter Island chants that have survived and are trotted out on all official occasions. I think I've recorded all of them.

"There is this marvellous old man called Papa Kiko, who is a warden at the Catholic church and he is like the Father of the Knowledge. He knows ancient songs and he sings them with his family who accompany him with clap-stones – just unaccompanied chants with stones beating together. It's a fantastic sound, but nobody knows now what they mean."

PAPUA NEW GUINEA

Papua New Guinea is a country of extraordinary ethnic and physical diversity. It has coral seas, great rivers, remote mountains and wild jungles as well as traffic jams and over a thousand tribal groups speaking nearly 700 different languages. Its music, too, is hugely diverse, with particular traditions in the highlands and lowlands, as Fanshawe discovered:

Solomon Island panpipers

"In the highlands the key thing is the **singsing**. This is where tribes from different villages come together to compete. I'd never heard anything like it. It's as if you turned up at the Royal Albert Hall to find the Royal Philharmonic, the London Symphony, the Bach Choir, the Liverpool and Bournemouth Symphony orchestras all doing their own thing, performing Mozart, Beethoven and Mahler – everything at the same time.

"Thousands of tribesmen arrive in full ceremonial costume to perform their particular music – it is usually unaccompanied chanting or yodelling originating in war-dances. Up until the 1930s many of the tribes were enemies and never met each other except in battle. Cannibalism was common. Now they are at peace, they like to come together to show off, to paint up and to perform."

The biggest singsings are in Goroka (in the Eastern Highlands, in even numbered years) and at Mount Hagen (in the Western Highlands, in odd-numbered years). Dates vary from year to year, although local singsings can occur anytime. Independence Day (Sept 16) is another popular time for festivals.

In the **lowlands**, the music is altogether different. "It is quieter and more sedentary with flutes and drums, notably the *kundu* (hour-glass drum) and the *garamut* (slit-log gong). These stay in the *haus tambaran*, the men's cult house, and each village will have a set of garamut drums. They are very heavy so you couldn't transport them if you were marching across the highlands for a singsing. They are traditionally played for initiations, when a village has been successful in a tribal dispute or to ask favours from the gods. Now they even bring garamuts into the church and they'll play them during the sung Eucharist!

"The other extraordinary instruments are the **bamboo flutes** of the **Sepik River** in the north west. At six foot, Sepik flutes are the longest in the world and they are kept in the rafters of the haus tambaran. They are very, very sacred, looked after by a special caretaker, and are played only by men – women aren't even allowed to see them. They are played exclusively for special blessings or dedications – never, like other instruments, on Independence Day out in the open. They are always played in groups with perhaps five or seven players, but never fewer than two. All this helps them preserve their magic and they have an extraordinary ethereal sound with interlocking tonalities from flutes of different lengths. Beautiful.

"Various sorts of pipes and flutes are important in Melanesia. There are glorious **panpipes** in the Solomon Islands which I recorded in Malaita. Like the Sepik flutes, they are related to the spirit world and are always played in groups, although they are not hidden in the same way. They can be played simply for entertainment. You also find them in Vanuatu, but no further, not into Polynesia.

"In PNG there is a very different society to those of Polynesia. Because it took so much longer to penetrate the highlands and the valleys deep in the heart of PNG, up until the Second World War much of the country was still untrodden by white men and so the old pagan rituals carried on until the middle part of this century. But all that is changing.

"When I went up the Sepik River I was looking for anything associated with initiation.

Did I actually see an initiation? No. All I ever saw was a re-enactment. The fact is I saw a different kind of initiation when I was there. The initiation of once-a-week performances taking place in the men's cult houses, the haus tamboran for the tourists.

"I got to hear quite a few traditional head-hunting songs in the remoter areas, though I wonder how long that'll be the case. The traditional ritualistic music of Melanesia is disappearing – it has lost its purpose and in the next twenty years people will forget the language and the customs of these rituals. The intensity of experience has gone out of these events. It becomes entertainment, something you perform for visitors at the Karawari Lodge up the Sepik River. Who can blame them? The villagers need electricity and they need to pay their bills."

FLIP FLOPS AND MODERN SOUNDS

The Solomon Islands and PNG are home to one of the most intriguing styles of modern music in the Pacific – **bamboo bands**. These are distantly related to the panpipe bands but are essentially an updated form of a traditional technique of stamping bamboo tubes of different lengths against the ground (Captain Cook described this in Tonga in the 1770s). In the modern bands the bamboo tubes are a good deal bigger, laid horizontally on the ground and sounded by striking them across the end with a pair of flip flops. Guitars are added to make the sound yet more funky.

Bamboo bands appeared after the Second World War. Just as the Americans left oil drums in Trinidad and the steel pans were tempered, it seems they left their flip flops around Honiara, the capital of the Solomon Islands, and kick-started the bamboo bands. They also left rock'n'roll rhythms, as David Fanshawe discovered: "You usually find the flip flops beating a bass-line on the bamboos and because you can't hear the guitars over the din of the bamboos they plug them into their transistor radios to amplify them and the more distorted it is the more they like it.

"I recorded the Wagi Brothers in Papua New Guinea who won a competition to celebrate the tenth anniversary of independence. But bamboo bands apart, the modern bands in the Pacific are pretty much stuck on the guitar, synthesizer and drum-kit syndrome with perhaps the odd ethnic instrument joining in.

"When I first went to the Pacific I was disappointed to find so many guitars and ukeleles – but these are classical instruments now. They have been there since the nineteenth

The Wagi Brothers giving it some flip flop

century and they are now the soul of the Pacific. Unaccompanied chant is very boring to the youth of today and it's the same everywhere in the world, not just in the Pacific.

"For me the most fervent and passionate guitar and ukelele bands are in the Northern Cook Islands where it's hypnotic with the fragrance of flowers. The songs are about flowers, the deep scent of the Pacific and the essence of sweet love juices flowing. When you travel through the islands and you have flowers in your hair, there's that intoxicating fragrance and only one sound can evoke it – a group of young people performing love songs and dances. There might be as many as seven guitars, a trio of ukeleles, slit-log gongs, and the ever-present cabin biscuit-tin beaten with sticks as loud as possible. The singing is in harmony above hypnotic, fast strumming which is usually the accompaniment to a wonderful dance."

In a region where music has always played a role in passing on oral history, it's not surprising that **contemporary events** have given rise to traditional songs. And it's not just Prince Charles visiting New Zealand. David Fanshawe has also recorded lyrics about the effects of the nuclear testing on Bikini Atoll in the Marshall Islands, Micronesia. This is where the first H-bomb was tested and from 1946–58 twenty-three nuclear tests were carried out here, leaving a continuing legacy of cancer, leukemia and deformity. The inhabitants were evacuated before the blasts, but many of the neighbouring islands received heavy doses of fall-out.

"I recorded these songs of radiation and fall-out in Rongelap and the one that moved me most was a very graphic description of how the sun rose twice, the sea turned purple and the water was hot. It was a simple, unaccompanied voice. Generally though, this sort of 'political' song is rare. There is still nuclear testing in French Polynesia and I can't say that I've heard songs about Mururoa – there's nothing like the protest songs about Aboriginal land rights in Australia. Pacific islanders enjoy themselves too much. They don't like a lot of what is going on around them, yet they still come up with jolly music. Being radical or political is not really their nature."

DISCOGRAPHY

A lot of discs of South Pacific music are bland grass-skirted tourist collections of poor-quality material. The recommendations below tend to the more ethnographic but are the real thing. Notable among them are the Pan Records series – an ambitious project with, so far, albums devoted to Tonga, Hawaii and Tuvalu – and David Fanshawe's releases on Saydisc and Arc. Fanshawe has set up a foundation to distribute royalties on his recordings to the local musicians.

GENERAL COMPILATIONS

ⓒ **Various** *Exotic Voices and Rhythms of the South Seas* (ARC, UK). The most far-reaching and most immediately accessible of David Fanshawe's Pacific collections. Ranging throughout the Pacific, the disc includes the Wagi Brothers bamboo band and Sepik flutes from PNG, panpipes from the Solomon Islands, and more from Fuji, Vanuatu, etc.

GOSPEL CHOIRS

ⓒ **The Tahitian Choir** *Rapa Iti* (Triloka, US). The extraordinary gospel singing of Tahiti and around is one of the most splendid musical hybrids of the Pacific. Recorded on the island of Rapa, this is an enjoyable introduction to Polynesian music – and spiritual too.
ⓒ **Tubai Choir** *Polynesian Odyssey* (Shanachie, US). Not as striking as the Tahitian Choir disc, to which this is a follow up, but a rich and powerful sound. Ancestral and Christian choral chants recorded on Tubai.

POLYNESIA

ⓒ **Cook Islands National Arts Theatre** *Drum Songs and Chants of the Cook Islands* (Manu, NZ). Showcase performances from the South Pacific Festival of Arts. Recorded live in Rarotonga.

ⓒ **Royal Folkloric Troupe of Tahiti** *Coco's Te Maeva* (Auvidis/Manuiti, France/Tahiti). Tahiti's foremost dance ensemble, led by Coco Hotahota. A Tahitian showcase.
ⓒ **Various** *Heiva i Tahiti* (ARC, UK). Fanshawe's atmospheric live recordings from the Tahiti July fête. Includes drum dances, polyphonic chants and popular songs.
ⓒ **Various** *Ifi Palasa* (Pan, Netherlands). Another of those bizarre Polynesian cultural fusions – Tongan music for brass band plus nose flutes and conch shells.
ⓒ **Various** *Mālie! Dance Music from Tonga* (Pan, Netherlands). Traditional and modern music, dance and poetry mainly for voices and percussion. Some cuts are sedate, others have rhythms beaten out on corrugated iron sheets.
ⓒ **Various** *Spirit of Polynesia* (Saydisc, UK). A fascinating collection of Fanshawe's Polynesian recordings including the wonderful Wagi Brothers flip-flop band, the famous Tahitian choir from Rapa Iti, a Maori haka and lots more from Tonga, Western Samoa, the Cook Islands and Easter Island.
ⓒ **Various** *Tuvalu: A Polynesian Atoll Society* (Pan, Netherlands). A cross-section of traditional musical life on Tuvalu on the cusp of Polynesia and Micronesia.

MELANESIA

ⓒ **Aborigines of Papua New Guinea** *Music from the Sepik Province* (Playasound, France). The wonderful world of Sepik flutes plus kundu and garamut drumming ensembles.
ⓒ **Various** *Polyphonies of the Solomon Islands* (Chant du Monde, France). A fine introduction to the islands' music, including panpipe ensembles, women's songs and sitting dances from Guadalcanal and Savo.

CONTRIBUTORS

ROB ALLINGHAM is archivist at Gallo (Africa) Records in South Africa, a music historian and a producer of re-issue compilations.

IAN ANDERSON is a musician, surfacing most recently with the Orchestre Super Moth. He also runs the Rogue Records label and is editor of the very wonderful *Folk Roots* magazine.

JAMES ATTLEE is a freelance writer, formerly a session guitarist and assistant editor of Gospel Music Magazine.

SAIRAH AWAN is a London-based music writer.

MAGNUS BACKSTRÖM is musiican and director of the Falun Folk Festival, Sweden.

NICK BARRACLOUGH plays guitar, five-string banjo and string bass and is a broadcaster specialising in American music.

COLIN BASS is a singer and multi-instrumentalist, resident in Berlin but often to be found in Jakarta.

MARCUS BREEN lives in Melbourne and has edited *Our Place, Our Music,* a collection of studies on Aboriginal music.

FERHAT BORATAV is a TV producer in Istanbul.

JOE BOYD is a record producer and creator of Hannibal Records, a label instrumental in bringing the music of eastern Europe to attention in the west.

KEN BRAUN is a New-York based freelance music journalist, and works at Stern's African Record Shop in London.

ROBIN BROADBANK is a proific sound recordist and a producer for Nimbus Records' world music CDs.

SIMON BROUGHTON is a music producer for BBC TV and a freelance writer.

RAMIRO BURR is writing a book on Tex-Mex music and reports for the *San-Antonio Express-News* and *Billboard*.

KIM BURTON is a pianist, accordion player and writer, specialising in Latin and Balkan music. He has participated in various GlobeStyle releases and field trips.

JENNY CATHCART is a journalist and TV producer, responsible for several of the BBC TV *Rhythms of the World* programmes. She is the author of *Hey You!,* a biography of Youssou N'Dour.

JOHN COLLINS runs Bokoor Studio in Ghana. He is the author of *Musicmakers of West Africa* (Three Continents Press, US) and *West African Pop Roots* (Temple University Press, US).

MIKE COOPER is a slide guitarist and composer. His most recent album, "Avant Roots", mixes rembétika, Hawaiian guitar sounds and blues.

DAVID CLEARY is a prophet of the Brazilian music and football scene; a writer and lecturer, he is based at the Centre for Latin American Studies at Cambridge University, England.

JOHN CLEWLEY is a music journalist and photographer based in Bangkok.

LOIS DARLINGTON is a journalist and works for Stern's African Record Shop in London, where she edits the *Tradewind* newsletter.

LUCY DURAN is a writer and broadcaster, and a lecturer at the School of Oriental and African Studies, London.

MARK ELLINGHAM was once weird music correspondent for the Irish paper *Hot Press* and is now Rough Guides series editor.

GRAEME EWENS is the author of *Africa O Yé* (Guinness, UK) and a biography of Franco, *Congo Colossus* (Buku Press/Stern's, UK).

JAN FAIRLEY is a writer and broadcaster with particular interests in Latin, Caribbean and Finnish music.

FRANCIS FALCETO is a record producer who divides his time between Paris and Addis Ababa.

DAVID FANSHAWE is a composer (African Sanctus) and global music recorder. He is currently working on his "Pacific Odyssey".

MARY FARQUHARSON is a freelance writer based in Mexico City, where she helps run the Corason record label.

ANDY FRANKEL is a producer and aspiring ethnomusicologist. Co-founder of Rakumi Arts, he lives in Seattle and works extensively with Nigerian music and musicians.

PAUL FISHER runs The Far Side music company in Japan and writes on Asian music for *The Japan Times* and *Folk Roots.*

RICK GLANVILL is an author and Chelsea fan.

RONNIE GRAHAM is the author of *Stern's Guides to African Music Vol 1* and *Vol 2* (Pluto Press, UK/De Capo, US). He works with HelpAge in Tanzania.

WERNER GRAEBNER is an ethnomusicologist and journalst. He is also a music broadcaster in Germany and the US.

JANE HAYTER-HAMES is an ex-farmer and is now a freelance writer and journalist, specializing in Africa.

STEPHEN HALLET is an independent film producer and China consultant.

JENNY HEATON studied gamelan in Bali and Solo and teaches gamelan in Britain and Germany. She is director of the London South Bank Gamelan,

SEAN HINTON was last heard of heading off to do musical research on the farthest reaches of the Mongolian steppe.

DAVE HUCKER is a London-based Latin DJ and a columnist for *The Beat* and *Straight No Chaser* magazines.

COLIN IRWIN wrote for *Melody Maker* for many years. Now freelance, his reports on Celtic and British music can be read most months in *Folk Roots* magazine.

HELEN M. JEROME is a journalist and freelance music writer.

STEPHEN JONES is a professional violinist and research fellow into Chinese folk music at the School of Oriental and African Studies, London.

NASREEN KABIR is a producer and director. She is producer of Channel 4's *Movie Mahal* series.

HIDEO KAWAKAMI is a popular music critic and jounalist based in Tokyo.

JUDY KENDALL worked in Zimbabwe for four years. She is a writer in residence at Shepton Mallet prison, England, and writes on music, film and women's issues.

ANDY KERSHAW is a broadcaster and BBC Radio 1 DJ, where he packs World Music sounds into his saturday afternoon show.

MARK KIDEL is an independent film maker.

JAK KILBY is a freelance photographer and writer, specializing in World Music.

PAUL LASHMAR is a freelance journalist and TV producer.

CHARLES DE LEDESMA is a music writer and co-author of *The Rough Guide to Malaysia, Singapore & Brunei.*

DAVID LODGE is a journalist and broadcaster in his latest incarnation. He lived in Egypt for several years and produced a compilation disc, "Yallah!", for Island Records.

JOHN LWANDA is a Malawian doctor, currently based in Scotland, from where he runs Pamtondo Records.

DAVID P. MCALLESTER has researched Navajo music and is professor emeritus of anthropology and music at Wesleyan University, US.

LOUISE MEINTJES is an anthropologist working in South Africa, with a special interest the relationships in a recording studio.

ANDY MORGAN is a QPR and Bulgaria supporter, and freelance journalist, based in Paris. He has worked with WOMAD and FNAC records.

DAVID MUDDYMAN is a writer, archive researcher and member of worldly dance band Loop Guru.

JEAN-VICTOR NKOLO currently works in the field of Mozambiquan reconstruction and is also a freelance journalist.

NUALA O'CONNOR is a Dublin-based TV producer. She researched the BBC TV series on Irish music, *Bringing It All Back Home*, and wrote the accompanying book.

PHILLIP PAGE runs the boundless shelves of the Digelius Music Shop in Helsinki.

DOUG PATERSON is an anthropology lecturer, freelance journalist and music promoter.

DAVID PETERSON lives in Utah, where he plays guitar in a reggae band and an Andean group (not at the same time).

TEDDY PEIRO is a tanguista and bandoneon player extraordinaire, based in London.

WILLIAM PRICE plays in a Welsh band.

GREG SALTER deejays a reggae club in Bristol, England, and is a freelance journalist and community worker.

CHRIS SHARRATT is a freelance rock journalist based in Manchester, England.

CAROLINE SHAW is a bibliographer, database manager and lecturer, specializing in African lusophone affairs.

JAMEELA SIDDIQI is a TV producer in current affairs with speciali interests in dance and musicology.

RUPERT SNELL is a lecturer at the School of Oriental and African Studies, London.

SUE STEWARD is a journalist, researcher and sometime DJ. She is a regular contributor on Latin and Caribbean music to *Straight No Chaser* magazine.

PHILIP SWEENEY is a journalist and broadcaster specializing in popular music from around the world. He wrote the *Virgin Directory of World Music.*

CAROL TINGEY is an anthropology lecturer at the School of Oriental and African Studies, London.

RAYMOND TRAVERS is an itinerant musician, who busks around Europe.

RICHARD TRILLO is publicity and rights manager at Rough Guides and author of the *Rough Guides* to Kenya and West Africa.

ART TROITSKY is head of popular music at Russian television and has written two books on the history of Russian rock.

PETER VERNEY is a writer and researcher and editor of *Sudan Update.*

PAUL VERNON is a freelance music consultant, specializing in vintage World Music.

CHRISTOPH WAGNER trained as a teacher and works as a music jounalist and promoter in the Alps. He is author of *Das Akkordeon*, a legendary accordion overview.

BROOKE WENTZ is a music journalist based in New York.

CHARLES B. WOLFF is an Andean music specialist at Cornell University, US.

PHOTO CREDITS

CHAPTER ONE
IRELAND: Crossroads dance (National Library of Dublin); Johnny Doran (Folk Roots archive); Sean Ó Riada (Jeffrey Craig/Claddagh Records); sharon Shannon (Solid Records); Dubliners (Folk Roots archive); Dolores Keane and Mary Black (Ian Anderson); Altan (Colm Henry/Green Linnet Records); De Dannan (Ian Anderson).
SCOTLAND: Scott Skinner (Topic Records); Aly Bain (Folk Roots archive); Capercaillie (Survival Records); Talitha MacKenzie (Triple Earth).
WALES: Bob Delyn (Crai Records); Gorky's Zygotic Mynci (Ankst Records).
BRITTANY: Kornog (Green Linnet).
ENGLAND: Blowzabella (Jak Kilby); Sidmouth session (Dave Peabody); Kathryn Tickell (Steve Gillett); Ashley Hutchings and Oyster Band (Dave Peabody); Leveller (China Records); Barely Works (Julian Boss/Cooking Vinyl); Eliza Carthy and Nancy Kerr (Dave Peabody).

CHAPTER TWO
SCANDINAVIA: Kantele group (FFF); JPP (Aki Paavola); Värttinä (Penntti Hokkanen); Hjort Anders (FFF); Mari Boine (Ola Røe).
ALPUNK: Bavario (Trikont); Hans Kegel (Christoph Wagner); Beergarden band (Christoph Wagner).
POLAND: Wedding band (Simon Broughton).
Hungary: Bartok (Hungarotron); Muszikas (Dave Peabody).
ROMANIA: Maramures dance (Simon Broughton); Sándor Fodor (Hungarotron); Taraf de Haïdouks (Klaus Reimer/Crammed Discs); Taragot player (Guy Le Querrec/Silex).
BULGARIA: Nadja Karadjova (Rogue Records); Trio Bulgarka (Hannibal); Village dancers (Folk Roots archive); Ivo Papasov (Hannibal).
FORMER-YUGOSLAVIA: Jova Stojiljkovíc (Annette Lesniewski/GlobeStyle); Gypsy musicians (Kim Burton).
ALBANIA: Sharki player (Kim Burton).
RUSSIA AND THE NEW REPUBLICS: Dmitri Potrovsky (Jak Kilby); Ukrainians (Volker Lenhard/Cooking Vinyl); Terem Quartet (Real World); Kaigal-ool Khavalyg (Clark Quin/Shanachie); Ashkabad (Stephen Lovell-Davis/Real World).

CHAPTER THREE
INSTRUMENTS: Abdel Aziz el-Mubarak (Jak Kilby); Rabab and lotar (Lyrichord).
MOROCCO: Ahouach (Moroccan Tourism Office); Gharnati Ensemble (Inedit/Auvidis); Mustapha Baqbou (Jak Kilby).
MAURITANIA: Dimi Mint Abba & Khalifa Ould Eide (Jak Kilby).
RAI: Chaba Fadhela & Cheb Sahraoui (Jak Kilby); Khaled (David Browne).
FLAMENCO: Camarón, Paco de Lucía & Juan Peña El Lebrijano (Elke/La Caña; Riverboat Records); Camarón (Vivire album/Philips); Pata negra (Hannibal Records); Juerga (Robin Broadbank/Nimbus).
FADO: Bairro Alto club (Paul Vernon).
GREECE: Yiorgos Mangas (GlobeStyle); Rosa Eskenazi, Rembetes at Pireás, Markos Vamvakaris, and Sailors (collection of Ilias Petropoulos/Kedros Publishers, Athens); Ross Daly (Marc S. Dubin).

CHAPTER FOUR
ARAB WORLD: Cairo cassette stall (David Lodge).

PALESTINE: Mustapha Al Kurd (Jak Kilby).
MODERN EGYPTIAN: Mulid folk band, Cairo wedding (David Lodge); Musicians of the Nile (Jak Kilby).
SUDAN: Sherhabeel Ahmed (SudaNow Magazine); Mohamed Wardi et al (Peter Verney); Hamza el-Din (Jack Nadelle).
ETHIOPIA: Police Force Band (Francis Falceto); Mahmoud Ahmed (Véronique Guillien/CramWorld); Alemayehu Eshete, Traditional musician (Francis Falceto); Tukul Band (Ilpo Saunio/Piranha).

CHAPTER FIVE
MAHFIL: Shruti Sadolikar and group (Robin Broadbank/Nimbus); Alla Rakha & Zakir Hussain, Sultan Khan (Jak Kilby); Hariprasad Chaurasia (Robin Broadbank/Nimbus); Sri Kumar Bose & Amjad Ali Khan (Jak Kilby); Shoba Gurtu (CMP); Vikku Vinayakram, Ali Akbar Khan (Jak Kilby); U Srinivas (GlobeStyle).
QAWWALI: Nusrat Fateh Ali Khan (Jak Kilby); Sabri Brothers (Piranha).
BHANGRA: Channi (Alaap); Achanak (Nachural).
NEPAL: Tailor-musicians, Beating the drum (Carol Tingey).

CHAPTER SIX
MANDING MUSIC: Mory Kanté (Jak Kilby); Tata Bambo Kouyaté (Tricia Chacon); Jalimadi Tounkara (Richard Trillo); Sékou Diabaté (Jak Kilby); Dembo Konteh & Kausu Kouyaté (Ian Anderson); Salif Keita (David Browne); Oumou Sangaré (John Mided).
ALI FARKA TOURÉ: Ali Farka Touré (Dave Peabody).
SENEGAL & THE GAMBIA: Orchestre Baobab (Balla Sidibé/World Circuit); Super Diamono (Jak Kilby); Ismael Lô (Catherine Millet/Mango); Youssou N'Dour & Assane Thiam (Jak Kilby); Baaba Maal (Dave Peabody); Baaba Maal portrait (Adrian Boot); Ibrahima Sylla (Rick Glanvill).
CAPE VERDE: Cesaria Evora, Bana (Pierre-René Worms).
SIERRA LEONE: SE Rogie (Steve Gillett).
GHANA: Joe Lamptey with fife band (collection of John Collins); ET Mensah (Jak Kilby); Kwaa Mensah (collection of John Collins), African Brothers, Koo Nimo (Jak Kilby); Alex Konadu (David Browne); Osibisa (Jak Kilby).
BENIN: Angélique Kidjo (Adrian Boot).
NIGERIA: IK Dairo (Andy Frankel), Ebenezer Obey (Jak Kilby); Sunny Ade (Richard Trillo); Barrister (Jak Kilby); Fela Kuti (David Browne)

CHAPTER SEVEN
ZAIRE: Kanda Bongo Man (Dave Peabody); Joseph Kabasele (collection of Graeme Ewens); Franco (Jak Kilby); Papa Wemba (WOMAD); Pepe Kalle (Graeme Ewens); Classic Swede Swede (Jak Kilby).
CAMEROON: Les Têtes Brulées (Stern's); Manu Dibango (Jak Kilby); Mystic Djim (Jane Hayter-Hames).
EQUATORIAL GUINEA: The Guinea Boys (Paul Lashmar).
SÃO TOMÉ & PRÍNCIPE: Danço Congo illustration (collection of Caroline Shaw).
KENYA: Fadhili Williams & Fundi Konde (collection of Graeme Ewens); DO Misiani (Earthworks); Abana Ba Nasary (Denis Lewis/GlobeStyle); Samba Mapangala (Ian Anderson).
TAARAB: Siti Bint Saad (collection of Werner Graebner); Culture Musical Group, Zuhurua Swaleh (Werner Graebner).
TANZANIA: Moro Jazz Band (collection of Werner Graebner); Maquis Original poster, Remmy Ongala (Werner Graebner); Hukwe Zawose (Jak Kilby).
MADAGASCAR: All illustrations (Ian Anderson).

CHAPTER EIGHT

SOUTH AFRICA: West Nkosi (Louise Meintjes); Mahlathini, Mahotella Queens (Jak Kilby); The Holy Brothers (Greg Salter); Ladysmith Black Mambazo (Warner Brothers); Zulu-Traditional Musicians (Harry Scurfield/Natal Newspaper); Sipho Mchunu & Johnny Clegg (Ralph Resnik/Safari Records).
SOUTH AFRICAN JAZZ: Miriam Makeba, Hugh Masekela, Dudu Pukwana (Jak Kilby); Abudullah Ibrahim (Tim Jarvis/Kaz Records).
ZIMBABWE: Posters, Dancers at Queens (Judy Kendall); Mbira (Jak Kilby); Stella Chiweshe (Richard Trillo); Thomas Mapfumo (Dirk Vandeberk/WOMAD); Biggie Tembo (David Browne); Runn Family, Dorothy Masuka (Judy Kendall); Black Umfolosi (Erik Sokkelund/World Circuit).
ZAMBIA: Alick Nkhata (collection of Graeme Ewens).
MALAWI: Kasambwe Brothers (John Lwanda/Malawi Information Office).
ANGOLA AND MOZAMBIQUE: Eyuphoro (Frank Drake/WOMAD); Ghorwane (Steve Gillett).

CHAPTER NINE

GAMELAN: Heavenly Orchestra (CMP Records); Javanese Court Gamelan (Elektra Nonesuch); Siter player (Jenny Heaton); Rebab player (CMP Records); Gamelan procession (Jenny Heaton).
INDONESIAN POP: Elvy Sukaeish (Wave Records); Jugala Orchestra (Colin Bass); Detty Kurnia (John Clewley); Nasida Ria (Piranha Records).
MALAYSIA: Blind musicians and Village musicians (Jak Kilby);
PHILIPPINES: Freddy Aguilar (John Clewley).
THAILAND: Bong lang (John Clewley); Fong Naam (Robin Broadbank/Nimbus records); Pompuang Duangjian, Pimpa Pornsiri (John Clewley).
LAOS: Taoboangern Chapoowong (John Clewley).
VIETNAM: Cai Luong and Thai Chau (John Clewley).
CHINA: Shawm band (Steve Jones); Suzhou Daoist group (Chen Pengshan/Asian Music Circuit); Ciu Jian (Graham de Smidt).
MONGOLIA: Ulan Bator ensemble (Hungarotron).
JAPAN: Shang, Shang Typhoon (John Clewley); Misora Hibari (Nippon Columbia); Miyako Harumi, Haruomi Hosono, Rinkenband, Dick Lee Band (John Clewley).
KOREA: Ancestors' Temple ensemble (Simon Broughton); Samulnori (CMP Records).

CHAPTER TEN

CUBA: Crossroads, Los Muñequitos de Matanzas, Celina Gonzalez (Lucy Duran); Orqusta Ritmo Oriental (Qbadisc); Elio Revé (Jak Kilby); Casa de la Trova (Simon Broughton).
SALSA: Celia Cruz (Jak Kilby); Joe Arroyo (Jak Kilby); Oscar D'Leon (Jak Kilby).
MERENGUE: Juan Luís Guerra (Arista).
HAITI: Dance (Steve Winter); Tabou Combo (John Clewley); Boukman Eksperyans (Steve Winter).
CALYPSO AND SOCA: The young Roaring Lion (from Roaring Lion's photo album); David Rudder (Adrian Boot); Arrow (Jak Kilby).
ZOUK: Jacob Desvarieux (John Clewley); Dédé Saint Prix (Jak Kilby); Malavoi (John Clewley).
REGGAE: Joseph Bennet (Jak Kilby); Lee Perry, Toots Hibbert, Bob Marley, and Burning Spear (Adrian Boot); Lucky Dube (Flame Tree); Chaka Demus & Pliers (David Hindley/Mango); Aswad (London Features International); Mad Professor (Ariwa).

CHAPTER ELEVEN

CUBA: Los Leones de la Sierra Xichu (Keith Dannemiller); Linda Ronstadt and Daniel Valdez (Bob Blakeman/Asylum Records); Mariachi Coculense "Rodriguez" (Marmolejo Family/Arhoolie); Banda del Recodo (J. Cruz Lizarraga); Poets' duel (Jessica Johnson).
COLOMBIA: Big Cumbia (Frané Lessac); Toto La Momposina (Jak Kilby); Peregoyo y su combo (Discos Fuentes); La Sonora Dinamita (Adrian Boot); Accordions logo (GlobeStyle).
BRASIL: Carmen Miranda (Harlequin Records); Os Ingênuos (Nimbus Records); Olodum (World Circuit); Margareth Menezes (John Clewley); Gilberto Gil (Jak Kilby); Caetano Veloso (John Clewley).
NUEVA CANCIÓN: Pablo Milanés (World Pacific); Mercedes Sosa (Jan Fairley); Silvio Rodriguez (Rigoberto Romero/Hannibal); Sandinistas (Uriel Molina/Rounder Records).
TANGO: Astor Piazzolla (Charles Reilly/American Clavé).
ANDES: Chicha drinkers (Mo Fini/Tumi); Rumillatja (Julio Etchart/Tumi); Belem (Mo Fini/Tumi); Awatinas (Narelle Autio/Heart Beat).

CHAPTER TWELVE

CUBA: Raymond Boley and Ed Lee Natay, and Southern Scratch (Canyon Records Productions).
OLD TIME AND BLUEGRASS: Carter Family (Country Music Foundation/Rounder Records); New York City Ramblers and The Dillards (Dave Peabody); Alison Krauss (Peter Nash/Rounder Records).
CUBA: Cleoma and Joseph Falcon (Cleoma and Joseph Falcon/Arhoolie); Iry LeJeune (Ace Records); Michael Doucet, Marc and Ann Savoy (Dave Peabody); Eddie LeJeune and D.L. Menard (Simon Broughton); Clifton Chenier (Howard Brainen/Arhoolie); Queen Ida (Jak Kilby); John Delafose and the Eunice Playboys (Mike Terranova/Rounder Records).
TEX-MEX: Narciso Martinez (Philip Gould/Arhoolie); Santiago Jimenez Jnr. and Flaco Jimenez (Dave Peabody); Lydia Mendoza (U.T. Institute of Texan cultures/Arhoolie); Texas Tornados (Mark Guerra/Reprise); Los Lobos (Caroline Greyshok/Warner Bros).
GOSPEL: Blind Willie Johnson (Robert Armstrong/Yazoo Records); Aretha Franklin (Rhino Records); Five Blind Boys of Alabama (Dave Peabody).
KLEZMER: Prewar klezmer band (Folk Roots archive); Violinist (Yivo Institute for Jewish research); Dave Tarras (Ethnic Folk Arts Center, New York); Giora Feldman (Simon Broughton).
HAWAII: Pahanui Brothers (BMG Records); Ray Kane (Paul Schraub/Dancing Cat Records); Rosa Moe (Rounder Records).

CHAPTER THIRTEEN

ABORIGINAL: Dancers (Jak Kilby); Ruby Hunter (Jacqueline Mitelman/Festival Records); Didgeridoo players (Larrikin Entertainment); Yothu Yindi (John W. McCormick/Festival Records); Archie Roach (Jacqueline Mitelman/Festival Records); Blek Bela Mujik (CAAMA/Mushroom).
OCEANIA: David Fanshawe (Jane Fanshawe); Tahitian drummer (Claire Leimbach); Tahitian choir (Michael Chansin/Triloka Records); Satawal stick dancers, Solomon Island panpipers (David Fanshawe); Wagi Brothers Band (Claire Leimbach).

INDEX

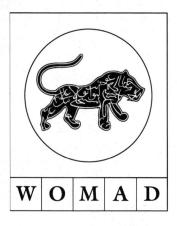

W O M A D

"The eclecticism of **WOMAD** works.
It has a **WONDERFUL** sense of the
unexpected, a BIZARRE melding of
musical and cultural styles
and a EUPHORIC sense of
peace and goodwill"

Rolling Stone Magazine

WOMAD - global music and dance festivals

The **EUROPEAN FORUM OF WORLDWIDE MUSIC FESTIVALS** presents

WOMEX

In 1991, 1992, 1993 there were the WORLDWIDE MUSIC DAYS (at BID) in Berlin.
Their successor is

WORLDWIDE
MUSIC EXPO

Conference
Showcases
Tradefair

The movable feast of worldwide, roots & traditional musics
EACH year, each autumn, a different host city

>1994 host: House of World Cultures, Berlin 13-16 October 1994<

Stay informed ! Year-round information about WOMEX WorldWide Music Expo from
EFWMF Network Office
Jan Frans Willemsstraat 10, B-2530 Boechout, Belgium
tel. (+32) 3 455 6944 fax: (+32) 3 454 1162
email: womex@global.pp.fi

C WORLD SOUN

C WORLD SOUNDS, is a series of 100 compact dis
featuring some the most exquisite and
xotic musical traditions from all corners of the glob
Superbly packaged and recorded with
ten breathtaking clarity, this highly acclaimed seri
is at last available to the world.

le throughout Europe (contact Japan office for details) and North A

VICTOR ENTERTAINMENT, INC.
26-18, JINGUMAE 4-CHOME
SHIBUYA-KU, TOKYO 150, JAPAN.
TEL.03-3746-5697 FAX.03-3746-5741

JVC MUSICAL INDUSTRIES, INC.
3800 BARHAM BLD, SUITE 305
LOS ANGELS, CA.90068 USA
TEL.213-878-0101 FAX.213-878-0202

REALWORLD

1 **REALWORLD PRESENTS...**

Six track sampler highlighting Realworld's 1994 releases.
Featuring Sheila Chandra, Nusrat Fateh Ali Khan, S.E. Rogie,
Doudou Ndiaye Rose, Shu-De and Raw Stylus.

2 **NUSRAT FATEH ALI KHAN** *The Last Prophet*

The greatest living Qawwali performs the traditional music
of mystical Islam. Nusrat's voice is a combination of uplifting
energy and haunting passion.

3 **SHEILA CHANDRA** *The Zen Kiss*

The former member of Monsoon uses her voice as the ultimate
instrument. The resulting album is an extraordinary and
diverse celebration of Sheila's unique vocal range and
poignant songwriting talent.

4 **S.E. ROGIE** *Dead Men Don't Smoke Marijuana*

The soothing sounds of palm wine music from the Sierra Leone.
Rogie's gentle acoustic guitar and mellow voice create a
wonderfully simple, beautiful album.

5 **A WEEK OR TWO IN THE REAL WORLD**

Collects the best performances from the 1992 and 1993
Realworld Recording Weeks. Features Mari Boine,
Karl Wallinger, Lucky Dube and Van Morrison with
the Holmes Brothers.

6 **U. SRINIVAS** *Rama Sreerama*

Enchanting classical Indian music performed on a five string
mandolin. The combination of Srinivas' skill and charm create
extraordinarily energetic and exotic music.

7 **SHU-DE** *Voices From The Distant Steppe*

A unique recording of traditional Tuvan 'throat-singing',
folk-songs, and ritual chants of shamen. An intimate glimpse
into a distant and mysterious world.

8 **DOUDOU NDIAYE ROSE** *Djabote*

Legendary master drummer leads fifty percussionists and
eighty singers in a mesmerising performance of power and
beauty. Truly unlike anything you have ever heard.